D1260461

A HISTORY OF CHRISTIAN MISSIONS IN CHINA

A HISTORY OF
CHRISTIAN MISSIONS
IN CHINA

By

KENNETH SCOTT LATOURETTE

*D. Willis James Professor of Missions and Oriental
History in Yale University*

NEW YORK / RUSSELL & RUSSELL

TO
MY FATHER AND MOTHER

FIRST PUBLISHED IN 1929
REISSUED, 1967, BY RUSSELL & RUSSELL
A DIVISION OF ATHENEUM HOUSE, INC.
BY ARRANGEMENT WITH KENNETH SCOTT LATOURETTE
L. C. CATALOG CARD NO: 66−24721
PRINTED IN THE UNITED STATES OF AMERICA

PREFACE

THE following pages are the attempt to tell the story of Christian missions in China and to do so in the light of the various factors, political, economic, intellectual, and religious, which have helped to shape the enterprise. The date chosen for the suspension of the narrative, the close of the year 1926, has been fixed arbitrarily as being the latest for which anything like complete material is available. The story of the last ten or twelve years, indeed, probably suffers from the fact that we are as yet too near the events to view them in true proportion.

It is impossible for any writer of history entirely to free his account from the influence of his own interests and convictions. In the following pages the effort has been made to view events objectively—to recount them as they actually occurred (if that can ever be done). It may seem, indeed, to some who have given their lives to carrying the Christian Gospel to China, that the author has at times forgotten that he himself has been a missionary. The author wishes to state frankly at the very outset, however, that he is thoroughly committed to the enterprise of Christian missions, and that his bias, therefore, is to interpret missionary activities in China more favorably than some who are not so committed believe that the facts warrant. He is, moreover, a Protestant, and while he has striven to narrate fairly the story of the efforts of Nestorian, Russian Orthodox, and Roman Catholic Christians, he has not been able to escape the uneasy feeling that he has not understood fully the convictions, the hopes, and the desires of the representatives of these communions. At times, on the other hand, the author has wondered whether the consciousness of his bias and the desire not to be influenced by it has not led him to be more restrained in his favorable estimate and more pronounced in his criticism of missions, and especially of Protestant missions, than accuracy warrants.

The writer, too, is a Westerner, and he has probably not given as much attention to the part of the Chinese in the life of the Church as would one of their own number. Nor has he been able to enter with complete understanding into the religious experience of the Chinese. For that reason the book has been purposely named "A History of Christian Missions in China," so stressing the part of the foreigner, rather than "A History of the Christian Church in China." It is to be hoped that a Chinese will sometime prepare a narrative from this latter angle.

The larger part of the material upon which the book is based consists of what historians choose to call primary sources—books and letters and reports of missionaries and of other eye-witnesses or participants. Much, however, is of a secondary character.

In the footnotes more than one reference is often given. This is usually for the purpose of facilitating the researches of those who may wish to use the book as a guide to further and more detailed study of the topics treated. Some of the accounts referred to, especially where more than one is given in a footnote, are of questionable authority. When, however, a statement in the text is based upon a dubious reference, that is usually indicated by some such qualifying word as "probably," "seems," "possibly," or "appears."

In the romanization of Chinese words the Wade system has been followed, except in the case of most geographical names and a few names of individuals. Here current usage has as a rule been adhered to. In quotations, naturally, the romanization of the writer has been reproduced. In those few instances where a word is used whose corresponding character is unknown, the romanization is irregular.

For their courtesy in facilitating his search for material, the author wishes gratefully to acknowledge his obligation to the Yale University, the Day Missions, the Cornell University, the Morrison, and the Missionary Research Libraries, to the North China Branch of the Royal Asiatic Society, to the late Professor F. Wells Williams, in whose excellent private collection the author has spent many happy hours, to Mrs. Charles W. Wason, who graciously made available the library of the late Mr. Wason while it was still in her home, to Mgr. Freri of the Society for the Propagation of the Faith, to the fathers of the Society of the Divine Word at Techny, Illinois, to Mr. J. H. Oldham for the use of a rare and valuable book, to Professor L. C. Goodrich for the privilege of examining and making use of the material in his manuscript, *American Catholic Missions in China,* and to the many others whose names there is no space to record, but whose kindly aid and interest have made pleasant the long days of research.

The author especially wishes to record his gratitude to Professor David Edward Owen and to Mr. Chauncey P. Williams, Jr., who by their assistance hastened the collection of material, especially that on Protestant missions before 1918, and to Mrs. C. T. Lincoln for her competent typing of the manuscript and her assistance in reading proof and in compiling the index.

The author also desires to acknowledge himself the grateful debtor of Dr. A. L. Warnshuis, and of Professors F. W. Schwager, H. P. Beach, E. D. Harvey, Lewis Hodous, Paul Pelliot, and the late F. Wells Williams, all of whom read extensive portions of the manuscript and made valuable suggestions. For any mistakes, however, the author alone is responsible.

K. S. L.

New Haven, Connecticut
May, 1928.

TABLE OF CONTENTS

		PAGE
PREFACE	. . . .	vii

CHAPTER

I.	INTRODUCTION	1
II.	THE RELIGIOUS BACKGROUND OF THE CHINESE . .	6
III.	THE OUTSTANDING CHARACTERISTICS OF CHRISTIANITY AND THE BEARING OF THESE UPON THE POSSIBLE ACCEPTANCE OF CHRISTIANITY IN CHINA . . .	25
IV.	CHRISTIANITY IN CHINA BEFORE THE MONGOL DYNASTY	46
V.	CHRISTIANITY IN CHINA UNDER THE MONGOLS . .	61
VI.	THE AGE OF EUROPEAN DISCOVERIES AND THE RESUMPTION OF ROMAN CATHOLIC MISSIONS . .	78
VII.	THE PROGRESS OF ROMAN CATHOLIC MISSIONS FROM THE DEATH OF RICCI TO THE REVERSES CAUSED BY THE CONTROVERSY OVER THE RITES (1610-1706) .	102
VIII.	THE BEGINNING OF RETARDED GROWTH: THE RITES CONTROVERSY	131
IX.	THE PERIOD OF RETARDED GROWTH: ITS BEGINNING (1707) TO ITS END (ABOUT 1839)	156
X.	METHODS AND RESULTS OF ROMAN CATHOLIC MISSIONS IN THE SIXTEENTH, SEVENTEENTH AND EIGHTEENTH CENTURIES	185
XI.	THE RUSSIAN ORTHODOX CHURCH IN CHINA IN THE SEVENTEENTH AND EIGHTEENTH CENTURIES . .	199
XII.	THE RENEWED EXPANSION OF EUROPE: THE INDUSTRIAL REVOLUTION, THE REVIVAL OF CATHOLIC MISSIONS, AND THE RELIGIOUS AND MISSIONARY AWAKENING AMONG PROTESTANTS	201
XIII.	THE BEGINNINGS OF PROTESTANT MISSIONS TO CHINA (1807-1839)	209
XIV.	THE FIRST WAR BETWEEN CHINA AND GREAT BRITAIN AND ITS AFTERMATH (1839-1855)	228
XV.	THE WAR WITH GREAT BRITAIN AND FRANCE AND THE SECOND GROUP OF TREATIES (1856-1860) . . .	271
XVI.	THE T'AI P'ING REBELLION	282

CHAPTER		PAGE
XVII.	THE GRADUAL PENETRATION OF CHINA BY MISSIONARIES, 1856-1897. INTRODUCTORY. ROMAN CATHOLIC MISSIONS	303
XVIII.	THE GRADUAL PENETRATION OF CHINA BY MISSIONARIES, 1856-1897. PROTESTANT MISSIONS	357
XIX.	THE GRADUAL PENETRATION OF CHINA BY MISSIONARIES, 1856-1897. METHODS OF PROTESTANT MISSIONS	416
XX.	THE GRADUAL PENETRATION OF CHINA BY MISSIONARIES, 1856-1897. RESULTS OF PROTESTANT MISSIONS	466
XXI.	RUSSIAN MISSIONS IN THE NINETEENTH CENTURY	486
XXII.	REFORM AND REACTION (1898-1900)	488
XXIII.	CHINA IN A TIME OF REORGANIZATION (1901-1926). INTRODUCTORY	527
XXIV.	CHINA IN A TIME OF REORGANIZATION (1901-1926). ROMAN CATHOLIC MISSIONS, 1901-July, 1914. THE MISSION OF THE RUSSIAN ORTHODOX CHURCH, 1901-1914	536
XXV.	CHINA IN A TIME OF REORGANIZATION (1901-1926). PROTESTANT MISSIONS, 1901-July, 1914	567
XXVI.	CHINA IN A TIME OF REORGANIZATION (1901-1926). PROTESTANT MISSIONS, 1901-July, 1914 (Continued). METHODS AND RESULTS	617
XXVII.	CHINA IN A TIME OF REORGANIZATION (1901-1926). CHANGES IN THE OCCIDENT AND IN CHINA, 1914-1926	686
XXVIII.	CHINA IN A TIME OF REORGANIZATION (1901-1926). ROMAN CATHOLIC MISSIONS, 1914-1926. RUSSIAN ORTHODOX MISSIONS, 1914-1926	705
XXIX.	CHINA IN A TIME OF REORGANIZATION (1901-1926). PROTESTANT MISSIONS DURING THE WAR, 1914-1918	743
XXX.	CHINA IN A TIME OF REORGANIZATION (1901-1926). PROTESTANT MISSIONS FROM THE CLOSE OF THE WAR TO THE CLOSE OF 1926	765
XXXI.	SUMMARY AND CONCLUSION	823
	BIBLIOGRAPHY	845
	INDEX	901

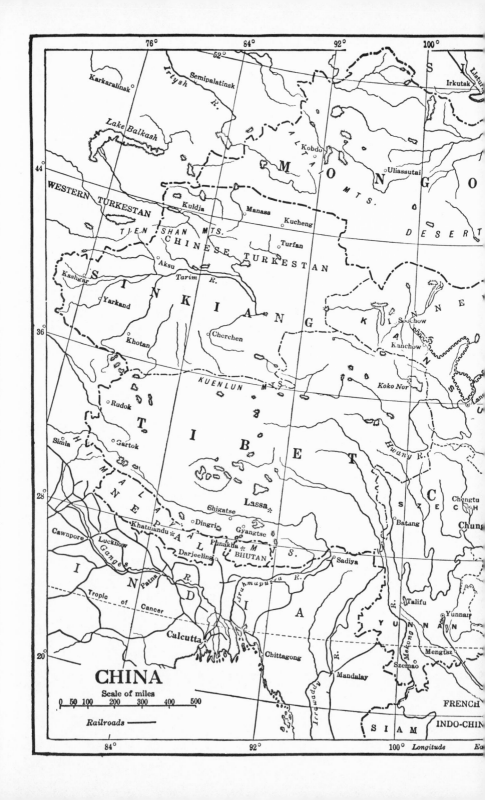

CHINA

Scale of miles

0   50 100   200   300   400   500

Railroads ⎯⎯⎯⎯

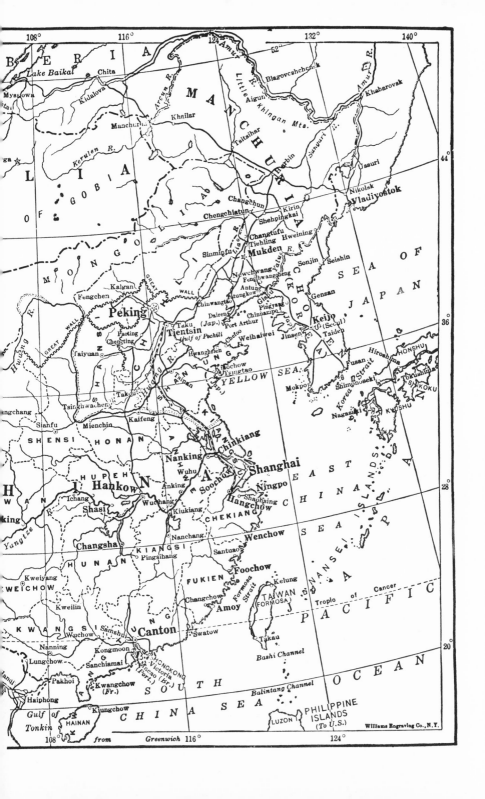

A HISTORY OF CHRISTIAN MISSIONS IN CHINA

CHAPTER I

INTRODUCTION

To the visitor to China in the year 1926 one of the most interesting and thought-provoking features of the landscape was the physical evidence of the activities of Christian missionaries. If the traveller entered the country by Shanghai, on the outskirts of the city his steamer passed the substantial buildings of an institution which he was informed was Shanghai College, maintained by American Baptists. Once in the city, if he were observant, he found buildings of the Young Men's and Young Women's Christian Associations, churches, Christian hospitals and schools, and a structure called the Missions Building in which were the headquarters of many national and local Protestant organizations. In the suburbs he discovered the well-equipped campus of St. John's University, the spacious buildings of the McTyeire School for girls, and the great Catholic plant at Zikawei, with its stately church, its commodious schools, orphanages, and seminaries, its library, its museum of natural history, its meteorological observatory, and its printing plant. If he came by way of Suez and Singapore, and if he paused at Hongkong long enough to visit Canton, the tourist saw, as his steamer carried him up one of the two principal channels toward the city, the extensive campus of Lingnan University, or, as it was formerly called, Canton Christian College. On the banks of the other channel he found the large building of a girls' boarding school—the True Light Seminary—and the smaller buildings of a Protestant union theological seminary. Long before he reached the city he saw rising in the distance the twin towers of the Roman Catholic cathedral, and on or near the bund he found a Protestant hospital, church

1

buildings, the salesroom of a Protestant publishing house, and the building of the Young Men's Christian Association. Just across from the city he discovered the first hospital in China for the insane, an institution begun and continued by missionaries. When the traveller went to Peking he saw from the city walls the towers of more than one Roman Catholic church, the substantial and completely equipped plant of the Peking Union Medical College—the best medical school in all China and closely allied to the missionary enterprise—many Protestant church and school buildings, and away in the northeast corner he discovered a large section given over to the work of the Russian Orthodox Church. On the wall itself he was shown the astronomical instruments constructed for the government by Roman Catholic missionaries centuries ago, and outside the wall to the west he found a Protestant university, a Roman Catholic theological college, a Roman Catholic normal school, a Roman Catholic memorial church bearing inscribed on its walls the names of several thousand Chinese martyrs of the stormy Boxer year, and a cemetery with missionaries' graves dating back to the seventeenth century. If the tourist pursued his way through the provinces, he saw in provincial capitals, in district towns and cities, and in country villages the physical proofs that the missionary had been there before him. In Changsha, the capital of Hunan, for example, there were much in evidence churches, schools, and the buildings of a Young Men's Christian Association, and as the visitor approached the city by boat the great hospital established by the Yale Foreign Missionary Society and the numerous structures on the campus of the middle school and college maintained by that same organization were among the first landmarks to greet him. The traveller also discovered, sometimes in the most remote districts, churches, chapels, preaching halls, schools, orphanages, hospitals, and dispensaries, and in them he met Europeans, Americans, and Chinese, serving as pastors, catechists, teachers, or physicians.

If he glanced at the statistics of the enterprise the traveller read that there were, at the middle of the third decade of the twentieth century, about three thousand Europeans and Americans giving their time as missionaries of the Roman Catholic Church, and that the Protestant foreign force, including the wives of missionaries, was about eight thousand. He saw that the Protestant communicants then numbered about four hundred thousand and had more than doubled in the preceding decade. He also found that there were estimated to be about two million two hundred thousand Roman Catholics, and that the number of the communicants of the Russian Orthodox Church was given as more than five thousand.

If the visitor sought for estimates of the enterprise he discovered the most diverse opinions. The majority of the missionaries, while awake to weaknesses in their work and the grave problems to be solved, proved unaffectedly enthusiastic—at least until the reverses of 1926. Some Chinese of the highest standing were earnest Christians; some intelligent non-Christian Chinese were warmly appreciative of what the missionary was doing; others were neutral; and still others, among them many able men of high character, were critical and even actively hostile. Some foreigners, both merchants and diplomats, the traveller learned, were violently anti-missionary; others were tolerant or indifferent; and now and then some business man or consul spoke in terms of the highest praise, even going so far as to say that of recent years practically every promising movement for moral and social betterment traced its origin to missionary activity.[1] The careful observer, then, would not have completed his journeys in China without becoming convinced that in the missionary movement he had one of the most interesting factors in the life of the country.

Whoever, indeed, would understand the China of 1928 and of the preceding hundred years must not only be familiar with the history of domestic politics, of intellectual movements, and of diplomatic and commercial contacts with the West, but must also know and appraise the missionary and his activities. How, he will naturally ask, did this movement come to be? Out of what conditions in the Occident did it arise? Were its roots purely religious, or did economic, political, and intellectual factors help to make it possible and mold it? How does it happen that the Roman Catholic, Russian Orthodox, and Protestant Churches were represented? What are the reasons for the relative proportions between them? Why, for example, was the Protestant missionary force so much larger than the Roman Catholic, and

---

[1] F. W. Stevens, public letter, Dec. 15, 1923. Mr. Stevens represented extensive American business interests in China.

yet Roman Catholic Chinese so much more numerous than Protestant Chinese? How shall one account for the presence of each of the bodies working in China, both Catholic and Protestant? Why were Dominicans in Fukien, Lazarists in Chihli, and Jesuits in Kiangsu; why had the London Missionary Society such widely scattered stations; and what was responsible for the origin and the strength of the great China Inland Mission? How did it happen that Anglo-Saxons so predominated in the Protestant movement, and why were so many of the Catholic missionaries from France? What was the reason for the rapid increase in the number of Catholic missionaries from America after 1918? Why had missionaries often undertaken such extensive educational and medical work? Why had Protestants done more of this than Catholics, and some Protestant societies more than others? What had been the results, both upon their respective Christian communities and upon the life of the nation, of the different policies and emphases of the various missionary groups? What effect had all this missionary activity upon China? To what extent had China become Christian? How far, if at all, had Christianity influenced political, social, religious, and intellectual movements and institutions? What changes of emphasis, if any, had the ethical, social, and religious background of China led missionaries and Chinese Christians to make in the interpretation of the Christian faith and the organization of the Church?

It is obvious that if one would understand the missionary enterprise in China he must see it both in its Occidental and its Chinese setting. He must be familiar, of course, with at least the general outlines of the religious history of Europe and America. But he must know more than that, for the missionary movement has been part of the impact of the West upon China, and it has been made possible and has been shaped not only by religious conditions but by economic, political, and intellectual factors: its story is inextricably bound up with the whole history of the Western invasion of China. Moreover, he who wishes to appraise Christian missions in China must seek to understand the Chinese reaction to the missionary and his message. He must constantly bear in mind Chinese religious, social, and political ideas and institutions, for it is by these that Christian missions were and are constantly being conditioned.

No one ought to attempt dogmatically to foretell the future.

We know only that under the impact of the West Chinese ideas and institutions are to-day being more rapidly and profoundly modified than at any other time in all the centuries of the nation's long history. Because of the extent of the missionary movement Christianity may well have an enduring and an increasing share in shaping the culture that is beginning to emerge. Should Christianity stamp its impress upon the new China even half as firmly as it has upon Europe and America, the future historian may see in missions in China one of the most important movements of the past three centuries.

CHAPTER II

CHRISTIANITY is, of course, a religion, and it is primarily as a religion that it comes to China. If one is to understand its history in China, then, one must know, first of all, the outstanding features of the religious life of the country during the time that the missionary has been at work. He must ask whether these have made the missionary's path difficult or easy, and to what extent they may be expected to mold the Chinese interpretation of Christianity.

The religious situation which the missionary found was the result of a development extending over thousands of years and had in it many strata of philosophy and of popular belief and practice. It is still impossible to reconstruct, except in general and debatable outline, the original religion of the Chinese. The oldest books have come to us in their present form largely from the Han dynasty, which began in B.C. 206, and were reëdited by scholars of that time. Enough of their contents goes back to the time of Confucius (the sixth and fifth centuries before Christ) to enable us to picture with a fair degree of accuracy the conditions and beliefs of that period; and some of them, notably the *Shu Ching* (the Book of History), and the *Shih Ching* (the Book of Poetry), in large part antedate Confucius and even contain passages which may have originated in the second millennium before the Christian era. It is certain, however, that before the songs and the rites had been put into writing and the historical records had begun to be composed, the culture of China was already old. Archæology has as yet done little except to show how much more ancient than our present written records is the beginning of the independent life of the Chinese and to illustrate the early documents and provide means of testing their reliability. Comparative religion, by describing the faiths of primitive peoples, helps us to guess, probably with some degree of accuracy,

6

at the main features of the religion of the earliest Chinese. There seems to have been a primitive matrix of animism out of which ancestor worship had arisen. This, at least, is the conclusion of a number of recent scholars. When, however, shortly before the time of Confucius, we first find ourselves on fairly solid ground, Chinese religious conceptions and practices were much more complex and were the result of an evolution over a much longer period than has since elapsed.

The outstanding characteristics of Chinese religion as the oldest books portray it can be briefly summarized. In the first place, in its objects of worship it was a mixture, showing evidences of various stages of religious development and perhaps of accretions from without. It was certainly in part animistic, probably polytheistic, and, although this is still open to debate, it was possibly in part approaching theism. Worship was paid to ancestors and to a great variety of spirits, among others those of mountains and rivers.[1] The worship of the spirits of ancestors was particularly prominent.[2] Some special gods were honored, as, for example, that of the hearth.[3] There was, as well, a belief in an overruling Power which was usually called *T'ien,* or "Heaven," but sometimes *Shang Ti,* or the "Emperor Above."[4] A clear distinction had probably once been made between these terms. It seems to have been largely obscured, however, by the time our oldest records were compiled in their present form, for in them the characteristics of the two were not carefully differentiated.[5] Over the significance of these words Occidental scholars have had prolonged and sometimes acrimonious discussion, but the debate appears to have proved only that there was originally a difference.[6] *T'ien* was the term most frequently employed. *T'ien* was intelligent, loved righteousness, and had

[1] Couvreur, *Chou King* (Shu Ching), p. 114; Couvreur, *Cheu King* (Shih Ching), p. 424.

[2] This is best seen by a cursory examination of the *Shu Ching* and the *Shih Ching.*

[3] *Analects,* 3:13 (Legge, *Life and Teachings of Confucius,* p. 130).

[4] See, for example, Couvreur, *Chou King* (Shu Ching), pp. 101-113.

[5] There are many passages to illustrate this. See, for example, Couvreur, op. cit., pp. 264, 283, 284.

[6] See, however, Schindler, *The Development of the Chinese Conceptions of Supreme Beings, in Hirth Anniversary Volume.* He claims that *Shang Ti, T'ien,* and *Tao* were originally local deities of separate royal houses, or *T'ien* may have been originally the material heavens, although it may have been anthropomorphic, and *Shang Ti* may have originated from ancestor worship as the father of the royal line. Harvey, *Chinese Daimonism* (MS.), has worked out the same idea on ethnological grounds.

regard for the welfare of the people. From *T'ien* the Emperor derived his authority, and when through injustice he had forfeited his right to continue on the throne *T'ien* removed its decree.[7] Men's lives were long or short as *T'ien* determined.[8] *T'ien* was compassionate and heard and saw as the people heard and saw.[9] This overruling Power had the characteristics of personality, for it was moral, intelligent, and could and did act. However, little or no attempt appears to have been made to think of it as having human form, and no evidence exists of any sense of mystical fellowship with it or of love for it. There was trust in *T'ien's* justice, compassion, and power, and there was reverence, but a sense of personal devotion was lacking.

The worship of this older China was largely ceremonial. There were sacrifices, music, and dancing, and on occasion announcements and petitions were made to the spirits and the superhuman powers.[10] The sacrifices were apparently not the bloody holocausts known in some nations, although offerings of animals were made, as well as of wine, grains, and other products of the earth.[11] It was a repast that was offered. In worship, correctness of form rather than purity of life was deemed of primary importance, but the ethical element was not entirely lacking.[12] A sense of joyous companionship with the objects of worship seems not to have existed, unless in a rudimentary form in ceremonies in honor of ancestors. Worship played a large part in the life of the people, for the unseen powers were believed to have an intimate concern with the affairs of man. The welfare of the social and political units—the family, the principality, and the Empire—quite as much as that of the individual, was held to be conditioned by the favor of the spirits and *T'ien,* so that worship was a social as well as an individual matter. The Emperor, surrounded by his court, performed ceremonies to *T'ien,* to *Shang Ti,* who was quite possibly regarded as his most remote ancestor, to his direct

---

[7] Couvreur, op. cit.. pp. 258-268, 283, 284.
[8] Man was not entirely without free will, however, for his life is shortened or prolonged according to his righteousness.—Couvreur, op. cit., p. 162.
[9] Couvreur, op. cit., p. 48.
[10] This is to be found repeatedly in the *Shih Ching, Shu Ching,* and *Li Chi.* See, for example, Couvreur, *Chou King* (Shu Ching), pp. 187-189; Couvreur, *Cheu King* (Shih Ching), p. 430.
[11] Couvreur, *Chou King* (Shu Ching), pp. 191, 192; Couvreur, *Cheu King* (Shih King), pp. 276, 277, 425.
[12] This is to be seen repeatedly in the *Shu Ching* and the *Shih Ching.* See, for example, Couvreur, *Cheu King* (Shih Ching), pp. 459, 460.

ancestors, and to a great variety of spirits.[13] The local princes and dignitaries of various ranks had their particular forms of worship, and the common man his.[14] There appears to have been no priesthood, although there were those who were experts in ritual and in the divination that was so common.[15] No clear convictions were held about the state of the dead. The departed were regarded as continuing to be interested in and to influence human affairs, and to be able to enjoy the sacrifices paid them, but no attempt was made at a complete description of what they were doing and no happy expectation of immortality was cherished.[16]

Out of this early faith there arose in the Chou dynasty (B.C. 1122-B.C. 249) several distinct schools of thought and practice. Two of these were to develop into cults [17] which were to have a permanent place in the life of the nation. The Chou dynasty was one of the major formative periods in the life of China. During the centuries that its representatives held the throne the race was expanding into fresh territories and culture was undergoing momentous changes. By the sixth century before the Christian era the power of the imperial house had perceptibly declined. The weak Chou Emperors were unable successfully to assert their authority over all the territory into which their nominal subjects had spread, and the many local principalities were all but independent; it seemed, in fact, that in the area at present occupied by China several nations with distinct cultures might arise. Between these incipient states warfare was frequent, and misrule and injustice were rife. Among the awakening minds of the more thoughtful Chinese the dominant interest became, then, the welfare of the race. How, they inquired, can we so reform the state that the prosperity of the people can be assured? They were not primarily concerned with nature or with metaphysics, but with human society. This interest in political and social welfare was to color their teaching and was to persist in much of future philosophy.

The most influential of the cults that trace their origin to the Chou period is what is known to the Occident as Confucianism

[13] Couvreur, *Cheu King* (Shih Ching), pp. 419 et seq.
[14] Couvreur, *Cheu King* (Shih Ching), pp. 419-469; *Analects*, 2:5; 2:24; 10:8; 10:13; 10:14 (Soothill, *Analects*, pp. 152, 177, 485, 495, 497).
[15] Couvreur, *Cheu King* (Shih Ching), pp. 224-226.
[16] Ibid., pp. 419-469.
[17] Confucianism and Taoism

and to the Chinese as *Ju Chiao,* or The Teaching of the Learned. Its dominant mind, as its foreign name indicates, has been Confucius. Confucius was born ca. B.C. 551 and died ca. B.C. 479. His life was spent partly in official service and partly in study, teaching, and writing. His outlook was always that of one who is primarily interested in social welfare and government, and he believed that the salvation of society depended upon a return to the principles and the practices of the best of the ancients. He was, therefore, a diligent student of all that had come down from antiquity, especially as disclosed in books and rituals. He felt that his function was that of a transmitter and not a creator, and rejoiced in being able to study, to edit, and to teach the earlier writings.[18] He emphasized ceremonies and ethics. The former he regarded as not confined to worship and court functions, although he gave these much attention, but as including all contacts between men. In ethics he set high store by principles which are rather crudely and inadequately translated as altruism or good-will (*jên*), filial piety (*hsiao*), righteousness (*i*), sincerity (*hsin*), loyalty (*chung*), reverence (*ching*), virtue (*tê*) and propriety (*li*). He talked much of the *chün tzŭ,* or gentleman, who was distinguished by the cultivation of these virtues. He was greatly interested in religious observances and insisted that these be maintained and carried out decorously, but he appears to have been concerned with religion chiefly as an aid to good government. He declined to discuss the supernatural,[19] but he seems to have accepted without serious question the beliefs about it that had come down from the past and he had a profound, even though rarely mentioned, confidence in the power, goodness, and protection of *T'ien.*[20] This faith had, indeed, an important part in giving stability to his whole life. He was very reticent about his inward religious experiences, however, and on the whole the effect of his teachings upon succeeding generations has been to encourage not theism but agnosticism.

In the centuries following his death, Confucius became more and more the dominant figure in the nation's past. Mencius (fourth and third centuries, B.C.) reverenced him and varied his teaching with an insistence upon the original goodness of human nature and its corollary, confidence in the voice of the people.

[18] *Analects,* 7:1 (Soothill, *The Analects of Confucius,* p. 325).
[19] *Analects,* 7:20 (Soothill, *Analects,* p. 353).
[20] *Analects,* 3:13; 6:26; 7:22 (Soothill, *Analects,* pp. 199, 317, 355).

Under the Han dynasties (B.C. 206-A.D. 214) official scholarship became thoroughly committed to Confucius and spent much time in studying and editing his works.   From that time on, indeed, Confucianism and the state for the most part were inextricably joined, the prevailing political and social theories being those of the Confucian school.   In the Sung dynasty (A.D. 960-1280) a succession of philosophers culminating in Chu Hsi (1130-1200) gave to Confucianism a much more ordered and philosophical form than it had yet achieved.   The philosophy of this school tended further to depersonalize *T'ien,* to make it even less an object of man's affectionate devotion, and so gave to Confucianism a further leaning toward religious agnosticism.   The school emphasized ethics, however, and had a profound confidence that the dominant force in nature was moral and benevolent.   The brilliant writings of Chu Hsi became the orthodox interpretation of Confucius and the ancient classics and remained so until the twentieth century.[21]

Since Confucianism was the orthodox philosophy of men of letters and since it usually enjoyed preferential treatment from the Emperors, it had a profound effect upon the entire life and thought of the nation.   In the main it tended to encourage the persistence of primitive religious beliefs and practices (including not only reverence for *T'ien* and *Shang Ti,* but animism and ancestor worship), to conserve and strengthen the family, to emphasize a high standard of ethics, to perpetuate religious ritual, and to discourage asceticism, mysticism, and theological speculation.   It helped to make the Chinese conservative, practical-minded, amenable to reason, appreciative of virtue, confident in the moral integrity of the universe, and interested in this present world rather than in the life to come.   It produced no Paul, no Francis of Assisi, no Augustine, no John Wesley, but it bred many high-minded administrators and scholars and it helped immeasurably to purify and stabilize society and to inculcate high ideals of loyalty, reverence, and righteousness.   While Confucius had little to say about women, in his example and teaching the mother shared in the respect paid to parents and in practice had a much higher position than in many other countries.   Confucianism, while intensely conservative, was so interested in social well-being that out of the ranks of scholars there arose from time to time

[21] See especially J. P. Bruce, *Chu Hsi and His Masters.*

radical reformers, who, while usually regarded as heterodox, owed their impulse largely to their orthodox background.

Next to Confucianism, the most influential school of thought that arose during the Chou dynasty was Taoism. Its reputed founder was Lao Tzŭ, a shadowy and perhaps an entirely mythical figure, who is said to have been an older contemporary of Confucius. To him is ascribed the *Tao Tê Ching,* a book which undoubtedly had later editing, but which probably is for the most part a product of the Chou period and of a number of authors who belonged to a single school of thought. Like Confucianism, the school represented by the *Tao Tê Ching* had as its chief interest not metaphysics but the salvation of society. Like Confucianism, too, it believed that the universe is moral. It differed from its rival, however, in finding social salvation not in ceremonies, in attention to the organization of government, in legal regulations, and in elaborately discussed ethics, but in simplicity and non-interference. It represented a protest against a civilization which was rapidly becoming complex, and held up as an ideal quietism, a return to a much simpler form of society, and conformity with nature. *Tao,* a term which comes out again and again in the *Tao Tê Ching,* is much older than the latter, but to it the latter gives its own meaning. It is held to be incapable of definition,[22] but in the main it seems to have been conceived as resembling what the Occidental scholar would call the Absolute. In one sense it is the orderly process of nature, in another it is being or becoming; but it is more than these, for while in no physical sense is it anthropomorphic, it is described as having the qualities which go to make up personality. It sustains and nourishes all.[23] It is, too, creative.[24] Conformity with *Tao* is the goal held up to man. This means self-forgetfulness, returning good for evil, the absence of pride, and peace of spirit.[25] The *Tao Tê Ching* is, then, highly moral, but it is opposed to ethical codes. It seeks to control society, to make it normal, and it would do this by a complete change and in accordance with a theory which is much like philosophical anarchism—an absence of all artificial restraint.[26]

[22] *Tao Tê Ching,* 1, 14 (*Sacred Books of East,* Vol. 39; Legge, *Texts of Taoism,* Part 1, pp. 47, 57).
[23] *Tao Tê Ching,* 34 (Legge in ibid., p. 76).
[24] *Tao Tê Ching,* 42, 51 (Legge in ibid., pp. 85, 93).
[25] *Tao Tê Ching,* 7, 8, 22 (*Sacred Books of East,* Vol. 39; Legge, *Texts of Taoism,* Part 1, pp. 52, 53, 65).
[26] *Tao Tê Ching,* 19, 29 (Legge in ibid., pp. 62, 72).

In many respects the *Tao Tê Ching* is at the opposite pole from Confucianism, but the two have in common a belief in the honesty and moral integrity of nature and a desire for the improvement of man's character.

The Chou dynasty saw several other thinkers who belonged in a general way to the school of thought represented by the *Tao Tê Ching*. The chief among these was Chuang Tzŭ, noted for his beautiful literary style. In the teachings attributed to him the desire to save society is less prominent than in the *Tao Tê Ching,* and in its place is a much greater attention to metaphysics. There appear passages which, by insisting on the superiority of the ideal man over matter, seem to encourage magic —that ever recurring belief of mankind. By the close of the Han dynasty there had arisen a cult which we know as Taoism. It looked upon the *Tao Tê Ching* and the books of Chang Tzŭ as classics, but it had degenerated from the standards set by them and its leading exponents directed their energies chiefly toward achieving immortality through the discovery of an elixir of life and by a special regimen in which physical practices played a large part. In this form Taoism represented a longing for immortality which we find absent in earlier writings and which may have helped to pave the way for Buddhism. It spoke—and speaks—much of *hsien,* human beings who have achieved eternal life through Taoist practices. Taoism was to be much influenced by Buddhism. Like the latter it was to develop temples, a pantheon, ritual, and a priesthood. It is, however, not as well organized as the latter, either in its philosophy or its monasteries, and it has been far more corrupted by magic and animism. In its popular aspects it is largely a means of expelling or warding off evil spirits and of obtaining good luck, and it has little that is elevating, either morally or religiously. Pure souls continue to emerge, however, who find in the earlier writings of the school food for meditation and in them seek inward peace.[27]

The Chou dynasty saw various incipient schools of thought which were not to achieve the popularity that attended Confucianism and Taoism and which have usually been frowned upon by official scholarship. They have not, however, been entirely

[27] Soothill, *The Three Religions of China*, London, 1913; de Groot, *The Religions of the Chinese*, New York, 1910; Maspero, *La Chine antique*, Paris, 1927.

without influence. Thus Yang Chu or Yang Tzǔ taught enlightened selfishness as the right principle of life and survived in the
memory of posterity largely because of the arguments with which
Mencius sturdily opposed him. More prominent was Mo Ti or
Mo Tzǔ, whose teachings have come down to us in much fuller
form. Like his contemporaries, he was interested in saving society.
He emphasized and developed the ancient belief that the world
is dominated by a T'ien that is moral and benevolent. He believed
that T'ien is good, that it loves the people, and that it looks after
their welfare by providing them with the seasons, with wood,
grain, and other necessities of life. Since T'ien takes this attitude
toward men, it must obviously be the will of T'ien, Mo Ti urged,
that men act toward each other with this same good-will. Universal love, then, should be the fundamental virtue in human
relationships. With this as his guiding principle, Mo Ti suggested
a reconstruction of human society that would eliminate war, concubinage, luxury in dress and eating, and costly ceremonies,
whether in honor of the gods, the living, or the dead. His was
distinctly a utilitarian view: whatever did not directly aid the
welfare of men must be eliminated. Much that he taught was
so diametrically opposed to prevailing customs and institutions—
to ancestor worship, for example, and even to the family as then
organized—that he was followed only by a minority and was
roundly condemned by the orthodox. He was remembered, however, and his works were not to be without fruitage, especially
in later days of transition.[28]

The early religion of China and the schools of thought that
developed from it were on the whole ethical and, with the exception of later Taoism, were primarily interested in improving
society. They had, however, very little to offer him who wished
definite assurance of personal immortality and who longed to
know what was beyond the grave. Neither did they give to the
worshiper any being with whom he could have joyous and personal fellowship. All of these cults, too, were primarily for the
educated minority or for officials and those of noble birth. The
masses were probably left to observances and beliefs which were
primarily animistic. During the Han dynasty there began coming

[28] See especially Forke, Mê Ti, des Sozialethikers und seiner Schüler Philoso-
phische Werke, Berlin, 1922; David, Le philosophe Meh Ti, London, 1907.

to China a new faith, Indian in origin, which agreed with the ethical emphasis of the native faiths, adjusted itself in part to the family system, was tolerant of the native religious beliefs, and yet at the same time brought in definite teachings about a future life and the offer of age long happiness or prolonged woe, a rich mystical life, an elaborate philosophy, an ornate ceremonial, and an extensive literature. It appealed, moreover, to both the educated and the uneducated. In other words, without running entirely counter to any of the fundamental native beliefs or institutions, it strengthened some of them and offered to fill a void.

Buddhism began, as is well known, as an outgrowth of the older Indian faith. Its founder, Sakyamuni, or Gautama Buddha, had sought earnestly for inward peace through the accepted channels of his time and had failed to find it. Enlightenment had at last come and for the remainder of a long life he gave himself to teaching his way of salvation. Salvation for him was a message of peace, of escape from suffering and the endless chain of reincarnations which contemporary Indian thought accepted as axiomatic. Suffering he held to be caused by desire, and desire he had found could be eliminated by the "eight-fold path." This eight-fold path involved chiefly the realization of the impermanence of all things, self-forgetfulness, meditation, and temperate, clean living. Its goal was the extinction of desire, a state which some held to be the cessation of personal existence.

As its founder taught it, Buddhism had neither temple nor worship. It did not reject the existence of the gods but it held that they, like men, were subject to change and for all practical purposes could be ignored. Buddhism began early to undergo great transformations which were in time to equip it with gods, temples, worship, and, in one of its two great branches, a belief in a future life of suffering or of joy. As it expanded geographically, in its northern territories it took a form that came to be known as Mahayana, or the Greater Vehicle, and in the south a form more like primitive Buddhism, which Mahayanists disparagingly dubbed Hinayana, or the Lesser Vehicle. Hinayana has as its ideal the *arahat,* or one who, having sought salvation for himself, has at last achieved it. Mahayana, on the other hand, glorified the *bodhisattva,* one who has undertaken to become a buddha for the sake not of his own salvation but that of the world, and who refuses to enter into Nirvana until every soul is freed from pain and sorrow.

Mahayana Buddhism developed in Northwest India and Central Asia. Since it was through Central Asia that the overland trade routes ran from the West to China, and since it was these, rather than the sea route to South China, that were most travelled during the Han dynasties and the times of their immediate successors, it was naturally the Greater Vehicle that made the deeper impression on China. Following the Han came four centuries when China was divided and when her culture was more in a state of flux than it had been since the earlier days of the Han. During these years the foreign faith firmly established itself and became one of the recognized factors in Chinese life. Naturally in the North it was still the Mahayana type that had full sway, and while the Lesser Vehicle made its contribution through the contacts of Southern India with the ports of South China, the Greater Vehicle remained dominant.

While Confucian scholars were never reconciled to Buddhism and Emperors sometimes persecuted it or strictly regulated it, it remained one of the chief faiths of the Chinese and has had a profound influence upon their life and religious outlook. Its time of greatest prosperity was just preceding and during the T'ang dynasty (618-907). In later days it lost some of its vitality, and although it still had many monastic communities, the life in these usually became decidedly formal. Meditation, where it existed, was as a rule a matter of ignorant routine. Few came into the monasteries in adult life or from a deep sense of religious or moral need, and the mass of the monks were recruited in childhood from the poorer classes and grew to manhood knowing little outside the cloister and with the haziest appreciation of the inner significance of the scriptures they chanted. Buddhism was, however, in many sections popular with the masses and often with the wealthy. The temples were many and there were sacred mountains, vows, and pilgrimages. The literature was extensive and much of it was for popular reading. The total effect of Buddhism was greatly to influence art and literature, to reënforce the native moral standards, to give to the masses some assurance of immortality and a conception of a future life of rewards and punishments, to provide objects of worship that awakened ardent devotion, and to introduce a philosophy that commanded the respect of many of the educated and that helped to mold philosophical thought.[29]

Still another foreign faith, Islam, has established itself in China. Mohammedans are to be found in nearly every province, but are especially numerous in the North and West. They are in large part, although by no means entirely, of foreign descent, and with some exceptions they attempt little or no direct missionary work. While not always easily distinguished in appearance from the non-Moslems, they have been and are a rather distinct and self-contained portion of the population. They have changed only slightly, if at all, the institutions and thought of China, but they have themselves been strongly influenced by their environment and in many respects have conformed to the life of the country.[30]

In addition to the underlying animism and to the recognized and widely spread religions that have so far been mentioned, there have been and are many minor religious sects and movements. Some of these are secret and some fairly public; some have been ephemeral and others have lasted, perhaps under different names, for centuries; some are for purely religious purposes and others have been organized for political ends and have been centers of sedition; some maintain a high moral tone, numbers prescribing for their membership asceticism in the mild form of vegetarianism or the more severe one of celibacy, and others demand but little ethical improvement; and a few are positively unwholesome. Members are usually from the lower classes, but some sects attract the educated and a few appeal almost exclusively to them. In many, perhaps most of the sects, Buddhist influences predominate, but in others Taoism has been potent. Confucian ethics have

---

[29] A full bibliography on Buddhism in China is outside the scope of this book. The following is suggested merely as introductory: R. F. Johnston, *Buddhist China*, New York, 1913; L. Hodous, *Buddhism and Buddhists in China;* J. Edkins, *Chinese Buddhism*, 2d edition, London, 1893; Legge, *A Record of Buddhistic Kingdoms, being an Account by the Chinese Monk Fa Hsien of his Travels in India and Ceylon (A.D. 399-414) in Search of the Buddhist Books of Discipline*, Oxford, 1886; Beal (translator), *Buddhist Records of the Western World*, 2 vols., London, 1906; Beal (translator), *The Life of Hiuen-Tsiang*, by the Shaman Hwui Li, new edition, London, 1911; Beal, *Buddhist Literature in China*, London, 1882; Beal, *A Catena of Buddhist Scriptures from the Chinese*, London, 1871; Wieger, *Bouddhisme chinois*, 2 vols., Shanghai, 1910, 1913; Wieger, *Moral Tenets and Customs in China*, Hokienfu, 1913; Reichelt, *Truth and Tradition in Chinese Buddhism*, Shanghai, 1927.

[30] Broomhall, *Islam in China;* de Thiersant, *La Mahometisme en Chine; The Christian Occupation of China*, pp. 353-358; d'Ollone et alii, *Mission d'Ollone, 1906-1909, Recherches sur les Musulmans chinois*.

entered into most of them to a greater or a lesser degree. Some sects have set out deliberately to combine the better elements of two or more religions. Because of the political activity of some, the government has usually been suspicious of all and occasionally has taken vigorous steps to suppress them. This has been particularly at the times when one of the sects has raised the standard of revolt and so has drawn to itself the attention of the authorities. While no single one has had any prolonged effect upon the life of the entire nation, taken together they have made an impression which is probably profound. They are indicative in part of the Chinese propensity to organize into groups, but they are also, and even more significantly, symptomatic of religious activity and hunger.[31]

The religious mind of China, then, during the period that the Christian missionary has had his most extensive contacts with it, has been the product of many movements, some of them indigenous, others from Central Asia, and some from India and Arabia. The man who would attempt dogmatic generalizations is either ignorant or foolhardy. However, out of all these contributions, native and foreign, there have emerged certain features which can probably, with proper reservations, be said to be characteristic. In the first place, the Chinese is usually tolerant on matters of religion. Persecutions have not been wanting, but of these the most ruthless and sanguinary have been instituted and conducted by the state either because a religious group had jeopardized the existing political order or because it was believed to have threatened the fundamental structure of society. Less frequently they have arisen because a particular sect was deemed to be immoral. The orthodox scholars of the Confucian school usually professed to regard other faiths as heretical and often led the state to frown upon them. Occasionally Buddhists or Taoists have induced a sympathetic Emperor to take action against their rivals.[32] On the pages of Chinese history, however, wars in which the religious element has entered as an important motive have been much less numerous than in the records of Mohammedanism or even of so-called Christian Europe. In practice the average Chinese is eclectic and without any sense of inconsistency is an

[31] de Groot, *Sectarianism and Religious Persecution in China*, passim; Hodous, in *The Christian Occupation of China*, pp. 29, 30.
[32] de Groot, *Sectarianism and Religious Persecution in China*, passim.

animist, a Confucianist, a Buddhist, and a Taoist. Any new religion coming to so numerous and so tolerant a people will inevitably find that its adherents from among them will tend to compromise with the older faiths. It will face the danger on the one hand of more or less complete absorption, and on the other of becoming a minority group cut off from the masses of the nation.

A second characteristic of Chinese religious life, and one related, perhaps, to its tolerance, is the persistence of beliefs that are usually associated with primitive peoples. The masses are convinced, as they were twenty-five hundred years ago, of the existence of myriads of spirits. Spirits are believed to be in trees, in rivers, ponds, and lakes, in hills, in houses, in timbers, in garments, and in many other natural objects. Some are held to assume the form of animals and even of men and women. Some are supposed to take up their abode at times in human beings and numberless incidents are similar to the stories of demon possession in the New Testament. At the doors of spirits are laid disease, many drownings, and a wide variety of accidents. There have not been lacking, indeed, those who hold that the dominant religion of the Chinese is neither Confucianism, Buddhism, or Taoism, but a kind of animism.[33] Certainly for the masses of the people spirits are an ever present fact. It is inevitable that many attempts should be made to expel the spirits and to ward them off. Charms and other devices for outwitting the ghostly world are legion,[34] and there are those who profess to be experts in their manipulation. The Taoist clergy are held to be particularly skillful and make their living in large part from demon exorcism.[35]

Closely allied to a belief in spirits is the conviction that there are lucky and unlucky days. Only the more daring or sceptical will embark on any important undertaking—marriage, or the burial of the dead, for example—without first determining whether the time is propitious. There is also an elaborate theory of wholesome and unwholesome sites, the so-called *feng shui,* or wind and water doctrine, by which the configuration of the land, including the presence or absence of bodies of water and the courses of the

---

[33] de Groot, *The Religion of the Chinese,* p. 3 et seq.
[34] See reproductions of many in Doré, *Researches into Chinese Superstitions,* passim.
[35] Ibid.

streams, is held to determine the peace and prosperity of the living and the dead. Graves, houses, and even cities must, according to this theory, be located by experts and with due regard for the influence of the surrounding landscape.[36]

Honors to ancestors have a large part in the lives of the Chinese and are intimately related to religion. More than in most countries the family is the outstanding social unit and tends to control and overshadow the individual. By the family is meant all the members of a clan, both the living and the dead. To a very large degree the individual has existed for the family. It is his duty to maintain the family reputation and to raise up sons to carry on the family name. The dead are to be honored by the virtuous lives of their descendants and by proper ceremonies. The great majority believe that the happiness of their progenitors depends upon the maintenance of the ancestral rites and that the dead can in part control the lot of the living. If, accordingly, burial has been improperly done or if ancestral rites have been neglected, the living will suffer, and, conversely, care in burial and faithfulness in continuing the observances for the dead make for the prosperity of the living. Hence funeral ceremonies are as elaborate as the family can afford, grave sites are carefully selected, tombs are scrupulously maintained, ancestral tablets are in the home and in halls built by the clan, and periodical offerings are made of food and of feasts. To some of the educated the honors to ancestors have been only a matter of propriety and custom, but to the masses and to many of the educated they have religious significance.[37]

It may be added that beliefs about life after death are very diverse. In Confucianism little is said about the future life: the Master, in fact, declined to discuss the question. "We do not know life," he said; "how then can we know death?" [38] Taoism speaks more of immortality, although originally as the achievement of the few rather than the privilege of the many. After the introduction of Buddhism it taught the existence of heaven and hell. In China Mahayana Buddhism has had little to say about the transmigration of souls, but it has talked much of a paradise and of a hell and it has profoundly influenced the thought of the

[36] Doré, *Researches into Chinese Superstitions;* de Groot, *The Religious System of China.*
[37] de Groot, *Religious System of China;* Doré, *Researches into Chinese Superstitions,* passim.
[38] *Analects,* 11, 11 (Soothill, *Analects,* p. 523).

nation. Seeing these conflicting teachings, the thoughtful Chinese cannot but be somewhat agnostic.

Not only are the Chinese tolerant and possessed of many animistic beliefs and practices, but they are also, in the third place, polytheists. Divinities are many, some of them of native origin and some the contributions of other peoples. They are often deified men. Some were, in the days of the Empire, honored by the state, either by the Emperor in person, by his deputies, or by provincial and local officials. For example, honors to Confucius and to the chief exponents of the Confucian school were paid by the state at regular intervals, and temples containing tablets to these worthies were maintained in government schools and in cities. Since Confucianism was, under the majority of monarchs in the Christian era, the state religion, and since that cult had grown out of the primitive life of China and tended to conserve many ancient beliefs and forms, it followed that the ceremonies frequently were attempted reproductions of those of early dynasties. There was a formally recognized hierarchy of "gods" which was in part a replica of the officialdom of the Empire. The Emperor could enter new names in the pantheon and could advance ones already there. Thus from time to time scholars were canonized and Confucius was promoted until in the early part of the twentieth century he was raised to the first rank and made the equal of Heaven and Earth.[39] In addition to the divinities of the state system, Buddhism and Taoism each had its own, Taoism often appropriating older native gods; and there were as well gods which were the property of no formal cult. The maintenance of temples and festivals was often a community affair in which all participated.

In the fourth place, in spite of the fact that the Chinese are both animists and polytheists, there is to be found, not only in their philosophies but in popular belief and in the practices of the Empire, a tendency toward theism. A persistent belief comes down from at least the Chou dynasty that an overruling, righteous, benevolent Providence exists. Definition may be vague or entirely lacking, but the belief is there. To some this Power may be the orderly process of nature and not at all personal, but the universe is held to be righteous and to make for the welfare of mankind. It was for the worship of *T'ien* that the stateliest of all the altars

[39] Soothill, *The Three Religions of China*, p. 34.

in the Empire was erected, and here at the capital, with imposing ceremony, the Emperor officiated in person.[40] Even here, however, ancestors and the spirits of the heavenly bodies shared in the honors.

Not only are the Chinese eclectic, not only are animism, polytheism, and a tendency toward theism all to be found in the land, but, in the fifth place, a strong ethical sense exists. Both Buddhism and Confucianism lay much emphasis on right conduct, and in this have joined some of the earliest Taoist writers and most of the philosophers whom Confucian scholars reckon heterodox. Ethics and religion are not divorced but are held to be closely interrelated. With all this respect for ethics, however, no such marked sense of sin against a personal Deity is found as in the writings of the greatest of the Hebrews and in the New Testament. A sense of guilt is not lacking, but there seems not to be the poignancy to it nor the joyous sense of release from it that one finds in Christian writings and experience. Moreover, many of the folklore stories connected with animism have much of the immoral and are undoubtedly debasing. From Confucius and other Chinese scholars has come, however, an insistence that ethics are the basis of all ordered human society, and Buddhism teaches that a man's conduct in this life helps to determine his fate after death. If, therefore, ethics lack the impulse of duty to and love for God, and are hampered by animism, they are not wanting in strong sanctions.

It is well to notice again that some of the early Taoist writings, nearly all the heretics of the Chou and of succeeding dynasties, and the Confucian scholars of all ages had this much in common: they were all interested in improving society. During at least part of their careers philosophers had usually been government officials and tended to look on the world through the eyes of those who are concerned with the welfare of the body politic and of existing civilization. They helped to create a frame of mind which tested systems of religion and ethics not so much by their absolute truth as by their social effects.

In the sixth place, the Chinese are not primarily a mystical people. Mystics some of them have been and are, and even for the vast majority the mystical is not without its appeal. The

---

[40] Williams, *Middle Kingdom*, Vol. 2, pp. 196, 197; Edkins, *Religion in China*, pp. 18-28. The imperial ancestors and the spirits of the heavenly bodies as well as *T'ien* and *Shang Ti* were honored at the same time.

mystical element is by no means as strong as it is in India, however, and there is lacking that union of exalted mysticism and passion for individual and social righteousness which is the outstanding characteristic of the greater Hebrew prophets and psalmists. Those who have done most to mold the thought of native Chinese religion have been primarily scholars and administrators, philosophers and men of affairs. Righteousness arises not from any compelling vision of God, but from a prudential regard for society, a sense of civic or family duty, a genuine concern for the welfare of the people as a whole, a desire for a life of bliss hereafter, or the wish to perfect one's own character.

In the last place, it is important to notice that the religions of China have been closely intertwined with the intellectual life and with the political and social institutions of the nation. Religion contained much of animism, but it had advanced far beyond primitive beliefs: some of the ablest minds that the race has known had devoted themselves to its development and interpretation. Confucianism especially was identified with scholarship, and was entrenched in the habits of thought, affections, and loyalties of the educated classes. Moreover, the state was committed to the existing faiths, especially to Confucianism. The Confucian classics were the basis of the education required of aspirants for civil office; many of the ceremonies associated with Confucianism were maintained at public expense; officials, including the Emperor himself, performed many of the duties usually assigned to a priesthood, and the very political theory on which the state rested derived much of its authority from Confucian teachings. Then, too, religion formed an integral part of village life. There were temples maintained by the village, and several of the festivals and processions in honor of particular divinities were community undertakings to which all were supposed to contribute. The guilds into which the industry and commerce of the country were organized usually had patron gods and religious features. Above all, the family, the strongest social unit in China, had as an integral part of its structure the honoring of ancestors by rites that were religious in origin and that for the vast majority retained a religious significance.

From what has been said it is obvious that any religion arriving for the first time in China would have no easy time in becoming established. It would find already in the field highly organized faiths with elaborate philosophies entrenched in the traditions and the institutions of the people. If it could meet a real need and if it could tolerate the presence of existing religions, ideas, and institutions, it might find a welcome. It would run the danger, however, of being absorbed and of losing its distinctive character- istics and even its identity. If, on the other hand, the new religion proved intolerant of native faiths and if its acceptance would involve any revolutionary changes in thought or in social, political, and economic institutions, its path would not be smooth. It would have to attack some of the outstanding features of the nation's life and thought and effect their destruction or transformation. This process would entail prolonged and extensive missionary work and even then might be unsuccessful unless other forces were to aid in the disintegration of the nation's life. Under the most favorable circumstances the conquest of China by a new faith would be the work of centuries and of thousands of earnest agents.

CHAPTER III

THE OUTSTANDING CHARACTERISTICS OF CHRISTIANITY AND THE BEARING OF THESE UPON THE POSSIBLE ACCEPTANCE OF CHRISTIANITY IN CHINA

WHAT are the outstanding characteristics of Christianity? To what extent are these in accord with existing religions and institutions in China? Has Christianity contributions for Chinese life which the older religions of the country have not been able to make and for which a need exists, either realized or unrealized? If it has these contributions, how important are they, and what changes will they probably work in the life of China? On the other hand, how far is Christianity antagonistic to existing beliefs and institutions, and what opposition may be expected? Under what conditions would it be likely to succeed? These are the questions which naturally arise as one turns from a study of the religious life of China to the history of the entrance of Christianity into that country. They may, too, be answered without passing judgment upon the validity of Christian beliefs.

It is apparent at the very start that many somewhat different descriptions of Christianity can be given, each of them true, for the faith has taken different forms in the course of its history. It is, however, possible to come at the question with some hope of a successful answer if one asks what Christianity was at its inception and then what it became in the various forms in which it entered China. Even with this method of approach the task is not easy, for it involves dealing with subjects which have long been controversial. He who would attempt a summary should do so with modesty and with the full realization of the danger of being guilty of serious omissions and of faulty generalizations.

The founder of Christianity arose out of a particular racial background and was heir to a national religious inheritance which was the accumulation of many generations of prophets, reformers, priests, and lawgivers, and of countless men and women, most of

25

them obscure, who had staked their all on their faith. This faith as he received it was, briefly, a belief in one God, who is the maker of heaven and earth. God could not be accurately represented by any physical image.[1]   He was often spoken of in anthropomorphic terms,[2] but in time the conception prevailed that God was so much greater than man that any attempt to portray him in the likeness of any visible being, even that of man, was hopelessly inadequate and hence should never be attempted.[3]   Yet, while God so far transcended man that he could not be represented by the human form, man was sufficiently akin to him to have fellowship with him and to find his greatest happiness and his highest duty in reverent, joyous love and devotion to him and to his will.[4] God, so many of the prophets said, took delight not in ritual, but in humility and in righteousness of life.[5]   This righteousness was not so much a formal ethical correctness as it was justice and mercy toward one's neighbor.

This conception of God had seemingly been developed by long, painful stages from a belief in a tribal or national divinity who protected his people against their rivals, who was jealous of his dignity, and who demanded bloody sacrifices and elaborate ceremonies.   With notable individual exceptions, the Jews as a people never succeeded in entirely emancipating their faith from these beliefs of their primitive days.

One effect of the work of Jesus was to make possible the freeing of the conceptions of God and of ethics from their nationalistic swaddling clothes and from their formalism and legalism.   He was at once the heir and the fulfiller of the prophetic desire; he accomplished that for which the noblest and most discerning of his race had been striving.   He did more than this, however.   By his words and his life he so interpreted and transmitted the best in the older faith that he made of it something new, a "good news" of great joy and peace.   Many, perhaps most, of the details of his teaching can be paralleled in the older writings of his race, but he so gave to the whole the stamp of a creative spirit as to make of it something different.   He talked of God not in terms of abstract monotheism, but as a powerful and loving father who was con-

---

[1] Exodus 20:4.
[2] Genesis 3:8; Exodus 33:18-23.
[3] Isaiah 40:18-31.
[4] Deuteronomy 6:5.
[5] Micah 6:6-8; Isaiah 1:11-17; Amos 5:21-24.

stantly active in the world, interested in everything both small and great—clothing the lily of the field, feeding the birds, causing the sun to rise, and sending the rain.[6]   God was to him morally perfect and worthy of the unreserved affection of men.[7]   He was not only forgiving and merciful, but he was constantly seeking to save even the humblest from waywardness, maladjustment, and sin.[8] He loved each man and woman, and all could find their highest joy in fellowship with him.   Man could trust God implicitly and could find in that trust freedom from anxiety.   This conviction about God was the keynote to Jesus' life.   To him, God transcended national boundaries.   Ceremony, too, was unessential, although Jesus participated in the simple services of the synagogue and never attacked directly the ornate ritual of the temple at Jerusalem: he seemingly, indeed, found ritual helpful.   Men could, however, come into intimate contact with God without the mediation of priest or the formality of sacrifices: when they prayed they were to enter into their closets and in the privacy of individual communion find God.   If they maintained a forgiving spirit toward those about them they could be sure of God's forgiveness, and the vision of God was possible to all who were pure in heart.[9]   This confidence in God gave to Jesus a power which in turn awoke faith in many of those whom he touched and led to healing in body and mind and to freedom from fear and from sin.[10]

Along with this belief in God there went naturally, so Jesus believed, certain convictions about the proper attitude of man to man.   Man was to have toward his neighbor active good-will— "love."   Since God forgave him so freely, each was to bear toward those who sinned against him an unfailing spirit of forgiveness [11] and was to be kind to the evil as well as to the good.[12]   Man should never hold his fellows in contempt, no matter how humble they might be.[13]   Jesus picked as an ideal example of one who had illustrated in action the law of love to his neighbor a nameless member of a race despised by the Jews, thus transcending racial

[6] Matthew 5 and 6.
[7] Luke 10:27.
[8] Luke 15.
[9] Matthew 5:8.
[10] See in the Gospels the accounts of Jesus' acts of physical healing, as, for example, Matthew 8:1-5, 16; and also of his moral healing, as Luke 7:36-50.
[11] Matthew 18:21-35.
[12] Luke 6:35.
[13] Matthew 18:10.

barriers. True greatness, he held, was disclosed in humble service: a man was to find his life in forgetting it. He placed the greatest value upon human personality: the outcast and the poor found with him as great a welcome as did the respectable and wealthy.[14] He reserved his anger only for the smug, the self-righteous, those who permitted formalism in law and institutions to displace mercy and justice, and those who preyed on their fellows. Prosperity might be a handicap and riches were a danger to a man's highest welfare.[15] Division of effort between a search for material prosperity and fellowship with God was impossible.[16] Man could not make both his chief goal. Ethics become not a matter of categorical commands, but an attitude of life.

Out of this active belief in God who is constantly working in the universe and who can be trusted and loved and out of this conviction that man's proper relationship to his fellows is active good-will, there naturally arose a conception of human society. The words, "the Kingdom of God," were often on Jesus' lips. The phrase was current among the Jews of his time, and, like many other popular slogans, often lacked clear definition and was given various meanings. In general it embodied the nationalistic hopes of "Israel" and meant independence from Rome and possibly dominion over neighboring peoples and even over all mankind. Many were expecting the attainment of this goal by a cataclysmic act of God. This popular phrase Jesus took over and gave a new meaning. He, like many of his contemporaries, believed "the Kingdom of God" to be "at hand," [17] but to his mind it was not coming suddenly as a visible state.[18] It was rather being achieved by the inward transformation of the lives of men.[19] He felt it would have fully come when all men did the will of God and he believed that men should give themselves unreservedly to the attainment of this goal.[20] Although this change worked from within and was to come about by the commitment to God of individual lives, it nevertheless inevitably followed that if enough lives were altered a new kind of social order would result. If God were the kind of being that Jesus conceived him to be and if

[14] Mark 2:15-17.
[15] Mark 10:23.
[16] Matthew 6:24.
[17] Mark 1:15; Luke 10:9, 11.
[18] Luke 17:20, 21.
[19] Ibid.; Luke 13:18-21.
[20] Matthew 6:10, 33.

enough men gave themselves to doing his will, there would be a transformation of human society. Jesus did not describe this in detail, but it is clear what would follow if his teachings were universally practiced. Injustice of all kinds, slavery, war, the exploitation of the weak by the strong, the strife for power, whether political or economic, would cease, and men would give themselves entirely to active, friendly coöperation in solving their common problems. In such a society poverty would at least be reduced and would probably be eliminated, and appreciation of all that is beautiful in human relations, in the human spirit, and in animate and inanimate nature would develop to the full and there would be a confidence in the universe that would lead to fearless investigation and to the utilization of all the forces of nature for the welfare of man. Art in its many forms, literature, and music would all come to flower, and honest scientific investigation would proceed and would not only enlarge man's horizon but, in its application to his physical needs, prove an unalloyed benefit. So far as we have records, of course, Jesus neither prophesied nor described all of these results, but they would logically appear if his teachings were followed.

Jesus seemingly gave no thought to the particular institutional molds that the ideal human society would take. Whether deliberate or not, this omission was fortunate, for organizations must change with the needs of different lands and centuries, and political, ecclesiastical, and economic machinery adapted to one age would have proved an incubus to succeeding generations. It is not clear—and is still a matter of debate—whether he believed that "the Kingdom of Heaven" would completely arrive by gradual transition or by cataclysm. Apparently he held that it was to be by a combination of both.[21] Whatever he expected the process to be, he felt no doubt about the ultimate realization of his vision. That confidence, indeed, was inevitable if he were loyal to his belief in God.

Jesus' conceptions of God and of man being what they were, an assurance of personal immortality almost inevitably followed. Jesus apparently spoke but very little about this and then usually —and necessarily—in figurative language.[22] That he held it is, however, certain.

[21] Matthew 13:24-33.
[22] Luke 16:19-31; 20:27-38.

Quite as important as Jesus' words was the man himself. He was so much the embodiment of what he spoke that he and his teachings could never be divorced but together made their impression, and that as a single whole, upon his contemporaries. What he preached, he lived. He taught as he did because he had first felt in his own life the certainty of what he spoke. This, at least, was the conviction of his followers of his own generation.[23] This integrity of life and teaching eventually cost him his life.

In the two generations that immediately succeeded Jesus the stream of religious experience that flowed through him took on certain characteristics that were to leave their indelible impress upon Christianity. Within a few weeks after his death there occurred momentous changes in the lives of his immediate followers. In the first place, they were persuaded that Jesus was alive and that they had seen him and talked with him. They became convinced, moreover, that he was still profoundly interested in his followers and could work and pray more effectively with them and for them than in the days of his flesh.

In the next place, the disciples found themselves in possession of a strange power that they had not known before, a power that they also observed to be acting in those who came in touch with their message. This power was sometimes associated with peculiar nervous manifestations.[24] Often in the strength of it men were enabled to make others whole physically in a way that reminded them of Jesus' acts of healing.[25] The greatest of the early Christian leaders valued it, however, chiefly because it led to revolutionary transformation in character. It freed men from enslaving and debasing sins and from debilitating inner conflict. It removed fear and gave men a new attitude of joyous confidence in God. It led men to forgive and to love each other and so lifted them out of themselves as to make of them transformed and ennobled "new creations." [26]

In the third place, there came confidence in the immortality of those who had shared in this transformation. As they had known the beginnings of the kind of life that Jesus lived, so it was believed that for them, like him, physical death was only the entrance into a richer personal development. Life beyond the

---

[23] Acts 10:37, 38.
[24] I Corinthians 14:1-28.
[25] I Corinthians 12:9.
[26] I Corinthians 13:1-13; Galatians 5:22, 23.

grave was not, so the early Christians held, a shadowy existence, nor one of sensual and selfish enjoyment, but for those who had begun the Christian experience it was continuous growth into the likeness of Jesus.[27] These convictions naturally brought with them great joy and those who entered most fully into them had a sense of discovery that could not be put into words.

In the fourth place, these experiences resulted in an altered conception of God. The early Christians naturally inherited the Jewish ideas of God. By the teachings and the life, death, and resurrection of Jesus they were now led to a belief about God which had in it much of the old but also much that was new. God was for them still the creator and the source of the moral law, but he was also a loving father who was seeking to transform men morally and spiritually. They felt that God was like Jesus, that they had seen God in the face of Jesus,[28] and that God had spoken through him as he had through no other.[29] They believed, too, that the strange new power which had wrought a revolution in their lives came from God and that it was actually God's spirit at work in men's hearts.

In the fifth place, they held that these new experiences of theirs were intimately associated with the death of Jesus and they saw in the cross the special work of God, God's way of "reconciling the world unto himself." The cross was the central point in their teaching,[30] and when they came to recount the story of Jesus' life it was to the events associated with the crucifixion that they gave their major attention.

From what has been said it is apparent, in the sixth place, that the early Christians held an exalted idea of Jesus. They saw in him the expected deliverer of the Jewish race, God's special messenger and representative, the Christ. They held that to him all the history of the nation pointed and that his coming, his life, death, and resurrection were foretold in the sacred writings of the Jews. Jesus was saviour and lord; he represented the eternal purpose of God;[31] he was the image of God.[32] The enthusiasms and experiences that led to this conviction were so fresh and so vivid that they precluded cool definition, but, whatever they

[27] Romans 8:15-17, 29, 38, 39.
[28] II Corinthians 4:6.
[29] Ibid.; Hebrews 1:1, 2; John 1:17; Acts 4:12.
[30] I Corinthians 1:23, 2:2; Hebrews 2:9, 10 and passim.
[31] Revelation 8:13; John 1:1; I Corinthians 2:7.
[32] Philippians 2:6.

believed about his exact relation to God, the early Christians agreed that Jesus was the center of their faith. It was not so much for his teachings that they revered him, although they preserved and treasured these, but it was Jesus himself and all that he was and did that they remembered and valued. It was not a system of ethics or of theology that had won them, but a person.

In the last place, this early Christianity quickly ceased to be purely Jewish and became a universal religion. It made its appeal to all races and classes. Christians discovered that the great experience that was theirs could be shared by all. Men did not need first to become Jews. The elaborate ritual and sacrifices of the older religion and the attendant priesthood had become unnecessary: more than that, they were now a hindrance. Jesus, so they felt, had made direct access to God possible without the mediation of man. He was the only priest that was needed.[33] The Jewish scriptures were preserved, but the legalistic ethics, the ceremonial worship, and the nationalism they contained were discarded or were held to be superseded.[34] The Gospel was not a statutory religion but a message of life based upon God's love for man. This freedom from law was not, however, to those who really understood the Gospel, an excuse for a lower plane of morality but an incentive to a higher type of life, the doing of righteousness not because of commandment but of love.

As Christianity spread through the ancient world it was inevitably altered. Since it was primarily an inner, personal experience resulting in profound moral and spiritual changes it could not be inherited and it could easily be misunderstood. The children of Christians might more easily come into it than those who had had non-Christian parents, but they often preserved the name and such forms as existed and failed to enter into the life that had given rise to them. Moreover, as large numbers joined the Christian fellowship, many partially or completely missed what Jesus and the leaders among the early Christians had held to be central. The process of misunderstanding began even during Jesus' lifetime and was accentuated as the years passed, especially when, as from the fourth century on, whole districts came into the Church en masse.

The society, or Church, which arose out of the Christian fellow-

[33] Hebrews, passim.
[34] Ibid. and Galatians and Romans, passim.

ship was profoundly influenced by its environment. To what extent the ensuing development was true to type is a matter of dispute. Many scholars—Protestants—hold that under the influence of Greek philosophy the Gospel was partially intellectualized and a theology developed. The Church conquered polytheism, but the place it gave the saints showed that the old system had not been completely displaced. The Church supplanted the mystery religions that were so popular in the world into which it came, but it took over some of their ideas and practices. Out of the simple rites of baptism and the Lord's supper, it made sacraments that had much of magic. An elaborate ecclesiastical organization grew up which in part paralleled the bureaucracy of the Roman Empire. Salvation for the world to come was regarded as the chief aim of the Church and was held to be achieved quite as much by assent to intellectual formulæ and by correct performance of ritual as by a life of holiness and faith. Monasticism arose and two standards of living were maintained, the one for the ordinary man, and the other, which was conceived of as higher, for the priest, the monk, and the nun. Christianity had, in other words, departed in many respects from the ideals of Jesus and held as important some ideas and practices against which he had vehemently protested. The process of adjustment was, however, so gradual as to be largely unconscious. The Church had, moreover, refused to compromise completely. It still preserved the writings of its first centuries and through them and through its teachings many men and women were entering into the life that Jesus held to be of supreme value.[35]

Out of this Church of the Græco-Roman world many separate bodies arose. Some of these have never touched China and so do not require our attention. The special characteristics of those that reached the Middle Kingdom, however, affected, obviously, both the success of the Christian message and the form which that message took. Three of these bodies, the Nestorian, the Russian Orthodox, and the Roman Catholic Churches, grew directly out of the Church of the Græco-Roman world and retained, in general, most of its main features. Like it, they made

---

[35] On the other hand, Roman Catholic scholars, and not a few Protestants, hold that Catholicism is present in germ in the New Testament, and that the Pauline Epistles and the Fourth Gospel show a definite sacramentalism existing from the beginning. Between these two positions are many intermediate ones. This entire question is, of course, extremely controversial.

much of the sacraments and of ritual. They had a priesthood and a hierarchy in whose hands were the administration of the sacraments and the organization of the Church. They possessed intellectual formulations of the faith and insisted upon the importance of assent to these. Each had monasticism and accordingly tended to hold that the highest type of Christian living could be entered upon only by those who had completely "renounced the world" through poverty, celibacy, meditation, and prayer. The chief purpose of the Church was usually conceived as being the salvation of individual men, and by salvation was chiefly meant a future life of bliss. In each of these churches were individuals, often many of them, who caught something of the meaning of Jesus and knew the joy and the moral and spiritual power of the early Christians. For the masses, moreover, membership in the Church undoubtedly meant a higher religious and moral life than their non-Christian forefathers had known. Much, however, in the accepted beliefs and practices of these bodies was utterly alien to what Jesus had taught.

Nestorianism had its stronghold in the Tigris-Euphrates Valley. Its official head, the Patriarch or Catholicos, claimed independence of all foreign ecclesiastical authorities and had his headquarters first at Seleucis-Ctesiphon and then at Bagdad. Its official formulations of belief were independent of the contemporary Hellenic creeds and were held by both Greek and Roman churches to be heretical. It spread eastward, as we shall see later, into Persia, India, and Central and Eastern Asia.[36]

The Russian Orthodox Church was the result of the missionary labors of the Greek or Orthodox Church and derived its creeds and organization from it. The Orthodox Church had developed in the Greek-speaking section of the Roman Empire and had its most prosperous years under the Eastern or Byzantine Emperors. It emphasized the creeds, believing that correct doctrine was essential to salvation. The Russians also made much of ritual and held closely to the forms in which this had come down to them. The Church was usually dependent upon and controlled by the state and acted in close conjunction with it. We shall see later how it entered China first in the closest alliance with, and indeed as an organ of, the Russian Government.

---

[36] Labourt, *Le Christianisme dans l'empire perse sous la dynastie sassanide,* passim.

The Roman Catholic Church was primarily that of the western or Latin-speaking section of the Roman Empire. The Bishop of Rome was naturally its head and he also, quite as naturally, claimed primacy in the entire Christian Church. This claim was not usually granted by the bodies in the eastern parts of the Empire, but in the West after the collapse of the imperial authority the Roman Pontiff took on civil as well as ecclesiastical duties and acquired a power greater than that enjoyed by the head of any other church. Partly under his leadership the barbarians of Western and Northwestern Europe were won to the Christian faith, and the Church, with him as its center, was their tutor in civilization. The Western Church perpetuated many of the features of the Roman Empire. Latin was its language, it claimed independence of and at times authority over secular governments, and over its hierarchy the Pope exercised the sway of an all but absolute monarch.[37] In addition to the creeds, the sacraments, the ritual, and the monasticism that it inherited from the Church of the Græco-Roman world, it developed, as was natural to the heir of the Roman tradition, an elaborate body of law. Thanks in part to Augustine, whose remarkable and deep religious conversion was a return to that of some of the greatest early Christians and whose writings profoundly influenced succeeding generations, the Roman Church has had a succession of those who have entered into the experience of the early disciples. The proportion of these to the total membership has possibly been greater than in any of the Eastern communions. Whatever its source, the Roman Catholic Church has possessed a vitality which has helped it to spread its message more widely than any faith or religious body the world has ever known.

Out of the Roman Church there arose, in the sixteenth century, the Protestant movement. Protestantism was in part the result of political causes and tended to develop into national churches. It was, moreover, in part the product of economic and intellectual forces. It was, however, primarily a religious movement, an attempt to return to the religious experiences of the first century of Christians, to find once more the secret of inward peace and of moral and spiritual power that the greatest of these had known. In its essence it laid chief emphasis upon this direct, personal,

[37] Papal absolutism, of course, did not develop quickly and was often contested by the civil authorities—the Holy Roman Emperor, kings, and the like—and by ecclesiastical officials. Even to-day in practice the Pope is not absolute.

transforming experience of God as found in and through Jesus. Hence Protestantism tended to abolish sacraments, formalism in worship, the priesthood, the elaborate hierarchy, and dependence on any other authority than the inwardly heard voice of the Spirit. The revolution was not always complete: most Protestants retained much that they had inherited from the older church. They usually preserved some of the sacraments in a modified form; most of them held either to the old creeds or formulated new and elaborate ones or did both; many of them preserved the liturgy and the ecclesiastical organization of the Roman Church in a more or less altered form. Many, indeed most of them, feared to rely entirely upon the inner experience of the individual Christian and sought authority in an infallible Bible. The more radical, however, rejected all sacraments—although they usually retained baptism and the Lord's Supper as symbolic and commemorative—abandoned all inherited ritual, developed new types of Christian bodies, democratically governed, and, while formulating statements of faith, held that adherence to these was not essential to salvation. From its very nature, Protestantism tended to develop many mutually independent groups and these at times were intolerant of each other. Only gradually did coöperation develop, and then never completely. With its flexibility and its insistence on the type of personal transformation that was found by the early disciples, Protestantism has from time to time passed through great emotional and moral reawakenings. As we shall see, Protestantism has been increasingly missionary and since most of the leading commercial powers of the last hundred and fifty years have been predominantly of that faith, it has sent its representatives to all continents.

This, then, is Christianity as it was as its beginning and as it has since developed. The summary is, obviously, greatly condensed. It may prove sufficient as an introduction, however, and as a basis for the answer to the questions propounded at the beginning of this chapter. To these we must now turn.

To what extent is Christianity like the religions that have been longer in China? In the first place, it is apparent that it has much in common with them. Christianity, like Buddhism and Confucianism, lays much emphasis upon ethics. It can appeal to the Chinese as "teaching men to do good" and hence as, in general, in accord with their own highest ideals. Christians, moreover, stress many of the virtues held important by the Buddha and Confucius. All have worked for a perfected individual. Then, too, Jesus' teaching about the Kingdom of God contains much that seems like the Confucian concern for an ideal social order. Confucius and his school, it will be recalled, have been interested in saving society—in building a perfect civilization. The Chinese have believed that social welfare must have its basis in ethics. They have held, too, that the ideal man will give himself in large part to the service of his fellow men. Much is found in Jesus' words which reminds them of this and which they naturally interpret as being congenial to their own ideals. Moreover, the idea of God has not been entirely alien to the Chinese and words and expressions are in existence which have some kinship with what the Christian means by God. Both Taoism and Confucianism have taught that the dominant forces in nature are moral, trustworthy, and benevolent. This, of course, is in accord with a fundamental Christian conviction. The idea of vicarious suffering and of salvation by faith in the one who has so suffered is to be found in both Mahayana Buddhism and Christianity. Buddhism, to a less extent Taoism, and to a still smaller extent Confucianism, speak, as does Christianity, of a life beyond the grave. Some sects of Buddhism, indeed, emphasize it. Moreover, much that is distinctive of the Nestorian, Russian Orthodox, and Roman Catholic Churches bears a striking resemblance to Mahayana Buddhism. All have monastic communities with attendant ascetic ideals. All have elaborate rituals. Christian saints have a likeness to bodhisattvas. To the Chinese these three churches do not come, then, as entirely strange. There is even the danger that because of the resemblances the Chinese may identify the ideas derived from Buddhism with the apparently similar but really different teachings of the Church.

In the next place, while Christianity contains much that is similar to the religions that have been longer in China, the likenesses are in no case complete identities. Confucian and Buddhist differ from Christian ethics in important respects. Jesus based his ethics, if a word which implies rules and system can be applied to his sayings about man's moral life, primarily upon the love of God. Man was to love his enemies because God was kind to both the evil and the good. Men were always to forgive each other because God forgives them. This, of course, was not like anything in Confucianism. Although the greatest and most influential thinkers of the Confucian school were convinced that the dominant force in the world was moral, they cherished no affection for God and did not conceive of him as loving individual men. Moreover, although Confucius believed in good-will, he would limit its operation, largely according to the class distinctions of the society with which he was familiar. He would not have men return good for evil. It is significant, too, that while Jesus said, "All things whatsoever ye would that men should do to you do ye even so to them," [38] Confucius said, "What you yourself do not wish, do not do to others." [39] The negative form is by no means as inclusive, nor does it call forth activity, as does the positive form: the one merely restrains from action, the other encourages it. Buddhism gives as the motive for conduct not love for God but the desire for one's own salvation. Now while to many Christians and to many Buddhists "salvation" chiefly connotes a future life of bliss, in the beginning it was not so. The Buddha's idea of salvation was the achievement of inward peace by the elimination of all that bound the individual together, including this very desire for immortality, while for Jesus salvation was the enrichment of individual personality, a more abundant individual life, through right relations to God and to one's fellows.

Buddhism has little to say of a new social order, for if all adopted its highest ideal and became celibates human society would come to an end in a generation. The Confucian goal for society did not involve a complete revolution. Neither Confucius nor his orthodox successors dreamed of any other type of government than a monarchy, or of a society without inequalities between classes and sexes. With his love for old institutions and customs, Confucius cramped the free development of civilization and hindered the removal of some long-standing injustices. His emphasis upon morality and public service has had an immeasurable influence for good, but he identified the ideal society with the perfect operation of a particular set of institutions. On the other hand, Jesus was not much interested in institutions, although he was respectful to the past and was no violent revolutionary: he believed it to be of primary importance that men

[38] Matthew 7:12.
[39] Analects, 12:2 (Soothill, *Analects*, p. 561).

should do the will of God. This latter, he held, was to love God and one's neighbor. If his teachings were followed, the result would be, as we have seen, a society in which all institutions would gradually conform to this ideal and would be valued only in so far as they promoted it. There was, too, in Jesus' teaching and way of life more of a passion for the oppressed than one finds in Confucius, more of a love that never fails, no matter how unworthy of affection the object might seem to be. Since Confucius and most of the leaders in his school were officials, they tended to think of services to their fellows as performed through the agency of a benevolent bureaucracy. For Jesus, however, love to one's neighbor was largely a personal matter and was not to be cramped by any institutional expression.

Even more different was the Christian conception of God. Mahayana Buddhism at times seemed about to develop such an idea, but the founder of Buddhism believed that gods, like men, were impermanent and could be of little or no assistance in man's search for salvation. Chinese Buddhism as popularly practiced tends toward polytheism rather than toward monotheism. Confucianism, moreover, contains much of polytheism and animism and such suggestions of theism as exist incline to be intellectualized to the exclusion of all warm sense of loving dependence. The early Christian conception of God was, however, as we have seen, of one who is constantly at work in the universe, righteous, loving each individual and seeking to win even the lowest to a right life and fellowship with him, caring for men more than a human father cares for his children, striving to make himself known to men and finally revealing himself in Jesus. God's love was believed to be seen at its best in the cross. In practice, animism and polytheism have at times crept into Christianity, but even those churches that have departed furthest from Jesus have never permitted his conception of God to be entirely obscured.

Not only does Christianity differ in part from the existing religions of China on the points where it seems to resemble them, but it has some features which are not to be found in the other faiths, or which, if they exist, do so only in rudimentary form. Most of these have already been hinted at. The Christian assurance of a God who at once sustains and pervades the universe and yet has shown his love for men in the suffering of Jesus on the cross, who is active in the orderly processes of nature and yet is portrayed by the life of Jesus, of a God with whom man can have fellowship, a fellowship that ennobles man and enriches life far beyond the most daring imagination—all this has been only in part paralleled in the other faiths known widely to the Chinese. Islam, which most nearly approaches it, has no conception quite like it and, besides, has had little effect upon the Chinese. Christians claim that there is in this conviction a moral dynamic and an incentive for noble living which are lacking in Confucianism.

Christianity is, moreover, so its adherents believe, supremely rich in the person of Jesus. Here is a figure of unquestionable historicity who exemplified all that he taught. In his conception of and sense of fellowship with God, in his complete dedication to the will of God, in his love for men, in his keen and delicate appreciation of all that is beautiful in men and in the world of nature, in his ideal for men, and in his power to heal and transform men, Christians feel that they have the unequalled and unsurpassable flower of the race. However much non-Christians may believe this estimate to be too enthusiastic, the fact remains that historically Jesus has been and is the central figure in Christianity and that the peculiar qualities of his life have indelibly molded it.

These, then, are the outstanding features of Christianity, the points in which it resembles the faiths that have been longer in China and the ways in which it differs from them. If the estimate that has just been made is correct, it is obvious that any extensive adoption of Christianity as it existed in the lives of the best of the early Christians and as it has been exemplified by the noblest of Christians since would work some very profound changes. It would give a more effective moral dynamic than China has yet known. It would enrich human life with its conception of God. It would result in a more definite view of personal immortality and by so much as it did that it would alter life here and now. It would bring about greater flexibility in the political, social, and economic structure of the nation and would promote the realization of a society in which all—men, women, and children—would have equal and full opportunities for the best that life has to offer and would live together in mutual and active good-will. It would stimulate intellectual activity and daring and all that is fine in art. The process would, of course, be slow and it might never be completed. Its progress would be conditioned by many factors—the attitude of the Chinese, the character and number of the representatives of the Christian faith, their zeal, their understanding or lack of understanding of the message and life of Jesus, the circumstances under which the faith had come to China, and a hundred and one other factors—but if at all extensive it would work profound changes, changes which would be of extreme importance to China and to the rest of the world.

It is obvious, however, that Christianity would not be without opposition in China. In the first place, it would have to meet religious systems that are entrenched in the institutions of the Chinese. Ancestor worship, for example, goes back to the earliest historic times and is intimately bound up with the most important social institution of China, the family. To attack it, or even to seek to modify it, would mean at least the partial recasting of the family, and this would be condemned as revolutionary, impious, and subversive to morals. The family, too, is the strongest agent for social control and any serious attack on it would be met by the prohibition of the state. Christianity could justify itself only if it could show that its adoption would lead to a richer family life and to a higher level of personal and civic morality. Moreover, certain religious ceremonies have been carried on by the state, and officials have been required to participate in or to officiate at them. These ceremonies include sacrifices to various spirits, divinities, and gods, among them Confucius. Failure to take part in these ceremonies would be regarded as a very serious matter, for neglect would earn the ill-will of the unseen powers upon whose coöperation the welfare of the community has been held to depend and so would bring disaster upon the people. Christianity could scarcely be true to its founder and tolerate either animism or polytheism: it would either have to be false to itself and compromise or run counter to deeply seated popular convictions and the opposition of the state. The Chinese state might well feel that to preserve its own existence it would have to exterminate the alien faith.

Not only would Christianity run counter to much in the existing family and state, but it would find itself accused of breaking up the life of the village and the city. Many religious festivals have been community undertakings, supported by popular subscriptions which are virtually obligatory. To refuse to contribute to these would be regarded as dereliction to civic duty and would be visited with public opprobrium. The merchant who declined to pay dues for the support of ceremonies connected with the older faiths would, moreover, be relieved of no little expense and so would be held to be taking an unfair advantage of his competitors. Since, too, the guilds had religious features, Christianity would find itself criticizing the prevailing organization of industry and commerce. Then the demand that the Christian observe the Sabbath was a handicap, for it meant monetary loss to the convert, who was living in a society which did not recognize the day.

In the next place, Christianity would meet opposition which arises from the fact that it is foreign. The Chinese have had a great pride in their own culture and a contempt for everything alien. This is not an exclusively Chinese trait: in any country to obtain condemnation for an idea or an institution it is frequently sufficient to say that it is of foreign origin—that it is un-American, for example. This is particularly true, however, where, as in China, a people has been isolated geographically from other advanced cultures and has itself been the source of most of the civilization of its immediate neighbors. Except for Buddhism and its attendant ideas and art, until the close of the nineteenth century the Chinese had not been aware of receiving any important cultural contributions from abroad. They had, on the other hand, given of their culture to all the peoples of the Far East. Christianity, then, would be confronted with all of the natural Chinese contempt for everything alien.

In the fourth place, Christianity would have to meet well organized religious systems and philosophies. Animism usually offers but a relatively feeble resistance to more mature religious faiths and if Christianity were confronted only by that its triumph would be comparatively easy. Taoism, as it was in later centuries, would prove a comparatively nerveless opponent. In China, however, Christianity would have also to face Confucianism and Buddhism, both of them highly developed and reënforced by elaborate philosophies. Both schools were, too, supported by an educated leadership whose place in society would be destroyed if the new faith were to triumph. The state rested largely upon the Confucian theory and Confucian scholars were its officials; communities of Buddhist monks dotted the land and depended for their support on the piety of the laity. Of these two groups the officials would offer the more effective opposition, but the Buddhists were not rivals to be despised.

In meeting this opposition Christianity might find its triumph delayed by its own intolerance. If it is to be consistent Christianity cannot compromise with other faiths. Individual Christians, if they have caught the spirit of Jesus, will never persecute their fellows, no matter how much they may differ from them, but for themselves they cannot be true to their faith and join in any worship of spirits or gods, nor will they, if they have found Christ's secret of life, accept the Buddhist or Taoist philosophy or the Confucian system. They can find much in all three that will enrich their lives, but they cannot be adherents of them. As has been pointed out, the older faiths of China have usually, with the exception of Islam, been fairly tolerant of each other. The bulk of the population is attached to all three with no sense of inconsistency. Christianity would naturally have a harder time than if it could make its peace with the older religions. The traditional easy-going eclecticism of the Chinese, too, would bring the danger that Christian converts would part lightly with the distinctive features of their new faith.

In most of its forms, moreover, Christianity has become more or less inflexible. In its development among various peoples and in various ages it has become set into distinct molds of doctrine, ritual, and organization. Missionaries naturally propagate their faith in the form in which they have received it, and as this is dear to them and has often become identified in their own minds with their Christian experience, they tend to feel that only thus can it be transmitted and received. Often, too, they have no choice in the matter, but are controlled by ecclesiastical authorities outside China who conscientiously insist upon the maintenance of the traditional system. This inflexibility is a serious and unnecessary handicap for it insists upon more of a dislocation of the older culture than is essential to an entrance into the Christian experience. It burdens Christianity with an enormous amount of baggage that is Græco-Roman, Russian, British, German, or American, and of which it must sometime rid itself if it is ever to be at home in China. This inflexibility is by no means the exclusive possession of any one church. At first sight it would seem to be more characteristic of Roman Catholic and Russian Orthodox missions, but most Protestant communions have in practice been almost as unyielding. However, since Protestantism has tended to hold that the inner witness and not an infallible church or an inerrant book must be the final authority, it will probably prove more elastic than the other branches of the Church. Its tendency, too, to form itself into national churches will very possibly be of assistance in helping the Chinese to make the Christian message their own.

Christianity as it has come to China, moreover, has suffered from schism. Nestorians, Roman Catholics, Russian Orthodox, and Protestants have shown little friendliness and much suspicion for each other, and the sects of Protestants are continually increasing in number. It has been a much divided witness that the Church has given the Chinese.

Since Christianity necessarily runs counter to so much that is an integral part of Chinese culture and, if its inward spirit is caught and its essential experience shared by many of the Chinese, would largely reshape that culture; since, moreover, it has become identified with certain ecclesiastical and doctrinal systems that are alien to Chinese experience, it is obvious that in China it can have no easily won triumph. It can succeed only by bringing enough forces to bear and for a sufficient period to work a revolution. This necessitates, under the most favorable circumstances, the presence of thousands of earnest representatives of the Christian faith scattered over the entire country and working for centuries. The nominal conversion of the Roman Empire was carried on from within and involved winning a much smaller population than that of China, and yet required over three hundred years. The decidedly superficial conversion of the peoples of Northern Europe was achieved by missionaries who had all the prestige of a superior civilization and who were often backed by the authority of the state, and yet was accomplished only in about a thousand years. It would be an experience utterly new in human history if the Chinese race were to be won even to a nominal acceptance of the Christian faith either quickly or easily. The progress of Christianity would be greatly hastened if China should be brought into intimate contact with peoples who are professedly Christian and it would be still further hastened if that contact were to bring about any general disintegration of Chinese culture. Christianity would then come with a certain amount of prestige and would find less solid opposition from existing institutions. If this situation should arise, Christianity would be handicapped by the inconsistencies of the nations who professed it, but it would have a great opportunity to bring its essential message to China and to influence the reshaping of Chinese civilization. In other words, should such a condition ever confront Christianity, it would face one of the greatest opportunities and challenges of its history.

CHAPTER IV

CHRISTIANITY IN CHINA BEFORE THE MONGOL DYNASTY

THE first entrance of Christianity into China was from the easternmost outposts of the Church. In Mesopotamia, Persia, Central Asia, and the northwestern confines of India, Christian communities early became numerous. However, the new religion completely supplanted its rivals in relatively few places and was usually the faith of the minority. Christians were often under political disabilities and were frequently persecuted.

Not much is known of the initial stages of the spread of the Faith into the Tigris-Euphrates Valley and eastward. By the close of the first century the Jewish-dominated city, Arbel, east of the Tigris, was the seat of a bishop.[1] It is clear that Edessa, the present Urfa, in Northwestern Mesopotamia, was early a Christian center. By the close of the second century it contained a strong church and for a few years Christianity was the state religion.[2] During the third century the new faith found lodgment at several places in Mesopotamia and Bactria and probably also in Persia.[3] It appears to have spread first among the numerous Jewish communities of the region,[4] but, as elsewhere, soon overflowed racial confines and became predominantly Gentile. Syriac, indeed, was the ecclesiastical language, and the Middle Persian, or Pahlawi, was used extensively by Persian Christians.[5] Christianity largely displaced the older faiths of the Aramaic-speaking peoples of Mesopotamia. The Church had great monastic schools at Edessa and Nisibis and established headquarters at the metropolis of

[1] Mingana, *The Early Spread of Christianity in Central Asia and the Far East*, p. 6. Mingana quotes Josephus, *Antiq. Jud.*, 1, xx; c, iv and Mshiha-Zkha, *History*, p. 77 of Mingana's edition.
[2] Harnack, *The Mission and Expansion of Christianity*, Vol. 2, p. 143.
[3] Ibid., Vol. 2, pp. 143-152; Mingana, op. cit., p. 6.
[4] Labourt, *Le Christianisme dans l'empire perse sous la dynastie sassanide*, pp. 6 et seq.
[5] Mingana, op. cit., p. 6, quoting *Chronique de Seert* in *Pat. Orient.* v, 328, 329, vii, 117.

the region, Seleucis-Ctesiphon.[6] The credal statements were somewhat different from those of the Græco-Roman world, and in time, although not without a struggle, the Church adopted the doctrine that is associated with the name of Nestorius (died circa 451) and whose chief feature is a belief that in Jesus the divine and the human existed as two distinct persons. It was not so much this or other beliefs, however, which gave distinctiveness to "Nestorian" Christianity. That came chiefly from its independence of the churches of the Græco-Roman world and from the fact that it became acclimated to the Tigris-Euphrates Valley.

From Mesopotamia the faith was carried eastward into Persia and Central Asia. By 424 there were bishops in Ray, Naishabur, Herat, and Merv.[7] Christianity was not without serious opposition, for the Sassanids (ca. 226-637 A. D.), the rulers of the Late Persian Empire, found it often under the protection of their great rival, the Roman Empire, and persecuted it as an agent of Roman imperialism. Pressure from Constantinople, indeed, compelled the Sassanids, in 410, to issue an edict of toleration.[8] The Church met with opposition, too, from the leaders of Zoroastrianism, the established religion of Persia. In Persia, therefore, Christianity was never the faith of the majority.

In the first half of the seventh century the Arabs, bringing with them Islam, overthrew the Sassanids, and Mesopotamia passed under their rule. For some time the Nestorian Church suffered greatly, not so much from persecution by its new masters as from the defection of adherents whose Christian faith had never been vital and who found attractive the greater privileges accorded to Moslems.[9]

The most prosperous days of the Nestorian Church were, however, still ahead. Under the Abbasid Caliphs, from the middle of the eighth to the middle of the thirteenth century, the Nestorians were not only tolerated but were treated with a favor that the Sassanids had never shown them. They held high office at court and introduced their rude masters to the learning of antiquity.[10] The Nestorian body moved its headquarters to Bagdad, the new capital built by the Abbasids on the Tigris, and its posi-

[6] Labourt, op. cit., pp. 327 et seq.
[7] Mingana, op. cit., p. 4.
[8] Labourt, op. cit., pp. 43 et seq.
[9] Labourt, Le Christianisme dans l'empire perse sous la dynastie sassanide, pp. 347 et seq.
[10] Ibid., pp. 347 et seq.

tion in what at its heyday probably was the largest city in the world offered a unique opportunity for the direction of missions.

It was natural that the Nestorians, forming an important element in the stream of traders that constantly came and went first from Seleucis-Ctesiphon and then from Bagdad, should carry their faith to distant lands. This was especially true because the efforts of merchants and officials were supplemented by those of earnest missionaries. Christianity seems to have followed the trade routes and to have been strongest in commercial centers, and its prosperity was largely bound up with that of Mesopotamia. It was also natural that, since they were always subject to rulers of an alien faith and were never dominant even in their headquarters, the Nestorians seldom won an entire land or people. In most places they remained a minority. The fortunes of politics had decreed that they should never be the rulers of an empire and that they should always remain one of several competing religious groups. They were zealous as missionaries, however, and were to be found scattered over a wider territory than were the members of any Christian communion before the thirteenth century. Had they been supported by powerful Christian monarchs, the entire religious map of Central Asia might have been altered. Even as it was, their churches were to be found from Mesopotamia to China and from South India to Mongolia.

Rumored Entrances of Christianity into China

The exact time when Christianity entered China is uncertain. One tradition attributes the first missionary work to St. Thomas the Apostle. The chief basis for this report seems to be the breviary of the ancient Syrian Church in Malabar. Here St. Thomas is twice said to have been responsible for the introduction of the Gospel to China.[11] However, one estimate places the date of the composition of this service book in or after the thirteenth

---

[11] Nicolas Trigautius, *De Christiana expeditione apud Sinas suscepta ab Societate Jesu*, 1615, quoted in Moule, *The Chinese People*, p. 308; Semedo, *The History of the Great and Renowned Monarchy of China*, p. 155 (he quotes the breviary of the Syrian church of India, translated by order of Archbishop Franciscus Ros as saying: "By the means of St. Thomas the Chinesses and Æthiopians were converted to the truth. . . . By the means of St. Thomas the Kingdome of Heaven flew and entered into China." ". . . the Chinesses . . . in commemoration of St. Thomas do offer their adoration unto thy most holy name, O God."); Huc, *Christianity in China, Tartary, and Thibet*, Vol. 1, p. 18; Cordier-Yule, *Cathay and the Way Thither*, Vol. 1, p. 101; Williams, *Middle Kingdom*, Vol. 2, p. 275.

century and suggests that the tradition may have arisen from the reports of envoys of the Malabar Church who visited Cambaluc (Peking) in 1282 and who may have met the Nestorian Christians who resided there under the Mongols.[12]

A well-known story assigns the introduction of Buddhism into China to a dream of the Emperor Ming of the Later Han dynasty which led him to send messengers to the West in search for a new faith. An interesting suggestion is that the dream was induced by reports of Christianity in Central Asia, and that the two missionaries who reached China in that reign (67 A. D.) were not Buddhists, as is commonly supposed, but Christians, disciples of St. Thomas.[13] The difficulty is that the entire story had its origin in the latter part of the second century A. D. and is without historical foundation.[14]

Still another suggestion, most alluring, is that Mahayana Buddhism, so influential in China, was in part the result of the contact of primitive Buddhism with Christianity, and is in many respects Christianity in disguise. The sponsors for this theory point out that the "Greater Vehicle" developed first in Northwestern India, that at the time of Christ contacts between India and the West were numerous, that Northwestern India heard Christian preaching at a very early date,[15] and that there is at so many points such striking resemblance between the two faiths that some historic connection between them is not impossible.[16] Whether Buddhism was influenced by Christianity, or Christianity by Buddhism,[17] whether they owe their likenesses to influences common to both or whether these are due to a parallel but unrelated development, is as yet impossible to say. Future archæological researches may shed light on the question, but at the present any connection between the two is entirely unproved. The best scholars are inclined to say positively that none existed.

Arnobius in his *Adversus Gentes,* about A.D. 300, makes mention of missions among the "Seres" but it is doubtful just

---

[12] *Encyclopædia Sinica,* p. 394.

[13] Lloyd, *The Creed of Half Japan,* passim.

[14] Maspero in *Bulletin ec. franc. Ext. Orient,* Vol. 10, pp. 95-130; Pelliot, in *T'oung Pao,* 1918/1919 (Vol. 19), pp. 255 et seq.

[15] It seems to be fairly certain that there were at least some Christian communities in Northwestern India by the early part of the third century.—Harnack, op. cit., Vol. 2, pp. 100, 152.

[16] Lloyd, op. cit., passim.

[17] Edmunds, *Buddhist and Christian Gospels,* passim, thinks that he finds strong evidence for Hindu and Buddhist influence upon Christianity.

how much credence should be given him.[18] As we have seen, it is fairly certain that there were Christian churches in Mesopotamia and Persia by the third century,[19] and it is possible that through Chinese intercourse with Central Asia, which we know to have existed during these years, some knowledge of Christianity may have reached the Middle Kingdom. It has been suggested that the monks who are said to have brought silkworms to Constantinople in A. D. 511 had resided in China,[20] but the best experts believe that they were from Persia, Western Chinese Turkestan, or Ceylon.[21] We have, too, an assertion that Archæus, Archbishop of Seleucis-Ctesiphon from 411 to 415, and Silas, Patriarch of the Nestorians from 505 to 520, created metropolitan sees in China,[22] but this comes to us from later centuries and is to be rejected as untrustworthy.[23] At the time of early Portuguese contact with India the Metropolitan of the Malabar Church is reported to have included China in his title.[24] The tradition, if it existed at all, was certainly of late origin.[25] This much is to be said, however: there was intercourse over the sea route between India and China at least as early as the Buddhist pilgrim Fa Hsien, in the fifth century of our era,[26] and the Nestorian community in India is probably at least as old as the fourth century.[27] It is entirely conceivable, then, that Indian Christians had made their way by sea to the ports of China by the fourth or fifth century and that the Metropolitan in India claimed ecclesiastical jurisdiction over them. Still, the presence in China at this early date even of individual Indian Christians cannot be proved and is a matter of conjecture.

In spite of all these interesting suggestions, no certain evidence is known of the existence of Christianity in China until the T'ang

[18] Cordier in The Catholic Encyclopedia, Vol. 3, p. 669.
[19] Harnack, op. cit., Vol. 2, pp. 150-152.
[20] Williams, Middle Kingdom, Vol. 2, p. 275.
[21] Pelliot. Letter to the author, March, 1926.
[22] Williams, op. cit., Vol. 2, pp. 275, 276; Huc, Christianity in China, Tartary, and Thibet, Vol. 1, p. 42; Cordier in The Catholic Encyclopedia, Vol. 3, p. 669.
[23] Pelliot. Letter to the author, March, 1926.
[24] Chinese Repository, Vol. 16, p. 153. It quotes from Thomas Yeates, An Accurate Relation of the First Christian Missions in China, London, 1818.
[25] Pelliot. Letter to the author, March, 1926.
[26] Hirth and Rockhill, Chau-ju-kua, pp. 6, 7. We know of travellers arriving by sea, possibly from as far distant a place as the Persian Gulf, as early as 166 A. D.—Hirth, China and the Roman Orient, pp. 42, 173. Hirth translates a passage from the Hou Han Shu.
[27] Richter, A History of Missions in India, pp. 30-32.

dynasty.[28] If there were Christian influences, they almost certainly made themselves felt either under the guise of Buddhism or were limited to small communities. If these latter existed, they were probably, if one may judge at all from similar bodies under the T'ang and Yüan dynasties, chiefly or entirely foreign in membership and had neither a great nor a permanent effect upon the Middle Kingdom.

NESTORIANISM IN CHINA UNDER THE T'ANG

The first reliable information of the presence of Christianity in China dates from the T'ang dynasty (618-907). Conditions under that ruling house were distinctly favorable to the introduction of a foreign faith. After a long period of division China was united under vigorous monarchs and her domain and political influence were more widely extended than at any time since the Han. The strongest man of the dynasty, and one of the greatest who ever sat on the throne of China, was T'ai Tsung (627-649). Under him and his immediate successors the power of the Empire was extended either in the form of direct sovereignty, temporary conquests, or political influence, over what is now China Proper, Manchuria, Mongolia, Northern Korea, Tibet, Sinkiang, part of Central Asia, Northern India, Tongking, and Annam. In the seventh century the T'ang Emperors ruled over the largest and probably the wealthiest empire of the time and under their beneficent sway trade flourished with many distant sections of the world. The Caliphs are said to have sought their friendship and a prince of the Sassanid line to have taken refuge at their court. Strangers came in large numbers and were hospitably received. Intercourse with India, Central Asia, Persia, and even Mesopotamia and the Near East was carried on directly or indirectly by overland trade routes across what is now Sinkiang and to the south by way of the sea. At the capital of the Empire were to be found visitors from lands as widely separated as Japan, Java, and Persia.

[28] Gaillard, in *Croix et Swastika en Chine,* gives interesting examples of a geometrical figure resembling the cross which is found in China in pre-T'ang days. He is able to show for it, however, no certain connection with Christianity or Christian symbolism. He also has some interesting remarks to make concerning the tradition that St. Thomas preached in China and of other attempts to push back the entrance of Christianity into China before the T'ang dynasty. He finds no proof of Christianity's existence in China earlier than the Nestorian missions recorded on the Hsianfu monument.

Under these circumstances it was not strange that representatives of alien faiths should make their way to China. Foreigners brought with them their religious observances and their priests attempted to win adherents from among the Chinese. Manichæism was represented by temples and was connected closely with the political fortunes of the Uighurs, a Turkish race in power in Central Asia from the beginning of the eighth century of our era.[29]   Moslems came to China [30]—although their numbers were not as great as they were to be later—and some Zoroastrians and Jews.[31]   When it is recalled that at this time there were Christian communities in Southern India and that in Central Asia the Nestorians were widespread and active, it is not surprising to find Christians in China. It would, indeed, be surprising if they had not been there.

The evidences of their presence are steadily accumulating. First of all is the famous monument of Hsianfu. This was uncovered in 1623 or 1625 [32] by workmen who were excavating for the foundations of a building. An official who had examined the stone soon after its exhumation sent a copy of the inscription to a friend in Hangchow. There it came to the attention of Jesuit missionaries and greatly aroused their interest. One of them, Semedo, saw the stone for himself in 1628.[33]   The discovery was quickly reported to Europe, and for many years Occidental scholars were divided over the question of its authenticity. Some held that the stone was a pious fraud perpetrated by the Jesuits to argue the early presence of Christianity in the Middle Kingdom. Others believed it to be genuine.[34]   Many years ago, however, the last doubter was silenced.[35]   Rubbings and models of the stone [36] are to be found in many places in Europe and

[29] Cordier-Yule, *Cathay and the Way Thither*, Vol. 1, p. 62; Saeki, *Nestorian Monument in China*, p. 65; Chavannes et Pelliot, *Un traité manichéen*, pp. 4, 137; *Encyclopædia Sinica*, p. 326.
[30] Cordier-Yule, op. cit., Vol. 1, pp. 89, 90, 92; Saeki, op. cit., p. 65.
[31] Cordier-Yule, op. cit., Vol. 1, p. 89.
[32] Parker, *Studies in Chinese Religion*, p. 276, says 1623. Semedo, *The History of the Great and Renowned Monarchy of China*, pp. 157-165, Havret, *La stèle chrétienne de Si-ngan-fou*, p. 39, Gaillard, *Croix et swastika en Chine*, p. 103. and Legge, *Christianity in China*, say 1625. See the discussion in Saeki, op. cit., p. 21. See also Thiersant, *Le catholicisme en Chine au VIIIᵉ siècle de notre ère.*
[33] Semedo, op. cit., pp. 157-165; Havret, op. cit., pp. 31, 32, 39, 82, 105.
[34] Havret, op. cit., pp. 192-228; Wylie, *Chinese Researches*, pp. 24-77; Cleisz, *Étude sur les missions nestoriennes en Chine*, passim.
[35] Saeki, op. cit., p. 34.
[36] Holm, *My Nestorian Adventure in China*, tells of the obtaining of the replica and models.

America and an excessive literature has been called forth.   No ancient Chinese inscription is better known in the West. The monument was erected in 781 A. D. and reviews the history of Nestorianism in China from its introduction.   It also contains a summary of the doctrines and practices of the missionaries. Its author was Ching-ching, or Adam, who is, interestingly enough, mentioned in a Chinese Buddhist record as joining a Buddhist scholar in the translation of a sutra of the latter's faith.[37]

Still other records of Nestorianism under the T'ang have come to light.   In the grottoes of Tun-huang in Northwest China not many years ago a hymn to the Holy Trinity was discovered.[38] This document also contains the names of a large number of Nestorian books or tracts, which had apparently either been composed in or translated into Chinese.[39]   Imperial edicts of A. D. 638, 745, and 845 which contain references to Nestorianism have been found in Chinese records.[40]   The name Messiah is in a Taoist compilation of about the ninth century, and in a geographical work of the same century is a reference to a Nestorian monument in Chengtu.[41]   Our chief source of information, however, is still the stone in Hsianfu.

According to the records that we have, Nestorianism owed its introduction to A-lo-pên of Ta-ch'in, who arrived in the capital in A. D. 635, in the reign of the great T'ai Tsung.   The term Ta-ch'in occurs in Chinese histories during several centuries, and while its users had no definite conception of the boundaries of the country it denoted, it evidently referred to parts of what we now designate with somewhat equal lack of exactness as the Near East, probably more specifically to Syria.[42]   Nestorianism itself was termed in the inscription "The Luminous (or Illustrious) Religion of Ta-ch'in."   If we may trust the monument, A-lo-pên was received with honor by the Emperor T'ai Tsung, translations of the "sacred books" of the new faith were made in the imperial library, and the Emperor himself studied the religion and gave

---

[37] Cordier-Yule, op. cit., Vol. 1, pp. 112, 113 (the authority given is Takakusu in T'oung Pao, 1896, pp. 589, 590) ; Inglis in Journal of the North China Branch of the Royal Asiatic Society, 1917, pp. 12-15; Gordon, Messiah, the Ancestral Hope of the Ages, p. 11; Chavannes et Pelliot, Un traité manichéen, p. 158.

[38] Chavannes et Pelliot, op. cit., pp. 7, 86, 158.

[39] Ibid., p. 158; Saeki, op. cit., pp. 68-70.

[40] Havret, op. cit., Part 2, p. 247; Parker, Studies in Chinese Religions, p. 276 et seq.

[41] Pelliot in T'oung Pao, Ser. 2, Vol. 15 (1914), pp. 623-644.

[42] Hirth and Rockhill, Chau-ju-kua, pp. 104, 105.

orders for its dissemination. A monastery was built in the capital, and in it was officially placed the Emperor's portrait. Under the vigorous but infamous Empress Dowager Wu, in 698-699, Buddhists raised their voices against the "Luminous Religion" and it seems to have been persecuted. There were difficulties again in 713. Several succeeding Emperors showed the faith marked favor, however, and from time to time missionary reënforcements came. Especial mention is naturally made of I-ssŭ, whose gifts appear to have been the occasion of the erection of the monument. He was a native of Balkh, in what is now Afghanistan, and in the eighth century was in high position under the Chinese Government and by helping to suppress a rebellion had earned the favor of the Emperor.[43] We hear, too, that sometime before 823 a metropolitan for China, David, had been consecrated.[44]

In later years the infant church fell upon evil days. In 845 the Emperor Wu Tsung, who was an ardent Taoist, issued an edict proscribing Buddhism and ordering its monks to return to private life. In this interdiction the Nestorians were included, and evidently suffered severely.[45] The Church apparently survived, although greatly weakened, for in 878 there perished in the capture by rebels of the port of Khanfu (Canton) a number of Christians as well as Jews, Moslems, and followers of the "Persian faith."[46] An Arab who visited the capital of China in the ninth century found that the Emperor knew about Noah, the prophets, Moses, and Jesus, and had portraits of them.[47] Christianity was, however, soon to disappear from purely Chinese soil. In 987 a monk who with five others had been sent seven years before to put in order the Church in China, told an Arab in Bagdad that he and his companions had found no Christians in the Empire.[48]

[43] Saeki, *Nestorian Monument*, pp. 167-172, 237, 238.
[44] Mingana, *The Early Spread of Christianity in Central Asia and the Far East*, p. 14. He quotes Thomas of Marga, who wrote ca. 840, and Thomas derived his information from letters of Patriarch Timothy, who died in 823. Mingana (op. cit., p. 31) believes that the metropolitan see in China was at least as old as the seventh century.
[45] Legge, *Christianity in China*, pp. 47, 48.
[46] Yule, *Cathay and the Way Thither*, Vol. 1, p. 113; Reinaud, *Relation des voyages faits par les Arabes et les Persans dans l'Inde et à la Chine dans le IXe siècle de l'ère chrétienne*, p. 64; Brinkley, *China*, Vol. 10, p. 141; Walsh in *The East and the West*, Vol. 7, p. 210; George Phillips, in the *China Review*, Vol. 8, pp. 31-34, gives the date of the capture of Khanfu as 877.
[47] Wylie, *Chinese Researches*, p. 90. The account is dated ca. 875.
[48] Huc, *Christianity in China, Tartary and Thibet*, Vol. 1, p. 101.

The foreign faith was not entirely forgotten, even though its followers had disappeared.   As late as the eleventh century a remnant of a Nestorian church building of T'ang times [49] was still pointed out in Ch'engtu, and in the eighteenth century there was in Peking a Syriac liturgical work of the same dynasty.[50] The Nestorianism of the T'ang dynasty disappeared, then, leaving few traces.   In addition to the scanty records in documents and monuments that have been mentioned, other physical survivals occasionally come to light, as, for example, in Chihli, where an ancient monastery has recently been found whose title contains the name of the cross and on whose foundation stones are two crosses resembling that on the Hsianfu monument.[51]   Some of the missionaries of the seventeenth and eighteenth centuries reported discoveries of crosses, but their testimony is of doubtful accuracy.[52]

It is doubtful whether this Nestorian missionary effort had any permanent influence on Chinese life and thought.   The assertion has been made that some theistic ideas in Chinese philosophy are due to it,[53] but this is as yet unproved.   One enthusiast claims to have identified the founder of the secret sect, Chin-tan Chiao—which may number some millions of members—with the scholar who wrote the ideographs of the Hsianfu stone, and it has been maintained that the teachings of the sect bear a striking resemblance to Nestorianism.[54] An attempt has been made to show a connection between Nestorianism and some of the divisions of Buddhism,[55] and it has also been suggested that the Nestorians were absorbed into the Chinese Moslem community.[56]   All of these guesses, interesting though they are, have yet to be verified. It is clear that the Church as such did not survive in China.

What was the nature of the faith that the Nestorians preached? To what extent did they transmit to China the impulse that came

[49] Walsh in *The East and the West*, Vol. 7, p. 211; Chavannes et Pelliot, *Un traité manichéen*, p. 270.   A Chinese work of the twelfth century quotes a book of the eleventh century as mentioning in Ch'engtu a "Temple of Ta Ts'in."—Cordier in *T'oung Pao* (1917), p. 63.
[50] Mingana, op. cit., pp. 42, 43.
[51] Christopher Irving in *The New China Review*, Vol. 1, pp. 522-533.   The monastery probably dates from much later times.—Pelliot.   Letter to the author, March, 1926.
[52] Gaillard, *Croix et swastika en Chine*, pp. 152-156.
[53] Saeki, *Nestorian Monument in China*, p. 200.
[54] Ibid., pp. 53-56.   Saeki also quotes Timothy Richard.
[55] Ibid., pp. 122-125.
[56] Ibid., p. 51.

from Jesus? How fully was Christian life and character, as the early disciples experienced it, reproduced before the Chinese? We know, of course, the chief tenets of the Nestorians. They believed in God as lord of heaven, earth, and sea. They held that God had made man in his own image, that he had given the law through Moses, had sent his spirit upon the prophets, and had finally sent his Christ into the world. They held to the resurrection of the dead and the mystery of baptism.[57] In addition to these main points, they believed there were two natures in Christ. They repudiated the worship of Mary as the "Mother of God" and the use of images. While opposed to the doctrine of purgatory, they prayed for the dead. They held to the real presence of Christ in the eucharist, although denying transubstantiation. Their ecclesiastical organization included eight orders of clergy, of whom the lower ranks could marry, and was headed, as we have noted, by a Patriarch who for some centuries lived in Seleucis-Ctesiphon and then in Bagdad.

Just what the Nestorians taught in China we do not certainly know. Our only detailed sources of information as to the main features of the faith as it was presented to the Chinese are the Hsianfu monument and the documents of the Tun-huang grottoes. The former contains an account of the creation of the world by God, the fall of man from his original state of sinlessness, the manifold errors that followed, and the Messiah's birth, teaching, ascension, and work in "opening" life and abolishing death. Curiously enough, the monument has no certain reference to the crucifixion—although the cross is mentioned and heads the inscription—and only vaguely hints at the resurrection. The Messiah is spoken of as purging human nature, perfecting character, and defeating the devices of the devil. Baptism by water and the spirit is referred to, and probably the New Testament. Quite a number of sacred books were translated, but it is uncertain whether these included the New Testament. The faith was said to make for the peace and tranquillity of the realm, the prosperity of the living, and the joy of the dead. The virtues extolled were love, mercy, kindness, the placing of all men on an equality, and the relief of suffering—including clothing the naked, feeding the hungry, and healing the sick. The priests were held to

[57] Labourt, *Le Christianisme dans l'empire perse sous la dynastie sassanide,* pp. 35 et seq.

exemplify these precepts by their lives. They were also described as refusing to amass wealth. They were said to keep no slaves and to make no distinction between the noble and the mean. Their religious observances were in part fasting and keeping "the vigil of silence and watchfulness." They met "seven times a day for worship and praise" and they offered prayers for the living and the dead. Every seventh day they had "a sacrifice"—probably the eucharist.[58] Although eulogistic inscriptions set up by the adherents of a faith are not always a trustworthy record of the impression made on outsiders, it seems fair to infer from the Hsianfu inscription that the message and practice of these Nestorian representatives of Christianity were as nearly true to the spirit of Jesus as were those of Roman Catholic and Greek Orthodox missionaries in Northern Europe during the period that the peoples of these regions were being won to the Christian faith.

Why did the Nestorian community disappear from the Middle Kingdom? Why did it apparently have so little permanent influence upon the culture of China? Nestorians were in China, probably continuously, for nearly two and a half centuries, or for almost the length of time that elapsed between the founding of the Christian Church and the acceptance of the faith by Constantine. Why was it that the fate of the same religion was so different in two empires which were probably so nearly equal in area, population, and culture? In China Christianity had certain advantages that it did not have in the Roman Empire until the time of Constantine. The state seems to have tolerated it for many years and even to have given it financial support.[59] Persecutions were infrequent and were probably not as cruel as were those that befell Christians in the Roman domains. Nestorianism came, too, not as a sect whose early adherents were chiefly members of despised and unlettered classes, but with the support of foreigners who were powerful at court and with the advocacy of at least

[58] See text of the Nestorian monument. The Chinese is in Saeki, *Nestorian Monument*, pp. 260-270. There are English translations in Saeki, op. cit., pp. 162-180, by Wylie in Williams, *Middle Kingdom*, Vol. 2, pp. 277-285, and by Legge in *Christianity in China* (or *The Nestorian Monument of Hsi-an Fu*). Legge also gives the Chinese text.

[59] From the Nestorian monument it is clear that several of the Emperors favored Christianity and even at times subsidized it. This does not mean that Christianity was singled out for the exclusive patronage of the state, for other faiths were also subsidized (Saeki, op. cit., p. 85). It does mean, however, that it had the sanction of the government. Without that it might have had much more difficulty in maintaining itself.

some men who were well versed in the Chinese language and literature.[60] Why was it that in spite of these advantages Christianity disappeared from one empire while without them it conquered in the other?

The answer must at best be conjectural, but certain facts which seem well established may shed light on the problem. In the first place, Nestorian Christianity appears never to have ceased to be primarily the faith of a foreign community. Its chief adherents were non-Chinese peoples who were resident in the Middle Kingdom under the powerful T'ang Emperors either as merchants, soldiers, or missionaries.[61] It is almost certain that there were at least some Christian Chinese, for the Nestorian monument speaks of numerous church buildings and of what may well have been missionary work among the Chinese. Some of the long list of names given on the monument may even have been those of Chinese converts. It is doubtful whether so many of the sacred writings of the Church would have been translated had there not been active work among the Chinese population and had there not been some native Christians. An imperial edict of 845 mentions "over three thousand monks of Ta-ch'in and Mu-hu-fu,"[62] and since those of Ta-ch'in were almost certainly Nestorians it is probable that a fair proportion of the three thousand were of that faith and that a lay community of larger size supported them. Such a community may well have been in part Chinese. Still, Nestorianism seems to have depended chiefly upon foreign leadership and support.

In the second place, Nestorianism arrived at a time when no especial need for a new faith was felt. When Christianity entered the Roman Empire it found a marked religious hunger for which the state faiths could do nothing and which was seeking satisfaction in various philosophies and in religions from the East. In the China of the T'ang dynasty, however, the older native faiths were popular and strongly entrenched, and the unfilled gaps were largely occupied by Buddhism. Had it not been for this latter

[60] This is clear from the Nestorian inscription. I-ssŭ, for example, was in high favor at court.
[61] See the names on the Nestorian monument. Recall, too, the numbers of Christians, evidently foreigners, who perished in the sack of Khanfu in 878.
[62] The Chinese text and translation are given in Saeki, op. cit., pp. 88, 281, 282. Pelliot says that the true reading is not Mu-hu-fu but Mu-hu-hsien, hsien meaning "The Celestial God" [of Fire] and that the whole is to be understood as the hsien religion of the Mu-hu (Magi).—Pelliot. Letter to the author, March, 1926.

faith, Nestorianism might have met with greater success, but the followers of Gautama had been carrying on missionary work in China long before the arrival of the Nestorians, they had become well established, and their faith was at the acme of its vigor. To the average Chinese, Nestorianism may have appeared to be another of the Buddhist sects that were so flourishing under the T'ang. The confusion may have been facilitated by the use of Buddhist phraseology by Nestorian translators and by a close association between some Nestorian and Buddhist leaders.[63] The Nestorians, in other words, in trying to clothe their faith in dress familiar to the Chinese, may have sacrificed in part its distinctiveness and defeated their own aim.

In the third place, the Nestorian missionaries were separated from the center of their church by immense distances and could look for little assistance and inspiration from the main body of their fellow believers.[64] This and the fact that in most countries the Nestorians were a minority group and that in Mesopotamia they were a subject people were serious handicaps to extensive missionary work in a land as vast as China. If Christianity were ever to make a profound impression it would have to be at a time when the older Chinese culture was more nearly in a state of flux than it was under the T'ang and when the Church could bring to the task greater resources than the Nestorians had at their command. When one remembers the political disabilities under which the Nestorians labored in most lands, including Mesopotamia itself, when one recalls that China was at the outermost fringe of the range of Nestorian influence and that under the T'ang monarchs she was the mightiest empire on earth, the marvel is not that the Nestorians did not win her to the Christian faith or found a permanent Chinese Christian community, but that they maintained themselves in the country for nearly two hundred and fifty years.

With the decline of the T'ang, the disappearance of the Nes-

[63] Saeki, op. cit., p. 15. Remember, too, that the author of the Hsianfu inscription collaborated with a Buddhist priest in the translation of a Buddhist sutra.— Chavannes et Pelliot, *Un traité manichéen*, p. 158. There is in the British Museum a picture which may be meant to be that of Christ or a Christian saint, but which, except for a cross on its forehead, is that of a Bodhisattva.— Arthur Waley in *Artibus Asiae* (1925), No. 1, p. 5.

[64] In the middle of the ninth century, for example, the Metropolitan of China is mentioned with those of India, Persia, Merv, Syria, Herat, Samarkand, and Arabia, as excused because of distance from attending the quadrennial synods of the Church.—Cordier-Yule, *Cathay and the Way Thither*, Vol. 1, p. 104.

torians was, under the circumstances, almost a foregone conclusion. The closing years of the dynasty were marked by extensive internal disorder which hampered foreign commerce, endangered the lives of foreign residents, and probably made missionary work difficult. When, finally, the dynasty collapsed, for over three and a half centuries none of its successors were able to unite all the country. First were five ephemeral dynasties (907-960) and almost constant civil war. Then came the Sung dynasty, during all of whose existence (960-1280) the country was subject to attacks from non-Chinese peoples on the north. The Khitan and then the Chin Tatars wrested part of the northern provinces from the hands of the native monarchs. Under the Sung dynasty Chinese culture flowered afresh, but the rulers and their subjects would not be inclined to look with favor upon a foreign faith, particularly if that religion were professed, as was Nestorianism, by some of the hated alien tribes of the north. Neither the Khitans nor the Chins were Christian, and while the faith persisted among some of their neighbors and non-Chinese subjects [65] there is no evidence of conversions among the Chinese. The revival of Christian effort in China was to wait for the reunification of the country under a new foreign dynasty.

[65] The biographies and genealogies of some of these non-Chinese Nestorian Christians are found in the *History of the Chin dynasty.*—Cordier, *Histoire générale de la Chine,* Vol. 2, p. 377; Pelliot, *T'oung Pao,* December, 1914.

CHAPTER V

THE MONGOL CONQUEST

IN the thirteenth century occurred one of those irruptions of peoples from Central Asia that from time to time have had so marked an effect upon the history of both Asia and Europe. For a brief period an empire was established which stretched from Eastern Europe to the Pacific Ocean and which was to make possible the exchange of cultural influences between the Far West and the Far East. The initiator of this series of invasions was one of the greatest military geniuses of history, Temuchin, or, as he is better known, Jenghiz Khan (ca. 1162-1227). Under his leadership a comparatively obscure Asiatic people, the Mongols, burst out of their home in the great stretches northwest of China Proper and within his lifetime made themselves masters of what is now a part or all of Northern China, Western Russia, Central Asia, and Northwestern India. Under his successor, Ogodai (died 1241), the overthrow of the Chin Tatars was completed, Northern China was annexed to the Mongol Empire, and Mongol armies invaded lands as widely separated as Korea and Hungary. Kuyuk (Khan 1246-1248) followed Ogodai and after an interval Mangu, a nephew of Ogodai, became Khan (1251). While Mangu was on the throne his brother Hulagu overran much of Western Asia, captured and sacked Bagdad (1258) and founded a dynasty in Persia. Mangu was succeeded by another brother, Khubilai (1216-1294). The latter completed the conquest of the Sung dynasty and so added the remainder of the Middle Kingdom to the Mongol domains. From his capital at Cambaluc, the modern Peking, he ruled an empire larger and more populous than had ever before acknowledged the authority of one man. All China, Central Asia, Persia, Mesopotamia, and parts of Europe as far west as Poland recognized him as sovereign.

61

The Mongol conquests facilitated the reëntrance of Christianity into China. In the first place, they brought about contact between the Chinese and Christian peoples. The Mongol rule made relatively safe the trade routes between China and Central and Western Asia. Commerce flourished, both by the overland routes and by sea. Not since the T'ang dynasty had the Middle Kingdom been so prosperous and never had it traded with such distant sections of the globe. Merchants came even from Europe, and for the first time the peoples of Italy and the Far Occident heard definitely of China—or Cathay, as they called it.

Missions were facilitated, moreover, by the attitude of the Mongol rulers. The Great Khans and their subordinates were usually tolerant of all faiths and subsidized the teachers and priests of Moslems, Buddhists, and Christians. Their attitude appears to have been that any god of any faith might harm their rule if he were not properly propitiated, and, on the other hand, that by honoring all religions no harm could come and some good might accrue. Whatever their motives, the Mongol Emperors gave to the many foreigners whom they brought into China the greatest latitude in the practice of their respective religions, and in accordance with this policy supported Christian priests and exempted Christians from at least some of the burdens of taxation.[1]

NESTORIANS UNDER THE MONGOLS

The Mongol conquests worked particularly for the benefit of Nestorianism. This church had suffered from the declining prosperity of Bagdad under the later Abbasid Caliphs. It was, however, by no means extinct. Not only in Mesopotamia, but in Central and Eastern Asia and even within the boundaries of China, Christian communities were in existence. Thus in the fourteenth century Friar Odoric found at Ormuz fifteen houses of Nestorians,[2] and in that same century other Europeans discovered Nestorians in Tartary, at Almalik in Central Asia, at Kashgar, Samarkand, Yarkand, Tangut (where there was a metropolitan), and Kamul[3] (where there seems to have been a bishop). Several of the non-Chinese peoples whose homes bor-

---

[1] Ch'ên Yüan, *Yüan Yeh-li-k'o-wên K'ao*, passim.
[2] Cordier-Yule, *Cathay and the Way Thither*, Vol. 2, p. 117.
[3] Ibid., Vol. 3, pp. 81-88.

dered on China and who were to be found even within the provinces had been Christian since the T'ang or earlier. Missionary activity had by no means ceased with the fall of the T'ang. The Keraits, a Turkish tribe whose home was southeast of Lake Baikal and whom we know to have been Nestorians in Mongol times, are said to have become Christian in 1007 through the efforts of the Bishop of Merv.[4] Rumors of a chief of this tribe may have been the basis of the strange story of Prester John that so gripped the imagination of Europeans of the Middle Ages.[5] This Kerait chief, Unc Khan, was defeated by Jenghiz Khan.[6] To seal the conquest and transform it into an alliance, Jenghiz married a Kerait princess (Soyorghactani-bagi) to his son Tuli. This princess became the mother of three of the most important of the Mongol leaders, Mangu, Hulagu, and Khubilai.[7] Hulagu had a Christian wife and through her influence a Nestorian chapel was attached to his camp.[8] Nestorian Keraits were high in the service of Jenghiz, Ogodai, and Mangu.[9] The Onguts, a people who lived north of the great northern bend of the Yellow River and whose lands commanded the route from China Proper to Mongolia, were Nestorians and used Christian names, such as Simeon, Paul, John, Jacob, and Luke. The Uighurs, a Turkish people, were in part Nestorians.[10] Their script was modeled on Syriac derived through the Nestorian Church and later became the basis of the Mongol alphabet.[11] Mark, son of a Uighur archdeacon and born at Koshang (in North China) in 1245, was, while travelling on a pilgrimage to Jerusalem, made Metropolitan of Cathay and then, in 1280, Patriarch of the Nestorians as Mar Yahballaha III. His bosom friend and companion, another Uighur, Rabban Çauma or Sauma, born in Peking, the son of a clergyman, and tonsured monk by the Metropolitan of

[4] Ibid., Vol. 3, pp. 15-24; Howorth in *Journal of the Royal Asiatic Society,* 1889, pp. 361-431; Cordier, *Histoire générale de la Chine,* Vol. 2, p. 195; Mingana, *Early Spread of Christianity in Central Asia and the Far East,* pp. 14-16.

[5] Cordier-Yule, *Book of Ser Marco Polo,* Vol. 1, pp. 231-237, Vol. 2, p. 244, Vol. 3, pp. 15-24; Pauthier, *Marco Polo,* pp. 176, 177; Rockhill, *William of Rubruck,* pp. 106-115.

[6] Cordier in *Catholic Encyclopedia,* Vol. 3, p. 669.

[7] Cordier in *Catholic Encyclopedia,* Vol. 3, p. 669.

[8] Montgomery, *The History of Yaballaha III,* p. 6.

[9] Pelliot in *T'oung Pao,* 1914, pp. 623 et seq.

[10] Rockhill, op. cit., p. 140; Bretschneider, *Medieval Researches from Eastern Asiatic Sources,* Vol. 1, pp. 236-263.

[11] Bretschneider, op. cit., Vol. 1, p. 14.

Cambaluc, visited Rome, Bordeaux, and Paris in 1287 and 1288 on a diplomatic mission from the Mongols.[12] Kuyuk, who, it will be recalled, was Khan of the Mongols from 1246 to 1248, chose his two chief ministers from among the Christians, used Christian physicians, and had a Christian chapel before his tent.[13]

Given all these facts, it is not surprising that under Khubilai and his successors Nestorians were to be found in China. In the latter part of the thirteenth century, during the conquest of China, a Nestorian engineer joined with a German in helping the Mongols with siege machinery in the beleaguerment of Hsiang-yang.[14] Some years before 1275 Cambaluc had become the seat of a Nestorian metropolitan.[15] In 1289 Khubilai established an office to supervise the Christians.[16] The Archbishop of Soltania, writing in 1330, declares that there were more than thirty thousand Nestorians in Cathay, that they "are passing rich, with very handsome and devoutly ordered churches and crosses and images in honor of God and the saints. They hold sundry offices under the . . . Emperor and have great privileges from him."[17] A center of Nestorianism was in Chinkiang. Here and in the vicinity a Mar Sergius or Sargis, a physician of Samarkand, who was appointed governor of the city in 1277 or 1278, built seven monasteries.[18] Chinese records of about 1333 speak of twenty-three Christian families in and around Chinkiang, with one hundred and sixty-six members and one hundred and nine slaves.[19] In the early part of the fourteenth century Yangchow had three Nestorian churches. One of these, "The Church of the Cross," had been founded near the end of the preceding century by a rich merchant named Abraham.[20] Hangchow also had a Nes-

[12] Mingana, op. cit., pp. 19, 20, quoting from *The History of Mar Yahh-Alāha;* Cordier-Yule, *Cathay and the Way Thither,* Vol. 1, pp. 119 et seq. See also Montgomery, *The History of Yaballaha III,* passim. Pelliot says that Mark was an Ongut.—*T'oung Pao,* 1914, p. 630.
[13] R. K. Douglas in *Encyclopædia Britannica,* 11th edition, Vol. 18, p. 713.
[14] Cordier, *Histoire générale de la Chine,* Vol. 2, p. 287.
[15] Moule in *The East and the West,* 1914, pp. 383-410; Montgomery, op. cit., p. 29.
[16] Pelliot in *T'oung Pao,* December, 1914, p. 637.
[17] Cordier-Yule, *Cathay and the Way Thither,* Vol. 3, p. 102.
[18] Pelliot in *T'oung Pao,* 1914, pp. 623-644; Palladius in *Chinese Recorder,* Vol. 6, p. 108; Moule and Giles in *T'oung Pao,* 1915, pp. 627-686; Mrs. Samuel Couling in *Chinese Recorder,* Vol. 55, p. 223.
[19] Moule in *The East and the West,* 1914, pp. 383-410. (Note the departure in the matter of slave-holding from the standard set in the Hsianfu monument.) Chinkiang, it will be recalled, is one of the chief trade routes within the Empire.
[20] Pelliot in *T'oung Pao,* 1914, pp. 623-644. See also Cordier in *T'oung Pao,* 1917, p. 63.

torian church,[21] and there were Nestorians in Yünnanfu, in Kansu, and in Hokienfu in Chihli.[22] They were known as Tarsa or Arkagun (Marco Polo's *agon,* in Chinese *Yeh-li-k'o-wên*).[23] As can be clearly seen from the above brief account, the Nestorians were largely if not entirely of foreign birth and owed their presence and influence in China to the favor of the Mongol conquerors. They were to be found only on the northern marches, in the capital, and in the cities on the main arteries of trade. They seem to have carried on some missionary work among the Chinese and to have aroused the opposition of Taoist and Buddhist leaders, but apparently very few of the native-born accepted their faith.[24]

Just how much the Nestorians deserved the name Christian is hard to say. William of Rubruck entertained a poor opinion of some whom he found on the edges of China. He complained that they did not know the language of their sacred books, that they chanted like the ignorant monks of Europe, were usurers, drunkards and polygamists. He said that the bishop came only once in eighty years and that when he made his visit all the male children were ordained priests. The Nestorians were, he declared, worse than the pagans around them.[25] This description was of only part of the Nestorians, however, and comes from a Roman Catholic who lived in an age when tolerance, especially toward Christians of heretical sects, was not regarded as a virtue. Even if some of the Nestorians had entered into the characteristically Christian experience, however, it is doubtful whether many Chinese were influenced by it, for, as we have said, the Christian community was almost or completely made up of foreigners.[26]

ROMAN CATHOLICS IN CHINA UNDER THE MONGOLS

The period of the Mongol conquest coincided with an era of great activity and expansion in Western Europe. The dark ages that followed the collapse of the Roman Empire had passed, and

[21] Moule, op. cit.; Cordier-Yule, *Book of Ser Marco Polo,* Vol. 2, p. 192.
[22] Cordier-Yule, *Book of Ser Marco Polo,* Vol. 1, pp. 220, 276, Vol. 2, pp. 66, 132.
[23] Pelliot in *T'oung Pao,* 1914, p. 636; Cordier in ibid., 1917, p. 63.
[24] Ch'ên Yüan, *Yüan Yeh-li-k'o-wên K'ao,* passim.
[25] Cordier-Yule, *Cathay and the Way Thither,* Vol. 1, p. 116; Rockhill, *William of Rubruck,* p. 157.
[26] A list of names of Christians given in Ch'ên Yüan, *Yüan Yeh-li-k'o-wên K'ao,* contains few characteristically Chinese names. Most of them are obviously foreign.

a new culture had dawned with abounding life—commercial, political, intellectual, artistic, and religious. The thirteenth century, with its beginnings of modern states, its vigorous cities, its increasing trade, its cathedral building, and its new universities, is one of the greatest in the history of Europe. The crusades had largely spent themselves, but they were still serving to direct the attention of Western Europeans to the East, and had encouraged the growth of the commerce of Italian cities with the Levant. It was but natural that merchants should make their way to distant Cathay.

Nor was it strange that Roman Catholic missionaries should seek to bear their message to the same distant realm. The crusades aroused in the ecclesiastical authorities of Europe an interest in all lands to the East and helped to establish Roman Catholic outposts along the coasts of Western Asia. The thirteenth century was marked by the rise of two great new religious orders, the Franciscans and the Dominicans, both distinctly missionary in purpose. St. Francis (died 1226) had as one of his dreams missions to the infidels, and before his death he had preached to the Moslems in Egypt and he and his companions had made their way to the Holy Land. The Dominicans (founded ca. 1214) grew out of a desire to win back to the Roman Catholic faith the heretic Cathari, but from the very beginning the purpose of the order was the prosecution of missions in the entire world. Members of both brotherhoods rapidly made their way throughout Roman Catholic Christendom and were eager to carry the banner of the Church to non-Christian peoples.

The Mongol armies, coming out of the unknown East with such sudden and irresistible success, terrorized Europe. Pope Innocent IV, as chief pastor of Christendom, sent friars to gain more definite information about them, to ask them to refrain from shedding Christian blood, and to prepare the way for their conversion. One mission, of which we know little, was headed by Friar Lawrence of Portugal.[27] Another was led by an Italian, John of Plano Carpini, who had been one of the immediate disciples of St. Francis. He left Lyons in 1245, accompanied by Friar Stephen, a Bohemian—who proved physically unequal to the trip and had to be left behind—and while passing through Silesia was joined by Friar Benedict, a Pole. He reached the

[27] Rockhill. *William of Rubruck,* pp. xxi-xxvi.

Volga in February, 1246, and arrived at the court of the Great Khan, Kuyuk, at Karakorum, in Central Asia, in July, 1246. He remained there until November of that year, when he was dismissed with a brief and haughty answer. Returning in the autumn of 1247, he reported to the Pope.[28] A third mission, made up of four Dominicans and headed by Anselm of Lombardy, went to a Mongol general in Persia and after being rudely treated was dismissed in 1247 with a curt reply.[29] None of these embassies reached China, but at least one, that headed by John of Plano Carpini, brought back reports of it.

During the latter half of the thirteenth century friars went on various errands, some partly political, others purely religious, to the Mongol chiefs in Central Asia and endeavored to found missions in that region. Thus the Franciscan, William of Rubruquis (or Rubruck), a Fleming, was sent (1253) by St. Louis of France to the court of the Great Khan, near Karakorum. He returned in 1255 and wrote an account of his experiences. He had found the Great Khan, Mangu, tolerant of the various faiths of his subjects, so tolerant, indeed, that he had held before him a disputation between the representatives of Christianity, Buddhism, and Mohammedanism, and, while not a Christian, attended Nestorian services. Friar William did not reach Cathay, but he had talked with some Chinese.[30]

The first Europeans of whose arrival in China we know were not missionaries, but merchants. In 1260 two Italians, brothers, Maffeo and Nicolo Polo, left Constantinople and journeyed as far as the court of Khubilai. In 1269 they reached Acre on their return journey. They were bearers of letters from Khubilai to the Pope asking that a hundred teachers of science and religion be sent to instruct the Chinese in the learning and faith of Europe. What motive lay behind this request we do not know. The Polos delivered their message to the papal legate in Syria, but they found the papal see vacant. The chair of St. Peter was still unfilled, when, two years later, they started for Cambaluc. Before

[28] Ibid., pp. xxi-xxvi; Cordier in *Catholic Encyclopedia,* Vol. 3, p. 669; Cordier-Yule, *Cathay and the Way Thither,* Vol. 1, p. 156; Daniel in *Revue d'histoire des missions,* Vol. 3, pp. 495, 496.

[29] Rockhill, op. cit., pp. xi-xxvi; Cordier, in op. cit., Vol. 3, p. 669; Huc, *Christianity in China, Tartary, and Thibet,* Vol. 1, p. 179.

[30] Cordier in op. cit., Vol. 3, p. 670; Cordier-Yule, op. cit., Vol. 1, p. 158; Huc, op. cit., Vol. 1, pp. 204-238; Rockhill, op. cit., passim; Parker, *Studies in Chinese Religion,* p. 271; Herbst, *Der Bericht des Franziskaners Wilhelm von Rubruck über seine Reise in das Innere Asiens in den Jahren 1253-1255,* passim.

they were fairly on their way, however, the legate who had received their message was elected to the vacant throne and recalled them. His messenger overtook them in Armenia and they retraced their steps to Acre. Armed with papal letters to Khubilai and accompanied by two Dominicans, Nicholas of Vicenza and William of Tripoli, and Marco, the son of Nicolo, the Polos made their second start in November, 1271. Before the party had proceeded far, a war so frightened the Dominicans that they turned back and left the Polos to go on alone. The latter continued their journey, and in due course of time reached Cathay.[31] Marco entered the service of Khubilai and remained in China for a number of years. The narrative of his experiences did much to arouse and keep alive in Europe an interest in Cathay and still makes delightful and informing reading.

Before the return of Marco Polo it was rumored in Europe that Khubilai had been baptized. Moved by this report, in 1278 Pope Nicholas III started toward Cathay a party of five Franciscans. Just what happened to them is uncertain, but they seem to have heard in Persia of the falsity of the information and to have halted there.[32]

The honor of being the first Roman Catholic missionary to reach China belongs, as far as we know, to a Franciscan, John of Montecorvino. John was born somewhere in Italy about the year 1246 or 1247. Of his early life we know little or nothing, but in 1272 he was already a member of the Franciscan order and was sent to the Eastern Emperor at Constantinople with a letter from the Pope. Soon after his return he was again sent east, this time with several companions. He remained in the East until 1289, when he appeared at the papal court with news of the progress of the Faith in Western Asia, a letter from the King of Armenia, and the information that a number of the princes and peoples of the region were eager to hear the Gospel. The Pope, encouraged, sent him back with letters to various notables, among them one to Khubilai.

Our knowledge of the succeeding events is derived from one of John's own letters written from Cambaluc and dated January 5, 1305. He left Tauris, so he says, in 1291, accompanied

---

[31] Lemmens, *Die Heidenmission des Spätmittelalters*, pp. 64-79; Cordier-Yule, *Book of Ser Marco Polo*, Vol. 1, pp. 15-26.

[32] Cordier-Yule, *Cathay and the Way Thither*, Vol. 2, p. 5; Lemmens, op. cit., pp. 64-79.

by a Dominican, Nicholas of Pistoia, and a merchant, Peter of Lucalongo. The party went out by way of India, where they remained for thirteen months. Here John baptized about a hundred persons, and here Friar Nicholas died. John arrived in Cambaluc in 1294, shortly after the death of Khubilai, and presented to the new Emperor (Timur, or Ch'ên Tsung) the Pope's letter. Although vigorously opposed by the Nestorians, he remained in the capital and won the favor of the court. By 1300 he had completed, so he says, a church with a bell tower and three bells. He had, by 1305, baptized about six thousand converts; he had bought a hundred and fifty young boys of pagan parents, had baptized them, had taught them Greek and Latin, and had written out for them psalters, thirty hymnaries, and two breviaries. Eleven of the boys had learned the service and took turns in helping in it. The Emperor from his palace could hear the chanting and, or at least so John optimistically reported, enjoyed it. A former Nestorian, Prince George of the Onguts, had been won to the Catholic faith and had been received into minor orders. The majority of his people had followed him into the Roman Catholic Church, but after his death, which had occurred in 1298 or 1299, his brothers had led most of the flock back to the old faith. The Onguts lived, as will be remembered, some distance west of Cambaluc, and John could evidently visit them only infrequently. John describes himself as having acquired "a competent knowledge of the language and character which is most generally in use among the Tartars" and as having "already translated into that language and character the New Testament and Psalter." Whether this tongue was Chinese is, however, decidedly doubtful; the court in Cambaluc was, it will be recalled, alien, and John would have been more likely to use its language than that of the subject race. John pathetically describes himself as old and gray, although he was but fifty-eight years old, and as having had no news of the papal court or of Europe for twelve years. For eleven years he had had no associate, but for nearly two years he had had with him a Friar Arnold of Cologne.

In a later letter, written in February, 1306, John speaks of a second church as being under erection some distance from the other but still near the palace. The ground had been given by his old travelling companion, Peter of Lucalongo, and the funds for the building were coming from various benefactors. The compound included houses, offices, courts, and a chapel which could hold two hundred people. John says that he had a place at the Emperor's court, a regular seat assigned him as a representative of the Pope, and that the Emperor honored him above the priests of all other faiths.[33]

The report of the success that had attended John's mission was brought to the papal court by a friar, Thomas of Tolentino, who for some years had been a missionary in Asia. The news created a sensation. Several Dominicans started for Cathay, but wars prevented them from getting through.[34] The Pope appointed John Archbishop of Cambaluc, probably in the spring of 1307, with powers that gave him great freedom of action and the authority of a patriarch. The archdiocese as delimited later (1318) included much of Asia east of Asia Minor. Seven Franciscans were named suffragan bishops and were ordered to proceed to Cathay. The journey to China was not easy, and of the party only three arrived at their destination. Three died in India, and of the seventh we know little except that he was later bishop in Corsica and in Trieste: whether he even began the journey is highly uncertain. Two of the three who reached Cathay, Andrew of Perugia and Peregrine, remained for a time in Cambaluc, and the third, Gerard, was made Bishop of Zaitun (Ch'üan-chow), the great medieval mart in Fukien. After the death of Gerard, Peregrine (died 1323) and then Andrew succeeded to this post. Apparently they were all supported by an allowance from the imperial treasury.[35]

Of the further history of the Franciscan mission we have only fragmentary information. In 1311 Pope Clement V sent out three more bishops, all of the Order of Brothers Minor. Only one of these, Peter of Florence, reached Cambaluc. In the early part of the fourteenth century an Italian Franciscan, Friar Odoric of Pordenone, possibly impelled as much by a roving disposition as by religious zeal, made an extensive journey to the East. He was in China for at least three years, sometime between 1322 and 1328. His trip out was by way of India, Ceylon, the East

[33] For the account of John of Montecorvino, see Cordier-Yule, *Cathay and the Way Thither*, Vol. 3, pp. 3, 4, 45-57; Hartig in *Catholic Encyclopedia*, Vol. 8, p. 474; Moule in *Journal of the Royal Asiatic Society*, July, 1914, pp. 583-599; Cordier, *The Book of Ser Marco Polo, Notes and Addenda*, p. 62.
[34] Lemmens, op. cit., pp. 64-70.
[35] Cordier-Yule, *Cathay and the Way Thither*, Vol. 3, p. 10; Lemmens, op. cit., pp. 4-70.

Indies and South China, and his return journey by the caravan routes from Northwest China to Central Asia, so that he had an opportunity to see quite thoroughly the work of his order in Cathay. In Zaitun he found, so he says, two houses of Franciscans. In Hangchow were friars who had won an official to the Christian faith, and at Yangchow was another house of the order.[36] Earlier than Friar Odoric's visit is a letter of doubtful authenticity, purporting to be written from Zaitun by Bishop Peregrine in 1318. This epistle states that in Cambaluc there were Archbishop John and two bishops, and that in Zaitun were the writer and three brothers. In Cambaluc, so Peregrine says, the Alani or Alans,[37] a body of foreigners numbering about twenty thousand and in the pay of the Emperor, had been won by John, and the Armenians, who disliked the Nestorians, were building a church which they planned to give to the Archbishop. In Zaitun the Franciscans had a church and a site given them by an Armenian lady of wealth.[38] A letter from one Andrew, dated at Zaitun in 1326, tells more of this gift of the wealthy Armenian. Andrew also speaks of himself as having been in that city since about 1318. In addition to the first church, he had built a second in a grove a short distance from the city. Here he resided, supported by an imperial grant.[39]

The exact date of Archbishop John's death is uncertain and is variously given as 1328, 1329, 1330, and 1333. Whatever the year, his passing was mourned by the city where he had spent more than three decades.[40] His life had been both eventful and courageous. He had, almost single-handed, established the

[36] Cordier-Yule, op. cit., Vol. 2, pp. 5-11, 183-239, 270, 271; A. C. Moule in *T'oung Pao,* Vol. 20, pp. 275-290, 301-322.

[37] The Alans were from the Caucasus and had been communicants of one of the Eastern churches before becoming Roman Catholics.—Cordier-Yule, *Book of Ser Marco Polo,* Vol. 2, pp. 178, 179, 493, 494.

[38] Moule in *The New China Review,* December, 1920, pp. 538-543; Moule in *Journal of the Royal Asiatic Society,* January, 1921, pp. 83-115.

[39] Cordier-Yule, *Cathay and the Way Thither,* Vol. 3, pp. 71-74. "Andrew the Frank" was a layman.—Pelliot. Letter to author, March, 1926.

[40] The date seems much in dispute.—Moule in *Journal of the Royal Asiatic Society,* July, 1914; Cordier-Yule, op. cit., Vol. 1, p, 169; Vol. 3, pp. 100, 101. If the dates given in the letter of the Alans are correct, the year is about 1328. This letter, presumably written in 1336, speaks of John as having been dead for eight years. The description of the funeral is in the "Book of the Estate of the Great Caan, Set forth by the Archbishop of Soltania," which was written about 1330. The year 1333 is, therefore, too late. If the date, moreover, had been 1333 the news of John's passing could scarcely have reached the Pope in time for the latter to have appointed a successor in that year, and this we know to have been done.

Roman Catholic faith in the capital of the mightiest empire of his time and to do so had journeyed farther from his home than ever any missionary of any religion is known to have done before him. When measured by the effect of his life upon his contemporaries and the succeeding generations, he is by no means the greatest of Christian apostles, but for single-hearted devotion and quiet persistence he deserves to be ranked with the foremost pioneers of all faiths and times.

In 1333 the Pope named as John's successor Nicholas, a professor of theology at the University of Paris. Nicholas started for China with a large party of friars, but seems to have died before reaching his post.[41]

In 1338 there arrived at the papal court an embassy from the Emperor of Cathay, consisting of Andrew [42] and fifteen others. It bore two letters. One was from the Christian Alans. They complained that since the death of John of Montecorvino they had been without spiritual guidance and asked that a "legate" be sent them. The other was from the Emperor himself, endorsing the request of the Alans and asking for the papal blessing. The Pope received the embassy graciously and promptly complied with its request. Only one of the legates appointed, John of Marignolli, reached Cambulac. He followed the overland route and arrived in 1342. John's reception was impressive. He went before the monarch in full vestments, with a procession, a cross, candles, and incense, and singing "I believe in one God." He gave the Emperor his benediction and presented him with warhorses, other gifts from the Pope, and the papal letters. John remained in Cambaluc for three or four years, returned by way of the Straits of Malacca, Ceylon, Bagdad, and Jerusalem, and arrived at Avignon in 1353. In his account of his journey he told how he was supported at Cambaluc by the Emperor's bounty, how he disputed there with the Jews and the adherents of other faiths, how he "made a great harvest of souls," how he found that the Franciscans had a cathedral and other churches in the capital and

[41] Moidrey, *La hiérarchie catholique en Chine*, etc., p. 3; Lemmens, *Die Heidenmission des Spätmittelalters*, pp. 64-79. Cordier, *Histoire générale de la Chine*, Vol. 2, p. 425, says that he reached China. He almost certainly did not reach Cambaluc or the Alans would not have written in 1338 that they had had no spiritual oversight since the death of John of Montecorvino.
[42] "Andrew the Frank," a layman, not Andrew of Perugia.—Pelliot. Letter to the author, March, 1926.

were fed by the Emperor, how on his departure the Emperor asked that a successor be sent with full episcopal powers and with the rank of cardinal, and how he found at Zaitun three churches of the Friars Minor, "passing rich and elegant." [43]

THE COLLAPSE OF THE MONGOLS AND THE DISAPPEARANCE OF CHRISTIANITY FROM CHINA

As far as we know, the mission of John of Marignolli was the last successful attempt of the Medieval Church to reach Cathay. In the latter half of the fourteenth century the Franciscan mission fell upon evil days. In Europe the Black Death depleted the houses of the order and so much energy was required to maintain and replenish them that scant resources were available for the distant and perilous mission to the Far East. More disastrous still was the break-up of the Mongol Empire. As it progressed the various routes to Cathay became unsafe. Fresh invasions, such as those of Timur (died 1405), wasted Eastern and Central Asia. Missionaries were martyred in Central Asia, [44] the Indian Ocean was dominated by Moslems, and the journey even to India became all but impossible to Europeans, whether merchants or churchmen. The Mongols were, moreover, driven from Cathay by uprisings of the Chinese. Their rule came to an end in 1368 and was replaced by that of a native dynasty, the Mings. When the Mongols were expelled there disappeared the foreign troops and officials who had been employed by them and the traders who had flourished under their protection. An anti-foreign reaction apparently set in and with it an active aversion to all that the hated alien had introduced.

Under these circumstances it was all but inevitable that the Franciscan mission should be terminated. During the nearly three-quarters of a century that had elapsed between the coming of John of Montecorvino and the collapse of the Mongols it is probable that many more friars came to China than those of whom we have record. The houses and churches mentioned in John of Marignolli's report were too numerous to have been staffed by

[43] Cordier-Yule, *Cathay and the Way Thither,* Vol. 3, pp. 177-215; Moule in *Journal of the Royal Asiatic Society,* January, 1917, pp. 1-36. There seems to be a little doubt as to the year in which the embassy started from Avignon.
[44] Brinkley, *China,* Vol. 10, p. 163; Cordier-Yule, op. cit., Vol. 1, p. 171, Vol. 3, p. 31.

those whose names have come down to us.   Even allowing for the unknown missionaries, however, there had almost certainly never been many friars in China at any one time, and these had apparently been supported by the Crown or by foreign residents. Apparently, too, they had ministered largely and perhaps entirely to non-Chinese, such as the Alans.   We know of no non-Europeans among the clergy and of no attempt to train any for that office.   When the dynasty collapsed and the non-Chinese communities were depleted or disappeared, it was but natural that the Church should cease to exist.[45]

The Papacy made some efforts to maintain the mission. Cosme, Archbishop of Sarai, was ordered transferred to the see of Cambaluc, but apparently did not assume his duties.[46]   In 1370 William of Prato, a Franciscan and a professor in the University of Paris, was named Archbishop.   He seems to have started for his post, accompanied by members of his order, but we do not know either his or their fate.[47]   In 1371 an apostolic legate, Francis of Podio, was dispatched to Cathay with twelve companions but was never heard of again.[48]   We have record of ten other Archbishops of Cambaluc, the last of whom was taken captive by the Turks in 1475, after seven years' detention was released, and shortly afterward (1483) died in Italy.[49]   It is not known that any of them reached China, and about some of the names that we have there is some question.[50]   The title appears to have existed as late as 1490, but for some years it had almost certainly been purely honorary.[51]

Of the fate of the Nestorian communities we have even less record than exists for that of the Roman Catholics.   Since the

[45] Lemmens, op. cit., p. 7; Semedo, *The History of the Great and Renowned Monarchy of China,* p. 156.   It is said that James of Florence, the fifth Bishop of Zaitun, was martyred in 1362.—Cordier in *Catholic Encyclopedia,* Vol. 3, p. 670. This martyrdom seems doubtful, however.—Pelliot.   Letter to author, March, 1926.
[46] Moidrey, *La hiérarchie catholique en Chine, en Corée et au Japon,* p. 3.
[47] Moidrey, op. cit., p. 93, and Cordier, *Histoire générale de la Chine,* Vol. 2, p. 426.
[48] Cordier, op. cit., Vol. 2, p. 426.
[49] Moidrey, op. cit., pp. 1-3; Cordier, op. cit., Vol. 2, p. 425.
[50] Moidrey, op. cit., pp. 1-3.
[51] Cordier-Yule, *Cathay and the Way Thither,* Vol. 1, p. 121.   There is a report quoted in Favier, *Peking,* Vol. 1, p. 119, that in 1391 the Franciscans of Cambaluc sent two of their number to the Pope to ask for reënforcements, and that they left for Cathay with twenty-four brothers and were never heard of again.   This report seems to be entirely without foundation in fact.   Probably equally open to question is the statement in Antonini, *Au pays de Chine,* p. 230, quoting from *Missions catholiques,* Jan. 29, 1886, that in 1399 there were martyred in North China a friar and one of his converts.

Nestorians were all or nearly all foreigners and were usually closely connected with the Mongols, they must have shared the fate of the latter. Most of such Chinese as had accepted the Faith probably apostatized once their foreign co-religionists had been expelled. We have a report that as late as 1490 and 1502 prelates were being sent to China and that in 1540 an anti-Nestorian persecution was instituted.[52] No certain traces of the Faith, however, were found by the Jesuits in the latter part of the sixteenth century.

Nestorianism, too, died out from the borders of the Empire. The mother communities in Mesopotamia and Central Asia suffered greatly from the conquests of Timur and the Turks and dwindled to small and powerless remnants. The nominally Christian tribes in what is now Mongolia and the New Territory could not look to them for fresh vision and spiritual oversight. Probably Christianity continued to exist in a corrupt form for some generations, but eventually the tribes that had professed it abandoned it for the more prevalent Islam and Lamaistic Buddhism. Whether the latter was influenced at all by the Nestorians who came over to it we do not know. From what we know of the Nestorianism of the region it seems fairly certain that it had become so decadent that little if any of the original Christian spirit and message could make itself felt.

Whether any Christian community in China, either Nestorian or Roman Catholic, long outlived the Mongol dynasty we do not know. In the early part of the seventeenth century some Jesuits then in China were told by a Jew that as late as the first half of the sixteenth century there had been those in North China who used the sign of the cross, but that they had been persecuted and had been absorbed either into the pagan community or into the Moslem and Jewish bodies. The Jesuits made diligent search for other traces but could find none.[53] The Jesuits also heard rumors of people in Kiangsi who used the sign of the cross, but who had inherited it without knowing its meaning.[54] It is entirely possible that the first of these reports is true, for if the numerous

[52] Mrs. S. Couling in *Chinese Recorder*, Vol. 55, p. 224. Mrs. Couling does not give exact references for these statements, simply saying that one comes from "Assyrian" and another from Chinese sources.

[53] Semedo, op. cit., p. 155; Favier, *Peking*, Vol. 1, p. 120, quoting from Trigault, Book I, Ch. 2. For other reports of Christians in Shensi and Honan, see a letter of Ricci, Nov. 12, 1607, in Tacchi Venturi, *Opere Storiche R. Matteo Ricci*, Vol. 2, p. 330.

[54] Semedo, op. cit., p. 155.

non-Chinese Christians of Mongol times left behind them any influence it would probably be strongest in the North. The latter report is more open to question, for we know of no Christian community in Kiangsi under the Yüan. Few physical relics of the Christian groups have come to light. In the sixteenth or seventeenth century three crosses were found in Fukien [55] and a Latin Bible is in existence which dates from the Franciscan mission.[56] We have no certain proof, however, that the Christianity of the Mongol period had any permanent effect upon the institutions and life of the nation. As far as we now know, the Chinese and their culture would to-day be no different had no Nestorians ever existed and had John of Montecorvino and his confrères never undertaken the long and arduous trip from Europe.

Again, as for the T'ang period, the question arises, why did the Christian communities disappear so completely? Why did they have so little effect upon the Chinese? Again, too, the answer must be given that we do not certainly know. The reasons were probably in part the same in both cases. Even more than in T'ang times the Christian community was foreign in its membership. It probably had little success and perhaps made little effort among the Chinese. Also, as under the T'ang, the Church did not have the way prepared for its message by any marked dissatisfaction with existing faiths. And, also, there were no extended, intimate contacts between the Chinese and any powerful people who professed the Christian faith. The Nestorian communities on the borders of China were relatively weak; Bagdad, the center of Nestorian power, was far away and its commercial and political importance was waning. For centuries the main body of Nestorians had been subject to rulers of an alien faith and it was soon to be all but wiped out by the devastations of Timur and the Turks. Western Europe was even more remote than Bagdad, and commercial and cultural intercourse with it, while spectacular, was slight. The Chinese were scarcely aware of the existence of such a region, and such ideas of it as they had were hazy in the extreme. Had China been subject to some such intimate and revolutionary relations with the Occident as

[55] Favier, op. cit., Vol. 1, p. 62; Moule in *The East and the West*, 1914, pp. 382-410; Gaillard, *Croix et swastika en Chine*, pp. 151-154.
[56] Moule, op. cit., pp. 382-410. See Mrs. S. Couling in *Chinese Recorder*, Vol. 55, p. 223, for other possible traces.

exist to-day or as were to be found between the peoples of Northern Europe and the Mediterranean world while the former were becoming Christian, or between Spain and the New World in the sixteenth and seventeenth centuries, the story might have been very different.

Moreover, Christianity labored under more disadvantages under the Mongols than under the T'ang. It had a much shorter time in which to effect a foothold—less than a century, as contrasted with at least two hundred and fifty years. While under both dynasties it usually had the favor of the monarch, in the one the ruling line was Chinese and in the other it was that of a foreign conqueror. Neither dynasty accepted it as its official religion or gave it undivided support. Moreover, in Mongol times, Nestorianism was probably less vigorous and more corrupt than under the T'ang, and its force was much more nearly spent. Even more than under the earlier dynasty it would have been a marvel had Christianity permanently established itself in China.

With the expulsion of the Mongols, Christianity disappeared from the horizon of the Chinese even more completely than it had after the fall of the T'ang. No non-Chinese Christian communities survived on the northern marches, ready to make their influence felt under more favorable circumstances. If Christianity were ever to become a permanent and influential factor in Chinese life, it could be only through movements much more powerful than any that had so far appeared.

CHAPTER VI

THE AGE OF EUROPEAN DISCOVERIES AND THE RESUMPTION OF ROMAN CATHOLIC MISSIONS

THE interruption of Christian missions in Cathay and of intercourse with the Occident which followed the collapse of the Mongol Empire was to continue long enough to lead the Chinese to forget almost entirely the existence of Europe and of Christianity, but it was only an interruption. In less than two centuries from the time when the last Franciscans disappeared from Cathay Roman Catholic missionaries were again knocking at the doors of China, this time with greater and more lasting effect. The Mongol invasions had but brought China into premature contact with a vigorous new life in Europe, and the Polos and John of Montecorvino were the forerunners of many thousands who in the course of the centuries were to penetrate the Middle Kingdom. The commerce of the Italian cities, the crusades, the rise of the Dominicans and the Franciscans, and the beginnings of universities were merely the precursors of geographic discoveries, economic and political expansion, religious awakenings and intellectual activity, which by the early years of the twentieth century were to affect the entire human race. The peoples of Western Europe, from being a relatively negligible factor in the world's affairs, were to become their arbiters.

As a result of the new life in Europe, China was in time to become partially subject to Western nations and was to undergo a revolution in ideas and institutions. Would this revolution be wholesome or unwholesome? Would it lead to misery for the masses of the nation or to a richer life? Would it weaken such ethical and religious values as the Chinese already possessed, or would it enrich, supplement, and transcend them? The answer, at least partly and perhaps chiefly, depended upon the Church. The Church was the chief agency for conserving and promoting such

78

moral and religious values as were to be found in the aggressive West. If it did not take active steps to give its message to China the impact of the Occident upon that country would be largely destructive of all that was best. Christianity, as the faith professed in the Occident, was to come with whatever prestige might be attached to the religion of the dominant race. It was to find the Chinese institutions opposed to it eventually giving way, and it was to have an opportunity such as no foreign faith, with the possible exception of Buddhism, had ever enjoyed.

It was in the sixteenth century that there began that continuous and increasing impact of an expanding Europe upon China which was to bring to the Church its great challenge and opportunity. This impact was to come in three rather distinct stages. The first was in the sixteenth, seventeenth, and eighteenth centuries. During these years the foreign merchant was confined to a few ports, usually one or two, little diplomatic intercourse was carried on, and the only foreigners living inland were missionaries. The Portuguese were the only Europeans having a territorial foothold and Christian missions were almost exclusively Roman Catholic.

The second stage coincided, roughly, with the nineteenth century. It was marked by the increasing pressure of European peoples on China, the forcible imposition of treaties, the partial opening of the country to the residence of foreigners, and the steady growth of foreign commerce. The dominant commercial power was Great Britain. Protestant missions had their inception, Roman Catholic missions continued, and the Russian Orthodox Church tentatively began reaching out among the Chinese. The foreigner was not yet accepted and Chinese culture remained intact.

The third stage began, approximately, with the twentieth century and was marked by the partial disintegration of Chinese civilization and institutions and the beginning of their reshaping under Occidental influences. The situation made, naturally, for increased openings for Christian missions and the Church grew apace.

Changes in Europe in the Fifteenth and Sixteenth Centuries

The Europe of the fifteenth and sixteenth centuries, as we have suggested, witnessed changes which were to introduce the first of these three stages and to determine its character. To understand what occurred in China we must describe these movements somewhat more fully. The age was, first of all, one of geographic discoveries. Under the direction of Prince Henry the Navigator (1394-1460) Portuguese exploring expeditions nosed their way along the west coast of Africa, and in time the southern cape of Africa was rounded (1497). India was reached (1498), the rich trade of the Indies was opened directly to Europe, and the Moslem commercial monopoly of the Indian Ocean was broken. Seeking another sea route to the rich marts of the East, Columbus daringly set sail to the westward and in 1492 found the edges of what was to prove to be a new world. These discoveries led to others. The globe was circumnavigated, islands, continents, and seas hitherto unknown to Europeans were explored and charted, European outposts were established in Africa, India, the East Indies, and the Far East, and conquests and settlements were made in the Americas.

In the second place, the fifteenth and sixteenth centuries were marked in Europe by the emergence of strong national monarchies. Under the leadership of dominant ruling houses, new states appeared and old ones were strengthened. Led by Ferdinand and Isabella, the Spaniards conquered the last Moslem stronghold in the Iberian Peninsula and laid the foundations of a united kingdom. Under an able royal family Portugal was prospering. France had in part recovered from the Hundred Years War with England and the powers and territories of the monarchy were being increased. Out of the Wars of the Roses had emerged a unified England. Ivan the Great was freeing his people from the remnants of Mongol domination and was beginning to build modern Russia. All these states were to have an important part in the new discoveries and conquests and were, with the exception of England, to encourage missions to China.

In the third place, there was an intellectual and artistic awakening. This had been foreshadowed by the rise of cathedrals, universities, and scholasticism, had shown itself in the Renaissance and the attendant Humanism, and it was to continue in the widespread use of printing, in discoveries in astronomy, and in the development of the scientific method. The mind of Europe was being remade and a new world was being opened to the intellect.

In the fourth place, the sixteenth century saw a religious

revival. In Northern Europe this took the form of the Protestant Reformation, and by the close of the seventeenth century there were attached to the new type of Christianity Northern Germany, Scandinavia, Holland, Scotland, most of England and Wales, parts of Ireland, of Southern Germany, and of the Swiss cantons, and a comparatively small group in France.

In Southern Europe the religious awakening effected a reform within the Catholic Church itself. The older religious orders displayed fresh activity and new ones came into existence. Out of a small group in the University of Paris, whom the burning zeal of Ignatius Loyola had attracted, arose the Society of Jesus. With its army-like organization, its complete devotion, the ability and learning of its members, and its appeal to the upper classes, it was a powerful agent in reforming the Church, counteracting Protestantism, and spreading the Faith to new lands. Even though it had lost great sections of Europe, the Roman Catholic Church had never been as rich in enthusiastic and devoted spirits.

THE REVIVED MISSIONARY ACTIVITY OF EUROPE

Out of these four movements in Europe arose a fresh missionary effort. The new geographic discoveries put the Occident into close touch with great non-Christian peoples. The rulers of the new states and the Church could not fail to be quickened into missionary activity by the sight of vast areas and numerous peoples now for the first time accessible to the Christian faith. Mining and commerce brought increased wealth and the means for the extension of the Church's work. Conquests in the Americas, in Africa, and in parts of Asia and the islands of the East placed thousands of non-Christians under rulers who professed to be Christians.

The kings of the new monarchical states often initiated or directly supported missions. Their aid probably arose from motives which were often, although by no means always, selfish, and national rivalries were frequently carried over into the religious sphere and led to controversies, jealousies, and competition which were far removed from the professed ideals of the Church. By one of the strange contradictions of history, however, the humble, self-sacrificing love and devotion of many of the missionaries who went out under this dubious patronage helped to bring at least individuals from the freshly discovered peoples into contact with the true fruits of the Christian Gospel, and some of the European monarchs were genuinely concerned for the spiritual welfare of their new subjects.

The intellectual awakening increased the knowledge of Europeans and so gave to them at times a certain prestige among non-European peoples.

The religious awakening led, as revivals within the Church nearly always have, to increased interest in missions. It was, after all, the religious purpose, and not the economic or political, that was dominant in the foreign enterprise of the Church. No one can read many of the letters and diaries of missionaries without realizing that their writers were actuated primarily by exalted devotion. At times unworthy motives emerged, but in the main the urge that sent representatives of the Church to the ends of the earth, often beyond the merchant, the warrior, the explorer, the scientist, and the diplomat, had its source in a profound conviction that in the Christian faith are spiritual values which are essential to the present and eternal welfare of men and which it is the duty and privilege of Christians to share with the entire world.

What European expansion would have been without the missionary can only be conjectured. With the economic and political factors left unbalanced by any religious elements, the results would have been far different and in all probability far worse. The missionary, with all his faults, has tended to make the expansion of Europe the means to a higher and richer spiritual life for the entire globe.

For over two hundred years the missionary activity which arose out of the new life of the fifteenth and sixteenth centuries was to be carried on almost entirely by Roman Catholics. The Eastern churches, with the exception of that of Russia, were suffering too much from the Turkish conquests to enter on any extensive program of expansion, and Russian energies, in so far as these were directed outward, were almost completely absorbed in Southwestern Europe and Siberia. Protestantism was late in becoming committed to foreign missions. Protestant countries took no very large part in the early discoveries and conquests and until the seventeenth and eighteenth centuries did not have any great importance as commercial and colonizing powers. Most of the sections of the Americas and Asia which were in contact with Europeans were controlled by Catholic nations and these would not have permitted Protestant missionaries to reside in their domains. Early Protestant leaders were too largely absorbed in defining and defending their theological positions, in reorganizing the Church, and in controversies among themselves and with Catholics to have time or energy for missionary activity outside of Europe. In the seventeenth and even the eighteenth century many Protestant theologians in Germany taught that Christians had no foreign missionary obligation. The command to preach the Gospel to the whole world was held to have been binding only on the Apostles.[1] Protestant rulers were, moreover, not as interested in missions as were their Catholic cousins and were sometimes even opposed to them. By the close of the eighteenth century there was some Protestant missionary work among nearly all the non-European races touched by Protestant peoples, but it was not until the nineteenth and twentieth centuries that Protestantism as a whole became committed to foreign missions.

Every reason, on the other hand, urged Roman Catholics to extend their faith abroad. The Spaniards and Portuguese, the leaders in discovery, conquest, and colonization, and for many years the wealthiest peoples in Europe, were ardently Catholic. They had but recently brought to a successful conclusion their struggle to drive the Moslem from the Iberian Peninsula and the crusading spirit still ran high. After the commercial and political power of Spain and Portugal declined, Catholic France became the strongest kingdom in Europe and made a determined effort to achieve maritime and colonial supremacy. In the great religious orders, moreover, the Catholics possessed large, earnest, and experienced missionary agencies. Particularly in the Franciscans, Augustinians, and Dominicans, the Church had great bodies, one of whose chief objectives had from the beginning been missions. Now, in the sixteenth century, were added the Jesuits. From its very inception the Society of Jesus had been strongly missionary and had attracted a large proportion of the earnest and able young men whom the Catholic Reformation had inspired

[1] Warneck, *Outline of a History of Protestant Missions*, pp. 8-31. Warneck gives many interesting quotations from the writings of Protestant leaders and theologians which clearly show their attitude.

to enter the religious life.   It was not strange, then, that the sixteenth and seventeenth centuries saw the Roman Catholic Church engaged in a missionary enterprise which for extent was unprecedented not only in Christian but in all history.   Catholic missionaries were to be found in the forests of Canada, in the valley of the Mississippi, on the distant shores of California, and in the West Indies.   In Mexico, Central America, Peru, and Paraguay they were winning the Indian populations.   They accompanied the Portuguese merchants to the factories in Africa, India, and the East of Asia.   They penetrated Abyssinia and the Near East.   They made of the Filipinos a Christian nation and carried their message to the Japanese.

The papal curia was, naturally, the coördinating center of all this activity.   It did not often initiate it, but it felt obligated to direct it.   So vast was the undertaking that some new supervising agency was needed, and after various experiments, in 1622 the Congregation for the Propagation of the Faith (often called, briefly, the Propaganda) was founded.   The Propaganda sent out few missionaries of its own, but it superintended and correlated the work of the various orders and societies.[2]   It was, however, greatly limited by the Spanish, Portuguese, and French protectorates, and only as the latter weakened—and that was a matter of centuries—could its authority be extended.   In China we shall find that for over two hundred and fifty years the Portuguese *padroãdo* greatly hampered the papal curia and the Propaganda. This *padroãdo,* or right to control the Church in the East, and especially the appointment of bishops, was held by the Portuguese to be based upon papal decisions and decrees, but there was room for wide latitude in the interpretation of these.   We shall see the dispute between Portugal on the one hand and on the other Rome and missionaries from nations other than Portugal emerging again and again to hamper the Church in China.   National rivalries and claims both within and without the missionary forces were to be one of the chief obstacles to coöperation among Roman Catholic missions, and Rome often found it difficult to assert its authority and establish harmony.[3]

[2] *Collectanea S. Congregatione de Propaganda Fide,* Vol. 1, pp. 1-4; Henrion, *Histoire générale des missions catholiques,* Vol. 2, p. 245; Schwager, *Die katholische Heidenmission der Gegenwart,* p. 17.
[3] See especially Jann, *Die katholischen Missionen in Indien, China, und Japan, ihre Organization und das portugiesische Patronat vom 15, bis ins 18. Jahrhundert.*

THE REOPENING OF CATHOLIC MISSIONS IN CHINA. XAVIER
When so large a part of the earth was being reached by an
expanding Europe and when Catholic missions were being so
zealously undertaken, it was to be expected that Christianity
would reënter China. The return occurred in the latter part of
the sixteenth and in the early part of the seventeenth century
and was effected, as might be expected, by Spaniards and Portuguese.
The finding of the sea route between Europe and India led
the Portuguese to undertake expeditions farther east. In 1511
they possessed themselves of Malacca and from there as an outpost merchants and adventurers made their way to the great
empire to the north. Just when they first reached China we do
not know, but it was apparently about 1514 or 1515.[4] They
were soon going in quite large numbers and quickly established
themselves in several of the southern ports.[5] A Portuguese envoy,
Pires, went to Peking in 1520, but he was unsuccessful in obtaining sanction for the commerce of his nation and was conducted
back to Canton.[6] The Chinese of the sixteenth century were not
hospitable to foreigners: they were disinclined to fare forth
beyond their boundaries and were satisfied to continue their
national life without intercourse with strangers. Japanese adventurers had recently ravaged the coast of China from north to
south [7] and had helped to create a deep-seated distrust of, and
contempt for, the alien. The Portuguese were received, therefore, in no very friendly fashion,[8] and the truculence with which
they treated the Chinese increased the antipathy. By 1550 the
Portuguese had been expelled from all the ports of China and
were carrying on a precarious trade from the island of Shang-
ch'üan,[9] south of Canton. Within a few years, however, they
were allowed to occupy a peninsula near Canton which commanded an excellent harbor. Here they built a city, Macao, for
nearly three centuries to come the main focus of European inter-

[4] Cordier, *Histoire générale de la Chine,* Vol. 3, pp. 118-124; Cordier in *Catholic Encyclopedia,* Vol. 3, p. 682.
[5] Montalto de Jesus, *Historic Macao,* pp. 2-16.
[6] Cordier, *Histoire générale de la Chine,* Vol. 3, pp. 118-124; Mendoza, *History of China* (R. H. Major's introduction), pp. xxxi-xxxiii.
[7] Cordier, *Histoire générale de la Chine,* Vol. 3, pp. 6, 59 et seq.
[8] Brinkley, *China,* Vol. 10, p. 170.
[9] Montalto de Jesus, op. cit., pp. 2-16.

course with China.[10] Macao was the only European settlement permitted by the Chinese and Canton was the chief and eventually the only port through which the Westerner was allowed to trade.

As has been suggested, Catholic missionary effort followed closely on the heels of Portuguese discovery and settlement. Henry the Navigator had been Grand Master of the Order of Christ—the successor of the Templars in Portugal—and many of his expeditions sailed under the flag of the order.[11] The Dominicans reached Goa in 1510. Aggressive missionary activity began in 1517, with the arrival of the Franciscans, and was extended by the Brothers Minor to Ceylon, Pegu, and the Malay Archipelago.[12] In 1534 Goa was made the seat of a bishop who was to have jurisdiction over all Portuguese possessions between the Cape of Good Hope and China. The right of patronage to the see was given the King of Portugal.[13]

Probably the inhospitable attitude of the Chinese prevented missionaries from early following the traders to the Middle Kingdom. Certainly the first serious attempt of which we know was not until 1552. It was made, fittingly, by the great Francis Xavier. This ardent soul had been a member of the group that initiated the Society of Jesus. He had been sent to the Indies to inaugurate the eastern mission of the Society and had arrived at Goa in 1542. Xavier possessed amazing energy, devotion, and courage, and an imagination that ranged over all the Far Orient. His own temperament and his position as papal nuncio and the official head of the Jesuits in the East made it impossible for him to remain long in one place, and after some years in and near India he went to Japan (1549) to begin there the work of evangelization. What he learned in the Far East made him eager to carry the Gospel to China. He had touched at Canton on the way out and while in Japan had heard more of the great empire. He found that the Japanese had drawn their civilization from

[10] Ibid., p. 17 et seq.; Cordier, *Histoire générale de la Chine*, Vol. 3, p. 129. The date of the first Portuguese settlement at Macao is uncertain, but it is probably about 1553. Apparently permission was obtained in 1557 to occupy Macao.— Servière, *Les anciennes missions de la Compagnie de Jesus*, p. 2. See also Cordier, op. cit., Vol. 3, pp. 129-133; Morse, *International Relations of the Chinese Empire*, Vol. 1, p. 43.

[11] Jann, op. cit., Chapters 1 and 2; C. R. Beazley in *Encyclopædia Britannica*, 11th ed., Vol. 13, p. 297.

[12] K. G. Jayne in *Encyclopædia Britannica*, 11th ed., Vol. 12, p. 160.

[13] Ibid. and Jann, op. cit., p. 89.

China and held that country in great respect. He believed that if the Chinese would accept the message of Christ, the Japanese would quickly follow. For him to think was to act. On his way back from Japan in the last weeks of 1551 he stopped at the island of Shang-ch'üan and there accepted the offer of his friend, Diego de Pereira, of passage to Malacca.

On the voyage Xavier elaborated with Pereira a plan for gaining access to China. Pereira was to be appointed to head a Portuguese embassy for which he was to defray part of the cost and from which he was supposedly to make a profit, and Xavier was to accompany him. The object of the embassy was to be the release of Portuguese held captive by the Chinese, an alliance between the Emperor of China and the King of Portugal, trade relations, and the opening of China to the Gospel.

At Malacca the friends separated, Pereira to make another voyage and Xavier to proceed to Goa to perfect arrangements for the embassy. At Goa Xavier obtained from the Viceroy sanction for his project and the appointment of Pereira as the royal representative. He made an elaborate outlay for presents and outfit, using for the purpose private subscriptions, a state grant, and funds with which Pereira had provided him. In April, 1552, he took his leave of India, accompanied by a priest, four lay brothers, and a young Chinese, Antonio by name, who had been educated in a Catholic college and was to act as interpreter.

At Malacca Francis was joined by Pereira, but here ill fortune met him in the person of the commandant, Don Alvaro de Ataide, a son of Vasco da Gama. Don Alvaro was vigorously opposed to the expedition—it is not certain why—and found a pretext for detaining it. In vain Xavier pleaded. In vain, when pleading had failed, he exercised his rights as papal nuncio and apostolic legate and excommunicated the refractory magnate. Goa and its Viceroy were far away and Lisbon and Rome were still farther. In Malacca Don Alvaro was supreme. He challenged the authenticity of Francis' credentials and stood resolutely by his prohibition. Xavier was not the kind of man to be easily thwarted and a compromise was finally effected. Xavier was permitted to embark for Shang-ch'üan on Pereira's ship, the *Santa Cruz*. He was, however, to go without his presents for the Chinese, Pereira was to remain behind, and the embassy was to be definitely abandoned.

Xavier, then, proceeded on his way, hoping still to enter China.

When he arrived at Shang-ch'üan the trading season had opened and the Portuguese merchants were already present in force. He erected a temporary chapel and began gathering the children for religious instruction. He endeavored to make arrangements to be taken to the coast of China, hoping that once there the way might open for him to remain. Toward this project the Portuguese merchants were none too cordial, for they had but recently been excluded from the mainland and feared that if Francis were detected in entering the country even their trade at Shang-ch'üan might be terminated. A Chinese ship captain finally engaged to perform Xavier's desire. He failed to appear, however, and the missionary had to remain on the island. The trading season at last closed, and all the Portuguese ships but the *Santa Cruz* departed. Still Francis lingered, hoping to find a way to effect his purpose. He fell ill, and as the motion of the ship distressed him he was, at his request, taken on shore. There, toward the close of the year (1552),[14] in a temporary shed, attended, appropriately, by the Chinese, Antonio, the end came. It was a dramatic and worthy close of a great career, this death of the Apostle to the Indies near the portal of the unopened empire of the Far East.[15] His body was later taken to Goa, but it might fittingly have been allowed to rest on this now half-forgotten island near the portals of China.

OTHER EFFORTS TO ENTER CHINA

The death of Xavier was a challenge to further efforts to enter the Middle Kingdom. By the close of the sixteenth century there were two centers of European power in the Far East. Both were in the hands of Catholic peoples and from both missionaries strove to penetrate China. One, Macao, the Portuguese outpost has already been mentioned. The other, the Philippines, was in the possession of Spain. The Philippines had been discovered by Magellan in 1521. During the latter half of the same century

[14] Probably the night of the second or third of December.—Pelliot, conversation with the author, May, 1926.

[15] The authorities consulted in the compilation of this account of Xavier's effort to enter China are as follows: Stewart, *Life of St. Francis Xavier*, pp. 311, 331; Kelly, *Life of St. Francis Xavier*, pp. 74, 204-234; Abelly, *Lettres de St. François Xavier*, pp. 455-573; Coleridge, *Life and Letters of St. Francis Xavier*, Vol. 2, pp. 232-571; *Chinese Recorder*, Vol. 27, pp. 517-525; Bowra, in *China Review*, Vol. 2, pp. 244-254; Brou, *St. Francis Xavier*, Vol. 2, pp. 245-366; Cros, *Saint François de Xavier*, Vol. 2, pp. 302-343; Halde, *China*, Vol. 2, p. 3; Luis de Guzman, *Historia de la Misiones la Compañia de Jésus*, pp. 47-51.

the Spaniards effected a permanent settlement and made Manila (founded 1571) the capital. From the beginning the occupation of the islands was as much for missionary as for commercial or political purposes. Augustinians, Dominicans, Franciscans, and Jesuits made their way thither and in the course of time won most of the population to the Christian faith. Ardent spirits early dreamed of using the Philippines as a base for missionary activity in Japan and China. Between missionaries coming from Macao and the Philippines there were often, unfortunately, bitterness and rivalry. The bull of Alexander VI in 1493, the treaty of Tordesillas (1494), and the treaty of 1529 which determined the ownership of the Moluccas delimited the Spanish and Portuguese spheres of influence. Portugal asserted an exclusive right to the East and only by a geographical fiction were the Philippines permitted to fall within the Spanish zone. The Portuguese, moreover, claimed under several other papal bulls [16] control over the Church in the East and objected to any poaching on their preserves. The Spaniards, on the other hand, were not inclined to observe either treaties or bulls when these proved inconvenient.

It was several years before either the Spanish or the Portuguese attempts to establish a permanent mission were successful. In 1553 Father Pierre d'Alcoceva resided for eight days on Shangch'üan and visited Xavier's tomb.[17] Apparently, however, he made no effort to enter China. In 1555 P. Melchior Nuñes Barreto, the Jesuit provincial for the Indies and Japan, spent two months in Canton attempting to ransom imprisoned Portuguese. He did some preaching and is said to have held a public disputation with a Chinese scholar. He left Etienne Goêz to study the language, but the latter fell ill and returned to Goa.[18] In 1555 or 1556 a Portuguese Dominican, Gaspar de la Cruz, arrived at Macao and possibly succeeded in entering Canton. He did not remain long, however, for we find him a little later at Ormuz and he returned to Lisbon in 1569.[19] Diego de Pereira—he who had

[16] Cordier, *Histoire générale de la Chine,* Vol. 3, p. 117.
[17] Ibid., Vol. 3, p. 246.
[18] Cordier, op. cit., Vol. 3. p. 246; Brou, *St. Francis Xavier,* Vol. 2, p. 347; Brucker in *Catholic Encyclopedia,* Vol. 13, p. 34; Colin (Pastells' edition), *Labor Evangélica de los Obreros de la Compañia de Jésus en las Islas Filipinas,* Vol. 1, p. 267.
[19] Cordier, op. cit., Vol. 3, p. 246; Brou, op. cit., Vol. 2, p. 347; Huc, *Christianity in China, Tartary and Thibet,* Vol. 3, p. 4; André-Marie, *Missions dominicaines dans l'Éxtrême-Orient,* Vol 1, pp. 178, 179.

in part financed Xavier's attempt to enter China—was finally named by the King of Portugal to head an embassy to Peking to obtain imperial sanction for missions. He preferred, however, the office of *Capitão de terra* at Macao. A relative of his was appointed to the other post and in 1562 started from Goa with some Jesuits as companions. For two years the party endeavored to enter the Middle Kingdom but was unable to proceed beyond Canton.[20] In 1562 or 1565 two of the group, François Perez and Texeira, established a Jesuit residence at Macao and made some converts among the Chinese.[21] In 1567 or 1568 Andrew Oviedo, a Jesuit with the title of Patriarch of Ethiopia, arrived in Macao and spent some years there.[22] Whether he did any work among the Chinese is not known. There were, of course, ecclesiastics in Macao, probably from the very beginning, who ministered to the Portuguese, and it is fairly certain that they carried on some Christian propaganda among the Chinese residents in the colony. In 1568 two priests, Jean Baptiste Ribeyra and Pierre Bonaventura Riera, arrived at Macao with instructions from their superiors to penetrate China, but they were unsuccessful.[23] In 1575 Martin de Herrada, a Spanish Augustinian, succeeded in reaching Fukien by way of the Philippines, but was not permitted to remain.[24] In 1579 further unsuccessful efforts were made from the Philippines by Franciscans and Augustinians[25] and possibly by Dominicans.[26] The Franciscan attempt was by one Italian and three Spanish priests and three lay brothers. The party reached Canton but found the language difficulty insuperable and propaganda in the interior impossible. One of the priests died, one returned to Manila, and two founded a cloister in Macao and persisted there in spite of Portuguese opposition. Other but no more fortunate attempts were made by Franciscans from the Philippines in 1582, and in 1585-1586.[27]

[20] Cordier, op. cit., Vol. 3, p. 246; Montalto de Jesus, *Historic Macao*, p. 30.
[21] Servière, *Les anciennes missions de la Compagnie de Jésus en Chine*, p. 2; Cordier, op. cit., Vol. 3, p. 246; Brou, op. cit., Vol. 2, p. 347.
[22] Moidrey, *La hiérarchie catholique en Chine*, etc., p. 175.
[23] Cordier, op. cit., Vol. 3, p. 246.
[24] Cordier in *Revue de l'Extrême-Orient*, Vol. 2, p. 61; Mendoza, *History of China* (Introduction by R. H. Major), Vol. 1, pp. lxvii-lxxiii; Colin (Pastells' edition), *Labor Evangelica*, etc., Vol. 1, pp. 303, 304. Luis de Guzman, *Historia de las Misiones de la Compañía de Jésus*, gives the date as 1565.
[25] Brou, op. cit., Vol. 2, p. 347; Luis de Guzman, op. cit., p. 185.
[26] Wieger, *Textes historiques*, p. 2037.
[27] Maas, *Die Wiederöffnung der Franziskannermission in China in der Neuzeit*, pp. 23-46.

The Jesuits Establish Themselves in China.

Valignani, Ruggerius, Ricci

The first permanent mission in China was due to the zeal and insight of Alessandro Valignani, an Italian Jesuit, who in 1573 was appointed by his Society Visitor to the Indies. While on his way to the prosperous missions in Japan, he was detained at Macao and had opportunity to study the problem of entering the Empire. He saw that if the enterprise were to be successful its agents would need to devote their lives to it and to learn the language. He accordingly arranged to have sent to Macao a Michael Ruggerius, an Italian of his Society, who had come to India in 1578. Ruggerius reached Macao in July, 1579, and began the study of the language, apparently not the local dialect but Mandarin. His task was not easy and both he and Valignani were at times almost discouraged. Ruggerius had difficulty in obtaining a teacher and even after he had made some progress with the language it seemed as though his efforts to obtain permission to reside outside Macao would be frustrated.[28] A story—which may or may not be true—has come down to us from an early chronicler that so dark was the prospect that "Father Valignani, looking one day out of a window of the College of Macao toward the continent . . . called out with a loud voice and the most intimate affection of his heart, speaking to China, 'Oh Rock, Rock, when wilt thou open, Rock.' "[29]

Father Ruggerius succeeded in making short visits to Canton when the Portuguese went there for the semi-annual fairs,[30] and he was, apparently, able to give some instruction to catechumens and to make a few converts.[31] Within a few years he received reënforcements in the persons of Francis Pasio and Matteo (Matthew) Ricci. Of these two, Pasio soon (1583) joined the mis-

[28] *Purchas, His Pilgrimes*, Vol. 3, p. 320; Huc, op. cit., Vol. 2, p. 36; Brucker in *Catholic Encyclopedia*, Vol. 13, p. 34; Trigault, *Histoire de l'expédition chretienne au royanne de la Chine*, pp. 230-232; Tacchi Venturi, *Opere Storiche del P. Matteo Ricci*, Vol. 1, pp. 107-109; Letters of Ruggerius in ibid., Vol. 2, pp. 396-413.
[29] Semedo, *The History of the Great and Renowned Monarchy of China*, pp. 170-172.
[30] *Purchas, His Pilgrimes*, Vol. 3, p. 320 (based largely on Ricci's account).
[31] Ibid. In 1582 and again in 1583 there was, too, in Canton, on a mission from the Philippines, Alonzo Sanchez, a Spanish Jesuit.—Luis de Guzman, op. cit., pp. 187-197.

sion in Japan,[32] but the other, Ricci, was destined to become one of the outstanding missionaries of the Church in China. Ricci was born at Macerata in the March of Ancona, October 6, 1552— a few months before the death of Xavier. His family wished him to enter the legal profession and he went to Rome to prepare for it. Here, like many of the able youths of his day, he was attracted by the Society of Jesus. During his novitiate he was under the direction of Valignani and it was apparently this influence that led him later to offer himself for work in the Orient. During his student days at Rome he had instruction in mathematics, cosmology, and astronomy, the latter under one of the greatest masters of that day. This knowledge was later to stand him in good stead and was to determine in part the method of approach of himself and his successors to the learned world of China. In 1577 he asked to be sent to the Orient and arrived at Goa in 1578, where he taught and where he completed his theological course. Summoned by Valignani, in 1582 he arrived at Macao and began the study of the language.[33]

The following year (1583) Ruggerius and Ricci succeeded in obtaining a permanent residence at Chaoch'ing, a city on the West River not far from Canton and then the capital of Kwangtung. While they made no secret of their faith, they deemed it wise not to press at first their missionary purpose. They spoke of themselves as having been attracted by the renown of the Empire and endeavored to win the interest and respect of the Chinese by their scientific attainments. Clocks were a never-failing source of attraction. Ricci prepared a map of the world which showed the location of the countries of Europe but discreetly put China in the center and pictured the rest of the earth as decorative fringes.[34] Ricci's mathematical attainments proved a useful introduction to educated circles. Before many months had passed he and Ruggerius had won the friendship of some of the scholars and officials of the city.

This effort to win the friendship of the ruling classes was in accord with a Jesuit policy that had been initiated by the

[32] *Avisi de Giapone degli Anni MDLXXXII, LXXXIII et LXXXIV, con alcuni altri della Cina dell' LXXXIII et LXXXIV,* pp. 178-188; Servière, op. cit., p. 4.

[33] Brucker in *Catholic Encyclopedia,* Vol. 13, pp. 34 et seq.; Abel-Rémusat in *Nouveaux mélanges asiatiques,* Vol. 2, p. 207; *Lettres édifiantes,* Vol. 3, p. 2.

[34] Pietro Tacchi Venturi, *Opere Storiche del P. Matteo Ricci,* Vol. 1, pp. 141-142; Huc, op. cit., Vol. 2, p. 68.

founder.[35] Loyola never spared himself in ministering to the poor. He apparently believed, however, that the Society could best promote "the greater glory of God" by reaching the upper classes: if the favor of these were secure, work for the poor would be on a more stable basis. In China this policy was undoubtedly wise. The missionaries were protected by no treaties and were in the Empire purely on the sufferance of the government. If they were to be permitted to remain and to prosecute their work, they would need to establish and strengthen their relations with that scholar class in whose hands were most of the offices of state. Fortunately the intellectual atmosphere of the time was not altogether unpropitious. In some quarters a restlessness, a dissatisfaction with the accepted philosophies, and a spirit of inquiry existed and promised a certain amount of receptivity to foreign ideas. The Jesuits first aroused the curiosity of the scholar class by the inventions of Europe and won its tolerance and at times its respect by demonstrating that in some branches they had intellectual attainments superior to those of the Chinese. The question would naturally follow whether they did not have philosophical and religious truth worthy of attention. The compilers of the Ming history recorded approvingly of the missionaries that "the majority of the books which they have written are what the Chinese have not yet treated of."[36] The first convert in Chaoch'ing was, however, not from the educated but from the poorer classes, an outcast whom the missionaries cared for and baptized shortly before his death.[37]

All was not smooth sailing in Chaoch'ing. This death of the first convert led the rumor mongers to declare that the man had a jewel in his hand and that the hope of obtaining it was responsible for the missionaries' attention.[38] The fathers were, too, accused of immorality and were thereupon threatened by a mob. Friendly officials exonerated them, however, and they were allowed to remain.[39]

The first opportunity to make their way farther into the Empire came to the missionaries in 1585. One of their acquaintances, an official, asked two of them, Ruggerius and Almeida (who had

[35] Sedgwick, *Ignatius Loyola*, p. 250.
[36] Translated by Moule in the *New China Review*, Vol. 4, pp. 450-456.
[37] *Purchas, His Pilgrimes*, Vol. 3, p. 329; Huc, op. cit., Vol. 2, p. 63.
[38] Huc, op. cit., Vol. 2, p. 64; *Purchas, His Pilgrimes*, Vol. 3, p. 329.
[39] *Purchas, His Pilgrimes*, Vol. 3, p. 332; Tacchi Venturi, *Opere Storiche del P. Matteo Ricci*, Vol. 1, pp. 166, 167.

recently joined the mission), to accompany him on a trip north, and they went as far as Hangchow, the official's family home.[40] Ruggerius seems also to have made a journey into Kwangsi.[41]

However, so many obstacles obstructed the free course of the Gospel that the fathers felt that it would be wise if an embassy could be sent by some of the European powers to obtain imperial toleration for the preaching of the Faith. Without such toleration the continuation of missionary operations would depend upon the favor of local officials, an extremely precarious and unsatisfactory status. In 1588 Ruggerius was, accordingly, sent to Europe to try to bring about an embassy. He was destined never again to see China, for his mission met with vexatious delays and he died at Salerno in 1607,[42] with the object that had taken him to the Occident unachieved.

After the departure of Ruggerius, the Chinese mission continued to progress, although slowly and irregularly. The missionaries were driven out of Chaoch'ing (1589), but were permitted to establish a residence at Ch'aochou in the same province.[43] Here again the Jesuits used their knowledge of mathematics, astronomy, and mechanics to win the respect of the educated. In 1594 Ricci and his colleagues decided to change their garb. They had heretofore dressed as Buddhist priests, probably to avoid attracting undue attention and to commend themselves as teachers of religion. They discovered, however, that Buddhist monks were not greatly respected and that the scholars were socially the dominant group. They accordingly altered their dress to that of the latter class.[44]

It was about this time that Ricci determined to push his way farther north and, if possible, to settle in Peking. Here he

[40] Huc, op. cit., Vol. 2, pp. 74, 75; Henrion, Histoire générale des missions catholiques, Vol. 2, p. 42; letter of Dalmeida (Almeida) in Avvisi della Cina et Giapone del fine dell' anno 1586.
[41] Servière, Les anciennes missions de la Compagnie de Jésus en Chine, p. 5.
[42] Brucker in Catholic Encyclopedia, Vol. 13, p. 34; Henrion, op. cit., Vol. 2, p. 42; Sousa, The Portuguese in Asia, Vol. 3, p. 83. Servière, op. cit., p. 5, gives 1606 as the date of Ruggerius' death. Ruggerius had apparently some years before given up all thought of returning to China.
[43] Purchas, His Pilgrimes, Vol. 3, p. 332; Huc., op. cit., Vol. 2, pp. 93-101; Servière, op. cit., p. 6.
[44] Semedo, The History of the Great and Renowned Monarchy of China, p. 175. It is interesting to note that in India, where the Brahmins were the dominant social class, the Jesuit Robert de Nobili was trying to win them, and through them India, by adopting their garb and many of their customs. The Jesuits believed it to be wise missionary policy to address themselves primarily to the most influential classes and through them to reach the nation.

planned to win the favor of the court and so to obtain for the mission legal recognition. In his first effort he succeeded in reaching Nanking, but persecution drove him back and he was perforce content with establishing himself at Nanch'ang, the capital of Kiangsi.[45] In 1598, after nearly twenty years of continuous effort, the Jesuit mission possessed outside of Macao only seven members and three stations.[46] The mortality had been heavy and no serious impression had yet been made on the Empire. Ricci, however, was undiscouraged and persevered in his endeavors to reach Peking. It is reported, although the story is of doubtful authenticity, that he and two companions attached themselves to the train of an official who was going to the capital to become the president of one of the boards of the central government; that they entered the city but found it impossible to remain; and that Ricci then reluctantly turned his face southward and took up his residence at Nanking, which was now (1599) opened to him.[47] It is certain that he established himself at Nanking, and here he was to spend some time. He still directed his attention to the scholars. Some of these he found singularly open-minded, perhaps because of the intellectual unrest which characterized so many in the last years of the Ming dynasty, and he succeeded in winning a number of converts, among them a man of distinction in official circles, Hsü Kuang-ch'i, known to the missionaries as Paul Hsü.[48] Hsü proved to be one of the most loyal and eminent converts that the Roman Catholic Church has had in China and by his outspoken friendship, his literary assistance, his influence at court, and his wise counsel, he was to be a tower of strength. His daughter, known in missionary annals as Candida, became an earnest Christian, and, left a widow at an early age, gave herself to good works and the spread of the Christian message. It was she who is said to have devised the method of teaching professional story-tellers the Gospel narrative, so that it might reach the more quickly the masses of the people. It is altogether fitting that the present center of Jesuit education in China should be in the home village of the Hsü family, Zikawei, and on land given by Hsü Kuang-ch'i.

[45] Huc, op. cit., Vol. 2, pp. 107, 110.
[46] Purchas, His Pilgrimes, Vol. 3, p. 343.
[47] Ibid., Vol. 3, p. 339; Servière, Les anciennes missions de la Compagnie de Jésus en Chine, pp. 9, 10.
[48] Huc, op. cit., Vol. 2, p. 142.

RICCI ESTABLISHES THE MISSION IN PEKING

Ricci's persistence was at last rewarded, and in 1601 he reached Peking and was permitted to remain.[49] In the capital Ricci used the methods which had proved successful in the other cities where he had resided. By his knowledge of European sciences he commended himself to the scholars: moreover, by diligent application he had acquired a remarkable proficiency in the Classics. He was, accordingly, given a stipend from the imperial treasury and assigned a house.[50]

The position of Ricci and his companions in Peking had its desired effect and opened doors in other parts of the Empire. The work at Ch'aochou progressed and was extended to outlying villages. Numerous conversions were made, and the state of public opinion was such that it was possible to administer baptism openly and with a good deal of ceremony. Before being admitted to the communion, too, the catechumen made public confession of his sins, either in a form suggested by the missionaries or in the words of his own.[51] At Peking there were conversions among some of the highest officials, even including two members of the Hanlin Academy and an imperial prince and some members of the latter's family.[52] By 1605 the Peking mission numbered more than two hundred neophytes.[53] More Jesuits entered the country and steps were taken to train a native clergy in a college at Macao.[54]

A temporary reversal in the fortunes of the mission occurred about 1606, when a rumor gained currency that the Portuguese were plotting with the Jesuits to conquer the country, that Macao was stored with arms, and that Cataneo, one of the missionaries, was to be made Emperor. For a time there was panic among the Chinese in and around Macao and some persecution followed. Unrest was felt even in Peking. The absurdity of the accusation

[49] Williams, *Middle Kingdom,* Vol. 2, pp. 289-295; *Purchas, His Pilgrimes,* Vol. 3, pp. 354-358; Huc, op. cit., Vol. 2, pp. 145-154. See the note in the *Ming Shih* on the reception of the Jesuits, translated by Moule in *The New China Review,* Vol. 4, pp. 450-456.

[50] Huc, op. cit., Vol. 2, p. 151.

[51] Huc, op. cit., Vol. 2, pp. 153-171.

[52] Letter of Ricci, February, 1605, in Tacchi Venturi, *Opere Storiche del P. Matteo Ricci,* Vol. 2, pp. 253, 254; *Huc, Christianity in China, Tartary and Thibet,* Vol. 2, pp. 175, 176.

[53] Huc, op. cit., Vol. 2, pp. 175, 176.

[54] Ibid., Vol. 2, p. 174.

quickly became apparent, however, and the fathers suffered only temporary embarrassment.[55] By 1610, indeed, through the kindly offices of Paul Hsü, a new mission had been inaugurated at Shanghai.[56]

Since the Portuguese rediscovery of the Far East, Europeans had not determined the location of the Cathay of which Marco Polo had told and on which the Franciscans had expended so much effort. By the time Ricci had obtained permission to reside permanently in Peking, he had procured information which led him to believe that China and Cathay were identical.[57] The final proof of the accuracy of his contention was, however, to come from another source. The Jesuits residing in India at the court of the Mogul Emperors heard from travellers of a great land to the north, Khitai or Xathai, where the population was said to be largely Christian. They thought it might be different from the China in which they knew their Society to be working and determined to investigate. Benedict of Goës, a lay brother, was instructed to make the perilous journey and left Agra in 1602. Aided by the Mogul Emperor Akbar and the Portuguese Viceroy, he went overland by way of Kabul, the Pamirs, Yarkand, and Turfan. He assumed the name and dress of an Armenian and was accompanied by an Armenian merchant, Isaac. Some time before he reached China Proper he met merchants who had just come from Peking and had there seen Jesuits. He knew, therefor, that Khitai, Cathay, and China were identical.[58] He pressed on, but died just within the borders of China shortly after the arrival of a messenger from the Peking mission. One of his Society summed up his venture in the words: "Seeking Cathay he found heaven." [59]

The first period of the Jesuit mission to China may be said to end in 1610 with the death of Ricci.[60] For the last several years

[55] Montalto de Jesus, *Historic Macao*, pp. 58-62; Bowra in *China Review*, Vol. 2, pp. 244-254.

[56] Huc, op. cit., Vol. 2, pp. 211, 212.

[57] Huc, op. cit., Vol. 2, pp. 186-208; Cordier-Yule, *Cathay and the Way Thither*, Vol. 4, pp. 170-288; Athanasii Kircheri, *China Monumentis*, p. 60; Ricci, *Lettere*, p. 227, and Ricci, *Commentari*, pp. 296, 297, quoted in Wessels, *Early Jesuit Travellers in Central Asia*, p. 6.

[58] Wessels, op. cit., pp. 14-41.

[59] Cordier-Yule, op. cit., Vol. 4, p. 171.

[60] Valignani, to whose wisdom and vigor was due the initiation of permanent work, had lived to see the success of the project. He died in 1606 and was buried at Macao.—*Catalogus Patrum ac Fratrum e Societate Jesu qui . . . in Sinis adlaboraverunt*, p. 3.

of his life Ricci had been the Superior of the China mission and it was due chiefly to his ability and courage that at his passing his Society had houses in Peking and in a number of other important centers and that it enjoyed the tolerance of the court and the adherence of influential officials. Ricci had made a profound impression on the Chinese. A local history records that he had "a curly beard, blue eyes, and a voice like a great bell." [61] He wrote voluminously in Chinese on theology and the teachings of the Church.[62] To him, probably more than to any other one man, was due that attempt to adjust the Christian faith to its Chinese environment which was later to bring about the famous rites controversy. He apparently saw that if Christianity was ever to have any large place in China either the culture and institutions of the country must be modified or the Church must in part adjust its teachings and practices to Chinese life. Since the former alternative seemed, at the time, impossible, he chose the latter. Measured by his ability and achievements, Ricci is undoubtedly one of the greatest missionaries whom the Church has had in China.

It is said that on his death-bed Ricci was asked by one of the Society: "Do you know, my father, in what position you leave us?" "Yes," said the dying man, "I leave you before a door which may be opened to great merits, but not without much trouble and danger." Whether or not the story is authentic, it accurately describes the situation and expresses the spirit of the great missionary.

Ricci was buried with imperial sanction in ground which had belonged to a eunuch of the court and which was obtained through the kindness of officials.[63] In fitting accord with his policy of conforming as far as possible to Chinese customs, his funeral and his grave approximated closely to native practices.[64] In death as in life he was seeking to conciliate rather than antagonize.

[61] *Records of Hangchow,* translated by Moule in *The New China Review,* Vol. 4, pp. 450-456.

[62] Wylie, *Notes on Chinese Literature,* pp. 172-174. In most if not all of his writings in Chinese he was aided by Chinese scholars.—Thomas, *Histoire de la mission de Pekin,* pp. 81, 82.

[63] Huc, op. cit., Vol. 2, pp. 213-220; *Purchas, His Pilgrimes,* Vol. 3, p. 407. Ricci's letters and some other accounts of the mission are to be found in Tacchi Venturi, op. cit.

[64] Blair and Robertson, op. cit., Vol. 14, passim; Brinkley, *China,* Vol. 10, p. 179.

SPANISH ATTEMPTS TO ENTER CHINA FROM THE PHILIPPINES

While the Jesuits were establishing themselves in the capital and the provinces other orders were by no means idle. The Philippines, it will be remembered, had been settled in the latter part of the sixteenth century largely as a missionary outpost,[65] and from them, as we have seen, Franciscans, Augustinians, and possibly Dominicans early attempted to make their way to China.

As time passed, these efforts multiplied. The Franciscans, when in 1586 they created a province for the Islands, gave it the significant name "S. Gregorii Philippinarum et Chinæ." [66] The Dominican Province of the Holy Rosary, founded in 1582, was defined as including the Philippines, China, and Japan.[67] It was not easy, however, for these orders to gain a foothold in the Middle Kingdom. The Portuguese claim to the right of patronage closed the route via Lisbon, the Cape of Good Hope, India, and Macao to all whom the Crown did not approve. When, in 1580, the Spanish monarch became also King of Portugal, Spanish missionaries flocked to Macao from Manila. We hear, foi example, of a Spanish Jesuit, Alonzo Sanchez, being there twice, and of several Spanish Franciscans—the Commissary Geronimo de Burgos and six companions—imprisoned in Canton by the Chinese, and of a letter from Philip II to the "King of China" asking permission for missionaries to labor in the Middle Kingdom.[68] Philip II was not minded, however, to jeopardize his rule by ruthlessly disregarding Portuguese sensibilities, and by his orders his new subjects were soon confirmed in their old privileges. At the command of the Viceroy of the Indies the Spanish friars left Macao and turned over their houses to their Portuguese brethren.[69] Although Spaniards kept filtering back,[70] they did not enjoy complete freedom of action. The Jesuits and the Portuguese made common cause. The former had sent their first missionaries to the East at the request of the King. A papal

[65] E. G. Bourne in Blair and Robertson, *The Philippine Islands*, Vol. 1, p. 48.
[66] Holzapfel, *Handbuch der Geschichte des Franziskanerordens*, p. 394.
[67] Blair and Robertson, op. cit., Vol. 30, p. 117; Moidrey, *Le hiérarchie catholique de la Chine*, p. 184.
[68] Colin (Pastells' edition), *Labor Evangelica*, Vol. 1, pp. 265 et seq.
[69] Montalto de Jesus, *Historic Macao*, p. 45; Colin (Pastells' edition), *Labor Evangelica*, Vol. 1, pp. 265 et seq.
[70] Civezza, *Histoire universelle des missions franciscaines*, Vol. 2, p. 238.

order of 1585 had opened China only to the Society of Jesus and it was not until 1600 that the head of the Church included the mendicant orders in the permission.   Even then missionaries were commanded to go out by way of Lisbon, a restriction which was not removed until 1608.   Not until 1633 did Rome grant full freedom to members of orders other than the Jesuits and the mendicants to go to non-Portuguese territories in the Far East, and only in 1673 was that permission extended to the secular clergy.[71]   It is not strange, therefore, that non-Jesuits were delayed in establishing missions in the Middle Kingdom.   Their chief agents were usually Spaniards and these had to come by way of the Atlantic, Mexico, the Pacific, and the Philippines.

Due to these difficulties, in 1610 only the Jesuits were to be found outside Macao and some years were to elapse before other bodies were to gain a secure foothold in the provinces.   However, many heroic attempts were made to enter China.   Sometime between 1581 and 1583 a party of Franciscans, probably seven in number, sailed from the Philippines and succeeded in landing on the coast of China.   They were apprehended, sent to Canton, and there imprisoned.   One died in confinement, but the others were released through the good offices of the Portuguese.   One of those so released, Martin Ignacio de Loyola, accompanied by a Father Lucarelli, returned to Europe, Lucarelli to seek permission from Rome to found seminaries to prepare missionaries for China, and Loyola to gather reënforcements.   The latter was back at Macao in 1587 and with his companions went to Canton to try once more to enter the country.   Again he was imprisoned and again Portuguese intervention obtained his release.   After this discouraging failure, for over a generation Franciscans made no further effort to penetrate the mainland.[72]

In 1586 there was sent to Philip II from the Philippines a remarkable document signed by the Governor, the Archbishop, and the superiors of the various religious orders, submitting a plan for the conquest of China.   It was estimated that the project would require ten or twelve thousand men from Spain and as many more Japanese and Filipinos.   The country was to be merely dominated, not ravaged, and its conversion was to be one of the

---

[71] Jann, *Die katholischen Missionen in Indien, China und Japan*, pp. 174-204.
[72] Maas, *Cartas de China*, pp. 4, 5; Mendoza, *History of China* (Introduction by R. H. Major), Vol. 1, p. lxxvi; Civezza, *Histoire universelle des missions franciscaines*, Vol. 2, p. 218.

prime objects of the enterprise. Nothing came of the proposal, but as an illustration of the temper of the Spaniards of that`day it is most illuminating.[73]

In 1587 three Dominicans came to Macao directly from Mexico, and one of them, Lopez, is said to have spent three years in China and to have baptized many converts.[74] In 1590 Jean de Castro, the founder of the Dominican Province of the Holy Rosary, landed in China with another member of his order, but was soon compelled to leave.[75] Other attempts by Dominicans, all unsuccessful, were made in 1593,[76] 1596, and 1598.[77] So popular, indeed, did it become to try to enter the Middle Kingdom that missions in the Philippines were threatened and in 1585 the state found it necessary to decree that no member of an order should go to China without the permission of the Governor and the Archbishop.[78] Apparently the command was not heeded, for it was repeated in 1596, 1621, 1635, 1636, 1638, and 1640.[79] In spite of zealous efforts, at the time of Ricci's death, of all the Catholic orders only the Jesuits had residences outside of Macao.

In the meantime members of the orders were not unmindful of the many Chinese in the Islands and were carrying on missions among them.[80] They were in part successful—at least as far as outward adherence to the Church was concerned. Fear and policy may have had a part in the conversion, however, for the relations between Spaniards and Chinese were often strained. Many of the latter were massacred in the first decade of the seventeenth century, and a limit was set on the numbers who could live in the Philippines.[81]

[73] Blair and Robertson, *The Philippine Islands,* Vol. 6, pp. 13, 197-226.
[74] André-Marie, *Missions dominicaines dans l'Éxtrême Orient,* Vol. 1, pp. 178, 179. (This work is not always dependable.)
[75] Ibid., Vol. 1, pp. 179-182; Aduarte, *Historia de la Provincia del Sancto Rosario de la Orden de Predicatores,* etc., in Blair and Robertson, op. cit., Vol. 30, pp. 246 et seq.
[76] Aduarte, op. cit., in Blair and Robertson, op. cit., Vol. 31, pp. 73-76.
[77] André-Marie, op. cit., Vol. 1, pp. 182-185; Savignol, *Les martyrs dominicains de la Chine au XVIIIe siècle,* pp. 13-16.
[78] Blair and Robertson, op. cit., Vol. 28, p. 67.
[79] Ibid., Vol. 28, p. 71.
[80] Ibid., Vol. 7, pp. 212-238.
[81] Thomas, *Histoire de la mission de Pékin,* pp. 80, 83.

CHAPTER VII

THE PROGRESS OF ROMAN CATHOLIC MISSIONS FROM THE DEATH OF RICCI TO THE REVERSES CAUSED BY THE CONTROVERSY OVER THE RITES
(1610-1706)

THE JESUITS IN CHARGE OF THE CALENDAR

THE death of Ricci had but little effect upon the progress of the enterprise he had helped to inaugurate. His Society had become so well established in China and possessed so many men of ability that even the loss of the leader worked no serious injury. Nicolo Longobardi, a Sicilian of noble family, quietly succeeded to the headship of the mission. He had been in China since 1597 and so had had extensive experience there. He had differed from Ricci on some fundamental missionary policies, but had been the latter's choice for the position.[1] The mission continued to prosper. Six new recruits joined the staff in 1610 and four in 1613.[2] In 1615 Nicholas Trigault journeyed through Europe, seeking to arouse the interest of princes in the China mission. He was so far successful that in 1616 the Duke of Bavaria promised an annual gift of five hundred florins and for at least a century the subvention was paid with a fair degree of regularity.[3]

Soon after the death of Ricci and because of his foresight, further official recognition was obtained. The calendar occupied an important place in China. Its acceptance by a conquered nation was recognition of the suzerainty of Peking and in other ways it was of political significance. It was used, too, throughout the Empire to determine lucky and unlucky days for weddings, funerals, and various events and transactions of social and business life. Ricci had noted its importance and the interest taken by the con-

---

[1] Huc, *Christianity in China, Tartary, and Thibet*, Vol. 2, pp. 226-229.
[2] Including Xavier, thirty-six missionaries had served in the China mission between 1552 and the close of 1613.—*Catalogus Patrum ac Fratrum e Societate Jesu qui . . . in Sinis adlaboraverunt*, pp. 2-11.
[3] Schneller in *Zeitschrift für Missionswissenschaft*, Vol. 4, pp. 176-189.

verts in a calendar which he had prepared for liturgical purposes. He therefore urged that the Society send out an expert astronomer.[4] In response to his request, in 1606 Father Sabbatino de Ursis arrived. It was not many years before a serious mistake in forecasting an eclipse was made by the Moslem mathematicians to whom were entrusted the calculations of the *Ch'in T'ien Chien*—the Imperial Bureau of Astronomy—and in 1611 an imperial decree ordered the missionaries to reform the calendar and to translate European astronomical books. De Ursis undertook the task, with the assistance of Paul Hsü and other Christian scholars.[5]

THE PERSECUTIONS OF 1616 AND 1622

The mission was not to enjoy uninterrupted prosperity, however, for in 1616 a severe persecution arose. The causes are somewhat obscure, but the chief instigator was an official connected with the Board of Rites who appears to have entertained a peculiar animosity for Father Alphonsus Vagnoni, then living in Nanking. He may also have been jealous of some of the Catholic Chinese scholars. Whatever the motives, the missionaries were denounced to the throne by the Board of Rites on the ground that they were seditious, like the White Lily and Wu Wei Societies, and were plotting with the foreigners at Macao. An imperial decree accordingly ordered the missionaries to Kwangtung to await deportation. The edict was partially enforced at Peking and Nanking: several missionaries were apprehended and sent to Macao, some of them in cages, but for the most part the foreigners hid among the Chinese Christians and secretly continued their ministrations.

Due apparently to the activity of the same hostile official, in 1622 the persecution was renewed and again the missionaries were forced either to flee or to go into hiding. Again the reason urged was that Christians were seditious. A rebellion instigated by the White Lily Society, moreover, helped to frighten the court into action. The dynasty was threatened by many rebellions and it is not strange that a sect led by aliens should fall under suspicion. However, the missionaries had powerful friends in the per-

---

[4] Letter of Ricci to Alvarez, 1605; Tacchi Venturi, *Opere Storiche del P. Matteo Ricci*, Vol. 2, pp. 284, 285.

[5] J. Brucker in *Catholic Encyclopedia*, Vol. 13, p. 520. The Board was not one of the six principal Pu, but had some sort of connection with the Li Pu, or Board of Rites.—*Encyclopædia Sinica*, p. 39.

sons of Hsü Kuang-ch'i and other scholars, the chief foe of the mission was removed from office and died, and the missionaries were recalled to Peking and honorably reinstated.[6]

RENEWED PROSPERITY

The next few years appear to have been comparatively uneventful. In 1624 it was reported that there were in the provinces six "colleges" or missionary centers, that at Peking there were three Jesuit fathers and a brother, and that many of the court had been baptized.[7] Nineteen joined the staff of the China mission between 1620 and 1629 inclusive.[8] A new station was opened as far west as Hsianfu in 1628 or 1629.[9] In 1629, thanks in part to the influence of Chinese Christians in high office, the Jesuits had been so far restored to favor that the task of revising the calendar was again committed to them. Ursis had died at Macao in 1620, a victim of the persecution of 1616,[10] but a capable successor, Terrentius, was at hand. Terrentius, or Schreck as he had been known before he became a Jesuit, had entered the Society in his middle thirties and was a physician, a botanist, a mathematician, and a friend of Galileo. He saw in his new position the one means of preventing the expulsion of the Society from China and gave himself unstintedly to it. In a little less than a year he was dead (May 13, 1630),[11] but again the Society had a man trained for the place, Johann Adam Schall von Bell. Schall was born near Cologne in 1591. He entered the Society of Jesus in 1611 and after his novitiate and further study was, at his own request, sent as a missionary. He arrived at Macao in 1619, but because of the persecution then in progress was unable to enter the interior until 1622. On the death of Terrentius he was summoned to Peking and soon became the leading figure in the mis-

[6] Moule in *The New China Review*, Vol. 4, pp. 450-456, has a translation from the *Ming Shih* which gives an account of the trouble. Other accounts are in Huc, op. cit., Vol. 2, pp. 234-285; Henrion, *Histoire générale des missions catholiques*, etc., Vol. 2, pp. 236, 237; Semedo, *The History of the Great and Renowned Monarchy of China*, pp. 205-226; Le Comte, *Nouveaux mémoires sur l'état present de la Chine*, Vol. 2, p. 158; *Chinese Repository*, Vol. 19, pp. 118-135

[7] *Histoire de ce qui s'est passe au royaume de la Chine en l'année 1624*, passim.

[8] *Catalogus Patrum ac Fratrum e Societate Jesu qui . . . in Sinis adlaboraverunt*, pp. 2-11.

[9] Cordier-Yule, *Cathay and the Way Thither*, Vol. 1, p. 236, quoting Semedo, *Relazioni della Cina*. Huc, op. cit., Vol. 2, p. 288, says 1629.

[10] *Encyclopædia Sinica*, p. 586.

[11] Brucker, in *Catholic Encyclopedia*, Vol. 13, p. 520.

sion.[12] Jacques Rho was associated with him for some years, but died in 1638.[13]

THE COMING OF THE MANCHUS

The second quarter of the seventeenth century saw the establishment of a new dynasty on the throne of China. Rebellions had been numerous, the Emperors were frequently weak, corruption was rife, and the influence of the palace eunuchs, always baleful, was increasing. It was apparent that Heaven was threatening to remove its decree from the Mings and that almost any astute adventurer might make himself master of the Empire. As it happened, there was on the northwestern borders a rising power. Repeatedly in the centuries past a non-Chinese northern people had broken through the barriers and had made itself ruler of part or all of the great fertile land to the south. The latest in this succession were the Manchus. For several decades an able family had been welding them together into a fighting force and had been threatening the northern marches. In 1644 the Manchu leaders took advantage of an unusually disastrous civil war in the northern provinces and occupied Peking. The Mings did not yield without a struggle but sought to retain a foothold in the South as the last native dynasty before them, the Sung, had done. Aided by Chinese allies, the Manchus pursued them, slowly driving them from province to province, until, in 1662, Kuei Wang, the last of the Mings to claim the imperial title, was captured and either was executed or committed suicide. The preceding year (1661) had witnessed the death of Shun Chih,[14] the first of the Manchus to be recognized as Emperor, and had seen the accession of the boy who was to be known to history as K'ang Hsi and who was to prove the ablest monarch of the dynasty and one of the strongest that China has known.

Missions might have been expected to suffer from the disorder of these stirring years. Strange to say, however, they flourished. There were, to be sure, some local persecutions,[15] but Manchus

---

[12] Ibid.

[13] *Encyclopædia Sinica*, p. 482.

[14] As all those familiar with China know, Shun Chih is a reign name, not a personal name or dynastic title. Foreigners, however, almost always refer to a sovereign by his reign name, and that custom is followed here and elsewhere in this work.

[15] Servière, *Les anciennes missions de la Compagnie de Jésus en Chine*, p. 29. There was a local persecution in Fukien in 1639.

and Mings were too intent on fighting each other to pay attention to Europeans and these were therefore much less molested than in years past.   Moreover, the Jesuits attached themselves to each court and were of substantial assistance to both without arousing the ire or the serious suspicion of either.   While the Mings were still at Peking, Schall, at their command, directed the casting of cannon for use against their enemies.[16]   When the Manchus occupied the city, Schall stayed on and speedily won their confidence.   Shun Chih employed him to arrange the calendar and gave him official rank.   Some of the Jesuits questioned whether one of their number should formally hold civil office and whether it was right to help arrange a calendar which in its published form contained references to lucky and unlucky days and so was used for pagan purposes.   The matter was eventually referred to Rome—although not until after the death of Schall—and a papal decision authorized Jesuits to hold the kind of office that had been conferred upon him.

In the meantime Schall had continued to perform his official duties and had won the warm personal esteem of the Emperor.[17] Shun Chih presented him with a site and a sum of money for a house and a church (later known as the Nan T'ang).[18]   Laudatory inscriptions, including an imperial declaration in praise of Christianity, were displayed in or near the edifice.   These declarations, while probably not a formal edict of toleration, had much the effect of one.[19]   Shun Chih also conferred honorific titles on Schall and, in accordance with Chinese custom, upon his parents.[20]

The Jesuits who attached themselves to the retreating Ming court were even more influential than was Schall at Peking.   Two of them, Andrew Koffler (also known as Andrew Xavier) and Michael Boym, were given official rank.   A concubine of a late Emperor, left by the death of the first wife with the position of Empress Dowager, was a Christian and is known in Jesuit annals

[16] Brucker in *Catholic Encyclopedia,* Vol. 13, p. 521; Schall, *Geschichte der chinesischen Mission,* pp. 119-134.
[17] Brucker in op. cit., Vol. 13, p. 521; Schall, op. cit., passim.
[18] The Jesuits had heretofore had in Peking only a private chapel attached to their residence.—Schall, op. cit., p. 353.
[19] Schall, op. cit., p. 359.   There is a statement (I have been unable to find the original text) that Shun Chih's declaration included a formal grant of toleration, but the authority is not given.—Brucker, op. cit., Vol. 13, p. 522; see also Abel-Rémusat, *Nouveaux mélanges asiatiques,* Vol. 2, p. 218.
[20] Brucker, op. cit., Vol. 13, p. 522; Thomas, *Histoire de la mission de Pékin,* pp. 102-105.

as the Empress Helen. Kuei Wang was himself not a Christian, but his heir, his mother, and the mother of his heir were baptized as Constantine, Mary, and Anne respectively. The Ming Governor of Kwangsi, the general-in-chief of the Ming forces, and Kuei Wang's highest court functionary, a eunuch, were also professing Christians. It may well be that this attachment to Christianity was at least in part due to a despairing hope that Europeans would come to the rescue of the rapidly waning Ming power. A Portuguese contingent from Macao seems for a time to have given a little aid. In 1650 Boym was sent to Europe with an embassy and letters to the Pope. He reached Italy in 1652 but was not given a formal reply until late in 1655. Boym died in Tongking on his return trip and Koffler perished in the disasters that overwhelmed the luckless Kuei Wang.[21] Whatever their hopes or motives, the Mings received no effective help from Christendom. Europe was not prepared to interfere in Chinese politics.

It was not only at the courts of the rival imperial houses that Christianity was making headway during these years of strife. Throughout the provinces similar progress was to be found. Statistics for the period are often extremely uncertain and we shall probably never know just the size of the Christian community or the exact location of all its members. It is certain, however, that the Church enjoyed a rapid growth and that its stronghold was in the lower part of the Yangtze Valley and in Peking. One estimate places the number of Christians in 1627 at 13,000, locates them in Kiangsi, Chêkiang, Kiangnan, Shantung, Shansi, Shensi, and Chihli,[22] and says that in ten years more it had increased to 40,000.[23] Another places the number in 1617 at 13,000 and says that this had risen to 150,000 in 1650 and to 254,980 in 1664.[24] Still another account says that by the end of the Ming dynasty there were missions in all the provinces except Yünnan and Kweichow, and that by 1663 there were 109,900 Christians in the Empire.[25]

[21] Backhouse and Bland, *Annals and Memoirs of the Court of Peking*, p. 222; Girard de Rialle in *T'oung Pao*, Vol. 1, pp. 99-117; *Encyclopædia Sinica*, p. 63; Thomas, op. cit., pp. 98-100.

[22] Martino Martinio, *de Statu et Qualitate Christianorum in Sina*, p. 16, quoted in Huc, *Christianity in China, Tartary and Thibet*, Vol. 2, p. 290.

[23] Huc, op. cit., Vol. 2, p. 290.

[24] Brucker in *Catholic Encyclopedia*, Vol. 13, p. 522; see also Schmidlin, *Katholische Missionsgeschichte*, p. 273, for slightly different figures.

[25] Servière, *Les anciennes missions de la Compagnie de Jésus en Chine*, pp. 31, 35.

Various scattered incidents show in what distant sections of the eighteen provinces the missionaries resided and how widely they had travelled. Sometime before or during the Manchu conquest two Jesuits began work in Szechwan and suffered severely during the disorders of the time.[26] A mission appears to have been begun on Hainan about 1630, although the date is uncertain.[27] Because in 1661 the Dutch had temporarily blockaded Macao, two Jesuits who were being sent to Rome in that year, Albert d'Orville and Johann Grueber, went overland and succeeded in crossing to India by way of Kansu, Tibet, and Nepal. Theirs was a remarkable feat, one not easily accomplished even to-day. Orville died at Agra but Grueber continued his journey and arrived safely in Europe.[28] Fourteen Jesuits joined the China mission in 1657 and twelve in 1659, but these were exceptional years, for the total from 1646 to 1663 inclusive was only thirty-six.[29]

THE SPANIARDS ESTABLISH MISSIONS IN CHINA

It was in the years just preceding and during the establishment of the Manchu dynasty that Spanish missionaries from the Philippines were at last successful in acquiring a permanent foothold in China. About 1625 or 1626 the Spaniards instituted a post on Formosa and followed it by another (at Tamsui) in 1629.[30] In 1642 they were driven out by the Dutch,[31] but in the brief interval both the Franciscans and Dominicans had seized the opportunity to use the island as a base for renewed efforts to enter China. In 1625 or 1626 a Dominican, Barthelemy Martinez, with five others of his order, founded in Formosa a house and a church and labored with some success for the conversion of non-Christians.[32] In 1630 two Dominicans, Angel Coqui or Ange Cocchi, a Florentine, and Thomas de Sierra, started from Formosa for the neighboring mainland of Fukien with an expedition which was seeking to open commercial relations with the Chinese. On

[26] Huc, op. cit., Vol. 2, pp. 343-349.
[27] Henry, Ling-nam, p. 337; China Mission Year Book, p. 208.
[28] Kircher, Monumenti Sinici, p. 64; Huonder in Catholic Encyclopedia, Vol. 7, p. 41; Wessels, Early Jesuit Travellers in Central Asia, pp. 164-202.
[29] Catalogus Patrum ac Fratrum e Societate Jesu qui . . . in Sinis adlaboraverunt, pp. 10-21.
[30] Encyclopædia Sinica, p. 192.
[31] Ibid., p. 192.
[32] André-Marie, Missions dominicaines dans l'Éxtrême Orient, Vol. 1, pp. 182-185.

the way the party was attacked, apparently first by the crew and then by pirates. Sierra and four others of the company were killed, but Coqui reached the mainland. He was ordered to leave, but by sending out in his garb a Christian Japanese he succeeded in eluding the authorities. He got in touch with some Christians, the fruits of Jesuit missions, and with an Italian Jesuit, Julio Aleni, who showed him much kindness. In the course of the next few years he made several converts. He wrote to the Philippines for reënforcements and in response to his request Juan Baptista de Morales was sent him.[33] Morales arrived in 1633 and was destined to have an important part in later controversies over missionary methods. Coqui died in November, 1633,[34] but the enterprise which he had established was to continue.

With Morales came a Franciscan, Antonio de Santa Maria (Anton Caballero), who also succeeded in remaining, the first of his order to reside in China outside of Macao since the disappearance of the Mongol dynasty.[35] He baptized as his first convert a Chinese, Lo Wên-tsao, who was to be known as Gregory Lopez. Lopez was to become a Dominican and was to be the first Chinese Roman Catholic bishop.[36] Others, both Dominicans and Franciscans, followed these successful pioneers and aided and continued their work.

Progress was not without its obstacles. In the first place, the journey from Europe by way of Spain, Mexico, and the Philippines was usually costly in life. For example, of twenty-eight Dominicans who in 1631 left Spain for the Far East, six died on the

[33] Aduarte, *Historia de la Provincia del Santo Rosario,* etc., in Blair and Robertson, *The Philippine Islands,* Vol. 32, pp. 13, 186 et seq.; Savignol, *Les martyrs dominicains de la Chine au XVIIIe siècle,* pp. 16 et seq.; Biermann, *Die Anfänge der neueren Dominikanermission in China,* pp. 27-39.

[34] Aduarte, op. cit., in Blair and Robertson, op. cit., Vol. 32, p. 225; Moidrey, *La hiérarchie catholique en Chine,* etc., p. 184, says 1634. Biermann, op. cit., p. 42, says November 18, 1633.

[35] Civezza, *Histoire universelle des missions franciscaines,* Vol. 2, p. 219 et seq.; Maas, *Cartas de China,* p. 7; Maas, *Die Wiederöffnung der Franziskannermission in China in der Neuzeit,* pp. 47-53.

[36] Maas, *Cartas de China,* p. 7. Lopez may have been a Eurasian. Huonder, *Der einheimische Klerus in den Heidenländern,* p. 178, says that his mother was Portuguese and his father Chinese. The life of Lopez in Quétif and Echard's *Scriptores Ordinis Praedicatorum,* Vol. 2, (1721), pp. 708, 709, translated by Moule in *The New China Review,* Vol. 1, p. 480 et seq., says that he was "a native of China, born in the city of Fogan [Fu-an, in Northeast Fukien] and embraced the Christian faith when he was grown up." Biermann, op. cit., p. 43, says that he was born of pagan parents in Lokchiahsiang ("the Village of the Family Lo") in 1611. Huonder, therefore, is probably mistaken.

way, although the voyage was described as "prosperous." [37] Then all the Jesuits in China were not as cordial to the representatives of the other orders as was Aleni and sometimes made difficulty.[38] Moreover, when in 1642 the Dutch drove the Spaniards out of Formosa, that island became impossible as a station between the Philippines and China. In the next place, when in 1640 the Kings of Spain ceased to wear the crown of Portugal, Spanish missionaries found Macao even more inhospitable than formerly. Spanish monks and nuns who were in Macao when the news of the separation arrived were apparently permitted to depart in peace,[39] but in 1644 there was a massacre of those Spaniards who persisted in remaining.[40] As late as 1697 we find Dominicans, Augustinians, and Franciscans sending from Manila a formal petition to the Spanish King asking him to use his influence at Rome to prevent the Portuguese and French bishops from expelling Spanish missionaries from China.[41] More serious than all other obstacles was the opposition of the Chinese authorities. In 1637 the three Franciscans and five Dominicans who that year entered Fukien found it necessary to hide in the mountains and most of them were arrested and taken to Macao.[42] In 1647 Capillas, a Dominican, who had been touring the villages of Fukien, preaching, was arrested and executed (January 15, 1648).[43]

Still the mendicant orders persisted. The news of the martyrdom of Capillas, indeed, proved an incentive and more men than ever offered for service in China.[44] About 1655 the Dominicans built a church at Foochow.[45] In 1654 Victorio Ricci, a Dominican and a relative of the great Matthew Ricci, went to China with four others of his order and labored there for some years.[46] In 160 Antonio de Santa Maria, the Franciscan who

[37] Letter of Fray Juan Garcia, O. P., 1632, in Blair and Robertson, op. cit., Vol. 24, pp. 275-278.
[38] Civezza, op. cit., p. 219 et seq.; Blair and Robertson, op. cit., Vol. 29, p. 37.
[39] Civezza, op. cit., Vol. 2, p. 238.
[40] Maas, op. cit., pp. 7, 9.
[41] Pérez, Origen de la Misiones Franciscanas en la Provincia de Kwangtung (China), p. 124.
[42] Civezza, op. cit., Vol. 2, p. 234. See also Blair and Robertson, op. cit., Vol. 29, pp. 36 and 150.
[43] Savignol, Les martyrs dominicains de la Chine au XVIIIe siècle, Vol. 2, pp. 377, 378; André-Marie, op. cit., Vol. 1, pp. 186-194.
[44] André-Marie, op. cit., Vol. 1, pp. 186-194.
[45] Ibid., Vol. 1, p. 195.
[46] Salazar, Historia de la Provincia de el Santissimo Rosario . . . de el Sagrada orden de Predicadores, 1669-1700, pp. 407-437.

had come to China with Morales, attempted to enter Korea but was turned back and settled in Shantung. Here, in 1650 or 1651, in Tsinanfu, he built a church and founded a mission which was to have a long and honorable history.[47] There are said to have been in Shantung by 1659 fifteen hundred baptized converts.[48] In contrast with the jealousies which so often disfigured the relations between the various orders, it is pleasant to record that the Franciscan success in Shantung was due in no small degree to the advice of Schall and to an introduction which he had given the Brothers Minor to an official in the province.[49]

As a result of all these many endeavors, by the time of the death of the first Manchu Emperor the prolonged Spanish efforts had been crowned with success: both Dominicans and Franciscans had established themselves firmly in China. It is said that by 1665 the Dominicans had eleven residences, about twenty churches, and approximately ten thousand Christians under their charge in Chêkiang, Fukien, and Kwangtung, and that the Franciscans had about four thousand neophytes in Canton.[50] The figures may well be incorrect, but both orders had undeniably begun to make their presence felt.

The Coming of the French
The Société des Missions Étrangères

Before the death of Shun Chih, plans had been begun in a third country, France, for Roman Catholic missions to China, and the foundations had been laid for one of the greatest of the missionary societies of the Church, the Société des Missions-Etrangères of Paris. By the middle of the seventeenth century Spain and Portugal had passed their zenith. The burst of energy which had made them the discoverers, the colonizers, and the missionaries of the fifteenth and sixteenth centuries was partly spent. Both countries still had great colonial empires and from both missionaries continued to go forth, but they were waning powers and their decay was becoming apparent even to the most careless observer. On the continent of Europe another monarchy, France, was seizing the hegemony, and in politics and culture

[47] Maas, *Cartas de China*, pp. 7-10, 52; Civezza, op. cit., Vol. 2, p. 240; Moidrey, *Le hiérarchie catholique en Chine*, etc., p. 181; Maas, *Die Wiederöffnung der Franziskannermission in China in der Neuzeit*, pp. 135-160.
[48] Bishop Giesen in Forsyth, *Shantung*, pp. 162 et seq.
[49] Ibid.
[50] E. H. Parker in *The China Review*, Vol. 18, pp. 163 et seq.

was to be the most important figure of the latter half of the seventeenth and of the eighteenth century. France was predominantly Catholic and, as had been the case with Spain and Portugal, its awakening energy was to lead in part to missionary activity. The sincere zeal of French missionaries was to be reënforced by the political and commercial ambitions of kings and ministers. Louis XIV (who reigned from 1643 to 1715) was not at all averse to supporting missions, especially if they contributed to the glory of his reign, and the great minister of his early manhood, Colbert, had among his chief aims the increase of French commerce and colonial possessions. The rulers of France were never to be as deeply interested in missions as were some of those of Spain and Portugal, their colonial possessions were not to be as large, and their preoccupation with continental affairs was frequently to prevent them from giving to missions as much substantial assistance as they might otherwise have done, but the state and its policies were often a direct aid to missions and the great vigor of the nation was to express itself in part in extending the Catholic faith. It is not surprising, then, that shortly after the middle of the seventeenth century the French began to share in missionary operations in China.

The first serious project for a distinctively French mission to the East of Asia was apparently due to a suggestion from a Jesuit, Alexander of Rhodes. Alexander had been for some years in the Far East. Persecution had driven him out of Cochin China and he had become convinced that the only effective method of planting the Church there was to raise up a native clergy. If this were to be done, supervision would be needed, and he suggested that this be given by foreign bishops.[51] He submitted the plan to the proper authorities in the papal curia (1649 or 1650)[52] and found them not entirely unresponsive. The Propaganda had already, in 1633, recommended the establishment of a hierarchy for Japan, China, Tongking, and Siam.[53] Alexander refused the episcopal honor for himself[54] and was then asked to seek fit candidates for the position (1653).[55] While engaged in this quest he came to Paris and found there in the

[51] Launay, *Nos missionaires,* pp. 12-20.
[52] Ibid., and Cordier, *Histoire générale de la Chine,* Vol. 3, .pp. 296-298.
[53] Launay, *Histoire générale de la Société des Missions-Étrangères,* Vol. 1, p. 9.
[54] Cordier, op. cit., Vol. 3, pp. 296-298.
[55] Launay, *Nos missionaires,* p. 14.

university a group of young men, clerical and lay, who were living under a rule drawn up by one of their number, François Pallu, and under the direction of a Jesuit, Bagot.[56]   Rhodes suggested that they assume the project.[57]   They received the proposal enthusiastically and in 1658 two of their number, Pallu and La Motte Lambert, were appointed vicars apostolic over Tongking and Cochin China and administrators of districts which included most of China south of the Yangtze.   A few months later a third, Cotolendi, was made vicar apostolic over Nanking and administrator of Korea and part of North China.[58]

The position of vicar apostolic, it may be noted, carries with it in cases such as these the same episcopal powers as that of bishop, for the holder of the office is made titular bishop of some extinct see.   However, while the bishop rules in his own name, the vicar apostolic rules in the name of the Pope[59] and the papal see may restrict his powers.   Vicars apostolic, then, are under the immediate jurisdiction of the Pope, who usually acts through the Propaganda.[60]   They were not subject to the control of Portugal nor to the Portuguese primate in the East, the Archbishop of Goa.   It was probably to avoid trouble with the King of Portugal that this plan was preferred to the creation of ordinary bishoprics.[61]   The Congregation of the Propaganda, now about a generation old, was naturally averse to recognizing the claims of a decaying monarchy to dominate the expanding missions in China: such a control would have crippled their growth.   The Propaganda was willing to grant that Portugal had a right to the nomination of bishops in regions actually under its rule, but it declined to concede that this prerogative extended beyond such regions.   However, it probably wished to arrange for an episcopacy in a manner which would as far as possible avoid needless conflict with Lisbon.   The Portuguese objected and raised obstacles which were not removed for many years.   Their claims again and again troubled the missions

[56] Launay, *Histoire générale de la Société des Missions-Étrangères*, Vol. 1, pp. 13-16.
[57] Launay, *Histoire générale de la Société des Missions-Étrangères*, Vol. 1, pp. 13-16.
[58] Jann, *Die katholischen Missionen in Indien, China und Japan*, pp. 217, 218.
[59] *Codex Juris Canonici*, Canon, 294, Sec. 1.   The vicars apostolic have the same rights as the bishops, "nisi quid Apostolica Sedes reservaverit."
[60] Moidrey, *La hiérarchie catholique en Chine*, etc., pp. 217, 218.
[61] Launay, *Histoire générale de la Société des Missions-Étrangères*, Vol. 1, pp. 20, 45.

in China and complicated the dissensions among the missionaries.

To continue with the account of the French missions, Lambert succeeded in reaching Siam in 1662,[62] but Cotolendi died in India on the way out.[63] Pallu remained for the time in Europe to insure the enterprise adequate support. In the attempt to reënforce French missions by promoting French commerce and political influence in the East, he formed a commercial company and the latter sent out a ship.[64] The vessel was wrecked (1660), but Pallu, undiscouraged, persevered with his plans to reach the Orient. He left France in 1662 and arrived in Siam two years later.[65]

In the meantime, in France friends and agents of the vicars apostolic were forming a permanent organization to support and perpetuate the new mission. Pallu and several others had already (1658) asked permission of the Propaganda to found a school to train agents for the spread of the Faith in Canada, China, Tongking, and Cochin China.[66] Now, in 1663, royal and ecclesiastical authority was obtained for the establishment of a seminary "for the conversion of the infidels in foreign states." [67] From this seminary and its friends at home and from the work of the vicars apostolic and missionaries abroad who looked to it for support, developed the Société des Missions Étrangères, or Society of Foreign Missions, which has had an extensive share in the activities of the Roman Catholic Church in the Far East and to whose work we shall have frequent occasion to recur. The Society was not, as are so many of the religious orders, the prolonged shadow of a great founder. It was to be an evolution, with an organization whose form changed from time to time, the result of the labors of many men. Its basic rule was not formed until 1700. Always it was to be a society of secular, not regular, clergy, with the seminary at Paris as the training school of its missionaries and the home nucleus of its activities. Its goal was to be the carrying of the Christian message to non-

[62] Alexander of Rhodes was soon after (1654) ordered to Persia and died there in 1660.—Launay, *Histoire générale de la Société des Missions-Étrangères*, Vol. 1, p. 17.

[63] Launay, *Nos missionaires*, pp. 19, 20.

[64] Launay, *Histoire générale de la Société des Missions-Étrangères*, Vol. 1, pp. 56-58.

[65] Ibid., Vol. 1, pp. 60, 75.

[66] Ibid., Vol. 1, pp. 39, 40.

[67] Ibid., Vol. 1, pp. 77-79.

Christians, the building of native churches, and the training of a native secular clergy which in time would be capable of self-maintenance.[68] It was believed that the emergence of a parochial system and of a hierarchy like that in old Roman Catholic lands and the transfer of control to native leaders would be easier than when the missionaries were members of great and dominating orders.

THE PERSECUTION OF 1664

The prosperity which had attended the work of the missionaries in China during the last years of the Ming and the first years of the Manchu dynasty was to be rudely interrupted. The death of the well-disposed Shun Chih brought no immediate reverse to the fortunes of the missions. The new Emperor, K'ang Hsi, was only a boy and was not yet in control of the government or old enough to have formed definite policies. The regents, while none too friendly to Schall, at first were not openly hostile and even gave him the title of preceptor of the young monarch.[69] Before long, however, a tempest of persecution broke out. The Moslem astronomers had not forgotten that the Jesuits had dispossessed them of the direction of the calendar, and in 1664 one of them took advantage of the change in rulers to launch an accusation against the missionaries. The regents, probably not unwillingly, heeded him, put him in charge of the calendar, and threw Schall and several of the latter's colleagues into prison. Schall was condemned to death but was freed, partly, so it is said, because a timely earthquake was attributed by the populace to the injustice done him, and partly because of the intervention of the Emperor's mother.[70] He was well past seventy years of age and did not long survive his release.[71] The persecution was not confined to Peking. Twenty-four or twenty-five missionaries of different orders were taken to Canton and imprisoned.[72] Others hid until the storm should blow over. There seem to have been no executions either of missionaries or of Chinese

[68] Launay, *Histoire générale de la Société des Missions-Étrangères,* Vol. 1, pp. 414-422. There is an interesting volume dating from the early days of the Society and showing in part its standards and ideals: *Instructiones ad Munera Apostolica Rite Abuenda Peritules Missionibus Chinæ, Tunchin, Cochin-Chinæ, atque Siam, Accomodatæ a Missionariis Seminarii Parisiensis Missionum ad Exteros, Juthiæ Regia Siami Congregatiis.*   Rome, 1665.
[69] Huc, *Christianity in China, Tartary and Thibet,* Vol. 3, p. 31.
[70] Ibid., Vol. 3, pp. 36, 37; Halde, *China,* Vol. 2, p. 15.
[71] Brucker in *Catholic Encyclopedia,* Vol. 13, p. 522.
[72] Halde, op. cit., Vol. 1, pp. 489, 490; Huc, op. cit., Vol. 3, p. 36.

Christians, but at least three of the missionaries died as a result of their sufferings [73] and the Christian faith was officially denounced.

RENEWED PROSPERITY

The persecution was not of long duration.   In 1669 K'ang Hsi fell out with the regents, dismissed them, and assumed the reins of government.[74]   The fact that the regency had been responsible for the persecution probably predisposed the young Emperor to give the Jesuits an opportunity to prove themselves worthy of his patronage.   Fortunately there was at hand a man sufficiently able and well-trained to rise to the occasion.   Verbiest, a native of the Low Countries, had been in China since 1658 and in 1660 had been ordered to Peking to assist Schall.[75]   He had shared the latter's imprisonment and so had remained in the capital.   In a series of tests which K'ang Hsi applied to Verbiest and the Moslem who had succeeded Schall, Verbiest demonstrated his superior knowledge of astronomy and mathematics and was promptly put in his rival's place.[76]   The Jesuits were thus once more in control of the calendar and in a position to win the favor of the Emperor and toleration for their faith.   In 1669 an imperial edict permitted Verbiest and his confrères to practice their religion but retained the prohibitions against the general dissemination of the faith.[77]

In 1671 the missionaries were given back their churches, Schall's titles were posthumously restored, and a mausoleum for him authorized.   Still, the Emperor was not ready to grant complete toleration and Chinese were forbidden to become Christians.[78]   As the years passed, K'ang Hsi became increasingly friendly to Verbiest.   He studied mathematics under his tutelage and was much in his company.   At the Emperor's command

[73] Blair and Robertson, *The Philippine Islands,* Vol. 24, p. 273; André-Marie. *Missions dominicaines dans l'Extrême Orient,* Vol. 1, pp. 198-207.
[74] *Encyclopædia Sinica,* p. 266.
[75] Brucker in *Catholic Encyclopedia,* Vol. 15, pp. 346, 347; Bosmans, *Ferdinand Verbiest,* passim; Bosmans in *Revue des questions scientifiques,* 3d Series, Vol. 21, pp. 195-273, 375-461, Vol. 24, pp. 272-298.   He was born October 29, 1623, at Pitthem.
[76] Brucker in *Catholic Encyclopedia,* Vol. 15, pp. 346, 347; Bosmans, *Ferdinand Verbiest,* passim; Mailla, *Histoire générale de la Chine,* Vol. 1, pp. 62, 63; Bosmans in *Revue des questions scientifiques,* loc. cit.
[77] Tobar, *Kiao-ou Ki-lio,* pp. 1, 2.
[78] De Groot, *Sectarianism and Religious Persecution in China,* pp. 271-276; Huc, op. cit., Vol. 3, pp. 63, 64; Joseph Suario in Leibnitz, *Novissima Sinica,* pp. 12-72.

Verbiest constructed astronomical instruments—a portion of those which still grace the walls of Peking—and prepared cannon for use against the rebel Wu San Kuei.[79]   Other Jesuits shared Verbiest's access to the court and were used extensively by the Emperor.[80] With some of the missionaries in such favor, officials in the provinces were inclined to wink at violations of the edicts against Christian teaching and worship.

With the persecution past and the missionaries once more enjoying imperial kindness, the Church prospered both in Peking and the provinces.   There were large accessions, for baptisms continued in spite of the prohibition.   The majority of the converts were not of the official classes, but a few were of high rank and some were Manchus.[81]   The Church was numerically strongest in the lower part of the valley of the Yangtze, in and around Nanking and Shanghai.   Here the Jesuits had now been at work for two generations.[82] Missionaries continued to come and reports of the renewed prosperity and the appeals of Verbiest[83] accelerated the movement.

In 1680 five Italian Franciscans were sent to China by the Propaganda.   They were headed by Bernardin della Chiesa, who had been created titular Bishop of Argolis and coadjutor to Pallu.[84]   The party reached China in 1684.[85]   They and succeeding Italian Brothers Minor were later to concentrate their efforts on some of the northern and central provinces, especially Shansi, Shensi, Honan, Hupeh, and Hunan.[86]   In the meantime the Spanish Franciscans were expanding their operations.   In 1662 Antonio de Santa Maria sent Bonaventura Ibanez to Europe for reënforcements, and by 1672 Ibanez was again in China with several recruits.[87]   In 1671 two Franciscans left the Philippines

[79] Huc, op. cit., Vol. 3, pp. 68, 78-80; Thomas, *Histoire de la mission de Pékin*, pp. 107, 108; *Encyclopædia Sinica*, p. 402.

[80] Grimaldi's annual letter of 1686, from Peking, describing the life of the Jesuits there, in translation in *Bibliotheca Asiatica*, Vol. 2, pp. 31-32.

[81] Huc, op. cit., Vol. 3, pp. 64, 65; Le Comte, *Nouveaux mémoires sur l'état present de la Chine*, Vol. 2, pp. 258, 259; Bosmans, opera cit.

[82] Le Comte, op. cit., Vol. 2, p. 259.

[83] Huc, op. cit., Vol. 3, pp. 89-92.

[84] Heeren in *Journal of the North China Branch of the Royal Asiatic Society*, 1923, pp. 182-199; Moidrey, *La hiérarchie catholique en Chine, en Corée, et au Japon*, p. 35.

[85] Moidrey, op. cit., pp. 35, 182; Civezza, *Histoire universelle des missions franciscaines*, Vol. 2, p. 260.

[86] Moidrey, op. cit., p. 182.

[87] Pérez, *Origen de la Misiones Franciscanas en la Provincia de Kwangtung*, pp. 6-27.

for China and in the succeeding year five more followed.[88]   In 1677 the Brothers Minor rebuilt in Tsinan the church which had been destroyed in the persecution of 1664.   By 1675 they had two chapels in Kwangtung.   They penetrated Kiangsi in 1687 and had work on the island of Hainan.[89]   By 1691 the Franciscans in China numbered seventeen.[90]   By 1698 there were twenty —in Shantung, Fukien, Kiangsi, Kiangnan, and Kwangtung.[91]

The Dominican mission likewise grew.   In 1673 four of the Order of Preachers were sent from the Philippines and the following year four more arrived.[92]   The order appears to have confined itself chiefly to Fukien, and the Christian communities that arose from its efforts were most numerous in and around Fu-an, in the northern part of the province.[93]

Augustinians also came from the Philippines.   They were never to be as active in China as the Franciscans and Dominicans, but by 1722 seventeen had entered the country.   They had endeavored to penetrate China in 1575 and 1580, it will be recalled, but had been unable to establish a firm foothold.   Their mission really began in 1680 when Benevente effected an entrance. From that time until the close of the century reënforcements came with a fair degree of regularity.[94]   In 1687 the order is reported to have had twelve hundred adult converts.[95]

It was to be expected that missions from France would grow rapidly, for the country was in the midst of the prosperous years of Louis XIV and the wars of the Grand Monarch had not yet seriously sapped its resources.   The first emissaries of the Société des Missions Étrangères, it will be remembered, had left France by 1662.   They found in Siam a more favorable reception than elsewhere, but sought entrance also into Tongking, Annam, and Cochin China.   Pallu, the outstanding figure of the early days of the Society, did not remain long in the Far East on this first

[88] Maas, *Cartas de China*, pp. 11, 12.
[89] Moidrey, op. cit., p. 181; Maas, op. cit., 2d series, p. 105.   A church and house had been built on Hainan in 1639.—Civezza, op. cit., Vol. 2, p. 282.
[90] Maas, op. cit., p. 178.
[91] Pérez, op. cit., pp. 160-207.   Fifty-two Franciscans had entered China by 1698, of whom twenty remained.   Of the fifty-two, six were Italian and forty-six were Spanish (some were from Mexico).—Ibid.
[92] André-Marie, *Missions dominicaines dans l'Éxtrême Orient,* Vol. 1, p. 207.
[93] Arias, *El Beato Sanz y Compañeros Mártires del Orden de Predicadores.* The map at the end of the volume shows this clearly.   Biermann, *Die Anfänge der neueren Dominikanermission in China,* pp. 129-136.
[94] Cordier in *Revue de l'Éxtrême-Orient,* Vol. 2, pp. 58-71.
[95] Maas, *Cartas de China,* 2d series, p. 172.

visit, but in 1665 left for Europe to further there the new organization.[96] He was interested not only in placing the Society on a firmer foundation at home and in procuring favor for it at Rome, but in encouraging French commerce and colonial projects. He kept, therefore, in close touch with Colbert.[97] In French commerce and imperialism he saw aid for his missionary projects and an effective counterweight to the Portuguese. These latter, including some who were missionaries in China, were offering serious opposition to the activities of Pallu and his colleagues.[98] They resented violently any trespassing upon what they claimed as their ecclesiastical preserves and perhaps also had apprehensions for their colonial possessions and dwindling commerce. At least one Jesuit, moreover, for a time feared that these French missionaries would introduce Jansenism into China.[99]

In 1670 Pallu again left France for the East,[100] this time accompanied by six missionaries. On his arrival he still gave his efforts chiefly to Siam and Indo-China.[101] In one of his journeys his ship was driven out of its course by a tempest and he was forced (1674) to land in the Philippines. Here he was kept virtually a prisoner,[102] for the Spaniards were no more cordial to French activities in the Far East than were the Portuguese, and Spain and France were at war during much of the reign of Louis XIV. Pallu eventually was returned to Europe by way of Mexico and the Atlantic. Undaunted by his hardships, in 1683 he once more left for the East, this time accompanied by Maigrot, a member of his Society who was destined to have an active part in future controversies with the Jesuits. The two went to China, where in spite of the fact that large sections were included in the jurisdiction of the French vicars apostolic there seems to have been as yet no resident representative of the Paris Society. They made their way to Fukien, for they appear to have been on friendly terms with the Dominicans, and here, at Mo-yang, resting in the arms of Maigrot, on October 29, 1684, Pallu finished his earthly

[96] Launay, *Histoire générale de la Société des Missions Étrangères,* Vol. 1, p. 114.
[97] Ibid., Vol. 1, pp. 188, 189.
[98] Launay, op. cit., Vol. 1, pp. 86-258.
[99] Letter of Father Anthony Thomas, ca. 1679, given in translation in *Bibliotheca Asiatica,* Vol. 2, p. 73.
[100] Launay, op. cit., Vol. 1, pp. 184, 185.
[101] Ibid., Vol. 1, pp. 186-223.
[102] Ibid., Vol. 1, pp. 224-227. On Pallu see also Pallu, *Lettres,* edited by Launay.

career. He had helped to establish French missions firmly in Siam and Indo-China, but it was fitting that he should die, as he had lived, opening up new territory, and that his body should rest in China, the country where his Society was to find its most extensive fields. The year of Pallu's death saw another missionary of the Paris Society, Le Blanc, enter China: [103] Maigrot was not left to carry on alone the enterprise which the great pioneer had laid down.

The Coming of the French Jesuits

French missions in China were not confined to the efforts of the Société des Missions Étrangères. In 1685 a company of six French Jesuits sailed for China. This undertaking seems to have been due in part to an appeal from Verbiest and in part to French colonial and commercial ambitions. Colbert had wished to send to China French members of the Society of Jesus, but his death (1683) temporarily delayed the execution of the project. Another of the ministers of Louis XIV, Louvois, continued the plans and brought them to a successful fruition. The General of the Jesuits was at first inclined to demur, for he foresaw difficulties with Portugal.[104] The idea, however, received the approval of the Jesuit procurator for China.[105] The missionaries chosen were skilled in mathematics and the Crown expected that they would give themselves to geographical observations for the benefit of the newly founded Academy of Sciences—later the Institut de France—as well as to the work of evangelization. They sailed on a ship that carried a French embassy to Siam and one of their number was detained in that country. Five—Bouvet, Le Comte, Visdelou, Fontenay, and Gerbillon—continued on their way in a Chinese junk. They were driven back to Siam by adverse winds but left again when the weather became more favorable and landed at Ningpo in July, 1687. It was well that they had not attempted to go by way of Macao, since the Portuguese would probably have hampered and possibly have ended their mission.[106]

[103] *Nouvelles lettres édifiantes*, Vol. 1, p. ix.
[104] Letter of the General, Charles de Noyelle, to F. La Chaise, Confessor of Louis XIV, Feb. 4, 1682. French translation in *Revue des questions scientifiques*, Vol. 21, p. 445.
[105] Harting in *Bibliotheca Asiatica*, Vol. 2, p. xiv.
[106] The Portuguese Jesuits in Peking apparently felt none too kindly toward these French Jesuits who had come out without the consent of Lisbon.—Letter of Bishop della Chiesa, Oct. 7, 1700, in *Journal of the North China Branch of the Royal Asiatic Society*, 1925, pp. 94-98.

Still at Ningpo they were not without opposition, for they were met by the suspicion of the Chinese officials. Through the good offices of Verbiest, however, they were summoned to court and arrived in February, 1688. They did not see their benefactor, for he had died a few days before their arrival, but they were in time for the elaborate funeral that was given him. Three of their number were permitted to go to the provinces—to Shansi, Shensi, and Kiangsu—but two, Bouvet and Gerbillon, remained at Peking to aid in the astronomical and other duties which had been assigned the Jesuits.

K'ang Hsi, with the intellectual curiosity which so characterized him, saw much of the two at the capital and put them many inquiries concerning European sciences. They seem to have won his confidence, partly through their scholarship, partly by help given him in negotiations with the Russians, and partly by the cure which they wrought in him with their imported cinchona bark. In 1697 Bouvet returned to Europe for reënforcements and bore with him gifts from the Emperor to the French King. These gifts, it is interesting to note, included some books which were the beginning of the great Chinese collection in the Bibliothèque Nationale.

Bouvet arrived in China in 1699 accompanied by ten more missionaries and a representative of Louis XIV. K'ang Hsi ordered five of the new recruits to remain at court, where they were to be employed in the mathematical, astronomical, and other scientific, diplomatic, and literary pursuits which had been assigned their colleagues, but the others were allowed to settle in the provinces and aid in the work of evangelization. In 1693 K'ang Hsi had given the French Jesuits a house near the imperial palace. Now, in 1699, he donated the ground and some of the funds for the erection of a church. Louis XIV also assisted, partly with funds and partly with vessels and furnishings. The building, later known as the Pei T'ang, or North Church, was dedicated in 1703.[107] It was constructed largely in European style, but, as if to sanction the alien intrusion into the heart of the Chinese capital, it contained tablets bearing inscriptions composed by K'ang Hsi. The French Jesuits had not only borne the name of their nation to Peking: by their scholarship they had enhanced the prestige of their faith and had aided in obtaining

[107] Neither the present structure nor location.

for all Catholic missionaries a hearing throughout the Empire.[108]
In 1700 the French mission was separated completely from that
of the Portuguese, and Gerbillon received from the General of
the Society the powers of a vice-provincial over all the French
Jesuits in China.[109]

At least one other European ruling house, the Austrian Haps-
burgs, strove to have an active part in missions in China.   There
were already German Jesuits in China, but these had come out
under Portuguese authority.   In the first decade of the eighteenth
century Leopold I (1705-1711) attempted to open for missionaries
to China a land route by way of Russia, as one which would be
free from Portuguese control and which could be placed under
the protection of the Holy Roman Emperor.   Charles VI (1711-
1740) attempted to effect connections with China through an East
Indian trading company.   These efforts, however, appear to have
been fruitless.[110]   Many Jesuits of Austrian and German birth
were in China, and several German princes aided in the financial
support of the missions, but no distinctively German mission was
established.[111]

A CHINESE BISHOP

Since the Jesuits had obtained the favor of K'ang Hsi and they
and the members of other orders were expanding the operations
of the missions, it was natural that the Holy See should make
efforts to extend the plan of ecclesiastical jurisdiction that had
been begun when Pallu, Le Motte Lambert, and Cotolendi had
been created vicars apostolic.   Even had Rome been content to
do nothing more or to draw back before opposition, the Société

[108] For this summary of the French Jesuit mission see Le Comte, *Nouveaux
mémoires sur l'état present de la Chine;* the letters of several of the missionaries
in Lockman, *Travels of the Jesuits,* Vol. 2; Halde, *China;* Thomas, *Histoire
de la mission de Pékin,* pp. 113-117; *Catholic Encyclopedia,* Vol. 2, p. 723, Vol. 3,
p. 673, Vol. 6, p. 471, Vol. 12, p. 489, Vol. 15, p. 347; *The Travels of Several
Learned Missionaries of the Society of Jesus,* pp. 198-200; Hering, *Roman Catholic
Missions in China,* 1692-1744, in the *New China Review,* Vol. 3; Cordier,
Histoire générale de la Chine, Vol. 3, pp. 312, 313; *Encyclopædia Sinica,* pp. 58,
259; Steinmetz, *History of the Jesuits,* Vol. 3, pp. 416-420; Huc, *Christianity in
China, Tartary and Thibet,* Vol. 3, pp. 107-175; Abel-Rémusat, *Nouveaux mélanges
asiatiques,* Vol. 2, p. 244.
[109] Cordier in *T'oung Pao,* Vol. 17 (1916), p. 273.
[110] Huonder, *Deutsche Jesuitenmissionäre des 17. und 18. Jahrhunderts,* pp. 43,
48, 49.
[111] Huonder, op. cit., pp. 49-62.   Huonder, op. cit., pp. 184-197, gives the
names of forty-six Jesuits of German birth who worked in China.   Two or three
of these had Slavic names.

des Missions Étrangères would have insisted on further action. It was a conviction of the founders of this Society, it will be recalled, that a native secular clergy should be rapidly built up. If this were to be done, they believed that adequate episcopal supervision would need to be provided as quickly as possible. Committed as they were to this program, these energetic Frenchmen would not acquiesce readily to objections raised in behalf of the decadent Portuguese Empire. Pallu dreamed of a native episcopate under the supervision of the vicars apostolic. He did not succeed in obtaining papal authorization for this, but he did urge as Cotolendi's successor to the Vicariate Apostolic of Nanking a Chinese, Gregory Lopez.[112] Lopez, as we have seen, had been baptized by a Franciscan, Antonio de Santa-Maria. He later studied at Manila, was admitted to the Dominican order, and in 1656 was ordained priest, the first Chinese of whose elevation to that office we have certain record.[113] In the persecution of 1664 he gave a good account of himself by remaining in China and ministering to the Christians during the absence of the missionaries. It was a Dominican, Navarette, who brought him to the attention of Pallu.[114] In accordance with Pallu's suggestion, Gregory Lopez was, in 1674, appointed Bishop of Basilea and Vicar Apostolic of Nanking. Lopez, with customary formal Chinese modesty, declined, but in 1679 a further papal decree ordered him to accept. To this bull the head of the Dominicans added his consent, with the provision that there should be associated with Lopez a wise and learned member of the order whose advice the new bishop should follow. Lopez, with interesting independence, refused to accept this condition, possibly feeling that if one of Chinese blood were to be bishop and vicar apostolic it should be on the same terms on which a European would be given the position. It is probable that the Dominicans suspected Lopez of leniency toward the Chinese practices which, as we shall soon see, were a matter of controversy and toward which the order took an attitude of uncompromising opposition. For his contumacy Lopez was refused consecration at Manila. It was

[112] Launay, *Histoire générale de la Société des Missions Étrangères*, Vol. 1, p. 187.
[113] Moule in *The New China Review*, Vol. 1, pp. 480-488. Jann, *Die katholischen Missionen in Indien, China und Japan*, p. 222, holds that Lopez was not entirely acceptable to the Paris Society.
[114] Launay, op. cit., Vol. 1, p. 187.

not until 1685, when he was well past seventy years of age, that he finally obtained it, and then at Canton and at the hands of the Italian Franciscan, Bernardin della Chiesa.[115] Five years later, in 1690, Lopez was appointed to the newly created see of Nanking, but he did not employ the title and died in February, 1691.[116] Not until the twentieth century did the Catholic Church repeat the experiment of appointing to the episcopate a Chinese priest.[117]

The Portuguese and the Vicars Apostolic

The agitation over the episcopate was by no means confined to the effort to obtain a position for a Chinese. The Portuguese continued to object to the vicars apostolic as infringements of their right of patronage and were ill content with a decision of a congregation of cardinals which in 1680 ruled against them at nearly every point.[118] In 1688 Lisbon showed its defiance by ordering that all missionaries to the East pass through Portugal and take oath to respect the royal patronage.[119] So strong was the pressure that Rome was forced to compromise and in 1690 created in China two sees, those of Peking and Nanking, in addition to the one already in existence, Macao, and gave to the King of Portugal the right of presentment to them.[120] Rome conceded to Portugal, indeed, the privilege of fixing the limits of these dioceses.[121] This settlement seemed to leave no room in the Middle Kingdom for the vicars apostolic, for the Portuguese divided practically all China among their three bishops. The question soon arose as to who had jurisdiction in Kwangtung and Kwangsi, the Vicar Apostolic or the Bishop of Macao, and was not settled for some years.[122] In 1696 the Pope again asserted himself against the

[115] Moule, op. cit.

[116] Moule, op. cit.; Moule in *The New China Review*, Vol. 3, pp. 138, 139; Moidrey, *La hiérarchie catholique en Chine*, etc., p. 22. See also Salazar, *Historia de la Provincia de el Santissimo Rosario de el Sagrado Orden de Predicadores, 1669-1700*, pp. 588-600.

[117] For a possible very doubtful exception see Moidrey, op. cit., p. 48.

[118] Ljunstedt, *An Historical Sketch of the Portuguese Settlements in China*, pp. 148, 149.

[119] Ibid., p. 150. No private ships were now going from Lisbon to the East and Portugal would not grant passage in the only means of conveyance, the state ships, to non-Portuguese missionaries.—Jann, op. cit., p. 192.

[120] Moidrey, op. cit., pp. 35, 36; Cordier in *T'oung Pao*, Vol. 17, p. 275; Jann, op. cit., pp. 253-256.

[121] Moidrey, op. cit., p. 489.

[122] Maas, *Cartas de China*, 2d series, pp. vi-viii.

Portuguese. He limited the dioceses of Nanking, Peking, and Macao to two or three provinces each[123] and created eight vicariates apostolic, apportioning among them Fukien, Chêkiang, Kiangsi, Szechwan, Yünnan, Kweichow, Hukwang, Shansi, and Shensi.[124] In three or four of these provinces there was as yet little or no missionary work. Rome had organized episcopal supervision sufficient for as many Christians as China was to have for many years to come. The reason given for this act was that the edict of K'ang Hsi (1692) granting toleration to Christianity had so increased the opportunity for missions that more adequate episcopal supervision would be required than that afforded by the existing three sees.[125] The King of Portugal demurred, but in vain.[126] The vicars apostolic were continued and were subject to direct control from Rome. They were not under Portugal or the primate of the Portuguese East.

Not all the missionaries were pleased with this provision for bishops and vicars apostolic, and not only Portuguese opposition but dissatisfaction among the Spaniards and some others of the regular clergy is reported. A papal decree (October 10, 1678) commanded[127] and the Propaganda insisted (January 29, 1680) that all missionaries take oath to obey the vicars apostolic in preaching and the administration of the sacraments and to abide by all bulls and letters of the Propaganda.[128] Against this order some of the missionaries vigorously protested[129] and one regrets to record that quite a number of them paid scant respect to their episcopal superiors. The trouble seems to have been chiefly on the ground of nationality. It was not strange that the Portuguese, with their claims under the *padroãdo,* should object to recognizing any bishops or vicars apostolic other than those of their sanctioning, and it would have been only a little less strange had French missionaries been content to serve under Portuguese

[123] Maas, op. cit., pp. 185-187; Jann, op. cit., pp. 260-262.

[124] Maas, op. cit., p. 201; Moidrey, op. cit., passim; Jann, op. cit., pp. 251-266. Each of the provinces named, with the exception of Shansi and Shensi, was made a separate vicariate. Shansi and Shensi together were made one vicariate.

[125] Jann, op. cit., p. 260.

[126] Jann, op. cit., pp. 263, 264.

[127] Jann, op. cit., p. 248.

[128] Maas, op. cit., pp. 147-151. Some of the Portuguese Jesuits were especially resentful, but all but four took the oath and these four left the country.—Noës, letter to the Duchess de Aveiro, Nov. 4, 1685, in *Bibliotheca Asiatica,* Vol. 2, p. 43.

[129] Maas, op. cit., pp. 147-151. See also Cerri, *An Account of the State of the Roman Catholic Religion,* pp. 121 et seq.

bishops, or had the Spaniards acquiesced in the appointment of the French vicars apostolic.[130]   The system worked best usually when the bishop or the vicar apostolic was of the nation of the missionaries in his vicariate or diocese.

THE EDICT OF TOLERATION, MARCH, 1692

Before this ecclesiastical organization was perfected—and, indeed, while deliberations were still in progress—an event occurred which may have hastened it and which was to give added impetus to the growth of the Church.   In 1691 the authorities of Chêkiang began a persecution of the Christians and closed all but one of the churches in the province.   Since the officials were clearly within their legal rights and could, in fact, plead that they were compelling compliance with existing edicts, it became necessary for the missionaries to obtain more formal imperial toleration than had yet been theirs.   K'ang Hsi was not unfriendly, but on the Board of Rites were those who, possibly because of the conservatism characteristic of Confucian scholars, were actively opposed to the foreign faith and who advocated further restrictions rather than greater liberty.   However, two of the Jesuits at Peking, Gerbillon and Pereyra, had recently been of distinct assistance to the court in negotiations with the Russians and had won the firm friendship of one of the Manchu princes.   With the aid of this prince an imperial decree was obtained (March, 1692) which protected existing church buildings throughout the provinces and permitted freedom of worship.   The privilege of teaching and baptizing was not explicitly granted, but the edict was so favorable that this would scarcely be denied by local authorities.   The decree cited as causes for the action the services rendered by the missionaries in correcting the calendar, in casting cannon, and in aiding in diplomacy.[131]   It was pointed out that the new faith held in it no danger of rebellion and that

[130] See for the difficulty that a bishop of Peking had with the Portuguese Jesuits, and in occupying his cathedral, a letter of Bishop della Chiesa, Oct. 6, 1700, in *Journal of the North China Branch of the Royal Asiatic Society,* 1925, pp. 88-94.   The French Jesuits seem to have sided with the Bishop against their Portuguese brethren.   We find, too, the Spaniards petitioning their King to prevent their expulsion from China by the Portuguese bishops and the French vicars apostolic.— Pérez, *Origen de las Misiones Franciscanas en la Provincia de Kwangtung,* p. 124.
[131] The decree is in *Kiao-ou Ki-lio,* pp. 2-5.   See also accounts in Halde, *China,* Vol. 1, pp. 496, 497, Vol. 2, pp. 23-29; a letter of Fontenay in Lockman, *Travels of the Jesuits,* Vol. 2, pp. 106, 107; and Gobien, *Histoire de l'édit de l'empereur de la Chine,* pp. 39-185.

similar privileges were accorded to the adherents of the Lama temples.

By their scientific attainments and their services to the state the Jesuits had at last obtained legal, if incomplete, toleration for the work of their Church. It was a triumph for the policy inaugurated by Valignani and Ricci, and the rapid growth of the Christian community seemed assured. The edict, however, had not been issued without opposition in influential quarters and specifically stated that the government had nothing to fear from the new religion. If Christianity should ever seem to prove subversive to the state the opposition would be quick to seize the opportunity to renew the attack. The position of the Church remained precarious.

QUIET AND PROSPERITY, 1692-1706

The fifteen years that followed the edict of 1692 were marked by the steady growth of the Christian community. Accurate statistics for all China are probably not to be had, but incidents and incomplete figures show that the Church prospered greatly. We have already seen the provision made by Rome in 1696 for the supervision of the enlarging constituency. Reënforcements came in rapidly. In 1698 fifteen Jesuits entered China and in 1701 sixteen more arrived. These were banner years: from 1694 to 1705 inclusive eighty-eight joined the ranks of the Society in China. A few of these were Chinese, but the large majority were Europeans.[132] In 1697 the Propaganda sent out at least ten missionaries, including two Lazarists—the first of their congregation to arrive in China—and six Franciscans.[133] The Propaganda wished one of the Lazarists, Appiani, to found a seminary for the training of a native clergy, but opposition seems to have been raised by some of the other missionaries, and Appiani, abandoning the project, settled in Szechwan.[134] In 1700 four Franciscans arrived who had been sent by the Propaganda and who had come by way of Poland, Russia, and Persia, and thence apparently by sea.[135]

[132] *Catalogus Patrum ac Fratrum e Societate Jesu qui . . . in Sinis adlaboraverunt*, pp. 20-33.
[133] Civezza, *Histoire universelle des missions franciscaines*, Vol. 2, pp. 262 et .seq.; Demimund, *Vie du François-Régis Clet*, pp. 97-104; Cordier in *Catholic Encyclopedia*, Vol. 3, p. 675.
[134] Demimund, op. cit., pp. 97-104.
[135] Civezza, op. cit., Vol. 2, p. 267.

Just how long the average length of missionary service was we do not know, nor are we able to say certainly how many missionaries were in China in any given year, but one estimate says that in 1695 there were in China seventy-five priests, of whom thirty-eight were Jesuits (thirty-two European and six Chinese), nine Spanish Dominicans, five Spanish Augustinians, seven representatives of the Missions Étrangères, twelve Spanish Franciscans, and four Italian Franciscans.[136]   Another estimate—contemporary— places the number of Jesuits in 1702 or 1703 at "upwards of seventy" and says that this was more than the total of all the other orders.[137]   Still another account states that in 1701 there were in China fifty-nine Jesuits, twenty-nine Franciscans, eight Dominicans, fifteen secular priests (nearly all of the Paris Society), and six Augustinians, a total of one hundred and seventeen.[138]   In 1703, so one missionary reported, Canton had seven churches—one belonging to the Portuguese Jesuits, one to the French Jesuits, two to the Missions Étrangères, two to the Franciscans, and one to the Augustinians.[139]   One of these was said to be the best building in the city.[140]

Between 1692 and 1707 there were, we know, missionaries or native Christians in all of the provinces but Kansu.[141]   Five hundred adults, it is said, were being baptized each year in Peking,[142] and in Kiangsi a missionary estimated that with the aid of a catechist a similar number could be won annually by each priest.[143]   Some of the Chinese were active in reaching non-Christians and we read of an organization of lay Christians for the spiritual oversight of their less instructed or less earnest fellow believers, for the baptism of children, for the care of the sick, and for the extension of the Faith among pagans.[144]

[136] Maas, Cartas de China, 2d series, p. 120.   Conde de Villa Humbrosa, Memorial Apologetica, p. 149, says that in 1664 the Jesuits had 30 priests, 41 houses of residence, 159 churches, and innumerable oratories.
[137] Report of Francis Noël to the General of the Jesuits, 1703, in Lockman, Travels of the Jesuits, Vol. 1, p. 447.
[138] Servière, Les missions anciennes de la Compagnie de Jésus en Chine, p. 55.
[139] Letter of Fontenay, Jan. 15, 1704, in Lockman, op. cit., Vol. 2, p. 205.
[140] Pere du Tartre to his father, Dec. 17, 1701, in Lettres édifiantes, Vol. 3.
[141] H. Cordier in Catholic Encyclopedia, Vol. 3, p. 675; Civezza, op. cit., Vol. 2, pp. 262, 267; Pourias, Huit ans au Yunnan, p. 19; Launay, Mission du Koung-si, p. 18; Maas, op. cit., p. 115; Cordier, docs. pour servir à l'hist. ecclès. de l'Extrême Orient, pp. 24-27; Lockman, Travels of the Jesuits, Vol. 2, p. 11; Hering, Roman Catholic Missions in China, 1692-1744.
[142] Noël in Lockman, op. cit., Vol. 1, p. 448.
[143] Premaire to Gobien, Nov. 1, 1700, in Lockman, op. cit., Vol. 1, p. 80.
[144] Huc, Christianity in China, Tartary and Thibet, Vol. 3, pp. 226-229.

The Christian community was still most numerous in the lower part of the Yangtze Valley.[145] How many Christians there were in all China we do not know, but by 1705 the total was almost certainly not more than 300,000 and it was possibly very much less.[146] Few Christians came from the educated classes, and—except for those attached to the astronomical bureau as assistants to the Jesuits—only a scanty number of officials had embraced the Faith.[147] The missionaries found trouble in reaching the women, for Chinese proprieties could not be ignored and separate chapels and churches had in some instances to be provided. Numbers of women were baptized, however, and some proved very zealous.[148] The rapid progress, however, was, after all, only a beginning.

The missionaries entertained great hopes for the future. They were enjoying the favor of the Emperor and this seemed to presage continued prosperity. In addition to the aid which he had given at Peking, K'ang Hsi contributed to the rebuilding of the church in Hangchow—in some respects the finest Christian temple in all China—and sent a personal representative to worship in this structure and in one in Nanking.[149] He commissioned some of the missionaries to undertake the mapping of a small section of the Empire,[150] and in 1708 the project was extended to the entire country.[151] This increasing imperial patronage appeared to give assurance of quiet and growth for years to come. However, as we have observed, the position of the missionaries remained insecure. They were foreigners and numbered less than one hundred. They were still looked at askance by most of the educated and official classes and for such tolerance as they enjoyed were dependent upon K'ang Hsi. His death or a change in his sentiments might at any moment bring swift disaster. They were, moreover, as we have often said, preaching a faith which, if it were adopted, would work a revolution in China and would

[145] Report of Noël in Lockman, op. cit., Vol. 1, p. 447.
[146] This figure must be at best a rough estimate. Noël (in Lockman, op. cit., Vol. 1, p. 447) says there were "upwards of . . . 100,000 Christians" in "the province of Nankin." This was in 1702 or 1703. Flores (Maas, op. cit., pp. 152, 153) says there were in Shantung in 1686 3,000 Christians.
[147] Report of Noël in Lockman, op. cit., Vol. 1, p. 449; letter of Chavagnac, Feb. 10, 1703, in Lockman, op. cit., Vol. 2, p. 309.
[148] Report of Francis Noël in Lockman, op. cit., Vol. 1, p. 447; letter of Chavagnac in Lockman, op. cit., Vol. 2, pp. 302-309.
[149] Letter of Bouvet, Nov. 30, 1699, in Lockman, op. cit., Vol. 1, p. 75.
[150] Lettres édifiantes, Vol. 3, pp. 156-160.
[151] Mailla, Histoire générale de la Chine, Vol. 11, pp. 314, 315. Mailla was himself engaged in the project.

overthrow or transform some of the most cherished institutions of the country. It is not strange, then, that the brief period of success was followed by several decades of disappointment and adversity, and that the growth of the Church, for a few years so promising, should suffer retardation.

CHAPTER VII

THE BEGINNING OF RETARDED GROWTH: THE RITES CONTROVERSY

WHILE all this growth was taking place and while outwardly the future of the Christian mission in China was bright, a controversy was in progress which was to bring reverses and persecution. From what was said at the close of the second and third chapters and at the conclusion of the one just completed, it is obvious that if the Catholic missionaries were to see any large proportion of the Chinese accept their faith they either would have to obtain extensive reënforcements over a prolonged period—a missionary body sufficiently large and working long enough to win at least a substantial minority of the nation from their existing religious practices and social institutions—or they would have to wait until other agencies, internal or external, had so influenced Chinese culture that it would offer less stubborn resistance to the entrance of a revolutionary religion.

Now reënforcements could not at that time be had from Europe in very large numbers. Distances were great, transportation and communication were uncertain and slow, and the home resources of the orders and societies were inadequate for an effort much greater than was already being made. The Europe of the eighteenth century, rich and growing though it was, did not have the means to send thousands of missionaries to China and, even had it possessed them, it was too distracted by wars and too lukewarm toward its professed faith to concentrate upon such an enterprise. Even if the impossible had been achieved and missionaries had in a few decades been multiplied ten or twenty-fold, the entrance of so many foreigners preaching a revolutionary doctrine could not have failed to arouse the active opposition of the Emperor and the ruling scholar class. No force was yet in sight to join with

Christianity in working a transformation in the structure of Chinese life and thought.

One method, however, offered some hope to the missionary—the effecting of such a compromise with Chinese culture that Christianity would cease to seem exotic and antagonistic to basic social and political institutions. If a Chinese, particularly a scholarly Chinese, could accept the Christian faith and remain loyal to the more important institutions and practices of his nation, if he could feel that the new religion was akin to Chinese thought and teachings at their best, the Church might achieve for itself a permanent and influential place in the life of the country. If, on the other hand, in becoming a Christian a Chinese would have to break radically with the social, economic, and political structure of his people, the Church would have small chance of success. Could a satisfactory adjustment be made without fatally denaturing Christianity? Could a type of Christianity that had taken form under a very different cultural environment, the Roman Empire, successfully make the change? In winning the ancient Mediterranean world Christianity had partly transformed it and had also adapted itself to it in organization, teaching, and practice. Was the resulting body, the Roman Catholic Church, sufficiently flexible to make a similar adjustment in China? The task would be at least extremely difficult, for not only was the Roman Church much more rigid than in its earlier centuries, but Chinese culture was much less plastic than that of the Roman Empire at the time of the Christian triumph.

The Jesuit Attitude Toward Chinese Rites and Nomenclature

From the beginning, as we have seen, some of the Jesuits had begun consciously to adapt their methods to Chinese prejudices. They had dressed first as Buddhist priests and then, when they learned of the contempt with which these were regarded by educated Chinese, they had put on the robes of the Confucian scholar. It was as scholars that they won the tolerance of much of officialdom and the court, for they had perceived that under existing conditions thus and probably only thus could they gain from the dominant classes a hearing for their message and permission to preach to the masses of the nation. As early as 1615 the Jesuits obtained the approval of the Pope for the use by native priests of the Chinese language in the liturgy and in the administration of the sacraments. This privilege was never used, perhaps because of the paucity of Chinese priests, and an attempt in 1681 to have it renewed proved unsuccessful.[1]

Before 1615 questions had arisen as to the proper attitude toward much more serious matters. These may in general be grouped under three heads. In the first place, what Chinese word or words should be used for God? Should the Church take from the older classical books the terms *Shang Ti* and *T'ien*, familiar to all Chinese scholars, and give them a Christian connotation—declaring that "whom ye ignorantly worship him declare we unto you"? Did these words, on the other hand, have either no theistic significance or so very little that others must be sought or new ones coined? There had been no uniformity in the practice of Moslems, Jews, and Nestorians, who before the Jesuits had attempted to discover in Chinese a name for God,[2] and Protestants were later to find the problem difficult and controversial. Ricci had used *T'ien Chu,* literally "The Lord of Heaven," a term which he found employed by Taoists and Buddhists and in orthodox Confucian literature, but he had also come to believe that both *Shang Ti* and *T'ien* originally had a theistic significance and could properly be adopted by Christians.[3] Some of the missionaries held that theism was to be found in Chu Hsi, who dominated orthodox Confucian thought. The new faith would certainly seem less strange if familiar words could be employed to express its leading concepts.

In the second place, should the ceremonies observed in honor of Confucius and of ancestors be condemned and Christians be

[1] *Catholic Encyclopedia,* Vol. 3, p. 40. It was for a time a mooted question whether the Chinese priests should be required to learn Latin at all. If the service could be said in Chinese and enough Catholic literature put into that language, Latin might possibly be dispensed with. The task of becoming sufficiently expert in classical Chinese to command the respect of the scholar class was so great that it was thought to preclude the possibility of becoming fluent in Latin. Rome believed, however, that only through Latin could the Chinese clergy be kept in touch with the life of the Church and be prevented from drifting off into heresy and schism.—Huonder, *Der einheimische Klerus in den Heidenländern,* pp. 157-172. In 1659, 1669, and 1673 the privilege was given the vicars apostolic to ordain to the priesthood natives who did not know Latin well. They were required, however, to know enough Latin to understand the sense of the mass and the sacramental formulas.—Jann, *Die katholische Missionen in Indien, China und Japan,* p. 219.

[2] Havret, *T'ien Tchou,* p. 2.

[3] Ibid., p. 9. Some missionaries also held that the *Li* and *T'ai Chi* of the Sung philosophers had theistic implications, for Chu Hsi and his school held them to be practically identical with *T'ien.*

forbidden to participate in them, or should they be regarded as not having a religious significance, or at least none contrary to Christian belief, and so be tolerated?   Or could the missionaries take still a third position, and while condemning some features, permit converts to perform the rites with modifications and trust to the Christian conscience eventually to abandon or still further to modify them?   It was obvious that if the rites were utterly proscribed the missionaries would be greatly handicapped.   Many religious customs they could not but condemn.   The worship of hills and rivers, of Taoist and Buddhist divinities, and of native gods was in clear contradiction to Catholic teaching.   If, however, missionaries included in the practices forbidden to Christians the ceremonies in honor of ancestors and Confucius, they would be denounced as attacking both the state and the family. Ricci, after prolonged study, took the moderate position, deciding that the rites in honor of Confucius and ancestors had only a civil significance and that Christians could engage in them in so far as the laws of the Empire required.   He would trust the Chinese Christians to decide eventually what they could and could not do, and he hoped that the Catholic practices concerning burial and honoring the dead would gradually supplant those of the older China.[4]

In the third place was a whole group of miscellaneous problems which were only slightly less important.   Should Christians be permitted to contribute to community festivals in honor of non-Christian divinities?   Could masses be said for the souls of the non-Christian ancestors of Christians?   Could priests, in administering the sacraments to women, omit those portions of the ritual which most offended the Chinese sense of propriety?[5]   Should the Chinese converts be made to conform immediately to all Catholic customs and doctrines as practiced in Europe, or should they only gradually be introduced to them?[6]

These questions were all of them thorny and on them a diversity of opinion was certain.   In general they were of the kind that the Christian missionary, and in a somewhat different way every Christian, has faced in all times and places: just how far should one who professes the Christian faith participate in the

[4] Mosheim, *Memoirs of the Christian Church in China*, pp. 14-16; Henrion, *Histoire générale des missions catholiques*, Vol. 2, p. 374.
[5] Le Comte, *Des cérémonies de la Chine*, pp. 122-128.
[6] Huonder, *Der chinesische Ritenstreit*, pp. 29, 30.

society in which he lives?   In the China of the seventeenth and eighteenth centuries, however, they seemed a matter of life or death to the Church, and missionaries could not discuss them calmly or be content with permitting Rome to do so.   Jealousies between orders and national rivalries [7] were interjected and prolonged and acrimonious controversy followed.   Eventually not only the missionary body in the Far East, but much of ecclesiastical and learned Europe took sides.   Only after more than a century of discussion did Rome stop the debate.

At the outset the Jesuits were not at all unanimous in supporting Ricci's views.   In China the majority of the Jesuits seem to have followed him.   The funerals and the graves of Ricci and some of his successors in Peking, for example, conformed largely to Chinese custom.[8]   In Japan, however, the majority appear to have taken the opposite position,[9] and their opinions were supported by Longobardi, Ricci's successor as head of the China mission.[10]   In 1628 representative Jesuits of the two schools of thought came together and after a discussion lasting several weeks failed to reach an agreement.[11]

MORALES ATTACKS THE JESUITS
THE DECREE OF 1645

When the members of other orders established themselves in China the situation became still more involved.   Some of the newcomers were none too kindly disposed toward the Jesuits [12] and were easily scandalized by what they deemed their easy-going compromises.   The Jesuits naturally resented what seemed to them the captious criticisms of those less acquainted than themselves with Chinese learning and customs and appear eventually to have rallied almost solidly in support of Ricci's views.   The Dominicans and Franciscans carried the question to the bishops

---

[7] Huonder, *Der chinesische Ritenstreit,* pp. 33-47.

[8] Thomas, *Histoire de la mission de Pékin,* pp. 80-85, 108, 110.

[9] Favier, *Peking,* Vol. 1, p. 134.

[10] Henrion, *Histoire générale des missions catholiques,* Vol. 2, p. 374; Brucker in *Catholic Encyclopedia,* Vol. 3, p. 671, Vol. 13, p. 37.

[11] Henrion, op. cit., Vol. 2, p. 374; Brucker in *Catholic Encyclopedia,* Vol. 13, p. 37; Joly, *Le christianisme et l'Éxtrême Orient,* Vol. 1, p. 120.

[12] As early as the sixteenth century there had been attacks on the Jesuits in Japan and China.—Valignano, *Apologia en quol se responde a diversas calumnias que se escrevieron contra los padres de la compañía de Jeſu de Japon y de la China.* MS. 1593.

in the Philippines and it was debated there for some time, the local Jesuits coming to the defence of their brethren in China.[13] In 1635 the Archbishop of Manila denounced the Jesuit practices to the Pope but in 1638 withdrew his accusation.[14]

Morales, a Dominican, who, it will be recalled, went to China in 1633 and who was, with some other missionaries, driven from the country by persecution in 1637, led in the opposition. On his expulsion from China, Morales laid his objections before the Jesuit Visitor, Emanuel Diaz, but obtained no satisfaction.[15] He then left for Europe and presented his case to the Propaganda (1643), putting it in the form of seventeen questions which purported to set forth the Jesuit practices. Were Chinese Christians, he asked, obliged as were other Catholics to go to confession and to take the communion at least once a year? Might missionaries in administering baptism to women omit the saliva and the salt, and might they be excused from giving to women extreme unction? Were Chinese to be permitted to charge an interest rate of thirty per cent,[16] and when those who made their living by lending money became Christians were they to be allowed to continue in their profession? Might Christians contribute to community sacrifices to pagan divinities? Might they be present at the required official sacrifices if they would conceal about their persons a cross and adore that while pretending to be worshiping the idol? Might they join in sacrifices to Confucius and at funerals? Might they join in honoring ancestral tablets and in making offerings to the dead at other times than at funerals? Should applicants for baptism be informed that their new faith forbade all idolatry and sacrifice? Might Christians apply to Confucius the term *sheng* or "holy"? Might they have in their churches tablets to the Emperor wishing him, as was customary, ten thousand years of life? Was it permissible to say masses for Chinese non-Christians who had died? Since some Chinese were scandalized by the crucifixion, was it necessary to speak to them of it or to show them a crucifix? [17] In due course of time a decree

[13] Brucker in *Catholic Encyclopedia,* Vol. 13, p. 37.
[14] *Encyclopædia Sinica,* p. 485.
[15] Henrion, op. cit., Vol. 2, pp. 374-376.
[16] This was probably not exorbitant for those times. The point seems to have been whether the Church should sanction interest.
[17] Le Comte, *Des cérémonies de la Chine,* pp. 122-128.

of the Propaganda was issued and approved by the Pope (September 12, 1645) whereby the practices as described by Morales were prohibited.[18] The decision was apparently meant to be only tentative for the decree contained the qualifying clause "until it shall be decided otherwise." [19]

THE JESUIT REPLY. THE DECREE OF 1656

The Jesuit missionaries in China were naturally alarmed by the news of the decision and determined to present to the papal authorities their side of the case. Accordingly in 1651 they sent to Rome one of their number, Martini. Through him they claimed that Morales had not accurately described their practices and presented to the Inquisition their version. After due consideration the Holy Office issued a decree approved by the Pope (March 23, 1656) giving sanction to the practices as described in the Jesuits' statement.[20] It granted missionaries a wide degree of latitude in the dispensing power; it gave to Chinese Christians the right to observe all ceremonies of a civil and political nature and allowed Christians a good deal of freedom in deciding what came under these categories; it said that if superstitious features were removed, ceremonies in honor of the dead might be performed even in the company of non-Christians; and it permitted Christians to assist in ceremonies of a superstitious nature if they made a protestation of their faith, if all fear of the subversion of their faith were removed, and if enmities could not otherwise be avoided.[21] This decision, too, was obviously tentative and the interpretation given it would determine whether its permissions contradicted the prohibitions of 1645.

THE DECREE OF 1669

The Dominicans were as little satisfied with the decree of 1656 as were the Jesuits with that of 1645 and in their turn declared that the Jesuit statement of the case did not conform to the facts. Morales submitted a new memorandum to the Holy Office (1651) but died (1664) before he was able to obtain a decision.[22] When

[18] Henrion, op. cit., Vol. 2, p. 377.
[19] Ibid.
[20] Thomas, *Histoire de la mission de Pékin*, p. 163.
[21] Jenkins, *The Jesuits in China*, pp. 20, 21.
[22] Cordier in *Catholic Encyclopedia*, Vol. 3, p. 671.

another Dominican, John de Polanco, asked whether the decree of 1656 annulled that of 1645 he was informed by the Holy Office (November 20, 1669) in a decree approved by the Pope that the first decree had not been cancelled by the second, but that both were to be observed "according to the questions, circumstances, and everything set forth in them.[23]   It was obvious that the Jesuits were getting the better of the controversy, for in the uncertainty much latitude would be allowed them.

THE INTENSIFICATION OF THE CONTROVERSY, 1669-1703

In the meantime an effort was being made in China to bring the differing parties to an agreement.   The persecution during the minority of K'ang Hsi brought into the same house in Canton for several years representatives of the Jesuits, Dominicans, and Franciscans, and so made possible unhurried discussion.   After a conference of forty days ending in January, 1668, all, with the possible exception of the one Franciscan, consented to a statement of forty-two articles, one of which was an engagement to follow the decree of 1656.[24]   However, the leader of the Dominican group, Navarette—who had come to China at the instance of Morales—soon afterward left for Europe and there renewed the attack on the Jesuits.   Innocent XI, so it is said, would have named him bishop and administrator-general of the missions in China, but Navarette declined the honor and never returned to the Far East.[25]   His attacks, however, added fuel to the controversy.   The Society had bitter enemies in Europe, even within the fold of the Catholic Church, and these welcomed such evidences of depravity as Navarette seemed to disclose.   In China nearly all Franciscans and Augustinians had been won to the Jesuit position[26] and only the Dominicans continued as a body to stand against it.   Even among these last there was division, and it is interesting—and perhaps significant of what a purely Chinese church would have done—that in 1681 and 1686 Gregory Lopez came out in opposition to the majority of his fellow members of the Order of Preachers with a work in defence of Ricci's position.[27]

[23] Thomas, op. cit., p. 165; Brucker in *Catholic Encyclopedia*, Vol. 13, p. 37.
[24] Brucker in op. cit., Vol. 13, p. 38.
[25] Thomas, op. cit., p. 165.
[26] Brucker in *Catholic Encyclopedia*, Vol. 13, pp. 38, 39.
[27] Moule in *The New China Review*, Vol. 1, pp. 480-488.

The entrance of the French missionaries further complicated the situation, for Maigrot of the Missions Étrangères condemned the Jesuit practices and some of the French members of the Society of Jesus came to the support of their brethren. In March, 1693, Maigrot as Bishop of Conon and Vicar Apostolic in Fukien issued a mandate to the priests of his vicariate which, while not mentioning the Jesuits by name, forbade the practices sanctioned by them. He interdicted the use of *T'ien* and *Shang Ti* and the placing in churches of tablets bearing the words *Ching T'ien* ("Adore Heaven"); he denounced as inaccurate the statements which had been the basis of the papal decree of 1656; he forbade missionaries to permit Christians to have any part in the customary honors to Confucius or to ancestors; he commended those missionaries who insisted on the removal of all ancestral tablets from the homes of Christians and said that if such memorials to the dead were permitted they should have on them only the names of the deceased and no exhortations to worship. He condemned remarks which tended to make Chinese believe that some of the Chinese practices and the classical books were in accord with Christian teaching, and he recommended that missionaries make sure that when Christian teachers read and explained Chinese books they should take care that their pupils did not imbibe the atheism and the superstition contained in them, but that they should emphasize what the Christian religion teaches about God and the creation and the government of the world.[28] The publication of this mandate created a sensation. Maigrot removed two Jesuits for disobeying it and their irate flock is said to have gone to the Vicar Apostolic and to have attacked and beaten him while he was saying mass.[29] Representatives sent to Rome by Maigrot and the Missions Étrangères saw to it that the mandate was presented to the papal authorities, and in 1697 the Pope ordered the Inquisition to reopen the entire question.[30]

Ecclesiastical circles were now more interested than ever and controversial books and pamphlets issued in streams from the

[28] The Latin text is in *Acta causæ rituum seu ceremoniarum sinensium complectentia*, pp. 1-12. There is a French version in Thomas, op. cit., pp. 166-170.
[29] Gonzalés de S. Pierre, *Relation abrégée de la nouvelle persecution de la Chine*, pp. 10-20.
[30] Brucker in *Catholic Encyclopedia*, Vol. 13, p. 38.

printing presses of Europe.[31]   The debate between the Jansenists and the Jesuits was just then acute and the former and their friends were not averse to this new weapon against their antagonists.[32]   The Protestant philosopher Leibnitz, fearing for the cause of Christian missions in China, published a defense of the Jesuits.[33]   In 1700 the theological faculty of the University of Paris formally disapproved the Jesuit position and censured some books that had appeared in its behalf.[34]

In 1700, on the other hand, K'ang Hsi came out with a public declaration upholding the Society.   The Jesuits had appealed to him for an opinion and he expressed himself as agreeing with them that honors were paid to Confucius only as a legislator, that those to ancestors were not for the purpose of asking protection but were merely a demonstration of love and a commemoration of the good the dead had done during their lives, and that the sacrifices to *T'ien* were not to the visible heavens but to the Supreme Lord, the creator and preserver of heaven and earth and of all that is contained in them.[35]   This opinion, together with similar ones from many Chinese scholars, was forwarded to Rome.[36]

THE DECREE OF 1704

After much deliberation, the Inquisition issued a statement, confirmed by Pope Clement XI (November 20, 1704), forbidding

[31] Martino, *L'Orient dans la litterature française au XVIIe et au XVIIIe siècle*, pp. 126 et seq.; Saint-Simon, *Mémoires*, Vol. 2, p. 335; *Catholic Encyclopedia*, Vol. 1, pp. 296, 297, Vol. 2, pp. 788, 789, Vol. 3, p. 414.   Cordier, *Bibliotheca Sinica*, pp. 869-925, gives a bibliography on the subject.   Some titles of books and pamphlets are: a number of tracts against the Jesuits published about 1700 under the back-title *Conformité des cérémonies chinoises avec l'idolâtrie grecque et romaine; Defense des nouveaux chretiens et des missionaires de la Chine, du Japon, et des Indes. Contre dux livres intitulez, la morale pratique des Jesuites et l'esprit de M. Arnauld*, Paris, 2d edition, two volumes, 1688; *Historia cultus sinensium seu varia scripta de cultibus Sinarum, inter Vicarios Apostolicos Gallos aliosque missionarios et Patres Societatis Jesu*, etc., two volumes, Cologne, 1700; *Apologie des dominicains missionaires de la Chine*, Cologne, 1700; *Difesa de 'Missionarii Cinesi della Compagnia di Giesu' in risposta All 'Apologia de' PP. Domenicani Missionarii della Cina, Intorno a gli onori di Confusio, e de Mortii opera di un Religioso Teologo della medesima Compagnia*, Colonia, 1700; *De Sinensium Ritibus politicis Acta seu R. P. Jacobi Le Favre Parisiensis è Societate Jesu Missionarii Sinensis, Dissertatio Theologico-Historia de avita Sinarum pietate praesertim erga defunctos, et eximia erga Confucium magistrum suum observantia*, Paris, 1700.

[32] Cretineau-Joly, *Histoire de la Compagnie de Jésus*, Vol. 5, pp. 64 et seq.

[33] Merkel, *G. W. Leibnitz und die China Mission*, pp. 100 et seq.

[34] Thomas, op. cit., p. 173.

[35] *Afgoden-Dienst der Jesuiten in China*, pp. 62-103; Mailla, *Historie générale de la Chine*, Vol. 11, pp. 302-304.

[36] Mosheim, *Memoirs of the Christian Church in China*, p. 27.

the use of *Shang Ti* and *T'ien* and approving *T'ien Chu;* forbidding in churches tablets bearing the characters *Ching T'ien;* forbidding Christians to take part in sacrifices to Confucius or to ancestors; proscribing ancestral tablets having on them characters calling them the throne or seat of the spirit of the deceased, but permitting tablets bearing merely the name of the dead.[37]   Rome had spoken, but it had yet to devise a wise method of enforcing its decree.   Could the announcement be made and the enforcement carried out in a way that would not bring disaster upon the work of the missionaries?   Would the Jesuits give unquestioning obedience, or would they find some reason, in spite of their avowed especial loyalty to Rome, to postpone acquiescence?

THE MISSION OF CHARLES MAILLARD DE TOURNON, 1704-1710

Even before the decree had been formulated the Pope had decided to send a special legate to the Far East.   Not only was there the China controversy to be settled, but a somewhat similar dispute had arisen in India over the Jesuit attitude toward what were known as the Malabar rites.[38]   The Holy See wished, too, to come into more direct relations with the growing Christian communities in the East and to supervise more carefully the work of the clergy and the vicars apostolic in that vast region.   Both tact and firmness would obviously be required on the part of whomever was appointed.   He would need to satisfy not only the missionaries and the native Christians, but he would have if possible to avoid offending European colonial powers, especially the Portuguese, and his would be the even harder task of convincing K'ang Hsi that the papal decree was not in contravention of imperial prerogatives and held no danger to Manchu rule.   For this delicate charge the Pope chose a man in his middle thirties,[39] Charles Maillard de Tournon, a younger son of the Marquis de Tournon of Savoy.   He seems to have been a lovable, earnestly religious man who was sincere in trying to dispatch his difficult mission with faithfulness, but he appears also to have been neither very wise in dealing with men nor of the stern sort who can override opposition by sheer force of character.

Late in 1701 Tournon was given the title Patriarch of Antioch,

---

[37] *Acta causæ rituum seu ceremoniarum sinensium complectentia,* pp. 50-60.

[38] Norbert, *Memoires historiques presentés au . . . Benoit XIV sur les missions des Indes Orientales,* Vol. 1, pp. 11-15.

[39] He was born in 1667.—Favier, *Peking,* Vol. 1, p. 171.

and to that was added a few months later the designation *Legatus a latere* to the Indies and China.[40]   Although Portugal was notified of the appointment, its approval was not obtained and the omission spelled trouble: Tournon's mission was regarded by Lisbon as a further infringement on the *patroãdo*.   The enmity of Portugal was further assured when Tournon sailed on a French ship.   In India the Legate stopped at Pondicherry—a French post—and there attempted a settlement of the Malabar rites.   In so doing he won the ill-will of the Jesuits and of the Portuguese Archbishop of Goa.[41]   The latter was already prejudiced against Tournon because of what he deemed the violation of Portuguese rights in the East and soon (May 12, 1706) issued a pastoral letter denouncing him.[42]

The Legate arrived at Canton in April, 1705,[43] and, reaching Peking early in December of that year,[44] was there about nine months.   His sojourn in the capital was stormy.   Even before arriving he had caused difficulty by ordering the vicars apostolic to visit their fields,[45] an act which could not fail to arouse opposition among the Portuguese clergy.   He chose for his interpreter Appiani, a Lazarist,[46] and later accepted the counsels of Maigrot, who in addition to being French was pronouncedly anti-Jesuit on the questions at issue.[47]   The Legate was already ill when he reached the capital and, a southerner, suffered greatly from the cold.[48]   He and the Jesuits irritated each other and since the latter had the Emperor's ear and the prestige acquired by long residence, Tournon often found himself blocked.   He discovered that the Jesuits were obtaining part of the support for their mission by money-lending, and although they charged a lower rate than that customary in the capital, he annulled all their contracts

[40] Favier, *Peking*, Vol. 1, p. 171.

[41] Cretineau-Joly, op. cit., Vol. 5, pp. 46-50; Jann, *Die katholische Missionen in Indien, China und Japan*, pp. 410-413.

[42] Jann, op. cit., pp. 416, 417.

[43] *Memoires pour Rome sur l'état de la religion chretienne dans la Chine*, pp. 6-9; *Lettres édifiantes*, Vol. 3, pp. 167-177.

[44] Jenkins, *The Jesuits in China*, p. 60.

[45] Ibid., p. 59.

[46] Appiani, it will be recalled, was the first Lazarist to come to China.   He had been sent by the Propaganda in 1697 as vice visitor apostolic.   He was accompanied by a party of thirty-two, some of them members of various orders and some of them secular priests.   One of the latter, Mullener, became a Lazarist while on the way out.—Coste in *Revue d'histoire des missions*, Vol. 3, pp. 328 et seq.

[47] Gonzalés de S. Pierre, *Relation abrégée de la nouvelle persecution de la Chine, pp.* 29-74; Thomas, op. cit., pp. 178, 179.

[48] Jenkins, op. cit., p. 60.

for interest.   He even removed two of the leading Jesuits from the office of missionary.[49]   His opinion on the rites was well known and the missionaries forbade Chinese Christians to come to his house, for fear, apparently, that they would be antagonized or perplexed by him.[50]   Some of the Christians had acted riotously toward those who forbade them their accustomed participation in the rites.   The Legate seems to have had his chief difficulty with the Portuguese members of the Society, for they could plead loyalty to Lisbon's right of patronage as a justification for questioning his authority.   They deemed it, indeed, a question whether Rome could give the Legate jurisdiction in China, or at least as much as he assumed.   The Legate's relations with the French Jesuits appear not to have been as acutely unpleasant.[51]

One's sympathies cannot but go out both to Tournon and to the missionaries.   Charged with the task of upholding the papal prerogatives and decrees in a distant land, ill, and with little experience in the East, the Legate found those contumacious whom he believed ought to be his supporters.   On the other hand, missionaries who had given their best years to establishing the Church in China saw the edifice built by over a century of sacrifice threatened by the tactlessness and obduracy of a young man who was ignorant of China and of whose authority they believed there was ground for question.

The Emperor received Tournon at first with courtesy, if not with cordiality, but he was more and more antagonized by him.[52]   The two could not agree on the question of the rites, for K'ang Hsi had already expressed himself and the Legate was under instructions which he could not alter.   K'ang Hsi was even more antagonized by Maigrot, for the latter dared to differ from him— who prided himself on being an expert Chinese scholar—on the interpretation of the Classics on the points at issue.[53]   Finally, in August, 1706, K'ang Hsi ordered Maigrot to leave Jehol—where their last interview had been held—and to go to Peking.   He also ordered the Legate to prepare for an early return to Europe.[54]

[49] Ibid., pp. 65-70.   Taking interest was contrary to the laws of the Roman Catholic Church.

[50] Ibid., p. 74.

[51] Ibid., pp. 59-69.   Visdelou, one of the French Jesuits, from the beginning espoused the cause of Tournon and was by the latter created Bishop of Claudianopolis and Vicar Apostolic in Kweichow.—Jann, op. cit., pp. 427, 428.

[52] Thomas, *Histoire de la mission de Pékin*, pp. 181-193.

[53] Ibid., pp. 191, 192.

[54] Cordier, *Histoire générale de la Chine*, Vol. 3, pp. 327, 328.

Tournon left the capital the latter part of the month, but halted for a time at Nanking.[55] The Emperor did not rest content with dismissing the Legate. The Manchus had had so constantly to face revolts that K'ang Hsi probably believed it to be wise to forestall the possibility of another one. Certainly he could not brook in his domains the presence of foreigners who regarded the authority of a non-Chinese ruler as superior to his own, even though that ruler was an ecclesiastical and not a civil official. Still less could he permit foreigners to teach their Chinese followers to accept the new allegiance. In the interests of internal unity, never too secure, the Emperor must be clearly recognized as supreme. In December, 1706, K'ang Hsi ordered Maigrot and two other missionaries banished from the Empire, commanded Appiani to be held for trial for alleged disorders in Szechwan,[56] and decreed punishment for some of the native Christians who had had connection with Maigrot and Mgr. de Tournon. He decreed that all missionaries, if they wished to remain in China, obtain an imperial *piao* or permit, and commanded that this be granted only to those who agreed to abide by the practices of Matthew Ricci.[57]

When the Legate learned of this edict he almost immediately (February 7, 1707) published at Nanking a decree of his own,[58] in which, on the strength of the papal decision of November, 1704, he condemned the use of *Shang Ti* and *T'ien,* participation in sacrifices to Confucius and to ancestors, and the current practices concerning ancestral tablets. He threatened the disobedient with excommunication—a more severe penalty than that indicated in the decree of November, 1704 [59]—and forbade all liberty of interpretation which might be claimed under the decree of 1656.[60]

The issue seemed squarely joined. The missionaries must choose between submission to the Emperor and obedience to the Pope's representative. Some of the Missions Étrangères refused

[55] Ibid.

[56] Appiani was held in prison for nearly twenty years. In 1726 he was released by the Emperor at the request of the Pope. He remained in Canton, pursuing his religious calling and died in 1732 from hardships endured in the persecution of that year.—Coste in *Revue d'histoire des missions,* Vol. 3, pp. 328 et seq.

[57] Thomas, op. cit., p. 196.

[58] The decree was dated January 15, 1707.

[59] Jann, *Die katholischen Missionen in Indien, China und Japan,* p. 430.

[60] Launay, *Histoire générale de la Société des Missions-Étrangères,* Vol. 1, pp. 477-480; Thomas, op. cit., pp. 207-209; Brucker in *Catholic Encyclopedia,* Vol. 13, p. 39.

to apply for the imperial permit in the prescribed form and were obliged either to leave for the coast or to go into hiding. Most of the Augustinians and Jesuits, however, chose to accept the *piao* for the time being on the Emperor's terms and hoped that an appeal to Rome, in which several of the vicars apostolic—formerly opponents of the rites—and twenty-two Jesuits joined, would bring about a modification of the Legate's edict.[61] The Franciscans of Shensi and Shantung seem to have abided by the Legate's decree but to have received special permission from the Emperor to remain in China on the condition that they would not leave the country without his consent.[62] K'ang Hsi commanded that Visdelou and Le Blanc, the latter Vicar Apostolic in Yünnan, be banished, and all preaching against the rites was forbidden on pain of death.[63] He ordered that Tournon be conveyed to Canton and thence to Macao and that he be detained in the latter port until a reply could be had from two missionaries whom K'ang Hsi had dispatched to Rome and the Christians in China could be restored to their accustomed quiet.[64] The messengers were sent at the instance of the Jesuits and in the hope of obtaining some modification of the decrees of 1704 and of Nanking.[65] The imperial order, by detaining the Legate in Macao, delivered him into the hands of the Portuguese and brought fresh trouble on his unfortunate head. Tournon and the civil and ecclesiastical authorities of Macao engaged in prolonged and unseemly wrangling over the question of whose authority should be recognized by the missions in China. The Legate was kept in his house in a kind of semi-imprisonment. The Bishop of Macao, by direction of the Archbishop of Goa, issued a pastoral forbidding the recognition of the Legate's powers.[66] The Legate in turn excommunicated the Bishop and later some of the clergy and the civil officials [67] and forbade either regulars or seculars to enter China as missionaries without his permission. Tournon also placed under an interdict the Jesuit college and cloister at Macao.[68] The

[61] Thomas, op. cit., pp. 203-205; Arias, *El Beato Sanz y Compañeros Martires del Orden de Predicadores*, p. 228; Jann, op. cit., p. 430.
[62] Thomas, op. cit., pp. 208, 209.
[63] Jann, op. cit., p. 431.
[64] Jenkins, *The Jesuits in China*, pp. 121, 122.
[65] Both messengers seem to have lost their lives on the way to Europe.—Huc, *Christianity in China, Tartary and Thibet*, Vol. 3, pp. 297, 298.
[66] Montalto de Jesus, *Historic Macao*, p. 123.
[67] Jann, op. cit., pp. 442-472; Jenkins, op. cit., pp. 126-129.
[68] Jann, op. cit., p. 450.

Portuguese civil and ecclesiastical officials naturally took action against such of the clergy as obeyed Tournon.

In the meantime the Pope, probably to give his legate greater prestige in the negotiations at Peking, had elevated Tournon to the cardinalate (August 1, 1707).[69]   The bearers of the biretta did not reach Macao until early in 1710 [70] and Tournon did not long survive his investiture with the insignia of his new dignity.   On June 8th of that year he was dead [71] and another chapter in the rites controversy had been concluded.   Rome had been bringing pressure on Lisbon in behalf of its Legate, but was helpless.   When the news of his passing reached Europe the Pope could only pronounce a eulogy over his memory and honor the clergy who had been loyal to him.[72]   The sad fate of the papal messenger, however, did not incline Rome to make more mild its attitude toward the Jesuits on the questions at issue.

THE BULL EX ILLA DIE, 1715

When Tournon's edict of Nanking and the Jesuit appeal arrived at Rome, the Inquisition (September 25, 1710) rejected the latter and affirmed that the former together with the papal edict of 1704 was to be regarded as in full force.   At the same time further discussion of the rites question through the press was prohibited.[73]   When this new decision reached China and the Bishop of Peking, the Franciscan Bernardin della Chiesa, sent one of his clergy from his residence in Shantung to publish it in the churches of the capital, the Jesuits offered such determined opposition that the messenger returned baffled.[74]

Rome was preparing to take still more vigorous action.   In March, 1715, Clement XI issued the bull *Ex illa die*.   This reaffirmed the prohibitions of the decree of 1704, upheld Tournon's edict of 1707, commanded obedience of all missionaries and ecclesiastical officers in China on pain of suspension, interdict, and excommunication, rejected all privileges, dispensations, or rights of interpretation that might be used to nullify or postpone obedi-

[69] Thomas, op. cit., p. 219; Jann, op. cit., p. 423.
[70] Thomas, op. cit., p. 223.
[71] Ibid.
[72] Mosheim, op. cit., p. 33; Jann, op. cit., pp. 457-471.
[73] Mosheim, op. cit., p. 34.
[74] Heeren in *Journal of the North China Branch of the Royal Asiatic Society*, 1923, pp. 182-199.

ence, required that all missionaries take oath before a commissioner, apostolic visitor, bishop, or vicar apostolic to obey the bull, and specified that these oaths, signed, be sent to Rome. However, one loophole was left: ceremonies which were purely civil or political and which had about them no taint of superstition were to be tolerated, and if any doubt arose as to whether a custom fulfilled these requirements, the question was to be submitted to the papal commissioner or visitor general or to a bishop or vicar apostolic.[75]

Bishop Bernardin della Chiesa had the greatest difficulty in getting this bull published in the churches of Peking.[76] When it was read, the Bishop's envoy was imprisoned by the Emperor and was released only on the condition that he take the decree back to the Bishop and engage in no further efforts to make known its contents.[77] The Jesuits found, moreover, reasons for questioning the finality of the decision and seem to have devised ways of partially carrying on their work without giving full obedience[78] —and this in spite of the fact that the Society's General had in 1711 promised submission to the then existing papal decrees on the subject.[79]

THE MISSION OF MEZZABARBA

The situation required that another legate be sent to China to obtain the full obedience of the missionaries and to mollify K'ang Hsi. The man appointed for the thankless task was Jean Ambrose Charles Mezzabarba. He was given the titles of Patriarch of Alexandria, Legate, and Visitor Apostolic, and he and his entourage left Rome in May, 1719. This time the mission went with the full consent of Portugal, the King attempting to safeguard what he deemed his rights by certain restrictions on Mezzabarba's powers. The Legate sailed from Lisbon in March, 1720, and the King of Portugal and the Senate of Macao bore his expenses.[80] In the meantime (1716) the Pope in appointing a new Archbishop of Goa had limited the jurisdiction of that see

---

[75] Thomas, op. cit., pp. 243-251.
[76] Mosheim, op. cit., pp. 38, 39.
[77] Ibid.
[78] Thomas, op. cit., pp. 256, 257, quoting Ripa's Journal.
[79] Cordier, *Histoire générale de la Chine*, Vol. 3, p. 329.
[80] Montalto de Jesus, op. cit., p. 126; Jann, *Die katholischen Missionen in Indien, China und Japan*, pp. 504, 505.

in a way which he hoped would leave no doubt as to the place and the authority of the vicars apostolic.[81]   Mezzabarba arrived in Macao late in September, 1720, and was received by the Portuguese authorities with every honor.   K'ang Hsi was at first not disposed to welcome another messenger, for he was wearied with the controversy and had no happy memories of Tournon.   Eventually he agreed to see Mezzabarba, however, and the latter reached the North late in December, 1720, and was received in formal audience on the last day of the year.   A number of interviews followed.   The Legate appears to have comported himself with dignity and discretion, but the Emperor treated him with ill-concealed contempt.   The Legate postponed the formal delivery of the bull *Ex illa die* as long as possible, but K'ang Hsi finally demanded to see the document, and on reading it became extremely angry, and is said to have pencilled on it a comment to the effect that Europeans were incompetent to sit as judges on the customs of the Chinese, that from the decree Christainity seemed to be like Taoism and Buddhism, and that its representatives had best be forbidden to preach their faith in China.

The missionaries at Peking were divided.   Those who had been sent by the Propaganda were willing to abide by the bull.   The Jesuits, however, were aghast and believed that the decree meant the ruin of the mission.   They besought Mezzabarba to suspend it, but this he declared he had no power to do.   He did, however, present to the Emperor a concession in the form of eight "permissions" which he hoped would obviate some of the most serious difficulties.   These were in the main an interpretation of the clauses which permitted ceremonies of a purely civil or political character.   By them Chinese Christians were to be allowed to have in their homes tablets to the dead inscribed with the names of the deceased, provided there was placed beside them a statement of the Christian belief about the soul and a disavowal of any superstition that might become a subject of scandal; all ceremonies of the Chinese in honor of ancestors which were neither superstitious nor suspected of superstition were permitted; honor to Confucius, in so far as it was purely civil, was allowed, provided that the tablet be purged of any superstitious inscription and that a declaration be made of the faith of the Church; the use of lights,

<hr>

[81] Jann, op. cit., p. 496.

incense, and viands before the tablet was sanctioned; genuflections and prostrations before the coffins and properly corrected tablets of the deceased, and incense and candles at funerals were allowed; food might be placed on tables before the tablets, provided a proper statement of Christian faith was made and the only object was to show respect to the dead; the customary prostrations might be performed before a properly corrected tablet; and incense and candles might be burned before tablets and tombs if the necessary precautions were observed.

These concessions were obviously open to various interpretations and might permit to Chinese Christians modified forms of the customary rites. They were, however, far from satisfactory to K'ang Hsi.[82] He saw Mezzabarba a number of times more, and often made him and the papal decisions a subject of scathing comment. He remarked, for example, that if the Pope's decree were inspired, Maigrot must be the Holy Spirit, for the document corresponded with Maigrot's position. He observed, too, that while the Pope insisted on the enforcement of the bull *Ex illa die* in a non-Christian empire, he was unable to obtain the acceptance of his bull *Unigenitus* against the Jansenists in Catholic France. The Legate failed to gain the sanction he had wished for the permanent residence in China of a papal officer who would supervise all the missions there, and in general made little headway with the Emperor. He had his final audience early in March and left soon afterward for Canton and Macao.

Before departing for Europe Mezzabarba issued in a pastoral letter to the missionaries the eight permissions, with the strict injunction that they be not translated into Chinese or Manchu or given out to the native Christians: they were purely for the guidance of the clergy. Some of the missionaries, among them the Vicar Apostolic of Shansi, declined to make use of the permissions, but the Jesuits welcomed them and are said to have disobeyed the Legate's command and to have translated them for the benefit of their flocks. On starting for Europe, Mezzabarba arranged to have carried with him the bones of Tournon. He had been more tactful than his predecessor, and he had handled

[82] The eight permissions could not modify the papal decision on the terms for God, which was one of the points on which K'ang Hsi and the Pope were at variance.

himself well in an extremely difficult position, but his visit had not brought peace to the missions in China.[83]

THE END OF THE CONTROVERSY
THE BULL EX QUO SINGULARI, 1742

When Mezzabarba made his report, the Pope, Innocent XIII, issued a decree (September 13, 1723) to the General of the Jesuits, charging the latter with not having obtained from the members of the Society in China the obedience to the papal orders which had been promised in 1711 and ordering him to do so now on pain of not being permitted to admit any more novices to his Society or of being allowed to send additional missionaries to China. The General responded, protesting the loyalty of the Society and promising to expel any member who was persistently disobedient. Innocent died before the reply of the General was answered and the final settlement of the controversy was passed on to his successors.[84]

In December, 1733, the Bishop of Peking, in two pastoral letters on the subject of the rites, ordered that the bull *Ex illa die* be observed in accordance with Mezzabarba's permissions and that Christians be instructed four times a year as to what was prohibited and what allowed. Contrary to Mezzabarba's commands, the permissions were thereby published. September 25, 1735, Clement XVI annulled these letters. He also believed that in view of the eight permissions and the varying practices in China the entire question needed reëxamination. He did not live to see the inquiry completed, but it was continued by the proper officials and on July 11, 1742, Benedict XIV, who was no friend of the Jesuits, sanctioned the findings by the bull *Ex quo singulari*. This rehearsed the history of the controversy and of the papal decisions, confirmed the bull *Ex illa die,* annulled the eight permissions of Mezzabarba, ordered all disobedient missionaries to be returned to Europe for punishment, and prescribed the form of

---

[83] There are accounts of Mezzabarba's embassy in Thomas, *Histoire de la mission de Pékin,* pp. 272-288; Mailla, *Histoire générale de la Chine,* Vol. 11, pp. 337-348; Huc, *Christianty in China, Tartary and Thibet,* Vol. 3, pp. 289-320; Mosheim, *Memoirs of the Christian Church in China,* pp. 4-46. Original documents are given principally in translation by Huc and Thomas. Nearly all accounts, even those written recently and after the controversy has been over these hundred and eighty years, show a decided bias. Jann, *Die katholischen Missionen in Indien, China und Japan,* p. 508, says that Mezzabarba died at Macao before returning to Europe, but in this he is mistaken.

[84] Thomas, *Histoire de la mission de Pékin,* pp. 361-364.

oath of obedience to the papal decrees which must be taken by all missionaries to China.[85]

THE AFTERMATH OF THE CONTROVERSY

This decree ended the long controversy. Some of the missionaries might still remain unconvinced, but Rome had spoken in such unmistakable terms that they had no recourse but obedience. K'ang Hsi's successors declined to become interested in the discussion and persecutions having little or no connection with the rites question absorbed the attention of the missionaries and their converts. The problem of interpreting and enforcing the decree continued to present itself from time to time, but the missionaries apparently always stood firmly by Rome. Thus in the last quarter of the century the question arose whether the custom of some Christians of preparing a piece of satin with the names and titles of their defunct parents and permitting pagans to perform prostrations before it was superstitious.[86] In 1769 the Holy Office forbade any contributions by Christians to a community enterprise for restoring or building temples or for sacrificing to idols, even though a vicar apostolic in Fukien had permitted them under certain conditions.[87] In 1777 the Holy Office in answer to an inquiry from Szechwan condemned prostrations before the dead.[88] In 1786 the Bishop of Peking found that not all Christians were obeying the bull of 1742 and had it published in the churches of the city and its enforcement decreed. This act provoked a tumult in the cathedral and one of the catechists shouted that the *k'ou t'ou* was not superstitious. A sermon on the subject by the Bishop aroused another storm, for some Christians among the officials and in the imperial family had apparently been compromising. The Bishop was firm and in time the opposition subsided.[89] In 1792 the Propaganda permitted the custom of cleaning the graves, but directed that it be done on another day than that adopted by the non-Christians.[90] The Roman Catholic Church had decided not to compromise its customs or to adapt

[85] Thomas, op. cit., pp. 364-374; *Collectanea S. Congregatione de Propaganda Fide*, Vol. 1, pp. 130-141; Grentrup in *Zeitschrift für Missionswissenschaft*, Vol. 15, pp. 100-110.
[86] Chaumont in *Nouvelles lettres édifiantes*, Vol. 1, pp. 464, 465. The practice was condemned.
[87] *Collectanea S. Congregatione de Propaganda Fide*, Vol. 1, p. 300.
[88] Ibid., p. 318.
[89] Dufresne, Feb. 8, 1788, in *Nouvelles lettres édifiantes*, Vol. 2, pp. 418-421.
[90] *Collectanea S. Congregatione de Propaganda Fide*, Vol. 1, p. 382.

itself to what it deemed superstitious in Chinese life, and by this determination it continued to abide.[91]

THE EFFECT OF THE CONTROVERSY AND THE DECISION

The story of the controversy is not a pleasant one. The jealousies, the mutual denunciations and recriminations, the evasions, all were contrary to that spirit which Christian missionaries supposedly came to China to exemplify. It must be remembered, however, that the missionaries on both sides of the question believed profoundly that the eternal welfare of souls was at stake. Moreover, the age was one when Europeans were intolerant and the missionaries were probably no more so than their contemporaries. To balance the picture, one must recall the heroism and devotion of the great majority of those who labored in China. They often had a perilous voyage to their field, they seldom saw Europe again, and they worked with the knowledge that persecution might at any moment break out and overwhelm them. Under such conditions it is not surprising that men felt strongly and acted vigorously.

What effect did the controversy and the final decision have upon the success of the Roman Catholic Church in China? This is impossible fully to determine and must always be a question on which judgments will differ. Many hold that the struggle and the papal decrees ruined the mission, and that but for them China would, in the eighteenth and nineteenth centuries, have become Roman Catholic. They believe that the Jesuits, if left to themselves, would have continued to win the friendship of Chinese leaders and would have worked out an attitude toward important Chinese customs and beliefs which, without sacrificing essential Christian and Catholic convictions, would not have unduly offended Chinese sensibilities—that they would have developed a Chinese Church which would have won the country.

This, it seems to the author, is highly doubtful. That during the reign of K'ang Hsi much harm was done cannot be denied.

[91] One would like to know just how far, if at all, national influences, jealousies between orders and factions in the Church, and the growing dislike for the Jesuits were factors in leading the papacy to its final decision. These may at times have had a part in bringing about the various decrees. Benedict XIV, for example, who issued the bull *Ex quo singulari*, was bent upon the more careful control and possibly the reorganization of the Society. There seems to be no clear proof, however, that these enmities were a determining or even an important element in the final decision. It seems probable, indeed, that had it not been for the strong Jesuit influence at Rome the decision would have been reached much earlier.

That, however, had the papal decision favored the Jesuits, the conversion of China would have been much more rapid is open to debate. It is true that in its inception the retardation was caused by the controversy. Because of the papal action K'ang Hsi changed his previously favorable attitude toward the Church and his disfavor was an encouragement to persecution. The decision on the rites, however, was only the earliest of a series of disasters, the majority of which would probably have come had the question never arisen. Most of the causes of the evil days of missions were connected only slightly, if at all, with the rites. The severe persecutions which, as we shall see, overtook the Church in the latter part of the eighteenth and the early part of the nineteenth centuries, while due in part to the papal stand on the rites, would probably have come had that never been taken. No large body of Christian missionaries could have lived and worked in China at this time, no matter what their attitude toward the term for God and the rites to ancestors and Confucius, without eventually arousing intense opposition. They would have been suspected of being agents of European powers, they would have had to forbid to their converts accepted practices of the community, and some of the fundamental institutions of the Catholic Church, such as confession, would have given rise to suspicion. The dissolution of the Society of Jesus, the waning energy of Spain and Portugal, the decline of religious zeal in France under Louis XV, and the disasters brought by the French Revolution were, with the persecutions, what nearly wrought the ruin of the China missions and could not have been averted or mitigated by a decision favoring the rites. It is significant that not only in China, but wherever Roman Catholics were engaged in missions among non-Christian peoples and where questions such as that over the rites never arose, the latter part of the eighteenth and the first two decades of the nineteenth century were marked by the decline and in places the collapse of missionary effort. It is at least doubtful, then, whether the continuation of the policy of Ricci would have led to any substantially greater increase in the Christian community than occurred in the eighteenth and nineteenth centuries. It is possible that in the latter part of the nineteenth and in the twentieth century, when other forces joined with missions in breaking down the resistance of Chinese culture, a more tolerant attitude toward established

customs might have been of advantage, but this also is doubtful.

The most serious indictment which can be brought against the
papal decision is that it established a tradition for making the
Church unadaptable to Chinese conditions and beliefs. It tended
and still tends to keep the Roman Catholic Church a foreign institution, one to which China must conform but which refuses to
conform to China. Among semi-civilized or barbarous peoples,
such as were those of Northern Europe before the advent of
Christianity, the Indians of South and Central America, and the
Filipinos of the sixteenth century, this relative inflexibility was
an advantage, for to them the Church came as the vehicle and
agent of an unmistakably higher and more powerful civilization
and the older cultures offered but a feeble resistance. What compromises were made led to decay in the quality of religious life.
It is significant, however, that in the only countries where Christianity has triumphed over a high civilization, as in the older
Mediterranean world and the Nearer East, it has done so by conforming in part to older cultures. Whether it can win to its fold
a highly cultured people like the Chinese without again making a
similar adaptation remains an unanswered question.

On the other hand, it must be said for the papal decrees that
they helped to keep the Church from losing its distinctive message and probably its vitality. Had the Church made its peace
with some of the more important existing religious practices of
China, deterioration would almost certainly have followed.
Whatever may be true of a few of the educated, for the great
masses the prohibited rites had in them much of animism. It may
not be feasible to lead a people all at once from animism to a
pure Christian faith, but conscious compromise with what is
avowedly lower and imperfect is dangerous. A Ricci might
safely permit it as long as he was living to guide it, but under less
able or less wise successors it probably would have gotten out of
hand. Moreover, in proportion to the Christians, the missionaries and native clergy have always been few, and the former,
without adequate supervision, instruction, and administration of
the sacraments, tend to drift back into a state little removed from
paganism. When, for example, during the evil days of the last
decades of the eighteenth and the first decade of the nineteenth
century the number of missionaries declined, the tone of the Chris-

tian community suffered marked decadence. This might well have been much greater had the compromises of Ricci been permitted. It is conviction and the sense of values not to be found elsewhere which in the last analysis must give the Church a permanent place in a community, and if the distinctiveness of its message or its loyalty to truth as it sees it be compromised, its vitality cannot but suffer. The papal decisions made the winning of nominal adherents more difficult, but they tended to keep high the standards of the Church. Numbers were sacrificed for vitality.

CHAPTER IX

DURING the century and a quarter which had elapsed between the time when Valignani, Ruggerius, and Ricci had obtained for the Jesuits a foothold outside Macao and the coming of Tournon's embassy, the growth of the Church had been rapid. Severe persecutions had occurred, some of them prolonged, but they had always been followed by renewed prosperity. With the visit of Tournon a series of misfortunes began which, although as a rule without causal connection with each other, were for over a hundred years greatly to retard the Church and then for a few decades to threaten it with extinction. In spite of these handicaps, however, missionaries continued to come and to labor heroically, and the Church, while it declined in some places, increased in others. Each fresh disaster was usually followed by a period of comparative quiet, with opportunity for recuperation. When, in the first and second quarters of the nineteenth century, new factors removed some of the obstacles and brought again a period of rapid growth, the number of Chinese Catholic communicants was probably almost as great as at the beginning of the era of adversity. The story of this century and a quarter is not easily woven into a continuous narrative. It is made up of numerous events, many of them unrelated, and the total effect is often confusing. Here and there, however, are events and movements which give a semblance of unity to the whole. The attempt will be made to arrange the incidents, large and small, into something approaching chronological order.

PERSECUTION UNDER K'ANG HSI, 1707-1723

The first serious reverse came, as we have seen, with the rites controversy. Before the arrival of Mgr. de Tournon the question of the rites, although it had attracted some attention, had not seriously interfered with the work of many of the missionaries and seems not to have affected the friendliness of the Emperor. With the coming of the Legate the Church began to suffer. Concentration upon the dispute was not conducive to progress in evangelization. Even more detrimental was the Emperor's decree of banishment for all who did not have the official permit. As we have seen, some missionaries were forced to leave China and others to remain hidden. K'ang Hsi was not, however, very strict in enforcing his edict. He persevered in his friendship for the Jesuits and he may have hoped that the appeal to the Pope would bring concessions. In 1711, when one of the censors brought an official accusation against the missionaries, the Board of Rites virtually reaffirmed the edict of toleration of 1692.[1]

The position of the Church was, however, much more precarious than before 1707. In 1714 there was in Honan a local persecution led by a *chih-fu* (county magistrate),[2] and that same year the Franciscans seem to have suffered annoyance in Shantung.[3] Late in 1716 and early in 1717 more serious difficulty arose when an official in Kwangtung denounced the presence of European traders at Canton and of European missionaries in the provinces. These might, he declared, prove pernicious, for they had brought sorrow in many neighboring countries, Manila and Batavia having actually become subject to the foreigner. Christian missions, he averred, had been used as a means to European aggressions both in the Philippines and in Japan. In response to this memorial and in spite of the efforts of the missionaries at Peking, it was commanded that all Chinese Christians should renounce their faith and that all missionaries who had not received the imperial permit should be conducted to Macao and ordered to return to their respective countries. Only the forty-seven who had received the *piao* were to be allowed to remain.[4] This decree seems not to have been enforced rigorously, but it may have deterred some of the more timid Chinese from embracing Christianity. Mezzabarba's embassy appears to have been followed by another persecution, for we hear in a letter of 1722 of

[1] Mailla, *Histoire générale de la Chine,* Vol. 11, p. 329.
[2] Domenge from Naniang-fu, Honan, July 1, 1716, in *Lettres édifiantes,* Vol. 3, p. 267.
[3] Mailla from Peking, June 5, 1717, in *Lettres édifiantes,* Vol. 3, pp. 270-286.
[4] Mailla from Peking, June 5, 1717, in *Lettres édifiantes,* Vol. 3, pp. 270-286.

churches ruined, Christians scattered, and missionaries exiled and confined to Canton.[5]

In spite of these unfavorable conditions the work of the Church continued. We hear of two missionaries reaching Lhasa in 1716 by way of India,[6] of Capuchins in Tibet from 1707 to 1742,[7] of one hundred thousand Christians under the care of the Franciscans in 1723,[8] and of fifty baptisms of adults in one month at Ching-tê-chên, the porcelain center in Kiangsi.[9] We have a list of one hundred and thirty-one churches known to have been in existence in 1722 in fifteen different provinces.[10] One missionary estimated that in 1724 there were in China more than three hundred churches and three hundred thousand Christians.[11] The Emperor, too, continued to employ missionaries. In addition to astronomical and other scientific pursuits, the task of mapping the Empire, as we have seen, was entrusted to them. The main portion of this mammoth undertaking seems to have been accomplished between 1708 and 1715, but that for some of the provinces and the outlying dependencies was not completed until several years later.[12] Then, too, in Peking missionaries (Parrenin and later Gaubil) were in charge of teaching Latin to Manchu youths who were preparing to participate in the intercourse with the Russians.

PERSECUTIONS BECOME MORE INTENSE UNDER YUNG CHÊNG 1723-1736

With the passing of K'ang Hsi (1723) and the accession of Yung Chêng the period of comparative quiet came to an end

[5] Gaubil from Canton, Nov. 4, 1722, in ibid., Vol. 3, p. 327.
[6] Desideri from Lhasa, April 10, 1716, in ibid., Vol. 3, pp. 531-535.
[7] Annales de la propagation de la foi, Vol. 4, p. 712.
[8] This is probably an over-estimate. It is found in Holzapfel, Handbuch der Geschichte des Franziskanerordens, p. 539.
[9] Letter of Entrecolles from Taochow, September 1, 1712. (MS.)
[10] Cordier, Doc. pour servir a l'his. ecclés. de l'Éxtrême-Orient in Rev. de l'Éxtrême-Orient, Vol. 2, pp. 66-71. There were sixteen in Anhui and Kiangsu, twenty in Kiangsi, twelve in Hunan and Hupeh, twelve in Chêkiang, fifteen in Fukien, twenty-six in Kwangtung outside of Macao, two in Kwangsi, five in Chihli (apparently outside of Peking), nine in Shantung, two in Shansi, seven in Shensi, three in Szechwan, and two in Honan.
[11] Mailla from Peking, Oct. 16, 1724, in Lettres édifiantes, Vol. 3, p. 365.
[12] Mailla, Histoire générale de la Chine, Vol. 2, p. 314; Mailla, August, 1715, in Lettres édifiantes, Vol. 3, p. 352; Huonder in Catholic Encyclopedia, Vol. 6, p. 303; Piolet, Les mis. cath. franç. au XXIe siècle, Vol. 3, p. 52; Brucker, La mission de Chine de 1722 à 1725, in Rev. des ques. hist., Vol. 29, pp. 515, 516.

and the Church was overtaken by a more severe persecution than
it had known since the minority of the late Emperor. Just what
led the new monarch to an anti-Christian attitude is not known.
It may have been dislike for the controversies among the missionaries and the wish not to be troubled by these as his father had
been. It may have been deep-seated distrust due to the papal
decisions on the rites controversy. It was possibly the desire for
the respect of the influential and conservative scholar class. It
may have been fear that the increasing numbers of missionaries
and Christians might lead to foreign aggression. It was very
possibly in large part because of intrigues over the succession: one
of Yung Chêng's brothers who had aspired to the throne had been
supported by a family of the imperial clan some of whose members were Christians.[13]

Whatever the cause of imperial disfavor, the persecution first
broke out as a local disturbance in Fukien. Here in Fu-an, the
strongest Dominican center, in 1723, several scholars, among them
a Christian apostate, denounced some missionaries to the *Chih-
hsien* (district official) on the ground that they were building a
church. The *Chih-hsien* reported the matter to the Viceroy. The
latter ordered vigorous action and turned the churches in the district into schools, ancestral halls, and meeting places for the local
scholars. The missionaries, through two high officials outside
the province, attempted to persuade the Viceroy to desist, but he
was obdurate. Late in December, 1723, he memorialized the
throne, asking that Christianity be exterminated. The memorial
was duly referred to the Board of Rites, and on recommendation
from the latter, Yung Chêng commanded (January 10, 1724) that
missionaries who were skilled in astronomy be sent to Peking,
that all the rest be conveyed to Macao, that church buildings be
confiscated, and that the Christians renounce their faith.[14] The
missionaries at Peking made every possible endeavor to have the
edict rescinded or modified, but the only alteration they could
obtain was authorization for their brethren to retire to Canton
rather than to Macao.

[13] Backhouse and Bland, *Annals and Memoirs of the Court of Peking,* pp. 247,
272; Boulger, *History of China,* Vol. 1, p. 647; Arias, *El Beato Sanz y Compañeros Mártires del Orden de Predicadores,* p. 256.
[14] A translation of the text is to be found in Cordier, *Doc. pour servir a l'his.
ecclés, de l'Éxtrême-Orient,* in *Rev. de l'Éxtrême-Orient,* Vol. 2, pp. 54, 55.

The edict seems to have been carried out fairly thoroughly. Churches were seized and turned into granaries or were used for schools or other public or semi-public enterprises. Missionaries were forced to leave their flocks, and a family of imperial blood which was largely Christian was sent into exile. None of the missionaries or their converts seems to have been killed, although some were roughly handled.[15] The days of formal toleration had passed, however, and in the future missionaries in the provinces were in constant danger of arrest and as a rule had to carry on their work secretly. No exception was made, as under K'ang Hsi, for those who took a lenient attitude toward Chinese customs. In 1727 a Portuguese envoy to Peking endeavored to obtain a modification of the decree, but although he was received with pomp, the persecution was renewed rather than relaxed.[16]

In spite of the persecution many missionaries found it possible, although often by dint of great heroism, to minister to their flocks. The churches in Peking remained open and Christians continued to attend them. In 1728 a missionary wrote from the capital that in that year the communion had been administered to more than four thousand, that three Chinese priests, six European priests, and one bishop were caring for the Christians in Shansi, Shensi, Hukwang, and Szechwan, that in the diocese of Nanking there were one bishop and eight priests, all in hiding, and that there were twenty-four or twenty-six missionaries in Kwangtung.[17] Other letters give vivid pictures of the way in which priests, both Chinese and foreign, travelled in secret to visit their flocks. These they often found hiding in the mountains. There seems, for example, to have been a large community in the hills of Hunan.[18]

In 1730 a fresh persecution broke out in Fukien and spread to other parts of the Empire. Great earthquakes in the Northeast partly diverted attention and the Emperor even aided in the

[15] Letter of Mailla from Peking, Oct. 16, 1724, in *Lettres édifiantes*, Vol. 3, pp. 360 et seq., gives a long first-hand account. See also Du Halde, *China*, Vol. 2, pp. 35-37; Brucker, *La mission de Chine de 1722 à 1735*, in *Rev. des ques. hist.*, Vol. 29, pp. 505-508.

[16] Mailla, *Histoire générale de la Chine*, Vol. 11, pp. 446-464; Cordier, *Histoire générale de la Chine*, Vol. 3, p. 343. It is interesting that the Pope was able to obtain from Yung Chêng the release of two priests imprisoned at Canton.— Bland and Backhouse, *Annals and Memoirs of the Court of Peking*, p. 308.

[17] Brucker in *Revue des ques. hist.*, Vol. 29, p. 512.

[18] Le Conteux, writing in 1730, tells of a trip begun from Canton in 1727 and extending into Hunan, Hupeh, and Honan.—*Lettres édifiantes*, Vol. 3, pp. 592-606.

repair of the churches in Peking.[19] By 1732 about thirty missionaries had been concentrated at Canton by the persecution and, apparently because they continued to pursue their vocation, nearly all of them were deported to Macao. Only four or five were left in Canton to transmit letters to the mission in Peking.[20] In 1734 a missionary wrote from Peking of two Dominicans who had been arrested in Fukien, one of them having been in hiding for two years. One was sent to Macao and the other to Manila.[21] Only in the capital were the missionaries allowed a certain degree of liberty.

Interestingly enough, in spite of the severe persecutions, twenty-six Jesuits, European and Chinese, are recorded as having joined the China mission during the reign of Yung Chêng (1723-1736).[22] These years, too, saw the founding at Naples of a college for the training of Chinese priests. This was the work of a certain Father Ripa. As a youth of eighteen Ripa had been converted from a profligate life and had entered the Church. About 1705 he became one of the first two students in a college which Clement XI had recently founded at Rome for instruction in the Chinese language. He was sent to China as one of the company which carried the cardinal's hat to the unfortunate Tournon, and remained in China, attached to the mission of the Propaganda in Peking, for over ten years. While in China he conceived the project of starting in Europe a school for the training of Chinese for the priesthood and to that end left Peking in 1723, taking with him four pupils and a Chinese teacher. The Propaganda at first demurred, partly because of the expense and partly because Ripa had left Peking without permission. At length official approval was obtained and in 1732 the college was opened.[23]

PERSECUTIONS UNDER CH'IEN LUNG

The death of Yung Chêng (1736) and the accession of Ch'ien Lung brought no relief to the harassed missionaries. The reign of Ch'ien Lung was nearly as long [24] and as brilliant as had been that

[19] Brucker in *Revue des ques. hist.*, Vol. 29, p. 525; Mailla, op. cit., Vol. 11, p. 494.

[20] Mailla, op. cit., Vol. 11, pp. 494-502.

[21] Parennin from Peking, Oct. 15, 1734, *Lettres édifiantes*, Vol. 3, p. 460.

[22] *Catalogus Patrum ac Fratrum e Societate Jesu qui . . . in Sinis adlaboraverunt*, pp. 33-45.

[23] Ripa, *Storia della Fondazione della Congregazione e del Collegio de'Cinesi*, passim; Prandi, *Memoirs of Father Ripa*, passim.

[24] It ended in 1796.

of his distinguished grandfather, K'ang Hsi, and during most of it the country was even more prosperous. Christian missionaries, however, were in much greater disfavor than they had been under either K'ang Hsi or Yung Chêng. The Peking missionaries had hoped that the new monarch would be less severe than his predecessor and attempted to obtain a modification of the anti-Christian decrees, but instead a new edict was issued ordering Chinese Christians to renounce their faith and specifically forbidding bannermen,[25] both Chinese and Manchu, to adopt the foreign religion.[26] We hear that the following year, 1737, the persecution was renewed with the arrest in Peking of a Chinese catechist who, in accordance with Roman Catholic practice, was administering baptism to infants in danger of death. We hear, too, of a Franciscan missionary coming from Shantung to Peking to attempt to procure relief for his converts and of a Christian family moving from Hsianfu to the capital in the hope of escaping persecution.[27]

The laws against Christianity were not, however, enforced with equal vigor over the entire Empire. In 1738 the Viceroy of Hunan and Hupeh, who is said to have been a Christian, did not widely publish the edict.[28] In 1738, in spite of the arrest of the catechist, three churches were open in Peking. Of the twenty-two missionaries in the capital—all Jesuits—only seven were required for the service of the Emperor, and the remainder, assisted by five Chinese Jesuits, pursued their ministry freely in and around the city. The French Jesuits were annually baptizing five or six hundred adults in Peking, Chihli, and "Tartary" (roughly Manchuria, Mongolia and the New Territory), and the Portuguese fathers were baptizing an even larger number. The Christians in Tartary alone were said to number thirty or thirty-five thousand.[29] In 1741 we hear of four young Christian "princes" and of the baptism of about twelve hundred adults in Peking.[30] Officials in the provinces knew that public worship continued in the capital and

[25] These were members of what were equivalent to permanent garrisons of occupation.
[26] Parennin from Peking, Oct. 22, 1736, in *Lettres édifiantes*, Vol. 3, pp. 469-472; Mailla, *Histoire générale de la Chine*, Vol. 11, pp. 512-517.
[27] *État de la religion dans l'empire de la Chine en l'année 1738*, in *Lettres édifiantes*, Vol. 3, pp. 726-736.
[28] Ibid.
[29] Attiret from Peking, Nov. 1, 1743, in *Lettres édifiantes*, Vol. 3, pp. 786-795. For scope of Tartary see map in Mailla, op. cit., Vol. 2.
[30] Gaubil from Peking, Oct. 29, 1741, in *Lettres édifiantes*, Vol. 3, pp. 766, 767.

often closed their eyes to the activities of the missionaries. From Honan in 1745 we hear of many conversions and baptisms and of the erection of a new chapel.[31] In Fukien especially there were many Christians and churches.[32]

It was in Fukien that severe persecution again broke out, and in the same district, Fu-an, where that of 1723 had begun. Several missionaries, Spanish Dominicans, were arrested and when the news reached Peking the Emperor ordered a search throughout the land for European priests and the punishment of officials who had allowed them to enter: the earlier edicts had been flouted too openly to permit of longer neglect. Missionaries and Christians were now dealt with much more severely than they had heretofore been. In 1747 Sanz, the Vicar Apostolic of Fukien, was executed at Foochow, and in the following year his coadjutor and three priests, all Dominicans, were strangled.[33] Numbers of native Christians were killed, and books, pictures, and church fittings were burned. Some Christians apostatized, but many—probably the majority—were true to their faith. Since the time of Ricci Nanking had been the home of a strong Christian community and at the outbreak of the new persecution was said to have had sixty thousand Christians under the care of eight Jesuits and a Franciscan bishop. Here and in the province the officials took drastic action and, among other victims, two European Jesuits were arrested, imprisoned, and strangled.[34] The two foreign priests in Szechwan were forced to leave, and only one clergyman, a Chinese, remained to minister to the Catholics in that great province.[35] We hear, too, of missionaries imprisoned or fleeing to Macao from other parts of China.[36] In Macao itself the Portuguese Government was constrained to agree (November 9, 1749) to a convention with the Chinese authorities forbidding the teaching of Christianity to Chinese or the acceptance of the

[31] Dugad, Aug. 22, 1745, in ibid., Vol. 3, pp. 796-799.
[32] Mailla, *Histoire générale de la Chine*, Vol. 11, pp. 524, 525.
[33] All five were beatified in 1893. Accounts of the persecution and the death of the five are in André-Marie, *Missions dominicaines dans l'Éxtrême Orient*, Vol. 1, pp. 212-219; *Los Dominicos en el Extremo Oriente*, p. 23; Chanseaume in *Lettres édifiantes*, Vol. 3, pp. 804-824; Savignol, *Les Martyrs dominicains de la Chine au XVIIIe siècle*, passim; Arias, *El Beato Sanz y Compañeros Mártires del Orden de Predicatores*.
[34] Forgeot from Macao, Dec. 2, 1750, in *Lettres édifiantes*, Vol. 3, pp. 825-830. The execution seems to have been at Soochow.
[35] Launay, *Journal d'André Ly*, pp. v et seq.
[36] Chanseaume in *Lettres édifiantes*, Vol. 3, pp. 804-824.

Faith by the latter.[37]   In Peking, however, missionaries and Chinese Christians were, as heretofore, free to pursue their normal life and to carry on their church services.[38]   The Emperor continued to employ Jesuits to supervise the astronomical bureau and to make for him a house, a fountain, paintings, and various other objects in European style.[39]   The foreigners were useful to him and he may have believed that in the capital, where they could be watched, no serious danger from them was to be anticipated.

Following the persecution of 1747 the edicts against missionaries and their converts continued to be strictly enforced for a much longer time than after the issuance of some of the preceding ones.   The presence of a Portuguese embassy in China in 1753 ameliorated conditions somewhat, although nothing was formally done on the Christians' behalf.[40]   In May, 1754, a Portuguese Jesuit was arrested in Kiangnan and tortured.[41]   From the same year an account comes to us of the banishment of a Chinese priest who again attempted to carry on work in Fu-an.[42]   In 1756 some missionaries appear to have been incarcerated at Nanking [43] and we hear that in 1757 one French and two Spanish missionaries had been in prison for the past two years.[44]   In 1768 and 1769 persecutions occurred in many parts of the Empire.[45]

As heretofore, however, persecution stimulated rather than dampened the ardor of the missionaries.   The training of Chinese for the priesthood continued, although some of it had to be done outside the Empire—at Bangkok for example.[46]   Late in 1753 there embarked for China François Pottier, who was to become the real founder of the great enterprise of the Paris Society in West China.   There had long been Christians in Szechwan, but

[37] Ljungstdet, *An Historical Sketch of the Portuguese Settlements in China*, p. 218.
[38] Chanseaume in *Lettres édifiantes*, Vol. 3, pp. 804-824.
[39] Amiot from Peking, Oct. 17, 1754, in *Lettres édifiantes*, Vol. 4, pp. 41-57.
[40] Brucker in *Catholic Encyclopedia*, Vol. 12, p. 489.
[41] Amiot, op. cit.
[42] Letter from Macao in *Lettres édifiantes*, Vol. 4, pp. 36-40; De Groot, *Sectarianism and Religious Persecution in China*, p. 289.
[43] De Groot, op. cit., p. 277.
[44] Dugad from Macao, Dec. 13, 1757, in *Lettres édifiantes*, Vol. 4, p. 84.
[45] Letter of Lamatthe, July 17, 1769, in ibid., Vol. 4, pp. 123-126.
[46] Letter from Macao, Sept. 14, 1754, in *Lettres édifiantes*, Vol. 4, pp. 36-40. The school at Bangkok was under the Missions Étrangères.

they had suffered severely from persecution. In 1746, as we have seen, all European priests had been driven out and only one Chinese father, Andrew Li, remained to minister to the faithful. In 1750 Andrew Li was joined by another Chinese priest, Luke Li.[47] In 1754 a missionary of the Paris Society, Lefevre, arrived, only to be arrested that same year and deported.[48] In 1752 the Paris Society was made definitely responsible for Southwest and West China—Yünnan, Szechwan, and Kweichow.[49] Its missionaries for the most part had been expelled from other parts of the country and for many years its chief efforts in China were to be directed to this difficult and distant region. Four men in succession were named as vicar apostolic, but did not reach their see.

Pottier was more fortunate. He arrived in Macao in 1754 and after a period of language study left in 1756 for Szechwan. He journeyed under the guidance of a Christian from the province and had to take extreme precautions to avoid detection by the authorities. For about ten years he was the only European in his vast parish. Once, in 1760, he was arrested and sentenced to banishment, but while being taken to the coast he escaped and returned to his post. In 1767 he was appointed Bishop of Agathopolis and Vicar Apostolic of Szechwan, but so slow was communication with Rome that he did not hear of his new office until 1769.

In 1767 reënforcements for Pottier reached China, but in 1769 one of the new arrivals, Gleyo, was arrested. The *Pai-lien Chiao,* or White Lotus Society, a seditious secret organization, was strong in Szechwan, and it was apparently on suspicion of being its agent that Gleyo was apprehended. He was imprisoned for eight years and his release was finally effected by one of the Peking missionaries who, travelling through Szechwan on an errand for the Emperor, interceded for him.[50] The arrest of Gleyo stirred the officials of Szechwan to a search for Christians and a seminary for the training of Chinese for the priesthood was destroyed. After his release Gleyo reëstablished the school in a small village

[47] Launay, *Journal d'André Ly,* pp. v et seq.
[48] *Nouvelles lettres édifiantes,* Vol. 1, p. iv.
[49] Launay, *Histoire générale de la Société des Missions Étrangères,* Vol. 2, pp. 72, 73. Missionaries of the Paris Society had first come to Yünnan and Szechwan a generation or so before 1752.—Ibid., Vol. 1, pp. 463, 464.
[50] Abridged narrative of Gleyo in *Nouvelles lettres édifiantes,* Vol. 1, pp. 44-88. See also ibid., Vol. 1, pp. 248-257.

on the borders of Yünnan and it was continued there for some years.[51]

It was not only in West China and by representatives of the Missions Étrangères that we hear of ministrations to Christians in the face of persecution. In 1759 Hunan and Hupeh had four French and three Chinese Jesuits and probably two or three thousand Christian families.[52] In 1764 the Franciscans of the Philippine province were still maintaining work in Shantung, Kwangtung, Kwangsi, and Fukien.[53] From 1773 comes a report that nearly one hundred Chinese had been baptized at one time in Nanch'ang in Kiangsi.[54]

THE DISSOLUTION OF THE SOCIETY OF JESUS, 1773

To persecutions was added in 1773 still another disaster, the abolition of the Society of Jesus. The dissolution of the Society, which so long had led in missions in China and which through its representatives in Peking had been the chief bulwark between the Church and persecution, could not but work grave harm to the Catholic community in the Middle Kingdom. The events which culminated in the suppression of the Jesuits did not have their origin in China and do not belong in this story. The Jesuit policies in China, the attitude of the majority of the Society toward the rites controversy, and the long delay in carrying out the papal decrees may have provided further arguments to the opposition and have strengthened the suspicions of the Papacy, but the chief causes must be sought in Europe and need not be recounted here. The struggle between the Jesuits and their foes was prolonged and the Society was driven out of several Catholic countries before it was finally abolished. Portugal expelled the Jesuits in 1759 and in 1764 France dissolved the Society within her boundaries. The forcible withdrawal of the Society from Macao naturally followed, although it was not until 1762 that the Jesuits were deported and their property confiscated.[55] It speaks well for the vitality of

[51] For accounts of Pottier and the Szechwan mission see *Nouvelles lettres édifiantes,* Vol. 1, pp. 27-39, 96-108, 109-127, 128-160, 167-169; Guiot, *La mission du Sutchuen au XVIIIme siècle,* passim; Launay, *Histoire générale de la Société des Missions-Étrangères,* Vol. 2, pp. 72, 78, 79, 161-163; Launay, *Mission du Kouy-Tcheou,* Vol. 1, pp. 16-25.

[52] Letter of Roy, Sept. 12, 1759, in *Lettres édifiantes,* Vol. 4, pp. 89-94.

[53] Civezza, *Histoire universelle des missions franciscaines,* Vol. 2, p. 275.

[54] Bourgeois from Peking, Sept. 18, 1773, in *Lettres édifiantes,* Vol. 4, p. 192.

[55] Cordier, in *Revue de l'Extrême-Orient,* Vol. 3, pp. 242-251; Montalto de Jesus, *Historic Macao,* p. 174.

the Society that in the eleven years, 1763 to 1773 inclusive, after the door by which most missionaries entered the Empire had been closed to them and the two countries which had been the chief support of their mission had turned against them, there were added to the Jesuits in China seventeen new recruits, Chinese and Europeans.[56]

The news of the dissolution of the Society by the Pope reached Peking in 1774 and while it brought sorrow and even protests the fathers had no choice but acquiescence.[57] They were, of course, priests of the Church as well as members of the Society, and in the former capacity they remained in the Empire. There were complications and heart-burnings over the disposition of the property, and some unhappy wranglings,[58] but the work went on. The last of the ex-Jesuits, Louis de Poirot, died in 1814.[59] Beginning with Francis Xavier, four hundred and fifty-six members of the Society, Chinese and Europeans, had labored in China.[60]

THE COMING OF THE LAZARISTS, 1784

The dissolution of the Jesuits made it necessary to find some organization to carry on in China the enterprise which the Society had so long maintained. Ch'ien Lung continued to employ the ex-Jesuits who remained in Peking and when, in 1775, one of their churches, the Nan T'ang, burned, he contributed toward its restoration.[61] With no possibility of reënforcements from the accustomed sources, however, the future was grave. The French ex-Jesuits repeatedly asked for help,[62] and Louis XVI, as the patron of their mission, requested in turn several different orders and congregations to take over the property and to carry on the mission, particularly that in Peking. The new body would have

[56] *Catalogus Patrum ac Fratrum e Societate Jesu qui . . . in Sinis adlaboraverunt*, pp. 33-45.
[57] Piolet, *Les mis. cath. françaises au XIXe siècle*, Vol. 3, p. 64; Cordier in *T'oung Pao*, Vol. 17, pp. 283-300.
[58] Cordier in ibid., Vol. 17, pp. 261 et seq., 561 et seq.
[59] Moidrey, *La hiér. cath. en Chine*, etc., p. 187; Servière, *Les anciennes missions de la Compagnie de Jésus*, p. 73.
[60] *Catalogus Patrum ac Fratrum e Societate Jesu qui . . . in Sinis adlaboraverunt*, pp. 1-47.
[61] Favier, *Peking*, Vol. 1, p. 189; Bourgeois in *Lettres édifiantes*, Vol. 4, pp. 267-272.
[62] Piolet, op. cit., Vol. 3, p. 65; Moidrey, op. cit., p. 190. The early suggestion of one of the French ex-Jesuits was that the Missions Étrangères of Paris take over the Peking mission.—Letter of Amiot quoted by Cordier in *T'oung Pao*, Vol. 17, pp. 287-299.

to possess men not only of religious zeal but of scholarly attainments, for upon the continuation of scientific and artistic services to the government largely depended the security of the rest of the Roman Catholic activity in China. No organization was eager to assume the burden, but after several had declined, the Congregation of the Priests of the Mission, or, as they are better known, the Lazarists, accepted, and on December 7, 1783, received the formal assignment from the Propaganda.[63]

The Lazarists are a congregation of secular priests and not an order, and arose in the seventeenth century out of the apostolic zeal of St. Vincent de Paul. They had as their primary charge the spiritual instruction of the neglected poor, but their large-visioned founder had never limited them to any one country and from the beginning foreign missions had been one of their objects.[64] A few of them, as we have seen, already had labored in China.[65] The Congregation numbered some scholars among its members and so could provide for the needs of the Peking mission.

The first three Lazarists designated for the new post arrived in China in 1784. In due course they proceeded to the capital, were received by the Emperor, and were given possession of the church of the French Jesuits, the Pei T'ang. In 1788 one of them, Raux, was placed in charge of the Bureau of Astronomy.[66] Lazarists of the Portuguese province also came to Peking,[67] and in time the Congregation sent priests to other districts formerly cared for by the Jesuits. Those at Peking were employed, as had been the Jesuits, as artists, mechanicians, mathematicians, astronomers, and as interpreters of the Court in the correspondence with Europeans—especially the Russians.[68]

The Lazarists had but just taken over the China mission when the French Revolution and the Napoleonic wars threw Europe into confusion and for a quarter of a century it was extremely difficult to find either money or men for the distant enterprise.

[63] Cordier in *Catholic Encyclopedia,* Vol. 3, p. 676; Demimund, *Vie du François-Régis Clet,* pp. 74-90.

[64] *Catholic Encyclopedia,* Vol. 10, pp. 357-367.

[65] There had been five all told, chief among them Appiani, interpreter to Mgr. de Tournon, and Mullener, who from 1716 to 1742 was Vicar Apostolic in Szechwan. There were also two Chinese priests who had been trained by Mullener. —Coste in *Revue d'histoire des missions,* Vol. 3, pp. 328 et seq.

[66] Favier, *Peking,* Vol. 1, p. 194.

[67] Moidrey, op. cit., p. 193; Coste in *Revue d'histoire des missions,* Vol. 3, p. 334.

[68] Richenet, letter of 1817 in *T'oung Pao,* Vol. 20, p. 121.

From 1784 to 1820 only twenty-eight priests were sent and in the decade from 1820 to 1830 only four more. Of these, fourteen seem to have been assigned to Macao and only eighteen to the rest of China.[69] While the energy and sacrifice required to make possible even this number were not inconsiderable, it is obvious that so few priests could not hope to continue adequately the task left by the Jesuits. It was but natural, then, that the mission in Peking declined and that the Christian communities in the North and in the lower and middle parts of the Yangtze Valley deteriorated.

THE FRENCH REVOLUTION AND THE WARS OF NAPOLEON, 1789-1815

As has just been suggested, the suppression of the Society of Jesus was not the only event in Europe in the latter part of the eighteenth century which proved a handicap to missions in China. It seemed, indeed, as though enemies were conspiring to ruin the Roman Catholic foreign missionary enterprise at its very source. Spain and Portugal had long been in decline and their ability and energy in foreign missions suffered correspondingly. France, which had begun so energetically to step into the breach, was weakened by the exhausting wars of Louis XIV and the further wars and the incompetent reigns of Louis XV and Louis XVI, and her zeal was chilled by the religious lethargy and the scepticism which characterized large sections of the nation during much of the eighteenth century.[70] In Germany the *Aufklärung* had partially dried up the springs of religious enthusiasm.[71] Even before the intellectual questioning had begun, emphasis on the state control of the Church and various religious controversies had diverted interest from foreign missions.[72]

To these adversities was added the upheaval of the French Revolution and the Napoleonic wars. All Europe was thrown into turmoil greater than it had known for centuries. The Church suffered at the hands both of the revolutionaries who looked upon it as part of the old régime and of the masterly and irreligious Napoleon. For the time being it was crippled even more

[69] *Catalogue des prêtres, clercs et frères de la Congrégation de la Mission qui ont travaillé en Chine depuis 1697*, passim.
[70] Launay, *Histoire générale de la Société des Missions-Étrangères*, Vol. 1, pp. 497-501.
[71] Schmidlin, *Katholische Missionsgeschichte*, p. 420.
[72] Ibid.

than it had been by the Protestant revolt. Not for some years after 1815, when Napoleon was sent into permanent exile and the forces of reaction and of order combined to restore peace, did the Church recover sufficiently to renew energetically its foreign missionary efforts. So far as China is concerned, the disheartening story is quickly told. The Revolution in France early cut off much of the income of the Paris Society and in 1792 the directors scattered, two going to Rome, three to England, and three remaining hid at Amiens.[73] Efforts were made to reëstablish the seminary outside of France, but without success.[74] A few of the students accompanied the three directors to England and there finished their course. It was difficult, however, to obtain for them passage to the Far East, and between 1793 and 1796 only three succeeded in carrying out their missionary purpose.[75] The Lazarists were somewhat more successful in sending recruits: from 1791 to 1800 inclusive ten new priests arrived in China.[76]

During the early days of the Empire Napoleon sought to revive missions as a support to French influence and trade. He reëstablished the seminary of the Paris Society (1805), although he placed it and the Lazarists under very close state supervision.[77] In 1809, however, he broke with the Pope and dissolved the religious foundations.[78] One director of the Missions Étrangères went to England and one to Rome, and when in 1812 the latter had again to flee, only the one in England could carry on the business of the Society.[79] Between 1804 and 1815 the Paris Society sent to China only one missionary and the Lazarists six.[80] About 1815 there were said to be in Hupeh two French Lazarists, but in Honan, Kiangnan, Chêkiang, and Kiangsi the care of the Christians—at least those under the French Lazarists—seems to have been entrusted largely if not entirely to the Chinese clergy.[81]

[73] Launay, op. cit., Vol. 2, pp. 258-277.

[74] Ibid., Vol. 2, pp. 343-347.

[75] Launay, op. cit., Vol. 2, pp. 297-302.

[76] *Catalogue des prêtres, clercs et frères de la Congrégation de la Mission qui ont travaillé en Chine depuis 1697.* At least two of these, Dumazel and Richenet, came out on a ship of the English East India Company.—Morse, *The East India Company Trading with China,* Vol. 3, p. 16.

[77] Launay, op. cit., Vol. 2, pp. 377, 419-422.

[78] Ibid., Vol. 2, p. 424.

[79] Ibid., Vol. 2, pp. 424-430.

[80] *Catalogue des prêtres, clercs et frères de la Congrégation de la Mission qui ont travaillé en Chine depuis 1697;* Launay, op. cit., Vol. 2, p. 421.

[81] Richenet, who had left China in 1815, writing in 1817 from Paris, in *T'oung Pao,* Vol. 20, p. 122.

Recruits from Italy must have been partly cut off, but we know of one Italian Franciscan who reached China (1805).[82] Spanish and Portuguese missionary efforts were also curtailed by the Napoleonic wars.[83] Once during this period the Philippines contained only one bishop, but in China the Dominican mission fared somewhat better, for reënforcements seem to have reached Fukien and in the province were both a vicar apostolic and his coadjutor.[84] The missions of all orders and societies were badly depleted when after Waterloo Europe once more settled down to a period of comparative peace.

RENEWED PERSECUTION, 1774-1781

Simultaneously with the dissolution of the Society of Jesus and the disturbances in Europe, the Church in China was visited with recurring and severe persecutions. To tell of all these would unduly prolong this chapter. Merely a condensed outline can be given and that only of the more serious outbreaks. In 1774 a revolt in Shantung led to an imperial edict against all seditious sects. The Christians were not mentioned by name, but in many provinces the officials extended the proscription to them.[85] In 1774 Moye of the Missions Étrangères was seized in Szechwan while saying mass. He was held for ten days and numbers of Chinese Christians in the province were persecuted.[86] Still, in 1778, a missionary reported that a Christian community of about six hundred had grown up in a place three days' journey from Chengtu where three years before there had been only one Christian family,[87] and in 1783 we hear of one Chinese Christian in Szechwan who in the two years since his conversion had won more than three hundred to the faith.[88]

In 1781 an anti-Christian edict went out from Peking, and in the capital itself pickets were stationed to keep converts from entering the churches.[89] The Church in Peking was troubled, too,

[82] Moidrey, *Le hiér. cath. en Chine*, etc., p. 54; Civezza, *Hist. universelle des missions françiscaines*, Vol. 2, p. 304.
[83] Schwager, *Die katholische Heidenmission in der Gegenwart*, p. 27.
[84] Moidrey, op. cit., p. 76.
[85] Letter of Bourgeois in *Lettres édifiantes*, Vol. 4, pp. 267-272.
[86] Letter of Moye, Aug. 6, 1774, in *Nouvelles lettres édifiantes*, Vol. 1, pp. 180-203; letter of Saint-Martin in ibid., Vol. 1, pp. 204-229.
[87] Letter of Saint-Martin, October, 1778, in ibid., Vol. 1, p. 277.
[88] Letters of Saint-Simon, April 1 and May 29, 1782, in ibid., Vol. 1, pp. 298-301.
[89] *Nouvelles lettres édifiantes*, Vol. 1, pp. 332-346.

by a schism over the succession to the episcopate, and three or four years elapsed before unity was restored.[90] On the other hand, in 1784 a prince of Korea was converted while visiting Peking with the annual tribute-bearing embassy[91]—the beginning of the stormy history of the Church in the peninsular kingdom. In 1785 in Peking, we hear, were four churches—two for the Portuguese ex-Jesuits, one for the French Lazarists, and one for Italians of various orders and more directly under the Propaganda. This last was small, but the others were large and were said to be higher than any other buildings in the city.[92]

THE PERSECUTION OF 1784

In 1784 an unusually severe persecution broke out. In the summer of that year four Italian Franciscans who had been sent to China by the Propaganda were on their way from Macao to their field in Shensi, when, in Hupeh, they were betrayed by an apostate Christian and handed over to the authorities. A recent Moslem revolt in Shensi made the Peking government especially watchful against possible rebellion in that region and a vigorous imperial edict was issued ordering the destruction of churches, the arrest of European and Chinese priests, the punishment of the officials who had permitted the foreigners to penetrate the country, and the renunciation by Christians of their faith. As a result of the edict sixteen European and ten Chinese priests were apprehended in various parts of the Empire—Szechwan, Kiangsi, Shensi, Shansi, Shantung, and Kwangtung—and were conveyed to Peking and cast into prison. Others of the missionaries succeeded in hiding from the officials, and still others believed that they could lessen the danger to their converts by withdrawing, and so escaped to Macao. Thirty catechists were banished and condemned to perpetual slavery, and in many places Christians were arrested and either banished or enslaved. Officials in Kwangtung were degraded and fined. The lot of the prisoners in Peking was pitiable: six European and two Chinese priests succumbed to the hardships of their confinement, and La Roche, an aged ex-Jesuit, died while he was being taken to the capital. Among the dead

[90] Cordier, *Doc. pour servir a l'hist. ecclés. de l'Éxtrême-Orient,* in *Rev. de l'Éxtrême-Orient,* Vol. 2, pp. 298-304; Cordier, *Histoire générale de la Chine,* Vol. 3, pp. 398, 399; Cordier in *T'oung Pao,* Vol. 17.
[91] Letter of Ventavon, Peking, Nov. 25, 1784, in *Lettres édifiantes,* Vol. 4, p. 306.
[92] Dufresse in *Nouvelles lettres édifiantes,* Vol. 2, pp. 321, 322.

were the Vicars Apostolic of Shensi and Shansi—Magi and Sacconi—and the Procurer (business agent) of the Propaganda at Canton. In 1785 the surviving prisoners were released, but under the condition that they either remain at Peking or accept deportation. Most of them chose deportation, apparently hoping that they might thus more quickly make their way back to their flocks. Two of the missionaries of the Paris Society—one of them Dufresse, later Vicar Apostolic in West China—went to Manila, and, after many adventures, by 1789 succeeded in reëntering Szechwan. We know of at least two or three others who returned to their respective fields. The government, having exerted itself vigorously, now felt it safe to relax its efforts and by 1786 or 1787 those priests who remained in the provinces were able to continue their activities if they were careful not to do so too publicly.[93]

For nearly twenty years after 1786 no severe general persecution was instituted. There were, however, many local ones in which individual Christians suffered.[94] In 1795 Aubin, a Lazarist, was arrested on the frontiers of Shensi and died in prison in Hsianfu.[95] In 1797 Paul Souviron, a newly arrived missionary of the Paris Society, started from Macao for Chengtu but when seven days on the road was detected and thrown into prison and there died of fever. Two of his Chinese companions were condemned to perpetual exile and slavery in Ili and Tartary, and persecution in Kwangtung and Fukien followed.[96]

In the comparative quiet and in spite of the paucity of missionaries, in some places progress was recorded. In Szechwan, Yünnan, and Kweichow in 1786 there were 469 baptisms of adults, in 1792 1,508, in 1795 1,401, in 1800 1,250, and in 1804 2,143.[97] In 1756 there are said to have been about four thousand Christians in Szechwan, in 1792 the number was estimated at twenty-five thousand, and in 1801 it is reported to have

---

[93] For accounts of the persecution of 1785 see numbers of contemporary letters, among them some by the victims, in *Nouvelles lettres édifiantes,* Vol. 2, passim, and in *Lettres édifiantes,* Vol. 4, pp. 330 et seq.; Launay, op. cit., Vol. 2, pp. 209-226; Civezza, *Hist. universelle des missions franciscaines,* Vol. 2, pp. 297, 298; Wegener, *Heroes of the Mission Field,* pp. 35-49; Guiot, *La mis. du Sutchuen au XVIIIme siècle,* pp. 347-362; Du Guignes, *Voyages à Peking, Manille et l'Île de France . . . 1784 à 1801,* Vol. 2, pp. 334-342; Lys, *Un vrai frère mineur,* etc., p. 95; Morse, *The East India Company Trading with China,* Vol. 2, p. 107.
[94] See *Nouvelles lettres édifiantes,* Vol. 3, passim.
[95] Raux, from Peking, in 1796, in ibid., Vol. 3, pp. 238-241.
[96] Letondal from Macao, Feb. 6, 1798, in ibid., Vol. 3, pp. 270-287.
[97] *Nouvelles lettres édifiantes,* Vol. 1, p. xiii.

been forty thousand.[98]   In 1799 Kweichow is said to have contained six hundred Catholics.[99]

Now and then the thin ranks of the clergy were reënforced by the advancement of Chinese to the priesthood.[100]   In the first decade of the nineteenth century the Paris Society opened on the island of Penang a school for the training of Chinese for holy orders, an institution which was later to draw students from many countries and races of the Far East.[101]   For the preparation of Chinese for the priesthood the French Lazarists had a small seminary at Peking and the Portuguese one at Macao.[102]   In 1793 the English embassy under Lord Macartney was of some assistance in smuggling two missionaries into China and had as interpreters two Chinese on their way back from Ripa's school at Naples.[103]

Macartney found the Peking mission fairly prosperous, although its younger members were not entirely satisfied with their enforced exile.[104]   Father Raux told Macartney that there were about five thousand Christians in the capital and put the numbers in all China at about 150,000.[105]   At least one Christian was of high official rank.[106]   In 1798 the Peking Lazarists sent two Chinese priests to care for the Christians who had begun to gather in Mongolia north of the Great Wall.[107]

In spite of occasional encouraging local gains, in many places the Christian community was declining in numbers and morale. This was particularly true in Hunan and Hupeh and in the lower part of the Yangtze Valley.[108]   No other fate could, indeed, be expected, for adequate spiritual supervision was more and more lacking.   The see of Nanking was vacant for fourteen years after 1790.   It did not have a resident bishop until the nineteenth

[98] Launay, *Hist. gén. de la Société des Missions-Étrangères*, Vol. 2, p. 393.

[99] Letter of Dufresse, Oct. 7, 1799, in *Nouvelles lettres édifiantes*, Vol. 3, p. 425.

[100] Saint-Martin, October, 1793, and Sept. 5, 1796, in ibid., Vol. 3, pp. 125-130, 242, 243; Guiot, *La mission du Sutchuen au XVIIIme siècle*, p. 395; Demimund, *Vie du François-Régis Clet*, pp. 203, 204.

[101] Launay, op. cit., Vol. 2, pp. 406-412.

[102] *Abridged account of the State of Religion in China, 1806-1807*, p. 30; Richenet, letter of 1817, in *T'oung Pao*, Vol. 20, p. 121.

[103] Prandi, *Memoirs of Father Ripa*, p. iii; Barrow, *Travels in China*, p. 108.

[104] Staunton, *Lord Macartney's Embassy*, Vol. 1, pp. 44-47, Vol. 2, pp. 6-8, 17, 192, 197-200, Vol. 3, p. 135; Robbins, *Our First Ambassador to China*, passim.

[105] Robbins, op. cit., p. 287.

[106] An imperial censor.—*Chine, Ceylan, Madagascar*, March, 1904, p. 245.

[107] Piolet, *Les mis. cath. françaises au XIXe siècle*, Vol. 3, p. 69.

[108] Demimund, op. cit., pp. 147-155.

century was well advanced and only part of the time was supervised by resident administrators.[109]   The last Spanish Franciscan
in Shantung is said to have died in 1797 and the province appears
to have been left without a resident priest until sometime in the
nineteenth century.[110]   In 1803 only five Lazarists were left in
Peking, three of them Chinese and two Europeans.[111]   The
Church seemed to be on the way to extinction.

Under the two Emperors who succeeded Ch'ien Lung—Chia
Ch'ing (1796-1820) and Tao Kuang (1820-1851)—China was
distraught by rebellions.   The Manchu dynasty had begun to
decay and although it was to survive into the twentieth century,
the remainder of its course was to be punctuated by devastating
insurrections.   The feeble Christian community of the early part
of the nineteenth century found this disorder a serious embarrassment, for on the one hand it suffered from the general lawlessness,
and on the other it was suspected of sedition.   Most of the rebellions were led by sects with a religious background and the
Church, with its strange rites administered secretly, was often
confused with them.[112]

THE PERSECUTION OF 1805

After nearly two decades of freedom from a nation-wide persecution, in 1805 an extremely serious one broke out.   On all the
many occasions on which the anti-Christian edicts had been
enforced in the provinces, the Christian community in the capital
had been relatively unmolested.   Since the minority of K'ang
Hsi, nearly a century and a half before, the missionaries attached
to the court had enjoyed almost complete toleration for their
local religious activity.   Now a persecution was centered primarily
upon the Christian community in the capital.   The immediate
occasion appears to have been the capture of a map which was
being sent by Adeodat, an Augustinian in Peking, to the Propaganda at Rome to elucidate a dispute between priests of different
orders and nationalities over the ecclesiastical supervision of a dis-

[109] Moidrey, *La hiér. cath. en Chine,* etc., pp. 30-34.
[110] Bishop Giesen in Forsyth, *Shantung,* p. 163.
[111] Lamiot from Peking, Sept. 16, 1803, in *Nouvelles lettres édifiantes,* Vol. 4,
pp. 82-91.   There were some priests in the city who were not Lazarists.
[112] Fortunately, in the earlier part of those rebellions of the *Pai-lien Chiao*
which began in 1794 and continued intermittently for two decades in Central
and West China, the Church does not seem to have been seriously disturbed.—
Dufresse, Oct. 20, 1805, in *Nouvelles lettres édifiantes,* Vol. 4, pp. 182-206.

trict which included a village near the capital. The authorities believed this map to betoken sedition and possible plans for an invasion. Dimly understood reports of the European wars may have made them especially suspicious of foreign encroachments. In spite of the fact that Adeodat was attached to the court as a clockmaker, he was exiled to Jehol. Christian books and the blocks for reproducing them were ordered destroyed. Christians were commanded to abjure their faith, but the majority, among them members of official and princely families, remained true. Many were tortured and a number were exiled to the far borders of the Empire. The missionaries were closely watched, their correspondence was censored, and they were restricted in their intercourse with both Chinese and Manchus. There seems even to have been some thought of substituting Russians for the missionaries employed in the Bureau of Astronomy.[113]

It may be that from this time dates the determination to attach no more Roman Catholics to the service of the government. It is certain that Mgr. de Souza-Saraiva, who in 1804 had been appointed coadjutor to Bishop Gouvea of Peking, was not permitted to come to the capital and that when in 1808, at the death of Mgr. Gouvea, he succeeded to the title, he had still to remain in Macao.[114] It is also certain that two new French Lazarists, Richenet and Dumazel, who for four years had been waiting at Macao or Canton for passports and who in 1805 had received permission to proceed to Peking and had already reached the borders of Chihli, were ordered back to the coast. Dumazel, who was assigned to Hukwang, was undiscouraged by this initial reverse, and in 1810 after persistent efforts succeeded in reaching his field by way of Tongking and Yünnan.[115]

Salvetti, an Italian Franciscan, had a somewhat similar experience. He arrived in Macao in 1804, started for the interior in

[113] For accounts of the 1805 persecution see Timkowski, *Travels of the Russian Mission . . . 1820-1821*, Vol. 1, p. 363; Létondal from Macao, Nov. 23, 1805, in *Nouvelle lettres édifiantes*, Vol. 4, pp. 207-211; Lamiot from Peking, Oct. 10, 1807, in ibid., Vol. 4, pp. 135-162; the imperial edict of 1805 in ibid., Vol. 4, pp. 219-224. There are a good many secondary accounts, some of them excellent and some full of mistakes.

[114] Moidrey, *La hiér. cath. en Chine*, etc., p. 38; *Nouvelles lettres édifiantes*, Vol. 4, p. 370.

[115] *Nouvelles lettres édifiantes*, Vol. 4, p. 371, editor's note; De Montgesty, *Two Vincentian Martyrs*, p. 54; Morse, *The East India Company Trading with China*, Vol. 3, p. 16.

March, 1805, was arrested, taken to Canton, beaten, and condemned to prison for three years. His prison sentence was remitted and he was conducted to Macao and threatened with death if he ever again entered the Empire. He, too, persevered, succeeded in entering by way of Tongking, and arrived on his field—Shansi —in 1810.[116] This feat is almost matched by that of Vincent d'Osimo, another Italian Franciscan, who entered China by way of Tongking and, although ignorant of the language, was conveyed by a Tongkingese who had never before been in the country, and arrived safely in Shansi in 1818.[117] Such devotion and courage need no comment.

Outside Peking the persecution of 1805 appears not to have been particularly severe. In Szechwan the officials had certified to the central authorities that there were no priests in the province and for fear of being accused of misrepresentation dared not later arrest any. The sacraments, including mass, had still to be administered secretly, but the Vicar Apostolic of West China reported in September, 1807, that during the year there had been eighteen hundred and forty-eight baptisms of adults, over two thousand baptisms of children of Christians, and that he had thirty-seven schools for boys and fifty-seven for girls.[118] A few were baptized in Yünnan and Kweichow.[119] West China seems to have been at this time the most prosperous mission field in the Empire.[120]

THE PERSECUTION OF 1811

In 1811 an imperial edict gave rise to one more general persecution. This time the exciting cause appears to have been the arrest in Shensi of a Chinese priest. Even greater restrictions were now placed on the missionaries in Peking. Four of those sent by the Propaganda—two of the Congregation of St. John the Baptist and two Augustinians, among them Adeodat—either chose to leave rather than comply with the new regulations or were expelled from the Empire. About seven Europeans—six

[116] Civezza, *Hist. universelle des missions franciscaines,* Vol. 2, p. 304; Hamel, Aug. 29, 1808, in *Nouvelles lettres édifiantes,* Vol. 4, p. 292.
[117] *Nouvelles lettres édifiantes,* editor's note, Vol. 5, p. 240.
[118] Dufresse from Szechwan, Sept. 29, 1807, in *Nouvelles lettres édifiantes,* Vol. 4, pp. 268-291; letter of Dufresse, Sept. 8, 1808, in *An Abridged Account of the State of Religion in . . . China . . . 1807-8-9.*
[119] *Nouvelles lettres édifiantes,* Vol. 1, p. xv.
[120] See also letters in ibid., Vol. 4, pp. 346-353, 354-369, 545-550.

Lazarists and one aged ex-Jesuit—were permitted to remain.[121] The church of the Propaganda, the Hsi T'ang ("West Church") was destroyed [122] and not long afterward the Tung T'ang ("East Church") shared its fate.[123] The Pei T'ang ("North Church") and the Nan T'ang ("South Church") continued to be occupied for some years longer, the former being razed about 1827.[124] In Szechwan 1810 had seen some persecution and the imperial edict of 1811 seems to have aggravated it. A number of catechists and other Chinese Christians were arrested in Chengtu and were exiled to distant Ili.[125]

MORE PERSECUTIONS

The year 1811 appears to have been the last in which a general edict against Christianity was issued,[126] but it by no means marked the end of persecution. The imperial will toward the foreign faith had been repeatedly indicated, and in the unsettled condition of the Empire all strange sects were under suspicion. Magistrates became more and more severe in their enforcement of the laws and at Peking no large missionary group strong in the favor of the court now exercised a moderating influence. The Christian community in West China, so long relatively exempt, suffered severely. In 1814 the school for the training of a native clergy, although it had been hidden in remote mountain fastnesses, was sought out and destroyed.[127] In 1814 Dufresse, the heroic Bishop of Tabraca and Vicar Apostolic in West China, was captured, taken to Chengtu, and beheaded. Others of the missionaries had either to hide or to flee, one or two of the Chinese priests died in prison, and at least one catechist was killed.[128] In 1816 a Franciscan, John Lantrua of Triora, was executed in

---

[121] Letter of Richenet from Macao, March 25, 1812, in ibid., Vol. 4, pp. 551, et seq.; Dufresse from Szechwan, Sept. 23, 1812, in ibid., Vol. 5, pp. 3-14; de Groot, *Sectarianism and Religious Persecution in China*, pp. 399-401; Piolet, *Les mis. cath. franç. au XIXe siècle*, Vol. 3, p. 70; Morse, op. cit., Vol. 3, p. 164.

[122] Piolet, op. cit., Vol. 3, p. 70.

[123] Ibid.

[124] Ibid.

[125] Dufresse from Szechwan, Oct. 20, 1811, Sept. 23, 1812, Sept. 28, 1813, Nov. 21, 1814, in *Nouvelles lettres édifiantes*, Vol. 4, pp. 430-544, Vol. 5, pp. 15-17, 33-58, 93-108.

[126] On his accession (1820) Tao-kuang renewed the edicts against Christianity but there does not seem to have been any new one issued.—*Annales de la propagation de la foi*, Vol. 20, p. 10.

[127] Escodeca, Sept. 20, 1815, in *Nouvelles lettres édifiantes*, Vol. 5, pp. 132-161.

[128] *Nouvelles lettres édifiantes*, Vol. 5, pp. 108-119, 120-131, 162-171, 175-180; *Annales de la propagation de la foi*, No. 4, p. 44.

Hunan, at Changsha. Because of his garb he had been mistaken for a *Pai-lien Chiao* rebel and had been captured near Hêngchow in that province. A Chinese arrested at the same time was exiled.[129] In 1817 and 1818 two Chinese priests, Joseph Yüan and Paul Liu, were strangled in Szechwan.[130] In 1821 still another of the native clergy was executed.[131] In 1819 an aged Lazarist, François-Régis Clet, who had been in hiding for some time with a price fixed on his head, was captured in Honan, imprisoned for some months, and then strangled (at Wuchang, February 18, 1820). A Chinese priest confined in the same prison was exiled.[132] There was further persecution in 1824,[133] another (in Szechwan) in 1830,[134] and in 1834 a Dominican was arrested and released only on payment of a bribe.[135] In 1835 another persecution visited West China, with the usual accompaniment of executions and exiles.[136] At the end of 1836 the Christians in Fukien were in great difficulty.[137] The government was making a determined effort to stamp out the European religion.

On behalf of the Chinese Government it must be said that in the earlier persecutions executions had been rare. The authorities were eager merely that the missionaries should leave the country and that their converts should renounce the Faith. It was only when, after repeated attempts to enforce the edicts against them, missionaries continued to carry on their activities and Chinese Christians to hold to their faith that more drastic measures were adopted. Both missionaries and Chinese Christians were persistently violating laws of the Empire which had been clearly and frequently promulgated, and from the standpoint of the officials they were criminals. It must be remembered, moreover, that, as we have repeatedly said, to the orthodox Confucian scholars who made up the governing class, Christianity was subversive to much that was best in Chinese civiliza-

---

[129] *Nouvelles lettres édifiantes*, Vol. 5, pp. 181-207; Moidrey, op. cit., p. 87; Lys, *Un vrai frère mineur, vie et martyre du Bienheureux Jean de Triora*, passim.
[130] *Nouvelles lettres édifiantes*, Vol. 5, pp. 208-245.
[131] Launay, *Hist. gén. de la Société des Missions-Étrangères*, Vol. 2, p. 490.
[132] *Annales de la propagation de la foi*, No. 6, pp. 19-25; Demimund, *Vie du François-Régis Clet*, passim; Montgesty and Gilmore, *Two Vincentian Martyrs*.
[133] *Annales de la propagation de la foi*, Vol. 2, pp. 248-253.
[134] Ibid., Vol. 6, pp. 497-499.
[135] Ibid., Vol. 9, pp. 63, 66.
[136] Ibid., Vol. 9, pp. 449-453.
[137] Ibid., Vol. 11, p. 58.

tion.   In the so-called Sacred Edict as it was elaborated for
purposes of popular instruction, Christianity was pilloried among
the heretical sects.[138]   Then, too, some officials may have dimly
suspected that missionaries, as forerunners of Western civilization,
might presage other and even stranger perils to Chinese culture.
The barbarians had better be kept at arm's length.   Under the
circumstances the government was certainly more lenient than
might have been expected.   The wonder is, not that Christianity
was persecuted, but that it was allowed to exist at all.

The State of the Church in the First Third
of the Nineteenth Century

In spite of the growing intensity of persecution and the declining power of the mission at Peking, the Church continued.
The revival in Europe of interest in Catholic missions which,
as we shall see in a later chapter, came after 1815, started
reënforcements for China.   Not until about 1840 was the number of recruits very large, but it was an increase over the discouraging years of the French Revolution and the Napoleonic
wars.   Between 1820 and 1838 Szechwan received twelve missionaries.[139]   In 1831 two Lazarists entered China and seven
others embarked for Macao.[140]   About 1829 a representative of
the Missions Étrangères entered Fukien to reopen the work of
his Society in that province, an enterprise which had been discontinued probably since before the Revolution.   He was accompanied by a Spanish Dominican designated for Fukien and an
Italian Franciscan for Shansi.[141]

There was, too, a native priesthood which, while small, was
larger than the missionary body, was devoted, and was being
maintained and even increased from various schools in and outside of China.   Thus in 1810, when the European missionaries
in the Empire numbered only thirty-one, eighty Chinese priests
are reported.[142]   The Dominicans had a preparatory school in
Fukien, apparently at the old Christian center Fu-an, and sent
their candidates for the priesthood to Manila to complete their

[138] See Baller's edition of the *Sacred Edict,* pp. 84, 85.
[139] Launay, op. cit., Vol. 3, p. 58.
[140] *Annales de la propagation de la foi,* Vol. 5, p. 560, Vol. 6, p. 330, Vol. 10,
p. 70.
[141] Ibid., Vol. 4, p. 422.
[142] Marchini's map of Catholic missions quoted in *Chinese Repository,* Vol. 1,
p. 443.

course.[143] The Lazarists maintained a seminary in Macao which in 1831 had about seven Chinese as resident students.[144] As late as about 1815 Peking had two colleges for the training of priests, one maintained by the French Lazarists and one by the Portuguese of the same congregation.[145] In the Lazarist center in Northern Chihli—where the headquarters of the mission were established after they had been removed from Peking—was a school preparatory to the priesthood.[146] A preparatory school for West China was maintained on the borders of Yünnan and graduates from it were sent to the more advanced institution at Pulo Penang.[147] By means of these priests, foreign and Chinese, the Church was kept alive and in some places growing. Even in some of the darker years, thousands of confessions were heard and there were baptisms of adults as well as of children of Christians and of children of non-Christians at the point of death.[148] Converts were being made, too, among the Chinese outside the Empire, in Siam,[149] and in the vicinity of Malacca.[150]

These encouraging features, however, must not be allowed to obscure the fact that in the first quarter of the nineteenth century the future of the Church was very dark. The Peking mission, the former center of the Church's strength, all but disappeared. The last European to serve the government in the Bureau of Astronomy was Pires. On his death in 1838 no European priest was left in the capital.[151] The institution which had been begun by Ricci and which had had so prominent a part in the activity of the Church came to an end. The headquarters of the Lazarists

[143] *Annales de la propagation de la foi*, Vol. 9, pp. 196 et seq. In 1836 Perboyre said there were two seminaries in Fukien.—Montgesty and Gilmore, *Two Vincentian Martyrs*, p. 148.
[144] Medhurst, *China, Its State and Present Prospects*, p. 245.
[145] Richenet, memorandum written in Paris July 30, 1817, in *T'oung Pao*, Vol. 20, p. 121. Richenet had been Procurer of the Mission in Peking and had returned to France in 1815. During its existence Ghislane's seminary in Peking supplied twenty priests to the China missions.—Montgesty and Gilmore, op. cit., p. 52.
[146] Moidrey, *Le hiér. cath. en Chine*, etc., pp. 190, 191.
[147] *Annales de la propagation de la foi*, Vol. 3, p. 239, Vol. 5, p. 645. There had been a college on the Coromandel Coast to which candidates had been sent, but this was closed in 1782.—*Nouvelles lettres édifiantes*, Vol. 1, pp. 358-361
[148] See figures for 1831 in *Annales de la propagation de la foi*, Vol. 6, pp. 530-533.
[149] Letter of Brugiere from Bangkok, 1829, in ibid., Vol. 5, p. 135.
[150] Letter in ibid., Vol. 8, pp. 124-127.
[151] Joly, *Le Christianisme et l'Extrême-Orient*, Vol. 1, p. 131; Piolet, *Les mis. cath. franç. au XIXe siècle*, Vol. 3, p. 75.

in the North had already been moved to Hsiwantzu in Northern Chihli, about thirty miles northeast of Kalgan and not far outside the Great Wall. Here was a Christian settlement and here a Chinese Superior with the aid of other Chinese priests held the work together.[152] It was not until about 1836 that a European, Mouly, arrived to relieve him.[153] In many parts of China the spiritual tone of the Church was a cause for anxiety. Christians often went for years without an opportunity for confession or instruction and as a result were conforming to their non-Christian environment. Frequently they were poverty-stricken and some had apostatized.[154] Even in Macao the Chinese Christians were sometimes neglected and were said by one observer to be religiously in a deplorable condition.[155] The Portuguese authorities, too, made Macao uncomfortable for priests of other nationalities and occasionally even for the members of the religious orders of their own people.[156] There were but scant intimations of the great changes which were soon to usher in more prosperous days for Catholic missions. One era was approaching its end and only faint traces were to be seen of the dawn which was to inaugurate a new one.

Just how many Catholic Christians were in China at the close of the old era will probably never be known. They were scattered in so many communities and over such a large part of the country, and their supervision was necessarily so imperfect, that accurate statistics were out of the question. In some districts a fairly careful record of baptisms and confessions was kept, but attempts to give the number of Catholics must at best have the value only of rough estimates. One author places the number of Christians in 1800 at 202,000 and in 1850, after a decade of revived growth, at 330,000.[157] A map of 1810 (which apparently did not include Macao) puts it at 215,000.[158] Still another

[152] *Annales de la propagation de la foi,* Vol. 19, p. 19.
[153] Moidrey, op. cit., p. 140.
[154] Letter of Rameaux from Hupeh, July 4, 1833, in *Annales de la propagation de la foi,* Vol. 7, pp. 248, 349; ibid., July 18, 1834, in ibid., Vol. 9, pp. 58, 59; Perboyre from Hupeh, Sept. 12, 1838, in ibid., Vol. 13, p. 146; Servière, *Histoire de la mission du Kiangnan,* Vol. 1, pp. 20, 21; Montgesty and Gilmore, op. cit., passim.
[155] Letter of Thiou from Macao, Dec. 8, 1837, in *Annales de la propagation de la foi,* Vol. 12, pp. 174-179; Mouly from Macao, Nov. 15, 1834, in ibid., Vol. 9, pp. 70-75.
[156] *Chinese Repository,* Vol. 2, p. 382, Vol. 3, p. 301.
[157] Louvet, *Les mis. cath. au XIXe siècle,* p. 234.
[158] Map of Marchini quoted in Medhurst, *China,* p. 244.

estimate places the number "at the beginning of the nineteenth century" at 290,000.[159]   An estimate of 1840 gives the total in 1839 as 313,000.[160]   In 1836 a missionary said that the largest estimate of the Christian community was 220,000 and that this was probably excessive.[161]   From a comparison of these totals with scattered figures from many districts it seems probable that in 1800 there were about two hundred or two hundred and fifty thousand Roman Catholics in all China and that this number remained fairly constant until about 1835 or 1840.   Increases were registered in some districts, but these were probably offset by decreases in others.   This figure may be in error by several thousands, but the true one was probably slightly above rather than below it.   Christians were apparently to be found in all of the eighteen provinces, with the possible exception of Kansu, and in Formosa, Mongolia, the New Territory, and possibly Manchuria. Szechwan, with about sixty thousand, seems to have had more than any other one province, but Fukien, Chihli, Kiangsu, and possibly Shensi and Shansi, each had more than twenty thousand.[162]   The foundations were laid in widespread Christian

---

[159] Schmidlin, *Katholische Missionsgeschichte,* p. 465.

[160] *Annales de la propagation de la foi,* Vol. 12, p. 333.   The difference is only partly accounted for by the fact that he includes Macao.

[161] Perboyre, quoted in Montgesty and Gilmore, *Two Vincentian Martyrs,* p. 150.   Perboyre said there were then in China eighty native and forty European priests, thirty of the latter having come in the past ten years.

[162] The map of Marchini [sic?] quoted in Medhurst, *China,* p. 244, says that in 1810 there were in Kwangsi, Kwangtung, and Hainan 7,000 Christians; in Chihli, Shantung, and Eastern Tartary 40,000; in Kiangnan and Honan, 33,000; in Fukien, Chêkiang, Kiangsi, and Formosa, 30,000; in Szechwan, Kweichow, and Yünnan, 70,000; in Shansi, Shensi, Kansu, Hukwang, and Western Tartary 35,000. *Les annales de la propagation de la foi,* Vol. 12, p. 333, gives for 1839 52,000 Catholics for the diocese of Macao, 40,000 for that of Nanking, 50,000 for that of Peking, 9,000 for the vicariate apostolic of Chêkiang and Kiangsi, 60,000 for the vicariate apostolic of Shansi, Shensi, and Hukwang, 40,000 for the vicariate apostolic of Fukien, and 52,000 for that of Szechwan. *An Abridged Account of the State of Religion in . . . China in . . . 1806-1807,* p. 53, says there were then 7,000 Christians in Hukwang. Rameaux in 1833 said there were 8,000 or 9,000 Christians in Hupeh (*Annales de la propagation de la foi,* Vol. 7, p. 348). He says that in 1834 there were 500 Christians in Honan, and that in 1820 there were 12,000 in Hukwang (in ibid., Vol. 9, p. 58).   A smaller figure is given in *Annales de la propagation de la foi,* Vol. 9, pp. 57 et seq., where the number of Christians in all the Lazarist missions in 1836 is put down at 40,000.   The district includes Peking, Hukwang, Honan, Kiangsi, Chêkiang, and Kiangnan. *An Abridged Account of Religion in . . . China in . . . 1807-8-9,* p. 210, gives the number of Christians in Szechwan in 1799 as 37,000, in 1804 as 47,867, and in 1809 as 56,165.   In 1836 Perboyre, passing through Fukien, said that there were there seven or eight churches, "open to all the world and known to the Mandarins," and forty thousand Christians in the diocese.—Montgesty and Gilmore, op. cit., p. 148.

groups for rapid growth if ever conditions in Europe and China should make that possible. When China should be opened to the foreigner and both zeal and resources in Europe increased, the Church was to grow by leaps and bounds.

CHAPTER X

METHODS AND RESULTS OF ROMAN CATHOLIC MISSIONS IN THE
SIXTEENTH, SEVENTEENTH, AND EIGHTEENTH CENTURIES

ANY account of Roman Catholic missions from the coming of Xavier to the eve of the new era would obviously be incomplete without a summary of the methods that were used and of the results which followed. The topic naturally arranges itself around six queries: what means were employed for bringing the Christian message to the Chinese; on what did the missionaries' teaching lay emphasis; what activities of the Church were stressed; what was the organization of the Church; what was the financial cost of the missions and how was support obtained; and what results followed the work of the missionaries? This last question in turn divides itself into four others: what success did the missionaries have in attaining the ends sought; what changes did acceptance of the message of the Europeans work in the lives of the Chinese; what part did the Church have in the life of the country and what effects, if any, were there upon the nation as a whole; and what reflex influences were there upon Europe?

MISSIONARY METHODS

The methods by which the missionaries approached the Chinese were various. We have seen how the Jesuits emphasized the fact that they were scholars and demonstrated that in certain branches of knowledge they were better informed than were the Chinese. They took pains, too, to learn the language and were thus able by word and pen, with the assistance of native scholars, to do what was quite as important—put their message in a literary form which was acceptable to the educated classes. They were, too, experts in Chinese etiquette and refrained as far as possible from offending Chinese sensibilities. When they presented their Christian message they emphasized its similarities

185

to the existing beliefs of the educated classes, pointing out the passages in the classical books which seemed to teach of God, and conformed as far as possible to Chinese religious conventions. They endeavored, in other words, to come as those who would fulfil and not destroy the best of the nation's heritage. They hoped by so doing to make contacts with the dominant class, to obtain its respect, and by winning the nation's leaders to gain access to the masses.

No better form of introduction could have been devised to a people which held in such honor learning, literary form, and courtesy, and had such pride in its culture and its past, and which had so acknowledged through the centuries the leadership of its educated men.

In the course of time this approach was confined almost exclusively to the missionaries in Peking. After the papal decision on the rites it became in part impossible and after the dissolution of the Society of Jesus its remaining features were less and less stressed. The declining influence of the missionaries at court and the increasing severity of persecution must probably be ascribed in part to the gradual abandonment of this method.

The branches of knowledge most emphasized by the missionaries were astronomy and the attendant science, mathematics. Map-making, painting, architecture, and the construction of mechanical devices as diverse as clocks, fountains, and cannon, all played their part.[1] The majority of the Chinese and Manchus at court probably looked upon most of the missionaries as interesting barbarians who in some matters displayed an amusing and even useful skill, but who in religious and other questions were not to be taken too seriously. A few Chinese and Manchus were, however, more impressed, and occasional missionaries of outstanding vigor and intelligence—Ricci, Schall, Verbiest, and a few others—apparently commanded the respect of the majority of those about them.

To the masses of the Chinese the missionary usually made his approach through the native catechist and through Chinese women who had dedicated themselves to a life of celibacy in the

[1] Van Braam, *The Embassy of the Dutch East India Company . . . 1794-1795,* Vol. 1, p. 251, Vol. 2, p. 69; *Lettres édifiantes,* passim; *Catholic Encyclopedia,* Vol. 2, p. 61, Vol. 6, p. 393; Pelliot, *À propos du Keng Tche T'ou,* in *Memoires concernant l'Asie Orientale,* Vol. 1, p. 65. For a list of works on astronomy, mathematics, etc., prepared by the missionaries, see Wylie, *Notes on Chinese Literature,* pp. 108-125.

service of the Church. It was these who frequently and perhaps usually first interested the non-Christians and in their hands was nearly all the instruction preliminary to and a good deal of that which followed baptism. The priests were so few that they had their time largely engrossed in the administration of the sacraments, in the instruction of catechists and candidates for the priesthood, and in other tasks which only they could perform. Sometimes the approach to non-Christians was made by laymen, and one approved method appears to have been to encourage a Christian family to move into a village where there were no other converts and to become a center of evangelization.[2] Public preaching was usually impossible because of the ever-present danger of persecution: the spread of the Christian message had nearly all to be through unobtrusive individual contacts, and the missionary, who was more likely to be detected than a Chinese, kept as far as possible behind the scenes.

The Substance of the Instruction Given

The substance of the instruction given to catechumens appears to have been the immortality of the soul, the acquisition of eternal blessedness by means of true religion, the duty of man to bend his energies to the attainment of this happy state, and the main doctrines and practices of the Church—the character of God, the Trinity, the incarnation, the life, death, and resurrection of Jesus, the Ten Commandments, the place of the sacraments, especially of penance and the eucharist, the function of the Church, and the use of symbolism.[3] There was, of course, a catechism for the purpose of teaching these and related doctrines, and, at least in theory, a fairly good knowledge of it was required before baptism. The catechumen was commanded, too, to destroy his idols and to cease from practices which the Church condemned as superstitious.[4]

The Missionaries' Activities

Among their activities the missionaries stressed the sacrament of baptism. Baptism of adults appears usually, except in emer-

[2] Guiot, *La mission du Sutchuen au XVIIIme siècle,* pp. 268, 269; *Collectanea S. Congregatione de Prop. Fide,* Vol. 1, pp. 350-356; *Nouvelles lettres édifiantes,* Vol. 1, pp. 347-357; *Lettres édifiantes,* Vol. 4, pp. 285 et seq.

[3] Guiot, op. cit., pp. 268, 269; Bishops Francis and Peter, *Instructiones ad munera apostolica rite obeunda perutiles missionibus Chinae,* etc., passim.

[4] *Nouvelles lettres édifiantes,* Vol. 1, pp. 347-357.

gencies, to have been reserved to the priest. Since oil was scarce, as a rule the rite was performed merely with water. At times confirmation was given by priests as well as bishops and because of the persecutions was not infrequently administered even to young children.[5] It sometimes fell badly into abeyance.[6] Much effort was devoted to the baptism of dying children of non-Christians, for it was believed that the sacrament insured the moribund infant the joys of heaven and that without it he could probably never be admitted to the beatific vision of God. The infant mortality rate in China was so high, particularly among poor and abandoned children and in time of famine, and it was so relatively easy, according to Catholic belief, to make possible eternal salvation for those about to die, that much stress was placed upon this use of the sacrament. Chinese Christians, particularly women and those possessing some knowledge of medicine, were taught the proper formula and method and were encouraged to gain access to sick infants and to baptize those *in articulo mortis.* In Peking some catechists were especially assigned the duty of seeking out children who were exposed to die, and others obtained permission from physicians to follow the latter on their rounds.[7] The statistics reported regularly included the number of children who were baptized while at the point of death. To non-Christian Chinese the practice was mystifying and later gave rise to credulously believed rumors of sinister practices. To most Protestants it seems an unavailing and magical use of a beautiful Christian rite. It can at least be said for the custom, however, that it tended to place a higher value upon the worth of the individual. When it was persistently taught that even an abandoned and dying infant might be assured an eternal life of bliss and when such care was taken to make that possible, there must have followed, at least among Christians, a higher conception of the dignity of man.

Baptism marked only one step in the Church's care of the Christian. For the children of Christians there were, as far as possible, provided schools where girls were taught the catechism and religious books, and boys were instructed not only in religion

[5] Betrand, from Szechwan, Aug. 10, 1840, in *Annales de la propagation de la foi,* Vol. 14, pp. 73-79.
[6] Letter of Mgr. della Chiesa, Oct. 22, 1701, in *Journal of the North China Branch of the Royal Asiatic Society,* Vol. 56, p. 102.
[7] Entrecolles, from Peking, Oct. 19, 1720, in *Lettres édifiantes,* Vol. 3, p. 292; Launay, *Hist. gén. de la Soc. des Mis. Étr.,* Vol. 2, p. 198.

but in writing and in some of the Chinese Classics.[8] Regular services were arranged for the Christians, even when a priest or a catechist could not be present. The priest came if possible at least once a year, heard confessions, said mass, preached, gave instruction, and administered baptism and at times confirmations. Religious books, rosaries, medals, statues, the veneration of the Cross, and the adoration of the Sacred Heart of Jesus, were all utilized to strengthen the religious life of the Christians.[9]

For approach to non-Christians and for the instruction of catechumens and Christians and of candidates for the priesthood, a fairly extensive Christian literature was provided. The early Jesuits, including Ricci, prepared a number of works to introduce the non-Christian Chinese to Christian teachings.[10] Prèmare (ca. 1666-ca. 1734), for example, wrote a pamphlet on God which has been used by Protestants as well as Catholics and which has been said by some of the former to be "the only really sublime piece of writing in Chinese Christian literature." [11] The "Imitation of Christ" and Loyola's "Exercises" were translated. Books were also prepared on the imitation of the Virgin, on theology, on moral and religious virtues, and on the use of the sacraments. Translations of prayers and hymns were made and there were lives of Christ and expositions of the Gospels. Thanks chiefly to the labors of Buglio, by the end of the seventeenth century the Roman missal, breviary, and ritual, and even the *Summa Theologiæ* of St. Thomas Aquinas had been put into Chinese.[12] No complete translation of the Bible seems ever to have been published and it is not certain that one was made, but there were versions of parts of the Scriptures, especially the Gospels, both in print and manuscript, and in Manchu as well as Chinese.[13] Emmanuel Diaz's homilies and translation of the

---

[8] Letter of Dufresse, Oct. 26, 1800, in *Nouvelles lettres édifiantes,* Vol. 3, pp. 446 et seq. The same, Oct. 28, 1803, in ibid., Vol. 4, pp. 62-71.

[9] *Lettres édifiantes,* Vol. 3, pp. 187-195; *Nouvelles lettres édifiantes,* Vol. 1, pp. 347-357.

[10] Wylie, *Notes on Chinese Literature,* pp. 172-180.

[11] *Edinburgh Conference Reports,* Vol. 2, p. 250.

[12] Huonder, *Der einheimische Klerus in den Heidenländern,* p. 160; Huonder, *Die Verdienste der katholischen Heidenmission um die Buchdruckerkunst in überseeischen Ländern vom 16-18 Jahrhundert,* pp. 70-80. Louis Buglio had put the liturgy into Mandarin.—Brou in *Revue d'histoire des missions,* pp. 523, 530.

[13] Le Comte, *Nouveaux memoires sur l'état present de la Chine,* Vol. 2, pp. 199, 200; Wylie, *Chinese Researches,* pp. 94, 95-97; Edkins, *Manchu Christian Literature,* in *China Review,* Vol. 24, pp. 72, 73.

Scripture lessons for Sundays and feast days may still be in use.[14] As we shall see later, a Catholic translation of part of the New Testament introduced the first Protestant missionary, Robert Morrison, to the study of Chinese. It undoubtedly influenced his own translation of the Bible, and so, to a certain extent, many later Protestant versions.[15]

THE ORGANIZATION OF THE MISSIONS

The organization of the Church was fairly simple. In the preceding chapters we have seen something of the bishops, of the vicars apostolic, and of the various orders, congregations, and societies. Each body usually had a business agent, or procurer, in Macao or Canton.[16] The priests, as we have seen, usually led—especially in the years of persecution—an arduous life of almost constant travel and danger. Those in Macao, Peking, and some of the other large cities, and the few engaged in teaching were probably the only exceptions. Chinese priests as a rule were recruited from the children of Christians [17] and were given a long training. Their education was sometimes completed outside of China—at Penang, in Siam, in India, and even in Europe.[18] The Jesuits, it will be recalled, had wished permission for the native priests to use their own tongue in the liturgy and this Rome at first granted. Older men were to be ordained and were not to be required to learn Latin. Later the use of the language

[14] Wylie, op. cit., p. 94; Brouillon, *La Mission du Kiangnan, 1842-1855*, p. 124; Dahlmann, *Sprachkunde und Missionen*, p. 157.

[15] Possible reasons for the failure to put the entire Bible into circulation in Chinese and Manchu were the fear of strange interpretations of the Scriptures by the uninstructed, the offense which the style of nearly all translations into Chinese gives to the educated, and the conviction that the Chinese could be better taught through summaries of the Faith adapted to their background than by the straight Bible text. Most of this literary work of the early Catholics seems to have been in the classical style and not in the vernacular. This would tend to win the respect of the scholar class but would render the writings unintelligible or difficult of understanding to the common people. This would be especially unfortunate in the case of the prayers and the Scripture portions.

[16] Launay, *Hist. gén. de la Soc. des Mis. Étr.*, Vol. 2, p. 473.

[17] This was not always true. For example, Ou Li Yu-chan, known better by his Portuguese name, Simon A. Cunha (1631-1718), was a painter of some distinction, was baptized in middle life, entered the Jesuit novitiate at the age of fifty-one, and was ordained priest at the age of fifty-seven.—Tchang et de Prunelé, *Le Père Simon A. Cunha, S. J. (Ou Li Yu-chang)*, pp. i-iv.

[18] Brou in *Revue d'histoire des missions*, Vol. 4, pp. 391-406. The French Jesuits often sent their Chinese novices to Paris to complete their education.—Ibid.

of the Church was insisted upon.[19] Sometimes, especially during the years of severe persecution, the standard of education for the priesthood was lowered and an occasional older man, perhaps a catechist who had been found faithful, was ordained with only a short course and with merely enough knowledge of Latin to enable him to repeat the services of the Church—at times without understanding them.[20] The great majority of both native and foreign priests seem to have been men of high character. The Europeans had, of course, to be conversant with the language. A few became masters of it, but some had at least to begin their work with only a slight knowledge of it.[21]

Catechists were given less prolonged training than were priests. They bore, however, the brunt of teaching and instructing the non-Christians and of caring for the Christians during the absence of the priest. Each Christian community, as far as possible, had one or more catechists in residence.[22] Work for women and children was entrusted largely to Christian women who remained unmarried and gave their lives to the Church. In a land where celibacy, especially in women, was regarded with suspicion and might easily bring the Church into disrepute, this institution required careful regulation. The women were not allowed to take vows until they were twenty-five years of age, and then only for a period of years, and they almost always lived with their families.[23]

The number of Christians in any one place seems usually to have been small, seldom more than five or six hundred, and as a rule very much less. In West China, at least, it was the practice to appoint, in Chinese style, several elders or head men to supervise the community and to take charge of the services: even when no priest or catechist was present there was worship and instruction.[24]

[19] In the papal decree of March 16, 1615.—Brou in ibid., Vol. 3, p. 520; Paschal d'Elia in *Chinese Recorder*, Vol. 58, p. 351.

[20] Pottier, Oct. 18, 1782, in *Nouvelles lettres édifiantes*, Vol. 1, pp. 358-361; Paschal d'Elia in *Chinese Recorder*, Vol. 58, p. 352.

[21] *Nouvelles lettres édifiantes*, Vol. 1, pp. 401-449.

[22] Jacques from Canton, Nov. 1, 1722, in *Lettres édifiantes*, Vol. 3, p. 316; Pottier from Szechwan, Oct. 18, 1782, in *Nouvelles lettres édifiantes*, Vol. 1, pp. 347-357; Demimund, *Vie du François-Régis Clet*, pp. 251-261.

[23] *Collectanea S. Congregatione de Prop. Fide*, Vol. 1, pp. 350-356; Launay, op. cit., Vol. 2, pp. 147, 165; Servière, *Hist. de la mission du Kiangnan*, Vol. 1, pp. 20, 21. We hear of at least one separate church building for women.—Arias, *El Beato Sanz*, etc., p. 181.

[24] Launay, op. cit., Vol. 2, pp. 156, 157.

MISSION FINANCES

The cost in money of the work of the missions is difficult to ascertain. It is also not easy to find out just how and where the funds were obtained. The yearly cost to the order or society for each priest was small. In Szechwan in the eighteenth century each foreign missionary seems to have been allowed annually thirty taels.[25] From this he not only supported himself but subscribed to the maintenance of the school for the training of native priests, to the poor, and to couriers to and from Macao, and paid for wine for the mass.[26] The native priests were usually supported by their Chinese flocks, but sometimes their stipend had to come in whole or in part from Europe. The allowance for each in West China in the eighteenth century is given as twenty taels a year.[27] An account from the early part of the nineteenth century says that the allowance for each European priest was one hundred and forty dollars (silver) besides travelling expenses.[28] The women dedicated to the service of the Church seem to have been maintained either by their families or by fees from the schools which they taught.[29] The cost of the passage of missionaries from Europe to China was large. In the early part of the nineteenth century it is said to have been four thousand francs per person from France to China.[30] It was exceptional, however, for a missionary to return to Europe, so this expense had as a rule to be met only once for each foreigner. Since in the first quarter of the nineteenth century the total number of foreign priests in China at any one time was less than forty and of Chinese priests about eighty, it is probable that the total annual cost to European bodies was then about twenty-five or thirty thousand dollars (gold).[31] In the early

[25] Guiot, *La mission du Sutchuen au XVIIIme siècle*, pp. 206, 266. This at to-day's rate of exchange would be about forty dollars. It would probably have been at least fifty or sixty dollars gold in the eighteenth century.
[26] Bertrand from Szechwan, Aug. 10, 1840, in *Annales de la propagation de la foi*, Vol. 14, p. 78.
[27] Guiot, op. cit., pp. 206, 266.
[28] Medhurst, *China*, p. 247.
[29] Piolet, *Les mis. cath. franç. au XIXe siècle*, pp. 249, 250. Occasionally the (English) East India Company had granted Roman Catholic missionaries free passage on its ships.—Morse, *The East India Company Trading with China*, Vol. 1, p. 179.
[30] *Annales de la propagation de la foi*, Vol. 1, p. 66.
[31] Yet Medhurst, in *China*, etc., p. 247, says that Roman Catholics cashed annually bills on Europe to the sum of £40,000.

part of the eighteenth century, before the beginning of the reverses, the cost may have been greater.

The sources of these funds must be in part a matter of conjecture. Some money came from Europe. We know that for many years the rulers of Bavaria made an annual contribution to the China mission of the Jesuits and that Louis XIV gave financial assistance to the Seminaire des Missions Étrangères.[32] In the earlier days, part of the expenses of the Peking mission was defrayed by the French monarch and by the Emperor of China.[33] At least a portion of the support of the Spanish missions came from the royal treasury.[34] In China the Jesuits engaged in lending money. It was only during crises, such as the abolition of the Society of Jesus and the French Revolution, however, that the problem of support appears to have loomed particularly large in the minds of the missionaries. In the published letters from China during most of the seventeenth and eighteenth centuries occur only occasional references to the inadequacy of funds.

THE RESULTS OF MISSIONS

What results followed the expenditure of so much labor and sacrifice? Had this question been put to him, the Catholic missionary would have pointed at once to the many thousands of souls who, he believed, had been assured an eternal life of bliss. He would have called attention to the fact that the two hundred thousand or more Catholics who were to be found in China in any one year in the eighteenth and the early part of the nineteenth century were only a fraction of those who, in the two and a half centuries since Ruggerius and Ricci had entered China, had died in the Faith. He would have pointed, too, to the many hundred thousands of children who had been baptized as they were dying and had thus been assured of heaven. The great

[32] Cordier, *Histoire générale de la Chine,* Vol. 3, p. 302.

[33] Richenet, Procurer of the French Lazarist mission in Peking, wrote in 1817 that the French Jesuits, in addition to aid from the Society and other sources, had 22,000 livres of fixed revenue in France. When Lazarists were substituted for the Jesuits, there were assigned to the former 12,000 francs a year, but with the coming of the Revolution this was not paid them.—*T'oung Pao,* Vol. 20, p. 128.

[34] In Manila in the middle of the eighteenth century some Chinese studying for the priesthood were maintained at royal expense.—Huonder, *Der einheimische Klerus in den Heidenländern,* p. 178. In 1696 the twelve Spanish Franciscans in China were also maintained by grants from the Spanish King.—*Pérez, Origen de las Misiones Francescanas en la Provincia Kwangtung (China),* p. 174.

multitude of souls who had—so he was convinced—been saved to life eternal would to him have been more than ample recompense for the toil and the suffering that had been undergone.

If, however, the questioner had continued by asking what changes the Faith had wrought in the lives of Christians, the answer might not have been as emphatic. Certainly from the surviving records it is not clear just how far a new religious and moral dynamic entered into the lives of the converts. It seems certain that most Christians, especially after 1742, broke fairly completely with their older religious practices. The decision on the rites controversy had made that duty clear. The Christian was required by the Church to abandon his domestic shrines and his participation in the family, clan, guild, and community religious ceremonies in which he had been accustomed to share. Conversion brought no material advantage and might involve contumely and persecution.

To become a Christian, then, must have required a decision of character and have involved a wrench with the past which probably led, under the guidance of the Church, to an improvement in other phases of life. We read that where persecution had been severe and priests had been unable to visit their flocks the tendency was to lapse into the religious practices of the non-Christian community. Some apostasy is reported , but we hear of so many Christians standing firm under persecution that we are led to suspect that the majority held to their faith even when they only imperfectly understood it. Difficulty was encountered in preventing Christians from marrying outside the Church and from betrothing their children to non-Christians.[35] The Church, however, insisted that believers must not be wedded to unbelievers and this restriction must have helped to keep the Christian community distinct and to hold its children true to the Faith.[36] The enforcement of the observance of Sunday was difficult, and the rule against labor on that day was in part relaxed.[37] Conversion appears often to have brought relief from the distressing and degrading malady known as demon possession.[38] Chinese doubtless entered the Church from a mixture

[35] *Lettres édifiantes*, Vol. 4, p. 292; *Collectanea S. Congregatione de Prop. Fide*, Vol. 1, p. 335.
[36] Ibid. and *Nouvelles lettres édifiantes*, Vol. 3, pp. 244-264.
[37] Guiot, op. cit., pp. 268, 269.
[38] *Nouvelles lettres édifiantes*, Vol. 1, pp. 157-159.

of motives, some of them unworthy,[39] and brought with them many of their earlier religious conceptions. So far as there is evidence, however, it seems clear that conversion, on the whole, worked moral and religious improvement. Second and third generations of Christians, those who from childhood had been nourished in the Faith, were as a rule markedly different from their non-Christian neighbors. Heroism certainly existed. Chinese priests, for instance, year after year faithfully ministered to their flocks, often in face of persecution and without a foreign colleague.[40]

The Church was far from having an assured part in Chinese life. While an occasional official and a person of means and consequence became a Christian, the bulk of the membership was from the poorer classes. We hear, for example, of Catholics among the despised barbers.[41] Early in the nineteenth century the Christians in Hunan and Hupeh were mostly outside the cities and were gardeners or small farmers.[42] The bulk of the support for the clergy seems to have come from Europe, and while by the beginning of the nineteenth century the Chinese priests outnumbered those of foreign birth, only one Chinese bishop had been consecrated. The Church possessed few schools and those of higher grade were supported largely or entirely from abroad. It is obvious that so small and widely scattered a body, drawn chiefly from the less influential portions of the community, dependent upon foreign leadership and financial support, and subject to almost unremitting persecution from the state, had so far obtained only an extremely precarious foothold.

On China and its culture as a whole the missionaries had made almost no impression. The new faith had wrought no important modification in the ethical standards and religious ideas of the nation, and social and political institutions, except among the

[39] One man is reported to have become a Christian to be cured of a severe toothache.—Ibid., Vol. 1, pp. 292-301.

[40] See the story of Andrew Li in Launay, *Journal d'André Ly, Prêtre Chinois*, passim. Li was born in 1692 or 1693 in Shensi, of a Christian family, was educated for the priesthood in Macao and Siam, and was ordained priest in 1725. He labored first in Fukien and was later sent to Yünnan and then to Szechwan. In 1746 the two foreign priests in Szechwan were driven out, but Li remained, ministering to the Christians, the only priest in the province for six years. He was arrested at least twice, but always remained true.

[41] *Nouvelles lettres édifiantes*, Vol. 3, pp. 288-350; De Groot, *Sectarianism and Religious Persecution in China*, p. 525; *Annales de la propagation de la foi*, Vol. 2, p. 35.

[42] Clet, quoted in Montgesty and Gilmore, *Two Vincentian Martyrs*, p. 69.

small body of Christians, were unaltered. However, the missionary had familiarized some of the scholar class with a few phases of European science and had helped to acquaint them with the existence of the Occident. He was possibly in part responsible for the rather active intellectual life of the seventeenth and eighteenth centuries.[43] He perhaps contributed to the thought of those who were daring to depart from the orthodox scholarship of the past, were examining critically the texts of the Chinese Classics, and in other ways were showing indications of vigorous fresh life. The missionary is said by at least one eminent later writer to have stimulated this group by opening to it a hitherto unknown world of ideas and by providing it with a better logical method than China had yet known.[44] These heterodox scholars, few in number and scorned by the orthodox, were the forerunners of the intellectual awakening which in the twentieth century was to stir the nation to its foundations. However, the fact of this foreign influence is somewhat doubtful,[45] and upon the nation as a whole this radical school had as yet no effect. The average official may have acquired slightly more respect for the peoples of Europe because of the missionary, but this respect was probably offset by irritation at the proselyting zeal of the foreigners. Had missionaries after 1835 gradually ceased coming to China instead of increasing in numbers, the Church would probably have passed out of existence within a few generations, leaving behind it no permanent mark.[46]

Strangely enough, missions seem to have had a greater immediate effect on Europe than on China. It was through them that Europe first became really acquainted with the Middle Kingdom. The letters, journals, and travels of missionaries were published and were widely read. Missionaries corresponded extensively with savants. They wrote books and provided material which

[43] Liang Ch'i-ch'ao believes that Christianity had some effect.—In *Chinese Social and Political Science Review*, Vol. 8, p. 38.
[44] Liang Ch'i-ch'ao, *Ch'ing Tai Hsüeh Hsiu K'ai Lun*, p. 46; Hodous in *Chinese Recorder*, Vol. 58, pp. 422-425.
[45] Hu Shih believes that Liang Ch'i-ch'ao is mistaken in crediting missionaries with this influence upon this school.—Conversation with the author, Feb. 16, 1926.
[46] There are a few evidences of a slight influence of Christianity outside the Church. For example, in the *Shêng Hsien T'ung Chien*, a Taoist work of about 1700 published in 1787, is an account of the life, death, and resurrection of Jesus (*Chinese Repository*, Vol. 18, pp. 498-502). In the *Sacred Edict*, Christianity was considered of sufficient importance to be ranked with Taoism and Buddhism as a heterodox religion against which Chinese were warned.—Baller, *Sacred Edict*, pp. 84, 85.

became the basis of other books. Mendoza's work on China, for instance, written in Spanish and first published in 1585, was translated into Italian, French, and English.[47] Halde's *China,* made up of extracts from the writings of missionaries, was first written in French and by 1741 had passed through two English editions.[48] Antoine Gaubil, one of the French Jesuits, who was in China from 1722 until his death, 1759, was probably more expert in Chinese than was any European before the nineteenth century. He translated the life of Jenghiz Khan, some of the T'ang Annals, and the *Shu Ching,* he prepared a treatise on Chinese chronology, and left behind him many unpublished manuscripts.[49] The largest history of China ever published in a European language is that to which is attached the name of Joseph Anne Maria de Moyriac de Mailla, who served in the Jesuit mission in Peking in the eighteenth century.[50] The missionaries prepared dictionaries,[51] wrote descriptions of Chinese plants,[52] sent or brought to Europe the first large collections of Chinese books,[53] translated some of the classical writings, and introduced Europe to the Chinese philosophers.[54] The very forms of the words by which two of the greatest of the sages, Confucius and Mencius, are known to the Occident are due to the missionaries and bear permanent witness to Europe's debt to them.[55]

Rococo art was influenced by Chinese models. Chinese gardens, pagodas, and pavilions were reproduced by the wealthy, largely from information derived from the missionaries, sedan chairs came into use, true porcelain was for the first time produced in Europe, lacquer, incense, tea, Chinese colors, and the Chinese style of painting were popular, and by a process of evolution, in an attempt to copy China, the first wall papers

[47] *Encyclopædia Sinica,* p. 348.
[48] Halde, *A Description of the Empire of China,* etc., 2 vols., London, 1741.
[49] Cordier in *Catholic Encyclopedia,* Vol. 6, p. 393.
[50] Mailla, *Histoire générale de la Chine,* 13 vols., Paris, 1777-1780.
[51] Cattaneo translated a Chinese dictionary, Verbiest prepared a Manchu grammar, Christian Herdtrich prepared a Chinese-Latin dictionary, there was a lexicon by Basilius of Clemona, and several others by other missionaries. Prémare's *Notitia* was well known to an earlier generation of sinologues.—Dahlmann, *Sprachkunde und Missionen,* pp. 30 et seq.
[52] Michel Boym, *Flora Sinensis,* Vienna, 1656.
[53] Cordier, *La Chine en France au XVIIIe siècle,* p. 113.
[54] Couplet translated parts of Confucius' writings, Noël translated Mencius, and Amiot prepared a *Vita Confucii.*—Dahlmann, op. cit., pp. 23-55.
[55] For books written by the missionaries, see Cordier, *Bibliotheca Sinica,* passim.

appeared.[56] One enthusiastic writer declares that by the latter part of the seventeenth century the missionaries had succeeded in making China better known in France than were many of the provinces of Europe.[57] They laid the foundations for the scientific study of China by Europeans and so of an intelligent appreciation of that country.

One interesting feature of this knowledge in Europe of China was the influence of the Middle Kingdom upon the liberal thought of the eighteenth century. For a time it was the fashion in the circles in which Voltaire and the encyclopædists moved to glorify Chinese culture.[58] Particularly was this so in the realm of religion. Many of the educated Europeans of the eighteenth century were deists and so upholders of "natural" as against "revealed" and ecclesiastical religion. The Jesuits by their translations of the Chinese Classics and their endeavor to find in the honors to T'ien and Shang Ti a belief in God akin to that in Judaism and Christianity had opened to the "enlightened" intellectual of the Occident a civilization in which he saw a confirmation of his views. Here was, so he believed, a monotheism which had grown up apart from the Jewish and Christian revelations, was adhered to by the educated, and was free from the domination of clerical superstition. Naturally he was intensely interested and was loud in his praises. Deism did not owe its origin to Chinese influence nor was it much modified by it, but its adherents were often strengthened in their convictions by what they thought they saw in China. It is just possible that an increased use of the word Heaven for God in the literature of the time had its origin here. By the end of the eighteenth century the adulation of China had largely subsided, but the nineteenth century still heard occasional echoes of it.[59] The missionaries had been largely responsible for initiating a cross-fertilization of cultures.

[56] Cordier, La Chine en France au XVIIIe siècle, passim; Reichwein, China and Europe, passim.
[57] Martino, L'orient dans la litterature française au XVIIe et au XVIIIe siècle, p. 107.
[58] Cordier, La Chine en France au XVIIIe siècle, pp. 114-126.
[59] For an excellent treatment of this general topic see Söderblom, Das Werden des Gottesglaubens, pp. 324-360. For echoes of this admiration for China in America, see Writings of Thomas Jefferson, Lipscomb, ed., Vol. 5, p. 183. The salutatory of the first volume of the American Philosophical Society expressed the hope that the United States might be "so fortunate as to introduce the industry of the Chinese, their arts of living, and improvements in husbandry."—Oberholtzer, Robert Morris, p. 223.

CHAPTER XI

IT was not alone by sea that in the sixteenth, seventeenth, and eighteenth centuries China came in touch with an expanding Europe. While the Portuguese, the Spaniards, the Dutch, the English, and the French were establishing their traders in the ports on the south coast and Roman Catholic missionaries were gaining followers in practically all the provinces, Russians were occupying Siberia and were forming commercial, diplomatic, and religious contacts with the Middle Kingdom.

The first Russian agents reached Peking in the latter part of the sixteenth century, but were not officially received. Russians continued to push their way eastward and by the middle of the seventeenth century had outposts in the portion of Siberia which drains into the Pacific. This activity on their northern borders alarmed the Manchus and they laid siege to Albazin, the principal Russian fort on the Amur River. Of the check to the Russian advance and of the treaty of Nerchinsk (1689)—the first formal agreement between China and a European power and negotiated in part with the aid of Roman Catholic missionaries —there is no need to go into detail here. What concerns us is that at the first siege of Albazin, in 1685, thirty-one prisoners were captured by K'ang Hsi's forces and were taken to Peking. They were given a residence in the northeast corner of the city and in time were incorporated into one of the "banners" and were given charge of the defense of their section of the capital. They were apparently members of the Russian Orthodox Church —so far as we know, the first of that communion to reside within the Eighteen Provinces—and with them had been taken captive a priest, Maxime Leontiev.

Leontiev ministered to his flock according to the customs of his church, first in a temple assigned to him and then in a chapel built for that purpose. In the course of time the Metropolitan of Tobolsk recognized the community by sending it a communion cloth, and ordered that preaching among the Chinese be begun. The cloth was accepted but the command was not obeyed. Leontiev died in 1712, and in 1715 there were sent to carry on his work, probably by Peter the Great, the Archimandrite Hilarion, a priest, a deacon, and seven clerics. They, too, apparently confined their ministrations to the Albazinians. It is interesting that they called their church by a Chinese word for temple, *miao,* that they used the Buddhist term *fo* for God, and called their clergymen *lama.*

Growing intercourse between the Chinese and Russians made necessary a suplementary treaty, that of Kiakhta, in 1727. This document, besides regulating trade, diplomatic relations, and the frontier, provided for the residence in Peking of four priests and of six students of Chinese and Manchu. As soon as they had completed their studies the latter were to return to Russia to aid in the conduct of the relations between the two countries. This ecclesiastical mission was supported at the expense of the Chinese and Russian governments. It was primarily for the purpose of giving spiritual care to the descendants of the Albazinians and to the Russians who visited or lived in the capital, and of providing a means for the study of Chinese. Its members carried on no activities among the Chinese, but in the twentieth century the group of Albazinians which they continued to nourish in the Faith became a center of evangelism among the Chinese, and the portion of the city assigned to the captives so long before remained for years the base of the mission's activities.[1]

[1] The authorities for this brief chapter are: Archimandrite Innocent in *Chinese Recorder,* Vol. 47, pp. 678 et seq.; Baddeley, *Russia, Mongolia and China,* Vol. 2, passim; Cordier, *Hist. des rel. de la Chine avec les puis. occid.,* Vol. 1, p. 87; Cordier, *Hist. générale de la Chine,* Vol. 3, pp. 270-278, 340-342; Cordier in *Catholic Encyclopedia,* Vol. 3, p. 679; Prandi, *Memoirs of Father Ripa,* p. 89; Timkowski, *Travels of the Russian Mission,* Vol. 1, pp. 1-3; Smirnoff, *A Short Account of the Historical Development and Present Position of Russian Orthodox Missions,* p. 75; *Chinese Recorder,* Vol. 4, pp. 68, 96, Vol. 23, p. 151; *Encyclopædia Sinica,* pp. 10, 287, 490.

CHAPTER XII

THE RENEWED EXPANSION OF EUROPE

THE INDUSTRIAL REVOLUTION, THE REVIVAL OF CATHOLIC MISSIONS, AND THE RELIGIOUS AND MISSIONARY AWAKENING AMONG PROTESTANTS

DURING the closing years of the eighteenth and the opening decades of the nineteenth century, missions in China, as we have seen, marked time. Advance had stopped and retreat seemed impending. When the outlook appeared darkest, however, new movements were beginning in the Occident which were to bring about a larger growth than the Church had yet known. The expansion of Europe which had commenced in the Middle Ages with the crusades, the commerce of the Italian cities, and the Franciscan and Dominican missions, and which had revived with the discoveries, commerce, conquests, and missions of the fifteenth, sixteenth, and seventeenth centuries, was to receive an additional impulse in the nineteenth and twentieth centuries and the entire race was to feel the effects.

The primary cause of this renewed expansion was the Industrial Revolution. Growing scientific knowledge brought increased mastery of man over his physical environment. Machinery, factories, railways, steamboats, and, later, telegraphs and telephones, airplanes and radios, worked startling changes. Populations multiplied, great migrations of peoples flowed into the vacant spaces of the earth, wealth accumulated, education became widespread, the globe was searched for raw materials and markets, commerce and travel increased to enormous proportions, the governments of the Occident controlled nearly all the planet, and every non-Occidental people began the reshaping of its culture under the influence of the civilization of Europe and America.

Modern industry began in Great Britain in the eighteenth cen-

201

tury and it was here and in the Low Countries, Northern France, Germany, the North of Italy, the United States, and Japan that by the end of the first quarter of the twentieth century it was to have reached its highest development. These regions profited most by the increase in wealth and power and, with agricultural Russia, were to dominate the world. Particularly did the Anglo-Saxon peoples gain in strength. The British Empire spread over great sections of the globe, and nations of British speech, blood, and institutions arose in Canada, Australia, and South Africa. The United States, English in speech and predominantly Anglo-Saxon in ancestry, rapidly moved its western boundary across the richest areas of the New World and in time became the wealthiest of nations. As Spain and Portugal had been the leading commercial and colonial powers of the sixteenth and seventeenth centuries, so the countries of Northern Europe and North America, and especially Great Britain and the United States, were to be preëminent in the expansion of the nineteenth and twentieth centuries.

Both in the thirteenth and in the sixteenth and seventeenth centuries, economic and political expansion had been accompanied in Europe by a religious revival. Similarly in the eighteenth, nineteenth, and twentieth centuries, in the lands most affected by the Industrial Revolution, the Church was to experience a great re-awakening. It is fortunate for the race that this was so. The decay in morals, the materialism, and the ruthlessness that accompany sudden increases of wealth and power might otherwise have brought disaster to all that is finest in mankind and in civilization. If the new economic movements were to prove beneficent, it could be only because they were accompanied by heightened spiritual and moral energy. This need was present, of course, in Europe and America. It was to be equally urgent in lands where, like China, the old culture was to be altered by the economic and political impact of the West. The peoples of the West would owe it to China to bring the best of their spiritual resources to counteract the evils attendant upon their commerce, industry, and use of force. When once the old barriers were down, an unprecedented opportunity would come to present to the Chinese the Christian faith. With it would go the privilege and obligation of contributing to Chinese culture and institutions in their day of transition the best that Christianity has to offer.

THE REVIVAL OF CATHOLIC MISSIONS

In Roman Catholic countries the religious awakening was not spectacular. No great need existed for the kind of moral reformation that the Church had undergone in the sixteenth century. The Roman Catholic Church had, however, suffered from the intellectual indifferentism of the eighteenth century, and had been dealt especially severe blows by the European upheaval which ushered in the nineteenth century. The new era inaugurated by the Congress of Vienna brought it peace and renewed strength. In the lands which had been most affected by the French Revolution the old régime was partially restored and governments and peoples sought to make good the losses which the Church had suffered. New congregations and societies were founded; old orders and societies were revived, among them those primarily interested in foreign missions. Louis XVIII aided in the resuscitation of the Missions Étrangères and in 1816 there sailed for the mission field the first recruit sent since 1807.[1] In 1816 the Lazarists were reëstablished in France.[2] In 1814 the Propaganda, which had been discontinued in 1808, was revived, and in 1817 the Pope ordered three cardinals to complete the work of reconstruction.[3] The new romanticism aided in the renewal of devotion to the Church. Even the democratic movement may have helped.[4] There began to appear in various cities of France societies and groups started by lay people for the collection of money for missions,[5] in 1817 the Missions Étrangères inaugurated an association for prayer,[6] and in 1822 these culminated in the Society for the Propagation of the Faith (*L'Œuvre de la Propagation de la Foi*).

This organization, while prepared for by earlier movements, owed its inception chiefly to a devout laywoman, Marie Pauline Jaricot of Lyons, to Bishop Dubourq of New Orleans, and to Father Inglesi, the Vicar General of New Orleans. Its purpose was to enlist Catholics the world over to give and to pray for missions. Members were to say daily the Lord's Prayer, a "Hail Mary," and an invocation to St. Francis Xavier, and were to

---

[1] Launay, *Hist. gén. de la Soc. des Mis. Étr.,* Vol. 2, p. 499.
[2] Henrion, *Hist. gén. des mis. cath.,* Vol. 2, p. 651.
[3] Schwager, *Die katholische Heidenmission der Gegenwart,* p. 19.
[4] Schmidlin, *Katholische Missionsgeschichte,* p. 426.
[5] Launay, op. cit., Vol. 2, p. 508.
[6] Ibid., Vol. 2, p. 504.

contribute two centimes a week. This sum was small enough to be within the reach of all, and many of the early members were workers in the factories at Lyons. The Society did not send out missionaries under its own auspices, but the funds raised were distributed among various orders and societies for their activities abroad.[7] At first it drew its membership chiefly from France, but in the course of time it expanded to other countries.[8] The French, however, long continued to contribute to it more than any other people. It was not until the twentieth century that they were outstripped by the Catholics of another country (the United States). The sums raised increased rapidly. In the first three years of the life of the Society they were 154,662 francs [9] and in 1839 they were 1,895,682 francs.[10]

The Society for the Propagation of the Faith was supplemented by the Association of the Holy Childhood (*L'Œuvre de la Sainte-Enfance*). This was founded in 1843, partly through the inspiration of Mlle. Jaricot but chiefly by the energy of Bishop Jansen of Nancy. It had for its goal the succor of children in non-Christian lands. Infants in danger of death were to be baptized, and whenever possible children were to be rescued, reared in the Catholic faith, and educated, either in Christian homes or in orphanages. The Association was to assist and to extend the efforts which for many years had been carried on for dying infants. It sought its contributors from among children and so did not conflict with its older sister society. Like the latter, it asked support from all parts of the Catholic world.[11] Like it, too, it experienced a rapid growth of income—from 129,944 francs in 1845-1846 to 712,401 francs in 1853-1854, 2,100,391 francs in 1873-1874, and 3,143,169 francs in 1883-1884.[12]

Organizations similar to these two, but smaller, were formed in Austria, Bavaria, and Cologne.[13]

It was clear that more missionaries and funds could be expected for Catholic work in China. France was to bear the brunt of

---

[7] Ibid., Vol. 2, p. 511; *Annales de la propagation de la foi,* Vol. 50, pp. 315 et seq.

[8] It was organized in Italy in 1837-1841.—Schwager, *Die katholische Heidenmission der Gegenwart,* p. 27.

[9] *Annales de la propagation de la foi,* Vol. 2, p. 30.

[10] Ibid., Vol. 12, p. 237.

[11] Schwager, op. cit., p. 37; Antonini, *Au pays de Chine,* p. 263; Launay, op. cit., Vol. 3, p. 123; Tragella, *L'Infanticidio e la S. Infanzia,* pp. 106-113.

[12] Tragella, op. cit., pp. 136, 137.

[13] Alzog, *Manual of Universal Church History,* Vol. 3, p. 922.

the support of the advance, but aid was to come from Catholics in other lands which had profited in wealth and population from the Industrial Revolution—Germany, Austria, Belgium, Northern Italy, and, in the twentieth century, the United States. Catholics in less prosperous regions—Spain, Portugal, and Southern Italy— were also to help, although to a less extent, especially since to poverty were often added civil war and revolution, and, in Italy, a long struggle for national unity.

THE RISE OF PROTESTANT MISSIONS

In Protestant lands the religious awakening was to be more spectacular than in Catholic countries. The revival in Protestant-ism was the logical outgrowth of the Reformation, the continua-tion of the fresh religious experience and enthusiasm of that movement. It was, however, less theological than the former, less associated with the state, and more spiritual and moral. Its immediate foreshadowings were the German Pietism of the seven-teenth and eighteenth centuries, but its largest early manifesta-tions were the Great Awakening in the English colonies in Amer-ica and the Evangelical Movement in England. It continued into and through the nineteenth century, its course being marked by revivals in America and by new life in Protestant churches in Great Britain, Ireland, France, Switzerland, Holland, and Scan-dinavia. It was to affect all Protestant communions, but it was strongest in the English-speaking nations.

The movement placed its greatest emphasis upon an individual religious experience—conversion, following usually a period of unhappiness and conviction of sin—a joyous sense of forgiveness, victory over temptation, and new life through faith in Christ. It had much to say of Christ's sufferings, death, and resurrection, and it was in part a return to Paul, with his emphasis upon the Cross of Christ, and a new and eternal life begun here through repentance, faith, and union with Christ.

The awakening was not confined to any one denomination or school of theological thought. To a certain extent, too, it appealed to all classes, although its leaders sought out partic-ularly the religiously neglected among the factory towns of Eng-land and on the frontiers in America.

Those who had experienced the new life were encouraged to lead others into it: by its very nature the awakening was missionary. With the emphasis upon individual conversion was usually associated an active desire to help others, not only by introducing them to a new spiritual and moral life, but by promoting their welfare in intellectual, physical, and material ways, by removing and redressing social injustices, and by educational and philanthropic enterprises.

To further and give expression to these convictions great leaders arose and new denominations and societies sprang into existence. Whitefield, Wesley, Wilberforce, Finney, Moody, Booth, and thousands of others were at once the children and the creators of the movement. The various Methodist and Wesleyan bodies, the Salvation Army, the Young Men's and Young Women's Christian Associations, the Sunday School, the numerous young people's societies, are a few of the many organizations which had their origin in the Evangelical Awakening. The anti-slavery agitation, world peace programs, the campaign against intemperance, demands for greater justice to women, and popular education were often closely associated with and sometimes sprang out of it. Children of their age, Protestant missionaries, particularly those from the Anglo-Saxon world, usually combined a personal religious experience and a passion to lead others into it with the ardor of the social reformer.

Until the close of the eighteenth century, Protestants, as we have seen, had had very little part in the foreign missionary enterprise. Among them had been many earnest men who had labored for the evangelization of the Indians of North America and for the non-Europeans in the Dutch colonial possessions, and under the inspiration of the Pietist and Moravian groups there had arisen, in the eighteenth century, heroic beginnings of missions in nearly every non-Christian region accessible to Protestants. These were the activities of small minorities, however, and the mass of Protestant Christendom remained indifferent to the spiritual welfare of the non-Christian world. Now, out of the Evangelical Movement sprang society after society for foreign missions. By the close of the nineteenth century nearly every denomination and national church was thoroughly committed to helping spread the Gospel through the entire world.

The first of the modern missionary societies was organized in 1792 by English Baptists. The London Missionary Society, at the outset undenominational and later the agent of English Congregationalists, followed in 1795; the Church Missionary Society was founded in 1799 by Evangelicals in the Church of England; the Wesleyans, who for many years had carried on missions without a society, formed one in 1818; in 1804 the British and Foreign Bible Society was organized for the purpose of distributing the Scriptures at home and abroad; and many other similar bodies came into existence in Great Britain.

On the continent of Europe the first few decades of the nineteenth century saw the foundation of a number of missionary societies and schools for the training of missionaries, among them those which bore the name of Basel and Berlin.

In the United States the enthusiasm and conviction of a few students in Andover Seminary led in 1810 to the formation of the American Board of Commissioners for Foreign Missions, which, like its prototype, the London Missionary Society, was in the beginning undenominational, and later, with the withdrawal of other groups, became the organ of the Congregational churches. In the next few decades the organization of other societies followed, until eventually nearly every denomination was provided with its foreign missionary agency.

Not only did these societies first come into existence in Great Britain, the country which profited earliest by the Industrial Revolution, but they were to continue to draw their most extensive support from it and from its daughter-nation, the United States. It was Anglo-Saxons of the Evangelical school who were to predominate in the Protestant foreign missionary enterprise and upon it they were to leave the indelible impress of their character and convictions.

China and the Missionary Awakening

While eventually this new missionary enthusiasm in Catholic and Protestant communions was to make itself powerfully felt in China, for the moment the Middle Kingdom presented great obstacles to it. Christian missions were proscribed by the state, such Catholics as were in the country were subject to frequent persecution, and missionaries entered at peril of their lives. At the beginning of the nineteenth century European merchants were permitted to reside and carry on their business at only a few points. Those who came overland, the Russians, enjoyed a limited trade in the North, and merchants from the rest of the

Occident, who were forced to come by sea, had open to them only Canton and Macao. At Canton Chinese were forbidden to teach them the language of the country; they were not allowed to go inside the city wall, but could reside only in a restricted district along the water front, the "Thirteen Factories," and there supposedly only for the part of the year known as the trading season; their commercial intercourse with the Chinese was through an officially designated monopoly of merchants, the Co-hong; customs duties were arbitrarily collected according to no published schedule; they were subject to Chinese laws and law courts; consuls were not recognized by the government, and special ambassadors sent from time to time by Occidental powers were regarded as conveyors of tribute from subordinate nations. Only in Macao did the European have a permanent residence, and even here Chinese officials claimed suzerainty.[14] It was obvious that under these conditions Catholics would not find it easy to strengthen their missions, and that Protestants, with their married clergy and with no previous foothold in the country, would have great difficulty in effecting an entrance. To add to the obstacles, British trade, which predominated, at the beginning of the nineteenth century was the monopoly of the East India Company, and that organization was hostile to missionaries.

[14] Latourette, *Early Relations between the United States and China, 1784-1844*, pp. 20-26. For a fuller bibliography see the footnote references there. The books most useful are Morrison, *A Chinese Commercial Guide*, Hunter, *The Fan Kwae in Canton before Treaty Days*, Roberts, *Embassy to Eastern Courts*, Morse, *International Relations of the Chinese Empire*, Vol. 1.

CHAPTER XIII

THE BEGINNINGS OF PROTESTANT MISSIONS TO CHINA
(1807-1839)

EARLY PROJECTS FOR PROTESTANT MISSIONS TO CHINA

DURING the years that Catholic missionaries had been laboring in the Middle Kingdom Protestants had not been entirely unmindful of the country and had had various projects for missions to it. During their occupation of Formosa in the seventeenth century (c. 1624-1662) the Dutch carried on missions among the aboriginal peoples and several thousand converts were made, but it is not certain that any Chinese became Christians. The Chinese had only begun to settle on the island, they were relatively few, and if any of them made a profession of the Christian faith it was apparently to obtain the permission of the Dutch to marry Formosan Christian women. When the Dutch were driven out, the Church collapsed, leaving no permanent traces of its existence.[1] In 1661 George Fox, it is said, exclaimed: "Oh, that some Friends might be raised up to publish the Truth in China."[2] Whether or not this wish was ever expressed, Fox records in his journal that in 1661 three Friends, John Stubbs, Richard Costroppe, and Henry F. Fell, were "moved to go towards China and Prester John's country." With the courage characteristic of their group, they started for the Middle Kingdom. After many difficulties, Fell and Stubbs, so Fox reported, got as far as Egypt. From here apparently they were banished through the efforts of the British consul.[3] The great Leibnitz had become

[1] Campbell, *Sketches from Formosa*, pp. 336-359; Campbell, *Missionary Success in Formosa*, Vol. 1, passim; Campbell, *Formosa under the Dutch, Described from Contemporary Records,* passim; *Chinese Recorder,* Vol. 20, p. 114, Vol. 35, pp. 166, 169; Good, *Famous Missionaries of the Reformed Church,* pp. 37-48; Morse, *International Relations of the Chinese Empire,* Vol. 1, p. 565. For possible Chinese converts see Campbell, *Formosa under the Dutch,* pp. 139, 202.

[2] Davidson and Mason, *Life in West China,* p. 136.

[3] Penney (ed.), *The Journal of George Fox,* Vol. 2, p. 8.

interested in the Catholic enterprise in China and in the last decade of the seventeenth century proposed that Protestants undertake a mission there. He hoped that in the Middle Kingdom an undenominational church might arise and that several Christian groups might aid in giving birth to it. Leibnitz's proposal attracted favorable attention but no missionaries were sent.[4] With the Evangelical Awakening and the quickening of interest in missions, projects for work in China multiplied.[5] In 1798 William Moseley, a non-conformist clergyman in England, issued a circular pleading for the translation and circulation of the Scriptures in Chinese [6] and calling attention to the existence in the British Museum of a manuscript containing a translation into that language of part of the New Testament. In 1801 representatives of the Church Missionary Society talked over the possibility of a mission to China, but found the way closed. They resolved, however, to start a fund for the purpose of initiating the project at some future time.[7] The British and Foreign Bible Society in its first report called attention to the British Museum manuscript and considered printing and circulating it.[8]

MARSHMAN'S CHINESE BIBLE

The honor of actually beginning Protestant work specifically for the Chinese must be divided between the famous trio in Serampore, India, and Robert Morrison of the London Missionary Society. At Serampore earnest men led by the saintly Carey were founding missions in various parts of India and translating the Bible into several of the Eastern tongues. Marshman, one of the group, wished to study Chinese and sought the assistance of an Armenian, Lassar, who had been born in Macao and had learned both to speak and to read the language. Lassar had gone to Calcutta in 1806 and was there employed by Claudius Buchanan, an earnest clergyman in Bengal, to translate the New Testament into Chinese. Marshman, at Buchanan's expense,

---

[4] Merkel, *G. W. von Leibniz und die China Mission,* passim.
[5] The Emperor's reply to Lord Macartney, in 1793, stated that "the propagation of the English religion is a matter which can by no means be allowed." Why this was put in is not clear, as Macartney seems not to have raised the question.—Morse, *The East India Company Trading with China,* Vol. 2, pp. 227, 251.
[6] Taylor, *China's Spiritual Needs and Claims,* passim; Stock, *History of the Church Missionary Society,* Vol. 1, p. 464.
[7] Stock, op. cit., Vol. 1, p. 464; Moule, *Story of the Chehkiang Mission,* p. 8.
[8] *Chinese Repository,* Vol. 4, p. 251.

began studying Chinese with him early in 1806. Marshman was also aided by a Catholic missionary who had been in China and by a Chinese who had lived in Peking and had come to Calcutta as teacher to a Mr. Manning. Lassar removed to Serampore with two Chinese and here, under Marshman's direction, the work of translation was done. The translation of the New Testament was finished in 1811 and that of the entire Bible in 1822 or 1823. After the first version of the Gospels, the printing was done by the then novel device of movable metallic type arranged according to radicals, with the characters most frequently used nearest the compositor. The translation, made outside of China and without the help of expert Chinese scholars, was necessarily crude. It was never extensively circulated except in some of the early Baptist missions, but it was of some help in the preparation of at least one later version.[9]

ROBERT MORRISON

The first Protestant missionary to reside in China was Robert Morrison. In 1805 the London Missionary Society, then barely ten years old, began planning for a mission to the Chinese. Since the country was all but closed to foreigners, it was believed that the mission could best be begun among Chinese emigrants in islands to the southeast of Asia which were under European control.[10] At first the Society planned to send an older man, J. T. Vanderkemp, a missionary in South Africa, but Vanderkemp believed—wisely as the event proved—that he ought not to leave the country of his first choice. The directors of the Society next asked a Mr. Brown, but he also declined.[11] Finally only Robert Morrison was sent and for five years he was to carry on the enterprise alone.

Morrison was born in 1782 in Northumberland. He was reared in a religious home and at fifteen or sixteen passed through the experience of conversion and joined the Presbyterian Church. He was very studious and by his reading had his attention directed to missions. In 1804 he offered himself to the London Missionary

[9] *Chinese Repository*, Vol. 4, p. 252; *Dictionary of National Biography*, Vol. 3, p. 183; Abel-Rémusat, *Mélanges asiatiques*, Vol. 1, pp. 14-26, 133 et seq.; Wherry in *Records of the Shanghai Conference, 1890*, pp. 49, 53; J. C. Marshman, *The Life and Times of Carey, Marshman and Ward*, Vol. 1, pp. 244, 245, Vol. 2, p. 63.
[10] *A Century of Protestant Missions in China*, pp. 1, 2; Lovett, *The History of the London Missionary Society*, Vol. 2, p. 403.
[11] Medhurst, *China, Its State and Present Prospects*, p. 253.

Society, and the earnestness of his purpose is shown by the fact that while still a student in London he began the acquisition of the Chinese language through the manuscript in the British Museum and with the aid of a Chinese. Because of the English East India Company's hostility to missions [12] he was obliged to go to the United States and seek passage to the East on an American ship. Armed with a letter from Madison, the American Secretary of State, to the American Consul in China, he set sail from New York and arrived in Canton in September, 1807. There he continued his study of the language with the help of two Chinese Roman Catholic Christians, and after some months (1809), to make his position in China more secure, became a translator of that same East India Company which at first had been so inhospitable. In 1816 he made the round trip to Peking as an interpreter in the ill-starred Amherst embassy. As Xavier had attempted an entrance to the Middle Kingdom in alliance with Portuguese commerce and diplomacy, so the first Protestant missionary to China became closely associated with a British trading company and the government of England. Morrison, however, always thought of himself as primarily a missionary and never allowed his service to the Company to take precedence over his first calling. It was fortunate that he was by disposition a student, for with the other avenues to the Chinese so nearly closed, it was through preparing literature that the foundations for his successors could best be laid. He had an unusual capacity for hard work and so was able successfully to carry on his two tasks. To the printed page, then, Morrison chiefly devoted his attention. By 1819, with the aid of Milne, he had completed the translation of the Old and New Testaments, and in the course of his life he wrote pamphlets, translated the shorter catechism of the Church of Scotland and part of the prayer book of the Church of England, and prepared a Chinese-English dictionary and a grammar. With necessarily restricted intercourse with the Chinese, and with so much time given to literary labors, it is not surprising that he made few converts. He baptized his first, Tsae A-ko, July 16, 1814, "at a spring of water issuing from the foot of a lofty hill by the seaside, away from human observa-

---

[12] The English East India Company had previously, however, on several occasions granted to Roman Catholic missionaries a free passage from Europe to China and its representatives in China had often received free advice and help from them.—Morse, op. cit., Vol. 1, p. 179.

tion." [13]   In the first twenty-five years of the mission he and his colleagues baptized only ten Chinese.[14]

REËNFORCEMENTS

To Morrison there came in time encouraging support from England.   The British and Foreign Bible Society helped with the publication of his translations of the Scriptures.[15]   His own society sent as large reënforcements as could well be used.   The first to come was William Milne, a Scotchman, and, like Morrison, a man of scholarly tastes and linguistic ability.   Milne and his wife arrived in Macao in July, 1813, and were almost immediately ordered by the authorities to leave, an action possibly taken at the request of the Roman Catholic clergy.[16]   Milne went to Canton, and then, at the end of the trading season, to Java and the East Indies with New Testaments and tracts.   Later, at the advice of Morrison, he made his home at Malacca, where British control and a Chinese population numbering about four thousand gave opportunity for language study and missionary activity.[17]   In 1817 Walter Henry Medhurst, a printer, arrived at Malacca, sent out, like Morrison and Milne, by the London Missionary Society.   He later left for Penang and then for Batavia for work among the Chinese emigrants.   Energetic, vigorous, and an earnest student of Chinese, he was a prominent figure among the early Protestant missionaries.[18]   By the close of 1832, when Morrison had been in China for a quarter of a century, the foreign staff of the Society's mission to the Chinese numbered five—Morrison, Medhurst, Samuel Kidd (ill in England), Jacob Tomlin, and Samuel Dyer.[19]   Several others had seen service in the intervening years, but climate and living conditions had taken

[13] Morrison, *Memoirs of Robert Morrison,* Vol. 1, p. 409.   Tsae remained true to his new faith.   He died in 1818.—Medhurst, op. cit., p. 262.

[14] Morrison, op. cit., passim.   This is the main published authority for Morrison's life and contains much first-hand material.   See also Broomhall, *Robert Morrison.*   The style of Morrison's Bible was between the colloquial and the classical.   The translation of the New Testament was in part based upon the Roman Catholic version.—Broomhall, op. cit., pp. 115-118.

[15] Canton, *History of the British and Foreign Bible Society,* Vol. 1, p. 300.

[16] Medhurst, *China,* p. 260; Milne, *A Retrospect of the First Ten Years of the Protestant Mission to China,* pp. 97 et seq.; Wylie, *Memorials of Protestant Missionaries to the Chinese,* pp. 122-125.

[17] *Chinese Repository,* Vol. 1, pp. 316-325.

[18] Wylie, *Memorials of Protestant Missionaries to the Chinese,* pp. 25-40; *Encyclopædia Sinica,* p. 344.

[19] Morrison, op. cit., Vol. 2, p. 471.

a heavy toll in ill-health and death.[20]   There were a number
of Chinese assistants, chief among them Liang A-fah, a printer
won to the Christian faith through Milne and apparently the first
ordained Chinese Protestant evangelist.[21]

THE ANGLO-CHINESE COLLEGE AT MALACCA

Morrison was eager to have some sort of permanent center
for the mission and since neither Canton nor Macao was available,
he decided (1814) on Malacca, which before the foundation of
Singapore (1819) was probably the chief city east of India under
British control.   Here Milne began a school for Chinese and
here, in 1816, land was obtained.[22]   Here, too, in 1818 Morrison's Anglo-Chinese College was launched.   This institution had
the double purpose of acquainting the English with Chinese culture and of putting in touch with Western culture "those nations
in which the Chinese written language is employed."   This was
to be done, of course, under Christian auspices and with Christian
worship and instruction as part of the daily program.   The original plan contemplated provision for six European and six "native"
students.   Chinese was to be taught and Chinese and others who
used the Chinese written language were to be instructed in
English and in Occidental sciences.   It was Morrison's hope that
"the light of science and revelation will, by means of this institution, peacefully and gradually shed their lustre on the Eastern
limit of Asia and the islands of the rising sun."[23]   Here was a
daring and noble project for educating jointly representatives of
the East and the West in such a way as to promote reciprocal
respect.

At its inception the institution gave a fair degree of promise.
Morrison contributed an initial £1,000 and £100 a year for five
years, and the East India Company for a time made an annual
subscription.   Building was completed in 1820 and several Chinese and two "of European extraction" were received for instruction.   During the opening year the student body ranged in number from about twenty to sixty.   The first class studied geography, Euclid, astronomy, ethics, English, and Chinese.   The gifted

[20] Milne, op. cit., pp. 211-215.
[21] Morrison, op. cit., Vol. 2, p. 224; Medhurst, op. cit., p. 270.
[22] Milne, op. cit., pp. 136-183.
[23] Morrison, *Memoirs of Robert Morrison,* Vol. 1, pp. 426, 512 et seq., Vol. 2,
pp. 39-56; Milne, op. cit., pp. 17 et seq.; *Chinese Repository,* Vol. 3, p. 138,
Vol. 4, pp. 98, 99.

Milne was in charge. The school was, however, ahead of its time and did not fulfil its founders' expectations. Very few of English blood seem to have studied in it and there was no demand from the educated and official classes of China for the type of training which it gave. Apparently only those Chinese who planned to engage in business with the foreigner or to seek employment under him found the school desirable. The institution soon confined its instruction to subjects of elementary grade. It had, however, an honorable history. In the first fifteen years of its existence forty completed its course and fifteen of its students were baptized.[24] Milne died in 1822 but others succeeded to his place and after 1842 the school was moved to the new British colony at Hongkong.

In connection with the Malacca mission there was, in addition to the Anglo-Chinese College, a press on which much of the early Protestant literature was printed, and for a time two periodicals were issued, a monthly in Chinese and a quarterly in English.[25] The latter, *The Indo-Chinese Gleaner*, apparently came to an end with the death of Milne.[26]

Morrison lived long enough to be appreciated in Great Britain and by the British community in China. While on a visit home he sought both to stimulate among the churches an interest in missions and to lay the foundations for a more extensive study of Eastern languages. Worn out by his excessive labors in an alien climate, he died (August 1, 1834) while yet in middle life. As was fitting, he was buried at Macao, in the China to which he had given himself so unsparingly.[27] His was not the brilliant genius of a Xavier or a Ricci, but he possessed unusual breadth of vision, integrity, singleness of purpose, devotion, scholarship, and sound judgment, and was one to whom Protestant missionaries and Chinese Christians can look back with pride.

THE MISSION TO THE MONGOLS

The London Missionary Society approached the Middle Kingdom from another direction, the North, and in 1817 began a mission to the Buriats. Edward Stallybrass and Cornelius Rahm, by

[24] Report of Anglo-Chinese College for 1834 in *Chinese Repository*, Vol. 4, pp. 98, 99. Most of the graduates became clerks. There were thirty-five students at this time, apparently studying only elementary subjects.
[25] *Chinese Repository*, Vol. 1, pp. 316, 325.
[26] Ibid., Vol. 2, p. 186.
[27] Broomhall, *Robert Morrison*, pp. 220, 221.

special permission of the Czar, went out across Russia. After a few years the ill-health of his wife compelled Rahm to leave Siberia, but the mission was reënforced in 1820 by Swan, Yuille, and later by Abercrombie. The Bible was translated into Mongolian and published, and a few converts were made. The Russian Government, however, eventually ordered the work stopped and in 1841 the mission was closed.[28]

OTHER BRITISH MISSIONS

Only two British Christian organizations besides the London Missionary Society sent representatives to China in these pre-treaty days. In 1836 the British and Foreign Bible Society dispatched to Macao as its agent G. Tradescant Lay, and he served until about 1839.[29]   Morrison asked the Church Missionary Society to enter the China field, but it felt that it had not the funds. In 1834, however, it granted Gützlaff £300 and in 1836 it sent out E. B. Squire. After a brief stay at Macao Squire went to Singapore and soon afterward returned to England.[30]

GÜTZLAFF

To the Protestant forces from England were added two missionaries from the Continent. The first and more prominent was Karl Friedrich August Gützlaff. Gützlaff was born in Prussian Pomerania in 1803. He was prepared for a missionary career, at royal expense, in a school maintained in Berlin by Jänicke, preacher in the Moravian church of that city.[31]   Appointed by the Netherlands Missionary Society to the East Indies, he sailed in 1827. Batavia was his first home, and there he came in touch with Medhurst and studied Malay and Chinese. He was assigned to Sumatra, but war prevented his entrance to that island and he spent some time at Riouw, a port southeast of Singapore. Thence he went to Bangkok to learn more Chinese and, later, to Singapore. In the eighteen thirties he made several trips along the coast of China to distribute Christian literature and was as

[28] Gilmour, *Among the Mongols,* pp. 56-70; Lovett, *The History of the London Missionary Society,* Vol. 2, pp. 585-597.
[29] Canton, *History of the British and Foreign Bible Society,* Vol. 2, pp. 391, 392.
[30] Stock, *History of the Church Missionary Society,* Vol. 1, pp. 467, 468.
[31] Ledderhofe und Knak, *Johann Jänicke,* pp. 93 et seq.; Warneck, *Outline of a History of Protestant Missions,* pp. 116, 117.

far north as Tientsin. He was a versatile linguist and succeeded Morrison as Chinese secretary to the British authorities in Canton and Macao.[32] The other missionary from the Continent, Herman Röttger, was sent out by the Dutch society which had originally supported Gützlaff. He arrived at Riouw (Rhio, on the island of Bintang) in 1832 [33] and was there as late as 1835 and probably until 1846,[34] working apparently among the Chinese. We hear little of him, however.

THE BEGINNING OF AMERICAN MISSIONS TO CHINA

From their inception American foreign missions had a close connection with the enterprise in Great Britain. The founders of the American Board of Commissioners for Foreign Missions desired at first to be auxiliary to the London Missionary Society and news of the latter's agents was eagerly read in missionary circles in the United States. In 1822 or 1823 the American Bible Society began helping in the distribution of the Scriptures among the Chinese and in 1833 and 1834 it used Liang A-fah as a colporteur.[35] The American Board was, however, the first organization in the United States to send a missionary to the Chinese. In 1829 there sailed from America two men, David Abeel, representing the American Seaman's Friend Society, to be chaplain to the many American sailors in Chinese waters, and Elijah C. Bridgman, under the American Board, for work among the Chinese. They were given free passage and other assistance by an American merchant engaged in the China trade, D. W. C. Olyphant,[36] whose earnest religious convictions were so well known that his rooms in the Canton factories were dubbed "Zion's Corner." [37] It was, indeed, because of Olyphant's aid that they had been sent at this time.[38]

Abeel and Bridgman arrived in Canton in February, 1830.[39]

[32] Ledderhofe und Knak, op. cit., pp. 93 et seq.; *Chinese Repository*, Vol. 1, passim, Vol. 2, pp. 20-32; *Encyclopædia Sinica*, p. 51; Kesson, op. cit., pp. 221-232; *Chinese Recorder*, Vol. 56, pp. 376-378; Wylie, op. cit., pp. 54-66.
[33] Dean, *The China Mission*, p. 161.
[34] Bridgman, *Life and Letters of Bridgman*, p. 97; Dean, op cit., p. 161; Wylie, op. cit., p. 75.
[35] *China Mission Hand-book*, Pt. 2, p. 298.
[36] Abeel, *Journal*, pp. 31, 32.
[37] Hunter, *Bits of Old China*, p. 166.
[38] Bridgman, op. cit., pp. 11, 12.
[39] Abeel, *Journal*, pp. 31-33; Bridgman, op. cit., pp. 1-37; Williamson, *Memoir of Abeel*, pp. 49-67.

By the end of the year Abeel's term of service had expired, and after a tour of investigation southward for the American Board he returned to the United States. His brief stay in the Far East had quickened his interest in China and he became a convincing advocate of missions. He was to help give the incentive to his own denomination, the (Dutch) Reformed Church in America, to initiate a mission in and around Amoy and he was to aid in stimulating the women of America and Great Britain to missionary activity.[40] Bridgman settled down in Canton to learn the language. He soon had a small school for Chinese boys and began literary work.[41] A press was sent him in 1831 and in May, 1832, he commenced the publication of *The Chinese Repository*.[42] This famous periodical had as its purpose the dissemination among foreigners not only of missionary news but of information concerning the laws, customs, history, literature, and current events of the Empire. It performed the useful task of interpreting China to Westerners, especially to the Western merchants who lived within her gates and who were all too often grossly and contemptuously ignorant of her. Bridgman was joined in 1832 by Edwin Stevens, Abeel's successor as chaplain for the American Seaman's Friend Society,[43] and in 1833 by Ira Tracy and Samuel Wells Williams, representatives of the American Board.[44] Williams was sent out as a printer. He was to prove one of the great scholars of the missionary body and was later to give his government years of service on its diplomatic staff.

The year 1834 saw the arrival of the first medical missionary to the Chinese, Peter Parker, also an agent of the American Board. The medical skill of the Occident had not been entirely unknown

[40] He appealed in 1834 in England for women to serve abroad. In 1837 there was formed, possibly in part in response to that appeal, The Ladies' Society for Promoting Female Education in China and the East. This went out of existence in 1890.—Underhill in *International Review of Missions,* Vol. 15, p. 250. In America Abeel interested a Mrs. Doremus who was the first president of the Women's Union Missionary Society (formed 1861).—Underhill in ibid., Vol. 14, p. 380. The plan for women's denominational missionary societies suggested by Abeel was killed for the time being by the opposition of the existing mission boards.—Ibid.
[41] *Correspondence of the American Board of Commissioners for Foreign Missions, China,* Nos. 21, 35, 37, 41; Bridgman, op. cit., pp. 43-57.
[42] *Correspondence of the American Board, etc., China,* Nos. 6, 89; Bridgman, op. cit., p. 74.
[43] *Chinese Repository,* Vol. 1, p. 243.
[44] *Correspondence of the American Board, etc., China,* No. 78; Williams, *Life and Letters of S. W. Williams,* p. 49.

to the Chinese.   The Jesuits, as we have seen, had introduced quinine.   Since at least 1805, the surgeons of the East India Company in Canton had been ministering intermittently to the Chinese. One of them, Dr. Pearson, seems to have been the first to teach the Chinese vaccination for smallpox, and another, T. R. Colledge, a man of earnest religious life, had for a time a dispensary in Macao.[45]   Morrison and Gützlaff had each done a little medical work.[46]   Parker, however, was trained in medicine as well as in theology, and his time was assigned entirely to the Chinese. He was in Singapore for a year studying the language and while there practiced his profession.   On his return to Canton, in 1835, he opened an ophthalmic hospital, possibly because he believed that he could be of most service by specializing on the eye troubles which he found so prevalent, and possibly, too, because Colledge had already had a similar establishment and so had helped to remove prejudice.[47]   Any suspicions the Chinese may have had were soon disarmed, and after the first year Howqua, one of the members of the *Co-hong,* gave the hospital free quarters.[48]

Still another American missionary agency, the "General Missionary Convention" of the Baptists, entered the China field.   In 1833 John Taylor Jones reached Bangkok from Burma and in that year baptized four Chinese.[49]   In 1835 William Dean arrived in Bangkok and in December organized a small church among the Chinese.[50]   In 1836 there arrived at Macao J. Lewis Shuck and his wife, the first Baptist representatives in China Proper.   They had an unhappy time, for their first convert apostatized, their salary was inadequate, and they were not popular with the other missionaries.[51]   They were joined in 1837 by the eccentric but earnest Issacher J. Roberts.   Roberts came out at his own

[45] *Encyclopædia Sinica*, p. 345; Lockhart, *The Medical Missionary in China,* p. 120; *Chinese Repository,* Vol. 3, p. 364; Balme, *China and Modern Medicine,* pp. 36-41.
[46] *Encyclopædia Sinica*, p. 345; Tatchell, *Medical Missions in China in Connexion with the Wesleyan Methodist Church,* p. 52.
[47] *Chinese Repository,* Vol. 2, p. 271; *Encyclopædia Sinica,* p. 124; Stevens, *The Life, Letters, and Journals of . . . Peter Parker,* etc., pp. 106-119.
[48] Williams, *The Middle Kingdom,* Vol. 2, pp. 333-337.
[49] Gammell, *History of American Baptist Missions,* p. 187.
[50] Dean, *The China Mission,* p. 233.
[51] Jeter, *Memoir of Mrs. Henrietta Shuck,* etc., passim; *Correspondence of the American Board,* Foreign Vol., p. 37; *Correspondence of the American Baptist Foreign Mission Society,* Shuck to Peck, Feb. 21, 1837.

charges,[52] but a few years later became a regular missionary of the Baptist board.[53]

The third American organization, and the first of the Anglican communion to send missionaries to the Chinese, was The Domestic and Foreign Missionary Society of the Protestant Episcopal Church in the United States. Its earliest two representatives, Henry Lockwood and Francis R. Hanson, arrived in Canton in 1835. They soon left for Singapore to study the language, and then after a few months went to Batavia. By the close of 1838 both retired because of ill-health. The real founder of the China mission of the Society was William J. Boone. He arrived in Batavia in 1837 and was later to move to China.[54]

One other American denomination, the Presbyterian, sent missionaries in pre-treaty days. It had coöperated with the American Board, but in 1837 formed its own board of foreign missions. From the beginning, the new board had as one of its chief objectives a mission to China, and in 1838 its first representatives, two men and their wives, arrived in Singapore.[55] Walter Lowrie, the great early secretary of the board, who resigned from the United States Senate to devote his time to foreign missions, gave two sons to China.[56]

MISSIONARY ORGANIZATIONS AT CANTON

In Canton itself organizations arose for missionary and philanthropic activity among the Chinese. Among the foreign merchants were those who, like Olyphant, were deeply interested in the welfare of the Chinese. The foreign residents at Canton and Macao in pre-treaty days were necessarily a very compact if not always an harmonious community, and joint enterprises were to be

[52] Letters of Roberts, Feb. 18, 1841, and Jan. 25, 1837, in *Correspondence of the American Baptist Foreign Mission Society;* Wylie, *Memorials of Protestant Missionaries to the Chinese,* p. 94; Hervey, *The Story of Baptist Missions,* pp. 512, 513.

[53] Letters of Roberts, Feb. 18, 1841, and April 19, 1841 in *Correspondence of Am. Bap. For. Mis. Soc.* He separated again from the board (this time of the Southern Convention) in 1851.

[54] Cutter in *History of American Missions to the Heathen,* p. 590; *Spirit of Missions,* Vol. 2, p. 219, Vol. 3, pp. 66, 210, Vol. 4, pp. 267, 596, Vol. 7, p. 130.

[55] *A Century of Protestant Missions in China,* p. 379; Garritt, *Historical Sketch of the Ningpo Station,* p. 1, in *Jubilee Papers of the Central China Presbyterian Mission.* There had earlier been the Western Foreign Missionary Society. The four missionaries were Rev. and Mrs. Robert W. Orr and Rev. and Mrs. John A. Mitchell. Mitchell died in October, 1838, and Orr left in 1839 because of ill-health.—Wylie, op. cit., p. 107.

[56] Speer, *Presbyterian Foreign Missions,* p. 14.

expected. The first of a specifically missionary nature seems to have been "The Christian Union at Canton." It was formed in the latter part of 1830 with a charter membership of seven, among whom were Morrison, Abeel, and Bridgman. It established a depository and library, published "Chinese scripture lessons for schools," and guaranteed the first year's expenses of the *Chinese Repository*.[57] The Union seems not to have had a very long existence, for we soon cease to hear of it. A second organization was the "Society for the Diffusion of Useful Knowledge in China," formed in December, 1834, or January, 1835. Its announced purpose was "to prepare and publish, in a cheap form, plain and easy treatises in the Chinese language on such branches of useful knowledge as are suited to the existing state and condition of the Chinese Empire."[58] In four years it issued almanacs, some of Æsop's fables in a modified form, a universal history, and a history of England.[59] Like the Christian Union, it did not have a long existence.

More important and longer-lived was the Morrison Education Society. Shortly after Morrison's death some of his friends undertook to raise a memorial to him. Believing that this could take no more appropriate form than a Christian educational project, early in 1835 they formed a society bearing his name and with the object of establishing and supporting schools in China to teach English and, through the medium of that language, the learning of the Occident, including the Bible and books on the Christian religion.[60] An initial sum of $4,860 was raised and almost immediately aid was begun to existing schools, among them one which Mrs. Gützlaff was conducting at Macao. Steps were taken to establish a separate institution under the control of the Society,[61] and a teacher, Samuel R. Brown, was obtained from America. Brown reached China in February, 1839, and almost immediately opened a school[62] which continued, first in Macao and then in Hongkong, until 1849.[63] One of the students to

[57] Bridgman to Evarts, Jan. 27, 1831, and Bridgman to Anderson, April 5, 1833, in *Correspoondence of the American Board, China, 1831-1837*.
[58] *Chinese Repository*, Vol. 4, p. 354; Williams, *Middle Kingdom*, Vol. 2, p. 340.
[59] *Chinese Repository*, Vol. 7, pp. 399-410.
[60] Ibid., Vol. 5, p. 373.
[61] *Chinese Repository*, Vol. 6, p. 229, Vol. 7, pp. 301-310.
[62] Ibid., Vol. 7, pp. 301-310.
[63] Ibid., Vol. 12, pp. 607-630; Williams, *Middle Kingdom*, Vol. 2, pp. 341-345; Griffis, *A Maker of the New Orient*, pp. 57-104.

whom the Society had made possible an education was Yung Wing. He had been first in Mrs. Gützlaff's school and was later under Brown's instruction. He was to be the first Chinese to graduate from an American college and, as we shall see, was to be chiefly responsible for the Chinese Educational Commission which, in the latter half of the century, sent several scores of Chinese to the United States.[64] There also studied under Brown Wong Fun, for whom foreigners were later to provide means for going abroad and who, as a graduate in medicine of the University of Edinburgh, was probably the first Chinese to acquire a medical training in the Occident.[65] Thus were some of Morrison's dreams for Christian education realized.

A fourth organization in Canton was the Medical Missionary Society in China, formed in 1838, with T. R. Colledge as president and as vice-presidents Peter Parker, W. Jardine, G. T. Lay, and Bridgman. Its purpose was to assist medical service undertaken gratuitously for the Chinese. The Society aided a hospital in Macao and the one maintained by Parker in Canton. The former was under the supervision first of Parker and then of William Lockhart of the London Missionary Society.[66] Lockhart was appointed in 1839 and by that time the disorders were in progress which were to bring to an end the peculiar life of the Canton community. The conditions which had made possible the Morrison Education Society and the Medical Missionary Society had come to an end and only the endowments which had been accumulated assured the continuation of the work which had been begun.

PROTESTANT METHODS

In the meantime, in the relatively quiet years of the eighteen thirties, the Protestant foreign missionary forces, under the impulse of the religious awakening and the added interest in missions, were increasing their pressure on China and in several different ways were endeavoring to gain access to the Empire and its inhabitants. First of all, as we have recorded, they were adding to their forces at the only accessible ports in China, Canton and Macao. Here they were fairly cautious and were able

[64] Yung Wing, *My Life in China and America*, passim.
[65] Ibid., pp. 19-33.
[66] *Chinese Repository*, Vol. 7, pp. 33-44, 411-422, 551.

to conduct their enterprise without much interference from the Chinese or Portuguese authorities.   Before the disorders which culminated in the first war with Great Britain, the most serious interruption was the raiding by official order, in 1834, of the American Board's press in Canton.   Liang A-fah and several other Chinese were seized, and while they were soon released they deemed it best to leave the city.[67]   In 1836 a slight flurry was caused by a proclamation of the local officials against the distribution of literature.[68]   In Macao the Portuguese in 1813 ordered Milne to leave, once in 1833 they stopped a press which was publishing a religious paper, *Miscellanea Sinica,* and in 1839 they hinted to an American missionary that no tracts should be distributed or public congregations held.[69]   On the whole, however, they were remarkably tolerant of Protestant activities and offered little serious opposition to them.

Protestants were, in the second place, trying to penetrate the Empire with literature.   Since resident work was out of the question except in Canton and Macao, and even there had to be carried on quietly, the printed page seemed the only approach possible.   Several presses, as we have seen, had been set up, and much of the time of the first missionaries was given to preparing literature.   Many pamphlets and tracts were issued, one of the best being Milne's *The Two Friends,* which in 1907 was still regarded as one of the most useful Christian books in Chinese.[70] The first book prepared by a Protestant woman for her Chinese sisters seems to have been a Christian trimetrical classic by a Miss Martin.[71]   In addition to the translations of the Scriptures by Marshman and Morrison, Medhurst, Bridgman, and Morrison's son made a revision of Morrison's New Testament,[72] and Gützlaff and Medhurst worked at the Old Testament.[73]   The Bible was still the center of Protestant literary activities.

Many efforts were made to circulate the literature so prepared. Liang A-fah and a colleague distributed books and pamphlets

[67] Williams, *Middle Kingdom,* Vol. 2, p. 328; Tracy, *History of the American Board,* etc., p. 246.
[68] *Chinese Repository,* Vol. 16, p. 49.
[69] Williams, op. cit., Vol. 2, p. 345.
[70] Darroch in *China Centenary Missionary Conference Records,* p. 197.
[71] *Chinese Repository,* Vol. 1, p. 77.
[72] Bridgman, *Life of Bridgman,* p. 100.   Perhaps Gützlaff also joined in this.— Williams, op. cit., Vol. 2, p. 363.
[73] Bondfield in *China Mission Year Book,* 1915, p. 469.

among the students who were congregated in Canton for the civil service examinations and made at least one trip of two hundred miles or more into the interior.[74]   It was a set of books given out at Canton which was later to bear fruit spectacularly in the leader of the T'ai P'ing Rebellion.   Gützlaff, as we have seen, made several voyages along the coast to China in the eighteen thirties.   In 1835 Medhurst and Stevens cruised along the coast in the brig *Huron,* which had been provided partly through the generosity of Olyphant.   They were as far north as Shantung, whose dialect Medhurst could speak, and there succeeded in making several trips overland, distributing literature as they went.   At Shanghai they were treated rather roughly and were followed for some distance by war junks, but these did them no harm.[75]   While literature was one of the few ways in which the Chinese could be reached and some of it accomplished its purpose, the method of distribution appears to have been wasteful and only a small proportion of the vast quantities circulated was given careful reading.

In the third place, Protestants were sending missionaries to ports and districts outside the Empire where there were Chinese either under Protestant powers or relatively tolerant native governments.   At Bangkok, Malacca, Penang, Singapore, Riouw (or Rhio), Batavia, a part of Burma, and in a section of Borneo missions were conducted for the Chinese.   The Dutch were not always cordial to British and American missionaries [76] and the King of Siam sometimes made them trouble, but in the main missionaries found it possible to reside in these places, to study the language, and to conduct various forms of religious activity.   It was hoped that some of the converts won would return to China to propagate their faith and penetrate the interior as the foreigner could not yet hope to do.[77]   It was expected, too, that the foreigner would obtain a preparation which would make him more effective when residence in the Empire should become possible. We have seen how under Morrison the London Missionary Society centered at Malacca its work for the Chinese.   At Malacca,

[74] Williams, *Life and Letters of* . . . *Williams,* p. 65; Williams, *Middle Kingdom,* Vol. 2, p. 328; *A Century of Protestant Missions in China,* p. 3; *Missionary Herald,* Vol. 30, p. 192.
[75] Medhurst, *China,* pp. 363-503; *Chinese Repository,* Vol. 4, pp. 308-335.
[76] *Missionary Herald,* Vol. 36, p. 11.
[77] Medhurst, *China,* pp. 361, 362.

too, lived one of the first unmarried Protestant women missionaries to the Chinese, Miss Newell, later Mrs. Gütlaff,[78] and here came from time to time representatives of other boards. Singapore was occupied the year it was founded (1819) by Milton, of the London Missionary Society.[79] It soon displaced Malacca as the chief British commercial center in the Southeast, and other missionaries found it a strategic place in which to live. The London Missionary Society from time to time had several other representatives there and the American Board possessed quite an establishment with a press and a school.[80] It was there that the (American) Presbyterian Board of Foreign Missions sent its first missionaries to the Chinese and it was there that Miss Grant began what seems to have been the first Protestant school for Chinese girls.[81] Penang did not prove to be as important a place as Singapore or Malacca, although Medhurst was there for a time [82] and in the course of the next few years his society had several resident representatives.[83] Röttger of the Rhenish Missionary Society was, as we have seen, at Riouw. Batavia was for a number of years the residence of Medhurst. Here came Miss Aldersey, who was to have a distinguished part in beginning in China Protestant education for women.[84] Here, too, came representatives of various American societies. About 1836 the Dutch Government discouraged the coming of any more American and British missionaries to other of its East Indian possessions than Borneo. To this island, then, went some of the representatives of the American Board, but before they had been there long the treaties of 1842 and 1844 made China more accessible and they transferred their mission to Amoy.[85] In Bangkok, as we have seen, was a mission of the American Baptists, of which Dean was the most prominent early figure. He was to be reënforced by Alanson Reed in 1836, only to lose him by death the following

[78] *A Century of Protestant Missions in China*, p. 457. The first may have been the one by Miss Grant, in Singapore.—Ibid.

[79] Medhurst, *China*, p. 327.

[80] *Correspondence of the American Board, China, 1831-1837.*

[81] *A Century of Protestant Missions in China*, p. 457.

[82] Medhurst, *China*, p. 329.

[83] *Chinese Repository*, Vol. 1, p. 376, Vol. 6, p. 549. John Ince was appointed to Penang in 1819 (Ibid., Vol. 3, p. 222) and in 1827 Mr. and Mrs. John Dyer settled there (Ibid., Vol. 3, p. 227).

[84] *A Century of Protestant Missions in China*, p. 457.

[85] Wylie, *Memorials of Protestant Missionaries*, pp. 97, 99; *Missionary Herald*, Vol. 35, p. 11, Vol. 36, p. 11; *Chinese Repository*, Vol. 16, pp. 12, 13.

year,[86] and by Josiah Goddard in 1840.[87]   The American Board also had a mission at Bangkok, its first representative being a physician, Bradley.[88]   In Burma, Boardman, an American Baptist, baptized a Chinese in 1828 and there seems to have been organized not long afterward a Chinese church of twenty members.[89]   In all these outlying Chinese communities Protestant missionaries, then, were learning the language, and from them they were to move into China Proper when more ports were opened. The permanent location of some of the missions and hence the later denominational map of China were to be determined in part by the dialects which the early missionaries had learned from emigrants in pre-treaty days.

SUMMARY

By 1840 the pressure of foreign trade on China had become so great that a war had broken out which was to alter the conditions of foreign residence and to inaugurate a new period in China's intercourse with the Occident.   The first stage in Protestant missions had passed.   In the little more than three decades which had elapsed since Morrison had landed at Canton the foundations of Protestant work had been laid, many of its methods had been outlined, and some of its characteristic features had made their appearance.   A missionary body numbering more than a score had begun the acquisition of the language and of a knowledge of China and the Chinese.   These missionaries were largely—as Protestant missionaries were mostly to be in the succeeding years —British and Americans of the type which had as a background the Evangelical Awakening.   The winning of Chinese to the Christian faith had been begun.   Some of this was by personal touch outside any institutional connection, but many of the first converts were either employees, like Liang A-fah, or students in Christian schools.   The total number of baptized was less than a hundred.[90]   They were largely from the classes which had commercial contact with the foreigner and were not from the group which ruled the Empire.   It was a humble beginning, but among

[86] Dean, *China Mission,* p. 359.
[87] Ibid., p. 279.
[88] Tracy, *History of the American Board,* p. 257.
[89] Sisson in *Missions,* Sept. 1924, p. 448; King, *Memoir of George Dana Boardman,* etc., pp. 181-186.   I have been unable to find other evidence than Sisson for this church, but Boardman records the baptism of at least one other Chinese.
[90] Medhurst, *China,* pp. 361, 362.

these early Protestant Christians were men of good quality. The most prominent, Liang A-fah, appears to have been an eminently worthy and devoted pioneer. A beginning had been made in the preparation of literature. The Bible had been translated, and while revision of the existing versions was urgently needed and would have to be done again and again, the preliminary steps, while necessarily imperfect, had been taken. Much other literature in Chinese had been prepared and already it was being widely distributed. Literature on China, too, was being produced in English, a foretaste of the part which Protestant missionaries were to have in interpreting China to Great Britain and America. Dictionaries and other materials were being prepared which were later to be of great service in introducing missionaries to China. Hospitals and schools had been founded. Even at their inception medical and educational activities were not maintained entirely or even always chiefly for the purpose of leading Chinese to accept the Christian faith. They had also as objectives the introduction to the Empire of those phases of Occidental culture which would make for the improvement of the physical and intellectual condition of the nation. The religious purpose was placed first, but, whether rightly or wrongly, the Christian message was believed also to include the other. Already it was possible dimly to foresee the large institutions which Protestants were to establish and the many angles from which they were to touch Chinese life.

CHAPTER XIV

THE FIRST WAR BETWEEN CHINA AND GREAT BRITAIN AND ITS AFTERMATH (1839-1855)

THE WARS AND TREATIES OF 1839-1844

FROM the vantage point of nearly a century it is apparent that the restrictions under which intercourse was carried on between foreigners and Chinese in the early part of the nineteenth century were foredoomed. The Occidental nations, expanding under the impulse of the Industrial Revolution, would demand greater freedom for trade, more privileges for their citizens, and diplomatic relations like those existing between themselves. Whether right or wrong, these demands were inevitable and resistance to them would be futile and possibly disastrous. Only the outlines of the struggle and those results which were important for the missionary enterprise need concern us here. The contest had, in the main, two stages. The first began in the eighteen thirties and culminated in a war between China and the chief commercial power, Great Britain, and in a series of treaties with Western nations. These treaties proved satisfactory neither to China nor to Westerners and another period of friction followed which, like the first, ended in war. The second war lasted from 1856 to 1860 and in it Great Britain and France joined forces against China. It led to another group of treaties (1858-1860), which proved fairly acceptable to Westerners and which, together with the earlier ones, defined the status of foreigners and the methods of intercourse with them which in their essential features remain largely in force to-day (1928). So far as missions have been protected by treaties, it is upon those of 1858 and 1860 that they have been chiefly dependent.

The underlying cause of the first war between Great Britain and China was, as has been suggested, the growing pressure of British trade and the dissatisfaction of British merchants with the conditions under which that trade was carried on. The British and Chinese differed in their conceptions of law and justice, and the former objected to the existing restrictions on residence and commerce and to the unwillingness of Chinese officials to deal on equal terms with the representatives of the British Government. The immediate occasion which brought these issues to a head was the attempt of the Chinese Government to stamp out the importation of opium. The difficulties over regulations of trade and residence had become acute early in the eighteen thirties, but the crisis over opium did not occur until 1839. War was begun in that year. It was almost entirely on the sea and was very one-sided. For months it was not waged vigorously and was interrupted by attempts at negotiations. The British seized several points along the coast, chiefly Hongkong and Chusan, and finally, in 1842, obtained the Treaty of Nanking, and in 1843 a supplementary treaty. Other Western powers, principally the Americans (1844) and the French (1844), took the opportunity to obtain treaties. The provisions of these documents which chiefly affected missions were as follows:

First. The Island of Hongkong was ceded to Great Britain, and five ports, Canton, Amoy, Foochow, Ningpo, and Shanghai, were opened to foreign residence and trade.

Second. Extraterritoriality was inaugurated. Henceforth foreigners were to be tried under their own laws and officials, and if they were plaintiffs their officials were to have the right of seeing that justice was done them in the Chinese courts.

Third. Foreigners were given permission to study the Chinese language.

Fourth. A most favored nation clause promised that privileges given to one treaty power would be granted to the others.

Fifth. If foreigners attempted to travel outside the ports, they were to be arrested and taken to the nearest consul.

Sixth. Little was said about religion, except that in the American and French treaties permission was given to foreigners to build houses, hospitals, schools, and places of worship in the open ports.

EDICTS OF TOLERATION

While nothing specific about missions was said in the formal treaties, the French envoy, Lagrené, had asked that a toleration clause be included. The French Government was making itself the champion of Catholic missions throughout the non-Occidental world and assumed in China the place once held by Portugal, not attempting, as had the other, to control the patronage to episcopal sees nor to dictate what missionaries should be allowed, but championing much more vigorously the cause of missionaries and insisting on the observance by the Chinese of such privileges as were granted.   Lagrené did not succeed in writing toleration into the French treaty, but he did obtain through the Chinese commissioner, Ch'i Ying, two imperial edicts which placed Roman Catholicism in a somewhat less unfavorable position than it had been in during the preceding century.   Ch'i Ying saw more clearly than did most Chinese and Manchu officials the necessity of making concessions to Europeans.[1]

The first edict, issued in December, 1844, gave consent to the erection of churches in the open ports and granted to Chinese permission to practice Roman Catholicism.   Foreigners were, however, forbidden to travel outside the five ports to propagate their faith.   If they disobeyed, they were, as the treaties provided, to be arrested and sent to one of their consuls.[2]   Ch'i Ying is said to have assured Lagrené that if missionaries were prudent, officials would not take notice of their presence in the interior.[3] The edict did not include Protestants, but the following year a supplementary decree was obtained which put them on an equal footing with the Roman Catholics.[4]   The second edict was issued in February, 1846.   It more specifically granted to Roman Catholics exemption from the previous penalties against them and confirmed them in the liberty of exercising their faith.   Those churches which had been built in the time of K'ang Hsi and had since been confiscated, except those transformed into temples and private dwellings, were to be restored to the Christians.   All attempts, however, to use the Catholic name to cloak crime or sedition were forbidden, and the prohibition on the travel of missionaries outside the treaty ports was reaffirmed.[5]

These treaties and the subsequent decrees obviously made conditions somewhat more favorable for missions and especially for those of Roman Catholics.   From the standpoint of the mission-

[1] *Chinese Repository*, Vol. 14, pp. 195-199.
[2] Morse, *International Relations of the Chinese Empire*, Vol. 1, pp. 91, 331, 692.
[3] Servière, *Histoire de la mission du Kiangnan*, Vol. 1, pp. 128-133.
[4] Morse, op. cit., Vol. 1, p. 332.
[5] Ibid., Vol. 1, pp. 91, 331, 692; *Chinese Repository*, Vol. 15, p. 155; Tobar, *Kiao-ou Ki-lio*, pp. 8, 9.

ary, to be sure, they were far from ideal. Both edicts and treaties were dependent for their enforcement largely upon the good-will of local officials and gentry, and since they had been the penalty for defeat in war there was at the most half-hearted compliance with them. Peking was not eager to enforce them and, especially after the accession of Hsien Fêng in 1850 and the degradation of Ch'i Ying, it was quite willing to have them ignored. In the interior persecutions still occurred and there were delays in opening some of the five ports. Even had the treaties and edicts been strictly observed, foreign missionaries had the legal right to live and to work only in five cities. However, toleration for Chinese Christians was at least promised, missionaries had been assured the privilege of residing and carrying on their activities in five centers, and in Hongkong, where a Chinese city was rapidly rising under the British flag, missions enjoyed complete freedom. Extraterritoriality, moreover, by putting the foreigner outside the reach of Chinese law and placing him under his own officials, gave him a certain assurance of safety.

It may be open to debate whether representatives of Jesus ought to have accepted privileges wrung from a nation by force of arms. It is probably even more a question whether they ought to have given their countenance to the negotiations which obtained these privileges for them. Missionaries and their advocates in Europe and America, however, appear to have been troubled little if any by these doubts. The opium traffic was vigorously criticized,[6] and, especially in the United States, condemnation was freely expressed for what was conceived as being the object of the war, the forcing of opium upon China.[7] No one, however, seems seriously to have challenged the right of the British to compel China to open her doors or the propriety of missionaries accepting the opportunities thus obtained. Missionaries or former missionaries served as interpreters and secretaries in negotiating

[6] *Chinese Repository*, Vol. 5, pp. 297-305, Vol. 8, pp. 310-317. An interesting example of this is D. Matheson, who came to China in 1837 as a merchant, was made a partner in the firm of Jardine, Matheson and Company, and then, in 1849, resigned from the firm because it was engaged in the opium traffic. He was later active in missions and was a member of the Committee of Foreign Missions of the English Presbyterian Church. In 1892 or so he was the chairman of the executive committee of the Society for the Suppression of the Opium Trade.— *State Papers of Great Britain, China*, No. 3, 1868-9, p. 24. *First Report of the Royal Commission on Opium*, London, 1894, pp. 57-59, 164.
[7] Latourette, *History of Early Relations between the U. S. and China*, pp. 125, 126.

each of the three main treaties—Gützlaff for the British, Bridgman and Parker for the Americans, and Callery for the French.[8]
In both Catholic and Protestant circles the treaties were welcomed
as marking a new era in missions and advantage was at once
taken of them.

ROMAN CATHOLIC MISSIONS

Under the impulse of revived religious life in Europe, Roman
Catholic work had begun, even before the treaties, to show signs
of growth.   Additional missionaries were sent.[9]   Rome recognized the need for better episcopal supervision and created new
vicariates apostolic—in 1838 one for Chêkiang and Kiangsi,[10]
one for the provinces of Hunan and Hupeh,[11] another for the
district north of the Great Wall,[12] and in 1839 one for Shantung.[13]   In 1840 a vicar apostolic was authorized for Mongolia,
and Yünnan was separated from Szechwan.[14]   In 1841 Hongkong
was made a prefecture apostolic.[15]   In 1840 three Jesuits came
out to revive the work of their Society.   In 1814 the Society of
Jesus had been restored by the Pope and for several years before
1840 the Chinese Christians in the lower part of the Yangtze
Valley, and Besi, the administrator of the diocese of Nanking, had
been requesting that the Jesuits take charge of this field of their
former triumphs.[16]   Both the Society and the Propaganda complied and the three pioneers of the renewed mission reached
Shanghai, after some delays, in 1841 or 1842.[17]

Persecution was by no means past, however.   The Chino-
British war revived official suspicion of foreigners and Chinese
Christians, and the imperial edicts of proscription are said to
have been renewed.[18]   In 1839 and 1840 the scattered groups in

[8] Encyclopædia Sinica, pp. 221, 284; Senate Documents 67, 28th Congress, 2d
Session, p. 38.   Callery seems to have ceased to be a missionary by this time, but
the others were still active as such.
[9] In 1836 two new Lazarists arrived in China, in 1831 one, in 1839 five, in
1840 two.—Catalogue des prêtres, clercs et frères de la Congregation de la Mission
qui ont travaillé en Chine depuis 1697.
[10] Moidrey, La hiér. cath. en Chine, etc., p. 135.
[11] Ibid., p. 85.
[12] Ibid., p. 114.
[13] Ibid., p. 62.
[14] Ibid., p. 117, 153.
[15] Ibid., p. 83.
[16] Moidrey, op. cit., p. 188; Brouillon, La mission du Kiangnan, 1842-1855,
p. 47; Piolet, Les mis. cath. franç. au XIXme siècle, p. 175.
[17] Ibid.
[18] Delamare from Szechwan, Sept. 12, 1840, in Annales de la propagation de
la foi, Vol. 14, p. 314.

Hukwang were set upon. Agatha Ho, who had dedicated herself to the Church, was, with two other Catholics, banished to Tartary,[19] and a Lazarist, the frail but heroic Perboyre, was executed in Wuchang (September 11, 1840).[20]   In 1838 persecutions occurred in Chihli and Shensi, and in 1842 Paul Yü, a member of the imperial family, died in prison for the Faith.[21]   From about 1836 to 1840 there was persecution of the Dominican mission in Fukien.[22]   The days of the martyrs were not yet done.

The treaties of 1842-1844 brought some relief and the decrees of 1844 and 1846 were partly put into force, both to the benefit and the detriment of Roman Catholic missionaries.   In Shanghai, Besi with the aid of the consuls obtained property in place of that once owned by the Church.[23]   At least two of the viceroys, those of Kwangtung and Kwangsi and of Kiangnan and Kiangsi, published the imperial edict of toleration.[24]   However, missionaries detected in the interior were sent to the coast as the edicts had specified.   Thus in 1847 or 1848 the Franciscans Rizzolati and Novella were expelled from Hukwang,[25] a Lazarist was deported from Chihli,[26] and the Lazarists Gabet and Huc, after making a remarkable journey across North China to Lhasa (1844-1846), were arrested and sent to the coast.[27]

GIFTS, NEW ORGANIZATIONS

With the interest created in Roman Catholic circles by the partial opening of China the sums allocated to the Empire increased and bodies heretofore not represented sent out missionaries.   In 1843 the Society for the Propagation of the Faith set

[19] *Annales de la propagation de la foi*, Vol. 20, p. 112.
[20] Wegener, *Heroes of the Mission Field*, pp. 257-298; *Catholic Encyclopedia*, Vol. 9, p. 746, Vol. 12, p. 490; Montgesty and Gilmore, *Two Vincentian Martyrs*, pp. 174, 175.
[21] Launay, *Les cinquante-deux serviteurs de Dieu*, pp. 388-390.
[22] Gentili, *Memoires di un missionario dominicano nella Cina*, Vol. 2, pp. 413-415.
[23] Piolet, op. cit., pp. 179, 180.
[24] Pauthier, *Proclamations du mandarin Ye et du vice-roi Ho*, passim.
[25] *Annales de la propagation de la foi*, Vol. 23, p. 53.
[26] Ibid., Vol. 19, pp. 73 et seq.
[27] Huc, *Journey Through the Chinese Empire*, passim; *Souvenirs d'un voyage dans la Tartarie et le Thibet pendant les années 1844, 1845, et 1846, par E. Huc. Nouvelle édition annotée et illustrée par J.-M. Planchet, Pekin, 1924.* The journey was apparently first directed toward Urga and then, due to a variety of circumstances, was diverted toward Lhasa. Huc later returned to France, left the Lazarists, and died in 1860. See a long article by Pelliot on Huc's trip and book in *T'oung Pao*, Vol. 24, pp. 133-177. Pelliot concludes that Huc's account is correct in its main features but is often inaccurate in details.

aside for China about 280,000 francs,[28] in 1845 about 304,000 francs,[29] in 1851 about 306,000 francs,[30] in 1854 about 311,000 francs,[31] and in 1859 about 540,000 francs.[32] In 1846 there arrived in Hongkong the initial contingent of what seems to have been the first European sisterhood to labor in China, the Sisters of St. Paul.[33] In 1847 twelve representatives of the Daughters of Charity sailed from France. Founded, like the Lazarists, by St. Vincent de Paul, it was fitting that this body should have in its initial company to China a sister of the Lazarist martyr Perboyre.[34] The first establishment of the Sisters of Charity was apparently in Ningpo, although they seem earlier to have gone to Macao. It was not until 1863 that they entered a second of the five ports, Shanghai.[35]

Representatives of a new organization of priests, the Seminary of Foreign Missions of Milan, also entered China. This body, modeled largely, as its name suggests, after the Missions Étrangères of Paris, was partly the outgrowth of the desire of Pius IX to have prosperous North Italy assume a larger share of the missionary burden of the Church. The chief founder was Angelo Ramazzotti, Bishop of Pavia, and under his leadership the seminary was opened in 1850. Like its Paris prototype, the Society was an association of secular priests and had for its center a training school for missionaries. Hongkong was assigned it by the Propaganda and its first representatives arrived in 1858.[36] Awakened Italy was taking a larger part in missions.

In addition to these two foreign organizations two new Chinese sisterhoods appeared, that of the Presentation, founded in 1855 with its mother house at Zikawei in Kiangsu, and that of the Holy Heart of Mary, founded in 1858 in Manchuria.[37] Thus did the long established custom of having Chinese women devote themselves to the Church begin to take more elaborate form.

[28] *Annales de la propagation de la foi,* Vol. 16.
[29] Ibid., Vol. 18.
[30] Ibid., Vol. 24, p. 155.
[31] Ibid., Vol. 27, p. 164.
[32] Ibid., Vol. 32, p. 154.
[33] *International Review of Missions,* Vol. 4, p. 467.
[34] Manna, *The Conversion of the Pagan World,* p. 167.
[35] *Encyclopædia Sinica,* p. 179; *The Christian Occupation of China,* p. 460.
[36] *Catholic Missions,* Vol. 12, pp. 29-36; Moidrey, *La hiér. cath. en Chine,* etc., pp. 201, 202.
[37] Arens, *Handbuch der katholischen Missionen,* p. 144.

THE JESUITS

Thanks to the partial toleration obtained through the imperial decrees, to the freedom in Hongkong and in the newly opened ports, and to the added interest in Europe, the years between the first and the second group of treaties were marked by growth in all the chief fields occupied by Roman Catholics. The first party of Jesuits was rapidly reënforced. From 1843 to 1857 inclusive fifty-eight joined the Society's mission in China, most of them Europeans.[38] This was greater than the total strength of the staff in the latter year, however, for the mortality was heavy.[39] Among the Jesuits were those who wished to renew the scientific mission in Peking which through the seventeenth and eighteenth centuries had been of such assistance to the Church, but counsels were divided, and the anti-foreign reaction at court which came with the accession of Hsien Fêng (1850) made the project impracticable.[40] Whether, had the ancient Peking mission been renewed in a modified form—a center of scientific investigation and foreign Christian scholarship in the capital and a means of approach to the Chinese official world—the progress and status of the Roman Catholic Church would have been greatly modified, must remain an interesting but debatable question.

The Jesuits established their headquarters, not at Peking, but at Zikawei. Zikawei was a happy choice, for it was on the outskirts of what was to be the greatest center of foreign trade, Shanghai, and it was also the ancestral village of that noted Chinese Christian of the early days of the Jesuit mission, Hsü Kuang-ch'i. Here was begun a school for boys and—after a famine in 1850—an orphanage for some of those whom the missionaries had rescued from death.[41]

One of the first cares of the Jesuits was to raise the quality of the life and faith of the Catholics of Kiangnan. After the enforced neglect of clerical ministration during the preceding

[38] *Catalogus patrum ac fratrum e Societate Jesu qui . . . in Sinis adlaboraverunt*, pp. 50 et seq.

[39] Servière, *Histoire de la mission du Kiangnan*, Vol. 1, pp. 159-165, Vol. 2, p. 91. In 1849 or 1850 the Jesuits had in Kiangnan twenty-six priests, four teachers, and five lay brothers.—*Annales de la propagation de la foi*, Vol. 22, p. 403.

[40] Servière, op. cit., Vol. 1, pp. 179-185.

[41] Servière, op. cit., Vol. 1, p. 210; Piolet, op. cit., p. 180; Brouillon, *La mission du Kiangnan, 1842-1856*, p. 98.

decades, the Christians were often in a deplorable state spiritually and some had apostatized.   Many of the wayward were reclaimed, marriages were revalidated, care was taken to see that baptism was properly performed, the Christians were visited regularly, instructed, and given the sacraments, and child engagements were forbidden, together with the custom of having the girl live before marriage in the home of the boy to whom she was betrothed.[42] For a time, as earlier, in default of regular episcopal ministrations, priests had often to administer confirmation.[43]

Schools were established.   Apparently these were only for the children of Christians and were for the purpose of giving instruction in the Christian faith and in the rudiments of Chinese.   A higher school was maintained at Zikawei and a seminary for preparation for the priesthood.[44]   Little or no attempt was made to introduce the Chinese to Occidental learning beyond that directly connected with the essentials of the Catholic faith.   Such an effort at that time would have made education by the Church extremely difficult or impossible.   Pupils would have been lost by a program which would not have fitted them for the normal life of the nation and which would even have lacked the attraction of the language of foreign commerce, English.   Students were, accordingly, educated primarily for a Chinese environment.[45]   By 1852 there were in Kiangnan seventy-eight schools containing twelve hundred and sixty pupils.[46]

The Jesuits did not confine themselves to improving the Christian community, but reached out for those who had not accepted the Faith.   In twelve months during 1854 and 1855, for instance, nearly two thousand adults were baptized in Kiangnan.[47]   The devotion of the missionaries, indeed, could not fail of results. One hears, for example, of a Father Laquez who won the affec-

---

[42] Servière, op. cit., Vol. 1, pp. 128-133, 222-250; *Annales de la propagation de la foi,* Vol. 18, pp. 265-269, Vol. 22, p. 204; Brouillon, op. cit., p. 54; Becker, *Joseph Gonnet,* pp. 13 et seq.

[43] Becker, op. cit., p. 13.

[44] Brouillon, op. cit., pp. 116-127; Servière, op. cit., Vol. 1, pp. 173, 210-222; Moges, *Recollections of Baron Gros's Embassy to China and Japan, 1857-1858,* pp. 189 et seq.; Brine, *The Taeping Rebellion,* pp. 52-54.   The school at Zikawei was long under the direction of Angelo Zottoli (1826-1902) who became a noted scholar.   His best-known work was his *Cursus litteraturæ Sinicæ. Encyclopædia Sinica,* p. 622.

[45] Moges, op. cit., pp. 189 et seq.

[46] Brouillon, op. cit., p. 224.

[47] Fournier in *Annales de la propagation de la foi,* Vol. 28, p. 210 (Sept. 29, 1855); Becker, *Joseph Gonnet,* pp. 25 et seq.

tion of a section of the army by caring for the wounded,[48] and of a Neapolitan, Rene Massa, who had given up fortune and career to become a missionary and who died of typhus while ministering to famine sufferers in Wuhu.[49]   Chinese lay Christians often supplemented the work of the clergy and were zealous in winning others to the Faith.[50]

The Jesuits concentrated their forces chiefly on Kiangnan and did not attempt to cover as large a portion of China as in the seventeenth and eighteenth centuries.   They did, however, assume responsibility for one other section.   For a time a few of them were in Shantung, but on the decision of the Propaganda to intrust each vicariate apostolic to only one society and to give Shantung to the Franciscans, they withdrew.[51]   When, in 1856, the diocese of Peking was suppressed and Chihli was divided into three vicariates apostolic, the Jesuits were assigned the southeastern one.   As in Kiangnan, they found that because of the enforced absence of clerical care, the Christians had deteriorated badly and possessed neither schools, orphanages, nor seminaries. Here, too, they entered vigorously upon their task and before long conditions began to improve.[52]

THE LAZARISTS

The Lazarists, who had attempted so valiantly to care for the vast districts assigned them in the eighteenth century, were relieved of part of their burden by the return of the Jesuits, but several large and important provinces were left them and in these by the aid of large reënforcements they were able to purify and enlarge the Church.   From 1846 to 1859 inclusive fifty-two Chinese and foreign priests were added to their ranks.[53]   For a time they continued in places in Kiangnan, but the responsibility for that section was soon placed entirely upon the Jesuits.[54]   For a time also they had some responsibility in Hunan and Hupeh, but before long their efforts were concentrated entirely upon Honan, Mongolia, Kiangsi, Chêkiang, and the larger part of Chihli.   In

---

[48] Fournier in op. cit., Vol. 28, p. 210 (from Zikawei, Sept. 29, 1855).
[49] Clavelin from Wuhu, May 24, 1855, in ibid., Vol. 28, pp. 436-438.
[50] Fournier, in ibid., Vol. 28, p. 212.
[51] Servière, op. cit., Vol. 1, pp. 149-154.
[52] Leroy, En Chine au Tché-ly S. E., p. 191.
[53] Catalogue des prêtres, clercs et frères de la Congreg. de la Mis. qui ont travaillé en Chine depuis 1697.
[54] Servière, op. cit., Vol. 1, pp. 65-90.

Honan, where the Christian communities had been especially decadent and many Catholics had lapsed into idolatry, a few years showed a marked improvement, both in the fidelity of the professing Christians and in the accession of new converts.[55]   In Mongolia a fairly strong Christian community had gathered in the early years of the century and conversions continued, chiefly among Chinese immigrants.[56]   In Chihli, where the Church had once been so vigorous and where it was later to have again one of its strongest centers, the years between the first and the second group of treaties appear to have been barren: it was not until after 1860 that the missionary was to have much freedom.   Dani-court, later to be vicar apostolic, was in Chusan from 1842 to 1846, and from 1846 to 1851 in Ningpo.[57]   By 1849 there were four foreign and six native priests in Kiangsi and three foreign and six native priests in Chêkiang.[58]   Each of these two provinces was estimated to have in that year forty-five hundred Roman Catholics and twenty chapels.[59]

THE DOMINICANS

The Spanish Dominicans, who for two centuries through many adversities had nurtured the Christians in Fukien, began at last to see the dawn of more promising days.   Between the publication of the imperial decrees and 1859 they built thirteen churches, among them one in Foochow and probably one at Amoy.[60]   In 1859, too, they reported over three thousand Christians in Foochow, seven-eighths of them among the large population that makes its home in boats.[61]   The removal of their business agent from Macao to Hongkong [62] probably gave the Dominicans somewhat greater freedom, and the withdrawal in 1850 of the Missions Étrangères from Hinghwa, the one remaining post occupied by that society in Fukien, and in 1863 of the Franciscans from

[55] Delaplace from Honan, Aug. 26, 1848, in *Annales de la propagation de la foi,* Vol. 23, pp. 27-39.
[56] Daguin from Siwang in Mongolia, Sept. 12, 1857, in *Annales de la propagation de la foi,* Vol. 32, p. 149.
[57] Danicourt, *Vie de Mgr. Danicourt,* passim.
[58] *Annales de la propagation de la foi,* Vol. 22, p. 22.
[59] Ibid.
[60] André-Marie, *Missions dominicaines dans l'Éxtrême-Orient,* Vol. 1, pp. 237-254.
[61] André-Marie, op. cit., Vol. 1, pp. 237-254.
[62] *Los Dominicos en el Oriente,* p. 109.

their two stations, gave to the Order of Preachers the sole spiritual oversight of Roman Catholic work in the province.[63]   In contrast with the Franciscans, they concentrated on a small area.

La Société des Missions Étrangères de Paris

The Paris Society, long so active in China and now reinvigorated by increased religious zeal in France, showed marked growth and assumed responsibility for much new territory.   In addition to its older fields it was given charge of Manchuria, almost virgin soil, and of Kwangsi and Kwangtung, including the island of Hainan.   Extensive journeys were made in Manchuria and some converts won.[64]   The two southern provinces, outside of Macao and possibly Canton, seem to have contained very few Roman Catholics in 1840.   Particularly in isolated Hainan and in turbulent Kwangsi was the task of reëstablishing the Church difficult and dangerous.[65]   In the districts longer occupied by the Society progress continued.   Huc, on his famous journey in the forties, found the Church more flourishing in Szechwan than elsewhere in China and drawing its members from better social classes.[66]   In 1848 the Vicar Apostolic reported the baptism in the province of eight hundred and eighty-eight adults and of over eighty-four thousand children in danger of death.[67]   In Kweichow, in spite of recent persecution, some gains were recorded, although the Christian communities remained small and struggling.[68]   In Yünnan there were a few Christians, but travel among them had to be carried on circumspectly and about 1846 a missionary, Vachal, was arrested and died in prison.[69]   In the forties the distant and alluring Tibet was intrusted to the Paris Society[70] and many heroic efforts to penetrate the great closed land followed.   Two priests, Krick and Bourry, endeavored to enter by way of Assam

---

[63] Moidrey, *Le hiér. cath. en Chine,* etc., p. 185.
[64] *Annales de la propagation de la foi,* Vol. 20, pp. 194-222, Vol. 22, pp. 26-70, Vol. 28, p. 29.
[65] Launay, *Mission du Koung-si,* pp. 23-94; *Annales de la propagation de la foi,* Vol. 24, pp. 40-55.
[66] Huc, *Journey Through the Chinese Empire,* Vol. 1, pp. 217, 310-311.
[67] Perrocheau, Sept. 4, 1848, in *Annales de la propagation de la foi,* Vol. 22, p. 127.
[68] Lyons from Kweichow, Sept. 16, 1882, in ibid., 1883, pp. 141-155; Albraud from Kweiyang, Aug. 17, 1847, in ibid., Vol. 20, pp. 276 et seq.
[69] Chauveau from Yünnan, Aug., 1851, in ibid., Vol. 24, pp. 261-264.
[70] Launay, *Hist. gén. de la Soc. des Missions-Étrangères,* Vol. 3, p. 290.

and the Brahmaputra, but were killed (1854).[71]   An attempt in 1857 by way of the Indus was blocked by savage tribes.[72]   Renou tried first by way of Szechwan and reached Batang, only to be arrested and sent to the coast.   He returned to the attempt by way of Yünnan.   This time he was more successful and for some years established himself at Bonga.[73]   In all these fields the representatives of the Society remembered that one of the primary objects of their organization had been to train a native clergy, and from the seminary in Penang Chinese priests continued to go forth to share the burdens of their European colleagues.

THE FRANCISCANS

The Franciscans were responsible for their old fields in Hunan, Hupeh, Shansi, Shensi, and Shantung.   In all these their path was made difficult by persecutions and an insufficient number of priests.   In 1852, however, the Vicar Apostolic in Shantung could report the baptism of one hundred adults in the past year and could speak of progress during the preceding nine years.[74]   Little growth could be reported from the other provinces.

SUMMARY

By 1858, then, in Manchuria and Mongolia and in all the Eighteen Provinces, with the possible exception of Kansu and Anhui, there were Chinese Roman Catholics ministered to by Chinese and foreign priests.   Even in mountainous Kweichow, in insurrection-ridden Kwangsi, and in far Yünnan there were missionaries and converts.   Remote Szechwan contained large and well cared for Christian communities and Tibet was beginning to know the patient and courageous efforts of pioneers.

CATHOLIC ECCLESIASTICAL ORGANIZATION

For the steadily growing Catholic missions Rome believed it necessary to provide more episcopal supervision.   This should not have been difficult, but the Portuguese authorities, although more

---

[71] *Annals of the Propagation of the Faith*, Vol. 22, pp. 263-279.
[72] Ibid., Vol. 22, pp. 263-279.
[73] Ibid., Vol. 22, pp. 263-279, Vol. 26, pp. 356-358; Piolet, *Les mis. cath. franç. au XIXme siècle*, pp. 332-342.
[74] Costellazzo, June 15, 1852, in *Annales de la propagation de la foi*, Vol. 25, p. 116; Bishop Giesen in Forsyth, *Shantung*, p. 164, says there were only three priests in the province in 1850.

incompetent than ever to man adequately the missions in China, offered vigorous opposition. They objected when Hongkong was made a prefecture apostolic and spitefully ordered the newly appointed prefect, a Frenchman, to leave Macao within twenty-four hours.[75] They protested when various provinces were separated from the dioceses of Nanking and Peking and they appointed to these sees two Portuguese Lazarists who gave Rome much annoyance.[76] Fruitless attempts were made to adjust the differences between Lisbon and Rome and it was not until late in the century that Portugal at last acquiesced to what by that time had become an accomplished fact.[77]

In spite of the opposition of Portugal, Rome continued to create new vicariates apostolic. Honan was so designated in 1844 and Kweichow in 1846. Shansi and Shensi were separated in 1844, Kiangsi and Chêkiang in 1846, and Hunan and Hupeh in 1856. In 1856 the old bishoprics of Nanking and Peking were suppressed and vicariates apostolic were substituted, three in Chihli and one in Kiangnan. Szechwan was divided in 1858 and again in 1860. In 1857 Tibet was made a vicariate, and in 1858 Kwangtung and Kwangsi were detached from the diocese of Macao and created a prefecture apostolic.[78]

In 1848 the Propaganda considered bringing together in a synod the vicars and prefects apostolic for a discussion of the problems common to China, but because of the danger of arousing suspicion among the Chinese by the simultaneous travel of so many foreigners from the interior the project was abandoned. However, in 1851 an unofficial synod was held in Shanghai and a program was recommended to Rome for the creation of a hierarchy like that in Europe. It was proposed that there should be archbishops and bishops in whose election both the Chinese and foreign clergy should join, and that either natives or Europeans should be eligible for the offices. The suggestion did not, apparently, meet with favor at Rome.[79] The synod also consid-

---

[75] Servière, *Histoire de la mission du Kiangnan*, Vol. 1, pp. 48 et seq.
[76] Ibid., Vol. 1, pp. 93-109; Moidrey, op. cit., p. 33.
[77] Moidrey, op. cit., p. 178; Launay, *Mission du Koung-si*, p. 96. Some difficulty existed, too, in Jesuit territory in defining the relation of a vicar apostolic to the Society and defining clearly the functions of a vicar apostolic in relation to those of the superiors of the Society.—Becker, *Joseph Gonnet*, pp. 40-53.
[78] Moidrey, op. cit., passim.
[79] Servière, op. cit., Vol. 1, pp. 189-195.

ered literature, the promotion of schools, the interest rate, and the problem presented by opium.[80]

PERSECUTIONS

The growth in Roman Catholic missions was inevitably attended by persecution. Full toleration had not been obtained, and even had it been officially granted there would have been unrest against missionaries and converts which most magistrates would have been slow to repress. Not only was Christianity disturbing to well established and cherished institutions and customs, but Roman Catholic practice gave rise to misunderstandings and sinister rumors. The baptism of infants in danger of death, for example, was being more and more stressed since the formation of the Society of the Holy Infancy and was popularly believed to be actuated by the basest motives. The foreigner and his assistants must surely desire the children's eyes or hearts for medicine, and since the rite was frequently followed shortly by the death of the infant the Catholics' guilt was held to be clear.[81] The chief basis of official opposition, however, seems still to have been the fear that the Christians, like so many other religious sects, might start rebellions. The fact that their rites had to be performed at least semi-secretly strengthened the suspicion.

About 1845 two Chinese priests and some students for the priesthood were arrested in Hukwang,[82] and in 1852 the head of the seminary at Hankow, a Chinese, was arrested and with him eight of his students and two catechists.[83]   In 1846 M. de la Brunière of the Paris Society was killed near Saghalin.[84]   In 1849 a mob attacked the residence of the Vicar Apostolic in Manchuria.[85]   In troubled Kweichow, Christians were in almost constant danger: in 1849 ten were in prison in Kweiyang,[86] in

[80] Ibid., Vol. 1, pp. 189-195. It is interesting to note that, contrary to what was soon to become the Protestant practice, the vicars apostolic were not in favor of putting into the local vernaculars either the catechism or the prayers. It was held that these could be explained to the people, but that if they were not in the literary style they would provoke the contempt of scholars.

[81] Servière, op. cit., Vol. 1, p. 141; Danicourt from Ningpo, May 6, 1854, in Annales de la propagation de la foi, Vol. 26, p. 431.

[82] Rizzolati from Wuchang, Oct. 20, 1845, in ibid., Vol. 18, pp. 347-361.

[83] Ibid. from Hongkong, Oct. 18, 1852, in ibid., Vol. 25, pp. 126-138.

[84] Launay, Hist. gén. de la Soc. des Missions-Étrangères, Vol. 3, pp. 198, 199.

[85] Berneux from Manchuria, May 10, 1851, in Annales de la propagation de la foi, Vol. 24, p. 112.

[86] Alband from Kweiyang, Jan. 12, 1849, in Annales de la propagation de la foi, Vol. 22, p. 360.

1856 Agnes Tsao Kuei died in jail,[87] and in 1858 a missionary wrote that in fifty years the province had seen forty persecutions, that two hundred Christians had been banished and twenty of the exiles had perished, that five Christians had been executed, that others had succumbed to their chains, and that the Catholics had often to hide in caves to escape their tormentors.[88] In 1850 the Vicar Apostolic of Shensi wrote of continued persecutions, although these, he said, were not as severe as formerly, for Christians, while threatened and imprisoned, were released after a time.[89] In 1850 a missionary of the Paris Society was deported from Kwangtung because of the secret baptism of the daughter of a minor official.[90] About the same time some Christians were arrested in Hainan and regained their liberty only through the intervention of the French Minister, M. de Bourboulon.[91] About 1855 Jacquemin was imprisoned in Kwangtung for several months.[92] In 1851 Hsien Fêng was reported to have issued a secret order which virtually annulled the edicts issued through Ch'i Ying. Certainly the Governor of Honan published an edict denouncing Christians as enemies of the public good and much suffering among the Catholics in the province followed.[93] Late in 1851 or early in 1852 a severe persecution was instituted in Hukwang, perhaps because of the same imperial order.[94] In 1851 persecution spread to Yünnan,[95] and in 1856 in that province there still were Christians in prison.[96] In 1853, when Catholics were being threatened in Mongolia, the Vicar Apostolic, Mgr. Mouly, gave himself up to the authorities to obtain protection for his flock and was deported to Shanghai.[97] The T'ai P'ing Rebellion, as we shall see again later, proved embarrassing to the Catholics. On the one hand the rebels often molested them, and on the other the imperial authorities suspected them of having

[87] Du Lys, *Un vrai frère mineur*, etc., p. 329. She was beatified by Rome in 1900.
[88] Perney from Rome, Sept. 14, 1858, in *Annales de la propagation de la foi*, Vol. 31, pp. 7-18, and June 17, 1857, in ibid., Vol. 31, p. 132.
[89] Letter of Chiais from Shensi, Sept. 22, 1850, in ibid., Vol. 23, p. 227.
[90] Letordu from Hongkong, Nov. 17, 1850, in ibid., Vol. 23, pp. 234-253.
[91] Launay, *Les cinquante-deux vénérables serviteurs de Dieu*, pp. 391-393.
[92] Jacquemin from Hongkong, Dec. 15, 1855, in *Annales de la propagation de la foi*, Vol. 28, p. 272.
[93] Delaplace from Kueitêfu, Dec. 5, 1851, in ibid., Vol. 25, pp. 102-114.
[94] Rizzolati from Hongkong, Feb. 18, 1852, in ibid., Vol. 24, pp. 272, 273.
[95] Chauveau from Yünnan, Oct. 20, 1851, in *Annales de la propagation de la foi*, Vol. 25, pp. 5-8.
[96] Ponsat, July 7, 1856, in ibid., Vol. 29, p. 352.
[97] *Annales de la propagation de la foi*, Vol. 41, p. 244.

some connection with the movement. We shall see, too, that the execution of a French priest, Chapdelaine, in Kwangsi in 1856, was the immediate cause of bringing France into war with China.

Annoying as were these persecutions, those in the decade after the decrees of 1844 and 1846 were not as severe as were many of preceding generations, and relatively few Chinese Christians and only three or four missionaries lost their lives. The French authorities, too, were beginning to assert themselves on behalf of their fellow nationals, and while their protectorate, later to be extended greatly, was of doubtful value in the production of Christian character, it was at least affording some security. Catholic missions, while still badly handicapped by the Chinese state, enjoyed more freedom than they had known for many decades.

PROTESTANT MISSIONS

If the years during and just after the war of 1839-1842 witnessed the rapid recovery of Roman Catholic missions they saw an even more marked growth of Protestant activity. During the hostilities between Great Britain and China, Protestant operations were partly interrupted. Canton was abandoned for the time and conditions were unsettled at Macao. The losses in these localities, however, were more than offset by gains elsewhere. Parker took the opportunity to return to America and to plead for more help for missions in China. He spoke in many different places and aroused much interest.[98] When Hongkong was seized and other ports were occupied, missionaries moved to them. For a time in 1840 and 1841 Lockhart of the London Missionary Society maintained a hospital on Chusan.[99] Dr. Benjamin Hobson of the same society kept a hospital open intermittently in Macao and had some medical work at Hongkong.[100] In February, 1842, Boone and the saintly but frail Abeel, who at last had returned to China, established themselves on the island of Kulangsu opposite Amoy.[101] Boone did not believe that many missionaries could yet be used, but he asked that three or four be sent to aid

[98] *Chinese Repository*, Vol. 8, pp. 624-627, Vol. 12, pp. 191-206; Graves, *Forty Years in China*, p. 240; Stevens, *Life of Parker*, passim.
[99] *Chinese Repository*, Vol. 10, pp. 448-453.
[100] Ibid., Vol. 10, p. 465.
[101] Boone from Macao, Sept. 15, 1841, and May 11, 1842, in *Spirit of Missions*, Vol. 7, pp. 53, 310; *Chinese Repository*, Vol. 11, p. 505.

him.[102]   In 1842 Dr. William Henry Cumming, unattached to any board, began medical practice on Kulangsu.[103]   William C. Milne, son of the elder Milne, was at Tinghai on Chusan in 1842. He there made the acquaintance of men from Ningpo who helped him to visit the latter city in that same year.[104]   Early in 1842 Roberts and then Shuck of the American Baptists removed to Hongkong and soon were followed by Dean from Bangkok.[105] Walter M. Lowrie, son of the distinguished secretary of the board of the American Presbyterians, arrived in Macao in May, 1842, and while studying the language canvassed the possibilities of removing the mission of his denomination from Singapore to one of the newly opened ports.[106]   Bridgman removed to Hongkong in July, 1842.[107]   In 1835 a representative of the Basel Mission visited Gützlaff at Macao and wrote home urging that two men be sent to help penetrate the interior.[108]   Missionaries were not waiting for formal treaties to enter the doors now partly opened to them.

The war aroused much interest among Protestant missionary leaders both at home and in China.   Some were very sanguine,[109] and others, although they saw that Protestant missions were still circumscribed, were eager to take advantage of the opportunities created by the treaties.[110]   There was a general movement to occupy Hongkong and the five treaty ports.   The societies which had had representatives among the Chinese before the war, moved to China many of their missionaries from Singapore, Malacca, Bangkok, Batavia, and Borneo, and despatched reënforcements, and other societies now for the first time sent agents to China.

THE LONDON MISSIONARY SOCIETY

The London Missionary Society, after its many years of prepa-

[102] Boone from Macao, June 11, 1841, in *Spirit of Missions,* Vol. 6, p. 366.
[103] *Chinese Recorder,* Vol. 5, p. 140; *Correspondence of the A. B. C. F. M.,* Foreign Vol. 4, p. 244.
[104] Milne, *Life in China,* passim.
[105] *Baptist Missionary Magazine,* Vol. 23, p. 21; *Niles Register,* Vol. 65, p. 68.
[106] *Chinese Repository,* Vol. 19, pp. 491-498; Dean, *The China Mission,* pp. 298-302.
[107] Bridgman, *Life of Bridgman,* p. 115.
[108] Schlatter, *Rudolf Lechler,* p. 16.
[109] Shuck wrote Sept. 14, 1842, from Hongkong: "The great land of heathenised infidelity has at last been thrown open."—*Correspondence of the American Baptist Missionary Union.*
[110] Bridgman from Macao, July 1, 1841, in *The Missionary Herald,* Vol. 38, p. 101.

ration and waiting, was eager to approach China through all the newly opened channels. At a conference in Hongkong in 1843 the decision was reached to inaugurate operations in as many of the six cities as possible.[111] By 1850 beginnings had been made in Hongkong and in three of the five ports. The press and the Anglo-Chinese College were moved from Malacca to Hongkong.[112] With the college (1843) came James Legge, who was to become widely known as a scholar—the translator into English of much of the Chinese classical literature and later Professor of Chinese at Oxford—and who was to give less spectacular but no less devoted service in training Chinese leadership and in laying the foundations of an important independent Chinese congregation in Hongkong. Legge was born in Scotland in 1815 and early gave promise of exceptional scholarly ability. For a time he was tempted to qualify for a professorship in Latin, but he abandoned that plan to enter a theological college and while there decided to become a missionary. Physicians at first advised him not to go to China but eventually withdrew their objections. Legge sailed in 1839, and, arriving in Malacca in the following year, became the Principal of the Anglo-Chinese College. At Hongkong, on the advice of his fellow missionaries, he transformed the school into an institution to train a Chinese clergy, for he and his colleagues were eager to see developed a strong native leadership for the Church.[113]

In 1844 John Stronach removed from Singapore to Amoy.[114] For a time the number of converts in the new station was small, but in 1855 seventy-seven were baptized. Among the earlier accessions was a military official who resigned from the army and for thirty-eight years served as a preacher.[115] Work was resumed in Canton, in spite of unrest, but it was not until 1859 that the London Society established a permanent mission there.[116] For a few months in 1842 and 1843 W. C. Milne was at Ningpo, but that city did not permanently become a station of the Soci-

---

[111] Lovett, *The History of the London Missionary Society*, Vol. 2, pp. 449, 450; *Report of the London Missionary Society, 1844*, pp. 38, 39.

[112] *China Mission Hand-book*, p. 7.

[113] Legge, *James Legge*, passim; Wylie, *Memorials of Protestant Missionaries*, etc., p. 118; *Chinese Repository*, Vol. 10, p. 53.

[114] Macgowan, *Christ or Confucius, Which? The Story of the Amoy Mission*, p. 48.

[115] *China Mission Hand-book*, Part 2, p. 9.

[116] *A Century of Protestant Missions in China*, p. 4; Lovett, *The History of the London Missionary Society*, Vol. 2, pp. 467-472.

ety.[117]   Shanghai, destined to be the most important of the new ports, was reached by Medhurst and Lockhart late in 1843.[118] Others soon followed—Milne in 1846,[119] William Muirhead in 1847,[120] Joseph Edkins in 1848,[121] and Griffith John in 1855.[122] All were names which later became household words in missionary circles. Edkins was to write extensively on China and Griffith John was to be a pioneer in Central China. The group was not content to confine its efforts to Shanghai and preaching tours were made in the surrounding country.[123]

THE AMERICAN BOARD OF COMMISSIONERS FOR FOREIGN MISSIONS

The missionaries of the American Board, like those of the London Missionary Society, wished to enter all the ports. At a meeting in Hongkong in July, 1843, they asked for men for each of the cities except Foochow and outlined a program of preaching, of revision and distribution of translations of the Bible, and of primary and higher education.[124] Like the representatives of the older sister society, too, they did not see their hopes fully realized. However, they did continue at Canton and established themselves in two other of the ports, Foochow and Amoy, and temporarily in Shanghai.

Kulangsu, across the harbor from Amoy, was, as we have seen, occupied by Abeel in 1842. He and Boone made tours on the mainland as far as twenty-five miles west of the city.[125] In 1844 Doty and Pohlman, who for some time had been in Borneo, removed to Amoy.[126] Not long afterward, in January, 1845, Abeel was forced by increasing ill-health to return to the United States.[127] In 1847 the mission was reënforced by the most notable figure of its pioneer years, John Van Nest Talmage.[128] All the missionaries of the American Board at Amoy were mem-

---

[117] *Chinese Repository*, Vol. 13, pp. 14 et seq.
[118] Milne, *Life in China*, p. 496; *Chinese Repository*, Vol. 18, pp. 515-525.
[119] Ibid.
[120] *China Mission Hand-book*, Part 2, p. 11.
[121] *A Century of Protestant Missions in China*, p. 4.
[122] Thompson, *Griffith John*, passim.
[123] *A Century of Protestant Missions in China*, pp. 4, 7.
[124] Bridgman, July 31, 1843, in *Missionary Herald*, Vol. 40, p. 32.
[125] Pitcher, *Fifty Years in Amoy*, pp. 58-61.
[126] Pitcher, op. cit., pp. 58-61.
[127] Williamson, *Memoirs of Abeel*, p. 256. Abeel died in 1846.
[128] Fagg, *Forty Years in South China*, passim; Good, *Famous Missionaries of the Reformed Church*, pp. 235-243.

bers of the (Dutch) Reformed Church in America, and when, in 1857, that denomination formed an independent board, the station was transferred to it.[129]

For some time after the arrival of the first foreign consul (1844) Foochow did not have a Protestant missionary. In January, 1847, however, there came Stephen Johnson, for some years one of the representatives of the American Board at Bangkok.[130] By 1857 the Foochow mission of the American Board had increased to five,[131] among them Justus Doolittle, and that year a Chinese church of four members was organized,[132] apparently the first Protestant one in the city.

Bridgman moved to Shanghai in 1847 to assist in the revision of the Scriptures, but until about 1854 the Board did not have there a formally organized mission. Bridgman had returned in 1853 from a visit to America and in 1854 he was joined by Henry Blodget and William Aitchison.[133] For two years Aitchison lived in P'ing Hu in Chêkiang, seventy miles from Shanghai. He also did much travelling through Kiangsu and other provinces.[134]

THE AMERICAN PRESBYTERIANS

We have already seen that the American Presbyterians had first joined in supporting the American Board, but that before the first treaties they had formed a society of their own and had sent missionaries to the Chinese in Singapore. We have seen, too, that Walter M. Lowrie was only waiting for the opening of more cities to move the base of the Society's operations to China itself. The first occupation of the new ports was by a physician, D. B. McCartee, who in 1844 effected an entrance into Ningpo.[135] He was soon joined by others and in May, 1845, a church was organized,[136] possibly the first Protestant one on Chinese soil. By 1851 the missionaries had begun to establish centers outside the city.[137] In 1855 and 1856 Rankin

[129] Pitcher, op. cit., p. 18.
[130] *Chinese Repository*, Vol. 16, p. 483.
[131] C. Hartwell in *Chinese Recorder*, Vol. 28, p. 422.
[132] Doolittle, *Social Life of the Chinese*, Vol. 1, p. 33.
[133] Blodget in *Sketches of the American Board Mission in China*, p. 13; Bridgman, *Life of Bridgman*, pp. 191-207; Bush, *Five Years in China, Life of William Aitchison*, passim.
[134] Bush, op. cit., passim.
[135] Garritt in *Jubilee Papers of the Central Presbyterian Mission, 1844-1894*, pp. 1-3.
[136] Ibid., p. 4.
[137] Ibid., pp. 10, 12.

of the Presbyterian mission and Cobbold of the Church Missionary Society made two extensive tours of Chêkiang, visiting thirteen walled cities.[138] To Ningpo came various Presbyterian missionaries whose names were long to be remembered—Walter M. Lowrie, who met an untimely death in 1847, killed by pirates off the coast,[139] and was replaced by his younger brother, Reuben;[140] John L. Nevius, who with his wife arrived in 1854 and was later to have a prominent part in establishing his society in Shantung;[141] and W. A. P. Martin, who reached the city in 1850 and was to have an honored career as missionary, author, and head of the Government's T'ung Wên College in Peking.[142] Ningpo saw the beginnings of several noteworthy careers.

Much difficulty was experienced in maintaining any kind of foreign foothold in Canton in the years between the first and second treaties, and it was not until 1846 or 1847, after some years of waiting at Macao, that the American Presbyterians were able to enter the city. A. P. Happer, William Speer, and John B. French then gained admission.[143] In the course of the next few years Parker's hospital was transferred to the Presbyterians and John G. Kerr, who was to be notable as the pioneer in the care for the insane, was placed in charge.[144] Speer, it is interesting to note, was later sent to California as a missionary to the Chinese who after the discovery of gold in that region migrated there in large numbers.[145] For years activities in Canton were hampered by bitter anti-foreign feeling and were to be interrupted again by the second war with Great Britain. It was against handicaps that Presbyterianism was planted in that city.

In 1850 Shanghai was entered for the American Presbyterians by Wight and Culbertson and here in time was to be moved the mission's press.[146]

---

[138] Moule, *Story of the Chehkiang Mission of the C. M. S.,* p. 7.
[139] *Memorials of Protestant Missionaries,* No. 67.
[140] Farnham in *Jubilee Papers of the Central China Presbyterian Mission.* The successor to Walter M. Lowrie may have been Henry V. Rankin.—*Memorial of Henry V. Rankin,* passim.
[141] Nevius, *Life of Nevius,* passim; Nevius, *Our Life in China,* passim.
[142] Martin, *A Cycle of Cathay,* passim.
[143] *China Mission Hand-book,* Part 2, p. 187.
[144] *A Century of Protestant Missions in China,* p. 380.
[145] Trumbull, *Old Time Student Volunteers,* pp. 169-175; *China Mission Year Book, 1915,* p. 552. See also, Noyes, *History of the South China Mission of the American Presbyterian Church,* pp. 7-20.
[146] *Jubilee Papers of the Central China Presbyterian Mission, 1844-1894,* pp. 38-45, 12; Robinson, *Missions in China,* p. 10.

THE PROTESTANT EPISCOPAL CHURCH IN THE UNITED STATES

It will be recalled that for some years the American Episcopalians had had representatives among the Chinese and that Boone, the only one remaining in the East at the time of the first treaties, had gone with Abeel to Amoy in 1842. In 1843 and 1844 Boone was in the United States, arousing interest in China. Six new missionaries were appointed by his board [147] and in 1844, after consultation with the Archbishop of Canterbury, he was consecrated missionary bishop.[148] When, in 1845, he arrived once more in China, he decided to move his mission to Shanghai, partly because the climate was more favorable than in Amoy, and partly because the latter city seemed already well occupied by Protestants.[149] In his report for 1850 Bishop Boone announced twelve baptisms during the previous year and a total of twenty-two in Shanghai. In Shanghai, too, was a school attended by about fifty children.[150] In September, 1851, the first deacon, Wang Chi, was ordained in Shanghai and three candidates for Holy Orders were reported.[151] Before 1860 the home board was already beginning to look toward the lower basin of the Yangtze with its populous plains and great cities as its future field.[152]

THE AMERICAN BAPTISTS

The missionaries of the American Baptists, like those of the London Missionary Society and the American Board, were eager to have representatives in Hongkong and in each of the five treaty ports. In May, 1843, they appealed to the Baptist churches in six American cities to send one missionary family to each of the six cities in China. The home board found its funds too curtailed to endorse the project.[153] Moreover, the Baptists in the Southern States withdrew from the general society in 1845 and formed their own board, and a division, although in China apparently an entirely amicable one, appeared in the Baptist

[147] *Spirit of Missions,* Vol. 9, p. 502.
[148] *Spirit of Missions,* Vol. 2, pp. 114, 146, Vol. 9, pp. 334, 507, Vol. 10, pp. 28, 250; Smith, *Narrative of an Exploring Visit to . . . China, 1844-1846,* p. 110.
[149] Smith, op. cit., p. 110; *Spirit of Missions,* Vol. 11, p. 85.
[150] *Spirit of Missions,* Vol. 16, p. 383.
[151] Ibid., Vol. 17, p. 403.
[152] Ibid., Vol. 24, p. 46.
[153] *Baptist Missionary Magazine,* Vol. 23, p. 315.

ranks.[154]   Four of the six centers were, however, occupied by 1856.

Roberts, Shuck, and Dean, as we have seen, moved to Hongkong. In May, 1843, a Baptist church was organized in Victoria —the new settlement on the island.[155]

To Ningpo in 1843 came D. J. MacGowan, a physician, and opened a hospital. He was there for only a few months, however, and when later he returned it was under another society.[156] The real founders of the Baptist mission in Ningpo were Mr. and Mrs. Edward C. Lord, who arrived in 1847, and Josiah Goddard, who came from Bangkok in 1848.[157] A church was organized about 1847, Goddard translated into the local dialect the New Testament and part of the Old Testament, and outposts were established at various points.[158]

Hongkong and the adjoining mainland and Ningpo became centers for the Northern Baptists. Canton and Shanghai on the other hand were occupied by Baptists from the Southern States. In 1845 Shuck moved from Hongkong to Canton and began with T. T. Devan a mission which was later to grow to large proportions.[159]   Here among others came R. H. Graves (in 1856), who was to do extensive literary work.[160]   In Shanghai the pioneers, Shuck, Toby, and Matthew T. Yates, and their wives, arrived in 1847.[161]   Yates was to have many years in China and was to be the outstanding figure in his denomination in Kiangsu. Of him Dr. Angell, President of the University of Michigan and American Minister to China, is reported to have said that "more than any other man in China, he has shown what the Gospel can do for the Chinese." [162]   Shuck, the pioneer in so many cities, was transferred in 1854 to California for service among the Chinese immigrants.[163]   To Shanghai there came in 1852 T. P. Crawford, who was later to move to Shantung and still

[154] Titterington, *A Century of Baptist Foreign Missions,* pp. 163-169. The Southern Baptists took over the work in Canton and the Northern Baptists that in Hongkong and Tie Chiu.—Ashmore, *The South China Mission of the American Baptist Foreign Mission Society,* p. 8.
[155] Ashmore, op. cit., p. 6.
[156] *Encyclopædia Sinica,* p. 321.
[157] Titterington, op. cit., pp. 171-178; *Memoirs of Lucy T. Lord,* passim.
[158] Titterington, op. cit., pp. 171-178.
[159] Ibid., pp. 163-169.
[160] *China Mission Hand-book,* Part 2, p. 241.
[161] Foster, *Fifty Years in China,* p. 55.
[162] Taylor, *The Story of Yates the Missionary,* passim.
[163] Graves, *Forty Years in China,* p. 169.

later was to share in a novel experiment in mission administration and the self-support of Chinese churches.[164]

THE CHURCH MISSIONARY SOCIETY

In 1836 the Church Missionary Society had begun an attempt to reach the Chinese in Singapore, but its representative, E. B. Squire, was compelled by his wife's health to return to Great Britain and the Society did not resume its mission among the Chinese until after the first treaties. In December, 1842, a committee of the Society issued a statement of the needs of China and the following March an anonymous gift of £6,000 came for work in the Empire.[165] In 1844 two men, George Smith and McClatchie, were sent to survey the field.[166] McClatchie settled in Shanghai[167] and Smith returned to Great Britain, partly because of ill-health.[168]

In 1848 two representatives of the Society, R. H. Cobbold and W. A. Russell, arrived in Ningpo and established the mission in that port[169] which was later to be extended to other parts of Chêkiang. They were aided by Miss Aldersey, who had removed from Batavia to China with the opening of the ports. Miss Aldersey served independently of any denominational board, but two of her adopted daughters married men who were later bishops,[170] and upon her retirement from China in 1860 she transferred part of her enterprise to the Society.[171]

In 1849 George Smith was consecrated Bishop of Victoria and sailed that year for China with a group of new recruits.[172] A station was begun at Foochow in 1850, but ill-health and death worked havoc with those sent, converts were slow in coming, and for a time there was thought of discontinuing it. It was not until after 1860 that permanency and success were assured.[173]

The other foreign missionary agency of the Church of Eng-

---

[164] Foster, *Fifty Years in China* (the life of T. P. Crawford), passim.
[165] Stock, *History of the Church Missionary Society*, Vol. 1, p. 472; Smith, *Narrative of an Exploratory Visit to . . . China . . . 1844-1846,* passim.
[166] Stock, op. cit., Vol. 1, p. 472; Smith, op. cit., passim.
[167] Stock, op. cit., Vol. 1, p. 472.
[168] Ibid., Vol. 1, p. 472.
[169] *China Mission Hand-book,* Part 2, p. 27.
[170] Nevius, *Life of Nevius,* p. 133.
[171] Stock, op. cit., Vol. 2, p. 307.
[172] Stock, op. cit., Vol. 1, p. 473.
[173] Headland, *Brief Sketches of C. M. S. Missions,* Part 2, pp. 55-69; *China Mission Hand-book,* Part 2, p. 29.

land, the Society for the Propagation of the Gospel in Foreign Parts, did not at this time undertake a mission for the Chinese. In 1843, however, it sent a chaplain for the English in Hongkong [174] and it aided in raising funds for the Bishopric of Victoria and for Bishop Smith's missionary projects.[175]

GÜTZLAFF AND GERMAN SOCIETIES

Gützlaff, after sharing in the negotiation of the Treaty of Nanking, made his home at Hongkong and there elaborated a plan for the evangelization of China. He wished to have a German astronomer and mathematician gain access to Peking, perhaps to revive in a Protestant form the Roman Catholic scientific center of past centuries.[176] More especially, however, he hoped to penetrate the Empire by the agency of the Chinese themselves, and to establish in each province Christian bodies, or unions, which would be assisted by unions or associations in Europe.[177] This bold plan for having China reached rapidly by the Gospel and chiefly through the Chinese was most appealing, and to its execution Gützlaff brought devotion and enthusiasm. He gathered about him a group of Chinese, who first began work in Hongkong and on the adjoining mainland. By 1850 he had a staff of several scores of preachers and colporteurs and these were bringing him reports of the distribution of Scriptures and the formation of Christian nuclei in all the Eighteen Provinces except Kansu.[178]

Gützlaff wrote voluminously to Germany, describing his enterprise and urging support for it. Response came with remarkable promptness. In 1844 Dr. Barth of Calw began a monthly paper, *Morgenrot in China's Nacht,* presenting the needs of China and calling attention to Gützlaff's project.[179] The Rhenish Missionary Society sent Köster and Genähr, who arrived in 1847,[180] and in that year Rudolf Lechler and Hamberg [181] of

[174] Norris, *China*, p. 28.
[175] Pascoe, *Two Hundred Years of the S. P. G.*, Vol. 2, p. 704.
[176] *Geschichte der Missionen in China von ältesten Zeiten bis auf Gützlaff*, p. 72.
[177] Ibid. tells of how the Pomeranian "Verein für evangelische Missionen in China," formed in 1850, took Shansi as its special field; Gützlaff, *Abschiedswort an alle Chinesischen Vereine Europa's.*
[178] *Geschichte der Missionen in China*, etc., pp. 41-76.
[179] Schlatter, *Rudolf Lechler*, pp. 16 et seq.; Burkhardt, *Die evangelische Missionen in China und Japan*, p. 179.
[180] Letter from Gützlaff in *Geschichte der Missionen in China*, etc., pp. 34 et seq.   [181] Schlatter, op. cit., passim.

the Basel Missionary Society reached Hongkong. Some years earlier the Basel Society had considered appointing missionaries to China, but the war between China and Great Britain was in progress and not until after the first treaties did the time seem opportune.[182] A Berlin Missionary Society for China came into being to aid Gützlaff and in 1850 dispatched its first agent.[183] A Berlin Women's Missionary Society for China was also formed at the instance of Gützlaff and in 1851 sent a representative to Hongkong who began a mission for girls abandoned by their parents[184] which has continued to this day. In 1849 and 1850 Gützlaff was in Europe, giving an account of his activities, preaching, and organizing unions among which he divided responsibility for the various provinces of China.[185]

Unfortunately, while Gützlaff was proving so successful at home, in China it transpired that he had been the victim of his own enthusiasm and credulity. Those sent from Germany to aid him early suspected that many of his Chinese helpers were not really Christian, and while he was in Germany, Hamberg, who had been left in charge in Hongkong, discovered that he had been thoroughly deceived. The great majority of the "preachers" turned out to be opium-smokers and criminals, who, far from touring the Empire, were spending their time and Gützlaff's money in low dives. Literature, instead of being distributed, was usually sold to the printer and then resold to Gützlaff. Little if any travelling had been done outside Hongkong and the vicinity,[186] and only a small minority of the helpers were honest. On his return Gützlaff was confronted with the disheartening facts and planned more adequate supervision by Europeans. He did not live to retrieve his mistake, however, but died in 1851.[187]

Gützlaff's life had by no means been a failure, for much that was enduring came out of his efforts. Among his Chinese con-

---

[182] Schlatter, *Geschichte der Basler Mission,* Vol. 2, pp. 271-276; Schlatter, *Rudolf Lechler,* p. 16.
[183] *A Century of Protestant Missions in China,* p. 484.
[184] Ibid., p. 490.
[185] Burkhardt, op. cit., pp. 183-186. Some of Gützlaff's sermons are in Gützlaff, *Die Mission in China.*
[186] Burkhardt, op. cit., pp. 183-186; Foster, *Fifty Years in China,* p. 214; Schlatter, *Rudolf Lechler,* pp. 37 et seq.
[187] Schlatter, *Geschichte der Basler Mission,* Vol. 2, p. 285.

verts were some earnest and sincere men.[188]   He had, moreover,
been the means of bringing to China a number of able Germans
who were to lay the foundations of continuous and growing
missions.   By Christmas of 1850 there was a church in Hongkong with twenty-six communicants.[189]   By 1855 there had been
collected at Pukak a church of eighty-seven members.[190]   Lechler
and Hamberg decided to concentrate on the Hakkas, a distinct,
extensive, and vigorous group in South China.   They came in
touch with some of these in Hongkong and planned through
them later to reach the parent stocks on the mainland.[191]   By
1854 the Basel missionaries were maintaining one head station
and three outstations outside of Hongkong and had reported
two hundred and thirteen baptisms.[192]   Hamberg died in 1854
but Lechler was to live on into the next century and was to see
many of the dreams of the pioneers fulfilled.[193]

The various German groups whom Gützlaff had interested in
China, then, continued to labor after his death, although by
methods different from his.   Most of the home organizations
called into being by him eventually passed out of existence, but
the ones that antedated his efforts and whose attention he had
called to China—the Rhenish and the Basel Societies—continued
their operations and in time were joined by others.

While Gützlaff was in Germany in 1849 and 1850 he urged
the Moravian *Unitas Fratrum* to undertake work among the
Mongols.   This devoted body, so long experienced in missions
to the most difficult and remote regions, issued an appeal for
volunteers, and out of thirty who responded selected three.
These left Europe in 1853.   Their original plan was to reach
their field through Russia and Siberia, but they were unable to
procure passports and went instead by way of England and India
They arrived in Calcutta in 1853, but, blocked in their repeated
efforts to enter Tibet, they settled down in the Western Himalayas
to learn Hindustani, Tibetan, and Mongolian, against the time
when they might effect their original purpose.[194]

[188] Bentley, *Illustrious Chinese Christians,* p. 32.
[189] Burkhardt, op. cit., pp. 183-186.
[190] *Chinese Recorder,* Vol. 8, p. 48.
[191] Schlatter, *Rudolf Lechler,* passim.
[192] Ibid.   [193] Ibid.
[194] Schneider, *Working and Waiting for Tibet,* pp. iii-vi, 50-58; Hamilton, *A History of the Missions of the Moravian Church,* pp. 134, 135.

ENGLISH GENERAL BAPTISTS AND SEVENTH DAY BAPTISTS

Other Protestant societies of Europe and America were attracted by the opportunities brought by the first treaties and sent missionaries to China.   In 1845 the English General Baptists sent two representatives to Ningpo and began an enterprise which in the eighteen seventies they turned over to the English Methodists.[195]   Representatives of the Seventh Day Baptist Missionary Society, an American body, arrived in Shanghai in 1847 and by 1850 had organized a Chinese church.[196]

AMERICAN METHODISTS, NORTH AND SOUTH

The denominations which dated their origin from John Wesley were eventually to have a large part in missions in China, but they were the last of the major divisions of Protestantism to enter the country.   In 1835 or 1836 at Wesleyan University in Connecticut some American Methodists urged that a mission to the Chinese be begun and preliminary steps were taken to obtain funds.[197]   It was not until 1847, however, that the first missionaries were sent.   In that year J. D. Collins and M. C. White and their wives went to Foochow.[198]   Reënforcements followed, but there were many discouragements and a heavy toll of illness. It was not until 1857 that the first convert was baptized [199] and it was nearly as long before the first church building was erected.[200]   By the close of the second decade of the mission, however, a church membership of four hundred and fifty-four had been gathered.[201]   No other provinces were entered by the Methodists of the Northern States until well along in the eighteen sixties.

The Methodists of the Southern States separated from those of the North in 1844.   In that year they began planning for China and in 1846 at their first general conference a mission to

[195] *A Century of Protestant Missions in China,* p. 69.
[196] Ibid., p. 344.
[197] Reid and Gracey, *Missions and Missionary Society of the Methodist Episcopal Church,* Vol. 1, pp. 411, 412.
[198] Ibid., Vol. 1, pp. 411 et seq.
[199] Ibid., Vol. 1, pp. 428-436.
[200] Ibid., Vol. 1, pp. 428-436.
[201] Hart, *Virgil C. Hart,* pp. 43, 44.

the Middle Kingdom was unanimously endorsed.[202]   The first missionaries, Charles Taylor and Benjamin Jenkins, arrived in Shanghai in 1848.[203]

ENGLISH WESLEYANS

The English Wesleyans first entered China when in 1850 George Piercy came to Hongkong at his own expense, hoping that his denomination might later undertake missions in the Middle Kingdom.   He went to Canton in 1851 and, the Wesleyan Methodist Missionary Society having decided to begin operations in China, he was accepted by that body (1853).   In 1853 the Society sent out, also to Canton, W. R. Beach and Josiah Cox.   Beach soon (1856) withdrew and became an Anglican chaplain, but Piercy and Cox, aided by reënforcements, laid the foundations of a permanent mission.   After 1860 Cox was to extend to Central China the activities of the Society.[204]

ENGLISH PRESBYTERIANS

The Presbyterians of England organized themselves into a national body between 1836 and 1845.[205]   One of their earliest undertakings as a united organization was foreign missions, and since Hongkong and the five ports had recently been opened and the Church of Scotland and the Free Church were burdened with commitments elsewhere and the problems attendant upon the recent separation of the two bodies, the English Presbyterians decided to send to China their first missionaries.[206]   Their initial appointee, William C. Burns, sailed in 1847.   The son of a minister, at the age of sixteen or seventeen Burns had given himself completely to the Christian way of life, and, abandoning his earlier plans for a legal career, had decided to enter the ministry.   This decision was followed in his early twenties by a determination to become a missionary.   While waiting for the

---

[202] *Work and Progress in China of the Methodist Episcopal Church, South,* p. 5; Cannon, *A History of Southern Methodist Missions,* p. 95.   In 1848 there was formed The Ladies' China Missionary Society of Baltimore, primarily to help raise funds.—Underhill in *International Review of Missions,* Vol 14, p. 381.

[203] *Work and Progress in China of the Methodist Episcopal Church, South; A Century of Protestant Missions in China,* p. 411; Cannon, op. cit., p. 96.

[204] Cornaby, *The Call of Cathay,* p. 116; Findlay and Holdsworth, *The History of the Wesleyan Methodist Missionary Society,* Vol. 5, pp. 432-439.

[205] Johnston, *China and Formosa,* pp. 2, 3.

[206] Ibid., p. 4.

way to open to go abroad, a religious awakening broke out under his preaching and for about eight years he was a travelling evangelist in Scotland, Ireland, and Canada. He did not forget his purpose, however, and asked his church to send him to India. No opening appeared there, and since for some time the English Presbyterians had been looking in vain for a man to open their mission to China, he accepted appointment under them.

Now began what must often have been for Burns irksome and discouraging years. From great audiences, popularity, and large visible results, in his early thirties he had to settle down to the patient study of a difficult language and to years of seemingly fruitless effort. His courage and faith met the test; he achieved a remarkable fluency in Chinese and laid the foundations for the main centers of the work of his board in China. He always remained a wanderer. For a time, while learning the language, he was at Hongkong. He was not content to remain there, and after a survey of part of the neighboring mainland he followed James H. Young, a medical missionary, to Amoy. From there he began to itinerate in the adjoining country and after seven years in China without a convert, at last he saw results and by 1854 had baptized a score or more in several places not far from Amoy.[207]   In 1854 he and Young visited Scotland. Young died[208] but in 1855 Burns returned, bringing with him Carstairs Douglas.[209]   David Sandeman, who followed in 1856, died of cholera in 1858.[210]   Burns, under the urge of his roving spirit, first attempted to go to Nanking to visit the T'ai P'ing rebels— that group so strangely influenced by Christian teachings—and then, when he was turned back by the Manchu forces, went to Swatow (1856) and began preaching there and in the neighboring Ch'aochou. It was at Ch'aochou, it will be recalled, that the Jesuits, more than two and a half centuries before, had founded one of their earliest missions. Here Burns was arrested with two Chinese assistants and was sent to the British Consul at the nearest open port, Canton. He returned to Swatow to obtain the release of the two Chinese,[211] but was not there long.

[207] Burns, *Memoir of W. C. Burns,* passim; Johnston, op. cit., pp. 7-10; Matheson, *Narrative of the English Presbyterian Mission,* pp. 1-21; Smith, *Uplift of China,* pp. 131-136.
[208] Matheson, op. cit., pp. 17, 18.
[209] Ibid., pp. 17, 18.
[210] Bonar, *Memoir of David Sandeman,* passim.
[211] Matheson, op. cit., p. 26.

He remained in and near Amoy and Swatow until 1863, when he went to Peking. He died in 1868 at Newchwang, where he had gone in 1867 in an attempt to establish a mission in Manchuria.[212]

Although Burns, with all his devotion and ability, had never been content to stay long in any one place, the foundations had been well enough laid by him to be built upon successfully by his successors. Those in and around Amoy patiently nourished the Christian communities in the effort to make them as soon as possible self-governing, self-supporting, and self-propagating. To this end they endeavored to train a Chinese ministry and, at Amoy, to labor in close coöperation with the other Protestant bodies.[213]

As we shall see later, it was at Amoy, earlier than anywhere else in China, that the goal of independence was attained for a fairly large group of Christians. Continuous work at Swatow was begun in 1858 [214] and in Manchuria Irish and Scotch Presbyterians were later to enter the door which at his death Burns was trying to open.

OTHER SOCIETIES

The other societies which entered China during these years were either to go out of existence or to postpone permanent efforts. Partly as a result of a visit of Gützlaff to England in 1849 or 1850 a Chinese Evangelization Society was formed. This organization, like most of those which arose in response to Gützlaff's appeal, was short-lived. Even more than the others, however, it was to be a precursor of extensive and permanent effort, for under it there went out, in 1853, J. Hudson Taylor, who was to prove one of the greatest missionaries that the Church has known.[215]

The Norwegian Missionary Society sent a representative to China in 1847, but after a short time it decided to concentrate on Africa. Not until 1889 or 1890 did it make further attempts to establish itself in the Middle Kingdom.[216] The Missionary Society of Lund entered China in 1849, but one of its agents was

[212] Burns, op. cit., passim.
[213] Johnston, op. cit., pp. 120, 198, 206.
[214] Ibid., p. 148.
[215] A Century of Protestant Missions in China, p. 135.
[216] Gotteberg, Ti Aar i Hunan, p. 7.

killed and the other returned home in 1850 or 1851.[217]   For a time in the fifties the Cassel Missionary Society had a representative in China.[218]   The Netherlands Chinese Evangelization Society sent a man to China in 1855, but in 1858 he resigned and joined the (English) Baptist Missionary Society.[219]

Coöperation Among Protestants
Translation of the Scriptures

The coming of these many Protestant societies to Hongkong and the five open ports might have been expected to be attended by unfriendly and wasteful competition and by confusion in the minds of the Chinese.   Some little of these there probably was, but by no means as much as might be supposed.   The six cities were fairly large and in the pioneer days of Protestant effort offered ample room for the activities of all who came.   Moreover, in spite of distinct names and differing forms of ecclesiastical organization, there was, in the main, agreement as to what was essential in the Christian life.   Since Protestant foreign missions arose largely out of the Pietist and Evangelical movements, with few if any exceptions missionaries were agreed that becoming a Christian involved an experience of conversion.   Missionaries were unanimous in the conviction, too, that true conversion must be the introduction to a definite type of life, a life in which spiritual and moral transformation was being wrought.   Not only was there accord arising out of the common background of the Pietist and Evangelical movements, but numbers of the societies had similar polities and doctrines.   The London Missionary Society and the American Board represented churches which were practically identical in all except nationality.   The (Dutch) Reformed and the various Presbyterian societies could easily coöperate, and in theology they and the two Congregational bodies were practically agreed.   At Amoy, for example, from almost the beginning close coöperation existed among the three bodies working there—the London Missionary Society, the (Dutch) Reformed Mission, and the English Presbyterians.   The two latter strove to build one Chinese church.   The German societies had much in common, and so did the two Anglican organizations.   Sharp differences over home issues put a gulf

[217] *A Century of Protestant Missions in China,* pp. 521, 645.
[218] Ibid, p. 645.
[219] Ibid., p. 645.

between some of the Baptists and between some of the Methodists, but two of the differing societies were seldom to be found in the same port.

In spite of the community of interest and purpose among Protestants, little attempt was made to approach China unitedly. No conferences were held to discuss common problems and to plan a campaign for reaching the entire country. In one field, however, that of Bible translation, some coöperation was obviously essential. Uniformity in the terms used for God, for example, was highly desirable, so that Protestant missionaries might not seem to be talking about different deities. Missionaries who knew Chinese well were, moreover, not so numerous but that it was important to have the collaboration of all the best scholars in the production of a version in the literary style. The vernaculars in the regions in and around the five ports were so different that a uniform version in the language of every day was out of the question, but the literary language was the same throughout the Empire and all the educated could be reached by means of it. The literati were so exacting in matters of style that a translation of the Scriptures, if it were not to repel them as hopelessly barbarous, must be the fruit of the labor of all the best scholarship that the missionary body could provide.

In 1843 a meeting was held in Hongkong at which various American and British societies were represented.[220] Here a plan was devised for coöperation. In each of the six cities the missionary body was to perform specific portions of the task, each part was then to be sent to the other centers for correction, and the manuscripts were to undergo a final revision at the hands of a committee to which the missionaries in Hongkong and in each of the five ports were to elect delegates.

The project was not fully carried out. Not all the local committees made rapid progress. Then, too, some differences developed over terms. At the outset the Baptists had wished a word for baptism which would definitely connote immersion, and the others disagreed. All concurred, however, in a decision to proceed together to produce a version uniform except for this word and to leave each group to publish an edition with its own rendering of the term.[221] The delegates were eventually chosen

---

[220] *Chinese Repository*, Vol. 12, pp. 551 et seq.
[221] Ibid., Vol. 12, pp. 551 et seq.

and met in Shanghai in 1847. The committee had as members during all or some of its existence Medhurst, J. Stronach, Milne, Bridgman, Boone, Shuck, Lowrie, and Culbertson, most of them men of long experience in China.[222] Not all were active and most of the burden was carried by Medhurst, Stronach, Milne, and Bridgman.[223]

On many matters the delegates were of one mind, but even before they met a decided difference developed over the proper Chinese terms for God (the Hebrew *Elohim* and the Greek Θεός) and the Holy Spirit, especially the former. Like the Roman Catholics, the Protestants found it difficult to agree as to which term had a sufficiently theistic significance to be taken over by the Christian Church. Various characters were proposed for God, but in time the discussion narrowed down to *Shen* and *Shang Ti*. The debate called forth a flood of articles and pamphlets, but led to no unanimity. When in 1850 the New Testament was finished, the committee decided to leave the terms Θεός and Πνεῦμα untranslated and to permit the various societies or agencies to fill in the Chinese term that each preferred.[224] The English on the whole favored *Shang Ti* and the Americans *Shen*.[225] The edition subsidized by the American Bible Society accordingly had the latter term and the ones aided by the British and Foreign Bible Society the former.[226]

The version of the Old Testament, like that of the New, was to have been undertaken by a committee made up of delegates chosen by Protestant missionaries in Hongkong and the five open ports. The group met, but such disagreement arose over the principles of translation that in the end two versions were produced, one by Medhurst, Stronach, and Milne, and another, in a somewhat simpler style and which aimed at accuracy rather than ease, by Bridgman and Culbertson. The former version was completed in 1852 or 1853.[227] The style was of the kind to appeal to the Chinese scholar, but it sacrificed accuracy for literary grace and was too classical for the majority of the church members.

[222] Williams, *Middle Kingdom,* Vol. 2, p. 364.
[223] Canton, *History of the British and Foreign Bible Society,* Vol. 2, p. 399.
[224] *Chinese Repository,* Vol. 19, p. 545.
[225] There were some who preferred the Catholic term, *T'ien Chu.* This was quite largely used in North China.
[226] Canton, op. cit., Vol. 2, pp. 398, 399.
[227] Williams, *Middle Kingdom,* Vol. 2, p. 364; Dwight, *Centennial History of the American Bible Society,* Vol. 1, p. 244.

The latter version, more exact in its translation and more easily comprehended by those of little education, but not having the literary elegance of the former, was completed in 1862.[228] Bridgman, with the aid of others, also completed an edition of the New Testament to correspond to that of the Old.[229]

Thus the hoped-for uniformity in a version of the Scriptures was not achieved. It was further disturbed by a revision of Marshman's translation. This was undertaken at the suggestion of the society of the Northern Baptists and was chiefly the work of Goddard, Lord, and Dean. The New Testament was published in 1853 and the Old Testament later.[230]

If, however, the project for a "Union Bible" was not entirely successful, it at least prevented an endless multiplication of effort, and the "Delegates' Version" of the New Testament was in much better literary taste than any which had preceded it and remains in use to-day.

METHODS OF PROTESTANT MISSIONARIES

If complete coöperation among the various societies had not been attained, the methods employed showed a striking similarity. These were largely an outgrowth of the ones that had been in use before the first treaties. Emphasis, of course, was placed upon means of winning Chinese to the Christian faith and of building up a responsible church membership. Within Hongkong and the treaty ports greater freedom of preaching and of personal approach to Chinese was now to be found than in Canton or Macao in pre-treaty days, and Protestant churches began to appear. Occasional journeys were made, too, as we have seen, outside the six cities.

Much attention continued to be paid to the preparation and distribution of literature, for not only were books and pamphlets needed for the rising churches, but the printed page was still the only channel of approach open to the vast majority of non-Christians. Some of this literary effort, the translation of the Bible into the book language, has just been recounted. Portions of the Scriptures were also translated into several dialects of the spoken language. The vernacular varied in each of the five treaty ports and access was already to be had to Mandarin-speak-

[228] Williams, op. cit., Vol. 2, p. 364; Dwight, op. cit., Vol. 1, p. 244.
[229] Bondfield in *China Mission Year Book, 1915*, p. 471.
[230] Ibid., p. 471; Foster, *Christian Progress in China*, p. 41.

ing peoples. Considering the small number of Protestant missionaries, then, the task of translation was by no means light. It had to be performed, however, for if the Scriptures were to be confined to the classical language they would be a closed book to the vast majority of the nation. Since, too, the Chinese character is vastly more difficult to learn than an alphabet, missionaries attempted to facilitate teaching Christians to read by writing the dialects with Roman letters. Medhurst and Stronach put the New Testament into Mandarin, using the Chinese characters, but their version was imperfect.[231] A romanization for the Amoy colloquial was devised in 1850 and the succeeding three years.[232] About the same time Crawford invented a phonetic system for the Shanghai dialect, but it was little used.[233] Shortly after 1850 the Ningpo dialect was romanized and parts of the Gospels and the liturgy of the Church of England were translated into it.[234] The full Bible seems not to have been translated as yet into any of the colloquials, either through the character or Roman letters.

By putting the Christian sacred book into the language of every day, and especially by employing romanization, the missionary was incurring the contempt of Chinese scholars, if, indeed, the latter ever deigned to notice the efforts of the barbarian priests. It was a daring and noble innovation, however—this attempt to introduce Christian literature to the masses who would never have the leisure to learn the complex literary language and to whom even the characters were a serious barrier. As an experiment in popular education it was unique in the history of China and it was indicative of one of the contributions which the nation might expect from the Protestant form of the Christian faith.

Other literature than the Bible was prepared in Chinese. There were, of course, religious books and pamphlets. Burns, for example, translated *Pilgrim's Progress* and prepared a number of hymns.[235] His years of intimate life with the Chinese had given him an unusual command of the language of the common

[231] Wherry in *Records of the Shanghai Conference, 1890*. The version was made about 1854.
[232] Pitcher, *In and About Amoy*, pp. 77, 197; *A Century of Protestant Missions in China*, p. 377.
[233] Foster, *Fifty Years in China*, p. 66.
[234] Moule, *Story of the Chehkiang Mission*, p. 34.
[235] Burns, *Memoir of W. C. Burns*, pp. 256, 257, 330.

people and his version of *Pilgrim's Progress* was to be long and deservedly popular.   Books for acquainting the Chinese with the Occident and its science and civilization were also translated or written.   Hobson put into Chinese a popular digest of European astronomy,[236] Muirhead translated Milner's *History of England* and prepared a geography, and Alexander Wylie published a compendium of arithmetic.[237]   At least one almanac was gotten out.[238]

Missionaries, too, were preparing dictionaries and grammars, works on special phases of Chinese life, and general books on the country.   These not only helped to introduce the younger missionaries to the people, the customs, the language, the history, and the religious beliefs of the Empire, but aided the non-missionary foreign resident to a more intelligent appreciation of the Middle Kingdom and increased the knowledge of China in the English-speaking world.   In 1848 S. Wells Williams published the first edition of what was long to be the standard general book in English on China, *The Middle Kingdom*,[239] and a few years later completed a dictionary of the Canton dialect Joseph Edkins began a career of distinguished scholarship.[240] The *Chinese Repository* was continued through 1851 and is a mine of information concerning China.   In 1847 Alexander Wylie came to Shanghai.   Wylie was salaried by the British and Foreign Bible Society and had charge of the press of the London Missionary Society.   Before sailing he had begun the study of Chinese, and in his thirty years of residence in the country of his adoption he was not only to achieve marked familiarity with the language, but he was to learn something of Manchu and Mongolian, to acquire an extensive knowledge of Chinese literature, and to be the author of many books, pamphlets, and articles both in English and in Chinese.[241]

Presses to make possible the publication of this literature were continued or founded.   The American Board and the London Missionary Society each maintained the printing establishments which they had earlier begun.   For a number of years the Lon-

[236] Wylie, *Notes on Chinese Literature*, p. 129.
[237] Lockhart, *Medical Missionary*, p. 342.
[238] *Chinese Repository*, Vol. 14, p. 136.
[239] Williams, *The Middle Kingdom*, Vol. 1, preface.
[240] *L. M. S. Chronicle*, Vol. 14 (New Series), pp. 242-244.
[241] Thomas in Wylie, *Chinese Researches*, pp. 1-18.

don Missionary Society had presses both in Hongkong and in Shanghai.[242] In 1844 the American Presbyterians started a press at Macao. It was soon (1845) transferred to Ningpo and in 1860 it was again moved, this time to Shanghai. William Gamble, who came out in 1858 to supervise it, was chiefly responsible for placing it firmly on its feet.[243]

Great emphasis continued to be placed upon the distribution of literature, especially the Bible. China was more accessible than it had been and yet, as we have said, was still so far from being opened that the printed page remained the only means of access to the major portion of the population. The British and Foreign and the American Bible Societies enlarged their subsidies to literature and eleven editions of the Delegates' Version appeared before 1859.[244] In the eighteen fifties, when the British and Foreign Bible Society was celebrating its semi-centennial and when many missionaries still believed that the T'ai P'ing Rebellion presaged a greatly expanded opportunity for Christian missions, over fifty thousand pounds were raised in Great Britain to print and distribute a million copies of the New Testament. Several hundred thousand of these were printed in Shanghai on huge presses driven by bullocks.[245] However, difficulty was encountered in circulating so large a number of Christian books, even though the rule was, as with all Protestant distribution of the Scriptures in China at this time, that they were to be free to all who were willing to accept them. The total number of New Testaments made possible was, therefore, not printed at once, and for twenty years the entire expenditure of the Society in China was covered by the fund.[246] The American Bible Society had its energies so engrossed in giving the Scriptures to the rapidly growing population of the United States that it could not make as large donations to China as did its sister society, but it contributed generously toward the cost of the revised Bible.[247]

Schools, as we have seen, were one of the earliest methods

[242] *A Century of Protestant Missions in China,* p. 625.
[243] Smith, *Rex Christus,* p. 196; Robinson, *Missions in China,* p. 13; *The Mission Press in China,* Chapters I-IV.
[244] *British and Foreign Bible Society Historical Catalogue of Printed Bibles,* Part 2.
[245] *A Century of Protestant Missions in China,* p. 635.
[246] Canton, *History of the British and Foreign Bible Society,* Vol. 2, pp. 448-450, Vol. 3, p. 434.
[247] Dwight, op. cit., Vol. 1, p. 244.

employed by Protestant missionaries and had been begun long before the treaties of 1842 and 1844. Under the new conditions some of the older institutions disappeared. The London Missionary Society permitted the general work of the Anglo-Chinese College—that not continued in the theological college—to be absorbed into the educational system planned by the British authorities for Hongkong,[248] and the school maintained by the Morrison Education Society passed out of existence about 1849.[249] Other schools were founded, however, and even more emphasis was placed upon education than before 1842. Miss Aldersey began in Ningpo a school for girls, and when she retired from active service her institution was merged into the educational program which by that time had been started by the American Presbyterians.[250] In 1845 the Presbyterians began in Ningpo a boarding school for boys, and apparently decided to teach English in it and to lay down as a qualification to those training for the ministry the ability to read that language easily.[251] The romanization which was early devised for the Ningpo colloquial seems to have been taught in all the mission schools in the city.[252] In 1845 the American Presbyterians began a boarding school for boys in Macao but soon removed it to Canton.[253] In 1850 the Church Missionary Society began in Hongkong a school, later St. Paul's College, for the training of catechists and clergy.[254] In 1851 the American Methodists opened in Foochow a day school for girls. A foundling hospital followed, and in 1859 a boarding school for girls.[255] In the same city the American Board had a school from almost the inception of its mission. About 1851 the Protestant Episcopalians began in Shanghai an institution for boys which was later to be the foundation of St. John's University.[256] In Amoy there arrived in 1853 a Mr. Johnston whom the English Presbyterians had sent with the hope

[248] *A Century of Protestant Missions in China,* p. 11.
[249] Yung Wing, *My Life in China and America,* pp. 19-33; Lockhart, *The Medical Missionary in China,* p. 142.
[250] Martin, *A Cycle of Cathay,* p. 207; Milne, *Life in China,* p. 257; Speer, *A Missionary Pioneer in the Far East,* pp. 73, 93; Garritt in *Jubilee Papers of the Central China Presbyterian Mission,* p. 5. Part of her other work, as we have seen, was taken over by the Church Missionary Society.
[251] Garritt, op. cit., p. 5.
[252] Ibid., p. 9.
[253] *China Mission Hand-book,* Part 2, p. 189.
[254] Stock, *History of the Church Missionary Society,* Vol. 2, p. 293.
[255] Maclay, *Life among the Chinese,* pp. 242, 255.
[256] Luella Miner in *China Mission Year Book, 1918,* p. 322.

that he might begin the type of education that Alexander Duff had initiated in India. The time was not ripe for that kind of experiment in China, but education was carried on in Amoy in other forms.[257]

This list, while by no means exhaustive, indicates the place that the missionaries gave to the school. As a means of winning converts, of educating Chinese assistants and clergy, and of training the Christian community, it was already an integral part of the Protestant missionary program. A church of literate members, able to read the Bible for themselves, was one of the earliest objects of the missionaries' endeavors.

Since the schools were maintained by the distrusted foreigner and were not preparatory for the coveted degrees obtained through the civil service examinations, it was but natural that for the most part only those who could not afford the more desired training sent their children to them.[258] The day was far in the future when education by Occidentals was to prove a recognized asset. The education conducted by Protestant missionaries was, however, emphasizing certain features which were to be prominent in the China of the twentieth century—literacy for all and by means of the vernacular, and schools for girls as well as for boys.

Side by side with the teacher the medical missionary was frequently to be found. Before the last of the treaties of 1842-1844 had been signed, medical practice had been begun either permanently or intermittently in Canton, Macao, Hongkong, Amoy, Chusan, and Ningpo. In 1843 the report of the Medical Missionary Society for China showed that Parker had reopened his hospital at Canton (November 21, 1842), that Lockhart had opened a hospital at Shanghai (January, 1844), that Hobson had inaugurated one in Hongkong (June, 1843), that Macgowan had begun medical practice at Ningpo (November, 1843), and that J. C. Hepburn, an American Presbyterian, had undertaken similar work at Amoy.[259] In 1844 D. B. McCartee, a physician, entered Ningpo.[260] In 1846, 1847, or 1848, Hobson opened a hospital in Canton outside the foreign concessions.[261] Happer, a repre-

[257] Johnston, *China and Formosa*, pp. 80-92.
[258] Brine, *The Taeping Rebellion*, p. 61.
[259] *Chinese Repository*, Vol. 13, pp. 111, 369-376.
[260] Speer, *A Missionary Pioneer in the Far East*, passim.
[261] *Chinese Repository*, Vol. 19, pp. 253-280; Smith, *Rex Christus*, p. 138.

sentative of the American Presbyterians, had already, in 1851, begun a dispensary there.[262]   In 1850 Welton of the Church Missionary Society arrived at Foochow, the first medical missionary in that port.[263]   Hobson published at Canton in 1851 a treatise on anatomy—a precursor of the many books on Western medical science which Protestant missionaries were to put into Chinese—and followed it later with books on surgery, medicine, and midwifery.[264]   With these came the beginning of a new medical nomenclature.[265]   The medical missionary was conceiving of his function as being the removal of prejudice against his clerical colleagues, bringing Chinese in touch with the Christian message, the relief of some of the physical distress in China, and making accessible to the Chinese the best of Western medical science.[266]

As compared with Roman Catholic missions, the Protestant enterprise met relatively little active persecution.   There was, to be sure, opposition, and many petty annoyances were placed in the way of the missionary and his Chinese followers and associates.   Dr. Happer, for example, attempted to enter Canton in 1844 but was unable to obtain a building or even to remain in the city.   For two years he had to content himself at Macao as best he could.[267]   Burns was repeatedly hampered, partly because he often went outside the treaty ports.   Little actual violence was offered to the persons of missionaries, however. The most noteworthy exception was in 1848, when Medhurst, Lockhart, and Muirhead, while distributing tracts near Shanghai, were attacked by a mob and were all three injured.   They were probably violating at least the spirit of the treaties by being outside the port, but the Chinese authorities were under legal obligation to give them protection.   The British consul acted vigorously, for he believed the future security of other foreigners to be at stake, and in time some of the culprits were brought to justice.[268] As a rule, however, Protestants, unlike Roman Catholic mission-

[262] China Mission Hand-book, Part 2, p. 190.
[263] Stock and McClelland, For Christ in Fuh-kien, pp. 2-9; Lockhart, Medical Missionary in China, p. 216.
[264] China Mission Hand-book, Part 2, p. 5; Balme, China and Modern Medicine, pp. 46-48.
[265] Balme, op. cit., pp. 46-48.
[266] Lockhart, op. cit., p. 134.
[267] Trumbull, Old Time Student Volunteers, p. 165.
[268] Chinese Repository, Vol. 17, p. 151; Lane-Poole, The Life of Sir Harry Parkes, Vol. 1, pp. 126, 127; Scarth, Twelve Years in China, p. 135.

aries, kept within the limits of the treaty ports and so were relatively safe.

SUMMARY

The treaties of 1842 and 1844 had helped to make possible greater prosperity for both Roman Catholic and Protestant missions. Partial toleration throughout the Empire, freedom in six cities for missionary activity, and the extraterritorial status for the citizens of treaty powers, had partially opened the door. To the Roman Catholic the years between the first and second group of treaties were a time when the faith of the older Christian communities was being revived and purified and active attempts were being resumed to reach the non-Christian population. With the advantage of the many centers in the interior founded and maintained by missionaries of preceding generations, he could look for a larger numerical growth in membership than could the Protestant. The Protestants, although confined almost exclusively to Hongkong and the five treaty ports, were preparing for further expansion by producing literature, experimenting with missionary methods, and acquiring a body of foreign agents trained in the language and experienced in the customs of the country. The Protestant communities, while totalling only a few hundred, were increasing rapidly. Starting from such small beginnings, Protestants were making proportionately a more rapid growth than were Catholics. They were touching Chinese life at more angles and were the interpreters to China of more phases of Western civilization. In spite of the short time that they had been in China, they already gave promise of having not only an active part in the inevitable alteration of the older Chinese culture, but of helping in many wholesome ways in the process of transition. It was to be many years, however, before the accumulating pressure of the Occident was to bring about the transformation of the fabric of Chinese life. For more than a generation missionaries were to face the opposition of a political, intellectual, social, and religious structure which seemingly had in it no room either for them or for their message.

CHAPTER XV

ALTHOUGH, under the treaties of 1842 and 1844, missionaries were rapidly extending their operations, they still labored under severe handicaps. They possessed no legal right to purchase property or to reside or even to travel outside Hongkong, Macao, and the five treaty ports. While they might evade the notice of officials or enjoy tacit toleration, any foothold beyond these seven cities was insecure. Work in the interior and even on the coast north of the Yangtze was uncertain and perilous. Toleration had been obtained for the Christians, but this rested upon imperial edicts and at any time a strong anti-foreign reaction at court might annul it and initiate fresh persecution. Between the close of 1855 and the close of 1860 events were to occur which were to make it possible to extend missions throughout the Empire and to place under the guarantee of treaties the activities of the missionary and the faith of the Chinese Christians.

In the friction and the war which brought about these changes, missions had only a comparatively minor part. The major causes were the growing pressure of the trade of the Occident and the dissatisfaction of both foreigners and Chinese with the treaties of 1842 and 1844. With the industrial expansion in Europe, commerce with China, as with the rest of the world, increased rapidly. Foreign merchants wished more open ports and greater privileges and were impatient with the reluctance of the Chinese to fulfil the promises already made. Diplomatic intercourse, too, could never be carried on satisfactorily while the imperial government insisted on regarding all foreign nations as tributary and declined to receive at Peking or to send to other capitals resident official representatives. The Chinese, on the other hand, remembered that the treaties had been granted under duress and were often reluctant to carry out their provisions. The importation of opium continued, to the annoyance of some of the authorities. At Canton particularly there were many difficulties, and the patience of both foreign and Chinese officials was often near the breaking point. Because of her large commerce, Great Britain was naturally more concerned than were the other powers.

With relations so strained, almost any incident might have precipitated a war, and it chanced—as has so often been the case under similar circumstances—that hostilities broke out over a trifling occurrence. From a Chinese-owned craft, the lorcha *Arrow*, which was under Hongkong registry, the Canton authorities, while professing to look for pirates, on October 8, 1856, hauled down the British flag, and removed twelve of the crew, all Chinese. The case was one which in more quiet times and with better provisions for inter-governmental intercourse could easily have been peacefully settled. However, the British were in no temper for further delay or compromise and made demands which the Chinese, who were equally obdurate, refused to grant. Hostilities followed, but they were not pursued whole-heartedly by either country and for the time were confined largely to the vicinity of Canton.[1]

The United States, but for a resolutely pacific policy at Washington, would probably have been drawn into the war. Many Americans were engaged in commerce with China, some of them wished vigorous action, and late in 1856 the forts below Canton fired on the American flag and in return were silenced by the guns of the American squadron. Authorities at Washington, however, were unwilling to sanction a further use of force and contented themselves with sending a plenipotentiary, William B. Reed, to watch developments and to obtain, if possible, a revised treaty with China.[2] Russia, who had been extending her power in the north, also preserved the appearance of friendship, but, fishing in the troubled waters, sought treaty concessions.

It remained for France to join with Great Britain. The two powers had been allies in the war which was just closing in the Crimea, and the French Emperor, Napoleon III, was quite willing

---

[1] Morse, *The International Relations of the Chinese Empire,* Vol. 1, pp. 418-437.

[2] Morse, op. cit., Vol. 1, pp. 432-434, 485, 486; Dennett, *Americans in Eastern Asia,* pp. 292-306. Revision after twelve years had been provided for in the American treaty of 1844.

to see further coöperation. He was, moreover, eager to enter on any policy abroad which promised prestige for his reign, and was happy if, at the same time, he could demonstrate his loyalty to the Roman Catholic Church and so insure the continuation of its powerful support. France, then, associated herself with Great Britain in the war. A *casus belli* was found in an unfortunate incident which had occurred before the *Arrow* affair, the judicial murder of a French priest, Auguste Chapdelaine, in Kwangsi in February, 1856. Chapdelaine was a missionary of the Missions Étrangères of Paris and had been in Kwangsi for a little over two years. That province was notoriously turbulent and for some years had been overrun by rebels. The T'ai P'ing insurrection had recently arisen there and was devastating some of the best provinces of the Empire. If the local authorities knew of the connection between Christianity and the rebellion, they might well be excused if they viewed with suspicion the presence of a missionary. Whatever their reasons, they arrested Chapdelaine and tried, tortured, and executed him.[3] When the French asked for the punishment of the offenders, the Viceroy of Kwangtung and Kwangsi gave them no satisfaction, and Paris and London were already contemplating joint action to obtain redress and a revision of the treaties when the *Arrow* crisis led Great Britain to open hostilities. From the beginning of the war, therefore, the two powers stood by each other.

Various reasons, among them the Sepoy Mutiny in India, led Great Britain and France to postpone a serious attack for over a year. Late in 1857, however, Canton was taken by assault, and the following spring the joint fleets moved northward to the mouth of the Peiho, the nearest accessible sea approach to Peking, to insist upon the revision of the treaties. When Peking still temporized, the Taku forts at the mouth of the river were stormed (May, 1858). The French and British ambassadors and the Russian and American envoys then proceeded to Tientsin and there met the imperial representatives whom the danger to the capital had at last induced the court to appoint.

THE TREATIES OF 1858

Of the negotiations which followed there is no need to tell

[3] Morse, op. cit., Vol. 1, pp. 480-483; *Annales de la propagation de la foi,* Vol. 43, pp. 171-207. The place was Silin. See also Wegener, *Heroes of the Mission Field,* pp. 51-69.

the full story. Some of the provisions of the treaties framed were, however, of great importance to missionaries, for by them was made possible the greatly increased activity of the Church. Those that most directly affected missions and missionaries were as follows:

First. A number of additional ports were opened to foreign trade and residence: Newchwang in Manchuria, Chefoo in Shantung, T'aisan and Tamsui in Formosa, Swatow in Kwangtung, Kiungchow in Hainan, and Nanking in Kiangsu. The issuance of passports to Nanking was to be delayed until the imperial authorities had taken the city from the T'ai P'ing rebels. The Yangtze River was opened to foreign trade, and it was provided that as soon as the revolt had been subdued, three cities, later to be determined, were to become "ports of entry and discharge." [4] The three decided upon were Hankow, Kiukiang, and Chinkiang. [5] All of them were strategically located.

Second. Foreigners were accorded the privilege of travelling in the Empire outside the treaty ports.

Third. The treaty powers were permitted to have diplomatic representatives in Peking.

Fourth. Indemnities were exacted (increased for Great Britain and France by the Conventions of 1860) and portions of them were later assigned by the respective governments to missions and missionaries. [6]

Fifth. Each of the four treaties contained a guarantee of the toleration of Christianity and a promise of protection in the exercise of their faith, not only to missionaries, but either explicitly or by implication to Chinese Christians. The Russians seem to have led the way. [7] In the treaty with them the Chinese Government agreed "not to persecute its Christian subjects for the exercise of the duties of their religion" and to give permission to a

[4] *Treaties between the Empire of China and Foreign Powers,* p. 13.
[5] Morse, op. cit., Vol. 1, p. 538.
[6] Morse, op. cit., Vol. 1, pp. 570, 615. Out of a total of $489,694.78 allowed to claimants from the indemnity allocated to the United States, $57,019.71 went to missionaries and missionary societies. This was chiefly for property destroyed in Canton in 1856.—United States *Executive Documents,* 3d Session, 40th Congress, pp. 14, 156 et seq. Out of the large indemnity paid to the British for losses in Canton, $2,466.63 was given to the Wesleyan mission, $18,464.20 to the Church Society, $2,839.98 to Rev. J. H. Gray, and $8,680.00 to the Seaman's Bethel.— Great Britain, *Accounts and Papers. State Papers,* 1871, Vol. 70. *China. Return Relative to Claims for Indemnity under the Convention of Peking, 1860.*
[7] Williams, *Life and Letters of S. Wells Williams,* p. 270.

fixed number of missionaries to travel in the interior to propagate their faith. There was also some regulation of the long established Russian ecclesiastical mission in Peking.[8] A section on Christianity was placed in the American treaty at the instance of the interpreters, S. Wells Williams and W. A. P. Martin, both of whom had come to China as missionaries. This declared that ". . . Any persons, whether citizen of the United States or Chinese convert, who . . . peaceably teach and practise the principles of Christianity, shall in no case be interfered with or molested."[9] The Chinese negotiators at first demurred on the ground that Protestant missionaries had their families with them and so must be restricted to the open ports, and Reed, the American envoy, was not disposed to be insistent. The interpreters, however, persisted and the paragraph was finally agreed upon.[10] A somewhat similar section, an abridgment of that in the American document,[11] was included in the British treaty.[12] The French treaty provided that "the members of all Christian communions" should "enjoy entire security for their persons, property, and the free exercise of their religious practices," and that protection should be given to missionaries travelling in the interior. It recognized the right of any person in China to embrace the Christian faith and provided for the abrogation of all edicts against Christianity.[13] Articles supplementary to the French treaty also promised punishment for the murderers of Chapdelaine.

It proved easier to draft and sign the treaties than to obtain their execution. When, in 1859, the representatives of the powers returned to exchange ratifications, the Chinese authorities, under pressure from recalcitrants at Peking, wished to modify the documents, especially those of the British and French, and to prevent the residence of foreign ministers in Peking. The Russians and Americans, by conforming in part to Chinese procedure, retained their treaties intact and exchanged ratifications. The

[8] Text of the Russian treaty in *Treaties between the Empire of China and Foreign Powers*, p. 103.

[9] *Treaties between the Empire of China and Foreign Powers*, p. 92.

[10] Williams, op. cit., pp. 270-282. Williams was, apparently, the one chiefly responsible for the clause. The form given in the text, an extract from the one finally adopted, differs quite a little from the one first proposed by the Americans.

[11] Williams, op. cit., p. 271.

[12] *Treaties between the Empire of China and Foreign Powers*, p. 12.

[13] Ibid., p. 62.

British and French envoys, however, were not willing to compromise, and the British forces attempted to open a way for them to Tientsin and Peking. The fleet was repulsed at the Taku forts, but in 1860 the French and English returned to the attack and fought their way through to the capital, capturing the city and sacking and destroying the summer palace.

THE CONVENTIONS OF 1860

At Peking additional conventions were agreed upon between China and the two powers. Most of the provisions of these documents, like those of 1858, did not particularly affect missions. Those of importance to missions were: first, the cession of Kowloon, a section of the mainland opposite Hongkong, to Great Britain; second, the opening of Tientsin to foreign trade and residence; and third, the affirmation in the French treaty of the imperial edict of 1846 which had promised to restore to the Catholics the religious and benevolent establishments that had been confiscated from them. The Chinese text of this last paragraph differed materially from the French. It promised that the toleration of Catholicism would be promulgated throughout all China, that those who illegally arrested Christians would be punished, that churches, schools, cemeteries, lands, and buildings taken from Catholics would be handed over to the French representative at Peking for the Christians in the localities concerned, and that it would be "permitted to French missionaries to rent and purchase land in all the provinces and to erect buildings thereon at pleasure." [14] The most important difference was the assurance to French missionaries of the privilege of acquiring land and erecting buildings anywhere in the provinces. Since the chief interpreter for the French was a missionary, Delamarre, it is supposed that he introduced the changes,[15] perhaps surreptitiously. The Chinese authorities agreed to the convention only because they could not help themselves, and they can scarcely be blamed for objecting later to carrying out provisions which appeared in but one version of the document—especially since the treaty of 1858 had given them ground for contending that the

[14] *Kiao-ou Ki-lio,* pp. 50, 51.
[15] Favier, *Peking,* Vol. 2, p. 227. For the question of responsibility for the Chinese version, see Gaillard, *Nankin port ouvert. Variétés sinologiques* No. 18, pp. 162-172. This is, of course, a Jesuit publication.

French and not the Chinese text was authoritative.[16]   Here was a source of friction which was not to be removed for many years.

Several of the treaties with other European governments that followed in the next few years included toleration clauses somewhat similar to those of 1858—that with Prussia in 1861, with the Netherlands in 1863,[17] with Denmark in 1863, with Holland in 1863, with Spain in 1864, with Belgium in 1865, with Italy in 1866, and with Portugal in 1887.[18]   None of them, however, contained any important additions to those in the treaties with the four major powers.

THE EFFECT OF THE TREATIES UPON MISSIONS

The treaties of 1858 and the conventions of 1860 revolutionized the status of missionaries and Chinese Christians and made possible a large expansion of the Church.   In the first place, the newly opened cities gave to the missionary additional centers at which he could reside and from which he could extend his activities into the surrounding country.   Since these were as far inland as Hankow and as far north as Newchwang, the main body of China and the Chinese for the first time was made really accessible to Protestants.   Now it was the central and northern regions that were the heart of the country, and here, if China was ever to be profoundly influenced by Christianity, the Church must be well established; the nation could never be adequately reached from ports on the south coast.   Protestants, therefore, found their opportunity more than doubled.   To the Roman Catholic missionary, too, the new ports were a boon, although, since he had long been in most of the provinces, their opening was not of such great importance.

In the second place, the permission to travel in the interior was a direct reversal of the earlier arrangement by which foreigners

[16] Article III of that treaty said: "Les communications officielles des agents diplomatiques et consulaires français avec les autorités chinoises seront écrites en français, mais seront accompanées pour faciliter le service, d'une traduction chinoise aussi exacte que possible. . . . Il est convenuqu jusqu'là, et en cas de dissidence dans l'interpretation à donner aux texte français et au texte chinois, au sujet des clauses arrêtées d'avance dans des conventions faites de commun accord, se sera le texte français qui devra prévaloir."—*Maritime Customs, Treaties, Conventions, &c., between China and Foreign States,* Vol. 1, p. 816.
[17] Hertslet, *China Treaties,* p. 409.
[18] *Kiao-ou Ki-lio,* pp. 51-55.

found beyond a certain distance from the treaty ports were to be arrested and conveyed to the nearest consul. Under this new provision, missionaries, both Roman Catholic and Protestant, were to cover in their itineraries the Eighteen Provinces and large portions of the dependencies. They might meet opposition from the populace, the local gentry, or even the officials, and Peking might at best give them only half-hearted support, but back of them were their governments. Western consuls and merchants were often lukewarm toward or antagonistic to the missionary, but if the Chinese denied him rights guaranteed to all foreigners, the security of the whole of foreign intercourse would suffer. Consuls and ministers had, therefore, even though often reluctantly, to insist that his treaty rights be respected.

In the third place, the missionary often found it possible to effect a residence and to acquire property not only in the open ports but in other cities and towns. These privileges were not specifically guaranteed in the treaties, but neither were they explicitly forbidden. The interpolated clause in the French convention of 1860 was a reed of dubious strength. In the Berthemy convention of 1865, as we shall see later, the Chinese authorities partially assented to it, but difficulty was frequently encountered in obtaining its enforcement. The government of the United States did not support Protestant missionaries in claiming under the most favored nation clauses the extension of its privileges to themselves.[19] The British authorities, moreover, declined to countenance the attempts to construe the clause in the treaty of 1858 which gave to English subjects the privilege of buying land and building or opening "houses, warehouses, churches, hospitals, or burial-grounds," "whether at ports or at other places," as a guarantee of that right outside the treaty ports. However, the

[19] For example, E. C. Lord, American Consul at Ningpo, said to Southern Presbyterian missionaries when the question was up of Chinese objections to a site which they owned in Hangchow: ". . . It is a settled question, so far as the Government of the United States is concerned, that missionaries have no treaty right to reside in China elsewhere than at the open ports. The matter has to some extent been misunderstood. But it is known now that the clause in the French treaty, from which it was supposed the right of missionaries to reside in the interior was derived, does not exist in the French text, which alone, in cases of discrepancy, is to be regarded as authoritative. Moreover, irrespective of the French treaty or any other, our Government has decided that it is impolitic to claim from the Chinese government rights for missionaries not claimed for other citizens. The right of missionaries to reside in Hangchow is only such as the Chinese give you. We are willing and pleased to have you reside there if you can do so with their consent."—Lord to Houston and Helm, Aug. 15, 1873, in *House Executive Documents, 2d Session, 43d Congress*, Vol. 1 (Foreign Relations), pp. 232-246.

treaties clearly promised missionaries and Chinese Christians protection in the propagation and practice of their faith, and in many localities the Chinese authorities permitted even Protestant missionaries to rent or buy land, sometimes in the name of a Chinese convert, sometimes in the name of their mission, and sometimes in their own names. The governments of Great Britain and the United States, while recognizing that such action was not specifically authorized by the treaties and originally discouraging it, came more and more to hold that, when Chinese officials had permitted the purchase of land outside the ports, missionaries were entitled to the aid of consuls and ministers in obtaining justice. British and American officials, therefore, often gave support to missionaries in maintaining a residence once effected and in retaining property leased or purchased.[20] While, then, until the American treaty of 1903, Protestant missionaries possessed no formal legal right to buy land in the interior (technically, "to rent and to lease in perpetuity"), and while a similar right claimed by French missionaries rested upon doubtful grounds, in practice foreign missionaries of both branches of the Church established themselves in the interior far outside the treaty ports.[21]

In the fourth place, the treaties placed not only missionaries but Chinese Christians under the ægis of foreign powers. This gave to converts a certain assurance of protection and stimulated the numerical growth of the Church. The provision had, however, implications and results which were, to say the least, unfortunate. It tended to remove Chinese Christians from the jurisdiction of their government and to make of Christian communities *imperia in imperio,* widely scattered enclaves under the defense of aliens. To be sure, it was only as protectors of the faith of the converts that a foreign power could legally intervene, but in almost any lawsuit persecution might be set up as the motive of the Christian's opponent, and the consul or the minister could, if he were so disposed, find occasion to interfere. Many Chinese, seeing the advantage to be obtained from powerful foreign backing, feigned conversion. More than an occasional missionary

[20] United States, *Foreign Relations, 1st Session, 44th Congress,* Vol. 1, p. 332.

[21] See Morse, *International Relations of the Chinese Empire,* Vol. 1, p 565, Vol. 2, pp. 220 et seq.; Koo, *The Status of Aliens in China,* pp. 315-334; Rawlinson in *Chinese Recorder,* Vol. 56, pp. 716-728; Willoughby, *Foreign Rights and Interests in China,* pp. 192-207; Tyau, *Legal Obligations Arising out of Treaty Obligations between China and Other States,* pp. 151-154, 182-185.

promised Chinese the support of his government to induce them to enter the Church, hoping that when once within its fold they—or at least their children—could be trained to lead worthy Christian lives. Chinese assistants, too, often without the missionary's knowledge, used the desire for foreign aid to swell the numbers of converts and so to present to their superiors the appearance of success.

The French Government was more disposed to take advantage of this provision than were the other powers, for it had a definite policy of enhancing its prestige by protecting Catholic missions. The representatives of Great Britain and the United States were, indeed, often reluctant to give support to missionaries, even when the latter were undoubtedly within their treaty rights. Catholic missionaries, too, were more willing to attract Chinese by the advantage of the foreign protectorate than were those of Protestant communions. However, Protestant missionaries and their agents were by no means entirely innocent.[22]

The results of the toleration clauses, then, were far from being always creditable to the name of Christ. It is scant comfort to point out that in other lands and ages—in the Roman Empire, for instance, and in Western Europe—converts had been attracted to the Church from motives which were a mixture of good and evil. Nor is it entirely satisfying to say that those drawn by unworthy motives may in time have become fairly creditable Christians. Moreover, even at its best, this foreign protectorate was a serious blow to the prestige and integrity of the Chinese state: in all of the provinces there were to be within a few years Christian converts and communities, and each of these was partially removed from the jurisdiction of the Chinese Government. Missionaries, especially Roman Catholic missionaries, in time exercised almost the authority of civil officials over their converts. The political disintegration that marked the beginning of the twentieth century would have come had the protectorate never existed, but to the latter must be laid in part, even if in very small part, responsibility for the anarchy of the third decade of the twentieth century. The Church had become a partner in Western imperialism and could not well disavow some responsibility for the consequences.

In the last place, the provision for the restoration to the Catho-

[22] See, for example, articles by Sheffield and Hoste in *Chinese Recorder*, Vol. 39, pp. 657-675, and Gibson, *Mission Problems and Mission Methods in South China*, pp. 299-312.

lics of confiscated buildings and lands was to prove a source of much irritation and ill-will. The property involved had often passed into the hands of innocent purchasers or had long been in public use. The restoration was brought about by pressure from the French authorities under the provisions of a treaty that had been extracted by force and could not but misrepresent the spirit of the founder of the faith for whose uses the property was held.

The treaties of 1858 and 1860, then, helped to make possible the foreign penetration of China by Occidental culture. In the treaty ports foreign communities arose, partly missionary, partly official, but usually chiefly commercial, and from them irradiated influences which within fifty years were to bring about a startling alteration in all phases of Chinese life. From 1860 to 1898 there was little rapid outward change in China or in her relations with Occidental culture. During these decades, however, the Empire was being quietly honeycombed, and under the ever accumulating pressure from without its resistance was eventually to crumble.

CHAPTER XVI

THE T'AI P'ING REBELLION

WE have said that missions were at times to prove a disintegrating factor in Chinese life. Before the second war with Great Britain had broken out there was already well in progress what was at once a spectacular example of this influence and one of the strangest incidents in the entire history of the spread of Christianity. This is not the place for a detailed account of the T'ai P'ing Rebellion, of its organization, its military operations, and its dramatic end. Enough of the story must be given, however, to show the part which the missionary enterprise played in the origin and progress of the revolt and in shaping the policies and the beliefs of leaders and followers.

HUNG HSIU-CH'ÜAN AND HIS VISIONS

In 1813, six years after Morrison arrived in China, there was born in Hua-hsien, in Kwangtung, about thirty miles from Canton, a man by the name of Hung Hsiu-ch'üan. He was from the Hakkas, that large and widely scattered group in Southeast China which, probably originally immigrants from the northern provinces, still boasts distinctive speech and customs. Hung was of relatively humble birth, but, with the ambition so common among even the poor of China, his family managed to give him the education necessary to compete for the coveted literary degrees through which official preferment and honors were then attained. He tried several times to obtain the first degree, *Hsiu Ts'ai,* but always unsuccessfully. While in Canton on one of these attempts (probably in 1836) [1] he seems to have met a man who gave him

[1] Oehler, *Die Taiping-Bewegung,* pp. 88, 233; Meadows, *The Chinese and Their Rebellions,* pp. 75-78. The source of the account of the visions is the narrative of Hung Jên contained in Hamberg, *The Visions of Hung-Siu-tshuen,* pp. 1-48. The report, coming a good many years after the visions, is probably correct only in its main features. Even these may be subject to question. The account seems to be confirmed in its main outline by what we know of later developments. Lindley, in *Ti-Ping Tien-Kwoh,* Vol. 1, p. 31, says it accorded in

some pamphlets called "Good Words Exhorting the Age." These were by Liang A-fa, who, it will be recalled, was long in the employ of the London Missionary Society. They contained essays and Biblical selections, and constituted a kind of summary of the teaching of Protestant missionaries. At the time the young student did not, apparently, do more than glance them over, but, with the Chinese scholar's reverence for the printed page, took them home and preserved them.

In 1837, after another attempt for the degree, Hung returned home seriously ill. During his sickness he saw visions which largely determined his later career. He believed that he was taken to a beautiful and luminous place where he was washed clean, and then, in company with aged men, among whom were some of the ancient sages, he was conducted to a large building where his heart and other vital parts were excised and replaced by new organs. Afterward he was led to another hall, where he saw on the highest seat a venerable man with a golden beard and a black robe. The old man wept as he saw Hung and said: "All human beings in the world are produced and sustained by me; they eat my food and wear my clothing, but not a single one among them has a heart to remember and venerate me; what is, however, still worse, they take my gifts, and therewith worship demons; they purposely rebel against me and arouse my anger. Do thou not imitate them." He gave Hung a sword, commanding him to exterminate the demons, a seal by which he could overcome the evil spirits, and a yellow fruit. Hung thereupon began to exhort those in the hall to return to their duties to the venerable old man, but not with entire success. The old man encouraged him, promising him assistance, and, taking him to the parapet, bade him look down and behold the depravity and perverseness of the people on the earth. The visions continued for about forty days, and during them, among other incidents, Hung thought that he often met a man of middle age whom he called his elder brother and who instructed him and assisted him in exterminating demons.

most particulars with what he had learned independently from the T'ai P'ings themselves. A somewhat different account of Hung's first contact with Christianity, which says that for a time while a candidate for the examinations he lived in the home of Issacher J. Roberts in Canton and there first obtained Christian literature (given in Soothill, *China and the West*, pp. 139, 140, quoting from Rev. James Thomas, who obtained his story from Yates, and Yates from T'ai P'ings) is almost certainly inaccurate.

The source of the suggestion that gave rise to these visions is uncertain. We are not even sure that we have a trustworthy account of them, for our narrative, while coming from Hung Jên, a cousin and intimate friend of Hung Hsiu-ch'üan, dates from several years after their occurrence. It is possible that Hung's casual glance at the books of Liang A-fa had left upon his mind some impression of the contents. It seems more probable that the visions sprang primarily from the religious beliefs by which Hung had been surrounded from his youth. Whatever their origin, the dreams made a profound impression upon Hung. For the most part he did not speak of them but continued quietly his occupation of teaching school and was once more present at the examinations at Canton. His experience, however, appears to have changed him and to have left him ripe for later developments.

HUNG'S PREACHING AND THE RISE OF "THE WORSHIPERS OF SHANG TI"

In 1843, Hung Jên's account states, a cousin, Li, chanced to observe the books given Hung Hsiu-ch'üan so long before and asked to read them. Li became so interested that Hung also read them. In them, to his amazement, he found what seemed a complete confirmation and explanation of the visions of his illness. The old man of his dreams, so he believed, was none other than God the Father, the middle-aged elder brother was Jesus, and the demons were idols. His commission appeared clear. He and Li thereupon baptized themselves and Hung returned to his home and started on the mission of preaching to which he believed he had been sent. He soon won and baptized two intimate friends—a cousin, Hung Jên, and Fêng Yün-shan. He also turned his parents and brothers and their families from idolatry. In 1844 Hung Hsiu-ch'üan and Fêng Yün-shan left the former's home and, preaching as they went, made their way into Kwangsi, where they were kindly received by a kinsman of Hung. After a few months Hung returned to Kwangtung and for two years, 1845 and 1846, resumed his occupation of teaching school. He continued to preach in and near his native village, baptizing those who believed. In 1846 he and one of the early Baptist missionaries, Issacher J. Roberts, heard of each other, and the latter invited him to come and study further the Christian doctrine. Hung accepted the invitation and, accompanied by Hung Jên, went to Canton and was under Roberts' instruction for about a month. After a short visit to his native village, he was again for a time under Roberts' tuition, but through some misunderstanding he was not baptized. He thereupon went to Kwangsi to rejoin his friend, Fêng Yün-shan.

Hung discovered that in the two or three years since he had been in the province Fêng had continued to preach and with such marked success that a fairly large religious sect had sprung into existence. The members called themselves "The Society of the Worshipers of *Shang Ti*" (*Pai Shang Ti Huei*). All who joined the society threw away their idols and gave themselves to the worship of *Shang Ti,* the ancient Chinese deity whose name some of the Protestant missionaries had used as a translation for the Christian term God. Converts were baptized, and before the rite was administered a confession of sins was repeated by them, which, in accordance with Chinese practice, was presented to *Shang Ti* by burning the paper on which it was written. They also promised "not to worship evil spirits, not to practice evil things, but to keep the heavenly commandments." [2] The members of the society had communal worship with prayer, the singing of hymns, and an address. There were forms of prayer for use mornings and evenings and at meals. "Upon the celebration of festivals, as for instance at a marriage, a burial, or at the New Year, animals were offered in sacrifice, and afterwards consumed by those present." [3] Some of the members experienced trances accompanied by ecstatic utterances which were believed to be the work of spirits.[4]

Here was obviously arising one of those popular sects which in China flourish so abundantly. Like them, it was syncretic. It had apparently had its origin in the visions and work of Hung Hsiu-ch'üan and the activities of Fêng Yün-shan. In it were elements which had been derived from Christianity, but it also contained many distinctively Chinese practices and beliefs. It probably embodied, indeed, much more of older Chinese belief than of Christianity. Had it had intimate contact through missionaries with Christian communities in other lands, it is possible that in time it might have developed into a movement which,

[2] Hamberg, *The Visions of Hung-Siu-tshuen*, p. 35.
[3] Ibid., p. 36.
[4] Ibid., pp. 45, 46. Unless otherwise indicated, the account of the preceding pages is based on Hamberg.

while preserving many peculiarly Chinese features, would have caught the meaning of Jesus and have become a church which would have deserved both the adjectives Chinese and Christian. As it was, it is quite clear that even the leaders had never really understood the Christian message. The society owed its origin in part to Christian missions, but it was at best only superficially Christian and then only in some of its doctrines.

Hung's contact with the new sect was at first apparently very limited. He had been in Kwangsi for a few months in 1844, and possibly 1845. Now, in 1847, his sojourn was even briefer, for Fêng was imprisoned by the authorities on the charge of inciting revolt and Hung left for Canton to effect his release. Hung was unsuccessful in his quest and returned to Kwangsi, only to find that Fêng had obtained his freedom through other channels and had gone to Kwangtung to look for him. Hung thereupon returned to his old home in Kwangtung, and here, in 1848, the two friends found each other. It was not until 1849 that Hung was again in Kwangsi among "The Worshipers of *Shang Ti*."

THE BEGINNINGS OF INSURRECTION

In the meantime developments were in progress which were to make of the society an insurrectionary movement which was to threaten the existence of the Ta Ch'ing dynasty and lay waste some of China's fairest provinces.

The times favored revolt. The days of K'ang Hsi and Ch'ien Lung were past and the Manchu imperial family was losing its vigor. The indolent and narrow-minded Tao Kuang had succeeded the mediocre Chia Ch'ing and was to be followed in 1850 by the weak and contemptible Hsien Fêng. Unless the dynasty could soon produce a vigorous leader, the ever recurring cycle of Chinese history would once more be repeated and some rebel would prove by his prowess that he had received the mandate of *T'ien* and would found a new ruling house. The prestige and authority of the Manchus had been weakened by the first war with Great Britain and were soon to suffer still more from the second war with European powers. Bad harvests, seldom absent from some part of the Empire, fanned discontent. It is not strange, then, that the first half of the nineteenth century was marked by many revolts and that these increased as the century advanced. Nor is it remarkable that the most disastrous of these should arise in Kwangsi. That province was mountainous, remote from Peking, and was almost never entirely submissive to the central government.

Of the process by which "The Worshipers of *Shang Ti*" were transformed into an army which sought to overturn the Manchus and set up a new dynasty we have only the most fragmentary record. Any organization vigorously opposing the worship of idols and actively iconoclastic was certain very soon to clash both with the populace and the officials. Any group, too, chiefly made up, as was this, of Hakkas and Miao would quite naturally be attacked by their neighbors, the pure Chinese (sometimes called "Puntis") "natives." Further, if it possessed, as did "The Worshipers of *Shang Ti*," religious enthusiasm, it might readily be welded into an effective military machine. The general lack of order in Kwangsi and conflicts with neighbors and officials soon led to the arming of the new sect, but had it not possessed leaders of force and organizing ability it probably would soon have been suppressed. Hung himself apparently had little gift for organization or administration, and his contact with the formation of the sect had been slight. He may have contemplated an effort to oust the reigning dynasy,[5] but the genius which saw in the movement an opportunity for imperial power and was responsible for disciplining and training it in the art of war was probably not his. The real leader appears to have been a mysterious Chu Chiu-tao, a Hunanese who, like Hung, had been unsuccessful in the civil service examinations and who, while living the retired life of a monk, had planned revolt and had made a careful study of military organization and strategy. It seems fair to assume that he saw in the new religious sect an opportunity to further his ends and, adding to it other elements from the Triads, an old revolutionary group, began drilling it into formidable fighting units. He had, of course, to recognize Fêng and Hung. Fêng had been the real founder of "The Worshipers of *Shang Ti*" and apparently had early planned with a few others to make the movement political as well as religious, possibly keeping Hung in ignorance of the scheme. Whether Fêng's plotting began before his acquaintance with Chu is uncertain, but the latter would certainly have to concede to Fêng a leading posi-

---

[5] Hung Jên said that in 1845 and 1846 Hung Hsio-ch'üan talked to him of such a purpose.—Hamberg, op. cit., pp. 29, 30.

tion in the new army. Hung, too, as the source of the revelations to which "The Worshipers of ShSang Ti" owed their origin, had to be given a place of honored prominence.[6]

Whatever the steps by which the society became political, with designs on the throne, hostilities began in 1848, and by 1850 the imperial government had taken cognizance of the movement and had begun to act. Thanks partly to the incompetence of their opponents, the rebels were not crushed, and in 1851 Hung and his followers and associates captured Yungan in Kwangsi. Here, apparently, was set up the organization for the new dynasty. A name was chosen, T'ai P'ing T'ien Kuo, "Great Peaceful Heavenly Kingdom," or simply T'ai P'ing, "Great Peace"—a title which was to prove a melancholy misnomer. Chu and Hung may have been coördinate rulers, Chu as T'ien Tê or "Heavenly Virtue," and Hung as T'ien Wang, "Heavenly King," or T'ai P'ing Wang, "Great Peace King." Chu may have been the leader in name as well as in fact, or he may have had to give prominence to Hung, hoping that in time he could seize the supreme power for himself. The chief subordinates, among whom was Fêng, were raised to the rank of Wang, and the main outlines of military organization and civil administration were arranged. In Yungan friction appears to have developed among the leaders, perhaps between Chu and some of the direct followers of Hung. Apparently, too, Chu was here captured by the imperial forces, possibly through the treachery of Hung or his friends. Certainly there was taken and executed a prominent leader who claimed to have been Hung's instructor in the art of war. It is certain, too, that from now on the fanatical elements that surrounded Hung became prominent. Those that Chu had brought in either adopted the faith of Hung and his followers or withdrew or were expelled.[7]

THE PROGRESS OF THE REBELLION

In April, 1852, the rebels broke their way through the forces

---

[6] An illuminating and original analysis of the question of the origin of the rebellion, showing clearly the part played by Chu, has been made by W. J. Hail in Tsêng Kuo-fan and the T'aip'ing Rebellion, the best book that has yet appeared on the T'ai P'ings. Dr. Hail identifies Chu with the Hung Ta-ch'üan who was captured and executed outside of Yungan in 1852 and whose "confession," made shortly before his execution, appeared in the Overland China Mail, Aug. 23, 1852, and is copied from there by Brine in The Taeping Rebellion in China, pp. 131-136. The above account of the transformation of "The Worshipers of Shang Ti" into the T'ai P'ing Rebellion is based almost entirely upon Hail's work.

[7] Hail, op. cit.

that had penned them up in Yungan and laid siege to the provincial capital, Kueilin. They failed to take the city and, probably ten or twelve thousand strong, moved north into Hunan. They captured several cities in the valley of the Hsiang but were unsuccessful in their beleaguerment of Changsha. Before they reached Changsha the death of the able and level-headed Fêng had brought them a loss they could ill afford, but their victories had attracted to their standards large reënforcements. It was while besieging Changsha that Hung finally assumed imperial honors, being addressed as *Wan Sui,* "Ten Thousand Years," and adopting an imperial seal. The rebels turned westward from Changsha, apparently planning to make their headquarters at Changtê, but at Yiyang they captured several thousand boats and embarked in these for Yochow, at the mouth of the T'ung T'ing Lake. Yochow was almost undefended and its capture gave the T'ai P'ings vast military stores and additional boats. The insurgents easily captured Hanyang and burned Hankow. The Governor in Wuchang made a gallant but ineffectual defense and the city was taken by assault in January, 1853.

Instead of marching directly north toward Peking, the rebels now proceeded down the river, capturing Kiukiang, Anking, and Wuhu in rapid succession, and arrived before Nanking early in March. That city fell a few days later and the Manchu garrison was put to the sword. Again the rebels failed to go north and strike before the Manchus could organize resistance, but, using Nanking as a base, they captured some of the cities of Kiangsu, among them Chinkiang and Yangchow. They did not attempt at this time to take any of the coast ports.

An army now at last went north. It reached the walls of Kaifêng in June, but a rise in the Yellow River forced it to raise the siege. Hotly pursued by the imperial forces, it crossed the Huang Ho into Shansi and moved eastward into Chihli, being only thirty miles from Tientsin when at last checked. In spite of attempts from Nanking to reënforce and rescue it, the northern expeditionary force stopped here and was dispersed or annihilated. The rebels did not again seriously threaten Peking, but for more than a decade they were to hold Nanking and much of the lower part of the Yangtze Valley.[8]

[8] Morse, *International Relations of the Chinese Empire,* Vol. 1, pp. 444-446; Hail, op. cit.

The phenomenal success of the T'ai P'ings was due to a variety of causes—the incompetence and cowardice of many of the imperial officials, the weakness of the Manchus, a lack of military and civil machinery adequate for such emergencies, the organization and drill given the rebels (presumably by Chu), fanatical enthusiasm and confidence, and the terror inspired by the initial victories.

The Weakness and Failure of the Rebellion

The attempt of the T'ai P'ings to rule the Empire was almost certainly foredoomed. The only hope of enduring success lay in capturing the existing machinery of government and operating it intact, and in making no disturbance in the existing beliefs and institutions of the nation. This hope the T'ai P'ings consistently sacrificed. As a rule they contented themselves with retaining certain strongholds, such as Nanking, Yangchow, and Chinkiang. From these vantage points they sallied forth for raids on the surrounding country, destroying images and capturing and plundering cities and villages. They showed little or no capacity for organizing their conquests or giving them a permanent administration. Such political forms as they developed differed too greatly from those which had long been in use to be readily accepted. Their peculiar religious faith and their unwillingness to compromise antagonized the masses and were anathema to that scholar-official class without whose acquiescence and support no dynasty could hope long to endure. The T'ai P'ings declared that their doctrine was not new in China but that the ancient classics had taught it in part and later generations had departed from it. They carried over, too, some of the older practices, such as sacrifices of animals, tea, and rice. They could not, however, prevent their faith from appearing bizarre and offensive to their fellow-countrymen.[9]

Since the T'ai P'ings were so unfitted to rule the Empire permanently, their only chances of anything more than temporary and local success lay in the weakness of the Manchus and in the recognition and support of Western powers. These, too, were to be denied them. The Manchus, it is true, were incompetent, and the structure of the government and army were inadequate for the suppression of serious rebellions, but to the rescue came

[9] See Hail, op. cit., p. 365.

a remarkable Chinese, Tsêng Kuo-fan, and some lieutenants whom he discovered and trained—among them the young Li Hung-chang, later famous. Tsêng was primarily a scholar and administrator and was unskilled in military matters, but thanks chiefly to his ability and industry a force was eventually organized which began to make headway against the rebels. The imperial government proved still to have recuperative powers. Given time, it began to close in on the enemy.

In the early days of the insurrection it was uncertain what attitude would be taken by the Occidental powers. Some foreigners at first were disposed to regard the T'ai P'ings with favor. Among the Protestant missionaries were those who thought that the rebellion, because of its seemingly Christian features, would open the Empire to the preaching of the Gospel. A few merchants and officials were inclined to be at least neutral.[10] Had the T'ai P'ing leaders really wished it, they might have obtained

[10] Callery and Yvan, *History of the Insurrection in China,* written in 1853, is inclined to be favorable to the rebels. Gillespie, *The Land of Sinim,* 1854, p. 237, says of the T'ai P'ings that "there can be no doubt that if the new movement succeeds China will be thrown open throughout its length and breadth to the efforts of Protestant missionaries. . . . The movement is big with hope." Cox, of the Wesleyan Missionary Society, in notices of 1853, spoke of his anticipation of good results from the T'ai P'ings.—Findlay and Holdsworth, *History of the Wesleyan Methodist Missionary Society,* Vol. 5, p. 437. As late as 1860, Griffith John felt that the T'ai P'ings had "created a vacuum not only in the temples but also in the hearts of the people which remains to be filled. This is the missionary's work—a work which might be done immediately were it not for the unaccountable policy of the representatives of foreign powers at this port" (Shanghai). John says he had obtained from the T'ai P'ings full permission for missionaries "to enter into and live in the insurgents' territory for the purpose of carrying on mission work. . . . I fully believe that God is uprooting idolatry in this land through the insurgents and that He will by means of them, in connection with the foreign missionary, plant Christianity in its stead."—Report of Griffith John to the London Missionary Society, quoted in Lindley, *Ti Ping Tien Kwoh,* Vol. 2, p. 468. Scarth, a merchant in China between 1847 and 1859, in *Twelve Years in China* (published 1860), pp. 265, 266, expresses the opinion that if the British Government had not been unneutral, the rebellion would have afforded an opportunity for the country to have become Christian. Sir G. Bonham, the English plenipotentiary, visited Nanking in 1853 and recommended to his government strict neutrality.—Morse, op. cit., Vol. 1, pp. 453, 454. Some Americans were at first disposed to look with favor on the T'ai P'ings and believed that the movement might open the country further to Western intercourse.—See quotations in Dennett, *Americans in Eastern Asia,* pp. 212-214.

Some foreigners, however, were not so favorable, even in the earlier days of the rebellion. S. Wells Williams, writing in 1864, declares: "I had no faith in this rebellion from the first as likely to prove a means of promoting the truth."— F. W. Williams, *Life and Letters of Samuel Wells Williams,* p. 356. Scarth, writing in 1860, says that Sir John Bowring, the Governor of Hongkong, believed that British trade depended upon the continuance of the Manchu dynasty.—Scarth, op. cit., p. 265. The American commissioner Marshall, in 1853, came to favor the maintenance of the imperial government.—Dennett, op. cit., p. 216.

outside aid. By opening to foreign trade the cities in their control, by seeking diplomatic relations with and asking military
instruction and supplies from Westerners, by encouraging missionaries and declaring full toleration for all Christians, they quite
possibly might have won the assistance of the European and
American communities and of some of the Western governments.
Foreigners were so generally dissatisfied with the imperial government that it would probably not have been difficult to transform their neutrality into active support. Such support from the
West might have been insufficient to overthrow the Manchu
dynasty at once and to give the T'ai P'ings immediate control of
the entire country. It would, however, have enabled the rebels
to retain some of the provinces along the southern coast and the
lower part of the Yangtze Valley and possibly in time to master
the Empire. Had this mastery been achieved, the transformation
of China under Western influence might have begun a generation
earlier than it did and the Christian Church might to-day be
much stronger and more nearly Chinese in leadership and character.

Given the attitude of the rebels, however, this outcome was
impossible. The T'ai P'ing chiefs were no more aware of the
significance of the contacts which were beginning with Westerners than were the imperial authorities, and with their limited
opportunities for intercourse this could scarcely have been otherwise. They were, moreover, too fanatical and believed too firmly
in the supreme authority of the revelations of Hung to be amenable to foreign instruction. After the loss of Chu and Fêng
they were almost destitute of leaders who by any stretch of the
imagination might be called statesmen. It is not surprising, then,
that at best the T'ai P'ings gave to foreigners only a half-hearted
welcome and that they frequently assumed toward them the same
attitude of lofty superiority which made relations between Peking
and the Western powers so galling to the latter. To Sir George
Bonham, the English plenipotentiary who visited them in 1853,
they issued a "mandate" declaring that "Whereas God the Heavenly Father has sent our Sovereign down on earth, as the true
Sovereign of all nations in the world, all people in the world who
wish to appear at his Court must yield obedience to the rules of
ceremony." [11]   To the American Commissioner, Robert McLane,

[11] Meadows, *The Chinese and Their Rebellions*, pp. 259-271.

who came to Nanking in 1854, they said: ". . . If you do indeed respect Heaven and recognize the Sovereign, then our celestial court, viewing all under Heaven as one family and uniting all nations as one body, will most assuredly regard your faithful purpose and permit you year by year to bring tribute and annually to pay court, so that you may become the ministers and people of the Celestial Kingdom. . . ." [12] Missionaries were sometimes welcomed, but the T'ai P'ings usually made clear their conviction that Hung Hsiu-ch'üan had received further revelations than had been granted to Occidental Christians. In 1860 Edkins, of the London Missionary Society, visited the rebels in Soochow and was courteously received. Hung Jên, although one of the earliest converts of Hung Hsiu-ch'üan, at first did not join the rebellion and for some years was employed by the London Missionary Society as an evangelist. [13] It is possible that he also saw service with the English Wesleyans. [14] By 1860 he had attached himself to the T'ai P'ings, perhaps with the hope of elevating their faith, and had been given the title of *Kan Wang* or "Shield King." Hung Jên had known Edkins in Shanghai. Now, after the latter's visit to Soochow, he wrote urging him to come back "to instruct him more perfectly in the way of salvation." Edkins therefore went once more to Soochow, taking other foreigners with him, and had several interviews with the *Kan Wang*. He got as far as Nanking and obtained permission to settle there with his wife, but for a variety of reasons did not take advantage of the opportunity. [15] In 1860 there reached Cox, of the English Wesleyans, an invitation from Hung Jên to join in preaching the Gospel among the T'ai P'ings. Cox was then in England but when he returned to China he visited Nanking. He was refused freedom to preach in the city and departed thoroughly disillusioned. [16] Roberts, Hung Hsiu-ch'üan's old teacher in the Christian faith, had since 1853 been asked to come to Nanking. It was not until 1860 that he went, but he then remained for fifteen months. He left utterly opposed to the rebels, declaring that he believed Hung Hsiu-ch'üan to be insane and that any missionary who would

[12] United States, *Executive Documents*, 35th Congress, 2d Session, Vol. 22, Part 1, pp. 58-63.
[13] Legge, *James Legge*, p. 91.
[14] Cornaby, *The Call of Cathay*, pp. 156, 157.
[15] Edkins, *Chinese Scenes and People*, pp. 20, 201-206.
[16] Findlay and Holdsworth, *History of the Wesleyan Methodist Missionary Society*, Vol. 5, pp. 460, 461.

not admit Hung's divine commission would be in great danger in the city.[17] Muirhead, of the London Missionary Society, was in Nanking for a month early in 1861, and reported that the rebellion was destructive rather than constructive.[18] Some foreigners remained convinced, even after the collapse of the T'ai P'ings, that had missionaries and foreign governments handled the situation properly the rebellion might have succeeded and a more effective opportunity for missions have been obtained.[19] For the most part, however, whatever sympathy foreigners had entertained for the rebels disappeared by 1862. By 1861 Western governments had made their peace with Peking and were inclined to support the Manchus.

As a result of the failure of the T'ai P'ings to win the adherence of the nation and in consequence of the growing antagonism of foreigners and of the efforts of Tsêng Kuo-fan and his subordinates, the first few years after 1860 saw the imperial government slowly and with many reverses draw its cordons around the rebels and crush them. The insurgents were not without some brilliant military leadership, even in the days of their decline. For example, Li Hsiu-ch'êng, usually known by his title of *Chung Wang* (Loyal King), was a clear-headed, brave, and able strategist and remained faithful to the end. In 1860 the T'ai P'ings captured Hangchow, and in 1861 Ningpo. In 1862 they threatened Shanghai. They were, however, handicapped by dissensions, and Hung Hsiu-ch'üan did not leave his palace in Nanking to lead his followers and by his vagaries and lack of capacity for administration hindered their cause.

Foreigners at last began actively to assist the Manchu authorities. Frederick Townsend Ward organized a company to aid the imperialists, and the necessity of protecting their nationals in Shanghai and Ningpo led British and French naval officers to support the forces of the Peking government. Ward was killed in 1862, and after various experiments with a successor, his command, "The Ever Victorious Army," was turned over to the earnest and picturesque Major Charles George Gordon, a British officer who entered the Chinese service with the full consent of

[17] Roberts, Jan. 22, 1862, in *Papers Relating to the Rebellion in China;* Brine, *The Taeping Rebellion,* pp. 294, 295.
[18] Muirhead, in *Papers Relating to the Rebellion in China,* pp. 18-22.
[19] See, for example, Martin, *A Cycle of Cathay,* pp. 138-142, written long after the rebellion had collapsed.

his government. Late in 1863 Soochow capitulated and in July, 1864, Tsêng Kuo-fan took Nanking. Hung Hsiu-ch'üan committed suicide a few days before the fall of the city.

With the loss of its capital the rebellion collapsed. The *Chung Wang,* true to his title, attempted to convey the son of Hung Hsiu-ch'üan out of harm's way, but was captured and executed. For some time armed bands continued to give trouble in various parts of the country, but they were gradually suppressed.[20] The *T'ai P'ing T'ien Kuo* had come to an end. It had laid waste large and populous sections of the Empire and had cost millions of lives. While it was not as destructive as have been many other wars and internal dissensions from which China has suffered, it was probably the most desolating insurrection of the nineteenth century and because of its strange origin and of its proximity to the ports occupied by Occidentals it attracted wide attention.

THE T'AI P'INGS AND CHRISTIANITY

This, then, is the story of the T'ai P'ing Rebellion. It remains to ask how much resemblance to Christianity the rebels exhibited in their practices as finally developed, to estimate the responsibility of missions for the rebellion's origin and its destructive career, and to attempt to recount the effect of the uprising upon missions.

For the first of these questions, the extent of the similarity of the T'ai P'ings' doctrines and practices to Christianity, the answer is fairly easily obtained. Many documents have come down to us, both the writings of the rebels themselves and the reports of European observers, which shed light on the problem. The insurgents believed in a supreme God as father and in Jesus as his son. They also maintained that Hung Hsiu-ch'üan was the younger brother of Jesus and had revelations directly from God (*Shang Ti*). Hung, indeed, held that he and Jesus were born of the same mother.[21] Although, in accordance with the traditions of the Chinese family, God as father and Jesus as elder brother were regarded with reverence, Hung by virtue of his revelations was held to have the right to a certain authority over

[20] Hail, *Tsêng Kuo-fan and the T'aip'ing Rebellion,* passim; Morse, *International Relations of the Chinese Empire,* Vol. 2, pp. 64-112.
[21] Translation of a T'ai P'ing commentary on the third epistle of John, given by Forrest in *Journal of the North China Branch of the Royal Asiatic Society,* New Series, No. 4, Dec. 1867, pp. 187-208.

all peoples.[22]　Missionaries, therefore, while sometimes welcomed, were expected to acknowledge him.[23]　Yang Hsiu-ch'ing, known as the *Tung Wang* or "Eastern King," was likewise believed to be the mouthpiece of special revelations and was regarded as the Holy Ghost.[24]　To Hsiao Ch'ao Kuei, the *Hsi Wang* or "Western King," also came visions, but he perished in the siege of Changsha [25] and so had little permanent influence on the movement. The rebels were in possession of the Bible, read and honored it, and published commentaries on it. They gave prominence to the Ten Commandments and to a modification of the Lord's Prayer. They had a form of baptism, a ceremony which seems to have been only for adults, but they did not fully observe the Lord's Supper. Possibly as a substitute for the latter they partook of wine every fourth Sunday and had cups of tea on the altar.[26]　They were inexorably opposed to all idols and destroyed those that came into their hands. Lucky and unlucky days were eliminated from their calendar,[27] sacrifices to ancestors were forbidden, and the usual funeral rites were altered or abandoned.[28]　They made extensive use of the printing press and issued their teachings in many forms, including the time-honored one of a trimetrical classic.[29]　While cruel to their enemies and plundering and sacking many of the cities which they captured, they apparently advocated what in some respects was a fairly high moral code. They taught that disobedience to it led to hell, and that repentance and obedience were the way to heaven.[30]　They prohibited indulgence in opium and discouraged the use of wine and loose relations between the sexes.[31]　There

---

[22] Hail, op. cit., pp. 90-118; Forrest in *Journal of the North China Branch of the Royal Asiatic Society*, New Series, No. 4, Dec. 1867, pp. 187-208.

[23] Lindley, *Ti-ping Tien-kwoh*, Vol. 2, p. 469. Lindley had been among the rebels and his book in part embodies his observations. He was, however, so eager to present the T'ai P'ings in a favorable light that his descriptions must be discounted.

[24] Meadows, *The Chinese and Their Rebellions*, p. 441 (Meadows had some first-hand knowledge) ; Edkins, *Chinese Scenes and Peoples,* pp. 241 et seq.

[25] Hamberg, op. cit., p. 46.

[26] Meadows, op. cit., pp. 423-427; Lindley, op. cit., Vol. 1, pp. 315-317; Medhurst, *Books of the Insurgents;* Forrest in op. cit. They apparently used Gützlaff's translation of the Old Testament.—United States, *Executive Documents, 1st Session, 33d Congress*, Vol. 16, No. 123, pp. 147-155.

[27] Lindley, op. cit., Vol. 1, p. 300.

[28] Ibid., Vol. 1, p. 318.

[29] *Papers Respecting the Civil War in China*, pp. 35-44.

[30] Meadows, op. cit., pp. 423-427.

[31] *Papers Relating to the Civil War in China*, pp. 35-44; Scarth, *Twelve Years in China*, p. 163.

were women's companies,[32] and monogamy was the rule for the common soldier.[33] To the leaders, concubines were allowed;[34] this practice, however, could be justified both from the Old Testament and from current Chinese customs. The seventh day was observed by strict suspension of work and business and by three services, one just after midnight on Friday and two more on the following day. The services showed clearly their Protestant origin. Each opened with a doxology which was at first very much like that in use in Protestant churches[35] but which in a later form came to include praise to several of the *Wangs*.[36] The doxology was followed by a hymn, the reading of a chapter from the Bible, and the repetition of a creed. Then followed prayer by the leader, repeated by the congregation, and an address. Chinese musical instruments accompanied the singing. The services concluded with the repetition of the Ten Commandments, a hymn, the setting off of firecrackers, and the burning of incense.[37] There was also daily morning and evening worship.[38]

Outwardly, then, the T'ai P'ings showed markedly the influence of Christianity, although they had obviously modified what had come from the outside and had made it conform in large part to Chinese practice. Of the inner spirit of Christianity the insurgents knew little or nothing. They had, to be sure, broken with idolatry and the fear of spirits, and they had set up certain ethical standards. Probably some of them were as far advanced toward an understanding of Christianity as are many Chinese to-day when they are received into the Church, or as were many of the early Christian converts in the Roman Empire and Northern Europe. There were, however, apparently lacking any of those choice spirits which are to be found, even if in small numbers, in the Christian Church in nearly every land and age, who have comprehended the message of Jesus and have entered somewhat into the experience of Paul. Even Hung Jên, who had had years of association with the missionaries and who, after his arrival in Nanking, had apparently tried to make the faith of the T'ai

---

[32] Hail, op. cit., pp. 126 et seq.
[33] Lindley, op. cit., Vol. 1, p. 300.
[34] Ibid.; Meadows, op. cit., p. 443; Hake, *Events in the Taeping Rebellion*, pp. 112-114.
[35] Lindley, op. cit., Vol. 1, pp. 319-321; Meadows, op. cit., p. 427.
[36] Meadows, op. cit., Vol. 1, p. 441.
[37] Lindley, op. cit., Vol. 1, p. 321.
[38] *Papers Respecting the Civil War in China*, pp. 35-44.

P'ings approximate more nearly than formerly to what he had learned from his foreign friends, could not be said to be in any sense a mature Christian.[39] The lack of much intimate contact with missionaries, and the visions and vagaries of Hung, Yang, and some of the other leaders scarcely permitted the movement to become really Christian. At its close, as at its beginning, the T'ai P'ing movement was a Chinese sect, displaying some interesting results of contact with Christianity, but drawing most of its beliefs and characteristics from its Chinese environment and the erratic genius of its leaders.

Much more difficult of answer than the question of the extent of the resemblance of the T'ai P'ing system to Christianity is that of the accountability of missions for the rebellion. Our knowledge of the beginnings of the movement is too scanty and dubious to justify many positive statements. It is certain that missionaries and Chinese Christians connected with the Church did not have any share in planning or organizing the movement. The rebellion was probably largely the work of Chu, whose motives were political and personal and who seems not to have been particularly stirred by the religious message of Hung. After the insurrection was once well started, missionaries became interested in it, but they did not give it assistance. Hung Jên, the only leader of the T'ai P'ings who had had much intimate contact with them, apparently joined the movement without any encouragement from his foreign friends [40] and then had no very striking influence upon the policies of the *T'ien Wang*. Only a complete misunderstanding of the message of the New Testament could have led to so great a travesty on the doctrines of Christ as that which existed at Nanking.

On the other hand, but for the work of Morrison and his associates it is probable that Hung would never have conceived or undertaken his strange enterprise and the "Society of the Worshipers of *Shang Ti*" would not have come into existence. It is just possible that a brief glance at the contents of the books of Liang A-fa helped to determine the details of Hung Hsiu-ch'üan's visions and, if Hung Jên's narrative is to be trusted, it was a

[39] See account of Legge's relations with him in Legge, *James Legge*, pp. 91 et seq.
[40] Legge, *James Legge,* p. 22. Legge, indeed, tried to discourage Hung Jên from joining the rebels.

careful perusal of the little volumes that convinced the future *T'ien Wang* of his mission and decided him to undertake it.

It is certain that the influence of the missionary alone would not have given rise to the rebellion. It was other factors that were chiefly responsible—the illness of Hung, the inherited religious conceptions of Hung and his followers, local friction in Kwangtung and Kwangsi, the incompetence of the Manchu government, and the ambition and organizing genius of Chu. It is probable, however, that the books prepared and distributed by the missionary and his helpers furnished the initial impulse and that without them the religious convictions that gave driving power to the insurrection would not have come into existence. All unwittingly and unintentionally Occidental Christians helped to arouse forces which they could not control.

THE EFFECT UPON MISSIONS

The immediate effect of the rebellion upon the progress of Protestant missions was not great. Protestants had not yet spread much outside the port cities and their activities were accordingly but little disturbed. When in 1860 and 1861 the rebels overran Chêkiang and captured Ningpo the missionary was somewhat hampered, but by 1862 the worst of that particular crisis had passed.[41] At most the extension of Protestant activities outside the treaty cities was delayed no more than a decade.

Roman Catholic missions, on the other hand, suffered severely. Catholic communities were not confined to the open ports but were scattered throughout the provinces. They had not recovered fully from the persecutions of the eighteenth and the early part of the nineteenth centuries, and now they were frequently treated as enemies both by the T'ai P'ings and by the imperial authorities. In their religious practices Roman Catholics were very different from the rebels and they could not, of course, recognize as true the alleged revelations of Hung Hsiu-ch'üan. In some places, because of the resemblance of the two faiths for each other, the T'ai P'ings dealt considerately with the Roman Catholics.[42] For

[41] Moule, *Story of the Chehkiang Mission*, pp. 61-66; *A Century of Protestant Missions in China*, p. 24. J. L. Holmes and T. M. Parker, both American missionaries, were killed in 1861 in Shantung, but apparently by rebels called Neinfei rather than by T'ai P'ings.—Forsyth, *Shantung*, p. 171; Morse, *International Relations of the Chinese Empire*, Vol. 2, p. 73.

[42] Danicourt, *Vie de Danicourt*, p. 366.

the most part, however, they paid them scant respect. They may, indeed, have been antagonized by the Roman Catholic use of images.[43]   In Kiangnan some Catholics were killed by the rebels and others beaten.[44]   By 1853 most of the six hundred Catholics in Nanking, Yangchow, and Chinkiang were reported to be killed, lost, or captive.[45]   In Hangchow the Christian community experienced great hardships.[46]   In 1860 the Jesuit Louis Massa died of injuries inflicted by the T'ai P'ings,[47] and by the close of 1864 one more priest, Vuillaume, had been killed[48] and two or three others had perished from disease or exposure.[49]   In Shantung a missionary, Molina, was killed either by T'ai P'ings or by other rebels, and several others were beaten or threatened.[50]   Montels, a Lazarist, is said to have suffered death at the hands of the T'ai P'ings.[51]

The imperial authorities, on the other hand, because of the apparent similarity of the Roman Catholics and Hung's followers, often persecuted the former. Thus in Hunan, Huper,[52] and Yünnan[53] there were arrests, and in Shensi the populace looked upon Catholics with suspicion.[54]   An imperial decree ordered the removal of the cross that surmounted the Nan T'ang in Peking.[55] The judicial murder of Chapdelaine in Kwangsi in 1856 may have been due in part to a belief that he was connected with the rebels.

Even if Catholics were not singled out for attack by the belligerents, they often shared with the rest of the populace the distress brought by the general disorder. This was true, for example, in Kweichow,[56] and, of course, in all the provinces of Central

[43] Sykes, Tae Ping Rebellion, p. 26.
[44] Servière, Histoire de la mission du Kiangnan, Vol. 1, pp. 255-294.
[45] Servière, op. cit., Vol. 1, pp. 255-294; see also Becker, Joseph Gonnet, pp. 53-60.
[46] Annales de la propagation de la foi, Vol. 48, p. 44.
[47] Annals of the Propagation of the Faith, Vol. 22, pp. 40-47; Servière, op. cit., Vol. 2, pp. 24-27.
[48] Letter of Lemaitre from Shanghai, Nov. 14, 1862, in Annals of the Propagation of the Faith, Vol. 24, pp. 307-311.
[49] Ibid.; Piolet, Les missions cath. franç. au XIXme siècle, p. 183.
[50] Forsyth, Shantung, p. 164.
[51] Favier, Peking, Vol. 2, p. 211.
[52] Rizzolati in Annales de la propagation de la foi, Vol. 25, pp. 88, 289; Navarro, July 3, 1856, in ibid., Vol. 29, pp. 227-232.
[53] Letter of Huot from Yünnan, Sept. 6, 1854, in ibid., Vol. 28, pp. 131-139.
[54] Letter of Chiais, Sept. 6, 1856, in ibid., Vol. 29, pp. 371-376.
[55] Favier, Peking, Vol. 2, p. 211.
[56] Letter of Faurie from Kweichow, Oct. 19, 1860, in Annales de la propagation de la foi, Vol. 23, pp. 77-81.

China.[57]   Even from Manchuria it was reported that many Catholics were in the contingents that were being collected by the
government against the rebels.[58]

Occasionally the revolt seems to have aided the Catholics.
From Honan in 1856 it was reported that the houses of mission-
aries were crowded with those wishing to hear of the Christian
faith and it was thought that this might be due to the rebellion.[59]
On the whole, however, Roman Catholic missions fared badly and
Roman Catholic missionaries were even more critical of the T'ai
P'ings than were Protestants.

What ultimate effect the T'ai P'ing movement had upon missions is very difficult to determine. Because the doctrines of Hung
and his followers resembled Christianity there was undoubtedly
visited upon the latter some of the hatred felt for the former.
To those, too, who knew of the connection between Christian
missions and the origin of the rebellion, the latter must have
seemed a clear vindication of the long-cherished contention of
Chinese officialdom that Christianity would lead to the formation
of a religious, revolutionary sect whose existence would threaten
the integrity of the political and social structure of the Empire.
Thus in 1880 there was in Tientsin a general who had fought
against the rebels and who because of them was still bitter against
Christianity.[60]   Timothy Richard felt that half a century or so
after the insurrection had been suppressed Christianity was suffering from the legacy of ill-will.[61]   It is possible that the intense
anti-foreign and anti-Christian feeling in some provinces and cities,
such as Hunan and Changsha, was due in part to pride in having
expelled or repelled the rebels and to hatred for all that even
faintly resembled them.   On the other hand, it is also possible
that in the lower part of the Yangtze Valley—the section where
the power of the *T'ien Wang* was longest and most firmly established—the destruction of temples and monasteries, the decima-
tion of the more conservative elements of the community, and the
shock given to existing institutions weakened the resistance to

[57] Rizzolati from Hongkong, Aug. 4, 1853, in ibid., Vol. 26, pp. 109-117; letter
from Hongkong, March 10, 1853, in ibid., Vol. 25, p. 292.
[58] Letters of Verolles from Manchuria, May 20, 1852, in ibid., Vol. 26, pp.
289-308.
[59] Letters of Baldus, Vicar Apostolic of Honan, Nov. 14, 1856, in ibid., Vol.
29, p. 347.
[60] Bryson, *Mackenzie,* p. 186.
[61] Richard, *Forty-Five Years in China,* p. 185.

Christianity and so partly prepared the way for the foreign faith. Whatever its effects, however, the T'ai P'ing movement disappeared in the eighteen sixties, leaving behind it only a memory and the destruction it had wrought.

CHAPTER XVII

THE GRADUAL PENETRATION OF CHINA BY MISSIONARIES
(1856-1897)

INTRODUCTORY
ROMAN CATHOLIC MISSIONS

INTRODUCTORY

THE second war between China and Occidental powers and the second group of treaties were followed by about forty years of relatively uneventful intercourse between the Middle Kingdom and the West. Friction, to be sure, was frequent, and occasionally crises arose. Once, at the time of the Margary affair, in 1875 and 1876, war threatened with Great Britain. A few years later, in 1879, because of Kuldja, hostilities with Russia were narrowly averted. In 1884 and 1885 there was actual war with France. Some of China's outlying dependencies, never firmly attached to her rule, were seized by earth-hungry European powers. The trans-Ussuri region [1] and a part of Ili were lost to Russia, Chinese suzerainty over Burma was weakened by Great Britain, and that over Tongking was cancelled by France. The Loo Choo Islands passed to Japan, to be followed in 1895 by Formosa and the Pescadores. In 1895 the little remaining control over Korea was terminated. Occasionally, too, some new privilege within China was conceded to the foreigner, and now and again another city was added to the list of open ports. The pressure of Occidental commerce, governments, and culture continued to accumulate and foreign influences steadily penetrated the Empire. Ministers of foreign powers resided at Peking and consuls and merchants were to be found in growing numbers in the open ports. Foreign steamers plied the coastal waters and the lower reaches of the Yangtze. The Maritime Customs Service, organ-

[1] In 1860.

ized under foreign direction, not only collected the duties prescribed in the treaties but charted the coasts and began a postal department.

This growing contact with the West, however, was without a major crisis and effected but little apparent change in China. No thorough revision was made of the treaties which formed the legal basis of intercourse: relations between the Chinese and the peoples of the Occident continued largely on the terms of the agreements of 1842, 1844, 1858, and 1860. The question of altering the treaties was repeatedly raised, especially since the British document of 1858 provided that at the end of ten years revision could be requested by either China or Great Britain. In 1867 the Tsungli Yamen sought the opinions of the viceroys and provincial governors on the main issues to be discussed, among them the increase of privileges to missionaries. No fundamental modifications were made, however.[2] The Chefoo Convention (1876) made travel in the interior by foreigners, including missionaries, somewhat safer, and opened new ports to foreign residence, but it led to no great revolution in China's intercourse with the Occident. Under the vigorous but reactionary Empress Dowager the Manchu dynasty took on a new lease of life and opposed adjustment to the new conditions. Institutions and customs remained much the same as under K'ang Hsi and Ch'ien Lung. To be sure, legations were established in several Western capitals, an occasional telegraph line was built, a few miles of railway were constructed, iron works were opened at Hanyang, and at the urgent insistence of Yung Wing a few students were sent to America. There was little indication, however, of the upheaval which was soon to follow.

During the relatively quiet years between 1860 and 1897 both Protestant and Roman Catholic missionaries were steadily penetrating the country. They were soon scattered more widely than were the representatives of any other phase of Western activity, and had no small share in the transformation of Chinese culture which set in after 1897. As has been suggested before, this transformation would have occurred had never a missionary set foot in the land. Given the Industrial Revolution, it would have come as the result of the commercial and diplomatic pressure of the Occident and the consequent infiltration of new ideas. It is

[2] Morse, *International Relations of the Chinese Empire*, Vol. 2, pp. 204-206.

not even certain that the missionary hastened the process. What he did was to affect the quality of the transformation by bringing China into contact with the highest spiritual and moral forces of the West. As we have said before—and it cannot be repeated too often—but for him the Chinese would have seen in the main only the materialistic and selfish side of Europe and America. When the inevitable breakdown came in the structure of the older Chinese life, Christian missionaries were on hand to aid the elements that were struggling for the moral and spiritual well-being of the country. The missionary was sometimes associated with the imperialistic designs of European powers, occasionally he was narrow and bigoted, but he came to China at great personal sacrifice, he worked devotedly for the welfare of the Chinese as he understood it, and through him new forces were set in motion which were to be of unmeasured benefit to many millions in the land of his adoption.

Roman Catholics, with the advantage of work begun centuries before, in the years between 1856 and 1897 were to register a large numerical growth and to rejoice in numerous and widespread Christian communities. For Protestants the years were distinctly ones of pioneering, of traversing territory and of gaining footholds in provinces and cities which had heretofore not known them. Their churches showed a large proportional increase both in numbers and membership, although, since they had so recently been begun, measured in figures their gains were not as great as were those of the Roman Catholics. They were, too, founding and developing schools and hospitals and were adding to their literature, thus following in the main the methods that had been outlined in the years before 1858.

The Effect of the War of 1856-1860

During the war of 1856 to 1860 Roman Catholics, both foreign and Chinese, were occasionally persecuted by the local authorities, probably in part because of their supposed connection with the enemy. In 1858 a missionary was captured at Jehol but was later conveyed safely to Shanghai.[3] In the same year three Chinese Christians were killed in Kweichow[4] and a vicar apostolic

[3] Mesnard from Jehol, Jan. 18, 1858, and from Shanghai, Apr. 19, 1858, in *Annales de la propagation de la foi*, Vol. 3, pp. 209, 232.

[4] Launay, *Histoire des missions de Chine. Mission du Kuey-tcheou*, Vol. 1, p. 509.

was apprehended in Hêngchow, Hunan, and sent to Canton.[5] In December, 1859, an edict of persecution issued by Peking was put into effect in Chêkiang, Fukien, and Kiangsi, but not in Kiangnan.[6] In 1860 there was persecution in Hupeh.[7] During these years, however, the imperial and provincial authorities, perhaps because of the lack of national solidarity which was characteristic of China's attitude in the foreign wars of the period, were lenient with both missionaries and converts, and these did not suffer at their hands nearly as much as from the T'ai P'ings. The sympathy of the Catholics was naturally with the Allies. The editor of *Annales de la propagation de la foi* saw in the bombardment of Canton by the French and English in December, 1857, the punishment of God for the blindness of the city to the missionaries;[8] in March, 1859, a *Te Deum* was chanted in Hongkong in thanksgiving for the success of the British and French arms;[9] and in Chihli in 1860 at the news of the capture of the Taku forts by the Allies Christians went from village to village proclaiming their joy.[10]

THE FRENCH PROTECTORATE

As we have seen, one of the effects of the treaties of 1844, 1858, and 1860 was to place both Roman Catholic missionaries and their converts under the ægis of the French Government. The motive of the French in establishing this protectorate was, obviously, not so much zeal for the Faith as a desire for prestige and power. French trade with China was not large, and, as in Cambodia, Annam, and Tongking, the chief basis for insisting that France be heard by the authorities was the claim to the guardianship over Roman Catholic missionaries. Even when, under the Third Republic, the French Government at home became first suspicious of and then hostile to the Church, French representatives in China continued to support it. The French Government seems never to have claimed the privilege, as had the Portuguese, of nominating bishops or confirming their appointment. It did, however,

[5] *Annals of the Propagation of the Faith,* Vol. 28, p. 81.
[6] Servière, *Histoire de la mission du Kiangnan,* Vol. 2, pp. 15 et seq.
[7] Spelta from Hankow, May 16, 1861, in *Annals of the Propagation of the Faith,* Vol. 23, pp. 86-90.
[8] *Annales de la propagation de la foi,* Vol. 30, p. 338.
[9] Ibid., Vol. 30, p. 351.
[10] Lebourq, *Monseigneur Édouard Dubar,* pp. 150-154.

give to missionaries much more vigorous aid than Portugal had ever found it possible to do.

With the powerful backing of the French, Roman Catholics were able to insist upon the enforcement of those provisions of the treaties which so greatly favored them. Soon after the Allies captured Peking, passports authorized in the treaties of 1858 and assuring foreigners the right to travel in the Empire were obtained for the missionaries. Thus in December, 1860, Delamarre, the priest who had served as interpreter to the French, left Peking bearing the tricolor and carrying twenty-seven passports for the missionaries in Szechwan, Yünnan, and Kweichow.[11] The Vicar Apostolic for Tibet wrote in 1861 that his passport made it unnecessary to travel incognito as he had planned.[12] The contrast with conditions a decade earlier was marked.

The Chinese Government, moreover, in pursuance of the French treaties and probably at the instance of the French, soon issued an edict of toleration and instructions to the viceroys and provincial officials, commanding protection to Roman Catholic Christians so long as they obeyed the law, directing that they should be exempt from taxes to support local pagan festivals and celebrations, but cautioning against the interference of missionaries in extra-ecclesiastical questions.[13] In 1869 the French *Chargé d'Affaires* obtained from the viceroys of Kiangnan, Hukwang, and Szechwan edicts favoring Christianity.[14] When, in 1870, a new issue of the imperial code—the *Ta Ch'ing Lü Li*— appeared, the articles which had interdicted Christianity were stricken out and the decrees against it were specifically abrogated.[15] In an edition of the code published illegally in 1892 the ancient prohibitions were reaffirmed, but in 1895 a communication of the Tsungli Yamen to the French Minister formally declared that the version of 1870 was official and orders were given to destroy the issue of 1892.[16]

The French authorities, too, supported the Roman Catholic

[11] Delamarre from Szechwan, Apr. 8, 1861, in *Annals of the Propagation of the Faith,* Vol. 22, pp. 326-331.
[12] Mgr. T. Desmazures from Tibet, Oct. 27, 1861, in ibid., Vol. 23, pp. 261-272.
[13] Tobar, *Kiao-ou Ki-lio,* pp. 10, 65-72.
[14] Servière, op. cit., Vol. 2, pp. 170, 171.
[15] Cordier, *Histoire des relations de la Chine avec les puissances occidentales,* 1860-1900, Vol. 3, p. 326; Tobar, op. cit., p. 57.
[16] Cordier, op. cit., Vol. 3, p. 326.

missionaries in obtaining the restoration of confiscated property that had been promised by the convention of 1860. The return of buildings and land could not but be a source of friction, for often the property had passed through the hands of several purchasers [17] and there was strong popular objection to handing it over to the Church. However, in at least several places the transfer was made. By 1861 Mgr. Mouly obtained the ancient cemetery to the west of Peking where Ricci, Schall, and others of the early missionaries were buried, and the sites of four edifices within the city—the North, South, East, and West Churches (Pei T'ang, Nan T'ang, Tung T'ang, and Hsi T'ang). Of the buildings, only the South Church (Nan T'ang) remained intact; not since early in the century had any of the others been standing.[18] Mouly, in reopening the South Church, was accompanied by a French officer and a *Te Deum* was sung in honor of the French army and of Napoleon III.[19] In Shanghai a former church edifice, long used as a temple of the God of War, through the influence of General Montauban was returned to the Jesuits. The ancient residence of the missionaries in Shanghai had been transformed into a hall for the literati, and now through the same powerful friend and in spite of the protests of some of the Chinese it was handed over to the Roman Catholics.[20] The land at Zikawei once given the missionaries by Hsü Kuang-ch'i was restored to them. In Canton it proved impracticable to effect the return of all properties once occupied by churches, but, at the insistence of the French, there was selected and turned over to the Church a large centrally located tract of ground which, by a strange irony, had once been occupied by the yamen of Yeh Ming-shên, the bitterly anti-foreign Viceroy of the eighteen forties and fifties.[21] At Chingting in Chihli the site of an imperial palace, then a heap of ruins, was obtained and on it were soon erected a church, an orphanage, and schools.[22] In many other places either sites or money indemnities were obtained. Indemnities, too, were col-

    [17] Brinkley, *China*, Vol. 12, p. 114, quoting a decree of Prince Kung in 1871.
    [18] Cordier, op. cit., Vol. 1, pp. 54, 55. Cordier cites a letter of Mouly from Peking, Feb. 22, 1861, from *Annales Cong. de la Mission*, Vol. 26, pp. 234-244.
    [19] Favier, *Peking*, Vol. 2, p. 222.
    [20] Servière, *Histoire de la mission du Kiangnan*, Vol. 2, pp. 32-34.
    [21] Mgr. Guillemin from Canton, Nov. 25, 1860, in *Annals of the Propagation of the Faith*, Vol. 22, pp. 136-140; Cordier, op. cit., Vol. 1, pp. 63-67.
    [22] Mgr. Anouilt from Ching Ting, March 10, 1862, in *Annals of the Propagation of the Faith*, Vol. 23, pp. 291-295.

lected for damage to church property during the war of 1856-1860, and with these property was purchased.[23]

Trouble inevitably arose over the clause in the Chinese text of the French convention of 1860 which assured French missionaries the privilege of renting or buying land in the interior. The concession was of doubtful validity and the Chinese soon objected to it. Negotiations followed, and the clause was virtually affirmed in 1865 by the Berthemy convention. This was in part a restriction by definition of the privileges granted in the Chinese text. It provided that lands purchased in the interior should be held not in the name of a missionary or of the Christians but that they were to become part of the collective property of the Catholic mission of the locality.[24] It did not settle the question in a manner entirely satisfactory to the French, for local officials continued to raise many objections, possibly in pursuance of secret instructions which are said to have been issued by Peking when the Berthemy convention was transmitted to them. After at least one unsuccessful attempt (1882) there was obtained (1895) what amounted to a confirmation and further elaboration of the Berthemy agreement. The new convention provided for the holding of property as specified in the document of 1860: the Catholic mission was to pay the usual registration tax for recording the sale, but the seller was to be under no obligation to notify the officials before the transfer or to obtain their consent to the transaction.[25]

It is not surprising that with this support of the French Government Catholic missionaries interfered from time to time in lawsuits in which Christians were one of the parties. It was hard to know when a case at law arose out of persecution and when some other reason predominated. A missionary might be deceived into thinking that the point at issue was a convert's faith and the convert prove to be a consummate rascal. The missionary, too, naturally wished to be certain that full justice was done to Christians, for a convert's faith might easily prejudice the magistrate. Sometimes a mere gesture from a missionary—a

[23] Becker, *Joseph Gonnet*, p. 85.

[24] The text of the convention is in Cordier, op. cit., Vol. 1, pp. 70, 75. See also Willoughby, *Foreign Rights and Interests in China*, pp. 201, 202.

[25] Tobar, *Kiao-ou Ki-lio*, p. 73; Cordier, op. cit., Vol. 1, pp. 75, 76; Koo, *The Status of Aliens in China*, pp. 316-318.

visit or his card—was enough to obtain a decision in favor of a convert, for the official did not wish to become embroiled with foreigners who through their consuls and ministers could make trouble for him with his superiors. It is not strange, then, that individuals and families and even entire clans and villages professed conversion in the hope of obtaining support against an adversary.[26] Nor is it remarkable that the missionary and his assistants often avoided inquiring too carefully into the motives of those who applied for teachers, and that sometimes they espoused the cause of non-Christians on the condition that the latter would accept Christian instruction.[27] It seems fairly certain, indeed, that they even offered aid in lawsuits in order to obtain adherents.

It is impossibe to say just how extensive was this use of political influence to gain converts, but that it was employed and employed rather extensively there can be little doubt. Mgr. Faurie, Vicar Apostolic in Kweichow, wrote in 1864 that he had aided in sending to prison a man who had abused the Christians, but that he had obtained release for the culprit on the condition that the latter would return to his native town and make public and honorable reparation. Faurie says that the offender promised to do this and in addition offered to become a Christian. He adds—either naïvely or with dry humor—"It is worthy of remark that every one of the individuals who have been punished for reviling our religion have embraced with ardor the true faith on leaving prison."[28] A few days later the prelate writes of two families who had had a quarrel, each claiming to be Christian, to obtain his aid. They came before him accusing each other, but he asked for a few days' delay, had them instructed in the Christian faith, and then urged them to pardon each other. Faurie says that they took his advice and left in his hands a declaration of their reconciliation.[29] He also tells how the head of the rural national guard was imprisoned for anti-Christian activities, but was released through the good offices of the Vicar Apostolic and

[26] See instances of this in *Annals of the Propagation of the Faith*, Vol. 61, pp. 305-312; Becker, *Joseph Gonnet*, pp. 120 et seq.
[27] Becker, *Joseph Gonnet*, pp. 25 et seq.
[28] Faurie from Kweichow, July 20, 1864, in *Annals of the Propagation of the Faith*, Vol. 27, p. 72.
[29] Faurie from Kweichow, July 28, 1864, in *Annals of the Propagation of the Faith*, Vol. 27, p. 77.

"the same evening presented himself in the chapel to adore the true God." [30]

It is only fair to add that if the motive of the Chinese was open to question, it could be countered that by proper education and pastoral care the convert might in time become a good Christian and that at least his children or grandchildren could be so reared as to become exemplary Catholics. It must also be added that missionaries were not wanting who objected to dangling as a bait possible aid in litigation. Thus a vicar apostolic in Chêkiang wrote that in examining candidates for the catechumenate all must be rejected who came with lawsuits. [31]

For a good many years after 1858 both China and Europe appear to have acquiesced in the French protectorate of Catholic missions. The Chinese officials, of course, resented the interference of missionaries in the ordinary processes of the law courts and the endless trouble given them by what in effect was a rival and more powerful jurisdiction. After the Tientsin massacre (1870) they attempted to have restrictions placed on missionary activities and prerogatives. Their objections were, however, overruled. Portugal, the foreign country from which opposition might have been most naturally expected, seemingly entered no protest. In 1876, indeed, the Bishop of Macao asked the French Consul at Canton for a passport for a Portuguese missionary to Hainan. [32] Several Austrians were under French protection and the Spanish Dominicans in Fukien requested French passports. [33] When, in 1868, the Spanish Minister at Peking attempted to assume the protection of Spanish missionaries, the latter protested, and eventually the French resumed the issuance of passports to them. [34] During the Franco-Chinese war the Italian Minister endeavored to withdraw Italian missionaries from French protection but not with entire success. [35] In 1888 the German and Italian Governments tried to gain recognition of the right to issue passports to

[30] Faurie in ibid., Vol. 27, pp. 69 et seq. Simon, in *China,* p. 164, is very critical of the assumption of power and official insignia by Faurie and the Vicar Apostolic in Shensi. Schmidlin, in *Zeitschrift für Missionswissenschaft,* 1915, No. 1, speaks of the influence of missions as having been greatly extended formerly by the support of Chinese Christians in lawsuits and in defense against officials.

[31] Reynaud, *Another China,* pp. 65-70.

[32] Cordier, op. cit., Vol. 2, p. 637; Koo, op. cit., p. 298.

[33] Cordier, op. cit., Vol. 2, pp. 637, 638.

[34] Koo, op. cit., p. 299; Cordier, op. cit., Vol. 2, pp. 638, 639.

[35] Koo, op. cit., p. 299.

missionaries who were their subjects. The Chinese Government gave its consent, but France offered bitter opposition. Bishop Anzer, the head of the German missionaries in Shantung, sought the advice of Rome and eventually decided to accept the proffered support of Berlin.[36] The Italian bishops, however—because of the strained relations between the Quirinal and the Vatican—decided to remain under the protection of France [37] and in this decision they were supported by the Propaganda. The Propaganda, indeed, forbade the acceptance of the Italian protectorate.

While as a rule both China and the Papacy submitted to the French protectorate, they were at times restive. In 1885 the Franco-Chinese war seemed to offer some hope to those who wished to be rid of it. The Pope sent a letter to the Chinese Government thanking it for the imperial edict that was issued at the outbreak of the war promising protection to all missionaries. Probably at the instance of the Empress Dowager, Tzŭ Hsi, who was eager to have adjusted a question concerning the Pei T'ang, the Tsungli Yamen took the opportunity to send, through Li Hung-chang, George Dunn, a British merchant, as a semi-official messenger to the papal court. It was suggested that the Vatican appoint a legate to China, a step which would probably in time have brought to an end the special French relation to missionaries. Mgr. Agliardi was chosen for the post and had accepted when the French brought pressure on Rome and the plan was dropped.[38] In 1891 the Pope again contemplated sending to Peking a legate with a special letter to the Emperor, but because it might be considered unfriendly to the French protectorate the project was abandoned.[39] For the Chinese Government, the appointment of a papal legate to control Roman Catholic missionaries would have been a distinct advantage, for Rome could not have backed her demands by force. If the Church wished vigorous support, that could be obtained much more effectively from the French.

[36] Cordier, op. cit., Vol. 3, pp. 72-84; Brucker in *Catholic Encyclopedia,* Vol. 12, p. 491; Grentrup, *Jus Missionarium,* pp. 399, 400. The story is much more complicated than the above brief summary would indicate.
[37] Cordier, op. cit., Vol. 3, pp. 82, 83.
[38] Koo, op. cit., pp. 301-304; Cordier, op. cit., Vol. 2, pp. 647 et seq; Morse, *International Relations of the Chinese Empire,* Vol. 3, p. 160; Michie, *The Englishman in China,* Vol. 2, pp. 344-346.
[39] Cordier, op. cit.; Vol. 3, pp. 88, 89.

While the French protectorate probably led to an increase in adherents of the Catholic Church, it undoubtedly created much ill-will. It could not, moreover, but lead to a misunderstanding and misrepresentation of the true nature of the Christian Gospel. In justification of his action the Roman Catholic might point to the assistance given by the Carolingians to missionaries in the Low Countries, Germany, and Denmark in the days when these lands were being won to the Faith, and to many another instance where the support of missions by a foreign power had aided in at least the nominal conversion of a people. That the number of baptisms is considerably increased by such means cannot be denied and it may also be that after a few generations the results in Christian character are not entirely untoward. There can be no serious question, however, that the method is entirely contrary to the spirit of the founder of Christianity and that in the minds of many Chinese it led to the identification of the Faith with the imperialistic ambitions of the West. Happily by no means all Catholics approved the method [40] and after 1900 it tended to fall into disuse.

New Orders and Societies

The years between 1856 and 1897 saw the entrance into China of several additional congregations and societies. The increased opportunity afforded by the treaties of 1858 and 1860 stimulated the zeal of Catholics in Europe. In the regions made prosperous by the Industrial Revolution new organizations were arising for the undertaking of foreign missions and to many of these China seemed the most challenging field.

Among the first of the bodies to take advantage of the new conditions were societies of women. Work in the interior, heretofore all but impossible for them, was now feasible. Before 1856 the Daughters of Charity had had houses in China and they now proceeded to found a number of others. [41] In 1860 the Canossian Sisters—instituted in 1808 by the Marchioness of Canossa—opened a house at Hongkong, and by 1892 they had

[40] Louvet, *Les missions catholiques au XIXe siècle,* pp. 216, 217. Not all the French approved, moreover, even when they were interested in imperialism. Boell, *Le protectorat des missions catholiques in Chine et la politique de la France en Éxtrême-Orient,* Paris, 1899, is critical of the protectorate. See, too, article by Prof. G. M. Fiamingo, in *The Open Court,* Nov., 1900, pp. 692, 693.

[41] Planchet, *Les missions de Chine et du Japon, 1919,* pp. 45, 150, 173, 179.

established themselves in Hankow, Shensi, and Honan.[42]   In 1868 the first representatives of the recently founded Société des Auxiliatrices des Ames du Purgatoire reached Shanghai,[43] and in 1869 some Carmelite sisters arrived there.[44]   The Franciscan Missionaries of Mary, who were to assist both the Franciscans and the Paris Society, had a house in Chefoo as early as 1886 and in Ichang in 1889.[45]   There may also have arrived before 1897 the first representatives of the Dominican sisters, to aid in Fukien, and of the Society of the Servants of the Holy Ghost, the companion body of the Society of the Divine Word: certainly they were later to be in China.[46]   The women's bodies gave themselves principally to the care of orphans, children, the poor, and the sick.

The major part of the functions of the Catholic Church could not, of course, be performed by women, and several societies and congregations of priests, most of them of recent origin, were ambitious to supplement the efforts of organizations that had been longer in the country.

It was to be expected that among as strongly Catholic a people as the Belgians special bodies for missions would arise, particularly since the nation had so recently achieved independence and was a rapidly growing industrial center.   Somewhere between 1860 and 1863 there was founded at Scheutveld, on the outskirts of Brussels, the Congregation of the Immaculate Heart of Mary. The author of the enterprise, Theophile Verbist, was a young priest who had been director in Belgium of *L'Œuvre de la Sainte Enfance*—the association which, it will be recalled, had as its special charge children in non-Christian lands—and had himself wished to become a missionary.   The opening of China by the treaties of 1858 and 1860 further stimulated his desire and, with the permission and possibly at the instance of the Propaganda, he, with some companions, undertook the formation of a new congregation.   In 1865 an initial group of four missionaries, led by Verbist, went to China.   By 1868 Verbist—still in his early

---

[42] *Prospetti delle ricoverate e delle opere di carita esercitate nello stabilimento delle figlie della carità Canossiane in Hankow,* 1892, passim.
[43] Servière, *Histoire de la mission du Kiangnan,* Vol. 2, pp. 151-159; *Annales de la propagation de la foi,* Vol. 40, p. 400.
[44] Servière, op. cit., Vol. 2, pp. 151-159.
[45] Planchet, *Les missions de Chine et du Japon, 1919,* pp. 127, 196.
[46] *International Review of Missions,* Vol. 4, pp. 460, 466-464; *Catholic Encyclopedia,* Vol. 5, p. 54.

forties—and one other of the four were dead, but the survivors persevered. Mongolia, one of the most difficult of mission fields, was assigned them. Reënforcements came rapidly from both Belgium and Holland. In 1878 operations were begun in distant Kansu and in 1884 in still more remote Kuldja. The congregation later, indeed, became responsible not only for a large part of the frontiers of China, but also for portions of the Congo and the Philippines.[47]

In 1865, with the consent and possibly at the request of the Lazarists, the province of Honan was allotted to the Seminary of Foreign Missions of Milan.[48]

In 1879 a new vicariate apostolic was delimited in the northern part of Hunan and was entrusted to the Augustinians of the province of the Philippines. Representatives had arrived in China a few years before to begin operations and so, after an interruption of over a century, the order once more had an active share in the Roman Catholic enterprise in the Middle Kingdom.[49]

In 1867 there was established at Rome, for the training of priests for service abroad, a seminary to which was given the names of Peter and Paul. The project was first conceived by Pierre Avanzani in 1867, at the time of the centenary of the two apostles. Avanzani's early death nearly wrecked the undertaking, but in 1875 Pius IX refounded the school. For a few years the seminary contented itself with sending priests to China to reënforce the efforts of other agencies, but in the eighteen eighties the southern part of Shensi was assigned to it and made a vicariate apostolic.[50]

The Germans had at first no separate part in the Catholic missionary awakening of the nineteenth century. Their energies were largely absorbed by the task of unifying the nation, the Industrial Revolution did not have much effect until late, commerce was slow in beginning the growth that by the close of the century proved so phenomenal, and for some years the newly formed

[47] *Missions du Chine et aux Congo,* 1901, pp. 274-278; Schwager, *Die katholische Heidenmission der Gegenwart,* etc., p. 47; Moidrey, *La hiér. cath. en Chine, en Corée et au Japon,* p. 205; F. M. Rudge in *Cath. Encyc.,* Vol. 7, p. 167; Louvet, *Les missions cath. au XIXe siècle,* p. 218; *Annales de la propagation de la foi,* Vol. 45, p. 429; Cordier in *Cath. Encyc.,* Vol. 3, p. 676.
[48] Cordier in *Cath. Encyc.,* Vol. 3, p. 676; Moidrey, op. cit., pp. 81, 193; Schwager, op. cit., p. 32.
[49] Moidrey, op. cit., p. 89; Cordier, *Histoire des relations de la Chine avec les puissances occidentales,* Vol. 2, p. 139.
[50] Moidrey, op. cit., p. 208; Schwager, op. cit., p. 32; *Encyc. Sinica,* p. 50

Empire seemed without colonial ambitions. When, however, after 1870, national union was achieved, manufactures and commerce and with them wealth and population rapidly increased. Germany soon ceased to give its entire attention to Europe and looked eagerly outside the Continent for fresh activities and for a share in the world's affairs commensurate with its growing strength. Enthusiastic nationalism and the added resources of the country aroused in earnest Catholics a desire for a share in the work of the Church in non-Christian lands. The first separate foreign missionary undertaking affecting China that arose out of these conditions was the Society of the Divine Word, a congregation of regular clergy. The founder, and until his death (1909) the Father Superior, was the able and earnest Arnold Janssen. Because of the Kulturkampf—the struggle between Bismarck and the Roman Catholic Church which was then in progress—the headquarters were placed in Holland, at Steyl, not far from the German frontier, on land purchased in 1875. The congregation grew rapidly and before its semi-centennial it possessed houses for the training of missionaries in Rome, Germany, Austria, and the United States, and conducted missions in several widely separated parts of the world. Its first two missionaries to China, one of whom was Anzer, left Steyl in 1879 and went first to Hongkong. They were soon (1882) given as a field a section in Shantung and there began a mission which was not only to be important religiously but was to have significance for the extension of German power.[51]

In 1870, during the Vatican Council, Delaplace, the Vicar Apostolic of North Chihli, obtained a sum of money which he purposed using for the establishment of Trappists in the mountains of his vicariate. The approval of the Propaganda was obtained and after the project had been presented to several monasteries a prior, Seignal, accepted, and in 1883 left for China with one brother. Later in the year two priests and a brother followed. A location was chosen among the mountains at Yang-

[51] Cordier, in *Cath. Encyc.*, Vol. 3, p. 676; Moidrey, op. cit., pp. 64, 211; Schwager, op. cit., pp. 56-63; *Catholic Missions*, Vol. 11, pp. 77-82; *Pieper, Unkraut, Knospen und Blüten aus dem blumigen Reiche der Mitte*, p. 372; Fischer, *Arnold Janssen, Gründer des Steyler Missionswerkes, ein Lebensbild*, pp. 95-125, 221-284, 286-302; Cordier, *Histoire des relations de la Chine avec les puissances occidentales*, Vol. 3, pp. 73-75. Cordier, in the last named work, represents Janssen as being in part actuated by jealousy of the French predominance in foreign missions.

Chiapin, four days' journey west of Peking. Grape-vines were brought from Burgundy and the monks planned to introduce and acclimatize other European fruits. The founders hoped that the institution would not only maintain agriculture and a religious community, but that it would aid in the training of a native clergy and the foundation of a national church.[52]

As the years passed, two societies of teachers were added to the Catholic bodies in the Middle Kingdom. In 1891 the Marist Brothers of Saint Genis Laval, near Lyons, were asked to come to direct schools both for Chinese and for Europeans.[53] Sometime between 1894 and 1911 the Salesians, founded in 1857 for the education of boys, entered the country.[54]

THE GROWTH OF THE ORGANIZATIONS WHICH HAD PREVIOUSLY ENTERED CHINA

While these congregations and societies were gaining a foothold in China, the bodies that had earlier been there were by no means idle. Without exception they were adding to their staffs and were occupying more thoroughly the districts which had been entrusted to them.

The Jesuits confined their attention to Kiangsu, Anhui, and the southeastern part of Chihli. Particularly in Kiangsu and Anhui, where the presence of Shanghai and the concentration of foreign commerce gave to Westerners comparative security, they made rapid headway. During the T'ai P'ing Rebellion, to be sure, in large sections of the two provinces missionary activity was difficult or impossible, and in the general disorder Christians perished or were scattered. Recovery from the insurrection was, however, amazingly rapid, and, as has been suggested earlier, the relatively fluid state of the community that followed the insurrection seems to have given the missionaries a larger opportunity than they would otherwise have had.[55] Energetic Jesuits returned to the former T'ai P'ing strongholds almost on the heels of the

---

[52] Limagne, *Les Trappistes en Chine,* passim; Lemire, *Une Trappe en Chine,* passim. By 1895 there were forty Chinese living with the Trappists, and twenty-six had taken vows. They were extremely poor, obtaining about 2,000 francs a year from the sale of their products.—*Annales de la propagation de la foi,* Vol. 68, p. 73.

[53] Piolet, *Les missions catholiques françaises au XIXe Siècle,* Vol. 3, p. 91.

[54] *Catholic Encyclopedia,* Vol. 13, p. 399.

[55] Servière, *Histoire de la mission du Kiangnan,* Vol. 2, p. 117, says that the destruction of pagan shrines by the T'ai P'ings had made easier the work of evangelization.

victorious imperial armies. In 1864 Soochow was occupied and there, in 1866, in spite of the opposition of the military authorities, a house was purchased.[56] In 1865, with the support of a French gunboat, property was obtained and a resident foreign priest was installed at Chinkiang, and in the same year houses were bought at Tanyang and Yangchow.[57] In 1865, thanks to the efficient aid of a French ship, a foothold was acquired at Anking.[58] About the same time and with the same friendly offices an attempt was made to enter Nanking, but land could be purchased only at Hsia Kuan, on the river front outside the city wall. In 1866 the mission was given a site within the gates in exchange for property which had been confiscated years before and was now used as a state granary.[59] From Ningkohsien in Anhui it was reported in 1872 that among immigrants who were coming to cultivate the lands left desolate by the T'ai P'ings were Christians from Hupeh, and that the populace in general was open-minded to the missionaries' message.[60]

Not only were old centers reoccupied and new ones begun, but orphanages and schools were founded and enlarged and here and there dispensaries began to appear. Reënforcements helped to make possible the rapid extension: from 1864 to 1878 inclusive over a hundred priests joined the mission.[61]

Under these conditions it is not surprising to find the number of Christians growing. In 1856-1857 the Catholics in Kiangnan (Kiangsu and Anhui) are said to have numbered 74,286. By 1860-1861 they are reported to have increased to 77,418. Four years later, due to the ravages of rebellion, they are said to have declined to 71,184, although the baptisms of adults rose during these troublous years.[62] By 1874-1875 the number of Christians once more showed a gain, this time to the reported total of 88,869,[63] and during the same ten-year period the totals of

---

[56] Servière, op. cit., Vol. 2, pp. 146-148; *Annals of the Propagation of the Faith*, Vol. 28, p. 318.
[57] Servière, op. cit., Vol. 2, pp. 146-148.
[58] Ibid., Vol. 2, pp. 135-144; *Annales de la propagation de la foi*, Vol. 41, p. 427.
[59] Servière, op. cit., pp. 135-144.
[60] Ravary from Ningkohsien, March 28, 1872, in *Annales de la propagation de la foi*, Vol. 44, pp. 391-404.
[61] Piolet, op. cit., p. 194.
[62] Servière, op. cit., Vol. 2, p. 117. In 1859 there were reported in *Annales de la propagation de la foi* (Vol. 32, p. 226) to be 75,352 Christians and in 1869 (Vol. 42, p. 12) 77,449.
[63] *Annales de la propagation de la foi*, Vol. 48, p. 42.

confessions heard rose from 119,858 a year to 249,966, and communions from 108,894 to 267,835.[64] In 1866-1867 there were forty-two European and fourteen Chinese priests, and by 1878-1879 these totals had increased to fifty-five and twenty-six respectively.[65] In the latter year sixty-nine hundred orphans are said to have been supported. In 1890 there were reported in Kiangnan six hundred and fifty-five churches, seventy-seven chapels, two seminaries, one school for the preparation of Chinese officials, one industrial orphanage, twenty other orphanages, one hospital, a meteorological observatory, and six hundred and fifty schools enrolling over eleven hundred children.[66]

The district entrusted to the Jesuits in the southeastern section of Chihli also showed an encouraging growth. In 1854, when it was transferred to the Society, one estimate places the number of Christians at nine thousand [67] and another at only a little over three hundred and fifty.[68] By 1870 the number seems to have increased to about nineteen thousand,[69] by 1871-1872 to more than twenty thousand,[70] and in 1896 there were said to be 43,736 Catholics in the district.[71]

For many years the Franciscans had been caring for the provinces of Shantung, Shansi, Shensi, Hupeh, and Hunan. By 1897 a section of the southern part of Shantung had been transferred to the Society of the Divine Word, a portion of Shensi to the Seminary of Saints Peter and Paul, and a part of Hunan to the Augustinians, but the Friars Minor were still responsible for the major part of their former field. Many of the Franciscan missionaries were from Italy, but occasionally reënforcements came from other countries. In 1889, for example, of the eleven foreign priests in Shansi, four were Italian, two were French, and five were Dutch.[72] In most of the other provinces the proportion of Italians seems to have been larger.[73]

In Shantung in 1867 there were said to be seven missionaries,

[64] *Relations de la mission du Nankin,* Vol. 2, p. 13.
[65] Servière, op. cit., Vol. 2, pp. 321-322.
[66] Louvet, *Missions catholiques au XIXe siècle,* p. 223.
[67] Leroy, *En Chine au Tché-ly S.-E.,* p. viii.
[68] Lebourq, *Monseigneur Édouard Dubar,* pp. 171-175.
[69] Leroy, op. cit., p. viii.
[70] *Annales de la propagation de la foi,* Vol. 45, p. 98.
[71] Leroy, op. cit., p. viii.
[72] Ricci, *Barbarie e Trionfi,* p. 141.
[73] Moidrey, *La hiér. cath. en Chine,* etc., pp. 91, 92, 93; von Richthofen, *Tagebücher aus China,* Vol. 1, p. 407.

seven native priests, one hundred and twenty-three churches and chapels, one seminary, and a little over ten thousand Catholics.[74] At the capital, Tsinan, the mission regained (1865) the property within the walls that had once belonged to it and a cemetery outside the west gate.[75] A church and residence were soon erected,[76] and in the seventies a Protestant missionary described the cathedral as being one of the two most prominent buildings in the city "with its Western architecture and glittering cross." [77] In 1889, in the portion of Shantung occupied by the Franciscans, sixty churches, five orphanages, and seventeen thousand Catholics were reported.[78] In 1894 the eastern section of the province was made a separate vicariate apostolic and was entrusted to the French Franciscans.[79]

In Shansi in 1867 the number of Catholics was placed at 13,832 and these were ministered to by four foreign and sixteen native priests.[80] At least four of the Chinese clergy had passed some years at Rome.[81] In 1889 there are reported to have been in the province 19,065 Catholics, twenty native priests, and eleven missionaries.[82] By 1891 the Vicar Apostolic had erected about eight *li* southeast of T'aiyüanfu a monastery for the Chinese, and by 1893 the first three novices had been enrolled.[83] Here as elsewhere the effort was made to root the Church in the soil.

In Shensi in 1867 there were reported to be about twenty-three thousand Catholics ministered to by seven foreign and seventeen native priests.[84] In that year the number of Catholics in Hupeh was placed at 16,063, and there were fourteen foreign and fourteen native clergymen in the province.[85] In 1865 there was laid in Wuchang—only a few decades before the scene of noteworthy martyrdoms—the cornerstone of a cathedral.[86] When, in 1883, the Vicar Apostolic of West Hupeh, Zanoli, died, it was possible

[74] *Annals of the Propagation of the Faith,* Vol. 28, pp. 69-91.
[75] Giesen in Forsyth, *Shantung,* p. 165.
[76] Cosi, Oct. 17, 1873, in *Annales de la propagation de la foi,* Vol. 46, p. 28.
[77] Mrs. Williamson, *Old Highways in China,* p. 115.
[78] Antonini, *Au pays de Chine,* p. 263.
[79] Moidrey, op. cit., p. 65; Schmidlin, *Katholische Missionsgeschichte,* p. 470.
[80] *Annals of the Propagation of the Faith,* Vol. 28, pp. 69-91.
[81] Williamson, *Journeys in North China,* Vol. 1, p. 307.
[82] Ricci, op. cit., p. 141.
[83] Ibid., pp. 160-171.
[84] *Annals of the Propagation of the Faith,* Vol. 28, pp. 69-91.
[85] Ibid., Vol. 28, pp. 69-91. For the history of missions in South Hupeh, see also Nino, *Santo Storico de Vicariato Hupè Occ. Sett. in Cina,* passim.
[86] *Annals of the Propagation of the Faith,* Vol. 28, p. 78.

to have a public funeral.[87]   In 1873 persecution had sufficiently abated to permit of a large public procession in the northeastern section of the province.   Here, in the mountains, was a Christian community of fifteen hundred.[88]

Hunan was long bitterly anti-foreign and the progress of the Church was slow.   Only twenty-two hundred Roman Catholics were reported in 1867,[89] a number smaller by far than that in any of the other provinces administered by the Franciscans, and in 1885 the total was said to be only three thousand, or less than that in any of the Eighteen Provinces except Kansu and Kwangsi.[90]   Von Richtofen, who visited Hunan in the seventies, said that the chief function of the missionaries was usually the care of Catholics who were descendants of "old Christians." [91] In 1862 a church in Siangtan was destroyed by a mob, in Hêngchow the Bishop's residence, two churches, an orphanage, and sixty houses belonging to Christians were burned, and in Changsha the students in attendance on the annual examinations attacked the Christians.[92]   Still, in 1866 a church in Hêngchow was publicly consecrated and a new Christian community was reported in Siangtan.[93]

The Lazarists, who in the eighteenth century had manfully stepped into the breach left by the dissolution of the Society of Jesus and so long had spread their scanty forces over a large section of the country, were in 1897 still in charge of most of Chihli—including Peking—and all of Kiangsi and Chêkiang. For a time in the sixties, before it was transferred to the Milan Society, Honan was also under their care.   The number of priests, native and foreign, grew fairly rapidly.   From 1843 to 1859 inclusive, fifty-two were added to the ranks of the congregation, and from 1860 to 1899 inclusive the corresponding number was two hundred and thirty-five.[94]   We have seen that in Peking, through the good offices of the French, the sites of the four prin-

[87] Ibid., 1883, p. 354.
[88] Letter of Billi, May 20, 1873, in Annales de la propagation de la foi, Vol. 45, pp. 391-399.
[89] Annals of the Propagation of the Faith, Vol. 28, pp. 69-91.
[90] Werner, Katholischer Missions-Atlas.
[91] Von Richthofen, Tagebücher aus China, Vol. 1, p. 407.
[92] Navarro, Vicar Apostolic of Hunan, from Peking, Sept. 6, 1862, Nov. 10, 1862, Apr. 19, 1862, in Annals of the Propagation of the Faith, Vol. 24, pp. 342-351.
[93] Annals of the Propagation of the Faith, Vol. 28, pp. 82-87.
[94] Catalogue des prêtres, clercs et frères de la Congrégation de la Mission . . . en Chine, passim.

cipal churches of the eighteenth century had been restored. The Nan T'ang (South Church) had never been destroyed. A chapel was soon erected on the site of the Tung T'ang (East Church), in 1866 worship was reëstablished in the Hsi T'ang (West Church), and January first, 1867, Mgr. Mouly celebrated mass for the first time in the new building on the site of the Pei T'ang (North Church).[95] Much of the construction was by funds which the French authorities awarded the Vicar Apostolic, Mouly, from the indemnity collected from China under the treaties of 1858 and 1860.[96] Napoleon III was not content with providing money, but in 1862 sent out seven missionaries and fourteen Sisters of Charity, apparently entirely for the assistance of the Lazarists in North China.[97]

The Roman Catholics were not allowed to enjoy without protest their new properties in Peking. The Pei T'ang was a source of annoyance to the court, for the site was that given the French Jesuits by K'ang Hsi and the towers of the new structure overlooked the imperial palace. The Empress Dowager wished the building removed and the palace gardens extended to cover its location. In 1874 the Tsungli Yamen asked that this be done, but the Vicar Apostolic demurred and the death of the Emperor T'ung Chih (1875) postponed negotiations. The situation was complicated, because France, the Pope, and the Superior General of the Lazarists had each to consent. The request was renewed in 1886 and the assent of the interested parties was at length obtained. The Lazarists were given land at a greater distance from the palace and a sum for the construction of a new edifice. The completed building was dedicated in 1888.[98] Simultaneously with the transfer of the old site a remarkable natural history collection gathered by Armand David, a member of the Lazarist mission, was conveyed to the imperial government.[99]

In the meantime the Lazarists were able boldly to continue their activities and were prospering greatly. When, in 1868, Mouly died, he was buried with a pomp reminiscent of the palmi-

---

[95] *Annales de la propagation de la foi,* Vol. 41, p. 245.
[96] Favier, *Peking,* Vol. 2, p. 229.
[97] Ibid.
[98] Cordier, *Histoire des relations de la Chine avec les puissances occidentales,* Vol. 2, pp. 604-624; Favier, *Peking,* Vol. 2, pp. 243, 251; Little, *Intimate China,* p. 334; *Annales de la propagation de la foi,* Vol. 61, p. 231.
[99] Favier, *Peking,* Vol. 2, p. 231.

est days of the older Jesuit mission.[100]   The Catholics in the
central part of the province are reported to have increased from
4,585 in 1874 to about ten thousand in 1896.[101]   They seem, too,
to have been loyal to their faith, for in 1872 a group of them,
without solicitation from the missionaries, contributed nearly
twelve hundred francs to the Society for the Propagation of the
Faith.[102]   In all the parts of Chihli entrusted to the Lazarists
the number of Catholics is reported to have grown from about
thirty thousand in 1870 to about sixty-two thousand in 1890.[103]

Both in Kiangsi and in Chêkiang, the efforts of the Lazarists
were meeting with success.   It was estimated that in the former
province the number of Catholics had risen from about six
thousand in 1832 to nine thousand in 1856, had then, in T'ai
P'ing times, decreased to six thousand, by 1875 had increased to
about twelve thousand [104] and by 1885 to a little over thirteen
thousand.[105]   In 1890 there were said to be in Kiangsi one seminary, six schools, five orphanages, four churches, and twenty-one
chapels.[106]   In Chêkiang in the same year there were reported
to be two seminaries, sixty-four schools, eight churches, and forty-
three chapels.   Twenty-seven Sisters of Charity were in charge
of the hospitals and orphanages.[107]   In 1885 the province is said
to have contained twelve thousand Catholics and, in addition
to the Vicar Apostolic, eight European and six Chinese priests [108]
—a marked increase in the past three decades.

The Society of Foreign Missions of Paris had long been responsible for large areas—Szechwan, Kweichow, and Yünnan.   By
1897, as we have seen, to these had been added Kwangsi, Kwangtung, Hainan, Manchuria, and Tibet.   No other one Catholic
organization in China was attempting to minister to so vast a
territory.   Not until the twentieth century was any portion of
its field apportioned to other bodies, and then only when the
stress of the Great War had depleted its resources.   By 1872 the
Society was reported to have in China five bishops, seventy-eight

[100] Piolet, *Missions catholiques françaises au XIXe siècle*, Vol. 3, p. 80.
[101] Planchet, *Les missions de Chine et du Japon, 1917*, p. 60.
[102] *Annales de la propagation de la foi*, Vol. 49, p. 88.
[103] Louvet, *Missions catholiques au XIXe, siècle*, p. 218.
[104] *Annales de la propagation de la foi*, Vol. 48, p. 235, Vol. 52, pp. 13 et seq.
[105] Werner, *Katholischer Missions-Atlas*.
[106] Louvet, *Missions catholiques au XIXe, siècle*, p. 225.
[107] Ibid.
[108] Werner, op. cit.

other European missionaries, seventy-nine native priests, seven seminaries and colleges, three hundred and fourteen schools, and twenty-two orphanages.[109]

Manchuria suffered from disorder in the years immediately following 1860, probably in part as the result of the foreign war.[110] The Christians seem to have been troubled less than the non-Christians, however,[111] and the numbers of non-Christians applying for instruction increased.[112] By 1863 the advantages accruing to the Catholics because of the new treaties had become so apparent that pagans were applying to the Vicar Apostolic for protection against bandits. The Bishop responded and, riding with the flag of France above him and accompanied by his catechists, he was greeted joyously and addressed the suppliants on the teachings of the Christian faith.[113] By the close of 1861 a priest had crossed Manchuria from south to north.[114] The Franco-Prussian War delayed remittances from France and brought, as it did in at least one other place in China, embarrassment to the missionaries.[115] No permanent loss was suffered, however. There are said to have been about seven thousand Catholics in Manchuria in 1870,[116] in 1885 a little over eleven thousand,[117] and in 1890 almost fourteen thousand.[118] In 1890 the missionaries numbered thirty-five and the native priests eight.[119]

On the island of Hainan the progress of the Church was extremely slow, and as late as 1886 the number of Catholics was reported to be very small.[120] In the portion of Kwangtung on the mainland, however, progress was more rapid. Severe local persecutions occasionally broke out, but in and near Canton French protection secured a fair degree of toleration. In 1870 the number of Roman Catholics in Kwangtung outside of Macao

[109] *Annales de la propagation de la foi,* Vol. 44, p. 231.
[110] Verolles from Manchuria, March 23, 1861, in *Annals of the Propagation of the Faith,* Vol. 22, pp. 316-318.
[111] Verolles from Manchuria, Nov. 8, 1863, in ibid., Vol. 26, pp. 23-29.
[112] Verolles, March 23, 1861, in ibid., Vol. 22, pp. 316-318.
[113] Verolles, in *Annals of the Propagation of the Faith,* Vol. 26, pp. 29, 30.
[114] Franclet, Aug. 20, 1861, in ibid., Vol. 23, pp. 339-376.
[115] *Annales de la propagation de la foi,* Vol. 44, p. 95, Vol. 45, p. 85.
[116] Louvet, op. cit., pp. 218, 219.
[117] Werner, *Katholischer Missions-Atlas.*
[118] Louvet, op. cit., pp. 218, 219.
[119] Ibid.
[120] Henry, *Ling-nam,* p. 338.

is estimated to have been about twelve thousand and there were twenty-one foreign and three native priests; [121] in 1885 the number of Catholics was placed at 24,176,[122] and in 1890 at 30,500.[123] The great cathedral with its twin spires was the most prominent building on the sky-line of Canton.[124]   As was fitting in this day of revival of Catholic missions in China, a chapel was erected on Shang-ch'üan in memory of Xavier.[125]

It was to be expected that in Kwangsi the progress of the Church would be slow. So much of the province is mountainous, and disorder was so chronic that no very great gains were made. We have seen that the judicial murder in Kwangsi of Chapdelaine, a missionary of the Paris Society, had given the French authorities an excuse for active association with Great Britain in the latter's second war against China. Not until 1865 or 1867 did missionaries resume the enterprise which Chapdelaine's martyrdom had suspended.[126] A superior was sent into the province in 1868, but he died after three years. In 1878 Kwangsi contained about eleven groups of Catholics and about two hundred and fifty or three hundred and fifty Christians.[127] The officials offered stubborn opposition—which seems not unnatural in light of the turbulent state of the province and of the fact that the T'ai P'ing Rebellion took its rise there—and long delays were encountered in gaining access to the capital, Kweilin, and in obtaining the publication of the Treaty of Tientsin with its provisions in favor of missions.[128] The Franco-Chinese War of the eighties severely affected Kwangsi. During its progress over half of the scanty missionary force was compelled to withdraw, several stations were destroyed, and many Catholics, as was to be expected in Christian communities so young and so small, fell away from the Faith.[129] In 1891 there were only eleven priests in the prov-

[121] Louvet, op. cit., p. 231.
[122] Werner, op. cit.
[123] Louvet, op. cit., p. 226.
[124] Henry, *Ling-nam*, p. 38.
[125] *Annales de la propagation de la foi*, Vol. 40, p. 252, Vol. 41, p. 296. The cornerstone was laid Aug. 25, 1867, and the chapel opened April 25, 1869.
[126] Launay, *Mission du Koung-si*, pp. 102-109, says that it was in 1865 that the first priests were sent to the province. Bazin, a missionary to Kwangsi, in his journal of 1870 says that it was not until 1867 that the Christians were visited.— *Annales de la propagation de la foi*, Vol. 43, pp. 102-207.
[127] Launay, op. cit., pp. 102-166.
[128] Ibid., pp. 172, 206-243.
[129] Launay, op. cit., pp. 261-295.

ince and the Christians numbered only about eleven or twelve hundred.[130]

In Kweichow, as we have seen, French protection helped the Church to achieve a very remarkable growth. Severe persecutions had been launched in the fifties and early sixties. By 1864, however, the tide had turned. Thanks probably to pressure from the French authorities, the Viceroy came out positively in favor of tolerance and reparation was obtained from Peking.[131] What was almost a mass movement into the Church followed. In 1864 Faurie, the Vicar Apostolic, reported that one hundred large villages had recently been converted and that the Faith seemed to spread almost without the agency of the missionary. In one district alone, he said, forty thousand had taken the initial steps toward enrolling for instruction.[132] At least one temple was transformed into a church.[133] The officials entrusted the missionaries with a foundling home for boys and another one for girls and expressed a desire to turn over to them a hospital for the infirm.[134] This rapid growth could not continue. By no means all those asking for instruction persevered until they were received for baptism, and occasionally persecutions broke out. However, the number of Catholics reported rose from about six thousand in 1870 [135] to 16,443 in 1885 [136] and to 16,652 in 1890.[137] In the last named year there were thirty European and five Chinese priests.[138]

In Yünnan the missionary carried on his operations in the face of great unrest. During part of the fifties, all of the sixties, and the early years of the seventies the province was distracted by a rebellion of Moslems. When the revolt first began the only two missionaries in the province died of exposure and sorrow, a number of the Christians were killed, and the Church all but disappeared.[139] With the reëstablishment of the authority of the imperial government, however, better days came. In spite of

[130] Ibid., pp. 313, 315.
[131] Faurie, June 10, 1864, in *Annals of the Propagation of the Faith,* Vol. 26, pp. 31-42.
[132] Faurie, Dec., 1864, in ibid., Vol. 26, p. 352.
[133] Faurie, Aug., 1864, in ibid., Vol. 27, pp. 77-79.
[134] Faurie, June 10, 1864, in ibid., Vol. 26, pp. 31-42.
[135] Louvet, *Missions catholiques au XIXᵉ siècle,* p. 226.
[136] Werner, op. cit.
[137] Louvet, op. cit., p. 226.
[138] Ibid.
[139] Fenouil, Vicar Apostolic of Yünnan, writing in 1881 in *Annals of the Propagation of the Faith,* 1882, p. 195.

anti-foreign feeling and even before the rebellion was entirely suppressed, the Church began a rapid recovery. It is said that in 1870 the province contained slightly over eight thousand Catholics.[140] In the seventies a very successful mission among a non-Chinese people, the Lolos, was reported.[141] In the early eighties a visitor in Yünnanfu spoke of "the handsome palace of the French Bishop."[142] The number of Christians in 1885 is said to have been 10,798,[143] and in 1890, 10,620.[144]

Szechwan had been the scene of the chief triumphs of the Paris Society in China in the eighteenth century. As late as 1890 it seems still to have contained almost as many and perhaps more Catholics than did all the other provinces in charge of the Society. Growth was, however, not as rapid as in some of the other fields. Persecutions were frequent and occasionally severe, and the French authorities could not make entirely effective in so distant a region a protectorate that depended largely upon the fear of their arms. If the reported figures at all approach accuracy, in 1870 there were in the province about eighty thousand Catholics, and by 1890 the number had increased only to about eighty-three thousand. In 1870 the Christians were ministered to by forty-four foreign and sixty-six Chinese priests, and in 1890 by eighty-two foreign and eighty-six Chinese priests.[145]

Repeated and heroic efforts were made to penetrate Tibet. In 1861 the Vicar Apostolic of Tibet, Thomines Desmazures, sought to avail himself of the provisions of the new treaties and enter Lhasa. Before reaching his destination he was halted by the authorities and, leaving his companions to hold what had been gained, he went to Peking in an attempt to have extended to Tibet the privileges of travel and residence accorded to Catholic missionaries elsewhere in the Empire. He was unsuccessful, possibly in part because Peking realized its inability to afford protection to foreigners in a country upon which the rule of the Manchus sat rather lightly and where a bigoted and all-powerful

[140] Louvet, op. cit., p. 226.
[141] Pourias, *Huit ans au Yunnan*, passim.
[142] Hosie, *Three Years in Western China*, p. 55.
[143] Werner, *Katholischer Missions-Atlas*.
[144] Louvet, op. cit., p. 226.
[145] The Protestant missionary, Virgil C. Hart, in *Western China*, pp. 283 et seq., says that in 1888 there were in Szechwan 96 foreign and 86 native priests, and 88,445 Catholics. Werner, op. cit., puts the number of Catholics in 1885 at 149,936. *The Chinese Recorder*, Vol. 44, p. 618, says that in 1899 there were 82,879 Catholics in the province.

hierarchy was implacably opposed to the introduction of an alien faith.[146] The missionaries were forced to content themselves with stations on the frontier. Even here they were not always safe. In 1873 the mission at Batang was ruined, in 1881 a missionary was assassinated, and in 1887 the Chinese authorities ordered that all posts on the border be abandoned.[147] However, the missionaries would not cease their efforts. In Szechwan were Tibetans for whom they could labor and occasionally they penetrated in disguise the "great closed land." In 1870 Tibet was said to have about nine hundred Catholics and in 1890 a little over eleven hundred.[148]

For more than two centuries the Dominicans from Spain and the Philippines had maintained missions in Fukien and now that greater liberty had been granted Catholics they were naturally eager to reap the results of their long and patient sowing. Through the support of the French authorities they were able to regain some of the property that had been confiscated in the days of persecution and it is recorded that, with the countenance of the French Consul, the Vicar Apostolic, garbed in his official robes and carried in state, called on the Governor.[149] The district around Amoy was made a separate vicariate in 1883 [150] and new buildings were erected for worship and for instruction. Shortly after 1890 a part of the province witnessed what was almost a mass movement toward membership in the Church.[151] The Island of Formosa, apparently without resident missionaries for over two hundred years, was once more entered.[152] In 1870 Fukien was said to have about four hundred thousand Catholics and sixteen foreign and ten native priests, and in 1890, 34,250 Catholics and seventeen foreign and thirteen native priests.[153] The seeming decline in the number of Christians is probably due to an overestimate for the earlier years.

[146] Annales de la propagation de la foi, Vol. 41, p. 248. See also Annals of the Propagation of the Faith, Vol. 25, pp. 251, 264, Vol. 26, pp. 184-196.
[147] Louvet, op. cit., p. 230; Annales de la propagation de la foi, Vol. 41, p. 208. Marston, The Great Closed Land, p. 75, tells how the mission at Yerkalo was burned in 1887 by an uprising instigated by the Lamas. See also Annals of the Propagation of the Faith, 1882, pp. 178-192.
[148] Louvet, Missions catholiques au XIXe siècle, p. 226.
[149] Annals of the Propagation of the Faith, Vol. 28, pp. 178-186.
[150] Moidrey, La hiér. catholique en Chine, etc., p. 49.
[151] Cothonay, Deux ans en Chine, p. 131.
[152] Annals of the Propagation of the Faith, Vol. 28, pp. 178-186; Annales de la propagation de la foi, Vol. 61, pp. 35 et seq.
[153] Louvet, op. cit., p. 222.

SUMMARY OF GROWTH

These, then, are in brief survey the gains made society by society and province by province. As may easily be gathered, the statistics of growth, particularly in the number of Catholics, are inexact. One estimate puts the total number of Catholics in all China in 1870 at 369,441,[154] and another puts it at 404,530.[155] Both tables agree that about two hundred and fifty European priests were then in the country. An estimate in 1885 reckons 558,980 Catholics, thirty-five bishops, four hundred and fifty-three foreign and two hundred and seventy-three native priests.[156] The number of priests in this table seems to be approximately right, but the totals for the Catholic community are probably excessive.[157] By 1890 the Christian community appears to have increased to about half a million, the number of missionaries to six hundred and thirty-nine, and the Chinese priests to three hundred and sixty-nine.[158] The official tables of the Propaganda place the number of Catholics in 1896 or 1897 at 532,448 (catechumens not included), of European missionaries at seven hundred and fifty-nine, and of native priests at four hundred and nine.[159]

FINANCES

It seems impossible to determine the annual expense of main-

[154] Louvet, op. cit., pp. 218-231.
[155] *Bulletin des missions catholiques,* quoted in *Chinese Recorder,* Vol. 9, p. 118. Alzog, *Manual of Universal Church History,* Vol. 3, p. 932, says that in 1868 there were in China 325,000 Catholics, 153 European and 169 native priests.
[156] Werner, *Katholischer Missions-Atlas.*
[157] According to *Missiones Catholicae Ritus Latini Cura S. Congregationis de Propaganda Fide,* 1886, p. 36, there were in China in 1886 483,403 Catholics, 2,429 churches and chapels, 471 European missionaries, 281 native priests, 1,779 schools and 33 seminaries. On the other hand, *Annales de la propagation de la foi,* Vol. 50, p. 333, says that in China there were in 1878 772,412 Catholics. This figure is probably excessive. The *Chronicle of the London Missionary Society,* 1885, p. 135, says that in 1882 there were, according to official Catholic statements, 1,092,818 converts, 664 European priests, 41 bishops, and 559 native priests in China. This is almost undoubtedly a mistake.
[158] Louvet, op. cit., pp. 218-226. *Chinese Recorder,* Vol. 44, p. 618, says that there were in 1889 in China 542,664 Catholics. Huonder, in *Der einheimische Klerus in den Heidenländern,* p. 186, says the number of Chinese priests in 1890 was three hundred and seventy-one.
[159] *Missiones Catholicae Cura S. Congregationis de Propaganda Fide,* Rome, 1897. The 1895 edition of the same book (p. 311) placed the total number of Catholics at 581,575. Why there should be the apparent decline by 1896 or 1897 is not clear.

taining in China the work of the Church.[160]   In 1867 the Society for the Propagation of the Faith allocated to China 637,000 francs [161] and in 1882 861,000 francs.[162]   This, however, was probably very much less than half of the total budget of the missions.   Funds were obtained directly by the various orders and congregations or came to missionaries from abroad from private sources and as mass stipends, and some were raised in China itself.   Moreover, in many instances the orders and congregations acquired in China houses and lands which were not used for ecclesiastical purposes, but which were rented and the income used by the Church.   Probably much of the property obtained in exchange for lands confiscated in the eighteenth century was so employed.   At least part of the large Catholic holdings at Hsia Kuan, just outside Nanking, for example, and which are almost entirely leased for secular purposes, were obtained in this manner,[163] and in Shanghai, Tientsin, and in Szechwan the Church owned and rented much property.[164]   In the famine in the North in 1877 aid was sometimes given to non-Christians in the form of mortgages on the lands of those assisted.   The owner

[160] A possible clue to the annual expenditure is found in the estimate of the cost of maintaining each missionary. Mgr. Lions, Vicar Apostolic of Kweichow, writing Nov. 5, 1872 (*Annals de la propagation de la foi*, Vol. 45) said that two thousand francs were required for each missionary and that the latter with this must not only support himself but must employ catechists and school teachers, each of whom required about two hundred francs. If this was the scale of expense throughout China, the cost in 1890 for salaries alone would have been about two million francs. Mgr. Lions says that two thousand francs were required to build each chapel and about five hundred francs would erect an oratory.

[161] *Annales de la propagation de la foi*, Vol. 40, p. 184.

[162] *Annals of the Propagation of the Faith*, 1882, pp. 295, 296.

[163] Servière, *Histoire de la mission du Kiangnan*, pp. 135-144.

[164] Colquhoun, who had long travelled extensively in China, writing at the close of the century in *Overland to China*, p. 358, says: "Roman Catholic missions in China are enormously rich. Especially is this the case in Szechwan where they have accumulated real estate on a very large scale. This is the practice of Roman Catholic missionaries everywhere. The *procureur* is always a very keen man of business who through intimacy with family affairs is able to watch the decay of fortunes, the profligacy of sons, and the other factors which bring about the financial ruin of old families. . . . Property is thus continually passing into their hands and in some places, such as Tientsin for instance, the church is the principal landlord. It is this funded wealth which enables the Roman Catholic missions to extend themselves without requiring subsidies from Europe."

In 1851 the Propaganda forbade the Vicar Apostolic of Kweichow to invest with merchants money that had been sent him for current expenses—as had seemingly been his practice.—*Collectanea S. Congregatione de Propaganda Fide*, Vol. 1, p. 572.

In Shanghai the various procurers bought large tracts in the early days of the Settlements when land was cheap, and buildings were erected and rented and the proceeds used to support the missions.—Hagspiel, *Along the Mission Trail*, Vol. 4, pp. 24-26.

was allowed to continue to cultivate his farm and turned over part of the produce. The income thus obtained was assigned to the religious work of the Church.[165]   Land, too, was occasionally purchased outright in famine times, presumably at low prices.[166]

METHODS: THE MAKING AND TRAINING OF CATECHUMENS

The methods of the Roman Catholic Church between 1856 and 1897 did not vary greatly from those of the earlier years of the century. The chief innovations were the dependence on the French protectorate and the creation or expansion of certain types of institutions which had either been precluded or discouraged by the handicaps under which missionaries labored before the days of treaties. The major object of the missionary, so he would still have said, was the eternal salvation of souls. He continued to believe that this was to be achieved by leading men and women to become intelligent and sincere members of the Roman Catholic Church. The support of the French Government and the privileges granted by the treaties were, as we have seen, of great assistance in increasing the number of inquirers, both by reducing the danger of persecution and by affording in the yamens aid against adversaries. Missionaries, however, even while appealing to worldly motives to obtain adherents, recognized clearly the danger involved and the fact that true conversion must be an inward and spiritual process—a work of God. They therefore strove by education to purify and elevate motives.[167]   Other methods of attracting non-Christians were schools, to which some children of "pagans" were occasionally admitted, preaching halls, medical work which the missionary carried on as an incident to his other duties, the cure of opium addicts in refuges established for the purpose, and alms to the poverty-stricken.[168]

When a Chinese expressed a desire to learn the Catholic faith he was made to enter upon a course of instruction which, if he gave satisfactory proof of sincerity, eventually led to baptism. The steps in the preparation for baptism seem to have been much the same throughout China. The applicant was first told the main tenets of the Faith and was taught the sign of the cross.

[165] Becker, *Joseph Gonnet*, p. 126.
[166] Ibid., p. 128.
[167] Becker, *Joseph Gonnet*, pp. 131-137.
[168] Ibid., pp. 238-248.

Then, by a simple ceremony, he was enrolled as an adorer. Mgr. Faurie, Vicar Apostolic in Kweichow in 1864, described as follows this process as practiced in his province:

When a pagan has been told what he is to understand by the true religion and . . . declares his belief in one God and his desire to become a Christian, he is . . . taught the sign of the cross. As soon as he can do this without being prompted two candles are lighted on the altar and he is placed on his knees. He holds in his hands a paper on which is printed all that he has to repeat. An old Christian kneels near him, so as to be able to direct him how to answer. The ceremony commences by making the sign of the cross: then five prostrations while reciting the following words:

First prostration. "I believe in God. I abjure all my past errors."

Second prostration. "I hope that God, in His infinite goodness, will forgive all my sins."

Third prostration. "I love and adore God, all beautiful, almighty, more than anything else in this world."

Fourth prostration. "I detest with all my heart the sins of my past life and I firmly resolve never to commit them again."

Fifth prostration. "I pray the Blessed Virgin Mary, my mother, to obtain for me from God, by her powerful intercession, the grace of final perseverance."

After this the Apostles' Creed is recited, also Our Father, Hail Mary, and the Ten Commandments. Then is added this declaration:

"The commandments of God that I have just recited are contained in these two: To love God above all things and one's neighbor as oneself. These ten commandments have been dictated by God that all nations might observe them. Those who keep them faithfully will be recompensed with eternal glory in heaven. Those who disobey them will be condemned by Him to the eternal torments of hell."

The "adorer" then concluded with five thanksgivings—for the creation, nourishment, and preservation of his life, for redemption, for pardon for sins, for having been brought to a knowledge of the true religion, and for all other blessings. He then, Mgr. Faurie adds, regarded himself as a Christian and was expected to attend mass and observe all the laws of the Church. If, "after about a year" he knew "his prayers and" was "well instructed in the Christian doctrine," he was "advanced to the state of a catechumen," a step marked by more ceremonies. After another year of probation he was baptized.[109] Sometimes, as in Jesuit

---

[109] Mgr. Faurie in *Annals of the Propagation of the Faith,* Vol. 27, pp. 81, 82; *Collectanea S. Congregatione de Propaganda Fide,* Vol. 2, pp. 187-196; Reynaud, *Another China,* pp. 65-70.

territories, neophytes were gathered together in catechumenates for instruction. Here for several weeks, under the direction of a teacher, they gave their entire time to learning the doctrines and practices of the Faith.[170]

The official decrees of the Church ordered that no one should be enrolled as a catechumen who had not abandoned idols, who had not conformed his manner of life to the requirements of the Christian religion, and who had not begun the study of the Faith with the object of seeking baptism. No one was to be admitted to baptism unless, after long probation, he gave evidence of sincerity of heart and was Christian in his life. He was, of course, to know his catechism, the chief mysteries of the Faith, the more important Catholic symbols, the Lord's prayer, the Ten Commandments, the precepts of the Church, and the effect of baptism, and he must have forsworn the worship of his ancestors and all other ceremonies which in the decree of the eighteenth century terminating the rites controversy were declared to be superstitious. If he had concubines he was required to put them away. These regulations, it ought to be added, outlined the ideal of the Church; it is not certain that in practice they were always lived up to.[171]

The initial character of the converts was usually not promising. The assistance afforded in lawsuits probably tended to attract the baser and more turbulent elements of society. The extensive aid administered in the famine of 1877 was virtually given on the condition that the recipients accept Christian instruction,[172] and this tended to recruit the Church from the poorer elements of the community. The children who came in through the orphanages, and who in the course of time formed a not inconsiderable portion of the communicants, were probably for the most part from the lower economic and cultural strata of the nation. While the devotion expended upon these waifs was a

[170] Becker, *Joseph Gonnet,* pp. 241, 242.
[171] Mgr. Faurie in *Annals of the Propagation of the Faith,* Vol. 27, pp. 81, 82; *Collectanea S. Congregatione de Propaganda Fide,* Vol. 2, pp. 187-196; Caubrière, *Synthesis decretalium Sinarum,* pp. 96-102. To an applicant for instruction, Fenouil, Vicar Apostolic of Yünnan, summarized Christian beliefs and duties as follows: "To believe and hope in God, in one only God in three persons, to love and serve Him, to obey His law, to believe in Jesus Christ, our God and Saviour, to hope in His mercies, and to follow His counsels and to imitate His virtues."—*Annals of the Propagation of the Faith,* 1882, pp. 195, 196.
[172] Becker, *Joseph Gonnet,* p. 126; Kervyn, *Méthode de l'apostolat moderne en Chine,* pp. 429, 430.

striking example of Christian faith and charity, and although in caring for the outcast—often in the face of prejudice and gross misunderstanding—the Church was making a noteworthy contribution to Chinese life, the fact cannot be obscured that so large an accession from the poverty-stricken groups of the nation brought with it grave problems. It was not easy to build from such unpromising material a Christian community that could make a marked impression upon the nation. The Church was in danger of becoming a group which for generations to come would need to be under the tutelage of a foreign clergy. The Church did, however, draw occasionally from more promising classes. In more than one place it won leaders of those religious sects which have so often attracted some of the more earnest and upright.[173] The missionaries found difficulty in reaching the women, but frequently families came into the Church as a body,[174] bringing their women with them, and, as in the eighteenth century, there were women who had some of the functions of catechists and carried on active work among their sex.[175] Sometimes, too, an entire village or clan came into the Church.[176]

METHODS: THE CARE OF CHRISTIANS

With baptism the efforts of the Church had only begun. Converts needed to be strengthened in their faith, encouraged to maintain regular worship, and provided with the ministration of the sacraments. They must be taught to observe Sunday, to maintain family prayers, and to keep themselves from opium and from participating in the theatre.[177] Their children must be baptized, instructed, and, at the proper age, confirmed. Various means were employed to achieve these ends. Often Christians were gathered into villages, where, separated from too intimate contact with non-Christian neighbors, they could be kept from idolatrous community practices and their entire life be supervised by the Church.[178] Schools, too, were sometimes opened where, at the expense of the mission, adults as well as children were instructed in the Faith.[179] Apparently in adaptation of a

[173] Stenz, In der Heimat des Konfuzius, p. 200; Becker, op. cit., p. 25.
[174] Lemmens in Annales de la propagation de la foi, Vol. 64, pp. 20-25.
[175] Stenz, op. cit., p. 204.
[176] See examples in Becker, op. cit., pp. 122-124.
[177] Kervyn, op. cit., pp. 748 et seq.
[178] Lemmens in Annales de la propagation de la foi, Vol. 64, pp. 20-25.
[179] Becker, Joseph Gonnet, pp. 127, 128, 139.

familiar Chinese custom, each Catholic community normally had head men chosen by the Christians and approved by the vicar apostolic and the director of the district. These presided at public prayers, at weddings, and at funerals. When the priest was absent they administered baptism. They cared for the sick and dying, and they were charged with the propagation of the Faith among non-Christians.[180] Possibly also as an adaptation of Chinese custom, Catholics were sometimes provided with images of Christ, of the Virgin, and of a saint.[181] Much was made of the great festivals of the Church,[182] perhaps in part as a substitute for the holidays and processions of religious significance which for non-Christian Chinese do much to relieve the monotony of life. Pilgrimages, another feature of Chinese life combining recreation and religious duty, were encouraged and Christian shrines provided as objectives.[183] Christians were induced to maintain daily family worship,[184] a custom that among other values was a substitute for the former observances before domestic shrines. Among adaptations of Chinese customs that were clearly conscious were a feast of "inscriptions" on Christmas Eve, when honorific scrolls were presented to the church or chapel, the use of fire-crackers and the firing of cannon (to greet the priest, at the beginning and end of the mass and at the time of the elevation of the Host), and the greeting of the priest by prostrations.[185]

Most Catholic communities had no resident priest and, as in earlier years, the clergy spent much of their time on the road.[186] When a priest came to a village, he said mass, preached, heard confessions, catechized the children, inquired into the morals of his flock, and adjusted quarrels. He seldom made the initial approach to non-Christians to interest them in the Faith: this

[180] Caubrière, *Synthesis decretalium Sinarum*, pp. 69-80.
[181] Letter of Aubry from Kweichow, Aug. 6, 1886, in *Correspondence du Père J.-B. Aubry*, p. 116. In the Jesuit mission in Chihli representations of the last judgment, of hell, purgatory, and heaven, were used to impress the pagans. This may have been an adaptation of Buddhist and Taoist representations of hell.— *Annales de la propagation de la foi*, Vol. 40, p. 91.
[182] *Correspondence du Père J-B. Aubry*, p. 156.
[183] *Correspondence du Père J.-B. Aubry*, p. 156; *Relations de la mission de Nankin*, Vol. 2, pp. 111-113; Ricci, *Barbarie e Trionfi*, pp. 136-139.
[184] Von Richthofen, *Tagebücher aus China*, Vol. 2, pp. 71-74.
[185] *Annales de la propagation de la foi*, Vol. 66, p. 86; Kervyn, *Méthode de l'apostolat moderne en Chine*, p. 497.
[186] Gonnet, a Jesuit, writing from Kiangnan in 1845, said that the Christians were eager for extreme unction and asked for it at every illness. He said that visits to the sick Christians took more than half his time.—*Annales de la propagation de la foi*, Vol. 20, pp. 51, 58.

was usually done by Chinese, often the catechists. He did, however, have a part in the instruction of those who had not yet been admitted to baptism.[187]   The vicars apostolic had such vast territories to cover that sometimes, as previously, confirmation was delegated to priests.[188]   At least in the earlier days missionaries usually wore the garb of Chinese merchants and had nothing about them outwardly to indicate their ecclesiastical functions.[189]

Sincere efforts were made to lift the morals of the Christians above those of the surrounding community. The Propaganda forbade the sale and use of opium by Catholics.[190]   This prohibition was not always observed and at least once a vicar apostolic felt it necessary to issue a vigorous pastoral letter reminding his flock of its existence.[191]   The ruling was at times relaxed: the missionaries and the Vicar Apostolic in Kweichow declared that they would find it difficult to make converts if growers of opium were denied the sacraments and if old addicts of the drug were compelled to give it up at once, and the Propaganda accordingly made concessions.[192]   Vigorous orders were issued against admitting to the sacraments Catholics who had sold their wives or their infant daughters to pagans and were unrepentant.[193]   The minimum marriageable age was held to be twelve years for girls and fourteen for boys, and the reckoning was if possible to be after the Western manner.[194]   Converts were to restore goods taken wrongfully and were to make adequate reparation for other offenses.[195]

The change of life of those who had recently come into the Church was often not very marked. A priest writing from Kwei-chow in 1877 said that the new Christians were not full of zeal or free from their pagan superstitions and that baptism meant merely that a man had burned his idols and had declared himself a Christian. He believed that converts regarded the act of join-

[187] *Annales de la propagation de la foi*, Vol. 45, p. 83.
[188] *Collectanea S. Congregatione de Propaganda Fide*, Vol. 2, p. 137.
[189] Huc, *Journey Through Tartary, Tibet and China*, Vol. 1, p. 22.
[190] *Collectanea S. Congregatione de Propaganda Fide*, Vol. 2, p. 184. The order was dated March 10, 1852.
[191] Bishop Grassi of Shansi, Dec. 19, 1891.—Ricci, *Barbarie e Trionfi*, pp. 175 et seq.
[192] *Collectanea S. Congregatione de Propaganda Fide*, Vol. 2, pp. 118, 184.
[193] Ibid., Vol. 2, pp. 209, 210.
[194] Ibid., Vol. 2, p. 248. By the Chinese reckoning a child is one year old at birth.
[195] Ibid., Vol. 2, pp. 187-196.

ing the Church as having little if any more significance than obtaining membership in one of the many trade guilds or religious societies.[196] In this general opinion of the poor quality of recent converts, Von Richthofen, who had opportunity for wide observation, concurred.[197] It is significant, too, that as a rule candidates for the priesthood were accepted only from families that had long been Christian.[198] On the other hand, those who had been brought up from childhood as Christians appear to have been above the level of their non-Christian neighbors in morals and in personal cleanliness. So at least Von Richthofen believed.[199] Younghusband, too, commented on a Christian village in Manchuria, where he was impressed by "the really sincere and devout character" of the converts. They seemed, so he said, "like a different race from the cold, hard Chinamen about them." [200] A distinguished Protestant missionary, Christie, who spent many years in Manchuria, said of the Chinese Roman Catholics that they were "a well-behaved, clean, industrious part of the community." [201] W. H. Medhurst, the son of the Protestant missionary of the same name and for many years a consul in China, said that he had "often been struck by the quiet and respectability which prevails in . . . Catholic communities as compared to the heathen around them." [202] We hear, too, of the reconciliation of enemies [203] and of the healing of the strange and distressing malady called "demon possession," [204] an affliction which one missionary declared had never failed to disappear when the sufferer became a Christian.[205] On the whole, the Catholics appear as a result of their faith to have become distinctly better morally than their non-Christian neighbors of the same social strata.[206]

[196] Aubry from Kweichow, Dec. 1, 1877, in *Correspondence du Père J.-B. Aubry*, p. 222.
[197] Von Richthofen, *Tagebücher aus China*, Vol. 1, p. 144.
[198] A vicar apostolic in Chêkiang in Reynaud, *Another China*, p. 74.
[199] Von Richthofen, op. cit., Vol. 1, p. 144.
[200] Younghusband, *The Heart of a Continent*, p. 41.
[201] Christie, *Thirty Years in the Manchu Capital*, p. 18.
[202] Medhurst, *The Foreigner in Far Cathay*, pp. 33, 34.
[203] Mgr. de Marchi in *Annales de la propagation de la foi*, Vol. 67, pp. 328 et seq.
[204] Mgr. Anouilh from Chihli, Jan. 16, 1866, in *Annales de la propagation de la foi*, Vol. 28, p. 371; Leroy, *En Chine au Tché-ly S.-E.*, pp. 144-186.
[205] Becker, *Joseph Gonnet*, p. 23.
[206] Doolittle, a Protestant missionary, says of the Roman Catholics in Foochow that in their lives they could not be distinguished from the non-Christians.—*Social Life of the Chinese*, Vol. 1, pp. 37-40. He was not, however, unbiased.

METHODS: SCHOOLS

One of the methods upon which the Roman Catholic missionaries laid emphasis was the development of an extensive educational system.[207]   As in earlier years, schools were not primarily for the purpose of reaching non-Christians, but for providing the children of Catholics with religious as well as secular instruction, and for preparing Chinese leaders for the Church.   The Propaganda forbade the admission of pagans to the schools except with the consent of the missionary and commanded the vicars apostolic to endeavor to keep the children of the faithful from enrolling in other than Christian institutions.[208]   The Propaganda also directed that in the collections of Chinese writings used as texts in the mission schools there should not be anything encouraging to superstition or subversive to faith.[209]   The large majority of the schools were elementary, but a number of higher grade prepared priests, teachers, and catechists.   Every vicariate, indeed, seems to have had at least one seminary where a beginning of the preparation for the priesthood could be made, and there were a number of schools where the training could be completed.[210]   Sometimes, for fear of persecution, these institutions were hidden in the hills,[211] but they were also to be found in larger centers of population.[212]   The course of study required of candidates for the priesthood was long and exacting, for it had to equip the clergy with enough Chinese classical scholarship to command the respect of the educated and at the same time to give them the theological, historical, and liturgical knowledge necessary for the performance of their religious duties.   Candidates pursued for ten or twelve years the study of Chinese literature and acquired Latin, philosophy, and theology.   Their knowledge of Latin had to be adequate not only for the performance of the ritual, but for the perusal of books, for only thus could they keep in touch

[207] In Kiangnan in 1878-79 there are reported to have been 345 boys' schools with 6,222 pupils and 213 girls' schools with 2,791 pupils.   In 1897-98 the number of pupils is reported to have increased to 16,571.—Piolet, *Les mis. cath. franç. au XIXᵉ Siècle.*

[208] *Collectanea S. Congregatione de Propaganda Fide,* Vol. 2, pp. 193, 194.

[209] Ibid.

[210] Louvet, *Missions catholiques au XIXᵉ Siècle,* pp. 219, 221.

[211] As in Kweichow.—*Annales de la propagation de la foi,* Vol. 47, p. 35.

[212] As in Mukden (Ibid., Vol. 44, p. 84) and Shanghai (*Relations de la mission de Nankin,* Vol. 1, pp. 43, 56).

with the life and thought of the Church at large. In at least one vicariate candidates began their education at the age of ten or twelve and were not ordained priests until they were thirty-four or thirty-five.[213] Of those who started the course, apparently only a small proportion finished. The prejudice in China against celibacy, the physical strain of the prolonged preparation, and the privations and poverty incident to the profession weeded out all but the more hardy and persevering. Even then the product was by no means always satisfactory. The native clergy were said to be "pious and moral," and apt in settling difficulties among their countrymen,[214] but they had so long been kept in school and away from normal society that they were too timid and inexperienced to work alone for the conversion of souls,[215] and as a rule they were not physically robust.[216] It is pleasant to record, however, that Lord Elgin was favorably impressed with the Chinese in preparation for the priesthood whom he met in Shanghai in 1858. "They had an intelligent, cheerful look," he records, "greatly superior to that of the Roman Catholic seminarists generally in Europe." [217] In addition to the seminaries for the training of priests, there were schools for women pledged to virginity and who were to become schoolmistresses and to baptize and instruct members of their sex.[218] There were also schools for the training of catechists.[219] The catechists were most of them married. They were assistants to the missionaries, sometimes administering the Christian community, preaching at prayers and taking care of the church and its archives, sometimes preaching to non-Christians, sometimes teaching the prayers of the Church to children and the new Christians, and sometimes helping as secretaries in intercourse with Chinese

[213] *Annales de la propagation de la foi,* Vol. 45, pp. 85, 86.

[214] Poilet, *Les Missions catholiques au XIXe siècle,* p. 314.

[215] Leboucq, from Kiangnan, Jan. 18, 1870, in *Annales de la propagation de la foi,* Vol. 42, pp. 340-344; a vicar apostolic in Chêkiang in Reynaud, *Another China,* p. 74.

[216] Piolet, op. cit., p. 314.

[217] Walrond, *Letters and Journals of James, Eighth Earl of Elgin,* p. 242.

[218] *Annales de la propagation de la foi,* Vol. 45, p. 88. These virgins, accompanied by their parents, consecrated themselves before the priest, usually at the age of sixteen or eighteen. They were taught to repeat by heart the long prayers for morning and evening, for Sundays and feast days, and for the mass. They knew the catechism. They usually lived with their parents and did not wear a distinctive dress.—Werner, writing Oct. 20, 1847, from Haimen, in ibid., Vol. 21, p. 317.

[219] *Annales de la propagation de la foi,* Vol. 45, p. 87.

officials.[220] In a few institutions French was taught. A few schools of secondary grade gave a general education to non-clerical Catholics, and occasionally one was maintained for the foreign community.[221]

METHODS: SCIENTIFIC RESEARCH AND LITERATURE

As in the years between 1844 and 1856, some suggestions were made of reviving at Peking the group of Jesuit scholars that in the seventeenth and eighteenth centuries had played such an important part in obtaining a foothold for the Church. The proposal was not carried out, for the resources of the Jesuits were already strained by the responsibilities which they had undertaken in Kiangnan and Chihli. Then, too, for nearly a century Peking had been in the hands of the Lazarists, and, probably more important still, the changed situation in China seemed no longer to require this particular method.[222] Catholics were now protected by foreign treaties and were not in such need of the favor which a mission of scholars could win from the court and the official classes. Some research was maintained, however, by both Lazarists and Jesuits. Armand David, a Lazarist, was, at the request of the French Government, set apart by his superiors for the study of natural history. He travelled widely and gathered the museum which was transferred to the Chinese Government when the Pei T'ang was removed to its new site. The presence of the collection is said to have done something toward breaking down prejudice against foreigners.[223] As early as 1869 the Jesuits, true to their scholarly traditions, began to collect a museum of natural history as a means of approach to the Chinese.[224] In 1872 they decided to establish at Zikawei a center for scientific research.[225] The results are well known—an observatory with daily weather reports and forecasts, a large library, an ever-growing series of scholarly monographs on various phases of Chinese life (the

[220] Pieper, *Unkraut, Knospen und Blüten aus dem blumigen Reiche der Mitte*, pp. 502 et seq.; Brouillon, *La mission du Kiangnan, 1842-1855*, p. 104; Kervyn, *Méthode de l'apostolat moderne en Chine*, pp. 519 et seq.

[221] Favier, *Peking*, Vol. 2, p. 263; *Relations de la mission de Nankin*, Vol. 1, p. 73.

[222] Servière, *Histoire de la mission du Kiangnan*, Vol. 2, pp. 35-42; *Une université française en Chine*, extrait des *Relations de Chine*, April, 1925, p. 2.

[223] *Encyclopædia Sinica*, p. 139.

[224] Von Richthofen, *Tagebücher aus China*, Vol. 1, pp. 133, 134.

[225] Servière, op. cit., Vol. 2, pp. 192-198.

Variétés sinologiques),[226] an interesting museum of natural history, and a large printing establishment.[227] A member of the Jesuit mission in Southeastern Chihli, Seraphin Couvreur, prepared dictionaries and translated into French or Latin or both large sections of the Chinese classical literature.[228] Just how important this scholarly activity was in introducing and commending Christianity to the Chinese is difficult to say, but it clearly was not as prominent as had been the Peking mission in the former period of Jesuit history. Moreover, while Roman Catholic missionaries, especially Jesuits, were continuing in a scholarly way to interpret China to the Occident, the leadership in this field was passing into other hands.

Literature was prepared to aid the work of the Church. Much of what had been written in the seventeenth and eighteenth centuries was still useful and needed simply to be kept in print. Much more was added, including translations of parts of the Scriptures.[229]

METHODS: ORPHANAGES, HOSPITALS, AND FAMINE RELIEF

Catholic missionaries had as their primary objective the salvation of individual souls through the processes ordained by the Church. To this all their activities were designed to contribute. The zeal for souls, however, led to extensive humanitarian enterprises which in time were among the most prominent features of Catholic activity. The most important institutional philanthropy was the orphanage. In their origin and purpose, orphanages were closely associated with the baptism of infants who were in danger of death. If the infant died soon after baptism its soul was, so the Roman Catholics believed, assured of entrance to Heaven. If the child lived, it must, to insure its eternal welfare, be brought up in the Catholic faith. Thus for as many waifs as possible Christian orphanages were provided. Infants were, too, presented

[226] The first number appeared in 1892 and twelve had been published by the close of 1897.—Cordier, *Bibliotheca Sinica*, pp. 857, 858. It is interesting to note that several of the *Variétés sinologiques* and a number of other works were produced by a Chinese secular priest in Kiangnan, P. Huang Po-lu.—*T'oung Pao*, 1910, pp. 139-141.

[227] *Encyclopædia Sinica*, pp. 360, 413; *Relations de la missons de Nankin*, Vol. 1, p. 61; Cordier in *Catholic Encyclopedia*, Vol. 3, p. 674.

[228] See the bibliography of his works in *Encyclopædia Sinica*, p. 135.

[229] Bondfield in *China Mission Year Book, 1915*, p. 468. See also Henninghaus in *Zeitschrift für Missionswissenschaft*, 1911.

to the sisters by poor parents, often in exchange for a small sum—in one place about two hundred cash.   They were given out to Christian women to nurse and at about two years of age were taken into the orphanage to be reared.[230]   In the orphanages training was given not only in religion but in occupations which would enable the children later to become self-supporting. Before the treaties such institutions would not have been possible, but with the coming of guaranteed toleration they could safely be built.   They flourished especially in the shelter of the treaty ports —at Shanghai, Hankow, and Tientsin, for example—but they were also to be found in the interior.[231]   They seem usually, perhaps always, to have been in charge of some sisterhood—although a priest might be at the head.[232]   A few hospitals and dispensaries were maintained,[233] but they were not as numerous as those conducted by Protestants.   There were also a few homes for the indigent, especially the aged.[234]   Christian mendicant guilds were said to exist in West China, less barbarous and ill-behaved than the non-Christian ones.[235]   The belief in demon possession, so common in China, was shared by many missionaries, and the records are numerous of the healing of afflicted individuals through exorcism by a priest or a catechist or by the use of the rosary as an aid to faith.[236]

In the frequent famines which are so marked a feature of Chinese life the missionaries distributed relief.   Usually their resources were no more than sufficient for the Christians, but they saved as many children of pagans as possible and administered baptism to such of the dying as they could.   In the famine in North China in the latter part of the seventies, the resources of the Church were taxed beyond their limit.   Such funds as could be obtained from Europe and from foreigners in Shanghai were disbursed, but these were insufficient to relieve more than

[230] Cothonay, *Deux ans en Chine*, p. 258.

[231] *Annales de la propagation de la foi*, Vol. 44, pp. 84 et seq., Vol. 48, p. 1047; Louvet, *Missions catholiques au XIXᵉ siècle*, pp. 219, 221, 222; *The Chinese Recorder*, Vol. 10, p. 370, tells of an orphanage farm near Peking.

[232] Chamard, *Un missionaire poitevin en Chine*, passim, says that Father Louis Octave Barrois was head of an orphanage in Canton.

[233] Poilet, *Les missions catholiques françaises au XIXᵉ siècle*, p. 314.

[234] *Annales de la propagation de la foi*, Vol. 48, pp. 10-17, Vol. 60, p. 272; Favier, *Peking*, Vol. 2, pp. 247-250; Reynaud, *Another China*, pp. 94-97; Pieper, *Unkraut, Knospen und Blüten aus dem blumigen Reiche der Mitte*, p. 472.

[235] Piolet, op. cit., p. 316.

[236] Cothonay, *Deux ans en Chine*, p. 222, 461-517.

a fraction of the distress.[237]   Several missionaries died of disease contracted while ministering to the suffering,[238] and orphanages were crowded with children who had been abandoned or who had lost their parents by death.[239]   After the famine was over, the Church was seen to have profited.   In Shansi, for example, where the destitution had been most severe, in 1880 and 1881 large numbers of non-Christians flocked to the missionaries for instruction.[240]

THE CHARACTER OF THE MISSIONARY

Upon the quality of the missionaries depended to a large extent the character of the converts. The European priests seem, on the whole, to have been men of great devotion, but both their preparation and their manner of life in China narrowed their horizons. As a rule they had been educated from early youth in schools which were under the control of their order or congregation and which were largely cut off from the currents of thought of the non-ecclesiastical world.[241]   In China most of them knew little of what was happening outside their own station and province.[242] The Paris Society seems to have made an effort to keep its missionaries in West China in touch with the news of the world by sending them translations of items from the Shanghai papers,[243] but

[237] Ricci, *Barbarie e Trionfi*, pp. 62-66; *Annales de la propagation de la foi,* Vol. 49, p. 333, Vol. 50, pp. 83-90, 385, Vol. 51, pp. 9 et seq.; Leboucq, *Monseigneur Édouard Dubar,* pp. 428-470.

[238] Leboucq, *Monseigneur Édouard Dubar,* pp. 428-470; Piolet, *Les mis. cath. franç au XIXe siècle,* Vol. 3, p. 141; Leroy, *En Chine au Tché-ly S.-E.,* p. 266. At least six European priests died in Chihli. See also *Annales de la propagation de la foi,* Vol. 50, pp. 385 et seq.

[239] *Annales de la propagation de la foi,* Vol. 50, p. 392.

[240] Ricci, *Barbarie e Trionfi,* pp. 75-77. The accusation has been made (Duncan, *The Missionary Mail,* p. 66) that Catholic missionaries took the occasion of the famine to buy up at low prices lands and houses from pagans for the aggrandizement of the Church. Duncan also (ibid., p. 66) declares that during the Moslem rebellion in Northwest China the Catholics admitted many to the Church and that these converts were spared by the Moslems as "worshipers of the true God." These statements may be true, for they are from the pen of one who had opportunities for first-hand observation, but it must be remembered that Duncan, although living in and writing from Shensi, was a prejudiced observer.

[241] There were exceptions, of course, particularly among the Jesuits.

[242] Von Richthofen, *Tagebücher aus China,* Vol. 2, pp. 173, 218. Von Richthofen said (1869) that the Franciscans in Shantung had neither books nor maps and believed T'ai Shan the highest mountain in China. They knew nothing of the province except the names and situations of the mission stations. Even the bishop had been away from his vicariate only twice in twenty years and then not outside of China.

[243] Hosie, *Three Years in Western China,* p. 142.

at best life in the interior isolated the priests and confined their interests to the performance of their ecclesiastical duties.   The average quality of the missionaries was higher in some societies than in others.   Parker, for example, found the representatives of the Missions Étrangères of Paris not "so thoroughly grounded in scientific theology, or so admirably disciplined as the Jesuits" and in their methods "a little too aggressive and militant to meet our views of what charity and religion ought to be." [244]   Sometimes, in spite of their long life in the country, missionaries did not acquire a full knowledge of the vernacular, for their intercourse was chiefly with Christians and the latter tended to use only the vocabulary with which the missionary was familiar. [245] Some of the missionaries were not above believing in supernatural portents.   We find one of them reporting a cross in the air and another the appearance of a cross to a dying woman, and still another the vision of two radiant children on the altar which impelled a pagan to seek baptism. [246]   We have, too, a vicar apostolic solemnly reporting that the intercession of the Virgin had turned into another channel a stream which was threatening to undermine a village. [247]   We also have a missionary recording the appearance of the spirit of a deceased woman, a Christian, to her brother, to urge him to accept her faith. [248]   Missionaries as a rule came to China with no expectation of again seeing their native land and did not have the furloughs that served to keep Protestant missionaries in touch with events the world over and with the Church at home.   The life of the Catholic missionary was at best physically comfortless and tended to be mentally and spiritually depressing.   It is not strange that priests became homesick and that some returned to Europe. [249]   The wonder is that so many remained at their posts.   Numbers found in their faith resources which enabled them to grow into men who impressed travellers with the radiant strength and beauty of their lives.   Contact with them could not fail to be helpful to Christians.

[244] Parker, *John Chinaman*, p. 200.
[245] Huc, *Journey Through Tartary, Tibet and China*, Vol. 1, p. 232.   The Propaganda and the synods in China laid emphasis upon the importance of the missionary acquiring the language and a knowledge of the classics.—Becker, *Joseph Gonnet*, pp. 165 et seq.
[246] Cothonay, *Deux ans en Chine*, pp. 232, 233.
[247] Reynaud, *Another China*, p. 68.
[248] Bouchere in *Annals of the Propagation of the Faith*, Vol. 61, pp. 237-240.
[249] Little, *Intimate China*, p. 162.   Little says that the Italian priests often gave up and went home, but that not so many of the French priests did so.

CHURCH ORGANIZATION

Between 1855 and 1897 little change was made in the form of the organization of the Church. As the activity of the older missions expanded and additional congregations and societies entered the country, new vicariates apostolic were created. Almost no coöperation existed between the different orders and congregations, and none knew much of the achievements and difficulties of the others. To each the Propaganda had assigned territory and each was content to report directly to that body: coördination came almost entirely through Rome. In 1870 most of the vicars apostolic were in Rome for the Vatican Council and there held a number of meetings on the problems of China. A project was approved for the division of the Empire into five regional synods,[250] but the step was not formally taken by the Propaganda until 1879. In that year synods were ordered convened in each of these five regions once every five years.[251] The grouping was territorial and so brought together representatives of various bodies.[252] The synods met for the first time in 1880 and were held thereafter fairly regularly—although not always at the specified intervals. They considered chiefly such matters as the administration of the sacraments, the bishops and missionaries, the vocation and training of the Chinese clergy, the methods of conversion and of spreading the Faith, the spiritual oversight of the Christians, education, and regulations for Chinese priests and nuns.[253] Their scope, therefore, was fairly comprehensive.

Given existing conditions in China, not many steps could be taken toward freeing the Church from missionary control. The Church relied so much upon foreign treaties and the support of the French Government, its members were drawn so largely from the humbler and less desirable ranks of the nation, that dependence upon the foreign clergy was fairly complete. The Propaganda, remote from actual conditions, stressed the importance of training a Chinese clergy,[254] but the vicars apostolic were for the

---

[250] Servière, *Histoire de la mission du Kiangnan,* Vol. 2, pp. 183, 184.

[251] *Decreta Trium Synodarum regionalium annis 1880, 1886, et 1892 Pekini habitarum,* passim; Launay, *Mission du Koungsi,* p. 244; Caubrière, *Synthesis decretalium Sinarum,* pp. 41-43; Schmidlin in *Zeitschrift für Missionswissenschaft,* Vol. 13, pp. 87, 88. A synod had been held in West China in 1859 and in Hongkong in 1875, but these were only for local vicariates.

[252] Ibid.

[253] Ibid.

[254] *Collectanea S. Congregatione de Propaganda Fide,* Vol. 2, pp. 187-196.

most part rather pessimistic about any early success in building
up a native priesthood to which the Church could safely be
entrusted.[255] In their judgment the Chinese Church must for
an indefinitely long period remain under foreign tutelage. The
Chinese Christians were, however, not entirely without initiative
or active participation in the work of the Church. In addition
to the extensive activities of Chinese teachers, catechists, and
priests, Catholics often gave liberally toward the construction and
maintenance of churches.[256] As many as three religious societies
of men and nine of women were formed before 1899,[257] and
there were numerous associations for pious and philanthropic
purposes.[258]

PERSECUTIONS

It was inevitable that the progress of the Roman Catholic
Church should be marked by riots and persecutions. As has
been said more than once before in these pages, here was an
organization which, so the more respectable classes believed, was
subverting much of what was most dear to Chinese civilization.
Moreover, the Church was under the ægis of foreign powers and
by appealing to French officials was able to interfere in the conduct of the courts and the administration of justice. Missionaries
were rapidly increasing and were to be found in every province
and in some of the dependencies. The execution of an agent of
the Church had already been the occasion for one attack by a
foreign power and more missionaries might at any time come
to grief and embarrass the government. Among the masses,
moreover, sinister stories were widespread. Why should the
missionary and his assistants be so solicitous for young children?
Rumor had it that the "barbarian" desired their eyes and their
vital organs, perhaps to manufacture medicine. Suspicions, moreover, were aroused by the administration of extreme unction—
especially since the sacrament was usually followed almost imme-

---

[255] Servière, op. cit., Vol. 2, pp. 183, 184.
[256] Annals of the Propagation of the Faith, 1883, p. 27; Schwager in Zeitschrift für Missionswissenschaft, 1912, pp. 220 et seq.
[257] The Christian Occupation of China, p. 460; Arens, Handbuch der katholischen Missionen, pp. 134, 144; Annales de la propagation de la foi, Vol. 48,
p. 27.
[258] Servière, op. cit., Vol. 2, p. 262; Annales de la propagation de la foi, Vol.
63, p. 248, Vol. 48, p. 9; Relations de la mission de Nankin, Vol. 1, pp. 11-47.
The societies and associations seem often, however, to have been due originally to
the suggestion of a missionary.

diately by the death of the Christian—and by the celebration of the mass, which as a rule had to be non-public. Stories attributing to the foreigner the most inhuman and cruel practices persisted, indeed, well down into the twentieth century. Priests were accused of licentiousness, the assemblies of Christians were believed to be occasions for promiscuous relations between men and women, the eucharist was held to be a means of giving to the participants a kind of drug which made the recipient insensible to the afflictions of the evil spirits and invulnerable to persecution, and extreme unction was said to be a means of obtaining photographic materials.[259] Given these attitudes and popular beliefs, it is not remarkable that letters of missionaries are often devoted almost entirely to accounts of persecutions.

However, a marked difference existed between these attacks and those of pre-treaty days. Then, persecutions were nearly always begun and carried on by the state. Now, treaties and the protection of foreign powers usually prevented the government from openly taking an anti-Christian attitude. Peking might close its eyes to, and officials might secretly instigate or connive at, the harassing of Roman Catholics, but they did not often do it overtly. For the most part, injuries to Christians were the work of the populace and of the educated but non-office-holding classes. We have now to do with riots, feuds, and popular resentment rather than with official proscription.

Probably many of the persecutions have never been recorded, and even the briefest description of those of which we have mention would overpass the limits of this book. At the risk of tediousness, however, a number of typical instances must be catalogued. In the sixties and seventies, to other causes of difficulty were added the rebellions which for a time plunged much of the Empire into anarchy. Missionaries and their converts could not expect to pass scatheless through the violence of the times. In 1861 Fenouil, a missionary of the Paris Society in Yünnan, was held captive by one of the non-Chinese tribes.[260] That same year a missionary from Kwangtung spoke of the Christians in his district as having suffered in the general disorder wrought by rebels.[261] The Moslem rebels of Yünnan were bitterly anti-

[259] Kervyn, *Méthode de l'apostolat moderne en Chine,* pp. 274-277.
[260] Letter of Fenouil, July 18, 1861, in *Annals of the Propagation of the Faith,* Vol. 23, pp. 246-258.
[261] Letter from Philippe in ibid., Vol. 22, pp. 331-336.

Christian and the missionaries were often in danger.[262]   Kwei-chow was also affected.[263]   In 1861 Christians in Shantung suffered from the devastation caused by rebels.[264]   In 1862 a missionary, Octave, was robbed by bandits in Southeastern Chihli and a revolt drove from their homes several hundred Christians along with their non-Christian neighbors.   The central mission station in that section of the province was fortified as a permanent stronghold.[265]   In Kiangnan, as we have seen, much suffering was caused by the T'ai P'ing Rebellion.[266]   In Honan in 1863 missionaries were hampered by the armed bands which were devastating much of the province.[267]   The great rebellion of Moslems in the Northeast gave Christians some inconvenience,[268] even though the insurgents appear, at least in Shensi, purposely to have spared all Catholics.[269]

Most of the suffering of missionaries and their converts, however, was due to specifically anti-Christian opposition and not to the general disorder.   In 1865 Mabileau lost his life, apparently at the hands of a mob in a village in Szechwan,[270] and in 1869 Rigaud and a number of Chinese Christians were killed in the same village.[271]   In 1865 there were severe persecutions on the Tibetan frontier and Durand was drowned while trying to escape.[272]   In February, 1862, a missionary, Jean Pierre Noël,

[262] Pourias, Huit ans au Yünnan, pp. 70-77; letters from Huot, Dec. 1, 1861, and Chauveau, Sept. 5, 1862, in Annals of the Propagation of the Faith, Vol. 24, pp. 312-323.
[263] Launay, Histoire des missions de Chine. Mission du Kuey-Tcheu, Vol. 2, pp. 160-300.
[264] Louis de Castelazzo, Vicar Apostolic of Shantung, June 10, 1861, in Annals of the Propagation of the Faith, Vol. 24.
[265] Leboucq, Monseigneur Édouard Dubar, pp. 193-201; Leroy, En Chine au Tché-ly S.-E., p. 61.
[266] Letters from several missionaries in Annals of the Propagation of the Faith, Vol. 24, pp. 293-307.
[267] Letter of Baldus, Vicar Apostolic of Honan, Apr. 3, 1863, in ibid., Vol. 24, pp. 362-364.
[268] Letters in ibid., Vol. 28, pp. 69-91.
[269] Substance of a conversation with the Vicar Apostolic in Hsianfu in Williamson, Journeys in North China, p. 384.
[270] Launay, La salle des martyrs, p. 193; Morse, International Relations of the Chinese Empire, Vol. 2, p. 233; Letter of the Provincial in Eastern Szechwan, Oct. 21, 1868, in Annales de la propagation de la foi, Vol. 41, p. 260.   The village was Yuyangchow, and for some years there was strong feeling against the Christians.
[271] Morse, op. cit., Vol. 2, p. 233; Annales de la propagation de la foi, Vol. 41, p. 262.   After the killing of Rigaud an imperial commissioner was sent to restore the peace.—Annales de la propagation de la foi, Vol. 43, pp. 83-90.
[272] Cordier in Catholic Encyclopedia, Vol. 9, p. 747; Annals of the Propagation of the Faith, Vol. 27, pp. 245-261.

and three Chinese Christians were executed by an official in Kweichow.[273]   In 1865 a number of Christians were killed in the same province.[274]   In Kwangtung in 1867 Verchère was arrested;[275] in 1868 Dejean was the victim of an uprising; and a little later in the year Delavay was wounded, a chapel was destroyed, and a number of Chinese Christians were killed or injured.[276]   In Eastern Chihli in 1868 Christians suffered at the hands of brigands,[277] and a missionary was roughly handled by soldiers.[278]

In 1869 there were anti-Christian demonstrations in the Yangtze Valley, scurrilous placards denouncing Christians were circulated in Hunan,[279] the Viceroy at Wuchang issued an edict which was popularly interpreted as a condemnation of Christians,[280] the mission at Anking was pillaged,[281] and trouble was averted in Nanking only by the energetic action of the Viceroy.[282]   The French authorities took measures to exact reparation: the Chargé d'Affaires, escorted by two gunboats, went up the river as far as Hankow to enforce the treaty, and satisfaction was obtained for the Anking incident after the visit of a ship of war to the city.[283]

Of all the anti-Christian demonstrations between 1856 and 1897, the most spectacular occurred in 1870 in Tientsin. Here ill-will was quite naturally felt toward the foreigner who, in the preceding war, had so truculently forced himself on the city. The animosity seems to have been especially strong against the French. French troops are said to have left a bad name behind them

[273] Launay, *La salle des martyrs*, pp. 71-76; letter of Faurie, Vicar Apostolic of Kweichow, Feb. 23, 1862, in *Annals of the Propagation of the Faith*, Vol. 23, pp. 300-305; Cordier, *Histoire des relations de la Chine avec les puissances occidentales*, 1860-1900, Vol. 1, pp. 131, 262, 430.

[274] Launay, *La salle des martyrs*, p. 89.

[275] Letter of Verchère, Oct. 26, 1867, in *Annales de la propagation de la foi*, Vol. 40, p. 424.

[276] Cordier, op. cit., Vol. 1, p. 329.

[277] Letter of Guillon from Chihli, in *Annales de la propagation de la foi*, Vol. 40, pp. 348, 359.

[278] Leboucq, *Monseigneur Édouard Dubar*, pp. 262-268, 283; Leboucq in *Annales de la propagation de la foi*, Vol. 41, p. 79; Leroy, *En Chine au Tché-ly S.-E.*, pp. 243-246.

[279] Cordier, op. cit., Vol. 1, pp. 336 et seq.; Morse, op. cit., Vol. 2, pp. 235, 236. Morse gives a summary of the document, quoting from *The North China Herald*, Sept. 29 and Oct. 6, 1869.

[280] Cordier, op. cit., Vol. 1, p. 334.

[281] Ibid., Vol. 1, p. 342.

[282] Servière, *Histoire de la mission du Kiangnan*, Vol. 2, pp. 172-182.

[283] Morse, op. cit., Vol. 2, p. 234; *The Tientsin Massacre*, documents published by the *Shanghai Evening Courier*, p. vi.

after the occupation of the city, and a Catholic church—named, with strange disregard for Chinese feelings, *Notre Dame des Victoires*—and the adjoining French consulate were erected on the sites of a temple and government buildings. In an atmosphere so charged with rancor, anti-foreign rumors had easy currency. Neither the populace nor the officials were disposed to be critical when it began to be hinted that the sisters in charge of the Catholic orphanage were kidnapping children and were extracting the eyes and hearts of the unhappy waifs to manufacture charms and medicines. The deaths of those to whom baptism was administered *in articulo mortis* and an epidemic which visited the orphanage early in June, 1870, served to accentuate the reports. Some Chinese were accused of selling children to the sisters and were tried and executed: another confessed under torture that he had been guilty of the same offense. After some delay the Chinese authorities conducted an investigation and partially exonerated the orphanage. The populace, however, was in a dangerous mood and threatened to get out of hand. The needed incentive appears to have been supplied by the French Consul, who completely lost his temper and fired at the Imperial Commissioner and at one of the local officials, the *Hsien*. A mob thereupon destroyed the orphanage, the French consulate, and the adjoining church, and killed such Frenchmen as it could lay its hands on. Ten of the sisters, one foreign and one Chinese priest, the French Consul and his Chancellor, four other French men and women, three Russians, and a number of Chinese, including some of the orphans, were killed, and the bodies of most of the foreigners were badly mutilated.[284] The mob was through.

The news of the massacre spread rapidly and anti-Christian demonstrations were reported in Chihli, Shantung, Kiangsu, Kiangsi, and Kwangtung.[285] Throughout China foreigners of all nationalities were greatly alarmed. Protestant missionaries

[284] For excellent secondary accounts of the massacre, based on primary sources, see Morse, *International Relations of the Chinese Empire*, Vol. 2, pp. 241-258, and Cordier, *Relations de la Chine avec les puissances occidentales*, Vol. 1, pp. 324-390. See also Favier, *Peking*, Vol. 2, pp. 235 et seq., *The Tientsin Massacre*, documents published in the *Shanghai Evening Courier*, and *Notices et documents sur les prêtres de la mission et les filles de la charité de S. Vincent de Paul, massacrés, le 21 Juin, 1870, à Tien-tsin . . . par un prêtre de la mission.*

[285] *Annales de la propagation de la foi*, Vol. 43, p. 299; Morse, op. cit., Vol. 2, p. 247; Taylor, *Hudson Taylor*, p. 209.

sent their condolences to Catholic missionaries [286] and urged the representatives of their governments to take vigorous action.[287] Warships of several nations were dispatched to Tientsin and the foreign envoys in Peking sent a collective note demanding that justice be done and security be assured their nationals.[288] After some months of negotiations a settlement was effected whereby eighteen Chinese who were supposed to have been in the mob were executed, two of the officials were banished, the Viceroy, the famous Tsêng Kuo-fan, was transferred to Nanking, a mission of apology was sent to France, and an indemnity of 250,000 taels was paid (120,000 taels for the murder of non-ecclesiastical persons and 130,000 for the Church).[289] The sum allotted to the Church was expressly accepted by the Vicar Apostolic not as an indemnity for lives lost, but for the reconstruction of the buildings that had been destroyed.[290]

Chinese officialdom was much annoyed by missionaries and desired restrictions which would eliminate the most provocative features of their activity. Officials, indeed, regarded missions as one of the most troublesome and obnoxious features of intercourse with the West and would have been happy to be rid of them entirely. As early as 1867 Li Hung-chang presented to the throne a memorial with suggestions for the regulation of missionaries.[291] Now (1871), spurred by the Tientsin massacre, the Chinese Government presented to the representatives of the powers a memorial suggesting restrictions. The document was dignified and courteous but proposed a plan which would have radically curtailed missions, especially those of Roman Catholics. Orphanages were to admit only the children of Christians. Women were not to be allowed to enter churches, nor were members of sisterhoods to come to China. Missionaries were to conform to the laws and usages of China; they were not to interfere with the authority of the local officials and were not to assume official functions or intervene in lawsuits on behalf of Christians; Chinese Christians were to obey the law of the

---

[286] *The Tientsin Massacre*, documents published in the *Shanghai Evening Courier*.
[287] Morse, op. cit., Vol. 2, p. 250.
[288] Ibid., Vol. 2, p. 252.
[289] Morse, op. cit., Vol. 2, pp. 257, 258.
[290] Favier, *Peking*, Vol. 2, p. 240.
[291] Bland, *Li Hung Chang*, pp. 265-274.

land but were to be exempt from customary contributions to ceremonies and festivals which had a religious significance. Chinese and foreigners living together were to be controlled by identical rules; more specifically, excessive and unusual penalties were not to be demanded by foreigners for the murder of missionaries and Chinese Christians. Passports issued to French missionaries were to specify the province and prefecture to which the holders were to go and were not to be used for another province. Care was to be taken to admit to the Church only those of good character and to exclude those guilty of crime or rebellion: to make this effective, all conversions were to be reported to the officials and the latter were to make regular inspections of the missions. Missionaries were not to use official seals; they were to conform to Chinese usages when they visited officials and were not to demand consideration or privileges beyond those granted to the scholar class. In buying land, missionaries were first to consult the local officials and the latter were to see that the proposed purchase did not interfere with the *fêng shui* or meet opposition from the neighbors.[292]

These regulations probably seemed fair to the Chinese authorities. Since, however, if adopted they would as a rule have been executed by unfriendly officials, they would almost certainly have hampered the missionary and would probably have prevented his establishing himself in new localities. The powers would not accept the memorandum [293] and no compromise was reached. Before 1900 the only important diminution of the privileges granted Christians by the treaties was the Berthemy Convention (1865), which, as we have seen, laid down the rule that a deed for property bought by French missionaries should contain the name of the grantor and should specify the mission, and not individual missionaries or Christians, as the grantees. This helped to prevent secrecy in the transfer of land and in practice gave hostile officials an opportunity to embarrass sales. By the modification agreed upon in 1895, however, the grantor was relieved of the necessity of notifying the officials of his intention to sell or of gaining their consent.[294] So ended the most impor-

[292] *Kiao-ou Ki-lio,* pp. 77-90, contains a French version of the text.
[293] Morse, op. cit., Vol. 2, p. 260.
[294] Cordier, *Relations de la Chine avec les puissances occidentales,* Vol. 1, pp. 68-77.

tant attempt of Chinese officialdom to limit the legal privileges of the missionary.

The Tientsin massacre and its settlement by no means ended the troubles of Catholic missionaries and their converts. In February, 1873, Anne Lo suffered martyrdom in Kiangsi.[295] That same year Jean Hue, a French priest, and a Chinese priest, Tay, were killed in Eastern Szechwan.[296] The French authorities sent a representative to the province to demand reparation for Hue's death, and an indemnity of four hundred thousand francs was promised, some officials were punished, and one or two of the populace who were said to have been among the murderers were executed.[297] In 1874 Christians were robbed and wounded in Szechwan.[298]

In 1875 rumors against the Catholics spread through the lower part of the Yangtze Valley. Demons were said to be striking children and cutting queues. The Catholics were held responsible and were also accused of putting the souls of children into the foundations of new churches. In 1876 the agitation led to riots in Kiangsu and Anhui and a number of chapels and residences were destroyed and several Christians were killed. A Chinese priest, Huang, and his catechist were done to death, apparently at the instigation of one of the military officials. The French authorities again exacted an indemnity. By October, 1876, the riots had subsided.[299] The year 1876 also saw more trouble in Szechwan, with loss of life and the destruction of property.[300]

In 1880 there were riots in Kwangtung, and in Canton the property of the mission was for some months guarded by Chinese troops.[301] September 8, 1881, Brieux was killed on the Tibetan

[295] *Annales de la propagation de la foi,* Vol. 47, p. 235.

[296] Launay, *La salle des martyrs,* p. 194; letter of Provot from Yuyang, Szechwan, July 19, 1873, in *Annales de la propagation de la foi,* Vol. 46, pp. 79 et seq.

[297] *Annales de la propagation de la foi,* Vol. 49, pp. 92-109; Cordier, op. cit., Vol. 2, pp. 32, 33.

[298] Letters in *Annales de la propagation de la foi,* Vol. 47, p. 88, Vol. 49, pp. 92-109. Part of the trouble seems to have been caused by the hatred of the members of the Pai-lien Chiao for the Christians.

[299] Servière, *Histoire de la mission du Kiangnan,* Vol. 2, pp. 208-254; Cordier, op. cit., Vol. 2, p. 102; Piolet, *Les missions catholiques françaises au XIXe siècle,* p. 207; Seckinger from Anhui, March 20, 1876, in *Annales de la propagation de la foi,* Vol. 49, pp. 5-25.

[300] *Annales de la propagation de la foi,* Vol. 49, p. 241 et seq.

[301] *Annals of the Propagation of the Faith,* 1883, pp. 13 et seq.; Parker, *John Chinaman,* pp. 95-99.

frontier, near Batang.[302]   In 1882 a severe persecution broke out in Southern Shansi and the French legation intervened to stop it.[303]   That same year a priest who had purchased a house in Changtê, Hunan, was expelled from the city.[304]

The dispute over Tongking between France and China, which in 1883, 1884, and 1885 led to open hostilities, brought trouble to French missionaries and their converts.   In 1884 an imperial decree was issued which seemed in part to urge protection to Christians,[305] but in a number of places, especially in the southern provinces, where the war gave rise to brigandage and where the feeling against the French was most intense, missionary activities were greatly hampered.   In March, 1883, Terrasse and several Chinese Christians were killed in Yünnan, apparently by bandits.[306]   During the succeeding two years, five of the nine missionaries in Kwangsi were expelled from the province,[307] severe persecutions raged in Kwangtung, thousands of Christians took refuge in Hongkong and Macao,[308] and in Szechwan, Yünnan, Kweichow, Shensi, and Shansi, where officials were openly hostile, placards were posted on the walls of cities threatening Christians with extermination.[309]   With the conclusion of peace (1885) unrest against missionaries and Christians subsided and in September, 1885, an imperial edict ordered that the decree of 1884 be again prominently posted.[310]

In July, 1886, there broke out at Chungking in Szechwan riots for which the Catholics blamed the Protestants and in which both Catholics and Protestants suffered.[311]   An indemnity was paid by the Chinese for the damage to property,[312] but the authorities accused the leading Chinese Catholic of the city, Lo Pao-chi, of

---

[302] Launay, La salle des martyrs, p. 93.
[303] Ricci, Barbarie e Trionfi, pp. 79, 80.
[304] Broomhall, Pioneer Work in Hunan, p. 26.
[305] Favier, Peking, Vol. 2, p. 250.
[306] Launay, op. cit., p. 92; Fenouil from Yünnan, June 13, 1883, in Annales de la propagation de la foi, Vol. 56, pp. 22 et seq.
[307] Launay, Mission du Koungsi, pp. 261-295.
[308] Annales de la propagation de la foi, Vol. 57, pp. 11 et seq.; Chamard, Un missionaire poitevin en Chine, pp. 91 et seq.
[309] Annales de la propagation de la foi, Vol. 57, pp. 11 et seq.; Ricci, Barbarie e Trionfi, pp. 95-100.
[310] Annales de la propagation de la foi, Vol. 58, pp. 115, 211-217; Cordier, op. cit., Vol. 3, p. 14.
[311] Annales de la propagation de la foi, Vol. 59, pp. 144-175; Piolet, op cit., pp. 291-294.
[312] Anti-Foreign Riots in China in 1891, pp. 7-9.

responsibility for the death of a rioter who had been killed while attacking Lo's house, and in spite of the efforts of the French Minister the unfortunate man was condemned and executed.[313] In 1886 a dispute began which a little more than a decade later was to have serious results for the Catholics of Szechwan. A wealthy Chinese, Yü Man-tzu, became involved with a Catholic in a lawsuit over some land. Through the influence of a missionary—or at least so many in the community believed—the case was decided against Yü. The latter's son then collected a force of men and raided the Christians, but was surprised near Chungking by the Chinese authorities, captured, and executed. Yü thereupon became an implacable enemy of all Catholics and by 1898 had gathered several thousand Chinese who were making them their chief prey. It was reported that by 1898 he had destroyed houses and mission stations to the value of over four million dollars and that over twenty thousand Christians were homeless.[314]

In 1887 a riot in Fukien, said to have been incited by an official, pillaged several chapels and churches and only the energetic intervention of the French Consul prevented further disaster.[315] That same year a secret society led in anti-Catholic riots in Shantung,[316] and the Vicar Apostolic of Shansi declared that an imperial edict had been secretly issued excluding all Christians from the civil service examinations and ordering all Christians who were holders of literary degrees to renounce their faith.[317] In 1890 Bishop Anzer, of the Society of the Divine Word, appealed to the German authorities to compel the Chinese to open Yenchow in Shantung to missionaries. The German Consul at Tientsin made a trip through the province, but dealt so rudely with the officials that animosities were accentuated and it was not until 1896 that Anzer succeeded in establishing himself in the city.[318] In 1890 a society pillaged and burned Christian

[313] Parker, *John Chinaman,* p. 193.
[314] Beresford, *The Break Up of China,* pp. 140-142.
[315] Cothonay, *Deux ans en Chine,* pp. 169, 170; *Annales de la propagation de la foi,* Vol. 61, p. 143.
[316] Pieper, *Unkraut, Knospen und Blüten aus dem blumigen Reiche der Mitte,* p. 373.
[317] *Annales de la propagation de la foi,* Vol. 59, p. 318.
[318] Cordier, op. cit., Vol. 3, p. 85. For German accounts, presenting the actions of the Consul in a more favorable light, see Stenz, *In der Heimat des Konfuzius,* pp. 111-118; Pieper, op. cit., p. 374.

villages in Mongolia and killed several hundred Catholics, including a Chinese priest.[319]

In 1891 riots broke out in the Yangtze Valley and gave both Catholics and Protestants serious trouble. The chief cause seems to have been inflammatory anti-Christian literature from Hunan. In Wuhu, Anking, Kiukiang, Wusih, and Ichang mobs wrought much damage and unrest was widespread.[320] In 1893 there was trouble in Shensi.[321] In 1895 bandits attacked Christians in Kwangtung.[322] That same year Catholic Christians in West China suffered from brigands and the Vicar Apostolic in Southern Szechwan was held prisoner for a time.[323] In 1896, in Kwangsi, Mazel was killed by bandits only eight months after he had arrived in China. The French legation obtained from the authorities the punishment of the offenders and an indemnity of fifteen thousand taels for the Paris Society and the relatives of the victim.[324]

The Catholic faith was spreading, but it was meeting with serious opposition. The Church was being established at the cost of severe suffering to missionaries and Chinese Christians and of disturbance to society and state.

[319] Favier, *Peking*, Vol. 2, p. 261; Piolet, op. cit., Vol. 3, p. 90; *Annales de la propagation de la foi*, Vol. 64, pp. 147, 297, 379.
    [320] *Anti-Foreign Riots in China in 1891*, pp. 10 et seq.; letter of Tournade from Kiangnan in *Annales de la propagation de la foi*, Vol. 63, pp. 377-381. Piolet, op. cit., p. 218; Brinkley, *China*, Vol. 12, p. 173; Turner, *Kwangtung* (1894), pp. 168, 169.
    [321] *Annales de la propagation de la foi*, Vol. 65, p. 149.
    [322] Leuschner, *Auf Vorposten in China*, passim.
    [323] *Annales de la propagation de la foi*, Vol. 68, pp. 14-29.
    [324] Ibid., Vol. 69 (1897), p. 39, Vol. 70 (1898), p. 218; Launay, *La salle des martyrs*, p. 97.

CHAPTER XVIII

THE GRADUAL PENETRATION OF CHINA BY MISSIONARIES, 1856 TO 1897—PROTESTANT MISSIONS

INTRODUCTION: CONDITIONS IN EUROPE AND AMERICA

MARKED as was the expansion of Catholic missions in the forty years between 1856 and 1897, the extension of Protestant activity was even greater. Catholic missions had so long been in progress that their growth, while large, and in numbers of converts more impressive, was not as striking as that of Protestants. In 1856 Protestants had barely obtained a foothold in the country, so that even had their subsequent increase been small, proportionately it would have seemed remarkable.

This development was the outgrowth of forces which have been described in a previous chapter. In the sixteenth and seventeenth centuries Catholic powers had led in the expansion of Europe and a religious awakening within their borders had joined with their commercial and colonizing activities to give impetus to Roman Catholic missions. In the nineteenth century the new economic and religious life was chiefly in countries where Protestants predominated, and Protestant missions grew accordingly. The Industrial Revolution, by the middle of the nineteenth century nearly a hundred years old, continued to enrich Great Britain and was beginning to bring wealth to other countries in Northwestern Europe and to the United States. Particularly marked in the second half of the nineteenth century was the accumulation of riches in this latter country. Occupying virgin territory with vast undeveloped resources which were especially adapted to the new industrial processes, and inhabited by an enterprising people, the great American republic experienced a multiplication of material possessions which has seldom if ever been equalled. The Civil War (1861-1865) did not halt the westward movement of population and except for the southern states was not even an interruption in the progress of manu-factures and transportation.   On the continent of Europe—untroubled by a major war between 1870 and 1914—and espe-cially in Germany, the accumulation of riches was but a little less striking.

The amazing growth of wealth in lands predominatingly Prot-estant was paralleled, as we have seen, by a vigorous religious life.   The Christian bodies which had most profoundly felt the awakenings of the eighteenth and nineteenth centuries continued to be stirred by revivals and to give birth to new movements. The churches in Scotland, the Evangelical wing of the Church of England, the non-conformist groups of Great Britain, and the majority of the larger denominations of the United States were especially affected.[1]   Dwight L. Moody and other "evangelists" continued worthily the traditions of Wesley.   The Young Men's Christian Association, which just before 1856 had reached the United States from Great Britain, was in the early stages of its remarkable development and was stimulating the rise of Christian groups in colleges and universities.   These student organizations were to spread throughout the Protestant world and one of their primary concerns was to be foreign missions.   The Student Vol-unteer Movement for Foreign Missions, which began in the United States in 1886 and was quickly reproduced in several other countries, led thousands of students to devote themselves to the foreign missionary enterprise.   Many congregations held "monthly concerts of missions."   The young United Society of Christian Endeavor was thoroughly committed to missions. Almost invariably, indeed, the quickened religious life of the latter half of the nineteenth century, whether in the churches or in institutions of higher learning, had as one of its major expressions an increased interest in the world-wide propagation of the Christian faith.

INTRODUCTION: CONDITIONS IN CHINA

The rising tide of missionary enthusiasm of Protestant Chris-tendom found in the partial opening of China by the war of 1856-1860 and the resultant treaties of 1858 and 1860 one of its greatest outlets.   The naval and military operations of the

[1] On the continent of Europe there was in many quarters a new life—partly through Anglo-Saxon influence, but chiefly as an outgrowth of the older Pietism. It was, however, much less marked than that in Great Britain and North America.

war brought little inconvenience to Protestant missionaries. In and around Canton work was interrupted,[2] but this was the only port where it seems to have suffered severely. In Protestant missionary circles in the West and in China the war appears, indeed, to have been generally welcomed as a means of opening the country still further to the Gospel. No one of influence in the Church seems to have questioned seriously the consistency of entering the Empire in the wake of armed forces and under the protection of treaties. Some of the British deplored the fact that Christian missions and the opium traffic were both tolerated by the same treaty, and at least one American missionary believed extraterritoriality to be open to criticism.[3] No missionary, board secretary, or clergyman, however, seems to have objected to the toleration clauses. Most of the British Evangelical groups favored the policy of their government toward China—with the exception of the action on opium—and only one important paper in the Anglican Church denounced the war.[4] The attitude was very different from that of 1927.

While Lord Elgin, the British representative, was in Shanghai on his way to negotiate the treaty of 1858, the Protestant missionaries of the port presented him an address asking him to procure for Protestants toleration distinct from that which the French had obtained for Roman Catholics and liberty of travel and preaching in all parts of China.[5] The one voice of protest in Great Britain against the introduction of Christianity into China in the wake of force seems to have been that of a small journal, *The Free Press,* and of David Urquhart, a member of Parliament, who contended that British participation in the war had been piracy, that the English people had ceased to be Christian and were incapable of conveying Christianity to others, and that before missionaries were sent the people of England should repent and refound true Christianity in their own land. Urquhart, however, appears to have had little support in his criticisms and the clergy seem either to have ignored him entirely or to have

[2] Schlatter, *Rudolf Lechler,* p. 111; *A Century of Protestant Missions in China,* p. 251.

[3] Macgowan in *North China Herald,* Jan. 2, 1858. Macgowan termed the Chinese grant of extraterritoriality an "indirect suicidal act."

[4] Stock, *History of the Church Missionary Society,* Vol. 2, pp. 301, 304.

[5] Walrond, *Letters and Journals of James, Eighth Earl of Elgin,* p. 243. Lord Elgin replied to his petitioners that extending the privileges of foreigners was a delicate matter and that special foreign protection to Chinese converts would invite hypocritical professions of Christianity.

disagreed with him.[6] It was an attitude far different from that found in Protestant circles two generations later.[7] Some missionaries, indeed, were disappointed that the toleration clauses did not give them more.[8]

As has been pointed out in a previous chapter, the treaties of 1858-1860 made possible for the first time extensive Protestant activity. Heretofore Protestant missionaries had been confined almost exclusively to the five treaty ports and to Hongkong. Now they possessed the legal right to travel anywhere in the Empire

[6] *The Free Press,* September 22, 1858—February 23, 1859. *The New Heresy: Proselytism Substituted for Righteousness. Two letters to the Bishop of Oxford* by David Urquhart.

[7] An examination has been made for this period of the *Reports of the American Board of Commissioners for Foreign Missions* (1857-1861); the *Reports of the Directors of the London Missionary Society* (1856-1861); *Reports of the Wesleyan Methodist Missionary Society* for the years ending April, 1857, April, 1859, and April, 1860; *Proceedings of the Church Missionary Society,* 1857-1858, 1860-1861; *Reports of the Missionary Society . . . of the Methodist Episcopal Church,* 1859-1861; the *Missionary Magazine* (American Baptists), 1858-1860; and no disquietude of conscience has been discovered. Rather was there rejoicing that the Empire had been opened to the preaching of the Christian Gospel. Such expressions as the following are typical: "We are constrained to believe that the God of the whole earth is about preparing the way here for messengers of his Son to all the inhabitants of the 'land of Sinim' " (Statement of China Mission of the American Board in *Forty-Ninth Annual Report of the A. B. C. F. M.,* p. 106). The London Missionary Society's annual reports deplored the war but hoped that the new treaties might lead to safeguarding the missionaries. They did, however, express the hope that the illegal traffic in opium might be stopped (1857, p. 18). *The Proceedings of the Church Missionary Society for 1860* (p. 172) deplored the fact that "by the very instrument by which China is declared to have thrown open her gates to the free and unrestricted preaching of the Gospel . . . it is equally declared, although somewhat more covertly, that she has been forced by Christian England, at the very point of the bayonet, to throw open her gates to the free and unrestricted introduction of opium." M. J. Knowlton, one of the missionaries of the American Baptist Missionary Union in Ningpo, said (*The Missionary Magazine,* Vol. 39 [1859] p. 161): "The opening of China is undoubtedly one of the greatest among the great events of the present age. It is an event in which the hand of God is clearly manifest . . . leading forward the grand, yet gradually progressive movement of his kingdom." S. Wells Williams, who helped in drafting the American treaty and to whom, with a fellow missionary, Martin, was chiefly due the insertion of the toleration clause in that document, was "thankful to God that it was inserted." He added: "that if the Chinese had at all comprehended what was involved in these four toleration articles they would never have signed one of them" (Williams, *Life and Letters of S. Wells Williams,* p. 271). He also wrote: "The Christian and pagan nations of the earth never before stood in the same attitude to each other, and the forbearance and conscious power of the former made an impression at the time on the latter, a transitory one it may be, but not wholly useless." (*Fiftieth Annual Report of the A. B. C. F. M.,* p. 114.) The American missionaries in Shanghai on Nov. 4, 1858, sent a letter of congratulations to Reed, the American Minister, expressing their delight over the American treaty and the hope that the American Government "may in the future plainly declare that . . . the labours of missionaries . . . are to be sustained by all the *moral* influence of our land." The text of the letter is in the *Spirit of Missions,* Vol. 24, pp. 148-150.

[8] Williams, *Life and Letters of S. Wells Williams,* pp. 271, 281, 282.

and to propagate their faith without molestation from the state. They could own property in the new as well as in the old treaty ports, and in practice, although not strictly by treaty right, they acquired land in the interior.

GENERAL CHARACTERISTICS OF PROTESTANT MISSIONS, 1856-1897

Given conditions in the West and in China, then, it was almost inevitable that the four decades after 1856 should be years of rapid expansion of Protestant missionary activity. The period was, naturally, one of pioneering. Missionaries traversed the provinces, preaching, distributing literature, and spying out the land for future, permanent occupation. Provinces and cities hitherto impregnable to Protestant efforts were entered and new stations opened. In 1856 resident missionaries were found in only the four southern coast provinces and few had travelled beyond these. By 1898 all of the Eighteen Provinces and Manchuria had been traversed, some of them many times, and residential work had been established in each. After 1898 a good many new societies were to enter China and the older ones were to make some changes in their fields; but, with a few important exceptions, the Protestant ecclesiastical map of 1928 was largely that of 1898. In the four decades that succeeded the Tientsin treaties most of the societies and denominations had blocked out the main outlines of the territories in which they were to operate for at least the ensuing thirty years.

In all these pioneering efforts, Roman Catholic missionaries were practically ignored. To the Protestant it was as if the Catholics had never come to China. Protestants nearly always thought of themselves as the sole representatives of the Gospel and spoke of "opening" cities and provinces to the Christian message even when Catholics had been there before them. This was natural. By the average Protestant of the time Rome was thought of as anti-Christ. At best, Roman Catholicism was regarded as a corrupt form of Christianity from which the Reformers had, at great cost and suffering, escaped to restore the Gospel in its purity. The Roman Catholic, on the other hand, had nothing kind to say of the Protestants. They were, he believed, dangerous heretics who were hindering the work of Christ and who were introducing to China the multitudinous sects of Europe and America. One Catholic writer later spoke of them as leading China "from Confucius to confusion." [9] The gulf between the two divisions of Christians was deepened by linguistic and cultural differences. Roman Catholic missionaries were mainly from Latin lands and had French or Spanish or Italian for their mother tongue, while the Protestants were largely Anglo-Saxon and used English. Then, too, Roman Catholic and Protestant Chinese Christians were sometimes at swords' points, occasionally because warring factions or clans professed rival forms of the foreign faith in the hope of gaining support. The two great groups of Christians, far from coöperating, were like two different and rival religions.

For Protestants the period from 1856 to 1897 was one not only of pioneering, but of emphasis upon evangelism—the propagation of the Christian message by preaching, personal friendship, and the printed page. This was to be expected, both because the groups which sent missionaries for the most part were committed to that form of activity and because it seemed necessarily to precede any extensive institutional effort. However, Chinese churches were organized, and in some instances were nourished to the point of independence of foreign financial support and control. Schools were fostered, although they still were mostly of elementary grade. Literature continued to be produced. Medical work became more and more a normal feature of Protestant missions, and in a number of other ways efforts were made to better the physical lot of the Chinese.

The decades were marked by great missionary figures. The Chinese churches were as yet too small and weak to supply leaders to compare with the missionaries, and such as did appear were usually subordinate to the foreigner. The hour had not come for the prominence of educators and administrators: these were to have their day after 1900. It was the era of path-breakers, of men who travelled the highways and byways preaching and distributing literature, founding new stations, and introducing into whole provinces the Gospel as Protestants understood it. The years were biographical rather than institutional.

As was to be expected from the wealth and commerce of Great Britain and the part which the British played in the foreign relations of China, the majority of the outstanding pioneers were

[9] Wolferstan, *The Catholic Church in China*, p. 13.

British. The continent of Europe had as yet few representatives, and Americans did not have as important a place as they were to win after 1900.

The history of these years between 1856 and 1897 can best be told, first, by recounting the extension of the work of the societies which were in China before 1856, second, by sketching briefly the story of the bodies which entered China between that year and 1897, third, by describing the methods employed, and finally, by enumerating and evaluating the results which followed.

THE EXTENSION OF THE WORK OF THOSE SOCIETIES WHICH WERE IN CHINA BEFORE 1856

The societies which had work in China before 1856 saw in the conditions created by the treaties a challenge to expansion. The London Missionary Society continued most of its older centers and extended its efforts to both the central and northern portions of the country. In Canton the church maintained by the Society continued its growth and in Kwangtung several stations and outstations, among them one at Pok-lo, were opened.[10] After the retirement of Legge the most prominent figure in the Canton and Hongkong missions was John Chalmers—like his predecessor, a Scotchman.[11] Under Macgowan and Sadler the Amoy mission was extended inland.[12]

When, by the treaties of 1858, the Yangtze was opened to foreign trade, the Society's missionaries in Shanghai were eager to enter the freshly opened door. In that very year Muirhead accompanied the British squadron which was sent up the river to open the new ports.[13] In 1861 Griffith John and Robert Wilson founded the first permanent Protestant mission in Hankow.[14] Wilson died in 1863, but John continued, for many years one of the most prominent missionaries in Central China. From Hankow as a center, largely under John's leadership, preaching tours were undertaken over a radius of hundreds of miles and many outstations were established. In spite of the bitter oppo-

---

[10] L. M. S. Chronicle, Vol. 1 (new series), p. 7; China Mission Hand-book, Part 2, p. 6.
[11] Encyclopædia Sinica, p. 87.
[12] Macgowan, Christ or Confucius, Which? The Story of the Amoy Mission, p. 76; A Century of Protestant Missions in China, p. 7.
[13] China Mission Hand-book, Part 2, p. 15.
[14] L. M. S. Chronicle, Vol. 45, p. 75, Vol. 14 (new series), p. 103; Thompson, Griffith John, p. 174; John, A Voice from China, pp. 187, 188.

sition of officials, land was purchased in Wuchang in 1863,[15] and Hanyang, the third of the Wuhan cities, was occupied in 1867.[16] In 1868 John made a journey through Szechwan and for years urged that a mission be started there. Chungking was the natural place for the opening wedge, but various misfortunes intervened and it was not until 1888 that John's dream was fulfilled. In that year Mr. and Mrs. Wallace Wilson and a Chinese evangelist established a residence in the city.[17]

Hunan was more bitterly anti-foreign than any other section of the country and missionaries had extreme difficulty in entering or remaining within its borders. Perhaps for that reason John was especially eager to see missions established there. In 1880 and in 1883 and again in 1897 he journeyed into the province, and in 1891 and 1892 some converts of his society distributed Christian literature in the capital, Changsha. The opposition was too severe, however, to permit continuous activity.[18]

Among those who for shorter or longer periods joined in the work which John had begun in Central China, Arnold Foster was one of the most prominent. Appointed in 1871 to Hankow, he was to live until 1919 and so was to witness the changes of half a century. Uncompromisingly loyal to high ethical standards, vigorous of mind and speech, a tireless preacher, a man of vision and wide range of interest, he gave himself with tender and humble devotion to the relief of the destitute and lived with the utmost simplicity that he might have the more to share. His affectionate greeting to new missionaries was a benediction.[19]

The representatives of the London Missionary Society were eager to enter North as well as Central China. In 1860 and 1861 Edkins lived for some months in Chefoo. In the latter year he went to Tientsin and within a few months received his first converts.[20] In 1861 Dr. Lockhart gained entrance to Peking as a medical officer of the British legation and initiated Protestant missions in that city.[21] In 1862 Edkins paid several visits to Peking and in December baptized three men as members of

[15] John, A Voice from China, pp. 187, 188.
[16] Ibid.
[17] L. M. S. Chronicle, Vol. 48, p. 53; Bond, Our Share in China, p. 150.
[18] John, op. cit., p. 220; Thompson, Griffith John, pp. 482 et seq.
[19] Arnold Foster, Memoir, Selected Writings, passim; L. M. S. Chronicle, Vol. 19 (new series), p. 142.
[20] Edkins, Chinese Scenes and Peoples, pp. 22-30; China Mission Hand-book, Part 2, p. 18.
[21] China Mission Hand-book, Part 2, p. 18.

the first Protestant church in the capital.[22] In 1863 he obtained premises on which to reside and moved to Peking, leaving a successor in Tientsin.[23] From Peking and Tientsin the Society reached out into the surrounding country. The most distant extension was by James Gilmour, who for some twenty years labored indefatigably and heroically among the Mongols. He arrived in 1870 and in the face of indifference, misunderstanding, suspicion, a paucity of converts, and the faithlessness of some of the few won, continued his labors until his death, in 1891.[24]

So wide an expansion by a society with undertakings in several other parts of the world and with far from unlimited resources prevented the thoroughgoing occupation of any one province or even of any one city. However, in each of the larger centers where stations were established, the members of the Society left their impress in transformed lives and in churches, and often in schools and hospitals.

The American Board of Commissioners for Foreign Missions did not attempt to cover as much territory as did its British sister organization. It discontinued some of its efforts, indeed, but maintained stations in Kwangtung and Fukien and extended its activities into North China. The mission in Canton, the oldest of the Board, was suspended in 1866, for death had depleted the staff and several other societies had entered the city.[25] As the Congregationalists pursued work among the Chinese in the United States, however, they decided to conserve the results by keeping in touch with converts who returned to their native land. For this purpose C. R. Hager, who had had experience among the Chinese in San Francisco, was sent to Hongkong (1883) and itinerated from that city and established outstations on the mainland. Reënforcements did not come for eight years and progress was relatively slow, but eventually results were very encouraging.[26]

As we have seen, in 1857 the Amoy station of the American

[22] Ibid., p. 18.
[23] Ibid., p. 19; *A Century of Protestant Missions in China*, p. 5.
[24] Muirhead, *China and the Gospel*, pp. 174-180; Bryson and Buckland, *James Gilmour and John Horden*, passim; Lovett, *James Gilmour of Mongolia*, passim; Hedley, *Tramps in Dark Mongolia*, pp. 33, 35; Gilmour, *Among the Mongols*, passim; Gilmour, *More About the Mongols*, passim.
[25] *Fifty-Sixth Annual Report of the American Board of Commissioners for Foreign Missions*, pp. 127, 128; *Fifty-Seventh Annual Report* of ibid., p. 113.
[26] Blodget and Baldwin, *Sketches of the American Board Missions in China*, p. 6; Smith, *Congregational Missions in the Heavenly Kingdom*, p. 37; *A Century of Protestant Missions in China*, pp. 292-294.

Board was turned over to the newly organized board of the (Dutch) Reformed Church in America. By 1863 the station in Shanghai had been discontinued, largely because of the transfer of missionaries to the newly opened North.[27] The mission at Foochow was strengthened, however, and by a slow but fairly steady growth was extended into several other parts of the province.[28]

In 1860 Henry Blodget accompanied the allied forces to Tientsin.[29] The Board quickly sent reënforcements and other cities in North China were occupied. Blodget removed to Peking in 1864, the Gulicks settled in Kalgan in 1865, and long before 1897 stations were opened in T'ungchow, and as far south as Shantung and Paotingfu.[30] In 1881 the first members of the "Oberlin Band" came to China. The Band arose out of classes in church history in Oberlin Theological Seminary, the students suggesting that like the missionary monks of medieval Europe they go out as a group to some foreign center. Shansi, only recently the scene of an appalling famine, was chosen, and by 1900 sixteen missionaries were on the ground.[31]

We have seen that before 1858 the two denominations that had once been associated with the American Board, the (Dutch) Reformed Church in America and the Presbyterians, had formed separate societies. The Reformed Church, unlike the parent board, concentrated its efforts on one section, that in and around Amoy. Here, in close coöperation with the English Presbyterians, it built up a Christian community notable for evangelistic zeal, self-support, and independence of missionary control.[32]

The American Presbyterians were a larger body and felt able to extend their activities more widely. An account has already been given of their entrance, before 1858, into Canton, Ningpo,

[27] *Fifty-First, Fifty-Second and Fifty-Third Annual Reports of the American Board of Commissioners for Foreign Missions.*
[28] *A Century of Protestant Missions in China*, pp. 253-259. In 1876 there were reported in Fukien 13 missionaries, 21 chapels, 13 outstations, 7 organized churches, and 162 communicants.—*Chinese Recorder*, Vol. 7, p. 254.
[29] Blodget and Baldwin, op. cit., p. 15; Smith, *Rex Christus*, p. 148.
[30] *China Mission Hand-book*, Part 2, p. 156; Forsyth, *Shantung*, pp. 207, 239; Ketler, *The Tragedy of Paotingfu*, p. 88; *A Century of Protestant Missions in China*, p. 267; *Chinese Recorder*, Vol. 18, p. 211; Williams, *By the Great Wall*, passim; Porter, *Mary H. Porter*, passim; Porter, *William Scott Ament*, passim.
[31] Blodget and Baldwin, *Sketches of the American Board Missions in China*, p. 5; *Oberlin Shansi Mission. Ten Years After*, passim; Smith, *Congregational Missions in the Heavenly Kingdom*, p. 32.
[32] *A Century of Protestant Missions in China*, pp. 366-372; Chamberlain, *Fifty Years in Foreign Lands*, pp. 19, 47, 48.

and Shanghai. From Canton, they penetrated the surrounding territory and by 1897 had established outstations even within the borders of Hunan.[33] In 1885 they undertook operations on the island of Hainan.[34] From Ningpo and Shanghai they branched out into several of the larger cities of Chêkiang and Kiangsu. After visits by various missionaries and an unsuccessful attempt at permanent occupation by Nevius in 1859, in 1864 a station was established at Hangchow and by 1879 there were in the city two churches and one hundred and forty-two converts.[35] Before 1881 Soochow and Nanking were permanent stations.[36]

Like the two Congregational bodies, the Presbyterians were attracted by the opportunities in the newly opened North and hastened to send missionaries. In 1861 Nevius and others went to Shantung and remained for a time in Têngchow.[37] In 1862 Chefoo was occupied.[38] The following year two men went to Shantung, Calvin W. Mateer and Hunter Corbett, who with Nevius were long to be outstanding figures. Mateer was assigned to Têngchow. In after years the school which he founded there to train Christian leaders was to become a college and still later was to be merged into the Christian university at Tsinan. His textbooks, his share in translating the Bible, and his *Mandarin Lessons*—which introduced a generation of missionaries to the Chinese language—are evidences of his literary versatility and diligence.[39] Corbett spent most of his life in Chefoo.[40] Both Mateer and Corbett were indefatigable preachers and pastors and travelled widely in Shantung spreading the Christian message and building up churches. Tsinan, the provincial capital, was occupied by McIlvaine in 1872.[41] From Chefoo, Têngchow, Tsinan, and later from other cities, the Presbyterians itinerated and established a network of small churches.[42] Peking was

[33] *A Century of Protestant Missions in China*, p. 387.
[34] *China Mission Hand-book*, Part 2, p. 188; *China Mission Year Book, 1915*, p. 209; *Chinese Recorder*, Vol. 21, p. 274.
[35] *Jubilee Papers of the Central China Presbyterian Mission*, pp. 25, 76-90; *A Century of Protestant Missions in China*, p. 382; Nevius, *Life of Nevius*, pp. 164-190.
[36] *Jubilee Papers of the Central China Presbyterian Mission*, pp. 98-106.
[37] *A Century of Protestant Missions in China*, p. 382; Robinson, *Missions in China*; Nevius, *Our Life in China*, p. 327.
[38] *A Century of Protestant Missions in China*, p. 382.
[39] Fisher, *Calvin W. Mateer*, passim; Mateer, *Character Building in China*, passim.
[40] Craighead, *Hunter Corbett*, passim.
[41] Richard, *Forty-Five Years in China*, p. 58.
[42] *A Century of Protestant Missions in China*, pp. 389-391.

occupied for the Presbyterians by W. A. P. Martin in 1863 [43] and he was followed by others who gradually built a strong center and carried their activities into the surrounding country. [44]

Under Bishop Boone the Protestant Episcopal Church made Shanghai its chief center in China. For a short time it placed men in Chefoo and Peking, but it withdrew to concentrate its efforts upon the Yangtze Valley. [45] In 1868 it entered Wuchang and Hankow. [46] Stations were later opened as far west as Ichang, but it was in the populous cities from Shanghai to Hankow that the American Episcopalians found their main field. [47] Bishop Boone died in 1864. He was succeeded first by Channing Moore Williams, and then by Samuel Isaac Joseph Schereschewsky. [48]

Schereschewsky was an outstanding figure. Born in Russian Lithuania, a Jew, and given a strictly orthodox Jewish education, he went to America and, by gradual steps which began before he reached the New World, became a Christian. In 1859 he went to China as a missionary of the Protestant Episcopal Church. He acquired a remarkable mastery of the language and became notable for his translations of the Prayer Book and the Scriptures. Although he had once before declined the office, in 1877 he was made bishop, and in this capacity, among other achievements, founded at Shanghai St. John's College, which later was to be for many years the foremost Christian institution of higher education in the Empire. In 1881 he was prostrated by a sunstroke and was partially paralyzed. He was in Europe for several years for treatment, then in the United States, and still later in Shanghai and Japan. Strength never more than partially returned and he felt it wise to resign his bishopric. Undaunted, however, he gave himself to the translation of the Bible. Although able to write only by operating a typewriter with one finger, he revised his edition of the Mandarin Old Testament, turned the entire Bible into the literary language, and was engaged on the Apocrypha at the time of his death (in Japan, in 1906). [49]

[43] Ibid., p. 383.
[44] Ibid, pp. 388, 389.
[45] Ibid., p. 297.
[46] Ibid., p. 297; *Chinese Recorder,* Vol. 7, p. 423.
[47] *Historical Sketch of the China Mission of the American Protestant Episcopal Church,* passim.
[48] *American Church Mission in Shanghai and the Lower Yangtze Valley,* p. 5.
[49] *Missionary Review of the World,* Vol. 20, p. 86; *Spirit of Missions,* Vol. 42, p. 665, Vol. 46, p. 30, Vol. 68, pp. 233-238, Vol. 69, p. 392, Vol. 71, p. 1021; Norris, *China,* p. 117; *Encyclopædia Sinica,* p. 499.

Another devoted representative of the Episcopal Church was James Addison Ingle, who came to China in 1891. After a year and a half he was left the only missionary of his society in Hankow, but by means of Chinese laymen whom he trained he was able to carry on an extensive work not only in the city but in the outlying country. Even when reënforcements reached him from America, he continued to place great emphasis upon Chinese participation in the spread of the Faith and the support of the Church. In 1901 he was made bishop of a new diocese with headquarters at Hankow, but died in 1903.[50] His early demise was a great loss to his mission.

The other Anglican body in China before the treaties of Tientsin, the Church Missionary Society, concentrated primarily on the regions adjacent to the centers that it had first occupied— Hongkong, Foochow, Ningpo, and Shanghai. The story of its growth, like that of most other societies, is one of effort extending over decades. Space forbids going into it at all in detail. Mention must be made, however, of the Dublin University Mission in Fukien. As early as 1885 two or three members of Trinity College, Dublin, began to dream of a foreign missionary undertaking by the men of their university. The Church Missionary Society, to which they turned for counsel, suggested Fukien as a possible field, partly because one Trinity graduate was already there. The first agent of the new mission, Stratford Collins, arrived in 1888. A second was sent in 1891 and a third in 1894. In 1896 a prefecture, Fu-ning—not far from the ancient Dominican stronghold, Fu-an—was assigned them.[51] They were the second of the university missionaries in China.

Nor must the record be omitted of the Church of England Zenana Missionary Society. This organization, as its name suggests, was one of women for women and at first confined its efforts to India. Since for many years the Church Missionary Society did not appoint women as missionaries, and needs existed which only women could meet, in 1881 the women's society placed a representative in Fukien. In succeeding years it sent many others, even after the older society changed its policy and appointed members of both sexes.[52] Nor must there be forgotten

[50] Jefferys, *Ingle*, passim; Smith, *Uplift of China*, pp. 137-144; *Memorial Service for the Late Right Rev. James Addison Ingle*, passim.
[51] *A History of the Dublin University Fuh-kien Mission*, pp. 2-10.
[52] Stock, *History of the Church Missionary Society*, Vol. 4, p. 306.

a gift, in 1882, by W. C. Jones, of £72,000 for training and supporting native agents in China and Japan.[53]

Probably the most distinguished family connected with the Church Missionary Society in China during these years was the Moules. The first in China of that name, G. E. Moule, went out in 1857, in 1864 began a permanent residence for his Society at Hangchow, and was later Bishop in Mid-China. His brother, Arthur E., arrived in 1861 and was later archdeacon.[54]

The one departure from the Church Missionary Society's policy of expanding only from its older centers was the entrance in 1891 into Szechwan. Several members of the Church of England had been stationed there under the China Inland Mission. J. H. Horsburgh, a missionary of the Society, visited West China in 1888, and on his return urged formal participation by his board. A party was accordingly formed and, with the cordial coöperation of the China Inland Mission, was sent out to the distant field to begin permanent work.[55]

The growing enterprises of the Society necessitated an increasing number of missionaries. In the years 1883 to 1886 inclusive seven men were sent to China,[56] and in the years 1895 to 1899 inclusive ninety-three new recruits were appointed.[57]

The American Baptists, both of the Northern and the Southern States, undertook operations in several widely separated sections of the country. In 1856 the northern branch of the denomination had representatives in Hongkong and Ningpo. The station at Hongkong, as we have seen, had been started by Dean, who had begun his missionary career among the Chinese in Bangkok. Since in Siam Dean had learned the dialect of the prefecture of which Swatow is the port, in Hongkong he centered his efforts upon those who used it, and when, by the treaties of Tientsin, Swatow was opened to foreign residence, the mission was removed to that place (1860).[58] From this city the Baptists reached out into the *hinterland,* both among those of the dialect with which

[53] Ibid., Vol. 3, p. 233; *China Mission Hand-book,* Part 2, p. 28.
[54] Stock, op. cit., Vol. 4, p. 317.
[55] Stock, op. cit., Vol. 3, p. 576; A *Century of Protestant Missions in China,* pp. 45-48. The first party arrived in 1891.—Broomhall, *Bishop Cassels,* p. 143.
[56] Stock, op. cit., Vol. 3, p. 560.
[57] Ibid., Vol. 3, p. 769.
[58] Ashmore, the earliest Baptist missionary to visit Swatow, was there first in 1858, but the permanent occupation by the mission did not take place until 1860.— Ashmore, *South China Mission of the American Baptist Foreign Mission Society,* p. 14.

the missionaries had first become acquainted and among the Hakka-speaking peoples.[59] At Swatow, for the major part of the forty years after 1863, labored William Ashmore, the most distinguished missionary of his board in China.[60]

From Ningpo, under the energetic leadership of missionaries, and sometimes in part through the agency of Chinese Christians, churches were established in several of the chief cities of the northern and central portions of Chêkiang.[61]

Not content with its great fields in Kwangtung and Chêkiang, in 1889 the American Baptist Missionary Union entered Szechwan,[62] and between 1892 and the close of 1894 sent missionaries also into Central China, opening a station at Hanyang.[63]

The American Baptists from the Southern States were badly handicapped during the American Civil War and in the difficult *post bellum* years. Remittances were usually either curtailed or cut off. In Shanghai, Crawford and Yates were forced to support themselves.[64] At Chefoo, to which two missionary families went in 1860, one man, Holmes, was killed by bandits not far from the city, and the other, Hartwell, was supported in part by a friend who had been a missionary and had returned home soon after the outbreak of the war.[65] In spite of discouragements the Southern Baptists held on, and when recovery from the war enabled them to do so, they vigorously prosecuted the enterprise that had been maintained at such sacrifice.

By 1891 in and around Canton were thirteen stations and outstations, seven schools, and a church membership of five hundred and thirty.[66] In Shanghai Mr. and Mrs. Yates were left alone for a number of years after 1863, but eventually reënforcements arrived and stations were established in a number of the cities of Kiangsu.[67] In Shantung, Têngchow was for many years the center of operations. Few reënforcements came until the eighties,

[59] Ashmore, op. cit., pp. 14-76; *A Century of Protestant Missions in China,* p. 332; *Chinese Recorder,* Vol. 7, p. 42. Work among the Hakkas was begun ca. 1882.—Ashmore, op. cit., p. 76.

[60] Ashmore went to the East in 1849 and served in Bangkok and Hongkong before removing to Swatow.—*A Century of Protestant Missions in China,* p. 332.

[61] Ibid., pp. 336-339.

[62] Merriam, *Baptist Missions in China,* p. 21.

[63] *A Century of Protestant Missions in China,* p. 339; Merriam, op. cit., p. 22.

[64] Foster, *Fifty Years in China,* pp. 129 et seq.

[65] Ibid., pp. 129 et seq.; *A Century of Protestant Missions in China,* pp. 322. 323; Forsyth, *Shantung,* pp. 182, 229 et seq.

[66] Titterington, *A Century of Baptist Foreign Missions,* Chapter 24

[67] *A Century of Protestant Missions in China,* pp. 317-320

but with the revival of prosperity in the Southern States additional missionaries were sent and new stations were opened.[68] The board had staked out a fairly large territory for occupation.

In 1892 a division over methods led to the formation of the Gospel Baptist Mission. Several, among them one of the pioneers of the Shantung mission, Crawford, came to feel that a new organization of missions was needed, an organization which on the one hand would more quickly promote the self-support and independence of the Chinese churches and on the other would bring the individual missionary into closer touch with the local congregations in America. They believed that the existing method, that of receiving money from a central board and subsidizing Chinese workers, sacrificed the autonomy of both the American and the Chinese local churches. Accordingly they severed their connection with the Foreign Mission Board of the Southern Baptist Convention and depended for support directly upon individual congregations at home. To avoid possible collision with those who remained under the old board, they removed to a new center in Shantung. Recruits came from time to time and the activities of the new mission were extended to fresh districts.[69]

The one other Baptist body that had entered China before 1856, the Seventh Day Baptist Missionary Society, had many years of struggle and difficulty. The American Civil War cut off support, for a time the feeble church that had been organized in Shanghai was left in charge of a native pastor, and it was only by slow degrees that reënforcements came.[70]

The German societies which, under the influence of Gützlaff, had sent representatives to Hongkong and Kwangtung, with characteristic thoroughness continued to concentrate on this region, and until the occupation of Kiaochow by their government (1897) did not seek to expand into new sections. These societies were, it will be recalled, the Basel German Evangelical Society, the Berlin Missionary Society for China, the Rhenish Missionary Society—sometimes known by the name of its headquarters, Barmen—and the Berlin Women's Missionary Society for China. The last named organization pursued its special task of main-

[68] Ibid., pp. 322-328.
[69] Ibid., pp. 330, 331; *China Mission Hand-book*, Part 2, p. 255.
[70] *A Century of Protestant Missions in China*, pp. 344-346.

taining in Hongkong a home for Chinese girls but did not enter upon additional enterprises.[71]

The Basel Society found its field among the Hakkas, first in Hongkong, and then, as the way opened, on the mainland and well into the interior of Northeastern Kwangtung. One of its two pioneers, Rudolf Lechler, served the mission for over fifty years—for forty years as its director—and retired to Germany in 1908.[72] By 1899 the Society was occupying eleven stations and had 3,100 converts.[73] Early in its history the Basel Mission sent a Chinese boy to Europe to be educated. He returned in 1869 as an ordained missionary[74] on an equal footing with his European colleagues. The experiment appears to have been unsuccessful, however, and it was abandoned after a few other Chinese had been so trained.[75]

The Berlin Society, like most of the other bodies founded under the stimulus of Gützlaff's enthusiasm, did not persist. It sent out a few missionaries at intervals of several years, but at least one of them died on the field, others returned to Germany, and about 1872 it transferred its work to the Rhenish Society.[76]

The Rhenish Society seemed to have a promising future in China, but in 1880 a serious difference between some of the missionaries and between the home board and some of the missionaries led to the resignation of seven of the nine on the field.[77] Among the dissentients was Ernst Faber, a master of the Chinese language, and the author of many works in Chinese, German, and English.[78] After this disaster, the mission was confined to a small district east of Canton.[79]

[71] *A Century of Protestant Missions in China,* p. 490.
[72] *Encyclopædia Sinica,* p. 295. Another member of the society was E. J. Eitel, later distinguished as a sinologue. He was with the mission from 1862 to 1865, then joined the London Missionary Society, and after 1879 served the Hongkong Government for several years.—Ibid., p. 157.
[73] *The Missionary Year Book, 1889-1890,* p. 267.
[74] Oehler, *China und die christliche Mission,* p. 251.
[75] *A Century of Protestant Missions in China,* p. 481. The Berlin Missionary Society for China seems also to have had this policy to a limited extent.—Richter, *Geschichte der Berliner Missionsgesellschaft,* pp. 516, 517.
[76] There is difference of opinion about the date. *A Century of Protestant Missions in China,* p. 485, gives the dates as 1872 and 1873, and on p. 495 as 1875. Oehler, op. cit., p. 190, says 1873. Richter, *Geschichte der Berliner Missionsgesellschaft,* pp. 504, 517, gives the date as 1872.
[77] Oehler, op. cit., p. 192; *China Mission Hand-book,* Part 2, p. 274.
[78] *A Century of Protestant Missions in China,* p. 495.
[79] Ibid., p. 496; Oehler, op. cit., p. 189.

In 1882 the Berlin Missionary Society, a body which had been in existence for many years, came into Kwangtung as heir of part of the work which the Rhenish Society had been forced to surrender—including that of the Berlin Missionary Society for China.[80]   There passed to the Berlin Missionary Society a head station at Canton and several outstations with between four hundred and fifty and six hundred and fifty Christians—apparently all Hakkas.[81]   During the next decade and a half, increasing funds were allocated to the China field and in spite of persecutions and the death of some of the missionaries new centers were opened in the interior.[82]

By 1856 three Methodist bodies were represented in China—the Methodist Episcopal Church of the Northern States, the Methodist Episcopal Church of the Southern States, and the Wesleyan Missionary Society (British).   Before 1856 the Northern Methodists had begun in but one city, Foochow.   As the years passed they developed in that center the usual features of a Protestant mission, particularly the evangelistic and educational, and reached out into other sections of Fukien.[83]   They were not content with one province, but, with characteristic enthusiasm and enterprise, founded missions in Central, North, and West China.   In 1867 Virgil C. Hart, the outstanding pioneer of his board in the Middle Kingdom, with one colleague opened a station in Kiukiang.[84] Two years later Hart was made the first Superintendent of the newly formed Central China Mission, and under his supervision footholds were obtained in Wuhu, Chinkiang, Nanking, and Nanch'ang.[85]   In Nanking, the old "Southern Capital," Hart, with statesmanlike foresight, wished to establish medical work and a university.[86]   In 1869 Peking was entered by two representatives of the Board and, as reënforcements came, Tientsin and other

[80] Oehler, op. cit., p. 193; Richter, op. cit., p. 520.
[81] Richter, op. cit., p. 520; A Century of Protestant Missions in China, p. 484; China Mission Hand-book, Part 2, p. 281.
[82] A Century of Protestant Missions in China, pp. 484, 485; Richter, op. cit., p. 525.
[83] Reid and Gracey, Methodist Episcopal Missions, Vol. 1, pp. 454-462.   In 1876 there were 14 missionaries, 80 outstations, 80 organized churches in 26 circuits, 70 native preachers and 7 Bible women, and 1,089 members.—Chinese Recorder, Vol. 7, p. 257. A Century of Protestant Missions in China, pp. 430-440; Sites, Nathan Sites, passim.
[84] Hart, Virgil C. Hart, passim.
[85] Ibid., passim.
[86] Ibid., pp. 124-143.

places in Chihli were occupied.[87]   In 1882, through the generosity of Rev. J. F. Goucher, who gave ten thousand dollars for
the purpose, Szechwan became a mission field of the Board, with
the first station at Chungking.   A severe reverse was early encountered, for, in 1886, the property at Chungking was destroyed by
riots.   Chungking was not abandoned, but not until 1891 was a
second city, Chengtu, entered.[88]

The Southern Methodist Board was badly handicapped by the
American Civil War and the period of reconstruction.   Young
J. Allen, who had arrived in Shanghai in 1860 and was to be the
most prominent representative of his board in China in the nineteenth century, was forced to support himself.[89]   Until 1876 all
but one of the few missionaries who came out derived their living
either by extra-mission work in China or from contributions from
small groups in the United States.   No until after Bishop Marvin
visited China in 1876 did the home board begin vigorously to aid
the struggling mission.[90]   Even after prosperity came, the Southern Board, in marked contrast with its northern sister, confined its
efforts to one section, Kiangsu and a part of Chêkiang.   In this
densely populated region it found more than ample scope for its
resources.

The Wesleyan Methodist Missionary Society had, as we have
seen, entered Canton before the treaties of Tientsin.   Interrupted
by the war of 1856-1860, with the coming of peace, activities were
resumed and were maintained in and near that city.[91]   Josiah Cox,
driven out of Canton by the war, after some years in Singapore,
the East Indies, England, and East China, in 1862, at the suggestion of Griffith John, moved to Hankow.[92]   It was from this
beginning that the Society found its second field in China, Hupeh
and Hunan.[93]   Because of the intense anti-foreign feeling, no residence could be established in Hunan before 1900, but Cox seems

[87] *A Century of Protestant Missions in China*, pp. 447, 448; *Chinese Recorder*,
Vol. 26, p. 414.
[88] *A Century of Protestant Missions in China*, pp. 444, 445; Hart, *Virgil C.
Hart*, pp. 150, 180-184; Hart, *Western China*, pp. 290-296.
[89] *Missionary Review of the World*, Vol. 25, p. 648; Cannon, *History of
Southern Methodist Missions*, pp. 102, 103.
[90] Cannon, op. cit., pp. 106, 107.
[91] *A Century of Protestant Missions in China*, p. 411.
[92] *Bulletin No. 27 of the Wesleyan Methodist Missionary Society*, pp. 1-3;
Findlay and Holdsworth, *History of the Wesleyan Methodist Missionary Society*,
Vol. 5, p. 463.
[93] Clayton, *Methodism in Central China*, pp. 15-20.

to have been, by virtue of a visit in 1863, the first Protestant missionary to enter the province.[94]

It was to the Central China field of the Wesleyan Methodists that there came, in 1865, one of the most prominent and greatly beloved Protestant missionaries of the half-century, David Hill. Possessed, through his father's generosity, of an independent income, he remained unmarried, lived much of the time as simply as the humbler Chinese about him, and devoted his means to the Church and to the destitute, the aged, and the blind. His unselfishness and singleness of purpose made a profound impression upon both Chinese and Europeans. It was he who won to the Faith the devoted Pastor Hsi, and it was the spell of his life that attracted to China the majority of the members of his mission. It was characteristic of him that the great famine of 1877-1879 called forth his active help and led him to spend several years in Shansi, and it was also in keeping with his career that he should meet his death (1896) in his adopted home, Central China, of typhus, probably contracted while distributing among refugees alms entrusted to him by the Governor of Hupeh.[95]

The English Presbyterians continued their activities in and near the two centers to which Burns had introduced them, Amoy and Swatow. While the policy of the mission was one of concentration—of establishing strong stations rather than opening many weak ones—there was the expansion characteristic of all missions staffed by able and energetic men. Villages and cities around Amoy and Swatow were penetrated and efforts were made not only for those speaking the local dialects, but for the numerous Hakka peoples. Work was more formally started among these latter about 1871.[96] The field of the mission grew in another direction with the coming of agents of the "Women's Mission," who, among other activities, cared for deserted infants and deformed boys.[97]

It was a logical expansion that took the English Presbyterians into Formosa and Singapore. In 1859 missionaries had begun visiting Formosa and had discovered that on the island were many Chinese speaking the Amoy dialect and that among these were

[94] Ibid., passim.
[95] Barber, *David Hill*, passim.
[96] Paton, *The "Stranger People,"* p. 33.
[97] Johnston, *China and Formosa*, pp. 235, 236.

some Christians. A permanent enterprise was accordingly begun in Formosa in 1865. As a native church was established, it began a mission of its own on the neighboring Pescadores Islands.[98] After the London Missionary Society withdrew from Singapore to the newly opened ports of China, that city was left with very little Protestant effort for the Chinese. The Chinese population was increasing, however, both in the city and the adjoining peninsula—chiefly by emigration from South China. Since many of the immigrants spoke the Amoy and Swatow dialects and often had close connections with the home land, the English Presbyterians felt an obligation to aid them religiously and in 1881 formally began a mission among them—a mission which was not confined to Singapore but which was extended to a number of adjoining centers and to the Malay Peninsula.[99]

Among the organizations that had entered China before 1856 mention must not be omitted of the two pioneer Bible societies, the British and Foreign and the American. These will be spoken of more in detail later, but it must be noted that their agents, especially those of the British society, travelled widely and were often the first Protestants to penetrate many of the cities of the Empire.

The Entrance of New Societies

The thirty years after 1856 witnessed the coming of many societies which either had not been in existence or had not been represented in 1856. In general these will be mentioned in the chronological order in which they entered China: the exceptions are usually groups affiliated with each other. Because of the opening of the country by the treaties of 1858 and 1860, the late fifties and the sixties saw the arrival of many new bodies. Then came a lull: few new societies appeared between 1871 and 1885. In the late eighties and in the nineties, however, the movement began again on an even larger scale.

The first society to be noted was one which Gützlaff had called into existence, a Pomeranian organization, the Mission Union for the Evangelization of China. Its initial representatives, Mr. and

[98] *China Mission Hand-book*, Part 2, pp. 53-67; Johnston, op. cit., pp. 169, 177, 316; Duncan, *The City of Springs*, p. 60; Campbell, *Missionary Success in Formosa*, pp. 215-330.
[99] Johnston, op. cit., p. 337; *A Century of Protestant Missions in China*, pp. 194, 195.

Mrs. H. E. J. Vögler, reached Hongkong in 1858, but the mission appears not to have had a long life.[100]

Much more important was the enterprise founded by that historic board which had been organized by the heroic Carey and his supporters, the (English) Baptist Missionary Society. We have earlier seen that the English Baptists, through Marshman's translation of the Scriptures, shared in the beginnings of Protestant efforts for the Chinese. The Baptist Missionary Society, however, did not formally enter China until 1859. In that year it took over two men who had served with the short-lived Chinese Evangelization Society. These went to Chefoo, but within a year one was dead and ill health soon forced the other to return to Great Britain.[101] Although others filled the vacant places, disaster overtook most of them and in 1875 only one remained.[102] This lone representative, Timothy Richard, was, however, one of the greatest missionaries whom any branch of the Church, whether Roman Catholic, Russian Orthodox, or Protestant, has sent to China. Born in Wales in 1845, he was converted in his teens during a great revival, and, after studying theology, offered himself for China, and arrived in 1870. Left alone in 1875, he went to Tsingchow, in the very heart of Shantung. There, in the face of bitter opposition, he began what was to be a permanent, soundly organized mission. Reënforcements arrived and as the years pass we shall find him in various parts of the country, and always with a widening vision of the task of the Christian missionary. Warmly appreciative of the excellent features of Chinese civilization, Richard dreamed of reaching the nation by what he believed to be more expeditious and natural methods than those usually employed by missionaries—now by winning the most devout and high-minded souls, especially those in some of the strictest of the religious sects, and now using in the presentation of the Gospel the terms with which the "worthy" among the Chinese were familiar. He thought in terms of the entire Empire and of all phases of its life. To his mind Christian missions were under obligation to aid in the reconstruction of the country for the benefit of all the Chinese. Stirred to his depths by what he saw in the great famine of the seventies, he longed to see a China

---

[100] *Mittheilungen aus China,* p. 33; *A Century of Protestant Missions in China,* p. 645.
[101] Forsyth, *Shantung,* p. 208.
[102] *A Century of Protestant Missions in China,* p. 69.

so transformed by contact with the best elements and appliances of Western civilization that the recurrence of such a disaster would be impossible. In time he separated from his board, and by literature, eventually issued through the Society for the Diffusion of Christian and General Knowledge among the Chinese, he strove to broaden the outlook of the educated classes and so to aid in nation-wide reform. He was, as we shall see, the friend and adviser of Chinese liberals in the nineties, and after the Boxer outbreak suggested, as a novel "retaliation" for the martyrdoms in Shansi, a university which by enlightment would remove the prejudice that had helped give rise to anti-foreign feeling. He was to live until 1919 and so was to witness many changes. Fellow missionaries often differed from him on doctrine and method and on his interpretationos of Chinese religious life, but none could long doubt his enthusiasm, his devotion, his vigor, or his deeply religious nature. Like Ricci, he dreamed of reaching China through its dominant classes, but, less committed than Ricci to an inflexible dogma and a stereotyped ecclesiastical organization, he was much more free to choose his methods. His purpose was not so much to obtain the salvation of the Chinese by bringing them within the fold of a church as to transform wholesomely every phase of China's culture and so to make possible more abundant life—economic, intellectual, and spiritual—for the nation's millions. While unique, he was representative of a type of Protestant missionary which increased in numbers as the years passed.[103]

Reports of the great famine of 1877-1879 led Richard, as it did several other missionaries, to Shansi, at the heart of the destitute region. Richard was not content merely to distribute food, but suggested to the officials means of relief far more extensive than an unaided foreigner could undertake. After the famine had

[103] Richard, *Forty-Five Years in China,* passim; Soothill, *Timothy Richard of China,* passim; Reeve, *Timothy Richard,* passim. W. G. Walshe, Secretary of the Christian Literature Society, said of Richard that he "is a remarkable blending of shrinking modesty and vaulting ambition, of benignity of expression interrupted by occasional flashes of flaming indignation, of self-abnegation approximating to servility combined with a restlessness of contradiction and an indomitable self-will. . . . His seeming ambition amounts to this, that he wishes to serve all, but is conscious that he can only do so by serving the few—i.e., those in the highest places of authority and dignity."—Reeve, op. cit., pp. 156, 157. See also *A Century of Protestant Missions in China,* pp. 69, 70; Fullerton and Wilson, *New China,* pp. 200-206.

passed, he remained in Shansi for eight years and during at least part of that time centered his attention upon those groups which controlled Chinese opinion and which so far had been but little touched by Protestants—the officials and scholars. By literature and lectures he strove to break down prejudice against his faith and to pave the way for the application of Western science to the bettering of the economic conditions of the masses. However, he and his colleagues of the Baptist Missionary Society found tangible results very slow and after thirteen years had only about thirty converts.[104]

In the meantime other members of his society succeeded Richard in Shantung and by diligent efforts in and around Tsingchow saw the beginnings of a vigorous church. In 1899 during a famine in Shantung several families of converts joined in a great migration of their fellow provincials to Shensi. Here some of the Christians gathered themselves into a separate village and asked for missionaries. Two were sent them, and from this beginning a prosperous mission arose.[105]

From its rather unpromising beginning in Shantung, then, the Baptist Missionary Society had provided China with one of its greatest missionaries and had started permanent enterprises in three provinces—Shantung, Shansi, and Shensi. It gave, too, the opportunity in China for a sister organization, the Baptist Zenana Missionary Society, which, originally founded for the women of India, in 1893 began sending representatives to China.[106]

A small denomination in England, the Methodist New Connexion,[107] was stirred by the news of the opening of China by the treaties of 1858 and decided to begin a mission there. W. N. Hall, who was chiefly responsible for arousing interest in the undertaking, was sent, together with John Innocent, in 1859. For a time the two considered making Soochow their center, but that city was then virtually closed because of the T'ai P'ing rebels. In 1860 they went to Tientsin and here they remained. Hall died in 1878 but Innocent stayed on until 1897. The mission was

[104] Richard, op. cit., pp. 124-143; A Century of Protestant Missions in China, pp. 78-80; China Mission Hand-book, Part 2, p. 46.
[105] China Mission Hand-book, Part 2, p. 48; Duncan, The Missionary Mail, pp. 12, 13; Glover, Herbert Stanley Jenkins, p. 26.
[106] A Century of Protestant Missions in China, p. 75.
[107] The China Mission Year Book, 1911, p. 244, said that the denomination had at that time (1910 or 1911) in Great Britain only 25,000 members.

early successful in winning some able converts and branched out beyond the city and into Shantung.[108]

The Society for the Propagation of the Gospel in Foreign Parts was later in entering China than was its companion Anglican body, the Church Missionary Society, and it was not to undertake as extensive an enterprise. In 1859, however, it proposed sending men to China,[109] and in 1863 its two first missionaries arrived. They went to Peking, but the following year both retired, one to Shanghai for other work and the other recalled because of financial indiscretion.[110] After this inauspicious beginning the Society remained unrepresented for ten years. In 1872, however, as the result of a day of prayer for foreign missions, support for two missionaries for five years was offered, and in 1874 the two, one of them Charles Perry Scott, were sent out. These settled in Chefoo, and in 1880 Scott was consecrated bishop.[111] The mission grew but slowly. In the eighties much energy was expended upon an unsuccessful attempt at Chefoo to train as missionaries young men from England. From 1869 to 1891 inclusive only fifty Chinese were baptized. Better days dawned, however, and from 1892 to 1898 inclusive there were two hundred and thirty baptisms.[112] By 1900 there were missionaries both in Shantung and in Chihli.

The Evangelical Missionary Society of Paris sent two missionaries in 1860, but the effort was not long pursued.[113]

There must be noted here, although it will be mentioned again, the National Bible Society of Scotland. This was formed in 1860, and in 1863 its first agent, Alexander Williamson, landed at Chefoo. Williamson had previously served in China under the London Missionary Society, but his health had broken and he had been in Great Britain for about six years. For this new society he travelled extensively over the Empire, distributing Christian literature. He was later to be the chief founder of what was to grow first into the Society for the Diffusion of Christian and

---

[108] Candlin, *John Innocent*, passim. In 1877 there were in the mission three missionaries, six organized churches, and 276 church members (*Chinese Recorder*, Vol. 8, p. 460) ; Hedley, *Our Mission in North China*, p. 1; *China Mission Handbook*, Part 2, p. 104.
[109] Stock, *History of the Church Missionary Society*, Vol. 2, p. 306.
[110] Pascoe, *Two Hundred Years of the S. P. G.*, Vol. 2, pp. 704, 705.
[111] Pascoe, op. cit., Vol. 2, pp. 705-709; Norris, *China*, pp. 145-150; *North China Mission of the Church of England*, p. 5.
[112] *A Century of Protestant Missions in China*, p. 64.
[113] *Nos champs de mission*, 3d ed., 1922, p. xiii. Annual reports of the Société des Missions Évangéliques de Paris, for 1860, 1861, 1862, and 1863.

General Knowledge among the Chinese and then into the Christian Literature Society.[114]

Next in chronological order to enter China was one more of the numerous bodies that had its roots in the work of Wesley, the English Methodist Free Church Mission, supported by the United Methodist Free Churches. Its first missionary arrived in Ningpo in 1864. In 1878 another center in Chêkiang, Wênchow, was made a station and in and around these two cities the society was to find its field. Its most distinguished missionary, W. E. Soothill, was to have a long and varied career, first in pioneer endeavors at Wênchow, then as an educator and author, and still later as Professor of Chinese at Oxford in the chair once held by Legge.[115]

In 1865 all Protestant societies, both old and new, were confining their efforts to the coast provinces and to a few cities in the Yangtze Valley. In eleven provinces no Protestant missionaries were residing, and most of the eleven had never seen one. In the seven provinces with resident missionaries, the bulk of the population had not yet been approached. No concerted plans, moreover, were being made for giving to all China the Gospel as Protestants understood it.

Now, in 1866, there entered the Empire a body, the China Inland Mission, which was to attempt the unprecedented, the presentation of the Gospel by Protestants to all the Chinese, and on a systematic plan which would supplement rather than conflict with existing missions. This society was in time to have in China more missionaries than any other single agency, Protestant or Roman Catholic. Its beginnings and its development are in some respects the most remarkable chapter in all the history of Christian missions in China. The founder, James Hudson Taylor, usually known as Hudson Taylor, was, if measured by the movement which he called into being, one of the greatest missionaries of all time, and was certainly, judged by the results of his efforts, one of the four or five most influential foreigners who came to China in the nineteenth century for any purpose, religious or secular.

Taylor was born in 1832 at Barnsley in Yorkshire. His father and mother were devout people who before his birth prayed that

[114] *A Century of Protestant Missions in China*, p. 567.
[115] *A Century of Protestant Missions in China*, pp. 129-133; *China Mission Hand-book*, Part 2, p. 107; Soothill, *A Typical Mission in China*, passim.

if they were given a son, he should become a missionary to China. With rare wisdom and faith, however, they did not tell him of their hope until he had been for years fulfilling it. Reared in such a home, it is not remarkable that Taylor was profoundly religious. After several boyhood years of unhappiness and religious uncertainty he experienced a spiritual rebirth. Not long afterward he felt impelled to prepare himself for missionary work in China and to this end began the study of medicine. It was characteristic of his later life that he believed that his preparation should be not only in the science of healing, but in learning complete dependence upon God. With this conviction he laid before God in prayer all phases of life and all his interests, including the seemingly trivial. A growing faith, confirmed most remarkably by experience, that if he were doing what he believed to be God's will, God would, when asked, supply his every need, physical as well as spiritual, was to be one of the outstanding characteristics of his life and of the mission which he founded.

In 1853, at the age of twenty-one, Taylor sailed under the Chinese Evangelization Society, which was, it will be recalled, a relatively short-lived organization that owed its beginnings in part to Gützlaff. He landed at Shanghai, but spent the following six years in several different sections of the country. Some of the time, when that meant grave personal danger, he was engaged in itinerant preaching in Kiangsu, Chêkiang, and Kwangtung. For months he was thrown into close fellowship with William C. Burns and this earnest pioneer had a profound influence upon his inner life. Then for three and a half years he lived in Ningpo. In 1857 he severed his connection with the Chinese Evangelisation Society because that body was going into debt and because he believed that debt was unscriptural and implied a lack of faith in God. Cut off now from the support of any society, he lived in even more complete trust that God would provide for his needs. Old Testament phrases that were later to be much quoted in the China Inland Mission—*Jehovah Jireh,* "the Lord will provide," and *Ebenezer,* with its suggestion of the assurance "hitherto hath the Lord helped us"—became his watchwords and his comfort.

Taylor had never enjoyed robust health, and in 1860 illness forced him to return to England. Many would have felt that such an outcome had fully discharged their obligations to the Chinese,

but not so Taylor.   On his way home he and his wife [110] prayed
that their stay in Great Britain might be made the means of
raising up at least five missionaries for Ningpo and Chêkiang.
Two sailed in 1863 and four more in 1865.

While in England Taylor felt the burden of inland China
pressing ever more heavily upon him.   True to the convictions of
the school of Protestantism in which he had been reared, he
believed that Roman Catholics were not meeting the spiritual
needs of China—although he cited the presence of their missionaries in the interior as proof that it would be possible for Protestants to live there.   To his mind the major part of China was
entirely without an opportunity of hearing the true Gospel message.   Brought up, as he had been, to believe in the inconceiv-
ably and eternally unhappy state of those who died without
accepting the Christian message, the thought of the hundreds of
millions of Chinese passing out of this life without a chance of
hearing the New Testament way of salvation weighed upon his
sensitive spirit with crushing intensity.   The burden was increased
by the belief that God did not wish these millions to perish, but
that He could remedy their need only when His servants were
willing to draw in faith upon his infinite resources.   The societies
already in China felt unable to spread their activities much further than they were then doing and so, in June, 1865, Taylor
decided that he must and would be willing to undertake what
he believed to be God's will for the great Empire.

It was a daring decision for one man, without financial
resources, without the support of an organization, and always in
precarious health.   More nearly than is given to most men, however, Taylor lived to see his vision realized.   At the time of his
death (1905) the China Inland Mission counted on its rolls
eight hundred and twenty-eight missionaries, Protestant missionaries of various societies were living in each of the Eighteen
Provinces and in Mongolia and Manchuria, and in several provinces the initial pioneering had been done by members of the
organization which he had called into existence.   Fittingly enough,
he was to die in Changsha, the capital of that province which was
for many years the most bitterly anti-foreign and anti-Christian
center in China.

Many circumstances contributed to the success of Taylor's

[110] He had married in 1858.

efforts. Freedom to travel in inland China and full toleration to missionaries and Chinese Christians had been recently guaranteed by foreign treaties; for the Protestant world the four decades from 1865 to 1905 were a period of growing prosperity and comparative peace; there were, too, in nearly all Protestant denominations large numbers who believed, as did Taylor, in the imperative necessity of giving the Gospel to the non-Christian world and who rallied to his support; Taylor, moreover, developed unusual powers of organization and administration. All of these favoring conditions would have been ineffective, however, had it not been for Taylor's daring, simple faith, utter sincerity, and completely unselfish devotion.[117] This one man, frail in body and of no unusual intellectual powers, called into being a mission which, consecrated to one great task, the giving of the Faith to all Chinese who had never heard it, was to bear witness to the Gospel in every inland province in China.

It is a temptation to linger over the history of the China Inland Mission, but the story must be told quickly and all too briefly. In 1865 Taylor, in pursuance of his new and momentous decision, began asking in prayer for "twenty-four willing, skillful workers"[118]—two for each of the eleven provinces which at that time had no Protestant missionary and two for Mongolia. To support these he began an organization which he called the China Inland Mission. The main features of the Mission's policy, most of them announced at the outset or early in its history, were:

(1) The Mission was to be undenominational. Members of any Protestant denomination were accepted if they gave promise of being good missionaries. While persons of education were preferred, those were also welcomed who were without much learning but who were otherwise qualified. As time went on, missionaries were grouped denominationally by provinces or districts: for example, in Szechwan the members of the Mission were Anglicans. Taylor was always eager to assist, not to compete with denominational societies. He welcomed all agencies that would help give to the Chinese a knowledge of the Christian Gospel. As time passed and liberal theological opinions began to

[117] For the facts in these last four paragraphs see Taylor, *A Retrospect,* passim; Broomhall, *The Jubilee Story of the C. I. M.,* passim; Guinness, *The Story of the China Inland Mission,* passim.
[118] Taylor, *Hudson Taylor,* pp. 21-32. In a pamphlet, *China's Spiritual Needs and Claims,* issued about this time, Taylor asked for twenty-four European and twenty-four native evangelists.—Ibid., pp. 33-40. New editions of the pamphlet were published in 1866, 1868, 1872, and 1884.—Preface to the 1884 edition of Taylor, *China's Spiritual Needs and Claims.*

make their appearance, the Mission remained conservative.[119]   However, while some members were intolerant, the Mission's official policy, although firm, was usually irenic.

(2) As the years passed, the Mission became international and drew support in personnel and money from most of the countries where Protestants were strong.

(3) In accordance with Taylor's experience and profound conviction, the members of the mission had no guaranteed salary but were to trust God to supply their needs.   Moreover, also in accordance with one of Taylor's fundamental principles, the Mission was never to go into debt. A very efficient system of administration was developed, so that the funds which came to the Mission were made to accomplish the most possible.   Taylor did not allow faith to be an excuse for slovenly business methods.

(4) No personal solicitation for funds was to be made and no collections were to be taken at meetings.   This was in part to avoid unnecessary competition with existing denominational missionary agencies.

(5) Missionaries were to conform as nearly as possible to the social and living conditions of the Chinese, and until well after 1900 were for the most part to wear Chinese dress.

(6) The direction of the Mission was to be in China and not by a board in Great Britain.   For nearly forty years Taylor was the head, as Director or General Director, and in time there developed a council of senior missionaries who were advisers of the Director and superintendents of specified districts.

(7) Finally, the main purpose of the Mission was not to win converts or to build up and educate a Christian community, but to diffuse as quickly as possible a knowledge of the Gospel throughout the Empire. To this end, when a new province was penetrated, the capital city was, when at all feasible, made the seat of the first station, then, if practicable, stations were opened in the prefectural or *fu* cities and only later in the less important towns.   The Mission did not disparage the efforts of those who held it important to build up and educate a Christian community.   It believed, however, that the proclamation of the Gospel was the special task which had been assigned it and that it was of secondary importance by whom the sheaves were gathered.   The Mission, accordingly, laid little emphasis on schools, although—perhaps because of Taylor's training—it maintained medical work.[120]

Taylor and Timothy Richard were outstanding exponents of

[119] The first candidates were accepted only if they believed in (1) the inspiration of the whole Scripture; (2) the Bible as the ultimate and only rule and guide of the Christian; (3) the Trinity; (4) the pollution of the whole race through the fall of Adam; (5) the atoning merit of the death and resurrection of Jesus Christ; (6) future rewards and punishments; (7) the limitation of probation to this life.—Hulbert, in *Missionary Review of the World,* Vol. 2, p. 256.

[120] This statement of policies can be found in whole or in part in each of the following: Taylor, *Hudson Taylor,* pp. 41, 42, 52; *China Mission Hand-book,* Part 2, pp. 111, 147, 148; *A Century of Protestant Missions in China,* p. 136; Broomhall, *The Jubilee Story of the C. I. M.,* pp. 30, 31, 291, 292, 303, 316-319;

different and in time conflicting conceptions of the missionary's function. They had much in common. Richard, indeed, originally applied to the China Inland Mission, but was advised to go out under the society of his own denomination. Both dared to think in terms of all China and to attempt to formulate methods for reaching the whole of the nation much more expeditiously and effectively than was being done by their contemporaries. They were unlike in that Richard dreamed of seeing all phases of China's life transformed by the introduction of every wholesome feature of Western civilization, while Taylor confined his efforts to the proclamation of the Gospel as understood by the Evangelicals of the time. Richard's theology was the more flexible and he was quicker to recognize all that was good in the non-Christian faiths of China. Each was a great missionary, and it witnesses to the inclusiveness of Protestantism that both were usually recognized as in good and regular standing in missionary circles.

Taylor's initial appeal for twenty-four new missionaries and for funds to send them met with a gratifying response.[121]   In 1865 three left for China, two of them being Mr. and Mrs. J. W. Stevenson, later prominent in the Mission.   In 1866 there sailed on the *Lammermuir* a party of twenty-two, including the Taylors.[122]   The significance of this company was in part its size, for in March, 1865, there are said to have been only ninety-one Protestant missionaries in all China.[123]   The group landed at

China's Millions, 1877, pp. 30, 43, 1882, pp. 40, 126; Little, *In the Land of the Blue Gown*, p. 112; *Missionary Review of the World*, Vol. 2, p. 258.

The China Inland Mission was the first to inaugurate language schools for new missionaries.   About 1885 or 1887 training schools for new missionaries were opened by Taylor, one for men at Anking and one for women in Yangchow.— *China Mission Year Book, 1912*, pp. 233-235; *China's Millions*, 1898, p. 115.

The Mission, too, in 1880 started a school in Chefoo for the children of its missionaries.—*China's Millions*, 1892, p. 75, 1893, pp. 9, 46, 1895, p. 31, 1897, p. 25.

The home department examined, accepted, and trained candidates, promoted missionary interest, received contributions, made remittances, and audited and published reports and accounts.—*The Jubilee Story of the C. I. M.*, p. 314.

[121] In 1865 there came to Taylor applications from forty volunteers.—Broomhall, op. cit., p. 29.   George Müller, who was supporting in England many hundreds of orphans, helped Taylor greatly.—Taylor, *Hudson Taylor*, p. 60.   A Mr. Berger undertook to manage without salary the home end of the work.—Broomhall, op. cit., p. 24.   It is interesting to note that Barnardo, who was later to do memorable service among the London waifs, originally hoped to go to China under the China Inland Mission and was advised by its leaders to study medicine. —Taylor, *Hudson Taylor*, p. 56.

[122] Broomhall, op. cit., p. 38.

[123] Guinness, *Story of the China Inland Mission*, Vol. 1, pp. 215-224.

Shanghai and Taylor proceeded as soon as practicable to begin activities outside the treaty ports. Hangchow in Chêkiang was chosen as the Mission's first center, and by 1870 other cities in Chêkiang, Kiangsi, Kiangsu, and Anhui were occupied, among them Soochow, Nanking, Wênchow, Chinkiang, Yangchow, Anking, and Kiukiang.[124]

Taylor did not lack for difficulties. Occasionally missionaries of other societies were none too cordial;[125] some of Taylor's own company became disaffected and a few even left the Mission;[126] one of Taylor's children died;[127] serious opposition was encountered in Chinkiang and Anking; in 1868 Taylor and some of his party were driven out of Yangchow by a riot,[128] and while ultimately the British authorities brought about the reinstatement of the Mission in that city, the affair aroused much criticism in Great Britain[129] and for a time the income of the Mission fell off; income was further unfavorably affected by the Franco-Prussian War;[130] the Tientsin massacre seemed to threaten all missionaries in China, both Catholic and Protestant;[131] Taylor's own health was precarious and news came from England that Berger, who was generously managing the home organization, was ill;[132] and in 1870 Mrs. Taylor died.[133]

Yet Taylor was undismayed and prayed and planned for the expansion of the Mission. In 1869 he reported to his friends that he had found greater joy and faith than ever before.[134] In 1871 he was on his way to England to relieve Berger and to strengthen the home support.[135] While in Great Britain he further elaborated the home organization, placed it in new hands, and mar-

[124] Taylor, *Hudson Taylor*, p. 125; Broomhall, op. cit., pp. 54-69; Guinness, op. cit., pp. 286 et seq.; Scott, *Twenty-Six Years of Missionary Work in China*, p. 10.

[125] Taylor, *Hudson Taylor*, pp. 86-102.

[126] Ibid., pp. 104 et seq.

[127] Ibid., p. 118.

[128] Ibid., pp, 138-152; Broomhall, op. cit., pp. 55-65.

[129] Taylor, *Hudson Taylor*, pp. 154-164; Broomhall, op. cit., pp. 58, 59. The Mission accepted indemnity for damage to its property. It had a uniform rule never to accept an indemnity for lives lost in riots and in later years it generally refused compensation for damage to property.—Broomhall, *The Jubilee Story of the C. I. M.*, p. 60.

[130] Broomhall, op. cit., p. 73.

[131] Ibid., p. 69.

[132] Ibid., p. 74.

[133] Taylor, *Hudson Taylor*, p. 195.

[134] Taylor, *Hudson Taylor*, pp. 168-180.

[135] Broomhall, op. cit., pp. 77-79.

ried again.[136]   In 1872 he once more left for China.[137]   In 1874 a station was opened in Wuchang.[138]   In 1875, in spite of the fact that a fall had recently so injured his spine that he was in danger of being a cripple for life, Taylor sent out an appeal for prayer for eighteen missionaries for the nine provinces still unopened, and it was characteristic of him that the funds to finance the new workers came largely from a legacy that had been left to Mrs. Taylor.[139]   For a year or more he had been praying for these eighteen and for "fifty or one hundred native evangelists and as many foreign superintendents as may be needed, to open up the *fus* and forty-eight *hsiens* still unoccupied in Chêkiang." [140] His was a faith that thrived on adversity.

The growth of the Mission continued to justify the faith of Taylor and his associates.   By 1876 the eighteen new missionaries prayed for had sailed and within a year sixty more applications had been received.[141]   In 1876 the organization had fifty-two missionaries—almost a fifth of the total Protestant force in China [142]—seventy-five native helpers, two hospitals, and ninety-two stations and outstations.[143]   The Mission, too, was stretching out into new provinces.   In 1875 some of its representatives were travelling in Honan, a fleeting residence had been effected in Yochow in anti-foreign Hunan,[144] and in spite of the recent murder of Margary on the Yünnan-Burmese border—a tragedy that was threatening the peace between China and Great Britain— J. W. Stevenson and Henry Soltau were establishing themselves in Burma, preparatory to penetrating the Empire.[145]   The Chefoo Convention (1876) made travel in the interior much safer, and in the following eighteen months members of the Mission journeyed thirty thousand miles.[146]   Shensi was opened in 1876, and representatives of the Mission were active in ministering to the

[136] Ibid., pp. 79-81.
[137] Ibid., p. 82.
[138] Ibid., pp. 99, 100.
[139] Ibid., p. 100.
[140] Taylor, *Hudson Taylor*, p. 252.
[141] Ibid., p. 268.
[142] Broomhall, op. cit., p. 95.
[143] *China's Millions*, 1887, p. 84.
[144] Broomhall, *The Jubilee Story of the C. I. M.*, pp. 102, 103; Broomhall, *Pioneer Work in Hunan*, pp. 5-7.
[145] Broomhall, *The Jubilee Story of the C. I. M.*, p. 103; Broomhall, *John W. Stevenson*, passim.   For eight years Stevenson was at Bhamo.
[146] Taylor, *Hudson Taylor*, p. 285.

sufferers from the great famine in Shansi.[147]   The Mission penetrated Kansu in 1876 and 1877,[148] Hunan was crossed late in 1876, Kweichow was entered in 1877, and Kwangsi, Yünnan, and Szechwan were traversed in 1877.[149]   At least one bold spirit reached the Tibetan marches.[150]   Before 1880 Protestant missionaries had been in every one of the Eighteen Provinces and by 1882 missionaries seem to have been residing in each,[151] with the probable exceptions of Honan, Hunan, and Kwangsi.

This encouraging progress was an incentive to further effort. From the beginning Taylor had made use of unmarried women as missionaries.   Between 1878 and 1881 he began to send them alone into the interior provinces,[152] a policy whose success testified both to the courage of the women and to the character of the Chinese.   In 1881 increased opportunities led Taylor to ask for seventy additional missionaries by the close of 1884.[153]   For a time it seemed that at last his hopes were to be frustrated: in 1882 only eleven were commissioned, funds were so meager that some members resigned from the Mission, and even Taylor was weighed down by forebodings.[154]   By the close of 1884, however, six more than the specified seventy had sailed and gifts had increased.[155] Emboldened by this new success and the ever present needs of the Empire, in 1886 the China Council (of senior missionaries)— at its initial meeting—asked for one hundred new recruits and an additional £10,000 a year.   The following year the one hundred left Great Britain and the income increased from £22,000 to £33,000.[156]   The all-China conference of Protestant missionaries of 1890, at the suggestion of a committee of which Taylor was

[147] Taylor, Days of Blessing in Inland China, introduction; Guinness, Story of the China Inland Mission, Chapter 19.
[148] Broomhall, The Jubilee Story of the C. I. M., pp. 108, 109.
[149] Ibid., pp. 106-113; Broomhall, Pioneer Work in Hunan, pp. 5-7; Clarke, Among the Tribes of Southwest China, p. 139; Davidson and Mason, Life in West China, p. 153; Guinness, Story of the C. I. M., Chapters 17 and 18.
[150] Edgar, The Marches of the Mantze, p. iii.
[151] Broomhall, The Jubilee Story of the C. I. M., p. 128.
[152] Taylor, After Thirty Years, pp. 11-20; Guinness, Story of the C. I. M., Chapters 23, 24; Letters from Geraldine Guinness in China, passim; Fishe, My Father's Business, passim; Taylor, Hudson Taylor, pp. 339 et seq.
[153] Taylor, Hudson Taylor, pp. 360-370.
[154] Ibid., pp. 360-370.
[155] China Mission Hand-book, Part 2, p. 117; Taylor, Hudson Taylor, pp. 271-384.
[156] Taylor, Hudson Taylor, pp. 419-433; Broomhall, The Jubilee Story of the C. I. M., pp. 172-174.

chairman, sent out to Protestant Christendom an appeal for one thousand more missionaries in five years to reënforce the various societies represented in China, and the appeal seems to have been fully answered.[157]

Many of the members of the China Inland Mission had but little formal education, but a number were university graduates. In 1880 Dr. Harold Schofield, an Oxford man, sailed for China. He went to Shansi and there, after three all too brief years, died of typhus.[158] A visit of Dwight L. Moody to Cambridge in 1882 led, in 1884, to the announcement that seven men, among them the stroke of the university crew and the captain of the cricket team, had been accepted by the China Inland Mission. The going of this "Cambridge Seven"—D. E. Hoste, Stanley P. Smith, W. W. Cassels, C. T. Studd, Montagu Beauchamp, and Cecil and Arthur Polhill-Turner, some of them socially prominent—made a great stir in Great Britain and America.[159] One of the seven, Hoste, was later to become the General Director of the Mission and another, Cassels, was in after years (1895) to be consecrated Anglican Bishop in West China.

As time passed and the news of the daring and success of the Mission spread, help came to Taylor from Protestants of other lands than England, and in several countries organizations auxiliary to the China Inland Mission sprang into being. In 1889 a council was formed in Glasgow to deal with candidates from Scotland.[160] In 1887 Henry W. Frost journeyed from the United States to England to offer himself to the Mission and to suggest that a North American council be formed. Rather reluctantly Taylor went to America. He found there the Student Volunteer Movement for Foreign Missions in the first flush of its enthusiasm and Moody with a strong convention center at Northfield. As a result of his visit, support for eight missionaries was offered and a number of applicants for appointment presented themselves.

[157] Broomhall, op. cit., p. 193.
[158] Schofield, Memorials of Harold A. Schofield, passim.
[159] Broomhall, op. cit., pp. 160-166; Taylor, Hudson Taylor, pp. 386-396; Broomhall, A Missionary Band, 1886; Broomhall, Bishop Cassels, pp. 40-59; Guinness, Story of the C. I. M., Chapter 29; Missionaries in the Witness Box, pp. 127, 128. Cecil Polhill-Turner was to organize a band and attempt to penetrate Tibet via India.—Marston, With the King, passim. The visit of one of the band to Cornell University in America was to be a large factor in starting John R. Mott on his distinguished career as a religious leader.
[160] Taylor, Hudson Taylor, pp. 458-472.

In 1889 Taylor again visited America and a permanent council was formed with Frost as the secretary and with headquarters at Toronto.[161]

In 1882 Josef Holmgren, from Sweden, came in touch in England with the China Inland Mission and by a subsequent chain of events Erik Folke was sent out by a Swedish group led by Holmgren. In time a Swedish Mission to China was formed which adopted the principles and practices of the China Inland Mission and which was allotted by Taylor a field in Honan, Shansi, and Shensi. In 1890 there sailed from Sweden the first two missionaries of what was to be the Swedish Holiness Union, later assigned by Taylor to a field in the northern part of Shansi.[162]

Another Scandinavian body, but recruited primarily from churches in the United States, was the Scandinavian Alliance Mission, begun about 1892 largely through the efforts of Frederick Franson. Franson was born in Sweden in 1852, came to America in 1869, and after a deep religious experience in 1872, became an itinerant evangelist, in the course of his career visiting and preaching in all the continents.[163] He had been greatly impressed by Taylor's work and by his appeal for a thousand missionaries for China and was also stimulated by contact with A. B. Simpson, the founder of the Christian and Missionary Alliance. Eventually the Alliance sent missionaries to Mongolia, Japan, India, Africa, and South America, and drew for support on Scandinavia as well as the United States, but it owed its beginning to the China Inland Mission and in China Proper was affiliated with that body.[164] Franson was also responsible for the formation at Barmen of the German China Alliance, a body which sent its first missionaries in 1890.[165]

About 1892, through the efforts of a German pastor, Coerper, who had been stirred by the story of Taylor's life, an organization was begun which was later to have headquarters at and take its

[161] Ibid., pp. 437-455; China's Millions, 1893, p. 45.

[162] Taylor, Hudson Taylor, pp. 473-476; Broomhall, The Jubilee Story of the C. I. M., pp. 357, 358; China's Millions, 1895, p. 117, 1915, p. 94; A Century of Protestant Missions in China, p. 140.

[163] Broomhall, op. cit., pp. 195, 360; Taylor, Hudson Taylor, pp. 500-502; Beckman, The Massacre at Sianfu, pp. 17, 23; A Century of Protestant Missions in China, pp. 504, 507; Mrs. Princell, Frederick Franson, World Missionary, passim.

[164] Broomhall, op. cit., pp. 195, 360; Taylor, Hudson Taylor, pp. 500-502; Beckman, op. cit., pp. 17, 23; A Century of Protestant Missions in China, pp. 504, 507; Mrs. Princell, op. cit., passim.

[165] Broomhall, op. cit., p. 361; China's Millions, 1900, p. 207; Mrs. Princell, op. cit., pp. 42, 43.

name from Liebenzell. Until 1906 it was affiliated with the China Inland Mission.[166] In 1895, likewise in Germany, the St. Chrischona branch of the China Inland Mission was formed.[167] In 1889, during a visit of Taylor to Norway, the Norwegian Mission in China came into being. It lapsed for a time through the failure of the health of its missionaries, but was reorganized in 1905. It was assigned territory in Shansi and Shensi.[168]

The Free Church of Finland, a small body, in 1891, in association with the China Inland Mission, sent to China its first missionary.[169] The Bible Christian Methodist Mission began in 1885 when two men were dispatched to China. For some years it worked in connection with the China Inland Mission and at the advice of Taylor chose the northeastern part of Yünnan as its field.[170] Toward the close of 1889 a young curate in Melbourne communicated to the Mission his desire to go to China and this and other developments led Taylor in 1890 to visit Australia. He made a profound impression, an associate council was eventually formed, and from each of the Australian colonies missionaries went to China.[171]

The eighties and nineties, then, witnessed rapid expansion. In 1895 the Mission counted six hundred and forty-one missionaries, four hundred and sixty-two native helpers, two hundred and sixty stations and outstations, and five thousand two hundred and eleven communicants.[172] Taylor and his associates continued to conceive of their task as primarily that of giving a knowledge of the Gospel to as many as possible. Much itinerating was done and pioneers constantly pushed out into new districts. For example, Miss Annie R. Taylor, after attempting to penetrate Tibet from India, in 1892 entered from the Kansu border and when within three days' journey of Lhasa was turned back by the authorities;[173] an extensive mission was begun among the non-Chinese peoples in Kweichow and Yünnan;[174] and in 1887

[166] *China's Millions,* 1903, p. 57; Broomhall, op. cit., p. 362.
[167] Broomhall, op. cit., p. 365.
[168] Ibid., p. 361; *A Century of Protestant Missions in China,* p. 514.
[169] Broomhall, op. cit., p. 364; *China's Millions,* 1900, p. 208; *A Century of Protestant Missions in China,* p. 501.
[170] Broomhall, op. cit., p. 174; *A Century of Protestant Missions in China,* p. 125.
[171] Taylor, *Hudson Taylor,* pp. 488-499; *China's Millions,* 1900, p. 132.
[172] *China's Millions,* 1906, p. 124.
[173] Taylor, *Pioneering in Tibet,* passim.
[174] Broomhall, *Some a Hundredfold,* passim; Broomhall, *Jubilee Story of the China Inland Mission,* pp. 274-278.

Younghusband found a missionary and his wife in Mongolia west of Kalgan and commented on their zeal and energy.[175]   However, although this expansion continued, it was more and more from settled stations in the Eighteen Provinces that the Mission was carrying on its program.   Always welcoming any group which would share in the missionary task, from time to time it withdrew from centers as these were entered by other societies, and concentrated its attention upon districts still unoccupied by Protestants.

This, then, was the China Inland Mission, its origin and its growth to 1898.   Some might believe its theology narrow and antiquated and its definitions of "evangelization" too mechanical and restricted, and others might object that its methods were too wasteful of the health and life of its missionaries—and the toll was unquestionably great—but none knowing its history could question that the Mission had remained true to the purpose that had called it into existence.

To continue the enumeration of the societies which entered China in the forty years following the treaties of Tientsin:

The main body of Presbyterians in the United States divided in 1861, shortly after the outbreak of the Civil War.   During the years of that conflict the southern branch of the Church was unable to begin an independent mission in China, but in 1867 Elias B. Inslee, who had been a missionary there before the division, offered his services, was accepted, and sailed.   He and his wife settled in Hangchow and in 1868 three men left America to join him.   Other reënforcements arrived and in 1872 a station was opened in Soochow.   For nearly two decades the growth of the mission was necessarily slow.   During some of the worst of the *post bellum* years of financial stringency, for instance from 1875 to 1879 inclusive, no new missionaries were sent.   At the end of 1887 there were only four stations and twenty missionaries. From 1888 to 1896 the returning prosperity of the Southern States was reflected in the funds of the board, and forty-seven new missionaries were sent and six new stations opened.   The mission, however, continued to concentrate its efforts upon East Central China.[176]

In 1860 there was formed in New York City, partly from an

[175] Younghusband, *The Heart of a Continent*, p. 66.
[176] Woodbridge, *Fifty Years in China*, pp. 31-55; *China Mission Hand-book*, Part 2, p. 213; *A Century of Protestant Missions in China*, pp. 395-398.

impulse given by David Abeel and partly as a consequence of the growing independence of women in and out of the Church, the Women's Union Missionary Society of America. It was undenominational and for some years contented itself with supporting women, both Chinese and American, appointed by other agencies. In 1868, however, it sent three missionaries of its own to open in Peking a boarding-school for girls. In 1881 a bequest from Mrs. E. C. Bridgman led to the removal of the institution to Shanghai. In 1885 the Society also opened in Shanghai the Margaret Williamson Hospital for women and children. Women were later sent to begin evangelistic work and a Bible training school was founded, but the Society devoted its energies chiefly to educational and medical activities.[177]

As the years passed, women very generally organized societies independent of, but closely related to, the major denominational boards. Thus the Church of England Zenana Missionary Society, as we have seen, in 1883 began appointing representatives to work in connection with the Church Missionary Society.[178] At first they went only to Fukien, but later they were sent to other provinces. We hear, for example, of two representatives of the Society opening Mienchow in Szechwan when missionaries of the other sex were not allowed in the city.[179] The Women's Foreign Missionary Society of the Methodist Episcopal Church was organized in 1869 and sent its first missionaries to China in 1871.[180] In 1868 a Woman's Board of Missions was organized to work in coöperation with the American Board, and there later followed two other women's organizations for the same purpose.[181] The Women's Missionary Association of the Presbyterian Church of England was established in 1878 and sent representatives to supplement those of the general board of the church in and around Amoy.[182] The Baptist women of the Northern States had societies which supported women in China in conjunction with the appointees of the American Baptist Missionary Union.[183]

From 1869 to 1878 inclusive four Presbyterian bodies entered

---

[177] *A Century of Protestant Missions in China*, pp. 468-471.
[178] Barnes, *Behind the Great Wall*, p. 6. See also on work of the society, Marshall, *For His Sake*, the biography of Elsie Marshall.
[179] Luella Miner in *China Mission Year Book*, pp. 325, 326.
[180] *A Century of Protestant Missions in China*, p. 459.
[181] Strong, *The Story of the American Board*, p. 311.
[182] *Missionary Year Book, 1889-1890*, p. 197. See, too, Johnston, *Jin Ko-Niu*, passim.
[183] Merriam, *A History of American Baptist Missions*, p. 96.

China. The devoted William C. Burns, while dying (at New-chwang, in 1868), issued an appeal which deeply touched many. In 1869, in answer to it, the Irish Presbyterians sent two representatives to Manchuria and in the course of time others followed. They extended their activities over much of the eastern part of this great virgin land, reaching north almost as far as Harbin.[184]

In 1862 the United Presbyterian Church—later the United Free Church of Scotland—opened a mission at Ningpo, but discontinued it in 1872. For a time after 1871 Alexander Williamson, who had already spent some years in China, first under the London Missionary Society and then under the National Bible Society of Scotland, represented the United Presbyterian Church at Chefoo. Colleagues were sent him, but in 1886 Williamson removed to Shanghai to inaugurate another enterprise and his confrères were transferred from Shantung to Manchuria. While an agent of the Bible Society, Williamson had traversed Manchuria (1866-1868), but it was not until 1872 that John Ross crossed the gulf from Chefoo to Newchwang and began in Manchuria the work of the United Presbyterian Church. Early in the history of the mission the policy was adopted of centering first on the cities. About 1874 Mukden was entered, in spite of opposition from some of the scholar class, and Liaoyang in 1861. To Mukden in 1892 came Dugald Christie, who was to become famous as a physician. As time passed, the Irish and the Scotch societies divided Manchuria between them and in 1891 united their efforts to found one Presbyterian church in the region. When, in 1894 and 1895, Manchuria became a battleground for the Chinese and Japanese, some activities of the mission suffered, but the missionaries were able to be of much service to the wounded in Newchang, and in the year after the war a remarkable increase began in the numbers of those seeking admission to the Church. This access of members continued until 1900, when the Boxer outbreak brought it to a tragic halt and tested the fidelity of those who had declared themselves Christians.[185]

The Church of Scotland devoted its efforts chiefly to other lands than China, but beginning with 1878 it founded a station

[184] *A Century of Protestant Missions in China*, pp. 223, 224; *China Mission Hand-book*, Part 2, p. 86.
[185] *A Century of Protestant Missions in China*, pp. 206 et seq.; *Chinese Recorder*, Vol. 8, p. 385, Vol. 18, p. 255; Ross, *Missionary Methods in Manchuria*, p. 50; Christie, *Thirty Years in the Manchu Capital*, p. 19.

at the recently opened port of Ichang and there and in the immediate neighborhood supported a mission which was only scantily reënforced and which consequently grew slowly.[186]

The Presbyterian Church of Canada appointed as its first missionary to the Chinese a most remarkable man, G. L. Mackay. He was sent in 1871 and chose for his field the northern part of Formosa. Here for many years he labored—part of the time without a foreign colleague—both among the Chinese and the aborigines. He laid the foundations of a church and trained native assistants, founding in 1881 and 1882 Oxford College for the preparation of preachers. In 1887, as the result of an awakening of missionary interest in two of the colleges in Canada, a mission was projected on the mainland of China. Several were soon sent, among them Jonathan Goforth, who was later to be noted as a leader in evangelistic meetings, and D. MacGillivray, who was to be prominent in the preparation of literature. In spite of serious opposition from local officials, residence was established in Honan and the force there fairly rapidly increased.[187]

In 1884 Chinese in San Francisco organized the China Congregational Society for the purpose of spreading the Christian Gospel among their fellow countrymen in Kwangtung. They did not send out many missionaries, but by 1910 they had five outstations and were expending eighteen hundred dollars (silver) a year.[188]

The English Friends were stirred to an interest in China by Hudson Taylor and in 1883 the Friends Foreign Mission Association decided to act. Taylor suggested West China as a field, and in 1884 the first representative, a single lady, went out with a party of the China Inland Mission. On her arrival at Hankow she found that the British Consul was not then permitting unmarried women to go into Szechwan. She remained in Hankow, therefore, and in time severed her connection with the Association. Two men were commissioned in 1886, but not until 1889 did they obtain a foothold in Szechwan.[189]

[186] Weir, *A History of the Foreign Missions of the Church of Scotland*, pp. 113, 114; *A Century of Protestant Missions in China*, pp. 201, 202.
[187] Mackay, *From Far Formosa*, passim; Keith, *The Black Bearded Barbarian, The Life of George Leslie Mackay*, passim; *China Mission Hand-book*, Part 2, p. 286; *A Century of Protestant Missions in China*, pp. 232-242.
[188] *China Mission Year Book, 1910*, p. 117.
[189] Davidson and Mason, *Life in West China*, pp. 161-170; *China Mission Hand-book*, Part 2, p. 151; *A Century of Protestant Missions in China*, p. 164. The first station was at Chungking.

The Ohio Yearly Meeting of Friends sent a missionary to Nanking in 1887, and other representatives of the American Friends followed. Until 1900 these were all women.[190]

In 1884 an organization with the ambitious title, The General Evangelical Protestant Missionary Society, was formed at Weimar, in Germany. Its announced purpose was to present the Christian Gospel undenominationally to the educated classes, "building upon the elements of truth already prevalent" among non-Christian peoples. It was liberal theologically and specialized on literature, using the printed page to spread its message. In 1885 Ernst Faber, who had originally come to China under the Rhenish Mission, entered the service of the Society as its first agent in China and in 1892 was joined by Kranz. The staff was never large, but in addition to writing and publishing extensively it conducted schools and hospitals.[191]

The Disciples of Christ, an American denomination dating from the first half of the nineteenth century and with its stronghold in the Mississippi Valley, was rather late in organizing effectively for foreign missions, and not until 1886 did the Foreign Christian Missionary Society have a representative in China. This agent, Dr. W. E. Macklin, had been appointed to Japan, but on reaching that country decided that medical missionaries were not greatly needed there and asked leave to go to China. Upon his request being granted he went to Shanghai, and, after acquiring the rudiments of the language, moved to Nanking. Reënforcements were sent him, among them E. T. Williams, who after some years severed his connection with the Society, rose to prominence in the diplomatic service of the United States, and later became known as a writer on China and head of the Department of Oriental Languages and Literature of the University of California. As still other missionaries were sent, new stations were opened, but until after 1897 all of these remained confined to the lower part of the Yangtze Valley.[192]

In 1897 the Christian and Missionary Alliance was formed by the union of two previously affiliated organizations, the Christian

[190] Williams, *Ohio Friends in the Land of Sinim*, pp. 1-62; *A Century of Protestant Missions in China*, p. 528.

[191] *A Century of Protestant Missions in China*, p. 498; Warneck, *Outline of a History of Protestant Missions*, p. 126.

[192] McLean, *History of the Foreign Christian Missionary Society*, pp. 13-97; Garst, *In the Shadow of the Drum Tower*, passim; *A Century of Protestant Missions in China*, pp. 347 et seq.

Alliance and the International Missionary Alliance. These owed their origin chiefly to A. B. Simpson (1845-1919). Simpson was a Canadian by birth and education who removed to New York in 1881. As pastor of the undenominational Gospel Tabernacle in New York City he proved a remarkable preacher of an ardently evangelistic type and an excellent organizer. He wrote and published voluminously, and partly through a training school which he maintained at Nyack, New York, conducted an extensive missionary enterprise in America and in other lands. In their foreign policy the Christian and Missionary Alliance and its predecessors somewhat resembled the China Inland Mission, for they were undenominational and sought to send representatives to districts previously unoccupied by Protestants. Unlike the China Inland Mission, however, they did not confine their efforts to one country. The first Alliance missionary reached China in 1888. Ten years later, Alliance representatives were to be found in Anhui, Hupeh, Hunan, the Tibetan frontier of Kansu, Shansi, Mongolia, Kwangsi, Peking, Shanghai, and Tientsin. With the exception of Anhui and the three cities named, these districts, it will be noted, were among the most difficult in which to maintain missions. In Kwangsi the Alliance was apparently the first Protestant body to establish a permanent station, although that had been attempted by members of at least three other societies. The prolonged effort to penetrate Tibet by way of Kansu was made in the face of almost continuous danger and entailed great heroism. In Northern Shansi and Mongolia the missionaries, who were Swedish and by 1897 numbered about sixty, were entirely beyond the Great Wall. As a rule the Alliance representatives had only a scanty education and attempted, with but imperfect adaptation to the Chinese environment, to reproduce the revivalism to which they usually owed their own religious experience. The majority were in deadly earnest, however, and lived courageous and self-denying lives.[193]

In the late eighties two small missions opened in Canton. The American Swedish Free Mission Society dates its first efforts there from January first, 1888.[194] The United Brethren in Christ and the affiliated Woman's Missionary Association of the United

[193] *New York Times*, Oct. 30, 1919, p. 13; *A Century of Protestant Missions in China*, pp. 356 et seq.; *China Mission Hand-book*, Part 2, p. 295; Ekvall, *Outposts, or Tibetan Border Sketches*, pp. 32-48; Glover, *Ebenezer*, p. 12.
[194] *A Century of Protestant Missions in China*, p. 527.

Brethren in Christ sent out their first representatives in 1889. The United Brethren had a Chinese church in Portland, Oregon, and since the emigrants there were from South China it was natural that the first missionaries to go abroad should seek out Canton. Some of the Portland staff were, indeed, among the pioneers in China.[195]

Just when the first of the Christian Missions in Many Lands, or Plymouth Brethren as they are usually called, entered China is not clear, but as early as 1885 two centers in Chihli were occupied and before 1898 Brethren were to be found in Kiangsi and Shantung.[196]

The year 1890 saw three Scandinavian societies enter China. The Swedish Evangelical Missionary Covenant of America and the Swedish Missionary Union, the former with headquarters in Illinois and the latter with its home office in Stockholm, each sent its first emissaries in that year. Neither was to have a large staff and both were confined to portions of Hupeh.[197]   In 1893 the Swedish Missionary Union also began work in the western part of Chinese Turkestan. There it attempted to reach both Moslems and Chinese and set up in Kashgar a school for the latter.[198]   In 1890 what was later to be known as the American Lutheran Mission, the agent of some of the Norwegian Lutheran churches in the United States, sent out three men, and these, too, chose Hupeh.[199]

In 1890 the Norwegian Lutheran China Mission Association was organized at Bergen in Norway, and its first missionaries arrived in China the following year. They also chose Hupeh but later extended their stations northward into Honan.[200]

In 1890 a group of women was formed at Hildesheim, Germany, to aid in the relief of blind girls in China. Before long this had grown into the German Mission to Blind Females in China. The suggestion had originally come from the Berlin Foundling House in Hongkong and when, in 1896, the new organization sent its first missionary, she went to that city. The

[195] Ibid., p. 530.
[196] Directory of Protestant Missions in China, 1926, pp. 117-119.
[197] A Century of Protestant Missions in China, pp. 519, 524; China Mission Hand-book, Part 2, pp. 293-295; Chinese Recorder, Vol. 23, p. 273.
[198] Högberg, Ett Och Annat Från Kinesiska Turkestan, pp. 53-60.
[199] A Century of Protestant Missions in China, pp. 532, 533.
[200] A Century of Protestant Missions in China, pp. 512, 513; Gotteberg, Ti Aar i Hunan, p. 11.

purpose of the Mission was to found a home where blind girls who were threatened with slavery or prostitution could be reared in a wholesome environment for an honorable future.[201]

In 1890 the General Board of Missions of the Canadian Methodists accepted an offer of men and of money that had been made it for founding a mission in China. To lead the new enterprise it called upon Virgil C. Hart, who had already been a pioneer of the Northern Methodists in the lower part of the Yangtze Valley. In 1891 a party of nine, headed by him, arrived in Shanghai, but because of anti-missionary disturbances in the Yangtze Valley did not go inland until early in 1892. They then proceeded directly to Chengtu, the capital and natural center of the province, and by the middle of the year had succeeded in establishing themselves there. In 1895 their plant was wiped out by an anti-foreign riot, but they obtained an indemnity from the government, returned to the city, and started afresh.[202]

The Swedish Baptist Mission, supported by a small denomination in Scandinavia, sent its first representative in 1891 and chose Shantung as its field.[203] The Bible and Soul-Winning Prayer Union, a Scotch organization which seems to have had only a short career in China, had a missionary there in 1891.[204]

In 1893 the Misses E. A. and L. M. Hopwood of England commenced in Ningpo[205] one of those missions which from time to time have been begun apart from the auspices of any society or denominational board. Unlike most undertakings of that type, it was able to survive the changes of the years and to build up a fairly large physical equipment.[206] One of the interesting and at times picturesque features of Protestant activity in China has, indeed, been these "unconnected," "independent," or "faith" missionaries. Sometimes they have been supported by individual friends and sometimes by congregations. Usually they have come into their religious life through a highly emotional type of evangelism. Frequently eccentric and uneducated and displaying a mixture of intolerance and humble faith, they have often proved amusing, and sometimes annoying to their missionary brethren

[201] *A Century of Protestant Missions in China,* pp. 589-593.
[202] Ibid., pp. 13 et seq.; Hart, *V. C. Hart,* pp. 227-301; Bond, *Our Share in China,* pp. 56-58; Wallace, *The Heart of Sz-chuan,* pp. 37-49.
[203] *A Century of Protestant Missions in China,* p. 515.
[204] Ibid., p. 645.
[205] Ibid., p. 541.
[206] *Encyclopædia Sinica,* p. 113.

of the larger societies. Almost always they have been thoroughly devoted and self-sacrificing. Frequently their stay in China has been short, but in a few instances they have founded enduring institutions. Some, indeed, have been men and women of notable ability, breadth, and sanity of mind, and have ranked among the great missionaries: Hudson Taylor, it will be recalled, was for a time "unconnected." Protestantism in China has been, on the whole, decidedly stronger for their presence.

For a time after 1890 and 1891 the number of new societies entering China diminished. Most of the major Protestant denominations had begun work and many of the smaller ones were represented. With a few notable exceptions, it was only smaller bodies who entered after that time. In 1895 the Reformed Presbyterian Church (Covenanter) in North America sent missionaries to Kwangtung.[207] In 1894 Dr. and Mrs. Petrus Rijnhart and two others, all unconnected with any missionary society, left America with the purpose of penetrating Tibet. Dr. Rijnhart had previously (1892) crossed China and had lived for a time on the Tibetan frontier. For some years the Rijnharts remained on the border, then in seeking to penetrate to Lhasa Dr. Rijnhart disappeared, and his wife escaped only after great hardships.[208] In 1896 a Danish Lutheran mission was begun in Manchuria.[209] That same year there came from America to Tientsin, unconnected with any society, Horace W. Houlding and his wife, and in the following ten years, from that beginning, the South Chihli Mission arose, with forty-five missionaries.[210] In 1897 the American Advent Mission Society began operations in the lower part of the Yangtze Valley.[211] In 1897, too, the first representatives of the Cumberland Presbyterian Church came to China. They were later to make their center at Changtê, one of the important cities of anti-foreign Hunan, and still later, when the home body had merged with the Presbyterian Church of the Northern States (1906), they were united with the latter's mission in that prov-

[207] *A Century of Protestant Missions in China*, p. 408.
[208] Mrs. Rijnhart, *With the Tibetans in Tent and Temple*, passim. Other efforts to enter Tibet were made in these years. In 1890 G. M. Bullock of the London Missionary Society in North India began work for a part Tibetan people. By 1868 Jaeschke, a Moravian missionary on the Indian frontier, had translated the New Testament into Tibetan, and Redslob, another Moravian, continued his translation of the Old Testament.—Marston, *The Great Closed Land*, pp. 76, 81.
[209] *A Century of Protestant Missions in China*, p. 526.
[210] Ibid., p. 535.
[211] Ibid., p. 540.

ince.[212]   The Kieler Mission, with headquarters at Kiel, Germany, entered Kwangtung in 1897.[213]

In 1895 the first resident representative of the Young Men's Christian Association was sent to China.   This movement, begun in England shortly before the middle of the century, quickly spread to the United States and there attained its most extensive development.   In its inception led by young men, some of whom combined religious fervor with originality and a genius for organization, and always a lay body and free from control by older and stereotyped religious bodies, it had a remarkable growth and initiated many new methods of religious and social activity.   It was committed to the theological position held by the great majority of Protestants in the middle of the nineteenth century, but it was undenominational and could bring into its service men from almost all Protestant groups.   It specialized on meeting the needs of young men—particularly those in industry, business, and transportation—for wholesome religious, physical, and intellectual development.   To obtain support for current expenses and equipment it called to its aid the better elements of the well-to-do and wealthy classes.   The United States was being rapidly transformed from a rural and agricultural into an industrial and urban nation and the Young Men's Christian Association was an attempt to cope with some of the moral and social problems which arose from the transition.   It was an expression of American business genius in religious and philanthropic activity.

Early in its history in the United States, too, the Young Men's Christian Association spread to the colleges and universities and soon became almost the exclusive medium for the expression of the voluntary religious activity of men students.   The student branch developed many able leaders and sent a constant stream of them into the direction of the other branches of the movement.

The Association first entered China as a student organization, and when it began to have full-time secretaries these came largely from the United States and from the Student Department.   While city Associations soon began to appear, it was to the new student class which in the nineties was already emerging that most attention was directed.   The Association leaders believed that students held in their hands the future of China and that by centering

[212] *A Century of Protestant Missions in China,* pp. 406, 407.
[213] Ibid., p. 545.

upon them, the whole country could be most quickly reached by the Christian faith. The Association's foreign leaders were carefully selected and were deliberately placed in those cities from which their influence could most quickly be extended. They were American lay Protestant Christianity at its best, seeking to mold the entire life of the community by the Christian Gospel as they understood it—emphasizing democracy and, as a corollary, Chinese leadership.

The first Associations in China were organized in 1885 in the Anglo-Chinese College at Foochow, an institution maintained by the American Methodists of the Northern States, and in the school supported in T'ungchow, Chihli, by the American Board.[214] Between 1888 and 1892, Luther D. Wishard, the first Student Secretary of the (North American) International Committee of the movement, spent parts of two years in a visit to China, and in 1895 D. Willard Lyon, who had also been trained in America and primarily in the Student Department, was sent to China by the International Committee to supervise the Associations throughout the nation. In 1896 John R. Mott, one of the greatest religious leaders and organizers that Protestantism has produced, and who was then Student Secretary of the International Committee and General Secretary of the recently organized World's Student Christian Federation, visited China. As a result of his efforts the number of Associations, nearly all of them still among students, increased from five to twenty-seven, and a national organization was formed. The only Associations other than student were one in Shanghai, formed in 1889, and one in Hankow, which existed from 1893 to 1895. From these beginnings the Young Men's Christian Association was to enjoy a phenomenal growth in the new era that followed 1900.[215]

The sister organization, the Young Women's Christian Association, was slightly later in entering China. Its first units among the Chinese were in schools and came into existence about 1888. In succeeding years a few others followed. No national organization was formed until 1899.[216]

[214] Professor Harlan P. Beach, who founded the Association at T'ungchow, tells the writer that the date was September, 1885, and that the one at Foochow came into existence in the same year. He is not sure which was the earlier.

[215] A Century of Protestant Missions in China, pp. 597 et seq.; Wishard in Records of the Shanghai Conference, 1890, p. 142; Smith, Uplift of China, p. 176.

[216] A Century of Protestant Missions in China, p. 609; Dennis, Christian Missions and Social Progress, Vol. 3, p. 158.

Another undenominational Protestant movement, the Young People's Society for Christian Endeavor, came from America to China in the eighties. Its first unit was organized in Foochow in 1885 and others rapidly sprang up.[217] Less separate from the churches than the Young Men's and Young Women's Christian Associations, and without the extensive full-time secretaryship that these developed, it was not to have as prominent a part in China as they.

This concludes the list of Protestant organizations which entered China between 1856 and the close of 1897. It is incomplete, for some societies have quite possibly been overlooked and several of the women's societies which sent out representatives in connection with denominational boards have not been mentioned.[218] It includes, however, all the major and most of the smaller boards.

THE MISSIONARY BODY

The coming of all these societies to China, and the growth which most of them experienced, meant a rapid increase in the number of missionaries in the Empire. In 1858 there were said to be in China eighty-one Protestant missionaries representing twenty societies.[219] In 1864 all China contained twenty-four

[217] *Chinese Recorder,* Vol. 23, p. 573; *A Century of Protestant Missions in China,* p. 610.

[218] Some of the women's societies were: in the United States, The Woman's Foreign Missionary Society of the Methodist Episcopal Church (formed 1869), the Women's American Baptist Foreign Missionary Society (as it is now—1928) preceded by several societies, among them one of the East and one of the West, both formed in 1871, three American Congregational societies, the Women's Auxiliary of the Board of Missions of the Protestant Episcopal Church, the Women's Board of Foreign Missions of the Methodist Episcopal Church, South, formed in 1878; in Great Britain, the Women's Auxiliary of the Wesleyan Methodist Missionary Society, formed in 1858, the Women of the English Presbyterian Church, organized in 1878, and of the Irish Presbyterian Church, in 1873—Underhill in *International Review of Missions,* Vol. 14, pp. 380 et seq., Vol. 15, pp. 248-255.

Still other women's societies were the Woman's Foreign Missionary Society of the Free Methodist Church of North America; the Woman's Board of Foreign Missions of the Presbyterian Church (North) (U. S.) (seven societies); Woman's Board of Missions of the Reformed Church in America; Southern Baptist Convention (U. S.), Women's Missionary Union; Women's Missionary Association of the United Brethren in Christ; Baptist Zenana Mission (English); Woman's Auxiliary for China of the Methodist New Connexion Missionary Society (English); Church of Scotland Woman's Association for Foreign Missions; Woman's Foreign Missions of the United Free Church of Scotland; Woman's Missionary Society of the Methodist Church in Canada; Presbyterian Woman's Foreign Missionary Society in Canada.—*A Century of Protestant Missions in China,* pp. 456, 457.

[219] *The Missionary Magazine,* Vol. 39, p. 287, quoting a list by Bridgman. Two hundred and thirteen Protestant missionaries in all were said to have served the Chinese up to this time.

Protestant societies and one hundred and eighty-nine mission-aries.[220] In 1874 the number of Protestant missionaries was given as four hundred and thirty six,[221] in 1876 the totals reported were twenty-nine societies and four hundred and seventy-three missionaries (including wives),[222] in 1881 six hundred and eighteen missionaries (including one hundred and three wives),[223] and in 1889 forty-one societies and twelve hundred and ninety-six missionaries (five hundred and eighty-nine men, three hundred and ninety-one wives, and three hundred and sixteen single women).[224] The proportion of nationalities represented in the Protestant missionary body varied. In 1874 forty-eight per cent. were Americans, forty-four and a half per cent. British, and seven and a half per cent. Germans.[225] In 1889 fifty-six and a half per cent. were British, thirty-nine and a half per cent. Americans, and four per cent. from the Continent of Europe.[226]

It is very difficult to determine just how many Protestant missionaries went to China during these decades. Some were there for only a few months or years. Others remained for half a century or more. The most nearly complete record that has appeared lists about fifty-six as having arrived before 1842, about one hundred and forty-two from 1842 to 1857 inclusive, about one hundred and fifty as landing in China in the decade 1858-1867, about two hundred and one in the decade 1868-1877, about five hundred and sixty-seven between 1878 and 1887 inclusive, about twelve hundred and seventy-two between 1888 and 1897 inclusive, and several hundred whose dates of arrival are unknown.[227] The list is certainly incomplete, for it does not enumerate the wives of missionaries, but it probably gives a fairly accurate picture of the rapid increase of the missionary force.

By 1877 Protestant missionaries were to be found in each of the six coast provinces, in Manchuria, and in three inland provinces, Kiangsi, Anhui, and Hupeh.[228] By 1890 Protestant missionaries were residing in all of the provinces, with the possible

[220] Jonathan Lees in *Chinese Recorder*, Vol. 9, p. 5.
[221] *Chinese Recorder*, Vol. 6, p. 342.
[222] *A Century of Protestant Missions in China*, p. 667; *Chinese Recorder*, Vol. 9, p. 6.
[223] *Chinese Recorder*, Vol. 12, p. 395.
[224] *Records of Shanghai Conference, 1890*, p. 732.
[225] *Chinese Recorder*, Vol. 6, p. 342.
[226] *Records of the Shanghai Conference, 1890*, p. 733.
[227] Compiled from *A Century of Protestant Missions in China*, Appendix II.
[228] Lyon, *Sketch of Protestant Missions in China*, p. 25.

exception of Hunan.[229] In 1860 there were thirty-five mission stations in fourteen different residential centers. Most of these latter were cities. Two-thirds of the stations were in the five ports opened by the treaties of 1842-1844—Canton, Amoy, Foochow, Shanghai, and Ningpo—and in Hongkong and Swatow.[230] Between 1861 and 1880 inclusive sixty-five new residential centers were opened—usually in cities—and the number of mission stations (there were sometimes more than one in a city) increased to one hundred and thirty-two.[231] From 1881 to 1900 inclusive Protestant foreign missionaries established themselves in two hundred and seventy-seven additional centers and the number of mission stations increased from one hundred and thirty-two to four hundred and ninety-eight.[232]

This long chronicle of societies and these figures must of necessity be a somewhat dry catalogue of names, dates, and statistics. It must never be forgotten, however, that the few missionaries who have been mentioned at some length were only the most prominent and that by far the larger proportion of the achievement of these years was due to hundreds of obscure men and women. Whatever may be one's opinions of the doctrines they taught, even a casual reading of their biographies cannot but bring the conviction that those who laid the foundations of the future Protestant churches did so usually with heroism and often at the sacrifice of comfort, health, and even life. If to a later age some of the beliefs of the pioneers seem antiquated and narrow, against these should be set the difficulties of learning a new language, the adjustment to unfamiliar and usually unsanitary living conditions, the long struggles with ill health, the inconvenience of travel in an alien land, and the frequent unfriendliness and hostility of the populace and officials.

Because the brief biographical notices of missionaries on the preceding pages have been almost exclusively of men, it must not be supposed that the latter predominated in Protestant missionary circles or that all the burden was borne by them. Fully half— by 1890 more than half—of the missionary force were women.

[229] Ibid., p. 30.
[230] *The Christian Occupation of China*, p. 286. These figures may not be entirely accurate.
[231] Ibid., pp. 283-286. In 1876 there were ninety-one stations where missionaries resided and five hundred and eleven outstations.—*Records of the General Conference of Protestant Missionaries, Shanghai, 1877*, p. 486.
[232] *The Christian Occupation of China*, pp. 283, 286.

Slightly more than half of these women were wives and so had much of their time consumed by the care of children and of the household. The majority of wives, however, were considered to be missionaries as truly as were their husbands. In addition to the influence of the Christian home—which in itself was no small factor in introducing influential ideals of conduct and family life [233]—the wife often had a large share in the activities of the mission. Given the Chinese ideas of propriety, without her and her unmarried sisters the Church's approach to women and girls would have been much more difficult and at times impossible. All through the records of these years are stories, often preserved only in private letters and journals, of women who in addition to the strain of bearing and rearing children in a climate and amid sanitary conditions which were always trying and often fatal,[234] maintained Christian homes and gave valiant assistance to their husbands in the Church. Equally heroic were hundreds of unmarried women who, by their voluntarily assumed task denied the privileges of a home, devoted themselves unsparingly to furthering the Christian cause. Sometimes, indeed, they were its sole foreign representatives in inland cities and districts.

Most of the British missionaries came from the middle class. Relatively few had a university training.[235] For the most part, theirs was the education of the middle class physician or the non-conformist clergyman. By 1897 university-trained men had begun to arrive, but their numbers were still relatively small. Most of the Americans were from the farm and the small town. Usually the men were graduates of a denominational college and, if ordained, of a theological school. Both the British and the American missionaries were from stock which physically and mentally was sturdy and self-reliant. They were usually from earnestly religious families. Brought up in contact with secular society, their only formal vocational training being at most that

[233] One instance of this is in Ross, *Mission Methods in Manchuria*, pp. 193-195.

[234] The toll of disease, both for men and for women, was lessened by the beginning of the summer resorts which after 1900 were to play so large a part in missionary life. By 1897, for example, Kuliang, on a mountain ridge a few miles above Foochow, was offering relief from the heat of the valleys.—*L. M. S. Chronicle*, Vol. 6 (new series), p. 211.

[235] In 1862, eight out of the ten men the Church Missionary Society then had in China were university men. In 1872, out of the new men who had come in the meantime, not one was a university graduate.—Stock, *History of the Church Missionary Society*, Vol. 2, p. 579.

received in a medical school or in three years in a theological college, they were more nearly in touch with the non-ecclesiastical world than were Roman Catholic missionaries.   Furloughs in their native lands, while not as frequent as in the years of easy transportation that succeeded 1900, came to most missionaries and helped to keep them familiar with the thought, religious and secular, of the Occident.   Their outlook, then, tended to be broader than that of the Roman Catholic priest and it is not strange that they became interested not only in changing the religious and moral life of the Chinese but in altering the intellectual and social structure of the nation.

Protestant missionaries did not, as a rule, begin special preparation for their life in China until after reaching the country. Practically all of them studied the language, both written and spoken, and while many of them remained ignorant of the wider reaches of Chinese institutions, literature, and thought, and looked upon the culture around them with critical and unappreciative eyes,[236] the majority who remained any length of time[237] came to know intimately the life of the city or district in which they resided, and some of them made themselves experts in special phases of Chinese civilization and became ardent admirers of the best features of their adopted home.[238]

The major mission boards had rigorous requirements of character, purpose, and ability, and in intellectual vigor and training

[236] As an example of this see some (not all) of the comments in *Records of the Missionary Conference, Shanghai, 1890,* pp. 609-660.

[237] The length of service of Protestant missionaries in China cannot be determined, but in one mission in South China the time spent by fifty-one missionaries on the field varied from half a year to thirty-nine years and the average was seventy-eight months.—Ashmore, *The South China Mission of the American Baptist Foreign Mission Society.*

Wylie, in *Memorials of Protestant Missionaries in China,* pp. iii, v, says that the average length of residence in China of the three hundred and thirty-eight missionaries who up to that time (1867) had served there was seven and a half years, that of those not then on the field being seven and a quarter years.

[238] A. E. Moule, of the Church Missionary Society, in 1872 was urging missionaries to acquire a more intimate knowledge of Chinese customs and literature and to have a more sympathetic attitude toward them.—*Chinese Recorder,* Vol. 5, p. 41.   Timothy Richard, noted for his warm appreciation of the best in Chinese life and thought, was in 1880 urging that examinations be held for the newer missionaries to guide them in their study of Chinese culture and life.—*Chinese Recorder,* Vol. 11, p. 293.   In 1870 the study of the Chinese Classics was urged by a speaker at the annual meeting of the North China Mission of the American Board.—*Chinese Recorder,* Vol. 3, p. 55.   John Ross of Manchuria was in 1887 urging that Confucianism could be made a valuable help to Christianity.—*Chinese Recorder,* Vol. 18.   This attitude, however, was not by any means universal.

the missionary was above the average of the class from which he came. His occupation called out whatever ability was in him. The demands on him were many and varied. He was usually preacher, teacher, physician, administrator, architect, and builder,[239] and could scarcely avoid growing if he kept pace with his task. The missionary body was not without its bigots and fanatics,[240] but as a rule Protestantism was giving to China of its choicest sons and daughters.

Between the missionary and his fellow countrymen in business and government service a great gulf was usually fixed. Some on both sides succeeded in crossing it, but as a rule the foreign merchants and consuls were severely critical of the missionary and his work, while the missionary looked with thorough disapproval upon the life led by the average non-missionary foreigner. This was unfortunate, but it is not surprising. Most of the foreign community had no sympathy with the missionary's purpose, often thought of him as hampering trade by stirring up riots, and regarded the entire group as fanatical and narrow.[241] For many of the non-missionary body the Ten Commandments did not extend to China and morals were accordingly easy. The missionary, usually with the Puritan's standard of conduct, could not but disapprove. Some social intercourse there was, and among the merchants and consuls were men deeply and sympathetically interested in missions. As a rule, however, in each port the foreigners were in two reciprocally suspicious camps.[242]

COÖPERATION AMONG PROTESTANT MISSIONS

A natural inference from the entrance of so large a number of denominations and societies into China would be that serious overlapping of effort followed—an evil which might have been avoided by a unified church. That some unnecessary repetition

[239] See a description in Leuschner, *Aus dem Leben und der Arbeit eines China-Missionars,* passim.

[240] See in the *Missionary Magazine* (American Baptist Missionary Union), Vol. 37 (1857), pp. 33-38, an article by Edw. A. Stevens called "The Heathen Justly Condemned." This was by a missionary to Burma and not to China, but seems to have met with enough acceptance by his constituency in America to be published in its magazine. For a contrary view see Richard, *Conversion by the Million* and Martin's paper in *Records of the Shanghai Conference, 1890,* pp. 619-631.

[241] As an example see Parker, *John Chinaman and a Few Others,* and Lin Shaoyang (a foreigner writing under a Chinese name), *A Chinese Appeal to Christendom Concerning Christian Missions.*

[242] See a plea for breaking down this barrier in the *Chinese Recorder,* Vol. 27, p. 517.

and unfortunate competition and dissension resulted is certain, and it is probable, too, that at times the multiplicity of sects wrought confusion in the Chinese mind. However, these defects can easily be exaggerated. They were, indeed, very little in evidence. To be sure, in each of the chief treaty ports and the larger cities several societies were usually represented.[243] On the other hand, in at least the pioneer years, the great centers of population afforded ample scope for all the effort of all the missionaries and we have no evidence that any city was overchurched. Outside the main cities, moreover, as a rule only one society was represented in a district or town. Usually each mission kept out of territory previously occupied by another.[244] Moreover, as before 1856, most Protestant missionaries were the spiritual children of the movements which traced their origin to Pietism and to the Evangelical Awakening of the eighteenth century. They thought of themselves as "Evangelical" Christians and were generally agreed as to what constituted the essentials of the Christian faith. With some important exceptions, a common terminology for Christian doctrines was employed, and, although each denomination had its own Chinese name, Protestants were often known by one generic title. Vigorous and sometimes acrimonious controversies were waged, as, for example, those over the proper Chinese words for baptism and God. The divisions over these issues were, however, by no means always by denominational lines, but were sometimes quite as marked within societies and missions as between them. Within Protestant ranks no controversy approached

[243] In 1882 there were represented in Peking, for example, the London Missionary Society, the American Board, the (American) Northern Methodists, the (American) Northern Presbyterians, and the Society for the Propagation of the Gospel in Foreign Parts.—*L. M. S. Chronicle*, Vol. 40 (1882), p. 99.

[244] In the southern part of Fukien, the London Missionary Society, the Reformed Church in America, and the English Presbyterians agreed to a division of the field.—*A Century of Protestant Missions in China*, p. 367.

The Committee on Comity of the Shanghai Conference of 1890 recommended that as a rule only the large cities should be open to one or more missions, that societies wishing to begin new work or extend that already begun take into consideration unoccupied territory, "so as speedily to cover the whole field," that in case of disagreement as to territory arbitration be resorted to, that applicants for baptism in one church be not received as candidates in another, that the acts of discipline of the various churches be respected, that the right of every church member to transfer his membership to another denomination be recognized but that caution be recommended in dealing with such cases, and that no members of other churches be taken into mission employ without consulting the missionary in charge. —*Records of the General Conference of Protestant Missionaries held at Shanghai, May 7-20, 1890*, pp. xlix and l. These suggestions may indicate some of the evils which it was found advisable to remedy. There was no body to enforce them and only public opinion could see that they were conformed to.

in severity the earlier one of Roman Catholic missionaries over the question of the rites.

Moreover, a good deal of actual coöperation was to be found among Protestants—more than between Roman Catholics of different societies and orders. As before 1860, thorough-going coördination was not imperative. The country was large, there was ample room for all, and a central agency would probably not have distributed the missionaries much more strategically or widely than they distributed themselves. However, as missions became better established, need for common action developed in an increasing number of fields—in literature, for example, and in education. Joint efforts, accordingly, multiplied and the foundations were laid for the more extensive coördination of the years after 1900.

One form of coöperation was the actual union of some of the churches which were the fruits of the efforts of missions of closely related denominations. For instance, in 1862 members of the missions of the Reformed Church in America and the English Presbyterian Church in and around Amoy joined in a single presbytery, and a Chinese church grew up which was neither American nor English.[245] In Manchuria the Irish and the Scotch Presbyterians, while keeping their mission organizations distinct, united in building up the Chinese Presbyterian Church.[246] The possibility was discussed of organizing a Presbyterian Church for all China.[247] Among the majority of missions, however, even of different branches of the same denomination, no union existed and each kept on its own way with no organic fellowship with the others. Many missionaries desired closer coördination[248] but their dreams were slow of realization.

Another form of coöperation was in union religious services for

[245] Matheson, *Our Mission in China*, p. 28; Johnson, *China and Formosa*, p. 128. The General Synod of the Reformed Church in America opposed the union, but later withdrew its objections.—Fagg, *Forty Years in South China*, pp. 173 et seq.

[246] Ross, *Mission Methods in Manchuria*, pp. 123, 124. The first presbytery was formed in 1891.

[247] This was especially at the General Missionary Conferences at Shanghai in 1877 and 1890.—*Agendum voor de Synode der Christelyke Gereformaerde Kerk, 1926*, pp. 185, 186; *Missionary Review of the World*, Vol. 3, p. 693.

[248] See articles in *Chinese Recorder*, Vol. 1, p. 10, Vol. 5, p. 134, Vol. 12, p. 118, Vol. 20, pp. 25, 75, 181, Vol. 21, p. 209, Vol. 22, p. 10, Vol. 24, p. 130, Vol. 11, p. 449. In 1885 one writer urged that Western forms of church organization be not transferred to China, but that Chinese Christians be formed into union congregations with as simple an organization as possible and with no specific denominational bias.—*Chinese Recorder*, Vol. 16, p. 28.

foreigners. A large majority of Protestant missionaries owned English as their mother tongue and most of those who did not were at home in it. In many centers, therefore, representatives of all societies joined in a weekly English service of worship and preaching. In some of the larger ports union churches arose. At Tientsin, for example, a union chapel was opened in 1864.[249] There was, too, a union church in Shanghai.[250]

Most of the coöperation on a national scale centered around the two conferences of Protestant missionaries which were held in Shanghai in 1877 and 1890. The first of these, that of 1877, was an unexpected success. One hundred and forty-two missionaries were in attendance from practically all the fields then occupied by Protestants. The thorny term question which had so hampered the preparation of a uniform translation of the Scriptures was avoided by common consent, but nearly every other problem which confronted the missionary was presented and discussed—education in all its forms, medical work, literature, the attitude toward the native religions, toward such customs as footbinding and the honors paid to ancestors, and toward indulgence and traffic in opium, the methods of presenting the Gospel, the standards for church membership, the means of promoting self-support and greater activity on the part of the Chinese churches, and other similar topics. The Conference passed a number of resolutions and provided for several committees to continue its work. Among the resolutions were ones appealing to the churches, colleges, and mission boards in Europe and America for more missionaries and asking the Bible societies to add explanatory notes (unsectarian, of course) to their Chinese editions of the Bible and to permit the sale of tracts along with the sale of the Scriptures. Among the committees was one on literature, which was to find what books were being written and to prepare a series of textbooks for use in mission schools. It was planned to hold another conference in ten years.[251]

The next conference was held, not ten years after its prede-

[249] Candlin, *John Innocent*, pp. 117-123.
[250] The Missionary Conference of 1890 met in the building of this church.
[251] *Records of the General Conference of the Protestant Missionaries of China, Shanghai, 1877.* Of the 142 present, 74 were men, 52 were women, 72 represented American societies, 49 British societies, 1 a German society, 4 were unconnected with societies, and 16 were honorary members. See also *Chinese Recorder,* Vol. 6, p. 66, Vol. 8, p. 239. In interesting contrast with the conferences of 1912 and 1922, there were no Chinese delegates.

cessor, but in 1890. Like that of 1877, it was primarily for missionaries: the Chinese Protestant churches were not yet sufficiently strong in numbers or in leadership to require a share in the deliberations.[252]   Four hundred and forty-five delegates were present, or a little more than a third of the Protestant missionary force in China, representing thirty-seven different societies.   Like the Conference of 1877, that of 1890 met in Shanghai, and, like it, its time was largely spent in considering missionary methods and problems.   Much of the work of the Conference was done by committees, but there was free discussion of reports and papers.   The harmony is said to have been marked, even on the term question. A number of continuing committees were appointed, chief among them being those "to secure an easy Wen-li version," "a Mandarin version," and a "High Wen-li version" of the Scriptures, one to prepare an "annotated Bible" and "explanatory notes and comments on the Scriptures," another to develop romanized vernacular versions of the Bible, another on Christian literature, another to promote anti-opium societies, and still another on work for the blind and deaf and dumb.

Of the nine resolutions adopted, the most important seem to have been one urging "that in view of its paramount importance the evangelistic work be pushed forward with increased vigor and earnestness, in order, if possible, to save the present generation," and one dissenting from a paper which held that missionaries "should refrain from any interference with the native mode of honoring ancestors" and affirming the belief of the conference "that idolatry is an essential constituent of ancestor worship." Protestant missionaries, with a few exceptions, still viewed with entire disapproval the religious systems of China and believed that the eternal salvation of each Chinese depended upon his hearing and accepting the Christian message.   Since the Conference held such convictions, it was natural that, as its most impressive act, it should publish "an appeal to all Protestant churches of Christian lands . . . to send to China . . . one thousand men within five years from this time," and that the women of the Conference should issue a special call to their sisters in Protestant

[252] A brief account of the conference was, however, ordered prepared in Chinese and a committee appointed for that purpose.   This seems to have been a further step toward the recognition of the Chinese churches than any made by the Conference of 1877.   There were two Chinese members of the Conference, the Rev. and Mrs. Y. K. Yen.

countries to undertake work for women in China. Missionaries were primarily not to condemn but to save.

A plan was suggested by a "committee on union" for a permanent committee on correspondence "to communicate with missionaries on all subjects of common interest, to collect and publish missionary information and statistics, and to seek the views of the missionaries in the different parts of our common field on any subject where they may think united action desirable, including provision for the next Conference" and urging "the missionaries in the various missionary centers who have not already done so to unite in local conferences or associations, and that such bodies select one of their number to correspond with the Shanghai Committee." [253]

More than before, Protestant missionaries had been led to regard their task as one, to feel that their body had a spiritual, even if not an organic unity, and to see that there were specific enterprises which they must undertake as a unit. The Conference of 1890 left behind it more tangible organization than did that of 1877, and missionaries were coming to think of these gatherings as periodical events. In other words, beginnings had been made which might in time lead to one organic Protestant Christian Church for China, beginnings which in the twentieth century, as we shall see in later chapters, were to lead, while not to complete organic union—at least before 1928, to extensive coöperation which might sometime culminate in union.

[253] This account of the conference of 1890 is taken from *Records of the General Conference of the Protestant Missionaries of China held at Shanghai, May 7-20, 1890*. Of the 445 members of the Conference, 233 were men and 212 were women; 230 were from American societies, 193 from British societies, 4 from German societies, and 18 were unconnected.—Ibid., p. xxiii. See, too, other notices of the conference in *Chinese Recorder*, Vol. 21, p. 409, *Missionary Review of the World*, Vol. 3, p. 712, and Smith, *Rex Christus*, p. 190. It is interesting to note that 1,153 recruits came during the five years after the Conference, partly in response to the appeal for the thousand. Of these, 481 were men and 672 were women.—Smith, op. cit., p. 190.

CHAPTER XIX

THE GRADUAL PENETRATION OF CHINA BY MISSIONARIES, 1856-1897

METHODS OF PROTESTANT MISSIONS

GENERAL CHARACTERISTICS

FROM an account of the extension of the activities of the societies in China before 1856 and the entrance of new societies, the number and character of the missionaries, and the extent of coöperation, we naturally turn to the means by which Protestants pursued their task.

The methods employed were determined in large part by the missionary's conception of his purpose. On this point there was a fair degree of unanimity: as before 1856 missionaries thought of themselves as being in China primarily to proclaim the Christian message and to lead the Chinese into the Christian experience. They believed that the possession of this experience was evidenced not so much by the ability to repeat with accuracy and intelligence a summary of Christian doctrine—although they usually held this to be important—as by certain qualities of life. Parallel with the desire for an inward transformation of character was the purpose of alleviating much of the physical distress and of correcting what the missionary deemed the social and intellectual evils of China. Institutions grew up, therefore, for the relief of suffering, schools for the education of Christians and non-Christians arose, literature for introducing new ideas was prepared, and movements against opium, and, to a lesser extent, against foot-binding, were fostered. The institutions were usually believed to be of value only as they contributed to leading the Chinese into the Christian life, but here and there were indications that in time missionaries might conceive of this purpose as secondary.

On the whole the methods employed were a development of those introduced before 1856. The major emphasis was still upon spreading the Faith by preaching, personal contact, and the printed page, and upon nourishing Chinese Christian groups toward maturity. The other main branches of endeavor continued to be education, medical work, and the preparation and distribution of literature. All of these were, however, developed and modified, and some new, although relatively minor, types of effort were introduced.

ITINERATION

As we have seen, the treaties of 1858 legalized foreign travel in the interior, and the Chefoo Convention (1876) made it less dangerous. Following them, the Protestant missionary traversed the length and breadth of the Eighteen Provinces and Manchuria, proclaiming the Gospel. Much of the proclamation was by the spoken word, the missionary seeking a hearing wherever he could get it, usually in a street. With oral presentation went the distribution of the printed page—portions of Scripture (usually Gospels or chapters from the Gospels) and simple introductions to Christian doctrine. Part of the itineration arose from a literal interpretation of the Scriptural command to "preach the Gospel to every creature," but most of it was for the purpose of gaining a knowledge of the country, and as a preliminary to permanent stations and outstations. Much of the travelling was by young, unmarried missionaries. How lasting an impression was made on the minds of the Chinese was a matter of dispute.[1]

THE MISSION STATION

The major part of the work of the missionary was performed not by itinerant preaching, but in and from a permanent residential center, a mission station. These mission stations were usually in cities, some of them "ports," where the residence of foreigners was permitted by treaty, and others where the residence of Protestant missionaries depended upon the permission of the neighbors and of the Chinese officials. Difficulty was fre-

[1] On itineration see H. H. Lowry in *Chinese Recorder*, Vol. 6, pp. 241-245; John, *Sowing and Reaping*, passim; Ross, *Mission Methods in Manchuria*, p. 32; Graves, *Forty Years in China*, p. 277; Davies, *Among Hills and Valleys in Western China*, pp. 61-74, 19-202 (here the itineration was by women); Ashmore, *The South China Missior of the American Baptist Foreign Mission Society*, pp. 85, 86.

quently experienced in renting or buying property outside and
even in the treaty ports, and the missionary sometimes called upon
his government for support.   The governments of the United
States and Great Britain, as we have seen, took the attitude that
the treaties did not guarantee to Protestant missionaries the right
of residence outside the "open" ports, but that if the missionary
had acquired an entrance, and especially if he had obtained a
house or land either by lease or by purchase, he had by that act
come into possession of quasi-legal rights in which he must be
protected.[2]

The mission station was usually made up of a preaching hall,
a church building, a school or schools, a dispensary and perhaps
a hospital, and residences for missionaries and their Chinese colleagues and assistants.   Not all these buildings and institutions
were necessarily within one enclosure or even in the same part
of the city.   The residences, usually in Occidental style and surrounded by a wall, were, with their gardens and lawns, attractive
even if unpretentious bits of the West set down in China.

The street chapel was often a shop that had been rented or
bought.   It opened, as its name indicates, on a public thorough-
fare.   In it the missionary or his Chinese assistants spoke infor-
mally on the Christian message and answered questions.   The
audience came and went at will, but some personal contacts were
made which led to sustained interest and conversion.[3]   The street
chapel helped, too, to dispel the air of secrecy and mystery which

---

[2] Lord to Helm and Houston, Aug. 15, 1873, in *House Executive Documents,*
2d Session, 43d Congress, Vol. 1, pp. 233-246; Avery to Fish, June 1, 1875, in
Foreign Relations, 1st Session, 44th Congress, Vol. 1, pp. 332-335.   The Secretary of State wrote to the American Minister to China, March 7, 1889 (*Foreign
Relations, 1888,* Part 1, p. 266): "It cannot be contended that the treaties grant
to citizens of the United States an unlimited right to buy or lease land in the
interior of China. . . . On the other hand, if . . . missionaries, with the consent
of the local authorities, effect a lodgement, they should be protected."   In 1869
Clarendon wrote to Alcock that the British Government would not insist on
obtaining for British missionaries the privileges conceded to Roman Catholic missionaries of acquiring land in the interior.—*Parliamentary Papers,* 1870, Vol. 69,
China No. 9, p. 4.   There is in this document a lengthy official correspondence
on the question of the relation of the British Government to missionaries.   The
British Government was inclined to advise the missionary not to attempt to locate
outside of treaty ports, especially if the effort created violent opposition.   It was
held that mission work did not prosper by the consequent appeal to force, and that
commerce was adversely affected.
[3] Dubose, *Preaching in Sinim,* p. 49; Nevius, *China and the Chinese,* p. 328;
Ross, *Mission Methods in Manchuria,* pp. 45-67; Soothill, *A Typical Mission in
South China,* p. 38.

to many Chinese was a sufficient reason for opposing the Christian faith.

Somewhere near the street chapel or the missionary's residence was usually a reception-room in Chinese style in which guests could be welcomed in accordance with the etiquette of the country.

The church building was primarily for Christian services and was usually distinct from the street chapel. At first it might be a Chinese building made over and refitted for the purpose, but in time a special building was erected, either purely Western in architecture or with attempts at adaptation to Chinese style. Nearly all church buildings were bare of adornment, and services were, as a rule, almost innocent of any appeal to the æsthetic side of man's nature. In deference to Chinese conceptions of propriety, men and women sat on opposite sides of the room, sometimes separated by a high screen. Services were often held each night of the week and on Sundays. They were for Christians and catechumens and consisted of preaching, oral instruction, prayer, and the singing of hymns. Nearly all the hymns were translations and the tunes those in use in the Occident. Since Chinese were unaccustomed to Western music, the singing frequently left much to be desired. Congregational singing was, moreover, an innovation in China. The prayers, except in the denominations which had liturgies, were usually extemporaneous. Most of the missionaries came from bodies which had reacted against the elaborate ritual of the Church of the Middle Ages and reproduced the simple services to which they had been accustomed.

From the central stations journeys were made to neighboring cities and villages and in time a network of congregations, each with its chapel and often with its school, came into existence. Sometimes a congregation arose from the visits of a missionary or one of his Chinese assistants, and sometimes from the efforts of a former patient in the hospital or a visitor in the street chapel, or of a Christian who had moved to the locality. Each of these Christian groups, as it grew, was given a pastor and became partially or entirely free from the financial support of the missionary. The missionary attempted to visit each congregation one or more times a year, examining, baptizing, instructing, admonishing, and helping to solve problems and to adjust disputes. Some of the groups were opening wedges for the foundation of stations with resident missionaries.[4]

INSTRUCTION TO AND REQUIREMENTS OF CONVERTS

As has been suggested, the first approach to non-Christians was made by different types of persons and in a variety of ways— sometimes by the missionary, frequently by an unsalaried Christian Chinese, often by a Chinese in the employ of the Church, some-times through street preaching or the street chapel, often through the regular services of the Church, sometimes through the hospital or dispensary, and occasionally, as educational institutions developed, through the school. The initial contact with women was usually made by women, either foreign or Chinese.[5]

The substance of elementary instruction and of public addresses to non-Christians was, as a rule, God the creator and sustainer of all, man's sinfulness, Jesus as the Saviour sent by God to save men from sin, Jesus' perfect life, his crucifixion and resurrection, salvation from sin through faith, and eternal life.[6]   Methods for further instruction to those interested varied from mission to mission.   Some maintained that all who desired baptism should be given it, no matter how little knowledge of Christian truth they possessed or how little information the missionary had of their character.   They trusted to education after baptism to ensure an intelligent and worthy Christian life.   The majority of mission-aries, however, required a period of probation varying from sev-eral months to several years.   The candidate was taught, often in a weekly, sometimes in a daily class, the main tenets of the Christian faith, and was required to renounce idolatry and to show indications of Christian character.   More emphasis was placed on the quality of life than on the ability to answer correctly questions in a weekly, sometimes in a daily class, the main tenets of the

[4] This picture of a mission station and the activities radiating from it is drawn chiefly from three books which portray conditions as they were toward the close of the nineteenth century in three different parts of the country:—Gibson, *Mission Problems and Mission Methods in South China* (1901), depicting conditions in and around Swatow; Soothill, *A Typical Mission in China* (1906), describing con-ditions in and around Wênchow in Chêkiang; and Ross, *Mission Methods in Manchuria* (1903).   All three were men who had a leading part in the work of which they wrote.   On ways in which Christian communities grew up, see also Gordon-Cumming, *Wanderings in China*, Vol. 1, pp. 148-150.

[5] On some of the difficulties in approaching women, see *Chinese Recorder*, Vol. 26, p. 299.   On some of the problems of mission work for women, see Stod-dart, *The Life of Isabella Bird*, p. 257.

[6] Gibson, op. cit., pp. 150-168; Ross, op. cit., pp. 77-90; Soothill, op. cit., p. 55.

approved either by the missionary or by the proper officers of the Chinese church, or by both, he was baptized.[7]

Tuition by no means ceased with baptism. Classes and services were held, daily or weekly or both, and sometimes for several weeks in a central place in the slack season after harvest. Missionaries usually attempted to teach all Christians, both adults and children, to read, either the Chinese character or a romanized form of the vernacular, that they might study for themselves the Scriptures and other Christian literature.

Members as well as catechumens were held to a high standard of morality, discipline in the form of suspension or expulsion being administered, often rather strictly. Missionaries and churches were especially stern against sexual immorality, polygamy, gambling, any part in opium—either consuming it or growing the poppy—and any participation in idolatry. All forms of soothsaying and of observing lucky and unlucky days were discouraged, and some form of observing Sunday, often by complete cessation of labor, was enjoined. Early marriage and divorce were frowned upon or forbidden.[8] Becoming a Christian involved breaking with much of Chinese society, with the religious practices of the land, and with the customary forms of honors to ancestors. Keeping one day in seven for rest and worship was for many a serious handicap, and declining to grow the opium poppy entailed for others a serious loss of income. It is not strange that Christians were frequently regarded by their neighbors as bewitched by the foreigner and as having forsworn their nationality.

The Missionary and Litigation

It would not have been remarkable had the Protestant missionary followed the example of the Roman Catholics and under the ægis of the toleration clauses acquired adherents by interfering in lawsuits. Some missionaries held positions in the consular service,[9] Protestant converts were often persecuted by their neigh-

[7] Gibson, op. cit., pp. 200, 205, 206; Nevius in *Records of the Missionary Conference, Shanghai, 1890*, p. 171.
[8] Soothill, op. cit., pp. 92 et seq.; Ross, op. cit., p. 129; Faber, *Problems of Practical Christianity in China*, pp. 66 et seq.
[9] Ashmore was American Vice-Consul at Swatow.—*Foreign Relations*, 3d Session, 41st Congress, p. 380. McCartee was much in the American consular service.—Dennis, *Christian Missions and Social Progress*, Vol. 3, p. 396; Speer, *A Missionary Pioneer in the Far East*, passim.

bors, Chinese frequently sought enrollment as Christians in the hope of obtaining the support of the foreigner against their enemies,[10] and the missionary could easily have used his privileged position to add to his following.   As we shall see later in some detail, he repeatedly invoked the aid of his government in gaining protection for himself and his property and in obtaining and keeping a foothold in inland cities.   Occasionally his Chinese assistants without his knowledge used their connection with him as a club over the heads of officials[11] and as a bait to attract adherents. Occasionally, too, from an imperfect knowledge of a case and on the mistaken supposition that a Christian was being persecuted, the missionary appealed to the courts and became embroiled in long-standing controversies between families or clans.[12]   On the whole, however, Protestant missionaries seem scrupulously to have avoided even the appearance of gaining "converts" by such dubious methods.   At least one Chinese pastor, moreover, deliberately declined to appeal to the magistrate against persecution.[13]

That many inquirers came from a mixture of motives is certain,[14] and now and again missionaries through their consuls brought pressure to bear upon Chinese officials in what they regarded as cases of persecution or injustice.[15]   As a rule, however, Protestant missionaries attempted to keep out of the courts and brought action in them only as a last resort.   The majority of the leading missionaries looked with thorough disapproval on what they believed to be the Roman Catholic practice.[16]   The problem was, however, one which the missionary had almost constantly with him.   On the one hand he ran the danger of

---

[10] See instances in Ross, *Mission Methods in Manchuria*, pp. 163-168.

[11] In the sixties a Mr. Tso, connected with the Southern Baptist Mission in Têngchow, Shantung, made money by saying that he had influence with the missionaries and that these in turn could influence officials in the settlement of lawsuits.   He had the magistrates cowed and in one instance, under false pretenses, induced a missionary to interfere in a lawsuit.   When Tso's tactics were discovered he was expelled from the Church.—Foster, *Fifty Years in China*, pp. 164, 165.

[12] Gibson, *Mission Problems and Mission Methods in South China*, pp. 294-298.

[13] This was Pastor Hsi.—Hoste in *Chinese Recorder*, Vol. 55, pp. 247, 248.

[14] Ashmore, *South China Mission of the American Baptist Foreign Mission Society*, pp. 40, 48.

[15] Gibson, op. cit., pp. 298-309; Ross, op. cit., pp. 173-176.

[16] Gibson, op. cit., pp. 294-309; Ross, op. cit., pp. 160-176; Soothill, op cit., pp. 80-90; *Foreign Relations*, 2d Session, 42d Congress, pp. 97-111.   About 1870 Ashmore and his colleague decided not to appeal to the American Consul on behalf of Chinese Christians.—Ashmore, op. cit., pp. 40, 48, 56.

failing to interfere in cases of genuine injustice to Christians and of incurring ill-will for his seeming callousness, and on the other of being deceived into advocating an unrighteous cause.

Organizing and Nourishing the Chinese Church

The avowed purpose of most Protestant missionaries was not only to give to each Chinese an adequate knowledge of the Gospel and to lead as many as possible into the Christian experience, but to help bring into existence a self-supporting, self-propagating Chinese Church which should become as vigorous and independent as its sister bodies in the West. Naturally the missionary tended to reproduce the polity and creed of his denomination. There were often adaptations to Chinese institutions—the custom of having head men, for example, usually being taken over under the guise of vestrymen, deacons, or elders. Some contended that the Church should not be held either to the forms found in the New Testament or to those in use in the West, but should work out its own organization. In the main, however, Anglicanism, Congregationalism, Methodism, Presbyterianism, and the other types of Protestantism duplicated themselves in the Middle Kingdom.

Some missionaries believed that no foreign money should be paid to a Chinese for preaching the Gospel, and that from the very beginning the Church should be self-supporting. Several fairly large missions, indeed, put this principle into practice.[17] Others subsidized the Chinese rather freely, unintentionally encouraging them to depend entirely upon the foreigner and to postpone indefinitely the day of independence.[18] The majority of missionaries, however, endeavored to follow a middle course, putting Chinese agents on salary and aiding the Chinese congregations, but attempting gradually to reduce the proportion of foreign con-

---

[17] This was the principle on which T. P. Crawford of Shantung worked.— Foster, *Fifty Years in China,* pp. 226-257. In 1877 Crawford said that in twenty-five years in China he had never paid assistants or given a dollar of mission funds to any Chinese to preach the Gospel.—*Records of the General Conference of Protestant Missionaries of China, 1877,* p. 295. See, too, *The Christian Occupation of China,* p. 198. The English Baptist Mission in Shantung had a somewhat similar principle.—*China Mission Hand-book,* Part 2, p. 44. Nevius, too, was opposed to the payment of Chinese evangelists. His insistence on financial independence was widely known and was very influential, not only in China but in Korea.—See his *Methods of Mission Work* and an article by him in *Chinese Recorder,* Vol. 16, p. 461.

[18] Gibson, op. cit., pp. 192-196.

tributions. Once established, the subsidies were difficult to discontinue. However, contributions from Chinese increased quite steadily, and the number of congregations entirely independent of foreign aid rose with each decade.[19]

Closely related to the problem of self-support was that of freedom from foreign control. Complete independence could be brought about in denominations with a congregational or presbyterian form of organization more rapidly than in those episcopally governed. Missionaries under all types of polity, however, early took steps looking toward this goal. Nearly all local groups had from the beginning, or from near the beginning, officers chosen by the congregation or appointed by the missionary. On the shoulders of these office-bearers was placed much of the responsibility for holding services, supervising the local church property, raising money, and maintaining among the members standards of Christian faith and living.[20] Presbyteries were formed in various places—in the Amoy region in 1863, in Shan-

[19] In 1877 there were reported to be 18 churches which were wholly self-supporting and 243 that were partially self-supporting.—*Records of the General Conference of Protestant Missionaries of China, 1877,* p. 486. About 1893 there were reported to be 137 churches which were wholly self-supporting and 490 that were partially so.—*China Mission Hand-book,* Part 2, p. 324. On plans for increasing self-support and discussions of them, see *Records of the Missionary Conference, Shanghai, 1890,* pp. 415-447; *Chinese Recorder,* Vol. 1, p. 73, Vol. 2, p. 211, Vol. 3, p. 310, Vol. 10, p. 105, Vol. 15, p. 254, Vol. 26, p. 303; *China Mission Hand-book,* Part 2, p. 55; Nevius, *Life of Nevius,* p. 404; Duncan, *The Missionary Mail,* p. 24. In 1882 in Amoy 750 church members gave $1,877.32; in 1886, 804 members gave $2,076.29; in 1892, 1,008 members gave $3,894.80—Pitcher, *Fifty Years in Amoy,* p. 132. In 1874 the churches associated with the London Missionary Society in the Amoy region had a membership of 612 and gave to central funds £166. In 1911 a membership of 3,458 gave £1,328.—Bitton, *Our Heritage in China,* p. 63. It must be remembered that compared with Western standards not only were incomes of members low but salaries of native workers were meager. In 1877 the highest salaries paid to Chinese under the American Presbyterian Mission in Shantung were 6,000 cash a month to teachers and 4,500 cash a month to preachers.—*Records of the General Conference of Protestant Missionaries of China, 1877,* p. 294. About 1895 the American Board paid preachers from $5 to $10 a month, ordained pastors from $6 to $10 a month, and other pastors from $3 to $8 a month.—*China Mission Hand-book,* Part 2, p. 154. Judged even by Chinese standards, these stipends were not large. A particular type of self-supporting mission was the Chefoo Industrial Mission. This was begun in 1893 by Mr. and Mrs. James McMullan, formerly connected with the China Inland Mission, "with the set purpose of demonstrating that we could work for our support and at the same time do effective mission work." Lace-making was taught and a brush factory was added later. In 1896 a school was opened to lead the pupils to a Christian faith, to give them a sound education, and to teach them to support themselves.—Forsyth, *Shantung,* pp. 277 et seq.

[20] See examples of this in Ross, op. cit., pp. 108-143; Gibson, op. cit., pp. 169-232; Soothill, op. cit., pp. 57-74; Ashmore, *South China Mission of the American Baptist Foreign Mission Society,* p. 52.

tung in 1865,[21] and in Manchuria in 1891,[22] for example—in which it was planned to increase the Chinese element and in time to dispense with the foreigner. In the Shantung presbytery the discussions were, from 1866, entirely in Chinese.[23] In the seventies the churches which had arisen in and around Amoy out of the efforts of the London Missionary Society were formed into a "Congregational Union" in which missionaries, Chinese workers, and delegates from each church had seats.[24] In 1876 the Church Missionary Society created its first Chinese church committee for a local congregation in its Chêkiang-Kiangsu field,[25] and in 1882 steps were taken toward putting into operation a plan of Chinese church councils with delegates from the various pastorates and probably the first. Another, much talked of in its day and more successful, was developed in Hupeh by the American Episcopalians.[27]

Many ambitious plans were projected for reaching the Chinese through their fellow countrymen under the supervision of a minimum number of foreigners. Gützlaff's ill-starred enterprise was probably the first. Another, much talked of in its day and more successful, was developed in Hupeh by the American Episcopalians.[27]

Christians were also encouraged to spread the Faith without the assistance of the foreigner. Most of this "home missionary work" was performed by individuals and by single congregations.[28] In time, however, there began to be organized for this purpose societies in which a number of churches joined, the precursors of the larger movements after 1900.[29]

The earliest Protestant missionaries had realized that if the Chinese Church was ever to be vigorous, truly independent, and self-propagating, it must have trained Chinese leadership. They realized, too, that all the nation could never be reached with the

---

[21] Fisher, *C. W. Mateer*, p. 199.
[22] *A Century of Protestant Missions in China*, p. 178; Ross, op. cit., p. 123.
[23] Fisher, *C. W. Mateer*, p. 199.
[24] *L. M. S. Chronicle*, Vol. 15 (new series), p. 51.
[25] *A Century of Protestant Missions in China*, p. 28.
[26] Stock and McClelland, *For Christ in Fuhkien*, p. 26.
[27] Jefferys, *Ingle*, pp. 64, 65, 268-272.
[28] Soothill, *A Typical Mission in China*, pp. 58-60. The *L. M. S. Chronicle*, Vol. 34, p. 263, tells of a church in Fatshan supported in part by the Canton church.
[29] The Congregational Union of Amoy began a mission of its own in an adjoining prefecture in 1892.—*A Century of Protestant Missions in China*, p. 8. The Hing-hwa (Fukien) Home Missionary Society was formed in 1895.—*Chinese Recorder*, Vol. 34, p. 170.

Christian message by foreigners alone.[30]   Consequently, even
before 1856 Chinese were employed to help spread the Faith and
to shepherd the Christian communities, and some instruction had
been begun for them.

The creation of a body of well-prepared, able men and women
who would give full time to the Church was, however, no easy
task and not one to be accomplished in a few decades.   Outside
the Roman Catholic communities, nothing existed in China corresponding to the profession of the minister and pastor.   The
Buddhist and Taoist monks and nuns were probably the nearest
approach to it, and these were popularly in ill repute.   Most
of the early Christians were, moreover, men and women of scanty
education, and high standards of education could not quickly be
achieved.   The communities of Chinese Christians were small,
and their members were usually not far removed from poverty
and were unaccustomed to contributing to the support of a
church.   A larger body of converts would have to be gathered
and schools of higher grade would need to be established before
able Chinese leadership could be expected.   Missionaries gave
much thought to the problem, and many attempts were made to
solve it.[31]   After 1900, especially after 1914, these efforts were
to bear fruit in a rapidly growing body of competent leaders,
but, as a rule, before 1900 Chinese remained subordinate to the
missionaries.   The Chinese were "helpers," and the missionary,
often against his will, dominated the Church.

Chinese were in the service of the Church in various capacities.
There were "Bible women," [32] used to spread the message among
members of their own sex.   There were men who were colporteurs, others were "evangelists," travelling, like the former,
much of the time, others were teachers, and still others were
resident pastors.   Missionaries were usually slow in ordaining
Chinese, for they wished to maintain standards of preparation
somewhere nearly equal to those that obtained for the ministry
in Europe and America.   However, by 1897, in nearly every

[30] See an earnest plea on this ground for more training of Chinese workers, in
Doolittle, *Social Life of the Chinese*, Vol. 2, pp. 403-410.
[31] As typical of these discussions see *Chinese Recorder*, Vol. 2, p. 74, Vol. 3,
p. 315 et seq., Vol. 4, p. 118, Vol. 5, p. 137, Vol. 17, pp. 149, 213, 228, Vol.
22, p. 395, Vol. 23, p. 299.
[32] The Reformed Church at Amoy began in 1878 to employ Bible women to
go out two by two to outlying villages.—Chamberlain, *Fifty Years in Foreign
Fields,* p. 22.

mission were some who had been fully admitted to the ministry or priesthood of the Church.[33]

In the earlier days, naturally, there were few who had been trained from boyhood for the Church. It was from the adult converts who showed unusual zeal, ability, and Christian character that those were picked who were asked to give their entire time to the mission.[34] As the Christian communities became older, and members grew up in the Church from childhood, promising youths were selected and given a longer education. Stipends were meager—mere pittances in comparison with those paid in Europe and America—and since they were higher for teachers than for pastors,[35] the former profession tended to attract men of better training. Teachers, moreover, were traditionally held in higher respect in China than were priests. Salaries were sometimes paid entirely from foreign funds, in other instances by the Chinese Christians, and frequently were derived from both sources.

Many attempts were made to educate leaders for the Church. Some of these took the form of classes for those in active service, the kind that might be given to apprentices in a trade. Ashmore, for example, had the practice of bringing the Chinese evangelists together for study one week in every two months.[36] As the years passed, special schools were established. In 1866 the English Presbyterians opened a theological college at Amoy,[37] in 1869 a building for the same purpose was erected there by the (Dutch) Reformed Church,[38] and in 1884 or 1885 the two schools were united.[39] In 1876 twenty theological schools were reported, with two hundred and thirty-one students.[40] In 1878 the Church Missionary Society founded a divinity college at Foochow.[41] In 1862 Nevius was urging on the American Presbyterians the estab-

[33] In 1876 there were reported to be 73 ordained Chinese ministers, 511 "assistant preachers," 76 colporteurs, and 90 Bible women.—*Records of the General Conference of Protestant Missionaries, 1877*, p. 486.
[34] Soothill, op. cit., pp. 100-120; Ross, *Mission Methods in Manchuria*, pp. 91-107.
[35] *Records of the General Conference of Protestant Missionaries, 1877*, p. 294; *China Mission Hand-book*, Part 2, p. 154.
[36] Ashmore, *South China Mission of the American Baptist Foreign Mission Society*, p. 38.
[37] *A Century of Protestant Missions in China*, p. 177.
[38] Ibid., p. 373.
[39] Ibid., p. 374; Pitcher, *Fifty Years in Amoy*, p. 177.
[40] *Records of the General Conference of Protestant Missionaries of China, 1877*, p. 486.
[41] *A Century of Protestant Missions in China*, p. 35.

lishment of a theological school for China [42] and in 1864 Mateer began an institution with preparation for the service of the Church as one of its objectives. [43]   St. John's College was founded in Shanghai in 1879 by the American Episcopalians, [44] and in 1880 thirteen students were reported in its theological department. [45] These are merely important examples of what was being undertaken by many missions. [46]

In the beginning theological schools were of elementary grade, for the amount of preliminary education required was small.   In some missions standards were raised as the years passed.   For example, in 1896 St. John's began theological education with English as the medium of instruction. [47]   As a rule, however, by 1897 the amount of formal preparation given to Chinese in the ministry was still much less than that of their foreign colleagues. The ministry did not appeal to many of the better educated younger Christians who were beginning to graduate from the mission schools of higher grade, and there was danger that a Chinese ministry would grow up inferior in training and unable to take advantage for the Church of the years of opportunity ahead.

Of the delicate task of adjusting to Chinese culture Christian practices, organization, and convictions as they had developed in the West there was some appreciation.   Timothy Richard, for example, repeatedly urged that Christianity must be adapted to the Chinese background. [48]   A few believed that the Church should not utterly proscribe the Chinese form of honoring ancestors and that much of Chinese religious belief and practice, far from being antagonistic, had kinship with Christianity.   The time had not yet come, however, for any extensive adaptation of Protestant Christianity to China.   Here and there were timid beginnings—in the organization of local congregations, and in Chinese roofs on mission structures, but most missionaries either regarded all forms of indigenous religious practice as erroneous or held that contamination of the purity of the Christian faith could best

[42] Nevius, *Life of Nevius*, p. 231.
[43] *A Century of Protestant Missions in China*, p. 383.
[44] Ibid., p. 298.
[45] *Spirit of Missions*, Vol. 44 (1880), p. 209.
[46] A number of these are mentioned in Leger, *Education of Christian Ministers in China*, pp. 8-10.
[47] Leger, op. cit., p. 19.
[48] See Richard in *Records of the Missionary Conference, Shanghai, 1890*, pp. 412, 413.

be avoided by erring on the side of condemning rather than condoning Chinese customs. Such native leadership as existed leaned too heavily on the missionary to venture on the debatable paths of syncretism.

If the Church were ever to be a permanent and influential factor in Chinese life, a certain amount of intolerance of existing institutions and practices was necessary. The Church, after all, had a distinct message and wisely, especially in the days when Christian communities were young and feeble and made up of those newly and only partially emerged from non-Christian beliefs, avoided any risk of losing its justification for existence by an easy conformity to the culture about it.

The Preparation and Distribution of Literature

As before 1856, so in the four decades that followed, one of the major activities of Protestant missionaries was the preparation and distribution of literature. Before 1856 it was only through the printed page that most of the Empire could be penetrated by the Protestant presentation of Christianity. Now that the Empire was more nearly open, Protestants still emphasized the written word. Much more than the Roman Catholics, they used the pen and the printing press. Christian books were useful in spreading a knowledge of the Faith and were indispensable in the maintenance and improvement of the Church. Great emphasis was placed upon perfecting the translations of the Bible and making it available in additional forms of the vernacular, upon preparing tracts, hymnals, and religious books, and upon writing and translating textbooks for the growing schools. Books and articles were also composed to present to the Chinese other phases of Western thought and knowledge. Then, too, missionaries compiled manuals to introduce their younger colleagues to China and its language, they edited periodicals in Chinese and English, and they wrote books to place China before the English-speaking part of the Occident. To circulate this literature, existing agencies, such as the great Bible societies, expanded their organizations, and new societies came into existence.

The major emphasis was still upon the translation of the Scriptures. As we have seen in earlier chapters, by 1856 several translations of the Bible had been made, both in the literary style and in the vernacular. A number of new translations were now added.

As early as 1877 there were reported portions or all of the Bible in eleven "dialects." [49]   In 1862 Bridgman and Culbertson, as we have seen, completed a translation of the Bible which in some respects was an alternate to the Delegates' Version. [50]   Portions of the Bible were also put into the literary language as follows: Acts in 1860 by Charles W. Gaillard; Mark and Acts in 1862 by John L. Nevius; the New Testament, 1850-1866, by T. H. Hudson; Matthew and Mark by Ho Chin-shan, revised by James Legge, in 1860; John's epistles in 1870 by F. S. Turner; the Gospel of John in 1874 by Hobson and Muirhead; Psalms one to forty by John Macgowan in 1875; Colossians by Muirhead in 1875; Hebrews by Samuel Dodd, also in 1875; and the New Testament by Chalmers and Schaut in 1897. [51]   The opening to Protestant missionaries of the Yangtze Valley and the North necessitated a translation of the Bible into Mandarin, the vernacular of the greater part of these sections of the Empire.   A Mandarin version of the New Testament by Medhurst and Stronach appeared in 1857, but was unsatisfactory. [52]   After 1860 a committee was formed of Messrs. Burdon, Blodget, Martin, and Schereschewsky, representing some of the larger societies then in Peking.   The Mandarin New Testament produced by these men, assisted by Chinese, was issued about 1870 or 1872 [53] and rapidly came into extensive use.   A Mandarin version of the Old Testament, largely the work of Schereschewsky, appeared in 1873, 1874, or 1875. [54]   W. A. P. Martin made a Mandarin translation of the Gospel of John. [55]   Griffith John, at the request of the British and Foreign Bible Society and of the National Bible Society of Scotland, prepared a translation of the New Testament in Mandarin. [56]   He also began on the Old Testament. [57]   A translation was needed

[49] Baldwin in *Records of the General Conference of Protestant Missionaries of China, 1877*, p. 207.

[50] Canton, *History of the British and Foreign Bible Society*, Vol. 3, p. 445; Wherry in *Records of the Missionary Conference, Shanghai, 1890*, p. 53.

[51] *The Christian Occupation of China*, p. 452, based on *Historical Catalogue of Printed Editions of Holy Scriptures in the Library of the British and Foreign Bible Society, Translations of the Scriptures into the Languages of China and her Dependencies*, by J. R. Hykes, and Broomhall, *The Chinese Empire*.

[52] Wherry in *Records of the Missionary Conference, Shanghai, 1890*, p. 55.

[53] Wherry in ibid., pp. 54, 55; Woodin in ibid., p. 90; Soothill, *A Typical Mission in China*, p. 197; Canton, op. cit., Vol. 3, p. 445.

[54] *Spirit of Missions*, Vol. 68, p. 235; Woodin in *Records of the Missionary Conference, Shanghai, 1890*, p. 90; Soothill, op. cit., p. 197.

[55] *The Christian Occupation of China*, p. 452.

[56] Thompson, *Griffith John*, pp. 428, 441, 442.   The request was made in 1887.

[57] Ibid., p. 428.

which, while not as offensive to the scholar as that in the despised vernacular, would be fairly intelligible to the less educated and could be used in districts speaking Mandarin or dialects closely akin to it.   Versions were, therefore, produced in what was called "easy Wen-li," a less condensed form of the literary style.   Griffith John made one of the New Testament (begun in 1883 and finished in 1886),[58] and Blodget finished one, also of the New Testament, in 1889.[59]

None of these versions was entirely satisfactory, nor was it likely that any would ever be until the revision could be made by Chinese thoroughly at home both in the original languages and in their own.   Until such Chinese Christian scholarship should emerge, it was necessary for foreigners, with the aid of Chinese, to continue the task, and at the Shanghai Conference of 1890 committees were, as we have seen, appointed to undertake it.

Versions of part or all of the Scriptures were appearing in the forms of the spoken language which were found in such variety in the coast provinces south of the Yangtze.   Some of these were printed in the Chinese character, some in Roman letters, and some in both.   Roman letters, while by no means fully adapted to represent Chinese sounds, possessed the advantage of being more quickly learned than were the Chinese characters.   Then, too, in at least some forms of the vernacular were words for which no characters existed.   The use of Roman letters might seem barbarous to the scholar, but it was a courageous attempt to facilitate the literacy of all church members.   In several dialects no literature had previously appeared: the missionary was the first to reduce them to writing, and the portions of the Bible he translated were the earliest printed books to be issued in them. Portions of the Scriptures had been translated into some of the vernaculars before 1856.   Among the editions of part or all of the Bible that appeared between 1856 and 1897 were the Gospels and the Acts of the Apostles put into the Wênchow vernacular in romanized form by Soothill and printed in 1893;[60] the New Testament in the Hakka colloquial by members of the Basel mission and issued both in Roman letters and in the Chinese character

[58] Gibson, *Mission Problems and Mission Methods in South China*, p. 208; Bonfield in *China Mission Year Book, 1915*, p. 472; Thompson, op. cit., p. 428; Canton, op. cit., Vol. 5, p. 170.
[59] Bondfield in *China Mission Year Book, 1915*, p. 472.
[60] Soothill, op. cit., pp. 199, 200.

about 1883; [61] parts of the New Testament in the Canton colloquial by various missionaries by 1881, and later part of the Old Testament in the same vernacular; [62] the New Testament in the Foochow vernacular about 1867; [63] an edition in the Swatow dialect, prepared by members of both the American Baptist and the English Presbyterian missions; [64] the Old Testament in the Amoy colloquial by 1884 [65] (the New Testament had appeared before 1856); the Gospel of John in the Kinwha colloquial; parts of the New Testament in the Hangchow colloquial; the entire Bible in the Soochow, Hinghwa, and Taichow colloquials; parts of the Bible in the Shaowu dialect; portions of the New Testament in one of the dialects of Hainan; the New Testament and part of the Old in the Kienning colloquial; and Matthew and Mark in that of Kienyang. [66]

The question of what Chinese terms to use for God, for Holy Spirit, and for baptism still vexed Protestant missionaries and complete agreement seemed as remote as ever. [67] The discussion was complicated by the use by Schereschewsky, Burdon, and some others of *T'ien Chu*, the term adopted by the Roman Catholics for God. [68] The other terms for God in common use by Protestants, it will be recalled, were *Shang Ti* and *Shen*. [69] When

[61] J. C. Gibson in *Records of the Missionary Conference, Shanghai, 1890*, p. 74; Woodin in ibid., p. 92. Matthew and Luke by Lechler in 1865-1866, Mark and Acts in 1874, John, Romans, and 1st and 2d Corinthians by Kang Fatlin, a Chinese educated at Basel, in 1879, Galatians, Ephesians, Philippians, and Colossians, by Kang Fatlin, in 1881. The rest of the New Testament was finished by C. P. Piton in 1883.—Canton, op. cit., Vol. 3, pp. 446, 455. In 1904 a revised version of the New Testament was issued.—Richter, *Das Werden der Christliche Kirche in China*, p. 194.

[62] Woodin in *Records of the Missionary Conference, Shanghai, 1890*, p. 92; Canton, op. cit., Vol. 3, pp. 445, 455.

[63] Gibson in *Records of the Missionary Conference, Shanghai, 1890*, p. 73; Woodin in ibid., p. 91; *A Century of Protestant Missions in China*, pp. 255, 560; *China Mission Hand-book*, Part 2, p. 155.

[64] Gibson in *Records of the Missionary Conference, Shanghai, 1890*, p. 74. By 1896 all of the New Testament was available in the Swatow dialect.—Ashmore, *South China Mission of the American Baptist Foreign Mission Society*, p. 138. See also Richter, op. cit., p. 195.

[65] Woodin in *Records of the Missionary Conference, Shanghai, 1890*, p. 92; Gibson in ibid., p. 71. Richter, op. cit., p. 195, says the New Testament appeared in 1873.

[66] *The Christian Occupation of China*, p. 452.

[67] See, for example, *Chinese Recorder*, Vol. 6 (1875), pp. 432 et seq.

[68] Faber, *Problems of Practical Christianity in China*, pp. 46 et seq.; Havret, *T'ien Tchou*, p. 11.

[69] *T'ien, Shang Chu, Chu* and *Shen Ming* were also suggested for God and perhaps had a limited use.—Faber, op. cit., pp. 46 et seq.; Havret, op. cit., p. 11; Blodget, *Why Protestant Missionaries in China Should Unite in Using the Term "Tien Chu" for God*.

in 1874 or 1875 Burdon became Bishop of Victoria (Hongkong) he insisted upon the use of *T'ien Chu* in place of *Shang Ti.* This aroused such distress among the Chinese Christians that the question was referred to the Archbishop of Canterbury, who, after going to much trouble, reached no satisfactory solution.[70] As time passed, the controversy faded into the background. For the most part missionaries agreed to disagree and different terms were employed in different editions, sometimes of the same translation.

Much other religious literature was produced. This had in the main one of two purposes, either to present the Gospel to non-Christians, or to aid the Christians in their faith. Some of it was in the literary style and for the scholars, and part of it was in one of the many vernaculars. Some terms were coined for Christian ideas, but others were taken over from Buddhism and Confucianism.[71] At the 1877 Shanghai Conference there were reported to be forty-three books or pamphlets of commentaries and notes, five hundred and twenty-one of theology and narrative, twenty-nine of sacred biography, eighty-two catechisms, fifty-four prayer books and rituals, sixty-three hymn books, seven periodicals, and one hundred and one sheet tracts. About three-fourths of these were in the literary style.[72] The amount of literature, naturally, increased as the years passed. Some publications, of course, had only a limited circulation, but others were widely used. A few of the more important books were *Evidences of Christianity* by W. A. P. Martin;[73] the Prayer Book of the Church of England, translated by Burdon and Schereschewsky;[74] a hymnal by Jonathan Lees with a circulation of over twenty thousand;[75] and a hymnal by Henry Blodget and Chauncey Goodrich, first published in 1872.[76]

When, at the 1890 Conference, a permanent committee on

[70] Stock, *History of the Church Missionary Society,* Vol. 3, p. 219; Norris, *China,* pp. 67-73. It is interesting to note, too, that Bishop Burdon suggested the substitution of rice and tea for bread and wine in the Holy Communion.—Norris, *China,* pp. 67-73.

[71] Faber, op. cit., p. 43.

[72] Baldwin in *Records of the General Conference of the Protestant Missionaries of China, 1877,* p. 206. For a list see Wylie, *Memorials of Protestant Missionaries to the Chinese,* passim.

[73] It was put into Mandarin by Burdon.—*China Mission Hand-book,* Part 2, p. 40.

[74] Ibid.; *Spirit of Missions,* Vol. 68, p. 235.

[75] Dennis, *Christian Missions and Social Progress,* Vol. 3, p. 196.

[76] Ibid.

Christian literature was appointed, the suggestion was made that it collect information on Protestant Christian books already published, "form a complete library of Protestant Christian literature in Chinese," prepare a classified catalogue and revise it from time to time, gather information about works in preparation, and maintain a "general depot at Shanghai for the store and sale of all books in circulation." [77]

Most of the Christian literature was produced by missionaries, although practically always with the help of Chinese. In spite of the hope of many missionaries that Chinese Christians would write an increasing proportion of it, but little came from their pens: there was as yet too little educated Chinese Protestant leadership, and Chinese Christians were still too much inclined to follow the foreigner.[78] Here and there were exceptions: for example, the well known Pastor Hsi composed a number of hymns, at least one of which was still being sung in the third decade of the twentieth century,[79] and in the eighties a tract in favor of the older faiths was answered elaborately by a Chinese Christian.[80] In the main, however, by 1897 the Chinese Protestant Christian communities had given birth to no important literature.

Protestant schools included in their curriculums the science of the West and knowledge concerning the world outside of China. In wide ranges of these fields they were pioneers, and missionaries had of necessity to prepare textbooks. Some had already appeared when the 1877 Conference appointed a permanent committee on "schools and textbooks." John Fryer, the general editor named

[77] *Records of the Missionary Conference, Shanghai, 1890,* pp. xlvii, lxi.
[78] Mateer in *Chinese Recorder,* Vol. 17, pp. 93 et seq.
[79] Mrs. Howard Taylor in *The Call of China's Great North-West,* pp. 126, 127, gives a translation of one of the hymns of Pastor Hsi which she says was still in use (a little after 1920):

"When thou wouldst pour the living stream
Then I would be the earthen cup,
Filled to the brim and sparkling clear,
The fountain thou and living spring.
Flow thou through me, the vessel weak,
That thirsty souls may taste thy grace.

"When thou wouldst light the darkness, Lord,
Then I would be the silver lamp,
Whose oil-supply can never fail,
Placed high to shed the beams afar
That darkness may be turned to light
And men and women see thy face."

[80] *Chinese Recorder,* Vol. 15, p. 455.

by the committee, reported to the 1890 Conference a long list of volumes that had been written or translated by him or under his supervision. The subjects included mathematics, chemistry, biology, physics, geography, music, physiology and hygiene, astronomy, history, philosophy, theology, education, and law.[81] Missionaries were, too, producing textbooks independently of this committee, as, for example, the many written by C. W. Mateer,[82] and others by members of the Southern Methodist Mission.[83]

Protestant missionaries were, moreover, introducing to China the knowledge of the West by translating or writing books other than those intended for schools.   Among these were Faber's *Civilization East and West,* an elaborate exposition of the fundamental principles underlying the civilization of the Occident and much read by those progressive Chinese who by 1897 were desiring the reorganization of China,[84] and W. A. P. Martin's translations of books on international law.[85] Protestant missionaries were aiding in preparing for the revolution in thought and institutions that was about to begin.

Much of this general literature was in the literary form of the language, for only thus could it win the respect of scholars. Some of the textbooks seem to have been in the vernacular, however, and a few religious books and school-books appeared in Roman letters.[86] The missionaries were attempting to reach the masses as well as the learned.

Protestant missionaries were not content with producing literature for the Chinese, but also prepared it for Westerners. Neither before nor after 1897 was there to the credit of any one

[81] *Records of the Missionary Conference, Shanghai, 1890,* pp. 715-717. At the 1890 Conference the committee recommended that its books, maps, blocks, and other assets be turned over to the Educational Association of China.—Ibid., p. xlviii. See also Graves, *Forty Years in China,* p. 269. See, too, reports of meetings of this committee before 1890 in *Chinese Recorder,* Vol. 10, p. 41, Vol. 11, p. 138, Vol. 12, p. 41.   These show it to have been vigorously at work. Uniformity was desirable in the Chinese terminology representing the new scientific words and ideas from the West, and Fryer urged that this be achieved.— *Records of the Missionary Conference, Shanghai, 1890,* pp. 531-549.
[82] Fisher, *C. W. Mateer,* p. 162.
[83] *China Mission Hand-book,* Part 2, p. 233.
[84] Smith, *Uplift of China,* p. 222.
[85] Martin, *A Cycle of Cathay,* pp. 234, 235; Martin, *The Awakening of China,* p. 288.
[86] Brewster, *The Evolution of the New China,* p. 106; *China Mission Handbook,* Part 2, p. 65; Johnston, *China and Formosa,* p. 260; Gibson in *Records of the Missionary Conference, Shanghai, 1890,* pp. 62-89.

mission any such long list of scholarly monographs on China as those issued from the Jesuit press at Zikawei. The total of important works by Protestants was, however, probably larger than that by Catholics in the nineteenth century. A number of dictionaries were compiled,[87] for example, that of the Amoy vernacular by Carstairs Douglas,[88] one of Cantonese and a *Concise Dictionary of Chinese* by John Chalmers,[89] and a Cantonese dictionary by Eitel.[90] Books were written to introduce foreigners to the language, such as the large volume used by a generation or more of students, Mateer's *Mandarin Lessons.*[91] There were, moreover, many books on China and Chinese subjects, some of them popular and semi-popular, such as Nevius' *China and the Chinese* and Doolittle's *Social Life of the Chinese,* and others of a more erudite nature, such as the monumental translations of classical literature by James Legge, volumes on Chinese religion by Edkins, the careful works of the self-effacing Wylie, one of the greatest of missionary scholars, the books on Confucius and Mencius and Chinese religion by Ernst Faber, and the numerous volumes by Eitel. Many of these were later to be superseded, but some are still the best of their kind in English, and they helped to create in the Occident, especially in the English-speaking portion of the Occident, a greater appreciation of the Chinese, and furthered the study of China by the scholars of the West.

Missionaries edited a good many periodicals. At the 1890 Conference thirteen (Protestant) Christian periodicals in Chinese were reported, the oldest being *The Children's News,* begun in Foochow in 1874.[92] One, *A Review of the Times,* started by Young J. Allen and later taken over by the Society for the Diffusion of Christian and General Knowledge among the Chinese, was designed to convey Western ideas to officials and scholars.[93] Some of the periodicals were in English and were primarily for missionaries. Of these, the leading one for the

[87] For a complete list see Cordier, *Bibliotheca Sinica,* 1588-1625, 3155-3157.
[88] Douglas, *Memorials of Rev. Carstairs Douglas,* passim.
[89] *Encyclopædia Sinica,* p. 87.
[90] Ibid., p. 157.
[91] Fisher, *C. W. Mateer,* p. 162. *The Mandarin Lessons* were first published in 1892.
[92] *Records of the Missionary Conference, Shanghai, 1890,* p. xlvi. A full list of periodicals, including those discontinued (of which there were a number), is given in ibid., pp. 720-724. See, too, Farnham, *Historical Sketch of the Shanghai Station* (in *Jubilee Papers of the Central China Presbyterian Mission*), p. 67.
[93] Cornaby, *The Call of Cathay,* p. 103.

entire missionary body was *The Chinese Recorder. The Chinese Repository,* in some respects its predecessor, had been discontinued in 1851. A gap of sixteen years followed in which no journal attempted to minister to all the Protestant missionary group. *The Missionary Recorder,* published at Foochow in 1867 by L. N. Wheeler, was suspended after the first volume and was followed in May, 1868, by *The Chinese Recorder and Missionary Journal.* This in turn lapsed in 1872, but reappeared in 1874, issued from Shanghai. By its news of the various missions and articles on China and missions in China it served to tie the Protestant missionary body together and to influence missionary thought.[94]

The printing and distribution of the literature prepared by Protestant missionaries were accomplished by various agencies. Several societies maintained presses. Ten were reported in 1895 [95] and another was added in 1897.[96] Of these probably the most important was the American Presbyterian Mission Press. First (1844) located at Macao, it was moved to Ningpo in 1845 and to Shanghai in 1860.[97] The other important ones were that of the American Board, destroyed by fire in Canton in 1856 and reopened in Peking in 1868, that of the London Missionary Society, discontinued in 1873, and that of the American Methodists in Foochow, opened in 1861.[98]

Much, perhaps most, of the distribution of literature was by denominational missions. Most of the printing and much of the distribution of the Scriptures were, however, by the British and Foreign Bible Society, the American Bible Society, and the National Bible Society of Scotland. The first two were in the Empire before 1856. About 1863 or 1864 the British and Foreign Bible Society appointed as its agent in China Alexander Wylie,

[94] *Chinese Recorder,* Vol. 1, p. 6, Vol. 2, p. 234, Vol. 5, p. 1, Vol. 11, p. 209; Wheeler, *The Foreigner in China,* p. 13; *China Mission Year Book, 1914,* pp. 468-471.

[95] These were the presses of the American Presbyterian Mission, of the American Board, of the Church Missionary Society, of the English Presbyterians, of the National Bible Society of Scotland, of the Society for the Diffusion of Christian and General Knowledge, of the Methodist Episcopal Mission at Foochow, of the Central China Press at Kiukiang, and of The China Inland Mission Press at Taichow.—*China Mission Hand-book,* Part 2, pp. 315-323. See also *Chinese Recorder,* Vol. 10, pp. 209, 210, 270.

[96] That of the Canadian Methodists in West China.—*A Century of Protestant Missions in China,* p. 640.

[97] *Chinese Recorder,* Vol. 1, p. 167, Vol. 10, p. 212.

[98] Ibid., Vol. 10, pp. 212 et seq., pp. 273 et seq.

who previously had been in charge of the press of the London
Missionary Society. Wylie, in addition to his work in the central
office, travelled widely. Under his direction, too, several foreign
and a number of Chinese colporteurs were employed and covered
a large part of the Empire, circulating the Scriptures. When, in
1877, because of failing eyesight, Wylie retired, he had seen
distributed the last of the million New Testaments provided by
the special fund in the fifties. Under his successor, Samuel Dyer,
the Society still further increased its circulation and the number
of its agents.[99]

Like the British Society, the American Bible Society appointed
a supervising agent, L. H. Gulick, in 1876, and its circulation
greatly increased, reaching a little over a quarter of a million
volumes in 1887.[100]

The National Bible Society of Scotland was formed in 1860
by the union of several older bodies, and in 1863 sent Alexander
Williamson as its first representative. Williamson remained with
the Society only until 1866, but other agents were employed, the
central office was moved from the North to Hankow, and by
1896 nine Europeans were reported on the staff with about one
hundred Chinese colporteurs.[101]

The original policy of the Bible societies was to distribute the
Scriptures without cost to the recipients, but in the sixties the
conclusion was reached that the Chinese would value the Scriptures more highly if they paid for them.[102] Even then the prices
were so low that many copies were wasted.[103] The major number

[99] *A Century of Protestant Missions in China*, pp. 556-562; *China Mission
Hand-book*, Part 2, p. 296. In 1889 the number of Chinese colporteurs was 116
and there was a circulation of 232,198 a year.—Canton, *History of the British
and Foreign Bible Society*, Vol. 5, pp. 163 et seq.
[100] *A Century of Protestant Missions in China*, pp. 577-580; Dwight,
The Centennial History of the American Bible Society, Vol. 2, pp. 401-409. Gulick
was agent for China and Japan from 1876 to 1881 and in 1881 was assigned to
China alone.
[101] *A Century of Protestant Missions in China*, pp. 567-569; *China Mission
Hand-book*, Part 2, p. 300.
[102] Wylie in *Chinese Recorder*, Vol. 1, p. 149. It was in 1868 that the British
and Foreign Bible Society made the change. See also ibid., Vol. 1, p. 106.
[103] Von Richthofen (*Tagebücher aus China*, Vol. 1, p. 176) heard from Roman
Catholics that Bibles sold by the Protestants were used as soles for shoes. Roman
Catholics had, however, no love for the Protestants and especially disliked their
distribution of the Scriptures. There were other criticisms of the extensive distribution of the Bible. F. H. Balfour, in the *Imperail and Asiatic Quarterly
Review*, Vol. 9 (1890), pp. 12-29, complained that some of the stories in the
Bible were revolting to the Chinese, that much of the book was unintelligible, and
that it contained precepts which seemed to the Chinese blasphemous.

of the volumes distributed were single books—usually one of the Gospels—and not entire Testaments or Bibles.[104]

With the aid of the various missions the Bible societies were gradually making the Scriptures known. The scholar might profess to despise them because of what he deemed the crudity of their style and because they were often put into the vernacular, but he was at least becoming familiar with their existence. They were even reaching the court, for a beautiful copy of the New Testament was presented to the Empress Dowager on her sixtieth birthday by the Christian women of China, and the Emperor, hearing of it, himself soon sent for a copy of the entire Bible.[105]

The Bible societies confined themselves to the printing and circulation of the Scriptures. However, undenominational "tract societies" were formed for the preparation and distribution of other Christian literature, partly at least on the model and with the financial assistance of similar societies in London and New York. Among these were the Central China Religious Tract Society, formed in 1884 (the successor of the Hankow Tract Society, formed in 1876),[106] the East China Tract Society, formed in 1885, the Chinese Religious Tract Society, organized at Shanghai in 1878, the North China Tract Society, the North Fukien Religious Tract Society, and the Kiukiang Tract Society.[107] These sold their literature to missionaries, usually at less than cost, and as a rule had few distributing agents of their own. Much of the material provided by the societies was for the purpose of introducing non-Christians to the Faith, but part of it was for the Christian constituency. Many of the publications were short and simple tracts for the relatively uneducated, but others were more substantial and erudite. Some of the books and tracts were in the literary style and some in the vernacular.

[104] For example, in 1894 out of a total of 989,720 published, 6,575 were entire Bibles, 30,395 were Testaments, and 952,750 were portions of Scripture. *Chinese Recorder,* Vol. 26, p. 508. About 1871 in a tour in Shansi a Mr. Wellman sold 900 Old Testaments, 548 New Testaments, and 3,858 portions of Scripture.— *Chinese Recorder,* Vol. 3, p. 212.

[105] Richard, *Forty-Five Years in China,* p. 224; *Chinese Recorder,* Vol. 26, p. 160.

[106] Thompson, *Griffith John,* pp. 330-338; John, *A Voice from China,* pp. 125-137.

[107] *China Mission Hand-book,* Part 2, pp. 302-306; *Chinese Recorder,* Vol. 23, p. 129; *A Century of Protestant Missions in China,* pp. 613-627; *Missionary Review of the World,* Vol. 3, p. 78; *Chinese Recorder,* Vol. 11, p. 214, Vol. 12, p. 379; *China's Millions,* 1879, p. 27.

A few periodicals were also issued.[108] A beginning in Christian religious literature in Chinese was being made.

Resembling the tract societies, but with a more inclusive purpose, was the Society for the Diffusion of Christian and General Knowledge among the Chinese, later (1906) the Christian Literature Society for China. This was in part an outgrowth of the School and Textbook Series Committee appointed by the 1877 Conference. The secretary of the committee was Alexander Williamson and while in Scotland in 1884 he formed a Chinese Book and Tract Society. The new organization raised money to found a publishing house in Shanghai and to increase the distribution of Christian literature. In 1887, to put into use the funds raised in Scotland, Williamson brought into existence in Shanghai the society whose long name heads this paragraph. Its purpose was partly indicated by its title. Williamson envisaged an organization which should seek primarily to speak to scholars and officials, which should do so not only by literature presenting Christianity directly, but by portraying the fruits of Christianity in Western civilization and by disclosing the elements which had made for progress in the Occident. It was based upon the conviction that China could best be reached through the most influential classes, and that Christian missionaries should seek not only to win individuals but to transform wholesomely the entire life of the Empire, using all that was good in the culture of the West.

Williamson died in 1890, before the Society was more than well begun. Fortunately there was at hand a successor of experience, enthusiasm, and large vision, Timothy Richard. Richard became secretary in 1891 and early outlined a comprehensive program which was to include the publication of periodicals; a series of books and pamphlets showing the bearing of educational and religious development on industry, trade, and national progress; prizes for essays on national progress; the stimulation of other means for the enlightenment of China, such as lectures, museums, and reading-rooms; depots for the sale of publications; coöperation with the Chinese; and the distribution of literature at the civil service examinations. Williamson and Richard were more confident that Western culture possessed excellencies from which China could benefit than was a later generation of missionaries.

[108] *A Century of Protestant Missions in China,* pp. 613-628.

Richard, however, was warmly appreciative, sometimes almost quixotically so, of the praiseworthy features of Chinese civilization. The time was opportune for such an organization. Many of the educated were beginning to talk of change and were eager for information about the West. Most of the program was carried out and part of it met with a cordial welcome. Material from the monthly *Wan Kuo Kung Pao* (freely translated as "Review of the Times") was copied widely in the newly emerging Chinese press; there was a periodical for Chinese Christians, the *Chung Hsi Chiao Hui Pao;* Richard's translation of Mackenzie's *History of the Nineteenth Century* was so widely sold, and still more widely pirated, that Richard believed that a million or more copies were in circulation; financial aid was received not only from Great Britain and America but from such prominent officials as the Viceroy Chang Chih-tung and the Shanghai Tao-t'ai Nieh; and the Society's publications were distributed at several provincial capitals among the scholars gathered for the civil service examinations. The organization had no small part in aiding and molding the earlier stages of the transformation of China.[109] The Protestants' lavish use of the printed page was beginning to have its effect.

SCHOOLS

A necessary companion of the printed page was education: if people were to be provided with literature they must be taught to use it. If the Bible was the authoritative witness to the Christian faith, as most Protestants believed, all Christians should at least be enabled to read it. In earlier chapters we have described how from almost the beginning of their efforts in China Protestant missionaries had been conducting schools. After 1856 schools increasingly became a feature of the missionary program. Mateer probably spoke for many when, in the 1877 Conference, he said that he believed the purpose of Christian education to be to provide a native ministry; to train teachers for Christian schools and "through them to introduce to China the superior education of the West"; to prepare men "to take the lead in

[109] Richard, *Forty-Five Years in China,* pp. 218, 221, 223, 230; (The Christian Literature Society) *Christian Literature and the Reform Movement in China; Missionary Review of the World,* Vol. 22, p. 113; *Chinese Recorder,* Vol. 23, p. 131; *China Mission Hand-book,* Part 2, p. 307; *A Century of Protestant Missions in China,* pp. 628-633. On this and an allied work for the educated classes see Duncan, *The Missionary Mail,* p. 18; Richard, *Conversion by the Million,* Vol. 2, pp. 101-107; Reeve, *Timothy Richard,* p. 152.

introducing to China the science and arts of Western Civilization" as "the best means of gaining access to the higher classes of China" (for Western science was already gaining in repute and many of the higher classes were eager to learn about it); and to "give the native church self-reliance" and to guard it from superstition within and from the attacks of educated sceptics from without. To fulfil this purpose Mateer advocated that the emphasis be upon advanced rather than primary schools.[110]

By no means all missionaries agreed with Mateer: many thought of schools as being for the purpose of giving a limited amount of education to Christians, of reaching non-Christians, and of training Chinese "assistants." [111] Some, indeed, maintained very few schools, believing their primary task to be the diffusion of a knowledge of the Christian faith by methods which would more quickly reach the entire nation. At the 1890 Conference the China Inland Mission, for instance, reported three hundred and sixty-six missionaries and only a hundred and eighty-two pupils in schools, while the London Missionary Society, with sixty-five missionaries, reported 2,124 pupils in schools.[112] On the whole, however, schools showed a rapid growth. In 1876 5,917 students were reported,[113] and in 1889 16,836.[114]

Educational institutions and methods were of many types. One was modeled after existing Chinese schools.[115] A missionary of the Basel Society subsidized the teachers in non-Christian schools to introduce Christian subjects and literature into their curriculums.[116] Some schools were entirely for Christians,[117]

---

[110] Records of the General Conference of the Protestant Missionaries in China, 1877, pp. 160-203.
[111] Lechler in Records of the General Conference of the Protestant Missionaries in China, 1877, pp. 160-203. See another statement of the purpose of the mission school by J. Jackson in Chinese Recorder, Vol. 23, pp. 557 et seq.; it was, so Jackson said, to give a good education, inculcate patriotism, develop conscience, and supplement the message of the pulpit. A. J. Gordon (Chinese Recorder, Vol. 25, pp. 71 et seq.) contended that education was not an aid to evangelization but a hindrance, for it secularized missions, exalted the intellect, and discouraged work among the poor. See also Chinese Recorder, Vol. 1, p. 132.
[112] Records of the Missionary Conference, Shanghai, 1890, p. 732.
[113] Chinese Recorder, Vol. 9, p. 115. In 1869 incomplete returns gave 4,389 pupils in the schools.—Ibid., Vol. 2, p. 63.
[114] Records of the Missionary Conference, Shanghai, 1890, p. 732.
[115] Ross, Mission Methods in Manchuria, p. 147.
[116] This was G. A. Hauspach of the Berlin Mission.—Lechler in Records of the Missionary Conference, Shanghai, 1890, p. 448.
[117] There were, too, Sunday Schools, in the main of the general type familiar in the West, and only for religious instruction. There were 475 in about 1893.— China Mission Hand-book, Part 2, p. 324.

others for non-Christians, and some were for both. Some were day schools, others boarding schools. The majority were for boys, but a considerable proportion were for girls. Most of the students were in the elementary grades, but there were numbers of higher schools, and, at the other extreme, the kindergarten was introduced (apparently in 1894).[118]

Curriculums differed greatly, but in the large majority both Chinese and Western subjects were to be found. The Chinese Classics were usually taught, for although here and there were those who believed that these had an unchristian influence, the majority of educators agreed that the Chinese youth should be well grounded in their national literature.[119] Some of the teachers, especially of Chinese subjects, were non-Christians, but their employment was deplored.[120]

English was taught in a large number of the schools of higher grade, and in some it was the medium of instruction for Western subjects. This practice was debated at length. The protagonists maintained that many Chinese wished to learn English and that if the missionary did not teach it they would get it elsewhere and under non-Christian auspices; that English was superior to Chinese in precision and clearness; that its possessor had open to him a vast field of Western literature which was not, and most of which would not be translated, and that he was in a position to keep abreast of modern thought. The opponents contended that few pupils remained in school long enough to acquire sufficient English to enable them to read it well, that its use reduced the time spent on Chinese, that it tended to separate the student from the masses of his fellow-countrymen, and that most of those seeking it desired it only as a means of obtaining employment in the customs service, in minor government positions, and in foreign business houses.[121]

[118] Smith, *Rex Christus*, p. 175.
[119] See discussion in the *Records of the Missionary Conference, Shanghai, 1890*, pp. 490-509. See also *Chinese Recorder*, Vol. 1, p. 132, Vol. 10, pp. 285 et seq., Vol. 24, pp. 573 et seq.; Faber, *Problems of Practical Christianity in China*, p. 51. (Faber was opposed to the use of the Classics in Christian schools except in those of higher grade.)
[120] See Kupfer in *Chinese Recorder*, Vol. 24, p. 107. See also *Chinese Recorder*, Vol. 26, p. 76.
[121] *Chinese Recorder*, Vol. 1, p. 249, Vol. 12, pp. 225, 233, Vol. 17, p. 417, Vol. 20, pp. 405, 469, 470; *Records of the Second Triennial Meeting of the Educational Association of China, 1896; Records of the Missionary Conference, Shanghai, 1890*, pp. 456-509; Fisher, *Mateer*, p. 229. Mateer was one of the leading opponents of the use of English as a medium of instruction. See, too, for criticisms

Whatever the relative proportion between the Chinese and Western portions of the curriculum, however, and whatever the medium of instruction, Protestant mission schools were bringing into China new subjects of study and new methods and ideals. They were forerunners of a revolution in education.

Roman Catholic missionaries were giving no such place to the school, especially to the higher grade of school, and except in the training of the clergy were not yet making any such extensive innovations in subjects and methods. Before 1897, moreover, government and private schools of a new type were very few. The Protestant missionary, then, by establishing a majority of the best schools in which Western learning was first taught, was able to exert a commanding influence on the new education and to gain for the Protestant community, trained in the new ways, a place in the China that followed 1900 quite out of proportion to its numerical strength.

Protestant missionaries not only reaped the benefits but paid the price of being pioneers. Their schools were by no means always popular. For centuries the goal of education in China had been success in the government examinations, with the coveted literary degrees, social position, and possibly office and wealth as the tempting reward. The mission institutions were popularly supposed, and probably correctly, not to be as good places in which to acquire preparation for the civil service examinations as were the schools maintained by the Chinese. As a result, in their earlier years they were patronized only by parents who were Christians, or who could not afford the usual Chinese education for their sons, or who desired to fit their sons for employment

of the use of English, Graves, *Forty Years in China*, p. 207. The general tendency was to lay emphasis on English. Many Chinese wished it for their sons, for it was the language of commerce, of the Imperial Maritime Customs Service, and of some of the consular services. It could usually be had only in Protestant schools, and those schools which offered it experienced less difficulty in getting pupils than did those which refused to teach it. Pupils in English-teaching schools came, too, from more prosperous homes and were able to pay a larger share of the expense of instruction than did those in schools where English was not taught or where it was not emphasized. English was used as a medium of instruction in St. John's in 1880 or 1882, in the Anglo-Chinese College at Foochow in 1881, in the American Board's boys' boarding school at Foochow in 1891, in Canton Christian College from the beginning, in Boone College from 1891, and in the Methodist Universities at Nanking and Peking from their foundation.—Leger, *Education of Christian Ministers in China*, pp. 16, 17.

On the growing demand for English in the seventies and eighties, see Henry, *The Cross and the Dragon*, pp. 451-481.

in the Imperial Maritime Customs Service or a foreign business firm. In many instances missionaries had not only to grant free tuition but to give food, lodging, and clothing.[122] As time passed, parents were required to pay part of the cost, but until after 1897, with few if any exceptions, the schools were not self-supporting.[123] Those that taught English, however, had a financial advantage over those that did not,[124] for in that language they possessed a subject with a monetary value. Mission schools were often poorly equipped and experienced difficulty in obtaining good teachers.[125] Chinese teachers of Western subjects, indeed, they had as a rule to train for themselves. They were beginning a new teaching profession which was later to be in demand.

In spite of obstacles, excellent educational institutions arose. The Basel Society, for example, as early as 1886 had a system of schools with seven years of elementary grade, then four years of middle school, and then, for those preparing for the ministry, a theological course of four years.[126] Several other missions maintained schools which gave instruction above the primary years. There were, for instance, several "Anglo-Chinese colleges," such as that maintained by the Northern Methodists at Foochow,[127] and that founded in Shanghai by Young J. Allen of the Southern Methodists.[128] These did not offer what in the United States would be called college training, but were boarding schools in which Western subjects and English as well as Chinese were taught and which carried their students on into secondary work. Much of their instruction was in English and they became popular with those to whom that language and a smattering of Occidental lore meant business advancement.

A number of "high schools" began to appear. Mateer's school at Têngchow in Shantung, for example, was raised to that rank

[122] Cowling in *Chinese Recorder*, Vol. 25, p. 86; Fisher, *Mateer*, pp. 132, 133; *China Mission Hand-book*, Part 2, p. 154.

[123] *Chinese Recorder*, Vol. 17, p. 15.

[124] *China Mission Hand-book*, Part 2, p. 154.

[125] *Chinese Recorder*, Vol. 23, p. 202, Vol. 25, p. 391.

[126] *Chinese Recorder*, Vol. 17, pp. 112 et seq.

[127] Founded in 1881, partly through the gift of $10,000 for the purpose by a Chinese.—*A Century of Protestant Missions in China*, pp. 433-435.

[128] Ibid., p. 417; *China Mission Hand-book*, Part 2, p. 232. It was founded in 1882 and its purpose was to meet the demand for English-speaking Chinese employees in government offices, the customs service, telegraph offices, and the like. By 1898 over 2,000 boys had been in it.—*Work and Progress in China of the Methodist Episcopal Church, South*, p. 51.

in 1864; [129] in 1879 the Ningpo presbytery began planning for one; [130] and in 1885 there arrived in Central China W. T. A. Barber, sent out by the Wesleyan Missionary Society to open a high school in Wuchang to give a Western education to the sons of officials and other wealthy Chinese.[131]   Most of the "colleges" conducted by English societies were of about the same grade as the high schools and Anglo-Chinese colleges.   Thus the Church Missionary Society had a college at Ningpo, founded in 1876.[132] At least one normal school was maintained, that opened in 1888 by the American Presbyterians at Chefoo.[133]

Higher education of what in the United States would be called college grade followed almost as a matter of course.   Of the American missionaries, a large proportion had been trained in church colleges and nearly all came from groups of Christians which regarded the founding and maintenance of such institutions as one of the normal functions of a denomination.   In the United States, where by the middle of the nineteenth century the state had taken over almost all primary education except Roman Catholic parochial schools, colleges and academies were usually the only portions of the educational system in which the churches shared.[134]   Before 1897 the greater part of the higher education of the nation was in colleges on ecclesiastical foundation.   Nearly every state had a number, sometimes thirty or more.   Some were christened "universities," although with rare exceptions that title was an expression of ambitious hope rather than a description of fact.   The course was of four years' duration and presupposed a preparation of from ten to twelve years, but to many, probably to most colleges, since before 1890 public high schools were few and often poor, a preparatory department was attached.   The curriculums were usually a combination of Latin and Greek, philosophy, mathematics, and, by 1897, sciences of various kinds, history, and English literature.   They were, accordingly, humanistic in their trend rather than technical and professional.

It is not surprising that American missionaries wished to repro-

[129] *A Century of Protestant Missions in China*, p. 389.
[130] Garratt, *Historical Sketch of the Ningpo Station*, in *Jubilee Papers of the Central China Presbyterian Mission*, p. 29.
[131] Foster, *Christian Progress in China*, p. 156.
[132] Stock, *History of the Church Missionary Society*, Vol. 3, p. 572.
[133] *China Mission Hand-book*, Part 2, p. 198.
[134] There were, too, many "academies," schools doing work of secondary and sometimes of primary grade, but by the last of the nineteenth century these were being crowded out by the state-supported high school.

duce the type of college with which they were familiar. Before
1897 a number of institutions were begun which the founders
hoped would be of a grade and have an influence comparable
to that of their prototypes. The promoters believed that the
Church would thus be provided with a well-trained leadership,
lay and clerical, and that Christianity would achieve a larger
influence in the life and thought of the nation. The curriculums
inherited from America were modified somewhat to meet Chinese
needs—principally by introducing Chinese literature—but in general their aim was to produce Christian leaders by teaching humanistic subjects in a strongly Christian environment. These Christian colleges were by no means utterly alien, however, for the
traditional education of China was humanistic, and in time they,
like the Chinese examination system, offered degrees. In large
measure, however, they were distinctly an innovation and bore
unmistakable indications of their American parentage. They
were unmistakably foreign institutions.

At the beginning most of the colleges were not, in practice,
above the grade of an American secondary school. To each,
moreover, as in the United States, a preparatory department was
attached, which sometimes extended down into the primary years.
After 1897, however, and especially after 1900, the colleges were
able to raise their standards.

Before 1897 those institutions which professed to be colleges
in the American sense of the term, or had announced their purpose of becoming so, were not numerous. In 1881 or 1882 the
Shantung presbytery formally voted to ask the home board to
sanction enlarging into a college the high school at Têngchow.
The board consented and sent out Mr. and Mrs. W. M. Hayes
to assist in the project.[135] In 1885 Timothy Richard, with his
customary breadth of vision, proposed to the English Baptist
Missionary Society that, as a means of influencing the leaders of
the Empire to accept the Christian faith, all societies unite in
establishing in each provincial capital, beginning with those of
the maritime provinces, a high class college. He asked permission, as a first step toward realizing this plan, to found one
at the capital of Shansi, but his fellow missionaries did not
approve. Later he went to Shantung, where he wished to open
such an institution at Tsinanfu, but his board refused its endorse-

[135] Fisher, *Mateer*, p. 207; Mateer, *Character Building in China*, p. 55.

ment.[136] In the latter part of the seventies Schereschewsky, recently consecrated bishop, appealed for $100,000 for the establishment of a college in China. A portion of the sum was obtained,[137] land was purchased at Jessfield on the outskirts of Shanghai, and in 1879 the first building of St. John's College was erected and instruction was begun.[138] The first class from the collegiate department graduated in the nineties.[139] On the advice of Bishop Fowler, who foresaw a demand in China for higher education of a partially Western type, in 1888 the Northern Methodists began two institutions, one in Nanking and one in Peking, each with the hopeful cognomen of university. John C. Ferguson was appointed president of the University of Nanking, and in 1889 a school was opened in his house. Medical and theological departments were begun a few years later,[140] but few advanced courses were offered until after 1900. Peking University was incorporated in 1890 by the legislature of the State of New York and a board of trustees was constituted in New York City. The following year a board of managers was formed in Peking and included, in addition to members of the Methodist Mission, representatives of the foreign community, the American Board, and the London Missionary Society—a prophecy of the later international and undenominational character of the institution. The first building was erected in 1892 and in that year the first class was graduated. By 1896 there were one hundred and twenty-five students and standards were held to be as high as those of colleges in the Occident.[141]

In 1884 the American Presbyterian Mission at Canton authorized B. C. Henry to go to the United States and inaugurate plans for a Christian college at Canton. Most of the initial funds were raised by Andrew P. Happer (who, it may be recalled, first came to China in 1844) and by the close of 1887 about $100,000 had been obtained. Happer was the first president, but because of

[136] Richard, *Forty-Five Years in China*, pp. 197-213.
[137] *Spirit of Missions*, Vol. 42, p. 307.
[138] Ibid., Vol. 49, p. 321, Vol. 44, p. 277; *A Century of Protestant Missions in China*, p. 298.
[139] *Educational Review*, Vol. 9, p. 127; Mosher, *Institutions Connected with the American Church Mission*, p. 2.
[140] *A Century of Protestant Missions in China*, p. 443.
[141] *Encyclopædia Sinica*, p. 429; *Chinese Recorder*, Vol. 23, p. 28; *China Mission Hand-book*, Part 2, pp. 222, 224; *China Mission Year Book, 1910*, p. 73; *A Century of Protestant Missions in China*, p. 449; *Educational Review*, Vol. 8, p. 155.

ill-health was early compelled to return to the United States. In 1893 the college was incorporated under the regents of the University of the State of New York as the "Trustees of the Christian College in China." Property was purchased and in 1895 one hundred and five students were reported, twenty-two of them in the collegiate and theological departments.[142]

In 1889 the high school maintained by the American Board at T'ungchow, a few miles east of Peking, was expanded into The North China College, with D. Z. Sheffield as president, and by 1900 several years of college work had been completed.[143] By 1896, too, the American Board's boarding school for boys at Foochow was called a college.[144]

Protestant missions not only led in developing new types of educational institutions for men, but they inaugurated new forms of training for women. The Chinese had not entirely neglected the education of women and took pride in noteworthy examples of accomplished scholars from among the fair sex. However, possibly because women could not compete in the civil service examinations, no provision was made for them in the usual school and very few were literate. The Roman Catholics had long maintained schools for girls, but these were chiefly for the purpose of teaching the catechism and usually did not give a general education except of the most elementary kind. Protestants early began schools for girls and regarded them as one of the main features of their educational program. Nearly every mission supported one.[145] Sometimes it was a day-school, but frequently it was a boarding school.[146] The curriculums of the girls' schools seem always to have included learning to read the Bible, either in the Chinese character or in Roman letters or both, and they appear usually to have added subjects useful in the

[142] Henry, *The Cross and the Dragon*, pp. 451-481; Trumbull, *Old Time Student Volunteers*, pp. 164-168; *Chinese Recorder*, Vol. 27, p. 136; *China Mission Hand-book*, Part 2, p. 189; Barton, *Educational Missions*, p. 251; Edmunds, *Canton Christian College*, p. 10; *A Century of Protestant Missions in China*, pp. 546, 547.
[143] *A Century of Protestant Missions in China*, p. 277; *Educational Review*, Vol. 18, p. 302; *China Mission Hand-book*, Part 2, p. 158; *Chinese Recorder*, Vol. 26, p. 224.
[144] *China Mission Hand-book*, Part 2, p. 154.
[145] Of 4,389 pupils in mission schools reported in 1869, 576 were girls.—*Chinese Recorder*, Vol. 2, p. 63. Of the 5,686 reported in 1876 or 1877, 2,084 were girls.—Ibid., Vol. 9, p. 115.
[146] In Hongkong, for example, the wives of the missionaries of the London Missionary Society started a school for girls beside the Anglo-Chinese College.—*L. M. S. Chronicle*, Vol. 3 (new series), p. 176.

home, such as needlework, housekeeping, hygiene, and the like, and perhaps music and Chinese literature.[147] A few schools taught English.[148]

Before 1897 the mission schools for girls seem as a rule to have been chiefly patronized by Christians and many of their graduates married pastors or became teachers or "Bible women," devoting their time to reaching members of their sex with the Christian message and helping those already Christian to grow in the Faith.[149] Schools for women were such an innovation and the distrust felt for the foreigner was frequently so lively that difficulty was often experienced in obtaining pupils. For years it seems to have been customary for the missions to defray all the girls' expenses.[150] A few among the girls' schools were one opened in Amoy in 1870 by the (Dutch) Reformed Church and moved in 1880 to the Island of Kulangsu, across the harbor;[151] a boarding school in Canton founded by the (Northern) American Presbyterians and later developed into The True Light Seminary;[152] The Bridgman School, begun in Peking in 1864 by Mrs. Bridgman and later moved to Shanghai;[153] boarding schools maintained at Swatow and Amoy by the English Presbyterians;[154] St. Mary's Hall, maintained by the American Episcopalians in Shanghai and formed in 1881 by the consolidation of two earlier schools;[155] The Baltimore Female Seminary founded by Methodists at Foochow in 1859;[156] and The McTyeire School in Shanghai, named after the bishop by that name, and opened in 1892 as the result of the untiring efforts of Laura Haygood. The

[147] Graves, *Forty Years in China*, p. 213; Chamberlain, *Fifty Years in Foreign Fields*, pp. 20-46; Ashmore, *The South China Mission of the American Baptist Foreign Mission Society*, p. 95. The Bridgman School at Peking taught the Bible, the Four Books (of the Chinese Classics), arithmetic, geography, physical geography, history, science, biology, and physiology.—*China Mission Hand-book*, Part 2, p. 189.

[148] Chamberlain, op. cit., p. 44; Burton, *Notable Women of China*, p. 23.

[149] *A Century of Protestant Missions in China*, p. 422.

[150] In return at least one mission required parents to sign a contract agreeing to leave their daughters in the school until they were twenty years of age and to give the missions a veto in betrothals.—Ibid., p. 422. In some schools the parents clothed the girls.—Burton, *Education of Women in China*, p. 57; *China Mission Hand-book*, Part 2, p. 58.

[151] Chamberlain, op. cit., pp. 21-46.

[152] *China Mission Hand-book*, Part 2, p. 189; Noyes, *A Light in the Land of Sinim*, passim.

[153] Burton, op. cit., pp. 50-57; *A Century of Protestant Missions in China*, p. 469; *Spirit of Missions*, Vol. 40, p. 512.

[154] *China Mission Hand-book*, Part 2, pp. 54, 58.

[155] *Spirit of Missions*, Vol. 65, p. 284.

[156] Burton, op. cit., p. 41.

McTyeire School was especially for girls of the higher classes whom their parents refused to send to the usual mission institution.[157]

There were a number of schools for special trades and professions. At least one industrial school was begun and several missionaries vigorously advocated education of that type. They held that it would fit pupils for life in China better than did much of the training ordinarily given in a mission school.[158] Of medical education more will be said later, and what has already been said concerning theological education need not here be repeated or amplifide.

Long before 1897 a need for coöperation in education was beginning to be felt. The School and Textbook Series Committee of the 1877 Conference was an early and important attempt to meet it. Missionary educators took the opportunity given by the 1890 Conference to form (in May, 1890) what they called The Educational Association of China. This ambitiously named organization stated its object, with equal comprehensiveness, to be "the promotion of educational interests in China and the fraternal coöperation of all those engaged in teaching." To it were turned over the materials gathered by the committee of the 1877 Conference. Its meetings were held triennially and were of growing importance.[159] Protestant missionaries were not only introducing new types of education: some of them were dreaming of the day when all schools of the new order would be coördinated into one fellowship.

[157] Gamewell, *The Gateway to China*, p. 245; *China Mission Hand-book*, Part 2, p. 232; Cannon, *History of Southern Methodist Missions*, pp. 108, 109. The school was under the Southern Methodist Mission. See also on the education of women, Walker, *Sophia Cooke*, the account of the work of a woman in the school for girls in Singapore maintained by the Society for Promoting Female Education in the East, and Piercy, *Love for China*, the account of the life of Mary Gunson, the first woman teacher of the (English) Wesleyan Missionary Society in Canton. She was invalided home after three years in China.

[158] This was especially exemplified by the Chefoo Industrial School.—*Chinese Recorder*, Vol. 25, pp. 130 et seq. See also *China Mission Hand-book*, Part 2, p. 267, for the decision of the Foreign Christian Missionary Society to start a department of manual training in its boys' boarding school at Nanking. For the report of a committee on industrial education see *Chinese Recorder*, Vol. 20, pp. 51 et seq. For a plea by Dr. Kupfer for the teaching of trades and professions, see *Chinese Recorder*, Vol. 17, p. 445. The (American Methodist) Hinghua Anglo-Chinese high school began industrial work in 1895 to enable students to pay their own way.—Brewster, *The Evolution of New China*, p. 90.

[159] *China Mission Hand-book*, Part 2, p. 311; *A Century of Protestant Missions in China*, pp. 582, 583; *Chinese Recorder*, Vol. 23, pp. 30, 213. By 1893 the Association had fifty-two members.

MEDICAL MISSIONS

With the founding of churches, the preparation and distribution of literature, and the maintenance of schools, the physician went hand in hand as a characteristic feature of Protestant missions. The Chinese possessed a large medical literature, an extensive pharmacopœia, and many physicians. They knew little of anatomy, however, and what information they had was not acquired by dissecting the human body. Their theories of the causes of illness were often bizarre, and their treatment of disease had more of quackery and superstition than of science. Western medicine, and especially Western surgery, with the enormous strides made in the last half of the nineteenth century through the development of anæsthetics and antiseptics, had much to contribute toward the alleviation, healing, and prevention of disease in China. It is not strange, then, that, beginning with Peter Parker medical men came to China under the auspices of Protestant missions. Physicians early found not only that they could relieve much suffering, but that they could often break down the prejudice against the Christian faith, and that in their hospital and dispensary they could combine the healing of bodies with the cure of souls.

Following 1856 a steady development was made in the medical branch of Protestant missions. In 1874 ten medical missionaries were reported,[160] and about 1881, nineteen.[161] About 1876 sixteen hospitals, twenty-four dispensaries, and 41,281 patients were reported,[162] and in 1889 the totals were sixty-one hospitals, forty-four dispensaries, and 348,439 patients.[163] It is manifestly impossible within the limits of these pages to do more than enumerate some of the main features of so large an enterprise and name a few of the more noteworthy examples of the many who had a part in it.

The work of the medical missionary, as may be gathered from these statistics, was performed chiefly in hospitals and dispensaries, and from these as centers. Judged by later standards in the West, hospitals were small and poorly equipped. As a rule, however,

[160] *Chinese Recorder,* Vol. 6, p. 342.
[161] Ibid., Vol. 13, p. 308.
[162] Ibid., Vol. 9, p. 115.
[163] *Records of the Missionary Conference, Shanghai, 1890,* p. 732.

they were the only ones of their kind. Since the religious purpose was held to be quite as important as the physical,[164] the physician in charge was sometimes theologically trained and to the staffs were attached Chinese whose duty it was to present the Christian message to the patients, and religious services were regularly held. Few patients left without some impression of the faith of those in charge. While no one was turned away because of his poverty, the cost of maintaining the hospitals was partially met by the income from fees and from gifts from friendly Chinese.[165] In the absence of a medically trained colleague the ordained missionary often dispensed remedies for the simpler disorders, but as time passed each of the main mission centers usually had at least one physician.[166] The foreign physician was regarded at first with suspicion,[167] and ugly rumors accused him of seeking the hearts and eyes of his patients for medicine. With many, however, this prejudice soon passed and the news of the cures wrought, especially by the surgeon's knife, brought to the foreigner all whom he could treat.

The Medical Missionary Society of China, founded at Canton in pre-treaty days, suffered from the passing, with the first war with Great Britain, of the peculiar foreign society in which it had had its birth. It continued, however, and in time seems to have given its support entirely to the hospital in Canton which, although not always on the same site or under the same control, was the successor to that opened by Peter Parker. For nearly half a century the hospital was directed by Dr. J. G. Kerr of the American Presbyterian Mission (North), and under him and his staff over a million patients were treated, medical literature was produced, and Chinese were trained for the profession.[168] To Dr. Kerr, too, was due an asylum for the insane, apparently the first in China. Kerr broached the project in 1872, but not until

[164] A paper at the 1877 Conference was fairly typical when it held that the purpose of the medical missionary was, first, to relieve suffering better than Chinese methods could do, second, to break down prejudice against Christianity, and, third, to win the patients to the Christian faith.—*Records of the General Conference of the Protestant Missionaries of China, 1877*, pp. 114-132.
[165] Douthwaite in *Records of the Missionary Conference, Shanghai, 1890*, pp. 268-279.
[166] Soothill, *A Typical Mission in China*, pp. 149-163.
[167] See, for instance, Bryson, *Mackenzie*, p. 47.
[168] *China Review*, Vol. 14, p. 363; *Chinese Recorder*, Vol. 1, pp. 118, 263, Vol. 7, p. 193; Henry, *Ling-nam*, pp. 35 et seq.; Graves, *Forty Years in China*, p. 238; *A Century of Protestant Missions in China*, pp. 653-655.

1892 was a site purchased—and then by the founder's personal funds—and not until 1898 were the buildings completed and open for patients.[169]

Dr. Lockhart of the London Missionary Society arrived in Peking in 1861, and by 1866 the Society opened in the capital a hospital which was to stand until the troubles of 1900.[170]

One of the largest pieces of medical work in China was for a time that begun at Swatow (ca. 1863) by William Gauld of the English Presbyterian Mission. In 1867 a new hospital was erected, built to accommodate fifty or sixty patients, and in 1874 it cared for seven hundred and eighty-six in-patients.[171]

Dr. John Kenneth Mackenzie of the London Missionary Society was very prominent. He went to China in 1875 and for a time was in Hankow, serving in a hospital erected by his society and by the gifts of Chinese and foreign residents. Because of his wife's health, within a few years he moved to Tientsin. There he won official favor by bringing the wife of Li Hung-chang, the Viceroy, through a serious illness. Through funds contributed by Li and his grateful wife, and by other Chinese, a hospital was erected (1880) and in connection with it Mackenzie began a small medical school, most of whose graduates went into government service. After Mackenzie's death (1888) official support was withdrawn from the hospital, but the institution was purchased by his society and his work was continued by Dr. F. C. Roberts, who for a time had helped Gilmour in Mongolia.[173]

Mention has already been made of Dr. Harold A. Schofield, the brilliant young physician who, abandoning his prospects for a notable career in Great Britain, at his own charges went to China in 1880 under the China Inland Mission to be the first

[169] *China Mission Year Book, 1915,* p. 544; *A Century of Protestant Missions in China,* p. 594.
[170] Lockhart, *Medical Missionary Practice in Peking in 1861-1862,* in *Chinese and Japanese Repository,* Vol. 1, pp. 472-480, 483-494; *L. M. S. Chronicle,* Vol. 30, p. 6; *Chinese Recorder,* Vol. 1, p. 51, Vol. 2, p. 113, Vol. 8, p. 209; *A Century of Protestant Missions in China,* p. 10.
[171] Lowe, *Medical Missions,* pp. 128, 129; *Chinese Recorder,* Vol. 1, p. 74, Vol. 7, p. 38.
[172] Bryson, *Mackenzie,* passim. On the Hankow hospital of the London Missionary Society, see *Chinese Recorder,* Vol. 7, p. 419, Vol. 2, p. 318; *China Mission Hand-book,* Part 2, pp. 17, 18. On Roberts see Bryson, *F. C. Roberts of Tientsin,* passim. Roberts died in 1894. A memorial hospital to Roberts was built at Tsangchow, near Tientsin, and here served Arthur D. Peill from 1899 to 1906.—Peill, *The Beloved Physician of Tsang Chou,* passim. On Gilmour's medical work among the Mongols see Gilmour, *More About the Mongols,* pp. 253-263.

medical missionary in Shansi, and three years later died of typhus.[173]

A much longer career was that of Dr. Dugald Christie of the United Free Church of Scotland's mission in Manchuria. Christie was preceded in Manchuria by Dr. Joseph M. Hunter,[174] but his was the most notable medical enterprise in the three great provinces. Beginning in Mukden in 1882, in the face of suspicion which reported him to be one of the vanguard of an English armed invasion of China, declared that his medicine contained a magic which compelled those who received it to follow the foreigner and his teaching, and accused him of using the hearts and eyes of children for photographic purposes, he overcame opposition, won the regard of officials, and, living on into the new day that followed 1900, he was to see his hospital equipment improved and enlarged again and again, Western medicine come more and more into favor, and a medical school established and prosper.[175]

Space is lacking for further details. Something of the extent and importance of the activities of the physician can be gathered, however, from the barest mention of a few other examples—the large hospital of the Church Missionary Society in Hangchow, the center of the notable enterprise of Dr. Duncan Main, who came to China in 1881 and who, like Drs. Christie and Kerr, was to have a long and honored career;[176] the work in and near Amoy by the English Presbyterians,[177] the Reformed Church,[178] and the London Missionary Society;[179] the hospital of the English Wesleyans at Hankow;[180] that built in Formosa by Dr. Maxwell of the English Presbyterian Mission;[181] that in Shanghai

[173] *Memorials of Harold A. Schofield*, passim; Balme, *China and Modern Medicine*, p. 54; *China's Missions*, 1890, p. 51.
[174] Balme, op. cit., p. 51.
[175] Christie, *Thirty Years in the Manchu Capital*, passim; Christie, *Ten Years in Manchuria*, passim; Brown, *The Mastery of the Far East*, p. 211.
[176] Stock, *History of the Church Missionary Society*, Vol. 3, p. 573; Gruchè, *Doctor Apricot of Heaven Below*, passim; Bishop, *The Yangtze Valley and Beyond*, pp. 44-48.
[177] Duncan, *The City of Springs*, p. 73; *China Mission Hand-book*, Part 2, p. 53.
[178] *A Century of Protestant Missions in China*, p. 376.
[179] *L. M. S. Chronicle*, Vol. 43, p. 119; *Chinese Recorder*, Vol. 1, p. 112.
[180] Tatchell, *Medical Missions in China in Connection with the Wesleyan Methodist Church*, pp. 80 et seq.; *Chinese Recorder*, Vol. 2, p. 236, Vol. 7, p. 421, Vol. 3, p. 305. The work in Hankow was begun by Dr. F. Porter Smith in 1864 and a hospital was commenced in that year in rented quarters. In 1866 a new hospital building was opened, apparently the first of its kind in Central China.
[181] *Chinese Recorder*, Vol. 5, p. 143.

begun by the London Missionary Society; [182] another in the same
city maintained by the American Episcopalians; [183] the work
begun in Peking in 1879 under the American Presbyterians by
Dr. B. C. Atterbury and expanded into a hospital—at Dr. Atterbury's expense; [184] the hospital of the American Board at Foochow; [185] the London Missionary Society's Alice Memorial Hospital in Hongkong, erected by a prominent Chinese Christian in
memory of his English wife; the Nethersole Hospital under the
same Society, also in Hongkong; [186] the pioneer efforts of Dr.
Pruen of the China Inland Mission in Chengtu in 1889 and in
Kweiyang in 1890-1894; [187] the hospital built by the Canadian
Methodists at Chengtu in 1894, destroyed by the riots of the
following year, and courageously rebuilt in 1896 and 1897; [188]
and the many years of service at Nanking of Dr. R. C. Beebe
of the (Northern) Methodist Mission. [189] All these efforts together form a noteworthy achievement.

Women physicians had no inconsiderable part in Protestant
medical missions. The first woman medical missionary to China
appears to have been Dr. Combs, who went to Peking in 1873
under the (Northern) American Methodists. With her was
associated Dr. Howard, who founded a hospital in Tientsin and
who treated members of the family of Li Hung-chang. [190] In
1874 a woman physician sent by the Woman's Foreign Missionary Society of the Methodist Episcopal Church arrived in
Foochow. [191] In 1885, as we have seen, the Margaret Williamson
Hospital was opened in Shanghai, largely through the efforts of
Mrs. Williamson, and was maintained by the Woman's Union
Missionary Society of America. [192] In 1896 physicians of the
Women's Foreign Missionary Society of the (Scotch) United

[182] Ibid., Vol. 8, p. 304; *A Century of Protestant Missions in China*, p. 9;
Memorials of James Henderson, M.D. Dr. Henderson was connected with the
hospital in Shanghai from 1859 to 1868.
[183] *Chinese Recorder*, Vol. 8, p. 312.
[184] *China Mission Hand-book*, Part 2, p. 202; Bryson, *Mackenzie*, p. 297.
[185] *Chinese Recorder*, Vol. 7, p. 256.
[186] Bitton, *Our Heritage in China*, p. 53; *L. M. S. Chronicle*, Vol. 45, p. 372,
Vol. 3 (new series), p. 28.
[187] Pruen, *The Provinces of Western China*, pp. 80 et seq.
[188] Bond, *Our Share in China*, p. 61.
[189] *A Century of Protestant Missions in China*, p. 442.
[190] *Chinese Recorder*, Vol. 8, p. 214; Smith, *Rex Christus*, p. 180; *L. M. S.
Chronicle*, Vol. 41, p. 25.
[191] *Chinese Recorder*, Vol. 7, p. 259.
[192] *China Mission Year Book, 1911*, p. 164; *Chinese Recorder*, Vol. 23, p. 83.

Presbyterian Church began in Manchuria medical service for their sex.[193] There are said to have been twenty-two women physicians in China by 1890.[194]

Because of their prominence in the Gospel narratives and the peculiar loathsomeness and hopelessness of their malady, lepers were given especial attention. Just how common leprosy is in China is unknown, for no reliable statistics have been compiled, but the disease is frequently found in the South, especially in the provinces of Fukien, Kwangtung, and Kwangsi.[195] The date of the erection of the first hospital for lepers is uncertain,[196] but provision was made for them fairly early. In 1874 one hundred and fifteen were reported under the care of the English Presbyterian hospital at Swatow.[197] In 1890 or 1891 a hospital for them was founded at Pakhoi by E. G. Horder of the Church Missionary Society.[198] Dr. Main opened a hospital for them at Hangchow in 1892,[199] and in 1895 the London Missionary Society began a leper asylum near Hankow.[200] None of these institutions was very large.

Even more than lepers, those in the clutches of the opium habit made an appeal to the sympathies of missionaries. The number of the sufferers was so great, their condition so pitiable, and their unhappy plight so clearly due in part to the greed of Westerners, that in mission after mission efforts were made to free them from their slavery. Often a missionary with no medical training established a refuge where by simple remedies, food, Christian teaching, and prayer, he sought, and often successfully, to effect a cure.[201] Probably every medical missionary gave treat-

---

[193] Robertson, *Our Mission in Manchuria*, p. 108.

[194] Luella Miner in *China Mission Year Book, 1918*, p. 335. See, too, on women physicians, Foster, *Christian Progress in China*, p. 193, and Dennis, *Christian Missions and Social Progress*, Vol. 2, p. 53.

[195] *Encyclopædia Sinica*, p. 298.

[196] The date 1890, given in Balme, *China and Modern Medicine*, p. 95, seems to be too late.

[197] *Chinese Recorder*, Vol. 7, p. 38.

[198] Balme, op. cit., p. 95; Dennis, op. cit., Vol. 2, p. 442. There seems to have been a special board first.—*Proceedings of the Church Missionary Society*, 1890, 1891, p. 179.

[199] Gruchè, *Doctor Apricot of Heaven Below*, passim; Stock, op. cit., Vol. 3, p. 573. At Hangchow by 1899 there were leper hospitals for men and women and a home for lepers' children.—Stock, op. cit., Vol. 3, p. 772.

[200] Dennis, *Christian Missions and Social Progress*, Vol. 2, p. 443.

[201] Soothill, *A Typical Mission in China*, pp. 59, 171-177; Drake, *Among the Dark-haired Race in the Flowery Land*, pp. 27-39.

ment for the opium habit,[202] and a number established refuges. An official who had been a government inspector of the manufacture of opium in India felt so keenly the guilt of his share in the traffic that he contributed the savings of his official career, amounting to over £3,000, for the relief of opium sufferers in China. Some of these funds led (1870 or 1871) to the establishment of an opium refuge at Hangchow under Dr. Galt of the Church Missionary Society, and support from the same source made possible similar work by the Society in Ningpo.[203] An opium refuge was opened in Peking in 1878.[204]

One of the earliest tasks which confronted the medical missionary was the training of Chinese assistants and before many years this expanded into preparation for the medical profession. Medical education was conducted in hospitals, usually by staffs of one or two men who were already heavily burdened: the students were apprentices who learned while assisting their teachers. In 1877 thirty medical students were reported.[205] The most notable beginnings of medical instruction were in Canton under the supervision of Dr. Kerr; [206] in Tientsin by Dr. Mackenzie; [207] at Têngchow in Shantung, where, in connection with Mateer's school, a medical department was begun by Dr. James B. Neal; [208] and at St. John's College in Shanghai.[209] At Hongkong a school of medicine opened about 1886 worked in close coöperation with the hospitals of the London Missionary Society.[210]

Compared with the schools established in the next century by

---

[202] There are interesting examples of this in Osgood, *Breaking Down Chinese Walls*, pp. 44 et seq., and Dukes, *Along River and Road in Fuhkien*, p. 208. See also Ashmore, *South China Mission of the American Baptist Foreign Mission Society*, p. 123, and Dr. H. T. Whitney in *Records of the Missionary Conference, Shanghai, 1890*, pp. 302-314.

[203] Gruchè, op. cit., p. vii; *China Mission Hand-book*, Part 2, p. 27; *Chinese Recorder*, Vol. 3, p. 256, Vol. 5, p. 258; *A Century of Protestant Missions in China*, p. 27.

[204] *Chinese Recorder*, Vol. 11, pp. 196, 206.

[205] Ibid., Vol. 9, p. 115.

[206] *The Christian Occupation of China*, p. 423. Medical students were first admitted in 1870.

[207] This was begun in 1881.—Balme, *China and Modern Medicine*, p. 112; *L. M. S. Chronicle*, Vol. 42, p. 365; Bryson, *Mackenzie*, pp. 229 et seq.

[208] Forsyth, *Shantung*, p. 323. Dr. Neal came to China in 1883.

[209] The medical department was opened in 1880.—*Spirit of Missions*, Vol. 46, p. 534.

[210] *China Mission Hand-book*, Part 2, p. 8; Balme, op. cit., p. 112. It was in this medical school that the famous Sun Yat-sen received his medical training.—Bitton, *Our Heritage in China*, p. 53.

missions and the China Medical Board, educational standards were low. However, the men prepared were forerunners of a new medical profession in China.[211] Moreover, several Chinese who obtained a medical training in Great Britain and America owed the beginning of their Western education to mission schools, and to missionaries their opportunity to study abroad. Wong Fun, who, as we have seen, graduated in medicine from the University of Edinburgh and was probably the first Chinese physician trained in the Occident, had been a student in the school maintained by the Morrison Education Society.[212]

Apparently the first Chinese woman to receive a medical diploma abroad was You Me-king, the orphaned daughter of a Chinese pastor, who was taken into the family of Dr. D. B. McCartee, then a Presbyterian missionary at Ningpo, was educated in the United States, and returned to China to practice under the Woman's Board of the (Dutch) Reformed Church.[213] The second seems to have been Hü King-eng, of Foochow, likewise the daughter of a Chinese clergyman. She graduated from the Woman's Medical College in Philadelphia in 1894 and, returning to Fukien, after several years in a mission hospital in Foochow, in 1899 became the head of the Woolston Memorial Hospital.[214] Probably more widely known was Shih Ma-yu, usually known to foreigners as Mary Stone. She too was the daughter of a Chinese pastor. Educated by missionaries, she was brought by one of them to the United States and graduated in medicine from the University of Michigan. Returning to China in 1896, she opened a hospital in Kiukiang.[215] Ida Kahn, another Chinese woman physician, was trained with Mary Stone in the United States and for a time shared the latter's work in Kiukiang.[216]

With such a part in the preparation of the pioneers, Protestant

---

[211] There was, for example, a Chinese who studied in the hospital of the London Missionary Society at Hankow and who was later in charge of a hospital of his own, erected by his fellow Chinese.—Bryson, *Child Life in Chinese Homes*, pp. 168-174.

[212] Yung Wing, *My Life in China and America*, pp. 19-33.

[213] Dennis, op. cit., Vol. 2, p. 192; Burton, *Notable Women of Modern China*, pp. 25, 33; Pitcher, *Fifty Years in Amoy*, pp. 163, 164. She soon went to Japan.

[214] Burton, op. cit., pp. 15-70; Smith, *Rex Christus*, p. 182; Dennis, op. cit., Vol. 2, p. 193.

[215] Burton, op. cit., pp. 161-218; Hart, *V. C. Hart*, p. 73; Perkins, *Glimpse of the Heart*, p. 12.

[216] Burton, op. cit., pp. 115-158; Hart, op. cit., pp. 114 et seq. Dr. Kahn was later in medical work at Nanch'ang in Kiangsi.

missionaries were making a deep impression upon the scientific and ethical standards of the future medical profession of the country.

Not only were medical missionaries training Chinese in their profession: they were preparing medical literature. Dr. Francis Hobson of the London Missionary Society wrote or translated several Chinese books on medicine and surgery.[217]   Dr. J. Porter Smith of the Wesleyan Missionary Society in Hankow and Dr. Kerr were each the author of a *materia medica* in Chinese.[218] Dr. Wilhelm Lobscheid of the Rhenish Mission prepared several medical treatises.[219]   D. W. Osgood of the American Board's mission in Fukien put into Chinese Gray's *Anatomy,* a revision and then a new translation being done later by Dr. Whitney of the same mission.[220]   These and other physicians were laying the foundations for a new medical literature and terminology for China.[221]

Before 1897 missionary physicians, like missionary teachers, discovered the need for coöperation, and in 1886 formed the China Medical Missionary Association.   The new organization began a journal in 1887 and held its initial meeting in 1890.[222] It was the first to attempt to bring to bear on all China Western medical science, and was probably the first group of any kind or of any school of medicine, either voluntary or state-initiated, to begin to plan for the health of the entire Empire.

VARIOUS FORMS OF RELIEF AND SOCIAL REFORM

Missionaries were not content with attempting to relieve some of the physical distress about them by means of hospitals and dispensaries and by creating a new medical profession and literature: they were deeply stirred by all the forms of suffering which they found and in many different ways were attempting both to alleviate them and to remove some of their causes.

They could not long be in China without noting the pitiable condition of the blind.   The earliest efforts of the first medical missionary, Dr. Peter Parker, were, as we have seen, centered

[217] *L. M. S. Chronicle,* Vol. 1 (new series), p. 6.
[218] *Chinese Recorder,* Vol. 4, p. 171, Vol. 5, p. 143.
[219] *Encyclopædia Sinica,* p. 346.
[220] *A Century of Protestant Missions in China,* p. 266.
[221] The Medical Missionary Association, at its first meeting (1890) appointed a committee on terminology.—*China Mission Year Book, 1911,* p. 162.
[222] *China Mission Year Book, 1911,* p. 162; *Spirit of Missions,* Vol. 52, p. 150.

chiefly on diseases of the eye. Gützlaff, too, rescued six blind girls in Canton and sent two of them to America and four to England.[223] In the forties a workshop for the blind was established in Shanghai by a representative of the Church Missionary Society.[224] The most noteworthy of the early efforts for those who had lost their sight was by William Hill Murray. Murray came to China about 1871 as an agent of the National Bible Society of Scotland. While in Peking he became impressed with the hapless lot of the blind and in time worked out a plan—an adaptation of the Braille system—for enabling them to read. He established a school for teaching by his method and met with encouraging success. He had various devices for training the blind in self-support, such as instructing them in music and in book-making, and under his supervision and inspiration something of a literature was prepared for them.[225] Several other systems of reading, one of them in raised forms of modified Roman letters, were worked out by missionaries.[226] A number of other schools for the blind were begun—by Dr. Mary Niles in Canton,[227] by W. Campbell in Formosa,[228] by a Miss Graham in Ch'üanchow (Fukien),[229] in Hongkong and Kowloon by the German Mission to Blind Females in China,[230] in Hankow by the large-hearted David Hill,[231] and in Foochow.[232]

What seems to have been the first serious attempt to educate the deaf was instituted in 1887 by Mrs. C. R. Mills of the American Presbyterian Mission. It was begun at Têngchow in Shantung, was discontinued for a time in 1896, and was reorganized at Chefoo in 1898.[233]

[223] *Encyclopædia Sinica*, p. 51.
[224] *Chinese Recorder*, Vol. 1, p. 138.
[225] Murray in *Records of the Missionary Conference, Shanghai, 1890*, pp. 302-306; Gordon-Cumming, *The Inventor of the Numeral Type for China*, passim; Gordon-Cumming in *The East and the West*, Vol. 2, pp. 249-268; Gordon-Cumming, *Wanderings in China*, Vol. 2, pp. 221-228; *Chinese Recorder*, Vol. 20, p. 128, Vol. 22, pp. 257 et seq.
[226] By W. Campbell in Formosa.—Hartman, in *Records of the Missionary Conference, Shanghai, 1890*, p. 300. There were in time a number of forms of the modified Braille.—*Encyclopædia Sinica*, p. 51.
[227] Luella Miner in *China Mission Year Book, 1918*, p. 326; Smith, *Rex Christus*, p. 183.
[228] *China Mission Hand-book*, Part 2, p. 65.
[229] Ibid., Part 2, p. 54.
[230] *A Century of Protestant Missions in China*, p. 589.
[231] Ibid., p. 91.
[232] *Encyclopædia Sinica*, p. 52.
[233] Mrs. C. R. Mills in Forsyth, *Shantung*, p. 280; *China Mission Hand-book*, Part 2, p. 200; *Chinese Recorder*, Vol. 21, p. 245.

Missionaries deplored greatly the suffering and the ill-health entailed by the nearly universal practice of binding the feet of girls. Some missionaries believed that the foreigner ought not directly to attack the custom and that conformity or non-conformity to it should be left to the conscience of individual Chinese Christians.[234] Others held that the Church should take a decided stand against it. About 1867 a mission school in Hangchow required all girls for whom it provided board and clothing to unbind their feet.[235] The Methodist girls' school opened in Peking in 1872 made permission to unbind the pupils' feet a condition for entrance,[236] and in 1874 a school was begun in Wênchow with the same prerequisite.[237] In 1874 missionaries and Chinese women organized an anti-foot-binding society at Amoy.[238] In 1878 the Presbyterian synod meeting at Hangchow, after extended debate, took official action against foot-binding.[239] Those who followed the injunctions of the missionary and abandoned the custom met with much criticism, for "natural feet" were to be found only among the Hakkas, the Manchus, and a few other minority groups, and by the majority of Chinese were regarded with scorn and as a hindrance to marriage. It is not surprising, then, that many, probably the majority, of Christian women and girls conformed to tradition. However, the nation-wide movement against foot-binding, although led largely by non-missionaries, received its inspiration from missionaries,[240] and most of those who put the new principles into practice seem to have been Protestant Christians.

Protestant missionaries were not content to deal with the opium question merely by attempting to cure those who had become addicts of the drug: they wished to prevent the formation of the habit by removing the temptation. On this there seems to have been no division of opinion. The missionary had never acquiesced

[234] Little, *Intimate China*, p. 99.
[235] Ibid., p. 99.
[236] Tuttle, *Mary Porter Gamewell*, pp. 65-68.
[237] Dennis, *Christian Missions and Social Progress*, Vol. 2, p. 353.
[238] Chamberlain, *Fifty Years in Foreign Fields*, p. 22; *China Mission Handbook*, Part 2, p. 11; Little, *In the Land of the Blue Gown*, p. 282; *A Century of Protestant Missions in China*, p. 375.
[239] *Chinese Recorder*, Vol. 9, p. 206.
[240] *Encyclopædia Sinica*, p. 30; Macgowan, *How England Saved China*, passim. See also on the anti-foot-binding movement, Richard, *Forty-Five Years in China*. p. 227; Little, *Intimate China*, pp. 102-105; *Chinese Recorder*, Vol. 28, pp. 320. 585, Vol. 31, p. 258; *L. M. S. Chronicle*, Vol. 7 (new series), p. 63.

in the legalization of the traffic.[241]   The importation of the drug was deplored, partly because, being largely conducted by so-called Christian peoples, it was an obstacle to the acceptance of the Christian faith,[242] but chiefly because of the moral and physical wreckage and economic waste by which it was followed.[243] Missionaries stood firmly against both the use of the drug and the growth of the poppy by Chinese Christians.[244]   The 1877 Conference was deeply interested in the problem.[245]   At the 1890 Conference resolutions were adopted urging the formation of anti-opium societies among the missionaries and Chinese Christians, expressing the conviction that Great Britain must act with China for the suppression of the traffic, and appointing a permanent committee "to promote anti-opium societies."[246]   The action of missionaries had not waited for the resolution of 1890, however, and before that year groups were being formed both in China and in Great Britain to bring the iniquity to an end. Churches at home might be slow to act,[247] but whatever weight the missionaries had was cast unanimously and actively against the evil.[248]

[241] Mr. Reed, who negotiated the American treaty of 1858, had been instructed by his government to reaffirm the prohibitions of the treaty of Wanghia (1844), but on his arrival in China he found the contraband trade so extensive that he came to the conviction that legalization offered better chances of control than did prohibition and so omitted the anti-opium clause. He urged his position on the British plenipotentiary, Lord Elgin. Lord Elgin was of the same mind and believed as well that since the drug was being imported anyway the Chinese Government had better derive revenue from it. A tariff on opium was, accordingly, placed in the tariff schedule (1858) prepared in accordance with the British treaty of Tientsin, and the regulation of the tariff was specified in the accompanying rules. Merchants of several nationalities, including Americans, engaged in the importation of the drug, but the British were the largest participants. In the course of time the domestic cultivation of the poppy greatly increased, so that when, in 1906, the Chinese inaugurated a new campaign against the drug, the British (1907) conditioned the abolition of importation upon the cessation of internal production.—Morse, *International Relations of the Chinese Empire*, Vol. 1, pp. 553-556, Vol. 2, pp. 436, 437; Mayers, *Treaties between the Empire of China and Foreign Powers*, pp. 23, 28.
[242] Thompson, *Griffith John*, p. 408.
[243] *Records of the Missionary Conference, Shanghai, 1890*, pp. 314-356.
[244] Soothill, *A Typical Mission in China*, p. 93; Ross, *Mission Methods in Manchuria*, p. 129.
[245] *Records of the General Conference of the Protestant Missions of China, 1877*, pp. 352-367.
[246] *Records of the Missionary Conference, Shanghai, 1890*, pp. li, lxi, 355, 356.
[247] Broomhall, *Heirs Together*, p. 105.
[248] Flad, *Zehn Jahre in China*, pp. 254-264; Muirhead, *China and the Gospel*, pp. 110-127; *Chinese Recorder*, Vol. 14, p. 108, Vol. 22, p. 371, Vol. 25, p. 306; Broomhall, *Heirs Together*, p. 105; *Missionary Review of the World*, Vol. 3,

Homes for orphans had no such prominence in Protestant activities as in the Roman Catholic program. This may have been in part because of the ill-repute in which Protestant missionaries found these institutions to be held by many of the Chinese.[249] Protestants could not, however, entirely disregard the misery of orphans, especially of girls, or the infanticide that they frequently found. Some waifs were rescued and supported in Chinese families[250] and a few orphanages and foundling homes were established, as, for example, the one maintained by German women at Hongkong.[251] Such institutions, were, however, small and comparatively rare.

Missionaries were unanimously opposed to the concubinage which they observed in many Chinese homes, to the nearly universal gambling, and to the lightness with which some forms of untruthfulness were regarded. They tried to hold the Chinese Church rigorously to their standards, but on the last point they often found great difficulty.[252] Against none of these practices did they yet attempt any extensive campaign outside the church membership.

Adequate famine relief was too large an undertaking for the comparatively small body of Protestant missionaries. However, missionaries in distressed districts made valiant efforts to give such aid as they could. The greatest famine between 1856 and 1897 was that which in 1876-1878 had its center in Shantung and Chihli and in 1877-1879 in Shansi. Protestants helped to gather funds from Shanghai and the West, and numbers of Protestant missionaries, as we have seen, left their regular work and went to Shansi to aid in the distribution of food. Of these latter at least three died from disease contracted while in the

pp. 435, 612. In 1855 The American Board mission in Foochow would receive no one for theological training who had not signed a pledge to abstain from opium, tobacco, and alcoholic drinks.—*China Mission Hand-book*, Part 2, p. 153. There seems to have been little if any action by missionaries against the great evils of the coolie traffic of the nineteenth century, another crime of Westerners against China. Some missionary voices were raised against the Chinese Exclusion Acts of the United States.—*Missionary Review of the World*, Vol. 3, p. 785.

[249] McNabb, *The Women of the Middle Kingdom*, p. 108.

[250] Ibid.

[251] *Chinese Recorder*, Vol. 1, p. 264, Vol. 7, pp. 26, 28, Vol. 8, p. 41; Dennis, *Christian Missions and Social Progress*, Vol. 2, p. 277; Broomhall, *Jubilee Story of the China Inland Mission*, p. 293.

[252] Graves, *Forty Years in China*, passim; Soothill, *A Typical Mission in China*, pp. 92-99; Ross, *Mission Methods in Manchuria*, pp. 129-132.

famine area and others were incapacitated by illness.[253]   Other lesser famines, especially in Manchuria in 1886, in 1888 in Honan and Anhui, in 1888-1889 in Shantung, and in 1893-1894 in Shensi, called forth the aid of missionaries.[254]   Some attempt was made to deal with the fundamental causes of famine. Richard, for example, wished, as we have seen, to help remove them by educating the leading classes in Shansi in Western science.[255]   In 1886 Gilbert Reid suggested to the Governor of Shantung a plan for the control of the Yellow River.[256]   Nevius and others introduced new kinds of fruits,[257] although not always with the prevention of famine as a primary object, and still others sought new ways of assisting the needy to self-support.[258]   The time had not yet come, however, for missionaries to deal effectively with the fundamental causes of Chinese poverty.

[253] Nevius, *Life of Nevius*, p. 311; *China Mission Hand-book*, Part 2, p. 43; Barber, *David Hill*, p. 190. Hill gave several hundred pounds from his own means and went in person to Shansi. Timothy Richard led the missionaries in the work of relief. The Shanghai committee, with Rev. James Thomas of the Union Church and Rev. William Muirhead as secretaries, forwarded about £50,000 to the various parties carrying on relief work. Muirhead, *The Great Famine*, passim. See also Forsyth, *Shantung*, p. 186; Foster in *Chinese Recorder*, Vol. 43, p. 82; Morse, *International Relations of the Chinese Empire*, Vol. 2, pp. 307, 309; Foster, *Christian Progress in China*, pp. 217-232; *China Mission Year Book, 1915*, p. 273; Drake, *Among the Dark-haired Race in the Flowery Land*, pp. 9, 14; Candlin, *John Innocent*, p. 195; Edkins, *Memorial Sermon for Dr. Muirhead;* Speer, *Missionary Principles and Practice*, p. 175.

[254] Robertson, *Our Mission in Manchuria*, pp. 124 et seq.; *A Century of Protestant Missions in China*, p. 209; Foster, *Christian Progress in China*, p. 233; Nevius, *Life of Nevius*, p. 437; Drake, op. cit., pp. 47-76; Mateer, *Character Building in China*, p. 129; Duncan, *The Missionary Mail*, p. 28.

[255] Richard in *Chinese Recorder*, Vol. 23, pp. 131, 132.

[256] Reid, *Glances at China*, p. 141.

[257] Nevius, *Life of Nevius*, pp. 429, 430; Brown, *New Forces in Old China*, p. 226; Dennis, *Christian Missions and Social Progress*, Vol. 3, p. 514.

[258] Fisher, *C. W. Mateer*, p. 246; *China Mission Hand-book*, Part 2, p. 8.

CHAPTER XX

UNREST, RIOTS, AND THE INTERFERENCE OF FOREIGN POWERS

THESE, then, were the methods which Protestant missionaries employed. The inquiry naturally follows: what results followed the use of these methods and all the labor and devotion which their initiation and maintenance involved?

Probably the Chinese official answer would have been that the activities of missionaries brought dissension, riots, the interference of foreign powers, and serious strain upon the governmental machinery of the Empire. Prince Kung is reported to have said to the British Minister, Sir Rutherford Alcock: "Take away your opium and your missionaries and you will be welcome." [1] To a certain extent the officials were right. The missionary travelled more widely in China than did the foreign merchant, he attempted to effect a permanent residence in many cities which were not treaty ports, his activities were often irritating and frequently misunderstood, riots broke out against him, and he could and often did appeal to the protection of Chinese officials and of his own government on the basis not only of the extraterritorial privileges which he shared with other foreigners, but of the special toleration which the treaties promised him.

The Protestant missionary probably caused the Chinese officials much less difficulty than did the Roman Catholic: certainly fewer riots against him and less persecution of his converts were

---

[1] Morse, *International Relations of the Chinese Empire,* Vol. 2, p. 220; Martin, *A Cycle of Cathay,* p. 449. The remark, especially in its present form, may well be apocryphal, but that the missionary was to the average high official who had to do with foreigners a most disturbing factor is indisputable. Edkins, in *Records of the Missionary Conference, Shanghai, 1890,* p. 573, mentions a Chinese book in which it is said that but for the opium trade and missions the foreigner would be welcomed by the Chinese.

reported.[2] This may be because Protestant missionaries did not interfere as much in lawsuits or because their converts were not as numerous, or both. The Empire was seldom free, however, from local difficulties—sometimes very serious—caused by the presence of Protestants.

The causes of this friction are not far to seek. The Protestant missionary, like the Roman Catholic, was a disturber of existing customs and institutions; the permission to travel and the protection promised him had been wrested from China by force; he journeyed farther from the treaty ports than did most of his fellow-countrymen, and so was often the only alien on whom anti-foreign spleen could be vented; he often sought to rent or purchase property in places where all foreigners were unwelcome; and his actions and his purposes seemed to many of the populace mysterious and gave rise to ugly rumors which, while to the Westerner preposterous enough, were believed by the credulous.[3]

[2] Dr. Schereschewsky believed that Protestants were regarded more favorably by the officials than were Roman Catholics.—*Spirit of Missions,* Vol. 30, p. 109. See, too, a similar opinion in Ross, *Mission Methods in Manchuria,* p. 171. The anti-Christian placards and pamphlets seem to have picked out for criticism features which were more characteristic of Roman Catholic than of Protestant practice, such as the vows of celibacy, the treatment of the dead and dying (presumably arising largely from a misunderstanding of the baptism of moribund infants and the sacrament of extreme unction, but also possibly from the medical work of Protestants), and interference in lawsuits. Low, an American Minister to China, said in 1871 that the complaints of the Chinese were chiefly against the Roman Catholics.—*Foreign Relations,* 2d Session, 42d Congress, pp. 97-111.

[3] See a description of an anti-Christian pamphlet in Wheeler, *The Foreigner in China,* pp. 175-183, in which among other things Christians are accused of scooping out the eyes at death to compound with lead to produce silver, of not honoring their ancestors, of making no distinction between rich and poor, and in which the dissensions between Roman Catholics and Protestants are held up to ridicule and the English are described as half human, half beast. In July, 1871, placards were posted in parts of Kwangtung and Fukien accusing foreigners of importing poison, hiring Chinese to distribute it, and refusing to administer an antidote unless the victims would embrace the foreigner's religion.—Pitcher, *Fifty Years in Amoy,* pp. 152-160. In Têngchow, Shantung, foreigners were reported to put into the tea served to guests a powder which made those who drank it come under a spell and become Christian.—Speer, *Presbyterian Foreign Missions,* p. 125. See also on causes of suspicion, *Spirit of Missions,* Vol. 40, p. 243; Morse, *International Relations of the Chinese Empire,* Vol. 2, p. 221; Morris, *A Winter in North China,* passim; Gilmour, *Among the Mongols,* passim. In the Chungking riots of 1886 the missionaries were taunted with the fact that Chinese were being ill-treated in America.—Hubbard, *Under Marching Orders,* pp. 83-97.

In the latter part of the sixties a mob (led by the gentry) in driving a missionary out of a city in Honan is said to have cried after him: "You burned our palace, you killed our Emperor, you sell poison to our people, and now you come professing to teach us virtue."—Protestant missionaries' memorandum to Alcock, July 14, 1869, in *Parliamentary Papers, 1870,* Vol. 69, China No. 9, pp. 4-12.

On an anti-Christian placard in Honan about 1866 the missionaries were held

The movements against the missionary were often fomented by the educated and persons of local importance,[4] and at times were directly or indirectly encouraged by officials.[5] Students gathered for the civil service examinations sometimes led in the disturbances.[6] To all these classes the missionary was peculiarly obnoxious, for he appeared to be threatening the established order to which their training and interests committed them—to be, in other words, little better than an anarchist.

We need not chronicle all the instances of persecution of Protestant missionaries and their converts, or every occasion of friction. Some, however, including most of the important ones, must be given. In 1864 an outbreak occurred in Foochow and the property of at least two missions was destroyed.[7] For about two decades subsequent to 1863 riots and other opposition prevented the representatives of the Church Missionary Society from occupying Chienning in Fukien, and in 1892, after an entrance had been effected, riots again came.[8] In 1866 the chapel of the English Presbyterians at Ch'üanchow in Fukien was dismantled.[9] In 1867, as we have seen, Hudson Taylor and his party were attacked at Yangchow by a mob instigated by the scholars and gentry and the trouble spread to Chinkiang. The British Consul at Shanghai, supported by four ships of war, presented an ultimatum to the Viceroy at Nanking, and as a result two of the Yangchow officials were cashiered, compensation was paid for property destroyed, and steps were taken to protect the Mission's premises from a repetition of the outrage.[10] In 1867 an agent of the British and Foreign Bible Society was killed in Anhui.[11] In 1868 a mob destroyed Roman Catholic and Protestant churches near Taiwanfu, in Formosa, and one of the Chinese Christians

up to ridicule because "although the adherents of the religion only worship Jesus, yet being divided into the two sections of Roman Catholics and Protestants these are continually railing at each other so that we have no means of determining which is right and which is wrong."—Quoted by Alcock in ibid., p. 26.
[4] There are many instances of this. See, for example, Richter, *Geschichte der Berliner Missionsgesellschaft*, pp. 532, 533; Taylor, *Pastor Hsi*, p. 263; Morse, op. cit., Vol. 2, p. 227; Duncan, *The City of Springs*, p. 69.
[5] Richard, *Forty-Five Years in China*, p. 187; Richard in *Chinese Recorder*, Vol. 15, p. 244.
[6] Hubbard, *Under Marching Orders*, pp. 83-97.
[7] Stock and McClelland, *For Christ in Fuhkien*, p. 11.
[8] Darley, *The Light of the Morning*, pp. 15, 16.
[9] Duncan, *The City of Springs*, pp. 66-69.
[10] Morse, op. cit., Vol. 2, p. 227.
[11] Foster, *Christian Progress in China*, p. 126.

was killed and his heart torn out and eaten by his persecutors—a method of transferring his courage to his adversaries.[12]

The year 1870 witnessed many anti-missionary disturbances, repercussions of the Tientsin massacre. Several Protestant chapels in or near Tientsin were destroyed,[13] rumors against missionaries were rife in Shantung,[14] uneasiness was noticed in South China,[15] and at least one anti-missionary mob was reported in Chêkiang.[16]   In 1871 in several places in the southern coast provinces anti-Christian riots broke out because of reports that missionaries had been distributing poisonous powders.[17]   In 1873 a mob drove Hunter Corbett from a district one hundred and thirty miles south of Chefoo and some of his property was destroyed.[18]   In 1874 the danger of war between China and Japan brought jeopardy to foreigners.[19]   That same year two American missionaries were attacked near Kiukiang.[20]

In 1876 rumors were widespread in the Yangtze Valley that queues were being cut by mysterious hands and that the victims would die, and a few months later other reports declared that paper figures were being sent up in the air, which, falling, became as heavy as lead and crushed all on whom they lighted. Neither group of rumors was specifically anti-foreign, but suspicion was sometimes directed against the Christians and rioting and looting of chapels followed.[21]

In 1878 a mob destroyed the buildings of the theological school of the Church Missionary Society at Foochow on the ground that the *fêng shui* of the city was being disturbed and that missionaries had been building on land which did not belong to them.[22]

[12] *State Papers of Great Britain*, 1868-9, China No. 3, p. 24; Morse, op. cit., Vol. 2, p. 224.
[13] *L. M. S. Chronicle*, Vol. 34, p. 234.
[14] Foster, *Fifty Years in China*, p. 162.
[15] Schlatter, *Rudolf Lechler*, p. 159.
[16] Moule, *Story of the Chehkiang Mission*, p. 138.
[17] *Chinese Recorder*, Vol. 4, p. 106; Stock and McClelland, *For Christ in Fuhkien*, pp. 18 et seq.
[18] The American Government vigorously interfered to have the offenders punished and redress made to Corbett.—*House Executive Documents*, 2d Session, 43d Congress, Vol. 1, pp. 274-296.
[19] Moule, op. cit., p. 138.
[20] *Foreign Relations*, 1st Session, 44th Congress, pp. 383 et seq.
[21] Moule, *Half a Century in China*, pp. 106-110; Barber, *David Hill*, p. 149; *Jubilee Papers of the Central China Presbyterian Mission*, p. 87.
[22] Gordon-Cumming, *Wanderings in China*, Vol. 1, pp. 343-351; *Foreign Relations*, 2d Session, 46th Congress, p. 183.

In the eighties several riots occurred in Tsianfu over the purchase and leasing of property by the American Presbyterians.[23]   The Franco-Chinese War brought persecutions to Protestants as well as to Roman Catholics, in Fukien, Chêkiang, and Kwangtung, and eighteen or more Protestant chapels were destroyed.[24]   In 1886 severe anti-foreign riots destroyed mission property in Chungking.   These seem to have been fomented by students who aroused a populace irritated by the high price of rice.[25]   In 1886 some Presbyterian missionaries were driven out of Kwangsi and their property destroyed.[26]

As serious a group of disturbances as affected Protestant missionaries before 1900 broke out in 1890 and 1891, chiefly in the Yangtze Valley.   Various causes were assigned, but the chief one seems to have been pamphlets issued from Changsha, Hunan, largely at the instigation of Chou Han, an official originally from Ninghsiang in that province.   These pamphlets, among other charges, accused missionaries of being the mainstay of Western powers in their designs on China, of using magic to corrupt the Chinese, of extracting unborn infants from their mothers' wombs, and of scooping out the eyes of the dead to make silver.   Jesus was said to have debauched the women of Judæa and to have been put to death for having violated the king's harem.   Christians were accused of worshiping a pig (a play on the word *chu* in *T'ien Chu*), of gross licentiousness, and of refusing to honor Heaven, Earth, the Sun, Moon, stars, ancestors, and the sages. The pamphlets were circulated widely, and in 1890 and 1891 riots broke out in a number of cities on the Yangtze—Ichang, Wuhsueh, Nanking, Wusih, Wuhu, and Chinkiang.   Considerable property was destroyed, and one Protestant missionary was killed.   Foreign governments sent gunboats to defend nationals and at their instance the imperial government ordered the prov-

[23] Reid, *Glances at China*, pp. 153-169; *Foreign Relations*, 1st Session, 47th Congress, p. 284.
[24] Stock and McClelland, op. cit., p. 28; Soothill, *A Typical Mission in China*, p. 107 (Protestant missionaries were rioted out of Wênchow); *Chinese Recorder*, Vol. 15, p. 445, Vol. 16, pp. 53-95; Foster, *Christian Progress in China*, p. 95; Morse, *International Relations of the Chinese Empire*, Vol. 2, p. 373; *A Century of Protestant Missions in China*, p. 257; Graves, *Forty Years in China*, pp. 285-288; Stott, *Twenty-Six Years of Missionary Work*, pp. 96-98; *Foreign Relations*, 1st Session, 49th Congress, pp. 147 et seq.
[25] Tuttle, *Mary Porter Gamewell*, pp. 131-138; *Foreign Relations*, 1887 (1st Session, 50th Congress), pp. 159-166.
[26] *Foreign Relations*, 1888, Part 1, p. 220.

incial authorities to protect the missionaries.[27]   Peking may not have been particularly eager, but it had no other choice.

In 1891-1892 a rebellion on the Mongolian border brought disturbance to missionaries.[28]   In 1893 two Swedish missionaries were mobbed about sixty miles from Hankow.[29]   The Chino-Japanese War (1894-1895) brought trouble to Christians, especially in Chihli, Shantung, and Manchuria, and in the latter region one missionary was killed by a passing troop of Manchus.[30]   On August 1, 1895, while at Huashan near Kucheng in Fukien, four missionaries of the Church Missionary Society were killed by members of a secret sect of "Vegetarians."[31]   In 1895 severe riots in Szechwan destroyed mission property.[32]   In 1895, too, books were widely circulated repeating many of the old calumnies,[33] and so numerous were the anti-missionary disturbances that an imperial edict was issued ordering the protection of missionaries and the suppression of idle stories about them.[34]   In 1896 some property of the (Northern) American Presbyterians was destroyed on the southern borders of anti-foreign Hunan.[35]   That same year, at Kiangyin in Kiangsu, the mission of the (Southern) American Presbyterians, established two years before in the face

[27] Richard, *Conversion by the Million,* Vol. 2, pp. 140 et seq.; *Spirit of Missions,* Vol. 55, pp. 181, 217, Vol. 56, p. 488; Morse, op cit., Vol. 2, p. 409; Christie, *Thirty Years in the Manchu Capital,* p. 83; *L. M. S. Chronicle,* Vol. 14 (new series), p. 108; Gundry, *China,* pp. 209 et seq.; Garst, *In the Shadow of the Drum Tower,* p. 66; Martin, *A Cycle of Cathay,* p. 446; Barber, *David Hill,* p. 299; Thompson, *Griffith John,* p. 468; Smith, *China in Convulsion,* Vol. 1, pp. 79-84; *Anti-Foreign Riots in China in 1891,* passim; Hertslet, *China Treaties,* p. 1136; Curzon, *Problems of the Far East,* p. 296; *Foreign Relations, 1891,* pp. 395-454.

[28] Bryson, *F. C. Roberts of Tientsin,* p. 134; Turner, *Kwangtung: 1894,* p. 169.

[29] Smith, *China in Convulsion,* Vol. 1, p. 85; *Foreign Relations, 1894,* p. 150.

[30] Forsyth, *Shantung,* p. 269; Smith, *Rex Christus,* p. 187; Porter, *William S. Ament,* pp. 128 et seq.; Christie, *Thirty Years in the Manchu Capital,* pp. 87-99; Ketler, *The Tragedy of Paotingfu,* p. 73.

[31] Stock and McClelland, *For Christ in Fuhkien,* pp. 38-44; Turner, *His Witnesses,* passim; *A Century of Protestant Missions in China,* p. 53; Stock, *History of the Church Missionary Society,* Vol. 3, pp. 582-589; Elsie Marshall, *For His Sake,* passim; Berry, *The Sister Martyrs of Kucheng,* passim; Watson, *Robert and Louisa Stewart,* passim; *A History of the Dublin University Fuhkien Mission,* p. 14. Mrs. Saunders, whose two daughters were killed in the massacre, came to China two years later as a missionary—in a spirit of forgiveness which is beyond praise.— Hawes, *New Thrills in Old China,* p. 174.

[32] *Foreign Relations, 1896,* pp. 47-63; Taylor, *Hudson Taylor,* pp. 539, 540; Cunningham, *History of the Szechuen Riots;* Little, *In the Land of the Blue Gown,* pp. 200 et seq.; Wallace, *The Heart of Sz-chuan,* pp. 65-71.

[33] Richard, *Forty-Five Years in China,* p. 246.

[34] *China Year Book,* 1916, p. 457.

[35] *Foreign Relations, 1896,* pp. 84-86.

of opposition, was destroyed.[36]   This list of persecutions is not complete, but these are probably the most prominent instances.

In spite of all these disturbances, before 1900 very few Protestant missionaries lost their lives at the hands of mobs, while hundreds, sometimes women unaccompanied by foreign men, lived and travelled safely in the interior remote from the protection of gunboats and consuls.   There were, to be sure, repeated instances of persecution of Chinese Christians, of growing crops destroyed, and of many other annoyances,[37] and missionaries were often received with anything but cordiality.   It is probable, too, that had treaties not guaranteed protection to the foreigner, and had it not been known that these treaties would be vigorously enforced by the powers, the lot of the missionary and of his converts would have been far harder.   Given the conservatism of the Chinese, however, and the extent of Christian activity and the revolutionary character of much of Christian teaching, it is remarkable that missionaries were greeted with no more active intolerance.

Protestant missionaries, while loath to interfere in lawsuits between Chinese, were, as a rule, quite willing to ask representatives of their governments for protection against riots and for redress of injuries.   Now and then missionaries questioned the advisability of appeals to foreign governments.   Legge, for example, on going to settle a case of persecution, said: "If news comes that I have been murdered, go at once to the English consul and tell him that it is my wish that no English gunboat should be sent up the river to punish the people for my death." [38] A few missionaries even suggested that the toleration clauses be abrogated.   The majority of missionaries, however, and among them some of the most prominent, believed that the clauses should be retained.[39]   Missionaries were, indeed, inclined to lay claim

[36] Ibid., *1896, pp.* 70-81.
[37] Soothill, *A Typical Mission in China,* pp. 89 et seq.; Ross, *Mission Methods in Manchuria,* pp. 168-170.
[38] Legge, *James Legge,* p. 116.
[39] See discussion in *Chinese Recorder,* Vol. 2, pp. 11, 52, Vol. 10, p. 139, Vol. 11, p. 65, Vol. 12, pp. 11, 12, Vol. 16, p. 189, Vol. 20, p. 420, Vol. 22, p. 102, Vol. 27, p. 323; *China Review,* Vol. 7, p. 399.   One of these articles by Ashmore, the most distinguished of the missionaries of the American Baptist Missionary Union in China, said: "In the treaties made with China by Western nations great breadth and enlightenment have been shown from the first.   They are, and were intended to be, commercial treaties; but they were something more than that.   They were indicators of the advancement made by those Western nations in all that pertains to intellectual emancipation.   They made their very

to their full rights under the treaties and repeatedly lodged with their consuls, and occasionally directly with Chinese magistrates, complaints of interference with their activities. They seldom asked indemnity for lives lost [40] or for damages to the possessions of Chinese Christians, but as a rule they believed that enough should be given them by the Chinese authorities to replace destroyed property.[41] They were disposed, too, to stretch some of their privileges to the limit and to claim the benefit of any doubt in the interpretation of the treaties. Especially were they insistent upon the purchase and rental of property outside the treaty ports, even though it was questionable whether the treaties permitted it.

On the whole, however, missionaries sought other means than force to assure religious liberty. The 1890 Conference, for example, appointed a committee which in 1895 presented to the Tsungli Yamen a memorial stating the case of missions and asking that the government try to understand the work of the Church by obtaining actual knowledge of it through conference with missionaries.[42]

The governments of Great Britain and the United States, under whose protection most Protestants naturally came, never supported the missionary as a means of furthering their influence in China. Often, indeed, their representatives were disinclined to allow him the privileges which he claimed [43] and advised him

highest achievement when they stipulated for freedom of opinion. It does not affect the issue that this came under the form of a provision for religious freedom. The right of free trade in ideas of every kind is contained in the principle laid down in these treaties."—Wm. Ashmore in *Chinese Recorder*, Vol. 27, p. 209.

[40] After the Kucheng massacre in 1895 the Church Missionary Society and the Church of England Zenana Missionary Society declined to accept an indemnity.—Stock, *History of the Church Missionary Society*, Vol. 3, p. 587.

[41] See the instances in *Foreign Relations* quoted on the last two or three pages. Some other instances are in Cornaby, *The Call of Cathay*, p. 163; *Chinese Recorder*, Vol. 1, p. 65. To this, however, there were notable exceptions. The China Inland Mission generally declined compensation for property.—Broomhall, *Jubilee Story of the China Inland Mission*, pp. 60, 61.

[42] *Records of the Missionary Conference, Shanghai, 1890*, p. 1; *Chinese Recorder*, Vol. 27, pp. 62, 116, 182; Richard, *Forty-Five Years in China*, p. 250; Smith, *Rex Christus*, p. 200. The French Minister objected to missionaries appealing directly to the Tsungli Yamen, probably because that might set a precedent which would militate against the French protectorate of Roman Catholic missions. —Reeve, *Timothy Richard*, pp. 91-94.

[43] At the time of the settlement of the troubles arising out of the Tientsin massacre, the American Minister complained: "Both the American and English missionaries appear to be impressed with the belief that they are somehow specially charged with diplomatic functions by their government."—*Foreign Relations*, 3d Session, 41st Congress, p. 372.

to restrict his activities.   As a rule, they backed the missionary in maintaining his obvious treaty rights, but they sometimes did this reluctantly and always distinctly because he was a citizen of their country and not because of his occupation.

Late in the sixties the question of what protection should be accorded the missionary first came prominently before the British Government.   British missionaries were rapidly extending their activities into the interior, especially under the recently organized China Inland Mission; some of them maintained that the right to purchase property outside the open ports was granted by the British treaty of 1858; others urged that in the next revision of the treaties this privilege be incontestably granted; [44] and the Yangchow riot of 1867 annoyed the British authorities.   In England the missionary was much criticized [45] and the government took the attitude that if it insisted upon the Church's purchase of land in the interior, British commerce would suffer.   The missionaries, so some of the spokesmen for the government declared, were not likely soon to succeed in establishing Christianity in the Empire, and in the meantime were arousing so much resentment in China that trade was threatened. [46]   Sir Rutherford Alcock, the British representative at Peking, told the missionaries that he believed that the cause of Christianity would be bettered if it did not have the support of foreign governments and that if the missionaries would have more patience and moderation in pushing their enterprise they would be viewed by the Chinese less as political instruments and agents of revolutionary propaganda and more as teachers of religion. [47]

As the British missionary persisted, however, in travelling and in purchasing and leasing property outside the treaty ports, the British authorities felt themselves under the necessity of insisting that as a British subject he and his property be protected. He was seldom *persona grata* with the consul or naval commander, but as time passed there seems to have been less disposition to visit him with official censure. [48]

[44] *Parliamentary Papers*, 1871, Vol. 70, China No. 5, pp. 116, 117.
[45] Bitton, *Griffith John*, p. 75; *Chinese Recorder*, Vol. 2, pp. 20-24, Vol. 4, p. 57.
[46] *Parliamentary Papers*, 1870, Vol. 69, China No. 9, pp. 1-12, 44.
[47] Ibid., 1870, Vol. 69, China No. 9, pp. 4-11. See also ibid., 1872, Vol. 70, China No. 1.
[48] See, for example, the reports of the Yangtze riots of 1891 in *Parliamentary Papers*, 1890-1891, Vol. 96, China No. 3. There was at least unofficial criticism of missionaries after the Yangtze riots of 1891.—See Michie, *Missionaries in China*, passim.

The government of the United States was more favorable than was that of Great Britain. Several missionaries and former missionaries were in the American consular and diplomatic service and there was less American commerce to be jeopardized by the ill-will which Christian propaganda excited.[49] Like the British, the American authorities maintained that the missionary had no explicit right to lease or purchase land outside the treaty ports.[50] Like them, too, however, they held that in practice a certain permissive right to acquire such property had developed and that, once in possession, an American citizen was entitled to security.[51] Although the American Government disclaimed any authority over "the natives of China"[52] and urged missionaries to bring as few cases to the consul as possible,[53] at least once the American Minister acted to obtain the exemption of Protestant Christians from contributions to festivals, processions, and theatrical performances in honor of non-Christian deities.[54]

Both the British and American governments, then, while they declined to interfere as actively in behalf of Chinese Christians as did the French, supported vigorously the obvious treaty rights of their nationals and often brought pressure on behalf of missionaries, sending gunboats and exacting indemnities.[55]

[49] Seward, American Minister to China in 1876, said that more than half the Americans in China were missionaries and that missionary cases called for a large share of the efforts of the legation.—Foreign Relations, 2d Session, 44th Congress, p. 47.

[50] Foreign Relations, 1st Session, 43d Congress, Vol. 1, p. 137.

[51] Secretary of State to Minister to China, March 7, 1889, in Foreign Relations, 1888, Part 1, p. 266.

[52] The American Minister to the Tsungli Yamen, March 20, 1871, quoted in Brown, New Forces in Old China, p. 235; Williams, Anson Burlingame, p. 69.

[53] The American Minister in a circular to the consul to be read to missionaries.—Foreign Relations, 2d Session, 44th Congress, p. 47.

[54] Foreign Relations, 1st Session, 47th Congress, p. 272.

[55] An interesting and not altogether creditable instance of this occurred at Chinkiang about 1885. A Chinese contracted with American Methodist missionaries to build some houses. He attempted to throw up the contract before it was finished, the missionaries tried to hold him to it by withholding some of the pay for work already done until the rest should be completed, the contractor retaliated by attempting to carry away the blinds of a veranda, and when one of the missionaries interfered and another came to his assistance, the contractor bound them and took them to the Tipao. The Consul interfered and the Taot'ai and Tipao released the missionaries. When the Consul demanded the punishment of the offenders, the Taot'ai declined to comply until he could examine the accounts of the parties to the dispute to determine who was originally in the wrong. The Consul would not agree to this, brought the matter to the attention of the Consul-General, a British gunboat and an American gunboat were sent, and the Taot'ai, cowed, ordered the Chinese offenders put in the cangue and beaten.—Denby to Bayard, Feb. 9, 1886, in Foreign Relations, 1887, pp. 74 et seq. There is no clear information as to how much indemnity was collected for missionaries. 4,785 19/100 taels were paid to the American Board for damage to property at the time of the Tien-

Protestant as well as Roman Catholic messengers of the Prince of Peace were being supported by a substantial show of force.

THE PREPARATION OF CHINA FOR IMPENDING CHANGE

Protestant missionaries are often said to have caused the revolution in Chinese culture and institutions which was to be so marked after 1897. That they had something to do with it is fairly clear. Undoubtedly they brought an extra load upon a decrepit and already overtaxed government. Undoubtedly also they helped to give currency to new ideas. Yung Wing, for instance, who owed his Western education to Protestant missionaries, returned from his college course in the United States convinced that China must adopt much from the Occident. He aided in the importation of Western machinery, translated Western books, and was responsible for the Chinese Educational Mission through which in the seventies the Chinese Government sent one hundred and twenty youths to the United States, the first considerable group to study in the Occident.[56] Wherever a missionary travelled and spoke, wherever he distributed a book, organized a school, or opened a hospital, he introduced conceptions which, if put into effect, would disrupt many old institutions. The Protestant missionary's attitude toward bound feet, toward the education of women, toward the content and method of all education, toward honors to ancestors, concubinage, religious festivals, and the use of the vernacular for literary purposes—to mention only a few of his most prominent innovations—could not but prove revolutionary. Everyone influenced by him was a threat to the older fabric of Chinese life.

On the other hand, the changes in China were due primarily

tsin massacre.—*Foreign Relations,* 2d Session, 42d Congress, p. 75. The American Baptist Missionary Union was paid 14,305 taels and the Northern Methodists 30,325 taels for expenses and damages caused by the riots in Szechwan in 1895.— *Foreign Relations, 1896,* pp. 47-55. The American published official documents have much more about missionary cases than do the British Parliamentary Papers. See *Foreign Relations,* 3d Session, 41st Congress, pp. 380-390; 2d Session, 42d Congress, pp. 97-111; 3d Session, 41st Congress, p. 372; 1st Session, 43d Congress, Vol. 1, p. 137; 2d Session, 43d Congress, Vol. 1, pp. 232-246, 274-296; 1st Session, 44th Congress, pp. 332-335, 383; 2d Session, 44th Congress, p. 54; 2d Session, 46th Congress, p. 234; 1st Session, 47th Congress, pp. 265-267, 272, 284-290, 308; 1st Session, 49th Congress, pp. 147-163; 1887, pp. 159-166; 1888, Part 1, p. 220; 1891, pp. 395-454; 1893, p. 236; 1894, pp. 143-150; 1896, pp. 47-87. See also *Spirit of Missions,* Vol. 38, pp. 637-639; *Shanghai Consular Despatches* No. 4, April 28, 1859.

[56] Yung Wing, *My Life in China and America,* pp. 137-223.

to other factors and they would probably have come just as quickly and have been quite as thorough had no missionary, either Protestant or Roman Catholic, ever entered the country. The primary cause was the commercial and political expansion of the West. The Chinese found themselves helpless before the navies and armies of the Occident, whose chief object in coming was to force them to admit the merchandise of Europe and America and who even before 1898 were beginning to seize their territory. It is significant that among the first attempts of the government to employ the new methods was the construction of arsenals, and that the first government school to teach Western learning was one for the preparation of young men for service as interpreters in the Tsungli Yamen—itself a creature of diplomatic intercourse with the West—and in legations abroad.[57] The first introduction of Western subjects into the civil service examinations came in 1885, following the war with France.[58] New thoughts were constantly entering through merchants, through the foreign organized and directed Imperial Maritime Customs Service, through the legations in Peking, and the Chinese representatives in foreign capitals. When the great transformation finally came, its immediate causes were the decisive defeat of China by a Japan newly empowered by Occidental appliances, threatened partition by the powers, and the overwhelming and humiliating disaster which in 1900 followed the effort to oust the foreigner and all his ways. The Chinese decided that if they were ever to cope successfully with the foreigner they must adopt many of his methods and machines.

What the missionary did do was to help give direction to the revolution. He prepared leaders and communities who were ready to assist in the reshaping of China when the inevitable arrived. Because Christian groups and individuals existed and had become partly adjusted to Western ways before the general change began, the chaos and bewilderment were not as great as they would otherwise have been and the readjustment could be made more quickly. Moreover, by bringing to China moral, religious, and intellectual factors of Western culture with which the Chinese otherwise could not have come into such intimate

[57] The T'ung Wên Kuan.—Morse, *International Relations of the Chinese Empire,* Vol. 3, p. 413.
[58] Pott, *The Emergency in China,* p. 148.

contact, the missionary helped determine the character of the new China. He was by no means faultless, and many non-missionary foreigners were of inestimable service to China in preparing her for the transition. Witness, for example, Sir Robert Hart of the Customs Service and many of his subordinates. By and large, however, it is safe to say that chiefly because of the missionary, China in the days of its transformation came into intimate touch with, and so was influenced by, not only the militarism, commercialism, and materialism of the West—the features most prominent in commercial and diplomatic intercourse—but by the spiritual and moral forces of the Occident. As we have so often suggested, when in the succeeding decades the constructive elements in their older culture declined or collapsed, fortunate it was for the Chinese that foreigners were present who exemplified the ethical and religious values of the Christian faith. In spite of all their weaknesses and shortcomings, every Christian community, every mission press, every mission school, and every hospital was a center of influences of which China was to stand sorely in need.

In this general effect on the life of the country, the Protestant groups, although smaller, were more potent than were the Roman Catholic communities. That was probably in part because Protestant missionaries were from the countries who had the largest proportion of the foreign trade of China and whose language and ideas the Chinese were accordingly most inclined to adopt, but it was also partly because Protestants laid more emphasis on schools, medicine, and the preparation and distribution of literature, and had among their number men who sought to mold the life and thought of the nation as a whole. Certainly a large proportion of the leaders of the new China, especially its physicians, educators, and publishers, received their training at the hands of Protestant missionaries. This will become more apparent in later chapters: here reference need be made only to such examples as the greatest publishing house in China, the Commercial Press, an institution whose founders learned their trade in the Presbyterian Mission Press; to the numbers of graduates of mission schools who taught in government colleges; and to the sons of Chinese Protestant clergy of this early period, like C. T. Wang and W. W. Yen, who were to become important in Chinese politics.

THE SIZE AND CHARACTER OF THE PROTESTANT CHRISTIAN COMMUNITY

To the average Protestant missionary the significant results of his activities were not riots and the actions of governments, nor even changes in Chinese institutions and culture, but the numbers who heard and accepted the Christian message, and the fruits of that message in lives.

Judged by statistics, in 1897 the Protestant Christian communities were still a negligible fraction of the population.   In 1893 Protestant communicants were estimated to number 55,093,[59] only about one in every seventy-five hundred of the inhabitants of the Empire, and most of these were in the provinces on the south coast, for here Protestant activities had been longest in progress.[60]   This figure represented, however, a very rapid growth.   In 1853 Protestant churches are said to have had three hundred and fifty communicants.[61]   By the summer of 1869 the number had increased to 5,753.[62]   In 1876, 13,035 communicants were counted,[63] of whom more than two-thirds seem to have been in Fukien, Kwangtung, and Chêkiang.[64]   In 1886, 28,506 communicants were reported,[65] in 1887, 32,260,[66] in 1888, 34,-555,[67] and in 1889, 37,287.[68]   In each of these years non-communicant members of the Protestant groups, Christians' children not yet admitted to full church membership, and those regularly under instruction, were probably at least as numerous as the communicants.

Much more important than the numbers of Protestants is the question of their character.   It was upon quality of life that Protestant missionaries placed the most emphasis in testing applicants for church membership and they believed that in the last analysis the evidence for the success or failure of their work rested upon it.   The majority of their converts were farmers,

[59] *China Mission Hand-book,* Part 2, p. 325.
[60] In 1893, 8,248 of the communicants were in Kwangtung.—*Chinese Recorder,* Vol. 26, pp. 82-83.
[61] *Chinese Recorder,* Vol. 23, p. 512.
[62] Ibid., Vol. 2, p. 63.
[63] *Records of the General Conference of the Protestant Missionaries of China, 1877,* p. 486.
[64] *China's Millions,* 1879, p. 9.
[65] *Missionary Review of the World,* Vol. 1, p. 143.
[66] *Chinese Recorder,* Vol. 20, p. 47.
[67] Ibid.
[68] *Records of the Missionary Conference, Shanghai, 1890,* p. 732.

shop-keepers, physicians, artisans, street-vendors, and laborers,[69] and so belonged to the substantial, although not the influential, rank and file of the nation. It required, moreover, a certain initiative to break with Chinese society and, as a result, in native vigor Christians were probably above the average of the groups from which they came: by a process which the anthropologist would call "selection" they tended to be a superior company. Very few of the scholar class came into the Church, although now and then one was reached,[70] and by 1897 special efforts were being made to approach them, notably by Timothy Richard and the society of which he was the head, and by Gilbert Reid.[71] The Church welcomed—to its credit—the very poor, but those who availed themselves of the invitation seem to have composed only a small minority of the membership.

In the earlier days of a Christian community men were in the majority and adults predominated,[72] but as the years passed women often formed more than half the church membership and children began to be reached through the homes and the schools.[73]

The motives which impelled those seeking membership in the Church were varied. Now a man wished to be freed from the opium habit and found release through his new faith;[74] often he hoped for the aid of the missionary in a lawsuit; occasionally some one who had been vainly seeking inward peace through the religious agencies known to him discovered it in the Christian Gospel;[75] sometimes the attraction was the moral emphasis of Christianity and the changed lives of those already Christians,[76] and sometimes what the applicant had seen and heard while in a hospital.[77] Occasionally the catechumen was drawn by intel-

[69] Graves, Forty Years in China, p. 289; Soothill, A Typical Mission in China, p. 100.

[70] Soothill, op. cit., pp. 100-120.

[71] In 1897 Reid was planning an institute for the higher classes.—L. M. S. Chronicle, Vol. 6 (new series), p. 276.

[72] Nevius, China and the Chinese, p. 373; Duncan, The City of Springs, pp. 89-91; Chinese Recorder, Vol. 24, p. 120.

[73] Nevius, op. cit., p. 373.

[74] Cable, The Fulfilment of a Dream, pp. 127-138; Ross, Mission Methods in Manchuria, pp. 25-28.

[75] Ross, op. cit., pp. 18 et seq.; Davies, Among Hills and Valleys in Western China, p. 240. There was little of the deep sense of sin as a compelling motive, such a sense as was to be found in some places in the West, especially in Calvinistic circles.—Nevius, op. cit., p. 379.

[76] Craighead, Hunter Corbett, pp. 137, 138.

[77] Pakenham-Walsh, Some Typical Christians, pp. 55-66.

lectual belief in the superiority of Christianity,[78] sometimes by the promise of eternal life,[79] and often by a conviction of the futility of idolatry as an aid in obtaining the goods of this life and by confidence that these could be secured through the Christians' God.[80]

Missionary literature of the period abounds in the life-stories of converts and probably better than anything else these give insight into the character of the Protestant community and of the changes wrought by the Faith. A few of the outstanding ones will serve as illustrations.

Pastor Hsi was a native of Shansi, a scholar who had taken the first of the three literary degrees. While in Shansi to aid in famine relief, David Hill sought to awaken interest in the Faith by prizes for the best essays on Christianity. Hsi, although not then a Christian, wrote the winning paper, and so came in touch with the Gospel. He soon became Hill's teacher in Chinese, his conversion followed (1879), and as a result of his newly found faith he was cured of the opium habit, was reconciled to his brothers, and brought back his stepmother whom he had driven away. His wife, afflicted with the strange malady described as demon possession, was healed through his faith. Hsi was earnest in seeking to win others and he was led, too, to open refuges— eventually more than a score of them—where by prayer and the use of medicine which he compounded he sought, often successfully, to free others from the clutch of the drug that had once enslaved him. Through his efforts many entered the Church and he came to have much influence with the Protestant groups in his vicinity. He lived a life of unremitting toil and prayer, and he and his wife denied themselves all but the barest necessities of life that the work to which they were dedicated might have the financial means to go on. He was largely independent of the missionary, whom, indeed, he tended somewhat to dis-

---

[78] Ross, op. cit., p. 29.

[79] Muirhead, *China and the Gospel*, p. 184; Stott, *Twenty-Six Years of Mission Work in China*, p. 142.

[80] Davis, *Ch'oh Lin, the Chinese Boy Who Became a Preacher*, passim; Voskamp, *Zerstörende und aufbauende Mächte in China*, pp. 47-55; Brown, *China in Legend and Story*, pp. 150-162. Two most interesting studies of converts among the Chinese in Formosa and which make much of this point are Moody, *The Heathen Heart*, and Moody, *The Saints of Formosa*. See also Moody, *The Mind of the Early Converts*, in which Chinese Christians are compared with Christians in the early days of the Church in the Roman Empire. The latter are shown greatly to resemble the former in many of their motives and concepts.

dain, although he labored in connection with the China Inland Mission. He died, worn out, in 1896.[81]

Tao Hsing, once the keeper of a gambling den and a house of ill-fame near Ningpo, was won in 1872 or 1873 through representatives of the China Inland Mission, turned out the inmates of his premises and transformed his largest room into a chapel.[82]

Of Wang Ching-fu, a pastor in Hupeh under the London Missionary Society, a close student of the Bible and a man of prayer, a non-Christian who knew him well is reported to have said: "There is no difference between Mr. Wang and the Book." [83]

A Mr. Ahok, a wealthy merchant in Foochow, hesitated long to become a Christian because that meant closing his stores on Sundays and his partners were unsympathetic. He finally announced himself as a Christian and suspended his business on the first day of each week. His wife was active in winning to the Faith women of the higher classes. His was the initial gift which made possible the Anglo-Chinese College in Foochow, and a son graduated from the school and became a member of its faculty.[84]

A Mr. Chu of Shansi came into possession of a Christian tract and a copy of one of the Gospels and sought out a missionary to obtain more light. After two years of instruction he was baptized and later served as pastor, without pay, and won to the Faith several hundred men.[85]

The name has come down, too, of Sia Sek-ong, the son of a Fukien farmer. He studied, taught school, then became the Chinese instructor of Nathan Sites of the Methodist mission in Foochow, and after an inward struggle found peace as a Christian. He soon began to preach and during nearly three decades of service in the Church declined any support from the mission's treasury, that he might give no ground for the accusation that he had eaten the foreigner's rice.[86]

Another of the early Christians, Cheng Mao, a native of Ch'üanchow, Fukien, did not come in touch with Christianity until he

[81] Taylor, *One of China's Scholars: Pastor Hsi,* passim; Hellier, *David Hill,* pp. 118-139.
[82] Taylor, *Hudson Taylor,* p. 242.
[83] John, *A Voice from China,* pp. 209, 210.
[84] McNabb, *The Women of the Middle Kingdom,* pp. 124-143; Burton, *Notable Women of Modern China,* pp. 73-111.
[85] Drake, *Among the Dark-Haired Race in the Flowery Land,* pp. 40-46.
[86] Baldwin, *Sia Sek Ong* in *The Picket Line of Missions.*

was in his twenties, and then it was several years before his doubts and questions were cleared up. He was not baptized until he considered himself free to observe Sunday by paying off his debts. By his devoted, humble life, he made a deep impression on Christians and non-Christians alike. He was employed by the mission as a colporteur and remained unmarried that he might give himself exclusively to his work. He won many to the Christian faith and to changed lives—among them opium sots, a woman of the streets, and a ne'er-do-well brother.[87]

Still another early convert was Wang Ying-ming, in Manchuria. At the time when he first came in contact with Christianity, Wang was a commission merchant who was in the grip of the opium habit. He came into possession of a copy of one of the Gospels, sought from a missionary an explanation of its teachings, believed, and after desperate struggles, through prayer broke off his use of opium. He was the first to be baptized in Manchuria by John Ross, and because of his earnestness was soon set apart as an evangelist, at a salary much lower than his former profits as a merchant. His new life led him to resume the broken connections with his family and so great was the change that his younger brother, impressed, became a Christian and an evangelist. He helped lay the foundations of the Protestant Church in Manchuria, giving of his slender means to his family and to those needier than he.[88]

Yen Yung-kiung was taken as a boy to the United States by Episcopalians, graduated with honors from Kenyon College, and, returning to his native land, spent his life in the service of the denomination that had educated him, part of the time at Wuchang, then on the staff of St. John's College, and finally as pastor of a church in Shanghai.[89] He and his wife were the only Chinese delegates at the Shanghai Conference of 1890 and one of his sons, W. W. Yen, was later to hold prominent offices in the government.

Then there was an opium addict who drifted into Amoy to find work, while there heard the Christian message, was cured of his drug habit, went back to his native town, and won so many to his faith that a small church was started.[90]

[87] Brown, *A Chinese St. Francis,* passim.
[88] Ross, *Old Wang,* passim.
[89] Norris, *China,* p. 37.
[90] Macgowan, *Christ or Confucius, Which?,* pp. 127-174.

The story, too, has come down of a boy converted while an apprentice in Canton in the despised barber's trade. He soon began preaching, but entirely at his own expense. Later he became interested in his countrymen who were going in large numbers as contract laborers to the plantations of Guiana, and, to win them to the Faith, went himself as a coolie under a contract for seven years. In time he gathered a church of over one hundred members which supported its own pastor and sent money to China for religious work. He established two coöperative stores, the profits of which he devoted to religious work in Guiana and China.[91]

Handed down from the early days of Protestant missions in Fukien is the story of a thief who, blinded by his confederates, became chief of the beggars of his village, first entered a Christian chapel to discover a method of robbing it, became interested in what he heard, was converted, and as one of the results of the change burned the accounts of the usurious loans which he held against his fellow beggars.[92]

The account might continue for many pages.[93] The lives whose records have come down to us were probably better than the rank and file of Christians. By no means all the converts were ideal, some of them were no especial credit to the Church, and the vast majority had at the beginning but an imperfect understanding of the faith they were adopting. Some showed an unamiable cupidity,[94] and others were made arrogant by their favored position under the treaties.[95] On the whole, however, compared with the non-Christian community about it, the Protestant community was less superstitious and freer from the current

[91] Graves, Forty Years in China, p. 154.
[92] Brown, China in Legend and Story, pp. 139-150.
[93] For other accounts of converts see Duncan, The Missionary Mail, pp. 48, 54; Brown, op. cit., pp. 150-162, 238-249; Speer, Missionary Principles and Practice, pp. 172, 376 et seq.; Stott, Twenty-Six Years of Missionary Work, pp. 114, 142; Foster, Christian Progress in China, pp. 56, 90-94; Porter, W. S. Ament, p. 112; Pakenham-Walsh, Some Typical Christians, passim; Bentley, Illustrious Chinese Christians, passim; Davis, Leng Tso, The Chinese Bible Woman, passim; Hu, Way of Faith, passim; Bryson, Child Life in Chinese Homes, pp. 138-147; Fields, Pagoda Shadows, passim; Allan, Chu and Lo—Two Chinese Pastors, passim; Darley, The Light of the Morning, passim; Dennis, Christian Missions and Social Progress, Vol. 2, pp. 21, 170, 171; Soothill, A Typical Mission in China, pp. 100-120; Gibson, Mission Problems and Mission Methods in South China, pp. 251-286; Blessing-Eyster, A Chinese Quaker, passim; Davies, Among Hills and Valleys in Western China, p. 124.
[94] Ashmore, The South China Mission of the American Baptist Foreign Mission Society, p. 55.
[95] Hoste in Chinese Recorder, Vol. 55, pp. 247, 248.

vices of opium smoking and gambling, less dishonest, less inclined to engage in litigation, and cleaner in speech. Woman had a higher status, family life was happier, and the relations between the sexes were more wholesome. Literacy was more nearly general among Protestant Christians than among non-Christians. Christians were more generous and more inclined to contribute to famine relief and to the succor of the afflicted. The churches that arose not only nourished these characteristics but were spreading the Faith and on the whole were tending to bear a larger proportion of their own expenses and to be less dependent on the foreigner. Only here and there had leadership independent of the foreigner begun to emerge, for the Church was still young, but firm and sound foundations had been laid for the years of opportunity ahead.

CHAPTER XXI

RUSSIAN MISSIONS IN THE NINETEENTH CENTURY

IN the rapid spread of the Christian faith in China that marked the latter half of the nineteenth century the Russian Orthodox Church had little share. Until the treaties of 1858, the mission begun at Peking in the sixteenth and seventeenth centuries confined itself to the care of the Albazinians and the training of interpreters for Russo-Chinese diplomatic intercourse. Just how large the Christian community was is uncertain, but in 1856 it seems to have numbered about two hundred.[1] No effort was made, apparently, to carry the Faith to the Chinese or Manchus. The scholarly activities of the mission continued to supply Russia with men who knew Chinese and could aid in the intercourse with China, and who by publications, especially translations from Chinese into Russian, acquainted their fellow-countrymen with the civilization of the Middle Kingdom. The personnel of the mission was changed periodically, theoretically every ten years, but in practice at longer intervals.[2] This meant a fairly regular, if intermittent, stream of scholars returning to Russia.[3] A few members of the mission became distinguished savants. Vasili Pavlovitch Vasiliev (1818-1900), for example, was eleven years in Peking, in 1851 became Professor of Chinese at Kazan University, and in 1855 was transferred to Petrograd.[4] Probably

[1] *Encyclopædia Sinica,* p. 490, says that there were 200 in 1860. Archimandrite Innocent said that in 1860 there were less than 200 Christians, including the descendants of the Albazin prisoners.—*Chinese Recorder,* Vol. 47, p. 680. About 1820 a visitor reported that approximately 22 of the Albazinians had been baptized and that only three appeared at church to celebrate Christmas.—Baddeley, *Russia, Mongolia, and China,* Vol. 2, pp. 430, 431, quoting Timkowski. In 1871 there were said to be about 500 Christians.—Dudgeon in *Chinese Recorder,* Vol. 4, p. 188.

[2] Dudgeon in *Chinese Recorder,* Vol. 4, p. 68; Timkowski, *Travels of the Russian Mission . . . 1820-1821,* Vol. 1, p. 3. Up to 1860, 155 missionaries are said to have served.—Archimandrite Innocent in *Chinese Recorder,* Vol. 47, p. 680.

[3] In 1820 a new mission arrived made up of six ecclesiastics and four laymen.— Timkowski, op. cit., Vol. 1, p. 2.

[4] *Encyclopædia Sinica,* p. 587.

the most important was the Archimandrite Palladius (1817-1878), who spent three terms in China, the first beginning in 1840, and the third in 1865 and ending in 1878. Few missionaries of any branch of the Church have deserved the title "sinologue" as much as he.[5]

With the Russian treaty of 1858 changes began to come. With the establishment of a Russian legation in Peking, the Russian clergy gave more attention to their purely religious duties, carrying on work among the Chinese as well as the Albazinians.[6] The New Testament was translated into Chinese, a school was maintained, at least two centers outside Peking were established,[7] a few converts were made,[8] and services, previously in Slavonic, began to be conducted at least in part in Chinese.[9] There was also a little missionary activity by the Russians among the Mongols—although apparently not by members of the Peking group.[10] The chief interest of the Peking mission, however, continued to be literary. It was not until the eve of 1900 that plans were made for a more active preaching of the Faith among the Chinese. In 1897 the Archimandrite Innocent instituted reforms. These, among other things, provided for daily services in Chinese, the establishment of a business to support some of the poorer Albazinians, the sending out of preachers, parish activities, and local works of charity.[11] The Boxer storm was to work a temporary suspension of all these projects, but in the twentieth century they were to be renewed and extended.

[5] Ibid., p. 420. Palladius was the religious name of Piotre Ivanovitch Kafarof.
[6] The Archimandrite Innocent in *Chinese Recorder*, Vol. 47, pp. 678-683.
[7] Wylie in *Chinese Recorder*, Vol. 1, p. 148.
[8] Dudgeon in *Chinese Recorder*, Vol. 4 (1871), p. 189, said that from ten to forty Chinese were converted yearly in Peking. Between 1860 and 1897 less than 500—possibly including Albazinians—are said to have been baptized.—The Archimandrite Innocent in *Chinese Recorder*, Vol. 47, p. 683.
[9] The Archimandrite Innocent in *Chinese Recorder*, Vol. 47, pp. 681-683.
[10] Williamson, *Travels in North China*, Vol. 2, p. 19. These Russian missions used school books and the translation of the New Testament into Mongol that had been prepared by Swan and Stallybrass of the London Missionary Society. See also *Spirit of Missions*, Vol. 36, pp. 290, 291.
[11] The Archimandrite Innocent in *Chinese Recorder*, Vol. 47, p. 681.

CHAPTER XXII

THE REFORM MOVEMENT

By the close of 1897 important movements were under way in China which within a few years were to bring about the vast changes that had long been impending. The pressure of the Occident was at last taking effect and the Chinese were beginning to adopt some of the methods of the West. The revolution did not come all at once. For years a few far-sighted Chinese had perceived that Europe and America, empowered by the mechanical and industrial revolution of the nineteenth century, were to bring irresistible pressure, and that not only could the Middle Kingdom learn much from the aggressors, but that she must do so if she were to hold them at bay. Yung Wing, for example, as we have seen, had induced the government to send a number of students to America, the great Viceroys Li Hung-chang and Chang Chih-tung had utilized Western methods and appliances, and a few Occidental subjects had been timidly introduced into the civil service examinations. Here and there, too, were radicals, often looked at askance by the government, who were advocating more extensive reforms. On the whole, however, the nation continued on its accustomed paths, led by an educated class which interest and training thoroughly committed to traditional ways. At times it was irritated by the foreigner, but it was still supremely confident in the excellence of its culture and oblivious to the importance of what was transpiring in the outside world.

Then came a series of rude shocks. In 1894 and 1895 the Japanese, long regarded with contempt by the Chinese, administered to the latter a decisive defeat and wrested from them an indemnity, the opening of four more cities as treaty ports, the acknowledgment of the independence of Korea, and the cession of Formosa, the Pescadores Islands, and the Liaotung Peninsula. The major European powers now began a series of aggressions which threatened to dismember China and to bring her into political and economic subjection. During the latter half of the nineteenth century the expansion of Europe had been rapid. Great sections of the world, among them the larger part of Africa, had been parceled out, and, with their earth-hunger still unappeased, the powers were looking with covetous eyes upon the Empire whose weakness had now become so apparent. Germany, France, and Russia induced Japan to retrocede the Liaotung Peninsula. Then, one by one, the powers demanded that certain ports in China be leased to them, that large sections of the Empire be recognized as their spheres of interest, and that concessions for railways be granted to foreign firms. Between the beginning of 1895 and the close of 1898 Russia was given a twenty-five year lease to a part of the Liaotung Peninsula, including Port Arthur and Talienwan (Dairen), the privilege of building the Trans-Siberian Railway across Northern Manchuria, and an agreement for the construction of the Chinese Eastern Railway south to the newly leased ports; Germany, taking advantage of the murder in Shantung of two German Roman Catholic missionaries, members of the Society of the Divine Word, seized Tsingtau, and forced from China a ninety-nine year lease to Kiaochow—including the port of Tsingtau—and exclusive railway and mining concessions in Shantung; Great Britain obtained a lease to Weihai-wei, an extension of the Hongkong territory and a contract for the Shanghai-Nanking Railway, a "declaration of the non-alienation" to any third power of the provinces adjoining the Yangtze, and the assurance that under certain conditions a British subject would be continued as Inspector-General of the Imperial Maritime Customs Service; France was promised that neither Hainan nor any part of the provinces bordering on Tongking would be alienated to a third power, was given a lease to Kwangchow-wan, and began to plan for a railway from Tongking to Yünnanfu; Belgians acquired a contract for a railway from Peking to Hankow, Americans a contract for the line from Hankow to Canton, and the Japanese a non-alienation declaration covering the province of Fukien. It looked as though the next few years might see the partition of China. The American move for the recognition of the "open door" (1899)—an attempt to obtain an international guarantee of equality of economic opportunity—was only another indication of the weakness of the Empire.

These many foreign aggressions naturally gave birth to unrest. Some Chinese wished to hit the foreigner wherever he was found, and if possible drive him from China. Saner heads saw that such an attempt could only bring fresh disaster and contended that the nation must adopt many of the methods of the Westerners. It was the reformers who first had their way and under their leadership extensive changes began to appear. In 1894 and 1895 memorials advocating reform were presented to the throne, one drawn up by the Cantonese radical, Sun Yat-sen, and the other by another Cantonese, K'ang Yu-wei. Numerous reform associations sprang into existence, some of them with an extensive membership among the educated and official classes and one of them sponsored by Chang Chih-tung, Viceroy at Nanking. K'ang Yu-wei's writings were widely read, and Chang Chih-tung endorsed some of the new methods in a book called *Learn,* of which a million copies are said to have been sold. By the beginning of 1898 many of the younger officials and gentry were committed to some sort of reorganization. In June, 1898, the young Emperor called to Peking K'ang Yu-wei, and by the middle of September a number of imperial decrees had appeared, ordering changes which, although mild when compared with those of a decade and a half later, at the time seemed revolutionary. Among other innovations, colleges and schools were ordered established, Peking University was created, the old style of essay—the highly artificial *wên chang* that had long been standard in the civil service examinations—was abolished, steps were to be taken toward the formation of a national army patterned on Western models and based on conscription, a new ministry was created, and a number of sinecure and redundant offices were discontinued.[1]

MISSIONS IN THE YEARS OF REFORM

The reform was actuated largely by nationalistic motives. The desire to stave off further concessions to foreigners and to regain those already given was dominant. Few believed that the West had anything of moral or spiritual value to teach China: it was in the realm of pure and applied science, of machinery, of armies,

---

[1] Morse, *International Relations of the Chinese Empire,* Vol. 3, pp. 129-141; Smith, *China in Convulsion,* Vol. 1, pp. 130-144.

of commerce, and possibly of political organization that the Occident was held to surpass the Middle Kingdom. The movement, therefore, brought with it a double opportunity to the missionary: with the eagerness to learn from the West there was less objection to listening to his message, and he·could try so to direct the current or reform that it would lead to religious and moral as well as to material and intellectual reconstruction.

Roman Catholic missions seem to have made little effort to profit from the new movements. Roman Catholics had few schools of the kind to attract those seeking Western knowledge and placed scant emphasis on the preparation of literature that would introduce to the scholar class the information which many were now seeking. The prevailing missionary methods differed profoundly from those employed by Ricci and his successors. Roman Catholics continued their activities, however, and while the number of their converts seems not to have increased more rapidly than before, the reports show prosperity. There were many baptisms and catechumens. In South Shantung, in the year ending Easter, 1898, 27,869 catechumens were reported, and 1,694 baptisms of pagans.[2] In 1899, in Kweiyang, the capital of Kweichow, a visitor found two churches and at one of them he saw a thousand or twelve hundred present at mass on Sunday.[3] We hear of the officials in one village in Fukien joining in the reception to the Vicar Apostolic.[4] We hear, too, that in the Pei T'ang in Peking a monument was erected to the Virgin for the protection which she was believed to have given the country during the Chino-Japanese War.[5] In 1899 the Dutch province of the Lazarists began operations in the eastern part of Chihli.[6] On the whole, however, the years of rapid change seem not to have been widely commented on by Roman Catholic missionaries nor to have brought any great alteration in their policies.

Protestants, however, heralded the days as a time of opportunity[7] and through their churches, schools, literature, and personal contacts sought to take advantage of them to increase the

[2] *Annals of the Propagation of the Faith,* Vol. 62, p. 213.
[3] Raquez, *Au pays des pagodas,* March 19, 1899.
[4] Cothonay, *Deux ans en Chine,* p. 177.
[5] Piolet, *Les missions catholiques françaises au XIXe siècle,* Vol. 3, p. 92.
[6] Schwager, *Die katholische Heidenmission der Gegenwart,* p. 50.
[7] See, as examples, articles by A. H. Smith and T. Richard in *China Mission Hand-book,* Part 1, pp. 83-90. The translation of *Learn* was published in the *Chinese Recorder,* Vol. 29, showing the interest of Protestants in it. See, too, *Missionary Review of the World,* Vol. 22, p. 27.

numbers of converts, and to influence wholesomely the China which they believed to be on the point of emerging.

Some Protestant missionaries were in close touch with the leading reformers, were consulted by them, and provided them with literature. Sun Yat-sen was a Protestant Christian and had received his education, including his training in medicine, partly at the hands of Protestant missionaries.[8]   Young J. Allen, Gilbert Reid, and especially Timothy Richard were frequently sought out by the liberals.[9]   Allen, in publications before and after the Chino-Japanese War, urged reform, and Richard had the ear of men like Chang Chih-tung and Li Hung-chang.[10]   Liang Ch'i-ch'ao, one of the most brilliant of the younger reformers, was for a time Richard's private secretary.[11]   Richard was invited to Peking to become one of the Emperor's advisers [12] and was often in consultation with K'ang Yu-wei.[13]   W. A. P. Martin was asked to head the faculty of the new Peking University,[14] and a girls' school begun in Shanghai by the chief of the Chinese Telegraph Administration sought the help of missionaries.[15]   The publications of the Society for the Diffusion of Christian and General Knowledge among the Chinese were widely read.   In its first journal the reform society led by K'ang Yu-wei reprinted much of the material which had appeared in the periodical of the Christian society and its *New Collection of Tracts for the Times* contained almost as many essays by Richard as by Liang Ch'i-ch'ao or K'ang Yu-wei.[16]   The Emperor himself read much Christian

[8] Morse, *International Relations of the Chinese Empire*, Vol. 3, p. 130; Linebarger, *Sun Yat-sen and the Republic of China*, pp. 123-131, 152-155, 197, 198; Cantlie and Jones, *Sun Yat Sen and the Republic of China*, pp. 36-38. The last two books give partly conflicting accounts of Sun's youth, but of the facts mentioned above there is no doubt.

[9] Martin, *The Siege of Peking*, p. 41; Reeve, *Timothy Richard*, p. 94. In Shensi, about this time, Moir Duncan of the English Baptist Mission suggested a plan for irrigation to relieve famine and had it sanctioned by the provincial and Peking authorities.—Glover, *Herbert Stanley Jenkins*, p. 39.

[10] Soothill, *China and the West*, pp. 173, 174. Soothill, who had personal opportunity to know whereof he spoke, says: "More than to any others was it due to these two men [Y. J. Allen and T. Richard] that the Chinese were led to see a way of escape from their peril. Their publications were read throughout the length and breadth of the land. From the Emperor on his throne to the village scholar on his hard stool they were awaited with an astonishing eagerness to which I can personally testify."

[11] Richard, *Forty-Five Years in China*, p. 255.

[12] Ibid., p. 263.

[13] Richard, op. cit., p. 253; Reeve, op. cit., p. 100.

[14] Martin, *The Awakening of China*, p. 289.

[15] Richard, op. cit., p. 261.

[16] Ibid., pp. 253, 261.

literature and especially that prepared by Richard's society.[17] Some of the reformers were friendly to Christianity [18] and it is said that one official suggested in a memorial to the throne that the foreign faith be made the state religion.[19]

Protestant schools were practically the only institutions in China where training in Western learning could be acquired. With the reform movement, then, the better ones speedily became popular. Missionaries, sensing the need, strengthened those already in existence and opened new ones. For instance, in 1897 the Methodist Free Church Mission began at Wênchow a high school in which English was taught; [20] three new teachers sent to Canton Christian College in 1898 helped to bring new life to that struggling institution; [21] in 1897 the high school maintained by the (Northern) American Presbyterians at Hangchow became the Hangchow Presbyterian College; [22] in Ningpo, at the request of influential Chinese, a school of high grade was planned under missionary auspices; [23] in 1889 the (Southern) American Methodists decided to found a university at Soochow, although it was not until 1901 that instruction was begun; [24] and in 1899 the London Missionary Society erected the Walford Hart Memorial College at Tientsin.[25]

The circulation of Christian literature showed a phenomenal increase.[26] New presses and tract societies were begun—the Canadian Mission Press in Szechwan in 1897,[27] the China Baptist Publication Society at Canton in 1899,[28] and the West China Religious Tract Society.[29] The reform years, moreover, saw the

[17] *Christian Literature and the Reform Movement*, p. 9; Dennis, *Christian Missions and Social Progress*, Vol. 3, pp. 252, 305.
[18] Chang Chih-tung, in *Learn* (translated as *China's Only Hope*, pp. 144-148), held that the upper classes should tolerate Christianity as they tolerated Buddhism and Taoism.
[19] Smith, *China in Convulsion*, Vol. 1, pp. 145-150; Forsyth, *China Martyrs of 1900*, p. 3.
[20] Soothill, *A Typical Mission in China*, p. 189.
[21] *The Making of a Christian College in the Orient*, p. 7.
[22] *A Century of Protestant Missions in China*, p. 386.
[23] Ibid., p. 385.
[24] Ibid., p. 416; *Chinese Recorder*, Vol. 34, p. 30; *Educational Review*, Vol. 11, p. 75.
[25] *L. M. S. Chronicle*, Vol. 7 (new series), p. 209; *A Century of Protestant Missions in China*, p. 12. The building was not opened until after the Boxer year.
[26] See figures in *A Century of Protestant Missions in China*, pp. 564, 618, 622, 634. The circulation of the British and Foreign Bible Society was 236,717 in 1895, 366,347 in 1896, 567,012 in 1897, 728,716 in 1898, and 856,156 in 1899.— Ibid., p. 564.
[27] Bond, *Our Share in China*, p. 87; *Chinese Recorder*, Vol. 36, p. 352.
[28] *A Century of Protestant Missions in China*, p. 625.
[29] It was originated about 1899.—*China's Millions*, 1899, p. 106.

foundation of the Commercial Press, destined to be the largest publishing house in China and one of the greatest of the purveyors of the new learning. While not a missionary enterprise, its founders, as we have seen, were Christians who had received at least part of their training in a mission press, and they attempted to conduct their business according to Christian principles and made it one of their rules never to publish anything of an anti-Christian nature.[30]

Protestants, too, met with rapidly increasing success in presenting their faith. Between the close of the Chino-Japanese War and 1900 Manchuria witnessed a marked ingathering of converts. Village after village sent requests for evangelists and teachers and the missionaries were embarrassed by the crowds seeking instruction. The number of Protestant church members in the three provinces rose from 5,788 in 1896 to 19,646 in 1899.[31] In 1896 a movement toward Christianity was reported in Fukien, so that while Protestant churches had only 17,012 members, the number of inquirers was 22,037.[32] In 1895 the London Missionary Society alone had at Amoy 2,000 inquirers.[33] In 1898 the China Inland Mission recorded a decided increase in the number of baptisms in its stations in Shensi, Shansi, Honan, and Anhui.[34]

Protestant missionaries, too, were taking advantage of the opportunity rapidly to expand their activities. A few new societies—all of them relatively small—entered China between the close of 1895 and the close of 1899—the South Chihli Mission in 1896,[35] the Danish Lutherans (in Manchuria) in 1896,[36] the Cumberland Presbyterians in 1897 [37] (at Ichang temporarily and then at Changtê, Hunan), the Kieler China Mission (at Canton) in 1897,[38] and the Reformed Church in the United States in 1899.[39] The recently introduced Young Men's Christian Association gave the major part of its attention to the rapidly growing

[30] Encyclopædia Sinica, p. 124; China Mission Year Book, 1911, p. 13.
[31] Christie, Thirty Years in the Manchu Capital, pp. 110-114; Graham, East of the Barrier, p. 148.
[32] Chinese Recorder, Vol. 27, p. 528; Stock and McClelland, For Christ in Fuhkien, p. 47.
[33] China Mission Hand-book, Part 2, p. 11.
[34] China's Millions, 1899, p. 83.
[35] A Century of Protestant Missions in China, p. 535.
[36] Ibid., p. 526.
[37] Ibid., p. 406.
[38] Ibid., p. 545.
[39] A Century of Protestant Missions in China, p. 409; Hoy, History of the China Mission of the Reformed Church in the United States.

new student groups, both those in mission schools and those in non-missionary institutions. In 1898, to the initial secretary, D. Willard Lyon, three were added, Robert R. Gailey, Fletcher S. Brockman, and Robert E. Lewis, all of them able and soon to be prominent in missionary circles. In 1897 the first building erected in China especially for the Young Men's Christian Association was opened in a student district in Tientsin.[40]

Most of the extension of Protestant missions during the early reform years was, however, not by societies newly arrived, but by those that had been longer in the country. Representatives of several organizations gained footholds in that center of anti-foreign agitation, Hunan.[41] Between 1895 both the Church Missionary Society and the Christian and Missionary Alliance established stations in turbulent Kwangsi.[42] In 1896 work was begun among the Miao, a non-Chinese people in the Southwest.[43] The German occupation of Tsingtau led the Berlin Missionary Society, the General Evangelical Protestant Missionary Society, and the American Presbyterians to send representatives to Kiaochow.[44] These are only typical of the fresh activities which the conviction of enlarged opportunity led Protestants to undertake.

With this expansion greater coöperation between Protestant missions became necessary and steps were taken to bring it about. About 1897 a conference of Anglican bishops attempted to coördinate the activities of the various societies of that communion.[45] A form of coöperation was suggested for missions in Shantung.[46] In 1899 a conference of the seven Protestant societies represented

[40] *A Century of Protestant Missions in China,* p. 598; *Chinese Recorder,* Vol. 27, pp. 569, 595; *Foreign Mail,* Vol. 3, No. 2, p. 11, Vol. 3, No. 4, p. 11, Vol. 4, No. 2, p. 13, Vol. 4, No. 3, p. 15, Vol. 7, No. 11, p. 7.
[41] Broomhall, *Jubilee Story of the China Inland Mission,* pp. 232-234; Broomhall, *Pioneer Work in Hunan,* p. 81; Hoy, *History of the China Mission of the Reformed Church in the United States,* p. 106; Glover, *Ebenezer,* pp. 25 et seq.; *L. M. S. Chronicle,* Vol. 7 (new series), p. 5; Beresford, *The Breakup of China,* p. 165; Taylor, *Hudson Taylor,* p. 577; *A Century of Protestant Missions in China,* p. 387. The energetic anti-Christian propaganda from Hunan made missionaries eager to enter the province. The (Northern) American Presbyterians had for several years possessed outposts across the southern border. Between 1896 and 1900 they, the London Missionary Society, the China Inland Mission, the Christian and Missionary Alliance, and the Cumberland Presbyterians sent representatives into the province from the north and succeeded in gaining a foothold.
[42] Lowe, *Gleanings,* p. 2; Farmer, *Ida Beeson Farmer,* p. 59; *A Century of Protestant Missions in China,* pp. 41-43.
[43] Clarke, *Among the Tribes of Southwest China,* pp. 140-150.
[44] Richter, *Geschichte der Berlinermissionsgesellschaft,* pp. 614 et seq.; Schlunk, *Durch Deutsch-Kiautschou,* p. 34; Forsyth, *Shantung,* p. 248.
[45] *Spirit of Missions,* Vol. 62, p. 443.
[46] *Chinese Recorder,* Vol. 30, p. 468.

in Szechwan met at Chungking and out of it came a division of the province to prevent duplication, a standing advisory committee to which matters of common interest could be referred, a tract society, and the monthly *West China Missionary News.*[47] Protestants were endeavoring to approach as a unit the task of reaching this western province, so vast and so isolated by mountains that it was almost an empire in itself.

All of this Protestant activity led to a rapid growth in communicants. The total rose from 55,093 in 1893 [48] to 80,682 in 1898,[49] an increase of nearly fifty per cent. in about five years. Quite as important was the position that Protestant Christianity was coming to have in the China that was beginning to emerge. Protestant missionaries and the Protestant community, while by no means of outstanding importance in the nation's life, were influential out of all proportion to their numbers. They were providing the best source in China for acquiring the new knowledge so eagerly sought, and to some extent they were helping to steady and to direct the occasionally bewildered and often inexperienced reformers as the latter attempted to guide a huge Empire into untried and dangerous paths.

The Beginning of Reaction
September, 1898—December 31, 1899

The reform movement, progressing so rapidly and bringing such increased opportunity to missions was not to proceed far without encountering serious reverses. Many of the reforms proved inconvenient to influential officials, those that abolished offices aroused the opposition of the incumbents and their friends, and against all of them were arrayed the majority of the older members of a powerful ruling class. The liberals were many of them young and inexperienced and their chief dependence was on the Emperor, who had little skill in governing and was neither mature nor astute. Moreover, foreign aggressions continued and conservatives could urge that the reformers had not succeeded in saving the country. One after another, powerful groups and individuals were alienated, and in September, 1898, the Empress

---

[47] *Chinese Recorder,* Vol. 30, pp. 157-160; Hart, *V. C. Hart,* p. 331; Wallace, *The Heart of Sz-chuan,* pp. 79 et seq.; Davidson and Mason, *Life in West China,* p. 157.
[48] *China Mission Hand-book,* Part 2, p. 325.
[49] *Chinese Recorder,* Vol. 30, p. 144.

Dowager, a convinced conservative and long the real power behind the throne, stung by a threat against herself and her old friend, Jung Lu, by a *coup d'état* reassumed the direction of affairs, made the Emperor a virtual prisoner, executed such of the leading reformers as she could lay her hands on, and cancelled many of the innovations. The rest of the country took its cue from Peking and the popularity of new ideas abated.[50]

Given the recent defeat by Japan, the aggressions by European powers, the talk of change, and now the conservative reaction, unrest of some description was inevitable. It was accentuated by floods and bad harvests—misfortunes seldom absent from some section of the Empire. Part of the unrest was anti-dynastic, some took the form of robbery and banditry, but much of it was directed against the foreigner, for the latter was held to be the source of most of the nation's woes.

Missionaries were more widely scattered than were foreign merchants or diplomats and so bore the brunt of the anti-foreign outbreaks. Moreover, the feeling against them was accentuated by the old causes with which we have become familiar. Disturbances against the missionary and his converts were not unknown in 1897 and the early part of 1898, but they became much more numerous in the latter part of 1898 and in 1899.

Roman Catholics suffered severely. On November first, 1897, two priests, Fathers Henle and Nies, of the Society of the Divine Word, were killed in a village in Shantung. The murderers seem to have been members of a secret order with the significant name of Ta Tao Hui, or "Great Sword Society," and the Governor of the province, Li Ping-hêng, was anti-foreign and is said to have encouraged secret associations whose objective was the extermination of Westerners. The murder gave the German Government an excuse for seizing Tsingtau and demanding the lease of Kiaochow and special privileges in Shantung.[51] It seems probable

[50] The sales of the Society for the Diffusion of Christian and General Knowledge among the Chinese fell from $18,457 in 1898 to $9,113 in 1899; the circulation of the Central China Religious Tract Society fell from 1,470,699 in 1898 to 1,209,647 in 1899 and 880,453 in 1900; the circulation of the British and Foreign Bible Society rose from 728,716 in 1898 to 856,156 in 1899, but it fell to 604,462 in 1900 and to 431,446 in 1901.—*A Century of Protestant Missions in China*, pp. 564, 618, 634.

[51] Morse, *International Relations of the Chinese Empire*, Vol. 3, p. 106; Cordier in *Catholic Encyclopedia*, Vol. 9, p. 747; Stenz, *In der Heimat des Konfuzius*, pp. 211 et seq.; *Annals of the Propagation of the Faith*, Vol. 61, pp. 52-87; Stenz, *Life of Richard Henle*, passim; Stenz, *Twenty-Five Years in China*, pp. 73-93.

that at least some of the Roman Catholic authorities were not displeased by this action, but the Church appears not to have had any important part in initiating it.[52]   In 1898 Kwangsi, so frequently turbulent, was the scene of pronounced unrest, and although most of the agitation appears not to have been directed against the missionaries and part of the province remained quiet,[53] two priests, Mazel [54] and Bertholet,[55] of the Missions Étrangères of Paris, and several Chinese Christians were killed.   In November, 1898, Father Stenz of the Shantung mission of the Society of the Divine Word, who had barely escaped when his confrères Henle and Nies were slain, was imprisoned for two days and the homes of a number of Christians were plundered.[56]   In Szechwan the anti-Catholic rebellion led by Yü Man-tze continued.   In June or July, 1898, two priests were captured, and one of them, Fleury, was not released until January, 1899.   Yü Man-tze's example encouraged other anti-Catholic uprisings in the province, and Catholic villages were plundered and no priest was safe.   While, as a result of French pressure, the authorities took action, the revolt broke out again in 1899.[57]

On October 14th, 1898, Father Chanès and thirteen Chinese Christians were killed in Kwangtung.   Chanès was slain at the altar after having given his fellow victims absolution and plenary indulgence.[58]   In December, 1898, a Franciscan, Father Victorin Delbrouck, was tortured and beheaded in Hupeh after eight neophytes had been done to death before his eyes.[59]   In Chêkiang in 1898 and 1899 a society burned chapels and persecuted Catholics.[60]   In 1899 in one district in the northern part of Shantung

[52] Graham, *East of the Barrier,* pp. 194-198, declares that Count von Bülow said in the Reichstag on Feb. 8, 1898, that Bishop Anzer "has told us in the most peremptory manner that the occupation of Kiaochow was a vital question not only for the prosperity but for the maintenance of the Chinese mission."
[53] Launay, *Mission du Koungsi, pp.* 388-404.
[54] Joly, *Le christianisme et l'Éxtrême Orient,* Vol. 1, p. 273.   An indemnity of 15,000 taels was exacted by the French Government.
[55] Cordier in *Catholic Encyclopedia,* Vol. 9, p. 747; *Annals of the Propagation of the Faith,* Vol. 61, p. 230.
[56] Pieper, *Knospen und Blüten aus dem blumigen Reiche der Mitte,* p. 377.
[57] Morse, op. cit., Vol. 3, pp. 165, 166; Colquhoun, *Overland to China,* p. 349.
[58] Letter of Bishop Chausse, Oct. 21, 1898, in *Annals of the Propagation of the Faith,* Vol. 62, p. 77.
[59] *Annals of the Propagation of the Faith,* Vol. 62, pp. 196 et seq.; Wegener, *Viktorin Delbrouck,* passim.   The Chinese, as a result of the demand of the French Consul, paid 10,000 taels indemnity for the murder of Delbrouck and 44,500 taels for the property destroyed in Hupeh.—Cordier in *Catholic Encyclopedia,* Vol. 9, p. 747.
[60] *Annals of the Propagation of the Faith,* Vol. 62, pp. 254-257, 367.

twenty-seven Roman Catholic communities are said to have been plundered and two thousand Christians left homeless.[61] In one place in the province Roman Catholic missionaries and their converts barricaded a church against members of the Great Sword Society and there successfully defended themselves from the aggressors.[62]

Probably partly as a result of French pressure, on January 15th, 1898, July 12th, 1898, and again on October 6th, 1898, imperial decrees were published ordering special protection for Christians.[63]

On March 16th, 1899, an imperial rescript was issued laying down rules for the approach of Chinese officials by Roman Catholic missionaries. Bishops were to have the privilege of seeking interviews with viceroys and governors and were to rank with them, provincials and head priests could ask for interviews with provincial treasurers and judges and with taot'ais, and other priests could ask to see prefects and district magistrates. Bishops were to furnish the provincial authorities with lists of the clergy entitled to transact business with the officials, and the privileges were to apply only to priests who were Westerners. In important cases the ecclesiastical authorities might ask the minister or consul of the nation entrusted by the Pope with the protection of Roman Catholics to arrange matters with the Tsungli Yamen or with the local officials.[64]

The rescript was apparently issued partly through the coöperation of Bishop Favier, the Vicar Apostolic in Peking,[65] but chiefly on the initiative of Chinese officials. The imperial government seems to have been endeavoring, as part of the reactionary movement, to restore the authority of the provincial officials as against the centralizing tendencies of the past few years. It may also have thought that by permitting the missionary to go directly to the officials, without the foreign consul as intermediary, disputes with the missionary and his converts could be taken out of the realm of international politics, the French protectorate be annulled, and the government be enabled in time

[61] Volling, *Die Christenverfolgung in Nord-Shansi in 1900,* p. 22.
[62] Stenz, *In der Heimat des Konfuzius,* p. 145.
[63] Hertzlet, *China Treaties,* p. 1150; Cordier, *Histoire des relations de la Chine avec les puissances occidentales,* Vol. 3, p. 464.
[64] MacMurray, *Treaties and Conventions With and Concerning China,* Vol. 1, pp. 717-718.
[65] Cordier in *Catholic Encyclopedia,* Vol. 3, p. 677.

to remove the extraterritorial status of Christians.[66] If this was
the purpose of the government, in operation the rescript had
an effect quite contrary to that originally contemplated. In actual
practice it permitted Roman Catholic priests and vicars apostolic
to assume official insignia [67] and recognized them as having
a certain civil jurisdiction over their converts: Roman Catholic
communities were more than ever *imperia in imperio*.[68]

From the beginning the decree provoked criticism, especially
by Protestants. Protestants and Roman Catholics had little love
for each other,[69] Protestant missionaries viewed with disfavor the
political status of Roman Catholic missionaries, and the large
majority deprecated any effort to obtain an extension of its privileges in favor of themselves.[70] The British Government for-

[66] Steiger in *T'oung Pao*, Vol. 24, pp. 215-246.
[67] This custom had apparently been growing after 1860. Reid asserts (*The
Sources of the Anti-Foreign Disturbances in China*, pp. 76-104) that the bishops
often adopted an official button, had a cannon fired when they arrived in a town,
had an umbrella—a Chinese sign of rank—carried ahead of them, and had issued
proclamations in forms similar to those used by officials, and that they had been
doing so since 1860. Wên Chang (*The Chinese Crisis from Within*, p. 303) says:
"In many places the missionary intrudes himself into the Chinese court and sits
beside the magistrate to hear a case between his convert and a non-Christian
native." It must be recalled, however, that Reid is Protestant and Wên Chang
bitterly anti-missionary and both reports may be colored by their prejudices.
[68] The edict was welcomed by at least some of the Roman Catholics. Mgr.
Grassi, Vicar Apostolic in Northern Shansi, sang the *Te Deum* and believed that
the edict promised the triumph of the Church.—Ricci, *Barbarie e Trionfi*, p. 237.
[69] Only a few examples need be given of the friction between Roman Catholics and Protestants. John, *Sowing and Reaping*, p. 44, says (Apr. 1, 1896) that
Roman Catholics are doing all they can to obstruct some of his work. *The Chinese
Recorder*, Vol. 4 (1871), p. 9, answered a criticism that had appeared in *Annales
de la propagation de la foi*, Sept. 1870, saying that Protestant work in Laoling,
Shantung, was a failure.
[70] *Chinese Recorder*, Vol. 30, p. 481; *Spirit of Missions*, Vol. 65, p. 266;
Broomhall, *Bishop Cassels*, p. 211. Sept. 1, 1899, the Anglican bishops in conference at Shanghai passed resolutions viewing with alarm "the rapidly growing
interference of French and other Roman Catholic priests with the provincial and
local government of China."—Pascoe, *Two Hundred Years of the S. P. G.*, Vol. 2,
p. 711. Broomhall, *Bishop Cassels*, p. 211. A missionary conference at Peitaiho,
Aug. 19, 1899, asked the British and American ministers to obtain for Protestants
the same privileges that had been granted to Roman Catholics by the decree, and
a few other Protestant missionaries took the same position. However, conferences
of the Methodist Episcopal Church and the American Presbyterians and the Shanghai Missionary Association took a contrary position, and Conger, the American
Minister, reported that nine-tenths of the Protestant missionaries were opposed to
an extension of the privileges to themselves. The American State Department had
first instructed Conger to obtain an extension of the privileges of the decree to
American Protestant missionaries, but Conger found the large majority of missionaries so opposed to this action that he did not undertake it. The Anglican bishops
believed such privileges to be undesirable. Steiger, in *T'oung Pao*, Vol. 24,
pp. 215-246, gives the documentary evidence for these assertions. Steiger holds
that at least some Protestants were already, and quite illegally, dealing directly
with Chinese officials and not through their consuls.

mally refused to recognize French jurisdiction over Roman Catholic missionaries of British nationality.[71] The rescript irritated many of the Chinese, and after a little less than ten years (March 12th, 1908) it was revoked.[72]

Protestants likewise suffered from the general unrest. In March, 1898, property rented by the American Methodists at Chungking was destroyed by a riot.[73] In 1898 Fleming, a missionary of the China Inland Mission, together with a Chinese Christian, was killed by militia in Kweichow.[74] In 1898 anti-Christian riots broke out in Ochowfu, Shantung.[75] In the autumn of 1898 fresh disturbances were reported in Szechwan, but this time they were promptly suppressed by the officials.[76] In the summer of 1899 missionaries were rioted out of Paoan on the Kansu border of Tibet.[77] In 1899 serious trouble occurred again at Ichowfu, both Protestants and Roman Catholics being attacked and numbers of Christians being reduced to beggary.[78] The Protestant mission buildings at Chienning, Fukien, a town long the seat of anti-Christian feeling, were burned in June, 1899, one Christian was killed, and three English missionaries barely escaped with their lives.[79] In October, 1899, the premises of the China Inland Mission in Hokow, Kiangsi, were destroyed, and that same year saw other uprisings in the province in which both Roman Catholics and Protestants suffered.[80]

The close of 1899 found all China seething. Not only missionaries but other foreigners were being attacked and in most of the provinces there were riots and incipient rebellions. The discontent might take almost any direction and at any time blaze up into a serious conflagration.

THE BOXER OUTBREAK, 1900

By the close of 1899 the situation became especially ominous

[71] Koo, *Status of Aliens in China*, p. 300.
[72] MacMurray, op. cit., Vol. 1, p. 718.
[73] *Foreign Relations, 1898*, pp. 191 et seq.. An indemnity of 5,000 taels was paid through the intervention of the American authorities.
[74] *Parliamentary Papers*, 1900, Vol. 105, China No. 1, pp. 4, 98. An indemnity of 22,000 taels was paid through the intervention of the British authorities.
[75] Morse, *International Relations of the Chinese Empire*, Vol. 3, p. 173.
[76] Wallace, *The Heart of Sz-chwan*, p. 79.
[77] Ekvall, *Outposts, or Tibetan Border Sketches*, p. 152.
[78] Smith, *China in Convulsion*, Vol. 1, pp. 155-161.
[79] Morse, op. cit., Vol. 3, p. 162; Darley, *The Light of the Morning*, p. 163.
[80] Morse, op. cit., Vol. 3, p. 167; Fiske, *My Father's Business*, pp. 32, 33.

in the North and in 1900 what is usually known as the Boxer uprising broke out.

The causes of the disturbances were many. Practically all the factors that made for unrest throughout the Empire were present —anger at the seizure of territory by the powers; resentment against the interference of missionaries in lawsuits; irritation at the acquisition of property in the interior by missions, at the proscription by missionaries of many time-honored Chinese institutions and customs, and at the Christians who embraced these disorganizing teachings; offenses by foreigners, including tactless missionaries, against Chinese susceptibilities; the scandal occasioned by misunderstood Christian customs; the discontent of those thrown out of employment by the railway, the steamboat, and the post office; the belief that the railways were interfering with *fêng shui* and rumors that at every curve of the iron roads a Chinese boy and girl were buried; conservatism, especially among the official and educated classes; the presence of "lewd fellows of the baser sort," ready to take advantage of any opportunity for slaughter and looting; and, finally, the reaction led by the Empress Dowager and many of the high officials.[81]

Most of these causes, as has been suggested, were present in all the provinces, but it was in Manchuria, Shansi, Chihli, and the parts of Mongolia bordering on these districts that the disturbances centered. The movement first arose in Shantung, but it was in the districts mentioned that it was most acute. Elsewhere the unrest would probably have subsided without a violent

---

[81] There are various analyses of the causes of the Boxer outbreak, each emphasizing certain causes or groups of causes. See Ketler, *The Tragedy of Paotingfu,* p. 191; Reid, *Sources of the Anti-Foreign Disturbances in China,* passim; Beals, *China and the Boxers,* p. 17; Smyth in *China against the World;* Broomhall, *Martyred Missionaries of the China Inland Mission,* pp. 4 et seq.; Forsyth, *China Martyrs of 1900,* p. 5; Morse, *International Relations of the Chinese Empire,* Vol. 3, pp. 175-177, 253; Edwards, *Fire and Sword in Shansi,* pp. 52-54; *Missionary Herald,* Vol. 97, p. 364 (answering the charge that the outbreak was due to missionaries) ; Miner, *China's Book of Martyrs,* p. 17; Martin, *The Siege of Peking,* p. 68; Steiger, *China and the Occident,* passim. For accounts accusing the missionaries of being the chief cause, see Wên Chang, *The Chinese Crisis from Within;* Thomson, *The Chinese,* p. 367; Davenport, *China from Within,* especially pp. 36, 37; Michie, *The Englishman in China,* Vol. 2, pp. 233-238.

Interesting light is thrown on the causes by a placard posted on the walls of Peking in Boxer times:

"Our Emperor is about to become powerful."

"The leader of the Boxers is a royal person."

"Within three months all foreigners will be killed or driven away from China."

"During forty years the Empire has become full of foreigners."

"They have divided the land."—Beals, *China and the Boxers,* p. 15.

outburst, and reform would soon once more have become the order of the day.

The reasons why the general unrest broke out in such violence just where it did are not far to seek. In the Northeast were most of the ports that had been seized by foreigners; here most of the railway building was taking place; here, moreover, was the court, now dominated by reactionary elements; and here were to be found a number of powerful and extremely anti-foreign officials. Here, too, the government ordered the I Ho Tuan, or local militia, to be placed in readiness to defend the country against further encroachments by the alien. Later the situation was aggravated by the maladroitness of the legations, and of foreign naval and military commanders.[82]

The initial mutterings of the storm were heard in 1899. The then Governor of Shantung was a bitterly anti-foreign Manchu, Yü Hsien, who encouraged the I Ho Tuan in their preparations. To these bands Westerners early gave the name Boxers, from I Ho Ch'üan, or "Righteous Harmony Fists," and from the gymnastic exercises which were practiced by the various units. The groups soon adopted the mottoes *Pao kuo, mieh yang*, "Protect the country, destroy the foreigner," *Li kuo, mieh yang*, "Establish the country, destroy the foreigner," and *Pao Ch'ing, mieh yang*, "Protect the Ch'ing (dynasty), destroy the foreigner."[83] Into these groups, too, came many rowdies, and disorderly secret societies joined them.

Very soon, perhaps from the beginning, the "Boxer" bands began to practice occult rites. In a country where belief in magic and spirits is widespread this was not remarkable, especially since the foreigner was popularly accused of using the black art and it was by more powerful forces of the same kind that he could best be resisted. The secret initiation and mystic ceremonies were thought to insure the protection of the spirits and to render the recipients invulnerable to sword, spear, or bullet.

Anti-foreign bands, some of them I Ho Tuan, some of them members of the Ta Tao Hui, were protected by Yü Hsien, and by the close of 1899 they were persecuting Christians, unrepressed

[82] The most interesting account of the genesis of the Boxer uprising and of its connection with the local militia is in Steiger, *China and the Occident*. See, too, Graham, *East of the Barrier*, p. 204.

[83] The last is given in Weale, *Indiscreet Letters from Peking*, p. 12. Another version was "Cherish the dynasty, destroy the foreigner."—Morse, op. cit., Vol. 3, p. 175.

by the provincial authorities.[84]   The legations brought pressure on Peking and in December Yü Hsien was replaced by Yüan Shih-k'ai.[85]   Before the new Governor could restore order, on the last day of the year, Brooks, of the Society for the Propagation of the Gospel in Foreign Parts, was killed about fifty miles south-west of Tsinanfu.   The British authorities acted vigorously, several men were punished, and an indemnity was insisted upon —with doubtful consistency with Christian principles—to erect a memorial church and tablet.[86]   At Peking reactionary counsels were gaining strength and although the legations protested against the anti-foreign agitation that was now so widespread, in January an edict was issued which, while pretending to deal with the situation, gave encouragement to the Boxers.   Moreover, Yü Hsien was received at court as a hero and in March, 1900, was appointed Governor of Shansi.[87]

In February and March, 1900, fresh steps were taken against the reformers,[88] throughout the late winter and spring the Boxers increased in Chihli, Tientsin was threatened by them,[89] and in May Bishop Favier told the French Minister that several villages had been looted, that seventy Christians had been massacred, and that over two thousand were homeless.   He expressed the belief that an attack on the foreigners in Peking was impending.[90] The last of May a number of railway engineers had to fight their way as they fled from Paotingfu to Tientsin.[91]   In June the buildings of the Presbyterian mission in Weihsien, Shantung, were destroyed by a mob;[92] the anti-foreign Li Ping-hêng was appointed Viceroy of Chihli and on his way North to assume office slaughtered over a thousand Roman Catholics in Hochienfu, the center of the Jesuit mission in Chihli;[93] two English missionaries were killed a few miles northeast of Paotingfu;[94] and the plant of the American Board Mission at T'ungchow, just outside of

[84] Martin, *The Siege of Peking*, p. 60; Morse, op. cit., Vol. 3, pp. 175, 176; Smith, *China in Convulsion*, Vol. 1, pp. 163-182.
[85] Smith, op. cit., Vol. 1, pp. 176-182.
[86] Morse, op. cit., Vol. 3, pp. 178, 179; Forsyth, *The China Martyrs of 1900*, p. 9; Norris, *China*, pp. 156-158.
[87] Morse, op. cit., Vol. 3, pp. 185, 186; Smith, op. cit., Vol. 1, pp. 188-195.
[88] Morse, op. cit., Vol. 3, pp. 188, 189.
[89] Roberts, *A Flight for Life*, p. 10.
[90] Smith, op. cit., Vol. 1, pp. 206, 207.
[91] Morse, op. cit., Vol. 3, p. 199.
[92] Hawes, *New Thrills in Old China*, pp. 88-108.
[93] Morse, op. cit., Vol. 3, p. 261.
[94] Ibid., Vol. 3, p. 199; Forsyth, op. cit., pp. 15-17.

Peking, was burned and many Christians were killed only a few hours after the foreigners had made their escape to the capital.[95] In June, too, anti-foreign riots broke out in distant Yünnan, where the French aggression had helped to bring on a crisis.[96]

By the early part of June the situation in the North had become so serious that an attempt was made to throw additional foreign troops into Peking. On June 10th an international body of about two thousand left Tientsin, but its advance was blocked and with great difficulty it made its way back to Tientsin. The foreign community at Tientsin was in jeopardy, and on June 17th the Taku forts, commanding the approach to the city from the sea, were taken by a storming party made up of six nationalities.

By the Boxers and the court these attacks by foreigners were interpreted as wanton assaults. The Empress Dowager, swayed by bitterly anti-foreign and bellicose advisers, regarded the capture of the Taku forts as a declaration of war. In spite of the moderate counsels of her old friend Jung Lu and the wishes of the Emperor, she gave every encouragement to the Boxers, and on June 24th an imperial decree ordered the killing of foreigners throughout the Empire. The groups dominant at Peking believed that the time had come to drive out the overbearing alien and to rid the Empire of him and all his hateful works. Many of those about the Empress Dowager, and possibly the "Old Buddha" herself, were convinced that the Boxer forces, aided by the magical powers to which they laid claim and by the imperial forces, would be able successfully to dislodge the Westerner. China had been led, in effect, to pit herself against the world.[97]

Throughout Chihli, Shansi, Manchuria, and parts of Mongolia,

[95] Morse, *International Relations of the Chinese Empire,* Vol. 3, p. 203; Mateer, *Siege Days,* pp. 40-63.

[96] Jack, *The Back Blocks of China,* p. 103.

[97] *The Diary of His Excellency, Ching-shan,* translated by Duyvendale, passim. Ching-shan was in a position to know what was taking place at court. It is not altogether clear just what motives lay behind the action of the Empress Dowager and the advisers who for the moment had her ear. It is quite possible that the fate of the dynasty was deemed at stake and that it was believed that if active steps were not taken against the foreigner the unrest would be turned against the Manchus. Nor is it certain that if the foreign authorities had not used force to protect their nationals the outbreak would not have occurred. Their action in starting the relief force and in capturing the Taku forts precipitated the crisis, but it would very possibly have come anyway. There were conflicting counsels at court and while the warlike actions of the foreign commanders aided in throwing the balance in favor of the more violent factions it is very possible that the scale would have turned in that direction had the aliens remained quiescent. See one theory in Steiger, *China and the Occident.*

the Peking authorities were able for the time to carry out their will. In Tientsin the foreign community was beleaguered but was protected by the international forces, now able to reach them from the sea. In Peking the foreign community, together with some of the Chinese Christians, was concentrated first in the Pei T'ang, the legation quarter, and the compound of the American Methodist Mission, and then, on June 20th, in the first two places. On June 19th the Tsungli Yamen, two days after the Taku forts had been stormed, notified the foreign ministers that because of the demand of the admirals that the forts be given up, China was at war with the countries they represented, and that they and all their nationals must quit the capital within twenty-four hours.[98]   On June 21st appeared a formal declaration of war.[99]   On June 20th Baron von Ketteler, the German Minister, while on his way to the Tsungli Yamen, was murdered by a Manchu bannerman, and the ministers decided not to trust a Chinese guard or to leave the city.

That day began the siege of the foreigners in their two refuges. Here, aided by a few foreign troops—four hundred and twenty-five in all—who had been in Peking before communications with the sea were cut, the foreign communities and some of the Chinese Christians held out until August 14th, when a strong force collected by the powers succeeded in fighting its way through from Tientsin and captured the city. The court fled west to Hsianfu, much of Peking was looted by the invading army—with a sordidness more despicable than the madness of the Boxers—and foreign troops sent into the countryside relieved such Westerners and Chinese Christians as had succeeded in defending themselves through the crisis, and with much severity put down most of such resistance as remained.

The repercussions of the Boxer explosion were, of course, felt throughout the Empire. Outside the Northeast, however, the officials in command saw the futility of combatting the entire Occident and Japan, and not only did not join in the war but exerted themselves to protect the alien and to maintain order. They were reassured, moreover, when on June 20th the foreign admirals off Tientsin formally declared that they were not waging war on China but were seeking merely to rescue their fellow-

[98] Martin, *The Siege of Peking,* p. 77.
[99] Morse, op. cit., Vol. 3, p. 236; Beals, *China and the Boxers,* p. 110.

countrymen. The position of the admirals was in the main that of their governments. Thus reassured, in Shantung Yüan Shih-k'ai suppressed the Boxers, Chang Chih-tung and Liu K'un-i, Viceroys at Wuchang and Nanking respectively, exerted their powerful influence on the side of peace, and Li Hung-chang, then Viceroy at Canton, strove to mediate between the powers and the imperial government. Other officials for the most part followed their example. Moreover, the imperial order of June 24th, "whenever you meet a foreigner you must slay him," before being sent out by telegram to the provinces, was altered—probably at the cost of the heads of the responsible officials—so that the word "slay" was made to read "protect." [100] Only infrequently was there loss of life or serious destruction of property. [101]

This in brief summary is the main outline of the events of the summer and autumn of 1900. What interests us here especially is the extent to which missionaries and Chinese Christians suffered. As has already been suggested, missionaries were in part, but only in part, responsible for the unrest which gave rise to the Boxer outbreak. The uprising was not primarily anti-Christian: it was anti-foreign. Missionaries and their converts were, however, the chief sufferers. By the nature of their calling missionaries were more widely scattered outside the ports and hence more exposed to attack than were other foreigners, and, for the reasons which have been made apparent in the preceding chapters, they were probably disliked more heartily than were the others. Chinese Christians were dubbed "secondary devils." They were believed to be traitors to their country and its culture, the protection that they enjoyed under the treaties of 1858 served further to identify them with the Westerner, and the lawsuits in which missionaries had interfered were remembered against them. The year 1900 became memorable, therefore, for the most severe persecution which Christians had yet encountered in China. In the centuries of their activities in the Middle Kingdom Roman Catholics had faced many reverses, but probably never at one time had they suffered the loss of so many lives. For Protestants the Boxer uprising was the first really serious blow, the first general persecution. For neither Roman Catholics nor Protestants

[100] Morse, op. cit., Vol. 3, pp. 237, 238; *Diary of Ching-shan*, pp. 60, 61. There is some doubt as to the authenticity of this incident.

[101] This summary is taken chiefly from Morse, op. cit., Vol. 3, pp. 193-259.

was the reverse to be more than temporary; it was even, because of the memories of the heroism and devotion of the martyrs, to deepen devotion.   To both, however, the year was long to be memorable and in their annals its events occupy a prominent place.

ROMAN CATHOLICS AND THE BOXER DISORDERS

Roman Catholics suffered severely, for their work was old and well established, their converts were numerous, and their interference in litigation had sowed for them a harvest of ill-will. The wrath of the Boxers seems to have been fiercer toward them than toward Protestants.   In Chihli, where the storm centered, the destruction was great.   Bishop Favier, the Lazarist Vicar Apostolic in Peking, was in Europe in the early days of 1900, but hearing of the growing unrest, posted back to China.[102]   By May Christians were being killed, and note after note from the Bishop to the French authorities obtained only inadequate or temporary protection.[103]   By the middle of June the Boxers had arrived in Peking, and before the end of the month the ancient Nan T'ang, dating from the eighteenth century, had been destroyed and many Christians killed in it and its compound,[104] the Tung T'ang had been burned and the Christians gathered there, together with one of their pastors, had been slain, the Hsi T'ang had been given to the flames, and, although the priests and sisters and some of the Chinese Christians had been brought into the legations by a rescue party, others of the refugees still in the church were massacred or, attempting to escape, were thrown back into the blazing building.[105]   A thousand or so of the Christians, the survivors of the massacres, were brought into the legations and joined in the defense.   Part way across the city, in the Pei T'ang and its surrounding compound and in the adjoining house of the Daughters of Charity, Bishop Favier gathered about him a group of his clergy, foreign assistants, and Chinese Christians, about thirty-four hundred in all—more than half of them women and children from the schools and orphanages—and with

[102] Favier, *The Heart of Pekin*, pp. 6 et seq.
[103] Piolet, *Les missions catholiques français au XIXe siècle*, Vol. 3, p. 104.
[104] Planchet, *Documents sur les martyrs de Pékin pendant la persécution des Boxeurs*, Vol. 1, p. 107.
[105] Weale, *Indiscreet Letters from Peking*, pp. 56-70; Morse, op. cit., Vol. 3, pp. 204, 205; Bland and Backhouse, *China Under the Empress Dowager*, p. 194.

the aid of a handful of French marines held the Boxers at bay for two entire months—from June 14th until the relief by the Allies on August 16th. The firing was often heavy, five mines were planted and exploded under the devoted band, food ran short, and over four hundred of the besieged perished, but the survivors valiantly held out, and at times drove back the attackers by sorties.[106] All other Catholic edifices in Peking were destroyed, and even the cemetery at Chala, to the west of the city, where were the graves of Ricci, Schall, Verbiest, and others of the missionaries of the seventeenth and eighteenth centuries, was desecrated.[107] Throughout Chihli much the same story was repeated. In the southeastern part of the province the Jesuits suffered severely. Several churches and chapels and the houses of over half the Christians were destroyed, and many Chinese Christians and at least four priests were killed.[108] Several of the Jesuits remained with their flocks and concentrated about eighteen thousand, approximately one-third of those in the mission, at several centers, where they fended off their persecutors until the storm blew over or until rescued by French troops.[109] Some Christians attributed their escape to the Virgin Mary and to the use of the rosary. The Virgin was reported to have appeared on at least one occasion to warn off the attackers.[110] Here and there elsewhere Christians defended themselves, as, for example, at a place south of Tientsin where eighteen hundred of them stood siege until relieved in October by French troops.[111] The Trappist monastery, hidden away in its hills, was not seriously molested, and there a group of converts found safety.[112] By the time the storm had passed, however, Bishop Favier estimated that in his vicariate alone—and there were then four in Chihli—three-fourths of the chapels had been destroyed and that at least fifteen or

[106] Conger, *Letters from China*, p. 166; Favier, op. cit., passim; Planchet, op. cit., Vol. 1, pp. 35 et seq.; Lynch, *The War of the Civilizations*, pp. 93-395; Brown, *New Forces in Old China*, p. 199.
[107] Planchet, op. cit., Vol. 1, pp. 195 et seq.
[108] Piolet, op. cit., Vol. 3, p. 145; *Chine et Ceylan*, No. 6, Dec. 1900, pp. 185 et seq., No. 8, Dec. 1901, pp. 27 et seq., Sept. 1901, pp. 412 et seq., 443.
[109] Journals and accounts of missionaries in *Chine et Ceylan*, No. 6, Dec. 1900, pp. 112 et seq., No. 7, March 1901, pp. 275 et seq., No. 8, Sept. 1901, pp. 381 et seq.
[110] Albert Vinchon, S. J., in *Chine, Ceylan, Madagascar*, March, 1905, pp. 130-133.
[111] Morse, op. cit., Vol. 3, p. 316.
[112] Limagne, *Les Trappistes en Chine*, pp. 57 et seq.

twenty thousand Christians had lost their lives.[113] In the historic cemetery just to the west of Peking, in grounds in which evidences of Boxer desecration are still visible, lie buried the remains of six thousand or more martyrs of that one fateful year,[114] and in the memorial chapel on stones encircling the building are engraved the names of such as are known, mute witnesses to the suffering and the heroism of the Christian community.[115]

In Shantung the Governor, Yüan Shih-k'ai, prevented such excesses as were committed in Chihli, but in the vicariate of Northern Shantung two Christians were killed and from two to three hundred Christian communities wrecked.[116]

In Shansi, where the truculent Yü Hsien was in power, the Christians could expect little mercy. Here at the outbreak of the troubles were about eighteen foreign priests, including Gregory Grassi, the Vicar Apostolic, and his coadjutor, Francis Fogolla, all Franciscans, about twenty Chinese priests, about fifteen thousand Christians, and five orphanages maintained by the Franciscan Sisters of Mary.[117] By the close of June the work of extirpation was already well under way.[118] In T'aiyüanfu the mission property was destroyed, and on July 9th Bishops Grassi and Fogolla, several other priests, four or five students for the priesthood, a lay brother, several sisters, and nine servants of the mission were haled before the Governor's tribunal and killed. Yü Hsien himself dealt the aged Fogolla the first blow.[119] The massacre spread to the rest of the province and by the end of the year about two thousand Christians had perished.[120]

In Mongolia at the beginning of 1900 over a hundred missionaries of the Congregation of the Immaculate Heart of Mary were ministering to about forty thousand Christians and had numbers of schools. Here, too, were orphanages maintained by the Franciscan Sisters of Mary.[121] As in Shansi, the devastation began in June and continued during the summer. Bishop Hamer, Vicar

---

[113] Favier in *Annals of the Propagation of the Faith*, Vol. 64, pp. 18, 19. There were in the vicariate at the beginning of 1900 about 46,894 Christians, so that about a third of these had perished.—Planchet, op. cit., Vol. 1, p. 32.
[114] Considine, *The Vatican Mission Exposition*, p. 159.
[115] Clement, *Some Aspects of Chinese Life and Thought*, p. 186.
[116] Chardin, *Les missions franciscaines en Chine*, p. 61.
[117] Ricci, *Barbarie e Trionfi*, p. 19.
[118] Völling, *Die Christenverfolgung in Nord-Schansi*, pp. 28 et seq.
[119] Ricci, op. cit., passim; Völling, op. cit., passim.
[120] Holzapfel, *Handbuch der Geschichte des Franziskanenordens*, p. 541.
[121] *Missions du Chine et au Congo*, 1901, p. 279.

Apostolic in the Ordos country, after a valiant resistance, was captured, his fingers and toes were cut off, and he was taken from village to village until death ended his sufferings. In another place two European priests were executed and their heads exposed. In still another, three missionaries were burned in a church. All through the eastern and southern parts of the region were slaughter and the destruction of property. In at least one locality Mongols led in the attack. Here and there bodies of Christians fortified their refuges and held off their persecutors: in one place alone four thousand or more Catholics were besieged. In some of these strongholds they were assisted by Russian soldiers, in another a group of Christians, hunters by profession, led in the defense, and in others the pastors became the captains of their flocks. Fifteen missionaries made their escape to Siberia by travelling forty-two days across the desert. Bandits succeeded the Boxers and it was months before the missions were again at peace. All told, in Mongolia nine missionaries and three thousand Chinese Christians are said to have been killed and many others of the Chinese Christians died of privation, a heavy toll from so young a mission.[122]

In Manchuria also Roman Catholics suffered severely, a native sect, the "Fasters," joining with the Boxers and the government in the orgy of extermination. Churches and chapels, residences, seminaries, schools, and orphanages were ruthlessly pillaged and burned. In Mukden by the order of the authorities the Vicar Apostolic, Bishop Guillon, one foreign and one Chinese priest, two sisters, and hundreds of Christians were burned in their church after a futile defense. The Bishop is said to have died in his robes, first wounded by a bullet and then decapitated. In all Manchuria fourteen or fifteen hundred Christians are reported to have been massacred.[123]

Outside the Northeast, as has been said, the year was less devastating. In extensive districts no loss of life occurred. In Kansu, for example, in October, 1900, the province was reported peaceful, and although the authorities ordered the missionaries

[122] *Missions du Chine et au Congo,* 1901, pp. 1-6, 13-19, 33 et seq., 38-41, 60-62, 67-71, 73-89, 97-108, 121-131, 145-157, 176-181, 202-208, 1902, p. 31, 1906, pp. 92-95; Burke, *The Church in Many Lands,* p. 54; *Annals of the Propagation of the Faith,* Vol. 68, pp. 61, 62.
[123] Morse, op. cit., Vol. 3, p. 242; Graham, *East of the Barrier,* p. 168; Christie, *Thirty Years in the Manchu Capital,* p. 144; *Annals of the Propagation of the Faith,* Vol. 63, pp. 83-98, 393-403.

to return to Europe, they remained at their posts.[124]   In September, 1900, a traveller in the far Southwest found a European priest who had not even heard of the Boxer outbreak and who, when apprized of the order of the consul that all French citizens leave Yünnan, declined to go, saying that he could not abandon his flock until he had heard from his bishop.[125]

However, the news from the North, added to the unrest already existing, could not fail to give birth to sporadic outbreaks. The most severe of these was in and near Hêngchow, the center of the Catholic community in Hunan. Here much property was destroyed, Bishop Fantosati and two other European priests, Franciscans, were killed, and many Chinese Christians perished.[126] Two foreign priests are said to have escaped, the one by being hidden by an old non-Christian woman in a rice bin, and the other by being carried by Chinese Christians a seven days' journey in a box which his bearers declared to the curious to be a coffin in which a corpse was being taken home for burial.[127] At Hsiang-yangfu in Hupeh the prefect himself is reported to have given on July 10th the order for destruction.[128] In October it was reported that in Kiangsi neither churches, residences, nor Christian communities remained—but this was probably an over-statement.[129] In Chêkiang many districts suffered and most of the missionaries in Yünnan took refuge in Tongking and Burma.[130]

The total loss of Roman Catholic missionaries was reported to be five bishops, thirty-one other European priests, nine European sisters, and two Marists.[131] The exact number of Chinese Cath-

[124] Letters from Kansu in *Missions du Chine et au Congo*, 1901, pp. 60-66.
[125] Jack, *The Back Blocks of China*, p. 172.
[126] *Annals of the Propagation of the Faith*, Vol. 64, pp. 20-24.
[127] Beals, *China and the Boxers*, p. 120.
[128] L'Œuvre de la Propagation de la Foi, *Dix années d'apostolat catholiques dans les missions* (1898-1907), pp. 52, 53.
[129] Ibid., pp. 52, 53.
[130] Ibid., pp. 52, 53.
[131] L'Œuvre de la Propagation de la Foi, *Dix années d'apostolat catholiques dans les missions* (1898-1907), pp. 52, 53. There is some uncertainty as to the numbers. One list gives as killed (aside from the bishops) thirty-one European priests, of whom eight were Jesuits, eleven were of the Société des Missions Étrangères of Paris, five were Franciscans, four were Lazarists, and three of the Congregation of the Immaculate Heart of Mary.—Ibid., pp. 52, 53. Another list gives, in addition to the five bishops killed, six Franciscans, four Jesuits, four Lazarists, eight of the Paris Society, and seven of the Congregation of the Immaculate Heart of Mary.—Cordier, *Catholic Encyclopedia*, Vol. 3, p. 671. Seven is probably the correct number for Mongolia, including the two killed in 1901. Huonder, *Die Mission auf der Kanzel und in Verein*, Vol. 1, p. 39, says that the killed were four bishops, forty-one missionaries, eleven seminarians, nine sisters, and more than twenty thousand Christians.

olics who were killed or who died from privation is unknown, but it was probably in excess of thirty thousand.

PROTESTANTS AND THE BOXER DISORDERS

Protestants, being much more recently arrived in China than the Roman Catholics, and having been in North China, the center of the Boxer upheaval, for only forty years, had a much smaller body of converts to undergo persecution. Among the Chinese Christians, therefore, fewer Protestants than Roman Catholics were killed. On the other hand, more Protestant than Roman Catholic missionaries perished.

In and around Peking the losses were great. We have already noted the destruction of lives and property at T'ungchow. We have also seen that Protestant missionaries and some of their converts gathered first in the compound of the American Methodist Mission in Peking, and then, on June 20th, were transferred to the British Legation. Here the missionaries shared the privations and labors of the siege. They were at the head of the committees on general comfort and on fortifications and aided in many other ways. Some of the foreign envoys at first considered abandoning the Chinese converts, but room was found in an adjoining palace, and here about seven hundred Protestants and about twice as many Roman Catholics aided in the defense. Chinese Christians—even the students among them—served as manual laborers, often in positions of great danger. Some of them, too, were interpreters, and others undertook the perilous mission of attempting to carry messages to Tientsin and to the relieving forces. A few of the besieged lost their lives, but the large majority lived to welcome the rescuing forces.[132]

Protestant missions in the rest of Chihli were all severely affected. Chinese Christians were killed and missionaries fled to the coast, often amid great perils.[133] The worst of the massa-

[132] On the siege see Morse, *International Relations of the Chinese Empire*, Vol. 3, pp. 232-277; Allen, *Siege of the Peking Legations*, passim; Mateer, *Siege Days*, passim; Weale, *Indiscreet Letters from Peking*, passim; Ransome, *Story of the Siege Hospital in Peking*, passim; Miner, *China's Book of Martyrs*; Mrs. Conger, *Letters from China*, pp. 109 et seq.; Smith, *China in Convulsion*, passim; Headland, *Chinese Heroes*, pp. 49, 52-73, 121-137; *Chinese Martyrs of 1900*, pp. 107-113. On the siege and the relief of the legations, see Brown, *China's Dayspring after Thirty Years*. Brown was with the relieving army.

[133] Green, *In Deaths Oft*, passim; Green, *Thrilling Experiences of C. I. M. Missionaries in Chihli, 1900*, passim. One hundred and seventy-eight converts of the American Presbyterian Mission were killed in Paotingfu and Peking.—*Reports of Presbyterian Board, 1901*, p. 11.

cries was at Paotingfu where on the last day of June and the first of July the missions of the American Board and the (Northern) American Presbyterians were destroyed and fifteen foreigners belonging to them and to the China Inland Mission together with a number of Chinese Christians were killed.[134] The calmness of the martyrs made a deep impression on some of the spectators.

In Shansi Yü Hsien had no more mercy on Protestants than on Roman Catholics. On June 27th during a riot in T'aiyüanfu a Miss Coombs was burned to death by the mob while trying to save two Chinese children.[135] On July 9th in T'aiyüanfu thirty-three foreign members of Protestant missions—ten men, fourteen women, and nine children—were killed by the Governor's orders.[136] On July 12th two men, five women, and five children, all foreigners, with five Chinese Christians, were killed at Tat'ung.[137] At Hsinchow, forty-five miles north of the capital, when the news of the death of Miss Coombs reached them, the members of the English Baptist Mission decided to flee. They hid in a cave, were captured, taken back to the city and imprisoned, and then on August 9th were brought out, ostensibly for the purpose of being conveyed to the coast, were met at the city gates by Boxers, stripped, and murdered.[138] At Hsiaoyihsien two unmarried missionaries of the China Inland Mission were dispatched while kneeling in prayer.[139] At T'aiku six missionaries of the American Board and eight Chinese were executed on July 31st and their heads taken to the Governor.[140] At Fênchow on August 15th seven representatives of the American Board and three of the China Inland Mission were killed.[141] The mission of the American Board, supplied by the graduates of one college, Oberlin, lost fifteen members—to whom a memorial arch was

[134] Forsyth, *The China Martyrs of 1900*, pp. 19 et seq.; Ketler, *The Tragedy of Paotingfu*, pp. 317 et seq. One of those killed at Paotingfu was Horace Tracy Pitkin, a self-supporting missionary of the American Board who had been in China less than four years. A sentence in his last message to his wife, saying that he hoped that when his son was twenty-five years of age he would return to China, was much quoted.—Speer, *A Memorial of Horace T. Pitkin.*
[135] Forsyth, op. cit., p. 33; Edwards, *Fire and Sword in Shansi*, pp. 59-82.
[136] Forsyth, op. cit., pp. 32-40; Edwards, op. cit., pp. 59-82; Pigott, *Steadfast Unto Death, Memorials of Thomas W. and Jessie Pigott*, passim.
[137] *Last Letters and Further Records of Martyred Missionaries*, pp. 51-53.
[138] Forsyth, op. cit., pp. 43-46; Fullerton and Wilson, *New China*, p. 107.
[139] Forsyth, op. cit., pp. 64-68.
[140] Ibid., pp. 68, 79; Dreyer, *The Boxer Uprising and Missionary Massacres in Central and South Shansi*, pp. 15-42.
[141] Forsyth, op. cit., p. 70.

later erected on the quiet campus in Ohio.[142] At Sopingfu all the missionaries of the Swedish Holiness Mission then on the field, ten in all, suffered martyrdom.[143] On August 30th six other foreigners were killed after wandering about for weeks in a vain search for safety.[144] All told, seventy-eight foreign members of Protestant missions in the province lost their lives, fifty-six of them adults and twenty-two children.[145] Some others made their way to points of safety after hardships to which death was almost preferable.[146]

In Mongolia the toll of life was also heavy. The blow fell particularly upon the Christian and Missionary Alliance. This body lost twenty-one of the thirty-eight missionaries which it had in China at the beginning of 1900, in addition to fourteen children of missionaries.[147] On September 1st four members of the Scandinavian Alliance Mission were killed and one more was murdered later.[148] Thrilling escapes were made from Kalgan and other centers north of Peking across the Gobi desert to Urga and Kiakhta.[149]

In Manchuria the uprising was late in beginning, but the events in Peking in the latter part of June, the declaration of war on the powers, and the command to exterminate the foreigners led to a fierce persecution. The Protestant missionaries had ample warning and escaped. The Chinese Christians were not so fortunate. The Protestant churches had just received a large accession of members, and it is not strange that many, perhaps a third of the Christians, most of them only recently baptized, took the easy ways of escape offered by tolerant officials and renounced their faith. The majority, however, remained true and about three hundred of them were slaughtered, some of them with great

---

[142] *Oberlin-Shansi Mission Ten Years After,* passim.
[143] Broomhall, *Jubilee Story of the China Inland Mission,* p. 359.
[144] Edwards, op. cit., pp. 88-90.
[145] *Chinese Recorder,* Vol. 31, p. 532; see also on massacres in Shansi, Campbell, *Through the Gates into the City,* passim; *Further News of the Massacres in Shansi,* passim.
[146] Glover, *A Thousand Miles of Miracle in China,* passim; Broomhall, *Martyred Missionaries of the China Inland Mission,* pp. 68-76, 89-101; Edwards, op. cit., pp. 84-88; Forsyth, op. cit., pp. 116-147; *Last Letters and Further Records of Martyred Missionaries,* pp. 53-93.
[147] Forsyth, op. cit., p. 82.
[148] Williams, *Across the Desert of Gobi,* passim; Roberts, *A Flight for Life,* passim; Forsyth, op. cit., pp. 85 et seq.
[149] Forsyth, op. cit., p. 81.

cruelty.[150]   One preacher, for example, was caught, urged to recant, and upon his refusal his eyebrows, ears, and lips were cut off, and then, since he still remained obdurate, his heart was cut out and exhibited for days in a theatre.   His fourteen-year-old daughter followed the heroic example of her father and perished.[151]

Outside the Northeast, the most severe persecution was in Chê-kiang.   Here the edict ordering the extermination of the foreigners seems to have come through unaltered.   After some hesitation the Governor published it, and although he soon countermanded it, in one place, Chouchoufu, on July 21st to 23d disorderly elements killed the magistrate for wishing to protect the foreigners, and massacred eleven representatives of the China Inland Mission.[152]   Elsewhere no Protestant missionaries seem to have lost their lives.   There were harrowing experiences and narrow escapes, but the larger proportion of the missionaries, at the advice of their consuls, made their way to treaty ports.   Many chapels were destroyed and Chinese Christians were roughly handled, but comparatively little blood was shed.[153]   Even in Shantung, where the Boxers had first emerged, Yüan Shih-k'ai, although he did not entirely preserve the Christians from molestation, prevented the death of any more foreigners,[154] and in Shensi, next to the violent Shansi, the Governor, Tuan Fang, was able to conduct the missionaries of Kansu and his own province safely beyond his jurisdiction into that of the friendly Chang Chih-tung.[155]

The number of the Protestants who perished is somewhat uncertain.   Of the foreign missionary body what seem to be the best figures give the number of adults as one hundred and

[150] Ross in *Missionary Review of the World*, Vol. 15, p. 817; Christie, *Thirty Years in the Manchu Capital*, pp. 133-150; Graham, *East of the Barrier*, pp. 143, 222 et seq.; Forsyth, op. cit., pp. 273-310.

[151] Graham, op. cit., p. 179.

[152] Smith, *China in Convulsion*, Vol. 2, p. 605; Forsyth, op. cit., p. 90; Morse, op. cit., Vol. 3, p. 243.

[153] Glover, *Ebenezer*, pp. 73 et seq.; Sellew, *Clara Leffingwell, A Missionary*, pp. 137 et seq.; Grist, *Samuel Pollard*, pp. 111-118; *A History of the Dublin University Fuhkien Mission*, p. 23; Pitcher, *In and About Amoy*, p. 143; Stock and McClelland, *For Christ in Fuhkien*, p. 36; Smith, op. cit., Vol. 2, p. 605; China Inland Mission, *A Modern Pentecost*, p. 24; Mackenzie, *Twenty-Five Years in Honan*, pp. 94-107; Gurr, *Bilder aus der Berliner Mission in Lukhang, Südchina*, pp. 32 et seq.

[154] Smith, op. cit., Vol. 2, pp. 602-604.

[155] Beckman, *The Massacre at Sianfu*, p. 42; Morse, op. cit., Vol. 3, pp. 241, 242.

thirty-four [156] or one hundred and thirty-five [157] and of children as fifty-two [156] or fifty-three,[157] a total of one hundred and eighty-six or one hundred and eighty-eight. Of these slightly more than a third were under the China Inland Mission and its associated societies.[158] The total of Chinese Protestants killed is still more uncertain, but one set of figures gives it as nineteen hundred and twelve, including three Mongols.[159] The young Christian churches had paid a high price for their faith.

The attention of the European and American recorders of the Boxer uprising was naturally attracted chiefly to the sufferings of missionaries. The steadfastness and heroism of these martyrs are beyond praise: there is no record of a single attempt at recantation or of wavering of purpose. It must not be forgotten, however, that the vast majority of those who lost their lives were Chinese. Under the tremendous pressure exerted some converts denied their faith [160] and others escaped by devices more or less dubious.[161] The majority, however, remained true, even when they might have saved their lives by some simple act of compromise. The records abound with instances of constancy. The cook in a household of the English Baptist Mission in Shansi, in spite of the protest of his employers, followed them to prison, prepared their food for them there, and took their last messages.[162] Ting Li-mei, later to achieve distinction, remained with his flock during the persecutions, and was once beaten and left for dead.[163] Pastor Mêng of Paotingfu, a graduate of the college at T'ungchow and the first Chinese ordained by the North China Mission of the American Board, on hearing of the danger to the missionaries, hurried to the city, kept the preaching chapel open while he could, declined to flee when he might have done so with safety, commanded his oldest son to escape to carry on his work after he should be gone, and was then tortured and killed.[164] Such stories

---

[156] *Chinese Recorder*, Vol. 32, p. 150.

[157] Smith, *Rex Christus*, p. 209. See other figures in *China's Millions*, 1901, p. 24; *Souvenirs des martyrs de Chine;* Broomhall, *Martyred Missionaries of the China Inland Mission*, p. ix.

[158] *China's Millions*, 1901, p. 24; Broomhall, op. cit., p. lx.

[159] *Chinese Recorder*, Vol. 38, p. 611.

[160] See mention of some in Forsyth, *Chinese Martyrs of 1900*, pp. 349, 350, 399-411; Miner, op. cit., p. 26.

[161] Planchet, *Documents sur les martyrs de Pékin pendant le persécution des Boxeurs*, Vol. 1, pp. 13 et seq.

[162] Lady Hosie, *Two Gentlemen of China*, pp. 27, 28.

[163] Mateer, *Character Building in China*, p. 87.

[164] Miner, *China's Book of Martyrs*, p. 99.

might be continued for many pages.[165]   Nor must those Chinese officials be forgotten who, although not Christians, always at the risk of imperial displeasure, often at the price of the perilous enmity of Boxers and populace, and in some instances at the cost of their own lives, attempted to protect foreigners within their jurisdiction.   Moreover, examples are not wanting of non-Christian Chinese with no official responsibility who, often at great risk, aided those who were attempting to escape.

In spite of the disorders of the Boxer year, Protestant missions did not cease to continue the rapid augmentation of their forces that had characterized their efforts in the preceding six decades. Twenty-two new workers were sent by the China Inland Mission.[166]   In 1900 the first two representatives of the Norwegian Alliance Mission sailed for China.[167]   In December, 1900, the first two missionaries of the United Evangelical Mission arrived. The following year these latter entered the capital of anti-foreign Hunan.[168]   In 1901 the first Chinese agents of the Wesleyan Methodist Missionary Society entered Hunan.[169]   In 1900 the Methodist Protestants sent two ladies, the initial representatives in China of their denomination.[170]   In 1900 Robert Arthington of Leeds, England, died, leaving a large fund for the extension of the activities of several of the missionary societies at work in China.[171]   Protestantism in China was not to be discouraged by the reverse it had suffered.

THE RUSSIAN ORTHODOX MISSION IN THE BOXER YEAR

The Russian Mission, so lately entered on a program of extension, suffered severely, for its work was entirely in the storm area.   Its buildings in Peking, Kalgan, and Tungtingan were destroyed, its valuable library was lost, and between two hundred and four hundred out of approximately seven hundred commu-

---

[165] See accounts in Bashford, *Journal,* Oct. 4, 1907; Brown, *New Forces in Old China,* p. 261; Mrs. Bryson, *Cross and Crown,* pp. 41, 49, 59, 84, 97, 144; Mateer, *Siege Days,* p. 315; *The Reign of Terror in the Western Hills, 1900;* Miner, *China's Book of Martyrs,* pp. 114-136, 137, 138, 328; Planchet, op. cit., passim.
[166] *China's Millions,* 1901, p. 7.
[167] Broomhall, *Jubilee Story of the China Inland Mission,* p. 361.
[168] *A Century of Protestant Missions in China,* p. 543.
[169] Ibid., p. 96.
[170] Ibid., p. 542.
[171] *Encyclopædia Sinica,* p. 36. The fund was to be used not only in China but in other countries as well.

nicants were killed.[172] When, after 1900, the mission entered on
a new period of expansion, it had to start almost afresh.

THE IMMEDIATE AFTERMATH OF THE BOXER UPRISING

So great an upheaval as that of 1900 could not subside without
an aftermath, and the immediate sequels were almost if not quite
as important as the uprising itself. Of some of these, especially
those affecting diplomatic and commercial relations, we need not
speak, but others were of intimate concern to the Christian
Church in China and must be at least mentioned.

In many places in the Northwest the reign of terror occasioned
by the Boxers was continued by the foreign troops. Only now
it was not the foreigners and the Chinese Christians, but their
enemies and the innocent bystanders who suffered. The Emperor
of Germany, addressing on July 27th, 1900, the first contingent
sent from the Fatherland to aid in suppressing the Boxers, is
reported to have said:

> "No quarter will be given, no prisoners will be taken. Let all
> who fall into your hands be at your mercy. Just as the Huns a
> thousand years ago, under the leadership of Etzel [Attila], gained
> a reputation by virtue of which they still live in historical tradition,
> so may the name of Germany become known in such a manner in
> China, that no Chinese will ever again dare to look askance at a
> German." [173]

These words were probably spoken under stress of the resentment
felt for the death of the German Minister. In large part, however, they are a picture of the conduct in North China of the
troops not only of Germany but of at least some of the other
powers. Peking was looted [174] and punitive expeditions were
sent into the surrounding country, partly to rescue Christians and
foreigners who were still beleaguered, and partly to exact reparation for the destruction already wrought. Northeastern China
was treated much like a conquered country by soldiers who often
gave rein to the passions so near the surface in European troops
"East of Suez." It was a sorry sequel to the heroism of Christian

[172] Smirnoff, *Russian Orthodox Missions,* p. 76; *Chinese Recorder,* Vol. 4,
p. 683.
[173] Morse, *International Relations of the Chinese Empire,* Vol. 3, p. 309, quoting *Weser Zeitung,* Bremen, cited in *Times,* July 30, 1900.
[174] See Brown, *China's Dayspring after Thirty Years,* pp. 166 et seq., for one
account.

martyrs, all the more so since most of the forces professed the faith that the missionaries and Chinese Christians had died to represent.

Missionaries were not entirely guiltless of taking advantage of the situation to further their interests. The extreme charges against them are fabrications of their critics,[175] but the accusations had some basis in fact. Although most Chinese Christians had a creditable record, a few succumbed to the temptations offered by the wealth abandoned by those who fled Peking on the coming of the relieving armies.[176] Some of the Protestant missionaries employed the loot so easily obtainable to relieve the necessities of Chinese Christians.[177]   On the other hand, Moir Duncan of the English Baptist Mission used his position as interpreter at British headquarters to preserve from destruction the Peking palace of the Governor of Shensi,[178] Dr. Westwater is said to have prevented the plunder of the city of Liaoyang in Manchuria by the Russian forces,[179] and Rev. S. Walter Lowrie, of the (Northern) American Presbyterians, returning to Paotingfu in October, 1900, as interpreter to one of the foreign generals, saved hundreds of lives from the vengeance of the punitive expedition.[180]

The story of the negotiations that led to the official settlement of the Boxer troubles does not belong in this narrative. The powers had the country at their mercy and only their jealousies and the moderating counsels of some of them prevented the terms of the final protocol from being more severe. Nor need all the articles of the protocol be enumerated. At least four, however, were of importance to Christian missions. One, the second, provided for the punishment of the officials who were "the principal authors of the outrages and crimes committed." This included the decapitation of Yü Hsien and the posthumous

[175] Lynch, The War of Civilizations, p. 182, contains some of the most violent of these charges. Brown, op. cit., pp. 166 et seq., seeks to exonerate the missionaries and disproves some of the charges.

[176] Scott, Answered Prayer in China, pp. 26-39; Sixty-Fifth Report of the Board of Foreign Missions of the Presbyterian Church in the U. S. A. (1902), p. 79.

[177] Martin, The Siege of Peking, p. 136; Martin in Missionary Review of the World, Vol. 14, p. 208.

[178] Glover, Herbert Stanley Jenkins, p. 43.

[179] Graham, East of the Barrier, pp. 169, 170; Robertson, Our Missions in Manchuria, p. 106.

[180] Sixty-Fifth Annual Report of the Board of Foreign Missions of the Presbyterian Church in the U. S. A. (1902), p. 83.

degradation of Li Ping-hêng. Missionaries, at least Protestant missionaries, seem in general to have approved.[181] Another article provided for the suspension for five years of the time-honored civil service examinations in cities "where foreigners had been massacred or submitted to cruel treatment," a penalty which was to pave the way for an educational revolution that was to give to Christian missions one of the greatest of their opportunities. Still another provided for the wide publication of imperial decrees prohibiting membership in anti-foreign societies, enumerated the punishments meted out to the guilty, and announced that provincial officials would be held personally responsible for anti-foreign troubles. Still another recorded the settlement of the vexed question of indemnities.[182]

The detailed demands of the missions for indemnities seem never to have been made public, nor is it certain just what proportion of the four hundred and fifty million taels, the total for all purposes finally agreed upon by the powers, was assigned to missionary organizations and Chinese Christians.[183] A good many settlements for indemnity to missions and Chinese Christians were made with the local or provincial authorities independently of the general fund. We hear that for the damages to Roman Catholics in Shansi a total of two and a quarter million taels was fixed upon and that a large college in T'aiyüanfu was turned over in indemnification for the cathedral and other buildings destroyed.[184] We hear, too, that Bishop Favier accepted compensation for destroyed buildings but none for lives lost.[185] We know that in May, 1901, before the signing of the protocol, a Chinese official in Shansi, in part to prevent a foreign invasion, agreed to pay eighty thousand taels to relieve suffering Roman Catholic Christians and to return such of the Christians' land as

[181] Resolutions of missionaries in Shanghai, noted in *Spirit of Missions,* Vol. 66, p. 560.
[182] MacMurray, *Treaties and Agreements With and Concerning China,* pp. 278 et seq.
[183] Rockhill said to Hay, March 14, 1901, that in the report of the commission on indemnities no special mention was made of "missions or missionaries on account of the refusal of France to waive in any wise its claimed protectorate over Catholic missions and native Catholics in China."—*Message of the President of the U. S., Dec. 12, 1901.* Of the American indemnity $2,819,030.43 went to satisfy the claims of American citizens, but how much of this went to missions and missionaries has not been made public.—*U. S. Senate, Calendar No. 264,* 67th Congress, 1st Session, Report No. 250, p. 2.
[184] Edwards, *Fire and Sword in Shansi,* pp. 164-172.
[185] Joly, *Le Christianisme et l'Extrême Orient,* Vol. 1, p. 136.

had been seized.[186]   In Hsienhsien, in the Jesuit vicariate in Chihli, the district official agreed with the missionary to levy a special land tax of between five and ten per cent. of the annual income to compensate the Christians.[187]   In another district in the same vicariate the indemnity levied locally was in the form of recompense for property destroyed.[188]   On April 21st, 1901, the Chinese plenipotentiaries reported that the Taot'ai of Hopei in Honan had agreed with the Vicar Apostolic that one hundred and seventy thousand taels should be paid to cover all the claims of the missionaries there and that three thousand piculs of rice should be given to relieve the needy Christians.[189]   The Milan Society, the Augustinians, the Lazarists of Peking, and the Société des Missions Étrangères of Paris invested at least part of the indemnity paid them in real estate in the European concessions in Hankow.[190]   As we shall see later, the Lazarists in Chihli used the proceeds of the indemnity greatly to increase the number of their catechumens.   These bits of information are obviously fragmentary and by no means give a complete picture.

Among Protestants the attitude toward indemnities varied. Hudson Taylor for a time believed that compensation should be refused for lives lost, but that it should be accepted for mission premises and property.   Later he decided that in light of the great sufferings of the Chinese Christians, to distinguish the missionaries from the representatives of "the temporal power" and to show to the Chinese "the meekness and gentleness of Christ," "not only not to enter any claim against the Chinese Government but to refrain from accepting compensation even if offered," [191] and this became the fixed policy of the society that had suffered more than any other.[192]   On the other hand, most of the Protestant missionaries of other societies favored reimbursement for destroyed property [193] and that in general became the attitude of

[186] Ricci, *Barbarie e Trionfi*, pp. 667-692.
[187] "Cet impot . . . de 100 à 400 sapèques par arpent de terre alors qu'un arpent rapporte de 2 à 4,000 sapèques par an."—Letter from Jules Gouveneur, S. J., April 12, 1901, in *Chine et Ceylan*, No. 8, Sept. 1901, p. 425.
[188] Ibid., p. 426.
[189] *Message of the President of the U. S.*, Dec. 12, 1901, p. 201.
[190] Schmidlin, *Missions und Kulturverhältnisse in Fernen Osten*, p. 61.
[191] Broomhall, *Jubilee Story of the China Inland Mission*, p. 257.
[192] Taylor, *Hudson Taylor*, p. 591.
[193] See articles in *Missionary Review of the World*, Vol. 14, pp. 106, 673; *Chinese Recorder*, Vol. 31, pp. 537, 540, 544, 548.

their boards. Claims were presented through the foreign governments and not directly to the Chinese.[194] The powers backed the
general opinion of the missionary body and included in the
demands indemnities for societies, private individuals, and Chinese who had suffered "in person or in property in consequence
of their being in the service of foreigners." [195]

The American societies made a united presentation of their
claims to the Department of State.[196] Eventually, however, the
American claims were passed on by a commission of three sitting
in China. The principle adopted by this body was to allow "for
buildings destroyed their actual cost whenever it could be ascer-
tained, and twenty-five per cent. additional for enhanced cost of
labor and materials in reconstruction, with a view to settling their
owners back in the position in which they would have been had
the destruction not occurred. In all claims for personal property
the Commission . . . endeavored to award compensation for the
actual value at the time of its destruction. . . . In the adjustment
of death claims the Commissioners . . . tried to measure the
pecuniary interest of heirs at law and next of kin in the lives of
those . . . killed . . . to estimate the reasonable expectation of
pecuniary advantage to claimants from the continuation of the
lives of the decedents, [and] the reasonable prospect of support or
endowment out of their accumulations and earnings had their
lives been spared." It speaks well for the restraint shown by the
boards that while the commission allowed to all Americans, missionary and non-missionary, claims amounting to $1,514,292 and
rejected claims totalling $1,804,385, the amount awarded to the
American societies was $570,983.75, a sum more than half again
as large as that asked by them. This was for property only. The
sum awarded to individual missionaries and to the heirs of those
massacred was considerably less, and a total of about $20,000 was

[194] *Chinese Recorder,* Vol. 32, pp. 400 et seq.
[195] *Foreign Relations,* 1900, p. 245. The Russians opposed including indemnities to Chinese Christians, but Hay favored it.—Ibid., pp. 223, 224. The
indemnity paid to Chinese Christians was later believed to have worked injury to
the Protestant churches by sowing the seeds of a mercenary spirit. Christian
leaders in some places laid more or less compulsory contributions on nominally
Christian recipients of indemnity money and used these as an endowment which
it was hoped would stimulate giving. The plan had the opposite effect, save where
the sum was devoted exclusively to educational purposes.—Bryson in *Chinese
Recorder,* Vol. 54 (1923), pp. 257 et seq.
[196] F. D. Gamewell, the agent of the boards in the negotiations, in conversation
with the author, September, 1926.

given to servants of missionaries. In response to repeated rumors that missionaries were making extravagant demands for indemnity, the Department of State declared that "the claims of the missionaries and their wives were not unreasonably exaggerated and specifically that there were no claims on account of jewelry or wardrobes large enough to attract attention." The compensation paid to the heirs of a martyred missionary was usually $5,000, although in a few instances it was larger. Later Congress permitted claims which had been disallowed by the commission to be reviewed by the Court of Claims, and the Department of Justice allowed a few others.[197]

As was the case with the Roman Catholics, some indemnities were paid to Protestants by local communities and officials apart from the large general fund.[198] This was done especially for the Chinese Christians. Except in the case of servants of missionaries, these were reimbursed entirely by arrangements with the local and provincial authorities, usually by levies on the non-Christian community.[199] Trouble often followed. One American official complained that two American missionaries were presenting their claims directly to the Governor of Shantung and that the latter, to avoid friction, had agreed to pay them. He also said that missionaries, usually accompanied by soldiers, had assessed damages on villages where Christians had been killed or property destroyed and in doing so had brought on themselves and their converts "no end of criticism and ill-feeling."[200] American missionaries wrote of the ill-will engendered by collecting indemnities from non-Christians, of the excessive requests of some Christians, and of the difficulty of arriving at a just settlement.[201] In Shansi the Governor set aside two hundred thousand taels to be divided between Protestants and Catholics.[202] In Chihli at least one hospital was rebuilt from funds collected by the magistrate, largely from the Boxers of the neighborhood.[203] Late in 1900 British

[197] This material is drawn from the manuscript archives of the United States Department of State.

[198] See, for example, Sixty-Fifth Annual Report of the Board of Foreign Missions of the Presbyterian Church in the U. S. A. (1902), pp. 80, 85.

[199] See following footnotes, also Ninety-Second Annual Report of the A. B. C. F. M., p. 126.

[200] Foreign Relations, 1901, pp. 97, 98.

[201] Hopkins and Walker in Eighty-Fourth Annual Report of the Missionary Society of the Methodist Episcopal Church, pp. 151-153.

[202] Foreign Relations, 1901, pp. 97, 98.

[203] Peill, The Beloved Physician of Tsangchow, p. 78.

troops laid an indemnity on a city for the murder of two English missionaries.[204]

It is pleasant to record that Timothy Richard, who, it will be recalled, had lived in Shansi years before and had wished to prevent famine by introducing the leaders to Western science, was called upon by the provincial authorities to help make the post-Boxer adjustment, and that at his suggestion half a million taels were set aside as an indemnity, not to be paid to foreigners, but to found in T'aiyüanfu a Chinese university in which Western learning should be taught. Richard believed that this would help to dispel the ignorance and prejudice which he held had aided in bringing about the outbreak and would also benefit the province in other ways. Richard was given full control of the institution for ten years and appointed Moir Duncan of the English Baptist Mission as the first principal.[205] It is also pleasant to be able to note that it was probably in part from a suggestion of a missionary that the first installment of the Boxer Indemnity returned by the United States was devoted to educational purposes in China [206] and that it was very largely as the result of the efforts of another missionary that the balance of the indemnity due America was eventually remitted.

The amendment of existing conventions between China and the powers was promised in the Protocol of 1901, for no thorough revision had been made since 1858. In the next few years several new general treaties followed, and these naturally mentioned missions. In the document with Great Britain (September 5, 1902) the British Government agreed "to join in a commission to investigate this [missionary] question and if possible to devise means for securing permanent peace between converts and non-converts, should such a commission be formed by China and the Treaty Powers interested." [207] The American treaty (October 8, 1903), in addition to repeating the toleration clauses in the document of 1858, contained permission for American missionary

[204] Satow to Marquis of Salisbury, Nov. 8, 1900, in *Parliamentary Papers*, 1901, Vol. 91, China No. 5, p. 155.

[205] Richard, *Forty-Five Years in China*, pp. 299, 300; Edwards, *Fire and Sword in Shansi*, pp. 111, 122-164; Reeve, *Timothy Richard*, pp. 106-122.

[206] Malone in *China Mission Year Book*, 1924, p. 103; Roosevelt to Arthur H. Smith, Apr. 3, 1906, and Arthur H. Smith to his wife, March 7, 1906, in *Missionary Herald*, Vol. 121, pp. 4, 5; Malone in *American Historical Review*, Vol. 32, pp. 64-68.

[207] MacMurray, *Treaties and Agreements With and Concerning China*, Vol. 1, p. 351.

societies "to purchase or to lease in perpetuity as the property of such societies buildings or lands in all parts of the Empire for missionary purposes." [208]   This was the first explicit treaty guarantee of that privilege to Protestants, but it simply sanctioned what had come to be the established practice.   Definite provisions were also included, outgrowths of experience since the toleration clause was first framed, that the fact of being a convert should not free the Christian from the consequence of an offence committed before being admitted to the Church, nor exempt him from paying taxes except those levied for the support of religious customs contrary to his faith; and that missionaries should not interfere with the exercise by the native authorities of their jurisdiction over Chinese subjects. [209]

[208] Ibid., Vol. 1, pp. 430, 431.
[209] MacMurray, op. cit., Vol. 1, p. 430.

CHAPTER XXIII

CHINA IN A TIME OF REORGANIZATION (1901-1926)

INTRODUCTORY

CONDITIONS THAT AFFECTED THE WORK OF THE MISSIONARY, 1901-1926

WITH the suppression of the Boxer outbreak a new era in the history of China began and with it a fresh chapter in the story of the Church. The new day was to be distinguished first and primarily by changes in China itself which were to give to Christian missionaries a greater opportunity to imprint their message upon its people than they had had in all the centuries of their presence in the Empire. The changes were so profound that they were to introduce little less than a revolution in Chinese culture in all its phases, intellectual, political, economic, social, and religious. The year 1926 in no sense marks their end: they seem only to have begun, and the epoch characterized by them, therefore, is merely in its inception. The historian must, however, content himself with telling what has actually happened, and unsatisfactory as it is to break off a story at a point where it appears only to have gotten well under way—ending the narrative with a comma—the close of 1926 must, for at least the time being, be our pausing place. Even for the years between 1901 and 1926 we are under the disability of being too near the events to be certain of seeing them in their proper perspective.

The quarter of a century that followed the Boxer troubles, while in many respects made a unit by the great changes in China, is divided, as is the history of so many other parts of the earth, by movements both in China and in the Occident which came with and followed the World War of 1914-1918. We will address our attention first to the movements which run through all the years between 1901 and the close of 1926, and second to those features which are characteristic of the years between 1901 and the outbreak of the World War. In the succeeding chapters we will take up the narrative of missions between 1901 and the summer of 1914, then note the alterations which came with the war and its aftermath, and, finally, sketch the developments in missions from the summer of 1914 to the close of 1926.

CONDITIONS IN CHINA, 1901-1926, WHICH AFFECTED THE WORK OF THE CHURCH

With the cessation of the Boxer disturbances and the complete and humiliating subjection of the imperial government to the demands of the victorious foreigner the resistance which China had so long presented to the culture of the West crumbled. The conservative groups which had so suddenly broken off the reforms of 1898 had been discredited. Even the thoughtless began to see that the aggressive West had demolished the old horizons of China's world and that the Chinese, if they were to escape subjugation and division, would have to adopt many of the methods, institutions, and ideas of races whom they had heretofore regarded as barbarians. Most of the older Chinese and Manchus still held the irritating foreigner to be uncivilized and only grudgingly made adjustments to his ways. Many of the younger generation were, however, swept off their feet by a passion for reform, heartily accepted Western ways and ideas, and entered light-heartedly upon the delicate task of abandoning or modifying the honored institutions of the past.

Of all the ensuing changes, the most significant were in the intellectual life of the nation. In 1905 the old system of civil service examinations was abolished and there passed into oblivion an institution which had been one of the strongest anchors to China's past. In that same year, too, a Ministry of Education was created and to it was entrusted the organizing of a new school system in which both Western and Chinese subjects were studied. Schools in China which had offered courses on Occidental learning suddenly became popular, and hundreds of new ones, often with woefully low standards and poor equipment, sprang up almost over night.[1] Many of the youths went abroad to acquire Western knowledge, either at its sources in Europe and America

[1] For the changes before 1914 see P. W. Kuo, *The Chinese System of Public Education*, pp. 85 et seq.

or, because of geographical and linguistic propinquity, in Japan. Literature, much of it in the form of translations, conveying Western science, history, philosophy, and political and social ideas, appeared in floods.

Attempts were made to reach the masses with the new ideas and to this end a phonetic script was developed as a substitute for the beautiful but difficult characters. After 1914, as we shall see, many younger scholars began to write extensively in a dignified form of the Mandarin instead of in the less easily understood classical style, and campaigns were inaugurated for teaching the populace to read. Newspapers and magazines multiplied, many of them irresponsible and of low grade, but all of them purveyors of the new thought.

Two results of the changes were the emergence of a new student class and an intellectual ferment such as the nation had not known since before the time of Christ. Students were naturally the group most affected by the innovations. Building on the traditional respect for the scholar, they were often active and occasionally very influential in local and national affairs. They were not content with superficial changes but insisted upon examining afresh and often upon renouncing the fundamental convictions and institutions not only of the West but of the older China. Under the leadership of the radicals, some of the basic features of traditional Chinese civilization were discarded or altered.

Parallel with intellectual and educational changes went political revolution. Led by the Empress Dowager, the Manchus, reluctantly recognizing the inevitable, attempted to guide the reform movement in such a way that they could maintain their position. Among other things, they entered upon a program of gradually introducing constitutional and representative government. For over a hundred years, however, the dynasty had been decadent, and the almost simultaneous death in November, 1908, of the Empress Dowager and the unfortunate Emperor Kwang Hsü, at once removed the one strong leader left it and placed an infant on the throne. In 1911 and 1912, more because of their utter weakness than the strength of their opponents, the Manchus were swept aside and a republic was set up.

In China the disappearance of a dynasty has always been the occasion for civil strife, sometimes prolonged, in which rival aspirants fight for the vacant throne. The situation was now complicated by the attempt of the radicals to abandon or modify the forms of government which the Chinese had developed and to which they had become accustomed, and to adopt and adapt those of the Occident, institutions with which they were quite inexperienced. Unless some strong man could early make himself master of the country and direct the changes which the radicals desired, prolonged internal strife would inevitably ensue. For a time Yüan Shih-k'ai, to whom the Manchus and the revolutionists had entrusted the country, maintained a semblance of unity and order. His attempt to assume the imperial title (1915) and his death (1916) brought his rule to an end and in the following decade the power of the central government rapidly declined and disorder spread. Military leaders made themselves masters of larger or smaller sections of the country. There was no year in which fighting was not recorded, and from time to time the more powerful chieftains engaged in conflicts which brought distress to great portions of the nation. Alliances were made and dissolved as between independent monarchs. The government at Peking was regarded either as a prize or a pawn, and while a nominal allegiance to it was sometimes acknowledged, it was often openly flouted. The revenues of the government, inadequate at best and in part pledged to foreign creditors, were largely absorbed by contending generals. In the disorder banditry increased and whole districts were plundered. Old political institutions, too, were passing, partly because of the increasing anarchy, and partly through the conscious action of those who wished to begin new ones modeled on those of the Occident. New constitutions with Western prototypes were formulated for the central government and for some of the provinces, new codes of law were compiled, new courts were organized, and new forms of city administration appeared. The machinery of government was being more extensively modified than at any time in the Christian era. In spite of all the disunion and strife a national consciousness was growing which bitterly resented encroachments on China's sovereignty by foreign powers.

Not only in the intellectual and political life of the country was there revolution, but economic changes were beginning. Railways, steamships on the coastal and inland waters, the telegraph, and a Western form of postal system were altering transportation and communication. Factories were being built and were initiating an industrial revolution, banks of a Western type and new forms of currency were multiplying, chambers of commerce, an evolution under Western influence from the older guild system, were springing up, prices were rising,[2] foreign commerce, although small when compared to that of other large countries, was growing,[3] and new commodities were coming on the market. From being a self-sufficient economic unit, or, rather, a self-sufficient group of economic units, China was forced into the stream of the economic life of the world and was experiencing both a dislocation and a modification in the structure which through the centuries had fed and clothed her millions. In the main that structure was still intact, but by 1927 strikes and labor unions were in evidence and the traditional guilds were here and there disappearing or being modified.

The social structure of the nation was largely unaltered, even at the close of 1926, but now and again rifts appeared in it. For the most part the family remained as it had been, but many, especially among the students and in the cities and towns most closely in touch with the West, rebelled against its time-honored forms.[4] Old social customs were passing, here and there women were asserting themselves and demanding a different status, the separation between the sexes was becoming less strict, coëducation was more and more the practice in the higher schools, and individualism was popular, especially among the student class.

In religion, too, changes were occurring. The masses of the nation kept to the practices of their forefathers. Confucianism, Buddhism, and Taoism remained dominant, and Islam continued to be the faith of a minority. Here and there, however, especially just after the Revolution of 1911, images and all that they stood for were for a time unpopular. The collapse of the imperial form of government and the coming of the Republic meant the collapse of the type of state to which the Confucian school had been committed and on which it depended. The hold of the Confucian philosophy upon the nation, especially upon the

[2] As an illustration, see Meng and Gamble, *Prices, Wages and the Standard of Living in Peking, 1900-1924,* supplement to the *Chinese Social and Political Science Review,* July, 1926.
[3] See Remer, *The Foreign Trade of China.*
[4] For the changes in the family system in one small village in Kwangtung, see Kulp, *Country Life in South China. The Sociology of Familism.*

younger classes, was, accordingly, weakened. Older philosophies, once denounced by scholars as heretical, were reëxamined, often with avidity. Confucianism had so long been accepted by the leading classes that its impress upon the ethical standards and the thought of the nation could not easily be erased. Its hold, however, was relaxing. Some of the older religious observances maintained by the state, including those carried on by the Emperors, notably the imposing ones in the Temple of Heaven, disappeared after abortive efforts to restore them. In one province, Shansi, the Governor formulated a state religion based largely on Confucianism but showing the influence of Christianity. New syncretic cults were born, taking the forms of the private religious associations which had so long been a feature of religious life, but also often showing the influence of the Occident.[5] Attempts were made to inject new life into Buddhism, and in parts of China, notably in Hangchow and other places in the Yangtze Valley, a Buddhistic revival was apparent.[6] Among the intellectuals the discussion of religious and philosophic questions was at times widespread and vigorous.[7]

These alterations in the older life and structure of China meant, as has been said, unprecedented opportunity for Christian missions. At last that fabric which had so far been impermeable was crumbling. Through the centuries Christian missionaries had faced the alternatives of adapting their message and framing the requirements made of their converts in such a manner that fundamental Chinese beliefs and practices would not be antagonized—a procedure which if thorough would hopelessly denature their message—or of overthrowing practically singlehanded some of the basic institutions of the country. As a consequence, after several centuries of effort only a small and uninfluential minority had been gathered into the Church. Now at last the barrier was crumbling, and because of other agencies than the missionary.

The missionary, moreover, profited, at least for a time, by his association with the forces which were chiefly responsible for the change. It was the nations from which he came, who, mainly

---

[5] See, for example, Hodous in *The Christian Occupation of China*, pp. 29, 30.
[6] Ibid., pp. 30, 31.
[7] For a brief description of some of the new movements in religion, see Vargas in *International Review of Missions*, 1926, pp. 3-20.

by their economic and political impact, had led to the collapse of the old walls. In many cities the missionary was the only representative of the peoples whose civilization was now the popular subject of study, and even in the ports his schools were usually the best places for the acquisition of the new learning.

Moreover, after 1900 the country was prostrate before the foreigner. Violations of his person and property had been visited by swift and disastrous vengeance, and he and his possessions enjoyed a security that they had never before known. Chinese Christians had been awarded indemnities for the injuries inflicted on them in the Boxer year, and these indemnities had been collected from their neighbors. Protected as they were, therefore, by the powerful alien, they were relatively free from persecution. This prestige had its unfortunate side: it meant that some would be led to seek membership in the Church from unworthy motives. It did, however, bring a greater open-mindedness to the missionaries' message.

Opposition there still was, and criticism. The old culture had by no means entirely disappeared: most of its fundamental institutions remained, indeed, largely intact. Before the close of 1926 the rising tide of nationalism was to make the close connection of the Christian enterprise with the aggressive imperialism of the Occident a handicap to the missionary and to the Church. In general, however, especially in the first two decades after 1900, the missionary had free course. Never before in the entire history of the Church had so large a body of non-Christians been physically and mentally so accessible to the Gospel. The missionary believed, too, that at no previous time had his message been so needed: if there were in the Christian Gospel spiritual and moral values which were not to be found in the older faiths of China, now, above all others, was the time when it was imperative that they be made available. For better or for worse, the nation had embarked on an uncharted voyage over seas which were certain to be stormy. If the adventure was to prove fortunate, if, indeed, it was not to terminate in shipwreck, there would need to come from that West whose economic and political enterprises had forced the country to leave the safe haven of its older customs all the assistance, and especially all the steadying, inspiring, and directing impulses possible.

CONDITIONS BETWEEN 1901 AND 1914 WHICH AFFECTED THE
MISSIONARY

Of the quarter of a century between the close of 1901 and the close of 1926, approximately the first half, or the years preceding the outbreak of the World War, was the time of greatest opportunity. During these years the younger Chinese were viewing rather uncritically everything from the West. The country was still prostrate before the foreigner, he was thought to be all-powerful, and the articulate classes were painfully conscious of the weakness of the nation and eager to learn the secret of the strength which the Occident seemed to possess. The missionary, as one who was deemed a representative of the West and who professed to know of spiritual and moral resources which, if applied, would work a regeneration in individuals and nations, was listened to attentively, or, if not always attentively, with less prejudice than formerly. Thousands of students, officials, and merchants came to hear the presentation of the Christian message by prominent religious leaders from the West and many of them enrolled in classes to study the Faith. The coming of the Republic brought with it religious liberty, and Christianity no longer depended so largely upon the treaties for toleration. Criticisms, both of the Occident and of Christianity, were not lacking, but they were not as widespread as before 1900 nor as virulent or disturbing as they were to be after the World War. Missionaries found more doors open than they could well enter.

Moreover, the conditions in the West which had led to the rise of the missionary movements of the nineteenth century and had given them strength were apparently unweakened. The wealth of Europe and America continued to accumulate and contributions to Christian missions increased.

In the Roman Catholic Church new missionary organizations were continuing to appear and the Roman Catholics in the United States, now a body numbering several millions composed largely of recent immigrants and their descendants, were beginning to accumulate property and to become subscribers to the work of the Church in non-Christian lands.

In Protestantism the momentum given by the religious awakenings of the eighteenth and nineteenth centuries was unabated. Questions which a few years later were to cause dissensions and to undermine convictions upon which the missionary enterprise had once rested were not yet prominently raised. Foreign missions, from being maintained by only a minority of the membership, had long since obtained the endorsement of the official organizations of most of the denominations and had become a major activity of the churches. The foreign missionary conference held at Edinburgh in 1910 was probably more representative of all Protestantism than any religious gathering ever held for any purpose: it not only inaugurated a new era of coöperation but showed how large a place the missionary enterprise had come to hold in Protestant circles. The countries that were predominantly Protestant continued to reap the major part of the profits of the new industrial processes. Particularly in the United States, where the Protestant elements, being older and in the ascendant, had come into possession of most of the wealth which was there mounting more rapidly than elsewhere on earth, did interest in missions thrive. No gatherings held for any purpose, secular or religious, brought together as many students from as many colleges and universities as did the quadrennial conventions of the Student Volunteer Movement for Foreign Missions, an organization which had for its watchword the ambitious slogan, "The evangelism of the world in this generation." The Laymen's Missionary Movement, which arose in part out of one of these conventions, strove to provide the mission boards with sufficient income to make that dream a reality. The World War had not yet devastated Europe or revealed the weaknesses of Western civilization. Never before had Protestants been as wealthy and never before had they been so much interested in spreading their faith into non-Christian lands.

Given these conditions both in China and in the Occident, it is not strange that the years between 1901 and the summer of 1914 were the most prosperous that Christian missions in the Middle Kingdom had yet seen.

CHAPTER XXIV

CHINA IN A TIME OF REORGANIZATION (1901-1926)
ROMAN CATHOLIC MISSIONS, 1901-JULY, 1914
THE MISSION OF THE RUSSIAN ORTHODOX CHURCH,
1901-JULY, 1914

RECOVERY FROM THE BOXER UPRISING

IN the general prosperity of the Church in China during the years between 1901 and the summer of 1914 the Roman Catholic communion had a very large share. In most places it quickly recovered from the devastation wrought by the Boxers. By the close of 1901 the majority of the missionaries had returned to their stations and were receiving adults for baptism.[1] Here and there, to be sure, squalls followed in the wake of the storm. On December 13th, 1901, houses were pillaged and two missionaries of the Congregation of the Immaculate Heart of Mary (Scheutveld), Fathers Van Merhaeghen and Bongaerts, and three other Christians were killed in the southwestern part of Mongolia by a band of roughs, some of whom were in military uniform. It was suspected that the assassins had been hired by Moslems who had taken umbrage at being compelled to return the Christian women and girls who had been carried off in 1900.[2] January 15th, 1902, Father Julien, a missionary of the Paris Society, and two Chinese Christians were killed.[3] In 1902 Boxers were reported still to be active in Szechwan, and several Christians, including a Chinese priest, were murdered.[4] However, the letter reporting the disturbances told of thousands in the province asking for instruction.[5]

[1] Annual report of the Foreign Missionary Society of Paris for 1901, in *Annals of the Propagation of the Faith,* Vol. 65, p. 200.
[2] Letter of Van Hecke, Superior of the Belgian mission, from Scheutveld, April 7, 1902, in *Annals of the Propagation of the Faith,* Vol. 65, pp. 165-167; ibid., Vol. 65, p. 98.
[3] *Annals of the Propagation of the Faith,* Vol. 65, p. 98.
[4] Letter from Bishop Durand, Vicar Apostolic in West Szechwan, Aug. 3, 1902, in ibid., Vol. 66, pp. 13-16. Also letter of a missionary in Szechwan in ibid., Vol. 65, p. 312.
[5] Letter of Bishop Durand, Aug. 3, 1902, in ibid., Vol. 66, pp. 13-16.

That seems to have been the experience in many other parts of the country. It could, indeed, scarcely have been otherwise when the government had outwardly so changed its attitude toward missionaries. In 1901, for example, an armed escort accompanied the Vicar Apostolic to Silin in Kwangsi to hold commemorative services for the first martyrs in the province [6] and in 1902 Bishop Favier and his coadjutor were received in audience by the Empress Dowager and the Emperor.[7]

NUMERICAL GROWTH, 1901-1914

In the years following 1900 the number of Roman Catholics rapidly rose. In 1901 there were said to be 720,540 baptized Roman Catholics in China; [8] in 1903 the total was reported as being 811,140; [9] in 1906, 888,131; [10] in 1907, 902,478; [11] in 1910 there were said to be 1,364,618 Catholic Christians; [11] and at the close of 1912, 1,431,258.[12] If these figures are correct—and they are based upon official reports—in the eleven years between 1901 and 1912 Roman Catholics had increased nearly one hundred per cent., as compared with a growth of about forty per cent. in the eleven years between 1890 and 1901.

A map for 1911 shows that at the time it was issued there were Christians in each of the prefectures of China Proper except those in the eastern and western parts of Kansu, two in the southwestern part of Shansi, four in Southern and four in Northwestern Hunan, four in Kweichow, four in Southwestern Kwangsi, six in Yünnan, and one in Western Szechwan.[13] In other words, the Church was represented in all the prefectures except a very few in the mountains and in the extreme Northwest. In 1911 the provinces having the largest numbers of Christians were Chihli (and a part of Mongolia) with 360,460, nearly a third of the total, Kiangsu with 160,280, Szechwan with 118,724, and Shantung with 104,790. Those having the smallest numbers were

[6] The Vicar Apostolic, in ibid., Vol. 65, pp. 233-241.
[7] L'Œuvre de la Propagation de la Foi, *Dix années d'apostolat catholiques dans les missions*, p. 65.
[8] *Missiones Catholicae Cura S. Congregationis de Propaganda Fide*, 1907, p. 44.
[9] *Missions en Chine, au Congo et aux Philippines*, 1913, pp. 62, 63, quoting from *Calendier-annuaire* (Zikawei).
[10] *Missiones Catholicae Cura S. Congregationis de Propaganda Fide*, 1907, Table 38.
[11] *Catholic Missions*, Vol. 6, p. 76.
[12] Hoffman in *Zeitschrift für Missionswissenschaft*, Vol. 4, p. 42.
[13] Moidrey, *Carte des préfectures de Chine et de leur population chrétienne en 1911*.

Kirin with 14,821, Yünnan with 13,200, Hunan with 13,112, Kansu with 4,836, and Heilungchang with 4,307.[14] None of the above figures include the number of catechumens. These were reported as being 390,619 in all China in 1907,[15] and 448,200 in 1912.[16]

The growth seems to have been particularly marked in centers near the coast, like Chihli, Shantung, and Kiangnan,[17] but apparently it was shared by all the missions. The Congregation of the Immaculate Heart of Mary, working in some of the most difficult sections, Mongolia and Kansu, reported that between 1905 and 1912 the number of Christians in the southwestern part of Mongolia had more than doubled and that in the other districts assigned it they had increased between fifty and sixty per cent. in the same period.[18] In Western Szechwan more baptisms of adults were reported for 1907 than in many years [19] and in the northern part of Manchuria more adults were baptized in 1903-1904 than in any previous twelvemonth.[20]

Bodies for the First Time Sending Representatives to China

In the publications which sought to arouse interest among their constituency in Europe and America, Roman Catholics did not have as much to say of the changes in China and of the opportunities these afforded as did Protestant books and papers.[21] They were, however, by no means blind to the new day that had dawned. The numbers of priests, foreign and Chinese, increased from 1,375 in 1901 to 1,574 (1,075 foreign and 499 Chinese) in

[14] Ibid.
[15] Krose, *Katholische Missionsstatistik* (1908) founded on *Missiones Catholicae Cura S. Congregationis de Propaganda Fide,* 1907.
[16] Hoffman in *Zeitschrift für Missionswissenschaft,* Vol 4, p. 42.
[17] Schmidlin in *Die katholischen Missionen in den deutschen Schutzgebieten,* p. 212, reports the number of Christians in Shantung under the care of the Society of the Divine Word to have been 26,315 in 1904, 46,151 in 1908, and 59,000 in 1910.
[18] *Missions en Chine, au Congo et aux Philippines,* 1906, p. 47, 1909, pp. 25-28, 1911, p. 56, 1913, p. 72.
[19] *Société des Missions Étrangères, Compte rendu* (1907), pp. 97-120.
[20] Letter of Bishop Lalouyer, Vicar Apostolic in Northern Manchuria, in *Annals of the Propagation of the Faith,* 1905, p. 68.
[21] *Annals of the Propagation of the Faith* in the years 1902 to 1910, inclusive, contain very little mention of the new movements in China. *Chine, Ceylan, Madagascar,* containing letters from the Jesuits in Chihli, has more to say of them, but not as much as the usual Protestant journal.

1903,[22] to 1,717 in 1906, and to 2,298 (1,469 foreign and 729 Chinese) in 1912.[23] This growth, while not as great proportionately as that of the Catholic community, was rapid. It is interesting and perhaps significant, moreover, that the number of Chineses priests rose more markedly than did that of the foreign clergy: the Church was stressing the training of a native priesthood.

Between 1901 and 1914 representatives arrived of a few organizations which previously had not been in China, and fresh allocations of territory were made. In 1903 German Franciscans took over from their Italian brethren the northern part of Shantung,[24] and in 1904 the eastern part of the same province was given them.[25]

In 1904 there arrived in Honan the first missionaries of the recently founded Seminary of St. Francis Xavier for Foreign Missions, a body with headquarters at Parma, and in 1906 the southern part of the province was made a separate vicariate apostolic and assigned to their care.[26] In 1902 the Servants of the Holy Ghost, or the Missionary Sisters of Steyl, entered China. A companion organization of the Society of the Divine Word, this sisterhood had its origin in 1881 but it did not send members to China until after the Boxer year.[27] In 1909 six French-Canadian nuns left for China, the first representatives of the Sisters of the Immaculate Conception. They established themselves in Canton.[28] The Franciscan Sisters of Egypt founded a house in the northwestern part of Hupeh in 1915.[29] The Salesians (Society of St. Francis de Sales, begun between 1840 and 1860 in Italy by Dom Bosco and approved by the Pope in 1874) came to China in 1902, landing at Macao. In 1911 the Bishop of Macao assigned them the civil prefecture in which Macao is located,[30]

[22] Missiones Catholicae Cura S. Congregationis de Propaganda Fide, 1907, Table 44.
[23] Missions en Chine, au Congo at aux Philippines, 1913, pp. 62, 63, from Calendaire annuaire (Zikawei).
[24] Schmidlin, Die katholische Missionen in den deutschen Schutzgebieten, p. 226.
[25] Schmidlin, Katholische Missionsgeschichte, p. 470.
[26] Moidrey, La hiérarchie catholique en Chine, en Corée et au Japon, pp. 82, 214.
[27] Catholic Missions, Vol. 11, pp. 100-103.
[28] Ibid., Vol. 4, pp. 75, 76.
[29] Planchet, Les missions de Chine et du Japon, 1919, p. 192.
[30] Relations de Chine, Vol. 19, p. 492.

and in 1912 they commenced activities in a district near Canton.[31] In 1911 the northern part of Shensi was erected into a separate vicariate and entrusted to the Franciscans of the Province of Catalonia.[32] In 1913 a section of Kwangtung, which was part of the diocese of Macao but was outside Portuguese political jurisdiction, was given as a mission to the Portuguese Jesuits who had been driven out of Macao following the revolution in Portugal (1910) in which the monarchy had been supplanted by the republic.[33]

The Roman Catholic body in the United States, which after the World War was to undertake so many enterprises in China, was as yet scarcely represented. In 1908 a Franciscan reported that he knew of only seven American Catholic missionaries in the Empire.[34] There were probably more than this, but the number was small and little organized effort was made as yet to increase it. It was only in 1908 that the Pope withdrew the United States from the jurisdiction of the Propaganda and thus proclaimed that it had ceased to be a foreign mission field.[35] The energies of the Church in the United States were too absorbed in making provision for the millions of its adherents whom the great wave of immigration from Catholic communities in Europe was bringing to America to permit of any great interest in foreign missions. Here and there, however, were indications that this neglect of other countries would soon be lessened. An American branch of the Society for the Propagation of the Faith had been organized in 1896;[36] the Society of the Divine Word was founding a college at Techny, on the outskirts of Chicago, for the training of missionaries; the Catholic Foreign Missions Bureau was formed in Boston in 1906 and issued a periodical;[37] reports of the quadrennial convention of the (Protestant) Student Volunteer Movement held during the Christmas holidays of 1913-1914 led to the suggestion that a somewhat similar organization—to take shape later as the Catholic Students' Mission Crusade—be instituted by Roman Catholics; and in 1911 the archbishops approved a plan for a national seminary for foreign missions, the Catholic

[31] Moidrey, op. cit., p. 215; *The Christian Occupation of China,* p. 460.
[32] Moidrey, op. cit., p. 70.
[33] *Catholic Missions,* Vol. 8, pp. 137, 138.
[34] Blesser in *Catholic Missions,* Vol. 2, p. 97.
[35] Powers, *The Maryknoll Movement,* p. xv.
[36] Ibid., p. 37.
[37] Powers, *The Maryknoll Movement,* p. 49.

Foreign Mission Society of America.[38] It was not until after 1914, however, that this foreshadowing of a missionary awakening among American Roman Catholics was to have results important for China.

GROWTH IN MISSIONS ALREADY ESTABLISHED

While the Roman Catholic mission press gave no very great prominence to the new conditions in China, and while few new societies and congregations began operations there, the bodies already established steadily and rapidly extended their activities. It is impossible here to picture this growth in detail, but the statistics given above and the scattered examples which follow, drawn from many different parts of China, may serve as an indication of what was occurring, with variations, throughout the country. In 1912 two missionaries of the Congregation of the Immaculate Heart of Mary obtained a foothold in Siningfu in Kansu, where years before efforts to establish a residence had been thwarted by the provincial authorities.[39] In 1907 a missionary of the same congregation reported a journey to distant Urumtsi, in Sinkiang, for the purpose of beginning work there.[40] In 1904 a representative of the Missions Étrangères of Paris reported that he knew of about two hundred families of aborigines in one valley in Kweichow that were accepting the Christian faith.[41] The Franciscan Missionaries of Mary founded houses in Chengtu in 1903 and 1906 and at Suifu in Szechwan in 1903.[42] In 1904, after an interruption of about twenty years, operations were resumed on the island, so dear to Catholic hearts, on which Xavier had died, and by 1908 the Christian community there was said to number over three hundred.[43] In 1902 Bishop Verhaeghen reported that the Faith was making progress in his vicariate, the southern part of Hupeh.[44] In the year 1912-1913, in the great Jesuit field in Kiangsu and Anhui, 54,127 baptisms were reported —5,105 of adults, 1,595 of adults in *articulo mortis*, 6,155 of

[38] McQuaide, *With Christ in China*, pp. 267 et seq.
[39] *Annals of the Propagation of the Faith*, Vol. 83, pp. 174-178.
[40] Lessons from Urumsti, June 7, 1907, in *Missions en Chine et au Congo*, 1907, pp. 265-268.
[41] Cavalarie from Kweichow in *Annals of the Propagation of the Faith*, Vol. 67, pp. 5-15.
[42] Planchet, *Les missions de Chine et du Japon*, 1919, p. 217.
[43] *Catholic Missions*, Vol. 9, p. 37.
[44] Bishop Verhaeghen in *Annals of the Propagation of the Faith*, Vol. 66, p. 204.

children of Christians, 989 of children of catechumens, 31,479 of children of non-Christians, and 8,804 of orphans—and 10,530 confirmations.[45] In Chihli in 1913 a growth in the number of Catholics in the past year of 51,047, or about twelve per cent., was reported, in Shansi of 3,233, or seven per cent., in Shensi of 928, or two and a half per cent., and in Honan of 3,913, or more than eleven per cent.[46] In 1907 ninety baptisms of adults were reported from Tibet, 663 from Yünnan, 2,037 from Kwangtung, and 592 from Kwangsi.[47]

New vicariates apostolic were created. Northern Shensi was, as we have seen, divided in 1911 and the northern section of it entrusted to the Spanish Franciscans,[48] and we have also seen that in the same year the western portion of Honan, since 1906 a prefecture apostolic, was erected into a vicariate apostolic for the Seminary of St. Francis Xavier of Parma.[49] In 1905 the southern part of Kansu was made a prefecture apostolic and remained in the hands of the Congregation of the Immaculate Heart of Mary.[50] In 1908 the Bishop of Macao turned over the Island of Hainan, previously under his control, to the Vicar Apostolic of Kwangtung, and received in exchange the civil prefecture of Chaoch'ing, inland from Macao, and this new territory he cared for through secular priests, Portuguese Jesuits, and the Salesians of Dom Bosco.[51] Kiench'ang in Szechwan was created a vicariate apostolic in 1910 and continued to be a field of the Missions Étrangères of Paris.[52] Chêkiang was divided in 1910.[53] The central section of Chihli was separated from the northern section in 1910 and Tientsin was detached in 1912, both new vicariates continuing under the supervision of the Lazarists.[54] In 1913 Formosa, previously under the Vicar Apostolic of Amoy, was made a separate vicariate and to Amoy were added three civil prefectures in Fukien.[55] In 1914 Swatow with the surrounding

[45] Schmidlin, Missions und Kulturverhältnisse im fernen Osten, p. 106.
[46] Ibid., p. 117.
[47] Société des Missions Étrangères. Comte rendu (1907), pp. 121-156.
[48] Moidrey, La hiérarchie catholique en Chine, en Corée, et au Japon, p. 70.
[49] Ibid., p. 82.
[50] Ibid., p. 96.
[51] Relations de Chine, Vol. 21, p. 152.
[52] Moidrey, op. cit., p. 104.
[53] Ibid., p. 139.
[54] Ibid., p. 140.
[55] Missiones Catholicae Cura S. Congregationis de Propaganda Fide, 1922, p. 233.

region was erected into a vicariate apostolic, remaining in charge of the Missions Étrangères of Paris.[56]

THE REVOLUTION OF 1911

The Revolution of 1911 brought added opportunity. In the disorder attendant upon the changes, to be sure, some of the missionaries and Chinese Christians suffered. In 1911, on the Yünnanese borders of Tibet, Father Castanet of the Missions Étrangères of Paris was killed and Christian communities were devastated;[57] in Chihli a priest was murdered;[58] another lost his life near Hsianfu, and elsewhere in Shensi bandits were prevalent and wrought destruction among Christians as well as non-Christians.[59] The Revolution was, however, the triumph of forces favorable to the culture of the Occident and, while here and there Christians suffered, very little anti-Christian sentiment was shown. Officials, indeed, made special efforts to protect the missionary; neither imperialists nor revolutionists could afford to have the foreigner arrayed against them. In Shantung, for instance, where only twelve years before the Boxer movement had taken its first toll of foreign life, the cry went out: "Protect the foreigner, protect the Christian."[60]

In several places missionaries were able to succor those who suffered from the Revolution, and especially the helpless Manchus. In T'aiyüanfu hundreds of Chinese, non-Christians as well as Christians, were allowed to take refuge in the mission compound;[61] in Nanking Father Gain gave shelter on the mission premises to about three hundred women and children;[62] in Kingchow in Hupeh Roman Catholic missionaries preserved several thousand Manchus, first from revolutionists and later from starvation;[63] in Yachow in Szechwan a missionary interceded with the republican forces and saved the life of a Manchu official.[64]

[56] Ibid., p. 237.
[57] *Au pays du dragon*, p. 77; *Catholic Missions*, Vol. 6, pp. 37-40; *Annals of the Propagation of the Faith*, Vol. 75, p. 38.
[58] Beckman, *The Massacre at Sianfu*, pp. 117, 118.
[59] Ibid., pp. 117, 118; *Catholic Missions*, Vol. 9, p. 94.
[60] Schmidlin, *Die katholischen Missionen in den deutschen Schutzgebieten*, p. 214.
[61] Lady Hosie, *Two Gentlemen of China*, p. 186.
[62] Farjenal, *Through the Chinese Revolution*, p. 109.
[63] *Annals of the Propagation of the Faith*, Vol. 76, pp. 5-7, Vol. 77, pp. 45-50.
[64] Ibid., Vol. 76, pp. 5-7.

Naturally many Manchus became peculiarly accessible to the message of the missionary: within a year and a half about two thousand of those at Kingchow had been baptized,[65] and in Foochow hundreds were coming for instruction.[66]

It was not only the Manchus who showed an inclination to favor the missionary. In May, 1912, Sun Yat-sen, the idol of the revolutionists and a Protestant Christian, was present at a service in Canton while a *Te Deum* was sung in thanks to God for the protection of Christians during the unrest.[67]   Christians, most of them Protestant, but at least one of them Roman Catholic, were prominent in the early months of the republican régime.[68]   A day was set aside by Yüan Shih-k'ai in April, 1913, on which Christians were urged to pray for the success of the new government, and in Roman Catholic as well as Protestant churches officials were present at the services which were held in response to this request.[69]   Christians were assured by Yüan Shih-k'ai that full religious liberty would be granted them by the Republic and the "Constitutional Compact" drawn up in 1914 under his supervision wrote that promise into law.[70]   It was no wonder that Chinese as well as Manchus listened attentively to the missionaries' instruction and that the rate of increase in the number of Roman Catholics was greater than it had been even in the decade immediately preceding the Revolution.

PERSECUTIONS, 1901-1914

This relative open-mindedness did not mean that missionaries prosecuted their work without danger.   The government, especially after the Revolution, made greater efforts to protect missionaries and their converts than before.   It did so probably chiefly because of the trouble which anti-foreign demonstrations were now certain to bring on the heads of officials and not from any decrease in dislike for the missionary,[71] but the change was

[65] Ibid., Vol. 77, pp. 45-50.
[66] Bishop Aguirre, Vicar Apostolic of North Fukien, in ibid., Vol. 76.
[67] *Zeitschrift für Missionswissenschaft,* Vol. 4, pp. 38-40.
[68] Ibid.
[69] *Annals of the Propagation of the Faith,* Vol. 76, p. 168.
[70] *China Year Book,* 1916, pp. 437, 458.
[71] The attitude of the official classes seems to be shown in a memorial given in Wolferstan, *The Catholic Church in China,* p. 240, and quoted from *Die katholische Missionen* of January, 1907.   The memorial was entitled *Min Chiao*

no less welcome. Here and there popular animosity continued and occasionally broke out in the form of riots, nor did the bandits, who became more and more numerous, always respect the foreigner and his Chinese adherents. In 1902 a Jesuit, Victor Lomüller, was killed in Chihli in an insurrection caused by a tax levy for which missionaries were held to be responsible.[72] In 1903 a Chinese priest and several other Christians were killed by brigands in Chêkiang,[73] while in this same year other bands made away with Christians in Kwangsi.[74] In 1904 Bishop Verhaeghen, Vicar Apostolic in the southern part of Hupeh, died a martyr.[75]

During the Russo-Japanese War travel was interrupted in South Manchuria and both there and in Eastern Mongolia bandits

Hsiang An (Good relations between the people and the Church) and is said to have been composed in 1905 by two members of the Ministry of Public Instruction and by order of Yüan Shih-k'ai to have been distributed secretly among all the officials of Chihli. Father Jansen, a missionary in Eastern Mongolia, obtained a copy. The contents are in substance as follows:

First, Confucianism, Buddhism, and Islam are said to live peaceably together, but the religion from Europe is held to be different. Religious wars are the order of the day in Europe and this characteristic has been brought to China. The former decrees against Christianity had for their purpose the cessation of quarrels between Christians and non-Christians. Christianity was tolerated under pressure from foreign powers, notably France.

Second. The treaties between China and foreign powers have always been detrimental to China. Christians have oppressed non-Christians, rousing the latters' hatred.

Third. Chinese officials must be polite to missionaries, since the treaties order it. They must allow them to preach and remember that they are guests. They must neither oppress nor fawn on missionaries. They should permit Chinese to become Christians, although there are difficulties arising from the fact that Christians are exempt from taxes levied to support non-Christian festivals.

Fourth. There is condemnation of Chinese Christians for using their influence with foreigners to oppress their neighbors and of the evils that have come in China from missions.

Fifth. An account of the history of Christianity.

Sixth. A description of the Christian religion showing the discrepancy between its principles and the practice of those who profess it.

Seventh. The litigation between Christians and non-Christians is described.

Eighth. The present state of religion in Europe and America is given, showing that to be a Christian does not necessarily mean disloyalty to the state and contending that therefore in China Christianity should not necessarily mean a lack of patriotism.

A letter from Jansen from Mongolia, March 2, 1906, giving this document, is in *Missions en Chine et au Congo,* 1906, pp. 241-248.

[72] *Annals of the Propagation of the Faith,* Vol. 65, p. 167; *Chine, Ceylan, Madagascar,* March, 1904, p. 267.

[73] Letter of Bishop Reynaud, Vicar Apostolic in Chêkiang, in *Annals of the Propagation of the Faith,* Vol. 67, pp. 55-60.

[74] Letter of Seguret, a missionary in Kwangsi, in ibid., Vol. 66, pp. 56-64.

[75] Wegener, *Victorin Delbrouck,* p. 19; Cordier in *Catholic Encyclopedia,* Vol. 9, p. 748.

plundered many of the populace.[76] In 1904 Ernest Trecul, a young missionary, was killed while trying to rescue a neophyte from the hands of robbers.[77] The Japanese, moreover, are said to have desecrated churches and chapels, defacing the images, and to have treated the French much as they did the Russians. The Russian forces are reported to have suspected the Chinese clergy of being spies.[78] On the whole, however, Christians seem not to have suffered as severely as did non-Christians,[79] and after the war, possibly in part for this reason, Manchuria witnessed a large increase of accessions to the Church.[80] The war was not entirely a curse.

In 1905 and 1906 on the Szechwan border in and around Batang an uprising of Tibetans occurred and two priests were killed while all their followers who would not recant were shot. In reparation the Catholics were given, through pressure from the French Government, a house and one hundred and twenty thousand taels.[81] In 1906 Protestant and Roman Catholic Chinese in a prefecture in Chêkiang fell to fighting and the Chinese authorities sent soldiers to restore peace.[82] That same year, in February, in Chiangpoo in Fukien, an anti-Christian riot arose out of the claim that in a dispute Roman Catholics had imprisoned two members of a secret sect.[83] In February, 1906, an uprising broke out in Nanch'ang, Kiangsi, in which Roman Catholics and Protestants were killed and much property was destroyed. The occasion seems to have been the suicide of a Chinese official who took that characteristic method of protesting against the pressure which Roman Catholics were bringing upon him to punish the murderers of Christians.[84] The French Government demanded an indemnity of four hundred thousand taels but later reduced

[76] Letter of Monnier from Manchuria in *Annals of the Propagation of the Faith*, Vol. 68, pp. 3, 4; Letter of Louis Janssens from Notre Dame des Pins, Mongolia, Feb. 11, 1906, in *Missions en Chine et au Congo*, 1906, pp. 153-157; *Société des Missions Étrangères. Compte rendu*, 1907, pp. 74-82.

[77] Letter from Monnier in *Annals of the Propagation of the Faith*, Vol. 68, pp. 3, 4.

[78] A. Damerval, S. J., writing of a visit to Manchuria in *Chine, Ceylan, Madagascar*, Sept., 1908, p. 249.

[79] Letter of Janssens in *Missions en Chine et au Congo*, 1906, pp. 153-157.

[80] *Société des Missions Étrangères. Compte rendu*, 1907, pp. 83-96.

[81] Shelton, *Sunshine and Shadow on the Tibetan Border*, pp. 26-28; Cordier in *Catholic Encyclopedia*, Vol. 9, p. 748.

[82] Smith, *The Uplift of China*, p. 194.

[83] Pitcher, *In and About Amoy*, p. 163.

[84] Thomson, *The Chinese*, p. 367; Smith, op. cit., p. 193; *Annals of the Propagation of the Faith*, Vol. 69, pp. 178-180.

the amount.[85]   In September, 1907, a missionary and sixty or more Christians were killed in the southern part of Kiangsi.[86] In 1909 a Father Soffroy was killed in Manchuria by brigands while on his way to minister to a sick fellow missionary.[87]   About 1910 a Chinese in Kwangsi was chained and beaten for selling land to missionaries.[88]   December 22, 1910, Merigot, a missionary in Yünnan, was murdered.[89]   In the spring of 1910 an antiforeign riot broke out in and around Changsha, Hunan, and Bishop Perez and two other Augustinians were drowned when the junk on which they were endeavoring to escape collided with a British gunboat.[90]   In 1911 a magistrate in Shansi made trouble because Christians refused to contribute to community pagan festivals.[91] In June, 1913, a Franciscan, Francis Bernot, was assassinated in Shensi.[92]   In 1914 a Jesuit was killed by bandits in Anhui.[93]   The lives of the missionary and his converts, though less frequently in jeopardy than before 1900, were not yet secure.   Perils still attached both to the propagation and to the profession of the Christian faith.

Friction, too, occasionally broke out between Protestant and Roman Catholic Chinese, and that in spite of an official decree of the Church which commanded missionaries to live at peace with Protestants and, while refuting in sermons what the Church held to be the latters' errors, not to denounce individuals but to treat them all with prudence and charity.[94]

METHODS OF ROMAN CATHOLIC WORK, 1901-1914

Roman Catholic missionaries still had as their chief goal the winning of Chinese to the Christian faith and to this end they continued to stress what Protestants would have called evangelism. Unlike their Protestant brethren, they did not greatly expand their educational and medical activities.   However, they modified their

[85] *Foreign Relations,* 2d Session, 59th Congress, p. 339.
[86] *Annals of the Propagation of the Faith,* Vol. 71, pp. 99-107.
[87] Letter of the Vicar Apostolic of South Manchuria, Sept. 15, 1909, in ibid., Vol. 73, pp. 17, 18.
[88] Letter of Bishop Du Coeur, Vicar Apostolic in Kwangsi, in *Catholic Missions,* Vol. 6, pp. 240-242.
[89] *Catholic Missions,* Vol. 5, p. 64.
[90] Ibid., Vol. 4, p. 128.
[91] *Annals of the Propagation of the Faith,* Vol. 74, pp. 235-248.
[92] Ibid., Vol. 76, p. 211.
[93] Ibid., Vol. 76, p. 77.
[94] Caubrière, *Synthesis decretalium Sinarum,* p. 45.   See an example of friction in Bashford, *Journal,* Jan., 1908.

methods, partially abandoning some and developing and adding to others.

Of the methods which tended to fall into disuse, the most notable was interference in litigation. After 1900 Chinese officials were fairly obsequious to missionaries, usually deciding lawsuits in favor of the side espoused by the foreigner. If they did not, foreign governments might bring pressure on their superiors and these in turn call the unfortunate subordinate to task: peace with the Westerner was held to be more desirable than exact justice.[95] Roman Catholic missionaries, however, while still occasionally giving support to Chinese in the courtst, apparently did not as much as formerly employ that method to attract adherents.[96] Since at least 1880 the Church had officially frowned on its use,[97] and in 1908 the prohibition was reiterated and amplified. Missionaries were commanded to refrain from intervening in quarrels on behalf of Christians and catechumens and to go to law only in case a Christian was persecuted for his faith.[98] This change of policy may have been in part because of a growing feeling that the older procedure was unchristian,[99] in part because of the decreased persecution of Christians, and in part because catechumens were easily gained by other methods.

The change seems also to have been associated with the French Separation Act of 1905. The Church objected to this deed of the French Government, diplomatic relations between Paris and the Vatican were severed, and neither the French nor the ecclesiastical authorities were inclined to coöperate in China as closely as formerly. In January, 1906, the French Minister at Peking notified the Chinese Government of the Separation Act and said that he had instructions to declare that thereafter the French legation would take care only of cases affecting French missionaries and that those involving missionaries from other countries should be referred to their respective ministers.[100] The French protectorate of non-French Catholic missions came to an end and even French missionaries were less vigorously supported than formerly. As a rule the protectorate of non-French missions was assumed by other powers. In 1902 Italy, for example, had undertaken that

[95] Brown, *New Forces in Old China*, p. 230.
[96] Ibid., p. 230.
[97] Caubrière, op. cit., pp. 321-328.
[98] Ibid., pp. 321-328.
[99] This was about the attitude of Louvet in *Catholic World*, Vol. 91, p. 438.
[100] Koo, *Status of Aliens in China*, p. 309.

for the Italian Franciscans in the northern part of Shansi and in succeeding years extended it to all missions which were committed to her citizens.[101]   Apparently, however, either the disposition was lacking to appeal as formerly to the consul for aid in the settlement of lawsuits or the consul was less willing to heed the appeal.   Then, too, some Chinese seemed to feel that with the rupture between the French Government and the Church the force which the latter could bring to bear was diminished and that the missionary need not be as greatly feared as formerly.[102] Moreover, in 1908 the decree of 1899 by which Roman Catholic missionaries of various grades were granted the privilege of conferring on terms of equality with Chinese officials was formally revoked.   The restriction of the French protectorate very possibly made its annulment easier.[103]

Lessened participation in lawsuits and the curtailment of the French protectorate, however, did not mean that Roman Catholic missionaries were willing to dispense with the treaty privileges accorded them or the support of their respective governments. Some still argued vehemently that the cancellation of special privileges and the withdrawal of the protectorate would mean ruin to the Church.[104]   To them the Chinese Government was the greatest enemy to missions and they did not hesitate to invoke the secular arm against it.   Nor was every Catholic missionary opposed to giving assistance in the courts to his converts.   Some argued that all Chinese belonged to groups which supported them against members of other groups, that in joining the Church the Chinese dissociated himself from his former group to enter another, and that this other, the Church, should provide him the aid of which he had voluntarily deprived himself.[105]

Contemporaneously with the decreasing inclination to attract adherents by interfering in lawsuits came new methods and a greater use of some that had been employed before.   As in earlier years, few from the educated and official classes were reached and the Church made its chief gains from among the poor—

---

[101] Grentrup, *Jus Missionarium*, p. 402.

[102] Bishop Chatagnon, Vicar Apostolic in Southern Szechwan, wrote Sept. 1, 1906, that Chinese newspapers were saying that the time had come to abolish the Catholic religion in China, since Europeans were abandoning it at home.— *Annals of the Propagation of the Faith*, Vol. 70, p. 56.

[103] Koo, op. cit., pp. 314, 315.

[104] Kervyn, *Methode de l'apostolat moderne en Chine*, pp. 112-122.

[105] Ibid., pp. 122-126. He quotes others as being of the same conviction.

boatmen, fishermen, and peasants.[106] As formerly, too, and in distinct contrast to Protestant practice, isolated individuals were discouraged from becoming catechumens, for they would have difficulty in standing out alone against their non-Christian environment.[107] Emphasis was placed, rather, upon winning the natural social group, the family, and, when no Christians were found in a village or neighborhood, an effort was made to reach several families and to place all their members under instruction at the same time.[108]

The methods of instruction and the degree of progress in Christian knowledge and practice prerequisite to baptism varied from vicariate to vicariate, and even within individual vicariates.[109] The practice of the Jesuits in Kiangnan, of the Society of the Divine Word, and of the Congregation of the Immaculate Heart of Mary was usually to have a period of probation lasting two years or more in which the catechumens were taught in their own homes by resident catechists. Before they could be enrolled as catechumens they must remove from their homes all ancestral tablets and representations of non-Christian divinities. While catechumens they were required to learn the chief principles of the Catholic faith and the Pater, Ave, Credo, Confiteor, Ten Commandments, the acts of faith, hope, charity, and contrition, and the sign of the Cross.[110] They were then gathered into retreats for two or three months, where, away from their home villages and non-Christian associations, under the supervision of a priest and near to a church, domiciled perhaps in school buildings belonging to the mission, they were given the final preparation for baptism and their first communion.[111] While in these

[106] Servière in The Oxford and Cambridge Review, quoted in Chinese Recorder, Vol. 44, p. 614. Servière is speaking from personal observation.
[107] Kervyn, op. cit., p. 377.
[108] Servière, loc. cit., Vol. 44, p. 619.
[109] Ibid., p. 619.
[110] For the substance of the instruction given to catechumens see C. Daems [a missionary in Kansu], Le credo prêché aux neophytes, Hongkong, 1910. The instructions in this volume included the Catholic religion and false religions, the being and nature of God, the Trinity, the creation and fall of man, the promise of redemption, the Virgin Mary, "mother and redeemer," Jesus Christ and his nature, the purpose of the incarnation, original sin, the birth, life, miracles, passion, and resurrection of Jesus, the judgment, heaven, hell, purgatory, the human soul, the Church, baptism, confirmation and the other sacraments, and the Christian life.
[111] For an elaborate collection of cases illustrating problems arising in connection with baptism and of the solution given, see Payen, Casus de Baptismo in Missionibus ac Potissimum in Sinis, passim.

retreats their expenses were usually paid in part or in whole by the mission.[112] In 1893 there was begun at Tours, France, L'Œuvre des Catechumenats to provide the Jesuit missionaries with the means of conducting these retreats, and by 1923 ten catechumenates had been endowed at a cost of 6,000 francs each.[113]

The Lazarists in Chihli and the representatives of the Société des Missions Étrangères of Paris gave most of the instruction to the applicants for baptism in catechumenates lasting several months. The neophytes were taken aside in large groups, usually during the winter months when the work in the fields was the least exacting, and taught. Usually one winter sufficed, but sometimes attendance at more than one retreat was required. As a rule the expenses of the catechumen during these periods were paid by the mission. In Chihli this method was particularly prominent, for here the income from the Boxer indemnity provided the ecclesiastical authorities with fairly ample funds. In Peking the Vicar Apostolic gave the missionary six dollars for each Chinese who was shown to have been converted, one dollar after learning each of the four sections of the catechism and two dollars at baptism.[114]

Manifestly some Chinese were attracted by the prospect of support during the months when they might otherwise be out of work. A Jesuit in Chihli tells of giving succor in time of famine at the rate of a string of cash a month to a total of five strings per person to non-Christians who would agree to study Christianity under the direction of a catechist. In exchange for this sum he took pledges on their land. When prosperity returned, these mortgages were cancelled for three-fifths of the sum advanced and the proceeds were reinvested locally as an endowment for the new Christian community.[115] At least one other Jesuit missionary in Chihli, moreover, in the famine years of 1910 and 1911 gave a small monthly allowance to all non-Christians who would attend catechetical instruction, frankly recognizing the motives to which he was appealing but hoping that instruction

[112] Servière, loc. cit., pp. 619, 620; Schmidlin (also writing from personal observation), in *Zeitschrift für Missionswissenschaft,* Vol. 5, pp. 17-26.
[113] *Relations de Chine,* supplement for April, 1922.
[114] Schmidlin, loc. cit.
[115] E. Hopsomer, Jan. 26, 1909, in *Chine, Ceylan, Madagascar,* March, 1910, pp. 486, 487.

would bring good results.[116]   Some missionaries disapproved the method, holding that the "converts" thus won quickly drifted away if they moved into another vicariate.   Certainly it attracted adherents from the lower social and economic strata.[117]

The Franciscans and Dominicans, apparently because they lacked the funds necessary for paying the expenses of catechumens in these retreats, gave all their instruction preparatory to baptism while the applicant was in his own home.[118]

Sometimes only a slight amount of instruction was given before baptism and then more was required between baptism and the first communion: at other times most of the necessary instruction came as a preliminary to baptism and the first communion followed almost immediately.[119]

As in earlier years, little effort was made to obtain converts by the public preaching of the Christian message and only a limited number owed their first interest to the reading of Christian books: [120] most catechumens were secured through contacts with lay Christians and with the missionary or catechist.   The catechist seems to have been the chief agent used for reaching non-Christians.[121]   Public presentation of the Gospel to non-Christians by missionaries who never could know the language perfectly was believed to cheapen the message and breed misunderstanding, and the Protestant custom of broadcasting great quantities of literature was bitterly criticized.[122]

Missionaries frankly recognized that many non-Christians were first attracted by unworthy motives, but they contended that instruction tended to improve their purpose [123] and that in the second and third generations trained from infancy by the Church lay the hope of a Christian community of high character.[124]   As had long been the custom, Christians were usually formed into communities, sometimes within a non-Christian village or city, but frequently in separate villages.   These communities had their

[116] Hopsomer, telling of his work in *Annals of the Propagation of the Faith*, Vol. 75, p. 83.
[117] Schmidlin, loc. cit.; *The Christian Occupation of China*, p. 463.
[118] Schmidlin, loc. cit.
[119] Servière, op. cit., p. 620.
[120] DePreter, missionary in Eastern Mongolia, writing in *Missions en Chine et au Congo*, 1903, pp. 91-96.
[121] Schmidlin, loc. cit.; *Missions en Chine, au Congo, et aux Philippines*, 1912, p. 41.
[122] Kervyn, *Méthode de l'apostolat moderne en Chine*, pp. 417-419.
[123] DePreter, loc. cit.
[124] Schmidlin, loc. cit.

head men, and frequently a resident catechist or priest.[125] The Church could thus control the life of the Christian and make his continued adherence to and progress in the Faith more assured. Often, especially in Mongolia, where vacant land existed and Chinese were pressing in to occupy it, the Church bought large tracts of land and leased them to settlers. Sometimes the settlers were Christians: sometimes they were non-Christians, who, as a prerequisite to an allotment, were required to accept Christian instruction. In either case a Christian community resulted.[126]

As in previous decades, the missionary found his energies chiefly engrossed in the supervision of the Christian communities and the catechists, and in administering the sacraments. Missionaries usually attempted to visit every hamlet three times a year, remaining in each from four days to three weeks, administering the sacraments, holding services, and preaching.[127] The missionaries were treated with great deference and exercised much authority over the Christians.[128]

As in previous years, organizations sprang up among the Chinese Christians, usually at the suggestion of a missionary, either for some activity or for the purpose of nourishing the religious life of the members. Thus in 1910 or 1913, in Southern Shantung, one of the missionaries of the Society of the Divine Word founded the Oblates of the Holy Family, an organization for women;[129] in 1906 or 1907 Bishop Ferrant initiated in Kiangsi the Companions of Our Lady of Good Counsel;[130] in 1910 there was begun in Eastern Szechwan a body called the Servants of the Holy Ghost, also for women;[131] the Mariales of Yungpingfu had their inception in 1901, the Josephines of Paotingfu in 1910, the Josephines of Tientsin in 1912, the Josephines of Honan in 1914, the Daughters of the Sacred Heart in 1914 in Western Szechwan, the Servants of the Sacred Heart in 1910 in Eastern Szechwan, and the Tertiates (Franciscan) of the Holy Infancy in 1908 in Eastern Hupeh.[132] In 1911 the Brothers of the Sacred Heart

[125] Servière, op. cit., p. 614.
[126] Kervyn, op. cit., pp. 427-433.
[127] Leo Desmet, for thirteen years a missionary in Mongolia, in *Recent Developments in China*, pp. 378-387; Kervyn, op. cit., pp. 496-504.
[128] Trémarin, writing from Chihli in *Annals of the Propagation of the Faith*, Vol. 75, pp. 177-186.
[129] Arens, *Handbuch der katholische Missionen*, p. 146.
[130] Ibid., p. 145; Planchet, *Les missions de Chine et au Japon*, 1919, p. 162.
[131] Arens, op. cit., p. 145.
[132] *The Christian Occupation of China*, pp. 460, 461.

appeared in Eastern Mongolia.[133]   In Mongolia, too, was a con-
fraternity called the Xavierian Society, the members of which were
to pray for the conversion of their neighbors.[134]   A Jesuit in
Chihli described groups of *ling-ching-ti,* or cantors, whose function it was to lead the congregation when prayers were chanted
in unison.   They had a fixed place in church and were divided
into four or five groups of five or six each, each group serving a
week at a time.   Each had its aspirants, or novices.   The music
seems to have been of native origin and varied from place to place.
The Peking cantors' guild is said to have originated in the seventeenth century.[135]

In 1912 a movement of national proportions, the Union for
Chinese Catholic Action, came into existence.   It appears to have
arisen out of an Association for the Propagation of the Faith, an
attempt to encourage Chinese Christians to bring others into the
Church.   At the outset, in Yenshan, the "propagators" were each
to promise to try to win to the Faith at least three families a year,
and their fellow Christians were each to be encouraged to win at
least one non-Christian every twelvemonth.   At Yenshan within
a year the number of Christians is said to have risen from seven
hundred to more than five thousand.   A general congress of the
Association was held in Tientsin in 1911 and to aid it a new
periodical, the *Chiao-li-t'ung,* was founded.   In time this grew into
a Catholic weekly, the *Kung-i-lou.*[136]   The Union for Catholic
Action was formally founded at a congress held in Tientsin in
August, 1912, and was modelled partly on similar unions in
Europe.   Even before the 1912 meeting the movement had spread
and by 1915 it was represented in a score of vicariates.   A
women's auxiliary was formed to study the life of the Christian
family and the training of children.   The Union became a convenient agency through which Roman Catholic Chinese the nation
over later brought pressure to thwart the attempt to make of
Confucianism the established religion of the Republic and opposed
the resumption of the state sacrifices in the Temple of Heaven.[137]

Not only were there new organizations for joint action and for
nourishing the faith of the Christians, but other devices were

[133] *The Christian Occupation of China,* pp. 460, 461.
[134] *Annals of the Propagation of the Faith,* Vol. 74, pp. 135-139.
[135] *Chine, Ceylan, Madagascar,* Sept., 1903, pp. 22, 23.
[136] *Annals of the Propagation of the Faith,* Vol. 76, p. 83.
[137] *Annals of the Propagation of the Faith,* Vol. 77, pp. 99-104, Vol. 78,
pp. 95-104, 201.

introduced for aiding Catholics in their spiritual growth. Retreats were held for the laity.[138] About ninety miles west of Shanghai a church to Our Lady of Lourdes was built in 1901, in imitation of the famous shrine in France. Several miracles were soon reported and pilgrimages were made four times a year. So large did these become, indeed, that by 1914 a church was planned large enough to accommodate two thousand.[139]

In education, the Church was only here and there beginning to modify the policy long pursued. Most of the primary education was still for the purpose of teaching the children of Christians the catechism with the rudiments of reading and writing, and most of the secondary and higher education had as its objective the preparation of teachers, catechists, and priests. In all these branches of education, however, a more extensive program was beginning. Most of the primary schools—"prayer schools" as they were sometimes called—did not attempt to conform to the curriculum of the state system, but contented themselves with teaching the catechism, the sacred formulæ, and the most frequently used characters.[140] They were chiefly for the children of Christians and were not much used for spreading the Faith among non-Christians. The Church directed, indeed, that non-Christians should be discouraged from entering Catholic schools and Catholics from attending non-Catholic schools.[141] Not infrequently, however, non-Christians were to be found in elementary institutions as well as in some of higher grade.[142] There were normal schools for the training of catechists and Christians of higher rank.[143]

As through most of the preceding centuries, the training of a Chinese clergy was stressed, and one of the constant features of the program of every vicariate was the maintenance of at least one seminary, either preparatory or advanced or both.[144] In 1906 sixty-four seminaries were reported, with 1,640 pupils.[145]

[138] Letter of P. Marcel Baecheroot, Oct. 29, 1909, in *Missions en Chine au Congo et aux Philippines*, 1910, p. 65.
[139] *Catholic Missions*, Vol. 8, pp. 87-99.
[140] Servière in *Chinese Recorder*, Vol. 44, p. 624; Schmidlin in *Zeitschrift für Missionswissenschaft*, Vol. 8, pp. 96-113.
[141] Caubrière, *Synthesis decretalium Sinarum*, p. 266; Kervyn, *Méthode de l'apostolat moderne en Chine*, p. 419.
[142] Servière, loc. cit.
[143] Ibid.
[144] Desmet in *Recent Developments in China*, pp. 378-387.
[145] Arens, *Handbuch der katholische Missionen*, pp. 225, 226.

As a rule the candidates for the priesthood came from families which had long been Christian, and for fear that relatives might later bring pressure on them to abandon their preparation, eldest sons, sons of widows, and sons of the poor were discouraged from applying.[146] Even then, difficulty was often encountered in breaking off the aspirants' betrothals which, in accordance with Chinese custom, had been contracted in childhood.[147] As formerly, the course that led to ordination was long, involving, in addition to the elementary education given to the masses of Catholic children, a careful preparation in Chinese literature, that the priest might have the respect of the educated among his fellow-countrymen; at least a smattering of European sciences—a requirement added or emphasized only after 1900; a great deal of Latin, not only because a knowledge of this language was necessary for the conduct of the services and the business of the Church, but because many of the higher studies were pursued through it as the medium of instruction; philosophy; and a thorough training in theology.[148] Usually—at least in the Jesuit missions—the course was broken by a period of two or three years of actual service in the work of the Church—hearing catechisms, teaching school, and preaching to the children on Sundays and feast days—under the direction of an experienced priest.[149] As previously, advancement to the priesthood did not generally take place until the candidate was between twenty-five and thirty years of age.[150]

It is no wonder that many—apparently the majority—who entered upon this prolonged program did not complete it and either dropped entirely out of the sacred profession or were content with becoming catechists, lay brothers, or teachers.[151] The long period of testing, moreover, enabled the ecclesiastical authorities to eliminate those whom they deemed of questionable worth. Most of the native priests obtained all their preparation

---

[146] Bishop Fatiguet, Vicar Apostolic in Kiangsi, in *Catholic Missions*, Vol. 8, pp. 153-155.
[147] Ibid.
[148] Servière in *Chinese Recorder*, Vol. 44, pp. 621, 622; Bishop Reynaud, Vicar Apostolic in Chêkiang, in *Catholic Missions*, Vol. 1, pp. 124, 125; Huonder, *Der einheimische Klerus in den Heidenländern*, pp. 188-191; Kervyn, op. cit., pp. 579, 580.
[149] Servière in *Chinese Recorder*, Vol. 44, pp. 622, 623; *Annals of the Propagation of the Faith*, Vol. 68, pp. 92-95.
[150] Servière in *Chinese Recorder*, Vol. 44, pp. 622, 623.
[151] Ibid.

in China, but a few were sent to Europe—thus bringing them in touch with the main currents of the Church's life.[152]

Generalizations about the character of the Chinese clergy are difficult to substantiate. Some were undoubtedly men of high character. One missionary, however, complained of their pride, their haughtiness, and their lack of the spirit of sacrifice.[153]

The Chinese clergy, while after 1900 increasing proportionately more rapidly than the foreign priests, in 1914, as we have seen, still were less numerous than the latter. They were often given a status inferior to that of European priests.[154] As yet, moreover, since the days of Gregory Lopez—now more than two centuries past—no Chinese had been raised to the episcopal dignity. One of the reasons given was that a foreign bishop enjoyed an extra-territorial status and was independent of Chinese authorities, while a Chinese bishop would be subject even to minor Chinese officials and would suffer in dignity and in efficiency.[155] A European bishop, moreover, would have more prestige in dealing with European naval, military, and diplomatic authorities than would a Chinese.[156]

Catechists were, at Wênchow, given a course of three years and were required to have a knowledge of Chinese literature. Occasionally they were recruited from recently converted *literati,* but usually they were obtained from country schools where during their preparation they had been obliged to assist their parents in the ordinary pursuits and had kept in close touch with the life of the people. Their instruction was continued by means of annual retreats.[157]

While, however, Roman Catholic missionaries still gave the major portion of their energies to the spreading of the Faith among non-Christians and to ministering to the spiritual needs of Christians, and, except in the religious instruction of Catholics and the preparation of catechists and the Chinese clergy, were relegat-

[152] In 1908 in the Collegium Urbanum de Propaganda Fide in Rome there were 120 students, of whom three were Chinese.—*Zeitschrift für Missionswissenschaft,* Vol. 12, p. 63. These may have been from Honan, as in 1906 three were reported as being from there in the College of the Propaganda.—*Annals of the Propagation of the Faith,* Vol. 69, p. 176.
[153] Kervyn, op. cit., pp. 586 et seq.
[154] Kervyn, op. cit.
[155] Servière in *Chinese Recorder,* Vol. 44, pp. 623; Kervyn, op. cit., pp. 592, 593.
[156] Kervyn, op. cit., p. 593.
[157] *Catholic Missions,* Vol. 11, pp. 152, 153.

ing education to a secondary place, they were not entirely blind to the opportunity which the new demand for Western education gave them or to the need, if the Church were to occupy an influential place in molding the thought and life of the nation, of affording more facilities to the Catholic laity for secondary and higher education in secular subjects. Some Roman Catholics saw clearly that their membership, drawn so largely from the poverty-stricken and ignorant, was in special need of education, and that higher schools conducted by missions could now be a means of reaching the upper classes.[158]

Dearth of funds and the greater importance of using for the direct spread of the Gospel such moneys as were available were given as the reasons for the comparative neglect of secular education.[159] Those were not lacking, indeed, who deplored diverting even a part of the income of missions from the urgent task of evangelization.[160] By 1914, however, the old policy was in process of modification. The quinquennial regional synods gave time and thought to education as well as to the other problems of the Church[161] and in 1914 special conferences on schools were held in various parts of the country.[162] At the latter gatherings a program was outlined which contemplated the establishment of a primary school in each head station, a higher school in each mission district, a secondary and normal school in each vicariate, and—although this was not approved unanimously—the foundation of a Catholic university for the entire country.[163]

[158] See, for example, Schmidlin in *Zeitschrift für Missionswissenschaft*, Vol. 8, ΓP. 96-113; editorial in *Missions en Chine au Congo et aux Philippines*, 1908, pp. 241-245.

[159] Desmet in *Recent Developments in China*, p. 385.

[160] Joly, *Le Christianisme de l'Éxtrême Orient*, Vol. 1, pp. 267-269. The author laments the secularization of the apostolate that he believes is to be found in some quarters and its diversion to archæology and teaching French instead of preaching purely and simply the Gospel by example and word.

[161] *Zeitschrift für Missionswissenschaft*, Vol. 13, pp. 84-87; *Missions en Chine au Congo et aux Philippines*, 1908, pp. 241-245.

[162] Schmidlin was a special visitor at these conferences and writes of them in *Missions und Kulturverhältnisse im fernen Osten*, pp. 93, 94, and in *Zeitschrift für Missionswissenschaft*, Vol. 4, pp. 134-140.

[163] Schmidlin in *Zeitschrift für Missionswissenschaft*, Vol. 4, pp. 134-140. Schmidlin says that there was a division as to whether there should be one or more than one university, whether there should be one in which several European languages should be taught, or several, each teaching one European tongue, or whether the university should be based entirely on the Chinese language. Some suggested sending Chinese to Europe for their university training, possibly to Louvain.

In a regional synod held in Peking about 1906 the bishops present unanimously recommended that a Catholic university be established in Peking.—*Missions en Chine aux Congo et aux Philippines*, 1908, pp. 241-245.

Here and there, moreover, higher schools were already begun. The following are examples but are not an exhaustive list. In 1908 a college in Central Mongolia had Western subjects on its curriculum.[164] As early as 1908 a college in Wuchang taught English and French.[165] In 1912 other high schools or colleges were reported at Zikawei, in Shanghai proper, in Canton, Hongkong, Tientsin, Peking, and Nanking.[166] In 1902 a school in which French was taught was started at Tamingfu in Chihli.[167] At Chichou in that province was another in which instruction in French was given.[168] St. Joseph's College, the only Catholic institution of its kind in the city, was erected in Foochow.[169] In 1913 the Society of the Divine Word maintained five Chinese-German middle schools in Shantung, and at Yenchow in the same province the Servants of the Holy Ghost conducted a school for manual training and domestic science.[170] In 1910 the Marists, a teaching brotherhood, founded a provincial house at Chala, just outside Peking, and were to have there a normal school and a novitiate.[171] In 1904 a school, L'Étoile du Matin, was started at Zikawei for girls from wealthy and official families.[172]

The one Roman Catholic institution of university grade was Aurora University, begun in Shanghai by the Jesuits in March, 1903. It was first conducted at Zikawei but in 1908 was moved to a site in the French Settlement. Much of the instruction was in French, but as a necessary concession to the popular demand, English was also taught. Faculties of arts, law, science, civil engineering, and medicine were established.[173] The university was not as large, however, either in equipment, teaching staff, or student body, as several of the institutions of higher grade maintained by Protestants.

[164] *Missions en Chine au Congo et aux Philippines,* 1908, pp. 241-245.
[165] Father Espelage writes of his work in this school in *Catholic Missions,* Vol. 2, p. 51.
[166] Desmet in *Recent Developments in China,* p. 385; Farjenal, *Through the Chinese Revolution,* pp. 89, 90.
[167] Paul Jung, in *Catholic Missions and Annals of the Propagation of the Faith,* Vol. 1, pp. 220-229.
[168] Paul Jung, in *Chine, Ceylan, Madagascar,* Sept., 1902, pp. 182, 183.
[169] *Catholic Missions,* Vol. 13, p. 90.
[170] Schmidlin, *Die katholische Missionen in den deutschen Schutzgebieten,* p. 220.
[171] Planchet, *Les missions de Chine et du Japon,* 1925, p. 18.
[172] *Relations de China,* Jan., 1904, July-Oct., 1918, May-Aug., 1923.
[173] *Encyclopædia Sinica,* p. 584; *Annals of the Propagation of the Faith,* Vol. 82, p. 153; *Une université française en Chine,* extrait des *Relations de Chine,* April, 1925.

In spite of the beginnings of a greater emphasis upon education of the laity, in 1914 Roman Catholics were still far behind Protestants in their general educational achievements. In the scholastic standards set for their clergy they were much in advance of the latter, and Protestants had nothing to equal the meteorological observatory and the library at Zikawei and the long list of erudite publications on China which continued to issue from the press there.[174] Nor did they have living a savant who had produced works on China equal either in quality or quantity to those from the pens of Father L. Wieger, and of the now aged Father Couvreur, members of the Jesuit mission in Southeastern Chihli.[175] In the general influence of their education upon the nation, however, Protestants were far in the lead. Roman Catholics had, rightly or wrongly, chosen to devote their energies chiefly to winning to the Faith as many souls as possible and to treat schools as of decidedly secondary importance.

Literature was not neglected. New works were prepared, some of them, interestingly enough, designed to refute Protestants, and the presses were kept going. Especially prominent were the printing establishments at Zikawei, Peking, Hsienhsien (Chihli),[176] and Hongkong. Not only books of devotion and instruction for Catholics and popular apologetics for non-Christians were issued, but more learned works, especially in French, were published.

As in previous years, Roman Catholics gave much time and money to charitable institutions, and especially to orphanages. These latter have so often been mentioned that no detailed description of them is again needed. It must be noted, however, that they increased in number and in size, and that from them came a constant stream of converts into the Catholic fold. These converts were naturally from the poorest classes, but the girls had been trained in needlework and in homemaking, the boys had been taught useful trades, and all had been reared in the Christian faith. As was to be expected in China where, to the poor, girls are often an economic liability, the large majority of the children

[174] The *Variétés sinologiques* continued to be issued—monographs by various authors, European and Chinese, treating of Chinese subjects in a scholarly way.
[175] L. Wieger was the author of such books as *Textes historiques*, 1903-1905, *Textes philosophiques*, 1906, and *Langue écrite, méchanisme, phraséologie*, 1908. Couvreur prepared translations of the Classics.
[176] *Chine, Ceylan, Madagascar*, Sept., 1903, pp. 28-34.

rescued by the Society of the Holy Infancy and placed in orphanages were of that sex.[177]

In contrast with Protestants, Roman Catholics maintained relatively few hospitals and usually these were not large. There was an excellent one at Hankow.[178] In 1905 the two municipal hospitals in Shanghai—one for foreigners and one for Chinese—had as their nursing staffs Sisters of St. Vincent de Paul.[179] In 1913 the Franciscan Missionaries of Mary founded in Shanghai a hospital for Europeans and a dispensary for Chinese.[180] In Shensi Bishop Goette opened a hospital, in part for the purpose of offsetting the influence which medical work was giving to Protestants.[181] As early as 1906 Father Conrady, a friend of the well-known Damien, although then sixty years of age, began collecting funds to build at Canton a home for lepers.[182] In time the Chinese Government entrusted to Conrady and his assistants a leper asylum at Sheklung which was said to have over one thousand inmates, and the Vicar Apostolic asked assistance of the Sisters of the Immaculate Conception in Montreal.[183] In August, 1914, Father Conrady died, but successors were at hand.[184]

Some Chinese Christians were trained in simple medical knowledge and were encouraged to use it as an aid in the spread of the Christian message.[185] In 1904 the Little Sisters of the Poor founded in Shanghai a home for the aged, which by 1919 had a staff of twenty-five, the majority of them French, and about three hundred inmates whom advancing years had left in poverty.[186] In Swatow special care was provided for young women whose husbands had deserted them to migrate overseas.[187] The epidemic of pneumonic plague, which in 1911 caused such loss of life in Mongolia and Manchuria and which Protestant missionaries, with their superior medical equipment, had so large a share in checking,

[177] In *Catholic Missions*, Vol. 1, pp. 141-143, it is said that over eighty per cent. of the children rescued were girls.
[178] Schmidlin, *Missions und Kulturverhältnisse im fernen Osten*, p. 60.
[179] Allen, a British consul, in *The East and the West*, Vol. 3, p. 204.
[180] Planchet, *Les missions de Chine et du Japon*, 1919, p. 153.
[181] J. W. Doolin, O.F.M., in *Catholic Missions*, Vol. 2, pp. 172, 173.
[182] *Annals of the Propagation of the Faith*, Vol. 69, pp. 148-155.
[183] Bishop Merel in *Annals of the Propagation of the Faith*, Vol. 76, p. 83; *Catholic Missions*, Vol. 8, pp. 60, 61; Walsh, *Observations in the Orient*, p. 201.
[184] McQuaide, *With Christ in China*, p. 254; Burke, *The Church in Many Lands*, p. 55.
[185] Kervyn, *Méthode de l'apostolat moderne en Chine*, pp. 422-426.
[186] Planchet, *Les missions de Chine et du Japon*, 1919, p. 154.
[187] *Annals of the Propagation of the Faith*, Vol. 78, p. 38.

was bravely, although less effectively, fought by Roman Catholics. At Chefoo two Franciscan Sisters of Mary, while ministering to sufferers, contracted the disease and died, and Father Bourles opened in Manchuria a hospital for plague patients, where he and two of his confrères, Delpal and Mutillod, while engaged in the work of mercy, lost their lives to the same dread enemy.[188] In the severe famines which visited parts of Central and North China the missionaries were active in the distribution of relief.[189] One missionary, a Jesuit in Anhui, died from typhus contracted while so engaged.[190]

SOURCES OF FINANCIAL SUPPORT

No complete figures have been published either of incomes or expenditures of Roman Catholic missions. The amount of money required for the support of an individual priest was not large: one statement—probably strictly accurate for only one locality— places it at one hundred and fifty dollars (seemingly gold) a year.[191]   In Mongolia a catechist was said to cost twenty-five dollars a year and a teacher for a Catholic school fifty dollars.[192] Just what the total cost of the work was, however, either vicariate by vicariate, or for the entire country, has not been made public, nor are all the sources of income known. Money was, of course, contributed to various organizations by the Society for the Propagation of the Faith and the Society of the Holy Infancy.[193] Some amounts were received by priests from mass stipends,[194] some were raised in Europe and America by the individual societies and orders, some came from indemnities,[195] and some, probably a good

---

[188] Letter of Verbois, March 4, 1911, from Mongolia, in *Missions en Chine au Congo et aux Philippines,* 1911; *Catholic Missions,* Vol. 5, p. 96.

[189] Hopsomer, in *Annals of the Propagation of the Faith,* Vol. 75, p. 83; *Missions en Chine au Congo et aux Philippines,* 1911, pp. 13-20, 201.

[190] Cochran, *Foreign Magic,* pp. 56-58.

[191] Sylvester Espelage, from Wuchang, Dec., 1905, in *Annals of the Propagation of the Faith,* Vol. 69, pp. 159-161.

[192] Burke, *The Church in Many Lands,* p. 52.

[193] The total amount raised by the Society for the Propagation of the Faith in 1913 for use in all the mission fields of the Church was $1,610,315.—*Annals of the Propagation of the Faith,* Vol. 69, p. 90. The amount allocated to China is not given. In 1917-1918 Walsh said (*Observations in the Orient,* pp. 310-318) that not every missionary received as much as a dollar a day from Europe and America.

[194] Mass stipends in China were set between the limits of 500 and 5,000 cash. —Caubrière, *Synthesis decretalium Sinarum,* p. 135.

[195] Walsh, *Observations in the Orient,* pp. 310-318.

deal in several of the missions, were derived from investments, chiefly in real estate in China.[196] Incomes varied from society to society and vicariate to vicariate, as the physical equipment and the extent of the work indicated; not all the missions were equally well supplied with funds.[197]

RESULTS OF CATHOLIC MISSION WORK, 1901-1914

Of the results of Roman Catholic missions in these fourteen years not a great deal more need be said. As has been stated earlier, the numerical increase was very marked. Whereas before 1900 it had required more than thirty years for the Church to double itself,[198] after 1900 the number of Catholics doubled in about eleven years.[199] Whether this great influx of Christians led to a lowering in the moral and spiritual quality of the Church is difficult to determine. The majority were, of course, from the humbler classes and had often sought baptism from very materialistic motives. Some, as we have seen, had been attracted by the financial support provided while they were under instruction, not

[196] Bard, in *Chinese Life in Town and Country*, p. 80, says that Catholic missions had important sources of revenue in the property that they had acquired in the open ports, and that some of this property had so increased in value that it yielded a yearly income greater than the original purchase price. Walsh, *Observations in the Orient*, p. 118, a report by a priest who had access to correct information, says that the money for the big enterprises of the Church in Peking and in China came largely from wise investments, and that land bought in Peking by the Church for $10 (gold) was "to-day" worth several thousands of dollars (gold). Little, in *Gleanings from Fifty Years in China*, p. 294, says that in West China the Roman Catholics were adding field to field and house to house at a rapid rate and that their revenues were steadily increasing. Thomson, in *The Chinese*, p. 370, says that: "The Missions d'Étrangères is one of the heaviest stockholders (holding half a million) in the lucrative Tanjong Pagar Wharves and Dock of Singapore."

[197] Schmidlin, in *Missions und Kulturverhältnisse im fernen Osten*, p. 247, says (1914) that the Jesuit Mission in Kiangnan and the Paris Society in Eastern Szechwan were well off financially and that the missions in Hankow possessed good houses, but that the missions in South China were poor. Father Leo Desmet (of Mongolia) in *Recent Developments in China*, p. 384, says that the missions in Eastern Mongolia received in 1906 about $3,000 from the Society for the Propagation of the Faith, and that $3,000 more came from friends and relatives; that there was in that year, in other words, $6,000 from abroad to support forty-eight priests, three boarding houses, fifteen residences, sixty-six schools, and a number of catechists.

[198] Louvet, *Les missions catholiques au XIXᵉ siècle*, pp. 218-231, gives the number of Catholics in 1870 as 369,441—the smallest figure given by any Roman Catholic source for that year; and Louvet, op. cit., gives the number for 1901 as 720,540.

[199] In 1912 the number given is 1,431,258.—Hoffman in *Zeitschrift für Missionswissenschaft*, Vol. 14, p. 42.

infrequently as the one way of avoiding starvation, and others, even though not as many as formerly, from a desire for assistance in litigation.[200] One Protestant missionary declared that many village "roughs" with grudges to revenge and promoters of lawsuits seeking prestige enrolled in the Roman Catholic Church, and that some who had been advised by Protestants to "study the doctrine" more fully before baptism became Catholics out of pique.[201] While his testimony must be discounted, it is not wholly to be disregarded. In Chêkiang it was found that Christians who had grown up in orphanages were not self-reliant enough to make good catechists. The same was true of the children of "old" Christians who had been brought up continuously in Christian schools.[202] We find one Roman Catholic missionary complaining that Chinese readily became catechumens but balked at baptism and its obligations.[203] Another wrote that the Chinese preserved something of their superstitious past, that they were particularly impressed by ritual and pious practices and not by the "essential foundations of doctrine," and that "newly made Christians consume an enormous amount of holy water." He also declared that conversion was often thwarted by material adversity, by the death of a buffalo or pig, or by sickness in the family.[204] Another Roman Catholic missionary reported that he knew of several instances in which a man fell ill shortly after becoming a Christian and therefore returned to his old gods.[205] Still another deplored the lack of faith of the newer Christians and found among the "old" Christians formalism, a willingness to conform unthinkingly to tradition, a rarity of real piety, a dearth of moral conviction, a willingness to compromise, and a want of the stuff from which martyrs are made.[206]

The Church, however, continued to make fairly stringent

[200] One man came into the Church because he had married a Catholic girl who had been sold to him by her dissipated brothers and had been given by the priest the choice of becoming a Christian or having the case brought before an official.—A. de Smedt in *Catholic Missions*, Vol. 12, p. 252.

[201] Scott, *China from Within*, p. 248.

[202] Cyprian Aroud in *Annals of the Propagation of the Faith*, Vol. 80, pp. 232-239.

[203] Preynot, writing in 1905, quoted in Joly, *Le Christianisme et l'Éxtrême Orient*, Vol. 1, p. 157.

[204] Thiollière, writing from Kwangtung, in *Annals of the Propagation of the Faith*, Vol. 76, p. 111.

[205] Bishop Fatiguet, Vicar Apostolic in Northern Kiangsi, in *Annals of the Propagation of the Faith*, Vol. 76, pp. 43-153.

[206] Kervyn, *Méthode de l'apostolat moderne en Chine*, pp. 790 et seq.

requirements of Christians.[207] Moreover, the devotion and noble character of many of the missionaries could hardly fail to be contagious and must have left their impress upon many.[208] One traveller reported that in a village in Szechwan which she visited the inhabitants had been Catholics for one hundred and fifty years and that they were cleaner than their non-Christian neighbors and had brighter, more intelligent eyes.[209] About 1913 it was reported that in Kiangnan two-thirds of the Catholics were "old Christians," descendants of seventeenth and eighteenth century converts, and that they were characterized by "deep faith, strict observance of traditional customs, and a lavish spirit of charity which it often requires some exercise of authority to keep within bounds." They were also said to keep themselves aloof from their non-Christian neighbors, regarding the latter as doomed to destruction, and conversions were reported to be relatively rare in districts where they were numerous.[210]

In spite of the rapid growth in the preceding thirteen or fourteen years, the Roman Catholic Church was having little if any appreciable effect upon the life of the country as a whole. Its membership and adherents numbered only about one-half of one per cent. of the population and were drawn chiefly from other groups than those which were leading the nation. Its educational, philanthropic, and literary enterprises were making but small impression upon the vast majority of the non-Christian community. The Church remained an activity by itself, still controlled by foreigners and largely under the ægis of foreign governments, and was apart from the main currents of thought that were shaping the changing China.

[207] In addition to regulations earlier in force, one finds the following: none were to be admitted to baptism who had not renounced all connection with secret societies; much was made of the purity of the marriage tie, and there was a rule against usury; servile labor was forbidden before noon on Sundays and feast days and entirely forbidden on four solemn days.—Caubrière, op. cit., pp. 215, 221. Girls betrothed to pagans could not be baptized until after the engagement was broken.—*Catholic Missions*, Vol. 11, p. 180. Christians who before their conversion had sold their daughters to non-Christians were required to buy them back.—Burke, op. cit., p. 53.

[208] A Protestant missionary's account of life on the Tibetan frontier speaks of a Catholic priest who after thirty years of labor had died of typhus in Tachienlu and says that: "Many of the natives went to see his face as he lay asleep, and as they looked at it, they said: 'If to be a Christian means to look like that when you die, I want to be a Christian.'"—Shelton, *Shelton of Tibet*, p. 68.

[209] Mrs. Archibald Little, *In the Land of the Blue Gown*, p. 98.

[210] Servière in *The Oxford and Cambridge Review*, quoted in *Chinese Recorder*, Vol. 44, pp. 614, 615.

THE MISSION OF THE RUSSIAN ORTHODOX CHURCH
1901—JULY, 1914

For the mission of the Russian Orthodox Church the years between the Boxer uprising and the outbreak of the World War were ones of marked prosperity. Before 1900, as we have seen, the work of the mission was primarily literary and little attempt had been made to approach with the Gospel the non-Christian population. Now for the first time a serious effort was put forth to bring Chinese into the Church and to reach out beyond Peking. Much of the energy of the ecclesiastics in China was, as heretofore, devoted to the spiritual care of those in communion with their Church, the descendants of the Albazinians—still to be found in Peking—and the Russians who in increasing numbers were entering Manchuria and some of the treaty ports of the Eighteen Provinces. Definite missions, however, were now opened for the Chinese.

In 1901 the Archimandrite Innocent was called to Petrograd. While there he made a report to the Holy Synod of the state of the mission in China, and as a result was consecrated Bishop of Peking and returned to his post with additional clergy.[211] Whether this enlargement of the mission was a part of the program of the Russian penetration of China which was now so important a phase of the Far Eastern situation is uncertain: the Imperial Government may have decided to extend Russian influence through cultural and religious as well as economic and political agencies. Whatever the motive, in 1909 the mission counted in China one bishop, two archimandrites, ten priests (of whom three were Chinese), six deacons (of whom two were Chinese), three psalm-readers, ten monks, and seven nuns.[212] In addition to the extensive plant in the northeastern corner of Peking which had long been its headquarters, it possessed a church in the legation, two conventual churches in Manchuria, churches in Hankow, Dalny, and Port Arthur, fifteen schools, two chapels, and five churchyards.[213] At the end of 1914 it counted thirty-two mission centers in Chihli, Hupeh, Honan, Kiangsu, and Mongolia, enrolled five hundred pupils in its schools, and claimed a Chinese baptized membership of 5,035.[214]

[211] *Chinese Recorder*, Vol. 47, p. 683.
[212] *China Mission Year Book, 1910*, pp. 425 et seq.
[213] Ibid.
[214] *China Mission Year Book, 1915*, pp. 583, 584.

CHAPTER XXV

CHINA IN A TIME OF REORGANIZATION (1901-1926)
PROTESTANT MISSIONS, 1901—JULY, 1914

INTRODUCTORY

IMPRESSIVE as was the growth of the Roman Catholic Church in China in the fourteen years after 1900, that of the Protestant bodies was proportionately more rapid,[1] and the influence of Protestantism upon changing China was much more marked than was that of the older and larger Roman Catholic body.

The reasons for the greater progress and influence of Protestantism were numerous. In the first place, Great Britain, predominatingly Protestant, still had a larger proportion of the foreign trade of China than had any other power, and in most of the ports of China outside the German, Russian, Japanese, and French spheres of influence the British consul continued to be the most important foreign functionary.

English, moreover, was the medium through which most of the foreign commerce of the land was conducted, the head of the Imperial Maritime Customs Service, for years one of the most influential, if not, indeed, the most influential foreigner, Sir Robert Hart, was a British subject, and the foreign language of that important branch of the government was English. English, too, was of use in the allied service, the Post Office. Partly for this reason, English was the Occidental tongue through which most of the progressive Chinese strove to acquire the new ideas which were

---

[1] While between 1901 and 1912 the number of Roman Catholics increased from 720,540 to 1,431,258 (*Missiones Catholicae cura S. Congregationis de Propaganda Fide,* 1907, p. 44; Hoffman in *Zeitschrift für Missionswissenschaft,* Vol. 4, p. 42), or a growth of not quite one hundred per cent. in eleven years, from 1900 to 1906 the number of Protestant communicants increased from 85,000 to 178,251, or a little over one hundred per cent. in six years, and to 235,303 in 1914. The growth in the latter year was really larger, for the 1900 and 1906 figures included some baptized non-communicants such as children and infants, and the figures for 1914 omitted these.—Rawlinson in *The Christian Occupation of China,* p. 38. The Catholic figures, of course, include all baptized persons.

becoming so popular. Now the Protestant mission forces of the world were drawn chiefly from the English-speaking countries, and since their schools were for years the best and in many places the only institutions in which English could be acquired, they soon found themselves much sought after.

Then, too, the Chinese came to the Protestant missionary more readily because the latter, while rarely possessed of as prolonged a training in theology as was the Roman Catholic priest, usually knew more of the Western science for which the Chinese were now eager.

In the fourth place, Protestant missions, much more than Roman Catholic, had at hand the beginnings of machinery for influencing the new China and quickly expanded them. The revolution in China was primarily one of ideas, for it was these which were to work the changes in the other phases of the nation's life. Protestants had emphasized in China the chief medium through which these ideas could be acquired, the press and the school. For a time, although for only a brief time, a large proportion of the literature in Chinese through which the new knowledge could be acquired was produced by Protestants. What soon became the greatest publishing house in the Middle Kingdom, the Commercial Press, was begun, as we have seen, by men who had been trained by Protestants and showed the effects of strong, although entirely extra-ecclesiastical, Protestant influence. As the years passed, Protestants more and more stressed their schools and as a rule admitted to them non-Christians as well as Christians. Moreover, they invested much of their resources in secondary and higher education, sometimes at the expense of primary education. It was in these Protestant higher schools, in most places the best of the new style, that a large proportion of the influential educators and an appreciable number of the prominent business men and leaders in public life received at least part of their formal training. In the Young Men's Christian Association, moreover, and in the less widely extended Young Women's Christian Association, Protestants developed a means of reaching the student, official, and merchant groups. Then, too, Protestant philanthropic enterprises, especially the hospital, with the avowed object of improving the physical as well as the moral and religious conditions of the Chinese, appealed to a nation that had been brought up on the

Confucian tradition of valuing that which made for the public weal.

In the fifth place, Protestants were able quickly to put into China a large number of new missionaries and to provide them with the necessary equipment. As we have said before, the wealth due to the Industrial Revolution accumulated more rapidly in the lands—Great Britain, the United States, and Germany—and in the groups—the middle classes—in which Protestantism had its stronghold, than in Catholic countries and constituencies, and while in comparison with the expenditure for other purposes the sums contributed to missions were a mere pittance, in total figures they were impressive and made possible a rapid expansion of missionary activities. Between 1900 and 1914, moreover, no major wars vexed Protestant countries, and the theological storms which after 1914 were to sweep across many denominations had as yet scarcely appeared above the horizon. Protestantism was free to give its attention to its foreign enterprises overseas.

In the sixth place, the opportunity brought by the great post-Boxer changes was widely heralded in Protestant circles. Both British and Americans had their eyes on China, the former because of their commercial and diplomatic connections and the latter because of their recent occupation of the Philippines and Hawaii and their enunciation of the Open Door Policy. Church circles were peculiarly responsive to appeals for the great Far Eastern Empire.

Moreover, the sufferings of missionaries and of Chinese Christians in the Boxer outbreak, the most severe persecution which Protestant missions had yet experienced in any country, focused the attention of the Protestant world on China. The appeal to the heroic, the challenge to carry on the work of the martyrs, seldom failed of a response. The religious literature of the time contains abundant evidences of this augmented interest. Church periodicals carried many an article on China, and book after book was written for the mission-supporting constituency.[2]

[2] See Broomhall, *Jubilee Story of the China Inland Mission,* p. 263, and a paper written by Richard in 1901 and mentioned in his *Conversion by the Million,* pp. 1-17. See also *Missionary Review of the World,* Vol. 24, p. 834, Vol. 19, p. 662; Martin, *The Awakening of China; Chinese Recorder,* Vol. 35, p. 295; Broomhall, *Present Day Conditions in China,* in which the author calls attention to the great changes in China and speaks of this as an opportunity for bringing the Gospel to the country; Brown, *New Forces in Old China,* in which the author

EXTENSION OF THE WORK OF THE SOCIETIES REPRESENTED BEFORE 1901

Given these advantages and the growing interest in China, it is not strange that the years between 1900 and the outbreak of the World War witnessed a rapid expansion of Protestant missions. The opposition of the Chinese, moreover, while by no means a thing of the past, was less vigorous than formerly, and the powerlessness of the country before the foreigner and the rapid spread of the reform movement produced a much nearer approach to open-mindedness than the missionary had yet met. As the years passed, receptiveness increased and at times became friendliness.[3]

For the societies represented in China before 1900 the recovery from the damage wrought by the Boxer disturbances was as a rule rapid,[4] and an extension of their operations followed. Before 1900 some of the societies had undertaken to cover as much territory as their resources justified, but they were now able to reach

speaks at length of the new China, takes up the relation of the missionary enterprise to it, and on the ground of the unparalleled opportunity makes a plea for more missionary work; Bond, *Our Share in China,* pp. 15-30, an appeal to Canadian Methodist laymen which speaks of conditions in China as "the greatest opportunity for the extension of Christ's kingdom that his church has ever had." In 1906 a week of prayer for China was held in Great Britain.—Broomhall, *Jubilee Story of the China Inland Mission,* p. 273.

[3] Bashford's *Journal,* April 8, 1907, records that Hunter Corbett, of Shantung, said that forty years ago he could scarcely obtain a hearing in Shantung but that in 1906 in a tour of five hundred miles in the province he spoke two hundred and sixty-five times and everywhere had large and attentive audiences. When Pollard returned to Chaoting in Yünnan in 1901 he was greeted by the chief officials, the people were friendly, and inquiries about Christianity were made by students and people of distinction.—Grist, *Samuel Pollard,* p. 127. In 1909 there was reported by one society "a more eager desire to hear the gospel message . . . and . . . a greater willingness to become associated with church life."—*Ninety-sixth Report of the Wesleyan Methodist Missionary Society,* p. 127.

[4] In and around Nanking, for example, the people were more responsive than before 1900.—Williams, *Ohio Friends in the Land of Sinim,* pp. 75 et seq. The Northern Presbyterians reported in 1903 that "the Boxer outbreak . . . did much to open the way for the preaching of the truth. Last year 1,282 were received into our China churches as against 681 the previous year. . . . The missionary outlook was never so bright."—*Report of the Presbyterian Board,* 1903, pp. 15, 16. There followed, indeed, in some places almost a mass movement toward Christianity. Thus in Szechwan wealthy Chinese subscribed money to open preaching halls, lands and buildings were offered for mission purposes, and crowds gathered daily to hear the Christian message. In 1905 Bishop Cassels reported for his field in that province that in the preceding seven years the number of central stations had increased fourfold and of outstations more than tenfold, and that the number of baptisms had risen from seven hundred a year in 1895 to twenty-five hundred a year in 1905.—Broomhall, *Jubilee Story of the China Inland Mission,* pp. 267, 268. In Kiangsi in 1901 and 1902 a single missionary is reported to have counted twenty thousand converts.—Ross, *The Changing Chinese,* p. 236. Much of this interest was, however, from the hope of gaining the support of the powerful foreigner in settling old scores with enemies and was not from any genuine religious conviction.—Broomhall, loc. cit.

more effectively the peoples in their fields. The bodies longer in China, indeed, concentrated their energies upon the stations previously opened, upon reënforcing these by new neighboring stations and outstations, upon building up the Christian communities already founded, and upon the development of institutions. Between 1901 and 1910 inclusive the thirty-two societies which had been most largely represented in China before 1900 increased by one hundred and eighty the number of their stations, as against two hundred and one in the preceding decade and one hundred and twenty-five in the decade between 1881 and 1890.[5] While not reaching out into many new provinces, they were expanding their activities geographically almost as rapidly as they had ever done, and, as we shall see, they were consolidating and greatly strengthening them in the cities which they had already occupied.

For many societies the pioneer stage was now past. Before 1900 the outstanding figures in missionary circles were almost entirely men who had broken new ground territorially—Morrison, Gützlaff, Taylor, John, Hill, Hart, and the long list of others enumerated in earlier chapters. After 1900 great leaders on the frontiers were by no means lacking, but the majority of the most prominent missionaries were those who in administration, education, and medicine were initiating new enterprises or were developing old ones. Here and there, moreover, prominent Chinese Christians were beginning to emerge. The day of the exclusive leadership of the foreigner was drawing to a close.

The older organizations need not be covered one by one in as much detail as in the chapters narrating events between 1856 and 1897, and a brief summary will serve to show what was taking place.

The pioneer Protestant body in China, the London Missionary Society, already with commitments in many provinces, established several stations in Hunan, the anti-foreign province which had been so resistant to the missionary and which Griffith John, largely through Chinese assistants, had long been attempting to penetrate.[6] Financial resources, however, proved inadequate for the maintenance of all the undertakings which the Society had

[5] *The Christian Occupation of China*, p. 313.
[6] *L. M. S. Chronicle*, 1901, p. 106, 1902, p. 212; *L. M. S. Chronicle*, 1907, p. 170; *A Century of Protestant Missions in China*, p. 6. Yochow was in 1900 a mission station.—*London Missionary Society, 1901, 106th Report*, p. 94. Hêngshow was opened in 1901.—*London Missionary Society, 107th Report, 1902*, pp. 76-80. In 1906 Changsha was occupied, and Siangtan in 1904.—*L. M. S. 112th Report, 1907*, p. 191.

initiated, other Protestant bodies were entering the province, and, for these and other reasons, before many years the representatives of the London Mission were withdrawn.[7] The Society found its strength more than taxed to occupy as it wished the territory that it had previously served.

The sister organization, the American Board of Commissioners for Foreign Missions, had been among the most severe sufferers from the Boxer upheaval: in Chihli and especially in Shansi the destruction of life and property had been great. In Chihli recovery was rapid. Missionaries went back to their stations, the scattered Christians were gathered, and before long the mission was more thriving than it had ever been.[8] In Shansi, where the devastation had been more nearly complete, the restoration was slower. Not until about 1905 did the first missionaries to settle anew in the province arrive at Taiku.[9] The beginning having once been made, however, progress was steady. About 1907 the graduates of Oberlin formed the Shansi Memorial Association and before many years they had on the field a number of representatives— engaged principally in education.[10] From Fênchow as a base and under the direction of Watts O. Pye, there began shortly after 1907 the most remarkable piece of pioneering done in China under the Board after 1900, and one of the most noteworthy ever undertaken under any society. In Shansi and Shensi, in districts previously practically untouched by Protestants, a thorough survey, geographic, economic, social, and religious, was made, and in the ensuing eighteen years numerous churches were founded, largely by Chinese under the inspiring guidance of their foreign leader, and plans were laid to make them centers of wholesome intellectual, economic, social, and religious influence in a region impoverished by frequent famines.[11]

Long before 1900 the Protestant Episcopal Church in the United States had concentrated on the Yangtze Valley east of the gorges, taking as centers Shanghai and Hankow. Here it developed strong

[7] The work in Hunan was turned over to the American Presbyterians (North) in 1912.—*L. M. S. 118th Report, 1913,* p. 165. See also *L. M. S., Report of Hawkins and Martin, 1909-1910,* pp. 176-205.
[8] Strong, *The Story of the American Board,* p. 380.
[9] Strong, op. cit., p. 381; *Annual Report of the A. B. C. F. M.,* 1905, p. 111. The work had previously been supervised from outside the province.—*Annual Report of the A. B. C. F. M.,* 1904, p. 116.
[10] *Oberlin-Shansi, Ten Years After;* Strong, op. cit., p. 381; *Annual Report of the A. B. C. F. M.,* 1908, p. 127.
[11] Watts O. Pye in *China Mission Year Book, 1919,* pp. 109-116.

Christian congregations and stressed education, especially schools of secondary and higher grade. In this populous area it opened, after 1900, new stations in important cities—Nanking, Soochow, Wusih, and Yangchow in Kiangsu, Kiukiang and Nanch'ang in Kiangsi, Changsha in Hunan [12]—and many outstations. Two new bishoprics were created, that of Hankow in 1901 and that of Anking in 1912.[13] Bishop Ingle, the first incumbent of the Hankow see, still a young man, died in 1903, leaving a record of noteworthy achievement.[14] He was succeeded (1904) by Logan H. Roots, who had come to China less than a decade before and was to be one of the outstanding Christians in China, a leader of saintly life and of far-seeing and contagious enthusiasm.[15]

The Church Missionary Society had already entered Chêkiang, Shanghai, Fukien, Hongkong, Kwangtung, and Szechwan. Before 1900 it planned to penetrate Central China by way of the South and in 1899 had a missionary and his wife in Kwangsi. Between 1899 and 1915 it increased its missionary force from one hundred and eighty to three hundred and fifteen,[16] it opened new stations in most of its fields,[17] in 1906 it made Fukien a diocese,[18] it entered Hunan, and in 1909 it created a diocese in Kwangsi and Hunan.[19]

The Society for the Propagation of the Gospel in Foreign Parts increased the number of its stations in Chihli and Shantung, provinces in which it had been before 1900,[20] and in 1901 Shantung was made a diocese.[21]

The several Presbyterian bodies that had entered China before 1900 had spread widely and had undertaken to cover such vast areas that before 1914 most of the growing resources placed at their disposal were required to cover with any degree of adequacy the fields for which they had made themselves responsible. Here and there, however, they entered new territory. The Presbyterian Church in the United States of America (North) extended its

[12] *Directory of Protestant Missions in China, 1926*, pp. 1-5; *Spirit of Missions*, Vol. 69, p. 798, Vol. 68, p. 96, Vol. 66, p. 794; *A Century of Protestant Missions in China*, pp. 302, 303.
[13] *Spirit of Missions*, Vol. 77, pp. 441-444, 455-457.
[14] Ibid., Vol. 66, p. 794; Jefferys, *Ingle*, pp. 246 et seq.
[15] *Spirit of Missions*, Vol. 69, p. 798.
[16] Stock, *History of the Church Missionary Society*, Vol. 4, p. 305.
[17] *Directory of Protestant Missions in China, 1926*, pp. 7-12.
[18] Stock, op. cit., Vol. 4, p. 293. Bishop Price was the first incumbent.
[19] Stock, op. cit., Vol. 4, pp. 303, 304; *China Mission Year Book, 1910*, p. 170.
[20] *Directory of Protestant Missions in China, 1926*, pp. 12, 13.
[21] Stock, op. cit., Vol. 4, p. 293. Bishop Iliff succeeded to it in 1903.

operations in Hunan, a province on whose outer fringes it had for some years been maintaining missions. It also pushed north into the Hwai River Valley in Anhui [22] and opened new stations in Shantung.[23] By the union (1906) in America of the Cumberland and the Northern Presbyterians, the mission which the former had begun in Hunan was joined to that of the latter.[24] The Presbyterian Church in the United States (South) concentrated on its old fields, Chêkiang and Kiangsu, but in these provinces, especially the latter, it placed missionaries for the first time in several important cities and it stretched across into Shantung.[25] The English Presbyterians confined their efforts to their old fields around Amoy and Swatow, cultivating them more intensively than formerly.[26] The Church of Scotland did not attempt to move far from its old base in Ichang, and the United Free Church of Scotland and the Irish Presbyterians found all that they could well undertake in the rapidly growing population and vast area of Manchuria.[27] In the Manchurian churches a missionary society was formed. Heilungchiang, the northern province, was chosen as a field and by 1914 a small Christian church was there emerging unsupported by foreign money.[28] In 1908, moreover, largely through contact with a revival in Korea, a remarkable religious movement broke out in Manchuria. The meetings were often accompanied by public confession of sin and by extreme emotional and physical manifestations reminiscent of the revivals in the frontier districts of the United States in the eighteenth and nineteenth centuries.[29] Permanent moral and spiritual transformations were recorded and many accessions to the Church.[30] Some con-

[22] In Hwaiyüan about 1909 there was organized by the Presbyterians what was believed to be the first Protestant Church in North Anhui.—*China Mission Year Book, 1910*, p. 125.
[23] *Directory of Protestant Missions in China, 1926*, pp. 67-75; *A Century of Protestant Missions in China*, pp. 384-394.
[24] *A Century of Protestant Missions in China*, p. 407.
[25] *Directory of Protestant Missions in China, 1926*, pp. 75-79.
[26] Ibid., pp. 64, 65; Paton, *The Stranger People*, passim.
[27] *Directory of Protestant Missions in China, 1926*, pp. 63 et seq.
[28] Christie, *Thirty Years in the Manchu Capital*, pp. 206-215.
[29] Webster, *Times of Blessing in Manchuria;* Webster, *The Revival in Manchuria.* (Webster was a leader in the movement.)
[30] Webster, op. cit.; *China Mission Year Book, 1910*, p. 144, *1911*, pp. 215-219. There was some reaction. In 1907 the number of baptisms in Manchuria had been 1,474. In 1908 it was 3,496, in 1909, 2,713, and in 1912, 1,867.— *Chinese Recorder*, Vol. 46, p. 100. In 1914 a committee investigated the results of the movement in Manchuria after the lapse of six years and recorded a permanent deepening in the religious life of the church.—*China Mission Year Book, 1915*, p. 45.

verts, however, slipped back into their old ways and in later years the results were believed to have been most lasting in individuals whose excitement had not been so extreme.[31] The movement spread to other parts of China, often with similar manifestations, and in places continued until the Revolution of 1911.[32]

The Reformed Church in America did not open any new important centers but confined its efforts to its old fields in Fukien. Here, however, it prospered, and in 1905 reported the greatest number of accessions on confession of faith that it had yet received in any one year.[33] The Presbyterian Church in Canada continued in Formosa and Honan, and, especially in the latter field, opened new stations and sent extensive reënforcements.[34] Jonathan Goforth of its Honan mission rose to prominence as a leader in the Manchurian revival and for many years thereafter was to be active in evangelistic services in many parts of China.[35]

The Swedish Missionary Society (Svenska Missions Förbundet) added four new stations in Hupeh to the three that it had already established in that province.[36] The Swedish Evangelical Mission Covenant of America, later the Covenant Missionary Society, which had also begun operations in Hupeh, between 1900 and 1914 doubled the number of its stations.[37] The Reformed Church in the United States had sent its first missionaries to China shortly before 1900, but it was not until after the Boxer uprising that they founded their initial station. This was in Yochow, and here and in other parts of Hunan the society was to continue, sending out many additional missionaries.[38] The Reformed Presbyterian Church in the United States of America (Covenanter), although its first representatives had arrived in China before 1900, commencing work in Kwangtung, west of Canton, counted the real

[31] Christie, op. cit., pp. 206-215.
[32] Broomhall, *Jubilee Story of the China Inland Mission*, pp. 269, 272; *China Mission Year Book, 1910*, p. 119; Beckman, *The Massacre of Sianfu*, p. 45; Goforth in *Chinese Recorder*, Vol. 39, p. 330, and elsewhere; Tatchell, *Booth of Hankow*, p. 73; Gasgoyne-Cecil, *Changing China*, p. 240.
[33] Pitcher, *In and About Amoy*, p. 120; Chamberlain, *Fifty Years in Foreign Fields*, p. 122.
[34] *A Century of Protestant Missions in China*, pp. 232-246.
[35] Webster, *The Revival in Manchuria*, pp. 48-50.
[36] *Directory of Protestant Missions in China, 1926*, p. 47.
[37] *Directory of Protestant Missions in China, 1926*, p. 37; *A Century of Protestant Missions in China*, pp. 524, 525. The number was increased from two to four.
[38] *A Century of Protestant Missions in China*, p. 409; *A Directory of Protestant Missions in China, 1926*, p. 78; Hoy, *History of the China Mission of the Reformed Church in the United States*.

growth of its mission as beginning after the interruption of 1900. Many reënforcements were sent and another station was added (1913) to that already existing.[39]

The German societies which had so long labored in South China still made that region their chief interest in the Middle Kingdom. All—the Berlin, the Rhenish, and the Basel societies—opened new stations.[40]   For many years Christians under the care of the German societies had been joining the stream of Chinese emigration to Borneo.   Here they were cared for by occasional visits of missionaries from China, but beginning with 1906 the Basel Society placed among them a resident representative.[41]   In 1898, shortly after the German occupation of Kiaochow, the Berlin Society sent representatives to Tsingtau, and after 1900 further stations were established in Shantung.[42]   Between 1906 and 1914 the territory in South China occupied by the Berlin Society was greatly disturbed by bandits, and at least in part for this reason between these years the number of baptized Christians registered no growth.[43]   The Weimar Mission (Allgemeine evangelisch-protestantischer Missionsverein) placed representatives in Kiaochow and specialized as previously on literature, education, and medicine, gathering no Christian communities of its own.[44]   The Berlin Women's Missionary Society for China quietly continued at Hongkong its home for foundlings, and for 1905 reported twenty-three baptisms and three former inmates who had gone out as leaders or as helpers to missionaries.[45]

Before 1901 other Lutheran bodies had begun operations in China and most of them were now to send large reënforcements. The Danish Lutheran Mission (Danske Missionsselskab), which had entered South Manchuria in 1896, founded new stations in each of the three Manchurian provinces.[46]   The Board of Foreign

[39] *Directory of Protestant Missions in China, 1926*, pp. 79, 80; *A Century of Protestant Missions in China*, p. 408.

[40] *Directory of Protestant Missions in China, 1926*, pp. 34-45.   Between 1900 and 1914 the Berlin Society opened seven new stations, as against a total of seven opened in all the years previous to 1900.—Beyer, *China als Missionsfeld*, Ch. 7, pp. 33-39.

[41] Oehler, *China und die christliche Mission*, pp. 261, 262; Schlatter, *Geschichte der Basler Mission*, Vol. 2, p. 421.

[42] *A Century of Protestant Missions in China*, p. 487; Oehler, op. cit., p. 194; Lutschewitz, *Alte und Neue Zeit in Tsimo*, pp. 64, 65.

[43] Richter, *Geschichte der Berliner Missionsgesellschaft*, pp. 572 et seq.

[44] *A Century of Protestant Missions in China*, pp. 498, 499; Schlunk, *Durch Deutsch-Kiautschou*, p. 16.

[45] *A Century of Protestant Missions in China*, p. 491.

[46] *Directory of Protestant Missions in China, 1926*, pp. 37-39.

Missions of the Norwegian Lutheran Church in America succeeded to the enterprise which, a little over ten years before, the American-Norwegian China Mission had commenced in Honan and Hupeh. Between 1901 and 1914 a number of new stations were opened, most of them in Honan.[47] The Hauge's Synodes Mission was closely associated with this society and had work in much the same section. It, too, sent out more missionaries after 1900.[48] The Norwegian Lutheran China Mission Association (Norsk Lutherske Kinamissionsforbund), with headquarters in Norway, in 1902 sent ten missionaries to reënforce its staff in Hupeh and Honan, and in the following years established residences in a number of cities and towns in the two provinces.[49] The Schleswig-Holstein Lutheran Mission (Schleswig-Holstein evang.-luth. Missionsgesellschaft zu Breklum) entered Shantung in 1900. It was never to have many agents in China, but it commenced at least three stations, all in that province.[50]

The various Methodist missions experienced a rapid growth. The Northern (American) Methodists did not enter other provinces than those they had occupied before 1900, for they had assumed large responsibilities in the North, South, East, and West. However, they sent out many new missionaries and developed greatly their educational and other institutional activities. Probably their most distinguished new representative was Bishop James W. Bashford. Since his student days Bashford had had a desire to go to China, but the way had not seemed to open, and he had entered upon an active life in America, first as pastor and then, for fifteen years, as president of Ohio Wesleyan University. In 1904 his church elected him a bishop. Although fifty-five years of age, he was assigned, at his own request, to China, and to that country he gave the remaining fourteen years of his life. Bringing to his task enthusiasm and ripe experience, he made an impression not only upon his own mission but upon the Protestant movement as a whole. He was a man of vision and was deeply interested in all the internal and foreign affairs of his adopted land.[51] The Southern (American) Methodists concentrated, as formerly, upon Kiangsu and Chêkiang, and especially upon Kiangsu. Here they

[47] Ibid., pp. 41, 42; *A Century of Protestant Missions in China*, pp. 532-534.
[48] *A Century of Protestant Missions in China*, p. 508.
[49] *Directory of Protestant Missions in China, 1926*, pp. 43, 44; *A Century of Protestant Missions in China*, pp. 512, 513.
[50] *Directory of Protestant Missions in China, 1926*, p. 46.
[51] Grose, *James W. Bashford*, passim.

were to register marked expansion, both in the number of converts and in their educational and medical institutions.[52]

The Wesleyan Methodist Missionary Society continued in Hupeh and in South China, and reported an encouraging increase in membership, in the willingness of Chinese Christians to assume the burdens of the Church, and in the readiness of non-Christians to listen to the Christian message.[53]   Even before 1900 the Society had made efforts to establish missions in anti-foreign Hunan, and here, after the Boxer year, in several cities and towns stations were opened.[54]   The United Methodist Church Mission added stations in Kweichow to those already established in Chihli, Chêkiang, and Yünnan.[55]   In Yünnan and Kweichow Samuel Pollard was leading a very prosperous enterprise among the Miao.   Pollard came to China in 1887 and died in 1915.   He spent the intervening twenty-eight years in the Southwest and between 1904 and 1910 witnessed what was almost a mass movement into the Church.   He reduced to writing the language of the Miao, devising a script and preparing literature in it.[56]   The English Methodist New Connexion Missionary Society continued in Chihli,[57] and the Bible Christian Methodist Mission in Yünnan and Kweichow.[58]   The laymen of the Canadian Methodists planned to raise one and a half million dollars for the mission of their church in West China,[59] several new stations were opened,[60] and in 1906 the women's society reported "uninterrupted progress."[61] The United Evangelical Church, whose first representatives, Rev. and Mrs. C. N. Dubs, had arrived in China in 1900, centered on Hunan, and in and near Changsha established a number of stations.[62]   The Methodist Protestants, who about 1900 had sent two ladies to China, opened a station in Kalgan in 1909.   They

[52] A Century of Protestant Missions in China, pp. 411 et seq.
[53] Ninety-fifth, Ninety-sixth, and Ninety-seventh Reports of the Wesleyan Methodist Missionary Society; Findlay and Holdsworth, History of the Wesleyan Methodist Missionary Society, Vol. 5, pp. 430-505.
[54] Findlay and Holdsworth, op. cit., Vol. 5, pp. 498-505.
[55] Directory of Protestant Missions in China, 1926, p. 60.
[56] Pollard, Tight Corners in China, passim; Grist, Samuel Pollard, passim; China Inland Mission, A Modern Pentecost.
[57] A Century of Protestant Missions in China, p. 104.
[58] Ibid., p. 125.
[59] Bond, Our Share in China.
[60] Directory of Protestant Missions in China, 1926, pp. 84-86.
[61] Platt, The Story of the Years, Vol. 2, p. 118.
[62] A Century of Protestant Missions in China, p. 543; Directory of Protestant Missions in China, 1926, p. 48.

seem never to have had more than three or four missionaries there at any one time.[63]

The various Baptist societies also registered growth. The Northern (American) Baptists continued in Kwangtung, Chêkiang, and Szechwan, entered Kiangsu,[64] but withdrew from Hupeh. The Southern (American) Baptists continued in Kwangsi, Kwangtung, Kiangsu, and Shantung, and began a new series of stations in Anhui and Honan.[65] The Seventh Day Baptists found the means to expand the enterprise which they had long maintained in Kiangsu.[66] The English Baptists, encouraged by the Arthington bequest of £500,000, entered upon a policy of extension, but confined it to the provinces in which they had previously been residing—Shantung, Shansi, and Shensi. Their growth seems to have been particularly marked in Shensi and Shantung. In Shensi, for example, where before 1900 the membership had been recruited largely from immigrants from Shantung, before 1909 accessions had begun to come from natives of the province, and Christian groups were to be found in about sixty towns and villages.[67] The Swedish Baptists extended somewhat their mission in Shantung.[68] The American Advent Mission Society, in spite of the fact that its young work—in Anhui and Kiangsu —had almost disappeared during the Boxer year, sent reënforcements, gathered together its scattered Chinese members, and in the following fourteen years opened two new stations in Anhui.[69]

The Foreign Christian Missionary Society continued to concentrate its efforts chiefly upon Kiangsu, where it was already well established. Here it did not begin many new stations, although it developed most of those which it had founded. It did, however, undertake a new and thoroughly pioneer mission on the Szechwan border of Tibet. Here, to Tachienlu, in 1903, it sent Dr. Susie C. Rijnhart, who, it may be remembered, had been an independent

[63] *Directory of Protestant Missions in China, 1926,* p. 33.
[64] Ibid., pp. 14-16.
[65] Ibid., pp. 22-26.
[66] Ibid., p. 26.
[67] Fullerton and Wilson, *New China,* p. 51; Glover, *Herbert Stanley Jenkins,* passim; Keyte, *Andrew Young of Shensi,* pp. 189-191; Borst-Smith, *Mandarin and Missionary in Cathay,* pp. 64-69; *China Mission Year Book, 1917,* p. 238; *A Century of Protestant Missions in China,* pp. 69 et seq.
[68] *A Century of Protestant Missions in China,* p. 515.
[69] *Directory of Protestant Missions in China, 1926,* p. 14; *A Century of Protestant Missions in China,* p. 540.

missionary in Tibet and there in a most tragic manner had lost both husband and child. To aid her the Society appointed Dr. and Mrs. Albert L. Shelton. Dr. Rijnhart's strength had been sapped by her earlier sufferings and her health soon began to fail. Dr. Shelton, however, proved a worthy leader, reënforcements came, and eventually a new station was opened at Batang, eighteen days nearer Tibet.[70]

The English Friends expanded somewhat their mission in Szechwan[71] and the American Friends Mission (from Ohio), a smaller body, sent out from time to time new representatives to Kiangsu.[72] The United Brethren in Christ reënforced their work on the delta of the Pearl River in Kwangtung and entered for the first time a number of towns and cities.[73] The Woman's Union Missionary Society of America maintained the enterprises which it had undertaken in Shanghai, sending out new missionaries but opening no new institutions.[74] A Swedish-American Mission continued in Kwangtung.[75] The Northwest Kiangsi Mission, which appears to have been begun in the eighties, seems to have opened no new head stations. It did, however, send out new missionaries.[76] The Christian Mission continued, as formerly, in Ningpo.[77] The Christian Missions in Many Lands, usually known as the Plymouth Brethren, or simply the Brethren, were already in Chihli, Kiangsi, and Shantung, and between 1900 and 1914 many new representatives came and numbers of cities in these three provinces were occupied.[78] The South Chihli Mission opened several new stations and extended its operations into Honan.[79]

Most of the organizations so far mentioned were concerned not only with spreading the Christian message into new regions,

[70] Shelton, *Shelton of Tibet,* passim; McLean, *The History of the Foreign Christian Missionary Society,* pp. 115-122, 202-289. Years later Dr. Shelton was killed by robbers.
[71] *Directory of Protestant Missions in China, 1926,* p. 111.
[72] *Directory of Protestant Missions in China, 1926,* p. 108; Williams, *Ohio Friends in the Land of Sinim,* pp. 73 et seq.
[73] *A Century of Protestant Missions in China,* p. 531.
[74] Ibid., p. 472.
[75] *Directory of Protestant Missions in China, 1926,* p. 134. It was apparently called either the American Scandinavian Christian Free Mission or the American Swedish Free Mission Society.—*A Century of Protestant Missions in China,* p. 527.
[76] *Directory of Protestant Missions in China, 1926,* p. 125.
[77] Ibid., p. 117.
[78] Ibid., pp. 117, 118; *Parliamentary Papers,* 1907, China No. 1.
[79] *A Century of Protestant Missions in China,* pp. 535-537.

but in nourishing the growing Christian communities and in founding institutions. Practically all of them conformed, with variations, to what had become the usual threefold program of Protestant missions—evangelistic, educational, and medical. There were, however, other bodies who gave major attention to spreading a knowledge of the Christian faith. So urgent did they believe to be the accomplishment of this task—so many, they contended, were passing through the gates of death unsaved— that they would leave to other bodies the building up of educational and philanthropic institutions and the nurturing of Christian communities for the permanent occupation of China. Many of their missionaries held, moreover, that Christ's second coming was imminent, that it would occur as soon as the Faith had been preached to all nations, and that any attempt to found institutions looking toward the long duration of the present world was unwarranted.

The most important of these bodies was the China Inland Mission, for not only did it have in China more missionaries than any other organization, but with it, as we have seen, were associated several other societies with similar objectives. Its founder, Hudson Taylor, although old and in failing health, lived long enough to see the recovery from the Boxer outbreak. On January 1, 1903, he formally retired from the office of Director and was succeeded by D. E. Hoste,[80] of that famous "Cambridge Seven" whose coming to China had been such an event. Taylor himself could not stay away from the country to which he had given so many years and returned in 1905. In a few weeks he was in Changsha, the capital of the province that had been most stubborn in resistance to the foreigner, and here on June 3, 1905, in the recently opened station of his Mission, he quietly breathed his last.[81]

The Mission did not lag after Taylor's death. True to its purpose, in the day of greater opportunity that had dawned, it kept its eyes on unoccupied areas. Even for this essentially pioneering movement, however, the rate of entering new cities and districts was slowing down. Between 1901 and 1910 inclusive it and its associated missions opened fifty-two new stations, as against seventy-eight in the preceding decade and fifty in the

[80] Broomhall, *Jubilee Story of the China Inland Mission*, p. 256.
[81] Taylor, *Hudson Taylor*, p. 605.

decade of the eighties.[82]   All the provinces and most of the chief
cities now had resident missionaries and from the standpoint of
geographical expansion the main unfinished task was to fill the
gaps between the major centers.   In 1901 a few great areas
remained into which missionaries of no society had yet gone in
force, and it was in these that the China Inland Mission had its
most important extension.   In Northeast Szechwan the number
of stations grew from five in 1896 to nine in 1901, and in the
latter year thirty-one missionaries were in the district.[83]   By 1904
the Mission had stations on the Tibetan border both in Kansu and
Szechwan,[84] and in that year the first baptisms on the Tibetan
marches were recorded.[85]   Beginning with 1905, itineration was
initiated in Sinkiang and before many years property was acquired
at Urumtsi, the capital.[86]

The revival which had begun in Manchuria spread especially
to the stations in charge of the China Inland Mission and its
associated societies: what seemed to be mass movements occurred,
and baptisms rose from about seven hundred a year in 1895 to
about twenty-five hundred in 1905 and to about forty-five hundred
in 1914.[87]   In Kweichow and Yünnan particularly and from the
non-Chinese peoples there were great numbers of accessions to
the Church.[88]

The societies associated entirely or in part with the China
Inland Mission for the most part increased their staff and opened
new stations.   This was true, for example, of the Scandinavian
China Missionary Alliance;[89] of the Norwegian Alliance Mission
(Det Norske Missionsforbund), whose first representatives sailed
for China in 1900 and which eventually made its center at Lungchüchai, Shensi;[90] of the Scandinavian Alliance Mission in Mongolia, all but one of whose missionaries had been killed
during the Boxer uprising;[91] of the Swedish Holiness Union
Mission in China, which also had lost all but one of its mission-

[82] *The Christian Occupation of China*, p. 313.
[83] Davies, *Among Hills and Valleys in Western China*, Chapter 35.
[84] *Missionary Review of the World*, Vol. 17, p. 642.
[85] Broomhall, *Jubilee Story of the China Inland Mission*, p. 284.
[86] Ibid., p. 288.
[87] Ibid., p. 269.
[88] Ibid., pp. 274-281.
[89] *A Century of Protestant Missions in China*, p. 504.
[90] Broomhall, op. cit., p. 361.
[91] *A Century of Protestant Missions in China*, p. 507.

aries at the hands of the Boxers; [92] of the Finnish Free Church
Mission; [93] of the Alliance China Mission, a German organization, which expanded from Chêkiang into Kiangsi; [94] of the
Norwegian Mission in China, which added a number of stations
in Shansi; [95] and of the Swedish Mission in China. [96] The Liebenzell Mission did not take its distinctive name until 1906, but arising out of an interest created in 1891 when Pastor Coerper, in
Germany, read Hudson Taylor's *Retrospect,* it began in 1897 with
headquarters at Kiel.   In 1902 its head office was removed to
Liebenzell, in the Black Forest.   In 1906 Hunan was decided upon
as its special field, and before long the China Inland Mission retired in its favor from all but two stations in that province.   In
April, 1914, it had sixty missionaries. [97]   In 1899 the German
Women's Missionary Union (Deutscher Frauenmissionsbund) had
been formed, at the outset chiefly for prayer.   In the course of
time it sent missionaries, first one to Ceylon, then one with the
Liebenzell Mission, and then several in association with the China
Inland Mission. [98]   Still others coöperated with the Rhenish Mission. [99]   After 1900 a branch committee of the Scandinavian China
Missionary Alliance, a body with headquarters in Chicago, was
formed in Sweden.   It was financially and administratively independent and in 1913 its name was changed to the Swedish Alliance Mission (Svenska Alliansmissionen).   Its field was in Shansi
north of the Great Wall and in Inner Mongolia. [100]   The St.
Chrischona Pilgrim Mission, an enterprise whose representatives
were regular members of the China Inland Mission, increased its
small staff. [101]

While the number of headstations opened by the China Inland
Mission and its associates did not grow as rapidly between 1901
and 1914 as in the decade before 1901, the outstations between the
leading mission centers showed an unprecedented increase.   In

[92] Ibid., p. 516.
[93] Ibid., p. 501.
[94] *Directory of Protestant Missions in China, 1926,* pp. 100, 101.
[95] Ibid., p. 104.
[96] Ibid., pp. 106, 107.
[97] Broomhall, op. cit., pp. 234, 235, 362, 363.
[98] Broomhall, op. cit., p. 363.
[99] *China Mission Year Book, 1911,* p. 278.
[100] Broomhall, op. cit., pp. 361, 362; *Directory of Protestant Missions in China, 1926,* p. 107.
[101] Broomhall, op. cit., p. 365.

the decade between 1885 and 1895 they had risen from 44 to 123, between 1895 and 1905 they grew from 123 to 521, and between 1905 and 1915 from 521 to 1,100. The number of organized churches at the close of each of these three decades was 149, 418, and 754, respectively. The number of Chinese helpers, paid and unpaid, rose from 417 in 1895 to 1,152 in 1905 and to 2,765 in 1915. The number of missionaries increased, but not as rapidly. It was 604 in 1895, 825 in 1905, and 1,063 in 1915. Between 1885 and 1895 the number of baptisms had been 5,411, between 1895 and 1905 it was 11,452, and between 1905 and 1915, 32,146.[102] If unoccupied districts were not being entered as rapidly as formerly, that was chiefly because so few were left. Within the areas already entered, the Mission and its associates were expanding as never before.

There were other missions entirely independent of the China Inland Mission but with similar purposes. The Christian and Missionary Alliance, which before 1900, as we have seen, had entered several provinces, usually in districts far from the treaty ports and little touched by Protestant missionaries,[103] greatly increased its staff and opened many new stations. Most of the latter, however, were in the provinces in which operations had been begun before 1900.[104] Moreover, like the China Inland Mission, it did not open as many stations in the decade after 1900 as in the ten years immediately preceding.[105] It, too, had passed the first stage of its pioneering activities and was having to devote the major part of its attention to districts for which it had already assumed responsibility.

After 1900 the most noteworthy pioneering was not in new geographical areas, but in organization, in methods, and in institutions. Two of the most remarkable examples were the Young Men's and Young Women's Christian Associations. Between 1901 and 1914, indeed, they exhibited greater proportionate growth in staff and influence than did any other of the large societies working in China.

It will be recalled that the first Young Men's Christian Associations in China had been organized in mission schools in 1885.

[102] Ibid., p. 372.
[103] In Kansu the Alliance was to share with the China Inland Mission the honor of being represented on the Tibetan marches.—Ekvall, *Outposts, or Tibetan Border Sketches*, p. 20; *A Century of Protestant Missions in China*, p. 359.
[104] *Directory of Protestant Missions in China, 1926*, pp. 108-111.
[105] *The Christian Occupation of China*, p. 313.

In 1900 there were forty-seven Associations in eight provinces and a national convention held in 1901 brought together one hundred and seventy delegates, over three-fourths of them Chinese.[106] The leaders of the Young Men's Christian Association proved especially sensitive to the conditions that followed 1900. They realized that a new China was beginning to emerge and that the Christian forces had the opportunity to leave their impress upon the culture that was to be. They were, moreover, young and untrammeled by time-honored methods and institutions. Then, too, as a rule they were men of unusual native gifts, for, as we have seen, they were carefully picked from the student Associations in the United States, and these Associations, possessing almost a monopoly of the voluntary religious activities in American colleges and universities, were attracting and training a large proportion of the outstanding students who were interested in the Christian life.[107] In no other mission, therefore, was the average ability of the foreign representatives so high. Moreover, the Associations early adopted the policy, then comparatively new, of giving the control to Chinese. Chinese were placed on local boards of directors and were usually soon in the majority, and Chinese secretaries were put in positions of leadership.[108] Being undenominational, the Young Men's Christian Association could, and by these policies did, attract to its offices many of the best men from all branches of the Protestant community. Its program, moreover, appealed to the imagination of the rapidly growing Association movement in the United States, and to the Foreign Department of the International Committee of the Young Men's Christian Association [109] John R. Mott devoted a large proportion of his great energy and organizing ability. Large funds were, accordingly, placed at the disposal of the Young Men's Christian Association in China.

With all these advantages, it is not surprising that after 1900 the Association quickly became prominent and that it initiated and developed a number of new and important types of work.

[106] *Chinese Recorder,* Vol. 32, p. 611.

[107] Bishop Bashford, a keen observer, wrote in his journal in 1907, "The Y. M. C. A.—the youngest and most vigorous organization of Christians in Protestantism."—Bashford, *Journal,* p. 49.

[108] By 1912 all the members of the Board of Directors of the Shanghai Association were Chinese, and of an employed force numbering fifty-two only four were foreign.—Edwards, *The Chinese Y. M. C. A.,* in *China, Social and Economic Conditions,* p. 110.

[109] It included the United States and Canada.

While the Young Men's Christian Association began in China among students and continued to direct most of its attention to them, city Associations with their familiar program of religious, educational, social, and physical activities early arose. A word often on the lips of the early leaders was "strategy" and the first of the city Associations were accordingly placed in the great port cities. Attention was paid to the young men of the foreign business community, for they were usually unmarried and were exposed to strong temptations to physical and moral degradation. Quickly, however, activities for the Chinese outstripped those conducted for Europeans and Americans. As was natural, the oldest city Association was in Shanghai. It was founded in 1889,[110] and by 1902 it had a membership of 679 Chinese and on its board of directors were some of the most influential men of the city.[111] In 1901 Associations were formed in Tientsin and Hongkong.[112] Experienced foreign secretaries were early sent to each of the three cities, and by 1907 Associations without such secretaries had sprung up in four other centers.[113] Foreign secretaries arrived in Foochow in 1905, and the following year the first steps were taken toward an organization.[114] In 1906 graduates and students of Princeton University sent two representatives, R. R. Gailey[115] and D. W. Edwards, to inaugurate in Peking a unit of the Association. By the end of 1909 five Princeton graduates were there, and by the time the undertaking had completed its first decade it was housed in a permanent building and in addition to its foreign (American) secretariat had a large Chinese staff.[116]

The rapidly growing body of students trained in the new education was early regarded as an extremely important field. The graduates of the old civil service examinations had ruled the Empire under the old régime, and so, it was believed, the product of the new education would be dominant in the age just on the horizon. As long ago Ricci had held that the country could be most quickly won by centering on the scholar-official class, so

[110] *A Century of Protestant Missions in China*, p. 601.
[111] *Foreign Mail*, Vol. 9, No. 3, p. 10.
[112] *A Century of Protestant Missions in China*, pp. 601, 602.
[113] Ibid., p. 602.
[114] *A Century of Protestant Missions in China*, p. 604.
[115] In his student days Gailey had been a notable athlete. He had come to China under the Y. M. C. A. in 1898.
[116] *Missionary Review of the World*, Vol. 29, p. 605; *China Mission Year Book, 1911*, p. 154.

the leaders of the Young Men's Christian Association maintained that the new students were the key to the China of the twentieth century. For a time access could be had only to mission schools, but it was early felt to be of vital importance to reach what must remain the most numerous and influential body of students, those in government institutions. It will be recalled that a building for this purpose had been erected in Tientsin in 1895.[117] Immediately after the Boxer year the Association opened in Tientsin a school for the sons of *literati* and toward the expenses Chinese made a substantial contribution.[118] In 1906 an Association was organized in the Imperial Polytechnic College in Shanghai, the first in a government school.[119]

After 1900 Chinese students were going by the thousands to Japan, and especially to Tokyo, there to acquire Western learning. In this new environment, and freed from the accustomed restraints, their moral plight was often pitiable. Seeing here an unusual opportunity and a great need, in 1908 the Association sent to Tokyo two secretaries, one foreign and one Chinese. The Chinese was Wang Cheng-ting, son of a clergyman at Ningpo and later to be National Secretary for China and still later to have an important part in Chinese politics and diplomacy.[120]

The flood of Chinese going abroad to study brought not only its tens of thousands to Japan but its thousands to Europe and America. By 1909 the Association established in Shanghai a hostel for students on their way overseas and placed in charge a secretary to give them advice and assistance.[121] Partly under the influence of the Association, a national organization of Christian Chinese Students was formed in the United States.

By 1909, moreover, the Association devised a plan for obtaining for government and private schools in China the teachers from the Occident who were now in such demand, and so to see that these were the type to exert a Christian influence over their pupils.[122] Conferences for students, usually held in the summer, lasting from six to ten days or more, and having a program of Bible study, addresses on religious and moral subjects, training in

[117] *A Century of Protestant Missions in China,* pp. 602, 605.
[118] Ibid., p. 606.
[119] Ibid., p. 606.
[120] Wallace in *China Mission Year Book, 1911,* pp. 417-422; Edwards, *The Chinese Y. M. C. A.,* in *China, Social and Economic Conditions,* p. 115.
[121] *Record of the Seventh Annual Conference of the Y. M. C. A., 1909.*
[122] Ibid.

Association methods, and recreation, were developed in the United States in the eighties and nineties, and after 1900 this method was introduced into China. In 1910 eleven such conferences were held for Chinese, three in the United States, one in Japan, and seven in China, with a total attendance of eight hundred and twenty-six.[123] The study of the Bible, then greatly stressed by the Association in America, and especially by the student Associations, was emphasized in China, and in 1911 there were reported 2,732 in Bible classes.[124] Literature suitable for the new student class was developed. Before 1911 a Chinese, H. L. Zia, was made educational secretary, a monthly periodical in Chinese was inaugurated, and numerous books and pamphlets were prepared, some of them translations or adaptations of publications which had been found useful in the Occident.[125] To reach the educated classes, moreover, plans were laid for lectures on Western science. To investigate this field and to test out the method, in 1902 C. H. Robertson was sent to Nanking, but it was not until 1910 that he began on a large scale the extensive program that had been conceived. In the following three years, under his direction, a staff was gathered, partly paid and partly voluntary, lectures and demonstrations on scientific subjects were given in more than twenty centers, and in nearly half of these the lectures were followed by "evangelistic campaigns"—the public presentation of the Christian message.[126]

While giving a large proportion of its attention to the educated, the Young Men's Christian Association by no means ignored the other groups corresponding to those to which in the United States and Canada it also directed its efforts. The Associations in the large cities addressed themselves not only to students but to boys,[127] clerks, and younger business men. There were day schools, night schools, Bible classes, and religious meetings. M. J. Exner was brought from the Kansas City Association to Shanghai

[123] Boynton in *China Mission Year Book, 1911*, p. 411.
[124] Edwards, op. cit., p. 119.
[125] *Work of the Y. M. C. A. for China and Korea, 1908*. In 1911 it was reported that 84,050 copies of new books and new editions had been printed during the year and that 6,528 copies of *China's Young Men* were being taken.— Pettus in *Foreign Mail*, Vol. 18, No. 6, p. 12.
[126] C. H. Robertson in *China Mission Year Book, 1913*, pp. 145-150, and in *Chinese Recorder*, Vol. 43, p. 410; *Y. M. C. A. Report for 1911*.
[127] The first boys' secretary for China, J. C. Clark, began work in 1913 (Y. M. C. A., *Another Year of Progress*, 1913, p. 16) and before long the boys' department of the Shanghai Association became the largest in the world.

to organize a school for the training of physical directors for Associations and colleges. He not only did this but took the initiative in bringing together for competition athletes from various parts of China and in other ways stimulated interest in sports and in physical education. In a country which had had no place for physical training in its educational program, the Associations were aiding in the introduction of wholesome outdoor play and the intelligent cultivation of a sound physique.[128]

With its resources in money and leadership and this many-sided program, the Young Men's Christian Association had a phenomenal growth. In 1907 there were in China and Korea eleven city and forty-four student Associations with memberships of 2,190 and 2,767 respectively.[129] By 1912 fourteen cities had fully organized general Associations with a membership of 4,631 and in seven more work was in its initial stages.[130] In 1911 there were ninety-three student Associations and seventy of these reported a total membership of 4,459.[131] In 1913 China and Korea held twenty-five city and one hundred and five student Associations.[132] Even in distant Chengtu an Association was organized.[133] The secretarial staff rapidly increased, rising from a body of seven foreigners and three Chinese in 1901 to twenty-eight foreigners and and sixteen Chinese in 1907, and to seventy-five foreigners and eighty-five Chinese in 1912.[134]

From the beginning the foreign leaders insisted that the Associations be predominantly Chinese in support as well as in leadership. No money was contributed from abroad for anything except the salaries of the foreign secretaries and for buildings and permanent equipment.[135] Even part of the money for buildings came from China.[136] Chinese prominent in official and business circles con-

[128] *The Work of the Y. M. C. A. of China and Korea, 1908.* In October, 1910, the Y. M. C. A. opened in Shanghai what was said to be the first properly equipped athletic field—from the Western point of view—in any city in China.—Pratt, *The Christianizing of China,* p. 63.
[129] *China Mission Year Book, 1913,* p. 63.
[130] Edwards, op. cit., p. 110.
[131] Pettus in *Foreign Mail,* Vol. 18, No. 6, p. 12.
[132] *China Mission Year Book, 1913,* p. 329.
[133] R. R. Service (one of the secretaries in Chengtu) in *Foreign Mail,* Vol. 18, No. 1, p. 16; W. Wilson in *China Mission Year Book, 1911,* pp. 173-180.
[134] *China Mission Year Book, 1913,* p. 330; *Five Years of Progress, 1907-1912.* The figures include China and Korea, but the bulk of the secretaries were, of course, in China.
[135] *A Century of Protestant Missions in China,* p. 604; Edwards, *The Chinese Y. M. C. A.,* in *China, Social and Economic Conditions,* pp. 110, 111.
[136] Edwards, op. cit., pp. 110, 111.

tributed to the budgets, President Yüan Shih-k'ai himself being of the number.[187]

The Revolution of 1911 for the moment brought grave problems. The income from Chinese sources fell off sharply and the Associations were in danger of being drawn into politics.[188] The reverse, however, proved temporary and enlarged opportunities soon came and even more rapid growth. The country quickly became more open-minded to the Christian message than it had yet been, and since the Associations were so largely Chinese in leadership and since both members and leaders were chiefly from those younger groups which were in sympathy with the ideas that had had so large a part in precipitating the Revolution and had been given such wide currency by it, the Young Men's Christian Association quickly became popular. By the end of 1912 requests for Associations had been made by a number of provincial governors, and the Provincial Assembly of Kirin had asked for the formation of one in every *hsien* city of the province.[189] The general convention of the Associations of China and Korea which met in Peking in December, 1912, was given a reception by President Li Yüan-hung, and addresses of welcome were made by the President, the Premier, and by the President and the Secretary of the National Assembly.[140] Six new city Associations were organized in 1913,[141] buildings were erected or enlarged in a number of the large centers, and sites for buildings acquired in others.[142] Secretaries were asked to lead in preparing Chinese athletes for participation in the Far Eastern Olympic Games in Manila in 1913.[143] The Lecture Department grew rapidly,[144] adding to its staff, among others, Dr. W. W. Peter. In 1913 Dr. Peter laid plans for public health education which within a few years were to lead to a nation-wide program. A Department of Conservation was also designed, and to render it effective the Famine Relief Committee appropriated fifteen thousand taels.

[187] Eddy, *How China's Leaders Received the Gospel*, p. 5.
[188] Y. M. C. A., *Five Years of Progress, 1907-1912*, p. 1; *China Mission Year Book, 1913*, pp. 327-330.
[139] *International Review of Missions*, Vol. 3, p. 25.
[140] Y. M. C. A., *Five Years of Progress, 1907-1912*, p. 3.
[141] F. S. Brockman in *China Mission Year Book, 1914*, pp. 472-477.
[142] Y. M. C. A., *Another Year's Progress, 1913*, p. 1; *Chinese Recorder*, Vol. 47, p. 111.
[143] Y. M. C. A., *Another Year's Progress, 1913*, p. 13. The Y. M. C. A. was largely responsible for initiating the Far Eastern Olympics.
[144] C. H. Robertson in *China Mission Year Book, 1914*, pp. 156-162.

There were other projects for physical education and for lectures on the fundamentals of government.[145] The Publication Department added to its output.[146] Increased attention was given to the Chinese who were going abroad to study—to making easy and pleasant their journey and to aiding them in the difficult process of adjustment to their new environment.[147] Student members of the Associations were reported to be conducting night classes for servants, lectures for the uneducated, and other forms of social service.[148]

The prominence of the social service phases of the Association's activity did not lead to a curtailment of distinctively religious activities. With increasing success the Association sought to present the Christian message to students. Several denominational missions, indeed, set aside men to give their entire time as special secretaries to students.[149] Associations were organized in government as well as in mission schools,[150] and churches were urged to provide Bible classes for students.[151] In 1907 John R. Mott conducted the first organized series of meetings for reaching government schools with the Christian message, and the Centenary Missionary Conference (1907) asked the Young Men's Christian Association to make a special effort for both government and mission students.[152] In 1911 George Sherwood Eddy held special evangelistic meetings for students in Hongkong, Tokyo, Shanghai, Hangchow, Taiyüanfu, Paotingfu, and Tientsin. Thousands were in attendance and several hundred signed cards agreeing to make a further study of Christianity.[153] In 1913 in several important cities Mr. Mott and Mr. Eddy held meetings at which they presented the Christian message. Admission was by ticket only and was limited chiefly to teachers, students, officials, and members of the local gentry. The attendance averaged more than two thousand a night. In Mukden the Governor presided and made possible the presence of four thousand government school students. As a result of the meetings the country over, more than six thousand signed cards indicating a desire to study Christianity and by

[145] Ibid., p. 159.
[146] Y. M. C. A., *Another Year of Progress, 1913*, p. 31.
[147] Ibid., p. 25.
[148] F. S. Brockman in *China Mission Year Book, 1914*, p. 474.
[149] Ibid., p. 473.
[150] Y. M. C. A., *Five years of Progress, 1907-1912*, p. 17.
[151] Arthur Rugh in *Chinese Recorder*, Vol. 48, p. 227.
[152] *China Mission Year Book, 1916*, pp. 226, 227.
[153] *Y. M. C. A. Report for 1911*, pp. 9-11.

the end of half a year a little over a thousand either had been baptized or had been enrolled in churches for further instruction.[154]   In 1914 and 1915 Mr. Eddy paid another visit to China with similar results: it was estimated that sixty-three thousand different individuals heard him and that nearly eight thousand entered Bible classes.[155]

Under the auspices of the Young Men's Christian Association, moreover, the Student Volunteer Movement for the Ministry came into existence.   In 1886, it will be recalled, there had begun in the United States, as an outgrowth of the Student Department of the Young Men's Christian Association, the Student Volunteer Movement for Foreign Missions, and in the ensuing years organizations with similar or identical names and objectives arose in several other countries.   Some time before 1900 a beginning was made in China toward a corresponding movement for recruiting young men for the ministry, and by the close of 1909 "volunteer bands" of students with that purpose had sprung up in several institutions.   Before 1910, however, these were not bound together by any common organization.[156]   This was to arise out of a series of awakenings in Christian schools.   In the spring of 1909 a strong religious movement broke out in Shantung Union College at Weihsien under the leadership of Ting Li-mei, and under its inspiration over one hundred boys decided to enter the Christian ministry.[157]   Ting Li-mei, a pastor in Shantung, had suffered for his faith during the Boxer uprising and through that and later developments had come into a deep religious experience.[158]   So great an impression did he make in Shantung Union College that he was asked to visit institutions in Tientsin, T'ungchow, and Peking.   As a result more than two hundred in these three centers also announced it to be their purpose to enter the ministry.[159]   At the annual North China Student Conference of the Young

[154] Y. M. C. A., *Another Year of Progress, 1913*, p. 27; W. E. Taylor, *Report on the Evangelistic Meetings for Government Students in China Conducted by Dr. John R. Mott and Mr. Sherwood Eddy, Jan. 30 to March 29, 1913* (in Library North China Branch Royal Asiatic Society); *North China Herald*, Nov. 29, 1913, p. 693.

[155] *China Mission Year Book, 1915*, pp. 165-170.

[156] *Record of the Seventh Annual Conference of the Y. M. C. A.*, 1909.

[157] *Report of the Presbyterian Board, 1910*, pp. 43-46; Pettus in *China Mission Year Book, 1911*, pp. 190-192.

[158] Scott, *China from Within*, pp. 288-293; *Missionary Review of the World*, Vol. 24, p. 125.

[159] *L. M. S. Chronicle*, Vol. 18 (new series), pp. 129, 175; Pettus in *China Mission Year Book, 1911*, pp. 190-192.

Men's Christian Association at T'ungchow in June, 1910, representatives of local groups not only from North China but from Hupeh, Anhui, and Kiangsu, formed the Chinese Student Volunteer Movement for the Ministry—with the motto, somewhat like that of the similar bodies in other countries: "The evangelization of our mother country and the world in this generation." [160] Ting Li-mei became the first travelling secretary and visited the Christian schools and colleges of the country, holding meetings, interviewing students, and organizing and nourishing local "bands." [161] At the general convention of the Young Men's Christian Association for China and Korea held in Peking in December, 1912, a permanent organization was effected with an executive committee appointed annually by the General Committee of the Young Men's Christian Association. [162] In 1915 it was reported that forty "volunteers" had already entered the ministry and that one hundred and seven had begun their theological studies. [163] In 1916 it was reported that these numbers had increased to one hundred and twenty-five and to two hundred and twenty-five respectively. [164] An important step had been taken toward recruiting educated Chinese for the service of the Church.

By 1914, then, the Young Men's Christian Association had brought to the country some very able men, it had reached thousands of Chinese, many of them students, it had set a new standard for turning Christian organizations quickly over to the support and control of the Chinese, and it had inaugurated many new methods. It was coming to have a great influence upon the entire Protestant body.

The sister organization, the Young Women's Christian Association, became only a little less prominent. By 1900 it had at least two units in mission schools. In 1899 the Young Men's Christian Association appointed a number of women to form a National Women's Committee. In 1903 the first secretary for China, Miss Martha Berninger, was appointed by the World's Committee of the Young Women's Christian Associations and a little later

[160] Pettus in *China Mission Year Book, 1911*, pp. 190-192; *Report of the Presbyterian Board, 1911*, p. 172.
[161] Boynton in *Foreign Mail*, Vol. 18, No. 3, p. 11; *Y. M. C. A. Report for 1911*, p. 15.
[162] Y. M. C. A., *Five Years of Progress, 1907-1912;* p. 3; *China Mission Year Book, 1915*, p. 533.
[163] *China Mission Year Book, 1915*, p. 533.
[164] *China Mission Year Book, 1916*, p. 422.

inaugurated work in Shanghai for the women employed in the factories that were beginning to make of that port an industrial center. The first general secretary of the National Committee of China arrived in 1905 and the first general secretary of the Shanghai Association came the following year.[165] In 1913 there were three Chinese and fourteen foreign secretaries, and three city Associations and thirty-three student Associations.[166] The program followed was much like that of the Young Men's Christian Association, although on a smaller scale.[167]

SOCIETIES WHICH ENTERED CHINA, 1901-1914

Before 1900 most of the larger denominations of Protestant Christendom had sent representatives to China. No diminution followed, however, in the number of organizations which now for the first time sent missionaries to the Empire. In 1900 sixty-one Protestant societies are said to have been at work in China. In 1906 this number is reported to have grown to sixty-seven, and in 1919 to one hundred and thirty.[168] These figures may not be complete, for the records of some of the smaller bodies may have escaped observation. The increase was in the main from three groups: (1) from branches of larger denominational groups or national churches which, for a variety of reasons, had been late in entering the country; (2) from smaller and sometimes younger denominations and Christian groups; and (3) from bodies which were organized for special tasks. These new societies did not greatly alter the character of the missionary force or of the missionary message. Most of them were from Anglo-Saxon countries and the majority were either a direct or an indirect outgrowth of that same general Evangelical movement which had been chiefly responsible for the rise and development of Protestant missions. While they wrought no fundamental changes, they did cause some important modifications, modifications which will become apparent as the narrative proceeds.

First, as to the groups related to those already represented in China. The one new Anglican body was the Missionary Society of the Church of England in Canada. For some years Canadian

[165] *A Century of Protestant Missions in China*, p. 609.
[166] *China Mission Year Book, 1913*, p. 350.
[167] Ibid. and *China Mission Year Book, 1911*, p. 423.
[168] Rawlinson in *The Christian Occupation of China*, p. 34.

Anglicans had been sending men and women to Fukien in connection with the Church Missionary Society. In response to an appeal by the Conference of the Anglican Communion in China in 1907, they undertook responsibility for a new diocese. Honan was chosen, and in 1910 William C. White, consecrated bishop the preceding year, came with several clergymen to Kaifeng, the center of the new mission.[169] The Swedish Independent Baptist Mission, with headquarters in Rättvik, occupied its first station, in Shensi, in 1913.[170] In 1901 there arrived in Canton the first missionary of the Presbyterian Church of New Zealand, armed with letters of introduction to Chinese. For more than twenty years his church had been ministering to Chinese immigrants in New Zealand and now wished an enterprise in the districts from which these had come.[171] For some years the Korean Presbyterian churches had been maintaining missions among the Chinese in Chosen. When, in 1907, a Korean Board of Foreign Missions was formed, it naturally planned to send missionaries to China and beginning with 1912 despatched several to Shantung.[172] The General Missionary Board of the Free Methodist Church of North America sent its first representatives to China in 1905. Clara Leffingwell, to whom the enterprise was primarily due, had been trained in Toronto under the China Inland Mission and it was under that body that she first went to the Middle Kingdom (1896). While on furlough she succeeded in arousing interest among the Free Methodists and in 1905 eight, including herself, were sent out. Miss Leffingwell died shortly after her return to China,[173] but the mission continued and in 1914 had eight men and women working from two centers in Honan.[174] In 1904 the Evangelical Association of North America sent its first missionaries to China and chose a part of Hunan as its field,[175] and in 1914 it had nine missionaries in Hunan and Kweichow.[176]

[169] *China Mission Year Book, 1911*, p. 20; *China Mission Year Book, 1912*, p. 208.

[170] *Directory of Protestant Missions in China, 1926*, p. 21.

[171] *A Century of Protestant Missions in China*, p. 249.

[172] Brown, *The Mastery of the Far East*, pp. 531, 532; *China Mission Year Book, 1915*, p. 48.

[173] Sellew, *Clara Leffingwell, A Missionary*, passim.

[174] *Proceedings of the General Missionary Board of the Free Methodist Church and of the Woman's Foreign Missionary Society, Oct. 1914*, p. 408.

[175] *A Century of Protestant Missions in China*, p. 541.

[176] *Missionary Year Book. Proceedings of the Board of Missions of the Evangelical Association for the Years 1913-1914*, p. 66.

About 1922 it joined forces with the United Evangelical Church, which had representatives in another section of the province.[177] The Friedenshort Deaconess Mission, a German organization associated with the China Inland Mission, sent its first representatives to China—to Kweichow—in 1912.[178]

Between 1900 and the summer of 1914 more societies entered China from the Lutheran bodies than from any other of the major denominational groups. From almost the earliest days of Protestant missions, as we have often seen, Lutherans had been in China, but the major bodies represented had been German and but few missionaries had come from the churches in Scandinavia and the United States. The Scandinavian churches had not been lacking in interest in foreign missions, but they had directed their energies toward other countries. They were stirred by the martyrdoms of the Boxer year, however, and now that to these were added the great changes in China they began to feel an obligation to aid in founding the Christian Church in that land also. As a rule the churches in the United States had been too engrossed in taking care of the Lutheran immigrants who had come from Northern Europe during the nineteenth century to have either resources or attention for other lands. By the beginning of the twentieth century, however, the stream of immigration from Northern Europe had dwindled, the older immigrant stock had accumulated wealth, and the great bodies of Lutherans began to have resources and interest for the needs of other countries. They, too, naturally became interested in China.

Most of the new Lutheran missions, both Scandinavian and American, chose territory in Central China, and in Hunan, Hupeh, and Honan a body of Lutherans began to arise which gave promise of becoming even stronger than the older one in South China. The first representatives of the Augustana Synod went to China in 1905 and, after a short stay with the Hauge's Synod Mission in Hupeh, selected Hsüchow, Honan, as a center.[179] Within the Evangelical Lutheran Synod of Missouri, Ohio, and Other States, usually known as the Missouri Synod, a society was organized

[177] *Missions of the Evangelical Church. Annual Report, 1922-1923*, pp. 85 et seq.
[178] Broomhall, *Jubilee Story of the China Inland Mission*, p. 364.
[179] Augustana Synod, *Our First Decade in China, 1905-1915*, pp. 9-18. The first representatives of the Synod were sent by the Swedish Evangelical Lutheran Foreign Mission Society of North America, a body within the Synod, and were later taken over by the Synod.—*A Century of Protestant Missions in China*, p. 518.

by Rev. E. L. Arndt and others and sent its first missionaries to China in 1913. They and those who followed them found a field in Hankow and in cities on the Yangtze as far west as Wanhsien. In 1917 the Synod officially took over the work of the society.[180] In 1898 the Finnish Missionary Society (Suomen Lahetysseura Finska Missionssalskapet) had contemplated beginning operations in Manchuria and Mongolia, but it did not send its first missionaries until 1901. These, after advising with Stevenson of the China Inland Mission, established themselves in the northwestern portion of Hunan.[181] The American Lutheran Brethren Mission, representing the Church of the Lutheran Brethren, sent its first missionaries to China in 1902, and they and their successors obtained locations in Hupeh and Honan.[182] The Independent Lutheran Mission appears to have begun about 1915 and to have had only one station,[183] in Honan. The Evangelical Lutheran Mission opened a center in Szechwan in 1913.[184] The Norwegian Missionary Society (Det Norske Misionsselskab) early began a mission in China but about 1848 discontinued it. It now (1901) resumed operations and partly at the recommendation of Griffith John its initial group of missionaries settled in Hunan, fixing their headquarters at Yiyang. The 1902 conference of Protestant missionaries in Hunan assigned them Yiyang and adjoining regions and Changsha, and here a number of stations were opened. By 1913 the Society had sent to China twenty-eight missionaries and in 1910 had in its employ sixty-three Chinese.[185]

The second group of societies entering China between 1900 and the summer of 1914, made up of those maintained by smaller denominations and by individual congregations, was very large. Some of the supporting denominations were old, but others were relatively young. Most of them were American in origin and headquarters. Nearly all clung tenaciously to the convictions which gave them a reason for their separate existence and some believed it their duty to propagate these among other Christians. Many of their representatives were men and women of little formal education and of narrow outlook. Often they did not

[180] Fuerbringer, *Men and Missions. IV. Our China Mission*, passim.
[181] *A Century of Protestant Missions in China*, pp. 502, 503.
[182] Ibid., p. 518.
[183] *Directory of Protestant Missions in China, 1926*, p. 40.
[184] Ibid., p. 120.
[185] Gotteberg, *Ti Aar i Hunan*, pp. 14-32.

follow the practice of the older and larger bodies and seek a city unoccupied by Protestants, but acquired property in centers where other boards were at work.[186]   Their coming made coöperation more difficult, reënforced those who held to a conservative theological position, and added to the complexity of Protestantism in China.   Missionaries of these societies were often regarded as eccentric both by their fellow foreigners and by the Chinese, but as a rule they lived lives of great devotion and often, because of small salaries, of privation.   No complete list of them or of their boards is available and at best only a partial picture of their activities can here be given.   That which follows is of necessity incomplete.

One of the largest was an American organization, the Seventh Day Adventist General Conference.   The decision to enter China was reached in 1901 and the first missionaries were sent soon afterward.   Conceiving it to be their duty to spread among Christians as well as non-Christians their distinctive tenets—the observance of the seventh day instead of the first and a belief in the early second coming of Christ—as a rule the Seventh Day Adventists established themselves first in the chief cities, usually where other Protestants had long been, and before many years they were to be found in ten provinces.[187]   In 1914 they had forty-two churches, 1,355 members (of whom 404 had been baptized during the year), and a staff of 312, foreigners and Chinese.[188]   Their major emphasis seems to have been upon reaching non-Christians, and to this end they not only preached in the large cities but travelled far and wide through the countryside:[189] they were indefatigable evangelists.

The Assemblies of God in the United States of America and Foreign Lands entered China somewhat later than did the Seventh Day Adventists.   They, too, at first chose cities where other Protestants had long been at work, but after 1914 they occupied

[186] Two-thirds of the new residential centers were opened by the older societies, which shows that the new bodies did not as a rule specialize on regions as yet unoccupied, but left most of these to older societies.—Rawlinson, in *The Christian Occupation of China*, p. 34.

[187] *A Century of Protestant Missions in China*, pp. 538, 539; *Directory of Protestant Missions in China, 1926*, pp. 131-134.   See, too, a statement by the Seventh Day Adventist General Conference Committee, Far Eastern Division, 1919, in *The Christian Occupation of China*, pp. lxxxviii, lxxxix.

[188] *52d Annual Statistical Report (Year ending Dec. 31, 1914), Seventh-day Adventist Conferences, Missions and Institutions*, p. 8.

[189] Lee, *Travel Talks on China*, passim.   Lee was a Seventh Day Adventist missionary.

what seems to have been new territory in Kansu.[190] The Broadcast Tract Press and Faith Orphanages was the name given to a
small enterprise in Changsha led by Allen N. Cameron. It was
begun about 1905 and was supported chiefly by a Baptist church
in Colorado.[191] The Metropolitan Presbyterian Mission, apparently with one representative, H. G. C. Hallock, was located in
Shanghai, and Hallock was also the head of what was ambitiously denominated the National Tract Society for China.[192]
The Church of God Mission entered Chinkiang, in Kiangsu, in
1910.[193] The Canadian Holiness Mission sent representatives,
two men and two women, to Changtê, Hunan, in 1910, and later
spread to two other centers.[194] The General Mission Board of
the Church of the Nazarene, with headquarters in Kansas City,
Missouri, sent its first missionaries to China about 1913 and opened
stations in Shantung and later in Chihli.[195] The Ebenezer Mission, with headquarters in Watertown, Wisconsin, occupied its
single center, Piyang, Honan, in 1907.[196] The Evangel Mission,
with headquarters in California, opened its only central station, in
Kwangtung, in 1904.[197] The Hebron Mission, also with headquarters in California, occupied Kunshan, in Kwangtung, in
1911.[198] A Faith Mission, made up apparently of two sisters
who came to China in 1895, entered Wuhu in 1901.[199] The
Mission Alliance, a Norwegian organization, seems to have sent
its first representative to China at least as early as 1911 and to
have opened its first station, in Chihli, in 1914.[200] The Mennonite Brethren Church had missionaries in China as early as 1911
and had its field of labor in Fukien.[201] The Board of Foreign
Missions of the Conference of the Mennonites of North America
had missionaries in China beginning at least with 1909, and
opened a station at K'aichow, Chihli, in 1911.[202] The Board
of Foreign Missions of the Mennonite Brethren in Christ (Penn-

[190] *Directory of Protestant Missions in China, 1926*, pp. 113, 114.
[191] Ibid., p. 116.
[192] Ibid., pp. 124, 160.
[193] Ibid., p. 116.
[194] *Directory of Protestant Missions in China, 1926*, p. 116.
[195] Ibid., p. 119.
[196] Ibid., p. 120.
[197] Ibid., p. 120.
[198] Ibid., p. 120.
[199] Ibid., p. 120.
[200] Ibid., p. 123.
[201] Ibid., p. 123.
[202] Ibid., p. 124.

sylvania Conference) had missionaries on the Kansu border of Tibet as early as 1911.[203]   The China Mennonite Mission Society, with headquarters at Hillsboro, Kansas, had representatives in Shantung by the close of 1905, and by 1914 had extended its work into Honan.[204]   The German Mennonites (Light and Hope Mission) began in Tsaohsien, Shantung, in 1905, and by 1912 had thirteen missionaries in the province.[205]   The National Holiness Mission, with headquarters in Chicago and apparently an offshoot of the South Chihli Mission, had two large centers in Shantung.[206] The Pentecostal Assemblies of the World, an American organization, commenced operations in Shansi as early as 1910.[207]   The Pentecostal Holiness Church sent its first representatives—to Hongkong—at least as early as 1914.[208]   The Pentecostal Missionary Union for Great Britain and Ireland chose Yünnan as its field of labor and beginning about 1912 sent representatives there.[209]   A number of men and women known as "Pentecostal missionaries" were found in Mongolia, in Chihli, in Kwangtung, Hongkong, Shanghai, and Chêkiang, and began coming as early as 1907 and 1908.[210]   In 1903 the South China Holiness Mission made Canton its initial center.[211]   The South China Peniel Holiness Missionary Society, in Hongkong, may have been started as early as 1910.[212]   The South Yünnan Mission, apparently created by one who came out under the China Inland Mission in 1912, recorded its single station as having been opened in 1915.[213]   The Tsehchow Mission, in Shansi, said to have been

[203] 27th Annual Report of the Board of Foreign Missions of the Mennonite Brethren in Christ (Pennsylvania Conference), 1911, pp. 8-10.
[204] Directory of Protestant Missions in China, 1926, p. 120. In 1922 it had 42 missionaries (of whom 9 were on furlough), 7 stations, and 32 outstations. Some of these missionaries were in Honan and three were in Mongolia.—Field Report of the China Mennonite Mission Society Located in Southern Shantung and Northern Honan, 1922.
[205] Forsyth, Shantung, p. 276.
[206] Directory of Protestant Missions in China, 1926, p. 124.
[207] Ibid., p. 125.
[208] Ibid., p. 126.
[209] Ibid., p. 127.
[210] Ibid., pp. 126, 127. China Mission Year Book, 1912, pp. 134-142, mentions six men from Canada as being in Mongolia. The Pentecostal Mission in Nashville was in 1902 contributing to work in China through the Christian and Missionary Alliance. W. A. Farmer was sent out in 1901 as its first missionary. He later joined the Christian and Missionary Alliance. The Pentecostal Mission in Nashville then felt that it should organize a separate board.—Farmer, Ada Beeson Farmer, pp. 73 et seq.
[211] Directory of Protestant Missions in China, 1926, p. 130.
[212] Ibid., p. 131.
[213] Ibid., p.135.

begun in 1903, seems to have had as its founder Stanley P. Smith, long with the China Inland Mission.[214] In 1908 the General Mission Board of the Church of the Brethren, an American organization with a German background, sent its first representatives, five in number, to Shansi. In 1916, as an outgrowth of a Sunday School among the Chinese in Chicago, the same board sent missionaries to Sunning in Kwangtung.[215] The Swedish Mongol Mission, with Prince Oscar Bernadotte as chairman, was established in 1905.[216] The Pacific Coast Missionary Society, with headquarters in Vancouver, B. C., founded its oldest station, in Hangchow, in 1913.[217] The Free Evangelical Missionary Union of Norway (Norges Frie Evangeliske Hedninge Mission) seems to have begun operations, in Chihli, about 1910.[218] The Tibetan Tribes Mission appears to have been begun by J. MacGillivray, who came to China in 1910.[219] We hear, too, although we do not know the date of their entrance into China, of the Christian Catholic Apostolic Church Mission, the Grace Evangelical Mission, and the Christians' Mission.[220]

A good many missionaries were not affiliated with any board. From almost the beginning of Protestant missions in China there had been such, but with the increasing ease of access to China and the growing interest in it in church circles in Europe and America, the number seems steadily to have mounted. Some came, as they said, on faith, with no assured income, and often were a charge upon missionaries who were supported by boards.[221] Others had independent incomes, and still others were backed by friends. Many remained in China for only a brief period, but others were there for years. They were usually picturesque, sometimes eccentric, and occasionally very able.

At first sight it might seem that these many small societies and independent missionaries had entirely altered the complexion of

[214] *Directory of Protestant Missions in China, 1926*, p. 136.
[215] Moyer, *A History of the Missions of the Church of the Brethren*, MS., pp. 268, 330.
[216] *China Mission Year Book, 1912*, pp. 134-142.
[217] *Directory of Protestant Missions in China, 1926*, p. 126.
[218] Ibid., p. 124.
[219] Ibid., p. 136.
[220] *China Mission Year Book, 1915*, statistical tables, p. ix.
[221] There is an autobiographical account of one such in an anonymous book, *A Saved Sinner, Faith Mission, China*. The author was converted in 1903 at the age of twenty-six, felt that he ought to go to China as a missionary, was rejected by a mission board, but with his wife and two children went out anyway, trusting God to supply his needs.

the Protestant forces in China. The missionaries falling under this category, however, only about equalled in number the representatives of one of the larger denominational groups, the Presbyterians, for example, or the Methodists. While some of them introduced a bizarre and often highly emotional type of Protestantism repulsive to the more intelligent and better educated Chinese, many held their converts to exacting moral standards and emphasized an inward religious experience and a complete change of life.

The third group of societies now entering China for the first time, those organized for some special task, displayed a variety of purposes, origins, and supporting constituencies. About 1897 religious work had been begun for the employees of the postal and telegraph services and in 1907 the International Postal Telegraph Christian Association appointed a representative to carry it on. The men were approached largely through copies of the New Testament, circular letters, and a periodical.[222] The South China Boat Mission, for the large population which lives on the water in and near Canton, was initiated in 1909.[223]

The Mission Among the Higher Classes of China dates from 1894. Its founder, Gilbert Reid, had been a missionary of the (Northern) American Presbyterian Board. After a number of years he became convinced that if China were to be reached effectively with the Christian message the influential and educated must be approached and the masses won through them. He believed, accordingly, that he should devote his entire time to this group, especially since Protestants had heretofore so largely neglected it. Since his board was unwilling to set him aside for this special task, he resigned and undertook it without the official aid of any denomination. Between 1894 and 1897, when, after the Chino-Japanese War, many officials were feeling the need of governmental reform, he gained the confidence of many of the more prominent, especially in Peking, and in March, 1897, obtained the approval of the Tsungli Yamen for an educational institution to be known as the International Institute. W. A. P. Martin, long in China as a missionary and teacher, and recently returned to Peking, agreed to aid, and Reid canvassed Europe and America for funds. The reaction of 1898 and the Boxer uprising brought

[222] *China Mission Year Book, 1911*, p. 450, *1915*, pp. 173-176; Dennis, *Christian Missions and Social Progress*, Vol. 3, p. 212.
[223] *The Christian Occupation of China*, p. 367.

delay, and in 1903 the decision was reached to inaugurate the undertaking in Shanghai rather than in the capital. With the assistance of Chinese as well as foreigners, property was acquired and buildings were erected in the French Concession. In 1909 the Wai Wu Pu (Ministry of Foreign Affairs) and in 1914 the corresponding ministry under the Republic repeated the official approval that had been given by the Tsungli Yamen. As the Mission developed, its purpose became not so much the direct winning of the higher classes to the Christian faith as the furthering among Chinese officials and merchants of a knowledge of the constructive features of Occidental civilization, and the promotion of friendship and better understanding between Westerners and Chinese. To that end, through the Institute in Shanghai, classes in special subjects were conducted for Chinese; lectures were given on various topics, including the more prominent faiths of mankind; literature was prepared, particularly on phases of Western learning; many calls of friendship were made; and receptions and other social gatherings were arranged at which foreigners and Chinese met.[224]

Another special mission in Shanghai, but for a very different class and for a quite different purpose, bore the inviting name, "The Door of Hope." Miss Cornelia Bonnell, a graduate of Vassar, while teaching in Shanghai in a private school for foreign children, became impressed with the unhappy condition of Chinese prostitutes. Accordingly she resigned her position and became the first superintendent of a home which in 1900 was founded by five women, all missionaries, to receive those who cared to escape from their unfortunate occupation. The enterprise was supported by foreigners, Chinese gentry, and the Municipal Council of the International Settlement. By the end of its first ten years it had received and cared for about a thousand women, had aided a large proportion of these to begin a wholesome life, and had founded and maintained a home for children who had been rescued from brothels.[225]

Another Shanghai mission, but again to a different class, was for the men who drew the rickshas by which much of the populace

[224] Gilbert Reid, *The International Institute*, the Sixth to the Thirty-fourth *Reports of the Mission Among the Higher Classes in Shanghai*, passim; *The Open Court*, June, 1915, p. 384.
[225] The Door of Hope, *Annual Reports*, Shanghai, 1901 et seq.; *Of His Planting, A Retrospect of Ten Years' Work in the Door of Hope;* Burton, *Women Workers in the Orient*, p. 165.

traversed the streets. It was begun in 1913 by George Matheson, a business man, and was supported largely by the Shanghai foreign community. It aided the sick, organized classes for elementary education, provided meals and lodging, and conducted a Sunday School and other religious services. In time it extended its activities to Peking, Canton, Nanking, Foochow, and Hangchow.[226]

Another and again a very different kind of enterprise was the Yale Foreign Missionary Society. Incorporated in 1902, it was the outgrowth of the purpose of recent graduates of Yale to initiate a foreign missionary undertaking. The decision was early reached to choose a field of labor in China and to found an institution for higher education. Largely in response to an invitation of the 1902 conference of Protestant missionaries in Hunan, the new institution was established in Changsha, the capital of that province. The first representative, J. Lawrence Thurston, who had gone out in 1902, died after less than a year of service, and another early representative, W. B. Seabury, was accidentally drowned in 1907, but others were sent. In 1906 a secondary school was opened and before many years a hospital, a school for nurses, a medical school, and a college were added.[227]

This Yale undertaking was the largest but not the first of its kind, for the enterprises maintained by graduates of Trinity College, Dublin, in Fukien, and by the Oberlin Band in Shansi, both antedated it. It was, however, more nearly independent of any of the denominational boards than was either of these. The students and graduates of many other colleges and universities, almost all of them American, formed organizations to support representatives in China. Most of these organizations were connected with the Christian Association on the campus and in China assisted some existing board or institution. For example, a University of Pennsylvania group sent Dr. J. C. McCracken first to Canton Christian College and then to St. John's University to aid with medical education. The Princeton undertaking in Peking has already been mentioned. The Harvard Medical School in China, an enterprise begun about 1912, was merged later with the China Medical Board.[228] Most of the college and university

[226] Matheson in *Chinese Recorder*, Vol. 45, p. 525; *The Christian Occupation of China*, p. 368.

[227] *The Yale Mission, Changsha, China, Annual Reports;* Wright, *A Life with a Purpose*, passim; Seabury, *The Vision of a Short Life*, passim; W. H. Sallmon in *Christian Activity at Yale*, Vol. 3, Part 4, pp. 73 et seq.

[228] *Chinese Recorder*, Vol. 46, p. 699.

missions, as was natural, gave themselves exclusively to the task of education.

GEOGRAPHIC EXPANSION, 1901-1914: SUMMARY

Although the years after 1900 were not primarily characterized by pioneering in regions heretofore untouched by Protestants, they were, as we have suggested, by no means lacking in geographic expansion. The outlying dependencies were more continuously approached, and some of the provinces where before 1900 a foothold had barely been obtained were covered with a network of stations. In the provinces where missionaries had been longer at work, numbers of new residential centers were established, and many a town and hamlet which until now had seldom or never seen a foreigner was visited and made the location of a chapel and school. Whereas between 1807 and 1890 two hundred and seventy and between 1891 and 1900 inclusive two hundred and twenty-five mission stations had been opened,[229] in the decade following 1900 two hundred and seventy-four were established.[230] The greatest increase was in Hunan, Honan, Kwangtung, Chihli, Shantung, Kiangsi, Szechwan, and Hupeh.[231] In Hunan, for instance, where before 1900 Protestants had scarcely obtained a foothold, in 1904 twelve societies were represented,[232] and in 1903 it was reported that with one exception every *fu* city was either occupied or was about to be occupied by missionaries.[233] Kaifeng, Honan, the last provincial capital to admit the Protestant missionary, was entered in 1902.[234] Great numbers of accessions came from the non-Chinese peoples in Kweichow and Yünnan, and work for the aborigines was begun in other provinces.[235] A good deal was being said about making a special effort to reach the Moslems,[236] and the interest was stimulated by the early death of William W. Borden, who had planned to give his life to them and

[229] There might be more than one in a city, for the name is used to indicate a residence established by a missionary or missionaries of a given society.

[230] *The Christian Occupation of China*, p. 286. About 1909 Kwangtung had the largest number of mission stations, 56. Szechwan was second with 47, Fukien third with 42, Kiangsi fourth with 37, Shansi fifth with 35. Kweichow was nineteenth and Mongolia twentieth.—*Edinburgh Conference Reports*, Vol. 1, p. 90.

[231] *The Christian Occupation of China*, p. 286.

[232] *Missionary Review of the World*, Vol. 17, p. 47.

[233] Ibid., Vol. 16, p. 954.

[234] Cochrane, *Survey of the Missionary Occupation of China*, p. 256.

[235] Clarke, *Among the Tribes of S. W. China*, pp. 264-285; *China Mission Year Book, 1911*, pp. 206-214, *1915*, pp. 200-207.

[236] Broomhall, *Islam in China*, passim.

had died in Cairo (1913) while studying Arabic.[237]   There were a few missionaries in Mongolia,[238] some had entered the New Territory, [239] and an added number were on the marches of Tibet, trying to penetrate that great plateau.[240]

With all this activity, however, some of the extreme inland provinces continued to have a few Protestant missionaries.   In 1911 Chêkiang had one to about every 38,000 of the population, but Yünnan had only one to every 326,000 and Kweichow one to every 332,000.[241]   Kwangsi and Kansu were also almost without missionaries.[242]

Numbers of Missionaries

The total number of missionaries increased very rapidly, and that of Chinese employed by the missions still more so.   In 1889 1,296 Protestant missionaries had been reported.[243]   In 1905 the number had risen to 3,445, of whom 1,443 were men, 1,038 wives, and 964 unmarried women.[244]   In 1905 the Chinese staff of the Church numbered 9,904.[245]   In 1910, 5,144 missionaries were reported, and the Chinese staff had increased to 15,501.[246]   In 1914 the number of missionaries was said to be 5,462, of whom 53 were short term appointees, 2,143 were men, 1,652 wives, and 1,614 unmarried women.[247]

Protestant Missions and International and Internal Political Disturbances

This remarkable expansion of Protestant missions was stimulated rather than retarded by the external and internal political

[237] Mrs. Taylor, Borden of Yale, '09, passim.
[238] Hedley in China Centenary Missionary Conference Records, pp. 129, 130.
[239] China Mission Year Book, 1912, pp. 131-134.
[240] Ibid., p. 127; Edgar, The Marches of the Mantze, p. 4.
[241] China Mission Year Book, 1911, p. 193.
[242] Edinburgh Conference Reports, Vol. 1, pp. 99-101.
[243] Records of the Shanghai Conference, 1890, p. 732.
[244] A Century of Protestant Missions in China, Appendix II, p. 1, and Statistical Chart in front of p. 1.
[245] A Century of Protestant Missions in China, Appendix II, p. 1, and Statistical Chart in front of p. 1.
[246] China Mission Year Book, 1912, Statistical Chart.   About 1909 Kiangsu ranked first among the provinces in numbers of missionaries, having 503, Kwangtung came second with 471, Szechwan third with 386, Fukien fourth with 378, Yünnan eighteenth, Kweichow nineteenth, and Sinkiang twentieth.—World Missionary Conference, 1910, Reports, Vol. 1, p. 90.
[247] China Mission Year Book, 1915, p. xiv.

disturbances which marked the years between 1900 and 1914. The Russo-Japanese War brought a partial interruption of the regular activities in the zone of conflict, South Manchuria, but as a rule missionaries were permitted to remain and some of them opened hospitals and in other ways attempted to relieve the suffering brought by the struggle.[248] After peace had been declared the missions rapidly recovered and within three years the remarkable religious awakening which we have already noted had broken out.[249] Throughout the rest of China the war served to accentuate reform. The younger Chinese felt it a disgrace that foreign nations could fight over Chinese soil while the Chinese Government stood helplessly by. They listened eagerly to any who seemed to speak intelligently about this Western culture which had helped to make Japan powerful. Protestants were quick to see their opportunity and some of them began using as subjects for public addresses current events and the principles which they believed must underlie reform.[250] Since the missionary was frequently the only person from whom a knowledge of the West could be obtained, his utterances were often listened to with a new respect and his faith was sometimes regarded as part of that Western civilization from which China must learn if she were to be strong. The growing nationalism of the younger Chinese expressed itself in the slogan, "China for the Chinese," and here and there Chinese Christians began to ask for a larger share in the control of the Church.[251]

Even more marked in its effects was the Revolution of 1911 and the establishment of the Republic. During the Revolution disorder was frequent, not only because of the contending armies, but because the rougher elements took advantage of the weakness of the government to rob their weaker neighbors. Some mission work was interrupted, and, at the advice of the consuls, the wives and children of missionaries and many of the unmarried women

[248] Ibid., p. 254; *A Century of Protestant Missions in China*, pp. 211, 226. During the Russo-Japanese War an international Red Cross Society was formed in Shanghai for the relief of sufferers in Manchuria. Timothy Richard was foreign secretary. Over 500,000 taels were raised, chiefly from Chinese.—Reese, *Timothy Richard*, p. 126.

[249] Webster, *Times of Blessing in Manchuria*, passim.

[250] After the treaty of Portsmouth the Chinese pastor in a Peking church began weekly meetings for the discussion of current events, and Ament adopted somewhat similar tactics. Crowds of students came to listen.—Porter, *W. S. Ament*, p. 339.

[251] Porter, op. cit., p. 302.

took refuge in Shanghai and other places of safety.[252]   In Honan
a missionary and his wife were assailed by robbers.[253]   In Shantung
a number of Chinese Christians were killed—as adherents to the
new ideas—by members of reactionary societies, and others were
roughly handled by soldiers loyal to the old régime.[254]   In Kwangtung robbers and pirates increased,[255] and at several points on
the Yangtze mission activities were suspended.[256]   The most acute
disturbance to Protestant missions was in Shensi.   Here rowdies
and the Ko Lao Hui, or Ancient Society of Elder Brothers, attacked
foreigners as well as Manchus.   They may have believed that the
two were acting together, but their chief motive was probably
plunder.   In Hsianfu, on October 22, 1911, two adults, Mrs.
Beckman and Mr. Vatne, and six foreign children, all connected
with the Scandinavian Alliance Mission, were killed by a mob.
Elsewhere in the province at least one other station was looted
and some of the missionaries were roughly handled or escaped only
by going into hiding.   A group of nine young foreigners left
Peking in November and brought to Hsianfu and thence to the
coast a number of the endangered Westerners.   Throughout
China, however, most of the missionaries remained at their posts.
In one city they climbed over the wall mornings and evenings to
keep their school going, and in other centers they endured hardships and danger to continue their work and to relieve the distressed.   Occasionally, moreover, they mediated between the
revolutionaries and officials of the old régime, and they saved the
lives of many Manchus.[257]   Even in Shensi some stayed on to

[252] In Hwochow in Shansi the missionaries closed their schools and sent the
children home, for they feared disorder, and the British Minister ordered all
women and children to the coast.—Cable, *The Fulfillment of a Dream*, pp. 189-195.
The American Board reported that its work, especially its school work, had been
interrupted.—*Annual Report of the American Board* (1912), pp. 110-113.   All
the missionaries of the Augustana Synod had to leave their stations.—Augustana
Synod, *Our First Decade in China, 1905-1915*, p. 81.   The Disciples missionaries
had to leave Batang on the Tibetan frontier.—Mrs. Shelton, *Sunshine and Shadow
on the Tibetan Border*, pp. 133-136.
[253] Beckman, *The Massacre at Sianfu*, pp. 117, 118.
[254] Scott, *China from Within*, pp. 199-209, 255.
[255] *Ninety-Eighth Report of the Wesleyan Methodist Missionary Society*,
pp. 2, 132, 133.
[256] Ibid.
[257] Keyte, *The Passing of the Dragon*, deals chiefly with events in Shensi at the
time of the Revolution.   So does Beckman (a survivor of the massacre), *The
Massacre at Sianfu*.   See also Hawes, *New Thrills in Old China*, p. 220; Keyte,
Andrew Young of Shensi, pp. 32 et seq., Meyer, *Memorial of Cecil Robertson of
Sianfu*, pp. 52, 71; Broomhall, *Jubilee Story of the China Inland Mission*, p. 323;
Borst-Smith, *Mandarin and Missionary in Cathay*, pp. 111-119; Glover, *Herbert
Stanley Jenkins*, pp. 99-103; Borst-Smith, *Caught in the Chinese Revolution*,
passim.

minister to the wounded and to those Manchus who survived the massacres.

The interruption was only temporary. Both Manchus and revolutionists were eager not to offend the foreigner for fear that the Western powers would support their opponents. The revolutionists especially were friendly to the missionaries and their converts. Through their connection with the Church, Protestant Christians had imbibed a desire for change and their sympathies were usually with the new régime. Some of the chief radicals were Protestants and the outstanding ones were usually favorable to Christianity. Sun Yat-sen, more than any other responsible for the movement leading to the Republic, the idol of the Republicans, and the Provisional President, had, as we have seen, received much of his education at the hands of Protestants in Honolulu, was known to be a Christian, and had been baptized in 1884 while living on the premises of the American Board Mission in Hongkong.[258] Many Protestant Christians were active in the new government, especially in Kwangtung.[259] One of the most prominent of the Republican generals, Huang Hsing, is reported by Bishop Bashford to have said to the latter in response to an inquiry as to what cause the revolutionary leaders attributed the fall of city after city and province after province before their forces:

"To Christianity more than to any other single cause. . . . Christianity is far more widespread than you missionaries realize. Its ideals have largely pervaded China. Along with its ideals of religious freedom it brings a knowledge of Western political freedom, and along with these

[258] Sun Yat-sen's father seems not to have been a Christian nor to have been in the employ of the London Missionary Society, as is said in Cantlie and Jones, *Sun Yat Sen and the Awakening of China*, pp. 36, 37. An article by Hager, who knew Sun Yat-sen in his youth in Hongkong, from about 1883 on, in the *North American Student*, May, 1913 (reprinted in *Spirit of Missions*, Vol. 78, pp. 385 et seq.) says that Sun obtained his first acquaintance with Christianity in Honolulu, where he was a student in a Christian school, that he was baptized in Hongkong in 1884, and was for a time an ardent preacher of Christianity. See also the somewhat imaginative biography by Linebarger, *Sun Yat Sen and the Chinese Republic*, pp. 123, 152, 153, etc., and Mathews-Hough, *The Call of China and the Islands*, pp. 21 et seq.

[259] *Ninety-Eighth Report of the Wesleyan Methodist Missionary Society*, pp. 132, 133. In 1912 in Kwangtung sixty-five per cent of the provincial officials were Christians or had been in mission schools.—*China Mission Year Book, 1912*, p. 97; see also Edmunds, *Canton Christian College*, p. 9. Professor Chung of Canton Christian College was commissioner of education for Kwangtung.— Mathews-Hough, *The Call of China and the Islands*, p. 28. Half the young men in the offices of the new government in Wuchang were said to be Christians or in sympathy with Christianity.—Macfarlane in *China Mission Year Book, 1912*, p. 107. In 1912 three members of the Cabinet were said to be decided Christians.— *International Review of Missions*, Vol. 2, p. 18.

it inculcates everywhere a doctrine of universal love and peace. These ideals appeal to the Chinese; they largely caused the Revolution and they largely determined its peaceful character." [260]

Li Yüan-hung, the Vice-President, is quoted as saying: "China would not be aroused today as it is were it not for the missionaries." [261]

Just how accurately these words reproduce the real convictions of the speakers is hard to say, and it is even more difficult to determine how far they accord with the facts. [262] That Protestant missionaries had some part in disseminating ideals of democracy cannot be denied. An important phase of their message was the value of the individual, the polity of many of their churches was democratic, the textbooks in their schools were often permeated with democratic teachings, and without having set out deliberately to alter the government, for several generations they had been spreading ideas which were revolutionary in character. Certainly many thoughtful Chinese, in facing the new day brought by the Revolution, looked hopefully toward Christianity as a possible source of the moral and spiritual dynamic which they believed to be needed if the nation was to pass safely through the period of reconstruction. [263] The Confucian tradition had led the educated to believe that the basis of every stable government must be moral, the older religious and moral systems of China were in some quarters discredited, and many of the Chinese were willing to examine Christianity to see whether it had something better to offer.

Whatever the motives and causes, the Revolution inaugurated a period of unprecedented open-mindedness to the Christian message and of friendliness to the messengers. Republican leaders ordered the protection of foreigners in general and of missionaries in particular. [264] Red Cross units, with their striking use of the

[260] Bashford in *China Mission Year Book, 1913*, p. 95. Lanning, superintendent of the public schools of the International Settlement in Shanghai, in *Old Forces in New China*, pp. 17 et seq., says that to missionaries "is due the new desire which is already reënergizing the old forces."

[261] Brown, *The Mastery of the Far East*, p. 476.

[262] As an interesting bit of evidence it is reported that the translation of Henry George's *Progress and Poverty*, by Dr. Macklin, of the Foreign Christian Missionary Society, had come into the hands of the reformers and was particularly appreciated by Sun Yat-sen.—Thomson, *China Revolutionized*, p. 13.

[263] Bashford gives a number of these incidents in *China Mission Year Book, 1913*. pp. 95-97.

[264] Thomson, *China Revolutionized*, p. 49.

Christian emblem, were organized by the Chinese. They frequently requested the coöperation of missionary physicians and here and there were under their direction.[265] In Yangchow, less than fifty years before the scene of the famous riot against the China Inland Mission, after the Revolution the chief magistrate asked Christian preachers to address his troops.[266] Officials often sought the advice of missionaries and Chinese pastors about methods of government.[267] Inquirers multiplied, in some places so rapidly that missionaries were unable to deal adequately with them.[268] Bible classes sprang up and the sales of Christian literature rose.[269] Sun Yat-sen spoke in the Presbyterian Church in Tsingtau,[270] Yüan Shih-k'ai received the delegates of the China Medical Missionary Association at their triennial meeting[271] and Sherwood Eddy during the latter's meetings in 1914, and was a contributor to the Young Men's Christian Association.[272] Li Yüan-hung expressed himself as strongly in favor of more missionaries coming to China.[273] During the course of his evangelistic campaign in 1914, Sherwood Eddy was given a hearing by governors and other officials, one of his interpreters was a grandson of the famous Tsêng Kuo-fan, and among the converts were the Salt Commissioner of Fukien and the Commissioner of Foreign Affairs of Chêkiang. In Peking the pavilion for Eddy's meetings was erected in the Forbidden City and covered with tents loaned by the Ministry of War, and the Ministry of Education declared a half-holiday to enable students to attend.[274] Most interesting of all the evidences of official favor was the setting aside of April

---

[265] Dr. Booth, in Hankow, was an officer of the Red Cross Society and his hospital was protected by the imperialists and was almost unharmed when Hankow burned.—Tatchell, *Booth of Hankow*, pp. 83 et seq. In Mukden Dr. Christie was director of the Red Cross.—Robertson, *Our Mission in Manchuria*, p. 108. The Chinese Red Cross and Vice-President Li Yüan-hung gave medals to Miss Cody of the American Baptists for her help as a nurse during the Revolution.—Cody, *Letters to Betsey*, p. 201.

[266] Pott, *The Emergency in China*, p. 202; A. R. Saunders in *Chinese Recorder*, 1913, p. 94; Broomhall, *Jubilee Story of the China Inland Mission*, p. 62.

[267] *China Mission Year Book*, 1914, p. 111.

[268] Various instances of this popularity of Christianity are in the *China Mission Year Book*, 1912, pp. 101 et seq., 1913, pp. 166, 167, 270-280, 1915, pp. 268, 348, 1917, p. 87; *Missionary Review of the World*, Vol. 23, p. 129; Borst-Smith, *Mandarin and Missionary in Cathay*, pp. 129-133.

[269] *China Mission Year Book*, 1913, pp. 166, 167.

[270] *Report of Presbyterian Board* (North), 1913.

[271] Broomhall, *Jubilee Story of the China Inland Mission*, p. 342.

[272] Eddy, *How China's Leaders Received the Gospel*, p. 5.

[273] Brown, *The Mastery of the Far East*, p. 476.

[274] Eddy, op. cit., passim.

27th, 1913, by the Cabinet as a day of prayer in which Christians were asked to meet and offer petitions for the new government. In response to the appeal, services were held throughout the Republic and in many churches in Europe and America.[275] In 1913 the Temple of Heaven in Peking was used for a series of evangelistic addresses.[276]

From this popularity a reaction was almost inevitable. It did not come in full force until after 1922, but by 1914 indications were appearing of a waning of the first enthusiasms. From several places a Buddhist revival was reported.[277] Attempts were made, too, to restore Confucianism to its old status. A Confucian society was formed in Peking, partly at the instance of Ch'ên Huan-chang, and agitation was begun to place in the new constitution a provision making Confucianism the state religion.[278] In June, 1913, the President, Yüan Shih-k'ai, urged the study of the Classics. In 1914 he came out in favor of the usual honors to Confucius and officiated at them in the temple in Peking. He also reconstituted the sacrifices at the Altar of Heaven at the winter solstice.[279] Chinese students, moreover, were reading sceptical literature from the West and were beginning to question all religions and to show marked tendencies toward a materialistic philosophy and religious indifferentism.[280] Then, too, peace did not come permanently with the abdication of the Manchus. The "Second Revolution"—

[275] *China Mission Year Book, 1913*, pp. 40-42; *1917*, p. 131; *International Review of Missions*, Vol. 3, p. 13; Wallace, *The New Life in China*, p. 84; *Chinese Recorder*, Vol. 44, p. 359; *99th Report of the Wesleyan Methodist Missionary Society*, p. 123; *100th Report* of ibid., p. 136; *North China Herald*, May 3, 1913, p. 305.

[276] *China Mission Year Book, 1914*, p. 137; Broomhall, *Jubilee Story of the China Inland Missions*, p. 325; *International Review of Missions*, Vol. 3, p. 15.

The churches in Europe and America responded to the new opportunity with reënforcements to the missionary body and with somewhat larger gifts of money, but were not as awake to the situation as missionary leaders desired.—*International Review of Missions*, Vol. 2, p. 16. As an Imperial Jubilee gift in behalf of missions in German protectorates, £245,000 was raised by the German public to be expended through existing missionary agencies, partly on the ground that "colonizing means missionizing."—Ibid.

[277] In Canton and Fukien,—*China Mission Year Book, 1914*, pp. 133-136, 387; in Yünnan,—*North China Herald*, March 15, 1913, p. 807; in Manchuria and Shantung,—*Allgemeine Missionszeitschrift*, Vol. 42, p. 502.

[278] H. K. Wright in *China Mission Year Book, 1914*, pp. 61-72; Ch'ên Huan-chang, *Economic Principles of Confucianism and His School*, passim; *101st Report of Wesleyan Methodist Missionary Society*, p. 119.

[279] H. K. Wright in *China Mission Year Book, 1914*, pp. 61-72; *100th Report of the Wesleyan Methodist Missionary Society*, pp. 122-124.

[280] *China Mission Year Book, 1911*, pp. 117-126, *1914*, p. 189; *North China Herald*, June 21, 1913, p. 857; ibid., Jan. 11, 1913, p. 74.

the expedition launched against Yüan Shih-k'ai in 1913 [281]—led to grave disorder and in 1913 and 1914 a notorious bandit, "The White Wolf," held Honan and some adjoining districts in terror.[282]

In spite of untoward circumstances which in places seemed to nullify the expectations aroused by the Revolution, the populace remained open-minded, great throngs came to hear Christian addresses, and applications for Church membership continued to increase.[283]   Popularity was not without its dangers.   Some Chinese became adherents because they believed the Church to be a useful agency for social and political reform, and acquired only an imperfect knowledge of the real message of the Church.   Missionaries were tempted to present Christianity as a panacea for China's political, social, and economic woes—an approach especially attractive because the missionary himself felt the gravity of the troubles about him, because it was of social and political needs that the Chinese were the most conscious, and because Confucianism led the nation to look upon religion as a means of saving society.   Some of the fundamentals of the Christian message might be minimized or ignored, however, hopes be awakened which could not quickly be realized, and disillusion bring loss.[284]

RIOTS, PERSECUTIONS, AND RELATIONS TO THE GOVERNMENT, 1901-1914

It must not be thought that because the old opposition to Christianity had weakened it had disappeared, or that the relations of missionaries to the government were entirely smooth.   Christianity was still an alien faith and missionaries and the Church remained under the protection of treaties.

Protestant missionaries, to be sure, continued to disclaim any authority in litigation, asked that in the courts Church members be

[281] Bashford in *China Mission Year Book, 1914*, pp. 37 et seq.; P. F. Price in ibid., pp. 110-115.

[282] *Annual Report of the American Bible Society*, 1915, p. 400; Borst-Smith, *Mandarin and Missionary in Cathay*, pp. 184-198; *China Mission Year Book, 1917*, p. 122; Broomhall, *Jubilee Story of the China Inland Mission*, p. 329.

[283] *Annual Report of the A. B. C. F. M.*, 1915, p. 157; Broomhall, op. cit., p. 326; *China Mission Year Book, 1917*, pp. 164 et seq.; Bishop Huntington, of Anking, in *The East and the West*, 1914, pp. 137-144; *International Review of Missions*, Vol. 4, p. 371; *British and Foreign Bible Society, Report for year ending March, 1914*, p. 321.

[284] This danger was recognized.   See article by Nelson Bitton in *The East and the West*, 1912, pp. 441-448.

treated exactly as were other subjects of the realm,[285] and forbade to Christians the use of the name of the Church or its officers when appearing before officials.[286]   In 1903 the British Minister issued a circular instructing consuls that in cases of persecution the missionaries were to take action through them and not go directly to the Chinese authorities.[287]   In Manchuria the Presbyterian mission ruled that no one known to be a party in an impending lawsuit was to be enrolled as an enquirer.[288]   The fact remained, however, that missionaries and their converts enjoyed a privileged status, and until the treaties were amended unworthy motives would move some Chinese to seek the shelter of the Church. Missionaries clearly recognized this unhappy situation[289] and reported that bodies falsely calling themselves churches had been formed to obtain the advantages accruing from the Christian connection.[290]   Most missionaries, however, believed that the time had not yet come for the annulment of the special protection guaranteed by the treaties,[291] and the missionary conference held in Shanghai in 1907 put itself officially on record as being of this opinion.[292]   Missionaries, moreover, continued to appeal to their consuls for aid in settling difficulties over the title to property they had purchased or leased.[293]

Under these circumstances it is not surprising that the Chinese Government still regarded the missionary and his converts as annoying.   It had to protect them, and in 1907 an edict was issued reiterating the duty of all officials to observe the treaties.[294]   However, while the government was not in a position to attempt the drastic curtailment of ecclesiastical privileges which it had desired a generation before, in 1911 the Wai Wu Pu issued regulations for the purchase of property by missions.[295]   It was reported that in government schools Christian students were compelled to par-

---

[285] Cornaby in *The Call of Cathay*, p. 102, says that in 1902 a missionary association took such action.
[286] Brown, *New Forces in Old China*, p. 233.
[287] Morse, *Trade and Administration of China*, pp. 430, 431; Hertslet, *China Treaties*, p. 1181.
[288] Graham, *East of the Barrier*, p. 69.
[289] *Edinburgh Conference Reports*, Vol. 2, p. 88.
[290] Ibid., Vol. 1, p. 95.
[291] *Edinburgh Conference Reports*, Vol. 7, pp. 8-15.
[292] *China Centenary Missionary Conference Records*, p. 722.
[293] Morse, *Trade and Administration of China*, p. 422.
[294] Bashford, *Journal*, Oct. 10, 1907.
[295] Sze, *China and the Most-Favored-Nation Clause*, p. 210.   (Quoting *Chinese Ministry of Foreign Affairs Red Book*, Oct., 1911.)

ticipate in ceremonies which violated their consciences,[296] and in 1909 and 1910 graduates of mission schools were denied admission to the newly organized provincial assemblies.[297] The Wai Wu Pu forbade any Chinese to organize an independent church.[298] Only a few years before the downfall of the Manchu dynasty, Confucius was elevated to the first rank in the official pantheon,[299] being declared the equal of Heaven and Earth.

In 1910, however, Chinese Christian leaders took preliminary steps toward an effort to have religious liberty written into the proposed constitution of China.[300] Then came the Revolution, with its temporary reaction against the old religions. The provisional constitution of the Republic accorded liberty of conscience and Yüan Shih-k'ai expressed himself as favoring the same policy.[301] To the movement to recognize Confucianism as the official religion [302] strong opposition was offered by Christians, both Protestant and Roman Catholic, and by representatives of some of the other faiths, and the project failed of ratification.[303]

The years between 1901 and 1914 witnessed little open or severe persecution of Protestants. In August, 1902, two British missionaries, J. R. Bruce and R. H. Lewis, were killed in Ch'enchow, Hunan, because of a popular rumor that a cholera epidemic was due to poison which they had distributed under the guise of medicine.[304] In 1902 a revival of the Boxer movement was reported in Szechwan and some Protestants were killed.[305] Petty persecution of Christians was frequently reported.[306] The anti-American boycott of 1905, brought on by resentment against the exclusion laws of the United States, led for a time to increased suspicion of American missionaries.[307] On October 28, 1905, Rev. and Mrs. John Peale, Dr. Eleanor Chesnut, and Mrs. Mackle and her daughter, all of the American Presbyterian Mission, were

---

[296] *Edinburgh Conference Reports,* Vol. 7, p. 19.
[297] Brown, *Report on a Second Visit to China,* pp. 110, 111.
[298] *Missionary Review of the World,* Vol. 22 (new series), p. 803.
[299] Soothill, *The Three Religions of China,* p. 34.
[300] *China Mission Year Book, 1917,* p. 297.
[301] Ibid., *1913,* p. 442.
[302] Ibid., *1914,* p. 30; Oldham in *International Review of Missions,* Vol. 3, p. 17; Oldham, *The Missionary Situation After the War,* p. 25.
[303] *Chinese Recorder,* Vol. 49, p. 687; Scott in *The East and the West,* Vol. 15, pp. 401-404.
[304] Conger in *Foreign Relations, 1902,* p. 174.
[305] Wallace, *The Heart of Sz-chuan,* pp. 89-91; Smith, *Rex Christus,* p. 213.
[306] *Chinese Recorder,* Vol. 35, p. 28.
[307] Martin, *The Awakening of China,* p. 248.

killed by a mob in Lienchow, Kwangtung.[308]   In February, 1906, some Protestants perished in Nanch'ang in an uprising which was directed chiefly against Roman Catholics.[309]   That same month the plant of the English Presbyterians in Chiangpoo, in Fukien, was looted by a mob whose animus was chiefly against the Roman Catholics.[310]   In April, 1910, Changsha and the surrounding country were the scene of anti-official riots and while no foreigners lost their lives more damage was wrought to mission property than in any disturbance in the preceding nine years.[311]   Three of the heaviest sufferers, the Wesleyan Missionary Society, the China Inland Mission, and the London Missionary Society, declined any indemnity.[312]   In 1910 a rebellion in the southwestern part of Yünnan placed missionaries and their converts in danger,[313] and in 1913 robbers attacked a party of Canadian Methodist missionaries in Szechwan.[314]   In 1913 there was local persecution in a village in Hunan.[315]   In 1912 and 1913, the destruction of mission property, the murder of Christians, and the occupation of a chapel by troops were reported from Kwangtung, but these unfortunate incidents were due more to the general disorder than to any marked anti-Christian sentiment.[316]   Even when there are added the losses due to the unrest attending the Revolution, missionaries met with surprisingly little interference.   The treaties, the severe punishment meted out for the Boxer outbreak, and the friendliness of the reformers united to place Christians, both foreign and Chinese, in a position of privileged security.

[308] *Report of the Presbyterian Board, 1906*, p. 11; *Missionary Review of the World*, Vol. 19, p. 87.   The missionaries asked $52,786.40 indemnity for the loss of foreign property, and $9,057.86 for the loss of Chinese property.   The United States legation asked 50,000 taels for the next of kin of those murdered. The Chinese Government paid 46,129.65 taels for the property destroyed and 50,000 taels for indemnity for the lives lost.—*Foreign Relations*, 2d session, 59th Congress, pp. 308-323.
[309] Smith, *The Uplift of China*, p. 193; Thomson, *The Chinese*, p. 367.
[310] Pitcher, *In and About Amoy*, p. 164; Pitcher in *Chinese Recorder*, Vol. 37, p. 172.
[311] Brown, *Report on a Second Visit to China*, 1909, pp. 110, 111; *Twenty-seventh Report of the Wesleyan Methodist Missionary Society*, p. 137; *China Mission Year Book, 1911*, pp. 63-65.
[312] *China Mission Year Book, 1911*, p. 23.   Various opinions about the propriety of accepting indemnities existed in the missionary body.—*Chinese Recorder*, Vol. 33, pp. 49, 217.
[313] Dingle, *Across China on Foot*, pp. 110-125.
[314] Sir John Jordan to Sir Edward Grey in *Parliamentary Papers*, China No. 1, p. 3.
[315] *China Mission Year Book, 1914*, p. 186.
[316] *Report of the Presbyterian Board, 1912*, p. 125; *Ninety-ninth Report of the Wesleyan Methodist Missionary Society*, p. 125.

CHAPTER XXVI

GENERAL CHARACTERISTICS

THE changed situation which followed the Boxer uprising led to an extensive modification of the methods of Protestant missionaries. No sudden break was made with the past. Foreigners and their Chinese assistants continued to traverse the countryside proclaiming their message, the mission station remained the center from which radiated the activities of the Church, and the instruction given to converts and the requirements for baptism were not greatly altered. The preparation and distribution of literature and the establishment and maintenance of schools and hospitals were now, as formerly, major features of the missionary program, and many attempts were made to relieve the suffering and to attack the vices which the Christian saw about him.

However, important innovations were introduced. In general, the missionary was able to undertake activities on a larger scale than formerly would have been dreamed possible. As we have seen, the foreigner was dominant in China and the Chinese were attempting to learn from him, Europe and America were at peace and were more prosperous than they ever had been, and contributions to missions, while only the merest fraction of the income of the membership of Protestant churches, were rapidly increasing. The far-sighted among the missionaries knew that conditions could not always remain so favorable and strained every nerve to take advantage of them. The result was the rapid expansion of all phases of Protestant activities.

Particularly marked were the rise of institutions and the additions to equipment. Church buildings, missionaries' residences, and especially schools and hospitals were erected on a far larger scale than the Chinese Christian community could hope to finance for years to come. The dangers were obvious. In the first place, the self-support of the Church was postponed. In the second place, it would be long before enough Chinese leaders of ability could be developed to conduct these institutions as efficiently as could foreigners. In the third place, foreign subventions and direction might postpone the time when the Church would cease to be alien, and so Protestant Christianity might suffer severely and even disappear before a strong wave of nationalism. In the fourth place, there was the possibility that Protestant Christianity would be swamped by institutions, that the energies of missionaries and Chinese Christians would be absorbed in the machinery of organization, and that the Church would forget that its primary function was to serve as a vehicle for a religious and spiritual message. This was especially perilous in China, where the dominant philosophic tradition conceived of religion as primarily concerned with relations of men to each other and minimized man's relations to God. Since this latter was the wellspring of Jesus' whole life, Christianity was in danger of being denatured. This tendency was reënforced by the fact that institutions more and more demanded specialists—teachers, nurses, and physicians —whose professional training had crowded out careful preparation in theology, philosophy, the Bible, and kindred subjects. Protestantism was threatened with secularization. In defence it could be urged that the time of opportunity might be short, and that only by great institutions could Christianity quickly make an impression upon the nation and train up leaders who could carry on when the hour of the foreigner had passed.

THE PROPAGATION OF THE FAITH BY PERSONAL CONTACTS, PUBLIC ADDRESSES, AND BIBLE CLASSES

In spite of the emphasis on institutions, many of the former methods of approaching non-Christians were still employed. The use of portions of the Gospel and other printed material, the informal address wherever a group could be induced to listen, meetings in the homes of Christians, calls on individuals, the street chapel, and the regular services of the Church were all continued.[1] In spite of an increasing diversification in methods, more missionaries were engaged in what was called evangelistic work than in any other one activity.

[1] *China Mission Year Book, 1914,* pp. 128-132, 137-141.

Important changes were, however, in progress. Protestant institutions were more and more being developed for other purposes than imparting directly to individuals a knowledge of the Christian message. As Timothy Richard pointed out, there were two ways of regarding the Gospel: as a means of saving the soul of each individual, and as a means of saving a nation through the collective efforts of regenerated souls.[2] The majority of the earlier missionaries conceived of their task in terms of the former alternative. Now, with the opportunity to help mold the new culture, an increasing number held that their function was in part, and perhaps chiefly, the latter. This change of emphasis was made easier by the fact that in many places the missionary was the only representative of that West to which the Chinese were now going to school, and by the Chinese tradition of emphasizing the social values of religion and philosophy. Moreover, the missionary believed that he must devote an increasing proportion of his energy to the training of Chinese Christian leaders.

As a result of these changes, by 1911 less than half the total missionary staff was engaged in direct evangelistic work and the proportion would have been still smaller had not the great majority of the members of the China Inland Mission—which had in China more missionaries than any other society—been in that type of activity.[3] American missions were especially affected, for in their hands was centered the larger part of the medical, social, and higher educational work of Protestants.[4] Even of those supposedly set aside for evangelism, many could give but little time to personal contacts with the Chinese, for the care of churches already organized and the operation of the rapidly increasing machinery of missions absorbed much of their energy.[5]

In theory practically all missionaries believed that the purpose of the Church had not been fulfilled until every individual had been given an opportunity intelligently to consider the Christian message. New plans were devised for achieving this end.[6] Mention has already been made of the religious awakening which, beginning about 1908, spread from Korea through Manchuria into China Proper. An earlier revival began in Weihsien in Shantung

[2] Timothy Richard in *Chinese Recorder*, Vol. 32, p. 124.
[3] *China Mission Year Book, 1911*, p. 355.
[4] Ross, *The Changing Chinese*, p. 224.
[5] *China Mission Year Book, 1910*, p. 185.
[6] *China Centenary Missionary Conference Records*, pp. 522-551.

in 1905 [7] and extended to adjoining regions.   Under its impulse
Chinese Christians became more active in seeking to win non-
Christians, and thronged meetings and remarkable conversions
were reported.[8]   The Centenary Missionary Conference (1907),
the successor of the gatherings of 1877 and 1890, devoted much
attention to the propagation of the Faith,[9] and out of it arose an
Evangelistic Association which in 1910 held in Hankow what was
called its first triennial meeting.   At the Hankow gathering plans
were enthusiastically proposed for reaching more effectively all
parts of the nation, including the rural districts and cities, for the
establishment of training schools for Chinese evangelists, and for
the holding of evangelistic meetings.[10]   In connection with it
special addresses were given for students in the government
schools of the vicinity.[11]

Mention has already been made of the meetings, chiefly for
students, officials, and other members of the influential classes,
held under the Young Men's Christian Association in 1907, 1911,
1913, 1914, and 1915 and addressed by John R. Mott and George
Sherwood Eddy.   These stimulated similar efforts.   In 1913 the
Protestant missions in Changsha united in meetings in the churches
and in the largest hall in the city.[12]   In 1914, partly in conjunction
with the campaigns conducted in Foochow and Amoy by Mr.
Eddy, series of lectures were given in eleven other cities of Fukien:
as a result over eight thousand enrolled in Bible classes for further
Christian instruction and nearly half of these were in attendance
for three months.[13]

These were not the only attempts to approach the educated.
In 1902 eighteen thousand portions of Scripture were distributed
in Chengtu among the candidates for degrees as they were leaving
the examination halls.[14]   In Hongkong in connection with the
university a hostel was built by two societies in which students
could reside and be brought under Christian influences.[15]   In

[7] Hawes, *New Thrills in Old China*, p. 152.
[8] Peill, *The Beloved Physician of Tsangchow*, pp. 232 et seq.; Porter, *W. S. Ament*, p. 309.
[9] *China Centenary Missionary Conference Records*, pp. 522-551.
[10] *Report of the Presbyterian Board, 1911*, p. 22; *Chinese Recorder*, Vol. 41, p. 37, Vol. 42, p. 151; *China Mission Year Book, 1911*, p. 368.
[11] H. A. Moran in *Foreign Mail*, Vol. 18, No. 2, p. 1.
[12] *One Hundredth Report of the Wesleyan Methodist Missionary Society*, p. 137.
[13] E. H. Munson in *China Mission Year Book, 1915*, pp. 144-160; Stock, *History of the Church Missionary Society*, Vol. 4, p. 290.
[14] Wallace, *The Heart of Sz-chuan*, p. 157.
[15] Cochrane, *Survey of the Missionary Occupation of China*, p. 21.

spite of these and of other endeavors, however, most of the members of the upper classes remained untouched by the Christian message and it is doubtful whether more than a small minority had an intelligent knowledge of its content.

The women of the higher classes were even less familiar with the missionary's message. Women missionaries were reaching their sisters of the middle classes,[16] but the wives and daughters of scholars and officials were but little approached.[17]

A few other methods of evangelism must be noted. In Mongolia the Scandinavian Missionary Alliance conducted a farm colony in which the Mongols were encouraged to begin a settled life under Christian influences.[18] Shortly before the Revolution a tent was set up at T'aianfu, Shantung, to present the Christian message to pilgrims on their way to T'ai Shan.[19] Before many years special efforts were begun to reach the pilgrims at Nan Yo, or the "Southern Peak," in Hunan. Mention has already been made of the methods of Watts O. Pye of the American Board in Shansi and Shensi. The American Baptist Foreign Mission Society, in place of its earlier policy of attempting to reach immediately many cities and villages with a somewhat superficial account of the Christian message, in 1912 adopted a program of concentrating on a few centers and there establishing and nourishing strong churches with competent Chinese leaders. The hope was that in time these would evangelize the districts in which they were situated.[20]

A notable modification was made in the form in which the Christian message was put. In some of the meetings most thronged by the leading classes, notably those conducted by Eddy, the Gospel was presented as a means of national regeneration. "What will save China?" was a question uppermost in the minds of thoughtful men and with it the addresses were introduced. Sometimes, to make it more poignant, the speaker first depicted the unhappy condition of the country. The fundamental cause of China's misfortunes was then declared to be moral and spiritual, and the Christian Gospel was presented as possessing the

[16] *Edinburgh Conference Reports*, Vol. 1, p. 91.
[17] *Spirit of Missions*, Vol. 67, p. 402. In some places women of the higher classes were being reached.—*China Mission Year Book, 1912*, pp. 144-152; *Chinese Recorder*, Vol. 44, p. 478.
[18] Cochrane, op. cit., p. 334.
[19] *China Mission Year Book, 1911*, p. 432.
[20] *China Mission Year Book, 1916*, pp. 65-68.

dynamic necessary for healing.[21]   This form of presentation was not without its dangers.   Some Chinese, impatient for immediate results, eventually turned against Christianity as having failed to save the Occident from war, moral corruption, and industrial injustice, and as having brought no solution for China's problems.   By no means all missionaries, however, used this approach. Probably the majority still strove to create in their hearers a sense of personal guilt and emphasized the Gospel as a means of the present and eternal salvation of the individual.

EDUCATION

While innovations were being introduced in the presentation of the Christian message, it was in education that the most marked developments occurred.   For the time being the Protestant missionary had almost a monopoly of the best schools in which the much desired Western learning could be acquired.   Government and private agencies, to be sure, opened institutions which in total attendance and budget surpassed any system of education that the missionary could hope to create.[22]   Many youths, too, went to Japan, Europe, and the United States—the largest student migration of history.[23]   However, in China trained teachers were not immediately to be had, and in government and private schools standards were usually low and discipline poor.   Institutions organized by missionaries usually offered better instruction, stricter discipline, and often more adequate equipment than any others in the neighborhood.   In Protestant schools, moreover, English could be learned much more quickly and accurately than anywhere else in the country.   That language was in great demand, both among those who desired positions in the post office, the customs service, and foreign firms, and among those who wished to pursue their studies in Western science, history, or philosophy.[24]

[21] Eddy, *How China's Leaders Received the Gospel*, pp. 10-15; Eddy, *The Students of Asia*, p. 83.
[22] In 1908, 1,013,571 students were reported in government schools and in 1910, 1,284,965.—*China Mission Year Book, 1911*, p. 79.   See also ibid., p. 136.
[23] In 1907 there were said to be 15,000 or more Chinese students in Japan, but by the end of 1910 the number sank to about 2,000.—C. T. Wang in *China Mission Year Book, 1913*, pp. 342-349.   The estimate of 15,000 for 1907 may have been excessive.   In 1907 the Chinese minister at Tokyo told Professor Harlan P. Beach that a careful census he had taken showed the number to be slightly over 13,000 and that some one was profiting by the sums paid for the remaining 2,000.—Letter of H. P. Beach to the author, Aug., 1927.
[24] *Chinese Recorder*, Vol. 40, p. 109; *Edinburgh Conference Reports*, Vol. 3, pp. 91-96.

In this situation Protestant missionaries saw an unexampled opportunity.[25] Through schools they could educate the Christian community and leaders for the Church, so enabling these more quickly to influence the entire country, and they could reach with the Christian message a fair proportion of those who were to reshape China.[26] Because of their freedom from government control, moreover, they could experiment and blaze new trails in education.[27] They realized that the schools established by the government and other secular agencies would claim an ever-increasing majority of the students and soon would be equal and perhaps superior in equipment to those maintained by the Church.[28] Accordingly they made every endeavor to take advantage of the opening while it was theirs.

A phenomenal growth ensued. In 1877, 5,917 pupils had been reported in mission schools.[29] In 1889 the number had risen to 16,836,[30] in 1911 it was 102,533,[31] and in 1915, 169,707.[32] The increased relative emphasis upon education is partly disclosed by a comparison with the number of Protestant Christians. While the communicant membership mounted rapidly, from 13,035 in 1877[33] to 37,287 in 1889[34] and to 268,652 in 1915,[35] and the number of baptized Christians—a more inclusive figure—was 195,-905 in 1910[36] and 331,000 in 1915,[37] the proportion of pupils to communicant members was forty-five per cent. in both 1877 and 1889, and sixty-four per cent. in 1915. In 1910 the number of pupils was fifty per cent. of that of baptized Christians and in 1915 sixty per cent. This expansion was paralleled and in part made possible by the changed attitude of the Chinese. Mission

[25] Bishop C. P. Scott in *The East and the West,* Vol. 7, pp. 153-161.
[26] *Edinburgh Conference Reports,* Vol. 3, pp. 65-72. It was held that the purpose of Christian education in China was: (1) provision for an educated ministry; (2) raising up Christian laymen; (3) educating the rank and file of the Church to make them more responsive to more highly educated leaders ("In a country like China a church of ignorant men cannot hope to have influence"); (4) the evangelization of non-Christians; (5) the spread of general enlightenment and a manifestation of the philanthropic spirit of Christianity.
[27] G. A. Stuart in *Records of the Sixth Triennial Meeting of the Educational Association of China,* p. 4.
[28] Bashford in *China Centenary Missionary Conference Records,* p. 484.
[29] *Records of the Missionary Conference, Shanghai, 1877,* p. 486.
[30] *Records of the Shanghai Missionary Conference, 1890,* p. 433.
[31] *China Mission Year Book, 1911,* Statistical Summary.
[32] *The Christian Occupation of China,* p. xcvi.
[33] *Records of the Missionary Conference, Shanghai, 1877,* p. 486.
[34] *Records of the Shanghai Missionary Conference, 1890,* p. 433.
[35] *The Christian Occupation of China,* p. xc.
[36] *China Mission Year Book, 1911,* Statistical Summary.
[37] *The Christian Occupation of China,* p. xc.

schools had once been despised and few if any Chinese of consequence would send their children to them. Missionaries had often, as we have seen, provided food and clothing as well as tuition. Now mission schools were popular.[38] They were usually crowded and tuition fees and contributions from Chinese not only met the cost of board and lodging but often bore a substantial portion of the salaries of teachers.

Primary education in some form was a phase of the program of practically every society. The Basel Mission ruled that all children of Christians must be given an education,[39] and the Berlin Evangelical Missionary Society had in each station a primary school.[40] In Szechwan the Canadian Methodists reported junior and senior primary schools [41] and in Fukien the Church Missionary Society had both day and boarding schools of primary grade.[42] Schools were established for the Miao in Yünnan and used literature prepared in an alphabet that had been invented by missionaries.[43] In 1913, among the Protestant missions in Shantung, for every four communicants there was one pupil in a primary school.[44] Even the China Inland Mission, whose chief purpose it was to reach as quickly as possible the untouched masses of China with a knowledge of the Gospel, decided to devote more attention than formerly to the education of the children of the Christians under its care.[45] In 1913 it reported one hundred and five boarding and two hundred and three day schools with a total of 6,817 pupils.[46] Here and there kindergartens were opened and training classes for teachers for this new type of institution were begun in Peking in connection with the North China Union Woman's College.[47] In primary schools there were less than half as many girls as boys.[48] Even this proportion, however, marked a notable departure from the Chinese tradition which made little provision for the formal education of women. By 1907, 42,546 pupils, boys and girls, were enrolled in 2,196 day

[38] Moore, *The Spread of Christianity in the Modern World*, p. 200.
[39] *A Century of Protestant Missions in China*, p. 478.
[40] Leuschner, *Aus dem Leben und der Arbeit eines China-Missionars*, p. 72.
[41] Bond, *Our Share in China*, pp. 70, 71.
[42] Stock, *History of the Church Missionary Society*, Vol. 4, p. 310.
[43] *China Mission Year Book, 1910*, p. 84.
[44] E. W. Burt in *Chinese Recorder*, Vol. 45, p. 442.
[45] *China Mission Year Book, 1910*, p. 151.
[46] *China's Millions*, 1913, p. 70.
[47] *China Centenary Missionary Conference Records*, p. 170.
[48] *China Mission Year Book, 1911*, Statistical Summary; *Spirit of Missions*, Vol. 71, p. 366.

schools.[49]   Four years later the numbers had increased to 56,732 and 2,557 respectively,[50] and by the close of 1914 there were 4,120 lower primary schools with 104,841 pupils, and 268 higher primary schools with 13,453 pupils.[51]   In addition, some effort was made outside these institutions to instruct adult Church members in the rudiments of reading.[52]

In an earlier chapter attention was called to the fact that Protestant missionaries, especially those from the United States, emphasized secondary and higher education.   Academies and colleges, we saw, were part of the program of practically every American denomination, while primary schools were left to the support of the state.   It was natural, then, we said, that American missionaries should believe that by reproducing this system in China they could best make a Christian impress on the country.   British missionaries, on the other hand, were more accustomed by their background to regard the support of primary and especially of boarding schools which prepared for the universities as a normal function of the Church.   It was equally natural, therefore, that in China they should lay their emphasis on secondary education and leave higher education to others.   Both Americans and British held primary schools to be less important than those of higher grade.   They contended that in the long run China would more quickly become Christian if a body of well-trained leaders, even if small in number, could be produced, than if a great mass of poorly educated people were gathered into the Church.   Such leaders, they held, could best be obtained through secondary and higher schools under Christian auspices.   It was to these institutions, therefore, that they chiefly devoted their efforts.

Nearly all the secondary schools opened before 1900 were continued, usually with added equipment and an increased enrollment.   New ones were founded.   In Tientsin, for example, an institution established by the Young Men's Christian Association was known, although inaccurately, as the parent high school of Chihli.[53]   In the Malay Peninsula and the East Indies eight Anglo-Chinese colleges were by 1919 under the direction of the American Methodists,[54] and the entire budget was met by local

[49] *A Century of Protestant Missions in China,* p. 674.
[50] *China Mission Year Book, 1911,* Statistical Summary.
[51] Ibid., *1914,* pp. xxii-xxvii.
[52] Ibid., *1914,* p. 228.
[53] Edwards, *The Chinese Y. M. C. A.,* p. 113.
[54] Dennett, *The Democratic Movement in Asia,* pp. 95, 96.

Chinese and the government.[55]   At Wênchow in Chêkiang a secondary school—called, as were many boarding institutions of that rank, a college—was opened by Soothill of the United Methodist Mission.[56]   The English Presbyterians had Anglo-Chinese colleges at Swatow and Amoy,[57] and the Presbyterians of New Zealand a college in Canton.[58]   On the outskirts of Hankow the London Missionary Society opened Griffith John College [59] and in 1904 in Shanghai the same society erected new quarters for Medhurst College, a development from an older Anglo-Chinese school.[60]   In 1906 the Church Missionary Society established at Foochow an Anglo-Chinese college later called St. Mark's.[61]   In 1903 the same society founded in Hongkong St. Stephen's College to prepare boys for the local university.   Since St. Stephen's drew the majority of its students from the wealthier classes, the fees covered most of the cost of the school, and new buildings were erected in 1909 by contributions from the scholars' parents.[62] At T'aiku in Shansi, one of the schools maintained by the Oberlin Shansi Memorial Association became an academy in 1907.[63]   In 1910 the Mary Porter Gamewell Memorial School, a Methodist institution in Peking, was said to be the largest for girls in the province.[64]   In 1914 one hundred and eighty-four Protestant middle schools were reported with 12,698 pupils,[65] and in 1915 two hundred and sixteen middle schools with 13,369 students.[66]

It was in higher education that the growth of missionary education was most spectacular.   By 1900 what Americans called college work was being given in six centers—by the American Board at T'ungchow and Foochow, by the American Methodists in Nanking and Peking, by the American Presbyterians at Hangchow and at Têngchow, Shantung, by the American Episcopa-

[55] Ibid.
[56] China Mission Year Book, 1910, p. 96.
[57] Ibid., pp. 98, 100; A Century of Protestant Missions in China, p. 184.
[58] China Mission Year Book, 1910, p. 102.
[59] Bitton, Griffith John, p. 135.
[60] L. M. S. Chronicle, Vol. 13 (new series), p. 186; Educational Review, Vol. 6, No. 3, p. 38.
[61] A History of the Dublin University Fuhkien Mission, p. 31.
[62] A Century of Protestant Missions in China, p. 39; Stock, History of the Church Missionary Society, Vol. 4, p. 301.
[63] China Mission Year Book, 1911, p. 158.
[64] Ibid., 1910, p. 298.
[65] Ibid., 1915, pp. xxii-xxvii.
[66] The Christian Occupation of China, p. xcv.

lians in St. John's at Shanghai, and by the Canton Christian College. These were all American institutions and most of those formed later bore the same national stamp.[67] The majority were chartered by one of the United States and hence their degrees were primarily American.[68] They represented, indeed, a curious extension of extraterritoriality and by a later generation of Chinese were regarded as part of the "cultural invasion" of the country. By 1906 fourteen institutions were said to be of college rank.[69] All of these still counted most of their students as preparatory, but each gave some instruction of college grade.

If in the spring of 1914 a traveller had made a tour of the country, he would have found in the south, at Canton, the Canton Christian College. In that year this institution had a campus of sixty acres on a commanding site on the river a few miles below the city. Its first building, erected there in 1904 or 1905, had been augmented by six permanent and twenty-six temporary structures valued at nearly half a million dollars. It enrolled four hundred students, it maintained horticultural and medical departments as well as one of arts and sciences, and it counted a foreign faculty of seventeen and a Chinese staff of thirty-eight. It was coëducational, an interesting prophecy of the China that was to be.[70]

At Foochow the traveller would have found the large Anglo-Chinese College (under the Northern Methodists), supported chiefly by the Chinese, and primarily a secondary school.[71] Across the Min River, within the walled city, he would have visited Foochow College, an institution maintained by the American Board and which included a large preparatory school and smaller medical, theological, and college departments.[72] He would have heard a suggestion that a union Christian university be formed for the province.[73] A constitution, indeed, had already

[67] Thomson, *China Revolutionized,* p. 460; Gascoyne-Cecil, *Changing China,* p. 200.

[68] F. L. H. Pott in *Records of the Sixth Triennial Meeting of the Educational Association of China,* p. 23.

[69] Brewster, *The Evolution of China,* p. 94, quoting Pott in *The St. John's Echo,* May, 1906.

[70] *China Mission Year Book, 1913,* p. 264; Cochrane, *Survey of the Missionary Occupation of China,* p. 19; Edmunds, *Canton Christian College,* p. 13; *A Century of Protestant Missions in China* p. 546.

[71] Brewster, *The Evolution of New China,* p. 86.

[72] *China Mission Year Book, 1910,* p. 96.

[73] Cochrane, op. cit., p. 51.

been approved by the missions and sent to the home boards for ratification,[74] and a few years later the project was to take tangible shape on a new site below the city.

At Ningpo the tourist would have found what was essentially a secondary school, Trinity College, maintained by the Church Missionary Society.[75]   At Hangchow he would have discovered, on a picturesque and recently occupied campus some distance from the city, a Presbyterian college which traced its beginnings to a boarding school opened at Ningpo in 1845 and later transferred to Hangchow.[76]   The college proper dated from 1897 and was a joint enterprise of the Northern and Southern Presbyterians.

In Shanghai the visitor would have seen St. John's University, maintained by the American Episcopalians.   Situated in a suburb of the commercial metropolis of China and under the leadership of its great president, F. L. Hawks Pott, this institution, built on foundations laid by the scholarly Schereschewsky, had become the most efficient of the mission colleges of the time.   It drew its students—numbering three hundred and seventy in 1913 [77]—largely from families of the well-to-do and maintained a middle school and faculties of arts and sciences, medicine, and theology.[78] From its halls went out not only merchants, but some of the ablest teachers, physicians, and statesmen of the new China, and outstanding leaders of the Christian Church.   Such names as Y. T. Tsur and Y. S. Tsao, presidents of Tsing Hua College, Wellington Koo, prominent in diplomacy and Minister of Foreign Affairs, W. W. Yen (not a graduate but once a member of the faculty), Minister of Foreign Affairs and Premier, two important physicians, F. C. Yen and Tiao Hsin-jeh, David Z. T. Yui, national secretary of the Young Men's Christian Association and chairman of the National Christian Council, T. Z. Koo, prominent in Christian work for students, and K. T. Chung, one of the secretaries of the National Christian Council, although by no means a complete roster of the distinguished alumni, serve to show something of the contribution of the institution to the new China.[79] On a site below the city and commanding a view of the shipping

[74] *Annual Report of the Board of Foreign Missions of the M. E. Church,* 1913, p. 213.
[75] *China Mission Year Book, 1915,* p. 401.
[76] *A Century of Protestant Missions in China,* p. 381.
[77] Ibid., p. 386; *China Mission Year Book, 1911,* p. 151.
[78] Cochrane, op. cit., p. 92.
[79] *China Year Book, 1926, Who's Who* section.

as it came and went, was the Shanghai Baptist College and Theological Seminary, a union undertaking of the Northern and Southern Baptists of the United States. The project dated from 1900, but buildings were not erected until 1907.[80] Founded as the capstone of the educational systems of the two boards, and in an advantageous position, the new institution grew rapidly and in 1914 reported sixty-six students in the college, forty-four in the academy, and twenty in the theological seminary.[81]

In the ancient city of Soochow the traveller would have visited a university by that name, maintained by the Southern Methodists. In 1901 the New Orleans Conference pledged $50,000 for the buildings and equipment of an advanced school to be erected on the site of the older Buffington Institute, and Chinese subscribed $25,000.[82] In 1911 the Anglo-Chinese College maintained by the mission was moved from Shanghai and merged with the University.[83]

At the old Southern Capital the tourist would have found a strong Protestant educational center. Since 1888 the Northern Methodists had maintained there an institution which they called Nanking University. In 1906 the Nanking Christian College of the Disciples of Christ combined with the Presbyterian boys' school to form the Union Christian College. In 1909 this in turn merged with the Methodist school to form the University of Nanking.[84] The new foundation was chartered by the University of the State of New York and a large campus was acquired. In 1913 the East China Union Medical College, operated by seven American missions, had become a department and the Hangchow Medical College of the Church Missionary Society had affiliated with it. A Language School and Missionary Training Department for foreigners newly arrived in China was opened in 1912. A Department of Normal Training and an Agricultural Department were initiated, and in close relation with the University was the Union Bible Training and Theological School.[85] In 1913

[80] *Prospectus of the Shanghai Baptist College and the Shanghai Baptist Theological Seminary* (1907).

[81] *Bulletin of the Shanghai Baptist College and Seminary*, June, 1917.

[82] *Work and Progress of the M. E. Church, South*, p. 54.

[83] Cannon, *History of Southern Methodist Missions*, pp. 110-116.

[84] *Educational Review*, Vol. 9, p. 226; *China Mission Year Book, 1913*, pp. 259-261.

[85] *The University of Nanking Special Bulletin, 1913-1914;* Cochrane, op. cit., pp. 90, 91; Barton, *Educational Missions*, p. 240; Goucher in *Recent Developments in China*, pp. 402-406.

there were nearly five hundred students and a faculty of forty.[86] In November, 1913, five missions organized a board of control for a college for women to which was given the old name for Nanking, Ginling. Mrs. Matilda C. Thurston, the widow of the pioneer of the Yale Foreign Missionary Society, was elected president of the institution, and instruction was begun in September, 1915, in rented quarters and with eight students and six teachers.[87] Before a decade had passed, Ginling had moved into buildings of its own, erected to conform to Chinese architecture, and its student body and faculty had been greatly augmented.

Proceeding up the Yangtze, the visitor would have passed, at Kiukiang, William Nast College, founded by the Northern Methodists, but primarily a secondary school.[88] By 1914 the Northern Methodists had purchased a site at Nanch'ang on which they purposed building a college.[89]

Not until he had reached Wuchang would the traveller have discovered another institution regularly maintaining college work. Boone University, supported by the American Episcopalians, was opened there in 1903. In 1909 incorporation as a university was achieved and in 1911 the first Bachelors of Arts degrees were awarded.[90] A noteworthy part of Boone's equipment was a public library to which was added a training school for librarians.[91] Not far away, outside the city wall of Wuchang, was Wesley College, which gave almost all its attention to middle school work. Across the river, in Hankow, Griffith John College, although primarily a middle school, began in February, 1914, a college course with four students.[92]

Wu-han, as the three cities, Hankow, Hanyang, and Wuchang, were called, was the proposed site of an ill-starred project for an undenominational Christian university. The promoters believed that if the Christian Church were really to make an impact upon the educated classes of the new China and so upon the country

[86] *China Mission Year Book, 1913,* p. 259.
[87] *Ginling College, A Six Year Review, 1915-1921; Ginling College. Report of the President, 1915-1916;* Burton, *Women Workers of the Orient,* p. 217.
[88] In 1912 there were in William Nast twelve students of college grade.— Cochrane, *Survey of the Missionary Occupation of China,* p. 130.
[89] *Annual Report of the Board of Foreign Missions of the M. E. Church,* 1913, p. 262.
[90] Mosher, *Institutions Connected with the American Church Mission,* p. 2; *Spirit of Missions,* Vol. 75, p. 836; *China Mission Year Book, 1913,* p. 258.
[91] *Spirit of Missions,* Vol. 72, p. 9, Vol. 74, p. 851, Vol. 75, p. 673.
[92] *L. M. S. Handbook, 1915,* p. 60.

as a whole, it could not be through a number of small colleges and so-called universities, none of them with sufficient financial backing to command the respect of the Chinese when once the government had completed the organization of its educational system.[93]   Unless all forces could unite in the support of a great Christian university, equal in equipment and faculty to the best that the government could hope to create, Christian higher education would eventually be overshadowed by that conducted by the state and the opportunity of having a permanent important influence upon the nation's intellectual life and ideals be lost. With a few exceptions, Americans, accustomed to denominational colleges and already committed to a number of institutions in China, were not particularly cordial to the suggestion.[94] English missionaries, however, having but little higher education in China and thinking of universities in terms of Cambridge and Oxford, were many of them active in an effort to bring the plan to fruition. In 1907 Arnold Foster of the London Missionary Society proposed such an institution and the idea was further discussed and in principle approved by the Centenary Conference (1907).[95] In 1907 a commission of five came to China—among them Lord William Gascoyne-Cecil, later to be Bishop of Exeter—which had been appointed by a China Missions Emergency Committee, and as a result of its report £100,000 was asked of Christians for normal and medical colleges and one of literature.[96] About the same time Cambridge and Oxford experienced an awakened interest in missions in the Far East.[97] Partly as a result of these suggestions and movements, a representative committee of tutors and lecturers of the two universities was formed and in 1909 Lord William once more went to China to study the situation. On his return to Great Britain he urged the formation of an undenominational Christian university, and before long the plan was enlarged into a United Universities project in which it was hoped

[93] Cochrane, op. cit., p. 360.

[94] Bashford, while endorsing the project (*Journal*, July 1, 1907), was not then in favor of Nanking University joining in any union project (*Journal*, sometime in 1907). Some Americans, however, did endorse the plan for a great union Christian university. President Pott, for example, at the Centenary Conference (*China Centenary Missionary Conference Records*, pp. 70-77) and Dr. Kupfer, the head of William Nast College (*Records of the Sixth Triennial Meeting of the Educational Association of China*, pp. 81 et seq.) favored it.

[95] *Chinese Recorder*, Vol. 38, pp. 219, 267; *China Centenary Missionary Conference Records*, pp. 70-77.

[96] Richard, *Forty-Five Years in China*, p. 328.

[97] Gascoyne-Cecil, *Changing China*, p. vii.

that American as well as British coöperation could be obtained. Wu-han was chosen as the most central location, one or two men were sent to begin instruction in existing institutions, and a president, W. E. Soothill, was elected. However, funds were not forthcoming in any large amounts, the proposal that a portion of the British share of the Boxer indemnity be allocated to the University failed of adoption, and the entire project was soon nothing but a memory.[98]

If from Hankow the traveller had pursued his way farther inland, he would have seen at Yochow, at the mouth of the Tungt'ing Lake, on a site four miles from the city, the Lakeside School, with primary departments, an academy, and a college.[99] In Changsha he would have found that Ya-li, the institution maintained by the Yale Foreign Missionary Society, had begun with a middle school and a hospital. Temporary quarters had been purchased and rented, a permanent site had been acquired outside the north gate, and plans were on foot for opening a college department in the spring of 1915. Under the able leadership of Doctors E. H. Hume and F. C. Yen a program for coöperation in medical education was in process of adoption by the Society and the provincial government.[100]

Had the visitor on his return to the Yangtze made his way through the gorges into Szechwan he would have found in the capital, Chengtu, the West China Union University. In 1906 the West China Christian Educational Union was formed to coördinate Protestant education in this great inland empire, and in 1910, as the capstone of the system, the University was opened. Four missions, the (Northern) American Baptists, the English Friends, the Canadian Methodists, and the Methodist Episcopalians (North), coöperated, and the Church Missionary Society was later to join. On a site of more than sixty acres not far from the east gate, where each mission was assigned a section for its

[98] Ibid., passim; Gascoyne-Cecil, *Report on Cambridge-Oxford University Scheme; China Mission Year Book, 1911*, pp. 22, 138; *Christianization of Education*, p. 108; *North China Herald*, July 26, 1913, p. 241; Leslie Johnston (sent out to China in 1910 in behalf of the plan), in *The East and the West*, Vol. 10, pp. 27-39; *Ninety-eighth Report of the Wesleyan Methodist Missionary Society*, p. 130.

[99] Hoy, *History of the China Mission of the Reformed Church in the United States*, p. 124. The college department was very small.

[100] *The Yale Mission (The College of Yale in China) Ninth Annual Report;* Brownell Gage in *Monthly Bulletin*, No. 9 (1908), p. 3; *China Mission Year Book, 1913*, p. 258; Wright, *A Life with a Purpose*, passim; Seabury, *The Vision of a Short Life*, passim.

buildings, in 1914 a student body of two hundred and fifty-eight had gathered. Relations with the government were very friendly, the Civil and Military Governors and President Yüan Shih-k'ai having each made substantial gifts.[101]

If the traveller, after retracing his steps to Hankow, had gone on to North China, he would have found at T'ungchow, not far from Peking, North China Union College, an outgrowth of the college of the American Board and now under the North China Educational Union. This Union had been formed about 1903 by the London, the American Presbyterian, and the American Board Missions, and the Woman's Foreign Missionary Society of the Methodist Episcopal Church.[102] Under it were also the North China Union College for Women, opened in 1905 and in part an outgrowth of Bridgman Academy,[103] the North China Union Medical College, the North China Union Medical College for Women, and the North China Union Theological College (founded in 1906).[104] In 1911 the missions concerned decided to unite the college at T'ungchow with Peking University—the Methodist foundation incorporated in 1889—and the theological school. In 1915 the project received the approval of the boards and was later to include the women's college.[105]

At Tientsin an Anglo-Chinese College, founded in memory of Walford Hart by his brother, Lavington Hart—who was also its first principal—was opened in 1902. It was especially strong in its scientific and engineering departments, and in 1915 had four hundred and sixty-five students, of whom over half were in higher primary grades. About a third of its students were from the wealthier classes and it received gifts from officials, so that while counted as an enterprise of the London Missionary Society it was self-supporting.[106]

[101] *China Mission Year Book, 1910,* p. 90; ibid., *1915,* pp. 188-196; Goucher in *Recent Developments in China,* pp. 396-402; *Chinese Recorder,* Vol. 45, p. 352, Vol. 48, p. 603; Bond, *Our Share in China,* pp. 75-77.

[102] Moore, *The Deputation of the American Board to China; China Mission Year Book, 1913,* pp. 265, 266; *North China Union College, Bulletin No. IV* (January, 1915), pp. 3, 4; *China Mission Year Book, 1910,* pp. 17, 77.

[103] *Peking University,* passim; *L. M. S. Handbook,* 1914, p. 83; *Educational Review,* Vol. 6, No. 4, p. 23; *China Mission Year Book, 1918,* p. 333; Davis, *Neighbors in Christ,* p. 98.

[104] *North China Union College, Bulletin No. IV* (January, 1915), p. 3.

[105] *Peking University,* passim; *Educational Review,* Vol. 8, No. 2, p. 158.

[106] Bitton, *Our Heritage in China,* p. 102; *L. M. S. Handbook,* 1914, p. 90; *Chinese Recorder,* Vol. 48, p. 581; Kemp, *The Face of China,* p. 31; *China Mission Year Book, 1910,* pp. 76, 77; *Educational Review,* Vol. 8, No. 2, p. 159.

In Shantung the tourist would have found the Shantung Christian University, a union undertaking of the (Northern) American Presbyterians and the English Baptists begun in 1903 and 1904. The Presbyterian college at Têngchow had been moved to Weihsien and now became the college of arts and sciences of the University, the Baptist theological college and normal school at Tsingchowfu became another unit, and, partly with the aid of the Arthington Fund, a medical college was opened at Tsinanfu. In 1917 all the colleges were to be brought together on a new site just outside of Tsinanfu and in the course of time a number of other missions were to participate in their support.   English was less used as a medium of instruction and a larger proportion of the students came from Christian homes than in some other Protestant colleges and universities.[107]

Finally, if the visitor had left China by way of Manchuria he could have visited at Mukden a college opened in 1902 and supported by the Irish Presbyterians and the United Free Church of Scotland.[108]

The courses of study of these colleges included both Chinese and Western subjects.   Some departments were technical and professional, but there was usually an arts college whose purpose it was to give the Chinese what corresponded to the general cultural training of the West rather than preparation for a special occupation.   The conception of higher education back of these arts colleges was not basically different from that of the older education which had prepared Chinese for the civil service examinations: both sought to train the student for leadership in society by bringing him into contact with the best of the intellectual heritage of the race and by subjecting him to the mental discipline necessary to its acquisition.   The curriculum of the American arts college had been transferred to China, with the elimination of Greek and Latin, a diminution of the time allotted to European languages and literature, and some readjustment of the courses in English and the social sciences.   Attendance at chapel was compulsory and enrollment in courses on the Bible was required. To this program courses were added in Chinese composition,

[107] *Chinese Recorder*, Vol. 33, p. 417, Vol. 35, p. 154, Vol. 37, pp. 95, 327, Vol. 45, p. 444; Fisher, *C. W. Mateer*, pp. 225, 226; *China Mission Year Book, 1910*, p. 79, 1913, p. 263; *Report of the Presbyterian Board, 1911*, pp. 18, 19; Cochrane, op. cit., p. 273; *International Review of Missions*, Vol. 2, p. 21.

[108] *China Mission Year Book, 1910*, p. 80, *1911*, p. 218; *Missionary Review of the World*, Vol. 24, p. 120.

philosophy, literature and history—substitutes for the classical education once universal in China.   Most of the Chinese subjects were taught by scholars trained in the old ways and not according to the better pedagogical methods in use in the West.   Partly for this reason and partly because in the two decades after 1900 foreign culture was at the height of its popularity and was the attraction which had led to the rapid growth of mission schools, students were disposed to concentrate on Western subjects at the expense of the Chinese side of the curriculum.   Missionary educators deplored the tendency but were powerless to correct it.   The extra-curriculum activities so familiar in schools in the United States but new in the educational life of China had a large place in the mission colleges.   Athletics, dramatics, debating societies, musical clubs, Young Men's Christian Associations, and self-government consumed much of the time of the student and became part of the educative process.

It was sometimes feared that these colleges which absorbed so substantial a proportion of the funds of some of the larger missions were not making a corresponding return in Christian lives and influence.   It was said, for example, that few ministers and teachers came from institutions like Soochow and St. John's Universities.[109]   However, statistics gathered in 1913 from fourteen of the leading mission colleges showed that eighty-seven and a half per cent. of the graduates were professing Christians, that sixty-five per cent. of these had entered the service of the Church, and that twenty per cent. had entered the ministry.[110]   A large number of former students became teachers, many of them in government institutions,[111] a few went into politics and rose to high position,[112] and some engaged in business.   Protestants, by their emphasis on higher education, were rapidly raising up a trained leadership for the Church and were in a position to have an influence upon the nation far greater than their numerical strength would have given reason to expect.   Their educational policy was being justified by its results.

[109] Brewster, *The Evolution of New China*, p. 88.
[110] *China Mission Year Book, 1913*, pp. 222, 223.   E. H. Munson found (*Chinese Recorder*, Vol. 44, p. 267) that up to 1913 ten of the largest missionary institutions had graduated 1,171 from college courses.   Of these 138 were in the ministry, 455 in other forms of Christian service, and 47 were still in theological seminaries.
[111] Lewis, *The Educational Conquest of the Far East*, p. 206.
[112] *Millard's Review*, Sept. 27, 1919, p. 152, gives one of these instances.

More than before 1900, Protestants were embarking upon specialized types of education. They naturally placed great emphasis upon theological preparation. From the very beginning, therefore, as we have seen, they had organized classes and schools for teaching the Bible and allied subjects. Before 1900 these attempts had been relatively elementary in character and had required little preliminary education for admission. Only one used English as a medium of instruction. After 1900 the number of students who were receiving special training as Bible women, catechists, evangelists, or pastors grew rapidly, and the grade of many of the schools was raised. In 1876 twenty theological schools were reported with a total enrollment of two hundred and thirty-one.[113] Shortly before 1906 sixty-eight theological and training schools were in existence with an enrollment of seven hundred and seventy-two men and five hundred and forty-three women.[114] In some missions the instruction given Bible women was informal and brief; in others as much as a four years' course was required, with church history, theology, and the study of the Scriptures.[115] For men the standards varied even more widely, ranging from instruction for a few weeks each year for catechists and evangelists, to theological courses of three years' duration which presupposed graduation from a middle school and even some work in college.[116] More and more frequently the conviction was expressed that a long and thorough education was indispensable if the Chinese clergy were to give adequate leadership to an independent Church.[117] Before 1907 the Basel Mission had made secondary education a prerequisite for admission to its theological seminary.[118] The Boone Divinity School of the American Episcopalians at Wuchang admitted its first class in 1906, and of the six members three were graduates from the College and the others had had one year of college work.[119] Of the ten who graduated in 1912 from the Theological College of Shantung Christian

[113] Records of the General Conference of Protestant Missionaries in China, 1877, p. 486.
[114] Dennis, Christian Missions and Social Progress, Vol. 3, p. 44.
[115] Miss Edith Benham in China Centenary Missionary Conference Records, p. 152.
[116] Barton, Educational Missions, p. 100.
[117] Edinburgh Conference Reports, Vol. 2, p. 197; Findings of the Continuation Committee Conferences in Chinese Recorder, Vol. 44, p. 222.
[118] A Century of Protestant Missions in China, p. 479.
[119] Ibid., p. 303.

University, eight had previously completed the course of the Arts College.[120]   Indeed, institutions of two grades arose—those usually known as theological schools, requiring considerable preliminary education for admission and as a rule having a course of three years modeled on that in use in the Occident, and others called Bible schools with lower standards of admission and with courses of study of varying lengths and with much practical training in field work.   Examples of the latter were the Blackstone Bible Institute opened at Wuchang in 1910 by the Christian and Missionary Alliance[121] and four Bible Training Institutes with a two years' course inaugurated by 1912 by the China Inland Mission.[122]

The number of institutions did not increase as rapidly as did students, for the missions were entering extensively upon union projects.   Thus in Nanking in 1910 a Union Bible School was formed by four missions, succeeding three older seminaries;[123] in 1913 there was dedicated the plant of a seminary at Shekow, Hupeh, supported by four Lutheran missions;[124] in 1914 eight missions united in a theological seminary in Canton;[125] in 1912 three boards joined in one in Foochow,[126] and in 1914 a union theological school was opened in Changsha.[127]   The union schools in Peking and Shanghai have already been noted.   Even in that most controversial of all fields, theology, missions were attempting to eliminate duplication.

Carefully trained teachers were needed for the rapidly growing Christian schools, and missionaries had a unique opportunity to influence the nation by providing Christian instructors for the newly organized government and private institutions.   Normal classes were accordingly instituted in some of the mission schools,[128] the Centenary Missionary Conference passed a resolu-

[120] *China Mission Year Book, 1913*, p. 263.
[121] *China Mission Year Book, 1911*, p. 326.
[122] Broomhall, *Jubilee Story of the China Inland Mission*, p. 294; *China's Millions*, 1913, p. 109.
[123] *Report of the Presbyterian Board*, 1905, p. 12; *Missionary Review of the World*, Vol. 24, p. 481; Williams, *In Four Continents*, pp. 46-49; Cochrane, op. cit., p. 91.
[124] *China Mission Year Book, 1915*, p. 36.
[125] *Annual Report of the A. B. C. F. M.*, 1915, p. 166; Leger, *Education of Christian Ministers in China*, p. 34.
[126] *Annual Report of the A. B. C. F. M.*, 1915, p. 166; Leger, op. cit., p. 34.
[127] *The Christian Occupation of China*, p. 416.
[128] Chamberlain, *Fifty Years in Foreign Fields*, p. 125.

tion calling for the organization of a union normal school in at least one center in each province,[129] and institutions of this kind were projected or actually begun in Amoy, Foochow, Soochow, Wuchang, and Hankow.[130]   In spite of these convictions and efforts, however, missions were not supplying nearly enough technically prepared teachers for their own needs.[131]   Fortunately many who had had no courses in pedagogy but who had been graduated from middle schools or colleges went into the profession and were often successful.   Missions were not giving the best possible education for the teacher, but what they offered was better than that obtained in most of the hastily organized government institutions.

Education in medicine was a prominent feature of the Protestant program.   From the time of Peter Parker the physician had been a recognized member of the missionary staff and no station was considered complete without a hospital or a dispensary. Medical missionaries, as we have seen, had begun early to train assistants and full-fledged physicians, and even before 1900 saw the opportunity of taking the lead in creating the future medical profession and of leaving upon it an indelible stamp of Christian ideals.   The China Medical Missionary Association recognized clearly that the foreigner physician had no permanent place in China and that if the Church were to have lasting influence medical education must be stressed.[132]   Some missionaries, indeed, maintained that the Christian Church could make a greater ultimate contribution to China by spending less on hospitals and more on medical schools.[133]   Much training continued to be given through hospitals, but both before and after 1900 specialized medical schools appeared.   All of them were small and in none of them were the standards as high as in Europe and the United States.   They were, however, better than anything else of their kind in China.   In 1912 the Mukden Medical College, an outgrowth of the work of Dr. Christie, was formally opened and offered a course of five years.[134]   In Peking a Union Medical

[129] China Centenary Mission Conference Records, p. 519.
[130] Edinburgh Conference Reports, Vol. 3, pp. 305, 306; Cannon, History of Southern Methodist Missions, p. 117; China Mission Year Book, 1910, p. 108; Chinese Recorder, Vol. 40, p. 565, Vol. 35, p. 400.
[131] Edinburgh Conference Reports, Vol. 3, pp. 305, 306.
[132] Resolution of the China Medical Missionary Association, Jan., 1913, in Chinese Recorder, Vol. 44, p. 595.
[133] Dr. Gillison in Chinese Recorder, Vol. 44, p. 602.
[134] Christie, Thirty Years in the Manchu Capital, pp. 270-277.

College was inaugurated in 1906. The Empress Dowager contributed to it and the government gave it recognition and permitted it to grant degrees.[135]   In Peking, too, the North China Union Medical College for women in 1914 awarded its first diplomas to a class of two.[136]   The Medical College of the Shantung Christian University has already been noted. In 1914 it reported twenty-five students and a teaching staff of four. For admission to its course of five years a year in the Arts College was prerequisite.[137]   A small school at Boone, opened in 1906 or 1907,[138] a union undertaking in Hankow begun in 1902,[139] and the foreshadowings at Changsha of the school of the Yale Mission, were the provision for Central China. The West China Union University included plans for a medical school.[140]   At Nanking several missions coöperated in a Medical College [141]— at first independent and in 1913 made a part of the University [142] —and a union nursing school was founded there in 1909.[143]   The medical departments connected with Soochow and St. John's Universities granted the degree of Doctor of Medicine.[144]   By 1915 a group of graduates of the University of Pennsylvania began coöperating with St. John's, supporting Dr. J. C. McCracken.[145] The medical school in Shanghai bearing the name of Harvard and supported in part by graduates of that university, was not officially a missionary undertaking, but it was initiated by men whose chief interest was missionary.[146]   In Hangchow Dr. Main of the Church Missionary Society continued medical instruction.[147]

[135] L. M. S. Chronicle, Vol. 15 (new series), p. 132; Barton, Educational Missions, p. 38; China Mission Year Book, 1910, p. 216.
[136] Peking Gazette, Feb. 14, 1914, p. 6; Educational Review, Vol. 6, No. 4, p. 24; China Mission Year Book, 1914, p. 326.
[137] Neal in China Medical Journal, Vol. 23, p. 316; Chinese Recorder, Vol. 46, p. 692, Vol. 45, p. 445.
[138] A Century of Protestant Missions in China, p. 304; China Medical Journal, Vol. 23, p. 318.
[139] China Mission Year Book, 1917, p. 142.   The teaching was done by members of the London Missionary Society and of the Wesleyan Mission, and the Reformed Church in the United States Mission at Yochow made a contribution of £50 a year.   In 1914 there were twenty-seven students.—L. M. S. Handbook, 1914, p. 59.
[140] China Medical Journal, Vol. 23, p. 296.
[141] Cochrane, op. cit., p. 91.
[142] Chinese Recorder, Vol. 46, p. 691.
[143] Williams, Ohio Friends in the Land of Sinim, p. 97.
[144] Jeffreys in China Medical Journal, Vol. 23, p. 298; Lincoln in ibid., Vol. 23, p. 308; Parker in ibid., Vol. 23, p. 300.
[145] China Mission Year Book, 1911, p. 159.
[146] Ibid., 1913, pp. 301, 302.
[147] Ibid., 1910, pp. 216-233.

In Foochow physicians were being trained,[148] and in 1910 a union medical college was established there which continued until 1921.[149] At Hongkong the missions contented themselves with hospitals and with hostels in connection with the medical department of Hongkong University.[150] In Canton were the South China Medical College in connection with the historic hospital maintained by the China Medical Missionary Society,[151] the medical department of the Canton Christian College,[152] and the Hackett Medical School for Women.[153] In 1913 in all China about five hundred students were receiving a medical training under missionary auspices.[154] A number of training schools for nurses were, moreover, in existence.[155]

The faults common to all these courageous beginnings were inadequate equipment and small teaching staffs. These defects became so obvious that shortly after 1914, as we shall see later, successful efforts were made to concentrate in a few centers the available resources.

A new development was schools for teaching the language to newly arrived missionaries. Before 1900 the China Inland Mission had inaugurated such an undertaking for its junior members, but most missionaries acquired the language with the aid of manuals, Chinese teachers who were without training in pedagogy, and the occasional advice of foreign friends. This method proved wasteful in time and energy, and with the rapid increase in the number of new arrivals various attempts were made at systematic and collective instruction. The most noteworthy of these were a language school at Peking, begun in 1910 by the London Missionary Society and in 1913 enlarged to a union enterprise;[156] another in Shanghai, conducted for a few weeks in 1912 while missionaries were gathered there because of the disturbances due to the Revolution;[157] a regular department of the University of

[148] Ibid., 1910, pp. 216-233.
[149] Lora G. Dyer in Anti-Cobweb Club, Fukien, p. 90.
[150] China Mission Year Book, 1912, pp. 153-157.
[151] China Medical Journal, Vol. 23, p. 303.
[152] Cochrane, Survey of the Missionary Occupation of China, p. 26. In 1912 it had three men and three women on its staff.
[153] Smith, Rex Christus, p. 183. It was begun by Dr. Mary Fuller and Dr. Mary Niles.—China Mission Year Book, 1918, p. 335.
[154] Cochrane, op. cit., p. 331.
[155] China Medical Journal, Vol. 23, p. 118.
[156] China Mission Year Book, 1912, pp. 230, 231.
[157] Ibid., 1912, pp. 236-238; International Review of Missions, Vol. 2, p. 24.

Nanking which arose in part out of the success of that experiment;[158] a school in Chengtu; and another in Canton.[159]

Another form of education was industrial schools, of which the outstanding examples were those maintained at Chefoo by Mr. and Mrs. McMullan for the manufacture of brushes and lace.[160] Industrial schools were also found at Shanghai, Hinghwa, Ichang, and Foochow.[161]

Still other types of education were self-help, which was sometimes given in connection with an existing school, such as a farm at T'ungchow on which the college students earned part of their expenses;[162] training in Western music, such as that afforded by the Chinese Choral Union at Foochow;[163] the popular addresses on scientific topics given by the Young Men's Christian Association under the leadership of C. H. Robertson;[164] schools for the children of missionaries;[165] and museums illustrating Occidental life and thought and scientific achievement—notably the Tsianfu Institute, maintained by the English Baptists, with exhibits of geography, architecture, chemistry, pathology, hygiene, and geology, a library and reading room, and lecture halls.[166] Attention has already been called to the beginnings of education in agriculture at Nanking and in law in Shanghai.

Before 1900 Sunday Schools had become a regular feature of the work of some missions. They were chiefly for the children of Christians but in places were also used to reach non-Christians.[167] In only about an eighth of the congregations, however, did classes for children exist, and in one-half no Sunday School was main-

[158] *The Christian Occupation of China*, p. 425; *Missionary Review of the World*, Vol. 27, p. 144.

[159] *China Mission Year Book, 1917*, p. 188; ibid., *1914*, pp. 499, 500.

[160] Dennis, *Christian Missions and Social Progress*, Vol. 3, p. 115.

[161] *Chinese Recorder*, Vol. 38, p. 436. Those employed were chiefly old women, young girls, slaves, and members of afflicted classes who stood in need of a means of livelihood. In 1906 a trade school for destitute boys was begun at Ichang by Rev. (later Bishop) D. T. Huntington of the American Episcopal Mission.—*China Mission Year Book, 1912*, pp. 349-352.

[162] Dennis, op. cit., Vol. 3, p. 115. About 40% of the boys' schools and 55% of the girls' schools had industrial employment by which students might in part or entirely support themselves.—*China Mission Year Book, 1910*, p. 394.

[163] Dennis, op. cit., Vol. 3, p. 135.

[164] Edwards, *The Chinese Y. M. C. A.*, p. 114.

[165] *China Mission Year Book, 1911*, p. xxxix.

[166] Ibid., *1910*, pp. 68, 69, 127; ibid., *1913*, p. 275; *Chinese Recorder*, Vol. 37, p. 200; Dennis, op. cit., Vol. 3, pp. 525, 526; *L. M. S. Chronicle*, Vol. 13 (new series), p. 174.

[167] *Edinburgh Conference Reports*, Vol. 2, p. 157.

tained for either children or adults.[168]   Adequate lesson material
in Chinese was, moreover, lacking, and there was no general
supervision of religious education.[169]   Accordingly, the Centenary
Conference (1907) appointed a committee to improve conditions,[170] and at the World Sunday School Convention in Washington, D. C., in 1910, arrangements were made to appoint a secretary to give his entire time to the newly formed China Sunday
School Union.   E. G. Tewksbury of the American Board was
chosen, and before long regional unions were organized, teachers'
training classes were held, and lesson notes prepared.[171]   The visit
of a group of Sunday School experts in 1914 gave further stimulus
to what was being done.[172]

In these varied educational activities it was becoming clear
that the best results could be achieved only through coöperation,
and that as far as possible a coördinated system of Protestant
schools must be built up, embracing all societies and according to
a program covering the entire country.   From the foregoing pages
it must be apparent that between 1900 and 1914 great strides
were made toward this goal.   Few missionaries spoke openly of
a unified nationwide program and still fewer were committed to
it, but the obvious needs of the situation led missions to enter
upon a path which, if followed, would lead to this destination.
Some missionaries were pleading for greater coördination.[173]
Uniform examinations for Christian schools, at least by regions,
were advocated,[174] and a general education board for the Orient
was suggested.[175]   The Educational Association of China, organized by missionaries in 1890, continued to hold triennial meetings
and attempted to draw up a standard course of study.[176]   The Centenary Missionary Conference gave much attention to education [177]

[168] D. W. Lyon in *China Centenary Missionary Conference Records*, pp. 286,
287.
[169] Ibid., pp. 286 et seq.
[170] Ibid., pp. 686-688; *L. M. S. Chronicle*, Vol. 19 (new series), p. 3.
[171] *Edinburgh Conference Reports*, Vol. 2, p. 157; *China Mission Year Book,
1910*, pp. 261-263; ibid., *1911*, p. 401; ibid., *1912*, pp. 327-331.
[172] Brown, *A Sunday School Tour of the Orient*, p. 266; *China Mission Year
Book, 1914*, p. 246.
[173] Barton, *Educational Missions*, p. 74; Bashford in *China Mission Year Book,
1914*, pp. 38-58.
[174] *Chinese Recorder*, Vol. 42, p. 210, Vol. 43, p. 215.
[175] J. T. Proctor in *Chinese Recorder*, Vol. 43, p. 385.
[176] Pott in *China Mission Year Book, 1911*, pp. 134-150.
[177] *Chinese Recorder*, Vol. 38, p. 381.

and urged upon the home boards the importance of developing secondary and higher schools. It also ordered the appointment of a General Education Committee to study the entire field, to present to givers at home the need of strengthening these institutions, and to devise means for establishing a union Christian university.[178] In 1907 the foreign missions boards of North America appointed a commission on Christian education in China, but beyond a report no results were immediately achieved.[179] An account has already been given of the coöperative enterprises in higher education. The Northern Methodists planned a general board of education for all their work in China and appointed an educational secretary.[180] The West China Christian Educational Union, inaugurated in 1906, arranged a uniform course of study with common textbooks and examinations for all primary and secondary Protestant schools in the province and E. W. Wallace was designated educational superintendent.[181] The attempt was made to coördinate under Nanking University all the schools of the missions which coöperated in that institution.[182] A union educational commission studied the problem of East China (Anhui, Kiangsu, and Chêkiang) and the East China Educational Association was formed.[183] The Central China Christian Educational Union was organized in 1909 and prepared a primary school curriculum and common examinations which in 1914 were in use in forty-one schools,[184] and educational associations came into existence in Fukien (1905) and Kwangtung.[185] The most effective of the regional associations was that in Szechwan: the others only partly achieved the ends which they had in view and did not succeed in welding the schools of their neighborhood into a unified system.

The problem of the relation of Protestant missions to the educational program which after 1900 began to be framed by the gov-

[178] *China Centenary Conference Records,* p. 520.
[179] *Report on Christian Education in China,* passim.
[180] Goucher in *Recent Developments in China,* pp. 388-409.
[181] *China Mission Year Book, 1910,* p. 85; ibid., *1915,* pp. 188-192; *Educational Review,* Vol. 6, No. 4, p. 9; *Chinese Recorder,* Vol. 45, p. 382; *International Review of Missions,* Vol. 2, p. 22.
[182] *International Review of Missions,* Vol. 2, p. 22.
[183] Cochrane, op. cit., p. 90; *China Mission Year Book, 1915,* pp. 392-394; *Continuation Committee Conference Findings,* p. 224.
[184] *China Mission Year Book, 1915,* p. 389.
[185] *Chinese Recorder,* Vol. 36, p. 573, Vol. 38, p. 578, Vol. 42, p. 209; *China Mission Year Book, 1915,* p. 394.

ernment early assumed importance.   Should missionary institutions seek registration with the state?   If they did not, would their diplomas be recognized in making official appointments and in framing the conditions of admission to government higher schools?   The government's attitude was not uniform.   In 1907 the national Board of Education decided that no schools established by foreigners would be registered nor recognition be vouchsafed their graduates for fear that the encouragement of foreign-controlled education would hinder the abolition of extraterritoriality.[186]   A few years later the Board returned a non-committal reply to an inquiry concerning the possibility of substituting the elementary education given by mission schools for that which the government was proposing to make compulsory for all children,[187] and parried the suggestion of assimilating the curricula of Christian schools to those of the state with the plea that the latter were not yet sufficiently fixed.[188]   Shortly after the Revolution, on the other hand, the new Commissioner of Education for Kwangtung, a Christian, gave official recognition to mission schools.[189]   In practice, moreover, the government elsewhere granted quasi-recognition: graduates of mission schools were employed in state institutions, competitive examinations for scholarships for foreign study were opened to students in Christian schools, and high officials gave the approval of their presence on formal occasions and expressed their good-will in the more substantial form of contributions toward the budget of missionary institutions.[190]   The state system of education was as yet in such rudimentary stages that the relatively excellent schools maintained by the foreigners were not seriously opposed.   The foreigner was, moreover, too powerful a personage to be insulted, even when his participation in education offended the patriotic.

Missionaries, like the officials, were of two minds.   The question was discussed at the Centenary Conference, but beyond recommending that friendly relations be established between Christian and tax-supported institutions no action was taken.[191]   Missions on the whole refrained from seeking governmental recognition for their schools.   Some of them feared the imposition of restrictions

[186] *Chinese Recorder*, Vol. 38, p. 104.
[187] *China Mission Year Book, 1911*, p. 99.
[188] *China Mission Year Book, 1910*, p. 16.
[189] Ibid., *1913*, p. 251; *Chinese Recorder*, Vol. 44, p. 464.
[190] *Chinese Recorder*, Vol. 43, pp. 743, 744, and author's personal knowledge.
[191] *China Centenary Missionary Conference Records*, p. 521.

which would weaken the Christian character of the institutions: [192] the state might, for example, forbid Christian religious instruction.[193] On the whole, however, they tended to favor conformity to the curricula laid down by the state and wished to aid and not to hinder the official educational program.[194] In 1906 the Educational Associatioin, on the advice of the American Minister, appointed a committee to confer on the question with the appropriate bureau; [195] and the conferences held in 1913 under the Continuation Committee of the Edinburgh Conference held that governmental recognition was desirable.[196] It was clearly perceived that when the state system of modern schools should become well established, the Christian institution would occupy a subordinate position.[197]

In the face of these divided counsels it was fortunate that the question of registration did not become acute. Relations with the government were, on the whole, friendly. In the absence of a sufficient number of trained teachers, indeed, the state not only employed the graduates of Christian schools but occasionally called upon missionaries to teach in and even to supervise its institutions. The most notable examples were the university in T'aiyüanfu, founded at the suggestion of Timothy Richard and under foreign supervision,[198] and the Shantung Provincial College at Tsinanfu which in 1901 was placed under the direction of Rev. W. M. Hayes of the (Northern) American Presbyterian Mission.[199] Some of the texts used by the state-supported institutions were, moreover, translations prepared by missionaries.[200]

Protestant schools were not without serious defects. Some of their most severe critics were, indeed, missionaries. Missionaries contended that the instruction too closely followed traditional Western models, that it was poorly adjusted to the local environ-

---

[192] *Chinese Recorder,* Vol. 37, p. 96, Vol. 43, pp. 199, 215. Fong F. Sec advised the missionaries to make their schools conform to the government system in course of study and textbooks and to open them to government inspection.—*Records of the Sixth Triennial Meeting of the Educational Association of China* (1909), pp. 66 ff.

[193] *China Mission Year Book, 1911,* p. 141.

[194] *China Mission Year Book, 1911,* p. 13; *Chinese Recorder,* Vol. 44, p. 225.

[195] *Chinese Recorder,* Vol. 37, p. 147.

[196] *China Continuation Committee Findings,* p. 224.

[197] A. J. Bowen in *Chinese Recorder,* Vol. 41, p. 45.

[198] *Chinese Recorder,* Vol. 34, p. 460; *China Mission Year Book, 1911,* pp. 111 et seq.; Gascoyne-Cecil, *Changing China,* p. 274.

[199] Martin, *The Awakening of China,* p. 285; *Chinese Recorder,* Vol. 33, p. 247; H. W. Luce in Forsyth, *Shantung,* p. 301; Fisher, *Mateer,* p. 214.

[200] Brewster, *The Evolution of New China.*

ment, and that it tended to denationalize its product.[201]   They held that not enough attention was paid to Chinese,[202] that there was a lack of system and continuity, and that the education given was not sufficiently practical.[203]   The staffs and equipment were, so they said, inadequate; insufficient training for teachers was provided; higher schools were too few in number; and churches did not make enough effort to keep in touch with those formerly students in Christian schools.[204]   Missionaries were, moreover, still of two minds as to the advisability of employing English as a medium of instruction.   The majority of educators believed the extensive use of that tongue to be wise, or at least unavoidable, but a minority claimed that while it might be taught as a language, all instruction in other subjects should be in Chinese.[205]   In spite of these weaknesses and problems, both Chinese and foreigners were generally of the opinion that much and perhaps most of the best education in China continued to be given by the Protestant missionary.[206]

The Preparation and Distribution of Literature

Protestant missionaries had made such extensive use of the printed page that, with the eager appetite for Western knowledge which the Chinese developed after 1900, the preparation and distribution of literature might naturally be expected to be even more prominent than before that transitional year.   Such, however, was not the case.   The press continued to be employed and in the volume of sales the growth was large, but literature did not have quite the place in the attention of the missionary which it had formerly commanded, nor did Protestants here maintain the position that they had won in the decade before the Boxer year in shaping progressive Chinese thought.   Some missionaries believed that in not retaining this leadership a notable opportunity had been irretrievably lost.

The one exception to this generalization was in the distribution

[201] Bishop Westcott in *Chinese Recorder,* Vol. 37, p. 25; *Christianization of Education,* p. 79.
[202] Soothill in *Chinese Recorder,* Vol. 40, p. 634.
[203] Pott in *Report on Christian Education in China,* p. 9.
[204] *Edinburgh Conference Reports,* Vol. 3, pp. 79-82.
[205] *Report on Christian Education in China,* p. 18; Du Bose in *Chinese Recorder,* Vol. 35, pp. 271, 343.
[206] E. D. Burton quoted in Barton, *Educational Missions,* p. 165.

of the Scriptures. The great era of translation—at least by foreigners—had almost passed. The task remained, however, of perfecting the editions in use and of preparing additional ones in the dialects into which the Bible had not yet been put. The committee appointed by the 1890 Conference to revise the easy Wênli version completed the New Testament in 1900,[207] but publication was delayed until 1908.[208] The corresponding committee on the version in what was known as high Wênli handed its manuscript of the New Testament to the Bible societies in 1906,[209] but the entire Bible seems to have been first published in 1919.[210] Bishop Schereschewsky completed his easy Wênli version in 1902.[211] The most noteworthy achievement was that of the committee on a Mandarin version. They suffered from many changes in membership, from differences of opinion as to the style of Mandarin to be used, and from other vicissitudes. A text of the New Testament was, however, completed in 1906[212] and was put on sale in 1907. It later underwent a further revision and was published, together with a version of the Old Testament, in 1920.[213] The editions produced by these committees were appropriately known as "union" versions and before many years almost monopolized the field.

Portions of the Bible continued to appear in the many vernaculars. For example, in 1904 the four Gospels were published in the Samkiong dialect.[214] The first copy of the entire Bible in the Ningpo dialect appeared in 1901.[215] In 1904 a version of the Taichow New Testament and Psalms was ready for the press and the first draft of the Taichow Pentateuch had been made.[216] In 1902 a revision of the Amoy Old Testament was printed.[217] In 1900 Genesis and Exodus in the Kienning colloquial were published and a Kienyang version of the Gospel of Matthew.[218] The entire Bible in the Shanghai colloquial seems to have been first published in 1908, in the Soochow dialect in 1908, in that

[207] J. C. Gibson in *China Centenary Missionary Conference Records*, p. 270.
[208] *The Christian Occupation of China*, p. 452.
[209] Sheffield in *China Centenary Missionary Conference Records*, p. 282.
[210] *The Christian Occupation of China*, p. 452.
[211] Ibid., p. 452; *Chinese Recorder*, Vol. 34, p. 148.
[212] *China Centenary Missionary Conference Records*, p. 281.
[213] *The Christian Occupation of China*, p. 453.
[214] Ibid., p. 452.
[215] Canton, *History of the British and Foreign Bible Society*, Vol. 5, p. 193.
[216] Ibid., Vol. 5, p. 193.
[217] Ibid., Vol. 5, p. 194.
[218] Ibid., Vol. 5, p. 195.

of Hinghwa in 1912, and in that of Taichow in 1914.[219] It was, however, into the languages of the non-Chinese peoples of the Empire, especially those of the tribes in the Southwest, that most of the fresh translations were made. The New Testament was put into the Hua Miao by means of a script invented by Pollard,[220] and portions of the New Testament were translated into Chung-kai, Laka, Lisu, Kopu, and, after 1914, Western Lisu, Chuan Miao, and Nosu.[221] An edition of Matthew in the Buriat tongue was issued in 1909 [222] and a revision of the New Testament in Tibetan was completed in 1903.[223]

The controversy over the terms to be employed in putting the Bible into Chinese passed into the background. Differences remained and varying expressions were used, but the debate, once so acrimonious, survived only as a memory. Other questions had come to the fore and the younger missionaries were but little interested in the problem that had so engaged their predecessors.

In the meantime the great Bible societies—the British and Foreign, American, and Scotch—found their sales rapidly mounting. Hykes of the American Bible Society declared: "Formerly our anxieties were occasioned by how to increase the circulation; now they are caused by how to restrict our sales." [224] The student class was reported to be unusually receptive.[225] In 1913 the British and Foreign Bible Society employed eleven sub-agents, four hundred and sixty-eight colporteurs, and thirty-six Bible women. It reported that distribution among railway employees had been begun and that during the Revolution twenty-five thousand portions had been circulated among soldiers of both camps.[226] The total sales of the three societies rose from 2,519,758 in 1905 [227] to 4,769,554 in 1911, and to 6,014,857 in 1914.[228] Less than ten per cent. of this enormous circulation was in the form of entire New Testaments and a still smaller proportion was made up of entire Bibles. The great bulk was of single books from the

[219] Richter, Das Werden der Christlichen Kirche in China, p. 195.
[220] Grist, Samuel Pollard, pp. 286-296.
[221] The Christian Occupation of China, p. 453.
[222] Ibid., p. 453.
[223] Ibid., p. 282.
[224] American Bible Society, Annual Report, 1913, p. 349.
[225] Annual Report of the American Bible Society, 1914, p. 360.
[226] Reports of the British and Foreign Bible Society, 1912, 1913.
[227] A Century of Protestant Missions in China, pp. 565, 573, 580.
[228] The Christian Occupation of China, p. 453.

Bible, mostly Gospels, the Acts, or one of the Epistles. Except for the Psalms and possibly Genesis, the Old Testament was not being extensively read: it was upon the New Testament that the Church was laying its emphasis.

Other agencies joined in distributing the Scriptures. The Bible House of Los Angeles became active in China. Its own colporteurs concentrated on the province of Hunan, but it made literature available for members of the China Inland Mission to give out as they saw fit.[229] Milton Stewart established a Distribution Fund of $15,000 a year for five years beginning with 1909, largely for the purpose of circulating the Scriptures in China, and committed the management to William E. Blackstone.[230] The Pocket Testament League, a movement which began in America about 1909 and whose object it was to promote daily reading in the New Testament, was introduced to China, and the Bible societies issued special editions to encourage it.[231]

The tract societies and the Society for the Diffusion of Christian and General Knowledge, now generally known as the Christian Literature Society, expanded their activities. In 1904, for example, the Religious Tract Society issued fifteen million pages of religious matter [232] and in 1912 published 667,000 copies of books, tracts, and magazines.[233] Hymnals were produced and in at least one of these half of the contents were by Chinese.[234] The Revolution of 1911-1912 caused for the moment a sharp decline in sales,[235] but before long the tide was once more rising. The Christian Literature Society continued to bring forth books and periodicals not only on religious topics but on other phases of life, such as home-making, child-training, the treatment of common diseases,[236] and the biographies of eminent statesmen.[237] It published at least three periodicals, including a magazine for women.[238] In 1910 it prepared and distributed information con-

[229] Cochrane, *Survey of the Missionary Occupation of China*, p. 169.
[230] *China Mission Year Book, 1912*, pp. 322, 323.
[231] Ibid., *1911*, p. 387.
[232] *A Century of Protestant Missions in China*, p. 386.
[233] Cochrane, op. cit., p. 95.
[234] *China Mission Year Book, 1912*, p. 244.
[235] *China Mission Year Book, 1912*, pp. 315-317.
[236] Richard in *The East and the West*, Vol. 3, p. 433; *China Mission Year Book, 1911*, pp. 393, 394; ibid., *1913*, p. 354.
[237] *International Review of Missions*, Vol. 2, p. 23.
[238] *China Mission Year Book, 1913*, p. 308; *A Century of Protestant Missions in China*, p. 631.

cerning Halley's Comet, which was then due to reappear, lest its coming occasion uprisings and riots among the ignorant.[239]

Mission presses increased both in number and output. By 1910 the Presbyterian Mission Press, in Shanghai, employed two hundred workmen.[240] The Methodist Publishing House was formed in 1902 by an amalgamation of the efforts of the northern and southern churches.[241] In 1914 nineteen presses were reported to be in operation. Three had recently been closed, but three had been founded or projected since 1910.[242]

Christian periodicals continued to play a fairly large part in the life of the Church. At the time of the Centenary Conference (1907) thirteen "chief newspapers," nine of them in Shanghai,[243] were being published by missionaries. At least two, the *T'ung Wên Pao* or *Christian Intelligencer,* begun in 1902 as the result of the Pan-Presbyterian Conference of the preceding year,[244] and the *Ta T'ung Pao,* or *Chinese Weekly,* commenced in 1904 by the Christian Literature Society under the editorship of the gifted W. A. Cornaby,[245] counted non-Christians as well as Christians among their subscribers.[246] At the Conference the suggestion was made that the periodicals published in Shanghai be superseded by others in which all the missions would unite and which would be designed to meet the specific needs of various classes. It was proposed, for example, that a Christian daily be published.[247] However, beyond recommending that the bodies concerned give consideration to the question, the Conference took no action.[248] A

[239] *China Mission Year Book, 1910,* Appendix X.
[240] *A Mission Press Sexagenary, 1844-1904,* passim; *China Mission Year Book, 1910,* pp. 351-362.
[241] *China Mission Year Book, 1910,* pp. 351-362.
[242] Ibid., *1915,* pp. 516, 517. The Commercial Press, by 1912 the largest publishing house in all Asia, with twenty branch presses and sales rooms in the principal cities of China, while not a missionary undertaking, was, as we have seen, under the management of Christians and was in part the result of the missionary's activities. A. J. Brown in *The East and the West,* Vol. 10, p. 17.
[243] *China Centenary Missionary Conference Records,* p. 195.
[244] Woodbridge, *Fifty Years in China,* p. 205; *A Century of Protestant Missions in China,* p. 403.
[245] Cornaby, *The Call of Cathay,* pp. 103, 104; Kernahan and Mrs. Cornaby, *Cornaby of Hanyang,* passim.
[246] About 1910 the *Ta T'ung Pao* had a weekly circulation of about 2,500 to 3,500.—Cornaby, op. cit., pp. 103, 104; *China Mission Year Book, 1910,* p. 343. Over half of these copies were subscribed to by officials.—*China Mission Year Book, 1910,* p. 343. Among the subscribers of the *T'ung Wên Pao* were many non-Christians.—George Douglas in *The China Centenary Missionary Conference Records,* p. 121.
[247] *China Centenary Missionary Conference Records,* pp. 104, 596-600.
[248] Ibid., p. 602.

daily paper independent of formal missionary organizations was projected by a group of Chinese, and the first number, under Chinese editorship, was issued February 8, 1913.[249] In 1913 and 1914 a beginning was made toward utilizing the secular press for the publication of Christian articles.[250]

A part of this Christian literature was issued in Roman letters, for it was believed that thus the illiterate could more quickly be taught to read.[251] However, although a system of Mandarin was devised by a committee of the Educational Association, and a literature was begun in it, the chief success of the romanized publications was in the dialects which could not easily be written with Chinese characters.[252]

Missionaries, moreover, continued to produce books to assist foreigners in understanding China and in becoming acquainted with its language and literature. Thus a Hakka-English dictionary was produced by Donald MacIver of the English Presbyterian Mission,[253] and F. W. Baller of the China Inland Mission wrote many books, not only in Chinese, but in English. Among the latter were a Chinese-English dictionary and translations from Chinese into English.[254] Frank H. Chalfant of the American Presbyterian Mission became an expert on the early forms of the Chinese written character and compiled an important monograph on the subject.[255] W. E. Soothill was the author of the best English edition of the *Analects* of Confucius.[256]

In spite of all these achievements and a Christian literature which was probably richer and more varied than that produced by Protestant missionaries in any other language,[257] what had been done was, as has been suggested, painfully inadequate. The Chinese held the printed page in great respect and in the transitional era no agency could be more effective in reaching the nation than the press. Yet much of Christian literature was in

[249] *China Mission Year Book, 1913,* pp. 356-362.

[250] MacGillivray in *The East and the West,* Vol. 13, pp. 212-217; *China Mission Year Book, 1915,* p. 180.

[251] W. A. P. Martin in *Chinese Recorder,* Vol. 33, p. 18.

[252] Brewster, *The Evolution of New China,* p. 112. In 1904 10,233 romanized publications were issued.—*Faith Triennial Meeting of the Educational Association,* p. 53.

[253] Paton, *The "Stranger People,"* p. 67.

[254] Broomhall, *F. W. Baller,* passim.

[255] *Encyclopædia Sinica,* p. 86.

[256] W. E. Soothill, *The Analects of Confucius.* Yokohama, 1910.

[257] So D. Z. Sheffield said.—*Edinburgh Conference Reports,* Vol. 3, pp. 339, 340.

inferior literary style,[258] not enough was of the kind to bring conviction to the new student class, and an insufficient number of foreigners and Christian Chinese of ability were devoting their time to its production.[259] Missionary gatherings were cognizant of these weaknesses but beyond bringing in "findings" did little to remedy them.

MEDICAL WORK

If in the field of the new literature Protestant missions did not maintain the lead which they had held before 1900, they continued to be all but supreme in modern medicine. Since the days of Peter Parker the physician had been a recognized member of the missionary body. In 1905, out of a total of 3,445 missionaries, 301 were physicians, 207 of them men and 94 women. Hospitals numbered 166, dispensaries 241, and during the year 35,301 in-patients and 1,044,948 out-patients were treated.[260] In 1915, out of a missionary body of 5,338, 525 were on the medical staff, 277 being men physicians, 106 women physicians, and 142 nurses.[261] In the ten years the number of hospitals had increased to 330, that of dispensaries to 223, of in-patients to 104,418 and of out-patients to 1,535,841.[262]

So extensive a work defies any attempt at a full picture in a book of this length. A few examples, however, will indicate something of the scope and the nature of what was accomplished. The very fact that they are scattering and apparently unrelated will serve to show how impressive a complete record would be. In fifteen years Dr. Elizabeth Reifsnyder, of Shanghai, ministered to more than two hundred thousand patients.[263] In Canton Dr. Kerr continued his hospital for the insane and by 1909 had treated in it 1,198 patients.[264] In 1907 the foundations for a new four-story hospital were laid in Chengtu.[265] Regular care for lepers was provided by the Church Missionary Society at Pakhoi, Foo-

---

[258] Darroch in *China Centenary Missionary Conference Records,* p. 205.
[259] For criticisms by missionaries, see Christie in ibid., p. 264; *Chinese Recorder,* Vol. 41, pp. 329, 579, Vol. 42, p. 337, Vol. 44, p. 230; *China Continuation Committee Conference Findings,* pp. 269-277.
[260] *A Century of Protestant Missions in China,* p. 674 and statistical tables.
[261] *The Christian Occupation of China,* Appendix, pp. xc, xcviii.
[262] Ibid., pp. xcviii, c.
[263] Taylor, *Social Work of Christian Missions,* p. 128.
[264] Brown, *Report on a Second Visit to China,* p. 133; *Chinese Recorder,* Vol. 40, p. 262.
[265] Bond, *Our Share in China,* pp. 63-66.

chow, Hangchow, and Hokchiang; by the Rhenish Missionary Society near Canton; and by the London Missionary Society at Siaokan, forty-five miles from Hankow.[266] The hospital of the Southern Methodist Mission at Soochow was supported by fees and local contributions except for the salaries of the foreign physicians and of the chaplain.[267] Both during the Revolution of 1911-1912 and the so-called Second Revolution of 1913, Dr. Macklin of the Foreign Christian Missionary Society remained in Nanking and ministered to the wounded while the city changed hands.[268] At Batang, on the Tibetan frontier, Drs. Shelton and Loftis of the same society used their medical skill to relieve suffering and to remove prejudice against the Christian message.[269] Dr. Clift, formerly of the Church Missionary Society and later of the Emmanuel Medical Mission, was a pioneer in turbulent Kwangsi.[270] Dr. Booth of the Wesleyan Methodist Missionary Society burned out his life in Hankow in superintending a hospital, conducting a medical school, and alleviating the suffering that the Revolution of 1911 brought upon the city.[271] In the distant and often lonely stations of the China Inland Mission the dispensary and the hospital were usually a part of the regular program,[272] and the pioneer missionary was often both evangelist and physician. The English Baptist Missionary Society had barely commenced medical work in Shensi when the Boxer uprising interrupted, and not until 1904 did Dr. H. Stanley Jenkins arrive in the province to lay the foundations anew.[273] Late in the following year he was joined by Dr. Andrew Young, who had been a missionary in the Congo, and then, his health failing, had, undaunted, returned to Scotland, acquired a medical education, and sought an appointment to China.[274] In 1909 he was again reënforced by the arrival of Dr. Cecil Robertson[275] and still

[266] Upward, *The Sons of Han*, pp. 171, 172; Gascoyne-Cecil, *Changing China*, p. 227; Martin, *One Hundred and Fifty Days in China*, p. 53; *China Mission Year Book, 1910*, p. 213, *1913*, p. 403, *1915*, p. 304.

[267] *A Century of Protestant Missions in China*, p. 419.

[268] McLean, *History of the Foreign Christian Missionary Society*, pp. 222, 265.

[269] Mrs. Shelton, *Sunshine and Shadow on the Tibetan Frontier*, passim; Loftis, *A Message from Batang*, passim.

[270] Clift, *Very Far East*, p. 10.

[271] Tatchell, *Booth of Hankow*, passim.

[272] See *China's Millions, 1912*, p. 42, for an instance.

[273] Keyte, *Andrew Young of Shensi*, p. 125.

[274] Ibid., passim.

[275] Meyer, *Memorials of Cecil Robertson of Sianfu*, passim.

later by that of Dr. Charter.   A hospital was opened in Hsianfu and three of the staff remained during the trying days of 1911, when massacre and fighting brought unusual need for their ministrations.   Late in 1912 Jenkins and Robertson succumbed to typhus, but Young, who was in Great Britain recuperating from an illness superinduced by the strain of the Revolution, at the risk of his own uncertain health returned and resumed the load.[276] Such heroism was typical.

Most of the service rendered was unrecorded or at best was reported only in letters or in periodicals with a limited circulation.   There was no extensive sale, for example, of the biography of Dr. Isabel Mitchell of the Irish Presbyterian Mission, who gave over ten years to Manchuria,[277] nor of that of Miss Li Bi Cu, a Chinese educated in the United States who served faithfully and efficiently under the Methodist Mission in Fukien.[278]   Medical missionaries, like their clerical colleagues, took adventures and perils and heroic deeds as part of the day's work.   An American missionary physician, the only skilled member of his profession in an inland city, was seized with an acute attack of appendicitis and started for the nearest fellow surgeon, three or four days' journey distant.   While on the way he became so much worse that his wife, who was not even a professionally trained nurse, under his direction operated where they were, on a Chinese houseboat, and saved his life.[279]   Yet the story was never widely heralded.   Some medical men, however, could not escape the limelight.   Especially was this true of the physicians who aided in combating the pneumonic plague. From this pestilence no one is known to have recovered.   It is harbored by the marmot and spreads southward into Manchuria and Mongolia by the trappers and traders who traffic in that animal's pelt.   In the autumn of 1910 an unusually severe epidemic broke out and against it the Chinese Government marshalled all possible forces.   At Mukden Dr. Christie with his new hospital was at the center where the greatest fight at isolation was conducted.   He and his colleagues gave themselves unstintedly, and one of the latter, the brilliant and attractive Dr. Arthur Jackson, who only a few weeks before

---

[276] Keyte, op. cit., passim.
[277] O'Neill, *Dr. Isabel Mitchell of Manchuria*, passim.
[278] Burton, *Comrades in Service*, pp. 101-114.
[279] The author knew personally of this incident.

had arrived in Manchuria, contracted the disease and died.[280] Two students in the Union Medical College at Peking also lost their lives [281] before the pestilence burned itself out.

To what has previously been said of medical education nothing need here be added. Something should, however, be recorded of the activities of the China Medical Missionary Association. That body, which had met first in 1890, held its second gathering in Shanghai in 1905 and subsequent ones in 1907, 1910, 1913, and 1915.[282] It was the pioneer national organization of modern physicians in China and conducted a journal and discussed and laid plans for the promotion of medical education and of public health, the preparation of medical literature, the fixing of a uniform terminology, and the conduct of research.[283] Under the auspices of the Association an English-Chinese dictionary of fifteen thousand medical and scientific terms was issued,[284] and a series of medical textbooks was projected in which the new nomenclature was to be employed.[285] A large book on the diseases of China was the work of two missionaries.[286] The first dissection of the human body in China for purposes of medical instruction seems to have been been made in the Harvard Medical School in the International Settlement in Shanghai in 1911 or 1912, a year or more before the practice was officially permitted by the government.[287] Autopsies had, moreover, long been performed in mission hospitals.[288]

Medical missionaries did not ignore the fact that they were sent to spread the Gospel by word as well as example, and not only discussed ways and means of improving the quality of their medical work as such, but the methods of evangelism.[289] Attached

[280] Christie, *Jackson of Mukden*, passim; *China Mission Year Book, 1912*, pp. 259-265; Costain, *Life of Dr. Arthur Jackson*, passim; Christie, *Thirty Years in the Manchu Capital*, pp. 204, 234-245.
[281] Armitage in *The East and the West*, Vol. 14, pp. 419-428.
[282] *Encyclopædia Sinica*, p. 101; *China Mission Year Book, 1913*, p. 287; *1911*, pp. 162-164; *China Medical Journal*, Vol. 24, p. 110.
[283] *The North-China Herald*, Jan. 15, 1913, p. 231; *China Medical Journal*, Vol. 22, p. 213, Vol. 26, p. 215, Vol. 27, p. 307, Vol. 28, p. 123.
[284] Henry Fowler in *The East and the West*, Vol. 5 (1907), p. 136.
[285] *China Mission Year Book, 1912*, pp. 266-268.
[286] W. Hamilton Jefferys and James L. Maxwell, *The Diseases of China, including Formosa and Korea*. London, 1914.
[287] For the government permission, see Gamewell, *New Life Currents in China*, p. 50.
[288] Balme, *China and Modern Medicine*, p. 132.
[289] G. A. Huntley in *China Medical Journal*, Vol. 25, p. 154.

to each hospital were Chinese who gave their entire time to bringing a religious message to the patients, and the foreigner himself usually took an active part in this side of the institution's activities.　Services were held daily and there was preaching and the distribution of literature in the waiting rooms of the dispensaries.[290]　Into many a community the Church first obtained access through a former patient in a mission hospital.[291]

Various Forms of Relief and Social Reform

Not only through Western medicine was the Protestant missionary striving to relieve suffering and to bring in more wholesome living: in a great variety of other ways he was seeking to minister to the physical and moral needs about him.　Before 1900 missionaries were too few and were confronted with too much opposition to attack more than an occasional outstanding evil. Now that their numbers had increased and resistance had declined, and now that Chinese culture was in process of change, they were attempting to bring to bear upon the nation's life what they believed to be Christian influences.　One missionary declared that the Church must address itself to the removal of opium, footbinding, gambling, concubinage and polygamy, official peculation, domestic slavery, vice, infanticide, the lack of respect for women, suicide, and the absence of individualism.[292]　Another held that the Church must concern itself with the relations of capital and labor and with interracial conflicts.[293]　A "Conference on the Social Application of Christianity" was held in Shanghai in January, 1914.[294]

As we have repeatedly said, to some missionaries this emphasis upon "the social gospel" seemed a departure from New Testament standards: they contended that the Christian's function was not to help build a better world, but that human society was to become more and more corrupt until Christ by his second coming should terminate the present age and should inaugurate his reign —a reign whose blessings the wicked, separated from the saved and suffering in hell, were to be eternally denied.　They accord-

[290] F. A. Keller in *Chinese Recorder,* Vol. 40, p. 314; *Chinese Recorder,* Vol. 32, p. 183.
[291] Osgood, *Breaking Down Chinese Walls,* p. 37; *China Mission Year Book, 1914,* p. 226.
[292] Bitton, *The Regeneration of New China,* pp. 127-145.
[293] Bashford, *Journal,* Sept. 22, 1907.
[294] *China Mission Year Book, 1914,* pp. 285-287.

ingly maintained that the missionary should limit himself to the proclamation of a gospel of personal salvation and strive to pluck from the burning as many brands as possible against the time when the Lord should appear. It is only fair to add, however, that even missionaries who held this view the most firmly were often active in works of mercy. Whatever the theories they propounded, in practice nearly all carried on forms of social relief. If missionaries were sometimes maladroit, or confused with the Christian Gospel social ideals and institutions to which their background committed them, they were undoubtedly earnest and devoted and were often farseeing and sagacious.

Even a bare catalogue of all the activities and institutions which were part of the missionary's labors would cover many pages. Only a few examples can be given and the chief types enumerated of what may rather loosely be termed the social phases of the Church's program.

In the first place, missionaries were often prominent in the community movements through which, after 1900 and especially after 1911, Chinese were attempting to readjust and reform their culture. In Chuchow in Anhui, for instance, Dr. E. I. Osgood initiated and became the president of a good citizenship league which set aside a piece of public land for a park and playground; he helped in the birth of a Red Cross unit; and at his suggestion these bodies introduced a street-cleaning department and conducted a campaign against gambling, immorality, and the use of wine and cigarettes.[295]   The Young Men's Christian Association sponsored the Peking Students' Social Service Club.[296]   In Changsha missionaries encouraged the formation of a Women's Social Service League [297] and a similar body sprang up in Nanking.[298]

In the second place, missionaries often took the sole responsibility for inaugurating changes. Thus in Shantung Alfred G. Jones of the English Baptist Mission introduced labor-saving machinery, especially that for the spinning of cotton, and experimented in improving the quality of silkworm eggs.[299]   Caldwell, an American Methodist in Fukien, used his expertness with the

[295] Osgood in *China Mission Year Book, 1914,* pp. 293-299.
[296] *China Mission Year Book, 1915,* pp. 322-336.
[297] *China Medical Journal,* Vol. 28, p. 331.
[298] *China Mission Year Book, 1915,* pp. 322-336.
[299] Dennis, *Christian Missions and Social Progress,* Vol. 3, pp. 115, 522.

rifle to rid the countryside of many a man-eating tiger.[300] Organized athletics of the kind familiar in the Occident were fostered by the mission schools and the Young Men's Christian Association.[301] The Chinese were not quick to adapt themselves to Western standards of sportsmanship, for the loss of a game or a meet meant also a loss of "face." With great rapidity, however, athletics became a regular feature of modern schools, non-missionary as well as missionary.

In the third place, missionaries sometimes acted as peacemakers between bandits and the authorities and between warring forces, and often relieved the distress which was an accompaniment of the civil strife that followed the Revolution. In 1913, for example, Dr. W. E. Macklin obtained a promise from Chang Hsun—violated later—not to loot Nanking.[302] In 1912 in the same city Dr. Gaynor of the Friends' Mission opened a hospital and refuge for the Manchus left destitute by the Revolution and died of typhus contracted from those to whom she was ministering.[303] Caldwell added to his prowess with the rifle noteworthy service as an intermediary between officials and bandits. He was, indeed, the means of inducing several bands of brigands to abandon their lawless occupation and to return to peaceful pursuits.[304]

In the fourth place, missionaries were constantly seeking to improve the status of women and girls. For years many missionaries, as we have seen, had been protesting against the custom of foot-binding. As time passed it became customary in some Christian communities for women on entering into church membership to unbind their feet.[305] This was, indeed, occasionally made obligatory.[306] In many mission schools no girl with bound feet was admitted.[307] With the death of Mrs. Archibald Little the general movement outside the Church for "natural feet" declined for a time, but within the Church it was more vigorous than ever.[308]

Missionaries did not confine their efforts on behalf of women

[300] Caldwell, *Blue Tiger*, passim.
[301] Speer, *The Gospel and the New World*, p. 227; *China Mission Year Book, 1912*, pp. 355-357.
[302] Dennett, *Democratic Movement in Asia*, p. 68.
[303] Williams, *Ohio Friends in the Land of Sinim*, p. 129.
[304] Caldwell, op. cit., passim.
[305] McNabb, *The Women of the Middle Kingdom*, pp. 100, 116.
[306] Ibid.; Ross, *The Changing Chinese*, p. 179.
[307] Ross, op. cit., p. 179.
[308] *The Peking Gazette*, June 8, 1914.

to an attack on this one custom.   The Conference of 1913 suggested that a Chinese Women's Alliance be formed to oppose early betrothals and marriages, the taking of secondary wives, and the employment of domestic slave girls, and to induce the government to incorporate these reforms in the laws of the Republic. It urged that Christian and non-Christian women unite in the study of child welfare, of healthful and modest dress for women and girls, and of the moral well-being of women employed in the factories.[309]   In a medical school for women maintained by the missions the physician in charge exhorted the students to shun marriage on the existing terms.[310]   Some missionaries, too, were exercised by the exploitation of women and girls in the new factories which were beginning to emerge.[311]   The Women's Christian Temperance Union organized women for the protection and betterment of their homes and for opposition to alcohol, opium, and cigarettes.[312]

In the fifth place, missionaries continued to combat opium. As formerly, they conducted refuges for the cure of addicts and forbade Church members to have any part in the production, sale, or use of the drug.   From one church in an opium-ridden district a missionary cast out a tenth of the membership for having grown the poppy.[313]   Moreover, the missionary was endeavoring not only to keep his own skirts and those of the Christians clean from all taint of the curse, but to free the nation from it.   Hampden DuBose, of Soochow, the president of the Anti-Opium League in China, while in the United States in 1904 stirred up the Department of State to send American consuls in China a circular of inquiry on the opium situation.[314]   This same Anti-Opium League prepared a memorial to the throne which was signed by twelve hundred missionaries from seventeen provinces.   That document, forwarded to Peking in 1906 through the good offices of the Viceroy at Nanking, appears to have been the incentive that led the not unwilling court to issue the edict of that year which

[309] *Continuation Committee Conference Findings,* p. 892; *China Mission Year Book, 1913,* p. 314.
[310] Ross, op. cit., p. 206.
[311] Burton, *Women Workers of the Orient,* pp. 51, 53.
[312] There had been a unit at Chinkiang for at least ten years before 1900 (Mrs. Chauncey Goodrich in *China Mission Year Book, 1911,* pp. 452-455) and several branches were later organized in Peking (Gamble, *Peking, a Social Survey,* p. 388).
[313] Ross, *The Changing Chinese,* p. 217.
[314] Pitcher, *In and About Amoy,* p. 125.

inaugurated a new and successful campaign against the drug.[315] The campaign is not properly a part of this story, for it quickly spread beyond missionary circles. Note, however, must be made of the fact that in 1908 Great Britain and China entered into àn agreement by which the two governments were to seek to bring the traffic to an end within a decade, the one by curtailing the importation of the Indian drug by one-tenth each year and the other by a proportionate reduction of the local production. Such unexpected progress did China make in carrying out her side of the agreement that in 1913 the Indian Government put an end to the sale of opium for the China market.[316] For the time China was practically rid of the vice. In the last stages of the battle the anti-opium forces were aided by the presence of the International Reform Bureau, a world-wide Christian organization of American origin which entered China in January, 1909, in the person of an energetic secretary, Rev. E. W. Thwing, and aided in the foundation of anti-opium societies.[317] The International Reform Bureau, it may be added in passing, also attacked gambling, impurity, the use of alcohol, and the rapidly growing consumption of cigarettes.[318]

In the sixth place, missionaries continued their attempts to ameliorate the lot of the blind, the deaf, and the dumb. In 1914 at least thirteen schools for the blind were in operation and over four hundred students had been graduated, and a union system for teaching the sightless to read had been evolved as a substitute for the several that were in use.[319] The school at Chefoo for deaf-mutes was strengthened and enlarged.[320]

A seventh activity was the relief of famine sufferers. In 1907 excessive rainfall brought an extensive crop failure in Anhui, Honan, and the northern part of Kiangsu. *The Christian Herald,*

[315] Ibid., p. 125; A. J. Brown in *The East and the West,* Vol. 10, p. 21; Ross, *The Changing Chinese,* p. 157.
[316] Pott, *The Emergency in China,* pp. 113, 114; *Ninety-Eighth Report of the Wesleyan Methodist Missionary Society,* p. 129; *International Review of Missions,* Vol. 3, p. 15; *L. M. S. Chronicle,* Vol. 18 (new series), p. 84; *China Mission Year Book, 1911,* p. 447; *1914,* pp. 25, 301-306.
[317] *China Mission Year Book, 1911,* pp. 17, 443; *1912,* p. 362; *1913,* p. 410.
[318] Ibid., *1912,* p. 362.
[319] *One Hundred and First Report of the Wesleyan Methodist Missionary Society,* p. 136; *China Missions Emergency Committee,* p. 228; Hume-Griffith, *Dust of Gold,* p. 16; Augustana Synod, *Our First Decade in China,* p. 88; *Chinese Recorder,* Vol. 40, p. 249; *China Mission Year Book, 1910,* pp. 380-384; *1911,* p. 275; *1913,* p. 410: *1914,* pp. 312-330.
[320] *China Mission Year Book, 1911,* p. 449; Brown, *New Forces in Old China,* p. 225.

an American periodical, raised and forwarded $450,000 gold [321] and the Methodists gave $42,607.23 [322] The Viceroy, Tuan Fang, at first objected to the distribution of relief by missionaries, saying that in case of anti-foreign disturbances an indemnity might be demanded which would be larger than the relief funds contributed. Protestant missionaries, however, assured him that under no circumstances would compensation be asked, and so were permitted to continue their work of mercy.[323] In the winter of 1910-1911 another famine, again due to floods, devastated much the same districts. A Central China Famine Relief Committee, officered by a former missionary and a missionary, appealed to Europe and America for help. Extensive funds came and were distributed largely by missionaries.[324] The following year floods brought a recurrence of distress in the same region and dearth in a few other sections of Central China. A new committee repeating the old name was formed, with Bishop Graves of the American Church (Episcopal) Mission as chairman but with a majority of non-missionary members. Over a million dollars were subscribed and more than one hundred missionaries aided in the distribution.[325]

An eighth and last activity, the care of orphans, was largely the outgrowth of famine relief. The orphan asylum was never as prominent a part of the Protestant program as it was of that of the Roman Catholics. However, so many children had lost their parents in the famine that mercy demanded that something be done for them. *The Christian Herald* was active in raising support, and after the new harvests had brought to an end the acute stage of destitution, committees were left with undistributed moneys which could be used for this purpose. Outside the famine areas, moreover, a few orphanages were maintained.[326] In 1914

[321] Broomhall, *Present-Day Conditions in China*, pp. 35-41.
[322] Bashford, *Journal*, 1908.
[323] Broomhall, op. cit., pp. 35-41; *China's Millions*, 1907, p. 154; Williams, *In Four Continents*, pp. 77-80; Bashford, *Journal*, May, 1907.
[324] *International Review of Missions*, Vol. 2, p. 17; *China Mission Year Book, 1911*, pp. 66-68.
[325] *China Mission Year Book, 1912*, Appendix, pp. 77 et seq.; *Chinese Recorder*, Vol. 43, p. 90; *Church Missionary Gleaner*, Aug., 1912, p. 139; Cody, *Letters to Betsy*, p. 170.
[326] Bashford, *Journal*, July 31, 1907; Broomhall, *Jubilee Story of the China Inland Mission*, p. 293; *A Century of Protestant Missions in China*, p. 438; Edinburgh Conference Reports, Vol. 3, pp. 97-104; Cochrane, *Survey of the Missionary Occupation of China*, p. 27; Davis, *Neighbors in Christ*, p. 91; *China Mission Year Book, 1911*, p. 457; *1918*, p. 327.

2,093 were reported to be in Protestant orphanages, and of these 1,005 were supported by *The Christian Herald*.[327]

COÖPERATION AND UNION

The rapid extension of Protestant missions necessitated a much larger degree of coöperation than had heretofore existed. In the earlier years when missionaries were comparatively few, institutions small, and most of the country yet to be occupied, little associated effort had been called for. Each society and mission could go its own way without serious danger of reduplicating the work of another. Even as late as the eighteen nineties joint action did not seem particularly imperative. There was, to be sure, as we have seen, coöperation in the translation of the Scriptures and in the preparation of textbooks, and the Educational and Medical Missionary Associations had been formed. Gatherings for fellowship, moreover, were held, notably the conferences of missionaries at Shanghai in 1877 and 1890. One journal, *The Chinese Recorder,* brought to the entire missionary body the news of the activities of its members and provided a platform on which common problems could be discussed. Here and there, as in the Amoy region, two or more missions had achieved close affiliation. In general, however, each Protestant mission acted independently of its fellows.

Before 1900 a change had begun to be foreshadowed, and after that year it came with surprising rapidity. By 1914 Protestant missionaries were to be found in practically all the chief cities and in many of the smaller ones. The number of different societies and of missionaries had increased greatly. Schools had multiplied and efficiency demanded that they be knit into a unified system. In secondary and especially in higher education the best results could be obtained only if the missions pooled their efforts. Through the entire missionary program closer coöperation had become imperative if Protestants were to employ economically the forces at their disposal.

Among the missionary body were those who viewed with disapproval attempts at union and even at coöperation. To their minds they would be disloyal to the distinctive and God-given tenets for which their branch of the Church stood if they were to consent to such movements. Some of the supporting con-

[327] *China Mission Year Book, 1914,* p. 249.

stituencies and boards in Europe and America shared this opposition. Missionaries were not wanting, however, who declared publicly and emphatically the necessity of joint effort and planning.[328] A circular sent out in 1903 to all missionaries in China elicited a wide response and nine-tenths of those replying favored some kind of federation of all the Protestant churches in the Empire.[329] As has been said earlier, in spite of the large number of different denominations and societies, the majority were in agreement as to what constituted the essence of the Christian message. Protestant missions were a phase of a general religious movement which had first become important in the eighteenth century, which was broader than any one religious body, and which, while varying in details in different ecclesiastical groups, was essentially one. It is not surprising, therefore, that Protestant missionaries found coöperation both possible and desirable.

The forms taken by the coöperative movement were many. We have already noted that the China Inland Mission, which had more missionaries in China than any other one organization, either Roman Catholic or Protestant, included on its roll members of many different denominations, even of such particularistic bodies as Baptists and Anglicans. We have seen, too, the extensive progress made after 1900 in coöperation in the translation of the Bible, in evangelism, in the Sunday School, in education, in medicine, and in such works of beneficence as the relief of famine.[330] Even in theological education, in which, to insure the adherence of their clergy to their distinctive beliefs, denominations would be inclined to be most insistent upon separate schools, union was becoming more and more common. Some of the most important of these joint undertakings dated from before 1900, but the majority had their beginnings after that year.[331]

A simple and frequent form of coöperation was the partition of territory, so that in rural districts there should not be that duplication of effort which had proved so wasteful in the United

---

[328] For examples of this and discussion of ways and means, see the several articles in *Chinese Recorder* for Feb., 1910; Cochrane in ibid., Vol. 37, p. 306; A. E. Moule in *The East and the West*, Vol. 4, pp. 361-372; Bishop Graves in *The Spirit of Missions*, Vol. 75, p. 361; and Bitton, *The Regeneration of New China*, pp. 174-180.

[329] Cochrane in *Chinese Recorder*, Vol. 44, p. 342.

[330] See a partial list in *Edinburgh Conference Reports*, Vol. 8, pp. 52-82.

[331] See another list in *China Mission Year Book, 1914*, pp. 200-207.

States. After 1900, for example, the (Northern) American Presbyterians generously offered to exchange their mission in Chihli, where the Congregationalists were strong, for the small work which the American Board conducted in Shantung, a province in which the Presbyterians were represented in force. The Congregationalists as generously declined—on the ground that Presbyterians had long been in Chihli and that the plan would seem to discourage comity.[332] In 1909 and 1910 the London Missionary Society transferred to the Canadian Methodists territory extending three hundred miles along the Yangtze below Chungking.[333] In Szechwan the various Protestant bodies divided the province among themselves.[334] These ecclesiastical "spheres of influence" might lay the missions open to the criticism of extreme nationalists, but they were preferable to senseless competition and overlapping.

A closer form of coördination was the union or federation of closely related bodies. Of this, one of the largest and earliest instances was the formation of the *Chung Hua Sheng Kung Hui,* or Holy Catholic Church of China, by representatives of the Church Missionary Society, the Society for the Propagation of the Gospel in Foreign Parts, the American Protestant Episcopalians, and the Canadian Anglicans. In 1897 most of the bishops together with some of the clergy met in Shanghai and in 1899 a larger and similar gathering convened. Subsequent conferences were held in 1903, 1907, and 1909. At the 1909 meeting a constitution was adopted for a united church and this having been approved by the authorities in England and America, the first General Synod met in 1912. Thus had come into existence a body counting about thirty thousand baptized members in eleven dioceses.[335] Even larger was the *Chung Kuo Chi Tu Sheng Chiao Chang Lao Hui,* or Presbyterian Church of China, formed by eight bodies, the American Presbyterians of the North and the South, the Reformed Church in America, the Presbyterian Churches of Ireland, of Canada, and of England, the Church of Scotland, and the

[332] Brown, *New Forces in Old China,* p. 290.
[333] Bond, *Our Share in China,* p. 148.
[334] *Edinburgh Conference Reports,* Vol. 8, p. 24.
[335] Bishop C. P. Scott in *The East and the West,* Vol. 16, p. 303; Stock, *History of the Church Missionary Society,* Vol. 4, pp. 294, 295; *Spirit of Missions,* Vol. 72, p. 556, Vol. 77, p. 503; Louis Byrde in *The East and the West,* Vol. 11, pp. 66-81; *Church Missionary Gleaner,* July, 1909; Gascoyne-Cecil, *Changing China,* p. 216; *China Mission Year Book, 1912,* p. 203; *Chinese Recorder,* Vol. 43, p. 378; *Edinburgh Conference Reports,* Vol. 2, p. 290.

United Free Church of Scotland. In 1901 from a preliminary gathering in Shanghai a Committee on Presbyterian Union emerged which met in 1902, 1903, and 1905. From its deliberations came a plan for an autonomous Presbyterian Church for China. Not until after 1914 was a General Assembly formed, but the organization of synods, a process which had begun before 1900, was encouraged, and a national Federal Council was authorized and met for the first time in 1907.[336] Suggestions were made looking toward a single body of Baptists, and among the Methodists were those who wished for a union of all the missions of Wesleyan origin. Both projects, however, proved abortive.[337] In Kwangtung the Basel, Rhenish, and Berlin societies achieved a type of federation.[338]

Only infrequently was there coalescence of widely different denominations. Almost unique was the union (1907) in Tsinanfu of the churches founded by the American Presbyterians and the English Baptists.[339]

On a much larger scale than any of these unions was the movement for the coördination and federation of all Protestant work in China. Before its adjournment the General Missionary Conference of 1890 appointed a committee to provide for its successor. The original plan had been to hold this gathering in 1900, but because of the World Missionary Conference of that year the time was postponed until 1901. Then came the Boxer outbreak and the date was changed to 1907 to make of the occasion a centenary celebration of the coming of Morrison.[340] The gathering assembled in Shanghai and had a total attendance of 1,170, of whom 500 were delegates and 670 visitors and representatives of the home boards.[341] It was more than twice as large as the 1890 Conference, but like the latter it was made up almost entirely of foreigners, only six or seven Chinese being enrolled.[342]

[336] *Agendum voor de Synode der Christelijke Gereformeerde Kerk*, p. 186; *Edinburgh Conference Reports*, Vol. 2, p. 305; *Chinese Recorder*, Vol. 32, p. 553, Vol. 34, p. 10, Vol. 42, pp. 682, 686, Vol. 45, p. 588; *Report of the Presbyterian Board, 1902*, p. 11, *1907*, pp. 44, 45; Fisher, *C. W. Mateer*, p. 205.
[337] *Edinburgh Conference Reports*, Vol. 8, pp. 88-102; Bashford, *Journal*, May 4, 1907, Oct., 1907, Feb., 1908.
[338] *China Mission Year Book, 1910*, p. 196.
[339] *Missionary Review of the World*, Vol. 24, p. 882; *China Council, Second Annual Meeting, 1911, Presbyterian Church in the U. S. A.*, p. 44; *The Christian Occupation of China*, p. 203.
[340] *China Centenary Conference Records*, Introduction.
[341] Ibid.
[342] Ibid., pp. 784 et seq.

Like its predecessors, too, the 1907 Conference heard papers on and discussed various phases of missionary work and adopted resolutions. It registered, however, a marked advance in coöperation and in plans for turning over the control of the Church to the Chinese. It suggested the union of the churches established by different missions of the same ecclesiastical order; looked forward to a Chinese Church; [343] urged the importance of recruiting and training a Chinese ministry; [344] stressed education, taking steps to strengthen the Educational Association by recommending provision for full-time secretaries; called attention to the importance of teaching Mandarin in the hope that the ability to read and write in that vernacular might become general; [345] appealed to the Christian world to realize more adequately its responsibility for giving a knowledge of the Gospel to every person in the Empire and proposed a committee "to consider the possibility of the formation of a National Missionary Society for China by the Chinese Churches"; [346] urged education for women, including the establishment of colleges and normal schools; [347] drew attention to the need for more and better Christian literature; [348] while holding that "the Worship of Ancestors is incompatible with an enlightened and spiritual conception of the Christian Faith," held that the Chinese Church must ultimately be the judge of what should be substituted for it, and stressed the necessity of encouraging reverence for parents and affectionate remembrance of the dead; [349] emphasized a high standard of preparation for the missionary physician, union medical schools, medical literature, the campaign against opium, and care for the insane and the lepers; [350] made provision, as we have seen, for union versions of the Bible, and inaugurated a movement for the extension and improvement of the Sunday Schools; [351] and, while holding "that the time had not yet come when all the protection to Christian converts provided in the treaties can safely be withdrawn," expressed the hope "that any intervention of missionaries

[343] Ibid., pp. 437-444.
[344] Ibid., pp. 473-477.
[345] Ibid., pp. 519-521, 758. The establishment of schools for the education of missionaries' children was also recommended.—Ibid., p. 758.
[346] Ibid., pp. 548-551.
[347] Ibid., pp. 587, 588.
[348] Ibid., pp. 602, 603.
[349] *China Centenary Conference Records*, pp. 623, 624.
[350] Ibid., pp. 656-658.
[351] Ibid., pp. 684-688.

in such matters may speedily become wholly unnecessary . . . an appeal to the authorities being the last resort," and exhorted "all missionaries to be vigilant, lest, in the present national awakening, the Christian Church should, in any way, be made use of for revolutionary ends." [352]

Finally, the Conference recommended "the formation of a Federal Union under the title, the Christian Federation of China." The methods suggested for attaining this goal were the organization in each province or group of provinces of a council consisting of delegates, both Chinese and foreign, representing all the missions in the area. The councils were to meet at least once in two years and each was to appoint a Chinese and a foreign secretary. A national council was projected to be composed of representatives of the provincial bodies and was to convene "once in three years or at least once in five years." The Conference appointed a committee of twenty-five missionaries to bring about the organization of the councils. The function of the federation was defined as being "to encourage everything that will demonstrate the existing essential unity of Christians . . . to devise . . . plans whereby the whole field can be worked most efficiently . . . to promote union in educational work [and] the encouragement of the consideration of all questions as to how the various phases of Christian work can be carried on most efficiently, e.g., translation and literary work, social work, medical work, evangelistic work, etc." [353]

The movement which expressed itself in these last resolutions had arisen in Peking in 1903 as the result of a paper read before the local missionary association by Dr. Thomas Cochrane. A letter sent out by a committee of this body asked the opinion of missionaries concerning the preparation of a union hymn-book, the adoption of a common designation for churches and chapels, the approval of common terms for God and Holy Spirit—reviving memories of earlier controversies—and the federation of all the Protestant churches in China. [354] The replies were encouraging, and a meeting of missionaries at Peitaiho in August, 1904, took steps to call at Peking a conference on federation to which every mission in each province was to be asked to send a representa-

[352] Ibid., pp. 743, 744.
[353] *China Centenary Conference Records*, pp. 719-721; *Edinburgh Conference Reports*, Vol. 8, pp. 103, 104; *Spirit of Missions*, Vol. 75, p. 359.
[354] *Chinese Recorder*, Vol. 35, p. 551, Vol. 44, p. 342.

tive. The Peking conference met in September, 1905, adopted further plans for inaugurating local and national councils, and paved the way for the project which the Centenary Conference approved two years later.[355]

So important an endorsement of the federation movement as that given by the Centenary gathering could not fail of large effect. The inertia of established methods and institutions and the criticisms of disapproving missionaries might retard but could not entirely prevent adoption. Several provincial councils were formed. The most marked progress was in West China. Here the Protestant missions had met in 1899 and had constituted an Advisory Board of Reference and Coöperation, and in 1905 had planned a union university.[356] Following the Centenary Conference, in January, 1908, another regional gathering convened, in Chengtu, and the goal was adopted of "One Protestant Christian Church for West China." The achievement of this aim would not be easy, for the extremes of Protestantism were represented—Quakers, Baptists, Methodists, and Anglicans. The territory could be amicably divided, but would Baptists receive into membership without immersion Christians moving from non-Baptist districts, would Anglicans admit to communion without confirmation those who had become Christians in non-Anglican territories, and would the non-Quakers welcome to full membership without baptism those whom the accident of territorial division had made Friends? The 1908 gathering bravely decided on the attempt and sealed its purpose with a communion service in which Baptists, Quakers, Methodists, and Anglicans joined.[357] While its entire purpose was not quickly achieved, progress was made, especially in a union hymnal, in a tract society, in education, in terminology, and in the conditions laid down for church membership. Moreover, the underlying unity of spirit was marked.[358]

In other sections of China advance was registered and by 1914 federation councils were either in existence or in process of

[355] Ibid., Vol. 35, p. 551, Vol. 37, p. 231, Vol. 44, pp. 343, 344; Brewster, *The Evolution of New China*, p. 271.
[356] *Chinese Recorder*, Vol. 36, p. 439; *Edinburgh Conference Reports*, Vol. 8, p. 24.
[357] *Chinese Recorder*, Vol. 45, p. 350; *China Mission Year Book, 1910*, p. 145; *West China Missionary Conference*, passim; Bashford, *Journal*, Feb. 2, 1908, May 1, 1908.
[358] *Edinburgh Conference Reports*, Vol. 2, p. 315; *China Mission Year Book, 1912*, pp. 275-277; *Chinese Recorder*, Vol. 45, p. 349.

formation in Chêkiang, Kiangsu, Kwangtung, Kwangsi, Man-churia, Chihli, Shantung, Honan, Kiangsi, Anhui, Hupeh, Hunan, and North Fukien, and a missionary conference cared for South Fukien.[359] Several of these councils were little more than paper organizations and met infrequently, and one, that in Hunan, had been succeeded by a continuation committee.[360]

While these local councils were in process of birth, the forma-tion of the national organization contemplated by the Centenary Conference was postponed. The delay proved permanent, for another body, the China Continuation Committee, came into existence and made the other unnecessary. The World Mis-sionary Conference held at Edinburgh in 1910 initiated a plan for the better coördination of Protestant missionary forces. Regional bodies for coöperative purposes were to be formed where they did not already exist, both in the countries from which mis-sionaries were sent and in those to which they went, and all were to culminate in an International Missionary Council.[361] The Continuation Committee of the Edinburgh Conference, which was formed to bring this program into effect, had as its chairman John R. Mott. Under Mr. Mott's leadership gatherings convened in various countries as a preliminary to permanent committees, and in time there followed the most inclusive and effective world-wide organization that Protestantism had yet developed.

Mr. Mott arrived in China in 1913, and with him as presiding officer five regional conferences were held and a national body made up of delegates from these was convened at Shanghai. A supplementary gathering met later in Manchuria. In marked contrast to previous national Protestant gatherings, Chinese were now included, between a third and a fourth of the nearly one hundred and twenty members of the national conference and a large proportion of each of the regional gatherings being of that nationality. The new movement did not seek to start afresh, however, but to build on and to consummate what had already been achieved. In each of the conferences, regional and national, a study of the field was made and findings were adopted. The

[359] Cochrane in *Chinese Recorder*, Vol. 44, pp. 342-351; ibid., Vol. 32, p. 218; Cochrane in *China Mission Year Book, 1912*, pp. 269-273; Cochrane, *Survey of the Missionary Occupation of China, 1913*, p. 295; *China Mission Year Book, 1914*, pp. 207-210, 218-220; *Edinburgh Conference Reports*, Vol. 8, p. 108.
[360] Box in *China Mission Year Book, 1914*, pp. 218-220.
[361] See plan for the Continuation Committee in *Edinburgh Conference Reports*, Vol. 8, pp. 202, 203.

findings of the national body included (1) a recognition of the strong plea to the Church presented by the districts in China still unoccupied by Protestant forces, a call for a survey to show the state of the occupation (later to lead to the preparation of a huge quarto volume), a suggested procedure for comity in entering new territory, a note of the need for work among Moslems, and an expression of the conviction that the missionary body should be heavily reënforced; (2) a statement of the unprecedented openmindedness of the Chinese to the Gospel, a declaration that much of the burden of evangelism could now be assumed by the Chinese churches, and that the work of evangelism should be pushed; (3) an expression of hope that "the Churches . . . be so developed that the Chinese themselves may recognize them as having become truly native," that "to manifest the unity that already exists among all faithful Christians in China" a common name be adopted, the one preferred being *Chung Hua Chi Tu Chiao Hui,* "the Christian Church in China," and suggested steps toward a larger unity and toward self-support; (4) emphasis upon the training of Chinese leaders; (5) standards for the selection and training of missionaries; (6) a plea for expansion in Christian education, especially in primary, secondary, and theological schools; (7) a statement of the next steps to be taken in Christian literature; (8) plans for more extensive union and coöperation; (9) medical work; (10) women's work; and (11) business efficiency.[362]

The steps toward federation, coöperation, and unity proposed by the Continuation Committee Conference were in the main a natural sequence to what had already been attained. The Conference urged "the uniting of Churches of similar ecclesiastical order planted in China by different Missions . . . the organic union of Churches which already enjoy inter-communion in any particular area, . . . federation, local and provincial, of all Churches, . . . the formation of a National Council of the Churches in accordance with plans which the Continuation Committee of this Conference shall devise if it deem such a Council necessary, . . . the reference to the China Continuation Committee of . . . the question of uniform terms for use in the Churches, . . . a hymn-book for common use, . . . [and] the

[362] See full texts in *The Continuation Conferences in Asia, 1912-1913,* pp. 321-367.

publication of a China Church Year Book, . . . the fresh study by all Christians of the faith and order held by those who differ from them, in order to promote cordial mutual understanding, . . . [and] prayer in public and private for the whole Church of Christ. . . ." The conference also stressed the need of greater coöperation of the mission boards at home, recommended "that medical, theological, and middle schools and colleges be conducted on union principles," that union summer Bible schools be held, and that there be more uniformity in nomenclature in Christian literature, and encouraged further consolidation of publishing and distributing agencies.[363]

The China Continuation Committee, organized to carry on the work begun by the Conference, was defined as having merely "consultative and advisory, not legislative or mandatory" functions. It was to be composed of not less than forty and not more than sixty members, of whom not less than one-third were to be Chinese.[364]

The Continuation Committee so constituted proved very active. It chose as full time secretaries two very able men, E. C. Lobenstine of the American Presbyterian Mission (North) and Ch'êng Ching-yi, pastor of an independent church in Peking formerly connected with the London Missionary Society.[365] In 1914 A. L. Warnshuis of the American (Dutch) Reformed Mission was called to the position of National Evangelistic Secretary.[366] While the Committee itself met only once a year, its executive committee convened more frequently and much additional work was performed by sub-committees appointed to carry into effect some of the mandates of the Continuation Conference.[367] In the summer of 1914 one of the sub-committees, that on a Forward Evangelistic Movement, held fourteen special conferences on evangelism.[368]

The impulse brought by the Edinburgh gathering had reënforced tendencies toward coöperation which were already strong

---

[363] *The Continuation Committee Conferences in Asia, 1912-1913,* pp. 328-348.
[364] *The Continuation Committee Conferences in Asia, 1912-1913,* pp. 348-350. For other accounts of the China Continuation Conferences, see *International Review of Missions,* Vol. 2, pp. 501-519, Vol. 3, pp. 18, 19; *Chinese Recorder,* Vol. 44, pp. 203-239; *China Mission Year Book, 1913,* pp. 60-80, 187-189, 212-215; *China's Millions,* 1913, p. 75.
[365] E. C. Lobenstine in *China Mission Year Book,* 1914, p. 485.
[366] E. C. Lobenstine in ibid., *1915,* p. 487.
[367] E. C. Lobenstine in ibid., *1914,* p. 490.
[368] *China Mission Year Book, 1915,* pp. 135-143.

and had prepared the way for that progress toward union which was to be so marked a feature of the years between 1914 and 1926. In spite of the multiplicity of societies and denominations, Protestants in China were beginning to work together. Criticism was not wanting, and as yet little organic union of churches had been achieved, but through joint enterprises a consciousness of being part of a single "Christian Movement"—a new and significant term—was being strengthened. Actual nation-wide union might never be attained and at best was probably far in the future, but greater strides toward it had been made than in Europe or America.

The consolidation of Protestantism in China was facilitated by the summer resorts which after 1900 came into prominence. At Peitaiho on the coast north of Tientsin not far from where the Great Wall touches the sea, in the mountain valley of Kuling just south of Kiukiang, on hill sites at Mokanshan in Chêkiang, Chikungshan in Hupeh, Kuliang near Foochow, and in a number of less frequented places, missionaries and their families took refuge from the summer's heat. In the larger centers missionaries of many different boards rested, played, worked, and worshiped together for a month or more in each year, and conferences for study and inspiration became the order of the day. The summer assembly, so popular in the United States and Great Britain, found here a congenial habitat. In seeking rest and health missionaries were unexpectedly strengthening bonds of fellowship: the summer resort was a social group which did not conform to ecclesiastical boundaries.[369]

THE GROWTH OF THE CHINESE CHURCH IN INDEPENDENCE AND SELF-SUPPORT

Closely associated with the movement toward coöperation and unity was that toward a Church Chinese in its maintenance and control. From the beginning, as we have so often seen, Protestant missionaries had set as a goal a Church self-supporting and self-propagating. In some areas great strides toward this objective had been made before 1900. Now, with the rapid growth of the Church and the emphasis upon education with the conse-

[369] *China Mission Year Book, 1911*, pp. xxiii-xxviii; *The Christian Occupation of China*, p. 395. For the legal problem involved in land-holding by foreigners in these resorts, see Clennell in *Parliamentary Papers*, 1903, Vol. 87, China No. 1.

quent emergence of young and well-trained Chinese leaders, progress was marked. The sentiment of patriotism, long present in the form of pride of culture, was being accentuated by contact with the nationalism which was so marked a characteristic of the Occident of the nineteenth and twentieth centuries. Chinese Christians sought to rid themselves of the odium of subserviency to the foreigner and of eating his rice and aping his ways, and desired a larger share in the direction of the Church.[370] Many missionaries encouraged the movement.[371] Even before 1900 self-support had been a fairly constant topic of discussion among missionaries, but after that year it became more prominent and Chinese as well as foreigners dwelt on its importance.[372] The Centenary Conference, although almost exclusively a missionary gathering, placed "The Chinese Church" at the forefront of its discussions and in its resolutions said:

"That in planting the Church of Christ on Chinese soil, we desire only to plant one Church under the sole control of the Lord Jesus Christ, governed by the Word of the living God and led by His guiding Spirit. While freely communicating to this Church the knowledge of Truth, and the rich historical experience to which older churches have attained, we fully recognize the liberty in Christ of the churches in China planted by the Missions and Churches which we represent, in so far as these churches are, by maturity of Christian character and experience, fitted to exercise it; and we desire to commit them in faith and hope to the continued safe keeping of their Lord, when the time shall arrive, which we eagerly anticipate, when they shall pass beyond our guidance and control.

"That in this view we cordially undertake to submit very respectfully

[370] *Edinburgh Conference Reports.* Vol. 1, p. 96. "Recently at an informal meeting of Chinese Christians, a symposium took place concerning the prospects of Christianity in the Empire. These men represented different groups and widely different interests and localities; yet they were all agreed that if Christianity is to succeed in China it must become less foreign and more Chinese; that stress must be laid on essentials of faith, rather than on formation of creed; that there must be a certain liberality which will not consider sinful the ceremonies of respect for ancestors, for the emperor, for Confucius and for the dead, but will tolerate these as national observances, and that Christian thought should be presented so as to appeal to all classes, not only of the people, but to their leaders as well."—Reinsch, *Intellectual and Political Currents in the Far East,* p. 185.
[371] *Missionary Review of the World,* Vol. 17, p. 268.
[372] As examples of the discussion, see C. T. Wang in *The East and the West,* Vol. 8, pp. 288-298; C. T. Wang quoted in Broomhall, *Present-Day Conditions in China,* p. 34; *Chinese Recorder,* Vol. 36, p. 275; E. L. Mattox in ibid., Vol. 37, p. 18; H. E. King in ibid., Vol. 43, p. 137; J. C. Gibson in ibid., Vol. 43, p. 352; C. E. Patton in ibid., Vol. 44, p. 432; J. G. Griffith in ibid., Vol. 45, p. 294; R. E. Chambers in ibid., Vol. 45, p. 559; H. S. Martin in ibid., Vol. 45, p. 626; Nelson Bitton in *The East and the West,* Vol. 10, pp. 436-440.

to the Home Churches which have sent us to China, the following recommendations:

"(a) That they should sanction the recognition by their missionaries of the right of the churches in China planted by them to organize themselves in accordance with their own views of truth and duty, suitable arrangements being made for the due representation of the missionaries on their governing bodies until these churches shall be in a position to assume the full responsibilities of self-support and self-government.

"(b) That they should abstain from claiming any permanent right of spiritual or administrative control over these churches." [373]

In the six-year interval between this gathering and that presided over by Mr. Mott the Revolution occurred, China became a republic, and the tides of nationalism rose. All over the world, moreover, missionaries were stressing the transfer of control to the "native" churches. The 1913 Conference, accordingly, not only included Chinese in its membership but had much more to say of the transfer of responsibility from mission to church than did that of 1907. A general statement of purpose was issued similar to that of the earlier gathering, but more detailed suggestions were adopted for the development of self-support, the sharing of administrative responsibility with the Chinese, the self-propagation of Chinese churches, and the discovery and training of Chinese leaders. The Conference favored Chinese churches independent of and separated from the missions. [374]

It was easy to outline a program for the formation of a Chinese Church independent of the foreigner, but it was quite another matter to put it into effect. There was always the problem of finding and educating enough Chinese of ability to lead the Church successfully. As we have said, nothing quite like the pastoral profession, except the Roman Catholic priesthood, had existed in China, and the nearest approach to it, the Buddhist and Taoist monks, had usually been regarded with contempt. Moreover, such Chinese as had heretofore given their full time to the Protestant Church, while often earnest and devout, had been relatively uneducated, had been looked upon as "helpers" of the missionary, and had been paid low salaries. [375] If highly educated

---

[373] *China Centenary Missionary Conference Records*, pp. 438, 439.

[374] *The Continuation Committee Conferences in Asia, 1912-1913*, pp. 326-334.

[375] *Missionary Review of the World*, Vol. 17, p. 270; J. R. Mott in *Chinese Recorder*, Vol. 34, p. 534; F. S. Brockman in ibid., Vol. 34, p. 447; R. M. Mateer in ibid., Vol. 39, p. 539; R. T. Bryan in ibid., Vol. 33, p. 321. In 1902 the Shanghai Missionary Association suggested as salaries for evangelists a scale running from $8.00 to $15.00 a month.—*Chinese Recorder*, Vol. 33, p. 325. See also ibid., Vol. 40, p. 367.

men entered the ministry, self-support might for a time be deferred, for they would need larger stipends and the Church might not quickly be able to pay these without assistance from abroad. Chinese pastors, moreover, while often devoted, were in some places said not to yearn over their charges and bear them on their hearts as would a good minister in Great Britain, and the tie between pastor and people was at times easily severed.[376]   More-over, as we have seen, it was highly doubtful whether the Chinese Church could soon assume the financial support of the great and expensive plants, evangelistic, educational, and medical, which the missionary had erected and which had become so marked a feature of Protestantism in China, and it was almost equally improbable that it could early supply enough men and women of adequate training and strength of Christian faith and character to conduct them.   Difficult though the task was, how-ever, missionaries and Chinese Christians undauntedly addressed themselves to it.

The means used and the steps taken in the solution of the problem were various, and space does not permit their complete enumeration.   A few examples, however, will indicate that prog-ress, and, on the whole, rapid progress, was made.   While between 1889 and 1905 the communicant membership increased fivefold, the contributions of the Chinese Church multiplied eight or ninefold.[377]   We have already noted the manner in which from the first the Young Men's Christian Association placed Chinese in positions of authority and insisted on local support.   In Mid-China the Church Missionary Society worked out a plan for vestries chosen by Christians worshiping in one chapel or room, of district councils composed of deputies elected by the vestries, and of departmental councils made up of representative deputies and of pastors.[378]   The Diocesan Conference of North China, composed of Chinese as well as foreign delegates, was given a voice in the choice of Bishop Norris for that see.[379]   In Swatow the English Presbyterians had a plan of church finance which contemplated aid from foreign funds for certain specific objects, such as the maintenance of the theological college, the purchase or rental of chapels and schools, and about twenty per cent. of the

[376] Moody, *The Saints of Formosa*, p. 196.
[377] *Chinese Recorder,* Vol. 43, p. 348.
[378] Ibid., Vol. 32, p. 171.
[379] *The Peking Gazette,* Jan. 19, 1914, p. 6.

salaries of teachers and preachers, and which provided for Chinese support of the remainder.[380]   At Wênchow, in Chêkiang, the Methodist Free Church Mission's program called for the progressive achievement of self-support by well-defined steps.[381]   In and around Amoy self-support and independence had long existed in many of the congregations which owed their origin to the Reformed (Dutch) Church in America and the English Presbyterian Church.   The two missions united in bringing into existence a church which was not to be a branch of any ecclesiastical body in the Occident and which was to frame its own creed and polity.   No pastor was ordained over any congregation which was not able and willing to support him, and the responsibility for the appointment and maintenance of unordained preachers was to be shared by the Chinese synod and mission.[382]   In that same district the representatives of the London Missionary Society had only an advisory relation to the Congregational Union.[383]   In West China, in spite of the youth of the Chinese Church, Chinese were appointed on an advisory council formed in 1913 and to the committee on church union.[384]   In Shantung both Baptists and Presbyterians made marked progress toward self-support and self-direction, the Baptists developing a form of government which resembled that of the Presbyterians and the Presbyterians one which was somewhat congregational.[385]   In Shaowu, in the back districts of Fukien, the churches established by the American Board were practically all controlled by the Chinese.[386]   The Foochow Council of Congregational Churches gave Chinese pastors and laymen a voice in the management of the Church.[387]   In the North China mission of the American Board Chinese shared in the deliberations and voting.[388]   In 1910 in Manchuria, in spite of the disorganization attendant upon

[380] J. C. Gibson in *China Centenary Conference Records*, p. 12; *China Mission Year Book, 1915*, p. 36.
[381] Soothill, *A Typical Mission in China*, p. 70.
[382] *A Century of Protestant Missions in China*, p. 372; *Chinese Recorder*, Vol. 32, p. 559, Vol. 45, pp. 289, 290; *Board of Foreign Missions of Reformed Church in America, Amoy Mission, Dec. 1913, Preachers' Salary Scheme Adopted by the Synod of the South Fukien Presbyterian Church.*
[383] *L. M. S. Chronicle*, Vol. 18 (new series), p. 131.
[384] *China Mission Year Book, 1915*, pp. 184-188.
[385] E. W. Burt in *Chinese Recorder*, Vol. 45, pp. 270-275.
[386] Moore, *West and East*, p. 334; *Annual Report of the A. B. C. F. M.*, 1911, p. 119.
[387] *Annual Report of the A. B. C. F. M.*, 1913, pp. 109-116.
[388] Ibid.

the Russo-Japanese War, in eight centers connected with the United Free Church of Scotland Mission the pastors were supported by their own congregations and nearly all the primary and much of the secondary education was at the cost of the Christians.[389]   In Chihli, with the Boxer year only a decade in the past, much progress was recorded toward the support and the control of the churches by the Chinese.[390]   In Hongkong most of the congregations under the Church Missionary Society became self-supporting in 1901 and the Church had its own constitution under the bishop.[391]

Many Protestant schools derived most of their income from tuition fees and from gifts of the Chinese: some, indeed, were independent of mission control.   Chinese liberality made possible the erection of buildings at Canton Christian College, at Boone, and at the Lowrie High School in Shanghai.[392]   In Amoy the management of the girls' school of the London Missionary Society was shared with a board of Chinese women.[393]   The Canton Baptist Academy was begun and controlled by the Chinese, and on July 1, 1914, all the boys' schools of the Southern Baptist Convention in Kwangtung were placed under the direction of a Chinese Education Board, the mission agreeing to contribute a dollar for every dollar raised by the Chinese, and the home board promising $25,000 for equipment.[394]

In many cities "Chinese Independent Churches" arose and a Chinese Christian Union was formed in Shanghai to unite these bodies and to carry the Gospel to unevangelized districts.[395] The movement was stimulated by the Revolution.[396]   The most successful of the Independent Churches were founded by missionaries and had been under the boards, but having achieved self-support were no longer controlled by foreigners.   Thus the one at Tientsin had as a nucleus a congregation once affiliated with the American Board.[397]   The one formed in Tsinanfu in 1912 was the outgrowth of the Presbyterian mission and included

[389] *China Mission Year Book, 1910,* pp. 189-194.
[390] Ibid.
[391] Norris, *China,* pp. 74-80; *A Century of Protestant Missions in China,* p. 39.
[392] *China Mission Year Book, 1910,* p. 122, *1911,* pp. 21, 22.
[393] *L. M. S. Handbook,* 1914, p. 29.
[394] *China Mission Year Book, 1915,* p. 37.
[395] Ibid., *1912,* pp. 216, 217.
[396] Ibid., *1913,* pp. 43, 44, 182 et seq.; A. H. Smith in *Missionary Review of the World,* Vol. 26, p. 839; *China's Millions,* 1913, p. 27.
[397] *Annual Report of the A. B. C. F. M.,* 1911, p. 119; 1912, p. 120.

not only a place of worship but schools and a dispensary.[398]   In Shanghai were several Independent Churches, largely on foundations laid by missions.[399]   In Hongkong, the notable To Tsai Church had its origin in a group that had moved from Malacca in 1842 and it had once been under the care of John Chalmers and James Legge of the London Missionary Society.[400]   In Hongkong and Canton were self-supporting churches which had arisen from the work of the American Board.[401]   In Peking an Independent Church gathered around Ch'êng Ching-yi, soon to be a secretary of the China Continuation Committee.[402]   In T'aiyüanfu an Independent Church was established in 1912 by men who had come into prominence in the Revolution, was housed in a temple and subsidized by the Military Governor, Yen Hsi-shan, and was assisted by a self-supporting missionary, E. Pilquist.[403]

Chinese were, moreover, organizing home missionary societies for the spread of the Faith.   While some of these were due in part to the encouragement of missionaries and took advantage of foreign counsel, they were primarily Chinese.   Thus the Presbyterian synod in Shantung in May, 1908, formed a missionary society which initiated an enterprise in Chihli.[404]   As early as 1901 congregations connected with the Church Missionary Society united in supporting a Chinese missionary organization.[405]   One of the earliest acts of the *Chung Hua Sheng Kung Hui* was the formation of a Board of Missions,[406] and Shensi was later chosen as a field.[407]   In Hongkong, Chinese Congregationalists joined with foreigners in the support of a society for the conduct of missions on the island, in Kowloon, and in outlying districts.[408]

---

[398] *The Christian Occupation of China*, p. 203.

[399] *L. M. S. Handbook*, 1914, p. 49.

[400] Bitton, *Our Heritage in China*, p. 50; *China Mission Year Book, 1912*, pp. 220-223.

[401] *Annual Report of the A. B. C. F. M.*, 1913, pp. 109-116.

[402] *International Review of Missions*, Vol. 2, p. 18; Cochrane, *Survey of the Missionary Occupation of China*, p. 296.

[403] *China Mission Year Book, 1914*, p. 411; Broomhall, *Jubilee Story of the China Inland Mission*, p. 325.   See notices of other Independent Churches, at Nanking in *China Mission Year Book, 1914*, pp. 265-270, and at Pingyüan in Shantung in ibid., *1914*, pp. 261-265.

[404] *Chinese Recorder*, Vol. 43, p. 285.

[405] *The Church Missionary Gleaner*, January, 1902; Stock, *History of the Church Missionary Society*, Vol. 4, p. 322.

[406] *Spirit of Missions*, Vol. 80, p. 472.

[407] Ibid., Vol. 81, p. 805.

[408] *L. M. S. Handbook*, 1914, p. 6.

The Chinese Christian Union of Shanghai, a purely indigenous organization which in its palmy days had eighteen hundred members in China, Hongkong, Japan, and San Francisco, in 1905 dispatched a missionary, its first, into the western part of Kiangsu, and the following year sent another.[409]   The Home Mission Board of Kwangtung and Kwangsi was a Baptist organization made up chiefly of Chinese and drew its funds in equal amounts from Chinese and the mission.[410]

This array of examples of an increasing share by Chinese in the support and direction of the Church becomes all the more significant when the fact is recalled that it is far from complete. Impressive though it is, however, it must not be interpreted as meaning that, taken the country over, the foreigner had yet turned over the control of the churches and affiliated institutions to the Chinese or that the Chinese had assumed the full support of the Church.   The great majority of leaders and executive officers, whether bishops, superintendents, principals and presidents of schools, or directors of hospitals, were still foreign, the bulk of the funds came from abroad, the forms of organization continued to be Occidental, and the expressions of religious life, whether in creeds, hymns, liturgies, architecture, or theology, were those brought by the missionary.   The Church was still a foreign importation.   The most that could be said was that it was taking root, that in many of its members the Christian experience was being repeated, and that it was beginning to give promise of a life which was not entirely dependent upon Western initiative and assistance.

The adaptation of Christianity to Chinese environment had as a rule not passed beyond the discussion stage.[411]   Most of the energy of missionaries and Chinese was directed toward achieving self-support, and with this still far in the distance, little energy was available for the other and more difficult task of adjusting Christian faith and life to the Chinese cultural environment in a

[409] *Chinese Recorder,* Vol. 43, pp. 286 et seq.
[410] Ibid.
[411] See a discussion of Chinese church hymnology and music, in *Chinese Recorder,* Vol. 40, pp. 189, 210 et seq.; of the need of a new type of apologetic, in ibid., Vol. 39, p. 680; of the probable future nature of Chinese Christianity and of Chinese Christian doctrines, in ibid., Vol. 33, p. 588, Vol. 37, p. 298, and in *The East and the West,* Vol. 4, pp. 373-382; and of the future organization of the Chinese Church, in *Chinese Recorder,* Vol. 33, p. 589.   See some of Timothy Richard's opinions on the necessity of adapting Christianity to China, in Bashford, *Journal,* April 9, 1907.

way that would enrich and strengthen rather than denature and dilute them. This was obviously a task for the Chinese and might be deferred for years: the age for the naturalization of the Christian message in China, with all the debates and strange heresies which would certainly be entailed, was still in the future.

RESULTS OF PROTESTANT MISSIONS, 1901-1914

The results of the extensive effort recounted in these two chapters must have become at least partly apparent as the story has progressed. The rapid growth of the numbers of pupils in the schools and of patients in the hospitals, an increase in mission stations, an improvement in the physical equipment of missions, the beginnings of a unified national Protestant Christian Church, and a progressive willingness of the Chinese to assume the support and direction of the Church, have all been noted. A few additional statements, however, must be made to summarize and complete the picture and may well be permitted to conclude this already over-prolonged portion of our narrative.

As was to be expected, the number of communicants greatly increased. The exact number of these can probably not be determined, but the best statistics available are as follows:

Year	Communicants	Baptized non-communicants	Others under Christian instruction	Total, Christian community
1898	80,682 [412]	.....	.....	......
1900	{ 95,943 [413]	.....	.....	......
	{112,808 [414]	.....	.....	......
1904	131,404 [415]	.....	.....	......
1905	178,251⎤	(Figures are for	78,528	256,779 [416]
1908-1909	195,905⎬	baptized Christian	49,172	278,628 [417]
1911	207,747⎦	community)	.....	370,114 [418]
1912-1913	235,303	49,742	59,106	356,209 [419]
1914	253,210 [420]	.....	.....	......
1915	268,652	62,274	190,958	526,108 [421]

[412] *Chinese Recorder*, Vol. 30, p. 144.
[413] *China Mission Year Book, 1915*, pp. 91, 92.
[414] H. P. Beach in *China's Millions*, 1905, p. 145.
[415] Ibid.
[416] *A Century of Protestant Missions in China*, statistical table.
[417] *China Mission Year Book, 1910*, p. lxxv.
[418] Ibid., *1913*.
[419] Ibid., *1914*, p. xvii.
[420] Ibid., *1915*, p. vii. This membership was divided denominationally as follows: Presbyterians 65,786, Methodists 52,200, China Inland Mission 35,150, Baptists 33,256, Lutherans 24,422, Congregationalists 21,828, Anglicans 14,541, others 6,027.—Ibid.
[421] *The Christian Occupation of China*, p. xci.

As will quickly be seen, these figures are incomplete, especially the last three columns, and even those of the communicants are probably below rather than above the true total. They are full enough, however, to indicate the rapidity of the growth of the Church.

More important than the number of Protestant Christians is the quality. From what classes did the Christians come? How nearly did they approximate Christian standards? What alteration had their Christian profession wrought in their lives? These questions are very difficult to answer accurately. As compared with the years before 1900 the Church seems to have attracted only a slightly greater proportion of the educated classes. Progress in literacy was marked, but was due more to the Church's schools than to any change in the groups from which Christians were drawn. As before 1900, the communicant membership seems to have been recruited chiefly from the superior elements of the middle and lower classes and to have been made up more of men than of women.[422] While fairly large churches existed in the cities, converts appear to have been more numerous and more easily obtained in the rural districts.[423]

The requirements for church membership seem not to have been appreciably different from those fixed in the years before 1900. The amount of pre-baptismal instruction remained about what it had been.[424] Now and again substitutes for the non-Christian honors to ancestors were suggested, that Christians might not seem to be failing in filial respect or in reverence for the memory of the dead,[425] and occasionally a voice was raised for the toleration of the forms customary in the non-Christian community.[426] On the whole, however, missions continued to refuse to Christians what they called ancestor worship.[427]

As before 1900, evidence is not wanting that the acceptance

[422] *The Christian Occupation of China*, p. xci; Ross, *The Changing Chinese*, p. 239; *Edinburgh Conference Reports*, Vol. 1, p. 94.
[423] Moule, *New China and Old*, p. 288; *China Mission Year Book, 1913*, pp. 323-326.
[424] *Edinburgh Conference Reports*, Vol. 2, pp. 54, 104; China Inland Mission, *Another Pentecost*, pp. 23 et seq. The home committee of the Berlin Missionary Society permitted, on recommendation from the field, the baptism of polygamists.— Schlunk, *Durch Chinas Südprovinz*, pp. 128 et seq.
[425] Schlunk, op. cit., pp. 125-127; *Edinburgh Conference Reports*, Vol. 2, pp. 67, 152, 328; Gascoyne-Cecil, *Changing China*, p. 124.
[426] W. A. P. Martin in *Chinese Recorder*, Vol. 33, p. 117.
[427] Schlunk, op. cit., pp. 125-127; *Edinburgh Conference Reports*, Vol. 2, pp. 67, 152,328; Gascoyne-Cecil, *Changing China*, p. 124.

of the Christian faith worked moral improvement. Some, to be sure, were drawn by unworthy motives. Protestant missionaries employed so large a proportion of the membership in the service of the Church that some were attracted by the hope of a liveli- hood. In many mission schools Christians or children of Chris- tians were given greater financial assistance than non-Christians, and as one student is reported to have said: "Who would not accept baptism for forty dollars a year?" Not all catechumens, however, sought instruction for selfish reasons, and even where mixed motives predominated, instruction and the fellowship of the Church often helped to purify them. An American scholar who travelled extensively through China, and who came with no special bias, observed that Christianity brought with it a change in fundamental values, and that its acceptance worked an alteration in character, leading converts to abandon opium, gambling, unchastity, lying, backbiting, and filthy language.[428] Among the fruits of the Gospel others enumerated the casting out of fear, especially the dread of the evil spirits that so beset the path of the Chinese, purity of speech, truthfulness, generosity, a Christian family life, patience under persecution, and the for- giveness of enemies.[429]   Missionary narratives continued to abound in the stories of transformed lives. Here was a man, reared as a Christian, who proved false to his boyhood's ideals, but was brought back to a life of rectitude and became an honored and earnest worker in the Church.[430]   Here was a carpenter who had run away with the wife of his employer, was a gambler, and had an atrocious temper, who after having been won to the Christian faith made restitution for his misdeeds, and in other ways became worthy of his new profession.[431]   Here, too, was a professional story-teller who first came in touch with the Gospel through purely Chinese agencies, because of it broke with opium, gambling, and wine, and developed into an earnest and devoted pastor, standing much reviling for his new faith.[432]   Here, again, was a devout Taoist nun who came to a Christian faith.[433] Another story is that of an ex-fortune-teller, tricky and despised,

[428] Ross, *The Changing Chinese*, p. 230.
[429] *Edinburgh Conference Reports*, Vol. 2, pp. 213-233; *China Mission Year Book, 1913*, pp. 121-125.
[430] Bashford, *Journal*, Oct. 4, 1907.
[431] Osgood, *Breaking Down Chinese Walls*, pp. 77-86.
[432] Osgood, *Shi, The Story-Teller*, passim.
[433] Burton, *Notable Women of Modern China*, pp. 221-230.

who embraced the Christian Gospel and was gradually transformed, offering to pay a forgotten debt, praying for a wayward
son until the latter mended his ways, and who at the price of a
beating by ruffians refused to use his influence with the mission
to induce it to buy a piece of land at an excessive price.[434]   In
one place in Hunan non-Christians entrusted the construction of
a road to Christians because they said that the latter would not
steal.[435]   Christian virtues were not quickly achieved, nor was
the full spiritual significance of the Faith immediately apprehended.   A sense of sin, reverence, and an insight which saw
beyond ritual and words were only slowly developed.[436]   They
did, however, come in time, even though in varying degrees.

The study of the effect of the Christian Gospel upon the
average Chinese which best combines the judicial attitude, intimate knowledge, and sympathetic insight, is recorded in three
books by Rev. Campbell N. Moody, a missionary among the
Chinese in Formosa.[437]   He held that Chinese were frequently
first attracted to the Faith by the preaching of the folly of idolatry
and the inefficacy of popular religion to accomplish what was
claimed for it.   Converts expected their new faith to do for them
what they had once believed their old religious observances would
achieve, namely, insure health to them and their domestic animals,
bring wealth, and afford protection against evil spirits.   Sometimes non-Christians were first attracted by the purity of life of
the members of the Church.   Chinese Christians, Moody maintained, were freer than non-Christians from vice, opium-smoking,
and gambling, and refused to admit to church-membership those
who were guilty of foul language or a bad temper, or who
quarrelled with their wives, or kept their ancestral tablets, or
were proud.   A good many inquirers, so he declared, did not
persevere until permitted to enter the Church, but those who had
once been admitted seldom fell away.   Moody observed, how-

[434] Wallace, *The New Life in China*, p. 69.   See other individual examples of
Christian living in Keyte, *Andrew Young of Shensi*, pp. 179-181, Johannson,
Everlasting Pearl, passim, Cody, *Letters to Betsy*, passim, Chapman, *Flood-Tide in
China*, pp. 60, 61.
[435] Hardy Jowett in *Ninety-Seventh Report of the Wesleyan Methodist Missionary Society*, p. 140.
[436] Bishop Hoare of Fukien, quoted in Stock, *History of the Church Missionary Society*, Vol. 4, p. 314; G. W. Greene in *Chinese Recorder*, Vol. 33, p. 595;
Graham, *East of the Barrier*, pp. 72-74.
[437] Moody, *The Heathen Heart, The Saints of Formosa*, and *The Mind of the
Early Converts*, and in *China Mission Year Book, 1913*, pp. 131-136.

ever, that what he believed to be the higher levels of Christian experience were but slowly reached.   A real sense of fellowship with and love for God, joy in private prayer, an appreciation of the spiritual and moral significance of the Cross of Christ, and a deep sense of inward renewal were relatively rare and late developments.   Christians, were, however, often earnest in propagating the Faith as they understood it.

As to the effect of Protestant Christianity upon Chinese life as a whole there was much difference of opinion, and an accurate appraisal cannot be made.   Here and there Christians such as C. T. Wang [438] and W. W. Yen [439] were prominent in political life, but whether they and their co-religionists were able to make any great impression upon that Augean stable is doubtful. Missionaries were again and again advisers to officials, but probably did not often influence profoundly or decisively the actions of these dignitaries.[440]   Bitter critics of the missionary, both Chinese and foreign, were not wanting.   Some foreigners insisted that missions were undermining the basic institutions of Chinese life,[441] that missionaries were intolerant,[442] that they relied too much on the protection of their governments,[443] and that they were attempting to plant in China a faith which was being abandoned by the more enlightened in the Occident.[444]   Some Chinese, moreover, maintained that in his representation of China to his home constituency the missionary, to obtain support for his work, spoke only of the dark sides of Chinese life and so lessened rather than promoted understanding of China in the Occident.[445] On the other hand there were those, not missionaries, who held that "every good work that has been started during the past fifty years for the advancement of the Chinese people has been carried out by missionaries, including that society to which the Progress Party in China owes its inception," [446] and one prominent Chinese official said: "Missionaries have borne the light of

[438] Bitton, *The Regeneration of New China,* p. 157.
[439] Ibid., p. 156.
[440] *Edinburgh Conference Reports,* Vol. 7, p. 20.
[441] (Dickinson), *Letters from a Chinese Official,* pp. 48-65.
[442] Little, *Gleanings from Fifty Years in China,* pp. 289-307.
[443] F. H. Nichols in *Atlantic Monthly,* December, 1902, pp. 773-782.
[444] Maxim, *Li Hung Chang's Scrap Book,* passim.
[445] Lin Shao-yang, *A Chinese Appeal to Christendom Concerning Christian Missions,* p. 65, quoting a Chinese student in America in *The American Journal of Sociology,* July, 1908.
[446] Little, op. cit., p. 307.

Western civilization into every nook and corner of the Empire. They have rendered inestimable service to China by the laborious task of translating into the Chinese language the religious and scientific books of the West. They help us to bring happiness and comfort to the poor and the suffering by the establishment of hospitals and schools. The awakening of China . . . may be traced in no small amount to the hand of the missionary." [447]

These latter statements, like the unfavorable ones, may give a distorted picture. On the whole, however, it was undoubtedly fortunate for the Chinese that during their years of transition the missionary was in their midst. As we have said before, the older Chinese culture would have passed had never a missionary landed on the shores of the Middle Kingdom. The missionary's distinctive achievement was to help determine the character of the impact of the West and the quality of the transformation which followed. Education was furthered, men and women were trained in wholesome surroundings to be leaders of the China that was to be, needed moral and social reforms were initiated or reënforced, institutions for the relief of suffering were founded, and family life and the lot of women and girls were improved. Every life transformed and ennobled was an asset to the new China, and the Christian communities which were beginning to arise, weak and imperfect though they were, had in them a promise of a new, growing, and permanent spiritual and moral dynamic of which the nation stood sorely in need.

[447] Tuan Fang, speaking in 1906, quoted in Bitton, op. cit., p. 89.

CHAPTER XXVII

CHINA IN A TIME OF REORGANIZATION (1901-1926)
CHANGES IN THE OCCIDENT AND IN CHINA, 1914-1926

THE years between 1900 and 1914, as we have seen, had witnessed an unprecedented growth in the Church in China. Both in the Occident and in China conditions had combined to further the expansion of the missionary enterprise and to obtain for its agents a favorable hearing. In Europe and America no major war interrupted the rapid accumulation of wealth, and within the churches no controversy or serious doubts arose to check the rising enthusiasm for foreign missions. Abounding prosperity afforded ample means, and a steadily increasing interest in missions provided the incentive for largely reënforcing missionary efforts in other lands. In China the outcome of the Boxer uprising had left the country prostrate and few dared openly resist the foreigner's activities, whether political, economic, or religious: the Westerner was enjoying all the prestige that attaches to a conqueror. Moreover, the older culture that had so long opposed the missionary was crumbling, and Western institutions and ideas were popular and, especially after 1911, were admired and accepted uncritically. Christian missionaries, all but inviolable in person and property because of the certain and swift vengeance wreaked by the powers on any who did violence to foreigners, and active representatives of the culture which the younger Chinese were now so avidly adopting, were given a ready hearing. Never, not even in the peaceful years at the close of the seventeenth century, had the Church enjoyed such prosperity or seemed so likely to win the nation to its faith.

Now, however, came a series of events, some of them catastrophic, which wrought great changes both in the Occident and in China. Some of the events were localized, but others were not confined to any one country. Together they profoundly affected the Church, both in the Occident and in China, and worked great alterations in the missionary enterprise.

THE WORLD WAR

First of all was the war whose outbreak made the summer days of 1914 forever memorable. Primarily a European struggle, in the slightly more than fifty-one months of its course it drew into its maelstrom most of the world and ushered in a new and troubled era for mankind. During the war itself missions in China were seriously curtailed. Since the majority of missionaries came from countries which were engaged in the conflict, foreign staffs were depleted by the absence in various forms of war service of many of their members and the number of new recruits fell off. In Great Britain and the Continent of Europe, moreover, contributions to many missionary societies either declined or ceased to gain At the same time a world-wide jump in prices greatly augmented the cost of maintaining missions.

The declaration of peace brought no complete return to *ante bellum* conditions. Europe was impoverished. Its currency was depreciated and in some countries which had once given largely to missions, notably Germany, was for a time almost worthless. At the same time prices in China continued to rise. Measured by their purchasing power, therefore, the incomes of many missionary societies and orders from the Continent of Europe did not fully recover. The changes in government that accompanied the war disestablished and so dealt a serious blow to some of the churches having missions in China. Notable sufferers were German Protestantism and the Russian Orthodox Church. Moreover, Great Britain and France, victorious, expelled some of the German societies and orders from lands where they had formerly worked, and several Roman Catholic bodies transferred their operations to China.

INCREASED RELATIVE IMPORTANCE OF THE UNITED STATES

A second accompaniment and sequel of the war was the increased importance of the United States in the missionary enterprise. This would have come in any event, for enormous natural resources, a growing population, and economic organization were rapidly making that land the wealthiest on earth. The war, however, by impoverishing Europe hastened and accentuated the process. Capital borrowed to develop American enterprises was repaid, huge sums were advanced to the governments associated with the United States in the war, and when peace came private capital was invested abroad at the rate of hundreds of millions a year. The banking center of the world shifted from London, Berlin, and Paris to New York. The missionary enterprise, both Roman Catholic and Protestant, had now to look to the United States for most of its funds. With financial support went reënforcements in missionary personnel and a somewhat, although not proportionately, greater voice in determining objectives, policies, and methods.

The Altered Status of the Westerner in China

In the third place, closely following the war and partly caused by it, was an alteration in the position of the Westerner in China. Both the prestige and the power of the Occident were badly shaken. The "Concert of the Powers," never very harmonious, had been shattered, and Europe could no longer act together to impose its will on the country: such a joint expedition as that which suppressed the Boxers was now impossible. China was a formal, although an almost entirely inactive participant in the World War, and from her new treaty with Germany the special status which she had once accorded all the major and many of the minor powers was omitted. Germans were permitted to reside, travel, and carry on business in all places in China to which citizens of other countries could go, but they were expressly declared to be subject to Chinese laws and courts with no greater privileges than those possessed by citizens of China,[1] and their concessions in the treaty ports were not returned. Their leaseholds in Shantung, seized by Japan during the war, were permanently taken away and after the Washington Conference (1921-1922) were restored to China. Moreover, the new government in Russia in time agreed to renounce extraterritorial rights,[2] and the citizens of the new states in Europe did not possess them.

These breaches having been effected in the favored position of foreigners, the Chinese pressed for complete restoration to what

[1] See the clauses from the treaty quoted in Grentrup, *Jus Missionarium*, p. 400. For the clause in the treaty of Versailles which affected German mission property in the leased territory in Shantung, see MacMurray, *Treaties and Conventions with and Concerning China*, Vol. 2, p. 1493.

[2] Willoughby, *Foreign Rights and Interests in China*, revised edition, Vol. 2, pp. 529-586. The extraterritorial rights were, however, not finally renounced—only the promise was made to do so when new treaties should be negotiated.

they deemed equality with other nations. At the Peace Conference and again at the Washington Conference the Chinese representatives asked for the termination of extraterritoriality and all other special concessions. When at Paris the powers turned a deaf ear, and when at Washington they contented themselves with promises about which the only certainty was that fulfillment would be delayed, restlessness in China increased, and by the middle of 1926 one of the slogans of the Nationalist Party, the abolishment of "the unequal treaties," had been taken up by practically the entire country. In 1925, following the shooting of some members of a mob of Chinese students by the police of the International Settlement in Shanghai on May 30th, and a subsequent clash (in June) between Chinese and foreigners at Shameen, in Canton, an anti-British boycott was instituted. During 1925, 1926, and 1927 agitation continued, directed primarily against the British but also against the Japanese and in time against the Americans. Russian influence intensified the uprising against the "capitalistic" and "imperialistic" powers. Vigorous retaliation by armed force, such as once had made the foreigner dominant, did not follow, partly because in a Britain staggering under war debts and weary from the late war public opinion would not permit it. In the winter of 1926-1927 the Chinese occupied, almost unopposed, the British concessions in Kiukiang and Hankow. Gunboats on the Yangtze aggravated the situation, especially when, as at Wanhsien in September, 1926, they fired on the Chinese. Whether, as in other years, the powers could have reduced China to submission by *force majeure* has been hotly disputed. They did not make the attempt, however, and, whatever the cause, the foreigner was no longer as secure or as deferred to as between 1900 and 1914. His loss of prestige was not markedly apparent until 1925, but after that year it was rapid.

The declining fear for the Westerner and the rising resentment against his domination was not, it must be recalled, confined to China. All over the world non-European races were restless, and books with such lurid titles as *The Rising Tide of Color* and *The Revolt of Asia* were only a few of the indications that for at least the moment Occidental imperialism was being threatened. Christian missions were not, as formerly, supported by the unquestioned prestige of the West. In time this change might free the Gospel from its association with the armed superiority of the Occident and so divest it of the false glamor lent by its affiliation with a conquering civilization and make clear its real message. The missionary faced, however, an altered status. More and more he had to heed the rumblings of discontent.

THE GROWTH OF NATIONALISM

A fourth new movement after 1914, closely associated with this last, was the rapid growth of nationalism. It, too, was not confined to China. In Europe and America nationalism had been one of the most powerful forces of the nineteenth century and was one of the major causes of the World War. Even before 1914 it had begun to be felt outside the Occident—in the Philippines, Japan, India, and Turkey, for example, as well as in China. The war greatly accentuated it. Because of it new states arose in Europe, Turkey cancelled the Capitulations, Egypt partly emancipated itself from British control, India was stirred by *swaraj*, the Philippines sought their independence, Koreans rose in revolt, and Africa gave birth to an Ethiopian movement.[3] It is not strange that the Chinese, long noted for their pride of race and culture, painfully conscious of their partial subjection to the powers, and smarting under the contempt with which they were often treated by foreigners, quickly became one of the most nationalistic of peoples.

In China nationalism showed itself in a variety of ways—in intense dislike and suspicion of the Japanese because of their aggressions during the war, in boycotts against the Japanese, the British, and the Americans, in repeated demands that the "unequal treaties" be abrogated, and in outcries against "imperialism." A nation-wide student movement with strong local units frequently took the lead in anti-foreign agitation. Educational institutions became centers of political discussion, often at the sacrifice of scholastic standards.[4] The majority of the members of the student movement were in secondary or primary schools and so were immature and lacked poise and judgment. Discontented elements in the community who saw in troubled waters an opportunity to better their lot usually joined in the demon-

[3] See C. J. H. Hayes, *Essays on Nationalism,* for an excellent account of nationalism.
[4] For an account of the movement of 1919 against Japan, see H. C. Hu in *Chinese Recorder,* Vol. 54, pp. 456-459.

strations and violence ensued. It was comparatively easy to blame the foreigner for China's woes and to unite an otherwise disorganized country upon a campaign against him.

Christian missions inevitably were affected. As we shall see later in more detail, in time Christianity was accused of being an agent of foreign "imperialism" and "capitalism" and nationalists demanded that Christian schools be made subject to the state. Christians, partly to free themselves from the odium of association with the alien, sought control of the churches, even before these bodies had become financially self-supporting, talked much about making Christianity "indigenous," and favored government registration of Christian schools. The problem of the transfer of authority to Chinese Christians became a major one both for Roman Catholics and Protestants. Moreover, the clauses in the treaties guaranteeing toleration to missionaries and their converts were more than ever abhorrent to the nation. Fewer arguments could be offered in their defence than formerly, for in spite of opposition in some Confucian quarters religious toleration was written into several of the attempts at national constitutions.[5] While these documents were more often ignored than followed, in theory they were the basic law of the land and their recognition of liberty of conscience seemed to render invalid some of the arguments that once had been advanced for treaty protection.

THE NEW TIDE

A fifth new movement which profoundly affected Christian missions was what is variously known as the Renaissance, New Thought, New Civilization, or New Tide. While only one phase of the transition through which China was passing, it was important because it dealt with ideas and affected primarily the intellectuals. The passing of the old examination system had removed most of the incentive for the former type of education. For the first time in many centuries the Chinese mind was free to roam afield unrestrained by the conventions of the past. The student mind, thus emancipated, was played upon by currents

[5] The constitution of March 11, 1912, said: "All citizens shall enjoy religious liberty." The constitution of May 1, 1914, said: "Within the limits of the law citizens shall enjoy religious liberty." The constitutional clause adopted May 14, 1917, declared: "Citizens of the Republic of China enjoy the liberty of venerating Confucius and within the limits of law of choosing their religions."—Grentrup, *Jus Missionarium*, p. 148.

from all over the world. Foreign books were translated in great numbers. The new schools which were so rapidly increasing gave instruction in Western as well as Chinese subjects. Thousands went abroad to study, and from Japan, Europe, and America they returned, enthusiastically bringing with them new conceptions. Lecturers from other lands, notably John Dewey from the United States and Bertrand Russell from Great Britain, were in the country for extended visits and were widely and enthusiastically heard.

By 1919 the movement was well under way. The National University at Peking, under the chancellorship of Ts'ai Yüan-p'ei, who, a Hanlin under the old régime, had been branded as a radical and had spent some years in Germany, became its center, but it was felt all over the country.

The Renaissance is not easily described, so many are the accounts of it given by its exponents and so numerous were its manifestations. Anything like a complete picture, moreover, is outside the scope of this book. In general it was the attempt to examine critically all that had come down from the past, whether of the Occident or of China. No institution, custom, or conviction was too sacred or too hoary to be questioned. New ideas were welcomed but—at least in theory—they were tested by the scientific method. Every infringement on freedom of thought or expression was resented and every curtailment of China's sovereignty and every disparagement of her culture by foreigners was vigorously opposed. Many clubs appeared to discuss and propagate the new spirit, prominent among them being The Young China Association, the Coöperative Study Society, the Philosophic Society, and the Renaissance Society. All young China was talking—and thinking.

The old classical style was displaced by the *pai hua,* a dignified Mandarin which could be understood wherever that form of the language was spoken, a revolution which was heralded as being as great as the substitution of modern European tongues for Latin. In 1917 Hu Shih and some of his friends began the innovation and, in spite of criticism, by 1920 the reform had gained such momentum that the Ministry of Education had ordered the *pai hua* to be taught in the primary schools. The *pai hua,* indeed, quickly became the literary medium of the new student class. In it appeared several hundred magazines, chief among them *La Jeunesse,* and many books and pamphlets. Closely associated with the production of literature in the vernacular, and necessary if that literature were universally to be understood, was the attempt to have adopted, especially in the non-Mandarin speaking sections, a form of Mandarin as the national tongue. It was taught in the schools in the hope that it would soon become current and aid in the unification of the country.

Other phases of the New Tide were the production of fresh forms of literature—including new types of poetry—the organization of numberless clubs, the eager discussion of philosophy—almost all schools, both Chinese and Occidental, coming in for examination—and a willingness to depart from established social institutions and customs. Women, especially among the students, demanded more freedom. Students often questioned the ethical standards of the older generation. They frequently insisted upon arranging their own betrothals, instead of having them made by their parents. They were often restive under the control of their teachers and demanded a voice in the management of the institutions in which they studied. Student strikes, indeed, became one of the most prominent and frequent features of school life. The intensely patriotic student movement which was so active in politics was closely associated with the Renaissance and, like it, found a stronghold in the National University at Peking.

The New Tide was characterized not only by an intolerance of foreign control but by a passion for internal reform. Its adherents were opposed to the rule of the military chieftains, found in Sun Yat-sen an ideal, and were ardent supporters of the Kuomintang or Nationalist Party. They professed a devotion to progress and desired greater economic, political, social, and intellectual opportunities for the masses. Some of them advocated democracy, others were attracted by Russian communism, and most of them favored universal education. The Renaissance was a seething new life, eager, questioning, intensely patriotic, hopeful, radical, seeking to build a new nation, freed from the old restraints and brooking no new ones, often unpractical, immature, and unstable, bewildering to the observer, by some foreigners praised and by others denounced.[6] Not for centuries, if ever, had Chinese culture been in so great a state of flux. Many of the rural districts and smaller inland centers were as yet but little affected, but in the great cities old sanctions, customs, beliefs, and institutions were disappearing and nothing stable had yet succeeded them.

THE ANTI-CHRISTIAN MOVEMENT

A sixth new factor confronting missions was the Anti-Christian Movement. Criticism and persecution of Christianity were, as we have repeatedly seen, nothing new in China. The majority of the scholar class had never been friendly. The literati had repeatedly sought to obstruct the entrance of missionaries, and sometimes, as in the Yangtze riots of 1890 and 1891, had fomented anti-Christian outbreaks. To them the missionary was a disturber of basic Chinese institutions, and through his extraterritorial privileges and the toleration guaranteed him and his converts by the treaties was a pestiferous agent of foreign imperialism. While after 1900 this opposition abated and students and older members of the educated class came out in numbers to hear the Christian message, some of them even joining the Church, criticism never entirely disappeared. Now, in 1922, it flamed up again and more fiercely and persistently than at any time since 1900.

The underlying causes of the outburst seem to have been the quickened spirit of nationalism and the attitude of destructive criticism which accompanied the Renaissance. Reënforcing these were the scepticism and agnosticism so widespread in the Occident and with which Chinese students came in contact as they studied abroad. To many, Christianity seemed an obstructive superstition from which science was emancipating the more enlightened in the West and which China would do well to shun. For centuries some schools of Chinese philosophy had had so strong a tendency to deny the existence of gods, spirits, and immortality,

[6] The literature on the Renaissance movement is voluminous. Among the accounts in foreign languages see Hodgkin, *China in the Family of Nations; China To-day Through Chinese Eyes* (First and Second Series); Wang, *The Youth Movement in China; Some Aspects of Chinese Civilization;* H. C. Hu in *Chinese Recorder,* Vol. 54, pp. 447-455; Wieger, *Chine Moderne;* John Dewey in *Asia,* 1921, pp. 581-586; Burgess in *The Survey,* 1921, pp. 238, 239. See T'ang Leang-li, *China in Revolt,* passim, as a sample of the attitude of exponents of the Renaissance.

that at least one leader of the Renaissance contended that the Chinese had never been truly religious and that the most enlightened among them had outgrown religion earlier than had any other group on earth. Breathing this atmosphere from childhood, Chinese students naturally lent a not unfriendly ear to the questionings of Europe and America. In 1920, for example, the Young China Association, formed by students in Peking and elsewhere, limited its membership to those who had no religious faith.[7] Bertrand Russell in his widely heard lectures attacked Christianity[8] and in 1920 at least one article appeared from a Chinese pen vigorously assailing Jesus.[9] Given these underlying conditions, some sort of anti-Christian movement was all but inevitable, and only awaited an exciting cause.

The occasion for the first outbreak came in 1922. In April of that year there convened at Tsing Hua College at Peking a conference of the World's Student Christian Federation, a Protestant organization. Delegates attended from most of the provinces of China, from all five of the continents, and from many of the islands of the sea. The gathering attracted wide attention in China and before it met, in March, 1922, a group of students in Shanghai announced the formation of an Anti-Christian Federation, on the ground that science and religion were incompatible and that Christianity was an ally of capitalism and imperialism, a means of oppressing weaker nations.[10] A few days later a group connected with educational institutions in Peking organized the Anti-Religious Federation, declaring that all religion was ruled out by science. While the objective was thus broadened, Christianity continued to be the chief target. The movement was given the tacit or open support of many of the leaders of the New Tide. A few outstanding scholars, especially Liang Ch'i-ch'ao,[11] criticized it, but for some months it was widespread and popular. In city after city branches were

---

[7] N. Z. Zia in *China Mission Year Book, 1925,* p. 52. For tendencies in Chinese religious thought among the leaders of the Renaissance, see Millican in *China Mission Year Book, 1926,* pp. 423-469, and C. S. Chang, *Kuo Nei Chin Shih Nien Lai Chih Tsung Chiao Ssu Ch'ao,* Part 1.

[8] *Chinese Recorder,* Vol. 52, p. 155.

[9] Ibid., Vol. 52, pp. 177-186.

[10] N. Z. Zia in *China Mission Year Book, 1925,* pp. 53, 54; Wieger, *Chine Moderne,* Vol. 3, pp. 9-94; C. S. Chang in *Chinese Recorder,* Vol. 54, pp. 459-467; *The Life,* Special Federation Conference Number, 1922.

[11] Liang Ch'i-Ch'ao, *The Anti-Religious Movement,* passim; *China To-day Through Chinese Eyes,* pp. 66-85.

formed and literature was issued, much of it crude, but all of it vigorous. Students, especially those in government schools, were the chief agitators.[12] The meetings of the World's Student Christian Federation were not seriously disturbed, but when, after the adjournment of the conference, the foreign delegates visited, by previous arrangement, several of the provincial capitals, in some they found it wise not to hold the large public meetings that had been planned.[13]

With the adjournment of the conference of the World's Student Christian Federation, the anti-religious and anti-Christian agitation gradually subsided. It did not, however, die out: here and there local groups continued and occasional articles appeared denouncing Christianity.[14] The quiet was only a lull before a still more violent outburst.

The next attack upon Christianity was directed primarily at mission schools. Although those enrolled in Christian institutions were only a minority of the total student body of China, in secondary and higher education Christians, and especially Protestants, held a very important position. In a number of provinces the best education was that given by them. Fairly large sums of money were, moreover, being expended on staff and equipment, and Chinese educators began to express fear of this "cultural invasion." Some of the former students in mission schools harbored grievances, usually because of the religious instruction, the strict dsicipline, and the high scholastic standards insisted upon. Occasionally teachers were jealous of schools which seemed to them competitors. The published report of a commismission sent from Great Britain and America in 1921 and 1922 to study Protestant education in China attracted wide attention and awakened apprehension lest, under foreign direction and independent of government control, a system of schools should grow up which would denationalize its students. To the distrust of mission schools was added resentment against Japanese educational activities in Manchuria. Nationalistic sentiment, then, united with anti-Christian sentiment and with personal

[12] Wieger, op. cit., Vol. 3, pp. 9-94; Philip de Vargas in *International Review of Missions,* Vol. 15, pp. 16, 17. C. S. Chang, op. cit., Part 2, contains several of the manifestoes.

[13] The author was in China for the conference and is writing partly from personal observation and memory.

[14] N. Z. Zia in *China Mission Year Book, 1925,* p. 54; Philip de Vargas in *International Review of Missions,* Vol. 15, p. 17.

jealousies and animosities to renew the agitation.[15] The rapidly growing influence of Communist Russia was, moreover, thoroughly anti-Christian.

The movement against Christian schools first became prominent in 1924. In July of that year the fifth annual conference of the Young China Association resolved: "That we strongly oppose Christian education which destroys the national spirit of our people and carries on a cultural program in order to undermine Chinese civilization." That same month the National Association for the Advancement of Education at its annual conference requested the government to insist upon the registration of foreign schools and colleges and to grant registration only upon condition that religious instruction be barred from the curriculum.[16] In August, 1924, the national conference of the Students' Union determined upon a movement for the "restoration of educational rights" and the denunciation of educational enterprises started by foreigners for the propagation of religion. The tenth joint meeting of the provincial educational associations in session at Kaifeng in October, 1924, recommended the separation of education from religion and the removal of the foreign control of schools.[17]

In the meantime the Anti-Christian Federation was again becoming active [18] and organizing new local branches. An extensive literature was published attacking Christianity, and Christmas week, 1924, was set aside for special anti-Christian demonstrations. Many other organizations took up the cudgels against the foreign religion and swelled the flood of periodicals and pamphlets. In a few places actual violence followed.[19] Christianity was condemned on the ground that it was the forerunner of imperialistic exploitation and was accompanied by demands for indemnities and territorial concessions; that it was allied with capitalism; that it destroyed the national spirit of the Chinese; that it had always existed for the strong and depended upon oppression; that converts were attracted by material rewards;

[15] *Chinese Christian Education*, pp. 5-7; Philip de Vargas in *China Mission Year Book, 1925*, p. 18.

[16] N. Z. Zia in *China Mission Year Book, 1925*, p. 54.

[17] Ibid., p. 55; translation of text in *China Weekly Review*, Vol. 30, pp. 385, 386, and in *Chinese Christian Education*, pp. 9, 10. See texts of various resolutions and proclamations in C. S. Chang, op. cit., Part III.

[18] It was revived as a national organization at Shanghai in August, 1924. —Wieger, *Chine Moderne*, Vol. 5, p. 233.

[19] N. Z. Zia in *China Mission Year Book, 1925*, pp. 55-57.

that Christians made use of prominent men and flattered the rich; that they were hypocrites; that they meddled in lawsuits and protected criminals; that Christian schools restrained freedom of thought and action, compelled attendance at worship, hindered the full development of individuals, suppressed patriotism, and were hopelessly conservative and old-fashioned; that Christian ethics and doctrines were untenable; and that Jesus himself was not perfect and was not particularly important.[20]

Fuel to the flames was added by the Shanghai incident of May 30, 1925, and by the subsequent events which aroused the Chinese, and especially the students, against the British, the "unequal treaties," and all forms of foreign aggression. On November 16, 1925, the Ministry of Education (of the Peking Government) promulgated regulations for the government recognition of educational institutions established by foreigners. These were less extreme than some which had been proposed, but they insisted that for registration a school must have a Chinese president or vice-president, that more than half its board of managers must be Chinese, that religious propaganda must not be its purpose, and that its curriculum must conform to that of the Ministry of Education and must not require instruction in religion.[21] Through the protest of the French Minister, on March 3, 1926, the Minister of Foreign Affairs ordered the Minister of Education to suspend the regulations on the ground that they were contrary to the treaties.[22] Peking, however, was by this time not listened to except in the Northeast and in most of the nation the agitation continued. The regulations issued by the Nationalist Government at Canton were more drastic than those of Peking.[23]

[20] C. S. Chang, op. cit., pp. 376 et seq.; N. Z. Zia in *China Mission Year Book, 1925*, pp. 58, 59; T'ang Leang-li, *China in Revolt*, pp. 57-78 (a typical and vigorous anti-Christian statement); *The Anti-Christian Movement* (translation of anti-Christian documents); *Chinese Recorder*, Vol. 56, pp. 72, 220-226, 231; *North-China Herald*, Dec. 26, 1925, p. 565.

[21] Philip de Vargas in *International Review of Missions*, Vol. 15, p. 18. The regulations of Nov. 16, 1925, are in *Information about China*, No. 20, Feb. 2, 1926, issued by the Foreign Missions Conference of North America. For earlier government regulations for registration (May, 1912, and April, 1921, the latter forbidding the curriculum to include anything in the nature of the propagation of religion and commanding that Christian and non-Christian students be treated alike) see *Educational Review*, Vol. 17, pp. 404-410. The regulations of 1925 are in ibid., Vol. 18, pp. 99-101. For regulations of the Nationalist and of provincial governments see ibid., Vol. 19, pp. 150-180, 413.

[22] Text in Planchet, *Les missions de Chine et du Japon, 1927*, Part 2, p. 84.

[23] *Information about China*, issued by the Foreign Missions Conference of North America, Jan. 5, 1925.

Special anti-Christian demonstrations were planned for Christmas week of 1925 and 1926 and in some cities were carried out.[24] Because of Russian influence the left wing of the Kuomintang was particularly bitter against the Church, and when, in the summer of 1926, the Nationalist forces moved northward, in some of the territory occupied, notably in Hunan, the extreme radicals entered upon an active campaign against missionaries as "imperialists" and "capitalists" and against Chinese Christians as the "running dogs of the foreign imperialists." In some centers, notably in Foochow, the early months of 1927 witnessed looting and the destruction of property and in Nanking (March 24th) the actual killing of missionaries. By the summer of 1927 a large proportion of the missionaries, especially the Protestants, had withdrawn from the interior, even from sections not yet occupied by the Nationalist forces, schools and hospitals were closing or were being left to the Chinese staffs, and the churches were confronted by the greatest dislocation of their work that they had experienced since 1900. Occasional attempts were made by the authorities to check the anti-Christian agitation[25] but they were often half-hearted and ineffectual.

CIVIL STRIFE

A seventh and last set of conditions which profoundly affected missions after 1914 was recurring civil strife and steadily increasing anarchy. With occasional halts, the years after the declaration of the Republic, and especially after 1917, were marked by a progressive disintegration of orderly government and an increase in banditry and lawlessness.

The reasons for this were, in the main, two. First, the Manchu dynasty had disappeared and with its end an old story began to be reënacted. Chinese political philosophy made no provision for the peaceful succession of one dynasty by another. It declared that the Emperor ruled by the mandate of Heaven, but it also held that through incompetence and misgovernment a ruling house might forfeit its trust. In practice the only way in which an aspirant for the throne could prove that he had the divine decree was to conquer his opponents. This meant that whenever a dynasty collapsed, as had happened many times in

[24] For examples see *The North-China Herald*, Dec. 12, 1925, p. 474.
[25] For an example see *The North-China Herald*, March 6, 1926, p. 414; Planchet, *Les missions de Chine et du Japon, 1927*, Part 2, pp. 86-88.

China's history, a period of civil strife ensued.   Sometimes it was prolonged for a century or more, and the country was divided among warring chieftains until eventually one, stronger than the others, eliminated his rivals.   The process naturally began to repeat itself after the abdication of the Manchus.

Complicating the situation was a second cause, the presence of the foreigner and of Occidental ideas.   In some respects the foreigner was an aid to union.   The Maritime Customs and the Post Office, the great administrative services which at the end of 1926 were, with the telegraph, the only pieces of government machinery that continued to function the country over, had been organized by and were still in part under the direction of aliens. Moreover, the one rallying cry on which the nation could be united was a denunciation of foreign encroachments.   However, the Westerner had made necessary a complete recasting of the political structure.   If China were to take her place as an equal among the nations of the world, her government must assume functions previously entrusted to private initiative and must become more highly centralized.   With contact with the Western world, too, came new ideas—representative government, democracy, socialism, communism, and the like. The Chinese would not if they could have been content with their former organization. New institutions were, therefore, necessary and inevitable, but the mammoth task of framing them and obtaining their acceptance and successful operation for four hundred million people could be accomplished neither quickly nor peacefully.   Long experimentation and partial anarchy would certainly be the unhappy lot of the nation.

Into the details of the troubled and confusing political history of these years there is no occasion here to enter.   The main outline, however, must be given if references in the ensuing chapters are to be clear.   From 1912 to his death in 1916 Yüan Shih-k'ai succeeded in holding the country together.   Banditry there occasionally was, and two serious rebellions arose, one in 1913 and the other in 1916, but the momentum acquired under Manchu rule was not yet spent.   Yüan was peacefully succeeded in the Presidential chair by the Vice-President, Li Yüan-hung, and for nearly a year comparative quiet reigned.   Then in 1917 the question of China's entry into the World War precipitated civil strife. After a brief and semi-comic restoration of the Manchu boy Emperor by the swashbuckling Chang Hsun (July, 1917), Li resigned the Presidency and a northern military group under Tuan Chi-jui became dominant. Fêng Kuo-chang, the Vice-President, was President from Li's retirement until September, 1918, when, because of his disagreement with Tuan, he was replaced by the elderly Hsü Shih-chang. In the meantime leaders of the Kuomintang, Sun Yat-sen's party, had retired, disgruntled, to Canton, and had set up a government which they declared to be the only legitimate one. A desultory war was carried on by the "South" against the "North." For a time strife in South China ousted Sun Yat-sen and his friends, but in 1921 Sun was reinstated at Canton by Ch'ên Ch'iung-ming and was elected "President of the Chinese Republic" by a few of the members of the Parliament of 1913. From time to time he attempted an expedition northward to make good his claims, but he was neither an organizer nor an administrator and was never complete master even of Kwangtung. The Peking Government, moreover, did not have smooth sailing, for in 1920 three of the major military leaders of the North, Wu P'ei-fu, Ts'ao Kun, and Chang Tso-lin, united to drive Tuan Chi-jui and his associates from power, leaving in the Presidential chair the pathetic Hsü Shih-chang. In 1921 Wu P'ei-fu and Chang Tso-lin fell out and in 1922 went to war with each other. Wu emerged victorious, Chang was driven back to his especial domain, Manchuria, Hsü was ousted, and Li Yüan-hung was recalled. Li found his position untenable and in June, 1923, once more fled from the capital and took refuge in his comfortable home in the foreign concessions in Tientsin. In October, 1923, Parliament was bribed into electing Ts'ao Kun to the vacant chair and a "permanent" constitution was promulgated.

For a year no major military action occurred. Then, in October, 1924, fresh civil strife broke out and Wu P'ei-fu and Chang Tso-lin were drawn into it. Fêng Yü-hsiang, a Christian general subordinate to Wu, suddenly deserted his superior, compelled the latter's withdrawal to the Yangtze Valley, and drove Ts'ao Kun from Peking. After a conference between Chang and Fêng, Tuan Chi-jui was called to Peking as "Chief Executive" (not President). An attempted "reorganization conference" for which Sun Yat-sen came North failed to bring unity to the distraught country, and in the autumn of 1925 the major figures once more went to war. For a time Fêng was master in Peking, but early in 1926 a coalition between Wu and Chang forced him to retire to Mongolia. Chang was now in control of Peking, but by the autumn of 1926 nearly every semblance of a national government, including the "Chief Executive," had disappeared from the city. Most of the country was divided between Chang Tso-lin in the Northeast (the Fengt'ien group), Fêng Yü-hsiang (leading the Kuominchun) in the Northwest, Yen Hsi-shan in Shansi, Sun Chuan-fang in Kiangsu, Wu P'ei-fu in the central part of the Yangtze Valley, and Yang Sen in Szechwan.

In the meantime Sun Yat-sen had died (March 19, 1925), leaving as his legacy to the nation a will summed up in three principles, the People's Nationalism, the People's Sovereignty, and the People's Livelihood, and a book, the *San Min Chu I,* setting these forth as the basis for the reorganization of the country.[26] His party, the Kuomintang, freed from his incompetent leadership, now proclaimed him as the nation's hero, and, aided by Russian advisers of the Communist group, perfected an organization at Canton, and in the summer of 1926 began a northward march which by·the early part of 1927 had all but eliminated Wu P'ei-fu and Sun Chuan-fang. Fêng Yü-hsiang championed Sun Yat-sen's principles and was sympathetic with the Kuomintang, but during 1926 and most of 1927 was prevented by the remnants of Wu's forces and the army of Chang Tso-lin from effecting a junction with the South. In April, 1927, a split occurred in the Kuomintang ranks between the moderates, led by Chiang K'ai-shek, and the Communists, in power in Hankow and Wuchang. The hopes of the intelligensia were pinned on the Kuomintang, and North and South wide sympathy was felt for its program, especially for its determination to be rid of the "unequal treaties." By the close of 1927 a vigorous anti-Communist agitation had set in and the Nationalists had broken off diplomatic relations with Moscow, but the Nationalist Government, theoretically with headquarters in Nanking, was divided and weak. In the spring and summer of 1928 the Nationalists, reorganized, pressed north and captured Peking. Chang Tso-lin was killed by a bomb as he was retiring to Manchuria, and his successor, Chang Hsüeh-liang, was prevented from aligning himself with

[26] *San Min Chu I, The Three Principles of the People,* by Dr. Sun Yat-sen. Translated into English by Frank W. Price, edited by L. T. Chen. Shanghai, 1927.

the Nationalists only by pressure from the Japanese. Much of the country claimed by the Nationalists, however, was still turbulent and owed only a nominal allegiance to them.

To all this internal strife between the major figures were added petty local wars, widespread oppression, and extensive banditry. Here and there a semblance of orderly government was maintained. In Shansi, for example, Yen Hsi-shan had held sway from the fall of the Manchus and until 1927 declined to become embroiled in national politics. In general, however, life and property were progressively less secure and government more unstable and oppressive. In 1926 and 1927 the Communist wing of the Kuomintang made matters still worse by inciting peasants and city laborers to rise against their landlords and employers. Ungoverned agrarian and labor agitation joined with the previous banditry to let loose the baser elements and added to the chaos.

Missions, missionaries, and Chinese Christians could not hope to escape the effects of the increasing disorder. For a number of years the foreigner and his property were comparatively immune and mission compounds were often a refuge from civil war and banditry. As anti-Christian agitation and the feeling against the "unequal treaties" spread, and as it became apparent that the powers would not use enough force to control the situation, the security of the foreigner declined. By the close of 1926 in many places his property and person had ceased to be inviolate and had even been singled out for attack. This was especially the case in territories professing allegiance to the Kuomintang. Sun Yat-sen had been baptized and, at his request, was given a (Protestant) Christian funeral service. His widow and a number of others in high position in the party were Protestants. However, the Kuomintang was so vigorously nationalistic and so opposed to any form of foreign control, and its left wing was so influenced by Russian anti-Christian Communism, that in 1926 and much of 1927 the Church usually faced opposition in regions controlled by it.

SUMMARY

The situation which confronted Christian missions in China after 1914 was, then, increasingly difficult. First the World War wrought great changes at the home base. Then the progress of the revolution in China brought fresh problems and obstacles.

Fortunately all these movements did not overtake missions simultaneously. Something of a breathing space intervened between the war and the crises in China. Until the autumn of 1926 both Protestant and Roman Catholic missions registered fairly steady and even remarkable growth. While, moreover, the path was rough and perilous, the challenge to the Church had never been greater. Here was a fourth of the human race on the march. Here was vibrant, though ungoverned, new life. Here, too, was uncertainty of outcome. China might find her way through her years of trial to a finer civilization than she had ever known, or she might utterly disintegrate with unparalleled suffering to her struggling masses and peril to the rest of the world. Could the Church build itself into this new nation and so present its message by deed and word that the scale would be swung to the side or order and wholesome progress?

The task was by no means as simple as before 1914. Movement was more rapid and the cross currents more numerous and powerful. Before 1914 in many parts of the country the Church had been almost the only representative of the new ideas. Now it was presenting only one of many ways of life which were contending for recognition and because of its association with Western imperialism and capitalism was often thought of as conservative and reactionary. The tide of radicalism was sweeping beyond it. It is too soon as yet to know the outcome, but the story of the years between 1914 and 1927, if only it can be told clearly, cannot fail to be of interest.

CHAPTER XXVIII

CHINA IN A TIME OF REORGANIZATION (1901-1926)
ROMAN CATHOLIC MISSIONS, 1914-1926
RUSSIAN ORTHODOX MISSIONS, 1914-1926

THE WORLD WAR AND ROMAN CATHOLIC MISSIONS

To Roman Catholic missions the outbreak of the European war immediately brought grave problems. Many missionaries, especially French and Belgian, were called to the colors. Some, of course, were exempted because of their age. Others could not pass the physical tests or were excused on the ground that they were indispensable to their mission.[1] Of the fifteen hundred foreign priests in China in 1914 about eight hundred and fifty were French.[2] Of these latter between two and three hundred, among them three bishops, were summoned home.[3] Numbers of the reservists were detailed to service in the Far East and of these a few made their way back to their flocks before the end of the war.[4] In 1916, however, the French missionary personnel in China had decreased by about two hundred and eighty.[5] By the end of 1914 sixty Lazarists had been claimed by the military authorities. In Eastern Kiangsi this meant nineteen out of the twenty-two European priests and in Eastern Chêkiang nine out of twenty-two.[6] Many went no farther than Shanghai and Tientsin, but by April, 1915, twenty of the sixty had gone to Europe.[7] Fourteen out of the forty-five representatives of the Missions Étrangères of Paris in Eastern Szechwan were called and six out of the twenty-one in Northern Manchuria.[8] In November, 1917, Bishop Choulet was the only European priest left at Mukden and since the beginning

---

[1] *Catholic Missions,* Vol. 9, p. 143.
[2] Krose, *Kirchliches Handbuch für das katholische Deutschland,* 1916-1917, p. 125.
[3] Schmidlin in *Zeitschrift für Missionswissenschaft,* Vol. 5, p. 73.
[4] Ibid.
[5] Krose, op. cit., p. 125.
[6] Krose, op. cit., p. 126.
[7] Schmidlin in *Zeitschrift für Missionswissenschaft,* Vol. 6, p. 246.
[8] Krose, op. cit., p. 126.

of the war no reënforcements had arrived even for the sisters in charge of the orphanage.[9] From the Jesuit mission in Chihli ten of the foreign staff reported to Tientsin and three joined the army in France. One of the three was killed in action, one saw extensive service and rose to the rank of lieutenant but did not return to China, and a third, after being wounded and awarded a *croix de guerre* and a *croix de la legion d'honneur,* at the close of the war came back to Chihli.[10]

Much of the German work was dislocated. While only one of the fathers seems to have served in Europe,[11] two of the German Dominicans in Fukien were required to report to their consul at Swatow,[12] in Shantung four of the fathers and two of the brothers of the Saxon Franciscans were made prisoners by the Japanese invaders, and nine priests and two brothers of the Society of the Divine Word assisted in the defense of Tsingtau.[13] Thirty-seven missionaries were in that city when it fell.[14] Once the Japanese occupation was completed, the missionaries were permitted to go about their usual duties and only the lay brothers who had actually borne arms were taken to Japan as prisoners.[15] China's entry into the struggle against the Central Powers wrought little change in the situation. The chief crisis came after the armistice. In December, 1918, and January, 1919, Entente influence endeavored to bring about the expulsion of all Germans from China, and nineteen members of the Society of the Divine Word were threatened with repatriation. Cardinal Gibbons of Baltimore appealed to the State Department at Washington on the ground that these missionaries were supported largely by American money, and exemption was granted to those "necessary to the continuity of the work." However, twelve of the Society of the Divine Word in Shantung were sent home, three Franciscans were compelled to leave the same province, and three Dominicans were forced out of Fukien.[16]

To the home base of missions the war brought important

[9] Walsh, *Observations in the Orient,* p. 99.
[10] *Chine, Ceylan, Madagascar,* No. 47, January, 1920, pp. 12-18.
[11] Planchet, *Les missions de Chine et du Japon, 1917,* p. 119.
[12] *Zeitschrift für Missionswissenschaft,* Vol. 5, pp. 162-164.
[13] *Allgemeine Missionszeitschrift,* Vol. 42, p. 202.
[14] Louis, *Katholische Missionskunde,* p. 121.
[15] *Zeitschrift für Missionswissenschaft,* Vol. 5, pp. 162-164.
[16] Louis, *Katholische Missionskunde,* p. 123; *Annals of the Propagation of the Faith,* Vol. 82, p. 111; *Catholic Missions,* Vol. 13, pp. 70, 178-180.

changes. With the outbreak of hostilities contributions fell off, the sum collected by the Society for the Propagation of the Faith in 1914 being only about two-thirds of that of 1913,[17] and the total gifts to the Holy Infancy declining from 4,373,981 francs in the year 1913-1914 to 1,694,686 francs in the year 1914-1915.[18] After the first sharp depression a slow recovery began. The Catholics in the United States were appealed to [19] and made a gratifying response. The income of the Society for the Propagation of the Faith, not including special funds,[20] rose from $1,118,528 in 1914 to $1,255,197 in 1915, $1,266,913 in 1916, $1,355,763 in 1917, and $1,601,140 in 1918.[21] Of the 1918 total $443,877 came from the United States and $704,926 from France, but American Catholics contributed $620,000 more to the special funds of the Society.[22] The income of the Holy Infancy, exclusive of that from the Central Empires, was 2,090,272 francs in 1915-1916, 2,468,273 francs in 1916-1917, and 4,139,663 francs in 1917-1918. In Germany over two and half million marks were contributed in 1917-1918. In spite of this partial recovery, the cost of conducting missions had so increased that the number of workers (in all lands) aided by the Holy Infancy declined from 4,550 in 1914 to 3,327 in 1916 and the number of baptisms from 459,603 in 1914 to 363,385 in 1916.[23]

Financial difficulties were only part of the problem. During the German occupation of Belgium the headquarters of the Congregation of the Immaculate Heart of Mary were removed from Scheutveld to Holland [24] and London.[25] The Champagne province of the Society of Jesus, supporting the mission in Southeastern Chihli, was badly disturbed. Its business office being at Lille, within the German lines, was cut off from the contributors, and the publication of its journal was discontinued.[26]

The sky was not utterly dark. As we shall see later, the

[17] *Catholic Missions*, Vol. 9, p. 191.
[18] Tragella, *L'Infanticidio e la S. Infanzia*, p. 136.
[19] *Catholic Missions*, Vol. 8 (1914). The reverse pages of the last two numbers for 1914 carry an appeal to Americans.
[20] In Italy a special fund was raised for missions and the same was true elsewhere.—Schmidlin in *Zeitschrift für Missionswissenschaft*, Vol. 9, p. 41.
[21] *Annals of the Propagation of the Faith*, Vol. 81, p. 91, Vol. 82, pp. 87, 186.
[22] Ibid.
[23] Tragella, op. cit., p. 136.
[24] Louis, op. cit., pp. 112-139.
[25] Schmidlin in *Zeitschrift für Missionswissenschaft*, Vol. 9, p. 41.
[26] *Chine, Ceylan, Madagascar*, No. 47, January, 1920.

United States was witnessing an awakening missionary interest among Roman Catholics, in Ireland and the United States a new society was arising, usually known by the name of Maynooth [27] and primarily for missions in China, and the *Unio cleri pro missionibus* (the Priests' Mission Union) was founded—in Italy in 1916. [28]

These harbingers of a new day, however, were not yet able entirely to dispel the night, and Catholic missions in China, as elsewhere, were suffering. In Szechwan two of the four colleges were closed [29] and in Southern Shantung lack of funds cut in half the student body of the school for catechists. [30]   The German Franciscans in Shantung were forced to give up most of their catechumenates and schools. [31]   Another mission reported the suspension of building and the abandonment of classes for catechumens and retreats for catechists. [32]   In Hongkong the bishop closed two schools and reduced the numbers in the orphanages. [33] The Spanish Dominicans in Fukien, who had only just recovered from the blow dealt by the American occupation of the Philippines, were seriously affected, [34] the bishop finding his funds reduced by half. [35]   In Mongolia many schools were shut [36] and the opening of new work was deferred because the needed recruits had been called to the colors. [37]

Added to the difficulties brought by the war in Europe were the increasing unrest and banditry in China. The notorious brigand, White Wolf, wrought havoc in parts of North China. Liuanchow in Anhui was sacked and a priest was shot, [38] and in Southern Kansu five residences were pillaged. [39]   No sooner had this miscreant been suppressed than in Kansu a revolutionary move-

[27] Schmidlin in *Zeitschrift für Missionswissenschaft*, Vol. 9, p. 41.
[28] Louis, op. cit., p. 33.
[29] *The Christian Occupation of China*, p. 228.
[30] Hesser in *Catholic Missions*, Vol. 9, pp. 114, 115.
[31] Schmidlin in *Zeitschrift für Missionswissenschaft*, Vol. 6, p. 245.
[32] Tisserand, of Chuchow, in *Catholic Missions*, Vol. 9, p. 262.
[33] Schmidlin in *Zeitschrift für Missionswissenschaft*, Vol. 6, p. 157.
[34] F. R. Noval, Procurer of the Dominicans at Hongkong, in conversation with the author, May 19, 1922.
[35] Schmidlin in *Zeitschrift für Missionswissenschaft*, Vol. 7, p. 311. See also *Die katholischen Missionen*, March, 1916, pp. 139, 140.
[36] Krose, *Kirchliches Handbuch für das katholische Deutschland*, p. 127.
[37] *Annals of the Propagation of the Faith*, Vol. 83, p. 87.
[38] Broomhall, *Jubilee Story of the China Inland Mission*, p. 330; *Die katholischen Missionen*, Dec., 1914, p. 65.
[39] Daems, Prefect Apostolic in S. Kansu, writing April 6, 1915, in *Annals of the Propagation of the Faith*, Vol. 78, pp. 236-240.

ment broke out with the motto: "Restore the Manchus, exterminate the foreigners."[40] In the Ordos region complete quiet had
not returned after the Revolution of 1911 and beginning with the
spring of 1916 bandits were an almost continuous nuisance.[41]
Few Christians were killed,[42] and some fortified their settlements
and even brought in the wounded brigands and nursed them,
but several mission stations were pillaged or burned, instruction
of catechumens was interrupted, and a missionary reported finding those who were able only to make the sign of the cross,
stammer a few prayers, and recite scattered scraps of the catechism.[43] Following the bandits came drought and pestilence, and
the latter caused the death of three hundred Chinese Christians
and three missionaries.[44] In Kwang tung in 1916 Christians were
pillaged in the unrest that accompanied the revolt against Yüan
shih-k'ai,[45] and a priest, Etienne, was wounded while on his way
to Swatow.[46] In Kwangsi, Hunan, and Honan, Christians suffered.[47]

Banditry and civil strife were not an unmitigated curse, for
missions were often able to afford protection to the non-Christian
population and so to win confidence and attract adherents. The
fear of the foreigner was still on the land and gave to church
compounds comparative immunity.[48] One priest wrote of the
eagerness of his neighbors to become Christians and so to obtain
security from brigands.[49] In Southwestern China missionaries

[40] *Annals of the Propagation of the Faith*, Vol. 79, pp. 183 et seq.
[41] Planchet, *Les missions de Chine et du Japon, 1917*, p. 93; Soenen, from
Mongolia, in *Annals of the Propagation of the Faith*, Vol. 83, pp. 3-7.
[42] Van Dyk, Vicar Apostolic, writing (1918) in *Annals of the Propagation of
the Faith*, Vol. 82, pp. 55, 56.
[43] Soenen, from Mongolia, in *Annals of the Propagation of the Faith*, Vol. 83,
pp. 3-7; *Die katholischen Missionen*, July, 1916, p. 238, Feb., 1917, p. 112.
[44] Soenen, from Mongolia, in *Annals of the Propagation of the Faith*, Vol. 81,
p. 169; Van Dyk, Vicar Apostolic, in ibid., Vol. 82, pp. 55, 56. Of these three
priests one contracted the disease while administering extreme unction.—*Catholic
Missions*, Vol. 12, p. 96. It is interesting, too, to note that services were held
to avert the plague, and that catechists, to reënforce their prayers for the termination of the pestilence, vowed to build a chapel to the Sacred Heart and to
make a pilgrimage to the shrine of the Sacred Heart in Shensi—a proceeding
reminiscent both of medieval Europe and of the practice of non-Christian Chinese.—*Annals of the Propagation of the Faith*, Vol. 81, p. 169.
[45] Planchet, *Les missions de Chine et du Japon, 1917*, p. 242.
[46] *Catholic Missions*, Vol. 10, p. 91.
[47] Ibid., Vol. 11, p. 183; *China Mission Year Book, 1918*, p. 32; Schmidlin in
Zeitschrift für Missionswissenschaft, Vol. 7, p. 159.
[48] In Canton, however, numbers of Christians were killed in the civil strife
of 1917.—Schmidlin in *Zeitschrift für Missionswissenschaft*, Vol. 7, p. 159.
[49] R. Gaudissart, S. J., writing from Chihli in *Catholic Missions*, Vol. 12,
pp. 272-274.

saved several cities from pillage[50] and this service was repeated in
the Southeast, where in 1917 P. Roudiére was intermediary between the Northern and Southern forces in Ch'aochou. In numbers of places in Kwangtung and Fukien both Christians and non-
Christians entrusted their valuables to priests for safe-keeping.[51]
Even the President, Li Yüan-hung, in the crisis of 1917 sought
refuge in St. Michael's Hospital in Peking.[52]

Nor was the World War able to prevent or even seriously to
check the growth of the Church. While the number of foreign
priests in China of the Missions Étrangères of Paris declined from
three hundred and forty-three in 1914 to three hundred and nineteen in 1918 and to two hundred and eighty-two in 1923, the Chinese Catholics in the charge of the Society rose from 240,148
in 1914 to 266,270 in 1918 and to 289,979 in 1923. This expansion was in part made possible by the rapid augmentation of the
staff of Chinese priests, from one hundred and eighty-four in 1914
to two hundred and seven in 1918 and to two hundred and forty-
two in 1923.[53] The record in the territories supervised by the
Paris Society was paralleled elsewhere. In Kiangsu and Anhui
the Catholic body increased from 220,069 in 1913-1914 to 227,917
in 1914-1915 and to 234,721 in 1915-1916.[54] In the vicariate
apostolic of Northern Chihli, manned chiefly by French Lazarists,
the growth was even more marked, the total number of Catholics in 1914 being 157,195, in 1915, 193,602, and in 1916,
204,861.[55] In the Shantung missions of the Society of the Divine
Word the numbers were 79,798 in 1914, 82,492 in 1915, and
86,150 in 1916.[56] All these missions, it will be recalled, obtained
most of their support from countries that suffered severely from
the war. Exact statistics for the entire Republic are probably un-
obtainable. One set of figures gives the total number of Roman
Catholics in all China as 1,615,107 in 1914, 1,750,675 in 1915,
and 1,827,172 in 1916.[57] In 1918 the total was reported to be
1,963,639.[58] It is interesting to note that between 1914 and 1916

[50] *Catholic Missions,* Vol. 11, pp. 112-114.
[51] Letters in *Catholic Missions,* Vol. 12, pp. 248-250.
[52] Schmidlin in *Zeitschrift für Missionswissenschaft,* Vol. 8, p. 55.
[53] *Zeitschrift für Missionswissenschaft,* Vol. 14, p. 227.
[54] Planchet, *Les missions de Chine et du Japon, 1917,* p. 152.
[55] Krose, *Kirchliches Handbuch für das katholische Deutschland,* p. 127.
[56] Ibid., p. 127.
[57] Krose, op. cit., p. 127; Planchet, op. cit., p. 301, says that in 1916 there
were 1,868,218 Catholics.
[58] Arens, *Handbuch der katholischen Missionen* (1920), pp. 162, 163.

the number of foreign priests of all societies increased only from 1,510 to 1,546, while that of Chinese priests rose from 745 to 834:[59] the preparation of a Chinese clergy was being stressed to compensate for losses in the foreign staff.[60] To complete the statistical picture of the last year of the war it may be added that in 1918 the staffs of the missions also included 195 foreign and 134 Chinese lay brothers, 986 foreign and 1,928 Chinese sisters, and about thirteen thousand Chinese catechists and teachers, and that there were 9,978 churches and chapels, 8,659 elementary schools with 179,546 students, and forty-nine seminaries of all grades with 2,448 students.[61]

These statistics may be made somewhat more vivid by a few specific and somewhat disjointed incidents culled from the records of these years. A normal school was opened by the Franciscans in T'aianfu in Shantung,[62] another was founded in Peking about 1915, and a school was begun at T'aiyüanfu.[63] In 1914 the French Sisters of St. Paul of Chartres acquired a large cotton mill in Hongkong and turned it into a hospital and orphanage, at an ultimate cost of $375,000 besides the purchase price of the land.[64] In South Hunan, a pagoda was converted into a church.[65] In Southern Shantung a new sisterhood, the Daughters of the Christian Doctrine, was founded in 1916 and the following year counted seventeen novices.[66] In 1917 Bishop Henninghaus wrote from Shantung that the Chinese were seeing more clearly the true purpose of the Church and were not associating it, as formerly, with European imperialism.[67] The Union for Catholic

[59] Krose, op. cit., p. 127.

[60] A plea for more native clergy to make good the losses of foreign clergy in the war is from the pen of Mgr. Freri of the Society for the Propagation of the Faith in *Catholic Missions,* Vol. 11, pp. 193-201.

[61] Arens, op. cit., pp. 162, 163. A list of the sisterhoods in China in 1917 shows Franciscan Missionaries of Mary in Manchuria, Kwangtung, Shensi, Shansi, Hunan, Hupeh, Shantung, Kiangnan, and Szechwan; Sisters of the Sacred Heart of Mary in Manchuria and Szechwan; Sisters of the Holy Ghost in Shantung; Carmelites in Kiangnan; Auxiliatrices du Purgatoire in Kiangnan; Sisters of St. Vincent de Paul, Little Sisters of the Poor, Presentadines (all Chinese), Daughters of Charity, Sisters of St. Anne (all Chinese), Daughters of Purgatory (all Chinese), Canossian Daughters of Charity, Sisters of the Third Order of St. Francis, Franciscan Sisters of Egypt, and Sisters of St. Paul de Chartres.—Planchet, op. cit., *1917,* pp. 77 et seq.

[62] Schmidlin in *Zeitschrift für Missionswissenschaft,* Vol. 6, p. 157.

[63] *Annals of the Propagation of the Faith,* Vol. 78, pp. 77, 123.

[64] Hagspiel, *Along the Mission Trail,* Vol. 4, p. 18.

[65] *Die katholischen Missionen,* Jan., 1918, p. 84.

[66] Arens, op. cit., p. 146.

[67] *Die katholischen Missionen,* Oct., 1918, p. 15.

Chinese Action continued to flourish,[68] and a Catholic Society, formed to offset the Young Men's Christian Association, was inaugurated in Chihli and spread to other parts of China.[69] In October, 1915, a Catholic daily newspaper, the *I Shih Pao*—"Social Welfare"—was begun in Tientsin,[70] and the following year *The China Sun* made its appearance under the editorship of a Chinese Catholic from Hawaii.[71] Between 1914 and 1916 several other Catholic sheets were inaugurated.[72] Father Lebbe, who in 1911 had commenced to preach directly to non-Christians rather than to trust to the private approach through catechists, was very successful. In 1914 and 1915 the Canton Guild Hall in Tientsin was rented for three days at a time and Lebbe spoke to great audiences. In 1916 nine halls were maintained for public addresses.[73] In France some religious work was done among the laborers who were brought from China to serve behind the Western front.[74] In Peking a new government hospital, staffed largely by Chinese physicians trained in the United States, was in 1918 put in charge of the Sisters of Charity.[75] This was not the only instance of official recognition of the Roman Catholic Church. On several occasions we hear of the decoration of missionaries for service in time of pestilence and flood and to the wounded in the civil wars.[76] In 1916, when Yüan Shih-k'ai was attempting to found a new dynasty, the Minister of Foreign Affairs asked the bishops to hold a solemn mass for the new régime.[77] The Church complied and at least one bishop sent felicitations to Yüan on his accession.[78]

On the horizon was beginning to appear promise of help from Roman Catholics in the United States. Added gifts from this

[68] McQuaide, *With Christ in China*, p. 225; *Catholic Missions*, Vol. 9, p. 216.
[69] *Catholic Missions*, Vol. 9, p. 176, Vol. 11, p. 240.
[70] Planchet, op. cit., p. 359. The same page contains a list of other Catholic periodicals in Chinese. See also *Die katholischen Missionen*, Apr., 1917, p. 162, June, 1917, p. 199.
[71] Walsh, *Observations in the Orient*, p. 109.
[72] Arens in *Die katholischen Missionen*, June, 1917, pp. 199-202.
[73] *Our Missions*, Vol. 21, p. 69.
[74] Planchet, op. cit., pp. 316-335; *Chine, Ceylan, Madagascar*, No. 48, pp. 97, 98.
[75] Walsh, op. cit., p. 123; *Catholic Missions*, Vol. 12, p. 144; *Annals of the Propagation of the Faith*, Vol. 81, p. 168.
[76] Planchet, op. cit., p. 344; *Annals of the Propagation of the Faith*, Vol. 77, p. 164, Vol. 82, p. 152; *Die katholischen Missionen*, Jan., 1915, p. 90.
[77] Planchet, op. cit., p. 346; *Die katholischen Missionen*, Oct., 1916, p. 20.
[78] Planchet, op. cit., p. 346.

source helped to atone for the loss of income from Europe.[79] In 1917 a section of Kwangtung was set aside for the Catholic Foreign Mission Society of America,[80] and American interest brought the Society of the Divine Word financial support. Not until after the close of the war, however, did extensive additions to the missionary staff come from America. The growth of the Roman Catholic Church in China during the war years was due almost entirely to the bodies represented there before 1914—those that had long been in the country.

The World War saw an attempt still further to weaken the French protectorate over Catholic missions in China. Two vicariates were already under German and seven under Italian protection.[81] Both the papal see and Peking desired direct diplomatic relations with each other. In November, 1914, Yüan Shih-k'ai gave formal reception to greetings sent by Benedict XV at the hands of Bishop Jarlin, Vicar Apostolic in Peking.[82] In 1918 China appointed a representative to the Vatican, and a nuncio was decided upon for Peking. A protest from the Entente, however, probably at the instance of France, was made to China, and the project was postponed.[83]

INCREASED ROMAN CATHOLIC INTEREST IN MISSIONS AFTER
THE WAR AND NEW MISSIONS IN CHINA

Peace inaugurated great changes in Roman Catholic missions in China. A much quoted generalization which can lay claim to some degree of accuracy declared that religiously the Roman Catholic Church won the war. Certainly the armistice was followed by an increase in the popularity of the Church in Europe. For this various reasons have been assigned—among them the heroism of priests who served in the armies, and the desire for authority displayed politically in Fascism. Whatever the causes, the Catholic revival was a fact and was accompanied by augmented missionary activity. November 30, 1919, a papal

[79] We have seen the gifts of American Catholics to the Society for the Propagation of the Faith. In 1916 an American branch was formed of the Missionary Association of Catholic Women.—*Our Missions,* Vol. 1, p. 65.

[80] Planchet, *Les missions de Chine et du Japon, 1919,* p. 262; Walsh, op. cit., p. 184.

[81] Planchet, *Les missions de Chine et du Japon, 1917,* p. 366.

[82] *Die katholischen Missionen,* April, 1915, p. 160.

[83] Reid, *China, Captive or Free,* pp. 137-139; *Zeitschrift für Missionswissenschaft,* Vol. 13, p. 39.

encyclical, *Maximum illud,* was issued (by Benedict XV). It approved the recently formed Union of the Clergy in Behalf of Missions and took occasion to stress the importance of the entire enterprise, and, while labelling nationalism as the most troublesome obstacle to the spread of the Faith, pleaded for the building up of a body of native clergy. It also reiterated the papal approval of the agencies that were collecting funds for and arousing an interest in missions.[84] By a papal edict of 1922 the Society for the Propagation of the Faith was reorganized in such a manner that French influence was not so predominant, and the headquarters were moved from Lyons and Paris to Rome.[85] The Jubilee Year of 1925 had as one of its main features a mission exposition at the Vatican, making vivid the work of the Church on its far-flung frontiers.[86] This was followed, March 1, 1926, by another encyclical, *Rerum Ecclesiæ,* in which the Pope (Pius XI) urged the Church, and especially the bishops, to further the cause of foreign missions by gifts and prayers and by encouraging vocations for a missionary career, and dwelt particularly on the importance of trusting the native churches and raising up a native clergy. The Pope insisted that native priests should not be held in subordinate positions. He also protested against the concentration of missionaries in a few great centers and institutions and advised that the forces of the Church be more widely dispersed. He directed, too, that missionaries give attention to winning the natural leaders of a nation, those of superior social position.[87] Thus did Rome seek both to stimulate an interest in missions and to adjust itself to the rapidly rising tides of nationalism.

This increased interest in missions was not confined to Rome. Throughout much of the Catholic world new missionary organizations were appearing. One list gives the names of thirty that arose between 1914 and 1922, most of them after the war, for the support of missions by prayer, giving, and education. They were to be found in Italy, Germany, Austria, Holland, Belgium, Spain, Great Britain, Ireland, Switzerland, Hungary, France, and

[84] Louis, *Katholische Missionskunde,* pp. 139-154; *Annals of the Propagation of the Faith,* Vol. 83, p. 160.
[85] *Annals of the Propagation of the Faith,* Vol. 85, pp. 161-164.
[86] Considine, *The Vatican Mission Exposition,* passim.
[87] Bishop Trollope in *The East and the West,* Vol. 25, pp. 1-20; *Les missions catholiques,* March 26, 1926, pp. 145 et seq.

the United States.[88] Beginning with 1923 an annual Week of
Missions was held at Louvain at which representatives of many
nationalities and organizations convened.[89] So marked was the
growth of the Society for the Propagation of the Faith that in
1925 the sums allocated to various missions were increased fifteen
and even forty per cent.[90]
Especially noteworthy was the growth in the United States.
The reasons for this have already been indicated. The Roman
Catholic body was here made up largely of late immigrants, most
of whom had come seeking larger economic opportunity and were
poor at the time of their arrival. Churches and schools had to
be erected and a clergy recruited and educated, and no surplus
energy was available for activities outside the country. By 1914,
however, the economic level of the Catholic population had
greatly risen, many Catholics were becoming wealthy, and after
that year the flood of immigration diminished, first because of
the war and then because of the new restrictions imposed by the
government. It was therefore possible to gain attention for
undertakings abroad. Thanks to the energetic work that had
been done among the immigrants, relatively few of them or their
descendants had broken away from the Church.[91] Here, then,
was a body of Roman Catholics, twenty millions strong, second
only to Italy in the number of its residential sees,[92] and rapidly
increasing in wealth. The United States bade fair to become the
treasure chest of the Church. In 1919 American Catholics were
said to be giving to foreign missions about three million dollars
a year.[93] By 1926 about half the income of the great organiza-

[88] Arens, *Die katholischen Missionsvereine*, pp. 10-25. See also on the
increased interest in missions Freitag in *Zeitschrift für Missionswissenschaft*,
Vol. 16, p. 293; Bekkers in *Revue d'histoire des missions*, Vol. 4, pp. 185-216;
Dahmen in *Revue d'histoire des Missions*, Vol. 4, pp. 334-358; Miss Underhill in
The International Review of Missions, Vol. 17, pp. 218-227.
[89] Miss Underhill in op. cit., Vol. 17, p. 224.
[90] *Zeitschrift für Missionswissenschaft*, Vol. 16, p. 288. The income for the
Society for 1925 was 49,183,342 lire, as against about forty-four million lire for
the preceding year. Of the 1925 total, 22,234,596 lire came from the United
States. To this must be added the gifts for mass intentions, which in 1925
for the United States alone were 27,056,016 lire. The 1925 receipts of the Society
of the Holy Infancy of Jesus were about twenty million francs, an increase of
about six million francs. The Union of Catholic Women and Girls in 1925
received 979,215 gold marks, of which 709,117 came from the United States.—
Ibid., Vol. 16, pp. 288-290.
[91] Shaughnessy, *Has the Immigrant Kept the Faith?* passim.
[92] Ibid., pp. 213, 268.
[93] *Our Missions*, Vol. 1, p. 12.

tions that raised money for missions came from the United
States,[94] and in 1925 a bequest of $1,200,000 was received from
an American by the Missions Union of Catholic Women and
Girls.[95] The contributions from the United States to the Society
for the Propagation of the Faith mounted from $366,460 in 1912
to $1,203,469 in 1922 and to $1,837,003 in 1924.[96] This assistance was badly needed, for the depreciation of the currencies
of Europe and the increased cost of living in China were embarrassing most of the congregations and orders. The Salesians, for
example, in 1920 begged for aid on the ground that unfavorable
exchange had reduced their income from Europe to almost nothing, and that same year a Lazarist vicar apostolic in Chêkiang
reported the curtailment of school work and the dismissal of half
his catechists.[97] Missionaries of the Society of the Divine Word
sold timber and grew mulberry trees and vegetables to help pay
expenses.[98] As we shall see more in detail when we come to the
part which they played in China, several new organizations arose
in the United States for the purpose of sending and supporting
foreign missionaries, and many older congregations, orders, and
societies began dispatching Americans to other lands. The
Catholic Students' Mission Crusade, contemplated before 1914,
was formally organized at St. Mary's Mission House at Techny,
just outside Chicago, in July, 1918,[99] and by the end of three
years had enrolled over thirty thousand members.[100] In December, 1920, an American Board of Catholic Missions was formed
to supervise both home and foreign missions.[101]

This fresh European and American interest in Catholic missions
was directed toward China more than toward any other country.
The ecclesiastical map of the Republic was, accordingly, greatly
altered. Societies and congregations, especially the French and
the Belgian, that had long borne the burden and heat of the
day were weakened by the war and needed assistance in covering
the vast regions for which they were responsible. Some German
bodies, excluded from former German colonies and from the

[94] Zeitschrift für Missionswissenschaft, Vol. 16, p. 290.
[95] Ibid.
[96] Catholic Missions and Annals of the Propagation of the Faith, Vol. 2, p. 70.
[97] Annals of the Propagation of the Faith, Vol. 83, p. 132.
[98] Hagspiel, Along the Mission Trail, Vol. 4, pp. 193, 232.
[99] Catholic Students' Mission Crusade, Bulletin No. 3, passim.
[100] Our Missions, Vol. 1, p. 91.
[101] Ibid., Vol. 1, pp. 2, 12, 18.

possessions of the Entente powers, were seeking new fields and were assigned by the Propaganda to sections carved from the territories of other organizations.

Like all the accounts of the entrance of new bodies to China which this story has so far included, the list that follows will necessarily present something of the arid aspect of a catalogue. Behind it, however, are hidden the ambitions, the dreams, the prayers, and the life-blood of many a man and woman, and it represents one of the greatest bursts of missionary energy that the Roman Catholic Church in China has known.

Because of their possible significance for the future, first in importance and interest were missionaries from the United States. Before 1914 the Society of the Divine Word, German in origin, was erecting missionary training schools in America, the chief being at Techny, Illinois. During the war much of the support for the Society's activities in China came from the United States, and by 1921 three American priests had joined its Shantung mission.[102] Thanks probably in part to the assistance assured from the United States, in 1923 the Society was entrusted with Western Kansu and Sinkiang and a section of Southern Honan,[103] the district in Honan being especially the charge of the American province.[104] The formation in 1911 of the Catholic Foreign Mission Society of America has already been noted. The organizer and head was the Rev. James A. Walsh and under his leadership, on the campus at Maryknoll, just outside of Ossining, New York, a large school for the training of missionaries began to take form. A companion body, the Foreign Mission Sisters of St. Dominic, also with headquarters at Maryknoll, received official sanction in 1920.[105] Walsh made a tour of the Far East in 1917 and selected a field in Southern Kwangtung and Eastern Kwangsi. The following year Rome formally approved his choice. In 1918 the first party of "Maryknollers," a group of four, left for China. Their leader was Rev. Thomas F. Price who, fifty-eight years of age, the son of converts from Protestantism, had been the first North Carolinian to be ordained priest, for years had been a pioneer home missionary, and had joined with Walsh in the foundation of the Society. He lived to see the land of his hopes,

[102] *Our Missions*, Vol. 1, p. 29.
[103] *Les missions catholiques*, 1923, p. 104.
[104] *Les missions catholiques*, Vol. 56, p. 281.
[105] Powers, *The Maryknoll Movement*, p. 113.

but in September of the following year he was dead. Undiscouraged by the loss of its Superior or by the bandits who infested Kwangtung and Kwangsi, the mission continued, and each year was sent reënforcements. The first sisters, six in number, sailed in 1921.[106] In 1925 an additional field in the vicariate of Swatow was assigned the Maryknollers,[107] and in 1926 they were given a district in the southeastern part of Manchuria.[108] Thus was this young body sharing the load that had so long been borne by the Paris Society.

Another organization that drew heavily from the United States was the Chinese Mission Society of St. Columban. It owed its origin to a Father Galvin, who, a graduate of Maynooth, Ireland, spent the four years from 1912 to 1916 in Chêkiang and there became convinced of the need in China for English-speaking priests. English, he discovered, was the language of commerce, and Protestant missionaries, largely native to that tongue, had an advantage over Roman Catholics in approaching the Chinese youth. Galvin therefore projected a new society and in 1916 his plans received the approval of the Irish bishops and in 1917 the papal blessing. The first theological seminary was opened at Dolgan Park, Galway, a preparatory school was begun in County Clare, and a little later a house was founded at Omaha, Nebraska, a preparatory college at Silver Creek, New York, and a branch in Australia and New Zealand with a house at Melbourne.[109] A companion body, the Missionary Sisters of St. Columban, was organized in 1922, and in its first year sent nine novices to China.[110] The first parties of men sailed in 1920, one from the United States and one from Ireland. They were assigned a section of Hupeh, with Hanyang as headquarters.[111] In 1923 the budget called for $125,000 for buildings and current expenses,[112] and by 1927 seventy missionaries were on the ground,

[106] Powers, op. cit., passim; *Father Price of Maryknoll*, passim; *Annals of the Propagation of the Faith*, Vol. 85, p. 172; *Millard's Review*, Oct. 4, 1919, p. 198; Walsh, *Observations in the Orient*, passim; *Maryknoll Letters, China*, Vols. 1 and 2, passim.

[107] *Catholic Missions and Annals of the Propagation of the Faith*, Vol. 2, p. 298.

[108] Powers, op. cit., p. 122.

[109] *Catholic Missions and Annals of the Propagation of the Faith*, Vol. 2, p. 279; *Catholic Missions*, Vol. 12, p. 71, Vol. 13, p. 166; *Annals of the Propagation of the Faith*, Vol. 81, p. 72.

[110] Arens, *Handbuch der katholischen Missionen*, 1925, p. 122.

[111] *Annals of the Propagation of the Faith*, Vol. 83, p. 71.

[112] Ibid., Vol. 86, p. 29; Hagspiel, *Along the Mission Trail*, Vol. 4, p. 352.

with a college, high school, and hospital in Hanyang, and over-sight over the Christians in the surrounding country.[113]   Aiding them were Sisters of Loretto, from Kentucky, the first party of whom arrived in October, 1923.[114]

American Lazarists of the eastern province came to the assist-ance of their French brethren and were apportioned a district around Nanchow in Kiangsi.   The pioneers of the new mission reached China in 1921.[115]   At Yukiang in Kiangsi were soon seven priests from the western province of the United States.[116] In 1921 the Propaganda gave the American provinces of the Passionists a section of the territory of the Spanish Augustinians in the northwestern portion of Hunan.   The first group arrived in March, 1922, and in 1923 and 1924 was followed by other contingents.   In 1925 the district was created a prefecture apostolic and in that year five Sisters of Charity from New Jersey went out to care for women and children.   The region was mountainous, contained very few Christians, and parts of it never had seen a Catholic missionary.[117]   The Dominicans of St. Joseph's Province in North America came to the help of the Spaniards who had so long been responsible for Fukien and in 1920 were assigned a section around Kienningfu.   The first group reached the field in 1923.[118]   To Fukien, too, came, about 1923, to aid their then recently arrived German brothers, Salvatorian fathers from St. Nazianz, Wisconsin.[119]   In 1920 the Vicar Apostolic of Eastern Honan visited the United States seeking assistance and in response to his appeal secular priests from the diocese of Philadelphia and several Sisters of Providence from St. Mary of the Woods, Indiana, went to Kaifeng.   Both groups began schools, the one for boys and the other for girls.[120]   On June 10, 1918, six members of the New York convent of the Franciscan Missionaries of Mary sailed for China,[121] and at

[113] Goodrich, *American Catholic Missions in China,* pp. 25, 26.
[114] *Relations de Chine,* Vol. 22, p. 367.
[115] *Annals of the Propagation of the Faith,* Vol. 84, p. 76.
[116] Goodrich, op. cit., pp. 31, 32.
[117] *Annals of the Propagation of the Faith,* Vol. 85, p. 225; *Catholic Mis-sions and Annals of the Propagation of the Faith,* Vol. 2, p. 276; *The Christian Occupation of China,* p. 460.
[118] *Zeitschrift für Missionswissenschaft,* Vol. 13, p. 175; *Annals of the Propa-gation of the Faith,* Vol. 83, p. 151.
[119] *Annals of the Propagation of the Faith,* Vol. 86, p. 30.
[120] Planchet, *Les missions de Chine et du Japon, 1925,* pp. 140, 529; Good-rich, op. cit., p. 39; *Annals of the Propagation of the Faith,* Vol. 83, p. 230.
[121] *Annals of the Propagation of the Faith,* Vol. 81, p. 166.

various times others of the same sisterhood went from Providence, Rhode Island. In May, 1924, two sisters of the Society of the Precious Blood from Portland, Oregon, and five from Manchester, New Hampshire, left to establish a convent at Hochienfu, Chihli.[122]   Theirs was a contemplative congregation and their especial purpose was to aid by continual prayer the conversion of China.[123]   In September, 1926, six from the convent of the Sacred Heart, in Albany, New York, sailed to open at Shanghai an academy for girls.[124]   Sisters of Charity from Maryland were also coming to China.[125]

The Rev. Remigius Goette, a Franciscan from Sacred Heart Province (St. Louis), went to Hsianfu in 1882 and in 1905 was created Vicar Apostolic of Northern Shensi.   Between 1882 and 1921 ten American Franciscans joined the Shensi mission.   After the close of the war American Brothers Minor awoke to an increased interest in China.   In 1922 a region around Wuchang was assigned them, and in 1923 this was especially entrusted to those from Cincinnati and Santa Barbara.   A prefecture in Shantung was apportioned to the St. Louis province and a section in Shensi to the New York province.   St. Joseph's Hospital, in Tsinanfu, was in charge of the Hospital Sisters of St. Francis, whose mother house was at Springfield, Illinois.[126]   By 1926, American Franciscans were to be found in several provinces.

Some American Capuchins went to the assistance of their German brethren who after the war were assigned part of Kansu,[127] and, as we shall see more fully later, American Benedictines were placed in charge of the project for a Catholic university in Peking.

Not only from the United States, but from Canada, missionaries began going in numbers to China.   We have already seen that before the war Canadian Sisters of the Immaculate Conception were aiding in the care of lepers in Canton.   They increased their staff and about 1918 took charge of an orphanage

[122] Goodrich, op. cit., p. 33.
[123] Letter from Lécroart, Vicar Apostolic of S. E. Chihli, in *Les missions catholiques*, Vol. 56, p. 521; Planchet, op. cit., *1925*, p. 515; *Chine, Ceylan, Madagascar*, No. 66, p. 271, No. 67, p. 6.
[124] *Die katholischen Missionen*, 1926, p. 317; Goodrich, op. cit., p. 33.
[125] Goodrich, op. cit., p. 32.
[126] Ibid., pp. 27-31; *Catholic Missions and Annals of the Propagation of the Faith*, Vol. 2, p. 290.
[127] Goodrich, op. cit., p. 57.

in that city.[128] The Sisters of Our Lady of the Angels had their inception in 1920 at Sherbrooke, primarily for work in China, and by the close of 1923 five of their number were in distant Kweiyang.[129] Canadian Ursulines received permission from the Propaganda to labor in Swatow and in June, 1922, the first contingent sailed.[130] A seminary for foreign missions, modeled after the famous one at Paris, was established at Montreal with Canon Avila Roch as its superior.[131] It was assigned (1925) a section of Manchuria.[132] In 1920 a mission college founded by Father Fraser at Almonte, Canada, sent Father Caralt to Spain to institute there a China Mission College, and as a result one was begun in the monastery of Leire, near the birthplace of St. Francis Xavier.[133] In 1921 the school at Almonte had twenty-two students and one graduate had already arrived in Kwei-chow.[134] Fraser changed the field of labor to Chêkiang, perhaps because from 1903 to 1917 he himself had been a missionary there, and in 1926 three priests under his leadership arrived at Chuchow, not far from Wênchow, in that province.[135] In 1924 Canadian Jesuits sent an initial contingent to aid the French members of their Society in Kiangsu.[136] Canadian Franciscans took charge of a portion of Shantung, near Chefoo.[137]

The Old World did not sit idly by and leave to the New World the honor of being the sole source of the new enterprises in China. The outcome of the war forced the Capuchins of the Rhenish-Westphalian province to leave the Caroline and Marianne Islands and they were assigned the eastern part of Kansu.[138] Near the close of the war the Vicar Apostolic of Northern Chihli asked the Provincial of the Irish Lazarists for priests to fill the vacancies in his staff. In 1920 four priests responded

[128] Catholic Missions and Annals of the Propagation of the Faith, Vol. 2, p. 95; Maryknoll Mission Letters, China, Vol. 1, pp. 52, 54.
[129] Arens, Handbuch der katholischen Missionen, 1925, p. 140; Planchet, op. cit., 1925, p. 536.
[130] Annals of the Propagation of the Faith, Vol. 85, p. 151.
[131] Ibid., Vol. 84, p. 188.
[132] Planchet, op. cit., 1927, Part 2, p. 28.
[133] Annals of the Propagation of the Faith, Vol. 86, p. 31.
[134] Our Missions, Vol. 1, p. 45.
[135] Planchet, op. cit., 1927, Part 2, pp. 30, 62.
[136] Relations de Chine, Vol. 23, p. 39.
[137] Planchet, op. cit., 1927, Part 2, p. 62.
[138] Die katholischen Missionen, 1926, p. 302; Planchet, op. cit., 1925, p. 108; Clemens a Terzorio, Manuale Historicum Missionum Ordinis Minorum Capuccinorum, 1926, pp. 217-219.

and took charge of part of Peking near the Tung T'ang and founded a middle school, St. Patrick's College.[139] It seemed probable that before many years a special vicariate in Chihli would be formed for them.[140] In 1922 the Irish Brothers of the Christian Schools came to the assistance of the Maynooth Mission and made their special task St. Columban's College, at Hanyang.[141] In 1922 Benedictines of St. Odele, Germans who had worked in Chosen, were allocated to a portion of Northern Manchuria into which Koreans had emigrated.[142] In 1926 the Conventuals, Franciscans, were assigned a vicariate in Shensi.[143] In November, 1926, the Priests of the Holy Stigmata, or the Stimatini, came to Chihli to a part of the vicariate of Paotingfu.[144] That same year members of the Society of Foreign Missions of Bethlehem, a Swiss organization, arrived in Manchuria, and it was expected that in time a part of Heilungchiang would be given them. They were to be aided by the Sisters of Ingenbohl and by lay brothers.[145] In 1923 the Society of the Hiltrup Missionaries of the Sacred Heart of Issoudon were planning to labor in Kweichow, in the difficult region once assigned to Fraser's mission.[146]

To the Jesuits already in China came fresh assistance from other groups of their Society. In 1926 the Austrian province sent two priests to Chihli, and to Chihli also came Jesuits from Hungary accompanying ten sisters from Kalocza, of the Congregation of Our Lady.[147] In 1922 Anhui was divided into three missions, that of Wuhu being entrusted to the Spanish Jesuits of Castile, that of Anking to those of the province of Leon, and the Northeast to Italian Jesuits of Turin.[148]

German Salvatorians who had been driven out of Assam in 1923 were appointed a portion of Fukien around Shaowu, where

[139] *Catholic Missions and Annals of the Propagation of the Faith,* Vol. 1, pp. 62, 63.
[140] *Relations de Chine,* Vol. 21, p. 148.
[141] Planchet, op. cit., *1925,* p. 221.
[142] *Relations de Chine,* Vol. 21, p. 148.
[143] Planchet, op. cit., *1927,* Part 2, pp. 59-63.
[144] Ibid.
[145] Planchet, op. cit., *1927,* Part 2, pp. 59-63.
[146] Ibid.; *Our Missions,* Vol. 7, p. 69.
[147] *Zeitschrift für Missionswissenschaft,* Vol. 16, p. 296; *Chine, Ceylan, Madagascar,* No. 73, p. 195.
[148] *Relations de Chine,* Vol. 21, p. 152. In September and October, 1921, there left for Kiangnan four Jesuits from France, one from Ireland, three from Turin, one from Malta, and three from Canada.—Ibid., Vol. 19, p. 109.

they were aided by Americans of their congregation.[149] The vicariate apostolic of Northern Shantung was given to the Franciscans of the Rhenish province,[150] Northern Shansi was transferred from the Italian Franciscans to those of Bavaria, and Eastern Hupeh from the Italian Brothers Minor to their confrères from the Tyrol.[151] To the Tyrolese Franciscans also went a portion of Southern Hunan,[152] their initial contingent being sent in 1919.[153] In 1922 the first representative of the Priests of the Sacred Heart of Jesus of Betharram (of Bayonne) reached Yünnan.[154] Spanish Augustinian-Recollets took over part of the vicariate apostolic of East Honan.[155] The Congregation of Picpus, or, to use its official name, the Congregation of the Sacred Heart of Jesus and Mary and of the Perpetual Adoration of the Very Holy Sacrament of the Altar, began a mission in the island of Hainan.[156] A priest came from Uruguay to join the Salesians of Dom Bosco.[157] The Ursulines (of the Roman Union) arrived in Swatow in July, 1922,[158] and the following year the "Soeurs Chanoinesses de S. Augustin," a Belgian body, reached Western Mongolia. In 1923, too, the vicariate apostolic of Eastern Mongolia received its first European sisters, members of the Congregation of the Daughters of Mary and Joseph, a body whose mother house was in Holland. The superior of the first band died of typhoid soon after reaching China.[159] It must also be noted that in 1926 the Foreign Mission Society of Saints Peter and Paul united with that of Milan and the work of the two was accordingly placed under a single administration.[160]

This list of new undertakings, bare chronicle though it is, indicates that the Roman Catholic world was looking toward China as its field of greatest opportunity. Never in any similar

[149] Louis, *Katholische Missionskunde*, p. 157.
[150] Ibid.
[151] Ibid.
[152] *Zeitschrift für Missionswissenschaft*, Vol. 13, pp. 42, 43.
[153] Ibid., Vol. 15, p. 51.
[154] Planchet, *Les missions de Chine et du Japon, 1925*, p. 305.
[155] *Die katholischen Missionen*, 1924-1925, p. 94.
[156] Planchet, op. cit., *1927*, Part 2, pp. 59-63.
[157] *Die katholischen Missionen*, 1924-1925, p. 94.
[158] Planchet, op. cit., *1925*, p. 329.
[159] Ibid., *1925*, p. 112.
[160] Arens, op. cit. (1920), pp. 162, 163. There were also in Hongkong, the date of their arrival not being given, the Brothers of Christian Doctrine, the Sisters of S. Paul of Chartres, and the (Chinese) Sisters of the Most Precious Blood.—*Missiones Catholicae Cura S. Congregatione de Propaganda Fide, 1922*, p. 232.

period of time had as many Catholic organizations entered the country. Between 1918 and 1927, indeed, almost as many began work there as in all the previous history of the Middle Kingdom. This did not mean, however, a proportionate change in the missionary body. In 1916 the number of foreign priests had been 1,668,[161] and in 1918 the number of foreign sisters 996, and of foreign lay brothers 195, a total of 2,727.[162] In 1926 there were 1,723 foreign priests, 1,088 foreign sisters, and 248 lay brothers, a total of 3,059.[163] The French, although not as predominant as formerly, were still more numerous than were the representatives of any other nation.[164] Nor did this addition of new missions immediately work any revolution in methods. Alterations there were, as we shall see in a moment, but in the main, except for the fact that Americans tended to stress education, these were not due to ideas introduced by the new congregations.

PROGRESS TOWARD MAKING THE CHURCH CHINESE IN LEADERSHIP AND CHARACTER

While the coming of so many new congregations brought no very great changes in the methods of Catholic missions, the movements afoot in China did so. No body of men as intelligent as those who directed the Roman Catholic Church could fail to be impressed with the nationalism which was mounting so rapidly in the great republic. If the Church were to remain primarily foreign and divided into districts worked by bodies which had relations with each other only through Rome, it could not hope to win the confidence of the Chinese and, should the nationalistic movement ever unite the country and gave birth to a strong government, it might be obliterated.

The Catholic Church could scarcely make its peace with China on matters of doctrine. Here it believed that it had a divine and

[161] Planchet, op. cit., 1917, p. 301.

[162] Arens, op. cit. (1920), p. 162.

[163] Planchet, op. cit., 1927, p. xv. This increase did not mean as many new missionaries as would have been the case fifty years before. In the Kiangnan mission (Jesuit) in 1842-1852 the mean life of the missionary was thirty-eight years and nine months, in 1863-1872 forty years and five months, and in 1913-1921 fifty-seven years and eight months. The turnover in the missionary body, therefore, was not as great as formerly.—Hermand, Les étapes de la mission du Kiangnan 1842-1922, pp. 13, 14.

[164] In 1922, of the 1,438 foreign priests in China, 680 belonged to French congregations, and of the 56 bishops 24 were French.—Relations de Chine, Vol. 21, p. 83. The French press complained of the declining French influence.

immutable message. The decision on the rites controversy had demonstrated that it was not disposed to compromise its teachings to avoid offending Chinese susceptibilities. In other ways, however, Rome could go far toward accommodating itself to nationalistic aspirations. It could increase the proportion of Chinese clergy and begin the creation of a native hierarchy, and it could bring in some kind of coördination among the separate missions and take steps toward creating an organization which could be national and at the same time remain in full fellowship with the Catholic Church.

In the creation of a Chinese clergy progress was rapid. In 1918 the number of native priests was 834, or thirty-five per cent. of the clerical body.[165] In 1923 it had risen to 1,088 or forty-one per cent.,[166] and in 1926 it was 1,184 or still forty-one per cent.[167] In 1916 Chinese made up sixty-six per cent. of the total number of sisters,[168] and ten years later seventy-two per cent.[169]

This change was due partly to the insistence of Rome. The papal brief of November 30, 1919, praised the Opus S. Petri which had been organized in 1889 to help create a native clergy in mission lands and emphasized the importance of that goal.[170] The brief of March 1, 1926, was even more forcible and earnest, and June 15, 1926, the Pope wrote especially to the bishops in China urging a national structure for the Church.[171]

The figures given above show that the missionaries were not entirely disobedient. New Chinese sisterhoods continued to be organized.[172] Occasionally, too, discussion arose over the adoption of Chinese architecture for ecclesiastical purposes, although the most conspicuous experiments in this direction resulted only in strange hybrids.[173] In appreciation of the Chinese love of the theatre, a passion play and other dramatizations of Bible stories

---

[165] Arens, *Handbuch der katholischen Missionen* (1920), pp. 162, 163.
[166] Ibid. (1925), p. 222. Of the 1,088, 938 were seculars. For the life of one of the prospective priests see Couturier, *Un séminariste chinois fidèle imitateur de St. Jean Berchmans, Barthélemy Zin, 1er Sept. 1903—4 Juillet, 1925*, passim.
[167] Planchet, op. cit., 1927, p. xv.
[168] Arens, op. cit. (1920), pp. 162, 163.
[169] Planchet, loc. cit.
[170] Louis, *Katholische Missionskunde*, p. 32.
[171] *Zeitschrift für Missionswissenschaft*, Vol. 16, p. 288.
[172] See examples in Arens, op. cit. (1920), p. 164, and Planchet, op. cit., 1927, pp. 103, 121, 156, Part 2, p. 34.
[173] Planchet, op. cit., 1927, Part 2, pp. 102-106.

were introduced.[174] Congregational chants of a Chinese type were a feature of the mass in as widely separated districts as Mongolia and Hankow.[175] Between 1920 and 1924, moreover, the names of most of the vicariates apostolic were changed from those of regions to cities. Thus the vicariate apostolic of Maritime Chihli became that of Tientsin. This was a step, even though a slight one, toward creating the type of hierarchy to be found in Europe and America.[176]

More significant than any of these attempts, however, was the beginning of a native episcopate. The experiment of the seventeenth century, when a Chinese, Gregory Lopez, had been created Bishop of Basilea and Vicar Apostolic of Nanking, and then, shortly before his death, Bishop of Nanking, had never been repeated. The reason often given, as we have seen, was that a native bishop, being under Chinese laws and officials, would be unable to maintain the dignity of the Church. He might, for example, be compelled to prostrate himself before the meanest magistrate. Certainly a foreign bishop could better appeal to France or some other power for protection against persecution. It was also urged that no Chinese clergymen had yet arisen with qualities of character and physique adequate to the exacting duties of the episcopate. The time was speedily approaching, however, when because of the temper of the nation foreign leadership would be as much a handicap as an asset, and Rome saw and took to heart the writing on the wall. Sufficient information has not yet been made public to enable the historian to assess the responsibility for the change. Whether the missionaries in China demurred and Rome insisted, whether the foreign clergy were divided on the issue, or whether the Chinese priests brought pressure is not yet publicly known. Rumor has it that some of the Chinese clergy organized to obtain greater privileges.

Whatever the sources of the movement, the first steps were taken in 1924 when Lihsien in Chihli and P'uch'i in Hupeh were created prefectures apostolic and entrusted to the sole care of the Chinese clergy. Melchior Sun was appointed Prefect Apostolic

[174] Chine, Ceylan, Madagascar, No. 54, pp. 242, 249, 255, No. 60, p. 106.
[175] Annals of the Propagation of the Faith, Vol. 84, pp. 40-45; Schmidlin, Missions und Kulturverhältnisse im fernen Osten, p. 59.
[176] Planchet, op. cit., 1927, Part 2, p. 11; Revue d'histoire des missions, Vol. 3, p. 604; Missiones Catholicae Cura S. Congregationis de Propaganda Fide, 1922, pp. 194-200.

of Lihsien and Odoric Ch'êng of P'uch'i.[177]   In 1926 the announcement was made that six Chinese were to be raised to the episcopate, and on October 28, 1926, the ceremony was performed in Rome, the Pope officiating in person. Much publicity was given the bishops-elect on their way to Europe. Rome seemed eager to demonstrate to the world and especially to China its desire for a truly Chinese Church. The six so honored were the two Prefects Apostolic, Melchior Sun, a Lazarist, being made titular Bishop of Esbon and Vicar Apostolic of Lihsien, and Odoric Ch'êng, a Franciscan, who had studied in Italy, titular Bishop of Catonna and Vicar Apostolic of P'uch'i. Philip Chao, a secular and the son of a martyr of the Boxer year, was created titular Bishop of Vaga and Vicar Apostolic of Hsuanhuafu, Chihli; Simon Tsu, a Jesuit and a member of a prominent Shanghai family which had been won to the Christian faith nearly three centuries before, titular Bishop of Lesbitana and Vicar Apostolic of Haimen, Kiangsu; Joseph Hu, a Lazarist, brought up in an orphanage, titular Bishop of Theodosiopolitana and Vicar Apostolic of Taichow; and Aloysius Ch'ên, a Franciscan, titular Bishop of Attudensus and Vicar Apostolic of Fêngyang, Shansi.[178]   To none of these bishops was a major vicariate entrusted. The most important positions continued to be held by the foreigner and nine-tenths of the bishops were still of alien birth and allegiance. However, the Church had taken a momentous step, one which might well be followed by other and even greater ones.

THE ATTEMPT TO GIVE THE ROMAN CATHOLIC CHURCH IN CHINA A NATIONAL ORGANIZATION

Not only had the new conditions made a Chinese episcopate imperative, but larger coöperation among the various bodies working in the country was eminently desirable. Only a nationally organized church could deal adequately with intensely nationalistic China. Protestants, for all their multiplicity of denominations,

[177] *Les missions catholiques,* Vol. 56, p. 34; Planchet, op. cit., *1925,* pp. 498, 499; *Catholic Missions and Annals of the Propagation of the Faith,* Vol. 1, p. 239.
[178] Planchet, op. cit., *1927,* Part 2, p. 10; *Catholic Missions,* 1927, pp. 16-19; *North-China Herald,* Sept. 25, 1926; D'Elia, *Catholic Native Episcopacy in China,* pp. 80-88. Bishop Chao died in October, 1927, from apoplexy induced by the strain of administering relief to Christians and non-Christians during the war of that year.—*Chinese Recorder,* Vol. 59, p. 192.

were better coördinated than were Catholics. From time to time, to be sure, local synods had been held and for several decades the country had been divided into regions for this purpose. No machinery existed for anything further, however.

In 1912 a general synod for China was projected but was deferred because of the war.[179] We have already noted the plan of 1918 to appoint a papal representative to Peking and a Chinese to the Vatican, a proposal which failed because of French opposition.[180] In 1919 Guébriant, Vicar Apostolic of Canton, was appointed Visitor of all the missions in China.[181] In 1922 a further step was taken. Celse Bénigne-Louis Constantini was created titular Archbishop of Theodosia and Apostolic Delegate to China. His jurisdiction was to cover all the country, including Macao. He arrived late in 1922 and on the first day of 1923 was officially received by President Li Yüan-hung.[182] Constantini's power was religious, not political, and he was not recognized by Peking as a diplomatic agent of the Vatican. Thus respect was paid to French feelings and the remnants of the French protectorate were preserved.[183]

Through the Apostolic Delegate was called the first national council ever held by the Roman Catholic Church in China. This may have been suggested by the national gatherings of Protestants, notably the one in 1922. Certainly the preparatory machinery and the organization bore a close resemblance to them. Whatever the origin of the idea, in 1922 seven regional synods convened. Each chose three consultors, two foreign and one Chinese, and seven sub-commissions were appointed. In 1923 these met in Shanghai and Peking under the presidency of Mgr. Constantini. In 1924 the General Synod was held in Shanghai. The public ceremonies were stately and colorful and with much pomp the missions in China were consecrated to the Holy Virgin. The business sessions of the gathering, however, were secret and

---

[179] *Zeitschrift für Missionswissenschaft*, Vol. 10, pp. 116-126.

[180] Planchet, op. cit., 1919, p. 348.

[181] *Annals of the Propagation of the Faith*, Vol. 82, p. 232; Planchet, op. cit., 1925, pp. 5, 481, 482. A conference of bishops he called to confer with him in Hankow met during the anniversary of the martyrdom of Clet and they went in procession through the streets of Wuchang, the magistrates coming to greet them.—*Our Missions*, Jan., 1921, p. 11.

[182] Planchet, op. cit., *1919*, p. 348. The Chinese minister to Spain acted also as representative to the Vatican.

[183] *Missions catholiques*, 1923, pp. 313-316; Grentrup, *Jus Missionarium*, p. 398.

the findings were not to be published until approved by Rome.[184] Roman Catholics did not, as did the Protestants, carry on their discussions in public. It may have been that their unhappy experience in the rites controversy had taught them caution. It was obvious, however, that the Church in China was thinking and planning together as never before.

EDUCATION

Not only in raising up a native leadership and in creating a national organization was the Roman Catholic Church seeking to adjust itself to changing China. In education it was pursuing the efforts initiated before 1914 to impress its message upon the influential classes.[185] Between 1916 and 1925 the number of students in its schools seems nearly to have doubled.[186] We hear of a plan for a higher primary school in Mukden, with more applicants than could be accommodated.[187] The Jesuits in Kiangsu and Anhui continued to have an educational system superior to that in any other of the vicariates. From their parish schools—combining catechetical and elementary instruction—through excellent secondary institutions, including St. Ignatius College at Zikawei, up through Aurora University, they could offer boys a complete preparation for almost any important occupation or profession.[188] New schools preparatory to Aurora were opened at Nanking and Yangchow,[189] and Aurora drew as well from institutions in other vicariates, and even from Penang and Saigon.[190] Provision was made at Zikawei for advanced education for women,[191] and in Shanghai the Marists conducted St. Francis Xavier College.[192] The Marists had excellent schools in

[184] Planchet, op. cit., 1925, pp. 482-488; *Relations de Chine*, Vol. 23, p. 193; *Les missions catholiques*, Vol. 56, pp. 380, 381; *Zeitschrift für Missionswissenschaft*, Vol. 14, pp. 187-193; *Die katholischen Missionen*, 1924/1925, pp. 3-10.

[185] See the importance of this emphasized in Considine, *The Vatican Mission Exposition*, p. 155.

[186] In 1916 the number was 194,219 (*Die katholischen Missionen*, Jan., 1918, p. 78) and in 1925 the number was about 310,000.—Arens, op. cit. (1925), p. 254.

[187] Planchet, op. cit., *1919*, p. 50.

[188] Schmidlin, *Missions und Kulturverhältnisee im fernen Osten*, pp. 94-98; *Relations de Chine*, Vol. 19, p. 468.

[189] *Relations de Chine*, Vol. 19, pp. 598-602; Serviére, *La nouvelle mission du Kiangnan*, 1840-1922, p. 45.

[190] *Une université française en Chine*, pp. 11, 12. The Dominican school at Foochow granted degrees (*Los Dominicos en el Oriente*, p. 112), but seems to have been of secondary rank and to have sent students to Aurora.

[191] Serviére, op. cit., p. 45.

[192] An interview with Brother Charles of St. Xavier's College, July 7, 1922.

a number of cities,[193] and in some of them used French as a medium of instruction and asked for support from home on the ground that they were introducing French culture into China.[194] They maintained, too, a normal school at Chala, just outside Peking.[195] At Kaifeng Americans and at Hanyang Irish were opening excellent new middle schools. In 1922 the Jesuits founded at Tientsin *L'Institut des Hautes Études Industrielles et Commerciales*. The preparatory course was opened in 1923 and the following March had fifty students. By 1926 the faculty had been enlarged and plans had been made for conducting advanced work.[196]

With the emphasis upon the preparation of a Chinese clergy, it was natural that the development in theological education should be marked. Regional seminaries were projected, that the efforts of several missions might be united and the grade of training improved.[197] At Ta T'ung in Shansi, for example, a seminary was formed for the aspirants for the priesthood from all the five Scheutveld missions,[198] and in 1923 the Lazarists opened at Chala a higher theological school for five vicariates in Chihli.[199] Some of the Paris Society's candidates were sent to Penang,[200] and the Jesuits occasionally dispatched Chinese members of their Society to Europe,[201] there to complete their education. The number of seminarians for all China increased from 1,638 in 1913 to 2,448 in 1918 and to 3,022 in 1923,[202] or more than twice as rapidly as the number of Catholics.

Most spectacular of all the educational developments, however, was the project for a great university. In June, 1917, Vincent Ying, a Catholic layman, addressed to the clergy an *Exhortation to Study* and in November of that year appealed to the Pope to found a university at Peking. He called attention to Protestant efforts and declared that in contrast Catholics had "no university,

[193] *Les missions catholiques*, 1923, pp. 117, 118.
[194] Ibid., 1923, pp. 117, 118.
[195] Planchet, *Les missions de Chine et du Japon, 1927*, p. 18.
[196] *Zeitschrift für Missionswissenschaft*, Vol. 14, p. 188; *Chine, Ceylan, Madagascar*, No. 63, pp. 5-9, No. 74, p. 266; *Revue d'histoire des missions*, Vol. 2, p. 185, Vol. 1, p. 471.
[197] *Annals of the Propagation of the Faith*, Vol. 53, p. 154.
[198] *Les missions catholiques*, 1923, pp. 481, 482.
[199] *Zeitschrift für Missionswissenschaft*, Vol. 14, p. 80.
[200] *Maryknoll Letters*, Vol. 1, p. 154; Arens, *Handbuch der katholischen Missionen* (1920), p. 210.
[201] *Les missions catholiques*, Vol. 56, p. 520.
[202] Arens, op. cit., pp. 211, 212.

no secondary schools," and that "new China does not see any Catholics capable of sitting in Parliament or in provincial and departmental assemblies." [203] He may have painted the picture too darkly but he aroused Rome. The Pope promised a subsidy and appealed to the American Benedictines to assume responsibility for the enterprise. In 1920 a professor from the seminary of the Archabbey of St. Vincent at Beatty, Pennsylvania, sailed for China on a reconnoitering expedition, and in June, 1924, two more monks followed. Property—an old Manchu palace—was purchased in Peking, and in August, 1925, the institution opened its doors. Its plans called for a number of departments and for the expenditure of several million dollars, and in fitting deference to the nationalistic wave in China the initial department was a school of Chinese studies. [204]

In spite of this increased interest in education, missionaries were not wanting who insisted that the hope of the Church was not in schools but in the direct work of evangelization. [205] Compared, too, with the two and a quarter millions on the rolls of the Church, the total number of students was still small, about three hundred and ten thousand in 1925, [206] much less proportionately than the Protestant figures. Nearly two-thirds of these pupils were in "prayer schools," whose chief function it was to teach the rudiments of Christianity. The majority of the students were Christian, to be sure, but in the higher schools a large proportion were non-Christian. The masses of Catholics were still without formal education and very few even of the literate had more learning than could be acquired in elementary institutions. Contrasted with the non-Christian population, however, the proportion was large, for while about fourteen per cent. of the Catholics were enrolled as students, less than two per cent. of the entire population of China were in school. [207] When it is recalled that

[203] *Catholic Missions and Annals of the Propagation of the Faith*, Vol. 2, p. 278.
[204] *Catholic Missions and Annals of the Propagation of the Faith*, Vol. 2, pp. 42, 278; *Revue d'histoire des missions*, Vol. 2, p. 184; *China Weekly Review*, June 14, 1924.
[205] *Catholic Missions*, Vol. 12, pp. 51, 52.
[206] Arens, op. cit. (1925), p. 254. This includes about 30,000 in the orphanages. *Missions, séminaires, écoles catholiques en Chine en 1922-1923*, gives about 260,000 in the schools in 1923, exclusive of orphanages. About 1924 the total number of pupils in Catholic schools was 258,953, of whom 197,834 were in "prayer schools," and only 5,593 in middle schools.—*Die katholischen Missionen*, 1924/1925, p. 30.
[207] *China Year Book, 1923*, p. 408.

the Catholics were drawn largely from the less favored portions of the community, the educational achievement of the Church becomes notable.

If the picture of the educational activities of Catholic missions is to be complete, mention must be made of the presses, of which fourteen were named in a 1926 list.[208] The most important of these were at Hongkong (The Nazareth Press),[209] at Zikawei, and at the Pei T'ang in Peking.[210] Fifteen or more periodicals were issued, nine in French, three in Chinese, one in Portuguese, one in Latin, and one in English.[211] Nor must there be forgotten the scientific work continued at Zikawei, and the geological explorations in Mongolia of a Jesuit, Edward Licent, who also built up a special museum in Tientsin.[212]

OTHER MISSION METHODS, 1914-1916

Aside from the greater emphasis on Chinese leadership, a national church, and the development of schools, Roman Catholic missionaries, as we have suggested, made little change in methods between 1914 and the close of 1926. We hear, to be sure, of a few alterations and innovations. A "Crusade of Prayers to the Sacred Heart for China" was inaugurated by the Jesuits in Chihli in 1921, and an "Association of Prayers and Masses for the Conversion of China, Japan, and the Adjacent States" was started by the Trappist monastery in the same province. The Propaganda gave its formal endorsement and the two were soon merged under the name of the movement begun by the Trappists.[213] In France and Belgium, too, efforts were made to reach the hundreds of Chinese students who went to those countries soon after the war, and in 1926 one hundred and sixty-five were reported to have received baptism during the preceding three years.[214] Interference in lawsuits continued to be

[208] Planchet, op. cit., 1927, p. xvi.
[209] Hagspiel, Along the Mission Trail, Vol. 4, p. 14.
[210] Planchet, op. cit., 1927, p. xvi.
[211] The Christian Occupation of China, p. 457.
[212] Catholic Missions, Vol. 4, p. 81; Chine, Ceylan, Madagascar, No. 66, p. 27, No. 67, p. 26, No. 71, p. 25, No. 73, pp. 170-176.
[213] Les missions catholiques, Vol. 56, p. 234; Annals of the Propagation of the Faith, Vol. 85, p. 194; Arens, op. cit. (1925), p. 338; Chine, Ceylan, Madagascar, No. 60, p. 100.
[214] L'apostolat missionaire de la France. Conferences données a l'Institut Catholique de Paris, second series, 1926, p. 252. A "Catholic Association of Chinese Students in France and Belgium" was formed. About fifty Chinese students were baptized in 1922.—Les missions catholiques, 1923, p. 29.

less frequent than before 1900 and, indeed, most bishops prohibited it if used to win converts.[215]
On the whole, however, the old methods were followed with but little modification. The attempt at direct preaching to non-Christians, and especially to the more influential, which before and during the war had been made with such seeming success by Lebbe in Tientsin, largely ceased. Associated with the movement had been the "Catholic Action" and a newspaper, the *I Shih Pao*. Both were enthusiastically nationalistic and participated in the anti-Japanese agitation. When, however, the *I Shih Pao* attacked the French for extending the boundaries of their concession, latent criticism in missionary circles awoke. Lebbe was forced to leave Tientsin, and the methods he had inaugurated lapsed.[216] In Chihli the process of "mass conversion" continued through subsidizing during the hard months of the winter those who would accept Christian instruction.[217] During the dearth that followed drought and floods in North China not long after the war, relief was distributed in such a manner that the number of catechumens greatly increased.[218] One vicar apostolic wrote: "The calamities in China are the great means used by Providence to put pagans in contact with missionaries and by that into contact with the Christian faith." [219] Occasionally wealthy families sought refuge in mission compounds during civil wars and afterwards accepted instruction.[220] Opinions as to the wisdom of these methods varied. Some missionaries declared that the converts so reached persevered, while others maintained that the quality was poor and that as a rule the Church was not claiming the influential classes.[221] Moreover, in the catechumenates of the Society of the Divine Word in one of the most destitute of provinces, Shantung, all but the very poorest were asked to pay for their food.[222]
The reports of missionaries indicate the pursuance throughout China, as in Chihli and Shantung, of methods that had been

[215] Stenz, writing from Shantung, in *Zeitschrift für Missionswissinschaft*, Vol. 15, pp. 196-206.
[216] Schmidlin in *Zeitschrift für Missionswissenschaft*, Vol. 13, pp. 114-118.
[217] Ibid.; *Maryknoll Mission Letters, China*, Vol. 1, p. 33.
[218] Mgr. de Vienne, from Tientsin, in *Annals of the Propagation of the Faith*, Vol. 84, p. 230; Lécroart, Vicar Apostolic in S. E. Chihli, in ibid., Vol. 86, p. 85.
[219] Mgr. Lécroart in *Les missions catholiques*, Vol. 56, p. 520.
[220] Planchet in ibid., 1923, p. 104.
[221] Albert Watterwald, from S. E. Chihli, in *Chine, Ceylan, Madagascar*, No. 48, pp. 86-92; *Zeitschrift für Missionswissenschaft*, Vol. 13, pp. 114-118.
[222] Hagspiel, *Along the Mission Trail*, Vol. 4, p. 183.

approved by long usage. In Kiangnan the Jesuits and in Mongolia the Scheutveld fathers continued the instruction of inquirers as the latter went about their daily tasks and then, before baptism, took them apart for several weeks in a catechumenate.[223] We hear of retreats in which Christians were gathered for the strengthening of their faith,[224] and of special preaching missions for the same purpose.[225] Priests went their usual rounds to hear confessions and to administer the sacraments.[226] Pilgrimages to special shrines were still promoted,[227] and Christians were encouraged, as formerly, to gather into separate villages.[228]

Works of relief and benevolence were continued, likewise without important modifications. Orphanages under the charge of sisterhoods remained the chief form of institution. In the vicariates of Fukien and Amoy, for example, fifteen hundred infants were reported in thirteen orphanages, and five hundred more were entrusted to selected homes. It was a commentary on the condition of the infants when they were rescued and perhaps on the type of care given them that of the six thousand girl babies gathered yearly in Fukien only about a third survived.[229] Elsewhere orphans were also supported in Christian families as well as in institutions.[230] In more than one locality, too, officials turned over to Catholic sisters the administration of the municipal *crèche* or the public orphanage.[231] We hear of homes for the aged and of a school for the blind.[232] Somewhat more emphasis appears to have been placed on medical work than previously, possibly because Catholics saw what effective use Protestants had made of that type of philanthropy. Hospitals were founded or enlarged, and dispensaries cared for thousands

[223] *Zeitschrift für Missionswissenschaft,* Vol. 15, p. 71; *Annals of the Propagation of the Faith,* Vol. 73, p. 194.

[224] Mgr. Lécroart in *Annals of the Propagation of the Faith,* Vol. 82, p. 114; ibid. in *Chine, Ceylan, Madagascar,* No. 56, pp. 96-106.

[225] Walthé, from Kiangsi, in *Annals of the Propagation of the Faith,* Vol. 83, p. 138.

[226] Watterwald in *Annals of the Propagation of the Faith,* Vol. 75, pp. 136-139.

[227] Champeyrol in *Catholic Missions and Annals of the Propagation of the Faith,* Vol. 2, pp. 36-39; *Les missions catholiques,* Vol. 56, p. 437.

[228] In Kwangtung, for example, one Chinese priest bought land and settled his parishioners in it.—*Maryknoll Mission Letters, China,* Vol. 1, p. 157.

[229] John Labrador, O. P., in *Catholic Missions,* Vol. 13, pp. 14-16.

[230] Planchet, op. cit., *1919,* p. 26.

[231] Ibid., *1927,* Part 2, p. 30; *Annals of the Propagation of the Faith,* Vol. 83, p. 31.

[232] Mrs. Butler, *Missions as I Saw Them,* pp. 139-143; *Les missions catholiques,* 1923, p. 128.

of patients.[233]   In some cities, as at Shanghai and Hankow, municipal hospitals were placed in charge of one of the sisterhoods.[234]   Roman Catholics, too, joined in the fight against opium,[235] although they did not give as much attention to it as did Protestants.   In the great famines in North China they shared in the work of relief, usually, as we have seen, in such a manner that non-Christians would be attracted to what the missionary believed of greater importance than physical life, spiritual instruction.[236]

EFFECTS OF THE DOMESTIC DISORDER AND THE NATIONALIST AND ANTI-CHRISTIAN MOVEMENTS

The Roman Catholic Church could not pass scatheless through the increasing political disorder and the anti-religious agitation. To be sure, civil war and bandits often left missions and missionaries untouched and compounds and churches frequently afforded safe refuge to a harassed populace.   As time passed, however, and fear of the foreigner declined and agitation against him increased, missionaries and Chinese Christians more and more shared in the sufferings of the nation.   Missionaries were killed or carried captive by bandits; Chinese Christians were pillaged and killed, probably both for the reasons that made the years such unhappy ones for their non-Christian neighbors and because enemies who had once been held in check by dread of the foreigner or of officials took advantage of the anarchy to even up old scores.

In July, 1920, a Jesuit, Chevallier-Chantepie, of Kiangnan, was five days in the hands of bandits.[237]   The following October, in the missionary district of Weichow in Kwangtung, the war between Kwangsi and Canton troops wrought the destruction of six churches and chapels, three schools, and several residences of missionaries, and the murder of a number of Christians.[238] Kwangsi, seldom fully at peace, was now almost constantly in

[233] *Revue d'histoire des missions,* Vol. 1, p. 292; *Annals of the Propagation of the Faith,* Vol. 85, p. 229; Keeler, *Catholic Medical Missions,* p. 201; *Les missions catholiques,* Vol. 55, pp. 148, 149, 198, Vol. 56, pp. 364, 460.

[234] Keeler, op. cit., pp. 60, 61.

[235] *The Christian Occupation of China,* p. 440.

[236] *Annals of the Propagation of the Faith,* Vol. 84, p. 32, Vol. 85, p. 32; *Relations de Chine,* Vol. 19, pp. 417-419; *Zeitschrift für Missionswissenschaft,* Vol. 12, p. 103; *Chine, Ceylan, Madagascar,* No. 51, pp. 1-24.

[237] *Relations de Chine,* Vol. 19, p. 623.

[238] *Annals of the Propagation of the Faith,* Vol. 84, p. 74.

turmoil. Christian villages were burned, chapels and mission residences were occupied by troops and looted, and in October, 1921, a Chinese priest, Louis Tsin, was murdered.[239]   Kweichow, almost mountainous and chronically turbulent, was likewise the scene of much violence. Brigands looted whole towns and villages, churches were destroyed, and priests were robbed. In 1921 Father A. Yang was kept captive for several months, and in 1923 Father Joseph Freyche was held for ransom.[240]   In Hupeh in 1923 Angelicus Melotto, a Franciscan, was captured by bandits, held for over eighty days, and then, in a moribund condition, was abandoned and, picked up by troops, died a few days after arriving at a hospital.[241]   In Hupeh, too, another Franciscan, Julien Adons, was killed by outlaws.[242]   In 1923 bandits kidnapped two priests of the Irish mission during the looting of a town.[243]   In Yünnan at various times brigands captured eight or nine missionaries, one of whom, Piton, perished in their hands. On July 25, 1926, a catechist, Huang Fu, was killed in Yünnan.[244]   In 1923 a bishop, Mgr. Wittner, and a priest were captured by bandits in Shantung.[245]

Mongolia was among the chief sufferers. Christian communities were plundered, priests were seized, and Catholics in desperation moved into central fortified communities where they could be protected by the authorities. On Christmas Day, 1923, Achille Soenen was killed, possibly because of his opposition to Christians joining a secret order, the Ko Lao Hui.[246]   A little later Van Praet, taken by bandits and freed after six months, died as a result of the hardships he had undergone.[247]   In the war between Fêng Yü-hsiang and his enemies in 1925 and 1926 mission property suffered at the hands of both belligerents, and a missionary, Lauwers, and several Chinese Christians were killed. Fêng seized and sold mission property, and that in spite of the protests of the

[239] *Les missions catholiques,* Vol. 56, pp. 430-452.
[240] Ibid., 1923, pp. 269, 304, 1924, pp. 421-422; *Zeitschrift für Missionswissenschaft,* Vol. 15, p. 290.
[241] *The China Weekly Review,* Sept. 29, 1923, pp. 174, 175.
[242] *Annals of the Propagation of the Faith,* Vol. 86, p. 31.
[243] Ibid., Vol. 86, p. 233.
[244] Planchet, op. cit., *1927,* Part 2, pp. 40, 41.
[245] Ibid., *1925,* p. 524.
[246] Ibid., *1925,* p. 518; *Les missions catholiques,* Vol. 56, p. 148.
[247] *Les missions catholiques,* Vol. 56, pp. 351, 352; Planchet, op. cit., *1927,* Part 2, pp. 21-27.

French and Belgian legations.[248]   In Chihli, too, during the civil strife in 1926, mission property was pillaged by the troops of Chang Tso-lin and by bandits, a cathedral was plundered, and several priests and many of the laity were mishandled.[249]   In December, 1924, two Passionists and two nuns were captured by bandits in Hunan,[250] and in Szechwan mission work was at times interrupted.[251]

As has been suggested, most of these outrages were not the result of specifically anti-foreign or anti-Christian feeling, but were a phase of the increasing anarchy from which the entire community suffered.   After 1922, however, and especially after the Shanghai and Shameen incidents of 1925, here and there missions were singled out for attack, partly because they were foreign and partly because they were Christian.   We hear of the residence at Yenanfu in Shansi plundered and closed by students,[252] and of churches and chapels in and around Swatow occupied by troops and used for military purposes.[253]   In 1925 considerable mission property in Kwangtung, the heart of the Nationalist movement, was seized by troops or blockaders, and in August of that year a missionary near Swatow was beaten by troops to the cry of: "Down with capitalism.   Kill the foreign devil."[254]   In Canton an effort was made to save the schools by conforming to the regulations,[255] but this did not prevent student strikes.[256]   Because of the concentration of the anti-Christian agitators upon Christmas week, that festival was not as elaborately celebrated in Canton in 1925 as in previous years, midnight masses were omitted, and weddings at the cathedral were interrupted by mobs.[257]   As the Nationalist armies moved northward, further anti-foreign and anti-Christian disturbances were reported. In Hupeh, late in 1926, several missions were attacked and the seminary at Kingchowfu, near Shasi, was looted.[258]   In at least

[248] Planchet, op. cit., *1927*, Part 2, pp. 27-29.
[249] Ibid., *1927*, Part 2, pp. 17-19; *Les missions catholiques,* Aug. 13, 1926.
[250] *New York Times,* Dec. 9, 1924.
[251] *Les missions catholiques,* Apr. 2, 1926, pp. 158, 159.
[252] *Zeitschrift für Missionswissenschaft,* Vol. 16, p. 220.
[253] Ibid., Vol. 16, p. 218.
[254] Planchet, op. cit., *1927*, Part 2, pp. 40-47.
[255] *Zeitschrift für Missionswissenschaft,* Vol. 16, p. 218.
[256] Wieger, *Chine Moderne,* Vol. 5, p. 137.
[257] *Les missions catholiques,* May 28, 1926, p. 258.
[258] *North-China Herald,* Jan. 8, 1927.

the early stages of the anti-Christian movement, however, Roman Catholics did not suffer as much as did Protestants, for the attack was directed chiefly against the higher schools, and Catholics were not as well equipped with these as were the Protestants.[259] We do hear, however, of one move to plant a non-religious school by the side of each Catholic institution of learning.[260]

An interesting phase of the friction between foreigners and Chinese was a telegram sent by teachers in the National University in Peking to Rome, appealing to the Pope "for the cause of justice and humanity which all the nation now feels against the odious massacre perpetrated on unarmed Chinese citizens in the international concession of Shanghai." The Pope directed the Apostolic Delegate to reply conveying his sympathy for the people of China, deploring the spilling of fraternal blood, and expressing the hope that the spirit of concord would soon be reëstablished.[261] July 19, 1925, also following the May 30th incident in Shanghai, the Apostolic Delegate issued an open letter to the Catholic youth, saying that the Church must not mix in politics and urging them to spread the Christian Gospel as the best way of serving their country.[262] The papal letter of June, 1926, to the bishops in China sought to defend Catholic missions against the claim that they were in the service of foreign powers.[263] The Pope, too, occasionally bestowed decorations upon high Chinese officials.[264]

In spite of the declaration of the Pope, foreign powers did not withdraw their protection from the Church nor cease their interest in it. As late as 1925 the French flag was raised by a missionary to prevent troops from occupying his church.[265] In 1926 the French legation protested to the Wai Chiao Pu against the anti-Christian agitation and it will be recalled that the Foreign Office, presumably because of French pressure, ordered the

---

[259] *Chine, Ceylan, Madagascar*, Sept., 1922, p. 193.
[260] *Zeitschrift für Missionswissenschaft*, Vol. 11, p. 111.
[261] Planchet, op. cit., *1927*, Part 2, p. 15; *Zeitschrift für Missionswissenschaft*, Vol. 16, p. 215.
[262] *Die katholischen Missionen*, 1926, p. 316.
[263] Planchet, *Les missions de Chine et du Japon, 1927*, Part 2, p. 15.
[264] *Annals of the Propagation of the Faith*, Vol. 86 (1923), p. 153. The Pope bestowed on a Chinese Minister of Foreign Affairs the cross of the Order of Pius IX and gave decorations to other officials.
[265] *Chine, Ceylan, Madagascar*, No. 73, p. 188.

Ministry of Education to suspend the regulations for mission schools.[266] Under Mussolini's direction, moreover, in 1924 the Italian Government gave to Italian missions in China a subsidy of ten million lire, as direct financial assistance by a state to Catholic missions as had ever been recorded.[267] It seems significant, too, that no public movement for the abolition of the toleration clauses in the treaties was to be found in Catholic circles.

The Chinese authorities were seldom openly unfriendly to Catholic missions, and they often specifically ordered the defense of Christian lives and property. At times this may have been lip service rendered under duress from the powers, but it was at least given. In 1923 the Tuchun of Shantung commanded his subordinates to protect foreigners.[268] Not long afterward the Military Governor of Heilungchiang sent a missionary an honorific inscription to be placed above the main door of his residence.[269] In fulfilment of promises made after the assassination of Melotto, the Hupeh authorities built a hospital in Hankow which they purposed placing under the direction of the Catholic mission.[270] Ts'ao Kun, shortly after his election to the Presidency, formally notified the Pope of his accession and promised to promote and maintain friendship between China and the Holy See.[271]

Nor must the record of the sufferings of missionaries and Chinese Christians given above be allowed to convey the impression that the comparative freedom from attack which had been the lot of foreigners since 1900 had entirely disappeared. Until late in 1926 the privileged position of the Westerner, although more and more resented, was usually a protection to the Catholic community. Sometimes bandits singled out the missionary for capture in the hope that his release would be an effectual argument in bargaining with the officials, but until well after the rise of the anti-Christian movement as a rule both foreign priests and Chinese Christians were partially exempt from the hardships of the non-Christians around them. On at least one occasion,

[266] Planchet, op. cit., *1927*, Part 2, p. 81.
[267] *Catholic Missions and Annals of the Propagation of the Faith*, 1924, p. 166.
[268] *Les missions catholiques*, Vol. 55, p. 511.
[269] Ibid., Vol. 56, p. 199.
[270] Planchet, op. cit., *1927*, Part 2, p. 33.
[271] *Catholic Missions and Annals of the Propagation of the Faith*, Vol. 1, p. 143; *Les missions catholiques*, Vol. 56, p. 125.

indeed, a missionary served as an intermediary between warring factions and prevented a serious battle, and, perhaps, the sacking of an important city.[272] A Catholic missionary, with fine disregard for the differences that separated the great wings of the Church, obtained the release of Dr. Shelton, a Protestant missionary, from bandits on the Tibetan frontier.[273] Often, moreover, mission compounds became a refuge to non-Christians as well as Christians.[274] In the midst of increasing chaos, until 1925 and 1926 the missionary and the Christian community were, then, fairly secure and the work of the Church proceeded with surprisingly few interruptions. Desire for safety from the anarchy may, indeed, have been a stimulus to the number of baptisms.

RESULTS OF ROMAN CATHOLIC MISSIONS, 1918-1926

In spite, then, of China's unsettled state, and perhaps in part because of it, the first few years after the World War were fairly prosperous. In 1918, it will be recalled, the number of Chinese Catholics was reported to be 1,963,639.[275] Although somewhat different figures are given elsewhere,[276] the total seems to have been somewhere between 1,900,000 and 2,000,000. In 1924 the number of Catholics was given as 2,244,366, and of catechumens as 553,201.[277] This, to be sure, was proportionately only about a third as rapid a gain as had been registered in the years just preceding the war,[278] and it appears likely that in 1925 and 1926 the increase was still smaller. Considering the conditions

[272] This was Ch'aochou in Kwangtung.—Mgr. Rayssac of Swatow in *Annals of the Propagation of the Faith*, Vol. 84, p. 191.
[273] Shelton, *Shelton of Tibet*, pp. 224-236.
[274] *Relations de Chine*, Vol. 23, pp. 181 et seq.; *Our Missions*, Vol. 7, pp. 53, 54; *Chine, Ceylan, Madagascar*, No. 60, p. 99; *Annals of the Propagation of the Faith*, Vol. 85, p. 81.
[275] Arens, *Handbuch der katholischen Missionen* (1920), pp. 162, 163.
[276] *Relations de Chine*, Vol. 22, p. 371, places it at 1,940,000 in 1916.
[277] *Revue d'histoire des missions*, Vol. 2, p. 272. In 1923 the total number of Chinese Catholic Christians was variously said to be 2,208,000 (*Zeitschrift für Missionswissenschaft*, Vol. 14, p. 189), 2,244,366 (Arens, op. cit. [1925], p. 254), and 2,225,000 (*Relations de Chine*, Vol. 22, p. 37).
[278] One set of figures declares that between 1903 and 1915 the total Catholic baptized body rose from 783,000 to 1,750,675, or an average gain of about 9 per cent. a year, and that in 1923 the number was 2,208,800, or a gain between 1915 and 1923 of only about 3 per cent. a year. By these tables the gain from 1920 to 1923 was from 1,994,483 to 2,208,800, or about 3 per cent. a year.— Kennelly's figures in *Revue d'histoire des missions*, Vol. 1, p. 89. This agrees substantially with the set of figures given in *Relations de Chine*, Vol. 22, p. 371. A chart of growth is given in *Relations de Chine*, Vol. 19, p. 541.

in the country, however, it was remarkable.[279]   Encouraging reports continued to come from many quarters.   From Kwangtung we hear of a single request for Christian instruction from over two hundred families,[280] and from Kweichow of a non-Chinese community of about a thousand villages wishing to become Catholic.[281]

Most of the converts were still in rural districts and from among farmers,[282] but a few prominent men were to be found among the communicants.   The chief of the Chinese delegation at the peace conference at Paris had married a Belgian and had received baptism.[283]   The delegation of the Shanghai Chamber of Commerce to the National Foreign Trade Convention at Seattle in 1925 had as chairman Joseph Lo Pa Hong, who was described as "China's most charitable man, supporting from twenty-five hundred to three thousand persons out of his own funds," and as teaching the catechism every Sunday and organizing a corps of three hundred Chinese co-workers.[284]   The body of the Church continued to be drawn from the humbler classes and had little education beyond the rudiments of the Faith, but its educational status was probably improving.   The turbulent times through which the nation was passing and the restlessness under foreign control had slowed up the growth but had as yet brought no major disaster to the Church.

The Russian Orthodox Mission, 1914-1926

To the Russian mission, which after 1900 had had so marked an increase among the Chinese, the World War appears not immediately to have brought any great changes.   In 1916 over twenty foreign missionaries were reported, twenty-one churches and chapels and forty evangelistic centers, twenty schools, and

[279] Between a third and a fourth of the Christians were in Chihli, about a tenth in Kiangsu, about a twelfth each in Shantung and Szechwan, and smaller numbers in other provinces.   The totals were, according to Planchet, *Les missions de Chine et du Japon,* 1927, p. 15, Chihli, 674,023; Kiangsu, 213,687; Shantung, 180,537; Szechwan, 172,711; Hupeh, 125,771; Mongolia and Ninghsia, 136,065; Kiangsi, 99,894; Chêkiang, 73,369; Fukien, 70,274; Shensi, 62,273; Hunan, 47,628; Kweichow, 35,442; Kirin and Amur, 33,458; Mukden, 30,714; Yünnan, 17,254; Kansu and Sinkiang, 13,836; Kwangsi, 4,463.   In Kiangsu the Christian population was densest in and around Shanghai.—Hermand, *Les étapes de la mission du Kiang-nan,* 1842-1922, p. 19.
[280] *Maryknoll Mission Letters, China,* Vol. 1, p. 149.
[281] *Annals of the Propagation of the Faith,* Vol. 84, p. 132.
[282] *Maryknoll Mission Letters, China,* Vol. 1, p. 149.
[283] Reid, *China, Captive or Free,* p. 170.
[284] *Catholic Missions and Annals of the Propagation of the Faith,* 1925, p. 202.

more than five thousand baptized Chinese members. The Russian revolution of 1917, however, and especially the Bolshevist régime, nearly wrought the ruin of the mission. Financial support from home was cut off, and, except in Peking, work among the Chinese was terminated. Many converts fell away. The property in Peking was retained, although threatened with confiscation by the anti-Christian Bolshevist Government, and around it about three hundred members still clustered. For the White Russians, refugees in large numbers in some of the main cities, a little spiritual ministration was maintained. Unless sweeping changes should occur in Russia, however, this two centuries old mission seemed doomed.[285]

[285] *The Christian Occupation of China*, p. 464; *China Year Book, 1924-1925*. p. 1197; Planchet, op. cit., *1927*, Part 2, p. 194; Y. Y. Tsu in *China Christian Year Book, 1926*, pp. 92, 93.

CHAPTER XXIX

CHINA IN A TIME OF REORGANIZATION (1901-1926)
PROTESTANT MISSIONS DURING THE WAR, 1914-1918

THE IMMEDIATE EFFECT OF THE WAR

THE World War affected the missions of Protestants less than those of Roman Catholics. This was to be expected, for the sources of most of the Protestant missionaries and funds, North America and Great Britain, were not as nearly exhausted as were the lands from which the major part of Roman Catholic support came. Protestant missions, however, could not be expected to pass unharmed through so great a cataclysm.

Missionaries from Germany were, naturally, greater sufferers than those from other lands. In Kwangtung, the most important China field of German Protestants, many of the schools could not be opened, salaries were reduced, projected building was postponed, some younger missionaries were called to the colors, and the number of baptisms declined.[1] The British Government early ordered out of Hongkong all German missionaries except three sisters in charge of the home for the blind.[2] In Tsingtau some of the missionaries were interned by the Japanese and two were taken as prisoners to Japan.[3] Only four of the foreign staff remained in Shantung, the work of these was restricted, and the number of Christians in charge of the Berlin Society declined nearly one-fifth.[4] While the presidential mandate of January, 1919, which ordered the repatriation of all enemy subjects and the sequestration of enemy property, led to the exclusion of only a minority of German missionaries, those who remained feared that their future was precarious.[5]

However, German Protestant missions were by no means de-

[1] *China Mission Year Book, 1915,* p. 250, *1916,* pp. 86, 90, 97.
[2] *Allgemeine Missionszeitschrift,* Vol. 42, pp. 70, 71.
[3] Ibid.
[4] Richter, *Geschichte der Berliner Missionsgesellschaft,* pp. 626-631.
[5] Reid, *China, Captive or Free,* pp. 151, 152.

stroyed. Among some British and American missionaries anti-
Teutonic feeling was strong, but funds were raised by the China
Continuation Committee to aid the German societies,[6] the American missionaries in Canton helped financially,[7] and in the stringency after the war American Lutherans came to the rescue.[8]
In Shanghai, too, in 1916 a German association was formed which
was of some assistance.[9] The China Inland Mission, in spite of
its own grave problems, aided the affiliated Liebenzell Mission
with men and money.[10] In spite of the 1919 mandate, moreover,
regulations were eventually made by which it was possible for
Germans to continue in China.[11]

While among Protestants the Germans were the chief sufferers from the war, other nationalities were not immune. Japanese military operations in Shantung embarrassed American and
British as well as German societies.[12] Many missionaries, especially physicians, went into war service, one incomplete list made
in 1919 giving a total of seventy-three British who were so
engaged.[13] The number of new missionaries from Great Britain
declined, although increases from the United States were so
large that the accessions to the missionary staff did not fall sharply
and in 1916 even rose. Because of the entrance of the United
States into the struggle, the numbers dropped again in 1917,
but within a little over a year the armistice had been signed and
the total of new recruits speedily reached unprecedented levels.[14]
Financially the situation was complicated by a rapid rise in the
price of silver, so that in 1919 it took two and a half times as
much gold, in which contributions came, to purchase a Mexican
dollar, in which mission expenditures were made, as before

---

[6] Mex. $28,933.52 was raised in 1915 and Mex. $25,414.21 in 1916, and this
in spite of the other heavy loads on mission budgets caused by the war.—*China
Mission Year Book, 1916*, pp. 11-21.

[7] *Allgemeine Missionszeitschrift*, Vol. 42, p. 168.

[8] Richter, *Geschichte der Berliner Missionsgesellschaft*, pp. 586 et seq.

[9] Beyer, *China als Missionsfeld*, Chapter 6, p. 18.

[10] *Allgemeine Missionszeitschrift*, Vol. 45, p. 294.

[11] Oldham, *The Missionary Situation after the War*, p. 16.

[12] *China Mission Year Book, 1915*, p. i.

[13] Ibid., *1918*, p. 409. See also Emery, *A Century of Endeavor*, p. 308.

[14] *The Christian Occupation of China*, pp. 287, 345. One set of figures for
Protestant missionaries gives 3,235 women missionaries in 1915 and 3,637 in
1917, and 2,103 men missionaries in 1915 and 2,263 in 1917.—W. R. Wheeler
and J. E. Williams in *The Missionary Outlook in the Light of the War*, p. 97.
These totals, however, are incomplete as there were on the rolls at least 5,978
Protestant missionaries in China in 1914 (of whom part were on furlough).—*China
Mission Year Book, 1915*, statistical tables, p. iv.

1915.[15] Fortunately, for the most part, incomes increased, even if not in proportion to the rise in exchange, and in the latter years of the war those in Great Britain, usually after an initial decline in 1914 and 1915, partially or entirely recovered. The China Inland Mission, with a larger force in China than any other society, and at the outbreak of the war chiefly British in its support, had an interesting record. In 1914 the income from Great Britain fell off sharply, but it recovered fairly steadily as the war progressed, and the increase from the United States was so great that the total about kept pace with the rise of exchange and no serious retrenchment of activities was made.[16] In 1914, for the first time in the Mission's history, a decline in the staff of foreign workers was recorded. An increase was reported for 1915, but 1916 and 1917 each showed a slight decrease.[17] Both 1917 and 1918, however, witnessed larger numbers of baptisms than had any preceding year.[18] Two of the leading Canadian societies showed an encouraging record of income and augmented staffs, the English Friends found that in 1915 more recruits had sailed for their mission than in any previous year, and no British society of importance seems to have been driven to any great curtailment of its program. The chief immediate effect of the war upon non-German Protestant missions was a suspension of some building projects and of plans for new enterprises.[19]

Until well after its close the war seemed not to have wrought any marked change in the attitude of the Chinese toward the

[15] *The Missionary Outlook in the Light of the War*, p. 98; Speer, *The Gospel and the New World*, p. 52.

[16] In 1911 the China Inland Mission received from Great Britain £47,640, in 1912 £36,549, in 1913 £51,089, in 1914 £36,872.—*China's Millions*, 1915, p. 24. In 1916 £37,608 was received from Great Britain (ibid., 1917, p. 64), in 1917 £40,344 (ibid., 1918, p. 64), and in 1918 £42,931 (ibid., 1919, p. 64). In 1914 £19,609 was received from North America and Australia (ibid., 1915, p. 85), in 1916 £30,025 from North America (ibid., 1917, p. 64), in 1917 £35,916 (ibid., 1918, p. 64), and in 1918 from North America £31,133 (ibid., 1919, p. 64). The average annual income of the Church Missionary Society in the five years before the war was £402,681. During the four years of the war the average annual income was £372,510.—*China Mission Year Book, 1923*, pp. 102-111.

[17] *China's Millions*, 1915, p. 85; 1916, p. 72; 1917, p. 64; 1918, p. 64. The net reduction in staff in 1914 was thirteen, the increase in 1915 was fourteen, bringing the total foreign staff to 1,077, one higher than at any other time. In 1916 the net loss in staff was eighteen and in 1917 eight.

[18] The number of baptisms in 1917 was 5,064 (*China's Millions*, 1918, p. 64) and the number for 1918 was about a thousand more (ibid., 1919, p. 64).

[19] *China Mission Year Book, 1916*, pp. 105, 119, 122, 156; J. H. Oldham in *International Review of Missions*, Vol. 5, p. 17; *China Mission Year Book, 1915*, p. i.; *International Review of Missions*, Vol. 4, p. 16.

Christian message. Here and there were comments on the inconsistency between the slaughter in Europe and the principles preached by the Christian messengers from the West,[20] and when the coolies who had served in the labor battalions in France returned they occasionally told of the wickedness they had seen in the Occident.[21] For the most part, however, the spectacle of so-called Christendom at war appears to have wrought little if any diminution in the willingness of the Chinese to hear the missionary. Indeed, in 1917, a series of statements of the situation reflected in general an attitude of hope and indicated that the open-mindedness of the Chinese toward the Gospel was increasing rather than diminishing.[22]

New Societies

In spite of the war a few new Protestant agencies entered China. In 1912, shortly before his death, the founder of the Salvation Army, General William Booth, pledged his successor, General Bramwell Booth, to begin operations there at an early date. The outbreak of the war brought delay, but in 1916 a group of officers came to Peking and by 1919 corps were in existence in Peking, Tientsin, and eleven other centers in North China. Evangelism was the main form of activity first attempted, but the social work for which the Army was famous was projected and during the floods of 1917 some assistance was given in the distribution of relief.[23]

During the war years the Stewart Evangelistic Fund, a large sum set aside by Milton Stewart of Los Angeles to assist missions in the Orient, first became available. The plan was chiefly to aid existing agencies to strengthen their evangelistic efforts. Under the direction of one of the trustees, J. H. Blackstone, subsidies were given to Bible schools, especially to the Union Theological Seminary in Nanking. Bible class helps were issued, institutes were held for pastors and other church workers, at Kuling and Peitaiho grounds were acquired and buildings erected for summer conferences, and a hundred or more new

[20] Lipphard, *The Second Century of Baptist Foreign Missions*, p. 25.
[21] Keyte, *In China Now*, p. 64.
[22] *China Mission Year Book, 1917*, pp. 63-283. Officials did not hesitate to come out publicly in praise of Christianity. We have, for example, such commendation from a Minister of Education.—*The Eastern Miscellany*, March, 1917.
[23] C. H. Jeffries (Commissioner for China of the Salvation Army) in *China Mission Year Book, 1918*, pp. 301-310; *Millard's Review*, Vol. 12, pp. 418, 419.

missionaries and about three hundred Chinese under various boards were financed.[24]

About 1914 the United Free Gospel and Mission Society came;[25] the Lutheran Board of Missions, with headquarters in Minneapolis, entered China about 1916, centering upon Honan;[26] the Mission of the Evangelical Free Church of Norway established its single residential station in 1918, in Shensi;[27] about 1918 the Church of Sweden Mission sent representatives to Hunan, where the Norwegian Lutherans had prepared the way;[28] the Assembly of God, a small "independent" mission, appears to have begun in 1916, with a station in Chihli;[29] in 1918 the Federal Foreign Mission Committee of Churches of Christ (Disciples) in Australia opened in Shanghai the first of its two stations. Shanghai was only a convenient stepping stone to the interior, however, and the real field of the new mission was in and around Hweilichow in Szechwan.[30] We hear, too, of the International Bible Study Association and of the Tongues Movement.[31] Most of these bodies were small and could not be expected to support extensive enterprises. A noteworthy exception, however, of which more will be said in a moment, was the China Medical Board, established by the Rockefellers, which, while not professing to be missionary, distinctly called itself Christian, and had great influence upon the medical programs of all Protestant missions.

METHODS AND PROGRESS

The small number of new societies entering China during the war years does not mean that non-German Protestant missions were marking time. Practically all the larger and most of the smaller groups of Protestants were now established in the country and the time for the coming of new boards had passed. Moreover, most of the missions had staked out as much territory as they could well occupy and were not finding it wise to open many new residential centers. More and more they were

---

[24] J. H. Blackstone in *China Mission Year Book, 1917*, pp. 366-371; J. H. Blackstone in ibid., *1918*, pp. 359-366; *The Christian Occupation of China*, p. 377.
[25] Richter, *Das Werden der christlichen Kirche in China*, p. 298.
[26] *Directory of Protestant Missions in China, 1926*, p. 40.
[27] Ibid., p. 43.
[28] Ibid., p. 46.
[29] Ibid., p. 115.
[30] Ibid., p. 116.
[31] China Mission Year Book, 1916, p. 347.

seeking to make effective such stations as they had, and through education to raise up a Chinese leadership which could take over the task of more extensive evangelization.

The network of Protestant agencies, however, did not yet cover all the territory of China. While in 1920 only one hundred and six out of the seventeen hundred and four *hsiens* in the twenty-one provinces remained unclaimed by any Protestant body, forty-five per cent. of the area of these provinces lay beyond thirty *li* (about eleven English miles) of any evangelistic center, and for more than a half of this "unoccupied" territory no Protestant society had as yet made itself responsible.[32] Especially were the provinces of Kweichow, Yünnan, Kwangsi, and Kansu neglected, and among the aboriginal tribes were those whose language no missionary had yet learned.[33] In the great groups of Chinese of "the dispersion," in Hawaii, Borneo, the Dutch East Indies, Siam, Burma, the Straits Settlements, and the Philippines, moreover, only a few hundred Protestant communicants were to be found, and in Siam, where the Chinese were extremely important, no Protestant mission was conducted specifically for them.[34]

While very few new residential centers for missionaries— scarcely a score, indeed, even including those of the societies recently arrived—were opened during the war years, several of the missions made surveys to determine the extent of their task and the best way of performing it,[35] and plans were laid for extension of other kinds. Thus in 1915 the Northern Methodists instituted a "Forward Movement" to cover a four-year period and calling for a doubling of the membership, a trebling of the enrollment in Sunday Schools and Bible classes, increased self-support, and added equipment.[36]

Moreover, the emphasis upon evangelism that had characterized the years immediately before 1914 continued. In 1914 and again in 1917 Sherwood Eddy was in China for addresses to non-

[32] *The Christian Occupation of China*, p. 308.
[33] *International Review of Missions*, Vol. 5, p. 19.
[34] Out of the million Chinese in Java about 800 were Christians; in Singapore out of 200,000 Chinese about 660 were members of churches; in Hawaii about 700 Protestant communicants were reported in two of the major denominations.—*China Mission Year Book, 1915*, pp. 570-577.
[35] *China Mission Year Book, 1916*, pp. 432-449; *International Review of Missions*, Vol. 6, p. 16.
[36] *China Mission Year Book, 1916*, p. 110.

Christians.[37] Ting Li-mei was still active.[38] A Forward Evangelistic Movement was planned in which all the Protestant forces should coöperate and in 1917 a national evangelistic week was set aside, in which special meetings were held throughout the country. Laymen and laywomen helped with the preaching and the secular press was utilized. The effort was especially successful in Honan, Peking, and Manchuria.[39] We hear, too, of unusual activity in presenting the Christian message to non-Christians in a number of rural districts and of extensive plans by the Presbyterians for evangelism in the cities of Shantung.[40] In 1918 in Peking through the initiative of the Young Men's Christian Association a union was formed for religious work for students and in it six of the larger missions joined.[41] The Hangchow Union Evangelistic Committee continued to function.[42]

New interest was shown for special classes. Partly because of a visit by a noted missionary to the Moslems, Samuel M. Zwemer, in 1917, plans were laid for reaching the Chinese Mohammedans, and, in characteristic Anglo-Saxon manner, the Continuation Committee appointed a sub-committee to promote interest in this relatively untouched field.[43] Progress was reported among the non-Chinese peoples in the South and Southwest and in 1918 a new enterprise was opened by the Northern Presbyterians among the Tai speaking people of Yünnan.[44]

The Young Men's and the Young Women's Christian Associations, in spite of heavy responsibilities undertaken for prisoners of war and soldiers, continued to grow in China. Some projects for buildings were postponed, but student conferences were held and the lecture bureaus on health and science were maintained. In one year the Young Women's Christian Association brought twelve new foreign secretaries to the country. It also

[37] Eddy, *Everybody's World*, p. 162; *Foreign Mail*, Vol. 22, No. 2, p. 18.
[38] *China Mission Year Book, 1916*, p. 338.
[39] Ibid., *1917*, pp. 336-347, *1918*, pp. 154-158; *Chinese Recorder*, Vol. 47, pp. 9, 342-380; *International Review of Missions*, Vol. 6, p. 13.
[40] *Chinese Recorder*, Vol. 47, p. 278.
[41] Gamble, *Peking, A Social Survey*, p. 386.
[42] *China Mission Year Book, 1916*, pp. 461-466.
[43] Ibid., *1915*, pp. 283-286, *1916*, p. 347; *China's Millions*, 1917, p. 139; *The Christian Occupation of China*, p. 358; *Chinese Recorder*, Vol. 46, p. 9, Vol. 48, p. 632.
[44] *The Christian Occupation of China*, p. 350; *China Mission Year Book, 1916*, p. 118, *1918*, pp. 123-128, 165-167; Marshall Broomhall in *International Review of Missions*, Vol. 6, p. 27, Vol. 7, p. 20.

opened a normal training school for physical directors. In 1916 the Young Men's Christian Association inaugurated a secretarial training department.[45]

The Protestant forces in China, moreover, found strength to aid in the activities that were being undertaken in the war zones to offset the evil effects of the conflict. The United War Work Campaign in which, largely under the leadership of the Young Men's Christian Association, were joined many of the Protestant, Jewish, and Roman Catholic agencies that were carrying on religious and welfare activities among soldiers, asked from China $100,000 and the surprising sum of more than $1,000,000 gold was pledged, non-Christians as well as Christians contributing.[46] When, beginning with 1916, between one hundred and fifty and two hundred thousand Chinese were recruited by the British and French for rough manual labor behind the fighting lines in France, the International Committee (North American) and the English National Council of the Young Men's Christian Association undertook to aid their morale, to help prevent or adjust strikes, to conduct educational classes and religious work, to carry on recreation, and to assist in forwarding letters and remittances. The majority of the secretaries were missionaries and Chinese Christian students. Missionaries, too, were commissioned as officers by the British Government to help manage the laborers.[47]

On the whole, then, the war had but little immediate adverse effect upon the spread of the Christian message by Protestants in China. The rate of increase of the body of Protestant Christians was about as great as in the years immediately preceding 1914. In the four years just before the war—that is, between 1908-1909 and 1912-1913—the baptized community rose from 195,905 to 285,045, or about eleven and a half per cent. a year.[48] Between 1915 and 1917 it grew from 330,926 to 398,760, or at the rate

[45] *L. M. S. Chronicle*, Vol. 24 (new series), p. 236; *Foreign Mail*, Vol. 21, No. 3, p. 14; Vol. 23, No. 4, p. 4; Gamewell, *The Gateway to China*, p. 247; *China Mission Year Book, 1915*, pp. 339-370, *1916*, p. 19, *1917*, pp. 494-502; Ward, *Shanghai Sketches*, pp. 30, 31, 36, 37; Y. M. C. A., *The Year 1916*, pp. 20-25; H. A. Wilbur, *Letter for Year Ending Sept. 30, 1914*, p. 3; C. W. Harvey, *Annual Report for Year Ending Sept. 30, 1914; China Mission Year Book, 1918*, pp. 279-290, 337.

[46] Eddy, *Everybody's World*, p. 160.

[47] *Service with Fighting Men*, Vol. 2, pp. 364-368; *China Mission Year Book, 1918*, pp. 52-59; Gamewell, *New Life Currents in China*, p. 23; Lipphard, *The Second Century of Baptist Foreign Missions*, p. 11; *L. M. S. Chronicle*, Vol. 26 (new series), p. 123.

[48] *China Mission Year Book, 1910*, statistical tables; ibid., *1914*, p. xvii.

of about ten per cent. a year.[49]   It was not until some years after the war that Protestant missions were to face their real crisis.

EDUCATION

Rapid as was the growth in church membership, and great as was the emphasis upon the widespread preaching of the Faith, the expansion in the educational side of Protestant missions was fully as marked. This need not surprise us, for, as we have repeatedly seen, from almost the beginning of their missions in China Protestants had placed the school beside the church and of late years had been bending every energy to take advantage of the popularity of Western education to reach through their schools the future leaders of the country and to train the Christian community.   Moreover, education, especially higher education, was primarily in the hands of Americans, and American missions were not as seriously affected by the war as were those of Great Britain and Germany.

Many were the forms of education continued or now undertaken for the first time. In the two years between 1915 and 1917 the Sunday School enrollment increased by a third and the number of teachers nearly doubled,[50] striking testimony to the effect of the national organization that had been initiated a few years before. Much literature was prepared, summer schools in methods were held, and a movement just then in vogue in the United States, the Adult Bible Class, was stressed.[51]

Efforts to teach the entire church membership to read were numerous. The Christian Endeavor Societies, which often included the entire congregation, adults as well as young people, added to their well-known pledge the sentence: "If unable to read the Bible, I will go to the instruction committee and diligently try to learn to read."[52] A Chinese member of the faculty of Shanghai Baptist College compiled a list of the six hundred characters in most frequent use and by 1916 two hundred or more schools had been opened to teach them to illiterates.[53] In 1917 in Southern Fukien the Foochow Methodist Conference and the churches

[49] *The Christian Occupation of China*, p. xci. Nearly three-fourths of this membership was in the seven coast provinces.—*China Mission Year Book, 1917*, pp. 53-57.
[50] *The Christian Occupation of China*, xci.
[51] *China Mission Year Book, 1915*, pp. 411-422, *1916*, p. 308.
[52] *China Mission Year Book, 1918*, p. 298.
[53] Ibid., *1918*, p. 349.

inaugurated campaigns to insure the reading of the Bible in the romanized colloquial by every church member.[54]   In 1918 the China Continuation Committee called a conference to consider the use of a phonetic script which had been prepared through government agency and which was being promoted by the National Board of Education.   This conference gave unanimous endorsement to the project and steps were taken—with the inevitable "executive secretary" to carry them out—to induce the churches to adopt it.[55]   As a result, the new script was employed much more widely by the missions than by the country at large. Moreover, at least one other form of phonetic writing was in use by some of the missions.[56]

As in other years, many kinds of schools were maintained. In one station, not at all exceptional, we hear of women's, day, girls' boarding, boys' boarding, and blind schools.[57]   Here and there in the port cities were schools, usually self-supporting, for the children of wealthy parents.[58]   While most mission schools were declared to be lacking in adequate provision for manual and industrial education,[59] efforts were not lacking to train the sons of the poor in useful trades.[60]   An exceptional undertaking was the Huchow Women's School, opened in March, 1917, the purpose of which was to prepare wives to be intelligent companions of educated husbands.   Many a man found that as he acquired a modern education his wife, or the girl to whom he had been betrothed by his parents, failed to keep pace with him and that a lack of sympathy ensued.   This institution attempted to aid the woman to bridge the gulf, and emphasized home economics and the care of children.[61]   As in other years, attempts were made to improve the quality of the normal training given to the teachers in Christian schools.[62]   Correspondence schools on religious topics were conducted for those who for some reason could not attend school or who wished thus to continue their education.[63]

[54] Ibid., *1918*, p. 143.
[55] Ibid., *1918*, pp. 142, 168-175, *1919*, pp. 176-183.
[56] *L. M. S. Chronicle*, Vol. 28 (new series), p. 2.
[57] Darley, *Corners of a Chinese City*, p. 22.
[58] *China Mission Year Book, 1916*, p. 45.
[59] Ibid., *1916*, pp. 132, 276-285; *Spirit of Missions*, Vol. 8, p. 864.
[60] *China Mission Year Book, 1916*, pp. 132, 276-285; *Spirit of Missions*, Vol. 8, p. 864.
[61] *China Mission Year Book, 1919*, pp. 173-175; *The Baptist*, Jan. 31, 1920, p. 17.
[62] *China Mission Year Book, 1917*, p. 320, *1918*, pp. 178, 191-196.
[63] Ibid., *1917*, p. 538.

A school for the deaf, modeled on that in Chefoo, was begun in Hangchow by Chinese Christians.[64]

Colleges and universities continued to flourish and absorbed much of the energy of Protestant, and especially of American, missions. The enrollment in the college of arts and sciences of Canton Christian College grew from thirty-seven in 1914-1915 to one hundred and twenty-one in 1918-1919.[65] Chinese coöperated more and more in the support of the institution: by 1919 two-thirds of the income came from Chinese sources as compared with less than forty per cent. in 1913-1914, and ten of the thirty permanent buildings were the gifts of Chinese.[66] In 1915 the Methodists opened a women's college in Foochow.[67] In February, 1916, the Fukien College of Liberal Arts, also at Foochow, began instruction with three missions actively participating and three others approving,[68] and in June, 1918, Fukien Christian University, an institution of which this was to be a part, and which had been projected for several years, was incorporated under the laws of the State of New York.[69] In 1915 Soochow University opened a law department in Shanghai.[70] The various institutions at Nanking flourished, much being heard of the new Ginling College (for women) and of the College of Agriculture and Forestry at the University.[71] West China Union University reported added buildings and enrollment, and a new department of education.[72]

A sub-committee of the China Continuation Committee made a special study of theological education. It reported that standards were rising, but it strongly recommended that they should be still higher, that more theological literature should be prepared in Chinese, and that at least one first grade union institution should be established in which instruction should be largely in a European language.[73] This last need was soon to be met, for about 1915 the Union Theological College in Peking became a

---

[64] Ibid., *1915*, p. 41.
[65] Edmunds, *Canton Christian College*, p. 42.
[66] Edmunds, *Canton Christian College*, p. 42.
[67] *China Mission Year Book, 1916*, p. 383.
[68] Ibid., *1916*, p. 254, *1917*, pp. 377-382; *Educational Review*, Vol. 7, p. 300.
[69] *China Mission Year Book, 1918*, pp. 182, 187.
[70] Ibid., *1916*, p. 273.
[71] Ibid., *1915*, p. 420; *Millard's Review*, Vol. 11, p. 188; J. Arnold in *Far Eastern Bureau Bulletin*, May 12, 1919.
[72] *China Mission Year Book, 1916*, p. 253, *1918*, p. 176.
[73] Ibid., *1915*, pp. 425 et seq.

department of Peking University [74] and maintained corresponding scholastic requirements. By 1917 three schools were using English as a medium of instruction, and of eighteen hundred and sixty-one students in sixty-four theological and Bible Schools, one hundred and twenty-eight were college graduates, and four hundred and two were of middle school grade.[75] The Chinese Protestant ministry was becoming better educated.

With the coming of the China Medical Board medical education in China entered upon a new era. John D. Rockefeller had long been a large contributor to missions, usually through the board of the Northern Baptists. In 1914 the Rockefeller Foundation, a creation of the millionaire and primarily for the promotion of public health and of medical education and research, sent to China a commission to study the medical situation. Upon the report of that commission the China Medical Board was organized as a subsidiary body of the Foundation and to it large funds were entrusted. In general the plan adopted was to concentrate upon the training of a medical profession, Chinese in personnel, and with as high technical and educational standing as was held up to the Occident. To accomplish this purpose, it was proposed to found two or more schools in which English should be the medium of instruction, to assist a few selected missionary agencies in maintaining pre-medical and medical education, to establish two model tuberculosis hospitals, to provide scholarships for medical missionaries and Chinese for study abroad, and to assist a few hospitals in which Chinese could continue their training and in which nurses could be prepared. The entire plan called for close coöperation with existing missionary agencies.

Almost immediately the effects began to appear of the coming of a body with such distinct aims and in command of such large funds. The China Medical Board purchased and discontinued the Harvard Medical School in Shanghai with the expectation, destined not soon to be fulfilled, of creating a new medical school in that center. The existing Union Medical College in Peking was taken over and a new Peking Union Medical College was created with a board of trustees made up of representatives of seven Protestant missionary societies and of the China

[74] Ibid., *1916*, p. 255.
[75] *China Mission Year Book, 1917*, pp. 399-402.

Medical Board. In 1917 a preparatory department for the pre-medical school was opened and the cornerstone was laid of a group of buildings, in semi-Chinese style, which for solidity of construction and completeness of equipment were superior to anything that China had ever known for medical work, and the equal of the best medical schools in the West. Assistance was given to the recently begun Hunan-Yale Medical School (a union undertaking, in Changsha, of the provincial government and the Yale Foreign Missionary Society and using a large new hospital building), to a number of hospitals, to the St. John's-Pennsylvania medical school in Shanghai, and to pre-medical science departments in some of the Christian colleges. Appropriations were made for the translation of medical literature and for scholarships for study abroad.[76]

Because of the paucity of medical literature in Chinese, the Peking Union Medical College was to carry on its teaching in English, but the Council on Medical Education of the China Medical Missionary Association believed that at least one first grade medical school should use Chinese as the chief medium of instruction. As a result, several missions in East and Central China, with substantial assistance from the China Medical Board, united in a medical school at Tsinanfu, and the existing institutions in Nanking and Hankow were closed.[77]

The coming of the China Medical Board did not mean the death of all the missionary medical schools that were not aided by it. Most of these were continued, partly because of a natural reluctance to end undertakings into which much sacrifice had gone, and partly because of the conviction that China would need many more physicians than the new foundation could provide.[78] A new school, indeed, was opened, the medical department of West China Union University.[79]

[76] China Medical Commission of the Rockefeller Foundation, *Medicine in China*, New York, 1914; R. S. Greene in *China Medical Journal*, Vol. 31, pp. 43, 191-198; *China Mission Year Book, 1915*, pp. 292 et seq., *1916*, pp. 320-325, *1917*, p. 430, *1918*, pp. 202-227; *Chinese Recorder*, Vol. 46, pp. 664, 683, Vol. 47, p. 32; *China Medical Journal*, Vol. 31, p. 36; *L. M. S. Chronicle*, Vol. 22 (new series), p. 42; Gamewell, *New Life Currents in China*, p. 48; Vincent, *Rockefeller Foundation Review for 1918*, p. 24.
[77] Balme, *China and Modern Medicine*, p. 122.
[78] *Chinese Recorder*, Vol. 49 (1918), p. 27, shows twelve missionary medical schools besides the Peking Union Medical College. Only three institutions in China, however, offered thorough medical training for women.—Burton, *Women Workers in the Orient*, p. 156.
[79] *China Mission Year Book, 1916*, p. 253.

With all of this attention to education, in 1917 Protestant schools enrolled only about 191,033 students,[80] a number but slightly more than that reported three or four years later by Roman Catholics,[81] about five per cent. of the total in schools of all kinds, government and private,[82] and an increase of approximately seven per cent. a year since 1915, or three per cent. less than the annual growth in baptized Protestant membership during the same two years, and less than half the percentage of the annual increase of students in the preceding quadrennium. The war was having an effect.

The importance of Protestant schools, aside from the religious training given, lay largely in their equipment and educational standards—usually better than those of government schools— and in the fact that a considerable proportion of the best secondary and higher education was given by them. Moreover, while only about a third of the students in Protestant schools were from Christian homes,[83] the percentage of Protestants who were being given some sort of education was much greater than that of the country as a whole. Since, too, a large number of students—in the case of colleges the great majority—avowed themselves as Christians before graduation,[84] the Protestant body was rapidly becoming better equipped with the type of education which Chinese were now demanding than was any other religious group in the country. It is not surprising that three of the five representatives of China at the Peace Conference in Paris were Protestant Christians and that four were said to be former students in mission schools.[85]

Inter-mission coöperation in education continued to grow. In 1916 the China Christian Educational Association reported six

---

[80] Ibid., *1918*, statistical summary.

[81] The number given in Planchet, *Les missions de Chine et du Japon*, for 1920 and 1921 was 144,344.—*Christian Education in China*, paragraph 53.

[82] *China Mission Year Book*, 1918, pp. 349, 350.

[83] Arthur Rugh in *China Mission Year Book*, 1917, p. 403.

[84] In 1914 97 mission academies and colleges reported that 836 of their students who entered as non-Christians had been baptized.—W. B. Pettus in *Educational Review*, Vol. 7, No. 1, p. 13. Of the 145 who up to 1918 had graduated from Nanking University 96% were Christians.—*Report of the President of Nanking University, 1917-1918*. In Canton Christian College few students were Christian when they entered, but 90% of those in attendance two or more years left the institution professing Christians.—Edmunds, *Canton Christian College*, p. 32.

[85] High, *China's Place in the Sun*, p. 192.

regional associations and a seventh in process of formation.[86] A unified, coördinated national system of Protestant schools was still a dream, but it was a dream which each year seemed nearer fulfillment.

With emphasis upon education for the Chinese went even more rapid progress in the training of missionaries. Except for the China Inland Mission, until after 1911 the boards had not taken seriously language schools for new missionaries. By the close of 1916, however, eight such institutions were being maintained, the two best and largest being at Nanking and Peking. Most of them were joint enterprises of several missions and so were accustoming the new recruits to think in terms larger than their own denominations.[87]

Protestant education was not without its problems, and very serious ones. Christian graduates of mission schools often felt out of place in their local churches, so superior were they in training to the mass of the members and to the average pastor, and it was necessary to take steps to enlist them in some sort of active coöperation with organized Christianity.[88] While because of the demand of Chinese for English that language was still the medium of instruction in Western subjects in most secondary and higher schools, the advisability of its use continued a moot question.[89] Christian Chinese, moreover, were beginning to criticize the institutions for the poor quality of the Chinese scholarship of the graduates.[90] Missionaries themselves believed that primary schools and normal training were being neglected,[91] that the aims of the education given by the Church had not been clearly enough defined,[92] and that the curriculum did not sufficiently fit students for life in China and was too Western in object and content.[93] In spite of the fact, moreover, that fees and gifts from Chinese met a large part of the cost of the schools,

[86] *China Mission Year Book, 1916,* p. 258.   See also on these educational associations, ibid., *1915,* pp. 377-397,*1918,* p. 180.
[87] *China Mission Year Book, 1915,* pp. 404, 534, *1916,* pp. 407-411, *1918,* pp. 145, 314-317; Augustana Synod, *Our First Decade in China, 1905-1915,* p. 93; *Chinese Recorder,* Vol. 47, p. 31.
[88] *Chinese Recorder,* Vol. 47, p. 673.
[89] Ibid., Vol. 46, pp. 1, 115, 119; *Educational Review,* Vol. 7, pp. 71-75.
[90] C. T. Wang in *Missionary Review of the World,* Vol. 29, p. 569.
[91] A. J. Bowen in *Chinese Recorder,* Vol. 46, p. 406.
[92] Ibid., T. H. P. Sailer in *Chinese Recorder,* Vol. 47, p. 385; Webster, *Christian Education and the National Consciousness in China,* passim.
[93] *Chinese Recorder,* Vol. 47, p. 587.

the higher institutions, with their expanding budgets and the constant need for new buildings and equipment, were for the mission boards an ever increasing problem.[94]

On the whole, Protestant schools were popular and the storm which within a decade was to burst upon them had not yet given even the first indication of its approach. Relations with the government and with government schools were usually friendly. Missionaries and Chinese Christians were often asked to teach in state institutions,[95] and in Shansi the American Board was offered entire charge of the public school system for eight counties, with a population of four millions.[96] In the light of later developments, however, it was significant that few missionary institutions were registered with the government and that the rules adopted by the Ministry of Education for the registration of Christian primary schools included the requirements that the name of the mission or church should not be attached to the school, that no religious teaching or ceremony should be compulsory, that non-Christians should be admitted, and that no distinction should be made between them and Christians.[97]

LITERATURE

The war years brought no very great change in the preparation or circulation of Christian literature. Tract societies were injured by the unfavorable exchange and the rise in the price of paper,[98] and missionaries, among other economies forced upon them, were unable to buy Christian literature as freely as formerly.[99] However, the circulation of the Scriptures about held its own,[100] and a rising interest in Christianity among the educated and a corresponding increase in the demand for Christian literature were noted.[101] A Christian Publishers' Association was formed in 1915,[102] and in 1918 the China Continuation Commit-

[94] R. E. Speer in *China Mission Year Book, 1916*, p. 256.
[95] Scott, *China From Within*, p. 103.
[96] *International Review of Missions*, Vol. 4, p. 16.
[97] *China Mission Year Book, 1916*, p. 349.
[98] *China Mission Year Book, 1918*, pp. 245-247.
[99] Ibid., *1916*, pp. 367-370.
[100] The British and Foreign Bible Society showed a decrease in 1915, but the increase of the American Bible Society and of the Scotch Society more than offset it. The circulation of the American Bible Society declined sharply in 1917 and 1918, but that of the British and Foreign Bible Society increased during these years.—*Annual Reports of the American Bible Society, 1915-1920; Annual Reports of the British and Foreign Bible Society, 1915-1920; China Mission Year Book, 1916*, pp. 372, 373.
[101] D. W. Lyon in *China Mission Year Book, 1918*, p. 218.
[102] Ibid., *1918*, pp. 241-244; *International Review of Missions*, Vol. 5, p. 28.

tee created a special committee on Christian literature.[103] Several new versions of parts or all of the Bible were begun or completed. The revised New Testament in the Amoy vernacular appeared in 1914, the Mandarin Union Version of Luke and Acts was transliterated into the Hainan dialect, the Hakka Old Testament was completed by Otto Schultze,[104] Ashmore took up the task of putting the Old Testament into the Swatow dialect,[105] Taichow, in Chêkiang, was given its version of the entire Bible,[106] and the New Testament was put into Kashgar Turkish, a Tatar dialect spoken in Chinese Turkestan.[107]

MEDICAL WORK

It was in medical work more than in any other branch of Protestant missions that the war made itself felt. Numbers of physicians left for the fighting fronts, their places could not be filled, and several hospitals were closed.[108] The rising cost of medical supplies was a burden upon missions already hampered by unfavorable exchange.[109]

Even in the field of medicine, however, the war years witnessed marked progress. The formation of the China Medical Board, already noted, would alone have made the quadrennium memorable. The extensive lecture campaigns on public health conducted by Dr. W. W. Peter under the Young Men's Christian Association led to the organization (in 1916) of a Joint Council on Public Health in which the China Medical Missionary Association and the National Medical Association coöperated with the parent body. A Chinese associate for Dr. Peter was engaged, and public health campaigns were conducted in a number of cities.[110] The National Medical Association, made up of the Chinese practicing Western medicine, was an outgrowth of the Medical Missionary Association, for it was brought into existence

[103] *Fifth Annual Meeting of the China Continuation Committee*, p. 13.
[104] *China Mission Year Book, 1916*, pp. 371, 372; *International Review of Missions*, Vol. 7, p. 19.
[105] Ashmore, *The South China Mission of the A. B. F. M. S.*, p. 139.
[106] *International Review of Missions*, Vol. 5, p. 27.
[107] Ibid.
[108] *China Mission Year Book, 1916*, pp. 311-316, *1917*, pp. 61, 414-421; *One Hundred and First Report of the Wesleyan Methodist Missionary Society*, p. 131.
[109] R. C. Beebe in *China Mission Year Book, 1916*, p. 311.
[110] Gamewell, *New Life Currents in China*, p. 96; *International Review of Missions*, Vol. 5, p. 27; *The Christian Occupation of China*, pp. 433-435; *China Mission Year Book, 1916*, p. 330, *1918*, pp. 211-216.

in 1915 by Chinese who were attending the triennial conference of the latter body.[111] Chinese were becoming more favorable to Western medicine and, largely as a result of missionary efforts, a new medical profession was being born.

RELIEF AND SOCIAL REFORM

Protestant missionaries, as formerly, were interested in ameliorating the lot of the Chinese in every way possible, and not only continued the activities by which they had previously sought to do this, but initiated new ones. A few instances, somewhat disjointed, may serve to make this vivid. Students in mission schools were more and more encouraged to undertake in the community about them some form of what was technically known as "social service."[112] "Institutional churches" multiplied rapidly. In general these attempted to do for both sexes and all ages what the Young Men's Christian Association was undertaking for young men. They had class rooms, recreation halls, libraries, reading rooms, parlors, auditoriums, religious exercises and addresses, lectures on secular subjects, and moving pictures. By 1917 such churches existed in at least seven of the larger cities.[113] The first "social survey" of a modern type ever made of a Chinese city was the undertaking of Protestant missionaries in Peking.[114] When, in 1917, floods left destitute part of the population of North China, missionaries and Chinese Christians aided in the distribution of relief, and in response to the appeal of the China Continuation Committee over one hundred thousand dollars were contributed through the Protestant churches of China.[115] The deplorable living and working conditions in the rapidly growing factory districts in Shanghai attracted the attention of missionaries and a survey was made and a social center conducted under the direction of a member of the faculty of Shanghai Baptist College.[116] From various places we hear of an "anti-tuberculosis drive," public playgrounds, child welfare

---

[111] *China Mission Year Book, 1916*, pp. 317-319.
[112] *Chinese Recorder*, Vol. 46, p. 96.
[113] *China Mission Year Book, 1917*, pp. 304-306.
[114] Gamble, *Peking, a Social Survey*. The data for the volume was gathered Sept., 1918 to Dec., 1919.
[115] *China Mission Year Book, 1918*, pp. 41-51; Gamewell, *New Life Currents in China*, pp. 107-109.
[116] D. H. Kulp, II, was the man in charge. Reports by him in *China Mission Year Book, 1916*, pp. 474-478, and *1918*, pp. 342-348, and in *The Baptist*, Vol. 1, pp. 1451-1456. See also *L. M. S. Chronicle*, Vol. 24 (new series), p. 23.

movements, "anti-fly campaigns," summer vacation schools, free schools for poor boys, boys' clubs, a street-cleaning department, and the introduction of a pure water supply—all the result of the efforts of missionaries.[117] Missionaries continued to care for those wounded in the recurring civil strife, and to settle disputes between officials and bandits.[118] The opium trade nominally came to an end in March, 1917,[119] but a revival in the cultivation of the poppy and an increase in the importation of opium derivatives were soon reported. Against these new forms of the old evil missionaries protested.[120] Missionaries had a large part in a committee in Shanghai which censored the films that were beginning to be widely shown.[121] Boy Scout troops were formed in connection with Young Men's Christian Associations and mission schools.[122] On China's international relations Protestant missionaries had decided opinions: the majority were earnestly opposed to Japanese aggression in China and did not hesitate to say so.[123]

All this activity for social betterment, it may be well to repeat, was in general accord with what their philosophical and religious background prepared the Chinese to welcome. It was an attempt to better the lot of mankind here and now.

COÖPERATION

The war did not halt the growth in coöperation which had been one of the marked features of the preceding fourteen years. In 1918 the Presbyterians formed a Provisional General Assembly, an outgrowth of the Council which had been in existence for more than a decade.[124] At the gathering were representatives of the American Board and the London Missionary Society, and an agreement—whose consummation was delayed—was entered

[117] A. J. Allen in *China Mission Year Book, 1919,* pp. 205-217; Dennett, *Democratic Movement* in Asia, pp. 124-127.
[118] Andrews, *Camps and Trails in China,* pp. 32, 207-211; Caldwell, *Blue Tiger,* passim.
[119] *International Review of Missions,* Vol. 4, p. 20, Vol. 7, p. 20.
[120] *China Mission Year Book, 1917,* pp. 38-42, *1918,* pp. 60-68.
[121] Ibid., *1916,* pp. 492-494.
[122] Boy Scout troops began to be formed before 1914 and the national organization was organized in 1913.—Ibid., *1916,* pp. 494, 495.
[123] Reid, *China, Captive or Free,* pp. 215-300; *The Missionary Outlook in the Light of the War,* p. 99. Bishop Bashford was very aggressive in urging Washington to act against the Twenty-One Demands.—Grose, *Bashford,* p. 141.
[124] *China Mission Year Book, 1918,* p. 82; Woodbridge, *Fifty Years in China,* p. 207; *The Christian Occupation of China,* p. 337.

into by all three groups for a federation looking toward ultimate union.[125] The Lutheran bodies in China represented six different countries and more than that number of societies. Steps preliminary to union, however, were taken by the bodies working in Hunan, Hupeh, and Honan, when in 1915 a constitution was drafted and a "Temporary Council of the Lutheran Church in China" was elected, and when in 1917 at a celebration of the quadricentennial of the Reformation the constitution was adopted.[126]

The Associated Mission Treasurers of China was formed (1916) to facilitate the operation of the many mission business offices in Shanghai and in it five of the larger boards joined.[127] Some of the provincial councils continued to function and in Shansi steps toward union were taken in the reciprocal recognition by missions of each other's membership and discipline.[128] Several city unions were organized or reconstructed to coördinate the efforts of the missions in the larger centers.[129] Some progress toward union in bookstores and publishing houses was also reported.[130]

As may be surmised from repeated references in the preceding pages, the China Continuation Committee came speedily to occupy a large place in the Protestant enterprise. Regular meetings were held, the secretariat provided unusually able leadership, and through a number of sub-committees important phases of the common task were studied.[131]

INDEPENDENCE AND SELF-SUPPORT OF THE CHINESE CHURCH

The war years witnessed fairly rapid progress toward self-support and the transfer of responsibility to Chinese leaders. The number of Chinese ordained ministers rose from seven hundred and sixty-four in 1915 to eight hundred and forty-six in 1917.[132] Chinese increased their contributions to the support of the

[125] China Mission Year Book, 1918, p. 85; The Christian Occupation of China, p. 334.
[126] Chinese Recorder, Vol. 48, p. 724; China Mission Year Book, 1918, pp. 87-92.
[127] China Mission Year Book, 1917, pp. 491-493, 1919, p. 296.
[128] Ibid., 1915, pp. 43, 94-99, 1917, p. 215.
[129] Ibid., 1916, p. 249, 1917, p. 92.
[130] China Mission Year Book, 1915, p. 443.
[131] Chinese Recorder, Vol. 47, pp. 369, 405, Vol. 48, pp. 351-357, Vol. 49, p. 357; China Mission Year Book, 1915, pp. 481-515, 1916, pp. 377-400, 1917, pp. 468-477, 1918, pp. 266-275.
[132] The Christian Occupation of China, p. xci.

Church [133] and several new home missionary societies were reported.[134] The year 1915 saw C. T. Wang succeed Fletcher Brockman as National General Secretary of the Young Men's Christian Association,[135] and the Young Women's Christian Association was steadily passing into the control of Chinese.[136] In 1914 the North China Mission of the American Board extended to all business matters Chinese-foreign coöperative control.[137] A meeting of Chinese leaders held at Kuling in 1918 adopted a program which involved the education of members in Christian patriotism, the promotion of evangelism by personal contacts and campaigns of preaching, and the appointment of a commission to study Yünnan as a possible field for united home missionary effort.[138] In 1918, moreover, Shen Tsai-sheng was consecrated Assistant Bishop of Chêkiang, the first Chinese to be raised by Protestants to the episcopal dignity.[139]

With all this "devolution," the Church remained primarily a foreign institution in both leadership and support, and observers commented on the fact that in independence and efficiency it was behind the Church in Japan.[140] Here and there, however, Christians were rising to prominence in national affairs and a few members of well-known families and men in official position were beginning to enter the Church and to assume leadership in it.[141] The Protestant Church was becoming a force with which the nation had obviously to reckon.

That this rising Church could exert itself vigorously and effectively was demonstrated when it was proposed to establish Confucianism as the religion of the state. Protestant Christians petitioned Parliament against the measure, and when, in 1916, a

[133] *China Mission Year Book, 1915.* p. 331, *1916*, p. 51, *1917*, p. 189.
[134] *The Christian Occupation of China,* pp. 386-390.
[135] *China Mission Year Book, 1916,* p. 164.
[136] Burton, *Women Workers of the Orient,* p. 198.
[137] *Chinese Recorder,* Vol. 48, pp. 79-81.
[138] *China Mission Year Book, 1918,* p. 150; Gamewell, *New Life Currents in China,* pp. 212-215.
[139] A. C. Moule in *New China Review,* Vol. 1, pp. 480-488; *Spirit of Missions,* Vol. 83, p. 304.
[140] *China Mission Year Book, 1917,* pp. 170, 313, 314.
[141] Ibid., *1916,* p. 351; Dennett, *The Democratic Movement in Asia,* p. 50; Poteat, *Home Letters from China,* p. 152. In Foochow in 1914 25% of the Protestants were merchants and shopkeepers, 25% students, 16% teachers, 15% workmen, 3% doctors, 3% government employees, 2% farmers, and 1% ministers. 45% of the members had a fair education.—*China Mission Year Book, 1917,* p. 114. In Manchuria 30% of the Protestant Christians were farmers owning land, 10% were skilled laborers, 10% unskilled laborers, and 6% were in business.—Ibid., p. 275.

milder form of the same suggestion was broached—to declare Confucianism the basis of moral instruction in the national educational system—a union of Roman Catholics, Protestants, Buddhists, Taoists, and Moslems succeeded in defeating it and liberty of religious worship was guaranteed.[142]

The war years, then, while slowing down growth, had not caused it to cease. Protestant Christians were as yet little disturbed by the rising disorder in the country;[143] persecution, except in petty forms, was unknown; and the prospects were that the return of peace to Europe and America would be the signal for the resumption of rapid expansion.

[142] Oldham, *The Missionary Situation After the War*, p. 25; *Missionary Review of the World*, Vol. 28, pp. 272, 273, Vol. 30, pp. 580, 581; *China Mission Year Book, 1917*, pp. 34-37, 98-109; *The East and the West*, Vol. 15, pp. 401-404.

[143] In 1916 in the war between the North and the South, some German mission property was destroyed.—Richter, *Geschichte der Berliner Missionsgesellschaft*, p. 582. In the Civil War of 1917, in Hunan, some mission property suffered.—*China Mission Year Book, 1918*, pp. 29-40.

CHAPTER XXX

CHINA IN A TIME OF REORGANIZATION (1901-1926)
PROTESTANT MISSIONS FROM THE CLOSE OF THE WAR TO THE CLOSE OF 1926

CONDITIONS IN EUROPE AND AMERICA

THE hope that the end of the World War would usher in a new day of rapid growth for Protestant missions at first seemed to be well grounded. In some cases, to be sure, recovery was slow. German societies especially were impoverished: the disestablishment of Protestantism necessitated retaining at home for reconstruction most of such funds as could be procured for church purposes, and the rapid fall of the mark brought financial ruin to many former contributors.[1] However, many Germans gave heroically, and assistance came from Switzerland and the United States.[2] German missions by no means ceased to exist.

In Great Britain the war was followed by financial and industrial depression, the cost of living did not subside, taxes were a staggering burden, and the middle classes, from whom a large proportion of the support of missions was drawn, were especially affected. However, incomes of societies rose. The annual receipts of the Church Missionary Society, for example, in the four years after the war averaged £479,464 as against £372,510 during the war and £402,681 for the five years just before the war.[3] The annual income of the London Missionary Society for the five years just before the war (1909-1913) averaged £186,673, for the five years spanning the war (1914-1918) £222,144, for the five years just after the war (1919-1923) £337,014, and for the next four years (1924-1927) £378,824. The increase was, however, partly traceable to growing contributions from the

---

[1] Keller and Stewart, *Protestant Europe, Its Crisis and Outlook,* passim.
[2] Beyer, *China als Missionfeld,* Chapter 16, p. 22.
[3] *China Mission Year Book, 1923,* pp. 102-111.

mission fields.[4] It is interesting, too, that while the amount appropriated to China by the London treasurer increased but little—the figures being £44,472 in 1918, £55,758 in 1921, and £48,182 in 1927—the amount received in China from contributions, school fees, and the like rose from £12,711 in 1918 to £47,728 in 1921 and to £71,528 in 1927.[5] For the five years just before the war (1910-1914) the Baptist Missionary Society had an average annual income (exclusive of the Arthington fund) of £93,648, for the five years spanning the war (1915-1919) the corresponding figure was £116,621, for the five years just after the war (1920-1924) it was £199,862, and for the three years 1925-1927 £215,433.[6] The Wesleyan Methodist Missionary Society reported an income averaging £199,198 annually in the five years before the war (1909-1913), £374,089 annually during the war (1914-1918), and £432,076 annually in six of the seven years after the war (1919-23, 1925, 1926).[7] The income of the China Inland Mission mounted from £87,879 in 1915 and £123,229 in 1918 to £156,217 in 1919, and to £184,116 in 1920.[8] In 1921 it fell to £158,173 and in 1922 to £152,786, but the decline was accompanied by a favorable turn in the exchange and in 1923 the figures again began to rise—to £155,911 in 1923, to £175,217 [9] in 1924, and to £185,492 in 1926.[10] The British Chamber of Commerce in China contributed a fund to assist British mission hospitals and schools there—with the frankly and naïvely avowed purpose of strengthening British influence.[11] However, prices in China continued to mount and exchange

[4] 123d Report of the London Missionary Society (1918), p. 122, 132d Report of the London Missionary Society (1927), p. cxlviii. These figures did not include the Arthington fund.

[5] 123d Report of the London Missionary Society (1918), p. 144; 126th Report of ibid. (1921), p. cxix; 132d Report of ibid. (1927), p. cxxxviii.

[6] Baptist Missionary Society Annual Report and Statement of Accounts for the 118th year ending March 31, 1910, p. 348; 1911, p. 356, 1912, p. 360, 1913, p. 378, 1914, p. 456, 1915, p. 532, 1916, p. 462, 1917, p. 414, 1918, p. 186, 1919, p. 190, 1920, p. 214, 1921, p. 202, 1922, p. 210, 1923, p. 216, 1924, p. 250, 1925, p. 264, 1926, p. 168, 1927, p. 184.

[7] 96th to 112th Annual Reports of the Wesleyan Methodist Missionary Society. The amount received from foreign mission districts (largely the "native" churches) increased from £26,107 in 1909 to £163,954 in 1926.

[8] China's Millions, 1925, p. 88. These figures included income from North America as well as from Great Britain.

[9] Ibid. These figures included income from North America as well as from Great Britain.

[10] Ibid., 1927, pp. 93 et seq. These figures include income from North America as well as from Great Britain.

[11] Mrs. Butler, Missions as I Saw Them, p. 115; C. G. Sparham in Chinese Recorder, Vol. 51, pp. 271-276.

remained adverse, until 1921 very much so. The increase in giving, therefore, permitted little expansion.

In the United States conditions seemed more favorable. The wealth of the country was now nearly equal to Europe and was rapidly mounting, in most sections the *post bellum* financial reaction was comparatively slight, and ecclesiastical leaders hoped that the idealism shown in the war and the unprecedented generosity which had met appeals to the Red Cross, the war work of the Young Men's Christian Association, the American Relief Fund for the aid of sufferers in Europe, and the Near East Relief could be directed to the peace-time activities of the Church at home and abroad. The Inter-Church World Movement, an ambitious undertaking to unite all denominations in such a program, proved a disastrous failure. For a time, however, denominational movements seemed to meet with success. Several of the larger groups outlined what they wished to achieve during a set number of years and solicited pledges for that period. This, for example, was the procedure of the Methodist Episcopal Churches, both North and South, and of the Northern and Southern Baptist Conventions. The Northern Baptists planned to increase their staff of missionaries in China by about two-thirds between 1919 and 1924 and largely to augment their equipment.[12] The Northern Methodists proposed to spend in China six and a half million dollars of their Centenary Fund [13] and more than to double their staff, Chinese and foreign, within five years.[14]

Subscriptions seemed to promise a large and permanent increase in giving. In the first years of the Centenary Fund, for instance, the Methodists reported that their disbursements in China had more than doubled, that many new church organizations and buildings had appeared, that nearly a hundred and fifty new missionaries had been sent and over two thousand Chinese workers added to the staff, that nearly twenty thousand members had come into the churches, and that the enrollment in the schools was nearly twice what it had been in 1918.[15] The income of some boards that did not embark on a "five year program,"

[12] *Survey . . . of the Northern Baptist Convention,* 1919, p. 25.
[13] *Millard's Review,* 1920, pp. 578-580.
[14] Hutchinson, *China's Challenge and the Methodist Reply,* p. 9; *Chinese Recorder,* Vol. 51, pp. 271-276.
[15] *Chinese Recorder,* Vol. 55, p. 202.

moreover, rose encouragingly. The American Board of Commissioners for Foreign Missions showed an augmentation of income from an annual average of $1,043,357 for the five years 1910-1914 to one of $1,486,331 for the years 1915-1919, and to one of $1,887,358 for the years 1920-1924.[16]

Since the American churches were more interested in China than in any other country, the proportion of Americans in the Protestant missionary body there increased. In 1905 about forty-five per cent. of the Protestant missionaries were from Great Britain and thirty-five per cent. from the United States.[17] In 1922 the corresponding percentages were eighteen and fifty-one.[18]

The great additions to income, however, in some instances proved of disappointingly brief duration. By the close of 1926 six of the major American boards showed a decrease of six and a half million dollars from the highest levels attained within the preceding decade.[19] The pledges to the Centenary Fund were not fully met, and for the year ending November, 1924, gifts to the Northern Methodist denominational budget diminished forty-two per cent. Receipts of the Board of Foreign Missions of the Methodist Episcopal Church (North) fell from $6,071,107 in 1920 to $3,101,359 in 1925, and in 1926 only $2,817,975 was available for appropriation.[20] In 1924 the Southern Methodists showed a decline of twenty-eight per cent. as against 1923 and of fifty-seven per cent. as compared with 1920.[21] In 1927 the Disciples of Christ suspended their College of Missions in Indianapolis, for giving had increased only slightly between 1922 and 1927, costs had risen, and more emphasis was being laid on financing "native work." [22] In 1922 the Northern Baptists sent to all their foreign fields only twenty-seven new missionaries as against an average of eighty-one in each of the three years immediately following the war. The receipts of the Foreign Mission Board of the Southern Baptist Convention fell from $2,404,988

[16] *110th Annual Report of the American Board of Commissioners for Foreign Missions,* p. 254.
[17] *A Century of Protestant Missions in China,* statistical table.
[18] *World Missionary Atlas,* 1925, p. 83. It may be noted that while the staff from the United States had increased about three and a half fold in the sixteen years, that from Canada had multiplied four and a half fold.
[19] C. H. Fahs in *International Review of Missions,* Vol. 16, p. 405.
[20] *Annual Report of the Board of Foreign Missions of the Methodist Episcopal Church for the Year 1920,* pp. 629, 630, 1926, p. 456.
[21] *Chinese Recorder,* Vol. 56, pp. 59, 65, 132.
[22] *The Christian Century,* July 21, 1927, p. 885.

in the year 1920-1921 to $1,556,236 in the year 1924-1925.[23] These were only typical.[24] Not all the boards suffered so severely. Some, indeed, showed a fairly steady increase. The Board of Foreign Missions of the Presbyterian Church in the United States of America (North), for instance, in the five years before the war (1910-1914) had average annual receipts of $2,022,526, in the five years of the war (1915-1919) of $2,480,255, in the four years immediately after the war (1920-1923) of $4,084,516, and in the three years 1924-1926 of $4,685,854.[25] In few if any instances did the *post bellum* income of an American society sink to *ante bellum* levels, but the decrease from the peaks reached after the war and higher prices saddled a number of boards with large debts and in other instances the added income was absorbed by rising costs.

After 1924, the number of those in North America deciding on a missionary career as a life-work suffered a sharp decline.

As to the causes of the decrease in the offering of money and life there was no general agreement. Among those prominently suggested were the increased cost of living, the augmented expenses of local churches, the unified denominational budgets which prevented givers from contributing specifically to foreign missions, a reaction against the high-powered financial "drives" which were the fashion during and just after the war, the multiplicity of appeals for benevolent undertakings, disillusionment and cynicism after the idealism of the war,[26] severe strictures on missions by foreign students in American universities, and criticisms of mission methods by younger church leaders. All these most certainly had a share in the result, but they were of such a nature that, given conviction as to the fundamental importance of missions, recovery could confidently be predicted.

Three other factors, however, were much more serious, for they cut at the very root of the missionary motive. One was the discovery forced home by the war that the West was far from Christian. With this came the conviction that the Occident must become more nearly Christian in its economic life, its race relations, and its international contacts before missionaries could

---

[23] *Annual Reports of the Foreign Mission Board of the Southern Baptist Convention,* 1921, 1925.

[24] F. M. North in *International Review of Missions,* Vol. 15, pp. 93-105.

[25] *89th Annual Report of the Board of Foreign Missions of the Presbyterian Church in the U. S. A.* (1926), p. 290.

[26] C. H. Fahs in *International Review of Missions,* Vol. 16, pp. 405-414.

dare go to other peoples. The Church itself was seen to be far below the standards of Jesus and many earnest Christians lost their zeal for reproducing abroad so imperfect an organization.

A second factor, closely allied to the first, was the belief that other obligations were now much more pressing than that of giving a knowledge of the Christian message to every human being. The idealism of Protestant youth was being less appealed to by the foreign missionary enterprise than in the preceding generation and was attracted by the imperative need of finding some solution for the international, social, and industrial problems of the day.

Accompanying these two factors was a third, still more threatening, a loss of assurance as to the validity of the Gospel and the superiority of Christianity over the other religions of the world. Christians were having to reconcile their faith with the vast flood of new knowledge that was pouring in upon them. Once the other religions were believed to be false and "the heathen in his blindness" to be bowing "down to wood and stone." Better acquaintance with the literature and some of the noblest representatives of the Orient disclosed unsuspected excellencies and Christians wondered whether they had anything at all to offer—whether one religion were not about as good as another. Modern science was disquieting. Was Christianity the truth, or had geology, the evolutionary hypothesis, sociology, and psychology bowed God out of the universe, made religion only a development from primitive "ghost fear," immortality a delusion, the Bible a faulty product of earlier and credulous ages, and Christian ethics obsolete? Some frankly became atheists or agnostics. Many were bewildered and while trying to cling to their earlier convictions did so without enthusiasm. Some attempted so to reframe the statements of their faith as to make them consistent with new discoveries and in doing so often departed widely from the historic creeds. Others, "fundamentalists," branded these attempts as destructive "modernism," maintained that the Bible was infallible, the older creeds final, and such of the scientific "discoveries" as were inconsistent with them false. The crisis was severe, and Protestantism, being less inflexible, was more distraught than was Roman Catholicism. Under these circumstances the Protestant campaign to spread the Christian message naturally suffered.

The Evangelical Movement out of which Protestant missions had arisen was broader than any one denomination and back of it were certain common and fairly definite convictions. As long as these were held, unity on the mission field was possible, for differences were largely over such relative details as polity and modes of baptism. By the end of the nineteenth century, moreover, the older theological battles had largely subsided and extensive coöperation had begun. Now came this new issue. Some great denominations were almost rent in two and their foreign boards spent much time examining charges of "fundamentalists" against "modernist" missionaries. As a rule, bodies with a Calvinistic background were more severely affected than those of Arminian antecedents, but few completely escaped. The controversy was, as we shall see, particularly acute in China and synchronized with other factors which were there distressing Christian missions.

Within less than a decade of the close of the World War, then, Protestant missions were facing at their home base the most disturbing set of problems that had confronted them in the century and a quarter since they had become a major movement, and in China were fighting for their life.

NEW SOCIETIES

Fortunately the new problems did not all come upon Protestantism immediately after the war. A breathing space intervened before the breaking of the storm. Until 1925, indeed, in spite of increasing difficulties, the story of Protestant missions in China is largely a continuation of that which had begun in 1900—of rapid expansion in membership and in all the main phases of the Church's activities. This growth may best be described before we turn to the reverses that all too soon were to bring dismay and to usher in a new era.

A few Christian bodies now for the first time sent representatives to China. The great majority of the larger denominations had long been at work, and these belated arrivals were usually emissaries of minor groups. Two German societies, the Njassabund and the Berlin Union for Medical Missions, had lost their field in German East Africa as the result of the war and turned to South China.[27] The Norwegian Free Baptists entered

---

[27] Richter, *Geschicte der Berlinermissionsgesellschaft*, pp. 591, 592.

in 1918 and the Pittsburgh Bible Institute in 1922 [28]—only to withdraw before 1926.[29] The United Lutheran Church in America, which years before had considered opening a mission in China, purchased the Shantung property of the Berlin Missionary Society and in January, 1925, assumed full control.[30] In 1919 the American-Chinese Educational Commission was organized in the United States, the result of the efforts of Rev. and Mrs. C. A. Nelson. The ultimate aim was to promote independent Chinese action in developing schools, and the immediate purpose was to assist an existing boys' school, Mei Wa, in Canton.[31] In 1922 the Christian Reformed Church, an American body with about fifty thousand members, began work in Kiangsu.[32] In 1920 the Baptist China Direct Mission opened in Shantung what appears to have been its first station.[33] The Krimmer Mennonite Brethren, with headquarters at Hillsboro, Kansas, occupied a section of Inner Mongolia and seem to have sent their first missionaries in 1921.[34] In 1919 the initial contingent of the Missionary Society of Örebro, Sweden, reached China, and two years later the first station, in Shansi, was opened.[35] The Woman's Foreign Missionary Society of the Methodist Protestant group joined in 1919 in the single station of the general society of the denomination, at Kalgan.[36] The Bethel Mission's one center, in Shanghai, dated from 1920.[37] The Christian Mission to Buddhists, an interesting attempt to reach Buddhist monks by methods congenial to their background, was opened in Nanking by K. L. Reichelt, formerly with the Norwegian Missionary Society in Hunan.[38] The Hepzibah Faith Mission, American in origin, penetrated to Chahar about 1922.[39]

[28] Richter, *Das Werden der Christlichen Kirche in China*, p. 299.
[29] *China Christian Year Book, 1926*, p. 151.
[30] Drach, *Forces in Foreign Missions*, p. 111; Speer and Kerr, *Report on China and Japan*, p. 79.
[31] Mary E. Elmore, *The New Idea in Chinese Education*, passim.
[32] *Agendum voor der Christelijke Gereformeerde Kerk*, p. 194.
[33] *Directory of Protestant Missions in China, 1926*, p. 17.
[34] Ibid., p. 21.
[35] Ibid., p. 21.
[36] Ibid., p. 33.
[37] Ibid., p. 115.
[38] Reichelt in *Chinese Recorder*, Vol. 51, pp. 491-497; the same in *China Mission Year Book, 1924*, pp. 73-77. See also O'Neill, *The Quest for God in China*, p. 187, and *Chinese Recorder*, Vol. 54, pp. 639-648. An interesting suggestion for still another type of mission in which Buddhists and Christians might exchange views and so Buddhism be Christianized is contained in Goddard, *A Vision of a Christian and Buddhist Fellowship*.
[39] *Directory of Protestant Missions in China, 1926*, p. 120.

The International Union Mission, another American undertaking, entered China in 1921 or earlier.[40]   An effort to reach the far frontiers, the Tibetan Forward Mission, occupied centers in Kansu in 1923 and 1925.[41]   The Bible Churchmen's Missionary Society, founded in 1922 by the extreme fundamentalist Evangelicals of the Church of England, in 1923 sent its first missionary to China, to Szechwan.   In 1923 it also took over the Nanning Medical Mission in Kwangsi and a little later established in Lungchow in Kwangsi a rescue orphanage for girls.[42]   Groups in several American colleges and universities began to support representatives, usually in educational institutions connected with one or more of the larger boards.[43]   Missionaries, too, continued to come out unattached to any board.[44]   This influx of new societies, interesting though it is, was by no means as important as that which was then occurring in Roman Catholic missions.   It may also be noted that between 1918 and 1925 about ten missions, all of them small, disappeared from China.[45]

EVANGELISM

Between 1918 and 1925 the missionary body increased from 6,395 to 8,158 or about four per cent. a year.[46]   This was only about half the rate of growth that had been registered between 1904 and 1914—partly because of the emphasis on Chinese

[40] *The Messenger* [New York], Vol. 5 (1926), No. 2.

[41] *Directory of Protestant Missions in China, 1926*, p. 135.

[42] Letter of the Honorary Secretary of the Bible Churchmen's Missionary Society, D. H. C. Bartlett, to the author, Jan. 31, 1928; *Bible Churchmen's Missionary Society, Record of a Fourth Year*, 1926.

[43] The graduates of Syracuse University, for example, established a unit at Chungking.—*Chinese Recorder*, Vol. 51, p. 364.   Williams students contributed $800 a year to Lingnan University, and students, faculty, and alumni of Dartmouth contributed $2,000 a year to an elementary school for boys in Paotingfu.— *The New England Intercollegian*, Dec., 1927, p. 3.

[44] Mrs. Howard Taylor reports finding on the Kansu border of Tibet a family, unattached to any board, consisting of a wife and husband and four small children, and living in four rooms.   The wife, in addition to doing most of the housework, was aiding in dispensing medicines and was preaching to the Chinese while her husband specialized on the Tibetans.—Mrs. Taylor, *The Call of China's Great North-West*, p. 144.

[45] S. J. Mills in *China Christian Year Book, 1926*, p. 151.   Those reported as no longer in China were the Angarrack Christian Mission (Japanese), the Baptist Missionary Association, the Christian Faith Mission, the China New Testament Mission, the Grace Evangelical Missions, the Grace Mission, the Hildesheim Mission for the Blind, the Kiel China Mission, the Pittsburgh Bible Institute Mission, the Pentecost Church of the Nazarene.

[46] S. J. Mills in *China Christian Year Book, 1926*, pp. 151-153.   Many of these were home on furlough, so the total number in China in any one year was considerably less—probably a sixth or a seventh—than these figures.

leadership and partly because of the rising costs—but it represented a large number of new missionaries. What employers of labor call the "turn-over" was extensive, for many missionaries spent only a few years in China: indeed, forty-four per cent. of the staff of 1925 had come to the country within the preceding seven years.[47] During this period the stations at which missionaries resided increased from 979 to 1,133,[48] a fairly large geographic expansion. However, they did not multiply as rapidly as the missionary body: proportionately the latter was being concentrated in larger and larger groups. Most of the new centers were opened by societies recently arrived or by older societies in districts for which they had already assumed responsibility. Here and there, however, a board branched out into an entirely new province, as when, about 1921, the Southern Methodists inaugurated a "Siberia-Manchuria mission" with the head station at Harbin.[49] We hear, too, of marked progress on the frontiers—of the baptism of nearly six thousand among the non-Chinese tribes on the Burmo-Chinese border by Baptist missionaries in 1924 and the first month of 1925,[50] of eighteen hundred Miao in Kweichow baptized in three months in 1919 or 1920,[51] of a large increase among the bodies connected with the Assemblies of God in Kansu,[52] of a mass movement among the Miao in Hainan and a rise in the number of Christians on that island of more than a hundred per cent. between 1917 and 1923,[53] and of the rapid expansion of the remarkable pioneer enterprise in Shansi and Shensi under Watts O. Pye of the American Board.[54]

Four-fifths of the missionaries, however, were in the coast provinces and the lower part of the Yangtze Valley, and in the coast provinces were nearly three-fourths of the Protestant church membership and two-thirds of the Chinese staff.[55] It was in these sections, therefore, that most of the extension took place. Until 1922 and even until 1925 progress was fairly steady. Late

[47] Ibid.
[48] Ibid.
[49] *Chinese Recorder*, Vol. 53, p. 215, Vol. 56, p. 200.
[50] Lipphard, *The Second Century of Baptist Missions*, p. 122; Letter from W. M. Young, the missionary in charge, Feb. 18, 1925 (MS.).
[51] *Chinese Recorder*, Vol. 51, p. 363.
[52] Ibid., Vol. 54, p. 57.
[53] Ibid., Vol. 55, p. 475; *China Mission Year Book, 1924*, pp. 230-234.
[54] Address of Watts O. Pye, heard by the author, Feb. 23, 1925; Pye in *Student Volunteer Bulletin*, May, 1925, pp. 10-13.
[55] *The Christian Occupation of China*, pp. 288-293.

in 1921, on the eve of the first outbreak of the Anti-Christian Movement, a well-informed writer declared that friendliness and the spirit of inquiry had replaced the old antagonism toward Christianity.[56] Even in 1923 a greater open-mindedness to the Christian appeal was noted in East China.[57] The examples of growth are numerous but there is space for only a few. The membership of the Young Men's Christian Association increased three hundred and fifty-nine per cent. between 1914 and 1922 and —an interesting detail in light of the later movement against the organization—the student membership lagged only a little behind.[58] Arthur Rugh, of the Student Department of the Association, in 1919 declared the Chinese students to be the "ripest field for evangelism on earth."[59] As late as May, 1921, T. T. Lew, a noted Chinese Christian, looked hopefully upon the New Tide or Renaissance as encouraging the study of Christianity and as preparing the way for the Gospel by sweeping out super-stition.[60] The Conference of the World's Student Christian Federation held just outside Peking in April, 1922, brought dele-gates from all over the Protestant world and especially students from many parts of China.[61] The publicity given it, even by the Anti-Christian Movement, and the teams which after its adjournment visited some of the leading cities, helped to bring Christianity prominently to the attention of the student class.

F. A. Keller wrote of the Biola Evangelistic Bands—named for the Bible Institute of Los Angeles and trained in the Hunan Bible Institute—that in ten years they had grown from one to twelve and were covering parts of three provinces with the proclamation of the Gospel.[62] Governor Yen Hsi-shan, of Shansi, the longest in high office of all the post-revolutionary military leaders, asked for Christian preachers for his troops and for a time contributed

[56] A. L. Warnshuis in *International Review of Missions,* Vol. 11, p. 13.
[57] W. P. Roberts in *China Mission Year Book, 1924,* pp. 100-126.
[58] *Chinese Recorder,* Vol. 55, p. 278. From Oct. 1, 1919, to Oct. 1, 1920, 14 Bible conferences had been held under the Y. M. C. A. with an attendance of 1,092; 11,319 students were enrolled in Bible study and 1,242 baptisms among students were reported.—*World's Student Christian Federation. Reports of Student Christian Movements, Oct. 1, 1919—Sept. 30, 1920,* pp. 14-21. The Y. W. C. A. reported 82 separate student associations with 4,039 members and 10 conferences with 756 in attendance.—Ibid., pp. 22-26.
[59] *China Mission Year Book, 1919,* pp. 140-146.
[60] T. T. Lew in *Chinese Recorder,* Vol. 52, pp. 301-323.
[61] *Chinese Recorder,* Vol. 53, pp. 318-326.
[62] Keller in *Chinese Recorder,* Vol. 55, pp. 568-573; *China Mission Year Book, 1917,* pp. 353-357, *1924,* pp. 175-179.

toward the Independent Chinese Church in T'aiyüanfu.[63] In Suifu, in Szechwan, we hear that a missionary had the friendship of most of the leading men of the city and that one of them had received baptism.[64] The Seventh Day Adventists conducted evangelistic meetings in tents in many centers, even in the Forbidden City in Peking.[65] From Kiukiang, as late as 1925, came the report that Wu Ching-piao, the Commissioner of Defense of Eastern Kiangsi, had been licensed as a local preacher of the Methodist Episcopal Church.[66] The Women's Christian Temperance Union held its first national convention in 1922 and reported sixty-three hundred members in eleven different provinces.[67] The "Week of Evangelism," begun before 1918, continued to be observed by many missions. In at least one large city the Christian community advertised it in a way dear to the heart of the Chinese, by a procession with flags bearing Christian mottoes.[68] The institutional churches numbered seventy in 1923 and in 1922 a national organization was formed for them.[69] Even the German boards showed growth, the Basel Society, while reporting that between 1914 and 1924 the number of missionaries had declined from forty-one to twenty-eight, recorded during the same decade an increase in the Chinese staff, a growth of twenty-five per cent. in the number of Christians, and one of nearly forty per cent. in school enrollment.[70]

In December, 1919, the China Continuation Committee called together a group of Chinese and foreigners to consider the question: "How can the Christian Church best help China?" As a result the "China for Christ Movement" was launched with David Z. T. Yui as chairman. The program was to include, in general, deepening the Christian life of the members of the Church and winning non-Christians to the faith, and, specifically, strengthening religious education in the home, the church, and the school, training Christian leadership, teaching every church member to read, and encouraging every Christian household to maintain family worship. Largely at its instance more than one large city-

[63] Watts O. Pye, conversation with the author, Feb. 23, 1925.
[64] Letter of D. C. Graham from Suifu, July 10, 1920 (MS.).
[65] Lee, Travel Talks in China, p. 16.
[66] Christian Century, Vol. 42, p. 933.
[67] Chinese Recorder, Vol. 54, p. 567.
[68] Ibid., Vol. 51, pp. 18-21, 276-278; China Mission Year Book, 1925, p. 188.
[69] China Mission Year Book, 1924, p. 143.
[70] Oehler, China und die Christliche Mission, p. 263.

wide campaign was held. The Movement was a call to an advance in all phases of church activity and before long was merged—logically—with the older and more representative China Continuation Committee.[71]

One of the most spectacular gains that Christianity had ever made in China, the large body of converts in the army of one of the major military leaders, Fêng Yü-hsiang, falls largely in these years. Fêng was born in Anhui in 1880 and when a flood reduced his family to penury, at the age of eighteen he enlisted in the army as a private. Several times he came in contact with Christians, notably when in 1900 at Paotingfu he saw Miss Morrill, before her martyrdom, offer her life to the Boxers if others would be spared. It was in 1913, when he had risen to the rank of major, that at one of Mott's meetings in Peking he made a profession of Christian faith. He was later baptized in the Methodist Episcopal Church. A forthright man of towering physique and great energy, he gave himself wholeheartedly to his new faith as he understood it. His contingent soon became known for its discipline and for the absence of the ordinary camp vices. Gambling and prostitution were forbidden, and his men were taught to read and write and were instructed in useful trades, that they might know how to make their living after returning to civil life. Schools were established, too, for the wives of the officers. He encouraged missionaries to preach to his troops, Goforth especially spending much time among them. Gailey, of the Young Men's Christian Association, became a trusted friend. Fêng rose rapidly in rank and influence and by 1922 was a national figure. Until about 1926, however, his zeal did not slacken. Thousands of his troops received baptism. Many of his officers were professing Christians and one of them, General Chang Chih-chiang, at one time wished to resign his command to organize a band of evangelists to go up and down the country preaching. In the army hymns were sung and grace was said before meals, and a daily religious meeting with Bible reading, prayer, and hymns was usual. Fêng himself often preached to his soldiers and is reported repeatedly to have confessed his sins publicly and with tears and to have encouraged his soldiers to do likewise. In 1925 he opened a school for the training of chaplains

[71] *Chinese Recorder*, Vol. 51, pp. 3-6, 420-421, Vol. 52, pp. 218, 654; *China Mission Year Book, 1919*, p. 59; *Millard's Review*, Vol. 11, p. 175; *West China Missionary News*, Vol. 22. No. 9.

for his army, having worked out a plan for the regular spiritual supervision of his troops.

Naturally Fêng was subjected to much criticism. In the foreign press he was usually dubbed the "so-called Christian general." His desertion of his superior, Wu P'ei-fu, in 1924, brought him much opprobrium, and his later connection with Russia was heralded as a conversion to Communism. After his visit to Russia, in 1926, his enthusiasm for Christianity cooled perceptibly, and by 1928 he hàd ceased to be aggressive in spreading the Faith and his troops were occupying mission buildings. Some of his officers, however, continued to be very pronounced Christians. It is too soon to pass final judgment upon him, but this much seems to be clear; for years he was intensely in earnest and thoroughly sincere. Among many other evidences was his adherence to monogamy and his rejection, upon the death of his first wife, of the thought of possible marriage alliances with some of his great military rivals, and his choice of a former secretary of the Young Women's Christian Association. The clue to many of his actions seems to lie in his intense nationalism. He appears to have longed for the unity, prestige, and peace of his country: to this end he trained his troops, for this purpose he espoused the program of Sun Yat-sen and called his forces the *Kuominchun,* "the National People's Army," and joined in the chorus demanding the abrogation of the "unequal" treaties. His patriotism undoubtedly colored his attitude toward Christianity. He probably looked upon the Gospel in part as a means of rescuing China from her ills: it may, indeed, have been that feature of Mott's appeal which finally won him. His public confessions of sin had as their point that his transgressions and those of his soldiers were hindering the welfare of his country, a characteristic Chinese conception. As the wave of nationalism took an anti-foreign turn, he sought to create in his army a purely Chinese Church, untrammeled by missionary advice or control. His beliefs were inevitably modified by his Chinese and military background. He prayed for rain. He prayed, too, for victory for his troops and would have had no comprehension of the ultra-pacificism which became fashionable in some liberal Protestant missionary circles after the World War. It may have been the failure of Christianity to achieve what he expected of it—constant victory for himself and the early unification of the country—which cooled his ardor.

Compared with the religion of the T'ai P'ings, his faith and that of his soldiers much more nearly approximated to the standards of the New Testament. Imperfect it doubtless was: he was not inaptly called an Old Testament Christian. He himself, however, and his army were evidence that Christianity was beginning to make itself felt, and felt profoundly, outside the circles in which missionaries were in control.[72]

The methods of approaching the Chinese with the Christian message did not greatly change. The street chapel was falling into disuse,[73] but itineration from village to village was still in vogue,[74] preaching in the streets was not unknown,[75] and many others of the means of earlier years continued to be employed. We hear more of "conferences" than formerly,[76] as was natural of an agency much esteemed in Great Britain and America. The great centers where missionaries congregated for the summers became favorite places for such meetings, both for foreigners and for Chinese. The custom grew of bringing each year distinguished preachers from the West to address the missionaries in their summer assemblies.[77] The word "retreat" now figured largely in the missionary vocabulary, as a designation for small gatherings which were not so much for a direct presentation of the Gospel as for an interchange of views, sometimes between Christians and non-Christians,[78] but more frequently between Christians. The teaching of the phonetic script, begun a few years before, was sometimes made a means of approach to non-Christians.[79] One missionary used to such good effect a special campaign for teaching the illiterate to read that three hundred enrolled as enquirers.[80]

The rate of growth of the Protestant community between 1918 and 1927 is not known, for between 1922 and 1927 there was no

---

[72] For material on Fêng Yü-hsiang and his army, see G. G. Warren in *China Mission Year Book, 1919,* pp. 281-286; *Millard's Review,* Sept. 20, 1919, p. 108; *Chinese Recorder,* Vol. 54, pp. 334-338, Vol. 57, p. 606; Broomhall, *General Fêng,* passim; Davis, *China's Christian Army,* passim; letter from Fêng's Chaplain-General, Nov. 4, 1925, in *The North-China Herald,* Dec. 19, 1925, p. 510; Address by Fêng in ibid., Dec. 12, 1925, p. 470; *Address Delivered by Fêng Yü-hsiang to the North China Union Language School, Peking, China, Feb. 27, 1923; The Christian Century,* Vol. 42, p. 1384.

[73] *Chinese Recorder,* Vol. 52, pp. 593-599.

[74] Ibid., Vol. 53, pp. 586-592, Vol. 56, pp. 147-152.

[75] Ibid., Vol. 52, pp. 386-397.

[76] Ibid., Vol. 54, p. 303.

[77] Ibid., Vol. 52, pp. 774-777, Vol. 55, pp. 671-674.

[78] Ibid., Vol. 51, p. 362.

[79] Keyte, *In China Now,* p. 73.

[80] *Chinese Recorder,* Vol. 55, pp. 769-774.

serious attempt to gather the figures for all China. The number of communicants rose from 312,970, in 1917 to 366,527 in 1920 [81] and to 402,539 in 1922.[82] That of the baptized non-communicants is uncertain. As reported, it sank a little between 1917 and 1920, from 85,790 to 85,140, so that the total of baptized Christians was about 398,760 in 1917 and 471,664 in 1920; [83] but another set of figures gives the total of baptized non-communicants in 1922 as 133,678 and the total number of baptized Protestants as 536,597.[84] Adding those under Christian instruction—234,448 in 1917 and 313,254 in 1920—the total Protestant Christian community was estimated at 654,658 in the former year and 806,926 in the latter.[85] The growth probably slowed down in 1925 and 1926. Indeed, in spite of accessions of 3,657 on confession of faith, the Northern Presbyterian missions reported a net decline of 2,028 in 1926, or from 50,005 to 47,977,[86] and what was true of this old and well-established communion may well have been true of others.

EDUCATION

Education continued to rank as one of the major activities of Protestant missions, and, if possible, was even more emphasized than formerly. While sixty per cent. of the men and forty per cent. of the women who were members of Protestant churches were sufficiently literate to read the New Testament in the vernacular with some degree of fluency,[87] a much higher proportion than in the nation at large and a noteworthy achievement, some missions continued to press for a program which would include teaching every church member to read and enroll in school every Christian child of suitable age. The Northern Methodists, for example, had that as part of their Centenary objective,[88] and their plans also included the coördination of their schools into one system under a China Educational Council of their own.[89]

[81] *The Christian Occupation of China*, p. xci.
[82] *World Missionary Atlas* (1925), p. 77.
[83] *The Christian Occupation of China*, p. xci.
[84] *World Missionary Atlas* (1925), p. 77.
[85] *The Christian Occupation of China*, p. xci.
[86] Speer and Kerr, *Report on Japan and China, 1927*, pp. 293, 328, 466.
[87] *The Christian Occupation of China*, p. 294. In the American Board district in Peking only 16 per cent. of the church group over ten years of age could not read, 15 per cent. had a middle school training, and 6 per cent. had attended some higher school.—Gamble, *Peking, A Social Survey*, p. 359.
[88] E. James in *Chinese Recorder*, Vol. 54, pp. 30-32.
[89] Hutchinson, *China's Challenge and the Methodist Reply*, p. 44.

Americans especially, as we have repeatedly seen, stressed education.[90] It is not surprising that, since the great growth after 1918 was in American missions, the enrollment in schools should jump by one-fourth between 1917 and 1920.[91] In connection with one city church, probably not at all exceptional, there were reported a night school for clerks and apprentices, a free night school for younger boys, a free afternoon school for girls in domestic service, boys' and girls' boarding schools, a primary day school, and a kindergarten.[92]

Many devices were employed to reduce illiteracy. The National Phonetic Script was widely used in Mandarin-speaking districts,[93] and the Phonetic Promotion Committee of the National Christian Council had as a motto: "Every Christian a Bible reader and every Christian a teacher of illiterates."[94] A Chinese member of the faculty of the Baptist seminary at Swatow worked out an adaptation of the system for the Swatow dialects[95] and a member of the Presbyterian mission in Hainan invented a script, partly of phonetic signs and partly of simple characters, which, in modified forms, would serve for several of the dialects not only on the island but in other parts of China.[96]

The most spectacular effort to teach illiterates was what came to be known as the Mass Education Movement. While a student in the United States, Y. C. James Yen volunteered to aid the Young Men's Christian Association among the Chinese laborers in France. In connection with his work there he compiled a list of the one thousand characters most commonly used in Mandarin, the language of his charges. By a series of lessons based upon these he began, with encouraging success, to teach the coolies to read. After the war Yen returned to China and there, still in connection with the Young Men's Christian Association, introduced the same method. His plan was to go to a city or a rural district, win the endorsement of some of the leading men, enlist

[90] In 1920, of those in mission schools, one-half of the lower primary pupils, two-thirds of the higher primary pupils, and over two-thirds of the middle school students were in institutions connected with American missions.—*The Christian Occupation of China*, p. 37.

[91] *The Christian Occupation of China*, p. xcvi.

[92] *Chinese Recorder*, Vol. 51, pp. 142, 143.

[93] Ibid., Vol. 51, pp. 517, 639-641, 856-858, Vol. 55, pp. 201, 270.

[94] C. Y. Cheng (Ch'êng Ching-i) in *China Today Through Chinese Eyes*, p. 131.

[95] Ashmore, *The South China Mission of the A. B. F. M. S.*, p. 92.

[96] *Chinese Recorder*, Vol. 54, p. 301. It is not clear that this was done after 1918.

as teachers a large number of the educated, especially students, and during an intensive campaign of several weeks enroll and instruct as many illiterates as possible. In the first city campaign, in Changsha in 1922, over one thousand were graduated, and the program was repeated so successfully in several other cities that in 1923 a National Popular Educational Association was formed, with many local committees, and others besides the Christian forces were drawn into it.[97]

Another innovation was the Daily Vacation Bible School. This institution was American in origin and had for its object recreation and religious instruction of children while the regular schools were not in session. It appears to have been introduced into China in 1918, enrolling in that year about seven hundred children. The method appealed to mission school students as a means of spending their summers in useful employment, and in 1923 over one thousand schools were reported, with more than five thousand teachers, and with fifty-five thousand pupils.[98]

"Religious education," another subject which was receiving much attention in the United States and which characteristic American enthusiasm was at times exaggerating into a fad, was inevitably discussed in China. Progress in it was declared to be decidedly unsatisfactory,[99] but here and there existing organizations were giving heed to it [100] and in 1924 the National Christian Council called a special conference on the subject.[101]

Higher education came in for much emphasis, for it was largely American money that was financing the new expansion of missions and, as we have often seen, Americans were inclined to devote a large part of their energies to institutions of this grade. No new colleges were founded, but existing ones were strengthened and many of them were given new buildings and even entirely new plants. In 1922 Fukien University moved to a commanding site on the Min River below Foochow and began the erection of permanent buildings.[102] In 1920 a campaign—one of the many

---

[97] Yen, *The Mass Education Movement in China*, passim; Yen in *China Mission Year Book, 1923*, pp. 205-215, *1924*, pp. 309-317; *Chinese Recorder*, Vol. 51, pp. 44-49, Vol. 54, pp. 596-600, Vol. 55, p. 613.

[98] *Chinese Recorder*, Vol. 51, p. 587, Vol. 55, p. 201, Vol. 56, p. 691; *China Mission Year Book, 1924*, p. 189.

[99] *China Mission Year Book, 1924*, pp. 278-282.

[100] *Christian Education in China*, sections 459-497; *Educational Review*, Vol. 17, pp. 29-32.

[101] *Educational Review*, Vol. 17, pp. 63-67.

[102] Beach and Ford in Anti-Cobweb Club, *Fukien*, p. 87.

post bellum money-raising undertakings—was begun in the United States for three million dollars for women's colleges in the Orient and in three years the fund was pledged. Ginling and Yenching and the Women's Medical College at Peking were the Chinese beneficiaries,[103] and new physical equipment followed. Yenching, the name now given to the Christian university in Peking, both men's and women's departments, acquired a new campus not far from the Summer Palace and, after a successful effort to raise money in the United States, began the construction of a new set of buildings. Canton Christian College received contributions to its faculty from at least three mission boards and added largely to its extensive plant.[104] New buildings, too, were rising at Tsinanfu for the Shantung Christian University, and St. John's celebrated its fortieth anniversary with the dedication of a gymnasium.[105] Most of the new structures of the Christian colleges were ingenious and beautiful combinations of Chinese style and Western convenience and solidity.

The Church of Sweden Mission, only recently arrived, decided to specialize on education and to lend its strength to the existing Lutheran college just outside of Yiyang in Hunan.[106] Concessions were made to the new tendencies in China when coëducation was introduced in Shanghai College and in the College of Yale in China.

Even more marked than the physical expansion was the growth in the attendance at Christian colleges. The total enrollment of students in Protestant institutions of college grade in 1924 was 3,901—of whom 3,450 were men and 451 women—as against 1,929 in 1920 and 267 in 1910.[107] In the four years between 1920 and 1924, in other words, the enrollment of college students in Protestant schools had doubled, a much more rapid rate of increase than in any other major phase of Protestant activity. About one-ninth of the college students of all China were in these mission institutions.[108] It is no wonder that Protestant schools attracted the attention and the envy of non-Christians.

[103] Mrs. Thurston, President of Ginling, in *China Mission Year Book, 1924*, pp. 307, 308.
[104] *Canton Christian College, 1919-1924, report of the President.*
[105] *Millard's Review*, Nov. 22, 1919, p. 488.
[106] *Chinese Recorder*, Vol. 55, p. 414.
[107] *Statistical Report of Christian Colleges and Universities in China, 1924* (*China Christian Education Association Bulletin* No. 8, 1925).
[108] *Bulletins on Chinese Education*, 1923, Statistical Summaries, p. 11.

Professional and technical education was also expanding. In 1918 the Union Normal School in Canton graduated its first class,[109] and in 1920 the Young Women's Christian Association dedicated the buildings of its National Normal School of Hygiene and Physical Education.[110] In Changsha both the Hunan Union Theological Seminary and the Hunan Bible Institute erected new plants.[111] Most of the theological education was still of a fairly elementary type, for the larger part remained in the hands of schools which required for entrance merely a primary education. Institutions of higher grade usually insisted upon a middle school preparation and three had as a prerequisite a full college course.[112] A new type of undertaking was an extensive "field trip" of students of the Nanking Theological Seminary in the summer vacation of 1926, in which, under the direction of Frank W. Price, a member of the faculty, practical instruction was given in meeting the rural problems of the Church.[113]

The buildings of the Peking Union Medical College were formally opened in September, 1921, in the presence of John D. Rockefeller, Jr.[114] As had been expected, one of the early effects of the institution and of the China Medical Board was to raise the standards of medical education throughout the country. Because of the cost of meeting these standards missions were usually discouraged from undertaking more schools, but in 1924 Dr. Main opened in Hangchow a new building for the instruction he maintained in connection with his great hospital under the Church Missionary Society.[115]

Agricultural education, which had been barely begun when the World War broke out, rapidly rose to prominence. Under its energetic Dean, John H. Reisner, the oldest school, the College of Agriculture and Forestry of the University of Nanking, expanded rapidly in 1925-1926, counting one hundred and ten students in its full college course as against sixty-seven two years

[109] Davis, Neighbors in Christ, p. 96.
[110] Chinese Recorder. Vol. 51, p. 145.
[111] Ibid., Vol. 56, p. 270.
[112] Leger, Education of Christian Ministers in China, pp. 41, 67; The Christian Occupation of China, pp. 414-418.
[113] F. W. Price, A Glimpse at Rural Needs and the Rural Church in China, passim.
[114] Chinese Recorder, Vol. 52, pp. 771-774; China Mission Year Book, 1919, pp. 184-189.
[115] Chinese Recorder, Vol. 55, p. 754.

before, and nearly a hundred in special courses.[116] It undertook many activities, among the chief being the improvement of cotton under a special subsidy from the Cotton Mill Owners' Association of China and the Shanghai Anti-Adulteration Association,[117] the improvement of seed wheat, conferences for Christian rural leaders and on agricultural education, the study of rinderpest and millet smut, the cultivation and distribution of disease-free silk-worm eggs, the stimulation of a national Arbor Day on which school children were encouraged to plant trees, and the organization and supervision of a coöperative credit and marketing society for farmers.[118] Agricultural schools were formed in connection with Canton Christian College and Yenching University [119] and a few middle and primary schools gave some instruction in the subject.[120] By 1925 some of the theological seminaries had organized rural work departments, the American Board had begun a rural training center at Kaifeng, the Central Teachers' College at Wuchang was requiring of its students courses in agriculture,[121] and at Changli, in Chihli, an agricultural department with extension work was opened in October, 1922, in connection with a Methodist middle school.[122] A great impetus was given to the colleges at Nanking and Peking when in 1923 the China Famine Fund assigned from its unexpended balance $675,000 to the former and $225,000 to the latter for the study of the causes of famine and the education of the Chinese in agriculture and forestry.[123]

Missionaries frequently wondered whether a disproportionate amount of money and men was not going into higher education. Since a large part of the running expenses came from the Chinese

[116] *Eleventh Annual Report of the College of Agriculture and Forestry and Experiment Station, University of Nanking.*
[117] *University of Nanking Agriculture and Forestry Series,* Vol. 1, No. 6.
[118] *Agriculture and Forestry Notes, University of Nanking, College of Agriculture and Forestry, Nanking, China,* edited by John H. Reisner, Dean, passim; Reisner in *China Mission Year Book, 1919,* pp. 158-172; *Chinese Recorder,* Vol. 55, p. 274.
[119] *Christian Education in China,* Section 342.
[120] *The Christian Occupation of China,* p. 421. An agricultural teaching station was reported at Shaowu, in Fukien, under the American Board (*Chinese Recorder,* Vol. 52, p. 581) and a class in agriculture was held for landowners by the Presbyterians at Nanhsuchow (ibid., Vol. 51, pp. 412-418).
[121] Reisner in *China Mission Year Book, 1925,* pp. 90-93.
[122] *Annual Report of the Board of Foreign Missions of the Methodist Episcopal Church,* 1923, p. 107, 1924, p. 56, 1925, pp. 83, 84.
[123] *Agriculture and Forestry Notes, University of Nanking,* etc., No. 2.

in fees, the load was not as heavy as might first appear,[124] but it was burdensome enough.

Protestant education was assuming such proportions and costs were mounting so rapidly that more coöperation was necessary, from the standpoint both of efficiency and economy. Most of the existing coördinating agencies expanded their activities. For example, the China Educational Association had a staff which included such men as F. D. Gamewell, who first came to China in 1881 and had been prominent in Methodist circles, E. C. Lobenstine, of the China Continuation Committee, and E. W. Wallace, who had achieved distinction in furthering educational coöperation in West China. Among its many activities was the publication of a series of bulletins on various phases of the educational problem.[125]   Under an energetic secretary, E. H. Cressey, the East China Christian Educational Association was studying its field and was improving methods and textbooks.[126] New bodies came into existence—the Association of Christian Colleges and Universities in 1919 [127] and a Council on Primary and Secondary Education.[128]

Much of the impetus for increased coöperation came from the China Educational Commission of 1921 and 1922. The China Christian Educational Association, the China Continuation Committee, the Committee 'of Reference and Counsel of the Foreign Missions Conference of North America, and the Conference of Foreign Mission Societies in Great Britain and Ireland appointed a Commission of sixteen educators, foreign and Chinese, headed by Professor, later President, E. D. Burton of the University of Chicago, to make a thorough study of Protestant education in China and to formulate recommendations for future development. The Commission spent between five and six months in visiting

[124] On the organization of mission colleges, see R. D. Wellons, *The Organization set up for the Control of Mission Union Higher Educational Institutions*, New York, 1927.
[125] These bulletins included *Criteria of a Standard College, College and University Finance, The Place of Private Schools in a National System of Education, A School Health Program, Tentative Standards in Christian Middle Schools, Bibliography of Text-Books for the Primary School, Costs of Higher Christian Education*, and a *Program of Worship in Schools and Colleges*.
[126] See a summary of its activities in *The Bulletin of the East China Christian Educational Association*, No. 28, Nov. 27, 1926.
[127] *Chinese Recorder*, Vol. 54, pp. 341-343, Vol. 55, pp. 182-185; *China Mission Year Book, 1919*, pp. 146-150; *Bulletin of the National Christian Council*, March, 1926, pp. 19, 20.
[128] *Chinese Recorder*, Vol. 56, p. 339.

most of the chief centers of China and in framing its report. The immediate result was the most careful investigation of the problem that had yet been made. The report defined the purpose and scope of Christian education; recommended that the participation of Chinese inteaching and administration be rapidly augmented, suggested the establishment of an Institute of Educational Research and an Institute of Economic and Social Research to investigate China's needs and the ways in which Christian education might help to meet them; and urged coöperation with the Chinese Government. The Commission was especially of the conviction that since Christian agencies could not hope to provide more than a small proportion of the schools needed by the Chinese, such institutions as were maintained should be of the best possible quality. It found, too, that missions were attempting more than their resources warranted, particularly in higher education. It was of the firm opinion that the entire body of Christian —meaning Protestant—schools in China should be coördinated into a system in which all societies would coöperate and that to this end primary education should be organized by provinces and by regions—a suggested map being submitted. Certain existing colleges and universities were encouraged to combine to form stronger institutions. More adequate supervision for the training of teachers and the introduction into middle schools of more occupational courses were stressed, and the foundation of professional schools for literature, commerce, and social science was recommended.[129]

The Commission and its report provoked much discussion and were not without results. Some existing institutions were reluctant to surrender their separate existence and denominational particularism did not easily die, but the beginning of a Central China University was made at Wuchang on the Boone campus, new life was injected into such agencies as the China Christian Educational Association, and as never before Protestants were brought to think of their educational task as one. An unexpected effect was upon non-Christian Chinese. As we have seen in a preceding chapter, the report attracted the attention of government educators to this system of schools—often better equipped and more efficient than anything else in a community—independ-

---

[129] *Christian Education in China. The Report of the China Educational Commission of 1921-1922.*

ent of the Chinese state and largely under foreign control. The intense nationalism of the day witnessed this development with a fear which was not unmixed with envy and before many years came the attempt to bring mission institutions under strict governmental supervision and to reduce to a minimum their foreign and religious character. The attempt would probably have been made had the Commission never existed, but the report gave it added stimulus.

LITERATURE

The great growth in education was not paralleled by a corresponding expansion in literature. The circulation of the Scriptures increased, to be sure. In 1921 the three Bible societies distributed 6,821,880 Bibles, Testaments, and single books of the Bible, a record-breaking total.[130] This was surpassed in 1923, and in 1924—in spite and perhaps because of the Anti-Christian Movement—all records were again eclipsed by a circulation of 9,488,260.[131] Christian periodicals were improving, especially interesting being a new paper, *The Life,* under purely Chinese auspices, whose purpose it was to present the Christian viewpoint to the student class which was being appealed to by so many conflicting philosophies.[132] Yenching University, too, looked forward to a school of journalism to help train Christians to influence wholesomely the new press.[133] However, most of the material on the shelves of the tract and literature societies was antiquated, and, in a day when the Chinese were inquiring and reading more avidly than ever before, there was a dearth of up-to-date books to appeal to their changing tastes. Missionaries were writing little of interest and as yet Chinese Christians had produced even less.[134] A great door of opportunity stood open, but unentered.

MEDICAL WORK

The coming of the China Medical Board was expected to stimulate marked growth in the medical side of Protestant missionary activity. In the field of education this hope was, as we have seen, fulfilled. Aside from that, however, the immediate effect was not marked. Even the large funds at the disposal of

---

[130] *China Mission Year Book, 1923,* p. 116.
[131] *China Mission Year Book, 1925,* pp. 369-373.
[132] D. M. McGillivray in *Chinese Recorder,* Vol. 53, pp. 525-529.
[133] *Chinese Recorder,* Vol. 56, p. 294.
[134] Ibid., May number, 1925, is largely given over to this topic.

the Board could not go far in so huge a country and the cost of building and maintaining the Peking Union Medical College was so great that not as many mission hospitals could be assisted as was at first planned.[135] Moreover, complaints began to be made that the Chinese physicians trained in the better medical schools now available were not as willing to serve in mission hospitals as their predecessors had been. Many of these hospitals were poorly equipped [136] and were unable to pay more than small salaries. They could not compete with the lure of the great port cities, where life was easier, facilities better, and Western medicine was beginning to prove popular and lucrative.[137] Some years were required, moreover, to recoup the medical missionary staff from the losses suffered through the World War.[138]

Progress was not entirely lacking, however. Some new hospitals were opened,[139] and a national mission to the lepers, with Chinese officers, was organized as the result of a visit of William M. Danner, the secretary of the International Mission to Lepers.[140] To unify all medical work in China, regardless of race or creed, in 1925 the China Medical Missionary Association, at its own request, was absorbed by the China Medical Association, and a division of the latter body was formed to take over the functions of the old organization.[141]

Outside the efforts of the China Medical Board the most spectacular progress was probably in the promotion of public health. The Council on Health Education, which had arisen out of the work of Dr. W. W. Peter of the Young Men's Christian Association, focused and stimulated an interest which, because of the current attention to the subject in the West, and particularly in the United States, was widespread in some missionary circles. In 1920 a city-wide campaign to prevent cholera was conducted in Foochow, with the result that the severe epidemic of the preceding year did not recur. The promotion of vaccination against small-

[135] Ibid., Vol. 51, p. 66.
[136] Dr. Balme in 1919-1920 discovered that most mission hospitals were poorly equipped, a third having no nurses, two-thirds no isolation block, a third no protection against flies or mosquitoes, two-thirds no screening in their kitchens or for their latrines, and half seldom or never bathing their patients.— *The Christian Occupation of China*, pp. 429-433.
[137] *Chinese Recorder*, Vol. 56, p. 6.
[138] *The Christian Occupation of China*, pp. xcviii-ci.
[139] *Chinese Recorder*, Vol. 55, p. 617; *China's Millions*, 1919, p. 55.
[140] *Chinese Recorder*, Vol. 58, p. 257.
[141] *China Mission Year Book*, 1925, pp. 301, 302.

pox, education in the prevention of tuberculosis, and the virtues of sunshine, soap, and water were stressed by lectures, posters, and lantern slides.[142] A reduction in the death rate without a corresponding diminution in the birth rate, if at all general, would bring fresh problems to China's overcrowded provinces, but the Christian physician could not be true to the standards of his profession if he callously neglected suffering which his skill could prevent.

An interesting illustration of the attitude of some of the missionary body toward medicine was the wide attention paid to the "healing mission" of James Moore Hickson, an earnest, devout English layman who toured China in 1921 and who used no other therapeutics than prayer and the laying on of hands.[143]

RELIEF AND SOCIAL REFORM

The World War increased the efforts of Anglo-Saxon Protestantism to remove the social evils that afflict the race. This attitude, so in accord with the best of Chinese ideals, was quickly reflected in missionary programs. The Northern Methodists, in the statement of their Centenary plans, voiced a conviction shared by many outside their ranks when they declared: "The church has emphasized evangelism through preaching. She must now emphasize evangelism through service. Not that there should be less preaching, but vastly more service." [144]

The old activities for ameliorating social and moral conditions were continued. Famine relief engaged the attention of many missionaries. The attempt to mitigate the intense suffering following the severe drought in North China in 1920 and 1921 was much of it their work: they were in charge of a large part of the distribution of relief, including the supervision of the building of roads by refugees, and their boards assisted in the collection and forwarding of funds.[145] At the time of the great earthquake in Kansu and Shensi they administered much of the foreign aid [146] and in 1924 they assisted in relieving destitution

[142] Peter, *Broadcasting Health in China*, passim; *Chinese Recorder*, Vol. 51, p. 588, Vol. 54, p. 244, Vol. 56, pp. 421-424.
[143] *Chinese Recorder*, Vol. 52, pp. 576-578.
[144] Hutchinson, *China's Challenge and the Methodist Reply*, p. 23.
[145] *Report of the China Famine Relief*, passim; *China Mission Year Book, 1923*, pp. 242-256; *Chinese Recorder*, Vol. 51, p. 806, Vol. 52, pp. 219, 580, 727, Vol. 55, pp. 589-591; *Millard's Review*, Feb. 26, 1921, p. 736.
[146] Mrs. Taylor, *The Call of China's Great Northwest*, p. 46.

from floods in Hunan, Kiangsi and Chihli.[147] Protestants, too, were carrying on an unremitting warfare against opium, the production and use of which had largely increased under many of the military chieftains.[148] Some missionaries were fighting the cigarette which, partly through the stimulus of the omnipresent British and American Tobacco Company, was coming into almost universal use.[149] Other enterprises of somewhat newer form were undertaken. As we have seen, institutional churches, "the church at work enlisting the support of the community in Christianizing the community life," increased in number.[150] The Church Federation Council of Hangchow attempted to obtain the discontinuance of lotteries in Chêkiang.[151] In Canton, under the local Christian Council, campaigns against gambling, prostitution, girl slavery, concubinage, and salacious literature were launched.[152] In 1919 a Fukien Moral Welfare Association was organized to oppose gambling and lotteries, and in Shanghai missionaries served on a Moral Welfare League which attempted the difficult and thankless task of eliminating brothels from the International Settlement.[153] A sub-committee of the China Continuation Committee issued an appeal against the reported plan of the American brewers to invade China after the Eighteenth Amendment had—supposedly—driven them out of the United States.[154] The antiwar agitation, because of the recent world catastrophe widespread in Anglo-Saxon Protestantism, aroused echoes in China. The Church was so small, civil strife so widespread, and the feeling against the "unequal treaties" so intense that little could be done toward the prevention of war as a whole.[155] As we shall see

[147] *China Mission Year Book, 1925*, pp. 363-368.
[148] Ibid., *1925*, pp. 330-344; *China Christian Year Book, 1926*, pp. 326-338; *The World Call of the Church, The Call of the Far East*, pp. 28, 29; *Chinese Recorder*, Vol. 56, pp. 45 et seq.; Gamewell, *New Life Currents in China*, pp. 100, 101. The National Christian Council formed an Anti-Narcotic Commission in 1923.—*Chinese Recorder*, Vol. 55, p. 174.
[149] Tinling, *Bits of China*, p. 16.
[150] *Chinese Recorder*, Vol. 51, p. 73; *The Christian Occupation of China*, pp. 379, 380.
[151] *Chinese Recorder*, Vol. 52, p. 439.
[152] *Chinese Recorder*, Vol. 53, pp. 341-344; *China Mission Year Book, 1923*, pp. 236-241.
[153] *China Mission Year Book, 1923*, pp. 236-241; Munson and Neely in Anti-Cobweb Club, *Fukien*, p. 96.
[154] *China Mission Year Book, 1919*, p. 190-195.
[155] Wieger, *Chine moderne*, Vol. 3, pp. 18-20; *Chinese Recorder*, Vol. 56, pp. 361-365, 407.

more fully later, such energy as Chinese Christians had for international affairs—and it proved to be surprisingly great—was directed toward assisting the nationalist protest against the position of the powers in China. Missionaries also were more and more engrossed in the same problem. In seeking to find a way through the particular international situation that confronted them, however, Protestants, both Chinese and foreign, were driven to consider what the Christian attitude should be toward the use of force in any and all relations between nations.

The coming of the Industrial Revolution to China, a movement accelerated during and after the World War, brought with it deplorable labor conditions which attracted the attention of many missionaries. Workers in the factories were probably no worse and in many instances better off than were hundreds of thousands of their fellows under the handicraft system. The factories, however, were new, they were concentrated in a few cities, and the evils which accompanied them were more noticeable than were those of the old economic order. Then, too, the Industrial Revolution was Occidental in origin and missionaries felt a certain responsibility to see that this importation from their native lands should be helpful rather than harmful. Conditions in many factories were bad enough—long hours, low wages, little or no ventilation, no protection against dangerous machinery, and the exploitation of children and adults. Numbers of attempts were made to deal with these evils. Under its Christian management the Commercial Press maintained a nine-hour day, one day of rest in seven, a savings department for its employees, and schools for children.[156] At least one former student in a mission school, on becoming manager of a cotton mill, sought to apply what he had heard in the college chapel by providing recreation and education for his workmen and in other ways seeking to make their lives more nearly wholesome.[157] In 1919 the social service section of the Federation of Women's Boards of Foreign Missions sent an industrial specialist to China and the following January at a conference of foreign and Chinese women in Shanghai a commission on social service recommended that the churches employ specialists on children and women in industry.[158] In May

[156] *Chinese Recorder*, Vol. 51, p. 217.
[157] Hart, *Education in China*, p. 15.
[158] Porter, *China's Challenge to Christianity*, p. 58; *China Mission Year Book, 1923*, pp. 225-235.

of that year (1921) an expert of this kind, Miss Agatha Harrison, was brought to China by the Young Women's Christian Association.[159] In 1922 the National Christian Conference put Protestants on record as opposing child labor and as advocating one day of rest in seven and provision for the health and safety of workers.[160] In the succeeding months the National Christian Council, charged with carrying out the will of the Conference, sought in a number of centers to have these standards put into practice, and in 1927 conducted in Shanghai a Conference on Christianizing economic relations.[161] The best immediate results were in Chefoo, where Chinese Christian managers and employers controlling several thousand laborers decided to put the recommendations into effect.[162] In Shanghai, partly through the persistence of the Young Women's Christian Association, regulations for the employment of children were drawn up by a commission and presented to the ratepayers of the International Settlement.[163] While they failed of adoption, they brought the problem to the attention of the city. The Young Men's Christian Association also sought to alleviate the lot of the workers.[164] In Shanghai it provided athletic directors, teachers, medical attention, lecturers, and entertainments,[165] and replaced a section of squalid huts by a model village.

The National Christian Conference gave consideration to rural conditions. China was primarily a nation of farmers, and three-fourths of the Chinese Protestants were in country churches.[166] Prior to 1922 scant study had been made of the possibility of improving the farming communities, but beginning with that year much attention was devoted to the problem.[167] Conferences were held in various places, the College of Agriculture and For-

[159] *Chinese Recorder*, Vol. 52, p. 438.
[160] *The Chinese Church, The National Christian Council, 1922*, p. 691.
[161] *Chinese Recorder*, Vol. 54, pp. 56, 60, 179; *Report of a Conference on Christianizing Economic Relations held under the auspices of the National Christian Council of China, Shanghai, August 18-28, 1927*, passim.
[162] *Chinese Recorder*, Vol. 54, p. 127; Tinling, *Memories of the Mission Field*, p. 94.
[163] *Threads, The Story of the Industrial Work of the Y. W. C. A. in China, 1925*, passim; *China Mission Year Book, 1925*, pp. 345-348; Anderson, *Humanity and Labour in China*, passim.
[164] *Chinese Recorder*, Vol. 57, p. 527.
[165] Ibid., Vol. 58, pp. 250, 251; Vera Kelsey in *The Survey*, Vol. 55, pp. 11-15, 55-59.
[166] *Chinese Recorder*, Vol. 57, pp. 381, 382.
[167] The December number of the *Chinese Recorder*, Vol. 55 (1924) was given over primarily to the rural problem.

estry at Nanking especially being active as host, and in North China and Fukien regional agricultural associations were formed for Christians.[168] Only a beginning had been made, however, before the disorders of 1925, 1926, and 1927 supervened. Even in the midst of the civil strife of 1927 and 1928, however, in Tinghsien in Chihli, south of Paotingfu, the Mass Education Movement was conducting an experiment in the remaking of a typical rural district.[169]

COÖPERATION

The growth and the steadily increasing activities of the Protestant churches and missions in China were, as heretofore, clearly making necessary ever greater coöperation. The task more and more became one which could be more effectively performed through joint planning and effort. Moreover, the rapidly rising passion for nationalism was making Chinese Christians increasingly impatient with divisions of foreign origin. It was to be expected, therefore, that the movements toward coördination and union in which the past thirty years had witnessed such progress, would rapidly go forward toward some sort of consummation.

Just as thoroughgoing coöperation was becoming urgent, however, and past achievements were seeming to make it a possibility, forces intervened which threatened not only the future but the disruption of what had been inherited from the past. We have already noted the rift which "fundamentalism" and "modernism" were bringing in Protestantism in Great Britain and America. The conflict was early carried to China and there became even more divisive than in the Occident. The reasons for this intensification of the struggle are not far to seek. Here were strongly represented the denominations in which the controversy

[168] Speer and Kerr, *Report on Japan and China, 1927,* pp. 170, 171; *Bulletin of National Christian Council,* March, 1926, p. 23; *Chinese Recorder,* Vol. 57, pp. 156-159; Hêng-ch'in Chang, *The Rural Church in China Today.* A Report of the Special Secretaries of the Committee on the Country Church and Rural Problems. National Christian Council, 1924-1925. Translated by R. E. Chandler, Nov., 1926; *The University of Nanking, College of Agriculture and Forestry, Bulletin No. 12.* Report of the Conference of Christian Rural Leaders, Nanking, Feb. 2 to 5, 1926, under the auspices of the College of Agriculture and Forestry of the University of Nanking. Report of the Conference on Agricultural Education, Nanking, Feb. 8 and 9, 1924, under the auspices of the Committee on Agricultural Education of the China Christian Educational Association.
[169] *Pacific Data,* April 15, 1928.

was most acute. Here, too, Christian colleges were prominent and growing rapidly, and in them, face to face as they were with the problem of adjusting religious belief to modern knowledge, liberalism was often strong. No one who knew the facts could deny that many missionaries had departed widely from the theological positions of their predecessors. Instead of the former stern criticism of the non-Christian faiths was coming an attitude more tolerant and appreciative.[170] At least one missionary publicly said that he did not believe the Bible to be infallible, nor Christianity the final religion to which all others must give place, nor Jesus perfect.[171] In China, on the other hand, conservatives were especially numerous. In addition to large denominations noted for adhering to the historic statements of the Faith was the great China Inland Mission which drew its missionaries from the conservative wings of most of the Evangelical bodies. Nearly all the smaller missions, too, of which China counted scores, were earnest supporters of the older Evangelical position. The stage was set for sharp conflict.

So strongly were the more aggressive among the conservatives convinced that "modernism" threatened the very life of the Church in China that in 1920 they organized under the name of The Bible Union. The Union's statement of faith expressed unqualified adherence to belief in the deity of Jesus, his virgin birth, atoning sacrifice for sin, and bodily resurrection, in the miracles of the Old and New Testaments, in the personality and work of the Holy Spirit, in the new birth of the individual as an essential prerequisite to Christian social service, and in "the whole Bible as the inspired Word of God and the ultimate authority for Christian faith and practice."[172] These convictions were not new, but were substantially the position always taken by the great body of Evangelicals and still held by the majority of missionaries in China. What was new was an organization "to present to our home boards and supporters the vital importance of accepting for missionary service only such candidates as accept the truths referred to above" and "to stand firm for faithful teaching of the whole Bible as of primary importance in the

---

[170] O'Neill, *The Quest for God in China*, is an illustration of this. Compared with Legge's volumes or Williams' *Middle Kingdom*, it is much more appreciative of other faiths.

[171] J. L. Childs, a Y. M. C. A. secretary, *The Evolution of a Missionary's Thought* in *The Life*, Vol. 5, July, 1925.

[172] *China Mission Year Book*, 1923, pp. 95-101.

work of all Christian schools and colleges."[173]   By January, 1921, the Union had enrolled seventeen hundred members, the great majority of them missionaries, and two years later the roster included over two thousand.[174]   Bulletins were issued, and the first national convention was held in Shanghai in May, 1922. Many, probably the majority of the members, were moderate and irenic, but some were acrimonious, and controversies followed.[175] New educational institutions were founded to teach the conservative views—a theological seminary in Shantung[176] and a university in Shanghai.[177]   The result was discord: Protestants were at odds with each other during the years when they were facing the most difficult situation which had yet confronted them in China.

In spite of divisions, however, progress toward coöperation continued, even if at times haltingly.   The outstanding achievements were the meeting, in the spring of 1922, of the National Christian Conference and the formation of the National Christian Council.   The National Christian Conference was the successor of the gatherings of 1877, 1890, 1907, and 1913.   Like them, it attempted to bring together all the Protestant forces of China, and, like them, it was held in Shanghai.   The preparation, directed by the China Continuation Committee, was extensive.   An elaborate survey of the status of Protestantism in China was made and was published in a massive quarto volume.[178]   Five commissions, each composed of foreigners and Chinese, presented carefully prepared reports.   These reports had as topics: "the present state of Christianity in China," "the future task of the Church," "the message of the Church," "leadership," and "coördination."   Their presentation and discussion consumed most of the time and determined the scope of the gathering.   In three respects the Conference differed markedly from its predecessors and was a significant picture of the changes in the Protestant churches.   First of all, the range

[173] Ibid., 1923, pp. 95-101.
[174] Ibid.; Leger, Education of Christian Ministers in China, p. 36.
[175] One of the most violent fundamentalist statements is Coates, The Red Theology in the Far East. London, 1926.
[176] Leger, op. cit., p. 38.   One fundamentalist held that of the thirteen theological seminaries in China only four were "safe," and that of the forty-eight Bible schools only nine or ten could be "depended upon."—Quoted in Coates, The Red Theology in the Far East, p. 142.
[177] The Christian Century, 1926, p. 1253.
[178] The title was The Christian Occupation of China.   There were two editions, one in English and one in Chinese.

of topics covered indicated that new phases of the Christian task were emerging. Old ones were there, and given prominence—evangelism, education, medical work, literature, and the distribution of the Scriptures. Some, however, which had loomed large in the discussions of earlier gatherings were absent or were passed over with brief mention. Thus ancestor worship, which had been a major topic in the Conferences of 1877, 1890, and 1907, was given only passing notice. Other subjects were appearing—the problems of the villages and of the cities, and economic and industrial conditions. In the second place, whereas the 1877, 1890, and 1907 gatherings had been almost exclusively foreign and that of 1913 predominatingly so, slightly more than half the members of this conference were Chinese, all reports and addresses of importance were in Chinese and English, and a Chinese, Ch'êng Ching-i (C. Y. Cheng), was the permanent chairman. In the third place, the attention of the gathering was chiefly devoted to the formation of a permanent body to take the place and extend the work of the China Continuation Committee: the crowning act of the gathering was the constitution of the National Christian Council.[179]

The National Christian Council, corresponding to similar bodies in India, Japan, and the Near East, was, like its predecessor, for the purpose of coördinating Protestantism in China. It was to have a membership of one hundred—a majority of them Chinese—representing the various Protestant groups in the country and elected by the Conference. Members were to serve until their successors were chosen by the next National Conference and this gathering was to meet within a period not to exceed ten years and was to be arranged for by the Council.[180] The Council did not have smooth sailing. One major group, the Southern Baptists (American) did not join it.[181] It was repeatedly subject to criticism for its alleged espousal of "modernism"[182] and its attention to social service.[183] In its fourth year the China Inland Mission and the Christian and Missionary Alliance withdrew from it.[184] The national crises of 1925, 1926, and 1927,

---

[179] *The Chinese Church as Revealed in the National Christian Conference . . . 1922,* passim, contains a full report of the commissions and of the actions taken.
[180] Ibid.
[181] *Chinese Recorder,* Vol. 53, p. 499, Vol. 55, pp. 455-460.
[182] Coates, *The Red Theology in the Far East,* p. 140.
[183] *National Christian Council of China, Annual Report, 1925-1926,* pp. 52, 55.
[184] Ibid., *1925-1926,* p. 20.

and the sharp differences of opinion in the ranks of missionaries and the Chinese churches which these years brought placed the Council in a most difficult position. It was looked to by many, especially among the Chinese, for an authoritative pronouncement, but the bodies it represented were far from having a single opinion. From time to time it attempted action and as this was usually representative of moderately radical Chinese Christian opinion, many, particularly more conservative foreigners, became increasingly distrustful.

Undeterred by the obstacles which confronted it, the Council met with regularity. Its membership included some of the ablest of the missionaries and Chinese Christians. Its chairman, David Z. T. Yui, the General Secretary of the National Committee of the Young Men's Christian Association, and its secretaries, C. Y. Cheng, K. T. Chung, Miss Y. J. Fan, H. T. Hodgkin, and E. C. Lobenstine, each possessed unusual ability. Bishop Logan H. Roots, as honorary secretary, gave it much of his time. The many sub-committees stimulated interest in the fields which were their especial charge. From the very nature of its organization and of Protestantism, the Council could not safely presume to dictate to the churches. It did, however, help to give direction to all Protestant effort. It was the one clearing house which Protestants in China possessed and in its influence marked an advance upon its predecessor, the China Continuation Committee.[185]

Coöperation was not confined to the National Conference and the National Christian Council. Protestants, in spite of their divisions, were more and more thinking of themselves as a unit, "the Christian Movement in China," as they increasingly called themselves—with serene but probably unintentional disregard of their Roman Catholic and Russian Orthodox brethren. Many forms of this coöperation, particularly in education, have been mentioned in preceding pages. Still other developments appeared. The first "Chinese Christian Conference" for the province of Hunan convened in Changsha in 1924 with a Chinese as chairman and Chinese as the only language of the proceedings.[186]

[185] National Christian Council of China, Annual Report, 1922-1926, passim; China Mission Year Book, 1923, pp. 60-65, 1924, pp. 147-153; Chinese Recorder, Vol. 56, pp. 345-348, 385-389; The National Christian Council, A Five Years' Review, 1922-1927.
[186] China Mission Year Book, 1925, pp. 135-138.

A Hunan Christian Council was then formed and held its second meeting in 1925.[187] In Chengtu, in January, 1925, Protestants in West China took a further step in the path in which they had long been pioneering and convened in the first General Conference of the Christian Churches of Szechwan. The chief difference between this and preceding gatherings in the province was that now the majority of the delegates and much of the leadership were Chinese.[188] In a number of cities local federations of churches—twenty-three by 1927—were formed for facing common problems.[189] The national organizations achieved by Anglicans, Presbyterians, and Lutherans continued. In 1922 both Methodists and Baptists conferred on possible national unions of their respective denominational groups, but no permanent organization was achieved. The attempt of Disciples of Christ missionaries to further Christian fellowship by admitting unimmersed Christians to their churches was forbidden by their American supporters.[190] In June, 1924, the Missions Building in Shanghai was formally opened, and at once became headquarters for many denominational and interdenominational organizations.[191] After the incidents of May 30, 1925, Chinese Christians formed many Christian Unions to deal with national and international issues of the day.[192]

The coöperative movements so far mentioned did not involve the surrender of denominational differences: they were "associations," "federations," "conferences," or "councils" for specific purposes, or coalitions of branches of the same communion. Now, however, came a noteworthy union of churches which were the fruits of several denominational missions. The first steps were taken when, in January, 1919, at the initial meeting of the Federal Council of the Presbyterian Churches in China, representatives of the London Missionary Society and the American Board joined with the Presbyterians in drafting a project for a "United Church of Christ in China." This plan outlined an ecclesiastical organization Presbyterian in form and having as a doctrinal

[187] China Christian Year Book, 1926, p. 106. Three conferences of Protestant missionaries in Hunan had previously been held.
[188] China Mission Year Book, 1925, pp. 143-146.
[189] China Christian Year Book, 1926, p. 103; China Mission Year Book, 1915, pp. 147-153, 1919, pp. 74-81, 1924, pp. 184-188.
[190] The Christian Century, Sept. 30, 1920; Chinese Recorder, Vol. 52, p. 869.
[191] China Mission Year Book, 1919, p. 62, 1925, pp. 238-243; Chinese Recorder, Vol. 55, p. 419.
[192] China Christian Year Book, 1926, pp. 111, 112.

basis faith in Jesus Christ as Redeemer and Lord, in the Bible as the "divinely inspired word of God and the supreme authority in matters of faith and duty," and in the Apostles' Creed "as expressing the fundamental doctrines of our common evangelical faith." [193] Before the year was out all the churches in Kwangtung on a Congregational or Presbyterian basis had joined in forming a divisional council of the United Church and steps toward that end were being taken by similar bodies in South Fukien.[194] A Provisional General Assembly convened in Shanghai in 1922 and adopted a constitution and a modified name, the Church of Christ in China (*Chung Hua Chi Tu Chiao Hui*).[195] By 1926 synods had come into existence in Kwangtung, where the churches associated with seven missions had united, in South Fukien, where those formerly affiliated with three missions had joined, and in Hunan and Hupeh, by churches which were the fruitage of four societies. In North Fukien two district associations had been organized by churches affiliated with the American Board.[196] By January first, 1927, sixteen denominational groups had attached themselves to the new body and three more were planning to do so.[197] The first General Assembly of the Church of Christ in China was held in Shanghai in October, 1927, its members—the large majority of them Chinese—coming from seventeen provinces and representing between a third and a fourth of the Protestant communicants of China. Ch'êng Ching-i was elected Moderator, A. R. Kepler, General Executive Secretary, a constitution and statement of faith were adopted, and various phases of the Church's task were considered.[198] Practically all the churches associated in the new organization were Calvinistic in background and Congregational or Presbyterian in polity. Anglicans and Lutherans, and most Methodists and Baptists, although numerous in the districts where the union was in progress, were conspicuous for their absence. However, the churches affiliated with the missions of the United

[193] *China Mission Year Book, 1919*, pp. 368-371.
[194] *China Mission Year Book, 1919*, p. 61; *Chinese Recorder*, Vol. 51, pp. 641-646.
[195] *Chinese Recorder*, Vol. 53, pp. 428, 669; *China Mission Year Book, 1923*, pp. 334-337.
[196] *China Mission Year Book, 1925*, pp. 123-129.
[197] *Chinese Recorder*, Jan. 1927; Speer and Kerr, *Report on Japan and China, 1927*, pp. 310-312; *China Christian Year Book, 1926*, p. 96.
[198] MS. letter of A. R. Kepler, the General Executive Secretary, Shanghai, Oct. 17, 1927.

Brethren and of the United Church of Canada—into which had gone Methodist churches—had joined,[199] and in December, 1927, the churches in Shantung connected with the English Baptist Mission cast in their lot with the new venture.[200] While the Church of Christ in China, like the Holy Catholic Church of China—the designation adopted by the Anglicans—was a name which as yet expressed a hope rather than a reality, it was more inclusive than any ecclesiastical union ever formed in any country.

THE MOVEMENT FOR AN "INDIGENOUS" CHURCH

Closely associated with progress toward coöperation and union was the movement to make the Church more nearly Chinese. As we have repeatedly seen, this was already well under way before 1918, but it was now greatly accentuated. The word "indigenous" became a slogan, and while, like many other popular watchcries, it did not easily lend itself to exact definition, it was usually taken to mean a Church led and supported by Chinese, and in doctrine, forms of worship, and organization conforming as far as possible to Chinese rather than to Occidental traditions.[201] The immediate emphasis was upon transferring leadership from foreigners to Chinese. In their efforts to reach quickly with the Christian message the entire country and to mold the changing nation with the Gospel, missionaries had built too extensive a structure of churches, schools, and hospitals to be supported by the half-million or so of Chinese Protestant Christians. The modification of polities, creeds, and rituals would take time. However, by their emphasis upon education and especially upon secondary and higher schools, Protestants had raised up in the service of the Church a fairly large body of energetic and sometimes able Chinese. In 1920 the number of ordained Chinese for the first time exceeded that of ordained foreigners, being 1,305 as compared with 1,268. It had risen to that figure from 764 in 1915, a seventy per cent. increase, while in 1915 the number of ordained foreigners had been 1,092. In these five years the total foreign missionary staff had increased from 5,338 to 6,204, a sixteen per cent. growth, but the Chinese personnel had more than doubled, rising from 836 to 1,745.[202] Even more than

---

[199] MS. letter of A. R. Kepler, Oct. 17, 1927.
[200] Ibid., Jan. 7, 1928.
[201] See Hodgkin in *International Review of Missions,* Vol. 14, pp. 545-559.
[202] *The Christian Occupation of China,* p. xc.

Roman Catholics, Protestants were increasing the proportion of Chinese leaders during the war and post war years. Most of these leaders were young, some of them were ambitious, and they nearly all smarted under the charge of their non-Christian fellows that they were adherents of an alien body, were restive under the control of foreigners, and were of the conviction that only a Church led by Chinese could hope to make headway in a strongly nationalistic China.[203]

Nationalism, then, accentuated by the World War and especially aggressive after May 30, 1925, greatly hastened the process of "devolution." From the beginning, as we have repeatedly seen, missionaries had expressed the hope that the Chinese would ultimately take over entire responsibility for the Church, and numbers of them were not quite as insistent as the "natives" that the transfer be made quickly.[204] Many, indeed, were more eager to pass over authority than were some of the Chinese to accept it.[205] Missionaries had become so enmeshed in administering the machinery which they had created that many of them were not averse to turning over the task to Chinese and so obtaining release for more direct personal contacts. After 1922, however, and especially after 1925, events moved more rapidly than some of the missionaries were prepared to approve, and while many hailed the changes with thanksgiving, others believed that the transition was being made more abruptly than was wise.[206]

The instances of the transfer of authority to the Chinese are too numerous to be catalogued fully here. Some have already been noted—for example, the National Christian Conference and the National Christian Council. These, by giving the Chinese the majority voice, marked the beginning of a new era. Even before 1922, Chinese were rapidly being placed on committees and boards of control, and missionaries, particularly younger missionaries, were displaying increased deference to the opinions of their Chinese colleagues.[207] After 1922 the process was accel-

[203] A few examples of this Chinese attitude are T. H. Koo in *Christian China*, March, 1921, pp. 201-206; C. T. Wang in *Chinese Recorder*, Vol. 52, pp. 323-329; ibid., Vol. 54, pp. 468-473, Vol. 56, pp. 496 et seq.
[204] An interesting example of this is in *Addresses on China at the Thirty-Fourth Annual Session, Foreign Missions Conference of North America . . . Jan. 11-14, 1926.* One set of opinions was expressed by Bishop Gilman and another by Dr. Robert E. Speer.
[205] F. W. S. O'Neill in *Chinese Recorder*, Vol. 57, pp. 315-322.
[206] See footnote 204, supra.
[207] J. L. Stuart in *China Mission Year Book, 1919*, pp. 65-73.

erated. A few examples of what was occurring, with varying degrees of rapidity, in practically all missions will serve to give a picture of the whole. In 1924 the Anglicans (*Chung Hua Shêng Kung Hui*) arranged for the creation of a diocese in Shensi—where their home missionary society had been active for some years—to be staffed entirely by Chinese.[208] In 1918 the Northern Baptist mission in East China reorganized its evangelistic work. The Association (of Chinese churches) was encouraged to appoint an executive committee of seven Chinese and two foreigners and to this were entrusted many powers heretofore reserved to missionaries, such as the appropriations for evangelistic work and the ordination and transfer of ministers. A few years later the mission made over to this executive committee all its work in one station.[209] In the South China mission of the same board the year 1925 saw a much more startling development: the Convention (of Chinese churches) asked and was given complete control of planning and administering all the activities, foreign and Chinese, of the denomination in that region. It requested the continuation of financial aid from America and appointed foreign as well as Chinese advisers, but missionaries were to be subject to its direction.[210]

Kwangtung, indeed, partly because Protestants had so long been active there and the Chinese churches were strong, and partly because the Nationalist movement focused in Canton, saw several marked steps toward devolution. In 1926 the Kwangtung Divisional Council of the Church of Christ in China proposed the transfer to itself of all the work of the coöperating missions, including missionaries, property, and financial subsidies.[211] This sweeping proposal was made partly at the instance of missionaries [212] and many of the foreign staff heartily welcomed it.[213] The United Brethren mission promptly approved the plan in its entirety and the other coöperating missions sanctioned it with reservations, for the most part slight.[214] The Ger-

[208] *The World Call of the Church. The Call from the Far East*, p. 36.
[209] A. F. Ufford of Shaoshing in *Missions*, Vol. 16, pp. 602-604; J. T. Proctor in *China Mission Year Book, 1925*, pp. 97-102.
[210] J. H. Franklin in *The Baptist*, Vol. 6, pp. 1208-1210.
[211] Speer and Kerr, *Report on Japan and China, 1927*, pp. 195-198; E. C. Lobenstine in *China Christian Year Book, 1926*, pp. 180-184.
[212] E. E. Barnett in *China Christian Year Book, 1926*, pp. 95, 96.
[213] *Chinese Recorder*, Vol. 57, pp. 14-21.
[214] *China Christian Year Book, 1926*, pp. 183, 184; Speer and Kerr, op. cit., pp. 198-210.

man missions in Kwangtung also took action, although not as immediately revolutionary, looking toward the independence of the congregations associated with them.[215] "Evaluation Conferences" held by the Northern Presbyterians in 1926 recommended drastic steps toward subordinating the mission to the Chinese churches.[216] In 1927 Methodist Episcopalians reported that of their fifty-one district superintendents forty-six were Chinese and only five Americans, and that in their nine conferences Chinese outnumbered Americans five to one.[217] In 1924, indeed, the Central Conference for Eastern Asia of the Methodist Episcopal Church asked for the power to nominate its own bishops.[218] In 1927 Ding Ing-ong was consecrated Assistant Bishop of the Fukien diocese of the *Chung Hua Shêng Kung Hui*.[219] In Shantung the English Baptists began the transfer to the associations of complete responsibility for church organization and finance,[220] and in Shensi put into effect a plan (ca. 1923) by which the mission would assist the Chinese Church rather than, as heretofore, be assisted by it.[221] About 1924 the mission and Chinese churches of the Disciples of Christ devised local and national organizations in which foreigners and Chinese would be equally represented.[222] In 1919 the (English) Friends Foreign Mission Association put into operation a somewhat similar plan.[223] In 1924 the North Fukien Anglican Conference decided to invite Chinese to become members of the committee which dealt with the location of the foreign staff and the requests for new missionaries.[224] In the Young Men's and Young Women's Christian Associations, which had taken the lead in putting Chinese in places of power, the process of devolution continued steadily. In student conferences especially it was noted that Chinese were replacing foreigners as speakers and executives.[225]

[215] Oehler, *China und die christliche Mission*, p. 194.
[216] Speer and Kerr, op. cit., passim.
[217] *The Christian Century*, March 31, 1927, p. 410.
[218] *Chinese Recorder*, Vol. 55, p. 42.
[219] *North-China Herald*, Nov. 5, 1927, p. 232.
[220] Baptist Missionary Society, *Annual Report and Statement of Accounts, for year ending March 31, 1924*, p. 55.
[221] Ibid., p. 62.
[222] Report of the China Mission of the United Christian Missionary Society, 1924-1925, pp. 13-19; *Fifth Annual Report of the United Christian Missionary Society* (in *Disciples of Christ Year Book*), p. 49.
[223] *Friends Foreign Mission Association, Fifty-third Annual Report*, pp. 13, 14.
[224] *Chinese Recorder*, Vol. 56, p. 200.
[225] J. W. Nipps in *Chinese Recorder*, Vol. 55, pp. 505, 508.

The government requirements for the registration of Christian schools and the popular "anti-imperialist" agitation hastened the creation of Chinese boards of trustees and the appointment of Chinese deans, principals, and presidents. Chinese, too, were rapidly replacing foreigners on the faculties. The years 1925 and 1926 especially were made noteworthy by these changes. The most striking single example was Canton Christian College. Early in 1927 the American trustees leased for a nominal sum the entire plant to a newly formed Chinese board and a Chinese president was appointed.

The year 1927, indeed, with the forced exodus of missionaries, witnessed the widespread assumption of leadership by the Chinese. In most places, if the churches were to go on at all, it had to be through Chinese, and positions and responsibilities were thrust upon Chinese shoulders with a rapidity which no one had foreseen. What the results would be, time alone would disclose.

Union and coöperation, the association of Chinese with foreigners in the management of the Church, and even the transfer to them of complete authority were only steps, although by no means unimportant ones, in the process of bringing into being a Chinese Church. If the funds were to continue to come from abroad and most of the propagation of the faith was still to be by the missionary or under his impulse and advice, the Church would obviously remain the creature of the Westerner, dependent upon artificial respiration.

The task of attaining self-support was rendered difficult by the flow of funds from what seemed to the Chinese the exhaustless spring of foreign benevolence. Why should the impecunious Chinese give to the Church when the wealthy foreigner was so willing to do so? Ought not the Church Universal to pool its funds, the most prosperous sections supporting the poverty-stricken ones? Chinese were not accustomed to regular, voluntary contributions for the maintenance of worship or of religious establishments, but usually provided for temples, monasteries, and ancestral halls by endowments given once for all.[226] Moreover, living costs were mounting fully as rapidly in China as in most of the Occident and internal disorder conspired with them to make the achievement of self-support either an extremely difficult or a seemingly impossible task.

[226] Speer and Kerr, op. cit., p. 286.

It is remarkable that in the face of these conditions substantial progress was made toward the desired goal. Examples are numerous. The Canadian Presbyterian mission in Honan adopted a plan whereby foreign grants to each local church were to be reduced at the rate of ten per cent. a year.[227] Another country district in North China reported that the past two decades had seen great improvement.[228] In Kwangtung Chinese congregations had become accustomed to raising much of their expenses. The major part of the budget of the leading Baptist academy in Canton came from domestic sources. What in 1926 was the largest Protestant church building in Canton was erected entirely by Chinese funds,[229] and several Presbyterian church structures in Kwangtung, some of them large, were put up without any aid from foreigners.[230] In 1926, indeed, the missions coöperating with the Kwangtung division of the newly-formed Church of Christ in China were contributing about one-third of the budget and the Chinese two-thirds, and the Council was denying full representation to non-self-supporting congregations.[231] Much home mission work, too, was being carried on by the South China churches.[232]

In 1927 the nearly ten thousand communicants of the South Fukien Synod of the Church of Christ in China contributed more than eight dollars per capita for the work of the Church.[233] About 1926 the Independent Church in Tsinanfu dedicated new buildings which had been erected entirely by Chinese gifts.[234] We hear, too, of a Chinese merchant in Szechwan donating property worth over one hundred thousand dollars to an orphanage, an independent Chinese church, and the Young Men's Christian Association.[235] In 1926, out of the two hundred and thirty-three churches associated with the Northern Presbyterian missions in China, thirty-two were self-supporting.[236] As against $1,650,000 gold contributed from the United States through these missions,

---

[227] W. A. Mather in *Chinese Recorder*, Vol. 53, p. 94, Vol. 54, pp. 338-340.
[228] A. G. Bryson in ibid., Vol. 54, pp. 258-261.
[229] *Chinese Recorder*, Vol. 57, p. 217.
[230] Speer and Kerr, *Report on Japan and China, 1927*, p. 189.
[231] Ibid., p. 319.
[232] *Chinese Recorder*, Vol. 53, pp. 787-789.
[233] A. R. Kepler, MS. letter, Jan. 7, 1928.
[234] *Chinese Recorder*, Vol. 57, p. 462.
[235] Ibid., Vol. 57, p. 226.
[236] Speer and Kerr, op. cit., p. 288.

$587,175 gold came from Chinese through school and hospital receipts alone.[237]

Chinese were more and more taking the initiative in spreading their faith among their fellows. The new Southern Methodist mission in Manchuria was almost entirely manned and financed by them.[238] The National Christian Conference was followed by a deepening sense of responsibility for the Church,[239] and the Shanghai Christian Council, formed as a result of the gathering, in 1923 held a series of evangelistic meetings.[240] In Chêkiang one of the twenty-one pastorates and districts under the Church Missionary Society was a home missionary enterprise supported by the Chinese of the diocese and fifteen of the others were in charge of Chinese clergy and were nearly self-supporting.[241] Between 1918 and 1924 the *Chung Hua Shêng Kung Hui's* Shensi mission, a purely Chinese undertaking, increased its staff from five to nineteen and its budget from $1,353 to $29,658.[242] The Independent Church in Tientsin grew steadily and by 1922 had started six branches in and near the city.[243] One of the most prominent of the Chinese attempts to propagate the Faith was the Chinese Home Missionary Society. It had its birth in Kuling in 1918 in a small group called to meet the Rev. Frank Buchman, who was then visiting China to promote evangelism by personal contacts. Undenominational, a purely Chinese organization with Dr. Chêng Ching-i as chairman, it grew rapidly. It first established a mission in Yünnan, where by the close of 1924 it had three stations and six missionaries. The home mission enterprise of the Manchurian Presbyterian churches joined with it, and the end of 1924 found it with seven stations and seven workers in Heilungchiang.[244] An interesting undertaking, especially encouraging to those who longed for the independence of Chinese Chris-

[237] Ibid., p. 325. No figures are given for the contributions from Chinese churches, but in 1920 these were $79,567 (Mex.).—*Christian Occupation of China*, p. xci.
[238] Cannon, *History of Southern Methodist Missions*, p. 121.
[239] *Chinese Recorder*, Vol. 54, p. 7.
[240] Ibid., Vol. 55, pp. 106-109.
[241] *The World Call of the Church. The Call from the Far East*, p. 64.
[242] *Chinese Recorder*, Vol. 55, p. 749.
[243] *The Christian Occupation of China*, p. 386.
[244] Letter of C. Y. Cheng, Dec. 25, 1924 (MS.); *Chinese Recorder*, Vol. 51, pp. 157-166, Vol. 52, pp. 653, 663, Vol. 55, p. 120, Vol. 56, p. 200; *China Mission Year Book, 1919*, pp. 62, 95-108, *1923*, p. 114, *1924*, pp. 172-174; C. Y. Cheng in *China Today Through Chinese Eyes*, p. 137.

tians, was the Ifang Girls' Collegiate School in Changsha.   It was distinctly Christian but had no official connection with any ecclesiastical organization, foreign or Chinese.   Its founder, Miss Tsêng Pao-suan, was a great-granddaughter of the famous Tsêng Kuo-fan.   While a student in a school of the Church Missionary Society at Hangchow she became a Christian and decided to give her life to the preparation of leaders among Chinese women. After study in England she, together with her cousin, Mr. Tsêng Beauson, in 1918 opened a school in Changsha.   The enrollment was purposely kept small—never much more than sixty—and was made up chiefly of girls from the upper classes.   The institution was remarkable for its strong Christian influence and for its successful student government.[245]

An interesting development was the appearance of new Chinese Christian sects entirely independent of the foreigner. Such, for example, was the "True Jesus Church" (*Ch'êng Yeh-su Chiao*). Its organizer was a Barnabas Tung who professed to have received a divine commission in a vision about 1909 or 1910, to have spent three years in quiet study, and then to have begun to preach.   The movement disclaimed any reliance on foreign money or personnel and denounced other Christian bodies as false.   It claimed to have returned to Apostolic doctrines and practices.   It rejoiced in poverty and persecution, practiced immersion, observed the seventh day, and believed in healing by faith and the laying on of hands, direct revelations through dreams and trances, speaking with tongues, the infilling of the Spirit, and the early second coming of Christ.   It was to be found in several provinces, but appears to have been especially strong in Fukien, where many pastors and members of the Anglican, Methodist, and Congregational churches were drawn into it.   It was said at one time to have about one thousand members, but by 1927 it had begun to wane.[246]   In Foochow, too, was a new congregation calling itself the *Ching Chiao,* from the Nestorians, and claiming to be purely Chinese.[247]

The Student Volunteer Movement continued and held its first

[245] *Chinese Recorder,* Vol. 58, pp. 425-430.
[246] Conversation with Peter Goertz, an American Board missionary in Fukien, Feb., 1928; *Annual Report of the Board of Foreign Missions of the Methodist Episcopal Church for the Year 1924,* p. 41; W. B. Call in ibid., *1925,* p. 64.
[247] Conversation with Peter Goertz, Feb., 1928.

national convention in 1922. By that time one hundred and thirty of its members were in the ministry and others were aiding the Church in indirect ways.[248]

In the process of making Christianity "indigenous" in China, the greatest delay was in the modification of the statements of faith and the practices which had come from the West. Various attempts were made, but few of them were widely accepted.[249] Some Buddhist terms had long been used in presenting the Christian Gospel,[250] although probably with no very deliberate intension of "accommodation." A Chinese musical setting for the Holy Communion was reported.[251] Many new buildings, most of them for schools but some for churches, were being erected in a style much more nearly Chinese than the former offensive hybrid of curved roofs and Western walls.[252] Christians were more and more trying to make their peace with that most widely observed Chinese religious custom, the honoring of ancestors. While forms that might be construed as worship were eschewed, memorial services were regularly held and many of these were observed at the graves at Ch'ing Ming—that festival when departed spirits are especially honored.[253]

While few positive readjustments of Christian creeds and forms were made, Chinese Protestants, especially among the students, were experiencing the spirit of inquiry which was so general. They were asking fundamental questions about the Christian faith. Many of them were at sea, and others were insisting upon thinking through for themselves the beliefs transmitted to them by the missionaries. There was less certainty but also less blind conformity.[254]

The question of the future of the missionary naturally arose. Was he still wanted by the Chinese Church? At least one mis-

[248] *Chinese Recorder*, Vol. 51, pp. 225, 518, Vol. 53, p. 46; *China Mission Year Book, 1924*, pp. 340-342.

[249] *Christian China*, May, 1921, p. 331. On the general problem see Rawlinson, *Naturalization of Christianity in China* (*A Study of the Relation of Christian and Chinese Idealism and Life*), Shanghai, 1927.

[250] Maclagan, *Chinese Religious Ideas*, Chapter 8.

[251] *Chinese Recorder*, Vol. 51, pp. 179-184.

[252] Ibid., Vol. 55, pp. 57, 270; H. K. Murphy in *The Oriental Engineer*, Vol. 7, No. 3.

[253] *Chinese Recorder*, Vol. 54, p. 308, Vol. 57, pp. 443-445; *China Christian Year Book, 1926*, p. 136; *Christian China*, Vol. 7, pp. 199, 200; C. Y. Cheng in *China Today Through Chinese Eyes*, pp. 124, 125.

[254] *The Life* contains many articles showing this attitude.

sionary urged that foreign staffs be not increased and that a date be fixed for the withdrawal of all alien workers.[255] Leading Chinese Christians, however, were practically unanimous in declaring that they wished missionaries to continue [256] and some asked that their numbers be increased.[257] Chinese and many foreigners were clear that the function of the missionary was changing, and that in the future he would be less a director and administrator and would be assigned his task by the Chinese. It was in certain phases of the activities of the Church, in conveying to Chinese Christians the experience of the churches of the West, in forming a friendly bond between Occidental and Chinese Christianity, and in pioneering in new territories that it was believed he would find his place.[258] He would, moreover, need to divest himself of what in the parlance of the times was called his "racial superiority complex" and be willing to adjust the practices of the West to Chinese conditions.[259]

With all the progress toward an independent, self-supporting, self-propagating, truly Chinese Church, the goal was still far from being reached. Protestantism in China was not as nearly independent of foreign financial aid as in Japan and Korea, the majority of Chinese Christians were inactive in spreading their faith, and complaints were not lacking that the tone of spiritual life was low and obscurity as to the central emphasis of Christianity widespread.[260] The immediate withdrawal of foreign money and

[255] *Chinese Recorder,* Vol. 55, p. 54.
[256] Statements of thirty-one prominent Chinese Christians in *Chinese Recorder,* Vol. 57, p. 310 et seq.; Findings of a conference called by the National Christian Council to meet John R. Mott in Shanghai, January, 1926, in *Bulletin of the National Christian Council.* March, 1926, pp. 3-9; David Yui in *China Her Own Interpreter,* p. 129.
[257] The Executive Committee of the Kwangtung Divisional Council of the Church of Christ in China, while asking for the transfer of the work of the Mission to the Church, in 1927 expressed itself as of the conviction "that the foreign missionary has a permanent place in the Chinese Church. We therefore request the Mission Board that for the next ten years they increase rather than diminish the total number of their present force."—Speer and Kerr, *Report for Japan and China, 1927,* p. 195.
[258] Findings of the conference of Jan., 1926, in *Bulletin of the National Christian Council,* March, 1926, pp. 3-9; Yui in *China Her Own Interpreter,* pp. 129, 130. See also, as the attitude of a former missionary, Keyte, *A Daughter of Cathay,* p. 258.
[259] David Yui in chairman's address to the National Christian Council, Oct., 1926, in *Bulletin of the National Christian Council,* Nov., 1926, pp. 9, 10; Bishop L. H. Roots in *China Christian Year Book, 1926,* pp. 162-173; *The Life,* July, 1925.
[260] See Rawlinson in *China Christian Year Book, 1926,* pp. 122-131.

personnel would certainly cause great reverses and might possibly be followed by the gradual disappearance of the Church.

PROTESTANTS AND THE REVISION OF THE TREATIES

The nationalistic movement not only hastened the realization of a truly Chinese Church, but brought home to missionaries the necessity of taking some attitude toward the treaties. The "anti-imperialist" agitators demanded revision and in the objectionable documents was written toleration of the missionary and his converts. No Chinese publicly defended the treaties and many were the utterances of Protestants demanding the elimination of all "unequal" features.[261] Missionaries were divided.[262] As early as 1923 they had begun actively to consider the question and several had announced themselves as opposed to any military pressure on behalf of their persons or property.[263] The Shanghai incident of May 30, 1925, precipitated discussion, and mission after mission, board after board, expressed itself in resolutions.[264] None explicitly favored the toleration clauses. A very few declined to offer any opinion, declaring that treaties were matters for governmental action and that the Church should not interfere. A few, too, said that they would be content with whatever arrangements the governments should reach. The great majority, however, specifically put themselves on record as desiring the removal of the toleration clauses and all special privileges to missionaries. A number, especially of American boards and missions, came out in favor of the abrogation, not only of the toleration clauses, but of extraterritoriality and the foreign control of the tariff. What was probably a fairly large minority of missionaries, however, believed that the time had not yet come for the removal of extraterritoriality and some even wished the retention of the toleration clauses.[265]

[261] *Chinese Recorder,* Vol. 56, pp. 505-517.
[262] Ibid., Vol. 57, pp. 322-328.
[263] *Chinese Recorder,* Vol. 54, p. 569.
[264] See texts of many of these actions in *China Christian Year Book, 1926,* pp. 483-534. See also *Chinese Recorder,* Vol. 56, pp. 705-715, 769-771, 834-838, Vol. 57, pp. 154-156, 447; *Bulletin of the National Christian Council,* Dec., 1926, March, 1926, pp. 10-18; *The Christian Century,* Vol. 42, pp. 1485, 1488; *Proceedings of a Conference of Administrators of the Mission Boards Having Work in China, October 2 and 3, 1925, at 25 Madison Avenue, New York City.*
[265] *Bulletin of the National Christian Council,* Dec., 1925; *American Relations with China,* passim.

NATIONALISM, THE ANTI-CHRISTIAN MOVEMENT, AND THE
ATTEMPT TO EXTEND GOVERNMENT CONTROL TO
MISSION SCHOOLS

Progress in devolution and the agitation for treaty revision were inextricably bound up with other phases of the nationalistic and anti-Christian agitation. So many were the currents and counter-currents and so rapidly did events move that an orderly, coherent narrative is almost impossible.

The incident of May 30, 1925, served to intensify all phases of the nationalistic agitation. Chinese indignation flamed against the massacre of unarmed students and the foreign control of the International Settlement. Students in Christian schools joined with those of government institutions in the nation-wide protest and in many cities Chinese Christian Unions were formed to add their voices to the demand for justice.[266] Many missionaries publicly expressed themselves as favoring an impartial inquiry into the shooting and as opposed to the treaties which had made it possible.[267] The National Christian Council issued a moderate appeal for a full investigation.[268] Some missionaries, however, were silent. In its inflamed state the popular mind tended to hold all foreigners responsible for the action of the police. To the Chinese the entire issue of the foreigners' privileged status seemed to be focused in this one outrage, and silence, hesitation, and even moderation on the part of their missionary colleagues appeared to "native" leaders as acquiescence in a crying injustice. In many places, therefore, a breach was wrought between foreign and Chinese Christians.[269] Before the year was out friendly relations were large restored, but it was clear that the foreigners' status in the Church was being threatened.

The first wave of the Anti-Christian Movement, that of 1922, had little adverse effect upon Protestant missions. For a time a few activities suffered but any loss was more than compensated

[266] *China Christian Year Book, 1926,* pp. 86-88; *The Peking Leader.—Special Supplement,* in June, 1925.
[267] *North-China Herald,* Oct. 10, 1925, p. 46; H. F. Ward, *Chinese Christians and the Shooting in Shanghai* (from National Committee of the Y. W. C. A., Shanghai).
[268] *Bulletin of the National Christian Council,* July, 1925; *Chinese Recorder,* Vol. 56, pp. 466 et seq.
[269] Speer and Kerr, *Report on Japan and China,* 1927, p. 78; J. S. Burgess in *The Survey,* Vol. 55, pp. 7-10, 49, 51; Broomhall, *Bishop Cassels,* p. 342.

by the attention drawn to Christianity.[270] The agitation advertised the Church and its message. Several thousand government school students were in Bible classes, some of them drawn by curiosity aroused by the attack. Many of them were deciding to follow Jesus, although very few were coming into the Church.[271] Chinese Christians, too, came out in defense of their faith and in doing so were forced to reëxamine it. They were, moreover, strengthened in their purpose to make the Church more distinctly Chinese and to purge it of the faults which the critics were denouncing.[272]

The renewed and more intense outbursts of the Anti-Christian Movement in 1924, 1925, and 1926 were followed by more serious results. Some Christians now found it difficult to reconcile their church allegiance with patriotism and decided in favor of their country.[273] Others, while continuing to call themselves Christians, either broke with the Church, as a Western institution, or, while remaining within it, found fault with it.[274] Still others, while silent, became uncertain and lukewarm.[275] Here and there were actual interference with Church activities and attacks on Christians. In 1925, after the May 30th incident, many schools declined in enrollment or closed before the end of the term and some did not reopen in the fall.[276] In some places public preaching became more difficult.[277] However, autumn found many Protestant schools with increased enrollments.[278] One missionary educator even hailed the Anti-Christian Movement as having strengthened the Christian cause "more than anything that has happened in the whole history of Christianity in China," for it had "sifted out some unworthy adherents . . . kept out of the Christian ranks all but the thoroughly convinced and . . . com-

---

[270] *Chinese Recorder*, Vol. 54, p. 3.
[271] E. E. Barnett in *China Mission Year Book, 1923*, pp. 80-87.
[272] T. C. Chao in *Chinese Recorder*, Vol. 53, pp. 743-748.
[273] Statement of Baxter, Acting President of Canton Christian College, Nov. 26, 1924.
[274] Rawlinson in *China Christian Year Book, 1926*, pp. xxx-xxxii.
[275] Rawlinson in *China Christian Year Book, 1926*, pp. xxx-xxxii; T. Z. Koo in *China Today Through Chinese Eyes, Second Series*, pp. 106-120.
[276] *Chinese Recorder*, Vol. 57, pp. 139-141; *Through Deep Waters, The Story of the C. E. Z. M. S. Abroad and at Home*, pp. 104-121; *China Christian Year Book, 1925*, pp. 224-235.
[277] *Chinese Recorder*, Vol. 57, p. 294.
[278] Ibid., Vol. 57, pp. 63-68; *University of Nanking, Report of the President for 1924-1925*, p. 4; *China Christian Year Book, 1926*, pp. 224-235.

pelled Christians to reëvaluate their religion and to take a firmer hold on God." [279]

The regulations for schools which from 1924 on were proposed or actually adopted by various governmental bodies brought many difficulties to Protestant educators. Criticisms that had long been current were now uttered more loudly and frequently. Mission schools, so it was complained, were not registered with the government nor organized in accordance with the Chinese educational system and were rivals of the state institutions; they made the Bible the most important subject of the curriculum, compelled attendance at religious exercises and had as their chief purpose not education but the propagation of Christianity; their teachers were not properly trained; they paid insufficient attention to Chinese literature and history; they suppressed the patriotic activities of students; and their tuition fees were inordinately high.[280] Even Christians declared that students in mission institutions were more protected from new ideas and did less thinking than those in government schools,[281] that they misunderstood what was taught in the Bible classes,[282] and only infrequently became leaders.[283]

Christian educators, both Chinese and foreign, were deeply concerned and devoted much time to the discussion of the regulations, particularly those of November, 1925. Foreigners and Chinese were fairly well agreed that ideally registration with the government was desirable, and in the main were quite willing to conform to the curriculum laid down by the Ministry of Education. There was general assent, moreover, to the principle that as rapidly as possible Chinese should be given a majority on the boards of control and on faculties and should displace foreigners in presidencies and principalships. Nor was there any doubt about the wisdom of greater emphasis upon China's cultural and literary heritage.[284] However, on the question of mak-

---

[279] F. J. White, *Annual Report of Shanghai College for 1925.*
[280] K. L. Ch'en in *The Chinese Christian Student*, Vol. 1, No. 4.
[281] *Chinese Recorder*, Vol. 53, pp. 49-113, Vol. 56, p. 10.
[282] *The West China Missionary News*, Vol. 22, No. 8.
[283] *Chinese Recorder*, Vol. 52, pp. 818-825.
[284] See the findings of a conference of Chinese administrators in Christian colleges and universities, held in Shanghai, Jan. 15-17, 1925, and of a conference held in New York, April 6, 1925, in *Chinese Christian Education*, pp. 18-20, 101-103, and of the conference of Christian colleges and universities in China held in Shanghai, Feb. 12 to 16, 1926, in *The Christian College in the New China*, pp. 76-81.

ing instruction in religious subjects and attendance at religious exercises elective, marked difference of opinion was discovered. Chinese Christian educators were almost solidly in favor of the voluntary principle.[285] Foreign educators were divided: some sided with their Chinese colleagues, but others contended that to yield would sacrifice the essential character of the schools and preferred closing to compromise.[286] The Anglo-Saxon, accustomed to the comparative independence of the churches to conduct schools in their own way, had a different background from the Chinese, whose government had possessed for centuries the unquestioned right to control education. In practice several institutions, including Yenching University and Canton Christian College, made participation in all religious activities optional; some insisted upon attendance at week-day Bible classes but not at chapel; others allowed a choice between ethical and avowedly Christian instruction; while still others retained the old requirements.[287]

The Kuomintang brought fresh difficulties, especially during its northward march in 1926 and 1927. Some of the locally-adopted variations of its regulations were more inimical to the Christian character of mission schools than were those of the Peking Government, and where the radical wing was in power, as in Hunan, strikes were fomented among students and servants. By the summer of 1927, most mission schools in Hunan and Hupeh had closed with no prospect of an early reopening. Even where the moderates were in control, institutions experienced much difficulty, and some, notably St. John's University, suspended until more favorable times should dawn.

BANDITS AND CIVIL WAR

The increasing civil strife and banditry, and the progressive breakdown of orderly government, which were the sad lot of China, could not but have an effect upon Protestant Christians, both Chinese and foreigners. Occasionally missionaries were able to act as intermediaries and peacemakers between warring

---

[285] *Chinese Christian Education*, pp. 18-20; *The Christian College in the New China*, pp. 76-81; *Chinese Recorder*, Vol. 57, pp. 340-344.
[286] *The Christian College in the New China*, pp. 76-81; *Chinese Recorder*, Vol. 56, pp. 565-570, 782 et seq.
[287] C. S. Miao in *China Christian Year Book, 1926*, pp. 242-246. See also on the status of Protestant education in 1927, E. W. Wallace in *International Review of Missions*, Vol. 17, pp. 205-217.

factions [288] and until late in 1926 and in some places even until 1927 enough shreds of the former prestige of the foreigner clung to him to make his compounds havens of refuge.[289] More and more, however, missionaries and Chinese Christians were sharing the sufferings of their non-Christian neighbors and at times were even being singled out for attack. Foreigners captured by bandits were held either for ransom or as a price for pardon by the authorities. On June 13, 1920, William A. Reimert, the Acting Principal of the Lakeside College at Yochow, was murdered by retreating soldiers of the notorious Chang Ching-yao.[290] In October, 1921, a Chinese Methodist district superintendent in Fukien was seized by Northern troops and held for ransom.[291] In December, 1921, W. H. Oldfield of the Christian and Missionary Alliance was taken by brigands in Kwangsi.[292] In 1922 Dr. Howard Taylor of the China Inland Mission was captured in Yünnan and four others of the same mission in Honan were carried off.[293] All were later released. In Honan, too, in that same year Forsberg and Lundeen of the Augustana Synod Mission were seized by part of a defeated army that had turned bandit and were released only after much delay.[294] In 1923 Christians in Hainan were kidnaped [295] and a station of the London Missionary Society in Hupeh was destroyed by brigands.[296] In August, 1923, F. J. Watts and E. A. Whiteside of the Church Missionary Society were murdered by robbers in Szechwan,[297] and a few months later four missionaries of the American Lutheran Mission were captured in Hupeh, and one, B. A. Hoff, died of wounds shortly after being released [298] In the autumn of 1923 two unmarried women of the China Inland Mission in Honan were abducted but after five weeks were freed through the interference of

[288] In 1922 Dr. Thompson of the Church Missionary Society negotiated an armistice between warring factions which saved Yünnanfu and other cities from pillage and which insured to wounded soldiers freedom from slaughter by the victors.—Stedeford in Mrs. Butler, *Missions as I Saw Them*, pp. 84-86; *Chinese Recorder*, Vol. 53, p. 69.
[289] *Chinese Recorder*, Vol. 55, p. 60; letter of E. J. Lee from Anking, Nov. 13, 1926, in *The Parish* (Worcester, Mass.), Dec. 26, 1926.
[290] Bartholomew, *The Martyr of Huping*, pp. 101-104.
[291] *Chinese Recorder*, Vol. 53, p. 137.
[292] Oldfield in ibid., Vol. 54, pp. 92 et seq.
[293] *Chinese Recorder*, Vol. 53, pp. 741, 742.
[294] Lundeen, *In the Grip of Bandits*, p. 13.
[295] *Chinese Recorder*, Vol. 54, p. 563.
[296] Ibid., Vol. 54, p. 624.
[297] Broomhall, *Bishop Cassels*, p. 326.
[298] *Chinese Recorder*, Vol. 55, p. 135.

Wu P'ei-fu's troops.[299] M. F. Strauss, of the affiliated Liebenzell Mission in Hunan, was captured in October, 1923, and held for three months.[300] E W. Schmalzried of the Missionary Society of the Evangelical Church was taken on the mountainous Hunan-Kweichow border and held until ransomed.[301] In January and February of 1924 several missions in Szechwan were looted, one member of the China Inland Mission was wounded, and several women of the Canadian Methodist Mission were removed from a steamer and released only on payment of a ransom.[302] The British and American Ministers thereupon advised the boards to send no new missionaries to the province for the time.[303] In March, 1924, a Chinese agent of the British and Foreign Bible Society was killed in Manchuria [304] and by the end of 1926 several colporteurs of the Society had lost their lives.[305] In 1924 Swedish missionaries were expelled from Urga[306] and a Swedish missionary and his converts were beaten and dragged through the streets of Yarkand in Sinkiang.[307] In 1924 a party of missionaries on their way to rescue colleagues besieged in Kwangsi were themselves taken captive, and one of the besieged, J. E. Cunningham of the Christian and Missionary Alliance, was killed by a stray bullet.[308] That same year George D. Byers, an American Presbyterian, was killed by bandits in Hainan.[309] In August, 1925, nine of the Church Missionary Society, including Bishop Howell, were carried off by brigands in Szechwan and held until ransomed by a magistrate.[310] In Honan in September, 1926, property of the China Inland Mission was destroyed by bandits and several missionaries were roughly treated and taken captive.[311] June 7, 1926, Mrs. Sibley of the Canadian Methodist Mission was murdered on the streets of Chengtu, probably at the instigation of the Red Lantern Society.[312] In the summer of 1926, in

[299] Ibid., Vol. 55, p. 132.
[300] Ibid., Vol. 55, p. 135.
[301] Ibid.; *The China Weekly Review*, Vol. 28, p. 110.
[302] *The China Weekly Review*, Vol. 28, p. 110.
[303] *Chinese Recorder*, Vol. 55, p. 202.
[304] *The China Weekly Review*, Vol. 28, p. 110.
[305] *Chinese Recorder*, Vol. 58, p. 385.
[306] Ibid., Vol. 55, p. 476.
[307] *The China Weekly Review*, Vol. 28, p. 110.
[308] *Chinese Recorder*, Vol. 55, p. 478.
[309] Ibid., Vol. 55, p. 485.
[310] Broomhall, *Bishop Cassels*, p. 347; letter of R. L. Simkin from Chengtu, Oct. 19, 1925, in *Information About China, Jan. 5, 1925*.
[311] *North-China Herald*, Oct. 16, 1926.
[312] *Chinese Recorder*, 1926, p. 608.

the course of one of the civil wars, Hsianfu was besieged for several months and by autumn the suffering in the city was intense. Food ran short and thousands succumbed to famine and disease. Christians shared in the distress and seven Protestant and several Roman Catholic missionaries remained, ministering to the afflicted as best they could.[313]

The above list is by no means exhaustive and makes little mention of the extensive losses by Chinese Christians. Being a missionary now in many parts of China was an extra-hazardous occupation and being a Christian did not carry as much immunity from attack as in the first years after the Boxer uprising.

In spite of all this provocation—more than had been given them since 1900—mission boards were disinclined to press for indemnities. The London Missionary Society refused to make any claim for damages to its mission in Hupeh, believing that participation in the Boxer Indemnity had done more harm than good.[314] The decision of the United States to return the balance of its share of the Boxer Indemnity, indeed, reached in 1924, was probably due to Miss Mary E. Woods of the American Church (Episcopal) Mission more than to any other one person, for she was untiring in urging the project upon members of Congress. Occasionally an indemnity was collected—$45,000 silver from the Governor of Hunan for the murder of Mr. Reimert and $20,000 silver by the Chinese general controlling Hainan for the death of Mr. Byers.[315] For the most part, however, little or no compensation seems to have been asked or given. Protestant missionaries usually refrained from claiming it for themselves and declined to request any for Chinese Christians.[316] Many were outspoken in their denunciation of the use of force by their governments. Theirs was an attitude different from that of many of their predecessors.

Until the summer of 1925 most of the destruction of property and actual violence suffered by missionaries and Chinese Christians had been at the hands of brigands or disbanded soldiers. With the revival of the Anti-Christian Movement, and especially after May 30, 1925, and the outbreak of the anti-British boy-

[313] *North-China Herald,* Aug. 7, 1926, Aug. 21, 1926, Oct. 9, 1926; *New York Times,* Dec. 10, 1926.
[314] *China Mission Year Book, 1924,* pp. 14, 15.
[315] *Archives of the U. S. Department of State.*
[316] *China Mission Year Book, 1924,* p. 14.

cott and the anti-treaty, anti-foreign agitation, local military and civil authorities, particularly in areas controlled by the Kuomintang, often winked at or even stimulated attacks on Christians, both foreign and Chinese. All British and most Americans were "imperialists," Chinese Christians were their "running dogs" and they and their property were fair prey for "patriotic" citizens. Servants were encouraged and at times compelled to organize into unions and to make demands which their employers deemed intolerable. If granted, the increased wages frequently went not to the servants but into the coffers of the unions, to the profit of the officers. Merely a bare list of the outrages, if complete, would prolong this book unduly, but a few of the more notorious will indicate the type of the others. The Canton Hospital, the famous institution dating back to Peter Parker and still owned by the venerable Canton Medical Missionary Society, was closed by the labor unions, and that in spite of the efforts of the government.[317] Later the hospital for the insane, founded by Dr. Kerr, was suspended for much the same reason. The Anglo-Chinese College at Swatow, belonging to the English Presbyterians, was seized under flimsy pretexts by a Chinese group headed by a former teacher in the school,[318] and in Kaying, in Kwangtung, the Baptist academy was sequestered under the leadership of the local magistrate.[319] In Wuchow, in Kwangsi, the control of the Stout Memorial Hospital, of the Southern Baptist Mission, was demanded by a body calling itself the "Kwangsi Chinese Christian Promotion Association" and the hospital servants submitted impossible requests. The foreigners in charge were obdurate and a boycott and strike were instituted which resulted in violence, the evacuation of the foreigners, and the seizure of the plant by the Chinese.[320]

When in the summer of 1926 the wave of the Kuomintang invasion moved northward, many Protestant missionaries were disposed to welcome it. Following and sometimes preceding the army, however, were Communist agitators. Radical labor, peasant, and student unions sprang into existence and made demands which could not be granted. Anti-foreign and anti-Christian

[317] Speer and Kerr, *Report on Japan and China, 1927*, p. 406.
[318] *North-China Herald*, Dec. 12, 1925, p. 474, March 6, 1926, p. 420; *Chinese Recorder*, Vol. 57, p. 448.
[319] *Chinese Recorder*, Vol. 57, p. 448.
[320] *North-China Herald*, April 17, 1926, p. 103, April 24, 1926, p. 154.

demonstrations were staged, in some places church services were forbidden, and Chinese pastors were paraded in disgrace through the streets. British and American missionaries in the danger zones were urged by their consuls to leave, and, after much hesitation, complied, partly to prevent the international complications which violence to them would entail and partly to save Chinese Christians the persecution that their presence might provoke. The situation was worst in Hunan, but it was not much better in several other provinces. Extreme violence, such as accompanied the Boxer uprising, was rare. Intimidation, the boycott, and popular agitation were the usual instruments chosen. Now and again, however, as at Liuyang, Hunan,[321] in October, 1926, and in Foochow in January, 1927,[322] mobs broke loose. The outstanding incident was at Nanking, on March 24, 1927, when the Nationalist troops, upon taking over the city, deliberately looted foreigners, killed the Vice-President of Nanking University, Dr. J. E. Williams, in front of his own home, and probably would have murdered others but for a barrage by foreign gunboats. In fear of a similar fate during the anticipated northward advance of the Nationalists, most Protestant missionaries withdrew from the interior. By July, 1927, about five thousand of the approximately eight thousand Protestant missionaries were said to be out of China, most of them in Great Britain and America, but some of them in Japan and the Philippines. Of the remaining three thousand, about fifteen hundred were refugees behind the guns of foreign troops in the foreign concessions in Shanghai, about one thousand were in other port cities where their governments could protect them, and only about five hundred were still in the interior.[323] Chinese Christians were suddenly left to shoulder responsibilities for which only a few weeks before many foreigners had deemed them unprepared. Occasionally mission buildings were occupied by troops or labor unions, but much of the work of the Church went on. Of one hundred and seventy hospitals in twelve provinces, only fifty-five were shut.[324] Of thirteen Christian colleges only three

[321] G. G. Warren in ibid., Nov. 20, 1926, p. 345. The North-China Herald was bitter in its denunciation of the Nationalists and accounts in it must be read with discrimination.
[322] New York Times, Jan. 17, 18, 1927.
[323] Chinese Recorder, Vol. 58, p. 359.
[324] Ibid., Vol. 58, p. 467.

were closed: six were maintained entirely by the Chinese members of the teaching staffs.[325]

One of the unfortunate accompaniments of the events of 1926 and 1927 was the accentuation of the divisions in Protestant ranks. Chinese Protestants were usually sympathetic with the Kuomintang—or at least with its moderate wing—and some held high position in it. All who were vocal favored the revision of the treaties and an altered status for the foreigner not only in general but in the Church. With feeling running high among both Chinese and foreigners, dissensions broke out. Many missionaries who were critical of the Kuomintang and opposed to the early revision of the treaties and the immediate transfer of leadership in the Church to the Chinese attacked the National Christian Council for expressing opposite views.

SUMMARY

The middle of 1927, then, found Protestantism in China in the worst plight in its history. It was, indeed, much more badly off than was Roman Catholicism. Most of the missionaries were out of the interior and a majority had left the country. Anti-Christian agitation was widespread and actual persecution frequent. The loss of life and property was by no means as great as in 1900 but it was more widespread and the prospect for an early restoration of orderly government seemed more remote. Nationalist sentiment was such that the missionary could not expect to recover his former status in the Church nor his privileged position in the country. Increasing anarchy added to the danger to life and property and to the difficulty of maintaining regular activities. In addition, the incomes of some boards were declining, criticisms of missions were frequent in Europe and America and were directed primarily against Protestant efforts, and widespread religious uncertainty was dampening missionary enthusiasm. In China itself the missionary body was divided on questions of doctrine and policy, many Chinese were estranged from some of their missionary colleagues, and others showed spiritual sterility and lack of conviction. A leading American religious journal spoke of "the missionary debacle in China." Protestant missions seemed about to enter a new stage whose outcome none could foresee. The days between

[325] Ibid., Vol. 58, p. 359.

1901 and 1914, when the opposition of the old structure of Chinese life was crumbling and no new enemies had appeared to thwart the rapid growth of the Church, seemed very remote. Dismay threatened even the stoutest hearts.

The facts would not all have been recorded were this narrative of Protestant missions in China to end in a note of defeat and foreboding. The very violence of the outbreak witnessed to the strength of the Church's foothold. Not all missionaries had left the interior and many of those in the ports, in Japan, and in Europe and America were expecting to return. By the close of 1927, indeed, a large number were back at their posts.[326] Missionary interest and conviction in the churches in Europe and America had far from died out, and, if Protestantism had permanent vitality, would continue. Some Chinese Christians had crumpled under the terrific strain, but others had risen to the emergency and were heroically standing by their faith. Protestants had greatly gained in numbers since 1900 and even since 1914, and the body of able, trained leaders had multiplied still more rapidly. Self-support had increased, and the Church probably had more of real conviction and inward vitality than ever. Reverses had simply disclosed weaknesses which had long been present and which probably were decreasing. Protestant churches in China might not yet be able to stand and continue to grow without help from their parent bodies in the Occident, but they were more nearly in a position to do so than they ever had been. No one could forecast events of even a decade ahead. The Church might be in process of disappearing. It had, however, a better chance of surviving and making a permanent impression than at any time during its presence in China.

[326] In May, 1928, about four thousand Protestant missionaries were in China, as against about sixty-five hundred actually resident in the country on Jan. 1, 1927.—*Bulletin of National Christian Council,* July, 1928, p. 18.

CHAPTER XXXI

SUMMARY AND CONCLUSION

THIS, then, is the history of Christian missions and of the Christian Church in China from the beginning into the critical year of 1927. It has been a long story. We have seen the efforts which, for more than three centuries, the Nestorians made on this, the remotest frontier of their church. We have watched the Franciscans, in the enthusiasm of the early years of their order, travel by desert and sea to Cambaluc and Zaitun. We have seen how, save for a few physical monuments and possible influences on non-Christian cults, all tangible results of the labors of Nestorians and Franciscans disappeared. With the sixteenth century came the Portuguese, and with them the Jesuits. We have watched, following the Society of Jesus, other representatives of the Church arrive, first more Roman Catholic congregations and orders, and, slightly later, a few Russian Orthodox clerics. We have witnessed the numbers of Roman Catholic converts rapidly increase, then become stationary. We have recounted how, when at the beginning of the nineteenth century the body of Christians were dwindling and seemed about to disappear, a fresh wave of the Occidental flood came, and with it the first representatives of Protestantism and reënforcements to the beleaguered Roman Catholics. We have watched pressure from the West continue and have seen how, as the nineteenth century wore on, missionaries rapidly increased in numbers and, under the ægis of treaties, established themselves even in the remotest provinces. We have witnessed, with the collapse after 1900 of the resistance of the old culture before the ever more aggressive West, the expanding missionary body begin to reap the fruits of the preceding century and the churches grow rapidly in numbers and influence. We have seen the World War shake the prestige and weaken the power of the Occident and we have watched the quickening spirit of nationalism rise against the foreigner and usher in for missionaries as well as merchants and

823

diplomats a new and more trying era. It remains now to appraise the movement whose history we have narrated, and to estimate its results and its effects upon the nation.

A fundamental fact, one which must always be borne in mind, is that the primary motives back of the missionary movement were unselfish. Selfish ones there undoubtedly were—the increase of the glory and power of a Western nation or of an order or a society, the desire for personal renown, and the urge to adventure. Missionaries were pioneers and were impelled in part, as are all pioneers, by a passion for achievement in a fresh environment. In the great majority of missionaries, however, the dominant motive had little of self: it was a feeling of obligation to share with others a message, a salvation, a way of life which the missionary believed of supreme importance. The merchants came from the West to China primarily for gain. While among them were high-minded men eager that the exchange should be of reciprocal benefit, very many were dissipated and none too scrupulous, ignoring the moral standards of their own people and of the land of their sojourn. Government representatives had as their chief concern the interests of themselves and their respective countries, although, fortunately, they not infrequently sought also what they deemed the best interests of China. Even the foreign members of the Customs, Post Office, and Salt Gabelle services, the administrators of as constructive non-missionary enterprises as the Westerner could show for himself in China, were most of them in the East for a livelihood, and in time the Customs service became a means of collecting debts due to foreigners, the chief of the obligations being indemnity for an unsuccessful effort of the Chinese to rid themselves of the alien. The missionaries were the one group of foreigners whose major endeavor it was to make the impact of the West upon the Middle Kingdom of benefit to the Chinese. Bigoted and narrow they frequently were, occasionally superstitious, and sometimes domineering and serenely convinced of the superiority of Western culture and of their own particular form of Christianity. When all that can be said in criticism of the missionaries has been said, however, and it is not a little, the fact remains that nearly always at considerable and very often at great sacrifice they came to China, and in unsanitary and uncongenial surroundings, usually with insufficient stipends, often at the cost of their own lives or

of lives that were dearer to them than their own, labored indefatigably for an alien people who did not want them or their
message. Whatever may be the final judgment on the major
premises, the methods, and the results of the missionary enterprise, the fact cannot be gainsaid that for sheer altruism and
heroic faith here is one of the bright pages in the history of
the race.

A second fact, also of importance, is that what was called
Christianity came to China under many forms and auspices. In
the attempt to evaluate the movement as a whole this variety
must not be lost sight of. Between the three great divisions of
the Church—Roman Catholic, Russian Orthodox, and Protestant
—marked differences existed, both in character and methods, and
within the two largest, particularly within Protestantism, great
diversity was to be found. The mission of the Russian Orthodox
Church and the body of its converts were so small that in esti-
mating the influence of Christian missions on China they can be
all but ignored. Only in its scholarship, in its interpretation of
China to Russia, was the Russian Mission really notable.

As we have repeatedly seen, in China Roman Catholicism and
Protestantism were so different as at times to make them seem
two separate religions. They were known by different names and
each had almost no dealings with the other. To other divisive
factors was added the barrier of nationality and language, for
the majority of Protestant missionaries were Americans and British
and the majority of the Catholics were from France, Italy, and
Spain. Only in famine relief, and then infrequently, did members of the two groups work side by side. Clashes between
Chinese Catholics and Protestants not infrequently occurred,
usually when clans long at loggerheads adopted the rival forms
of the new faith in hope of aid in their feud. To the Roman
Catholic the Protestant was a heretic who at best was giving the
perishing Chinese only half a loaf. Catholic book lists contained
numerous titles of tracts to counteract Protestant propaganda and
letters of Catholic missionaries often spoke with annoyance or
disdain and only infrequently in praise of their Protestant
brethren. Although Roman Catholics were so numerous, Protestants usually calmly ignored them. Occasionally they lost converts to and sometimes they won them from the rival fold. They
usually thought, spoke, and planned, however, as though they

were the only body of missionaries in China. The majority were not bitter toward the Catholics and when they recognized them were frequently tolerant and even friendly. As a rule they were simply unconscious of their existence. Still, Chinese in general recognized the two as wings of the one movement and any estimate of Christianity in China must include them both.

The chief differences between Roman Catholicism and Protestantism in China can be rather briefly summarized, especially as earlier in this work the history and general characteristics of the two, and some of the contrasts have been given.

In the first place, the body of Roman Catholics in China was between four and five times as large as and numerically was increasing more rapidly than that of Protestants. Proportionately, however, Protestants grew more rapidly than Roman Catholics, and the greater numbers of the latter were due in part to the fact that they had been in China nearly three times as long as had the former and had counted about two hundred thousand on their rolls when Robert Morrison landed.

In the second place, in some respects Roman Catholics were more united than were Protestants. They enjoyed uniformity of doctrine and in Rome they possessed a center not only of authority but for planning and coördinating their efforts. Rome, too, was a bond of fellowship and when the nationalization of the Church should be completed Chinese Catholics would not be as likely to drift away from the Church Universal as would their Protestant brethren.

In the third place, however, in other respects Roman Catholics in China, strangely enough, were not as near to being a unit as were Protestants. Protestants had had their controversies, but none had been as acrimonious or as prolonged as had that of Catholics over the rites. Protestants were earlier in achieving a national organization. Not until 1924 did Roman Catholics have a gathering which compared to those which Protestants had held in 1877, 1890, 1907, 1913, and 1922, and they were much slower in coördinating nationally their educational, medical, and literary activities.

In the fourth place, a marked difference existed in the methods of propagating the Christian message. Protestants spread it broadcast—by the wide dissemination of the printed page, by street chapels, street preaching, and other forms of public address.

With their emphasis upon private judgment and individual action they welcomed into fellowship any who seemed sincere in their profession of faith, whether from a Christian or from a non-Christian environment. Indeed, in 1918 two-thirds of the Protestants were said to live in homes in which the influence was predominantly non-Christian.[1] Roman Catholics, on the other hand, engaged in almost no public preaching to non-Christians, distributed little literature outside their own constituency, and made their first approaches to non-Christians through Chinese assistants. Much more than Protestants they held out as inducements aid in lawsuits and support of catechumens during an intensive study of the Faith. They attempted, moreover, to reach the group rather than the isolated individual and often collected their Christians into separate settlements. In this they were more in accord with the established social structure of China. Chinese had traditionally acted by families or villages rather than as individuals, and it was much easier to insure the perseverance of the convert when the entire natural unit was reached. Roman Catholics, as we have seen, usually declined to receive an individual apart from his family, or even a single family in a village.

A fifth difference between Roman Catholics and Protestants was in educational policy. The former stressed the religious training of both children and adults and maintained many catechetical schools. They devoted much attention, too, to the preparation of a Chinese priesthood, and for the candidates for holy orders they established many seminaries and insisted upon the completion of a long and fairly rigorous curriculum before ordination. Protestants on the whole paid less attention to the religious education of children. With their traditional emphasis upon the experience of conversion as the normal door into the Christian life, Evangelicals—of whom were most Protestant missionaries—tended to make less of "Christian nurture" than did Catholics.[2] Protestants, however, devoted much more energy to general education of a lay character, especially of secondary and higher grade. They did not shirk the training of the clergy but most of the theological preparation given was of the elementary type, more akin to that received by Roman Catholic catechists. They were constantly raising their standards, but even

---

[1] *China Mission Year Book, 1918,* pp. 294-296. The proportion may be excessive.

[2] G. M. Thomas in *International Review of Missions,* Vol. 14, pp. 412-420.

in 1927 they possessed only three theological schools of as advanced grade as were nearly all Roman Catholic higher seminaries, and these three did not have many students. However, the few Protestant Chinese clergymen who were well trained probably possessed a broader education than did any of the Chinese Catholic priests.

A sixth difference, closely related to this last, was that Protestantism in China was more nearly a lay movement than was Roman Catholicism. Nearly half the men among Protestant missionaries were unordained, while of Catholic male missionaries nearly nine-tenths were priests. Women—unordained, of course, and usually with little theological training—formed a much smaller proportion of the Roman Catholic foreign force than of the Protestant staff, even when wives are deducted from the totals of the latter, and for that reason also the Catholic movement had more of a clerical nature than did the Protestant. In this respect Protestants were probably more in accord with Chinese traditions and so better able to appeal to the educated Chinese mind, for Chinese society had never been dominated by a priesthood and the only professionally religious, the Buddhist and Taoist monks, were usually viewed with contempt. It was the lay scholar class that set the pace for the nation.

A seventh contrast, also allied to the fifth, was that in the time they were both in China Protestants gave much more attention to the educated than did Roman Catholics. This comparison would not be true if made with Roman Catholic methods of the seventeenth and the early part of the eighteenth century, for it was to the scholars that the Jesuits of these years chiefly directed their energies. In the nineteenth and twentieth centuries, however, Catholics did not especially exert themselves to win the intelligentsia, either of the old or of the new order. Protestants at first had little contact with scholars. Beginning with the eighteen nineties, however, and especially after 1900 they made great efforts to reach the new student class, for in this they thought they saw the leaders of the future China. Most of the first schools for the new learning were founded by Protestants, and even to the point where our story pauses much of the best secondary and higher education was in Protestant hands. As we have seen, the Christian Literature Society early devoted itself to the literati and the Young Men's and Young Women's Christian Associations made students a primary care. It was through educated leaders that Protestants thought most quickly to reach the nation.

Both Roman Catholics and Protestants established great institutions and were active in philanthropic projects. An eighth difference, however, was between the kinds of philanthropy undertaken. The chief Catholic institution was the orphanage, and it was regarded primarily as a means of saving souls. Catholics had few hospitals and had little energy to spare for the relief of woes outside the Christian community. Protestants, on the other hand, had few orphanages, but they emphasized the hospital and the school—and both were for non-Christians as well as Christians. In addition, Protestants were attempting to mitigate various kinds of suffering and attacked evils not only in the Christian community but in the nation at large. Famine relief, the campaign against opium, public health, popular education, the movement against foot-binding, education of the blind and the deaf, anti-gambling and anti-prostitution crusades, and efforts for better labor conditions are only a few of the many activities which were either begun or substantially supported by Protestants.

This leads directly to a ninth contrast between the two great branches of organized Christianity, a contrast both in method and in emphasis. Catholics concentrated upon building up a Christian community: Protestants divided their energies between that objective and attempting to influence the nation as a whole. Roman Catholics endeavored to bring as many as possible into the Church —an ambition natural to those who believed that in the Church is eternal salvation. They sought to win entire villages, or, where that was not possible, to found new villages in which all the population would be Christian. Through these groups the Church could direct the life of each Christian and make it easier for all to fulfill their Christian duties. Catholic missionaries did not make much attempt to modify the life of the non-Catholic portion of the nation. Protestants, on the other hand, as a rule did not create separate Christian villages. Nor were they of one mind about concentrating on building up a Christian community. Some gave themselves primarily to this task, and others devoted themselves to spreading broadcast the Christian message, conceiving it to be the main function of the missionary to convey a knowledge of the Gospel to as many individuals as possible. Still others— and they were an increasing proportion of the missionary body

—believed it to be their duty not only to win individuals to the Christian life and to build up the Church, but to influence as much as possible the culture which was so rapidly changing about them.

A tenth difference was in the method of financing the missionary enterprise. Figures are not available for the total amounts spent either by Protestants or by Roman Catholics. This much is clear, however: Catholic missions derived a large portion of their income from investments in China itself, usually made in lands and houses. Quantities of real estate in the chief cities and fairly extensive agricultural tracts were in their possession. This, it may be added, was the traditional Chinese method of maintaining religious establishments. Protestants, on the other hand, derived their revenues almost entirely from voluntary contributions from China and the Occident and from medical and tuition fees in China. Both, of course, depended largely upon supporters in Europe and America.

A last contrast was in the relative rapidity with which the two great branches of the Church were becoming acclimatized in China. Roman Catholics, on the whole, were slower than Protestants in turning over the control of the Church to the Chinese. Until 1926 they had raised only one Chinese to the episcopate, while Protestants had already placed Chinese in the majority on the National Christian Council and were making them district superintendents, secretaries of boards, and principals of schools. This difference was natural, for Roman Catholicism was less flexible than most forms of Protestantism and was therefore more insistent that before the natives of any country were given control of the hierarchy all serious danger of schism or of deviation from Catholic doctrine be obviated.[3] Protestantism, too, in its inception was in part the child of nationalism, while Roman Catholicism by its traditions and very name was imperialistic. Throughout its history, then, the latter had been less willing to accommodate itself to patriotic aspirations than had the former.

In the generalizations on the results of Christian missions which follow, these contrasts, even if not always expressly alluded to, must be borne in mind. The impact of organized Christianity

[3] Most of these contrasts appear, in a different form, in an article by the author in the April, 1927, number of *The International Review of Missions.*

upon China was varied and the two great branches of the Church differed in their fruits.

RESULTS OF MISSIONS

The task of determining accurately the effect of Christian missions upon China is most difficult. Some observers, usually non-Christian Chinese, have maintained that beyond aiding in the initial stages of the introduction of Western civilization, especially of the newer education, missions have made little impression upon the country as a whole.[4] Others have been of the conviction that the revolution which so transformed Chinese life was primarily due to the missionary. Some results are, however, fairly clear.

In the first place, a fairly large Christian community arose. In 1927 it probably numbered between two and a half and three million baptized persons, of whom somewhat more than four-fifths were Roman Catholics and a little less than one-fifth Protestants. If made to include those under Christian instruction, the total was not far from three and a half millions. While this number is fairly impressive and was about three times the total of 1900, it was not one per cent. of the population of China. Christians were still in a very small minority.

More important than quantity is the question of quality. How far and in what respects did Christians differ from their non-Christian neighbors? Generalizations here must be guarded and many exceptions to them can be found. In earlier chapters, however, enough examples have been given to establish some conclusions.

Chinese sought Christian instruction and baptism from a variety of motives. Some wished aid in a lawsuit, some were drawn by hope of employment, or by the support given—by some missions only—while in the catechumenate. Others hoped to find in Christianity a religion which would supply more effectively what they had expected from their old faiths—health for themselves or their cattle, protection against evil spirits, a happy immortality. In the twentieth century others came because they believed that China would find in the new faith a remedy for the national weaknesses which were so palpable, or because they

[4] See Hu Shih in *The Forum*, July, 1927, and Liang Ch'i-ch'ao in "The Introduction to the Learning of the Ch'ing Dynasty," quoted in *Chinese Recorder*, Vol. 54, p. 309.

were impressed by the philanthropic and reform activities of the Church. Others were first attracted by the quality of the lives of some Christians of their acquaintance. Still others sought release from vice, usually the opium habit, or craved inward peace and an answer to the riddle of life.

Among Roman Catholics the average of moral character seems to have been higher in some vicariates than in others. Among Protestants there were variations between societies and even between different missions of the same board. Christians unworthy of the name certainly existed. Many who had received baptism fell away. For those who lapsed no accurate statistics for all China are available, and apparently none whatever for Roman Catholics. One Protestant writer said that of every six added to the Protestant churches two fell away within five or ten years, and that two of the others were irregular in attendance on public worship.[5] An investigation of six Protestant colleges showed that of the graduates who were church members about fifteen per cent. lapsed, and this was said to be a smaller proportion than would have been found among rural Christians.[6] In one of the best Protestant parishes in Peking only about one-tenth of the members were engaged in any voluntary activity in the Church, and only about two-thirds attended a service as often as once a month.[7] A study made by the American Bible Society showed that out of about thirty-three hundred Protestant church members, less than one-eighth maintained family worship, only one-third read the Bible daily, and only two-thirds possessed a Bible or a New Testament.[8] Faithfulness in religious observances may not be an accurate barometer of moral or spiritual life, but it provides a fairly reliable gauge for interest in the Church and its message.

A Protestant missionary among the Chinese in Formosa—a most careful observer whom we have quoted before—describes the slowness with which the ordinary country and village folk of his district understood the Gospel. In their own words they were "like a duckling listening to thunder."[9] The ordinary convert summed up the duty of a Christian as "come to worship; observe

[5] *Chinese Recorder,* Vol. 56, p. 179.
[6] Ibid., Vol. 54, p. 379.
[7] Gamble, *Peking, a Social Survey,* p. 362.
[8] Speer and Moody, *Report on Japan and China, 1927,* p. 294.
[9] Moody, *The Mind of the Early Converts,* p. 117.

the Lord's day; give thanks at meal time; keep the ten commandments; obey the teaching of Christ." [10] To him God was neither very near nor very real, but Jesus was, and God and Jesus were regarded as interchangeable. He had no great sense of sin, and salvation to him meant deliverance from illness or distress, or escape from robbers, or a complete reformation of habits.[11] The inward life of fellowship with God was a slow development.

With occasional splendid exceptions, throughout China and among both Roman Catholics and Protestants, the Church was still dependent on the foreigner for ideas, leadership, and financial support. Little first-class Christian literature had yet appeared from Chinese pens. No outstanding apologia, no great work of devotion had yet been written by a Chinese. While here and there adaptation was being achieved, and Chinese were making rapid strides toward self-support, in propagating the Faith and in providing leadership, the Church was, as we have often seen, still predominantly alien in form and in control.

However, although the results in life were less than the missionary longed to see, they evidenced real progress. The requirements for admission to the Church made for improvement over the converts' pre-Christian state. As we have repeatedly seen in preceding pages, mission annals, both Roman Catholic and Protestant, abound in stories of moral transformation, of hope coming to despondent souls, of devoted, unselfish lives, and of loyalty to the new faith even at the cost of martyrdom.[12] Many Chinese Christians labored heroically as missionaries in their own or far distant provinces.[13] The family life of Christians was on the average more attractive than that of their non-Christian neighbors. One high official in Peking became a Christian because he found that without exception the homes which compelled his admiration were those of Christians.[14] Women found larger freedom, especially in Protestant circles, and received more respect from men. Christians had less part in the nefarious opium

[10] Ibid., p. 44.
[11] Moody, op. cit., pp. 17-23.
[12] See a few examples in Williams, *Ohio Friends in the Land of Sinim*, p. 178; *Missions*, Vol. 16, p. 596; Maclagan, *Chinese Religious Ideas, a Christian Valuation*, last chapter.
[13] So a Dr. Kao under the China Inland Mission, who gave up an opportunity for a lucrative professional career to undertake pioneer medical mission work in Kansu.—Mrs. Howard Taylor, *The Call of China's Great Northwest*, pp. 75 et seq.; Cable and French, *Through Jade Gate and Central Asia*, pp. 30-36.
[14] Porter, *China's Challenge to Christianity*, p. 100.

business than had non-Christians.[15]   A far greater proportion of Christians than of non-Christians were literate.[16]   Chinese Christians, too, were naturally among the first to be affected by Western civilization and through the missionary came in touch with its best features.   There seems to be no question that in morals and in education the Christian community, because of the fact that it was Christian, was above the average of the nation.

When we come to the influence of Christianity upon China as a whole—as distinct from the Christian community—we are on ground where conclusions cannot be as easily verified.   Even here, however, a few definite statements seen warranted.

In general it may be said that missionaries molded to some extent the revolution brought by the impact of the Occident. That this revolution would have come had never a missionary set foot in China, and probably about when it did, no one acquainted with the facts, as we have repeatedly said, can seriously question. Other forces, economic and political, were chiefly responsible for the changes and would have brought them about without the missionary.   It can scarcely be reiterated too often that what the missionary did was not to be the primary cause but to help to determine the course of the transformation.   The ways in which this influence was exerted and its results were about as follows:

First of all, the very presence in the nation of hundreds of thousands of Christians could not but have its effect.   The higher moral standards of the Christian community, the interpretation given to Western civilization of which Christians were often the forerunners, must have influenced those who saw them.   While Christians were most numerous in the coast provinces and along the Yangtze from Hankow eastward, scarcely a *hsien* in the country was without them and the contagion of their presence must have been very pervasive.   No other representatives of the new forces from the West were so widespread.

In the second place, it was due partly to the missionary that when the revolution came the nation had at least some leaders who were familiar with the learning to which it must now perforce adjust itself.   The first large group of Chinese to study abroad was sent at the initiative of Yung Wing, who through

---

[15] In Northwest China, for example, Protestant Christian farmers would not grow the opium poppy.—Cable and French, op. cit., p. 145.

[16] Statistics are lacking for Roman Catholics, but the generalization would probably hold true for them.   It certainly is true of Protestants.

the education that missionaries had made possible for him saw the necessity of a similar training for some of his countrymen. Mission schools and colleges were sending out graduates when Chinese government and private schools of the new type had barely gotten under way, and after the latter became numerous supplemented the all too meagre stream of well-prepared men who were trying to bring new vigor into the nation's life. Some of the most prominent of China's leaders received part or all of their training at the hands of missionaries. This was true of a number of nationally known educators—P. W. Kuo, the great President of Southeastern University at Nanking, for instance. Chang Po-Ling, President of an important school in Tientsin, was an earnest (Protestant) Christian. Three of the five Chinese delegates to the Paris Peace Conference were Christians, two being sons of Anglican clergymen. One of the latter was C. T. Wang (Wang Cheng-ting), formerly head of the Young Men's Christian Association in China. He filled many important diplomatic positions and was for brief periods Minister of Justice, Minister of Foreign Affairs, and Acting Premier.[17] ⸱Wang Ch'ung-hui, an outstanding jurist, chief judge of the Supreme Court, Minister of Justice, one of the three delegates to the Washington Disarmament Conference, for a time Acting Premier, and a member of the Permanent Court of International Justice, was the son of a pastor under the London Missionary Society.[18] W. W. Yen (Yen Hui-ch'ing), who held many diplomatic posts and was Minister of Foreign Affairs and Acting Premier and Premier during very trying periods, was the son of an Episcopal clergyman and a former student and later a member of the faculty of St. John's University.[19] Chang Ying-hua, Chief of the Salt Administration and Minister of Finance,[20] C. C. Wang and Yen Tê-Ching, important railway men, were also counted as Christians.[21] Wu P'ei-fu, although not a Christian, had for a time studied in Dr. Mateer's famous school at Têngchow.[22] Sun Yat-sen, probably more influential in China's transition than any other one individual, while critical of the Church, owed much of his education

[17] China Year Book, 1925, p. 1282a.
[18] China Mission Year Book, 1923, pp. 88-91; Keyte, In China Now, p. 143.
[19] Millard's Review, Vol. 14, p. 119.
[20] Keyte, op. cit., p. 143; China Year Book, 1925, p. 1222.
[21] China Mission Year Book, 1923, p. 90; China Year Book, 1925, pp. 1282-1293.
[22] Speer and Kerr, op. cit., p. 89.

to Protestant teachers and schools in Hawaii and Hongkong, and lived and died a professed Christian.[23] His second wife, who was high in the councils of the Kuomintang, was an avowed Christian and a graduate of a Christian school in the United States. In addition to these national figures, many others of local prominence owed their education in part or entirely to missionaries. One well known Protestant family, the father of which was picked out of poverty and educated by missionaries, numbered among its children, all trained in part in mission schools, a surgeon-general in the army, a prominent secretary of the Young Men's Christian Association, a pastor, and the head of a kindergarten.[24] We hear, too, of a graduate of and former teacher in mission schools who after years in business devoted his declining days to philanthropic and religious work, helping to found a girls' high school and a hospital and aiding in famine relief.[25] The list might be greatly extended. Not all the former students in mission schools or children of Christians who attained national or local eminence had characters which the Church could heartily endorse, but whatever the nation owed to them it owed in part to the missionary.

A third contribution, closely related to this last, was that of the missionary and of Chinese Christians to education. Many of the first text-books of the new learning were produced by missionaries and a large proportion of the teachers in government and private schools were trained in Christian institutions. Some dialects had never been reduced to writing until the missionary translated the Christian Scriptures into them. Everywhere the missionary, particularly the Protestant missionary, was emphasizing the use of a written form of the vernacular as an aid to universal literacy, and the Popular Education Movement had its birth in a Protestant organization.

In the fourth place, the missionary brought types of Western learning to China which without him would not have come as quickly, and, what was more important, by precept and example proclaimed the ideal that these should be used for the welfare of the community and not for private gain. At once there come to mind the scientific contributions of the Jesuits, both earlier and

[23] T. T. Lew in *The Life,* July, 1925; *Chinese Recorder,* Vol. 54, p. 242, Vol. 58, p. 242.
[24] Tinling, *Bits of China,* p. 61.
[25] *Chinese Recorder,* Vol. 58, pp. 276-278.

later, and of the Lazarists of the eighteenth century, the introduction of Western medical lore and the training of the pioneer Chinese members of the profession, the education of the blind and deaf, a better form of movable type, the conservation of public health, improvements in agriculture and forestry, better athletic sports, and personal hygiene.

A fifth contribution of the missionary to the changing nation was the reënforcement of Chinese ethical standards and the quickening of the Chinese public conscience. The missionary was active in fighting opium, gambling, and prostitution. He attacked whatever he believed cramped or harmed the best development of the individual—famine, poor labor conditions, concubinage, the custom of foot-binding, the exposure of infants. Against some of these evils high-minded men had labored long before the coming of the missionary. Missionaries, however, cast the weight of their efforts on the side of all movements toward righteousness and were the initiators of many of the protests against the open sores of the nation's life.

A sixth result, closely related to these others, was a heightened regard for the individual. No person was too lowly not to have, in the judgment of the missionary, an immortal soul of infinite value. No outcast girl infant, no beggar boy, no work-broken coolie, no opium sot, no leper, no bandit or prodigal son, but was worth saving. Jesus' followers must, as did he, "seek and save that which was lost."

All groups of Christians held to the pricelessness of every human being, but the larger proportion of Protestant denominations added to it an emphasis on democracy. Government of the Church by the majority, each communicant, whether man, woman, or child, having a voice, reënforced existing tendencies in Chinese life. Many Protestant missionaries, indeed, were so thoroughly convinced of the virtues of democracy that at times they might, with justice, be accused of confounding them with the Gospel.

A seventh contribution was the preparation and dissemination of literature which brought not only to Christians but to non-Christians new conceptions of ethics, of God, and of the religious life. Most influential were the Scriptures, to the translation and distribution of which Protestants devoted much of their energy, but pamphlets and books of apologetics and devotion all had their part.

An eighth effect was upon non-Christian faiths. On some of these, missions had only a disintegrating influence. Taoism as it was usually practiced, popular polytheism, and dæmonism crumbled where the Christian missionary had his way. A Christian might continue to believe that evil spirits existed, but he was convinced that he need no longer dread them and that former practices for their control either availed nothing or had been rendered unnecessary. Christians at times exorcised evil spirits and Catholics looked upon medals and other objects of devotion as amulets, but for the believer fear and with it the old customs and many of the old beliefs either had gone or were passing.

In Confucianism and Buddhism, however, competition with Christianity helped to stimulate reform. Various attempts were made to adjust Confucianism to the new day, and, while these were due to many factors, the presence of Christianity was among them. The same can be said of the new movements in Buddhism.

Most interesting of the influences upon religion outside the Church was the recognition given Christianity by new cults. For centuries sects had come and gone. Often they were in practice a syncretism of Taoism, Buddhism, and Confucianism. Here and there, from Nestorian times on, Christianity had possibly had some effect. Certainly the religion of the T'ai P'ings owed its inception and much of its form to it. In the cults which appeared after 1900 and especially after 1911 the influence of Christianity was often conspicuous. Thus the "Coöperative Goodness Association" (*T'ung Shan Shê*), an attempt to unite all leading religions, including Christianity, was to be found in many of the chief cities. It was a secret order, with several degrees, and showed strong Taoist and Buddhist proclivities.[26] The *Wu Shan Shê*—"Apprehension of Goodness Society"—was begun in Peking in 1918 and claimed to put equal emphasis upon Buddhism, Confucianism, Taoism, Islam, and Christianity.[27] The *Tao Yüan*, which first appeared in Tsinanfu in 1921 and later spread to numbers of other cities and drew its members largely from official circles, declared its purpose to be "the worship of the Most Holy Primeval Father" as the founder of the five religions. It made much of the planchette, for through it the members

---

[26] Twinem in *Journal of Religion*, Vol. 5, pp. 464-466; Hodous in *The Christian Occupation of China*, p. 50; *Chinese Recorder*, Vol. 55, pp. 372-379.
[27] Twinem in *Journal of Religion*, Vol. 5, pp. 467-472.

believed they received divine revelations, but it also devised modes of worship and encouraged works of benevolence and adherence to high ethical standards.[28] At least one prominent Christian joined it and claimed that by doing so he had not been disloyal to his faith.[29] The "Six Sages Union True Tao Society" (*Lu Shêng Chen Tao T'ung I Hui*) or "Union of the Religions of the Six Sages" was begun in Szechwan in 1921 by T'ang Huang-chang—formerly a member of the Methodist Church in Chengtu—and spread as far east as Nanking and Shanghai. It professed to combine Buddhism, Confucianism, Taoism, Islam, Christianity, and Judaism. Jesus was ranked as the first of the six sages and T'ang himself was said to be the seventh great religious leader. Commandments were given which showed Christian influence, and fasting and meditation were enjoined. The end of the world was declared to be at hand and membership in the society the way of avoiding destruction.[30] The *Tao Tê Hsüeh Hui,* the "Society for the Study of Morality," a cult founded in 1916 or 1917 and having branches in five cities, also strove to combine all religions, including Christianity.[31] In Shansi Governor Yen Hsi-shan maintained, as the state religion of the province, the *Tsung Shêng Hui* and the *Hsi Hsin Shê* ("Heart Cleansing Society"). In most respects both of these were an adaptation of Confucianism. The former maintained the semi-annual sacrifices to Confucius and the latter taught Confucian ethics of the people. The *Hsi Hsin Shê,* however, clearly showed the evidences of the Christian influences that had been potent in its formation. Services were held every Sunday in all cities and larger towns and occasionally Christian preachers were asked to speak. At T'aiyüanfu was a hall for meditation and worship.[32]

Except for the last two, none of these cults counted more than a few thousand members, but some of them were fairly prominent, and they were indubitable indications that Christianity was having religious fruit outside the Church. In general, the contribution of Christianity to them seems to have been the reënforcement

---

[28] Ibid., pp. 472-482; F. S. Drake in *Chinese Recorder,* Vol. 54, pp. 133-144.
[29] O'Neill, *The Quest for God in China,* p. 66.
[30] Twinem in *Journal of Religion,* Vol. 5, pp. 595-601; Donald Fay in *Chinese Recorder,* Vol. 55, pp. 155-159.
[31] Twinem in *Journal of Religion,* Vol. 5, pp. 601-606; Hodous in *The Christian Occupation of China,* p. 30.
[32] Hodous in *The Christian Occupation of China,* p. 29; *Chinese Recorder,* Vol. 51, pp. 482, 483.

of their ethical standards.   The methods for cultivating contact with the unseen were chiefly from other sources.

Upon the seething thought of the Renaissance and the new student class Christianity appears at first sight to have had practically no effect.   The Church had few scholars who commanded the respect of the leaders of the New Tide, and the bulk of the philosophical writings which for a time poured forth in such abundance usually did not take a Christian position.[33]   However, the picture has another side.   Christianity had become sufficiently prominent to attract the attention and to call forth the comments of all leading scholars, and the Anti-Christian Movement was unmistakable evidence that the new religion was important enough to evoke widespread and violent opposition.   Now and then some leader gave cautious approval to some phases of Christianity, and Ch'ên Tu-hsiu, one of the most prominent and radical of the intellectuals, at one time advocated the adoption by China of moral education based on the life and teachings of Jesus.[34]   Christianity, while not finding acceptance with the vast majority of the new scholar class, was at least engaging its attention.

In most of these impressions on China outside the Church, Protestantism had a larger part than did Roman Catholicism. When the non-Christian Chinese thought of Christianity, more and more he had in mind the former rather than the latter. That was probably chiefly because of the difference in methods. With their more public and more broadcast propaganda, with their greater emphasis upon secular education, and with their attempts to mold the life of the entire nation, non-Christian as well as Christian, Protestants were naturally more in the public eye.   Protestant missionaries, too, were more than twice as numerous as were those of Roman Catholics.

The question naturally arises whether missionaries had properly weighed the effects of widespread interference with long-established conditions and institutions.   Were they not well-intentioned but clumsy meddlers, who, while fighting one evil, were unintentionally opening the door to two others?   In pulling

[33] See an article by F. R. Millican on *Philosophical and Religious Thought in China*, in *China Christian Year Book, 1926*, pp. 423-469.
[34] Rawlinson in *Chinese Recorder*, Vol. 57, pp. 172 et seq., quoting from an article by Ch'ên in *La Jeunesse* for March, 1920.

up the tares were they not uprooting an unnecessary quantity of grain? In attacking idolatry, for example, were they not also weakening systems of ethics and social control which were of real use to the nation? In promoting greater liberty for women, in opposing the worship of ancestors, and in altering marriage customs and frowning upon concubinage, were they not adding to the disintegration which was threatening that most characteristic and stabilizing institution of the older China, the family? In introducing Western medical science, in promoting public health, and in relieving famines, were they not adding to an overcrowded population and so only postponing the day of reckoning and making more certain intense and widespread suffering? In advocating democracy and promoting social reform, were they not giving currency to ideas which, misunderstood, could be twisted to the nation's undoing?

That the missionary was at least partly destructive is indubitable. Of this the T'ai P'ing Rebellion, for which he was by no means entirely to blame but which without him would never have occurred, is undeniable evidence. As one of the agents of the impact of the Occident upon China he must share responsibility for the Revolution of 1911 and the subsequent chaos. The protection given him and his converts by foreign governments helped to bring about the breakdown of the Chinese state. If he were in part the means of Sun Yat-sen's education, he may have to assume a portion of the censure for the confusion as well as share the credit for the awakening which that unbalanced dreamer brought. It must again be reiterated, however, that revolution would have come to China without the missionaries. Had never one of their number left his native soil, the family would have disintegrated, the Manchus have fallen, and Renaissance dawned, and nationalism arisen.

For a few details of the destruction missionaries may have been chiefly to blame, but in the main they were more constructive than destructive. For the old family, which without them would have been shaken quite as much as it was, they were trying—and in Christian circles effectively—to substitute a better. They were reënforcing the excellent ethical standards of the old China. They were introducing moral and intellectual training which would help prepare leaders to grapple with the complex problems brought by the new day. They were endeavoring to improve agriculture and to increase the production of food as well as to prevent disease and to relieve famine. They were seeking to import sciences which would be of aid to the Chinese. Above all, they were the agents for creating in thousands of souls a courage, a faith, a hope, and an unselfish devotion without which the Chinese could never make their way through their distresses to a more stable, ordered life.

Before concluding this summary one other contribution of the missionary must be mentioned: he was an interpreter of China to the Occident. By no means all great sinologues were missionaries: the diplomatic services and European universities provided what was probably a majority of these. From the time of the earliest Jesuits, however, the missionary forces numbered great scholars in things Chinese.[35] More than any other group of foreigners resident in China, missionaries popularized in the Occident a knowledge of the country. Both with the object of enlisting the support of Christians of the West and from a desire to be channels of information they sent out countless letters and reports, prepared thousands of articles for church and secular periodicals, made tens of thousands of public addresses, and wrote hundreds of books. In general the information thus broadcasted was accurate and sympathetic. The best and almost the only language schools in China were those initiated by missionaries; nearly all missionaries had some use of the language and numbers were expert in it; and by the nature of their profession they had intimate contacts with the Chinese. They therefore knew whereof they spoke. Sometimes, to arouse pity or sympathy and so to obtain support for their work, they stressed the dark sides of Chinese life. Usually, however, their devotion and genuine love for the Chinese made them appreciative interpreters and even ardent champions. They were often active in opposing the traducers of China and in fostering organizations for mediating between the East and the West. The Institute of Pacific Relations, initiated and in its earlier stages fostered chiefly by the Young Men's Christian Association, is one of many instances. As they

---

[35] Missionaries who deserved the title of sinologue were by no means extinct in 1926. Bruce's translation of Chu Hsi, Soothill's presence in the chair at Oxford once held by Legge, and Wieger's voluminous publications are evidence of this. Couling, compiler of *The Encyclopædia Sinica* and editor of *The New China Review*, had only recently died.

were trying to bring to China the best that the Occident had to give, so they were endeavoring to make the Occident understand and respect China.

In conclusion, then, the historian does not cease to be impartial when he declares that the presence and the labors of the missionary were most fortunate for China. Defects the missionary enterprise undoubtedly had. Sometimes it did evil. On the whole, however, it was the one great agency whose primary function was to bring China into contact with the best in the Occident and to make the expansion of the West a means to the greater welfare of the Chinese people. If, when the Chinese have finally adjusted themselves and their culture to the new age, the revolution through which they shall have passed proves to have been more beneficial than harmful, it will be in no small degree because of the thousands of Christian apostles who counted not their own lives dear that to the Chinese might come more abundant life.

BIBLIOGRAPHY

SINCE Huc's well-known work, in its English title *Christianity in China, Tartary, and Thibet,* no general history of Christian missions in China has appeared. Huc brought the story down only to the close of 1706. Moreover, although very readable, Huc is not always dependable, and much new material has appeared since his day. Nor does there exist any general narrative of Roman Catholic missions in China. The work of some societies has been covered in whole or in part, notably in the detailed and scholarly tomes by Adrien Launay, *Histoire des missions de Chine* (of which have appeared *Mission du Kouang-si* and *Mission du Kouy-tchou*), and *Histoire générale de la Société des Missions Étrangères,* and Servière, *Histoire de la mission du Kiangnan 1804-1878.* No one has yet attempted, however, to tell at all at length the entire story. For Protestants the only efforts at a general history have been the work edited by MacGillivray, *A Century of Protestant Missions in China (1807-1907),* and Richter, *Das Werden der christlichen Kirche in China.* The former is an invaluable source of information, for it is chiefly a collection of histories of all the Protestant missions which up to that time had labored in China, each, wherever possible, compiled by a member of the mission, and it contains statistical tables and lists of missionaries. It is not, however, an attempt to weave the story of the separate societies into a connected whole. Dr. Richter, well known for his many histories of Protestant missions by both societies and countries, has collected much interesting information. His account is, however, somewhat briefer than that in the preceding pages, is based largely upon a limited number of periodicals and secondary works, and, while excellent, suffers from not being written from a thorough examination of the vast mass of existing literature. It is almost entirely lacking, moreover, in footnote references to the authorities consulted. It contains a brief summary of the earlier non-Protestant missions to China.

For the preparation of a general history the amount of available material is enormous. A few general periodicals, of which among the chief are *Lettres édifiantes et curieuses concernant l'Asie, l'Afrique et l'Amerique, etc., Nouvelles lettres édifiantes des missions de la Chine et des Indes Orientales, Annales de la propagation de la foi* (with editions in several languages), and *Catholic Missions and Annals of the Propagation of the Faith,* contain letters and articles by Catholic missionaries which cover nearly the entire range of our story. Protestants have *The Chinese Repository* and *The Chinese Recorder,* both published in China, with articles by missionaries and news items which, with one long gap from 1851 to 1867 and a shorter one from 1872 to 1874, give current information from 1832 to date. Protestants have *The China Mission Hand-book,* published in

1896, the *China Mission Year Book* (in 1926 the *China Christian Year Book*), published annually from 1910 through 1926 with the exception of the years 1920-1922, and the mammoth *The Christian Occupation of China* (1922). These contain articles, usually by participants in the events they narrate, on current phases of missionary activity, most of them have statistical tables, and several append lists of missionaries. They are invaluable source material for the Protestant movement. The corresponding publication for the Roman Catholics, Planchet, *Les missions de Chine et du Japon,* of which seven issues appeared between 1916 and 1928, has much fewer articles and documents than its Protestant contemporary, but has very full statistical tables and lists of the clergy. Nearly every society, congregation, and order, and several of the individual missions publish periodicals, chiefly for the purpose of arousing the interest of their constituency, with news items and letters "from the field." As a rule these give only what will serve that end—needs, encouraging news of progress or narratives of persecutions—but they are usually accurate, even if not well rounded. Most of the Protestant societies publish, as well, annual reports from each of their missions. For a few of the societies, Roman Catholic and Protestant, general histories have been written, some of them very voluminous. Launay's *Histoire générale de la Société des Missions-Étrangères,* already mentioned, Eugene Stock's four volumes, *The History of the Church Misisonary Society,* and Findlay and Holdsworth, *History of the Wesleyan Missionary Society* (five volumes) are among the best. Biographies and memoirs of missionaries are very numerous and are chiefly of value to the historian for the extracts from letters and other documents which they contain. Books of travel also are often important sources. So full are all these records, most of them based upon or made up largely of contemporary accounts by eye-witnesses or participants, that I have attempted no examination of the great masses of unpublished material in Rome, New York, London, and other places where headquarters of boards and congregations have preserved files of correspondence and reports. Such an examination would almost certainly not alter materially the majority of the main features and conclusions of the account given in the preceding pages. While they would prove indispensable to a complete study of many of the individual phases or incidents of missions, as a rule they would merely add more details to a general account which is already overlong. The archives of European governments doubtless contain material which would enlarge and complete the picture of the relations of governments to missions, but it has not been possible to examine them.

In the bibliography given below only those books and periodicals have been listed which have been actually examined in the preparation of this work. There has been no attempt to make it exhaustive. Many titles found in Cordier's monumental *Bibliotheca Sinica,* for example, are not given here. The converse is also true, and for a complete bibliography both Cordier and the list below will need to be used. The chief libraries in the United States, Japan, and China where material would most likely be found have been visited, but I have attempted no examination of libraries in Great Britain or Europe. Fortunately, the Day Missions Library at Yale University and the Missionary Research Library in New York City are the most nearly complete collections on Protestant missions to be found anywhere, and both, particularly the Day Missions Library, contain material on Roman Catholic missions. The Wason Library in Cornell University, the Morrison Library in Tokyo, and the collection of the North China Branch of the Royal Asiatic Society, in Shanghai, are excellent both for Protestant and for Roman Catholic missions. The material on Roman Catholic missions has been gathered from these and from a large number of other libraries, none of which contains a complete collection. For the mission of the Russian Orthodox Church the chief dependence has been upon the rather scanty material in English. Happily, some of this had as authors scholarly members of that mission. The Russian mission was, compared with those of Roman Catholics and Protestants, so small and had so relatively slight an influence on China that I have not attempted to overcome the language difficulty or to seek access to archives to obtain a more detailed picture.

In listing the bibliography the arrangement, as will quickly be seen, is alphabetical—by author in the case of books, by title in the case of periodicals, and by organization in the case of reports. No attempt has been made to classify the titles according to the familiar arrangement of primary and secondary authorities. Nor has any effort been made to give critical notes or to itemize the authors and titles of articles in the periodicals. For several of the periodicals fairly complete tables of contents will be found in Cordier, *Bibliotheca Sinica.* The purpose has been to provide a list to which the reader can quickly refer for more details as to author, date, and place of publication than are given in the footnotes.

Abeel, David. "Journal of a Residence in China and the Neighboring Countries with a preliminary Essay on the Commencement and Progress of Missions in the World." New York, 1836.

Abelly, M. Louys. "Lettres de S. François Xavier de la Compagnie de Jesus, apostre du Japon. Traduites de nouveau en Français." Paris, 1660.

Abel-Résumat. "Mélanges asiatiques, ou choix de morceaux critiques et de mémoires relatifs aux religions, aux sciences, aux coutumes, a l'histoire et a la géographie des nations orientales." 2 vols. Paris, 1825, 1826.

Abel-Rémusat. "Nouveaux mélanges asiatiques." 2 vols. Paris, 1829.

"Acta causæ rituum seu ceremoniarum sinensium complectentia." Venice, 1709.

"Addresses on China at the Thirty-fourth Annual Session Foreign Missions Conference of North America, Atlantic City, N. J., January 11-14, 1927." New York, 1927.

Aduarte, Don Fray Diego, and Gonzalez, Fray Domingo. "Historia de la Provincia del Santo Rosario de Filipinas, Iapon y China, de la Sagrada Orden de Predicadores. Escrita por el ilustrissimo señor Don Fray Diego Advarte . . . Añ Adida por el Muyr. P. Fray

Domingo Gonzalez." 2 vols. Zaragaca, 1693. Second volume is by Fr. Baltasar de Santa Cruz.

Alexander. "Conformité des ceremonies chinoises avec l'idolatrie grecque et romaine. Pour servir de confirmation à l'apologie des dominicains missionaires de la Chine." Cologne, 1700.

Allan, C. Wilfrid. "Chu and Lo, Two Chinese Pastors." London, 190–.

Allen, Roland. "The Siege of the Peking Legations." London, 1901.

"Allgemeine Missionszeitschrift. Monatshefte für geschichtliche und theoretische Missionskunde." Edited by Julius Richter, Joh. Warneck, founded by Gustav Warneck. Gütersloh, 1874-1894; Berlin, 1895 et seq.

Alzog, John. "Manual of Universal Church History." Translated, with additions from the ninth German edition, by F. J. Pabisch and Thomas S. Byrne. Cincinnati, 1903.

American Academy of Political and Social Sciences. "China, Social and Economic Conditions." Philadelphia, 1912.

American Baptist Missionary Union, Correspondence. [MSS.]

American Bible Society. Annual Reports. New York.

American Board of Commissioners for Foreign Missions. "China." Boston, 1867.

American Board of Commissioners for Foreign Missions, Correspondence. [MSS.]

American Board of Commissioners for Foreign Missions, Correspondence from the field. [MSS.]

American Board of Commissioners for Foreign Missions. Annual Reports. Boston, 1812 et seq.

American Church Mission. "An Account of the American Church Mission in Shanghai and the Lower Yangtse Valley." New York, 1898.

"American Church Review." September, 1883. New York, [?]

American Presbyterian Mission Press. "A Mission Press Sexagenary, 1844-1904." Shanghai, 1904.

American Presbyterian Mission Press. "The Mission Press in China." Shanghai, 1895.

American Red Cross. "Report of the China Famine Relief, American Red Cross, October, 1920—September, 1921."

"American Relations with China. Report of the Conference held at Johns Hopkins University, September 17-20, 1925." Baltimore, 1925.

American Seaman's Friend Society. Annual Reports, 1829-1844. New York.

American Tract Society, "Proceedings of the First Ten Years." Instituted in Boston, 1814. Boston, 1824.

American Tract Society. Annual Reports. Boston, 1833 et seq.

"An Abridged Account of the State of Religion in China and Cochin China during the years 1806-7." London, 1809.

"An Abridged Account of the State of Religion in Tonkin, Cochinchina, and China during the years 1807-8-9." London, 1811.

Anderson, Adelaide Mary. "Humanity and Labour in China. An Industrial Visit and Its Sequel (1923 to 1926)." London, 1928.

Anderson, Rufus. "Memorial Volume of the First Fifty Years of the American Board of Commissioners for Foreign Missions." Boston, 1861.

André-Marie. "Missions dominicaines dans l'Extrême Orient." 2 vols. Paris, 1865.

Andrews, Roy Chapman, and Andrews, Yvette Borup. "Camps and Trails in China. A Narrative of Exploration, Adventure, and Sport in Little-known China." New York, 1919.

"Annales de la propagation de la foi, recueil periodique. Collection faisant suite aux lettres édifiantes." Lyon, 1842 et seq.

"Annals of the Propagation of the Faith." Dublin and New York, 1838-1923.

"The Anti-Christian Movement." Shanghai, 1924. (Translation of anti-Christian documents.)

Anti-Cobweb Club, The. Foochow-fu, China. "Fukien, A Study of a Province in China." Shanghai, 1925.

"The Anti-Foreign Riots in China in 1891. With an Appendix." Shanghai, North China Herald Office, 1892.

Antonini, Paul. "Au Pays de Chine." Paris [1889].

"Apologie des dominicains missionaires de la Chine ou réponse au livre due Père le Tellier, Jesuite, intitule. Défense des nouveaux chrétiens et à l'éclaircissement du P. le Gobien de la même compagnie sur les honneurs que les Chinois rendent à Confucius aux morts." Cologne, 1700.

"L'apostolat missionnaire de la France. Conférences données à l'Institut Catholique de Paris." IIe série, deuxième edition, 1924-1925. Paris, 1926.

Appia, G. "Souvenirs des martyrs de Chine." Paris, 1901.

Arens, Bernard. "Die katholischen Missionsvereine. Darstellung ihres Werdens und Wirkens ihrer Satzungen und Vorrechte." Freiburg im Breisgau, 1922.

Arens, Bernard. "Handbuch der katholischen Missionen." Freiburg im Breisgau, 1920. Second edition, 1925.

Arias, Evaristo Fernández. "El Beato Sanz y Compañeros Mártires del Orden de Predicatores." Manila, 1893.

"Artibus Asiæ. Curant editionem Carl Hentze Antwerpiæ Alfred Salmony Coloniæ. MCMXXV, Part I." Dresden.

Ashmore, Lida Scott. "The South China Mission of the American Baptist Foreign Mission Society. A Historical Sketch of its First Cycle of Sixty Years." Shanghai (Foreword, 1920).

"Au pays du dragon." Paris, 1922.

Auber, Peter. "China. An Outline of Its Government, Laws, and Policy: and of the British and Foreign Embassies to, and Intercourse with that Empire." London, 1834.

Aubry, Père, J.-B. "Correspondance du Père J.-B. Aubry des Missions

Étrangères, missionaire au Kouy-Tchéou, docteur in théologie, ancien directeur au grand séminaire de Beauvais." Beauvais, 1886.

Augustana Synod. "Our First Decade in China, 1905-1915. The Augustana Mission in the Province of Honan." Rock Island, Ill., 1915.

"Avisi de Giapone degli Anni M.D.LXXXII, LXXXIII, et LXXXIV. Con alcuni altri della Cina dell' LXXXIII et LXXXIV. Canoti dalle lettere della Compagnia di Giesu. Riceunte il mese de Decembre, MD.LXXXV." Milan, 1586.

"Avvisi della Cina et Giapone de fine dell' anno 1586. Con l'arrivo delli Signori Giaponsi nell' India. Canoti dalle lettere della Compagnia di Giesu. Riceunte il mese d'Ottobre, 1588." Milan, 1588.

Backhouse, E., and Bland, J. O. P. "Annals and Memoirs of the Court of Peking." Boston, 1914.

Bacon, Bessie Blanchard. " 'With Heaps o' Love.' The Story of Four Years in China. Told in letters by Bessie Blanchard Bacon, edited by her father, Charles Blanchard." Des Moines, 1925.

Baddeley, John F. "Russia, Mongolia, China. Being Some Record of the Relations between Them from the Beginning of the XVIIth Century to the Death of the Tsar Alexei Mikhailovich, A.D. 1602-1676. Rendered Mainly in the Form of Narratives Dictated or Written by the Envoys Sent by the Russian Tsars, or their Vœvodas in Siberia to the Kalmuk and Mongol Khans and Princes: and to the Emperors of China," &c. 2 vols. London, 1919.

Baldwin, S. L. "Sia Sek Ong. On the Picket Line of Missions." New York, 1897.

Baller, F. W. (translator). "The Sacred Edict, with a Translation of the Colloquial Rendering." Shanghai, 1907.

Balme, Harold. "China and Modern Medicine. A Study in Medical Missionary Development." London, 1921.

"The Baptist." Published weekly by the Northern Baptist Convention. Chicago, 1920 et seq.

"The Baptist Missionary Magazine." Published by the Board of Managers of the Baptist General Convention. Boston, 1820 et seq.

Barber, Rev. W. T. A. "David Hill, Missionary and Saint." Second edition. London, 1898.

Bard, Émile. "Chinese Life in Town and Country." Adapted from the French by A. Twitchell. New York and London, 1905.

Barnes, Irene H. "Behind the Great Wall. The Story of the C.E.Z.M.S. Work and Workers in China." London, 1896. (Fifth edition, 1899.)

Barnes, Lemuel Call. "Two Thousand Years of Missions Before Carey." Chicago, 1900.

Barrow, John. "Travels in China." London, 1804.

Bartholomew, Allen R. "The Martyr of Huping. The Life Story of William Anson Reimert, Missionary in China." Philadelphia, 1925.

Barton, James L. "Educational Missions." New York, 1913.

Bashford, James W. "China and Methodism." Cincinnati, c.1906.

Bashford, James W. "China. An Interpretation." New York and Cincinnati, 1916.

Bashford, James W., "Journal." MS.

Batty, J. A. Staunton. "Our Opportunity in China." London, 1912.

Beach, Harlan Page. "Dawn on the Hills of T'ang; or, Missions in China." Revised edition. New York, 1905.

Beach, Harlan Page. "Princely Men in the Heavenly Kingdom." Boston and Chicago, 1903.

Beach, Harlan P. and Fahs, Charles H. (editors). "World Missionary Atlas, Containing a Directory of Missionary Societies, Classified Summaries of Statistics, Maps Showing the Location of Mission Stations Throughout the World, a Descriptive Account of the Principal Mission Lands, and Comprehensive Indices." New York, 1925.

Beals, Z. Charles. "China and the Boxers." New York, 1901.

Beazley, C. Raymond (editor). "The Texts and Versions of John de Plano Carpini and William de Rubruquis as Printed for the First Time by Hakluyt in 1598, Together with Some Shorter Pieces." London, 1903.

Becker, Émile. "Un demi-siècle d'apostolat en Chine Le Révérend Pere Joseph Gonnet de la Compagnie de Jésus." Third edition. Ho-kienfou, 1916.

Beckman, E. R. "The Massacre at Sianfu and Other Experiences in Connection with the Scandinavian Alliance Mission of North America." English edition. Chicago, 1913.

[Benedetti, G. B.] "Difesa de' Missionarii Cinesi Della Compagnia di Giesú in riposta All' Apologia de' PP. Domenicani Missionarii della Cina, Intorno à gli onori di Confusio, e de' Morti; opera di un Religioso Teologo della medesima Compagnia." In Colonia, per il Berges, Con Licenza de' Superiori, 1700.

Bentley, W. P. "Illustrious Chinese Christians." Cincinnati, 1906.

Beresford, Lord Charles. "The Break-Up of China." New York and London, 1899.

Berry, D. M. "The Sister Martyrs of Kucheng." New York [no date].

Beyer, Georg. "China als Missionsfeld." Berlin, 1923.

"Bible in China, The." (Read at the Quarterly Missionary Meeting in Union Chapel, Shanghai, in April, 1868.)

"Bibliotheca Asiatica, Part II. The Catholic Missions in India, China, Japan, Siam, and the Far East, in a series of Autograph Letters of the Seventeenth Century." (Maggs Brothers, publishers.) London, 1924.

Biermann, Benno M. "Die Anfänge der neueren Dominikanermission in China." Münster in Westfalen, 1927.

Bishop, Mrs. J. F. "The Yangtze Valley and Beyond." London, 1899.

Bitton, Nelson. "Our Heritage in China." London, 1913.

Bitton, Nelson. "Griffith, John. The Apostle of Central China." London [no date].

Bitton, Nelson. "The Regeneration of New China." London. Preface, May, 1914.

Blair, Emma Helen, and Robertson, James Alexander (translators and editors). "The Philippine Islands, 1493-1803."

Blakeslee, George H. (editor). "Recent Developments in China." Clark University Addresses, November, 1912. New York, 1913.

Bland, J. O. P., and Backhouse, E. "China under the Empress Dowager. Being the History of the Life and Times of Tzŭ Hsi, Compiled from the State Papers and the Diary of the Comptroller of Her Household." Boston, 1914.

Bland, J. O. P. "Li Hung-chang." New York, 1917.

Blessing-Eyster, Nellie. "A Chinese Quaker. An Unfictitious Novel." New York, 1902.

Blodget, Henry. "Why Protestant Missionaries in China Should Unite in Using the Term 'Tien-Chu' for God." [No date.]

Blodget, Henry, and Baldwin, C. C. "Sketches of the American Board Mission in China." Boston, 1896.

Boaz, Maud Elizabeth. "And the Villages Thereof." London [no date, ca. 1927].

Boell, Paul. "Le protectorat des missions catholiques en Chine et la politique de la France en Êxtrême-Orient." Paris, 1899.

Bonar, Andrew A. "Memoir of the Rev. David Sandeman, Missionary to China." London, 1862.

Bond, George J. (editor). "Our Share in China and What We Are Doing About It." Second edition. Toronto, 1911.

Boone, William J. "Address in Behalf of the China Mission." New York, 1837.

Borst-Smith, Ernest F. "Caught in the Chinese Revolution." London, 1912.

Borst-Smith, Ernest F. "Mandarin and Missionary in Cathay. The Story of Twelve Years' Strenuous Missionary Work During Stirring Times, Mainly Spent in Yenanfu, a Prefectural City of Shensi, North China, with a Review of Its History from the Earliest Date." London, 1917.

Bosmans, H. "Les écrets chinois de Verbiest." In Revue des questions scientifiques. Louvain, troisième série, tome XXIV, pp. 272-298.

Bosmans, H. "Ferdinand Verbiest, directeur de l'Observatoire de Peking (1623-1688)." (Extrait de la Revue des questions scientifiques, troisième série, tome XXI, pp. 195-273, 375-461.) Louvain, 1912.

Boulger, D. C. "The History of China." Two vols. London, 1898.

Bredon, Juliet. "Peking: A Historical and Intimate Description of Its Chief Places of Interest." Shanghai, 1920.

Brewster, William N. "The Evolution of New China." Cincinnati and New York, c. 1907.

Bridgman, Eliza J. Gillett (editor). "The Life and Labors of Elijah Coleman Bridgman." New York, 1864.

Brine, Lindesay. "The Taeping Rebellion in China: A Narrative of Its Rise and Progress Based upon Original Documents and Information obtained in China." London, 1862.

Brinkley, Captain F. "China: Its History, Arts and Literature." 4 vols. Boston and Tokyo, c. 1902.

British and Foreign Bible Society. "Historical Catalogue of Printed Bibles." London, 1911.

Reports of the British and Foreign Bible Society. London.

Broomhall, B. "A Missionary Band: A Record and An Appeal." London, 1886.

Broomhall, Marshall. "F. W. Baller, A Master of the Pencil." China Inland Mission, 1923.

Broomhall, Marshall. "W. W. Cassels, First Bishop in Western China." London, 1926.

Broomhall, Marshall. "Faith and Facts." London, 1909.

Broomhall, Marshall. "General Feng: 'A Good Soldier of Christ Jesus.'" China Inland Mission, 1923.

Broomhall, Marshall. "Heirs Together of the Grace of Life. Benjamin Broomhall, Amelia Hudson Broomhall." London, preface, 1918.

Broomhall, Marshall. "Islam in China: A Neglected Problem." London, 1910.

Broomhall, Marshall. "The Jubilee Story of the China Inland Mission." China Inland Mission, Philadelphia, Toronto, Melbourne, and Shanghai, preface, 1915.

Broomhall, Marshall. "Robert Morrison: A Master-Builder." New York [no date, 1924(?)].

Broomhall, Marshall. "Pioneer Work in Hunan by Adam Dorward and Other Missionaries of the China Inland Mission." China Inland Mission, preface, 1906.

Broomhall, Marshall. "Present-Day Conditions in China." New York, 1908.

Broomhall, Marshall. "Some a Hundredfold. The Life and Work of James R. Adam Among the Tribes of South West China." London [no date].

Broomhall, Marshall. "John W. Stevenson. One of Christ's Stalwarts." London, 1919.

Broomhall, Marshall (editor). "The Chinese Empire: A General and Missionary Survey." New York, 1907.

Broomhall, Marshall (editor). "Last Letters and Further Records of Martyred Missionaries of the China Inland Mission." London, 1901.

Broomhall, Marshall (editor). "Martyred Missionaries of the China Inland Mission. With a Record of the Perils and Sufferings of Some Who Escaped." Toronto, 1901.

Brou, A. "Saint François Xavier." 2 vols. Paris, 1912.

Brouillon. "Memoire sur l'état actuel de la mission du Kiang-nan, 1842-1855. Suivi de lettres relatives à l'insurrection 1851-1855." Paris, 1855.

Brown, A. J. "The Mastery of the Far East. The Story of Korea's Transformation and Japan's Rise to Supremacy in the Orient." New York, 1919.

Brown, A. J. "New Forces in Old China. An Unwelcome but Inevitable Awakening." New York, c. 1904.

Brown, A. J. "Report on a Second Visit to China, Japan, and Korea, 1909, with a Discussion of Some Problems of Mission Work." New York, 1909.

Brown, C. Campbell. "A Chinese St. Francis, or The Life of Brother Mao." London(?), 1911(?).

Brown, C. Campbell. "China in Legend and Story." Edinburgh and London, 1907.

Brown, Frank L. "A Sunday School Tour of the Orient." Garden City, 1914.

Brown, Frederick. "China's Dayspring After Thirty Years." London, 1914.

Brucker, Joseph. "La mission de Chine de 1722 a 1735. Quelques pages de l'histoire des missionaires français a Péking au XVIII° siècle, d'après des documents inédits. In *Revue des questions historiques,* Vol. 29 (1881), pp. 491-532.

Bryan, Robert Thomas. "Christianity's China Creations." Richmond, Va., 1927.

Bryson, Mrs. Mary I. "Child Life in Chinese Homes." London, 1885.

Bryson, Mrs. Mary I. and Buckland, A. R. "James Gilmour and John Horden: The Story of Their Lives." London, 1910.

Bryson, Mrs. Mary I. "Cross and Crown. Stories of the Chinese Martyrs." London, preface, 1904.

Bryson, Mrs. Mary I. "John Kenneth Mackenzie, Medical Missionary to China." New York [no date].

Bryson, Mrs. Mary I. "Fred C. Roberts of Tientsin, or For Christ and China." London, 1895.

Bulkley, Dr. L. Duncan. "Personal Impressions Regarding Missions in the Far East." New York [no date].

"Bulletins on Chinese Education, 1923." Issued by the Chinese National Association for the Advancement of Education. Shanghai, 1923.

Burgess, J. S. "New Tools in Old China." In *The Survey,* May 21, 1921, pp. 238, 239.

Burke, J. J. "The Church in Many Lands. A Trip Around the World." Baltimore and New York, c. 1915.

Burkhardt, G. E. "Die Evangelische Mission in China und Japan. Zweite Auflage, gänzlich ungearbeitet und bis auf die Gegenwart fortgeführt von Dr. K. Grundemann." Bielefeld and Leipzig, 1880.

Burns, Islay. "Memoir of the Rev. Wm. C. Burns, M.A., Missionary to China from the English Presbyterian Church." New edition, London, 1885.

Burton, Margaret E. "Comrades in Service." New York, 1915.

Burton, Margaret E. "Notable Women of Modern China." New York, c. 1912.

Burton, Margaret E. "The Education of Women in China." New York, c. 1911.

Burton, Margaret E. "Women Workers of the Orient." West Medford, Mass., c. 1918.

Bush, Charles P. "Five Years in China; or, The Factory Boy Made a Missionary. The Life and Observations of Rev. William Aitchison, Late Missionary to China." Philadelphia, c. 1865.

Butler, Mrs. Thomas. "Missions As I Saw Them. An Account of a Visit to the Important Centers of the United Methodist Missionary Society in China and Africa." London, 1924.

Cable, Mildred, and French, Francesca. "Through Jade Gate and Central Asia. An Account of a Journey in Kansu, Turkestan, and Gobi Desert." London, 1927.

Cable, A. Mildred. "The Fulfilment of a Dream of Pastor Hsi's. The Story of the Work in Hwochow." London, 1917.

Caldwell, Harry R. "Blue Tiger." Introduction by Roy Chapman Andrews, London, 1925.

Callery and Yvan. "History of the Insurrection in China, with Some Notices of the Christianity, Creed and Proclamations of the Insurgents. Translated from the French, with supplementary chapter, narrating the most recent events, by John Oxenford." London, 1853.

Campbell, Isabella C. MacLeod. "Through the Gates into the City. Memorials of Stewart and Kate McKee, Martyred Missionaries of the China Inland Mission." London [no date].

Campbell, William. "Sketches from Formosa." London, &c., preface dated 1915.

Campbell, William. "An Account of Missionary Success in the Island of Formosa. Published in London in 1650 and Now Reprinted with Copious Appendices." 2 vols. London, 1889.

Campbell, William. "Formosa under the Dutch. Described from Contemporary Records." London, 1903.

Candlin, G. T. "John Innocent: A Story of Mission Work in North China." London, 1909.

Cannon, James, III. "History of Southern Methodist Missions." Nashville, Tenn., 1926.

Cantlie, James, and Jones, C. Sheridan. "Sun Yat Sen and the Awakening of China." New York, 1912.

Canton, William. "A History of the British and Foreign Bible Society." 4 vols. London, 1904-1910.

(Canton Christian College.) "The Making of a Christian College in the Orient." New York [no date].

Canton Hospital, Canton. Reports for the Years 1919 and 1920. In Connection with the Canton Medical Missionary Society and the Canton Medical Missionary Union.

"The Canton Press." Canton.

"The Canton Register." Canton, 1827 et seq.

"Catalogue des prêtres, clercs et frères de la Congrégation de la Mission qui ont travaillé en Chine depuis 1697." Peking, 1911.

"Catalogus Patrum ac Fratrum e Societate Jesu qui a Morte S. Fr.

Xaverii ad annum MDCCCLXXII Evangelio Christi Propagando in Sinis adlaboraverunt." Shanghai, 1873.

"The Catholic Encyclopedia." 16 vols. New York, c. 1907-1913.

"Catholic Missions." A magazine devoted to home and foreign missions. Published by the Society for the Propagation of the Faith. New York, 1907-1923.

"Catholic Missions and Annals of the Propagation of the Faith." New York, 1924 et seq.

Catholic Students Mission Crusade. Bulletins Numbers 2 and 3. Techny, 1918.

"The Catholic World." New York, 1865 et seq.

Caubrière, J. M. (editor). "Synthesis Decretalium Sinarum e decretis regionalium synodorum ab anno 1803 ad annum 1910. Habitarum in Sinis, necnon aliquibus documentis ab anno 1784 ad annum 1884 a S. C. de P. Fide editis seu approbatis." Hongkong, 1914.

Central China Presbyterian Mission. "Jubilee Papers of the Central China Presbyterian Mission, 1844-1894." Shanghai, 1895.

Cerri, Mgr. "An Account of the State of the Roman Catholick Religion Throughout the World Written for the Use of Pope Innocent XI by Mgr. Cerri, Secretary of the Congregation de Propaganda Fide. Now first translated from an Authentick Italian MS. never publish'd to which is added a Discourse concerning the State of Religion in England. Written in French in the Time of K. Charles I and now first translated" (by Sir Richard Steele). London, 1715.

Chamard, Don François. "Un missionaire poitevin en Chine." Paris [no date].

Chamberlain, Mrs. W. I. "Fifty Years in Foreign Fields, China, Japan, India, Arabia. A History of Five Decades of the Woman's Board of Foreign Missions of the Reformed Church in America, 1875-1925." New York, 1925.

Chang, C. S. (compiler). "Kuo Nei Chin Shih Nien Lai Chih Tsung Chiao Shih Ch'ao." (Religious Thought Movements in China During the Last Decade—A Source Book—Specially Compiled for a Course of Study on Current Religious Thought in China for the Yenching School of Chinese Studies—North China Union Language School. Compiler: Neander C. S. Chang.) Peking, 1927.

Chang Chih-tung. "China's Only Hope." Translated by Samuel I. Woodbridge. New York, c. 1900.

Chapman, B. Burgoyne. "Flood-Tide in China." London, 1922.

Chardin, Pacifique-Marie. "Les missions franciscaines en Chine. Notes géographiques et historiques." Paris, 1915.

Chavannes, Eduard, et Pelliot, P. "Un traité manichéen retrouvé en Chine, traduit et annoté." Paris, 1913. (Extrait du Journal Asiatique, Nov.-Dec., 1911, et Jan.-Avril, 1913.)

H. de Chavannes de la Giraudière. "Les Chinois pendant une période de 4458 années." Tours, 1845.

Ch'ên Huan-chang. "The Economic Principles of Confucius and His School." 2 vols. New York, 1911.

Ch'ên Yüan. "Yüan Yeh Li K'o Wên K'ao." Third edition.

Chester, S. H. "Lights and Shadows of Mission Work in the Far East." Presbyterian Committee of Publication, 1899.

"China Against the World." (Articles by various authors.) New York, 1900.

"China Centenary Missionary Conference Records." New York [no date].

China Centenary Missionary Conference. "Conference Addresses." Shanghai, 1907.

China Christian Educational Association Bulletins, 1924 et seq. Shanghai.

"The China Christian Year Book, 1926. (Fourteenth Issue of the China 'Mission' Year Book.]" Frank Rawlinson, editor. Christian Literature Society, Shanghai, 1926.

China Continuation Committee, Minutes of Third Annual Meeting of. Shanghai, 1915.

China Continuation Committee, Fourth Annual Meeting of the. Shangai, 1916.

China Continuation Committee, Fifth Annual Meeting of the—1917 at Hangchow. Shanghai, 1917.

China Continuation Committee, Sixth Annual Meeting. Shanghai, 1918.

China Continuation Committee, Seventh Annual Meeting. Shanghai, 1919.

China Inland Mission. "China and the Gospel." China Inland Mission Reports, 1913-1916. London, 1913-1916.

China Inland Mission. "A Modern Pentecost. Being the Story of the Revival among the Aborigines of Southwest China." London [no date].

China Medical Commission of the Rockefeller Foundation. "Medicine in China." New York, 1914.

"China Medical Journal." Shanghai, 1887 et seq.

China Missions Emergency Committee. Report in *Contemporary Review,* February, 1908.

"The China Mission Hand-book." Shanghai, 1896.

"The China Mission Year Book, being 'The Christian Movement in China.' " 1910-1915 edited by D. MacGillivray; 1916-1919 edited by a committee appointed by the China Continuation Committee; 1923-1925 edited by a committee appointed by the National Christian Council. Shanghai, 1910-1919.

"The China Review, or Notes and Queries on the Far East." Hongkong, 1872-1901.

"China's Millions." London, 1875 et seq.

"China's Millions." American edition. Toronto, 1913 et seq.

"China To-Day Through Chinese Eyes" (First Series), by Lew, T. T., Tsu, Y.Y., Shih Hu, Cheng Ching Yi. London, 1922.

"China To-Day Through Chinese Eyes" (Second Series), by T. C. Chao, P. C. Hsu, T. Z. Koo, T. T. Lew, M. T. Tchou, F. C. M. Wei, D. Z. T. Yui. London, 1926.

"The China Year Book," 1913. By H. T. Montague Bell and H. G. W. Woodhead. London.

"The China Year Book, 1916. With a map of Mongolia." London.

"Chine et Ceylon. Lettres des missionaires de la Compagnie de Jésus. Province de Champagne." Abbeville, 1899-1914.

"Chine, Ceylan, Madagascar. Lettres des missionaires français de la Compagnie de Jésus. Province de Champagne." Lille, 1920—.

"The Chinese and Japanese Repository of Facts and Events in Science, History, and Art, Relating to Eastern Asia." Edited by the Rev. James Summers. London, 1863-1865.

"Chinese Christian Education. A Report of a Conference Held in New York City, April 6th, 1925, Under the Joint Auspices of the International Missionary Council and the Foreign Missions Conference of North America." New York, 1925.

"The Chinese Church as Revealed in the National Christian Conference Held in Shanghai, Tuesday, May 2, to Thursday, May 11, 1922." Editorial Committee, Rev. F. Rawlinson, Chairman, Miss Helen Thoburn, Rev. D. MacGillivray. Shanghai [no date].

The Chinese Government. "Memorandum on Christian Missions. Addressed by the Chinese Government to the Treaty Powers in 1871." Tientsin, 1872.

"The Chinese Recorder." Published at Foochow in 1867 as "The Missionary Recorder," at Foochow in 1868-1872 as "The Chinese Recorder and Missionary Journal," and at Shanghai, 1874 et seq. Beginning about 1911 the name was shortened to "The Chinese Recorder."

"The Chinese Repository." Canton, 1832-1851.

Ching-Shan. "The Diary of His Excellency Ching-Shan. Being a Chinese Account of the Boxer Troubles." Published and translated by J. J. L. Duyvendak. Ex Actorum Orientalium Volumine III excerptum. 1924.

"The Christian Century." Chicago, 1882 et seq.

"Christian China." New York, 1913[?].

"The Christian College in the New China. The Report of the Second Biennial Conference of Christian Colleges and Universities in China. Shanghai College, Feb. 12 to 16, 1926. China Christian Educational Association Bulletin No. 16." Shanghai, 1926.

Christian Literature Society for China. "Christian Literature and the Reform Movement in China."

(Christian Reformed Church.) "Agendum voor de Synode der Christelijke Gereformeerde Kerk. Te vergaderen te Englewood, Chicago, Ill., a Juni en volgende dagen. 1926."

Christie, Dugald. "Ten Years in Manchuria." Edinburgh [no date].

Christie, Dugald. "Thirty Years in the Manchu Capital. In and Around Moukden in Peace and War. Being the Recollections of Dugald Christie." Edited by his wife. New York, 1914.

Christie, Mrs. Dugald. "Jackson of Moukden." New York [no date].

Christie, Mrs. "The Chinese. A Study of Influences Operating in China with Special Reference to Manchuria." Edinburgh and Glasgow, 1927.

Chu, T. C., and Lo, P. H. (editors). "Some Aspects of Chinese Civilization." Shanghai, 1922.

"The Church Missionary Gleaner." London, 1850-1870, 1874 et seq.

(Church Missionary Society.) "Missionaries in the Witness Box. Personal Testimonies from the Foreign Field." London, 1897.

(Church of England Zenana Missionary Society.) "Through Deep Waters. The Story of the Years 1924-25 in the Work of the Church of England Zenana Missionary Society Abroad and at Home." London [no date].

de Civezza, T. R. P. Marcellin. "Histoire universelle des missions franciscaines. Ouvrage traduit de l'Italien et dispose sur un plan nouveau par le P. Victor-Bernardin de Rouen, O.F.M. Tome II. Asie." Paris, 1898.

Clarke, Samuel R. "Among the Tribes of South-West China." London, 1911.

Clayton, G. A. "Methodism in Central China." London, 190–.

Cleisz, Augustin. "Etude sur les missions nestoriennes en Chine au VII° et au VIII° siècles d'apres l'inscription syro-chinoise de Si-ngan-fu." Paris, 1880.

Clemens a Terzorio. "Manuale Historicum Missionum Ordinis Minorum Capuccinorum." 1926.

Clift, C. Winifred Lechmere. "Very Far East." London, ca. 1909.

Close, Upton (Josef Hall). "In the Land of the Laughing Buddha." New York, 1924.

Coates, Charles H. "The Red Theology in the Far East." London, 1926.

Cochran, Jean Carter. "Foreign Magic. Tales of Every-day China." New York, c. 1919.

Cochrane, Thomas. "Survey of the Missionary Occupation of China." Shanghai, 1913.

Cody, Jennie L. "Letters to Betsey." Philadelphia, c. 1915.

Coleridge, Henry James (S.J.). "The Life and Letters of St. Francis Xavier." 2 vols. London, 1872.

Colín, Francisco. "Labor Evangélica de los Obreros de la Compañia de Jésus en las Islas Filipinas por el Padre Francisco Colín de la misma Compañia. Nueva Edicíon Ilustrada con Copia de Notas y Documentos para la Crítica de la Historia General de la Soberanía de España en Filipinas por el Padre Pablo Pastells, S.J." 3 vols. Barcelona, 1900-1902.

"Collectanea S. Congregationis de Propaganda Fide, seu Decreta Instructiones Descripta pro Apostolicis Missionibus." 2 vols. Rome, 1907.

Colquhoun, Archibald R. "The 'Overland' to China." New York and London, 1900.

Commission on Christian Education. "Report on Christian Education in China." New York, 1916.

Committee of Reference and Counsel of the Foreign Missions Conference of North America. "The Present Situation in China and Its Significance for Christian Missions." December, 1925.

Committee on the War and the Religious Outlook, The. "The Missionary Outlook in the Light of the War." New York, 1920.

le Comte, Louis. "Nouveux mémoires sur l'état present de la Chine." 2 vols. Amsterdam, 1697.

le Comte, Louis. "Des ceremonies de la Chine." Liege, 1700.

Condit, Ira M. "The Force of Missions in New China." Oakland, Cal., 190–.

Conger, Sarah Pike. "Letters from China with Particular Reference to the Empress Dowager and the Women of China." Chicago, 1909.

Congregation du Cœur Immaculé de Marie, à Scheut lez Bruxelles. "Missions en Chine et au Congo." (Beginning with 1909, the Philippines were added to the title.) Bruxelles, 1899 et seq.

Considine, John J. "The Vatican Mission Exposition." New York, 1925.

"Continuation Committee Conferences in Asia, 1912-1913." New York, 1913.

"Findings of the Continuation Committee Conferences Held in Asia, 1912-1913." New York, 1913.

"Contra-Risposte. O sieno Esami di tutte de Scritture pubblicate dai Protettori de Riti condannoti della Cina. Intorno ad un fatto occudato in Scio nell' anno 1694, a riferito come di passaggio in aggiunta all seconda Edizione della Difesa del giudezio formate dalla Santa Sede Appostolica." Torino [no date].

Cooke, Sophia. "Forty-two Years' Work in Singapore." London, 1899.

Cordier, Henri. "Bibliotheca Sinica. Dictionnaire bibliographique des ouvrages relatifs de l'empire Chinois." Second edition, 4 vols. Paris, 1904-1907.

Cordier, Henri. "Histoire des relations de la Chine avec les puissances occidentales." 3 vols. Paris, 1901-1902.

Cordier, Henri. "Histoire générale de la Chine et de ses relations avec les pays étrangères depuis les temps les plus anciens jusqu'a la chute de la dynastie manchoue." 4 vols. Paris, 1920.

Cordier, Henri. "La Chine en France au XVIIIe siècle." Paris, 1910.

Cordier, Henri. "Ser Marco Polo. Notes and Addenda to Sir Henry Yule's Edition, containing the Results of Recent Research and Discovery." New York, 1920.

Cornaby, Wm. Arthur. "In Touch with Reality." London, 190–.

Cornaby, W. A. "The Call of Cathay." London, 1910.

Cornaby, Wm. Arthur. "China under the Search-Light." London, 1901.

Costain, Alfred J. "The Life of Dr. Arthur Jackson of Manchuria." London, 1911.

Cotes, Everard. "Signs and Portents in the Far East." London, 1907.

Cothonay, Bertrand. "Deux ans en Chine. Extrait du Journal." Tours, 1901.

Couling, Samuel. "The Encyclopædia Sinica." London, 1917.

Couturier, J. "Un séminariste chinois, fidele imitateur de St. Jean Berchmans. Berthélemy Zin, 1er Sep., 1903 4 Juillet, 1925."

Craighead, James R. E. "Hunter Corbett, Fifty-Six Years Missionary to China." New York, 1921.

Creighton, Louise. "Missions, Their Rise and Development." New York, 1912.

Crétineau-Joly, J. "Histoire religieuse politique et littéraire de la Compagnie de Jésus, composée sur les documents inédits et authentiques." 5 vols. Paris, 1844-1845.

Cros, P.-L. Jos.-Marie. "Saint François de Xavier. Sa vie et ses lettres." 2 vols. Paris and Toulouse, 1900.

Cunningham, Alfred. "A History of the Szechuen Riots." Shanghai Mercury Office, Shanghai, 1895.

Curzon, George Nathaniel. "Problems of the Far East." Westminster, 1896.

Cutler, William. "Missionary Efforts of the Protestant Episcopal Church in the United States." (In "History of American Missions to the Heathen.")

Daems, C. "Le credo prêché aux néophytes, ou série d'instructions familières et méthodiques, accomodées à un auditoire catéchumène et paien suivant les questions du catéchisme du baptême." Hongkong, 1910.

Daems, C. "Le décalogue prêche aux néophytes, ou série d'instructions familières et méthodiques, accomodées à un auditoire catéchumène et païen suivant les questions du catéchisme." Hongkong, 1922.

Dahlmann, Joseph. "Die Sprachkunde und die Missionen. Ein Beitrag zur Charakteristik der ältern katholischen Missionsthätigkeit (1500-1800)." Freiburg im Breisgau, 1891.

Danicourt, E. J. "Vie de Mgr. Danicourt de la Congrégation de la Mission, Éveque d'Antiphelles, Vicaire Apostolique du Tché-kiang et du Kiang-sy (Chine)." Paris, 1889.

Danton, George H. "The Student Movement in China" in School and Society. May 28, 1921.

Darley, Mary. "Cameos of a Chinese City." London, 1917.

Darley, Mary E. "The Light of the Morning." London, 1903.

Davenport, Arthur. "China from Within. A Study of Opium Fallacies and Missionary Mistakes." London, 1904.

Davidson, Robert J., and Mason, Isaac. "Life in West China Described by Two Residents in the Province of Sz-chwan." London, 1905.

Davies, Evan. "China, and Her Spiritual Claims." London, 1845.

Davies, Evan. "Memoir of the Rev. Samuel Dyer, Sixteen Years Missionary to the Chinese." London, 1846.

Davies, Hannah (of the China Inland Mission). "Among Hills and Valleys in Western China. Incidents of Missionary Work. With an introduction by Mrs. Isabella Bishop." London, 1901.

Davis, George T. B. "China's Christian Army. A Story of Marshal Feng and His Soldiers." Introduction by C. G. Trumbull. The Christian Alliance Publishing Co., 1925.

Davis, Grace T. "Neighbors in Christ. Fifty-eight Years of World Service by the Woman's Board of Missions of the Interior." Chicago, 1926.

Davis, J. A. "Choh Lin. The Chinese Boy Who Became a Preacher." Philadelphia, c. 1884.

Davis, J. A. "Leng Tso. The Chinese Bible-Woman. A Sequel to 'The Chinese Slave Girl.' " Philadelphia, c. 1886.

Davis, John Francis. "China, During the War and Since the Peace." 2 vols. London, 1852.

Davis, John Francis. "China: A General Description of That Empire and Its Inhabitants, with the History of Foreign Intercourse Down to the Events Which Produced the Dissolution of 1857." 2 vols. London, 1857.

"Days of Blessing in Inland China, being an account of meetings held in the province of Shan-si, etc., with an introduction by J. Hudson Taylor." London, 1887.

Dean, William. "The China Mission, embracing a History of the Various Missions of All Denominations among the Chinese." New York, 1859.

"Decreta Trium Synodarum regionalium annis 1880, 1886, et 1892. Pekini habitarum." Peking, 1904.

"Defense des nouveaux chretiens et des missionnaires de la Chine, du Japon, des Indes. Contre deux livres intitulez, La morale pratique des Jesuites, et l'esprit de M. Arnauld." 2 vols. Second edition. Paris, 1688.

Demimund, M. "Vie du bienheureux François-Régis Clet. Prêtre de la Congrégation de la Mission martyrisé en Chine le 18 Février, 1820." Paris, 1900.

Dennett, Tyler. "The Democratic Movement in Asia." New York, 1918.

Dennis, Rev. James S. "Christian Missions and Social Progress. A Sociological Study of Foreign Missions." 3 vols. New York, 1898-1906.

Dickinson, G. Lowes. "Letters from a Chinese Official. Being an Eastern View of Western Civilization." New York, 1906.

"Dictionary of National Biography," edited by Leslie Stephen and Sidney Lee. New York, 1908-1909.

Dingle, Edwin J. "Across China on Foot. Life in the Interior and the Reform Movement." Bristol and London, 1911.

"Directory of Protestant Missions in China, 1926." Edited for the National Christian Council. Shanghai, 1926.

" 'Doctor Robin.' What It Feels Like. Letters from a Doctor out East to a Colleague at Home." London, 1926.

Domestic and Foreign Missionary Society of the Protestant Episcopal Church in the United States of America at their first Annual Meeting, Proceedings of the. New York, 1836. Also for 1837-1841 inclusive.

"Los Dominicos en el Extremo Oriente Provincia del Santísimo Rosario de Filipinas. Relacions publicadas con motivo del séptimo cen-

tenario de la confirmácion de la sagrada Orden de Predicadores."
No date or place, probably ca. 1916.

Doolittle, Justus. "Social Life of the Chinese: with Some Account of Their Religious, Governmental, Educational, and Business Customs and Opinions with Special but not Exclusive Reference to Fuhchau." 2 vols. New York, 1867.

The Door of Hope. Annual Reports. Shanghai, 1901.

(Door of Hope.) "Of His Planting. A Retrospect of Ten Years' Work in the Door of Hope, A Rescue Mission for Chinese Girls." Shanghai [1910].

Douglas, John M. "Memorials of Rev. Carstairs Douglas, M.A., LL.D., Missionary of the Presbyterian Church of England at Amoy, China." London, 1877.

Drach, George. "Forces in Foreign Missions, with Special Reference to the Foreign Missions of the United Lutheran Church in America." Philadelphia, 1925.

Drake, Samuel B. "Among the Dark-Haired Race in the Flowery Land." London, 1897.

Dreyer, F. C. H. "The Boxer Rising and Missionary Massacres in Central and South Shansi, North China, with an account of a Missionary Band's Escape to the Coast." Toronto [no date].

Dubarbier, Georges. "La Chine contemporaine politique et économique." Paris, 1926.

(Dublin University Fuhkien Mission.) "A History of the Dublin University Fuhkien Mission, 1887-1911." Dublin [no date].

DuBose, Hampden C. "Preaching in Sinim, or The Gospel to the Gentiles. With hints and helps for addressing a heathen audience." Richmond, Va., 1893.

Dukes, Edwin Joshua. "Along River and Road in Fuh-kien, China." New York [no date].

Duncan, Annie N. "The City of Springs, or Mission Work in Chinchew." Edinburgh and London, 1902.

(Duncan, Moir B.) "The Missionary Mail. To Faithful Friends and Candid Critics." London, preface January, 1900.

Dwight, Henry Otis, Tupper, H. Allen, and Bliss, Edwin Munsell. "The Encyclopædia of Missions, Descriptive, Historical, Biographical, Statistical." Second edition. New York and London, 1904.

Dwight, Henry Otis. "The Centennial History of the American Bible Society." 2 vols. New York, 1916.

"The East and West. A Quarterly Review for the Study of Missions." Westminster, 1903 et seq.

(East China Christian Educational Association.) "The Bulletin of the East China Christian Educational Association." Shanghai.

Ecumenical Missionary Conference, Report of. 2 vols. New York, 1900.

Eddy, Sherwood. "Everybody's World." New York, c. 1920.

Eddy, G. Sherwood. "How China's Leaders Received the Gospel." New York [no date].

Eddy, Sherwood. "The Students of Asia." New York, 1916.

Edgar, J. H. "The Marches of the Mantze." London, preface 1908.
(Edinburgh Conference Report.) "World Missionary Conference, 1910." 7 vols. New York [no date].
(Edinburgh Medical Missionary Society, at first called Edinburgh Association for Sending Medical Aid to Foreign Countries, Instituted Nov. 30, 1841.) Annual Reports. Edinburgh, 1843-1845.
Edkins, Jane R. "Chinese Scenes and People. With Notices of Christian Missions and Missionary Life in a Series of Letters from Various Parts of China. With a narrative of a visit to Nanking, by . . . the Rev. Joseph Edkins. Also a memoir by her father, the Rev. William Stobbs." London, 1863.
Edkins, Joseph. "Memorial Sermon for Dr. William Muirhead." Shanghai, 1900.
Edmunds, Albert J. "Buddhist and Christian Gospels." Fourth edition, edited by Masaharu Anesaki. 2 vols. Philadelphia, 1908.
(Edmunds, C. K.) "Canton Christian College. Ling Naam Hok Hau. Its Growth and Outlook." New York, 1919.
The Educational Association of China. First Triennial Report. Shanghai, 1893-1896.
The Educational Association of China, Records of the Triennial Meetings. Shanghai, 1896, 1900, 1902, 1906, 1909.
Educational Association. "Monthly Bulletin." Shanghai, 1907-1908.
"The Educational Review." Shanghai, 1909 et seq.
Edwards, E. H. "Fire and Sword in Shansi. The Story of the Martyrdom of Foreigners and Chinese Christians." New York [no date].
Ekvall, David P. "Outposts, or Tibetan Border Sketches." New York, c. 1907.
d'Elia, Pascal M. "Catholic Native Episcopacy in China—Being an Outline of the Formation and Growth of the Chinese Catholic Clergy." Shanghai, 1927.
Elmore, Mary E. "The New Idea in Chinese Education. A Sketch of the beginning and progress of the work of the American Chinese Educational Commission in Canton, China." [Pamphlet. No date.]
Emery, Julia C. "A Century of Endeavor, 1821-1921. A Record of the First Hundred Years of the Domestic and Foreign Missionary Society of the Protestant Episcopal Church in the United States of America." New York, 1921.
d'Entrecolles. Original Manuscript Letters dated Tao tcheou, Sep. 1, 1712, and Kim te tchim, Jan. 25, 1722, with a translation by William L. Price. [MS. in Wason Library.]
Faber, Ernst. "Problems of Practical Christianity in China" (translated from the German by Rev. F. Ohlinger and edited by John Stevens). Prof. J. W. Jenks.
Shanghai and London, preface 1897.
Fagg, John G. "Forty Years in South China." New York, 1894.
"The Far Eastern Bureau Bulletin." Published in New York through
Farjenal, Fernand. "Through the Chinese Revolution. My Experiences in the South and North. The Evolution of Social Life. Inter-

views with Party Leaders. An Unconstitutional Loan. The Coup
d'État." Translated from the French by Dr. Margaret Vivian.
London, 1915.

Farmer, Wilmoth Alexander. "Ada Beeson Farmer. A Missionary
Heroine of Kuang Si, South China." Atlanta, 1912.

Farnham, J. M. W. (compiler). "Mary Jane (Scott) Farnham."
Shanghai, 1913.

Le Faure, J. "De Sinensium Ritibus politicis Acta seu R. P. Jacobi Le
Favre Parisiensis è Societate Jesu Missionarii Sinensis. Dissertatio
Theologico-Historica de avita Sinarum pietate praesertim erga de-
functos et eximia erga Confucium magistrum suum observantia."
Paris, 1700.

Favier, Bishop A. "The Heart of Pekin. Bishop A. Favier's Diary of
the Siege (May-August, 1900)." Edited by J. Freri. Boston, 1901.

Favier, Mgr. Alphonse. "Pékin, histoire et description." 2 vols. Lille,
1900.

Fielde, Adele M. "Pagoda Shadows: Studies from Life in China."
Boston, 1884.

Findlay, G. G., and Holdsworth, W. W. "The History of the Wesleyan
Methodist Missionary Society." 5 vols. London, 1921-1924.

Fischer, H. "Arnold Janssen, Gründer des Steyler Missionswerkes. Ein
Lebensbild." Steyl, 1919.

Fishe, Marian H. "My Father's Business, or a Brief Sketch of the Life
and Work of Agnes Gibson." London [no date].

Fisher, Daniel W. "Calvin Wilson Mateer, Forty-five Years a Missionary in Shantung, China." London, preface 1911.

Flad, I. "Zehn Jahre in China." Calw and Stuttgart, 1899.

"Foreign Mail" (of the International Committee of the Young Men's
Christian Association). New York, 1894 et seq.

Foreign Missions Conference of North America. "Information About
China." Number 20, Feb. 2, 1926.

Forsyth, Robert Coventry (compiler and editor). "The China Martyrs
of 1900. A Complete Roll of the Christian Heroes Martyred in
China in 1900, with narratives of survivors." New York [no date].

Forsyth, Robert Coventry (compiler and editor). "Shantung, the Sacred
Province of China. In Some of Its Aspects." Shanghai, 1912.

"Foster, Arnold. Memoir, Selected Writings, etc." [by various authors].
London Missionary Society, 1921.

Foster, Arnold (compiler). "Christian Progress in China. Gleanings
from the Writings and Speeches of Many Workers." London,
1889.

Foster, L. S. "Fifty Years in China. An Eventful Memoir of Tarleton
Perry Crawford." Nashville, 1909.

Francis, Bishop of Heliopolis, Vicar Apostolic of Nanking. Peter,
Bishop of Berytensis, Vicar Apostolic of Cochinchina. "Instructiones ad munera apostolica rite obeunda perutiles missionibus
Chinæ Tunchini Cochinchinæ atque Siami accomodatæ a missionariis S. Congregationis de Propaganda Fide iuthiæ regia Siami con-

gregatio anno domini 1665. Concinnatæ dicatæ summo pontifici Clement IX nova editio." Rome, 1807.

"The Free Press." London. (Vol. VI, pp. 170-233, Vol. VII, pp. 1-24. Sept. 22, 1858–Feb. 23, 1859. Used for criticism of missionaries in China.)

Fuerbringer, L. (editor). "Men and Missions. IV. Our China Mission." St. Louis, Mo., 1926.

Fullerton, W. Y., and Wilson, C. E. "New China: A Story of Modern Travel." London, 1909.

Gaillard, Louis. "Croix et Swastika en Chine." Second edition. Shanghai, 1904. (*Variétés sinologiques* No. 3.)

Gamble, Sidney D., assisted by Burgess, John Stewart. "Peking: A Social Survey. Conducted under the auspices of the Princeton University Center in China and the Peking Young Men's Christian Association." New York, 1921.

Gamewell, Mary Ninde. "The Gateway to China. Pictures of Shanghai." New York, c. 1916.

Gamewell, Mary Ninde. "New Life Currents in China." New York and Cincinnati, c. 1919.

Gammell, William. "A History of American Baptist Missions in Asia, Africa, Europe, and North America." Boston, 1849.

Garritt, J. C. (editor). "Jubilee Papers of the Central China Presbyterian Mission, 1844-1894, comprising Historical Sketches of the Mission Stations at Ningpo, Shanghai, Hangchow, Soochow, and Nanking." Shanghai, 1895.

Garst, Laura De Lany. "In the Shadow of the Drum Tower." Cincinnati, c. 1911.

Gascoyne-Cecil, Lord William (assisted by Lady Florence Cecil). "Changing China." New York, 1910.

Gascoyne-Cecil, Lord William. "Report on Oxford-Cambridge University Scheme." London, 1909.

General Association of Connecticut. "An Address of the General Association of Connecticut to the District Associations on the Subject of a Missionary Society, Together with Summaries and Extracts from Late European Publications on Missions to the Heathen." Norwich, 1797.

Gentili, Fra Tommaso Maria. "Memoire di un missionario domenicano nella Cina." 3 vols. Rome, 1887.

"Geschichte der Missionen in China von den ältesten Zeiten bis auf Gützlaff, herausgegeben von dem Pommerschen Hauptverein für Evangel. Missionen in China." Stettin, 1850.

Gibson, J. Campbell. "Mission Problems and Mission Methods in South China." New York, 1901(?).

Gillespie, William. "The Land of Sinim, or China and Chinese Missions." Edinburgh, 1854.

Gilmour, James. "Adventures in Mongolia." London, 1892.

Gilmour, James. "Among the Mongols." London [no date].

Gilmour, James. "More About the Mongols. Selected and arranged from the diaries and papers of James Gilmour by Richard Lovett, author of James Gilmour of Mongolia." London, 1893.

Ginling College. "A Six-Year Review, 1915-1921." Nanking, 1921.

Ginling College. "Report of the President, 1915-1916." Nanking, May, 1916.

Glover, Archibald E. "A Thousand Miles of Miracle in China. A Personal Record of God's Delivering Power from the Hands of Imperial Boxers of Shansi." London, 1904.

Glover, Richard. "Herbert Stanley Jenkins, M.D., F.R.C.S., Medical Missionary, Shensi, China. With Some Notices of the Work of the Baptist Missionary Society in That Country." London, 1914.

Glover, Robert (compiler). "Ebenezer, or Divine Deliverances in China." New York, c. 1905.

Gobien, Charles le. "Histoire de l'édit de l'empereur de la Chine, en faveur de la religion chretienne avec un eclaircissement sur les honneurs que les Chinois rendent à Confucius aux morts." Paris, 1698.

Goddard, Dwight. "A Vision of Christian and Buddhist Fellowship in the Search for Light and Reality." Los Gatos, California, 1924.

Gonzalés de S. Pierre, Francois (O.P.). "Relation abregée de la nouvelle persecution de la Chine tirée de la relation composée à Macao par les missionaires de l'Order de Saint Dominique, qui ou été chassis de cette mission." [1712].

Good, James I. "Famous Missionaries of the Reformed Church." Sunday School Board of the Reformed Church in the United States. 1903.

Goodrich, L. C. "American Catholic Missions in China." MS. prepared in 1926-1927. This appeared in *The Chinese Social and Political Science Review,* Vol. 11, No. 3 (July, 1927), pp. 413-441; No. 4 (October, 1927), pp. 414-434, Vol. 12; No. 1 (January, 1928), pp. 59-73. The references in my footnotes are to the MS.

Gordon, E. A. "Messiah, The Ancestral Hope of the Ages. 'The Desire of All Nations.'" Tokyo, 1909.

Gordon-Cumming, Constance F. "Wanderings in China." 2 vols. Edinburgh and London, 1886.

Gordon-Cumming, Constance F. "The Inventor of the Numeral-Type for China by the Use of Which Illiterate Chinese, Both Blind and Sighted, Can Very Quickly Be Taught to Read and Write Fluently." New edition, London, 1899.

Gorst, Harold E. "China." London, 1899.

Gotteberg, J. A. O. "Ti Aar i Hunan." Stavanger, 1913.

Graham, David C. Letter from Suifu, July 10, 1920. MS.

Graham, J. Miller. "East of the Barrier, or Lights on the Manchuria Mission." New York, 1902.

Graves, R. H. "Forty Years in China, or China in Transition." Baltimore, 1895.

Great Britain. "Parliamentary Papers." 1870, Vol. 69, China, No. 9,

Correspondence Respecting Inland Residence of English Missionaries in China; 1871, Vol. 70; 1872, Vol. 70; 1890-1891, Vol. 96, China, No. 3 (1891), Correspondence Respecting the Anti-Foreign Riots in China; 1900, Vol. 105, China, No. 1; 1901, Vol. 91.

Green. "Thrilling Experiences of C. I. M. Missionaries in Chih-li." Shanghai, 1900.

Green, C. H. S. "In Deaths Oft." Toronto, 1901.

Grentrup, Theodorus. "Jus Missionarium quod in Formam Compendii Scripsit P. Theodorus Grentrup, S.V.D." Vol. 1. Steyl, 1925.

Griffis, William Elliott. "A Maker of the New Orient. Samuel Robbins Brown." New York, 1902.

Grist, W. A. "Samuel Pollard, Pioneer Missionary in China." London [no date].

de Groot, J. J. M. "Sectarianism and Religious Persecution in China. A Page in the History of Religions." 2 vols. Amsterdam, 1903, 1904.

de Groot, J. J. M. "The Religious System of China, Its Ancient Forms, Evolution, History, and Present Aspect," etc. 4 vols. Leyden, 1892-1901.

Grose, George Richmond. "James W. Bashford, Pastor, Educator, Bishop." New York, Cincinnati, 1922.

Grose, George Richmond. "The New Soul in China." New York, 1927.

de Gruché, Kingston. "Doctor Apricot of 'Heaven-Below.' The Story of the Hangchow Medical Mission." Second edition. London and Edinburgh [no date].

Gützlaff, Charles. "The Journal of Two Voyages Along the Coast of China, in 1831 and 1832. The first in a Chinese Junk; The Second in the British ship Lord Amherst, With Notices of Siam, Corea, and the Loo-Choo Islands, etc." New York, 1833.

Gützlaff, C. "Die Mission in China." Berlin, 1850.

Gützlaff, Dr. K. "Abschiedswort an alle chinesischen Vereine Europa's." Stargard, 1850.

de Guignes. "Voyages à Peking, Manille et l'Ile de France faits dans l'intervalle des années 1784 à 1801." 3 vols. Paris, 1808.

Guinness, Geraldine. "In the Far East; Letters from China." London, 1890.

Guinness, Geraldine. "Letters from Geraldine Guinness [Mrs. F. Howard Taylor] in China, edited by her sister." New York, preface 1889.

Guinness, M. Geraldine. "The Story of the China Inland Mission." 2 vols. London, 1893.

Guiot, Léonide. "La mission du Su-Tchuen au XVIIIᵐᵉ siècle. Vie et apostolat de Mgr. Pottier, fondateur, évêque d'Agathopolis, vicaire apostolique en Chine, membre de la Société des Missions Étrangères de Paris." Paris, 1892.

Gundry, R. S. "China, Present and Past. Foreign Intercourse, Progress and Resources, the Missionary Question, etc." London, 1895.

Gurr, Paul. "Bilder aus der Berliner Mission in Lukhang-Südchina. Nach den Berichten des Missionars Rhein." Berlin [after 1900].

Guzman, Luis de. "Historia de las Misiones de la Compañia de Jesus en la India Oriental, en la China y Japon desde 1540 hasta 1600." Bilbas, 1891.

Hagspiel, Bruno. "Along the Mission Trail. Vol. 4. In China." Techny, 1927.

Hail, William James. "Tsêng Kuo-Fan and the Taiping Rebellion. With a Short Sketch of his Later Career." New Haven, 1927.

Hake, A. Egmont. "Events in the Taeping Rebellion. Being reprints of MSS. Copied by General Gordon, C.B., in his own handwriting." London, 1891.

du Halde, P. "The General History of China, Containing a Geographical, Historical, Chronological, Political, and Physical Description of the Empire of China, etc." London, 1736 and 1741.

du Halde, P. J. B. "A Description of the Empire of China and Chinese-Tartary, together with the Kingdoms of Korea, Tibet, etc." 2 vols. London, 1741.

Hall, R. O. "China and Britain." London, 1927.

Hamberg, Theodore. "The Chinese Rebel Chief, Hung-Siu-Tshuen, and the Origin of the Insurrection in China." London, 1855.

Hamberg, Theodore. "The Visions of Hung-Siu-Tshuen." Hongkong, 1854.

Hamilton, J. Taylor. "A History of the Missions of the Moravian Church." Bethlehem, Pa., 1901.

Hangchow Christian College. "Bulletin of Information."

Hart, E. I. "Virgil C. Hart: Missionary Statesman. Founder of the American and Canadian Missions in Central and West China." New York, 1917.

Hart, S. Lavington. "Education in China. Read before the China Society [London], April 24, 1923."

Hart, Virgil C. "Western China: A Journey to the Great Buddhist Centre of Mount Omei." Boston, 1888.

Harvey, Edwin Deeks. "Chinese Daimonism." [Manuscript book in Yale University Library.]

Havret, Henri. "La stèle chrétienne de Si-ngan-fou." 3 parts. Shanghai, 1895, 1897, 1902. (Varietes sinologiques, Nos. 7, 12, and 20.)

Havret, Henri. "T'ien Tchou 'Seigneur du Ciel' a propos d'une stèle bouddhique de Tch'eng Tou." Shanghai, 1901.

Hawes, Charlotte E. "New Thrills in Old China." New York, c. 1913.

Hawkins, F. H., and Martin, G. Currie. "London Missionary Society. Report of Mr. F. H. Hawkins and the Rev. G. Currie Martin, Deputation to China, November, 1909-April, 1910." London, 1910.

Headland, Emily. "Brief Sketches of C. M. S. Missions." London, 1890.

Headland, Isaac Taylor. "China's New Day. A Study of Events That Have Led to Its Coming." West Medford, Mass., 1912.

Headland, Isaac Taylor. "Chinese Heroes." New York, 1902.
Headland, Isaac Taylor. "Some By-Products of Missions." Cincinnati, 1912.
Hedley, John. "Our Mission in North China." London, 1907.
Hedley, John. "Tramps in Dark Mongolia." New York, 1910.
Hellier, J. E. "Life of David Hill. A new and revised edition of How David Hill Followed Christ." London [no date].
"Memorials of James Henderson, M.D., Medical Missionary to China." London, 1868.
Henrion, Le baron. "Histoire générale des missions catholiques depuis le XIII° siècle jusqu'a nos jours." 2 vols. Paris, 1846, 1847.
Henry, B. C. "The Cross and the Dragon, or Light in the Broad East." London [no date]. Introduction, 1885.
Henry, B. C. "Ling-nam, or Interior Views of Southern China. Including Explorations in the Hitherto Untraversed Island of Hainan." London, 1886.
Herbst, Hermann. "Der Bericht des Franziskaners Wilhelm von Rubruck über seine Reise in das Innere Asiens in den Jahren 1253-1255." Leipzig, 1925.
Hering, Hollis Webster. "A Study of Roman Catholic Missions in China, 1692-1744.' In New China Review, Vol. 3, pp. 107-126, 198-212.
Hermand, Louis. "Les étapes de la mission du Kiangnan, 1842-1922. Chine." Zikawei, 1926.
Hertsleb, Godfrey E. P. "China Treaties." 2 vols. London, 1908.
Hervey, G. Winfred. "The Story of Baptist Missions in Foreign Lands from the Time of Carey to the Present Time, with an introduction by Rev. A. H. Burlingham." St. Louis, 1885.
High, Stanley. "China's Place in the Sun." New York, 1922.
Hirth, Friedrich. "China and the Roman Orient. Researches Into Their Ancient and Medieval Relations as Represented in Old Chinese Records." Shanghai and Hongkong, 1885.
Hirth, Friedrich, and Rockhill, W. W. "Chau Ju-Kua. His Work on the Chinese and Arab Trade in the Twelfth and Thirteenth Centuries, entitled Chu-fan-chi." St. Petersburg, 1912.
"Histoire de ce qui s'est passé au royaume delle Chine en l'année 1624. Tirée des lettres écrites et adressées au R. P. Mutio Viteleschi, Général de la Compagnie de Jesus. Traduite de l'Italien en François par un pére de la mesme Compagnie." Paris, 1629.
"Historia cultus sinensium seu varia scripta de cultibus Sinarum, inter vicarios apostolicos Gallos aliosque missionarios, et Patres Societatis Jesu controversis, &c." Cologne, 1700.
Högberg, L. E. "Ett och Annat fron Kinesiska Turkestan (västra Kina)." Stockholm, preface 1907.
Holcombe, Chester. "The Real Chinese Question." New York, 1900.
Holzapfel, Heribert. "Handbuch der Geschichte des Franziskanerordens." Freiburg im Breisgau, 1909.
Hosie, Alexander. "Three Years in Western China: A Narrative of

Three Journeys in Ssu-ch'uan, Kueichow, and Yün-nan." London, 1890.

Hosie, Lady. "Two Gentlemen of China." Second edition. London, 1924.

Hoy, William Edwin. "History of the China Mission of the Reformed Church in the United States." Philadelphia, c. 1914.

Hu Yong Mi. "The Way of Faith. Autobiography." Chicago, 1896.

Hubbard, Ethel Daniels. "Under Marching Orders. A Story of Mary Porter Gamewell." New York, 1911.

Huby, Joseph, et alii. "Christus, Manuel d'histoire des religions." Paris, 1916.

Huc. "Christianity in China, Tartary, & Thibet." 3 vols. London, 1857, 1858.

Huc. "Recollections of a Journey Through Tartary, Thibet and China During the Years 1844, 1845 and 1846." New York, 1852.

Huc. "A Journey Through the Chinese Empire." 2 vols. New York, 1855.

Hume, Griffith M. E. "Dust of Gold. An Account of the Work of the C. E. Z. M. S. Among the Blind and Deaf of India, China and Ceylon. With a foreword by H. Tempest Reilly." London [no date].

Hunt, W. Remfry. "Heathenism Under the Searchlight." London, 1908.

Huonder, Anton. "Der Chinesische Ritenstreit." Aachen, 1921.

Huonder, Anton. "Deutsche Jesuitmissionäre des 17 und 18. Jahrhunderts." Freiburg im Breisgau, 1899.

Huonder, Anton. "Der einheimische Klerus in den Heidenländern." Freiburg im Breisgau, 1909.

Huonder, Anton (editor). "Die Mission auf der Kanzel und im Verein. Sammlung von Predigten, Vorträgen und Skizzen über die katholischen Missionen unter Mitwirkung anderer Mitglieder der Gesellschaft Jesu herausgegeben von Anton Huonder." 2 vols. Freiburg im Breisgau, 1912, 1913.

Huonder, Anton. "Die Verdienst der katholischen Heidenmission um die Buchdruckerkunst in überseeischen Ländern vom 16.-18. Jahrhundert." Aachen, 1923.

Hutchinson, Paul (editor). "China's Challenge and the Methodist Reply. Program of Advance of the Methodist Episcopal Church in China adopted at the Program Study and Statement Conference, Peking, Jan. 27–Feb. 10, 1920." Shanghai, 1920.

"The Imperial and Asiatic Quarterly Review and Oriental and Colonial Record." London, 1886-1900.

"Memorial Service for the Late Right Rev. James Addison Ingle, at All Saints Church, Frederick, Md., Jan. 31st, 1904, Conducted by Rev. J. Houston Eccleston, D.D., Rector of Emmanuel Church, Baltimore, Md."

"The International Review of Missions." Edinburgh, 1912 et seq.

Jack, R. Logan. "The Back Blocks of China. A Narrative of Experiences Among the Chinese, Lefans, Lolos, Tibetans, Shans and Kachins, Between Shanghai and the Irrawadi." London, 1904.

Jann, P. Adelhelm. "Die katholischen Missionen in Indien, China und Japan. Ihre organisation und das portugiesische Patronat vom 15. bis ins 18. Jahrhundert." Paderborn, 1915.

Jefferys, W. H. "James Addison Ingle (Yin Teh-sen). First Bishop of the Missionary District of Hankow, China." New York, 1913.

Jefferys, W. Hamilton, and Maxwell, James L. "The Diseases of China, including Formosa and Korea." London [1911].

Jenkins, Robert C. "The Jesuits in China and the Legation of Cardinal de Tournon. An Examination of Conflicting Evidence and an Attempt at an Impartial Judgment." London, 1894.

Jeter, J. B. "Memoir of Mrs. Henrietta Shuck, The First American Female Missionary to China." Boston, 1846.

Johannsen, Anna Magdalena. "Everlasting Pearl." London, 1913.

John, Griffith. "Sowing and Reaping. Letters from the Rev. Griffith John, D.D." London, 1897.

John, Griffith. "A Voice from China." London, 1907.

Johnston, Charles. "A Chinese Statesman's View of Religion." In Hibbert Journal, Oct., 1908, pp. 19-25.

Johnston, James. "China and Formosa: The Story of the Mission of the Presbyterian Church of England." London, 1897.

Johnston, Meta and Lena. "Jin Ko-Niu. A Brief Sketch of the Life of Jessie M. Johnston for Eighteen Years W. M. A. Missionary in Amoy, China." London, 1907.

Johnston, R. F. "Letters to a Missionary." London, 1918.

Joly (Chanoine) Léon. "Le christianisme et l'Extrême Orient." 2 vols. Paris [1908].

"Journal Asiatique." Paris, 1823 et seq.

"Journal of the North-China Branch of the Royal Asiatic Society." Shanghai, 1858 et seq.

"Journal of the Royal Asiatic Society of Great Britain and Ireland." London, 1834 et seq.

K'ang Hsi. Decree. A MS. translation in Latin of the imperial reply to a petition of Europeans, Apr., 1707. In Wason Library.

"Die katholischen Missionen." Aachen, 1873 et seq.

Keeler, Floyd (editor and compiler). "Catholic Medical Missions." New York, 1925.

Keith, Marian. "The Black Bearded Barbarian. The Life of George Leslie Mackay of Formosa." New York, 1912.

Keller, Adolph, and Stewart, George. "Protestant Europe: Its Crisis and Outlook." New York, 1927.

Kelly, M. T. (Miss). "A Life of Saint Francis Xavier, Based on Authentic Sources." St. Louis, 1918.

Kemp, E. G. "The Face of China. Travels in East, North, Central, and Western China, with Some Account of the New Schools, Universities, Missions, and the old Religious and Sacred Places of Confucianism, Buddhism, and Taoism." London, 1909.

Kernahan, Coulson, and Cornaby, Mrs. W. A. "Cornaby of Hanyang. A Great-Souled Missionary." London [1923].

Kervyn, Louis. "Méthode de l'apostolat moderne en Chine." Hongkong, 1911.

Kesson, John. "The Cross and the Dragon, or the Fortunes of Christianity in China: with Notices of the Christian Missions and Missionaries and Some Account of the Chinese Secret Societies." London, 1854.

Ketler, Isaac C. "The Tragedy of Paotingfu." New York, 1902.

Keyte, J. C. "Andrew Young of Shensi. Adventure in Medical Missions." London, 1924.

Keyte, J. C. "The Passing of the Dragon. The Story of the Shensi Revolution and Relief Expedition." London, 1913.

Keyte, J. C. "In China Now. China's Need and the Christian Contribution." London, 1923.

"Kiao-ou Ki-lio. Résumé des affaires religieuses. Publié par ordre de S. Exc. Tcheou Fou. Traduction, commentaire et documents diplomatiques, appendices contenant les plus récentes décisions, par le P. Jérôme Tobar, S.J." Shanghai, 1917.

King, Alonzo. "Memoir of George Dana Boardman, Late Missionary to Burmah." Boston, 1834.

Kircher, Athanasius. "Monumenti Sinici, Quod Anno Domini cbbcxxv terris, in ipsâ Chinâ erutum; Seculo verò Octavo Sinicè, ac partim Syriacè, in Saxo perscriptum esse, adeoque dogmatum & rituum Romanæ Ecclesiæ (ante annos quippe mille in extremo Oriente receptorum) antiquitatem magnoperè confirmare perhibetur Lectio seu Phrasis, Versio seu Metaphrasis, Translatio seu Paraphrasis. Planè uti Celeberrimus Polyhistor, P. Athanasius Kircherus . . . 1667."

Koo, Vi Kyuin Wellington. "The Status of Aliens in China." New York, 1912.

Krausse, Alexis. "China in Decay." London, 1900.

Krose, H. A. "Kirchliches Handbuch für das katholische Deutschland." [I have examined it for the years 1914-1920.]

Krose, H. A. "Katholische Missionsstatistik." Freiburg im Breisgau, 1908.

Labourt, J. "Le christianisme dans l'empire perse sous la dynastie sassanide (224-632)." Second edition. Paris, 1904.

Lane-Poole, Stanley. "The Life of Sir Harry Parkes, K.C.B., G.C.M.G. Sometime Her Majesty's Minister to China and Japan." 2 vols. London, 1894.

Lanning, George. "Old Forces in New China. An Effort to Exhibit the Fundamental Relationships of China and the West in Their True Light: Together with an Appendix Dealing with the Story of the Chinese Revolution Down to the End of June, 1912," etc. Shanghai and London, 1912.

Latourette, Kenneth Scott. "The History of Early Relations between the United States and China, 1784-1844." New Haven, 1917.

Launay, Adrien. "Histoire générale de la Société des Missions-Étrangères." 3 vols. Paris, 1894.

Launay, Adrien. "Histoire des missions de Chine. Mission du Kouy-Tcheou." 3 vols. Paris, 1907, 1908.

Launay, Adrien. "Histoire des missions de Chine. Mission du Kouang-si." Paris, 1903.

Launay, Adrien. "Journal d'André Ly, prêtre chinois, missionaire et notaire apostolique, 1746-1763. Texte Latin. Introduction par Adrien Launay." Second edition. Hongkong, 1924.

Launay, Adrien. "Les cinquente-deux vénérables serviteurs de Dieu, français, annamites, chinois, mis à mort pour la foi en Extrême-Orient de 1815 à 1856, dont la cause de beatification a été introduite en 1840, 1843, 1857." Paris, 1895.

Launay, Adrien. "La salle des martyrs du Séminaire des Missions-Étrangères." Paris, 1900.

Launay, Adrien. "Mémorial de la Société des Missions-Étrangères." Paris, 1912.

Launay, Adrien. "Nos missionaires, precédés d'une étude historique sur la Société des Missions-Étrangères." Paris, 1886.

Lavollée, M. C. "Voyages en Chine." Paris, 1853.

Lawrence, Edward A. "Modern Missions in the East." New York, 1895.

Leboucq, François-Xavier. "Monseigneur Édouard Dubar, de la Compagnie de Jésus, évêque de Canothe et la mission catholique du Tche-ly-sud-est, en Chine." Paris [no date; preface 1879].

Ledderhofe, Karl Friedrich, and Knak, G. "Johann Jänicke, der evangelisch-lutherische Prediger an der böhmischen—oder Bethlehems-Kirche zu Berlin, nach seinem Leben und Wirken dargestellt von Karl Friedrich Ledderhofe . . . und zum Besten der Mission für China herausgegeben von G. Knak . . ." Berlin, 1863.

Lee, Frederick. "Travel Talks on China." Washington, 1926.

Leger, Samuel H. "Education of Christian Ministers in China." Shanghai, 1925.

Legge, Helen Edith. "James Legge." London, 1905.

Legge, James. "Christianity in China. Nestorianism, Roman Catholicism, Protestantism." London, 1888.

L[eibnitz], G. G. "Novissima Sinica. Historium Nostri Temporis Illustrata In quibus de Christianismo publica nunc primum auctoritate propagate missa in Europa relatio exhibetur, deque favor scientiarum Europæarum ac moribus gentis et ipsius præsertim Monarchæ, tum et de bello Sinensium cum Moscis ac pace constituta, multa hactemus ignota explicantur." [1697].

Lemire, J. "Une Trappe en Chine." Paris, 1892.

Lemmens, Leonhard. "Die Heidenmission des Spätmittelalters. Festschrift zum siebenhunderjährigen jubiläum der Franziskanermission (1219-1919)." Münster in Westf., 1919.

Lennox, W. G. "The Health of Missionary Families in China. A Statistical Study." Denver [1921].

Lennox, W. G. "A Comparative Study of the Health of Missionary Families in Japan and China and a Selected Group in America." Denver, 1922.

Leroy, Henry-Joseph. "En Chine au Tché-ly S.E. Une mission d'après les missionnaires Société de Saint-Augustin." 1900.

Lesson. "Voyage autour de monde enterpris par ordre du gouvernement sur la corvette la Coquille, par P. Lesson." Bruxelles, 1839.

"Lettres édifiantes et curieuses, concernant l'Asie, l'Afrique et l'Amerique, avec quelques relations nouvelles des missions, et des notes geographiques et historiques. Publies sous la direction de M. L. Himé-Martin." Paris, 1843.

Leuschner, W. "Auf Vorposten in China. Aus dem Tagebuche einer Missionarsfrau." Berlin, 1913.

Leuschner, F. W. "Aus dem Leben und der Arbeit eines China-Missionars." Berlin, preface 1902.

Lew, Timothy Tingfang. "To the Members of the General Board, the Three Councils, Regional Associations, and Other Members of the China Christian Educational Association." [Open letter. No date, but in 1925, probably July or August.]

Lewis, Robert E. "The Educational Conquest of the Far East." New York, 1901.

Liang Ch'i-ch'ao. "The Anti-Religious Movement." A lecture to the Society of Philosophy. In *Liang Chin Ching Hsüeh Hsiu Chiang Yen Chi.*

"The Life." Peking, 1920 et seq.

Limaque, A. "Les Trappistes en Chine." Paris, 1911.

Lin Shao-yang. "A Chinese Appeal to Christendom Concerning Christian Missions." London, 1911.

[Lindley, A. F.] Lin-le. "Ti-Ping Tien Kwoh; the History of the Ti-Ping Revolution, including a Narrative of the Author's Personal Adventures." 2 vols. London, 1866.

Lipphard, William B. "The Second Century of Baptist Foreign Missions." Philadelphia, 1926.

Little, Archibald. "Gleanings from Fifty Years in China." London, ca. 1915.

Little, Mrs. Archibald. "In the Land of the Blue Gown." London, 1908.

Little, Mrs. Archibald. "Intimate China. The Chinese As I Have Seen Them." London, 1901.

Livingston, John H. "A Sermon delivered before the New York Missionary Society at their Annual Meeting, April 3, 1804, by John H. Livingston, D.D., S.T.D. To which are added an appendix, the Annual Report of the Directors and other papers relating to American Missions." New York, 1804.

Ljungstedt, Sir Andrew. "An Historical Sketch of the Portuguese Settlements in China and of the Roman Catholic Church and Mission in China." Boston, 1836.

Lloyd, Arthur. "The Creed of Half Japan." London, 1911.

Lockhart, William. "The Medical Missionary in China. A Narrative of Twenty Years' Experience." Second edition. London, 1861.

Lockman. "Travels of the Jesuits Into Various Parts of the World: Compiled from Their Letters. Now First Attempted in English. Intermix'd with An Account of the Manners, Government, Religion, &c., of the Several Nations Visited by Those Fathers. With Extracts from Other Travellers and Miscellaneous Notes." 2 vols. London, 1743.

Loftis, Z. S. "A Message from Batang." New York, c. 1911.

London Missionary Society. "Handbook of the China Mission." London, 1914.

(London Missionary Society.) "Missionary Magazine and Chronicle of the London Missionary Society." London.

(Lord, Lucy T.) "Memoirs of Lucy T. Lord of the Chinese Baptist Mission." Philadelphia, 1854.

Louis, Peter. "Katholische Missionskunde. Ein Studienbuch zur Einführung in das Missionswerk der katholischen Kirche." Aachen, 1924.

Louvet, Louis-Eugene. "Les missions catholiques au XIXᵉ siècle." Lyon, Lille and Paris [no date].

Lovett, Richard. "The History of the London Missionary Society, 1795-1895." 2 vols. London, 1899.

Lovett, Richard. "James Gilmour and His Boys." New York, 1892.

Lovett, Richard (editor). "James Gilmour of Mongolia. His Diaries, Letters and Reports." New York [no date].

Lowe, C. J. (editor). "Gleanings. The Mandarin Field, Kwei Lin, Kwangsi, China." 1920.

Lowe, John. "Medical Missions: Their Place and Power." London, 1895.

Lowrie, Walter M. "Memoirs of the Rev. Walter M. Lowrie, Missionary to China." Edited by his father. New York, 1850.

Lundeen, Anton. "In the Grip of Bandits and Yet in the Hands of God." Rock Island, 1925.

Lutschewitz, W. "Alte und Neue Zeit in Tsimo, der Kreistadt vom Hinterlande in Tsingtau." Berlin, 1910.

Lynch, George. "The War of the Civilizations. Being the record of a 'Foreign Devil's' Experience with the Allies in China." London, 1901.

Lyon, D. Willard. "Sketch of the History of Protestant Missions in China." New York, 1895.

du Lys, Antoine. "Un vrai frère Mineur. Vie et martyre du bienheureux Jean de Triora, béatifié le 27 Mai, 1900." Paris, 1900.

Maas, Otto. "Cartas de China. Documentos inéditos sobre misiones Franciscanas del siglo XVII." Seville, 1917.

Maas, Otto. "Cartas de China (Segunda Series). Documentos inéditos sobre misiones de los siglos XVII y XVIII." Seville, 1917.

Maas, Otto. "Die Wiedereröffnung der Franziskanermission in China in der Neuzeit. (Missionswissenschaftliche Abhandlungen und Texte, herausgegeben von Prof. J. Schmidlin, Münster, i. W.) Münster in Westfalen, 1926.

MacDonald, A. J. "The War and Missions in the East." London, 1919.

Macfee, K. J., and Codrington. "Eastern Schools and Schoolgirls. An Account of the Educational Work of the Church of England Zenana Missionary Society." London, ca. 1927.

MacGillivray, D. (editor). "A Century of Protestant Missions in China (1807-1907). Being the Centenary Conference Historical Volume." Shanghai, 1907.

MacGillivray, D. (compiler). "Descriptive and Classified Missionary Centenary Catalogue of Current Christian Literature, 1907, continuing that of 1901. (Wen-li and Mandarin.)" Shanghai, 1907.

Macgowan, John. "Beside the Bamboo." London, 1914.

Macgowan, John. "Christ or Confucius. Which? Or, The Story of the Amoy Mission." London, 1889.

Macgowan, J. "How England Saved China." London, 1913.

Mackay, G. L. "From Far Formosa." New York, 1896.

Mackenzie, Murdoch. "Twenty-five Years in Honan." Toronto, ca. 1913 or 1914.

Mackie, J. Milton. "Life of Tai-Ping-Wang." New York, 1857.

Maclagan, P. J. "Chinese Religious Ideas. A Christian Valuation." London, 1926.

Maclay, R. S. "Life Among the Chinese with Characteristic Sketches and Incidents." New York, preface 1861.

McLean, Archibald. "The History of the Foreign Christian Missionary Society." New York, 1919.

MacMurray, John V. A. (compiler and editor). "Treaties and Agreements with and Concerning China, 1894-1919." 2 vols. New York, 1921.

McNabb, R. L. "The Women of the Middle Kingdom." Cincinnati and New York, 1903.

McQuaide, Joseph P. "With Christ in China." San Francisco, 1916.

Magaillans, Gabriel. "A New History of China." London, 1688.

de Mailla, Joseph-Hune-Marie de Moyriac. "Histoire générale de la Chine ou annales de cet empire." 12 vols. Paris, 1777-1783.

Malcom, Howard. "Travels in South Eastern Asia Embracing Hindustan, Malaga, Siam, and China, with Notices of Numerous Missionary Stations and a Full Account of the Burman Empire." Philadelphia, preface 1853.

Manna, Paolo. "The Conversion of the Pagan World. A Treatise upon Catholic Foreign Missions. Translated and adapted from the Italian of Rev. Paolo Manna by Rev. Joseph F. McGlinchey." Boston, 1921.

Maritime Customs, The (III Miscellaneous Series: No. 30). "Treaties, Conventions, etc., between China and Foreign States." Second edition, 2 vols. 1917.

Marshall, Elsie. " 'For His Sake.' A Record of a Life Consecrated to God and Devoted to China. Extracts from the Letters of Elsie Marshall, martyred at Hwa-Sang, Aug. 1, 1895." New York, 1896.

Marshall, T. W. M. "Christian Missions, Their Agents and Their Results." Sixth edition, 2 vols. New York, 1901.

Marshall, T. W. M. "Christianity in China: A Fragment." London, 1858.

Marston, Annie W. "The Great Closed Land. A Plea for Tibet." London [no date].

Marston, Annie W. "With the King. Pages from the Life of Mrs. Cecil Polhill" (China Inland Mission). London, preface 1905.

Martin, G. Currie. "One Hundred and Fifty Days in China." London, 1910.

Martin, W. A. P. "The Awakening of China." New York, 1907.

Martin, W. A. P. "A Cycle of Cathay, or China, South and North, with Personal Reminiscences." New York, 1896.

Martin, W. A. P. "The Siege in Peking. China Against the World." New York, 1900.

Martino, Pierre. "L'Orient dans la littérature française au XVIIᵉ et au XVIIIᵉ siécle." Paris, 1906.

"Maryknoll Mission Letters. China. Extracts from the Letters and Diaries of the Pioneer Missioners of the Catholic Foreign Mission Society of America." Vol. 1. New York, 1923; vol. 2, 1927.

Mateer, Mrs. A. H. "Siege Days. Personal Experiences of American Women and Children During the Peking Siege." New York, 1903.

Mateer, Robert McCheyne. "Character-Building in China. The Life Story of Julia Brown Mateer." New York, c. 1912.

Matheson, Donald. "Narrative of the Mission to China of the English Presbyterian Church." London, 1866.

Mathews, G. M., and Hough, S. S. "The Call of China and the Islands." Dayton, Ohio, 1913.

Mauritius, Joannes. "Afgoden-Dienst der Jesuiten in China Waar over sy nog heden beschuldigt worden aan het Hof van Romen. Nevens hare Verandwoordinge, nu getrouwelijk uyt het Latyn vertaald, en met overtuygende Aanmerkingen over den verkeerden Handel, So der Europæaansche, als der Chineesche Jesuiten, voorgesteld door Joannes Mauritius. Eertyds Predikheer." Amsterdam, 1710.

Maxim, Sir Hiram Stevens (compiler and editor). "Li Hung Chang's Scrap-Book." London, 1913.

Mayers, William F. (editor). "Treaties between the Empire of China and Foreign Powers, etc." Fifth edition. Shanghai, 1906.

Meadows, Thomas Taylor. "The Chinese and Their Rebellions Viewed with Their National Philosophy, Ethics, Legislation, and Administration, to Which Is Added, an Essay on Civilization and Its Present State in the East and West." London, 1856.

Medhurst, W. H. "Books of the Tae-Ping-Wang Dynasty and some additional papers." Shanghai, 1853.

Medhurst, W. H. "China: Its State and Prospects. With especial reference to the Spread of the Gospel." London, 1842.

Medhurst, W. H. "Critical Review of the Books of the Insurgents." Shanghai, 1853.

Medhurst, W. H. "The Foreigner in Far Cathay." London, 1872.

Medical Missionary Society in China, 1845, 1846, Reports of the. Canton, 1845, 1846.

"Mémoires concernant l'Asie Orientale. Inde, Asie Centrale, Extrême-Orient. Publies par l'Académie des Inscriptions et Belles Lettres sous la direction de M. M. Senart, Barth. Chavannes, Cordier." 2 vols. Paris, 1913, 1916.

"Mémoires concernant l'histoire les sciences, les arts, les mœurs, les usages, etc., des Chinois. Par les missionaires de Pékin." 17 vols. 1777, 1778, 1779-1791, 1797, 1814.

"Mémoires pour Rome. Sur l'état de la religion chretienne dans la Chine avec le décret de nostre S.P. le pope Clement XI sur l'affaire des cultes chinois et le mandement de M. le Cardinal de Tournon sur le même sujet." 1709.

de Mendoza, Juan Gonzales (compiler). "The History of the Great and Mighty Kingdom of China and the Situation Thereof, edited by Sir George T. Staunton." London, Hakluyt Society, 2 vols., 1853.

Merkel, Franz Rudolf. "G. W. von Leibniz und die China-Mission." Leipzig, 1920.

Merriam, Edmund F. "Baptist Missions in China." Boston, 1894.

"Work and Progress in China of the Methodist Episcopal Church South, from 1848 to 1907." Prepared for the Young People's Dept., Board of Missions, M. E. Church South, July, 1907.

"The Methodist Review." (Used for Vol. CIII (1920), Fifth Series, Vol. 36.)

Meyer, F. B. "Memorials of Cecil Robertson of Sianfu, Medical Missionary." London, 1913.

Michie, Alexander. "China and Christianity." Boston, 1900.

Michie, Alexander. "The Englishman in China During the Victorian Era, as Illustrated by the Career of Sir Rutherford Alcock, K.C.B., D.C.L., Many Years Consul and Minister in China and Japan." 2 vols. Edinburgh and London, 1900.

Michie, Alexander. "Missionaries in China." London, 1891.

Millard, Thomas F. "Democracy and the Eastern Question. The Problem of the Far East as Demonstrated by the Great War, and Its Relation to the United States of America." New York, 1919.

"Millard's Review of the Far East." Shanghai.

Milne, William. "A Retrospect of the First Ten Years of the Protestant Mission to China, . . . accompanied with miscellaneous remarks on the literature, history, and mythology of China," etc. The Anglo-Chinese Press, Malacca, 1820.

Milne, William C. "Life in China." Second edition. London, 1858.

Miner, Luella. "China's Book of Martyrs. A Record of Heroic Martyrdoms and Marvelous Deliverances of Chinese Christians During the Summer of 1900." Philadelphia, 1903.

Miner, Luella. "Two Heroes of Cathay: Fay Chi Ho and Kung Hsiang Hsi." New York, 1903.

Mingana, Alphonse. "The Early Spread of Christianity in Central Asia and the Far East: A New Document." Manchester and London, 1925.

"The Mission Press in China. Being a Jubilee Retrospect of the American Presbyterian Mission Press with Sketches of Other Mission Presses in China, as well as Accounts of the Bible and Tract Societies at work in China." Shanghai, 1895.

"The Missionary Herald." Boston, 1820 et seq.

"The Missionary Review of the World." New York, 1888.

"The Missionary Year Book for 1889-90." New York, 1889.

"Missiones Catholicæ Cura S. Congregationis de Propaganda Fide Descriptæ Anno 1922." Florence, 1922.

"Missiones Catholicæ Ritus Latini Cura S. Congregationis de Propaganda Fide." Rome. [I have examined 1886, 1895, 1917.]

"Les missions catholiques. Bulletin hebdomadaire illustré de l'Œuvre de la Propagation de la Foi." Lyon.

"Missions of the Church of England to North China." January, 1893, Leeds.

"Missions, séminaires, écoles catholiques en Chine en 1922-1923." Shanghai, 1924.

de Moges, the Marquis. "Recollections of Baron Gros's Embassy to China and Japan in 1857-58." London and Glasgow, 1860.

Moidrey, J. "Carte des préfectures de Chine et de leur population chrétienne en 1911." Shanghai, 1913.

Moidrey, Joseph de (S.J.). "La hiérarchie catholique en Chine, en Corée et au Japon (1307-1914). Shanghai, 1914. (Variétés sinologiques No. 38.)

Monroe, Paul. "China, A Nation in Evolution." New York, 1928.

Montalto de Jesus. "Historic Macao." Hongkong, 1902.

de Montgesty, G. (adapted from the French by Florence Gilmore). "Two Vincentian Martyrs. Blessed Francis Regis Clet, C.M., Blessed John Gabriel Perboyre, C.M." Maryknoll, 1925.

Montgomery, James A. "The History of Yaballaha III, Nestorian Patriarch, and of His Vicar, Bar Sauma, Mongol Ambassador to the Frankish Courts at the End of the Thirteenth Century." New York, 1927.

Moody, Campbell N. "The Heathen Heart. An Account of the Reception of the Gospel Among the Chinese of Formosa." Edinburgh and London, 1907.

Moody, Campbell N. "The Mind of the Early Converts." London, preface 1920.

Moody, Campbell N. "The Saints of Formosa." London, 1912.

Moore, Edward Caldwell. "The Spread of Christianity in the Modern World." Chicago, 1919.

Moore, Edward Caldwell. "West and East. The Expansion of Chris-
tendom and Naturalization of Christianity in the Orient in the
Nineteenth Century. Being the Dale lectures, Oxford, 1913."
New York, 1920.

Moore, Edward C., and Barton, James L. "The Deputation of the American Board to China." Boston, 1907.

Morris, T. M. "A Winter in North China." New York, 1892.

Morrison, Mrs. Eliza A. "Memoirs of the Life and Labors of Robert
Morrison, D.D. [etc.]. Compiled by his widow, with critical notices of his Chinese works by Samuel Kidd." 2 vols. London,
1839.

Morrison Education Society, Report of the. Canton, 1837.

Morse, Hosea Ballou. "The Trade and Administration of China."
London, 1913.

Morse, Hosea Ballou. "The Chronicles of the East India Company
trading to China, 1635-1834." 4 vols. Cambridge and Oxford,
1926.

Morse, Hosea Ballou. "The International Relations of the Chinese
Empire." 3 vols. London, 1910-1918.

von Mosheim, John Laurence. "Authentick Memoirs of the Christian
Church in China. . . . Translated from the German." London,
1750.

Moshemius, Laurentius. "Historia Tartarorum Ecclesiastica." Helm-
stadt, 1741.

Mosher, Gouverneur Frank. "Institutions Connected with the American Church Mission in China." New York, 1914.

Moule, A. C. "Documents Relating to the Mission of the Minor Friars
to China in the Thirteenth and Fourteenth Centuries." In *Journal
of the Royal Asiatic Society,* July, 1914, pp. 583-599.

Moule, A. C. "The Failure of Early Christian Missions to China." In
The East and the West, 1914, pp. 383-410.

Moule, A. C. "The Minor Friars in China." In *Journal of the Royal
Asiatic Society,* January, 1921, pp. 83-115.

Moule, Arthur Evans. "The Chinese People. A Handbook on China."
London, 1914.

Moule, Arthur Evans. "Half a Century in China. Recollections and
Observations." London, preface 1911.

Moule, Arthur E. "New China and Old. Personal Recollections and
Observations of Thirty Years." Third edition. London, 1902.

Moule, A. E. "Personal Recollections of the Tai Ping Rebellion."
Shanghai, 1898.

Moule, Arthur E. "The Story of the Cheh-Kiang Mission of the Church
Missionary Society." London, 1891.

Moyer, Elgin S. "A History of Missions of the Church of the Brethren."
[MS.]

Muirhead, William. "China and the Gospel." London, 1870.

(Muirhead, W.) "The Great Famine." Shanghai, 1879.

"University of Nanking Bulletin. Eleventh Annual Report of the College of Agriculture and Forestry and Experiment Station, 1924-1925." Vol. 7, No. 4.

"The University of Nanking Special Bulletin, 1913-1914."

"Nanking University. Report of the President for 1917-18." Shanghai, 1918.

National Christian Council of China. Annual Reports. Shanghai, 1922-3, 1923-1924, 1924-1925, 1925-1926.

National Christian Council. "A Five Years' Review, 1922-1927." Shanghai, 1927.

"The Bulletin of the National Christian Council." Shanghai, 1924 et seq.

Nevius, Helen S. Coan. "The Life of John Livingston Nevius, for Forty Years a Missionary in China." New York, 1895.

Nevius, Helen S. C. "Our Life in China." New York, 1891.

Nevius, John L. "China and the Chinese." London, 1869.

Nevius, John L. "Methods of Mission Work." Second edition. New York, 1895.

"The New China Review." Shanghai, 1919-1922.

Nichols, Francis H. "Through Hidden Shensi." New York, 1905.

"Niles Weekly Register." Baltimore, 1811 et seq.

de Nino, Generoso. "Sunto Storico de Vicarioto Hupé occ. in Cina." Peking, 1924.

Norbert. "Mémoires historiques presentés au souverain pontife Benoit XIV sur les missions des Indes Orientales. Ou l'on fait voir que les PP. Capucins missionaires ont en raison de la séparer de communion des RR.PP. missionaires Jesuites qui ont refusé de se soumettre au decret de M. le Cardinal de Tournon, légat de S. Siège, contre les rits malabares." 4 vols. Luques, 1745.

Norris, Frank L. "China." London and New York, 1908.

North China Educational Union. "Register of the Union Colleges." Tungchou, 1907.

"The North-China Herald." Shanghai.

"North China Union College. Bulletin No. III. January, 1914. Course of Study and General Information." Tungchou, Chihli.

Northern Baptist Convention. "Survey of the Fields and Work of the Northern Baptist Convention by the Special Committee on Survey. Report of the National Committee of Northern Baptist Laymen, Section II, to the Northern Baptist Convention, Denver, May, 1919."

"Notices et documents sur les Prêtres de la Mission et les Filles de la Charité de S. Vincent de Paul massacrés le 21 Juni, 1870, à Tientsin . . . ou les premiers martyrs de l'Œuvre de la Sainte-Enfance. Par un Prêtre de la Mission." Paris, 1895.

"Nouvelles lettres édifiantes des missions de la Chine et des Indes Orientales." 8 vols. Paris, 1818-1823.

Noyes, Harriet Newell. "A Light in the Land of Sinim. Forty-five Years in the True Light Seminary." New York, 1919.

Noyes, Harriet Newell. "History of the South China Mission of the American Presbyterian Church, 1845-1920." Shanghai, 1927.

Oberlin-Shansi Mission. "Ten Years After." Shanghai [no date].

Oehler, W. "China und die christliche Mission in Geschichte und Gegenwart." Stuttgart, 1925.

Oehler, Wilhelm. "Die Taiping-Bewegung. Geschichte eines chinesisch-christlichen Gottesreichs." Gütersloh, 1923.

L'Œuvre de la Propagation de la Foi. "Dix années d'apostolat catholique dans les missions, 1808-1907."

Oldham, J. H. (editor). "The Missionary Situation After the War." Notes prepared for the International Missionary Meeting at Crans, near Geneva, June 22-28, 1920. New York, 1920.

O'Neill, F. W. S. "The Quest for God in China." London, 1925.

O'Neill, F. W. S. (editor). "Dr. Isabel Mitchell of Manchuria." Second edition. London, 1918.

d'Orleans, Pierre Joseph. "History of the two Tartar Conquerors of China, including the two Journeys into Tartary of Father Ferdinand Verbiest, in the Suite of the Empr. Kang Hi. From the French. To which is added Father Pereira's Journey in the Suite of the same Emperor. From the Dutch of Nicolaas Witsen. Translated and edited by the Earl of Ellesmere, with an introduction by R. H. Major." London, Hakluyt Society, 1854.

Osgood, Elliott I. "Breaking Down Chinese Walls. From a Doctor's Viewpoint." New York, 1908.

Osgood, Elliott I. "Shi, The Story-Teller. The Life and Work of Shi Kwei-piao, Chinese Story-teller and Pastor." Cincinnati, 1926.

Othon. "Trente mois en Chine. Le P. Apollinaire Dufrançois de Manciet, de l'Ordre des Frères Mineurs, missionaire apostolique, décédé a Tché-fou (Chine) le 21 Mai, 1904." Paris, 1905.

"Our Missions." Organ of the Society of the Divine Word. Techny, Ill., Jan., 1921 et seq.

Pakenham-Walsh, W. S. "Some Typical Christians of South China." London, 1905.

Pallu. "Lettres de Monseigneur Pallu . . . principal fondateur de la Société des Missions-Étrangères. Annotées par Adrien Launay." 2 vols. No place or date (preface 1904).

"The Panoplist and Missionary Magazine United," for the year ending June 1, 1809. New Series, Boston, 1809-1817. Called "The Panoplist, and Missionary Herald," 1818, 1819, 1820. Beginning with 1820, called "The Missionary Herald."

"Papers Relating to the Rebellion in China and Trade in the Yang-tze-kiang River. Presented to the House of Commons by Command of Her Majesty, in pursuance of their address dated Apr. 8, 1862."

"Papers Relative to Hospitals in China." Boston, 1841.

"Papers Respecting the Civil War in China [Tai Ping]. Presented to the House of Lords by Command of Her Majesty. 1853." London.

Parker, E. H. "John Chinaman and a Few Others." Second edition. London, 1902.

Parker, E. H. (translator). "History of the Churches of India, Burma, Siam . . . China . . . entrusted to the Society of the Missions Étrangères." In *China Review,* Vol. 18 (1890).

Parker, E. H. "Studies in Chinese Religion." London, 1910.

Parrenin, R. P. "Lettres de R. P. Parrenin, Jesuite missionaire à Pekin," edited by M. Dortous de Mairan of the French Academy. New edition, Paris, 1770.

Parsons, Reuben. "Studies in Church History." 7 vols. New York and Cincinnati, 1900.

Pascoe, C. F. "Two Hundred Years of the S. P. G.: An Historical Account of the Society for the Propagation of the Gospel in Foreign Parts, 1701-1900." 2 vols. London, 1901.

Paton, W. Bernard. "The 'Stranger People.'" London, ca. 1925.

Pauthier, M. G. (translator). "Proclamations du Mandarin Ye et du Vice-roi Ho, commissaire impérial et gouverneur-générale des deux-Kiang, ordonnant le liberté du culte catholique en Chine et la libre circulation des missionaires chrétiens dans tout l'empire; traduites sur les originaux chinois." Paris, 1860. (From *Revue de l'Orient,* Feb. [1860?]).

Pauthier, M. G. "Le livre de Marco Polo, citoyen de Venise, conseiller privé et commissaire impérial de Khoubilai-Khaan." Paris, 1865.

Payen, P. G. "Casus de Baptismo in Missionibus ac Potissimum in Sinis." Zicawei, 1920.

Peck, Solomon. "History of the Missions of the Baptist General Convention, prepared under the superintendence of Solomon Peck, Foreign Secretary of the Board." Worcester, 1840. In "History of American Missions to the Heathen."

Peill, Rev. J. (editor). "The Beloved Physician of Tsang Chou. Life-Work and Letters of Dr. Arthur D. Peill, F.R.C.S.E." London [no date].

"Peking Gazette." Peking, 1913 et seq.

"Peking University." (Pamphlet) ca. 1922.

Pène-Siefert. "Missionaries et le protectorat français en Éxtrême-Orient." Paris [no date (before 1902)].

Pérez, Lorenzo. "Origen de las Misiones Franciscanas en la Provincia de Kwang-Tung (China) extracto del Archivo Ibero-Americano, Nos. 20-23." Madrid, 1918.

Perkins, Edward C. "A Glimpse of the Heart in China." New York, 1911.

Peter, W. W. "Broadcasting Health in China. The Field and Methods of Public Health Work in the Missionary Enterprise." Shanghai, 1926.

Philip, Robert. "The Life and Opinions of the Rev. William Milne, D.D., Missionary to China." Philadelphia, 1840.

Pieper, R. "Unkraut, Knospen und Blüten aus dem blumigen Reiche der Mitte." Steyl, 1900.

Piercy, George. "Love for China: Memorials of Mary Gunson." London, 1865.

Pierson, H. W. (editor). "American Missionary Memorial, including Biographical and Historical Sketches." New York, 1853.

Pigott, C. A. "Steadfast Unto Death, or Martyred for China. Memorials of Thomas Wellesley and Jessie Pigott." London, 1903.

Piolet, J. B. (director). "Les Missions catholiques françaises au XIX⁺ siècle." 5 vols. Paris [no date].

Pitcher, P. W. "Fifty Years in Amoy, or A History of the Amoy Mission, China." New York, 1893.

Pitcher, Philip Wilson. "In and About Amoy. Some Historical and other facts connected with one of the First Open Ports in China." Shanghai and Foochow, 1909.

Planchet, J.-M. "Documents sur les martyrs de Pékin pendant la persécution des Boxeurs." 2 vols. Peking, 1922.

Planchet, J.-M. "Les missions de Chine et du Japon," 1917, 1919, 1925, 1927 [second, third, sixth, and seventh years). Peking, 1917, 1919, 1925, 1927.

Platt, Harriet Louise. "The Story of the Years. A History of the Women's Missionary Society of the Methodist Church, Canada, 1881-1906." 2 vols. Toronto, 1908.

Pollard, Samuel. "Tight Corners in China." London [no date].

(Pommerschen Hauptverein für Evangelisirung Chinas.) "Mittheilungen aus China. Herausgegeben vom Pommerschen Hauptverein für Evangelisirung Chinas." Stettin, 1858-1861.

(Pommerschen Hauptverein für Evangelisirung Chinas.) "Jahresbericht des Pommerschen Hauptverein für Evangelisirung Chinas." Stettin, 1851-1861. (7 numbers.)

Porter, Henry D. "William Scott Ament. Missionary of the American Board to China." New York, 1911.

Porter, Henry D. "Mary H. Porter. First Missionary of W. B. M. I." Chicago, 1914.

Porter, Lucius Chapin. "China's Challenge to Christianity." New York, 1924.

Poteat, Gordon. "Home Letters from China. The Story of How a Missionary Found and Began His Life Work in the Heart of China." New York, 1924.

Pott, F. L. Hawks. "The Emergency in China." New York, 1913.

Pourias, Émil-René. "La Chine. Huit ans au Yun-nan. Récit d'un missionnaire." Third edition, 1892.

Powers, George C. "The Maryknoll Movement." Maryknoll, 1926.

Pratt, Edwin A. "The Christianizing of China." London, 1915.

Presbyterian Church, Annual Reports of the Board of Foreign Missions of the. 1900-1914.

"Message from the President of the United States, transmitting report of William W. Rockhill, Late Commissioner to China, with Accompanying Documents, Dec. 12, 1901."

"Die Preussische Expedition nach Ost-Asien. Nach Amtlichen Quellen." 4 vols. Berlin, 1864-1873.

Price, Frank W. "A Glimpse at Rural Needs and the Rural Church in

China. Being a Report of a Field Trip Taken by the Senior Class, 1926, of the Nanking Theological Seminary." Nanking, 1926.

"A Short Sketch of the Life of Reverend Thomas Frederick Price, Missioner in North Carolina, Co-Founder of Maryknoll, Missioner in China. Compiled from letters to his friends by a priest of Maryknoll." Maryknoll, 1923.

Princell, Mrs. Josephine. "Frederick Franson. World Missionary." Chicago, ca. 1927.

"Proceedings of a Conference of Administrators of Mission Boards Having Work in China, Oct. 2 and 3, 1925, at 25 Madison Ave., New York City."

"Prospetto delle ricoverate e delle opere di carità esercitate nello stabilimento delle figlie della carità Canossiane in Han-kow (Hu-pe), China, 1892." Bergamo, 1893.

Protestant Episcopal Church in the U. S. A., A Historical Sketch of the China Mission of the. 1834-1892. New York, 1893.

Pruen, Mrs. "The Provinces of Western China." London and Glasgow, 1906.

"Purchas His Pilgrimes." London, 1625.

Ransome, Jessie. "Story of the Siege Hospital in Peking, and Diary of Events from May to August, 1900." London, 1902.

Raquez, A. "Au pays des pagodes. Notes de voyage, Hongkong, Macao, Shanghai, le Houpé, le Hounan, le Kouei-tcheou. Avec préface par le général Tcheng Ki-tong." Shanghai, 1900.

Rawlinson, Frank. "Changes in Missionary Effort and Thought in Two Decades." (MS.)

Rawlinson, Frank. "Naturalization of Christianity in China." Shanghai, 1927.

"Records of the General Conference of the Protestant Missionaries of China held at Shanghai, May 10-24, 1877." Shanghai, 1878.

"Records of the General Conference of the Protestant Missionaries of China Held at Shanghai, May 7-20, 1890."

Reeve, Rev. B. "Timothy Richard, D.D. China Missionary, Statesman and Reformer." London [no date].

Reichwein, Adolf. (J. C. Powell, translator.) "China and Europe. Intellectual and Artistic Contacts in the Eighteenth Century." New York, 1925.

Reid, Gilbert. "China, Captive or Free. A Study of China's Entanglements." New York, 1921.

Reid, Gilbert. "Glances at China." London [no date].

Reid, Gilbert. "The International Institute. Annual Reports of the Mission Among the Higher Classes in China." Sixth Report. Shanghai, 1906. (Several succeeding annual reports examined.)

Reid, Gilbert. "The Sources of the Anti-Foreign Disturbances in China, with a supplementary account of the Uprising of 1900." Shanghai, 1903.

Reid, J. M. "Missions and Missionary Society of the Methodist Episcopal Church, by J. M. Reid, revised and extended by J. T. Gracey, D.D." 3 vols. New York, c. 1895.

Reinaud. "Relation des voyages faits par les Arabes et les Persans dans l'Inde et à la Chine dans le IXᵉ siècle de l'ère chrétienne. Texte arabe imprimée en 1811 par les soins de feu langlès publié avec des corrections et additions et accompagné d'une traduction française et d'éclaircissements." 2 vols. Paris, 1845.

Reinsch, Paul S. "Intellectual and Political Currents in the Far East." Boston, 1911.

"Relations de Chine (Kiang-nan). Bulletin trimestriel." Shanghai, 1903 et seq.

"Relations de la mission de Nan-kin, confiée aux religieux de la Compagnie de Jésus." Vol. I, 1873-1874, Shanghai, 1875. Vol. II, 1874-1875, Shanghai, 1876.

"Report of the Conference on Christianizing Economic Relations held under the auspices of the National Christian Council of China, Shanghai, Aug. 18-28, 1927." Shanghai, 1927.

"Report on Christian Education in China. Its Present Status and Problems. The American-Canadian Commission. An Address by Professor E. D. Burton." New York, ca. 1909.

"Revue de l'Éxtrême Orient, publiée sous la direction de M. Henri Cordier." Paris, 1882, 1883, 1887.

"Revue d'histoire des missions." Paris, 1924 et seq.

Reynaud. "Une autre Chine." Abbeville, 1897.

Reynaud, Rt. Rev. Mgr. "Another China. Notes on the Celestial Empire as Viewed by a Catholic Bishop." Edited by M. T. Kelly. Dublin, 1897.

Ricci, Giovanni. "Barbarie e Trionfi ossia le Vittime Illustri del San-si in Cina nella Persecuzione del 1900." Second edition, enlarged. Firenze, 1910.

Richard, Timothy. "Conversion by the Million in China. Being Biographies and Articles." 2 vols. Shanghai, 1907.

Richard, Timothy. "Forty-Five Years in China. Reminiscences by Timothy Richard." New York, 1916.

Richard, Timothy (translator). "A Mission to Heaven. A great Chinese Epic and Allegory, by Ch'en Ch'ang Ch'un, a Taoist Gamaliel who became a Nestorian Prophet and Advisor to the Chinese Court." Shanghai, 1913.

Richter, Julius. "Das Werden der christlichen Kirche in China." (Allgemeine Evangelische Missionsgeschichte, Band IV.) Gütersloh, 1928.

Richter, Julius. "Geschichte der Berliner Missions-Gesellschaft, 1824-1924." Berlin, 1924.

Richter, Julius. "A History of Missions in India" (translation). New York, 1908.

von Richthofen, Ferdinand. "Tagebücher aus China." 2 vols. Berlin, 1907.

Rijnhart, Susie Carson. "With the Tibetans in Tent and Temple. Narrative of Four Years' Residence on the Tibetan Border and of a Journey into the Far Interior." New York, 1904.

Ripa, Matteo. "Storia della Fondazione della Congregazione e del Collegio de' Cinesi sotto il titolo della Sagra Famiglia di G. C. Seretta dello stesso fondatore Matteo Ripa e de' viaggi da lui fatti." 3 vols. Naples, 1832.

"Memoirs of Father Ripa. During Thirteen Years' Residence at the Court of Peking in the Service of the Emperor of China: With An Account of the Foundation of the College for the Education of Young Chinese at Naples. Selected and translated from the Italian by Fortunato Prandi." London, 1844.

Robbins, Helen H. "Our First Ambassador to China. An Account of the Life of George, Earl of Macartney, with extracts from his letters, and the narrative of his experiences in China, as told by himself. 1737-1806. From hitherto unpublished correspondence and documents." London, 1908.

Roberts, James Hudson. "A Fight for Life and An Inside View of Mongolia." Boston, c. 1903.

Robertson, Daniel T. "Manchuria. United Free Church of Scotland. The Story of Our Mission." Edinburgh, 1913.

Robinson, Albert B. "Historical Sketch of the Missions in China Under Care of the Board of Foreign Missions of the Presbyterian Church." Philadelphia, 1881.

Robinson, Charles Henry. "History of Christian Missions." New York, 1915.

Rockefeller Foundation. "The Rockefeller Foundation Review for 1918," by George E. Vincent. New York, 1919.

Rockhill, William Woodville. "The Journey of William of Rubruck to the Eastern Parts of the World, 1253-55, as narrated by himself, with two accounts of the earlier journey of John of Pian de Carpine." London, 1900. Hakluyt Society.

Ross, Edward Alsworth. "The Changing Chinese. The Conflict of Oriental and Western Cultures in China." New York, 1912.

Ross, John. "Mission Methods in Manchuria." New York, 1903(?).

Ross, John. "Old Wang, the First Chinese Evangelist in Manchuria. A Sketch of His Life and Work with a Chapter upon Native Agency in Chinese Missions." London, 1889.

Saeki, P. Y. "The Nestorian Monument in China." London, 1916.

Saint-Simon, duc de. "Mémoires du duc de Saint-Simon. Publies par MM. Chérvel et Ad. Regnier fils." 22 vols. Paris, 1873-1886.

Salazar, Vicente de. "Historia de la Provincia de el Santissimo Rosario de Philipinas, China, y Tunking, de el sagrado Orden de Predicadores." Third part, 1669-1700. Manila, 1742.

"A Saved Sinner. Faith Mission, China. A Story of My Conversion and Events that Followed." Shanghai, 1913.

Savignol, Marie-Joseph. "Les martyrs dominicains de la Chine au XVIII⁰ siècle." [No place given; introduction 1893.]

Scarth, John. "Twelve Years in China. The People, the Rebels, and the Mandarins." Edinburgh and London, 1860.

Schall, Johann Adam. "Geschichte der chinesischen Mission unter der Leitung des Pater Johann Adam Schall, Priester aus der Gesellschaft Jesu." Aus dem Lateinischen übersetzt und mit anmerkungen begleitet. Von Jg. Sch[umann] von Mannsegg." Vienna, 1834.

Schlatter, Wilhelm. "Geschichte der Basler Mission, 1815-1915." 3 vols. Basel, 1916.

Schlatter, W. "Rudolf Lechler. Ein Lebensbild aus der Basler Mission in China." Basel, 1911.

Schlunk, Martin. "Durch Deutsch-Kiautschou. Aus den Aufzeichnungen des Missionsinspektors Sauberzweig Schmidt über seine Visitation in Nordchina in Jahre 1905. 3 Heft. Seines literarischen Nachlasses." Berlin, 1909.

Schlunk, Martin. "Durch Chinas Südprovinz. Bericht über die Visitation des Missionsinspektors Sauberzweig Schmidt, in Südchina, 1904-1906. 2 Heft. Seines literarischen Nachlasses." Berlin, 1908.

Schmidlin, J. "Die katholischen Missionen in den deutschen Schutzgebieten." Münster in Westfalen, 1913.

Schmidlin, J. "Katholische Missionsgeschichte." Steyl, 1924.

Schmidlin, Josef. "Missions und Kulturverhältnisse im fernen Osten. Eindrücke und Berichte von meiner Missionsstudienreise im Winter 1913/14." Münster, 1914.

Schmidt, Elsa. "Father Paul's Story Box. Tales of a Chinese Missionary." Techny, 1915.

Schneider, H. G. (translated and revised by Arthur Ward). "Working and Waiting for Tibet. A Sketch of the Moravian Mission to the Western Himalayas." London [no date].

Schofield, A. T. "Memorials of Harold A. Schofield, First Medical Missionary to Shansi." London, 1898.

Schultze, O. "Lebensbilder aus der chinesischen Mission." Second edition, Stuttgart, 1922.

Schwager, Friedrich. "Die katholische Heidenmission der Gegenwart im Zuzammenhang mit ihrer grossen Vergangenheit." Steyl, 1907-1909.

Schwager, Friedrich W. "Kongregationale Missionsarbeit in China." Redfield, S. D., 1927.

Scott, Charles Ernest. "Answered Prayer in China. Some Prayer-Experiences of Present-Day Chinese Christians." Philadelphia, 1923.

Scott, Charles Ernest. "China from Within: Impressions and Experiences." New York, 1917.

Seabury. "The Vision of a Short Life. A Memorial of Warren Bartlett Seabury, one of the Founders of the Yale Mission College in China." Cambridge, 1909.

Sedgwick, Henry Dwight. "Ignatius Loyola." New York, 1923.

Selby, Thomas G. "Chinamen at Home." London, 1900.

Sellew, Walter A. "Clara Leffingwell, A Missionary." Chicago, 1907.

Semedo, F. Alvarez. "The History of the Great and Renowned Monarchy of China. . . . Lately written in Italian by F. Alvarez Semedo, a Portughess, after he had resided twenty-two years at the Court, and other famous Cities of that Kingdom. Now put into English by a Person of quality and illustrated with several Mapps and Figures, to satisfie the curious, and advance the Trade of Great Brittain. To which is added the History of the late invasion and Conquest of that flourishing Kingdom by the Tartars. . . ." London, 1655.

Servière, J. de la. "Les anciennes missions de la Compagnie de Jésus en Chine (1552-1814)." Shanghai, 1924.

Servière, J. de la. "Histoire de la mission du Kiangnan. Jesuites de la Province de France (Paris), (1840-1899)." Vols. 1 and 2, 1840-1878. Shanghai [no date (preface 1914)].

Servière, J. de la. "La nouvelle mission du Kiang-nan, 1840-1922." Shanghai, 1925.

Shanghai Baptist College and the Shanghai Baptist Theological Seminary, Prospectus of the. Shanghai, 1907.

Shanghai Baptist College and Seminary, Bulletin of the. Shanghai, June, 1917.

"The Reign of Terror in the Western Hills." Shanghai, in *Shanghai Mercury,* 1900.

"Further News of the Massacres in Shansi." Shanghai, in *Shanghai Mercury,* 1900.

Shaughnessy, Gerald. "Has the Immigrant Kept the Faith? A Study of Immigration and Catholic Growth in the United States, 1790-1920." New York, 1925.

Shelton, Flora Beal. "Shelton of Tibet. With an introduction by J. C. Ogden and the afterglow by Edgar DeWitt Jones." New York, 1923.

Shelton, Flora Beal. "Sunshine and Shadow on the Tibetan Border." Cincinnati, 1912.

Simon, G. Eng. "China: Its Social, Political, and Religious Life." London, 1887.

Sites, S. Moore. "Nathan Sites." New York, 1912.

Smirnoff, Eugene. "A Short Account of the Historical Development and Present Position of Russian Orthodox Missions." London, 1903.

Smith, Arthur H. "China in Convulsion." 2 vols. New York, 1901.

Smith, Arthur H. "Rex Christus. An Outline Study of China." New York, 1908.

Smith, Arthur H. "The Uplift of China." New York, 1907.

Smith, George. "A Narrative of an Exploratory Visit to Each of the Consular Cities of China and to the Islands of Hongkong and Chusan, in Behalf of the Church Missionary Society, in the Years 1844, 1845, 1846." New York, 1847.

Smith, Judson. "Congregational Missions in the Heavenly Kingdom." Boston, 1904.

Smith, Stanley. "China From Within." London, 1901.

"La Société des Missions-Étrangères." Paris, 1923.

Society for the Diffusion of Useful Knowledge in China, Proceedings Relative to the Formation of a. Canton, 1835.

Society for the Propagation of the Gospel in Foreign Parts, Classified Digest of the Records of the. 1701-1892. London, 1893.

Söderblom, Nathan. "Das Werden des Gottesglaubens. Untersuchungen über die Anfänge der Religion." Leipzig, 1916.

"Some Aspects of Chinese Life and Thought. Being Lectures Delivered Under the Auspices of the Peking Language School, 1917-1918." Shanghai and Peking.

Soothill, W. E. "China and the West. A Sketch of Their Intercourse." Oxford University Press, 1925.

Soothill, W. E. "A Typical Mission in China." New York, preface 1906.

Sousa, Manuel de Faria y. "The Portugues Asia: Or the History of the Discovery and Conquest of India by the Portugues." 3 vols. London, 1695.

Speer, Robert E. (editor). "A Missionary Pioneer in the Far East. A Memorial of Divie Bethune McCartee." New York, 1922.

Speer, Robert E. "The Gospel and the New World." New York, 1919.

Speer, Robert E. "A Memorial of Horace Tracy Pitkin." New York, 1903.

Speer, Robert E. "Missionary Principles and Practice. A Discussion of Christian Missions and of Some Criticisms upon Them." New York, 1902.

Speer, Robert E. "Presbyterian Foreign Missions. An Account of the Foreign Missions of the Presbyterian Church in the U. S. A." New York, 1901.

Speer, Robert E., and Kerr, Hugh T. "Report on Japan and China of the Deputation sent by the Board of Foreign Missions of the Presbyterian Church in the U. S. A. to visit these fields and to attend a series of Evaluation Conferences in China in 1926." New York, 1927.

"Spirit of Missions." Burlington, N. J., and New York, 1836 et seq.

Stauffer, Milton T. (secretary and editor). "The Christian Occupation of China." Shanghai, 1922.

Stauffer, Milton T. (assembler and editor). "China Her Own Interpreter. Chapters by a Group of Nationals Interpreting the Christian Movement." New York, 1927.

Staunton, Sir George. "An Authentic Account of an Embassy from the King of Great Britain to the Emperor of China." London, 1798.

Steiger, George Nye. "China and the Occident. The Origin and Development of the Boxer Movement." New Haven, 1927.

Steinmetz, Andrew. "History of the Jesuits." 3 vols. London, 1848.

Stenz, Georg Maria. "In der Heimat des Konfuzius. Skizzen, Bilder und Erlebnisse aus Schantung." Steyl, 1902.

Stenz, George M. "Life of Father Richard Henle, S.V.D., Missionary to China. Assassinated November 1, 1897." Second edition, Techny, 1921.

Stenz, George M. (compiler). "Twenty-Five Years in China, 1893-1918." Techny, 1924.

Stevens, George B. (with the coöperation of W. Fisher Markwick). 'The Life, Letters, and Journals of the Rev. and Hon. Peter Parker, M.D., Missionary, Physician, and Diplomatist, the Father of Medical Missions and Founder of the Ophthalmic Hospital in Canton." Boston, 1896.

Stewart, Edith Anne. "The Life of St. Francis Xavier, Evangelist, Explorer, Mystic. With translations from his Letters by David MacDonald." London, 1917.

Stock, Eugene, and McClelland, T. "For Christ in Fuh-Kien." London, 1904.

Stock, Eugene. "The History of the Church Missionary Society. Its Environment, Its Men, and Its Work." 3 vols., London, 1899; 4th vol., London, 1916.

Stoddart, Anna M. "The Life of Isabella Bird (Mrs. Bishop)." London, 1908.

Stott, Grace. "Twenty-Six Years of Missionary Work in China." London, 1904.

"Students and the Missionary Problem. Addresses delivered at the International Student Missionary Conference, London, Jan. 2-6, 1900." London, 1900.

Sun Yat-sen. "San Min Chu I. The Three Principles of the People." Translated by Frank W. Price, edited by L. T. Chen. Shanghai, 1927.

Sykes, W. H. "Tae-Ping Rebellion in China." A series of letters addressed to the Aberdeen *Free Press* and London *Daily News*. London, 1863.

"Synodus vicariatus sutchuensis habita in districtu civitatis Tchong King Tcheou. Anno 1803. Diebus secunda, quinta et nona Septembris." Rome, 1837.

Sze, Tsung-yu. "China and the Most-Favored-Nation Clause." New York, 1925.

Tacchi Venturi, Pietro, "Opere Storiche del P. Matteo Ricci, S. I., edite a cura del comitato per le onoranze nazionali con prolegomeni note a tavole dal P. Pietro Tacchi Venturi, S. I." 2 vols., Macerata, 1911.

T'ang, Leang-li. "China in Revolt. How a Civilization Became a Nation." London, 1927.

Tatchell, W. Arthur. "Booth of Hankow. A Crowded Hour of Glorious Life." London, 1915.

Tatchell, W. Arthur. "Medical Missions in China in Connexion with the Wesleyan Methodist Church." London [no date].

Taylor, Alva W. "The Social Work of Christian Missions." Cincinnati, 1912.

Taylor, Annie R. "Pioneering in Tibet." London [no date (after 1897)].

Taylor, Charles E. "The Story of Yates the Missionary." Nashville, Tenn., 1898.

Taylor, Mrs. Howard. "Borden of Yale, '09." China Inland Mission, London, &c., 1926.

Taylor, Mrs. Howard. "One of China's Scholars: Pastor Hsi." London, 1903.

Taylor, Mrs. Howard. "Pastor Hsi (of North China). One of China's Christians." New York, preface 1903.

Taylor, Mrs. Howard. "The Call of China's Great North-West, or Kansu and Beyond." China Inland Mission, London, &c. [no date (ca. 1923 or 1924)].

Taylor, Dr. and Mrs. Howard. "Hudson Taylor in Early Years." Philadelphia, 1912.

Taylor, Dr. and Mrs. Howard. "Hudson Taylor and the China Inland Mission. The Growth of a Work of God." London, 1919.

Taylor, J. Hudson. "After Thirty Years: Three Decades of the China Inland Mission, 1865-1895." London, 1896(?).

Taylor, J. Hudson. "China's Spiritual Need and Claims." Fifth edition. London, 1884.

Taylor, J. Hudson. "A Retrospect." Third edition. Philadelphia [no date].

Taylor, W. E. "Report on the Evangelistic Meetings for Government Students in China Conducted by Dr. John R. Mott and Mr. Sherwood Eddy, January 30th to March 29th, 1913."

Tchang, M. et de Prunelé. "Le Père Simon A. Cunha, S.J. (Ou Li Yu-Chau). L'homme et l'œuvre artistique." Shanghai, 1914.

Le Tellier, Michel. "Défense des nouveaux chrétiens et des missionnaires de la Chine, du Japon, et des Indes contre deux livres intitulez la morale pratique des Jesuits, et l'esprit de M. Arnauld." Second edition. Paris, 1688.

Thiersant, Dabry de. "Le catholicisme en Chine aux VIIIᵉ siècle de notre ère avec une nouvelle traduction de l'inscription de Sy-nganfou." Paris, 1877.

Thomas, A. "Histoire de la mission de Pékin depuis les origines jusqu'a l'arrivée des Lazaristes." Paris, 1923.

Thompson, R. Wardlaw. "Griffith John. The Story of Fifty Years in China." Popular, revised edition, London, 1908.

Thompson, Wm. "Memoirs of the Rev. Samuel Munson and the Rev. Henry Lyman, Late Missionaries to the Indian Archipelago, with the Journal of their exploring tour." New York, 1839.

Thomson, Edward. "Our Oriental Missions." 2 vols. Cincinnati, 1871.

Thomson, J. S. "The Chinese." London [no date].

Thomson, John Stuart. "China Revolutionized." Indianapolis, 1913.

"The Tientsin Massacre. Being Documents Published in *The Shanghai Evening Courier* from June 16th to Sept. 10, 1870. With an Introductory Narrative." Second edition, Shanghai [no date].

Timkowski, George. "Travels of the Russian Mission Through Mongolia

894 BIBLIOGRAPHY

to China and Residence in Peking, in the Years 1820-1821." Corrections and notes by Julius von Klaproth. 2 vols. London, 1827.

Tinling, Christine I. "Bits of China. Travel-Sketches in the Orient." New York, 1925.

Tinling, Christine I. "Memories of the Mission Field." London (ca. 1927).

Titterington, Sophie Bronson. "A Century of Baptist Foreign Missions." Philadelphia, 1891.

Tomlin, J. "Missionary Journals and Letters Written During Eleven Years' Residence and Travels Amongst the Chinese, Siamese, Javanese, Khassias, and Other Eastern Nations." London, 1844.

"T'oung Pao. Archives pour servir a l'étude de l'histoire, des langues, de la géographie et de l'ethnographie de l'Asie Orientale." Leyden, 1890 et seq.

Townsend, William John. "Robert Morrison, the Pioneer of Chinese Missions." New York [no date].

Tracy, Joseph. "History of the American Board of Commissioners for Foreign Missions." Worcester, 1840.

Tragella, P. G. B. "L'Infanticidio e la S. Infanzia con particolare riguardo alla Cina." Milan, 1920.

"The Travels of the Several Learned Missioners of the Society of Jesus, into divers parts of the Archipelago, India, China, and America . . . translated from the French original published at Paris in the year 1713." London, 1714.

Trigault, Nicolas. "De Christiana Expeditione apud Sinas Suscepta ab Societate Jesu ex P. Matthæi Ricii eiusdem Societatis Comentariis Libri V ad S.D.N. Paulum V. In quibus Sinensis Regni mores, leges, atq. instituta et nouae illius Ecclesiae difficillima primordia accurate et summa fide describuntur. Auctore P. Nicolao Trigaultio Belga ex eadem Societate, Augustae Vind. apud Christoph. Mangium. 1615."

Trigault, Nicolas. "Histoire de l'expedition chrestienne au royaume de la Chine. Entreprise par les PP. de la Compagnie de Jésus. . . . Tirée des comentaires du P. Matthaei Riccius et P. Nicolas Trigault de la mesme compagnie et nouvellement traduite en françois par le Sʳ. D. F. de Riquebourg-Trigault." Lyon, 1616.

Trumbull, H. Clay. "Old Time Student Volunteers. My Memories of Missionaries." New York, 1902.

Turner, H. F. "His Witnesses. Ku-cheng, Aug. 1, 1895." London [no date].

Turner, John A. "Kwang Tung, or Five Years in South China." London, 1894.

Tuttle, A. H. "Mary Porter Gamewell and Her Story of the Siege in Peking." New York, 1907.

Tyau, M. T. Z. "Legal Obligations Arising Out of Treaty Relations Between China and Other States." Shanghai, 1917.

United States. Consular Letters. Canton. Vol. 1, March, 1792, to Aug., 1834; Vol. 2, Sept., 1834, to April, 1839; Vol. 3, May, 1839-

49. MSS. in Bureau of MSS. and Archives, State Department, Washington.

United States. Executive Documents Printed by Order of the House of Representatives:

2d Session, 43d Cong., 1874-1875. Vol. 1, Foreign Relations.
1st Session, 33d Cong., 1853-1854. Vol. 16.
3d Session, 40th Cong., 1868-1869. Doc. No. 29.
3d Session, 41st Cong. Vol. 1, Foreign Relations.
2d Session, 42d Cong. Vol. 1.
1st Session, 43d Cong. Foreign Relations, Vol. 1.
1st Session, 44th Cong. Foreign Relations, Vol. 1.
2d Session, 49th Cong., Foreign Relations of the United States.
2d Session, 44th Cong., Foreign Relations of the United States.
2d Session, 46th Cong., Foreign Relations of the United States.
1st Session, 47th Cong., Foreign Relations of the United States.
1st Session, 49th Cong., Foreign Relations of the United States.
1st Session, 50th Cong., Foreign Relations of the United States.
2d Session, 50th Cong., Foreign Relations of the United States.
1st Session, 52d Cong., Foreign Relations of the United States.
2d Session, 53d Cong., Foreign Relations of the United States.
3d Session, 53d Cong., Foreign Relations of the United States.
2d Session, 54th Cong., Foreign Relations of the United States.
3d Session, 55th Cong., Foreign Relations of the United States.
2d Session, 56th Cong., Foreign Relations of the United States.
1st Session, 57th Cong., Foreign Relations of the United States.
2d Session, 57th Cong., Foreign Relations of the United States.
3d Session, 58th Cong., Foreign Relations of the United States.

United States. Senate Documents.

2d Session, 35th Cong., Vol. 1858-59, No. 22.
1st Session, 57th Cong., Sen. Doc. 67 (Affairs in China).

Upward, Bernard. "The Sons of Han." London, 1908.

Urquhart, David. "The New Heresy: Proselytism Substituted for Righteousness. Two Letters to the Bishop of Oxford by David Urquhart. To which are added
   "1. 'Change in a Nation imperceptible, being caused by a change in each man.'
   "2. Pledge given that the Troops should not be Employed Unlawfully. (Debate of August 11, 1848.)
   "3. Correspondence with Lord John Russell on its violation."
Fress Press Office. Whitefriars, Sept., 1862.

Valignano, Alexandro. "Apologia en la qual se responde á diversas calumnias que se escrevieron contra los padres de la compañia de Jesu de Japon y de la China. Hecha por el padre Alexandro Valignano de la misma Compañia en Henero de [15]98 ciudad de Amacao: y acrecentada por el mismo en Japon en Octubre de mismo año. Para N.R.P.G." 19th century MS. copy of the work. In Wason collection.

Van Braam, Andre Everard. "An Authentic Account of the Embassy of the Dutch East-India Company to the Court of the Emp^r. of China in the years 1794 and 1795 etc., taken from the journals of . . . Van Braam. Trans. by M. L. E. Moreau de Saint Mery." 2 vols. London, 1798.

"Verlags van de openbare vergadering der Nederlandsche vereiniging tot bevordering des Chrestindoms onder de Chinezan." Reports of various meetings held at Rotterdam; earliest, May 26, 1852; latest, May 27, 1858.

Verthamon. Letter to the Count du Dresnay, from Tching-tou-fou (capital of Se-tchouen), Aug. 3, 1745. MS. original and translation into English in Wason Library.

Villa-Humbrosa, Conde de, Presidente du Consejo supremo de Castilla. "Memorial Apologetico . . . de parte de los Missioneros Apostolicos de el Imperio de la China." Madrid, 1676.

Völling, Arsenius. "Die Christenverfolgung in Nord-Schansi (China) in Jahre, 1900." Trier, 1911. (Sixth volume of "Aus Allen Zonen. Bilder aus den Missionen der Franziskaner in Vergangenheit und Gegenwart.")

Voskamp, C. J. "Zerstörende und aufbauende Mächte in China." Berlin, 1898.

W——, L'Abbe Th. (des Missions Étrangères). "Les martyrs de l'Extrême Orient ou les 94 serviteurs de Dieu mis a mort pour la foi en Corée, en Cochinchine, au Tong-king et en Chine." Paris, 1859.

Wallace, Edward Wilson. "The Heart of Sz-chuan." Toronto, 1903.

Wallace, Edward Wilson. "The New Life in China." London, preface 1914.

Walrond, Theodore (editor). "Letters and Journals of James, Eighth Earl of Elgin, Governor of Jamaica, Governor-General of Canada, Envoy to China, Viceroy of India." Second edition. London, 1873.

Walsh, James H. "Observations in the Orient. The Account of a Journey to Catholic Mission Fields in Japan, Korea, Manchuria, China, Indo-China, and the Philippines (1917-1918)." Ossining, N. Y., 1919.

Wang, Tsi C. "The Youth Movement of China." New York, 1927.

Ward, Jane Shaw. "Shanghai Sketches." New York, 1917.

Ward, N. Lascelles. "Oriental Missions in British Columbia." Westminster, 1925.

Warneck, Gustav. "Outline of a History of Protestant Missions from the Reformation to the Present Time." Authorized translation from the seventh German edition. Edited by George Robson, D.D. New York, 1901.

Watson, Mary E. "Robert and Louisa Stewart." London, 1895.

Watthé, Henry. "La Chine qui s'éveille. Nouvelle édition des fleurs et épines du Kiang-si." Vichy, 1926.

Weale, B. L. Putnam. "Indiscreet Letters from Peking." New York, 1910.

Webster, James. "Times of Blessing in Manchuria. Letters from Moukden to the Church at Home, Feb. 17–June 10, 1908." Fourth edition. Shanghai and Edinburgh, 1909.

Webster, James. "The Revival in Manchuria." London, 1910.

Webster, James B. "Christian Education and the National Consciousness in China." New York, 1923.

Wegener, Herm. (translated by E. McCall). "Heroes of the Mission Field, or Abridged Lives of Famous Missionaries and Martyrs of Our Times." Techny, Ill., 1916.

Wegener, Rembert. "P. Viktorin Delbrouck ein Blutzeuge des Franziskanerordens aus unseren Tagen. Nach dem Französischen des Mgr. G. Monchamp." Trier, 1911. ("Aus allen Zonen: viertes Bändchen.")

Weir, Robert W. "A History of the Foreign Missions of the Church of Scotland." Edinburgh, 1900.

Wellons, R. D. "The Organization Set Up for the Control of Mission Union Higher Educational Institutions." New York, 1927.

Wen Ching. "The Chinese Crisis From Within," edited by G. M. Reith. London, 1901.

Werner, O. "Katholischer Missions-Atlas. Neunzehn Karten in Farbendruck mit Begleitendem Text." Freiburg, 1885.

Wesleyan Methodist Missionary Society. Annual Reports (examined from 1909 to 1915 inclusive).

Wesleyan Methodist Missionary Society, No. 27, Bulletin of the. Dec., 1906. London.

Wessels, C. "Early Jesuit Travellers in Central Asia, 1603-1721." The Hague, 1924.

"West China Missionary Conference." Chengtu, 1908.

"The West China Missionary News." Published by the West China Advisory Board. (Examined Vol. 22, Nos. 8, 9, 12—1920, Aug., Sept., Dec.)

Wheeler, L. N. "The Foreigner in China." Chicago, 1881.

White, F. J. Annual Report of Shanghai College for the Year 1925. (MS.)

White, Mary Culler. "The Days of June. The Life Story of June Nicholson." New York, 1909.

Wieger, Léon. "Chine moderne." 5 vols. Hsien Hsien, 1921-1924.

Wiley, I. W. "The Missionary Cemetery and the Fallen Missionaries of Fuchau, China. With an Introductory Notice of Fuchau and Its Missions." New York, 1858.

Wiley, I. W. "The Mission Cemetery at Fuchau. Memorials of Eight Fuchau Missionaries." New York, 1854.

Williams, Frederick Wells. "Anson Burlingame and the First Chinese Mission to Foreign Powers." New York, 1912.

Williams, Frederick Wells. "The Life and Letters of Samuel Wells Williams, LL.D., Missionary, Diplomatist, Sinologue." New York, 1889.

Williams, Henry F. "In Four Continents. A Sketch of the Foreign Missions of the Presbyterian Church, U. S." Richmond, Va., 1910.

Williams, Isabella Riggs. "By the Great Wall. Selected Correspondence of Isabella Riggs Williams." New York, 1909.

Williams, Mark. "Across the Desert of Gobi. A Narrative of an Escape During the Boxer Uprising, June to Sept., 1900." Hamilton, Ohio, 1901.

Williams, S. Wells. "The Middle Kingdom." Revised edition, 2 vols. New York, 1883.

Williams, Walter R. "Ohio Friends in the Land of Sinim. Being a Record of the Missionary Work in China under the Ohio Yearly Meeting of the Friends Church." Mt. Gilead, Ohio, 1925.

Williamson, Alexander. "Journeys in North China." London, 1870.

Williamson, G. R. "Memoir of the Rev. David Abeel, D.D., Late Missionary to China." New York, 1848.

Williamson, Isabelle. "Old Highways in China." London, 1884.

Willoughby, Westel W. "Foreign Rights and Interests in China." Baltimore, 1920.

Willoughby, Westel W. "Foreign Rights and Interests in China." Revised and enlarged edition. 2 vols. Baltimore, 1927.

Wilson, James Harrison. "China. Travels and Investigations in the 'Middle Kingdom.' A Study of Its Civilization and Possibilities. With a Glance at Japan." New York, 1887.

Wolferstan, Bertram. "The Catholic Church in China from 1860 to 1907." London, Edinburgh, St. Louis, 1909.

Woodbridge, Samuel Isett. "Fifty Years in China. Being Some Account of the History and Conditions in China and of the Missions of the Presbyterian Church in the United States there from 1867 to the Present Day." Written for Southern Presbyterians by the English editor of the *Chinese Christian Intelligencer* in 1918. Published 1919.

"The World Call to the Church. The Call from the Far East. Being a comprehensive statement of the facts which constitute the Call from the Far East to the Church of England prepared by a Commission appointed by the Missionary Council of the Church Assembly." London, 1926.

World's Student Christian Federation. Reports of Student Christian Movements, Oct. 1, 1919, to September 30, 1920. World's Student Christian Federation, 1921.

Wright, Henry B. "A Life with a Purpose. A Memorial of John Lawrence Thurston, First Missionary of the Yale Mission." New York, 1908.

Wylie, Alexander. "Chinese Researches." Shanghai, 1897.

Wylie, Alexander. "Memorials of Protestant Missionaries to the Chinese: giving a list of their publications, and obituary notices of the deceased, with copious indexes." Shanghai, 1867.

Wylie, A. "Notes on Chinese Literature." Shanghai, 1902.

Yale Mission, The. Changsha, China. Annual Reports.

Yen, James Y. C. "The Mass Education Movement in China." Shanghai. 1925.

Younghusband, Col. Francis Edward. "The Heart of a Continent. A Narrative of Travels in Manchuria, across the Gobi Desert, through the Himalayas, the Pamirs, and Hunza. 1884-1894." Second edition, London, 1904.

Young Men's Christian Association. "Record of the Seventh Annual Conference of the Secretaries of the International Committee of the Young Men's Christian Associations of China and Korea, July 23-29, 1909."

Young Men's Christian Associations of China and Korea During 1908, The Work of the. A Report of the General Committee by the General Secretary. Shanghai, 1909.

Young Men's Christian Association. "Service with Fighting Men. An Account of the Work of the American Young Men's Christian Associations in the World War. Editorial Board, Chairman, William Howard Taft. Managing editor, Frederick Harris. Associate editors, Frederic Houston Kent, William J. Newlin." 2 vols. New York, 1922.

"Among Young Men in the Middle Kingdom. A Report of the Work of the Young Men's Christian Associations of China and Korea." Shanghai, 1912.

Young Men's Christian Association. Correspondence of Secretaries in mimeographed form. H. A. Wilbur, letter for year ending Sept. 30, 1914; W. W. Lockwood, Annual Report for year ending Sept. 30, 1914; C. W. Harvey, Assistant National Secretary, Annual Report for year ending Sept. 30, 1914; D. W. Lyon, Assistant National Secretary, Annual Report for year ending Sept. 30, 1913.

Young Men's Christian Association. "Five Years of Progress, 1907-1912. A Report of the Work of the Young Men's Christian Associations of China and Korea, 1912, with a Review Covering the Period 1907-1912." Shanghai, 1913.

Young Men's Christian Association. "Another Year's Progress, 1913." Shanghai, 1914.

Young Men's Christian Association. "The Year Nineteen Sixteen." Shanghai, 1917.

Young Women's Christian Association. "Threads. The Story of the Industrial Work of the Y. W. C. A. in China, 1925." Shanghai.

Yule, Henry. "Cathay and the Way Thither." New edition by Henri Cordier. 4 vols. London, 1913-1916.

Yule, Henry. "The Book of Sir Marco Polo." Third edition, revised by Henri Cordier. 2 vols. London, 1903.

Yung Wing. "My Life in China and America." New York, 1909.

"Zeitschrift für Missionswissenschaft." Münster, 1911 et seq.

INDEX

A

Abbasid Caliphs, 47, 51, 62.
Abeel, David, 217, 218, 244, 247, 395.
Abercrombie, 216.
Adeodat, 175, 177.
Adons, Julien, 736.
Africa, 392, 489, 690, 771.
Agliardi, 312.
Agricultural education, 753, 784, 785, 793.
Ahok, 482.
Aitchison, William, 248.
Alans, 71, 72.
Albany, 720.
Albazin and Albazinians, 199, 200, 486, 487, 566.
Alcoceva, Pierre d', 89.
Alcock, Rutherford, 466, 474.
Aldersey, Miss, 225, 252, 267.
Aleni, Julio, 109.
Alice Memorial Hospital, 456.
Allen (British consul), 561.
Allen, Young J., 436, 445, 492.
Allgemeine evangelisch-protestantischer Missionsverein, 576, *see* Weimar Mission.
Alliance China Mission, 583.
Almalik, 62.
Almeida, 93.
Almonte (Canada), 721.
A-lo-pên, 53.
Altar of Heaven, 612.
Ament, 607.
America and Americans, 363, 368, 369, 391, 392, 394, 399, 404, 405, 427, 441, 459, 461, 488, 489, 523, 525, 528, 534, 538, 540, 562, 587, 597, 604, 612, 617, 625, 627, 629, 631, 643, 649, 654, 660, 661, 663, 664, 690, 695, 696, 720, 724, 726, 730, 743, 751, 753, 764, 765, 768, 772, 773, 779, 781, 791, 794, 799, 803, 805, 819-822, 830. See also, United States.
American Advent Mission Society, 402, 579.
American Baptist Foreign Mission Society, 621. *See* also Northern (American) Baptists.
American Baptist Missionary Union,

371, 395. *See* also Northern (American) Baptists.
American Benedictines, 731.
American Bible Society, 217, 262, 266, 377, 437, 438, 648, 832.
American Board Mission (Hongkong), 609.
American Board of Catholic Missions, 716.
American Board of Commissioners for Foreign Missions, 207, 217-219, 247, 248, 365, 366, 395, 404, 437, 448, 449, 456, 460, 504, 514, 517, 572, 608, 626, 627, 633, 642, 664, 677, 678, 758, 761, 763, 768, 774, 780, 785, 799, 800.
American-Chinese Educational Commission, 772.
American Church Mission (Episcopal), 661, 818.
American Civil War, 357, 371, 372, 375, 394.
American Department of State, 523.
American Government, 475.
American Minister (or Consul), 475, 645, 659, 817, 820.
American missions and missionaries, 615, 619, 625, 744. *See* also under the names of separate societies.
American-Norwegian China Mission, 577.
American Relief Fund, 767.
American Seaman's Friend Society, 217, 218.
American Scandinavian Christian Free Mission, *see* American Swedish Free Mission Society.
American Swedish Free Mission Society, 399, 580.
Amherst Embassy, 212.
Amoy, 229, 244, 246, 247, 259, 328, 363, 365, 366, 377, 395, 407, 412, 424, 425, 427, 432, 436, 450, 462, 494, 542, 574, 620, 626, 638, 647, 662, 676, 677, 734, 759.
Analects of Confucius, 651.
Anatomy, by Gray, 460.
Ancestor Worship, 7, 19, 41, 133-155, 797.
Ancient Society of Elder Brothers, *see* Ko Lao Hui.

Andrew the Frank, 71, 72.
Andrew of Perugia, 70.
Anglican Communion in China, Conference of the, 595.
Anglicans, 370, 385, 495, 594, 595, 663, 668, 680, 773, 799, 803, 808, 835, *see* also Church Missionary Society and Society for the Propagation of the Gospel.
Anglo-Chinese College: at Foochow, 404, 482, 627; at Malacca, 214, 215, 246, 267; at Shanghai, 629; at Swatow, 819; at Tientsin, 633.
Anglo-Saxon, 362, 815.
Anhui, 317, 318, 353, 388, 399, 406, **465, 468, 494,** 547, 561, 574, 579, 593, 643, 657, 660, 669, 708, 710, 722.
Animism, 7, 17, 19.
Anking, 318, 349, 356, 388, 573, 722.
Anselm of Lombardy, 67.
Anti-Christian movement, 694, 695, 697, 699, 737-739, 775, 788, 812, 813, 818, 821, 840.
Anti-Communist agitation, 702, 703.
Anti-Japanese agitation, 733.
Anti-Opium League, 659.
Anti-Religious Federation, 695.
Antonio, 87, 88.
Anzer, 312, 316, 355, 498.
Apostles' Creed, 800.
Appiani, 127, 142, 144.
"Apprehension of Goodness Society," 838.
Aquinas, St. Thomas, *Summa Theologiæ,* translated, 189.
Arabic, 606.
Arbel, 46.
Arbor Day, 785.
Archabbey of St. Vincent, 731.
Archæology, 558.
Archæus, 50.
Archimandrite, 487.
Arkagun, 65.
Arminian, 771.
Arndt, E. L., 597.
Arnobius, 49.
Arrow, lorcha, 272.
Arthington Fund, 634, 766.
Arthington, Robert, 518, 579.
Ashmore, William, 371, 427, 759.
Assam, 722.
Assemblies of God in the United States of America and Foreign Lands, 598, 747, 774.
Associated Mission Treasurers of China, 762.
Association of Christian Colleges and Universities, 786.
"Association of Prayers and Masses for the Conversion of China, Japan, and the Adjacent States," 732.
Association for the Propagation of the Faith, *see* Society for the Propagation of the Faith.
Astronomy, Bureau of. *See* Calendar.
Ataïde, Don Alvaro de, 87.
Atterbury, B. C., 456.
Attitude of missionaries toward opium, war, extraterritoriality, "unequal treaties," indemnities, and toleration clauses, 359, 472, 616, 659, 811, 818.
Aubin, 173.
Augustana Synod, 596, 608.
Augustana Synod Mission, 816.
Augustinian-Recollets, 723.
Augustinians, 89, 90, 118, 128, 138, 175, 177, 315, 319, 522, 547, 719, 723.
Aurora University, 559, 729.
Australia, 393, 718, 747.
Austria and Austrians, 122, 204, 311, 316, 714, 722.
Auxiliatrices du Purgatoire, 711.
Avanzani, Pierre, 315.

B

Bagdad, 47, 48, 54.
Balfour, F. H., 438.
Balkh, 54.
Baller, F. W., 651.
Balme, 789.
Baltimore, 706.
Baltimore Female Seminary, 450.
Bangkok, 164, 216, 225, 226, 251, 370.
Baptism, 188, 334, 350, 550-552, 734.
Baptist (American) "General Missionary Convention," 219, 225, 226, 251, 252. *See* also Southern Baptists and Northern Baptists.
Baptist China Direct Mission, 772.
Baptist Missionary Society, English, 206, 210, 260, 378, 380, 447, 766.
Baptist, Seventh Day, Missionary Society, 256.
Baptist Zenana Missionary Society, 380.
Baptists, 663, 665, 668, 676, 679, 680.
Baptists (American), 370, 432, 599, 611, 629. *See* also Southern Baptists and Northern Baptists.
Baptists (English), 514, 517, 520, 579, 634, 641, 653, 657, 665, 766, 801, 804.
Baptists, English General, 256.
Baptists (Norwegian), 771.
Baptists (Swedish), 401, 579.
Barber, W. T. A., 446.
Barmen, 372, 392.
Barnsley, 382.

Barreto, Melchior Nuñes, 89.
Barth of Calw, 253.
Basel Missionary Society and Basel Mission, 245, 254, 372, 373, 431, 442, 445, 576, 624, 636, 665, 776.
Bashford, Bishop James W., 577, 609, 761.
Batang, 240, 328, 353, 546, 580, 608, 653.
Batavia, 213, 216, 220, 224, 245.
Bavaria, 204, 723.
Bavaria, Duke of, 101.
Bayonne, 723.
Beach, Harlan P., 404, 622.
Beach, W. R., 257.
Beatty (Pa.), 731.
Beauchamp, Montagu, 391.
Beckman, 608.
Beebe, R. C., 456.
Belgium and the Belgians, 314, 315, 489, 705, 707, 714, 716, 723, 732, 737, 741.
Benedict, Friar, 66.
Benedict XV (Pope), 713.
Benedictines, 720.
Benedictines, American, 731.
Benedictines of St. Odele, 722.
Bergen, 400.
Berger, 388.
Berlin, 312.
Berlin Evangelical Missionary Society, 624.
Berlin Foundling House, 400.
Berlin Missionary Society, 374, 495, 576, 665, 681, 743, 772.
Berlin Missionary Society for China, 254, 372, 373, 374.
Berlin Union for Medical Missions, 771.
Berlin Women's Missionary Society for China, 254, 372, 576.
Bernadotte, Prince Oscar, 601.
Berninger, Martha, 593.
Bernot, Francis, 547.
Berthemy Convention, 309, 352.
Bertholet, 498.
Besi, 232.
Betharram, Priests of the Sacred Heart of Jesus of, 723.
Bethel Mission, 772.
Betrothals, of Catholics, 194, 236.
Bible, 76, 414, 439, 449, 588, 617, 634, 636, 647-649, 751, 752, 777, 781, 788, 795, 832. See also New Testament and Old Testament.
Bible, translated, 189, 211-213, 216, 251, 261-263, 368, 429, 430-432, 433, 647, 648, 759.
Bible, Delegates' Version of, 261-263, 266, 430.

Bible and Soul-Winning Prayer Union, 401 (Scotch).
Bible Christian Methodist Mission, 393, 578.
Bible Churchmen's Missionary Society, 773.
Bible classes, 813, 814.
Bible Training Institutes, 637.
Bible Union, 795, 796.
"Bible women," 426, 450, 636, 648.
Biola Evangelistic Bands, 775.
Bishop, first Chinese, 123, 124.
Bishop of Victoria, 433.
Bishoprics created, of Peking and Nanking, 124, suppressed, 241.
Bismarck, 316.
Black Forest, 583.
Blackstone Bible Institute, 637.
Blackstone, J. H., 746.
Blackstone, William E., 649.
Blanc, Le, 120, 145.
Blind, work for, 460, 461, 660.
Blodget, Henry, 248, 366, 430, 431, 433.
Board of Education (China), 644, 752.
Bolshevist régime, 742.
Bonga, 240.
Bonnell, Miss Cornelia, 603.
Boone Divinity School, 636.
Boone University, 630, 787.
Boone, William J., 220, 244, 250, 262, 368.
Booth, Dr., 611, 653.
Booth, General Bramwell, 746.
Borden, William W., 605.
Borneo, 576, 748.
Boston, 540.
Bourboulon, de, 243.
Bourles, 562.
Bourry, 239.
Bouvet, 120.
Boxer Indemnity, 521-525, 818.
Boxers and Boxer Uprising, 379, 396, 487, 501-526, 536, 543, 569-571, 582, 583, 592, 596, 615, 653, 665, 777.
Boycotts: anti-American, 615, 690; anti-British, 689; anti-Japanese, 690.
Boym, Michael, 106, 107.
Braille system, 461.
Brethren, General Mission Board of the Church of the (American), 601.
Breviary, translated, 189.
Bridgman, Elijah C., 217, 232, 245, 248, 262, 263, 430, 450.
Bridgman, Mrs. E. C., 395.
Bridgman School, 450, 633.
Brieux, 353.
British, see England and the English.
British and American Tobacco Company, 791.
British and Foreign Bible Society, 207,

210, 216, 265, 266, 377, 430, 437, 468, 648, 817.
British Chamber of Commerce in China, 766.
British Consul, see British Minister.
British Government, 474, 500, 743, 750.
British Legation, 513.
British Minister (or Consul), 397, 466, 468, 608, 614, 817, 820.
British missionaries, 615, 625, 631, 744.
British treaty of 1858, 474.
Broadcast Tract Press and Faith Orphanages, 599.
Brockman, Fletcher S., 495, 763.
Brooks, 504.
Brothers of Christian Doctrine, 723.
Brothers of the Sacred Heart, 553.
Brown, Samuel R., 221.
Bruce, J. R., 615.
Brunière, de la, 242.
Brussels, 314.
Buchanan, Claudius, 210.
Buchman, Frank, 807.
Buddhism and Buddhists, 15-17, 37-39, 42, 49, 54, 59, 426, 433, 531, 532, 612, 772, 838.
Buddhist terms, 809.
Buffington Institute, 629.
Buglio, 189.
Burdon, 430, 432, 433.
Burgos, Geronimo de, 99.
Burgundy, 317.
Buriats, 215.
Burma, 226, 389, 512, 748.
Burmo-Chinese border, 774.
Burns, William C., 257-259, 264, 383, 396.
Burton, E. D., 786.
Byers, George D., 817, 818.

C

Cairo, 606.
Caldwell, 657.
Calendar, administered by the Jesuits, 101, 102, 104, 106, 115, 116, 181.
California, 249, 599.
Callery, 232.
Calvinist, 771, 800.
Cambaluc. See Peking.
Cambridge, 391, 631.
"Cambridge Seven," 391, 581.
Cameron, Allen N., 599.
Campbell, W., 461.
Canada, 397, 722, 768.
Canadian Anglicans, 664.
Canadian Holiness Mission, 599.
Canadian Jesuits, 721.
Canadian Methodists, 578, 616, 624, 632, 664, 817.

Canadian Presbyterians, 397, 575, 664, 806.
Canadian Sisters of the Immaculate Conception, 720.
Canadian societies, 745.
Candida, 95.
Cannon, 106, 186.
Canossa, Marchioness of, 313.
Canossian Daughters of Charity, 313, 711.
Canterbury, Archbishop of, 433.
Canton, 1, 54, 85, 86, 89, 100, 111, 115, 159, 161, 176, 208, 212, 213, 217-223, 229, 244, 246, 249, 251, 257, 272, 282, 285, 308, 324, 325, 353, 359, 363, 365-367, 371, 373-375, 378, 399, 400, 407, 432, 437, 448, 453, 458, 460, 484, 489, 493, 494, 507, 539, 540, 544, 559, 561, 575, 595, 600, 602, 604, 626, 627, 637, 640, 641, 652, 678, 689, 698, 701, 702, 709, 720, 735, 737, 744, 772, 784, 791, 803, 805, 819.
Canton Baptist Academy, 677.
Canton Christian College, 1, 449, 493, 604, 609, 627, 640, 677, 753, 756, 783, 785, 805, 815.
Canton Guild Hall, 712.
Canton Hospital, 819.
Canton Medical Missionary Society, 819.
Cantonese, 436, 490.
Capillas, 110.
Capuchins, 158, 720.
Caralt, Father, 721.
Carey, William, 210, 378.
Carmelite Sisters, 314, 711.
Caroline Islands, 721.
Carolingians, 313.
Cassel Missionary Society, 260.
Cassels, W. W., 391, 570.
Castanet, 543.
Castile, 722.
Castro, Jean de, 101.
Cataneo, 96.
Catechists, 186, 191, 339, 557.
Catechumens, 187, 331-333, 550-552, 734.
Catechumenates, 550-552, 734.
"Catholic Action," 733.
"Catholic Association of Chinese Students in France and Belgium," 732.
Catholics, Chinese, character of, 194.
Catholic Foreign Missions Bureau, 540.
Catholic Foreign Mission Society of America, 540, 713, 717.
Catholic Students' Mission Crusade, 540, 716.
Catholics, numbers of. See Statistics.
Çauma, Rabban, 63.

Centenary Fund (Northern Methodist), 767, 768, 780, 790.
Centenary Missionary Conference (1907), 591, 614, 620, 631, 637, 642, 644, 650, 666, 668, 673, 796, 797, 826.
Central Asia, 47, 52, 63.
Central China Christian Educational Union, 643.
Central China Famine Relief Committee, 661.
Central China Mission, 374.
Central China Religious Tract Society, 439.
Central China University, 787.
Central Conference for Eastern Asia of the Methodist Episcopal Church, 804.
Central Teachers' College, Wuchang, 785.
Ceylon, 583.
Chahar, 772.
Chala, 509, 559, 730.
Chalfant, Frank H., 651.
Chalmers, John, 363, 430, 436, 678.
Champagne, 707.
Chanes, 498.
Chang Chih-chiang, 777.
Chang Chih-tung, 441, 488, 490, 492, 507, 516.
Chang Ching-yao, 816.
Chang Hsüeh-liang, 702.
Chang Hsun, 658, 701.
Chang Po-ling, 835.
Chang Tso-lin, 701, 702, 737.
Chang Ying-hua, 835.
Changli, 785.
Changsha, 1, 179, 289, 321, 364, 384, 470, 547, 573, 578, 581, 597, 599, 604, 616, 620, 632, 637, 657, 755, 782, 784, 798, 808.
Changtê, 289, 354, 402, 494, 599.
Chao, (Bishop) Philip, 727.
Chaoch'ing, 92, 93, 94, 542.
Ch'aochou, 94, 95, 258, 710.
Chaoting, 570.
Chapdelaine, 244, 273, 275, 325.
Charity, Daughters of. See Sisters of Charity.
Charter, Dr., 654.
Chefoo, 274, 314, 364, 367, 368, 371, 378, 381, 396, 446, 461, 469, 562, 641, 660, 721, 753, 793.
Chefoo Convention, 304, 389, 417.
Chêkiang, 107, 111, 125, 232, 237, 238, 241, 321, 323, 367, 371, 375, 382-384, 388, 389, 425, 469, 470, 479, 498, 512, 516, 542, 545, 546, 565, 573, 574, 577-579, 583, 600, 606, 607, 611, 626, 643, 668, 676, 705, 716, 718, 721, 759, 763, 791, 807.

Chen, L. T., 702.
Ch'ên, (Bishop) Aloysius, 727.
Ch'ên Ch'iung-ming, 701.
Ch'ên Huan-chang, 612.
Ch'ên Tu-hsiu, 840.
Ch'enchow, 615.
Cheng Mao, 482.
Ch'êng Ching-i (C. Y. Cheng), 671, 678, 797, 798, 800, 807.
Ch'eng, Odoric, 727.
Chengtu, 55, 171, 178, 375, 401, 456, 541, 589, 620, 641, 652, 668, 799, 817, 839.
Ch'êng Yeh-su Chiao, 808.
Chesnut, Dr. Eleanor, 615.
Chevallier-Chantepie, 735.
Ch'i Ying, 230.
Chia Ch'ing, 175.
Chiang K'ai-shek, 702.
Chiangpoo, 546, 616.
Chiao-li-t'ung, 554.
Chicago, 540, 583, 600, 716.
Chichou, 559.
Ch'ien Lung, 161-175.
Chienning, 468, 501.
Chiesa, Bernardin della, 117, 124, 126, 146.
Chihli, 55, 65, 107, 162, 182, 183, 233, 237, 238, 241, 308, 316, 319, 321, 323, 340, 341, 348-350, 375, 381, 400, 404, 464, 471, 491, 502, 504, 505, 508, 509, 513, 522, 524, 537, 538, 542, 543, 551, 554, 559, 560, 566, 572, 573, 578, 599, 600, 601, 605, 625, 664, 669, 677, 678, 706, 707, 710, 712, 720, 722, 726, 727, 730, 732, 737, 741, 747, 785, 791, 794.
Chikungshan, 672.
Childhood, Association of the Holy. See Holy Infancy, Association of the.
Children's News, The, 436.
China and the Chinese, 436.
China Baptist Publication Society, 493.
China Christian Educational Association, See Educational Association of China.
China Congregational Society, 397.
China Continuation Committee, 669, 670, 671, 744, 749, 752, 753, 758, 760, 762, 776, 777, 786, 791, 796-798.
China Council (China Inland Mission), 390.
China Educational Council (Northern Methodist), 780.
China Famine Fund, 785.
"China for Christ Movement," 776.
"China for the Chinese," 607.
China Inland Mission, 370, 382-394, 397, 399, 442, 454, 474, 482, 494, 501, 514, 516-518, 581-584, 595-597,

600, 601, 611, 616, 619, 624, 637, 640, 649, 653, 663, 680, 744, 745, 757, 766, 795, 797, 816, 817.
China Medical Board, 459, 604, 747, 754, 755, 759, 784, 788, 789.
China Medical Missionary Association, 460, 611, 638, 640, 655, 755, 759, 789.
China Mennonite Mission Society, 600.
China Missions Emergency Committee (British), 631.
China Sun, The, 712.
China Sunday School Union, 642.
China's Young Men, 588.
Chinese Book and Tract Society (Scotland), 440.
Chinese Choral Union (Foochow), 641.
"Chinese Christian Conference," 798.
Chinese Christian Union, 677, 679, 799, 812.
Chinese Eastern Railway, 489.
Chinese Educational Mission, 476.
Chinese Evangelization Society, 259, 378, 383.
Chinese Home Missionary Society, 807.
Chinese Recorder and Missionary Journal, The, 437, 662, 845.
Chinese Repository, The, 218, 221, 265, 437.
Chinese Telegraph Administration, 492.
Chinese Weekly, 650.
Ching Chiao, 808.
Ching-ching, 53.
Ch'ing Ming festival, 809.
Ching-shan, 505.
Ching-tê-chên, 158.
Ching T'ien, 141.
Chingting, 308.
Chinkiang, 64, 274, 318, 374, 388, 468, 470, 599, 659.
Chino-Japanese War, 471, 491, 494, 602.
Chosen, 595, 722.
Chou, Han, 470.
Chou dynasty, 8-14.
Chouchoufu, 516.
Choulet, Bishop, 705.
Christ, the Order of, 86.
Christian Alliance, 398.
Christian and Missionary Alliance, 392, 398, 399, 495, 515, 584, 637, 797, 816, 817.
Christian Catholic Apostolic Church Mission, 601.
"The Christian Church in China," 670.
Christian College in China, Trustees of the, 449.
Christian Endeavor, United Society of, 358, 405.
Christian Endeavor Society, 751.
Christian Federation of China, 667.

Christian Herald, 660-662.
Christian Intelligencer, 650.
Christian Literature Society, 382, 440, 649, 650, 828.
Christian Missions in Many Lands, 400, 580.
Christian Mission to Buddhists, 772.
Christian Publishers' Association, 758.
Christian Reformed Church, 772.
Christian Union at Canton, 221.
Christianity, outstanding characteristics of, 25-44.
Christians' Mission, 401, 580, 601.
Christie, Dr. Dugald, 337, 396, 455, 611, 638, 654.
Chu, 482.
Chu Chiu-tao, 287.
Ch'üanchow, 70, 71, 461, 468, 482.
Chuang, Tzŭ, 13.
Chuchow, 657, 721.
Chung Hsi Chiao Hui Pao, 441.
Chung Hua Chi Tu Chiao Hui, 670.
Chung Hua Sheng Kung Hui, see Holy Catholic Church of China.
Chung, K. T., 628, 798.
Chung, Professor, 609.
Chungking, 354, 355, 364, 375, 496, 501, 664.
Chung Kuo Chi Tu Sheng Chiao Chang Lao Hui, see Presbyterian Church of China.
Church Federation Council of Hangchow, 791.
Church Missionary Society, 206, 210, 216, 249, 252, 369, 370, 381, 395, 425, 427, 446, 455, 457, 458, 461, 468, 469, 471, 573, 595, 624, 626, 628, 629, 632, 639, 652, 653, 664, 677, 678, 765, 784, 807, 808, 816, 817.
Church of Christ in China, 800, 801.
Church of England Zenana Missionary Society, 369, 395.
Church of God Mission, 599.
Church of Scotland, 396, 574, 664.
Church of Sweden Mission, 747, 783.
Chusan, 238, 244, 245.
Cincinnati, 720.
Civil service examinations, 528.
Civilization East and West, 435.
Clare, County, 718.
Clark, J. C., 588.
Classics (Chinese), 443, 612.
Clergy, Chinese, 115, 123, 163, 173, 180, 191, 338, 339, 427, 428, 556, 557, 636, 637, 711, 725, 730, 753, 754, 762.
Clet, François-Régis, 179.
Clift, Dr., 653.
Cobbold, R. H., 249, 252.

Cochrane, Dr. Thomas, 667.
Cody, Miss, 611.
Coerper, 392, 583.
Colbert, 112, 119, 120.
Colledge, T. R., 219, 222.
College of Agriculture and Forestry of the University of Nanking, 753, 784, 793.
College of Missions (Disciples), 768.
Collegium Urbanum de Propaganda Fide, 557.
Collins, J. D., 256.
Colleges and Universities, Christian. See education.
Collins, Stratford, 369.
Cologne, 204.
Colorado, 599.
Colporteurs, 426, 438, 817.
Colquhoun, 330.
Columban, Missionary Sisters of St., 718.
Combs, 456.
Commercial Press, 478, 494, 568, 650, 792.
Commission on Protestant education in China, 786-788.
Committee of Reference and Counsel of the Foreign Missions Conference of North America, 786.
Communism, Russian and Chinese, 693, 697, 699, 702, 778, 819.
Companions of Our Lady of Good Counsel, 553.
Comte, Le, 120.
Concise Dictionary of Chinese, 436.
Conference of Foreign Mission Societies in Great Britain and Ireland, 786.
Conference of 1877, 413, 415, 433, 434, 440, 441, 451, 463, 796, 797, 826.
Conference of 1890, 390, 431, 433, 435, 436, 442, 451, 463, 473, 483, 635, 647, 665, 796, 797, 826.
Conference of 1907 in Shanghai. See Centenary Missionary Conference (1907).
Conference of 1913, 659, 674, 796, 797, 826.
Conference of 1922. See National Christian Conference.
Confirmation, 188.
Confucius, 6, 10, 133-155, 362, 436, 612, 615, 839.
Confucianism, 9-11, 37-39, 42, 433, 531, 532, 554, 612, 613, 615, 763, 838, 839.
Conger, 500.
Congo, 315, 653.
Congregation of the Immaculate Heart of Mary, 314, 510, 538, 541, 542, 550, 707, 730.
Congregation of Our Lady, 722.

Congregation of the Priests of the Mission. See Lazarists.
Congregation of the Sacred Heart of Jesus and Mary and of the Perpetual Adoration of the Very Holy Sacrament of the Altar. See Picpus, Congregation of.
"Congregational Union," 425.
Congregationalists, 365, 367, 664, 678, 680, 800, 808. See also American Board and London Missionary Society.
Congregation of the Daughters of Mary and Joseph, 723.
Conrady, 561.
Constantin, Celse Bénigne-Louis, 728.
Constantinople, 47, 50.
"Constitutional Compact," 544.
Continuation Committee of the Edinburgh Conference, 645. See also, China Continuation Committee.
Conventions of 1860, 276.
Conventuals, 722.
Coombs, Miss, 514.
Coöperation among Protestants, 260-262, 410-415, 662-672, 761, 762, 794-801.
"Coöperative Goodness Association," 838.
Coöperative Study Society, 692.
Coqui, Angel, 108, 109.
Corbett, Hunter, 367, 469, 570.
Cornaby, W. A., 650.
Cornell University, 391.
Cosme, Archbishop of Sarai, 74.
Costroppe, Richard, 209.
Cotolendi, 115.
Cotton Mill Owners' Association of China, 785.
Council on Health Education, 789.
Council on Medical Education of the China Medical Missionary Association, 755.
Council on Primary and Secondary Education, 786.
Couvreur, Seraphin, 341, 560.
Covenant Missionary Society, see Swedish Evangelical Mission Covenant of America.
(Covenanter) Reformed Presbyterian Church in North America, 402, 575.
Cox, Josiah, 257, 293, 375.
Crawford, T. P., 251, 264, 371, 372.
Cressey, E. H., 786.
"Crusade of Prayers to the Sacred Heart for China," 732.
Cruz, Gaspar de la, 89.
Culbertson, 249, 262, 430.
Cumberland Presbyterians, 402, 494.
Cumming, William, 245.
Cunha, Simon A., 190.

Cunningham, J. E., 817.
Customs Service, Imperial Maritime, 445, 477, 489, 567, 700.

D

Daily Vacation Bible School, 782.
Dairen (Dalny), 489, 566.
Damien, 561.
Danner, William M., 789.
Danske Missionsselskab, *see* Danish Lutheran Mission.
Daughters of Charity, *see* Sisters of Charity.
Daughters of Purgatory, 711.
Daughters of the Christian Doctrine, 711.
Daughters of the Sacred Heart, 553.
David, Armand, 322, 340.
David, Nestorian Metropolitan for China, 54.
Deaf, work for, 461.
Dean, William, 225, 245, 251, 263, 370.
Deism, influenced by China, 198.
Dejean, 349.
Delamarre, 276, 307.
Delaplace, 316.
Delavay, 349.
Delbrouck, Victorin, 498.
Delegates' Version, 261-263, 266, 430.
Delpal, 562.
Demon possession, 194.
Denmark, 313.
Desmazures, Thomines, 327.
Desmet, Leo, 563.
Deutscher Frauenmissionsbund, *see* German Women's Missionary Union.
Devan, T. T., 251.
Dewey, John, 692.
Diaz, Emmanuel, 136, 189.
Dictionaries, 265, 341, 436, 651, 655.
Ding Ing-ong, 804.
Diocesan Conference of North China, 675.
Disciples, 768.
(Disciples) Federal Foreign Mission Committee of Churches of Christ, 747.
Disciples of Christ, 398, 608, 629, 747, 768, 799, 804. *See* also Foreign Christian Missionary Society.
Dodd, Samuel, 430.
Dolgan Park, Galway, 718.
Dom Bosco, 539, 542, 723.
Domestic and Foreign Missionary Society of the Protestant Episcopal Church in the United States, 220, 250, 368, 425, 428, 450, 456, 483, 573, 626, 628, 630, 636, 641, 661, 664, 818, 835.
Dominican Sisters, 314.

Dominicans, 66-69, 86, 89, 90, 99-101, 108-111, 118, 123, 124, 128, 135-155, 159, 163, 171, 180, 233, 238, 311, 328, 552, 706, 708, 729.
Dominicans of St. Joseph's Province in North America, 719.
Doolittle, Justus, 248, 436.
"Door of Hope," 603.
Doty, 247.
Douglas, Carstairs, 258, 436.
Dublin University Mission, 369.
DuBose, Hampden, 659.
Dubourq, Bishop of New Orleans, 203.
Dubs, Rev. and Mrs. C. N., 578.
Dufresse, 173, 178.
Dumazel, 176.
Duncan, Moir, 520.
Dunn, George, 312.
Durand, 348.
Dutch, 108, 110, 209, 319, 491.
Dutch East Indies, 748.
(Dutch) Reformed Church. *See* Reformed Church in America.
Dyer, Samuel, 213, 438.

E

East China Christian Educational Association, 643, 786.
East China Union Medical College, 629.
East India Company, English, 212-214.
East Indies, 375, 625, 748.
Ebenezer Mission, 599.
Eddy, George Sherwood, 591, 592, 611, 620, 621, 748.
Edessa, 46.
Edinburgh, 669.
Edinburgh World Missionary Conference of 1910, 535, 669.
Edkins, Joseph, 247, 293, 364, 436.
Education, 195, 214, 215, 221, 222, 236, 267, 338-340, 427, 428, 447-451, 458, 459, 493, 551, 558-560, 622-646, 722, 730-732, 751-758, 780-788, 805, 814, 815, 827, 835.
Education, Ministry of, 528, 611, 692, 698, 739, 758, 814.
Educational Association of China, The, 452, 642, 645, 651, 666, 756, 786, 787.
Educational Commission (1921-1922), 786-788.
Edwards, D. W., 586.
Egypt, 690.
Eighteen Provinces, 361, 390, 394, 417, 566.
Eighteenth Amendment in U. S., 791.
Eitel, 436.
Elgin, 339, 359.
Emmanuel Medical Mission, 653.

Empress Dowager, 439, 502, 505, 529, 537, 639.
England and the English, 358, 359, 362, 363, 364, 365, 375, 381, 384, 392, 401, 403, 413, 428, 443, 450, 455, 461, 474, 493, 501, 504, 518, 524, 525, 559, 567, 568, 631, 646, 718, 732, 754, 757, 766, 796, 797, 808, 819. *See* also, Great Britain.
England, Church of. *See* Anglicans.
England in Canada, Missionary Society of the Church of, 594.
English Friends Foreign Missionary Association, 804.
English Methodist Free Church Mission, 382, 493, 676.
Episcopal Church, 368, 835. *See* also Domestic and Foreign Missionary Society of the Protestant Episcopal Church in the United States.
Episcopalians, American. *See* Domestic and Foreign Missionary Society of the Protestant Episcopal Church in the United States.
Etienne, 709.
L'Étoile du Matin, 559.
Europe, 357, 358, 363, 373, 427, 488, 489, 512, 528, 534, 538, 540, 554, 562, 587, 612, 617, 663, 687, 688, 690, 695, 705, 726, 730, 764, 765, 767, 821, 822, 830.
"Evaluation Conferences" (Presbyterian), 804.
Evangel Mission, 599.
Evangelical Association of North America, 595.
Evangelical Church, 817.
Evangelical Free Church of Norway, Mission of the, 747.
Evangelical Lutheran Mission, 597.
Evangelical Missionary Society of Paris, 381.
Evangelical Movement, 771.
Evangelicals, 773, 795.
Evangelism, Week of, 776.
Evangelistic Association, 620.
"Evangelists," 426, 427.
Evidences of Christianity, 433.
Exercises, Loyola's, translated, 189.
Exhortation to Study, 730.
Ex Illa Die, Bull, 146, 147.
Exner, M. J., 588.
Ex Quo Singulari, Bull, 150.
Extraterritoriality, 229, 689, 811.

F

Faber, Ernst, 373, 398, 435, 436.
Faith Mission, 599.
Famine relief, 464, 790.

Famine Relief Committee, 590.
Famine relief, 464, 465, 561, 562, 660, 661, 735, 760, 790.
Fan, Miss Y. J., 798.
Fantosati, Bishop, 512.
Far Eastern Olympic Games, 590.
Farmer, W. A., 600.
"Fasters," 511.
Faurie, 310, 326, 332, 333.
Favier, Bishop, 499, 504, 508, 509, 521, 537.
Federation of Women's Boards of Foreign Missions, 792.
Fell, Henry F., 209.
Fênchow, 514, 572.
Fêng Kuo-chang, 701.
Feng shui, 469.
Fêng Yü-hsiang, 701, 702, 736, 777, 778.
Fêng Yün-shan, 284-289.
Fenouil, 333, 347.
Ferguson, John C., 448.
Ferrant, Bishop, 553.
Finances, of Catholic missions in the eighteenth century, 192, 193, 234; in the nineteenth century, 329-331.
Finland, Free Church of, 393.
Finnish Free Church Mission, 583.
Finnish Missionary Society, 597.
Fleming, 501.
Fleury, 498.
Fogolla, Francis, 510.
Folke, Erik, 392.
Foochow, 110, 163, 229, 238, 248, 252, 256, 366, 369, 374, 404, 405, 407, 427, 432, 436, 437, 445, 449, 450, 456, 459, 461, 468, 469, 482, 544, 559, 586, 604, 620, 626, 627, 637, 638, 640, 641, 652, 699, 729, 753, 763, 782, 789, 808, 820.
Foochow College, 627.
Foochow Council of Congregational Churches, 676.
Foochow Methodist Conference, 751.
Foot-binding, 462, 658.
Forbidden City (Peking), 611, 776.
Foreign Christian Missionary Society, 398, 579, 610, 653. *See* also Disciples of Christ.
Foreign Mission Society of Saints Peter and Paul, 723.
Forestry, education in, 753, 784, 785.
Formosa, 108, 110, 209, 274, 328, 376, 377, 397, 455, 461, 468, 489, 542, 575, 832.
Forsberg, 816.
Forward Evangelistic Movement, 749.
"Forward Movement" (Northern Methodists), 748.
Foster, Arnold, 364, 631.

Fowler, Bishop, 448.
Fox, George, 209.
France, 80, 83, 111-114, 118-120, 167, 203, 204, 312, 322, 324, 351, 354, 477, 489, 551, 555, 687, 707, 712, 714, 716, 722, 726, 732, 750, 781. *See* also French Government.
Francis of Podio, 74.
Franciscans, 66-74, 86, 89, 90, 99-101, 108-111, 117, 118, 127, 128, 135-155, 158, 166, 175, 176, 180, 233, 238, 240, 314, 319, 320, 321, 498, 510, 512, 540, 547, 552, 553, 720, 722, 723, 727, 736, 823.
Franciscans (Canadian), 721; Franciscans (German), 539, 708; Franciscans (Italian), 549, 723; Franciscans (Saxon), 706, 711; Franciscans (Tyrolese), 723; Franciscans (Spanish), 542.
Franciscans of the Province of Catalonia, 540.
Franciscan Missionaries of Mary, 314, 510, 541, 561, 562, 711, 719.
Franciscan Sisters of Egypt, 539, 711.
Franco-Chinese war, 311, 312, 325, 470.
Franco-Prussian War, 324, 388.
Franson, Frederick, 392.
Fraser, Father, 721, 722.
Free Evangelical Missionary Union of Norway, 601.
Free Methodist Church of North America, General Missionary Board of the, 595.
Free Press, The, 359.
French, 307, 312, 318, 319, 322, 325, 326, 327, 349, 350, 352, 353, 362, 475, 505, 509, 512, 546, 548, 558, 559, 560, 561, 705, 716, 724, 730, 732, 733, 737.
French Consul. *See* French Minister.
French Convention of 1860, 309.
French Government, 309, 331, 340, 498, 546, 548, 549.
French Minister (and Consul), 328, 350, 498, 504, 548, 698.
French protectorate of Catholic missions, 306, 307, 311-313, 324, 326, 331, 346, 359, 499, 508, 538, 549, 713, 714, 728, 738.
French Revolution and its effects on Missions, 169, 170.
French Separation Act of 1905, 548.
French Sisters of St. Paul of Chartres, 711.
French, teaching of, 340-341.
French, John B., 249.
Freyche, Father Joseph, 736.
Friars Minor. *See* Franciscans.
Friedenshort Deaconess Mission, 596.

Friends, 209, 397, 398, 580, 658, 668, 804.
Friends (American) Mission (Ohio), 580.
Friends, English, 580, 632, 745, 804.
Friends Foreign Mission Association, 397.
Frost, Henry W., 391.
Fryer, John, 435.
Fu-an, 159, 163, 180, 369.
Fukien, 70, 90, 108, 110, 111, 118, 119, 125, 159, 160, 163, 166, 173, 179, 183, 233, 238, 314, 328, 355, 365, 369, 374, 395, 425, 457, 459-461, 468, 470, 471, 479, 482, 484, 489, 491, 494, 501, 542, 573, 575, 599, 604, 606, 611, 616, 620, 624, 643, 657, 669, 676, 706, 708, 710, 719, 722, 734, 751, 791, 794, 800, 804, 808.
Fukien Christian University, 753, 782.
Fukien College of Liberal Arts, 753.
Fukien Moral Welfare Association, 791.
"Fundamentalism," 794.
Fu-ning, 369.

G

Gabet, 233.
Gailey, Robert R., 495, 586, 777.
Gaillard, Charles W., 430.
Gain (Father), 543.
Galt, 458.
Galvin (Father), 718.
Galway, 718.
Gamble, William, 266.
Gamewell, F. D., 786.
Gasgoyne-Cecil, William, 631.
Gaubil, Antoine, 158, 197.
Gauld, William, 454.
Gaynor, Dr., 658.
Genähr, 253.
General Education Committee, 643.
General Evangelical Protestant Missionary Society, 398, 495.
George, Henry, 610.
George, Prince of the Onguts, 69.
Gerard, 70.
Gerbillon, 120, 122, 126.
German China Alliance, 392.
German Consul, *see* German Minister.
German East Africa, 771.
German Government, 311, 497.
German Minister (and Consul), 355, 506, 519.
German Mission to Blind Females in China, 400, 461.
German Women's Missionary Union, 583.
Germany and the Germans, 313, 315, 316, 355, 358, 372, 373, 393, 398, 400, 403, 464, 489, 495, 519, 569,

575, 583, 601, 612, 687, 688, 706, 707, 713, 714, 719, 720, 722, 743, 744, 751, 765, 771, 776, 803.
Gibbons, Cardinal, 706.
Gilman, 802.
Gilmour, James, 365, 454.
Ginling College, 630, 753, 783.
Girls' schools, 449, 450. *See also*, Education.
Glasgow, 391.
Gleyo, 165.
Goa, 86, 88, 90.
Goa, Archbishop of, 145, 147.
Gobi desert, 515.
Goddard, Josiah, 251, 263, 268.
Goës, Benedict of, 97.
Goêz, Etienne, 89.
Goette, Remigius, 561, 720.
Goforth, Jonathan, 397, 575, 777.
Goodrich, Chauncey, 433.
Gordon, Charles George, 294.
Gospel Baptist Mission, 372.
Gospel Tabernacle, 399.
Gospels, translated, 189, 341. *See also,* Bible, New Testament.
Gouvea, Bishop of Peking, 176.
Grace Evangelical Mission, 601.
Graham, 461.
Grassi, Gregory, 510.
Graves, Bishop, 661.
Graves, R. H., 251.
Gray, 460.
Great Britain, 325, 357-359, 362, 388, 389, 390, 391, 418, 441, 453, 454, 459, 463, 473, 475, 489, 525, 567, 569, 570, 654, 660, 687, 696, 714, 743-745, 751, 765, 766, 768, 779, 794, 820. *See also* England.
"Great Sword Society," 497, 499.
Great Wall, 399, 583.
Greek, 446, 634.
Griffith John College, 626, 630.
Grueber, Johann, 108.
Guébriant, 728.
Guiana, 484.
Guillon, Bishop, 511.
Gulick, L. H., 366, 438.
Gützlaff, Karl Friedrich August, 216, 217, 219, 232, 245, 253-255, 372, 373, 377, 383, 425, 461, 571.
Gützlaff, Mrs., 221, 222.

H

Hackett Medical School for Women, 640.
Hager, C. R., 365, 609.
Hainan, 118, 239, 243, 311, 323, 324, 367, 432, 489, 542, 759, 774, 781, 816, 818.

Hakka-English dictionary, 651.
Hakkas, 255, 282, 287, 371, 373, 374, 376, 431, 462, 759.
Hall, W. N., 380.
Halley's Comet, 650.
Hallock, H. G. C., 599.
Hamberg, 253-255.
Hamer, Bishop, 510.
Hangchow, 64, 71, 94, 129, 367, 370, 388, 394, 432, 455, 457, 458, 462, 493, 532, 591, 601, 604, 628, 639, 653, 753, 784, 791, 808.
Hangchow Medical College, 629.
Hangchow (Presbyterian) College, 493, 628.
Hangchow Union Evangelistic Committee, 749.
Hankow, 242, 274, 289, 314, 342, 349, 363, 364, 368, 369, 375, 397, 404, 438, 454, 455, 457, 460, 461, 471, 489, 522, 561, 563, 566, 572, 573, 597, 611, 620, 626, 630, 638, 653, 689, 702, 726, 735, 739, 834.
Hankow Tract Society, 439.
Hanlin, 692.
Hanlin Academy, 96.
Hanson, Francis R., 220.
Hanyang, 364, 371, 630, 718, 719, 722, 730.
Happer, Andrew P., 249, 268, 269, 448.
Harbin, 396, 774.
Harrison, Miss Agatha, 793.
Hart, Lavington, 633.
Hart, Sir Robert, 478, 567.
Hart, Virgil C., 374, 401, 571.
Hart, Walford, 633.
Hartwell, 371.
Harvard Medical School in China, 604, 655, 754.
Hauge's Synodes Mission, 577, 596.
Hawaii, 569, 712, 748, 836.
Hayes, Mr. and Mrs. W. M., 447, 645.
Haygood, Laura, 450.
"Heart Cleansing Society," 839.
Hebron Mission, 599.
Heilungchiang, 538, 574, 722, 739, 807.
Helen, Empress, 107.
Hêngchow, 179, 321, 512.
Henle, 497, 498.
Henninghaus, Bishop, 711.
Henry, B. C., 448.
Henry, Prince, the Navigator, 80, 86.
Hepburn, J. C., 268.
Hepzibah Faith Mission, 772.
Herat, 47.
Herrada, Martin de, 90.
Hickson, James Moore, 790.
Hilarion, Archimandrite, 200.
Hildesheim, 400.

Hill, David, 376, 461, 481, 571.
Hillsboro (Kansas), 600, 772.
Hinayana, 15.
Hinghwa, 238, 432, 641.
History of the Nineteenth Century, 441.
Ho, Agatha, 233.
Ho Chin-shan, 430.
Hobson, Benjamin, 244, 265, 268.
Hobson, Francis, 460.
Hochienfu, 65, 720.
Hodgkin, H. T., 798.
Hoff, B. A., 816.
Hokchiang, 653.
Hokow, 501.
Holland, 315, 316, 707, 714, 723.
Holmes, 371.
Holmgren, Josef, 392.
Holy Catholic Church of China, 664, 678, 803, 804, 807.
Holy Heart of Mary, Sisterhood of, 234.
Holy Infancy, Association of the, 204, 561, 562, 707.
Holy Rosary, the Dominican Province of the, 99, 101.
Holy Virgin, 728.
Honan, 157, 163, 179, 237, 241, 243, 314, 315, 321, 348, 389, 390, 392, 397, 400, 465, 494, 542, 557, 566, 575, 577, 580, 595, 596, 599, 600, 605, 608, 613, 660, 668, 709, 717, 723, 747, 749, 762, 806, 816.
Hong, Joseph Lo Pa, 741.
Hongkong, 1, 229, 234, 241, 244, 270, 313, 316, 354, 360, 363, 365, 369, 370, 372, 373, 378, 400, 407, 433, 456, 458, 461, 464, 489, 559, 560, 573, 576, 586, 591, 600, 609, 620, 626, 640, 677, 679, 708, 711, 723, 732, 743, 836.
Hongkong University, 640.
Honolulu, 609.
Hopei, 522.
Hopwood, Misses E. A. and L. M., 401.
Horder, E. G., 457.
Horsburgh, J. H., 370.
Hospitals, 452, 453. *See also,* Medical missions.
Hospital Sisters of St. Francis, 720.
Hoste, D. E., 391, 581.
Houlding, Mr. and Mrs. Horace W., 402.
Howard, 456.
Howell, Bishop, 817.
Hsi Hsin Shê, 839.
Hsi, Pastor, 376, 434, 481.
Hsi T'ang, 178, 308, 322, 508.
Hsia Kuan, 318, 330.
Hsianfu, 52, 53, 104, 173, 506, 543, 608, 654, 720, 818.

Hsianfu Monument, 52-57.
Hsiangyangfu, 512.
Hsiaoyihsien, 514.
Hsien Fêng, 231, 243.
Hsienhsien, 522, 560.
Hsinchow, 514.
Hsiwantzŭ, 182.
Hsü Kuang-ch'i, 95, 97, 104, 235, 308.
Hsü Shih-chang, 701.
Hsuchow, 596.
Hu (Bishop), Joseph, 727.
Hü King-eng, 459.
Hu Shih, 692.
Hua-hsien, 282.
Huang, 353.
Huang Fu, 736.
Huang Hsing, 609.
Huashan, 471.
Huc, 233, 239.
Huchow Women's School, 752.
Hudson, T. H., 430.
Hue, Jean, 353.
Hukwang, 125, 160, 176, 233, 242, 243, 307.
Hulagu, 61, 63.
Hume, E. H., 632.
Hunan, 160, 166, 174, 179, 195, 232, 237, 240, 241, 315, 319, 321, 349, 354, 356, 364, 367, 375, 389, 390, 399, 402, 407, 470, 471, 494, 495, 512, 518, 537, 538, 547, 571, 573, 574, 575, 578, 583, 595, 596, 597, 599, 604, 605, 615, 616, 621, 649, 669, 683, 699, 709, 711, 719, 723, 737, 747, 762, 772, 783, 791, 798, 800, 815, 817, 818, 820.
Hunan Bible Institute, 775, 784.
Hunan Christian Council, 799.
Hunan Union Theological Seminary, 784.
Hunan-Yale Medical School, 755.
Hung Hsiu-ch'üan, 282-302.
Hung Jên, 284-291, 297.
Hungary, 714, 722.
Huns, 519.
Hunter, Joseph M., 455.
Huntington, Bishop D. T., 641.
Hupeh, 166, 174, 195, 232, 237, 240, 241, 318, 319, 320, 375, 399, 400, 406, 425, 482, 498, 512, 539, 541, 543, 545, 553, 566, 575, 577-579, 593, 596, 597, 605, 637, 668, 711, 718, 723, 726, 736, 737, 739, 762, 800, 815, 816, 818.
Hupeh, Governor of, 376.
Hykes, 648.
Hwai River Valley, 574.
Hwaiyüan, 574.
Hweilichow, 747.
Hwochow, 608.

I

Ibanez, Bonaventura, 117.
Ichang, 314, 368, 397, 470, 494, 574, 641.
Ichowfu, 501.
Ifang Girls' Collegiate School, Changsha, 808.
I Ho Ch'üan, 503. *See also* Boxers.
I Ho Tuan, 503. *See also* Boxers.
Ili, 173.
Iliff, Bishop, 573.
Illinois, 400, 720.
Images, 189.
Imitation of Christ, translated, 189.
Imperial Polytechnic College, 587.
Indemnities, 274, 351, 356, 473. *See also* Attitude toward indemnities, and Boxer Indemnity.
Independence of Chinese churches. *See* Self-support.
Independent Chinese Church, 677, 678, 776.
Independent Church in Tientsin, 807.
Independent Church in Tsinanfu, 806.
Independent Lutheran Mission, 597.
India, 49-51, 380, 391, 392, 393, 690, 797.
Indian Government, 660.
Indiana, 719.
Indianapolis, 768.
Indo-China, 118-120.
Indo-Chinese Gleaner, 215.
Industrial Revolution, 201-203, 313, 315, 357, 792.
Infants, baptism of moribund, 188, 242.
Ingle, James Addison, 369, 573.
Innocent, Archimandrite, 487, 566.
Innocent, John, 380.
Innocent IV (Pope), 66.
Insane, first asylum for, 453.
Inslee, Elias B., 394.
L'Institut des Hautes Études Industrielles et Commerciales, 730.
Institute of Pacific Relations, 842.
"Institutional churches," 760.
Instruction to catechumens, Roman Catholic, 187, 331.
Inter-Church World Movement, 767.
International Bible Study Association, 747.
International Committee Y. M. C. A., 404.
International Institute, 602, 603.
International Missionary Alliance, 399.
International Postal Telegraph Christian Association, 602.
International Reform Bureau, 660.
International Settlement, Shanghai, 603, 610, 655, 689, 738, 793, 812.

International Union Mission, 773.
Ireland and the Irish, 708, 714, 718, 722, 730, 736.
Irish Brothers of the Christian Schools, 722.
Irish Lazarists, 721.
Irish Presbyterians, 396, 412, 574, 634, 654, 664.
I Shih Pao, 712, 733.
Islam, 17, 47, 52, 54, 326, 531, 838, 839.
I-ssŭ, 54.
Italian Government, 311, 739.
Italian protectorate, 312.
Italy and the Italians, 117, 176, 319, 362, 539, 548, 708, 713-715, 739.

J

Jackson, Dr. Arthur, 654.
Jacquemin, 243.
Jansen, Bishop of Nancy, 204.
Jansen, 545.
Jansenism and Jansenists, 119, 140.
Janssen, Arnold, 316.
Japan and the Japanese, 86, 89, 396, 398, 488, 489, 496, 506, 529, 546, 587, 588, 622, 679, 688, 690, 703, 706, 743, 744, 761, 763, 797, 810, 820, 822.
Jardine, W., 222.
Jaricot, Pauline, 203.
Jarlin, Bishop, 713.
Java, 213, 748.
Jenghiz Khan, 61, 64.
Jenkins, Benjamin, 257.
Jenkins, H. Stanley, 653, 654.
Jessfield, 448.
Jesuits, 75, 81, 86-89, 91-98, 102-108, 110-112, 115-117, 120-122, 126-130, 131-155, 166, 185-200, 232, 235-237, 309, 317, 319, 321, 322, 323, 340, 341, 344, 509, 522, 541, 542, 545, 547, 550, 551, 554, 556, 559, 560, 561, 563, 706, 707, 722, 727, 729, 730, 732, 734, 735, 823, 828, 836, 842.
Jesuits: French, 120-122, 143; Italian, 722; Spanish, 722.
Jesus, 25-32, 40, 470, 695, 698, 795, 800, 833, 837, 839, 840.
Jews and Judaism, 52, 54, 72, 75, 368, 750.
John, Griffith, 363, 364, 375, 430, 431, 571, 597.
John of Marignolli, 72, 73.
John of Montecorvino. *See* Montecorvino, John of.
Johnson, Stephen, 248.
Johnston, 267.

Jones, Alfred G., 657.
Jones, John Taylor, 219.
Jones, W. C., 370.
Josephines (of Paotingfu), (of Tientsin), (of Honan), 553.
Jubilee Year of 1925, 714.
Judæa, 470.
Jung Lu, 497, 505.

K

Kahn, Ida, 459.
K'aichow, 599.
Kaifeng, 595, 605, 697, 719, 730, 785.
Kalgan, 366, 394, 515, 518, 578, 772.
Kalocza, 722.
Kamul, 62.
K'ang Hsi, 105, 115, 116, 121, 125, 129, 140-153, 157, 158, 322.
K'ang Yu-wei, 490.
Kansas, 600, 772.
Kansas City, 588, 599.
Kansu, 65, 315, 321, 390, 393, 399, 501, 511, 516, 537, 538, 541, 542, 582, 598, 600, 606, 708, 717, 720, 721, 748, 773, 774, 790.
Karakorum, 66, 67.
Kashgar, 62, 400.
Kashgar Turkish, 759.
Kaying, 819.
Kazan University, 486.
Keller, F. A., 775.
Kenyon College, 483.
Kentucky, 719.
Kepler, A. R., 800.
Keraits, 63.
Kerr, John G., 249, 453, 455, 458, 460, 652, 819.
Ketteler, von, 506.
Khanfu, 54.
Khitans, 60.
Khubilai Khan, 61, 63, 67-69.
Kiakhta, 515.
Kiakhta, Treaty of, 200.
Kiangnan, 107, 118, 121, 164, 183, 232, 233, 235, 236, 237, 241, 307, 318, 319, 338, 340, 348, 538, 550, 563, 565, 711, 734, 735.
Kiangsi, 95, 107, 118, 125, 166, 232, 233, 237, 238, 241, 321, 323, 350, 353, 374, 388, 400, 406, 501, 512, 546, 547, 553, 570, 573, 580, 583, 605, 669, 705, 719, 776, 791, 819.
Kiangsu, 317, 318, 350, 353, 367, 371, 375, 388, 537, 541, 566, 573, 574, 577, 579, 580, 593, 599, 606, 643, 660, 669, 679, 702, 710, 721, 727, 729, 741, 772.
Kiangyin, 471.
Kiaochow, 372, 489, 495, 497, 498, 576.
Kidd, Samuel, 213.

Kiel (Germany), 403, 583.
Kieler Mission, 403, 494.
Kiench'ang, 542.
Kienning, 432, 647, 719.
Kienyang, 432, 647.
Kingchow, 543, 544, 737.
Kinwha, 432.
Kirin, 538, 590.
Kiukiang, 274, 374, 388, 459, 469, 573, 630, 689, 776.
Kiukiang Tract Society, 439.
Köster, 253.
Koffler, Andrew, 106, 107.
Ko Lao Hui, 608, 736.
Koo, T. Z., 628.
Koo, Wellington, 628.
Korea and the Koreans, 488, 574, 589, 593, 619, 690, 722, 810.
Korea, Prince of, converted, 172.
Korean Board of Foreign Missions, 505.
K'ou t'ou, 151.
Kowloon, 461, 678.
Kranz, 398.
Krick, 239.
Krimmer Mennonite Brethren, 772.
Kucheng, 471.
Kueilin, 289.
Kuei Wang, 105, 107.
Kulangsu, 244, 245, 247, 450.
Kuldja, 315.
Kuling, 672, 746, 763, 807.
Kulp, D. H., 760.
Kulturkampf, 316.
Kung, Prince, 466.
Kung-i-lou, 554.
Kunshan, 599.
Kuo, P. W., 835.
Kuominchun, 702, 778.
Kuomintang, 693, 699, 701-703, 815, 819, 821, 836. See also Nationalist Party.
Kuyuk, 61, 64, 67.
Kwangchow-wan, 489.
Kwang Hsü, 529.
Kwangsi, 166, 239, 241, 244, 284-289, 321, 323, 325, 354, 390, 457, 470, 495, 498, 537, 542, 545, 547, 573, 606, 653, 669, 679, 709, 717, 718, 735, 748, 773, 816, 817.
"Kwangsi Chinese Christian Promotion Association," 819.
Kwangtung, 111, 118, 157, 160, 166, 172, 173, 233, 239, 241, 243, 282, 323, 324, 347, 349, 350, 353, 354, 363, 365, 371-374, 383, 397, 402, 403, 457, 470, 479, 498, 531, 540, 542, 573, 575, 579, 580, 599-601, 605, 606, 608, 609, 616, 643-645, 669, 677, 679, 701, 709-711, 713,

717, 718, 735, 737, 741, 743, 800, 803, 804, 806, 819.
Kwangtung Divisional Council of the Church of Christ in China, 803.
Kweichow, 125, 165, 173, 174, 177, 239, 241, 242, 307, 323, 325, 330, 332, 336, 347, 349, 354, 390, 393, 491, 501, 537, 541, 578, 582, 595, 596, 605, 606, 721, 722, 736, 741, 747, 774, 817.
Kweilin, 325.
Kweiyang, 456, 491, 721.

L

Lagrené, 230.
La Jeunesse, 693.
Lakeside School and College, Yochow, 632, 816.
Lamas, 328.
Lambert, La Motte, 113, 114.
Lammermuir, 387.
Land, purchase of, 276, 278.
Language schools, 640, 641, 757.
Lanning, 610.
Lantrua, John, of Triora, 178.
Lao Tzŭ, 12.
Laquez, 236.
La Roche, 172.
Lassar, 210, 211.
Latin, 361, 446, 556, 634, 732.
Latin dictionary, 341.
Latin, in services of the Church, 190.
Lauwers, 736.
Lawrence, Friar, 66.
Lawsuits, interference in, 279, 280, 548, 549, 732.
Lay, G. Tradescant, 216, 222.
Laymen's Missionary Movement, 535.
Lazarists, 127, 167-170, 174, 175, 176, 180, 181, 203, 233, 237, 238, 315, 321, 322, 323, 340, 491, 508, 522, 542, 551, 705, 710, 716, 719, 721, 727, 730, 837.
Learn, 490.
Lebbe, Father, 712, 733.
Lechler, Rudolf, 253-255, 373.
Leeds, 518.
Lees, Jonathan, 433.
Leffingwell, Clara, 595.
Legge, James, 246, 363, 382, 430, 436, 678, 795.
Leibnitz, 140, 209, 210.
Leire, 721.
Leon, 722.
Leontiev, Maxime, 199.
Lepers in China, 457, 561.
Lepers, International Mission to, 789.
Lew, T. T., 775.
Lewis, H. R., 615.
Lewis, Robert E., 495.

Lhasa, 158, 233, 327, 393, 402.
Li, Andrew, 165.
Li Bi Cu (Miss), 654.
Li Hsiu-ch'êng, 294.
Li Hung-chang, 312, 351, 454, 456, 488, 492, 507.
Li Ping-hêng, 497, 504, 521.
Li Yüan-hung, 590, 610, 611, 700, 701, 710, 729.
Liang A-fah, 214, 217, 223, 283.
Liang Ch'i-ch'ao, 492, 695.
Liaotung Peninsula, 489.
Liaoyang, 396, 520.
Licent, Edward, 732.
Liebenzell, 393, 583, 744, 817.
Lienchow, 616.
Life, The, 788.
Light and Hope Mission, 600.
Lihsien, 726, 727.
Lille, 707.
Lingnan University. *See* Canton Christian College.
Lions, Mgr., 330.
Lisbon, 147.
Literature, Protestant, 261-266, 429-441, 493, 494, 646-651, 758, 759, 788.
Literature, Roman Catholic, 189, 216, 560.
Lithuania (Russian), 368.
Little, Mrs. Archibald, 658.
Little Sisters of the Poor, 561, 711.
Liuanchow, 708.
Liu K'un-i, 507.
Liu, Paul, 179.
Liuyang, 820.
Lo, Anne, 353.
Lo Pao-chi, 354-355.
Lobenstine, E. C., 671, 786, 798.
Lobschied, Wilhelm, 460.
Lockhart, William, 222, 244, 268, 269, 364, 454.
Lockwood, Henry, 220.
Loftis, 653.
Lolos, 327.
Lomüller, Victor, 545.
London, 439, 707.
London Missionary Society, 206, 210-216, 225, 244-247, 283, 363-365, 377, 381, 396, 425, 437, 438, 442, 448, 454, 456-458, 460, 482, 493-495, 571, 572, 609, 616, 626, 631, 633, 639, 653, 664, 671, 676-678, 761, 765, 799, 816, 818, 835.
Longobardi, Nicolo, 102, 135.
Lopez, Gregory, 101, 109. 123, 124, 138, 557, 726.
Lord, Edward C., 251, 263.
Los Angeles, 746.
Los Angeles, Bible Institute of, 649, 775.

Louis XIV, 112, 118-120.
Louis XVI, 167.
Lourdes, Our Lady of, 555.
Louvain, 558, 715.
Louvois, 120.
Low Countries, 313.
Lowrie High School (Shanghai), 677.
Lowrie, Reuben, 249.
Lowrie, Walter M., 220, 245, 248, 249, 520.
Loyola, Ignatius, 81.
Loyola, Martin Ignacio de, 100.
Lućarelli, 100.
Lund, Missionary Society of, 259.
Lundeen, 816.
Lungchüchai, 582.
Lu Shêng Chen Tao T'ung I Hui, 839.
Lutheran Board of Missions, 747.
Lutherans, 400, 402, 494, 576, 596, 597, 637, 680, 744, 747, 762, 783, 799, 800, 816.
Lyon, D. Willard, 404, 495.
Lyons, 317, 714.

M

Mabileau, 348.
Macao, 85, 86, 88-92, 96, 99-101, 103, 109, 110, 125, 146, 147, 149, 159, 161, 163, 172, 176, 177, 182, 208, 210, 213, 223, 238, 244, 249, 324, 354, 437, 539, 540, 542, 729.
Macao, Bishop of, 145, 311.
Macartney, Lord, embassy to China, 174.
MacGillivray, D., 397.
MacGillivray, J., 601.
MacGowan, D. J., 251.
Macgowan, John, 363, 430.
MacIver, Donald, 651.
Mackay, G. L., 397.
Mackenzie, John Kenneth, 454.
Mackle, Mrs., 615.
Macklin, W. E., 398, 610, 653, 658.
Magi, 173.
Mahayana, 15, 16, 37.
Maigrot, 119, 139, 142, 143, 144, 149.
Mailla, Joseph Anne Maria de Moyriac de, 197.
Main, Duncan, 455, 457, 639, 784.
Malabar Christians and Church, 48, 49, 50.
Malabar Rites, 141, 142.
Malacca, 87, 181, 213-215, 224, 225, 245, 678.
Malay Peninsula, 377, 625.
Malta, 722.
Manchester (N. H.), 720.
Manchuria and the Manchus, 105, 234, 239, 323, 324, 327, 337, 361, 384, 396, 402, 406, 412, 425, 455, 457, 462, 465, 471, 483, 486, 489, 494, 502, 503, 505, 506, 511, 515, 520, 528, 529, 538, 540, 544, 545, 546, 547, 561, 562, 566, 574, 576, 582, 607-609, 614, 619, 634, 654, 655, 658, 669, 676, 696, 699-703, 705, 711, 718, 731, 763, 807, 817, 841.
Manchuria, Southern Methodist Mission in, 807.
Mandarin, 414, 430, 529, 647, 651, 666, 692, 693, 759, 781.
Mandarin Lessons, 367, 436.
Mandarin New Testament, 264, 430.
Mandarin Old Testament, 430.
Mangu, 61, 63.
Manila, 89, 173, 180, 590.
Manila, Archbishop of, 101, 136.
Mapping the Empire, entrusted to the missionaries, 129, 158.
Margaret Williamson Hospital, 395, 456.
Margary Affair, 303, 389.
Mariales of Yungpingfu, 553.
Marianne Islands, 721.
Marignolli, John of. *See* John of Marignolli.
Marists, 317, 512, 559, 729.
Marriage of Catholics, 194, 236.
Marshman, 210, 211, 263, 378.
Martin, Miss, 223.
Martin, W. A. P., 249, 275, 368, 430, 433, 435, 492, 602.
Martinez, Barthelemy, 108.
Maryknoll, 717. *See also* Catholic Foreign Mission Society of America.
Maryland, 720.
Mary Porter Gamewell Memorial School, 626.
Massa, Louis, 300.
Massa, Rene, 237.
Mass Education Movement, 781.
Mateer, Calvin W., 367, 428, 435, 436, 441, 442, 445, 458, 835.
Matheson, George, 231, 604.
Maximum illud (Bull), 714.
Maxwell, 455.
May 30th, 1925, incident, 698, 737, 811-813.
Maynooth Mission, 708, 718, 722.
Mazel, 498.
McCartee, D. B., 248, 268, 459.
McClatchie, 252.
McCracken, J. C., 604.
McIlvaine, 367.
McMullan, Mr. and Mrs., 641.
McTyeire School, 1, 450, 451.
Medals, 189.
Medhurst, 213, 247, 262, 264, 269, 337, 430.
Medhurst College, 626.
Medical literature, 460.

Medical Missionary Society in China, 222, 268, 453.
Medical missions, 218, 219, 222, 268-269, 452-460, 561, 652-656, 734, 759, 760, 789, 790.
Mei Wa, 772.
Melbourne, 393, 718.
Melotto, Angelicus, 736, 739.
Mencius, 436.
Meng, Pastor, 517.
Mennonite Brethren Church, 599.
Mennonite Brethren in Christ, Board of Foreign Missions of the, 599.
Mennonites (German), 600.
Mennonites of North America, Board of Foreign Missions of the Conference of the, 599.
Merigot, 547.
Merv, 47.
Merv, Bishop of, 63.
Mesopotamia, 46, 50, 63.
Methodist (English) New Connexion Missionary Society, 380, 578.
Methodist Free Church Mission, 383, 493, 676.
Methodist girls' school, 462.
Methodist mission in Foochow, 482.
Methodist Publishing House, 650.
Methodists (American), 374, 437, 456, 501, 506, 513, 518, 578, 625, 626, 657, 661, 668, 680, 753, 767, 772, 776, 777, 785, 786, 804, 808, 838.
Methodists (Canadian), 401, 456, 578, 616, 624, 632, 664, 817.
Methodists (English), 256.
Methodists (Free), 595.
Methodists (Northern), 256, 374, 401, 456, 748, 767. See also Methodists (American), and Northern (American) Methodists.
Methodists (Southern), 256, 374, 493, 767. See also Methodists (American) and Southern (American) Methodists.
Methods, Protestant, 222-226, 263-269, 416-465, 617-685, 747-764, 781-794.
Methods, Roman Catholic, 185-193, 310, 331-342, 547-562, 724-735.
Metropolitan Presbyterian Mission, 599.
Mexico, 119.
Mezzabarba, Jean Ambrose Charles, 147-150.
Miao, 287, 495, 578, 624, 774.
Middle Kingdom, The, 265.
Mienchow, 395.
Milan, Seminary of Foreign Missions of, 234, 315, 321, 522, 723.
Mills, Mrs. C. R., 461.
Milne, William C., 212-215, 223, 245, 246, 262.

Min River, 627, 782.
Ming dynasty, conquered by Manchus, 105-107.
Minneapolis, 747.
Miscellanea Sinica, 223.
Missal, translated, 189.
Mission Alliance (Norwegian), 599.
Mission Among the Higher Classes of China, 602.
Missionary Recorder, The, 437.
Mission stations, 418, 419.
Missions Building, 1, 799.
Missions Union of Catholic Women and Girls, 716.
Mississippi Valley, 398.
Missouri, 599.
Missouri Synod (Lutheran), 596.
Mitchell, Dr. Isabel, 654.
Mo Ti (Mo Tzŭ), 14.
"Modernism," 794, 795, 797.
Mohammedanism. See Islam.
Mokanshan, 672.
Molina, 300.
Mongolia, 174, 232, 237, 238, 243, 315, 384, 385, 392, 394, 399, 454, 502, 505, 510, 511, 515, 537, 538, 545, 553, 554, 559, 561, 563, 566, 582, 583, 600, 606, 621, 654, 702, 708, 723, 726, 732, 734, 772.
Mongols, 61-77, 215, 255, 356, 487, 511, 517, 621.
Montauban, 308.
Montecorvino, John of, 68-72.
Montels, 300.
Montreal, 561, 721.
Moody, Campbell N., 683.
Moody, Dwight L., 358, 391.
Morales, Juan Baptista de, 109, 136, 137.
Moral Welfare League, Shanghai, 791.
Moravians, 255.
Morrill, Miss, 777.
Morrison, Robert, 190, 210-215, 219, 571, 665, 826.
Morrison Education Society, 221, 222, 267, 459.
Moscow, 702.
Moseley, William, 210.
Moslems, 116, 172, 347-348, 400, 605, 749.
Most favored nation clause, 229.
Mott, John R., 391, 404, 585, 591, 620, 669, 777, 810.
Moule, Arthur E., 370.
Moule, G. E., 370.
Mouly, 243, 308, 322.
Mo-yang, 119.
Moye, 171.
Muirhead, 265, 269, 294, 363, 430.

Mukden, 396, 455, 511, 591, 611, 634, 654, 705, 729.
Mukden Medical College, 638.
Munson, E. H., 635.
Murray, William Hill, 461.
Mussolini, 739.
Mutillod, 562.

N

Naishabur, 47.
Nanch'ang, 95, 166, 374, 546, 573, 616, 630.
Nanchow, 719.
Nanking, 95, 103, 117, 124, 129, 144, 160, 163, 274, 289-297, 318, 330, 349, 351, 367, 374, 388, 398, 448, 456, 468, 470, 490, 507, 543, 559, 570, 573, 588, 604, 626, 630, 637, 639, 653, 657-659, 678, 699, 702, 729, 753, 757, 772, 785, 820, 835, 839.
Nanking, Bishopric of, 124, 174, 241.
Nanking, incident, 820.
Nanking, Treaty of, 229.
Nanking Christian College, 629.
Nanking Theological Seminary, 746, 784.
Nanking University, 629, 640, 643, 756, 820.
Nanning Medical Mission, 773.
Nan T'ang, 106, 167, 178, 300, 308, 322, 508.
Nan Yo, 621.
Naples, Ripa's school at, 161, 174.
Napoleon and the Napoleonic Wars, 169, 170.
Napoleon III, 272, 308, 322.
Nashville, 600.
National Association for the Advancement of Education, 697.
National Bible Society of Scotland, 381, 396, 430, 437, 438, 461.
National Christian Conference (1922), 793, 796-798, 802, 807.
National Christian Council, 628, 781, 782, 793, 796, 797, 798, 802, 812, 821, 830.
National Foreign Trade Convention, 741.
National Holiness Mission, 600.
National Medical Association, 759.
National Normal School of Hygiene and Physical Education, 784.
National Popular Educational Association, 782.
National Tract Society for China, 599.
National University at Peking, 692, 693, 738.
Nationalist movement, 803.
Nationalist Party, 689, 693, 698, 702, 703, 737. See also Kuomintang.

Nationalist troops, 820.
Navarette, 138.
Nazarene, General Mission Board of the Church of the, 599.
Nazareth Press, 732.
Neal, James B., 458.
Near East Relief, 767, 797.
Nebraska, 718.
Nelson, Mr. and Mrs. C. A., 772.
Nerchinsk, Treaty of, 199.
Nestorian Monument. See Hsianfu Monument.
Nestorians and Nestorianism, 33, 34, 46-60, 62-65, 69, 74-76, 808, 823.
Netherlands Chinese Evangelization Society, 260.
Netherlands Missionary Society, 216.
Nethersole Hospital, 456.
Nevius, John L., 249, 367, 427, 430, 436, 465.
New Civilization, 691.
New Collection of Tracts for the Times, 492.
Newchwang, 259, 274, 396.
Newell, Miss, 225.
New Hampshire, 720.
New Jersey, 719.
New Orleans Conference, 629.
New Territory, 606.
New Testament, 56, 69, 190, 210, 264, 430, 487, 602, 648.
New Thought, 691.
New Tide, 691, 693, 695, 775, 840.
New York, 394, 399, 439, 448, 718, 719, 720, 753.
New Zealand, 595, 718.
Nicholas, succeeds John of Montecorvino, 72.
Nicholas of Pistoia, 69.
Nicholas of Vicenza, 68.
Nieh (Tao-t'ai), 441.
Nies, 497, 498.
Niles, Mary, 461.
Ninghsiang, 470.
Ningkohsien, 318.
Ningpo, 120, 229, 234, 238, 245, 246, 248, 249, 251, 252, 256, 266, 366, 367, 369, 371, 382-384, 396, 401, 407, 437, 446, 458, 459, 482, 493, 580, 587, 628, 647.
Nisibis, 46.
Njassabund Society, 771.
Noel, Jean Pierre, 348.
Norges Frie Evangeliske Hedninge Mission. See Free Evangelical Missionary Union of Norway.
Norris, Bishop, 675.
Norsk Lutherske Kinamissionsforbund. See Norwegian Lutheran China Mission Association.

Det Norske Missionsforbund. *See* Norwegian Alliance Mission.
Det Norske Missionsselskab. *See* Norwegian Missionary Society.
North America, 766, 769.
North China College, 449.
North China Educational Union, 633.
North China Student Conference (Y. M. C. A.), 593.
North China Tract Society, 439.
North China Union College, 633.
North China Union Medical College, 633.
North China Union Medical College for Women, 633.
North China Union Theological College, 633, 639.
North China Union Women's College, 624, 633.
Northern Baptist Convention, 767, 768.
Northern (American) Baptists, 579, 629, 632, 754, 767, 768, 803. *See also* Baptists (American).
Northern (American) Methodists, 577, 627, 629, 630, 632, 643, 767, 768, 780, 790. *See also* Methodists (American).
Northern (American) Presbyterians, 427, 450, 453, 471, 493, 514, 520, 570, 573, 574, 602, 628, 634, 645, 664, 671, 749, 769, 780. *See also* Presbyterians (American).
Northfield (Mass.), 391.
North Fukien Anglican Conference, 804.
North Fukien Religious Tract Society, 439.
Northwest Kiangsi Mission, 580.
Norway, 393, 400, 577.
Norway, Free Evangelical Missionary Union of, 601.
Norwegian Alliance Mission, 518, 582.
Norwegian Free Baptists, 771.
Norwegian Lutherans, 747.
Norwegian Lutheran China Mission Association, 400, 577.
Norwegian Lutheran Church in the U. S., 400, 577.
Norwegian Mission in China, 393, 583.
Norwegian Missionary Society, 259, 597, 772.
Notre Dame des Victoires, 350.
Novella, 233.
Nyack (N. Y.), 399.

O

"Oberlin Band," 366, 604.
Oberlin Theological Seminary, 366, 572, College, 514.

Oberlin Shansi Memorial Association, 626.
Oblates of the Holy Family, 553.
Octave, 348.
Odoric, Friar, of Pordenone, 62, 70, 71.
L'Œuvre de la Sainte Enfance, 314. *See* Holy Infancy, Association of the.
L'Œuvre des Catechumenats, 551.
Ogodai, 61.
Ohio, 515.
Ohio Wesleyan University, 577.
Ohio Yearly Meeting of Friends, 398.
"Old Buddha," 505.
Oldfield, W. H., 816.
Old Testament (in Mandarin), 430. *See also* Bible.
Olyphant, D. W. C., 217.
Omaha (Nebr.), 718.
Onguts, 63, 69.
Open Door Policy, 569.
Opium and opium traffic, 229, 231, 457, 462, 791.
Opus S. Petri, 725.
Ordos, 511, 709.
Örebro, Sweden, Missionary Society of, 772.
Oregon, 720.
Orphanages, 341, 342, 464, 560, 734.
Orville, Albert d', 108.
Osgood, D. W., 460.
Osgood, E. I., 657.
Osimo, Vincent d', 177.
Ossining (N. Y.), 717.
Oviedo, Andrew, 90.
Oxford College (Formosa), 397.
Oxford, 391, 631.

P

Pacific Coast Missionary Society, 601.
Padroãdo, the Portuguese, 84, 86, 89, 99, 113, 124, 125, 142-148, 241.
Pai-lien Chioa. See White Lotus Society.
Pai Shang Ti Huei, 285-288.
Pakhoi, 457, 652.
Palladius (Archimandrite), 487.
Pallu, François, 113, 114, 117-120, 123.
Paoan, 501.
Paotingfu, 366, 504, 514, 517, 520, 553, 591, 722, 777, 794.
Paris, 714, 721.
Paris, Society of Foreign Missions of. *See* Société des Missions Étrangères de Paris.
Paris, University of, 140.
Parker, Peter, 218, 219, 222, 232, 244, 268, 344, 452, 453, 460, 638, 819.
Parliament, 701, 763.
Parma, 539, 542.

Parrenin, 158.
Pasio, Francis, 91.
Passionists, 719, 737.
Patronage, Portuguese right of. *See* *Padroado*, the Portuguese.
Peace Conference, Paris (1919), 689, 756, 835.
Peale, Rev. and Mrs. John, 615.
Pearl River, 580.
Pearson, Dr., 219.
Peitaiho, 500, 667, 672, 746.
Pei T'ang, 121, 168, 178, 308, 312, 322, 340, 491, 506, 508, 732.
Peking, 49, 64, 69-73, 95-98, 103, 104, 115, 124, 146, 160, 162, 164, 167, 171, 172, 174, 175, 181, 241, 307, 312, 317, 321, 326, 327, 340, 347, 351, 364, 365, 366, 368, 374, 381, 395, 399, 430, 437, 448, 449, 450, 454, 456, 458, 461, 462, 474, 477, 486, 487, 489, 490, 491, 492, 497, 499, 504, 505, 506, 508, 509, 510, 513, 515, 518, 519, 520, 522, 530, 548, 551, 554, 558, 559, 560, 566, 586, 590, 592, 593, 602, 604, 607, 608, 611, 612, 624, 626, 638, 640, 655, 659, 668, 671, 678, 695, 701, 702, 710, 711, 712, 713, 722, 728, 730, 731, 738, 742, 746, 749, 753, 754, 757, 760, 775-777, 780, 783, 785, 823, 832, 833, 838.
Peking Government, 698, 701, 815.
Peking Students' Social Service Club, 657.
Peking Union Medical College, 1, 754, 755, 784, 789.
Peking University, 448, 490, 492, 633, 754.
Penang, 213, 729, 730.
Penang, Catholic seminary on, 174, 181.
Pennsylvania, 731.
Pennsylvania Conference, 600.
Pentecostal Assemblies of the World (American), 600.
Pentecostal Holiness Church, 600.
"Pentecostal missionaries," 600.
Pentecostal Missionary Union for Great Britain and Ireland, 600.
Pentecostal Mission in Nashville, 600.
Perboyre, 233, 234.
Peregrine, 70, 71.
Pereira, Diego de, 87, 89.
Pereyra, 126.
Perez, François, 90.
Perez, Bishop, 547.
"Permissions" of Mezzabarba, 148-150.
Persecution, of 1616 and 1622, 103; of 1664, 115; under K'ang Hsi, 156-158; under Yung Ch'eng, 158-161;
of 1784, 172; of 1805, 175; of 1811-1838, 178-181; under Ch'ien Lung, 162-175; persecution of Catholics, 1839-1840, 232, 233; 1845-1855, 242, 243; 1856-1897, 347-351; 353-356, 508-513, 544-547, 735-740; persecution of Protestants, 269, 513-518, 816-821.
Persia, 46, 47, 50, 51, 67, 68.
Pescadores Islands, 377, 489.
Peter and Paul, Seminary of, 315, 319.
Peter of Florence, 70.
Peter of Lucalongo, 69.
Peter, Dr. W. W., 590, 759, 789.
Petrograd, 486, 566.
Philadelphia, 459, 719.
Philip II of Spain, 99.
Philippines, 88, 90, 99, 108, 315, 328, 569, 690, 708, 748, 820.
Philosophic Society, 692.
Phonetic Promotion Committee, 781.
Phonetic writing of Chinese, 264, 752, 779, 781.
Piao, of K'ang Hsi, 144, 145, 157.
Picpus, Congregation of, 723.
Piercy, George, 257.
Pilgrim's Progress, translated, 264.
Pilquist, E., 678.
P'ing Hu, 248.
Pingyüan, 678.
Pires, 85, 181.
Pitkin, Horace Tracy, 514.
Piton, 736.
Pittsburgh Bible Institute, 772.
Pius IX (Pope), 315.
Pius XI (Pope), 714.
Piyang, 599.
Plano Carpini, John of, 66, 67.
Plymouth Brethren, 400, 580.
Pocket Testament League, 649.
Pohlman, 247.
Poirot, Louis de, 167.
Pok-lo, 363.
Polanco, John de, 138.
Polhill-Turner, Arthur, 391.
Polhill-Turner, Cecil, 391.
Pollard, Samuel, 570, 578.
Polo, Maffeo and Nicolo, 67, 68.
Polo, Marco, 68.
(Pomeranian) Mission Union for the Evangelization of China, 377.
Pope, 312, 322, 499, 539, 540, 714, 725, 727, 730, 731, 738, 739.
Popular Education Movement, 836.
Port Arthur, 489, 566.
Portland (Oregon), 400, 720.
Portugal and the Portuguese, 80, 83-90, 182, 311, 540, 542, 732, 823. *See also* Padroado.
Post Office, 567, 700, 824.

Pott, F. L. Hawks. 628.
Pottier, François, 164, 165.
Prayer Book, translated, 368, 433.
Prefecture Apostolic, 241.
Prèmare, 189.
Presbyterian boys' school, 629.
Presbyterian Church at Tsingtau, 611.
Presbyterian Church of Canada, 397, 575, 664, 806.
Presbyterian Church of New Zealand, 595, 626.
Presbyterian Churches in China, Federal Council of the, 799.
Presbyterian mission (in Weihsien, Shantung), 504.
Presbyterian synod, 462.
Presbyterians, 366, 367, 459, 614, 665, 676, 678, 749, 761, 781, 799, 800. *See also* Northern and Southern Presbyterians.
Presbyterians, American, 220, 245, 248, 249, 394, 427, 446, 448, 450, 453, 456, 461, 470, 471, 495, 573, 574, 615, 633, 651, 665, 804, 806, 817. *See also* Northern Presbyterians and Southern Presbyterians.
Presbyterians (Cumberland), 402, 494, 574.
Presbyterians, English, 257-259, 376, 377, 412, 427, 432, 450, 454, 455, 457, 468, 574, 616, 626, 651, 664, 676, 819.
Presbyterians (Irish), 396, 412, 574, 634, 654, 664.
Presbyterians (Korean), 595.
Presbyterians (Manchurian), 807.
Presbyterians (Scotch), 412.
Presentadines, 711.
Presentation, Sisterhood of, 234.
Press, Canadian Mission, 493.
Presses, Mission, 215, 246, 266, 437, 478, 650.
Press, Jesuit, 436.
Press, Nazareth, 732.
Press, Presbyterian Mission, 249, 266, 437, 478, 650.
Prester John, 63.
Price, Bishop, 573.
Price, Frank W., 702, 784.
Price, Thomas F., 717.
Priests' Mission Union, 708.
Priests of the Holy Stigmata, 722.
Priests of the Sacred Heart of Jesus of Betharram (of Bayonne), 723.
Princeton University, 586.
Procurer, 190.
Progress Party in China, 684.
Propaganda (the Congregation for the Propagation of the Faith), 84, 113, 117, 125, 161, 175, 177, 203, 232, 241, 312, 314, 316, 329, 330, 336, 338, 345, 540, 717, 719, 721, 732.
Propagation of the Faith, Society for the. *See* Society for the Propagation of the Faith.
Protestantism, 35, 36, 81, 82.
Protestant missions, 205-227, 244-270, 282-302, 357-485, 488-526, 567-685, 743-843.
Protestant statistics. *See* Statistics, of Protestants.
Protocol (Boxer), 520, 525.
Providence (R. I.), 720.
Pruen, 456.
Public Health, Joint Council on, 759.
P'uch'i, 726, 727.
Pukak, 255.
Puntis, 287.
Pye, Watts O., 572, 774.

Q

Quakers. *See* Friends.
Quinine, 121.
Quirinal, 312.

R

Rahm, Cornelius, 215, 216.
Ramazzotti, Angelo, 234.
Rankin, Henry V., 248, 249.
Rättvik, 595.
Raux, 174.
Ray, 47.
Red Cross Society, 607, 610, 611, 657, 767.
Red Lantern Society, 817.
Reed, Alanson, 225.
Reed, William B., 272.
Reformation, 762.
Reformed Church, 455.
Reformed Church in America (Dutch), 218, 248, 366, 412, 427, 450, 575, 664, 671, 676.
Reformed Church in the United States, 494, 575, 639.
Reformed Presbyterian Church in North America (Covenanter), 402, 575.
Registration of Christian schools with the Chinese Government, 645, 691, 697, 698, 758, 805, 814, 815.
Regulations for missionaries, 352.
Reichelt, K. L., 772.
Reid, Gilbert, 465, 480, 492, 602.
Reifsnyder, Dr. Elizabeth, 652.
Reimert, William A., 816, 818.
Reisner, John H., 784.
Religious Tract Society, 649.
Renaissance, 691, 692-695, 775, 840.
Renaissance Society, 692.
Renou, 240.

Republic (of China), 531, 534, 544, 607, 609, 612, 615, 699.
Rerum Ecclesiae, 714.
Retrospect, 583.
"Review of the Times," 436, 441.
Revolution of 1911, 531, 543, 590, 607, 610, 611, 615, 616, 640, 648, 649, 653, 654, 658, 709, 841.
"Revolution," of 1913, 612, 653.
Rhenish Missionary Society (and Mission), 253, 372-374, 398, 460, 576, 583, 653, 665.
Rhenish province (of Franciscans), 723.
Rhenish-Westphalian province (Capuchins), 721.
Rhio. See Riouw.
Rho, Jacques, 105.
Rhode Island, 720.
Rhodes, Alexander of, 112, 113.
Ribeyra, Jean Baptiste, 90.
Ricci, Matteo, 91-98, 133-155, 186, 308, 379, 491, 509, 586.
Ricci, Victorio, 110.
Richard, Timothy, 301, 378, 386, 428, 440, 441, 447, 465, 480, 492, 493, 502, 525, 607, 619, 645.
Richenet, 176.
Richthofen, Von, 321, 337.
Riera, Pierre Bonaventura, 90.
Rigaud, 348.
"Righteous Harmony Fists," 503.
Rijnhart, Dr. Petrus, 402, 580.
Rijnhart, Dr. Susie C., 402, 579.
Riouw, 216, 217, 225.
Ripa, 161.
Rites, Board of, 103, 159.
Rites controversy, 131-155.
Rizzolati, 233.
Roberts, Dr. F. C., 454.
Roberts, Issacher J., 219, 245, 251, 283, 284, 293.
Robertson, Dr. Cecil, 653, 654.
Robertson, C. H., 588, 641.
Roch, Canon Avila, 721.
Rockefeller Foundation, 754. See also China Medical Board.
Rockefellers, 747, 754, 784.
Rococo art, influenced by China, 198.
Röttger, Herman, 217, 225.
Roman Catholic Church, 33, 35.
Roman Catholic Missions, 1-3, 66-198, 231-244, 303-356, 488-526, 527-565, 705-741, 823, 825-831.
Roman Catholic methods, 330, 334, 335, 491, 825-831.
Roman Catholic statistics. See Statistics of Roman Catholics.
Romanized Chinese, 264, 267.
Rome, 312, 315, 316, 345, 361, 557, 714, 717, 724-727, 729, 731, 738.

Roots, Logan H., 573, 798.
Rosary, 189.
Ross, John, 396, 483.
Roudére, P., 710.
Rubruck, William of, 65, 67.
Ruggerius, Michael, 91-94.
Rugh, Arthur, 775.
Rural work, 784, 793, 794.
Russell, Bertrand, 692, 695.
Russia and the Russians, 121, 126, 158, 272, 350, 486, 487, 489, 511, 520, 546, 566, 688, 778.
Russian communism, 693, 697, 699, 702.
Russian Orthodox Church (and its mission), 1, 33, 34, 199, 200, 486, 518, 566, 687, 823, 825.
Russian Revolution of 1917, 742.
Russo-Japanese War, 545, 607, 677.

S

Sacconi, 173.
Sacred Edict, 180.
Sacred Heart, 709.
Sacred Heart Province (Franciscan, of St. Louis), 720.
Sadler, 363.
Saigon, 729.
St. Chrischona branch of the C. I. M., 393.
St. Chrischona Pilgrim Mission, 583.
St. Columban, Chinese Mission Society of, 708, 718, 722.
St. Columban's College, 721.
St. Francis Xavier College, 729.
Saint Genis Laval, 317.
St. Ignatius College, 729.
St. John's College. See St. John's University.
St. John's-Pennsylvania medical school, 755.
St. John's University, 1, 267, 368, 428, 448, 458, 483, 604, 627, 628, 635, 639, 783, 815, 835.
St. John the Baptist, Congregation of, 177.
St. Joseph's College (Foochow), 559.
St. Joseph's Hospital, 720.
St. Louis, 720.
St. Mark's College, 626.
St. Mary's Hall, 450.
St. Mary's Mission House, 716.
St. Mary of the Woods (Ind.), 719.
St. Michael's Hospital, 710.
St. Nazianz (Wisc.), 719.
St. Patrick's College, 721.
St. Paul's College, 267.
St. Stephen's College, 626.
St. Thomas, 48, 51.
Salesians. See Society of St. Francis de Sales.

Salt Gabelle service, 824.
Salvation Army, 746.
Salvatorians, 719, 722.
Salvetti, 176.
Samarkand, 62.
Samkiong, 647.
Sanchez, Alonzo, 99.
Sandeman, David, 258.
San Francisco, 365, 397, 679.
San Min Chu I, 702.
Santa Barbara, 720.
Santa Cruz, 87, 88.
Santa Maria, Antonio de, 109, 110, 117, 123.
Sanz, 163.
Sassanids, 47, 51.
Scandinavia, 392, 401.
Scandinavian Alliance Mission, 392, 515, 582, 608, 621.
Scandinavian China Missionary Alliance, 582, 583.
Schall, Johann Adam von Bell, 104, 106, 115, 116, 186, 308, 509.
Schaut, 430.
Schereschewsky, Samuel I. J., 368, 430, 432, 433, 448, 628, 647.
Scheutveld, 314, 707, 730. *See also* Congregation of the Immaculate Heart of Mary.
Schleswig-Holstein evang.-luth. Missions-gesellschaft zu Breklum, 577.
Schmalzried, E. W., 817.
Schofield, Harold A., 391, 454.
School and Textbook Series Committee, 440, 451.
Schools. *See* Education.
Schreck, 104.
Schultze, 759.
Scotland, 358, 363, 391, 440, 461, 653.
Scotland, Church of, 396, 574, 664.
Scotland, National Bible Society of, 381, 396, 430, 437, 438, 461, 648.
Scott, Charles Perry, 381.
Seabury, W. B., 604.
Seattle, 741.
Sec, Fong F., 645.
Seignal, 316.
Seleucis-Ctesiphon, 47, 48, 50.
Self-support of churches, 423, 424, 674-679, 762, 805-807, 822.
Semedo, 52.
Seminaries, 127, 161, 164, 165, 174, 180, 181. *See also* Clergy, Chinese.
Seminary, Baptist, Swatow, 781.
Seminary of St. Francis Xavier, for Foreign Missions, 539, 542.
Serampore Trio, 210.
Sergius or Sargis, Mar, 64.
Servants of the Holy Ghost, 539, 553, 559.

Servants of the Sacred Heart, 553.
Seventh Day Adventists, 598, 776.
Seventh Day Baptist Missionary Society, 372, 579.
Shameen, 689.
Shameen incident, 737.
Shang-chü'an, 85, 87, 88, 89, 325.
Shanghai, 1, 223, 234, 249, 250, 251, 266, 317, 330, 339, 342, 343, 359, 363, 366-369, 371, 372, 375, 381, 383, 388, 395, 396, 398, 399, 401, 404, 407, 413, 428, 434, 437, 439-441, 445, 448, 450, 455-457, 461, 464, 468, 483, 492, 555, 559, 561, 572, 573, 580, 586, 588, 591, 594, 599, 600, 603, 604, 608, 610, 626, 628, 629, 640, 641, 650, 652, 655, 656, 665, 677, 678, 695, 705, 720, 728, 735, 738, 744, 747, 753, 754, 760, 761, 762, 772, 791, 793, 796, 799, 800, 810, 814, 820, 839.
Shanghai Anti-Adulteration Association, 785.
Shanghai (Baptist) College, 1, 629, 751, 760, 783.
Shanghai Chamber of Commerce, 741.
Shanghai Christian Council, 807.
Shanghai conferences (Protestant), of 1877, 1890, 1907, 1913, 1922. *See* Conferences.
Shanghai-Nanking Railway, 489.
Shang Ti, 7, 8, 133, 262, 285-295, 432, 433.
Shansi, 107, 121, 125, 160, 172, 177, 183, 240, 241, 319, 320, 343, 354, 355, 366, 376, 379, 390, 393, 399, 447, 455, 464, 465, 481, 482, 494, 502, 504, 505, 510, 514, 516, 517, 521, 524, 532, 537, 542, 547, 549, 572, 579, 583, 600, 601, 604, 608, 626, 702, 703, 711, 723, 737, 762, 772, 774, 775, 839.
Shansi Memorial Association, 572.
Shantung, 107, 111, 166, 172, 175, 232, 237, 240, 312, 316, 319, 320, 347, 350, 355, 366, 367, 371, 372, 378, 380, 381, 396, 400, 401, 424, 425, 445, 447, 458, 461, 464, 465, 469, 471, 489, 491, 495, 497, 498, 501, 502, 503, 504, 507, 510, 516, 537, 538, 539, 543, 553, 559, 570, 573, 574, 576, 577, 578, 580, 592, 595, 599, 600, 605, 608, 619, 621, 624, 626, 634, 657, 664, 669, 676, 688, 706, 708, 710, 711, 717, 720, 721, 723, 733, 736, 739, 741, 743, 749, 772, 796, 801, 804.
Shantung Christian University, 634, 636, 639, 783.
Shantung Provincial College, 645.

Shantung Union College, 592.
Shaowu, 432, 676, 722.
Shasi, 737.
Sheffield, D. Z., 449.
Sheklung, 561.
Shekow, 637.
Shelton, Dr. and Mrs. Albert L., 580, 653, 740.
Shen, 432.
Shen Tsai-sheng, 763.
Shensi, 107, 121, 125, 160, 172, 177, 183, 233, 240, 241, 243, 314, 315, 319, 320, 348, 354, 380, 389, 392, 393, 465, 494, 516, 520, 540, 542, 543, 547, 561, 572, 579, 582, 595, 608, 653, 678, 709, 711, 720, 722, 747, 774, 790, 803, 804, 807.
Sherbrooke, 721.
Shih Ching, 6.
Shih Ma-yu, 459.
Shu Ching, 6.
Shuck, J. Lewis, 219, 245, 251, 262.
Shun Chih, 105, 106, 115.
Sia Sek-ong, 482.
Siam, 119, 181, 370, 748.
Siangtan, 321.
Siaokan, 653.
Siberia, 511.
"Siberia-Manchuria mission," 774.
Sibley, Mrs., 817.
Sierra, Thomas de, 108, 109.
Silas, 50.
Silin, 537.
Silkworms, 50.
Silver Creek (N. Y.), 718.
Simpson, A. B., 392, 399.
Singapore, 216, 219, 220, 225, 245, 375-377, 748.
Siningfu, 541.
Sinkiang, 541, 582, 606, 717, 817.
Sisterhoods, Catholic. *See under* Congregation, Sisters, and by separate names.
Sisters of Charity, 234, 313, 322, 323, 508, 711, 712, 719, 720.
Sisters of Ingenbohl, 722.
Sisters of Loretto, 719.
Sisters of Our Lady of the Angels, 721.
Sisters of Providence, 719.
Sisters of St. Anne, 711.
Sisters of St. Paul, 234.
Sisters of St. Paul of Chartres, 723.
Sisters of St. Vincent de Paul, 561, 711.
Sisters of the Holy Ghost, 711.
Sisters of the Immaculate Conception, 539, 561; Canadian, 720.
Sisters of the Most Precious Blood, 723.
Sisters of the Sacred Heart of Mary, 711.
Sisters of the Third Order of St. Francis, 711.

Sites, Nathan, 482.
"Six Sages Union True Tao Society," 839.
Slavonic, 487.
Smith, George, 252.
Smith, J. Porter, 460.
Smith, Stanley P., 391, 601.
Social Application of Christianity, Conference on the, 656.
Social Life of the Chinese, 436.
"Social Welfare." *See I Shih Pao.*
Société des Auxiliatrices des Ames du Purgatoire, 314.
Société des Missions Étrangères de Paris, 111-115, 118, 123, 128, 139, 164-166, 169-170, 174, 178, 180, 193, 203, 238-240, 314, 323, 326, 327, 343, 344, 347, 498, 522, 541-543, 551, 563, 705, 710, 718.
Society for the Diffusion of Christian and General Knowledge among the Chinese, 379, 381, 436, 440, 492, 649.
Society for the Diffusion of Useful Knowledge in China, 221.
Society for the Propagation of the Faith, 203, 204, 233, 323, 330, 540, 554, 562, 563, 707, 714-716.
Society for the Propagation of the Gospel in Foreign Parts, 253, 381, 504, 573, 664.
"Society for the Study of Morality," 839.
Society of Foreign Missions of Bethlehem, 722.
Society of Jesus. *See* Jesuits.
Society of St. Francis de Sales, 317, 539, 542, 716, 723.
Society of the Divine Word, 314, 316, 319, 355, 489, 497, 498, 539, 540, 550, 553, 559, 706, 710, 713, 716, 717, 733.
Society of the Hiltrup Missionaries of the Sacred Heart of Issoudon, 722.
Society of the Precious Blood, 720.
Society of the Servants of the Holy Ghost, 314.
Soenen, Achille, 736.
"Soeurs Chanoinsesses de S. Augustin," 723.
Soffroy, 547.
Soltau, Henry, 389.
Soochow, 318, 367, 493, 573, 629, 638, 653, 659.
Soochow University, 629, 635, 639, 753.
Soothill, W. E., 382, 431, 626, 632, 651.
Sopingfu, 515.
South America, 392.
South Chihli Mission, 402, 494, 580, 600.

South China Boat Mission, 602.
South China Holiness Mission, 600.
South China Medical College, 640.
South China Peniel Holiness Missionary Society, 600.
"Southern Peak," 621.
South Fukien Synod of the Church of Christ in China, 806.
South Yünnan Mission, 600.
Southeastern University (at Nanking), 835.
Southern (American) Baptists, 250, 371, 372, 629, 677, 767, 768, 797, 819.
Southern (American) Methodists, 433, 577, 629, 653, 807.
Southern (American) Presbyterians, 471, 574, 628, 664.
Souviron, Paul, 173.
Souza-Saraiva, 176.
Soyorghactani-bagi, 63.
Spaniards (and Spain), 80, 83, 88, 89, 328, 362, 714, 719, 721, 723.
Speer, Robert E., 802.
Speer, William, 249.
Springfield (Ill.), 720.
Squire, E. B., 216, 252.
Stallybrass, Edward, 215.
State Department, Washington, 706.
Statistics of Protestants, 226, 405, 406, 479, 680, 745, 750, 756, 765, 766, 773-776, 779, 780, 783, 801, 822.
Statistics of Roman Catholics, 128, 129, 158, 162, 173, 174, 182, 183, 318-329, 338, 537-542, 567, 710, 711, 725, 731, 740.
Status of missionaries, 809, 810.
Steiger, 500.
Stenz, 498.
Stephen, Friar, 66.
Stevens, Edwin, 218.
Stevenson, Mr. and Mrs. J. W., 387, 389, 597.
Stewart Evangelistic Fund, 746.
Stewart, Milton, 649, 746.
Steyl, 316. See also Society of the Divine Word.
Steyl, Missionary Sisters of, 539.
Stimatini. See Priests of the Holy Stigmata.
Stockholm, 400.
Stone, Mary, 459.
Stout Memorial Hospital, 819.
Straits Settlements, 748.
Strauss, M. F., 817.
Stronach, John, 246, 262, 264, 430.
Stubbs, John, 209.
Studd, C. T., 391.
Student Volunteer Movement for For-

eign Missions, 358, 391, 535, 540, 592, 808; Chinese, 592, 593.
Student Volunteer Movement for the Ministry, 592, 593, 808.
Suifu, 541, 776.
Summer Palace, 783.
Summer resorts for missionaries, 408. See also Peitaiho, Kuling, Mokanshan, Kuliang.
Sun Chuan-fang, 702.
Sun, Melchior, 726, 727.
Sun Yat-sen, 490, 492, 544, 609-611, 693, 701-703, 778, 835, 841.
Sunday, observance, 194.
Sunday Schools in China, 601, 604, 641, 642, 748, 751.
Sunning, 601.
Suomen Lahetysseura Finska Missionssalskapet. See Finnish Missionary Society.
Superstition of Roman Catholic missionaries, 344.
Svenska Alliansmissionen. See Swedish Alliance Mission.
Svenska Missions Förbundet. See Swedish Missionary Society.
Swan, 216.
Swatow, 258, 259, 274, 370, 371, 376, 377, 407, 432, 450, 454, 457, 542, 561, 574, 626, 675, 709, 718, 721, 723, 737, 759, 781, 819.
Sweden and Swedes, 392, 471, 583, 772, 817.
Sweden Mission, Church of, 747, 783.
Swedish Alliance Mission, 583.
Swedish Baptists, 401, 579.
Swedish Evangelical Lutheran Foreign Mission Society of North America, 596.
Swedish Evangelical Missionary Covenant of America, 400, 575.
Swedish Holiness Union Mission in China, 392, 515, 582.
Swedish Independent Baptist Mission, 595.
Swedish Mission to China, 392, 583.
Swedish Missionary Society, 575.
Swedish Missionary Union, 400.
Swedish Mongol Mission, 601.
Swiss missions, 722.
Switzerland, 714, 765.
Synods, Roman Catholic, 241, 345, 558, 728.
Synod, General, 664.
Syria, 53.
Syriac, 46, 55.
Szechwan, 108, 125, 127, 160, 164, 165, 171, 172, 173, 177-180, 183, 232, 239, 240, 241, 307, 323, 327, 328, 330, 348, 353, 354, 355, 364, 370,

371, 375, 385, 390, 395, 397, 471, 493, 496, 498, 501, 536-538, 541-543, 546, 553, 563-565, 570, 573, 579, 580, 582, 597, 605, 606, 615, 616, 624, 643, 664, 702, 705, 708, 711, 737, 741, 747, 773, 776, 799, 806, 816, 817, 839.
Szechwan, General Conference of the Christian Churches of, 799.

T

Tachienlu, 565, 579.
Ta-ch'in, 53, 58.
Ta Ch'ing Lü Li, 307.
Tai, 749.
T'aianfu, 621, 711.
Taichow, 432, 647, 759.
T'aiku, 514, 572, 626.
T'ai P'ing Rebels and Rebellion, 243, 258, 266, 273, 282-302, 317, 318, 325, 348, 779, 838, 841.
T'aisan, 274.
T'ai Shan, 621.
Taiwanfu, 468.
Taiyüanfu, 320, 510, 521, 525, 543, 591, 645, 678, 711, 776, 839.
Taku forts, 273, 276, 505, 506.
Talienwan, 489.
Talmage, John Van Nest, 247.
Taminfu, 559.
Tamsui, 274.
T'ang dynasty, 50-60.
T'ang Huang-chang, 839.
T'ang T'ai Tsung, 51, 53.
Tangut, 62.
Tanyang, 318.
Tao, 12.
Tao Hsing, 482.
Tao Kuang, 175.
Tao Tê Ching, 12.
Tao Tê Hsüeh Hui, 839.
Tao Yüan, 838.
Taoism, 12, 13, 42, 531, 838, 839.
Taoist monks, 426.
Taot'ai, 522.
Tarsa, 65.
Tartar, 759.
Tartary, 162.
Ta Tao Hui, 497.
Tat'ung, 514, 730.
Ta T'ung Pao, see Chinese Weekly.
Tay, 353.
Taylor, Mrs. Annie R., 393.
Taylor, Charles, 257.
Taylor, Howard, 816.
Taylor, James Hudson, 382-390, 468, 522, 571, 581, 583, 584.
Techny, 540, 716, 717.

Temple of Heaven, 532, 554, 612.
Têngchow, 367, 371, 445, 447, 458, 461, 626, 634, 835.
Term controversy, 262.
Terrasse, 354.
Terrentius, 104.
Tertiates of the Holy Infancy, 553.
Tewksbury, E. G., 642.
Theological Education. See Clergy, Chinese.
Thomas of Tolentino, 70.
Thompson, Dr., 816.
Thurston, J. Lawrence, 604.
Thurston, Mrs. Matilda C. (Mrs. J. Lawrence), 630.
Thwing, E. W., 660.
Tiao Hsin-jeh, 628.
Tibet and the Tibetans, 158, 239, 241, 307, 323, 328, 390, 391, 393, 399, 402, 501, 542, 543, 546, 579, 580, 600, 606.
Tibetan border, 582, 608, 653, 740.
Tibetan Forward Mission, 773.
Tibetan Tribes Mission, 601.
T'ien, 7, 8, 21, 133-155.
T'ien Chu, 133, 141, 432, 433, 470.
Tientsin, 217, 276, 330, 364-366, 374, 380, 399, 402, 413, 454, 456, 458, 469, 493, 495, 504-506, 509, 513, 542, 553, 554, 586, 587, 591, 592, 625, 633, 677, 701, 705, 712, 726, 730, 732, 733, 746, 807, 835.
Tientsin massacre, 311, 353, 388, 469.
Ting Li-mei, 517, 592, 593, 749.
Tinghai, 245.
Tinghsien, 794.
Toby, 251.
Tokyo, 587, 591.
Toleration clauses in treaties, 275, 277, 811.
Toleration, edict of 1692, 126.
Toleration, edicts of 1844 and 1846, 230.
Tomlin, Jacob, 213.
Tongking, 176, 177, 354, 489, 512.
Tongues Movement, 747.
Tordesillas, Treaty of, 89.
Toronto, 392, 595.
To Tsai Church (Hongkong), 678.
Tournon, Charles Maillard de, 141-146, 149.
Tours, France, 551.
Tracy, Ira, 218.
Trans-Siberian Railway, 489.
Trappists, 316, 509, 732.
Travel, forbidden in the interior, 229, 230.
Travel, right of, granted, 274.
Treaties, 199, 200, 229, 811.

Treaties of 1842-1844, 407.
Treaties of 1858, 274, 275, 325, 359, 361, 370, 375, 417, 486, 507.
Treaty of Portsmouth, 607.
Treaty ports, 360.
Treaty revision, agitation for. *See* "Unequal treaties."
Trecul, Ernest, 546.
Trigault, Nicholas, 102.
Trinity College (Dublin), 369, 604.
Trinity College (Ningpo), 628.
"True Jesus Church," 808.
True Light Seminary, 1, 450.
Tsae A-ko, 212.
Ts'ai Yüan-p'ei, 692.
Tsao Kuei, Agnes, 243.
Tsao, Y. S., 628, 701, 739.
Tsaohsien, 600.
Tsehchow Mission, 600.
Tsêng Beauson, 808.
Tsêng Kuo-fan, 291, 294, 295, 351, 611, 808.
Tsêng, Miss Pao-suan, 808.
Tsinan, 111, 118, 320, 367, 447, 470, 504, 634, 645, 677, 720, 755, 783, 838.
Tsianfu Institute, 641.
Tsin, Louis, 736.
Tsingchow, 378, 380, 634.
Tsing Hua College, 628, 695.
Tsingtau, 489, 495, 576, 611, 706, 743.
Tsu (Bishop) Simon, 727.
Tsungli Yamen, 304, 307, 312, 322, 473, 477, 499, 506, 602, 603.
Tsung Shêng Hui, 839.
Tsur, Y. T., 628.
Tuan Chi-jui, 701.
Tuan Fang, 516, 661.
Tuli, 63.
Tung, Barnabas, 808.
T'ung Chih, 322.
T'ungchow, 366, 404, 449, 504, 512, 517, 592, 593, 626, 633, 641.
T'ung Shan Shê, 838.
Tung T'ang, 178, 308, 322, 508, 722.
Tungtingan, 518.
Tungt'ing Lake, 632.
T'ung Wên Pao, see Christian Intelligencer.
Tun-huang grottoes, 53, 56.
Turin, 722.
Turkestan (Chinese), 400, 759.
Turkey, 690.
Turner, F. S., 430.
Two Friends, The, 223, 229.
Tyrol, 723.
Tzŭ Hsi, 312.

U

Uighurs, 52, 63.

Unc Khan, 63.
"Unconnected" missionaries in China, 401, 601, 773.
"Unequal treaties," 690, 698, 702, 703, 778, 791.
Union Bible School, Nanking, 637.
Union Bible Training and Theological School, 629.
Union Christian College, 629.
Union, Committee on Presbyterian, 665.
Union for Chinese Catholic Action, 554, 711.
Union Medical College (Peking), 638, 754.
Union Normal School, Canton, 784.
Union of the Clergy in Behalf of Missions, 713.
"Union of the Religions of the Six Sages," 839.
Union Theological College in Peking, 753.
Union Theological Seminary in Nanking, 746, 784.
United Brethren in Christ, 580, 800, 803.
United Church of Canada, 801.
"United Church of Christ in China," 799, 800, 801.
United Evangelical Church, 578, 596, 518.
United Free Church of Scotland, 396, 455, 574, 634, 665, 677.
United Free Gospel and Mission Society, 747.
United Lutheran Church in America, 772.
United Methodist Church Mission, 578, 626.
United Methodist Free Churches, 382.
United Presbyterian Church, 396.
United States, 272, 316, 357, 358, 365, 391, 392, 398, 403, 418, 445, 446, 448, 449, 459, 473, 475, 476, 483, 525, 535, 540, 569, 587, 615, 616, 625, 627, 635, 659, 663, 687, 688, 707, 708, 712, 715-719, 744, 745, 765, 767, 768, 772, 781, 783, 789, 791, 806, 836.
United Universities Project (at Wuhan), 631.
United War Work Campaign, 750.
University of California, 398.
University of Chicago, 786.
University of Edinburgh, 459.
University of Michigan, 459.
University of Pennsylvania, 604.
University of the State of New York, 449, 629.
Urga, 515, 817.

Urquhart, David, 359.
Ursis, Sabbatino de, 102, 104.
Ursulines, 723 (Canadian, 721).
Uruguay, 723.
Urumtsi, 541, 582.

V

Vachal, 239.
Vagnoni, Alphonsus, 103.
Valignani, Alessandro, 91, 92.
Vancouver, B. C., 601.
Vanderkemp, J. T., 211.
Van Praet, 736.
Variétés sinologiques, 341.
Vasiliev, Vasili Pavlovitch, 486.
Vassar, 603.
Vatican, 312, 316, 345, 548, 713, 714, 728.
Vatne, 608.
"Vegetarians," 471.
Verbiest, 116, 121, 186, 509.
Verbist, Theophile, 314.
Verchere, 349.
Verhaeghen, 541, 545.
Vicars Apostolic, 125.
Vicariates apostolic, created, 232, 241.
Vicars Apostolic, instituted in the Far East, 113.
Victoria. See Hongkong.
Victoria, Bishopric of, 252, 253.
Visdelou, 120, 145.
Vögler, Mr. and Mrs. H. E. J., 378.
Vuillaume, 300.

W

Wai Chiao Pu, 738.
Wai Wu Pu, 603, 614, 615.
Wales, 378.
Walford Hart Memorial Hospital, 493.
Wallace, E. W., 643, 786.
Walsh, James A., 717.
Wang, C. C., 835.
Wang Cheng-ting, 478, 587, 684, 763, 835.
Wang Chi, 250.
Wang Ching-fu, 482.
Wang Ch'ung-hui, 835.
Wang Ying-ming, 483.
Wanhsien, 597, 689.
Wan Kuo Kung Pao, 441.
War, Ministry of, 611.
War, First with Great Britain, 228-230.
War, with Great Britain and France, 1856-1860, 271-276.
War, World, 527, 528, 534, 687, 688, 700, 710, 713, 740, 741, 743, 765, 771, 778, 784, 789, 790, 792, 802, 823.
Ward, Frederick Townsend, 294.

Warnshuis, A. L., 671.
Washington, D. C., 642.
Washington Disarmament Conference (1921-22), 688, 835.
Watertown (Wisc.), 599.
Watts, F. J., 816.
Weichow, 735.
Weihaiwei, 489.
Weihsien, 504, 592, 619, 634.
Weimar Mission, 398, 576.
Welton, 269.
Wênchow, 382, 388, 431, 462, 493, 557, 625, 676, 721.
Wên-li, 414, 431, 647.
Wesley, 358, 382.
Wesleyan Methodist Missionary (and Mission) Society, 207, 257, 374, 375, 446, 455, 460, 518, 578, 616, 639, 653, 665, 766.
Wesley College, 630.
West China, 343, 370, 374, 391, 397, 668, 676, 786, 799. See also, Szechwan, Kweichow, Yünnan.
West China Christian Educational Union, 632, 643.
West China Missionary News, 496.
West China Religious Tract Society, 493.
West China Union University, 632, 639, 753, 755.
Western learning, 443, 444, 587, 588, 607, 622.
Western medicine and surgery in China, 452.
Westwater, 520.
Wheeler, L. N., 437.
White, M. C., 256.
White (Bishop), William C., 595.
White Lily Society, 103, 165, 179.
White Russians, 742.
Whiteside, E. A., 816.
"White Wolf, The," 613, 708.
Whitney, 460.
Wieger, L., 560.
Wight, 249.
William Nast College, 630.
William of Prato, 74.
William of Tripoli, 68.
Williams, Channing Moore, 368.
Williams, E. T., 398.
Williams, J. E., 820.
Williams, Samuel Wells, 218, 265, 275.
Williamson, Alexander, 381, 398, 438, 440.
Wilson, Robert, 363.
Wilson, Mr. and Mrs. Wallace, 364.
Wisconsin, 599, 719.
Wishard, Luther D., 404.
Wittner, Bishop, 736.
Woman's Board of the (Dutch) Reformed Church, 459.

Woman's Foreign Missionary Society of the (Scotch) United Presbyterian Church, 456.

Woman's Medical College in Philadelphia, 459.

Woman's Missionary Association of the United Brethren in Christ, 399.

Women, in service of Roman Catholic Church, 188, 191, 192, 334, 339, 539, 553, 718. *See also,* Sisterhoods, Societies, Sisters, Congregations.

Women medical missionaries, 456, 459.

Women missionaries, 390, 397, 398, 400, 407, 456, 518, 539, 621, 755, 792, 793.

Women of the Chinese churches, 480. *See also* "Bible women."

Women's Christian Temperance Union, 659, 776.

Women's Foreign Missionary Society of the Methodist Episcopal Church, 395, 456, 633.

Women's Medical College, Peking, 783.

Women's Missionary Association of the Presbyterian Church of England, 395.

Women's missionary organizations, 395 (Protestant).

Women's Social Service League, 657.

Women's Union Missionary Society of America, 395, 456, 580.

Wong Fun, 222, 459.

Woods, Miss Mary E., 818.

Woolston Memorial Hospital, 459.

World's Missionary Conference of 1890, 665.

World's Student Christian Federation, 404, 695, 696.

World's Student Christian Federation, Conference of the, 775.

"Worshipers of Shang Ti," 285-288.

Wu Ching-piao, 776.

Wu, Empress Dowager, 54.

Wu P'ei-fu, 701, 702, 778, 817, 835.

Wu Tsung, Emperor, 54.

Wuchow, 819.

Wuchang, 179, 233, 320, 349, 364, 368, 389, 446, 483, 507, 559, 609, 630, 636-638, 702, 720, 785, 787.

Wuhan, 364, 630, 632.

Wuhsueh, 470.

Wuhu, 237, 356, 374, 470, 599, 722.

Wu Shan She, 838.

Wusih, 470, 573.

Wu Wei Society, 103.

Wylie, Alexander, 265, 436, 437.

X

Xavier, St. Francis, 86-88, 325, 541, 721.

Xavierian Society, 554.

Y

Yachow, 543.

Yahballaha III, Mar, 63.

Yale (University), 604.

Yale Foreign Missionary Society (Yale in China), 1, 604, 630, 755, 783.

Yang, Father A., 736.

Yang Chu (Yang Tzŭ), 14.

Yang Sen, 702.

Yang-Chiapin, 316.

Yangchow, 64, 71, 318, 388, 468, 474, 573, 611.

Yangtze, 363, 431, 489, 597, 608, 630, 664, 689, 694, 701, 702, 774, 834.

Yangtze Valley, 129, 349, 353, 356, 368, 382, 398, 401, 402, 430, 469, 470, 532, 572.

Yarkand, 62, 817.

Yates, Matthew T., 251, 371.

Yeh-li-k'o-wên, 65.

Yeh Ming-shên, 308.

Yellow River, 465.

Yenchow, 355, 559.

Yen, F. C., 628, 632.

Yen Hsi-shan, 678, 701, 703, 775, 839.

Yen Hui-ch'ing, 835.

Yen Tê-ching, 835.

Yen, W. W., 478, 483, 628, 684, 835.

Yen, Y. C. James, 781.

Yen, Y. K., 414, 483.

Yenanfu, 737.

Yenching, 783, 785, 788, 815.

Yenshan, 554.

Yerkalo, 328.

Ying, Vincent, 730.

Yiyang, 597, 783.

Yochow, 289, 389, 575, 632, 816.

Yorkshire, 382.

You Me-king, 459.

Young, Andrew, 653, 654.

Young China Association, 692, 695, 697.

Young, James H., 258.

Younghusband, 337, 394.

Young Men's Christian Association, 1, 2, 206, 358, 403, 495, 568, 584-594, 604, 611, 620, 625, 628, 635, 641, 657, 658, 712, 749, 750, 759, 760, 761, 763, 767, 775, 777, 781, 789, 793, 795, 798, 804, 806, 828, 835, 836, 842.

Young Women's Christian Association, 1, 2, 206, 404, 568, 584, 593, 594, 749, 763, 778, 784, 793, 804, 828.

Yü, Paul, 233.

Yü Hsien, 503, 504, 510, 514, 521.

Yü Man-tzu, 355, 498.

Yüan, Joseph, 179.

Yüan Shih-k'ai, 504, 507, 510, 516, 530, 544, 545, 590, 611, 612, 613, 615, 633, 700, 712, 713.
Yui, David Z. T., 628, 798, 810.
Yuille, 216.
Yukiang, 719.
Yungan, 288.
Yung Chêng, 158-161.
Yung Wing, 222, 476, 488, 834.
Yünnan, 125, 165, 173, 176, 177, 181, 232, 239, 243, 307, 323, 333, 347, 354, 390, 393, 505, 512, 538, 542, 547, 570, 578, 582, 600, 605, 606, 616, 624, 723, 736, 748, 763, 807, 816.
Yünnanfu, 65, 327, 489, 816.

Z

Zaitun, 70, 71, 73, 823.
Zanoli, 320.
Zia, H. L., 588.
Zikawei, 1, 95, 234, 235, 236, 308, 340, 436, 559, 560, 729, 732.
Zoroastrianism, 47, 52.
Zwemer, Samuel M., 749.